© 2005, 2008 THOMSON/FOUNDATION PRESS
© 2012 By THOMSON REUTERS/FOUNDATION PRESS
© 2015 LEG, Inc. d/b/a West Academic
    444 Cedar Street, Suite 700
    St. Paul, MN 55101
    1-877-888-1330
Printed in the United States of America

ISBN: 978-1-60930-419-5

UNIVERSITY CASEBOOK SERIES®

SECURITIES REGULATION

CASES AND ANALYSIS

FOURTH EDITION

by

STEPHEN J. CHOI
Murray and Kathleen Bring Professor of Law
New York University School of Law

A.C. PRITCHARD
Frances and George Skestos Professor of Law
University of Michigan Law School

FOUNDATION
PRESS

Stephen Choi
To Un Kyung, Una, Sehan, and Sejin

Adam Pritchard
To Joan, Liza, and Ben

PREFACE

The United States enjoys the largest and best policed capital markets in the world. Since the Great Depression, the Securities and Exchange Commission ("SEC") has overseen the regulation of much of the securities markets, enforcing and interpreting the federal securities laws. Over this time period, the securities markets have seen great technological changes. And with these changes have come corresponding additions, reforms, and only rarely, subtractions, from the securities laws.

In revising for the fourth edition of *Securities Regulation: Cases and Analysis*, we have kept in mind the features that made the first two editions a success. We provide enough material for a three or four credit hour basic class in securities regulation offered at virtually every law school. The book is specifically not intended for more advanced classes in securities regulation. We have included only the topics covered in most basic classes, such as materiality, the definition of a security, public offerings, etc. Accordingly, some topics covered in other books, such as broker-dealer regulation and investment companies, are omitted. This allows us to produce a much shorter book than the average for the field without sacrificing depth of coverage for the topics that are included. Professors will find additional material relating to the book at our website, http://www.choipritchard.com.

Because securities regulation is constantly evolving, we start with the underlying business problem facing companies and investors. Each chapter begins with a brief essay laying out the economics of the subject of the chapter. Securities markets are all about money, so understanding the economic incentives of the various actors is essential to understanding the effects of the regulatory regime (and efforts to reform the regime). We have tried to present the economics in a way that appeals to common sense and intuition; we have scrupulously avoided bogging the book down with mathematical models and references to studies in finance journals. We also include in these discussions, and at various points throughout the book, insights from the field of behavioral law and economics.

The common sense approach is reinforced by organizing each chapter around a single "Motivating Hypothetical." The Motivating Hypothetical introduces a business, its principal officers, and a business problem or need. The scenario is chosen to be a typical situation that the students are likely to see in practice. We then present hypotheticals throughout the chapter that build on the Motivating Hypothetical. By relying on the Motivating Hypothetical throughout the chapter we avoid having to introduce a new set of facts for each of the hypotheticals. The hypotheticals challenge the students to apply the legal rules presented in the cases and materials and allow the professor to spend class time on a real-world problem, rather than simply going over the cases and statutes.

We also include questions in the introductory paragraphs that precede each of the cases. These questions are designed to focus the students on the main issue addressed by the case. We then include a series of questions after each of the cases to push the students to see the practical implications of the court's holding and reasoning. If you can answer the questions and hypotheticals, you are doing a good job with your reading. In addition to the hypotheticals and questions, we also include Notes that cover topics not found in the cases and other primary materials. Interspersing the Notes with the primary materials allows us to present important points in a logical order and a concise fashion.

We make extensive use of charts and tables to present the material in away that crystallizes the most important points. Many areas in the securities laws, such as public offerings and resales, involve a number of statutes and regulations intersecting to create the operative legal regime. It is easy for students to get lost in the dense language of the statutes and regulations; it only becomes worse when the need arises to understand how the rules and regulations interact. Our graphic presentations help focus students on those interactions. The PowerPoint slides available to accompany the materials offer even more graphics to help students understand this sometimes daunting field.

Finally, we present the material in a different order than is used in most books. Most books, after some introductory material, present the securities laws in their historical sequence, i.e., first covering the Securities Act of 1933 and then turning to the Exchange Act of 1934. We have reversed the usual order, presenting the Exchange Act first, and leaving the Securities Act for later in the book. Our rationale for presenting the Exchange Act first is that the law is more inclusive. The Exchange Act applies to all public companies (indeed, it defines what a public company is) and its antifraud provisions apply to all disclosures made by those companies and their affiliates. The individual chapters generally stand on their own, however, so professors who prefer the more traditional order can easily adapt the book to their needs.

STEPHEN J. CHOI
A.C. PRITCHARD

February 2015

EDITORIAL NOTE AND ACKNOWLEDGMENTS

As with other casebooks, in our editing of the cases, we omit most footnotes and case and statute citations without indication. Footnote numbers in cases are as in the original, with no renumbering to take account of omitted footnotes.

We have many people to thank for helping with this book at various stages. We are particularly grateful to the many law professors and students who have made suggestions and pointed out errors. We also thank Dexter Eng, Meg Holzer, Alice Kim, Mario Mendolaro, Serena Palumbo, Elgun Pashazade, Braden Robinson, and Yaman Shukairy for their invaluable research and editorial assistance. Three others deserve special thanks for contributions above and beyond the call of duty. Sahar Kianfar was our tech wizard, designing both our PowerPoint slides and our website. Janis Horning showed remarkable patience in word processing through multiple revisions. Un Kyung Park provided constant editorial revisions (particularly to Choi's sometimes uneven prose). Finally, Pritchard acknowledges the generous support of the Elkes Fund for Faculty Excellence in the Law, which allowed him the release time to complete this book.

We are grateful for permission to reprint copyrighted material from *Remarks of Milton Freeman, Conference on Codification of the Federal Securities Laws*, 22 Bus. Law. 793, 922 (1967). Copyright © 1967 by the American Bar Association. Reprinted with the permission of The Business Lawyer and the estate of Milton Freeman.

We are lucky enough to have made it to a fourth edition of this book; we plan to do a fifth. We would be delighted to hear from our fellow securities regulation professors with any criticisms or suggestions. We will do our best to make the fifth edition better for both students and professors. We hope you enjoy the book.

SUMMARY OF CONTENTS

PREFACE..V

EDITORIAL NOTE AND ACKNOWLEDGMENTS.................................... VII

TABLE OF CASES... XXVII

Chapter 1. Introduction to the Securities Markets and Securities Regulation..1
I.   The Basics...1
II.   Types of Securities 2
III. The Capital Market 8
IV.   Investment Decisions...15
V.   Who Provides Information to Investors? 20
VI.   The Regulatory Apparatus 33

Chapter 2. Materiality...47
I.   What Matters to Investors?..47
II.   Forward-Looking Information..49
III. Objective Tests of Materiality 57
IV.   The "Total Mix" 76
V.   Management Integrity..84

Chapter 3. The Definition of a "Security" 95
I.   Do the Securities Laws Apply?...95
II.   "Investment Contract" 98
III. "Stock"...142
IV.   "Note"..147
V.   Securitization 156

Chapter 4. Disclosure and Accuracy 161
I.   Mandatory Disclosure and Accuracy 161
II.   What Is a "Public Company?...163
III. When Must a Public Company Disclose? 169
IV.   Accuracy of Disclosure 182
V.   The Problem of Selective Disclosure....................................188

Chapter 5. Rule 10b–5 Antifraud 197
I.   The Economics of Securities Fraud and Private Rights of Action 197
II.   Who Can Sue Under Rule 10b–5?...205
III. Elements of the Cause of Action 227
IV.   Rule 10b–5 Defendants..289
V.   Damages 311
VI.   Transnational Securities Fraud 317

Chapter 6. Insider Trading 329
I.   Economics of Insider Trading...329
II.   Insider Trading at Common Law 331
III. Rule 10b–5 and the Classical Theory of Insider Trading....................336
IV.   The Misappropriation Theory 362

V.   Section 16 387

Chapter 7. Public Offerings **393**
I.   Economics of Public Offerings 393
II.   The Gun-Jumping Rules 406
III. Public Offering Trading Practices 452
IV.   Shelf Registration 458

Chapter 8. Civil Liability Under the Securities Act **467**
I.   Public Offerings, Uncertainty and Information Asymmetry 467
II.   Section 11 Liability 468
III. Section 12(**a**)(1) 522
IV.   Section 12(**a**)(2) Liability 530

Chapter 9. Exempt Offerings **549**
I.   Introduction 549
II.   Section 4(**a**)(2) Offerings 550
III. Regulation D 559
IV.   Regulation A 588
V.   Crowdfunding 605
VI.   Intrastate Offerings 612
VII. Regulation S 627

Chapter 10. Secondary Market Transactions **641**
I.   Introduction 641
II.   Transaction and Underwriter? 643
III. Control Persons' Resales 652
IV.   Rule 144 658
V.   Rule 144A 669

Chapter 11. Federal Regulation of Shareholder Voting **677**
I.   Introduction 677
II.   Solicitation of Proxies 679
III. Shareholder Democracy 699

Chapter 12. Gatekeepers **725**
I.   Gatekeeping 725
II.   Outside Directors 727
III. The Independent Auditor 736
IV.   The Role of Lawyers in Enforcing the Securities Laws 739
V.   Credit Rating Agencies 746
VI.   Whistleblowers 756

Chapter 13. Public Enforcement **765**
I.   SEC Enforcement 765
II.   Scope of SEC Enforcement 766
III. SEC Investigations 770
IV.   Enforcement Proceedings 789

INDEX 827

TABLE OF CONTENTS

PREFACE...V

EDITORIAL NOTE AND ACKNOWLEDGMENTS.. VII

TABLE OF CASES.. XXVII

Chapter 1. Introduction to the Securities Markets and Securities Regulation..1
    Motivating Hypothetical...1
I.   The Basics..1
II. Types of Securities...2
    A.   Common Stock...3
    B.   Preferred Stock...4
    C.   Bonds...7
III. The Capital Market 8
    A.   Primary Transactions...9
    B.   Secondary Transactions..11
        1.   Traditional Securities Exchanges 12
        2.   The Nasdaq Market 13
        3.   Alternative Trading Systems 15
IV. Investment Decisions..15
    A.   Present Discount Valuation 16
        1.   Interest..16
        2.   Present Value 17
        Hypothetical One 18
    B.   What Risks Matter..18
V.   Who Provides Information to Investors?...20
    A.   The Incentive to Provide Information..21
    B.   The Argument for Mandatory Disclosure.......................................24
        1.   Coordination Problems...25
        2.   Agency Costs..25
        3.   Positive Externalities...26
        4.   Duplicative Research 27
        5.   Costs of Mandatory Disclosure...28
    C.   How Does Disclosure Matter? 28
        1.   Filtering Mechanisms 29
        2.   The Efficient Capital Market Hypothesis..............................30
        a.   Weak ECMH...30
        b.   Semi-Strong ECMH 31
        c.   Strong ECMH 31
        d.   Implications of ECMH 31
VI. The Regulatory Apparatus 33
    A.   The Federal Securities Laws..34
        1.   Securities Exchange Act of 1934 34
        2.   Securities Act of 1933...35
        3.   Investment Company Act of 1940 and Investment Advisers Act of 1940 36
        4.   Trust Indenture Act of 1939 36

     5. Williams Act of 1968 37
     6. Sarbanes-Oxley Act of 2002...37
     7. Jumpstart Our Business Startups Act of 2012 38
  B. The Financial Crisis and the Dodd-Frank Act............................38
  C. The Securities and Exchange Commission 41
  D. Self-Regulatory Organizations...43

Chapter 2. Materiality...47
  Motivating Hypothetical..47
I. What Matters to Investors?..47
II. Forward-Looking Information 49
  Basic Inc. v. Levinson 49
  Notes 55
  Questions 56
  Hypothetical One 56
III. Objective Tests of Materiality 57
    SEC Staff Accounting Bulletin No. 99 57
    Litwin v. Blackstone Group, L.P. 58
    Questions 63
    Hypothetical Two 63
    In re Merck & Co., Inc. Securities Litigation 64
    Questions 68
    Matrixx Initiatives, Inc. v. Siracusano 69
    Questions 75
    Hypothetical Three 75
IV. The "Total Mix" 76
    Longman v. Food Lion, Inc. 76
    Notes 83
    Questions 83
    Hypothetical Four 83
V. Management Integrity...84
  In the Matter of Franchard Corporation 84
  Notes 91
  Questions 92
  Hypothetical Five 92
  Questions 94
  Hypothetical Six...94

Chapter 3. The Definition of a "Security" 95
  Motivating Hypothetical..95
I. Do the Securities Laws Apply? 95
  Hypothetical One 97
II. "Investment Contract" 98
  SEC v. W. J. Howey Co..98
  Notes 101
  Questions 102
  Hypothetical Two 102
  A. "A Person Invests His Money"...103
    International Brotherhood of Teamsters v. Daniel......................103

Notes 106
Questions 107
Hypothetical Three 107
B.   "[I]n a Common Enterprise" 108
SEC v. SG Ltd. 108
Questions 114
Hypothetical Four 114
C.   "[I]s Led to Expect Profits" 115
United Housing Foundation, Inc. v. Forman 115
Notes 120
Questions 122
SEC v. Edwards...122
Questions 124
Warfield v. Alaniz 125
Questions 129
Hypothetical Five 129
D.   "[S]olely from the Efforts of the Promoter or a Third Party" 129
SEC v. Merchant Capital, LLC 131
Questions 137
SEC v. Mutual Benefits Corp. 137
Questions 141
Notes 141
Hypothetical Six 142
III.   "Stock"..142
Landreth Timber Company v. Landreth 142
Notes 147
Questions 147
Hypothetical Seven 147
IV.   "Note" 147
Reves v. Ernst & Young..148
Notes 156
Questions 156
Hypothetical Eight...156
V.   Securitization 156

Chapter 4. Disclosure and Accuracy 161
Motivating Hypothetical..161
I.   Mandatory Disclosure and Accuracy 161
II.   What Is a "Public Company?..163
A.   Public Company Status 163
B.   Escaping Public Company Status 165
C.   Trading in the Stock of Private Companies 167
Hypothetical One 168
III.   When Must a Public Company Disclose? 169
A.   Form 8–K..170
In the Matter of Hewlett-Packard Company.........................173
Questions 176
Hypothetical Two 176
B.   Forms 10–K and 10–Q...177

Notes 179
Hypothetical Three 179
C.   Executive Compensation 179
D.   Emerging Growth Companies... 181
IV. Accuracy of Disclosure 182
In the Matter of Oil States International, Inc. 183
Notes 186
Questions.. 187
Hypothetical Four 187
V.   The Problem of Selective Disclosure... 188
SEC v. Siebel Systems, Inc.. 189
Questions.. 196
Hypothetical Five 196

Chapter 5. Rule 10b–5 Antifraud **197**
Motivating Hypothetical.. 197
I.   The Economics of Securities Fraud and Private Rights of Action 197
A.   The Rule 10b–5 Private Cause of Action................................... 199
1.   Genesis.. 199
2.   Overlap with Other Causes of Action 199
3.   Section 9 of the Exchange Act 200
4.   Overlap with State Law Causes of Action 201
B.   The Class Action Mechanism 202
Hypothetical One 202
C.   Sorting the Good from the Bad 203
Questions 204
II. Who Can Sue Under Rule 10b–5?... 205
A.   The "in Connection with" Requirement................................. 205
Blue Chip Stamps, et al. v. Manor Drug Stores............................ 205
Notes 210
Questions 210
Hypothetical Two 210
SEC v. Zandford 211
Notes 214
Questions 214
Hypothetical Three 215
B.   The Lead Plaintiff in a Class Action.................................... 215
In re Cendant Corp. Litigation.. 215
Notes 225
Questions 226
III. Elements of the Cause of Action 227
A.   Misstatement of a Material Fact.. 227
1.   Deception 227
Santa Fe Industries, Inc., et al. v. Green et al. 228
Notes 231
Questions 232
2.   Facts Versus Opinions 232
Virginia Bankshares, Inc. v. Sandberg.................................. 232
Notes 235

Questions 235
Hypothetical Four 235
3. The Duty to Update and the Duty to Correct 235
Gallagher v. Abbott Laboratories..................................236
Notes 238
Questions 239
4. Forward-Looking Statements................................239
Asher v. Baxter International Inc. 239
Notes 245
Questions 246
Hypothetical Five 246
B. Scienter 246
Ernst & Ernst v. Hochfelder..246
Questions 249
Hypothetical Six 250
Tellabs, Inc. v. Makor Issues & Rights, Ltd. 251
Notes 256
Questions 257
City of Livonia Employees' Retirement System v. The Boeing
Co...258
Questions 263
Hypothetical Seven 264
C. Reliance..265
Affiliated Ute Citizens of Utah v. United States 265
Questions 267
Halliburton Co. v. Erica P. John Fund, Inc. ("Halliburton
II")..268
Notes 282
Questions 283
Hypothetical Eight..283
D. Loss Causation 284
Dura Pharmaceuticals, Inc. v. Broudo...........................284
Notes 287
Questions 288
IV. Rule 10b–5 Defendants..289
A. Secondary Liability 289
Stoneridge Investment Partners, LLC v. Scientific-Atlanta,
Inc...291
Notes 299
Questions 299
Janus Capital Group, Inc., et al. v. First Derivative Traders 300
Questions 305
Hypothetical Nine 305
B. Control Person Liability 306
Lustgraaf v. Behrens 307
Notes 310
Questions 311
V. Damages 311
A. Open Market Damages 311

Hypothetical Ten 312
B.   Face-to-Face Damages 313
Garnatz v. Stifel, Nicolaus & Co., Inc. 314
Notes 316
Questions 316
C.   Proportionate Liability 316
Notes 317
Hypothetical Eleven 317
VI. Transnational Securities Fraud 317
Morrison v. National Australia Bank Ltd. 319
Notes 325
Questions 327

Chapter 6. Insider Trading 329
Motivating Hypothetical 329
I.   Economics of Insider Trading 329
II.   Insider Trading at Common Law 331
Strong v. Repide 331
Notes 334
Questions 335
Hypothetical One 335
III. Rule 10b–5 and the Classical Theory of Insider Trading 336
A.   Core Insiders 336
Chiarella v. United States 337
Notes 341
Questions 343
Hypothetical Two 343
B.   Tipper/Tippee Liability 344
Dirks v. SEC 344
Notes 350
Questions 350
United States v. Newman 351
Notes 361
Questions 361
Hypothetical Three 362
IV. The Misappropriation Theory 362
A.   The Misappropriation Theory 364
United States v. O'Hagan 365
Notes 371
Questions 371
B.   Duty of Confidentiality 371
SEC v. Rocklage 372
Questions 377
SEC v. Cuban 378
Notes 380
Questions 381
C.   Remedies 381
Hypothetical Four 381
Hypothetical Five 382

D. Alternatives to the Misappropriation Theory 383
 SEC v. Dorozhko 383
 Questions 386
V. Section 16 387
 A. Section 16 and Employee Compensation 388
 B. Special Issues with Large Block Shareholders 388
  Question 390
 C. Calculating Section 16(b) Damages 390
  Question 391

Chapter 7. Public Offerings **393**
 Motivating Hypothetical 393
I. Economics of Public Offerings 393
 A. A Brief Description of the Public Offering Process 395
  1. Different Types of Offerings 396
  2. The Underwriters 398
  3. The Underwriting Process 398
  4. Underpricing 400
  5. Capital Structure 401
 B. Public Offering Disclosure 403
  1. Plain English Disclosures 405
II. The Gun-Jumping Rules 406
 Securities Offering Reform 406
 A. Pre-Filing Period 411
  1. What Is an "Offer" 411
   Securities Act Release No. 3844 413
   Securities Act Release No. 5180 415
   Notes 416
   Questions 418
   Hypothetical One 419
  2. Putting Together the Offering 420
   Hypothetical Two 420
   Hypothetical Three 422
  3. Emerging Growth Companies 422
   Hypothetical Four 423
 B. Waiting Period 423
  1. Gauging Market Sentiment 424
   a. The Preliminary Prospectus 425
   b. The Free Writing Prospectus 425
   c. The Roadshow and Other Oral Offers 426
   d. Regularly Released Information in the Ordinary
    Course of Business 426
   e. "Tombstone" Advertisements 426
   f. Solicitations of Interest 427
    Hypothetical Five 427
  2. Free Writing Prospectuses 428
   a. Definition of a Free Writing Prospectus 429
   b. Issuer Requirements 429
   c. Disclosure, Filing and Retention Requirements 431

             d.   Antifraud Liability and Regulation FD
                    Implications 433
                    Hypothetical Six 433
                    Notes.. 434
           3.   The Process of Going Effective 435
           4.   Analysts 437
                Hypothetical Seven 440
      C.   Post-Effective Period.. 441
           1.   Forms of the Final Prospectus............................... 441
           2.   Traditional Free Writing 443
           3.   Prospectus Delivery Requirement.......................... 444
              a.   The Traditional Delivery Requirement......................... 444
              b.   Prospectus Delivery Period.................................. 445
              c.   Access Equals Delivery 446
                  Hypothetical Eight 448
            4.   Updating the Prospectus and Registration Statement........ 449
              a.   Updating the Prospectus...................................... 449
               b.   Updating the Registration Statement 451
                  Hypothetical Nine 452
III. Public Offering Trading Practices 452
      A.   IPO Allocations... 453
      B.   Market Manipulation... 455
               Hypothetical Ten 456
      C.   Stabilization 457
               Hypothetical Eleven 458
IV. Shelf Registration 458
      A.   Automatic Shelf Registration 462
      B.   The Base Prospectus 463
              Notes 464
              Hypothetical Twelve 465

Chapter 8. Civil Liability Under the Securities Act 467
             Motivating Hypothetical..467
I.   Public Offerings, Uncertainty and Information Asymmetry 467
II. Section 11 Liability 468
      A.   Standing... 468
              Krim v. pcOrder.com, Inc. 469
              Questions 475
              Hypothetical One 475
      B.   Statutory Defendants 476
              Hypothetical Two 476
               Questions 476
      C.   Elements of the Cause of Action 477
              Omnicare, Inc. v. Laborers Dist. Council Constr. Indus.
                 Pension Fund.. 479
              Questions 489
               Hypothetical Three 490
      D.   Defenses... 490
           1.   Due Diligence Defense 490

           Escott v. BarChris Construction Corp. 491

           Notes 501

           Questions 501

      2.   Due Diligence and Underwriters...501

           In re WorldCom, Inc. Securities Litigation 501

           Questions 512

           Hypothetical Four 512

    E.   Damages 514

      1.   Measuring § 11 Damages..514

           Beecher v. Able 514

           Notes 518

           Questions 518

           Hypothetical Five 518

      2.   Indemnification, Contribution, and Joint and Several
          Liability..519

           Eichenholtz v. Brennan...519

           Questions 521

           Hypothetical Six 521

III.   Section 12(a)(1)..522

    A.   Standing and Defendants..522

          Pinter v. Dahl 523

          Notes 527

          Questions 527

          Hypothetical Seven 528

    B.   Elements of the Cause of Action 529

    C.   Damages and Defenses 529

          Hypothetical Eight 529

IV.   Section 12(a)(2) Liability 530

    A.   The Scope of § 12(a)(2) 530

          Gustafson v. Alloyd Co., Inc. 531

          Questions 537

    B.   Implications of *Gustafson* 537

          Feiner v. SS & C Technologies, Inc. 538

          Notes 540

    C.   Elements of the Cause of Action 541

          Hypothetical Nine 541

    D.   Defenses...542

          Questions 542

    E.   Damages and Loss Causation 543

          Miller v. Thane International, Inc. 543

          Questions 546

          Hypothetical Ten..546

Chapter 9. Exempt Offerings...**549**

    Motivating Hypothetical..549

I.   Introduction...549

II.   Section 4(**a**)(2) Offerings..550

    SEC v. Ralston Purina Co. 551

    Questions 553

Doran v. Petroleum Management Corp...553
Questions..558
Hypothetical One 559
III. Regulation D..559
    A.   Aggregate Offering Price 561
        Hypothetical Two 561
    B.   Purchasers 562
        Hypothetical Three 564
        Hypothetical Four 566
    C.   General Solicitation 566
        In the Matter of Kenman Corp...567
        Questions 569
        SEC No-Action Letter Mineral Lands Research & Marketing
            Corporation..569
        Hypothetical Five...572
    D.   Disclosure 573
        Hypothetical Six...575
    E.   Resale Restrictions..575
        Hypothetical Seven 576
    F.   Integration..576
        Hypothetical Eight 578
    G.   Innocent and Insignificant Mistakes 578
        Hypothetical Nine 580
    H.   Disqualification 580
        Order Under Rule 506(d) of the Securities Act of 1933
            Granting a Waiver of the Rule 506(d)(1)(ii)
            Disqualification Provision In the Matter of Bank of
            America, N.A. and Merrill Lynch, Pierce, Fenner &
            Smith, Inc. 582
        Questions 584
    I.   Other Aspects of Regulation D 584
        1.   State Securities Regulation 584
        2.   Rule 504 585
        3.   Form D 586
        4.   Exchange Act Filing...586
    J.   The Private Placement Process..587
IV. Regulation A..588
    A.   Eligible Issuers and Securities..589
    B.   "Bad Actor" Disqualification 590
        Hypothetical Ten...591
    C.   Aggregate Offering Price 592
        Hypothetical Eleven..593
    D.   Investors 593
    E.   Disclosure 594
        1.   Offering 594
            Hypothetical Twelve 596
        2.   Periodic Reporting...596
    F.   Regulation A Gun Jumping..598
        1.   Pre-Filing Period 598

Hypothetical Thirteen 599
    2.   Waiting Period 600
Hypothetical Fourteen 600
    3.   Post-Qualification Period..600
Hypothetical Fifteen 601
  G. Continuous Offerings..601
  H. Insignificant Deviations..602
Hypothetical Sixteen 603
  I. Antifraud Liability 603
  J. Integration..603
Hypothetical Seventeen 604
  K. State Securities Law Requirements 605
V. Crowdfunding...605
  A. Disclosure 608
  B. Limits on Issuer Communication...........................609
  C. Periodic Disclosures 609
  D. Antifraud Liability 609
  E. Resales 610
  F. Disqualification 611
  G. Public Company Status 611
Hypothetical Eighteen 612
VI. Intrastate Offerings 612
  A. Section 3(a)(11) Offerings 613
Securities Act Release No. 4434 613
Busch v. Carpenter 616
Questions 619
Hypothetical Nineteen 620
  B. Rule 147 621
Exchange Act Release No. 5450 621
Hypothetical Twenty..626
VII. Regulation S 627
  A. Basic Regulation S Requirements...........................628
    1.   Offshore Transaction..629
Hypothetical Twenty-One..629
    2.   No Directed Selling Efforts 630
Hypothetical Twenty-Two...631
  B. Categories of Regulation S Offerings.....................631
    1.   Category 1 (Rule 903(b)(1)).......................................632
Hypothetical Twenty-Three..632
    2.   Category 2 Offerings (Rule 903(b)(2)) 633
Hypothetical Twenty-Four...635
    3.   Category 3 Offerings (Rule 903(b)(3)) 635
Hypothetical Twenty-Five 637
  C. Integration...637
  D. Resales 638
  E. Global Regulation S Offerings.................................640

Chapter 10. Secondary Market Transactions **641**
    Motivating Hypothetical 641
I.   Introduction 641
II. Transaction and Underwriter? 643
    Gilligan, Will & Co. v. SEC 645
    Notes 647
    Questions 647
    Hypothetical One 648
    SEC v. Chinese Consolidated Benevolent Ass'n, Inc. 649
    Questions 651
III. Control Persons' Resales 652
    A. Underwriters for Control Persons 653
        Hypothetical Two 653
        United States v. Wolfson 654
        Questions 655
    B. Section 4(a)(1 1/2) Exemption 655
        Hypothetical Three 657
IV. Rule 144 658
    A. Holding Period for Restricted Securities 660
    B. Current Public Information 661
        1. Applicability 661
        2. Information Required 662
        Hypothetical Four 663
    C. Additional Requirements for Affiliate Resales 665
        1. Limitation on Amount of Securities Sold 665
            Hypothetical Five 666
        2. Manner of Sale 666
            Hypothetical Six 667
        3. Notice of Proposed Sale 668
    D. Other Considerations 668
    E. Implications 668
V. Rule 144A 669
    A. Sales to a Qualified Institutional Buyer 670
    B. Purchaser Awareness of Exemption 671
    C. Fungibility 671
    D. Disclosure 671
        Hypothetical Seven 672
    E. Resales 673
        Hypothetical Eight 675
    F. Rule 144A and Registration Under the Securities Act ... 675

Chapter 11. Federal Regulation of Shareholder Voting **677**
    Motivating Hypothetical 677
I.   Introduction 677
II. Solicitation of Proxies 679
    A. What Is a "Solicitation"? 680
        Hypothetical One 682
    B. Proxy Disclosure 682
        1. Disclosure and Filing Requirements 682

2.   Testing the Waters 685
Hypothetical Two 686
C.   Rule 14a–9 Antifraud Liability 687
J.I. Case Co. v. Borak..687
Questions 689
Mills v. Electric Auto-Lite Co. 690
Notes 693
Questions 694
D.   Managing the Costs of Proxy Solicitations...........................694
Hypothetical Three 695
1.   Communicating with Shareholders 695
2.   Management Defensive Tactics.......................................698
3.   Reimbursement of Expenses 699
III.   Shareholder Democracy..699
A.   Shareholder Proposals 700
1.   Eligibility and Procedural Requirements 701
2.   Substantive Exclusions...702
Hypothetical Four 704
Lovenheim v. Iroquois Brands Ltd..705
Questions 708
Apache Corp. v. New York City Employees' Retirement
System 708
Questions 713
Hypothetical Five 713
B.   SEC Authority over Shareholder Voting 714
1.   Proxy Access 714
Business Roundtable v. SEC 715
Notes 721
Questions 721
2.   Say on Pay 722
Questions 723

Chapter 12. Gatekeepers 725
Motivating Hypothetical...725
I.   Gatekeeping...725
II.   Outside Directors 727
In the Matter of W. R. Grace & Co. 729
Questions 735
Hypothetical One 735
III.   The Independent Auditor 736
Hypothetical Two 738
IV.   The Role of Lawyers in Enforcing the Securities Laws.............739
Questions 740
Hypothetical Three 741
Pacific Inv. Management Co. LLC v. Mayer Brown LLP 741
Questions 746
V.   Credit Rating Agencies 746
Securities Fraud Liability of Secondary Actors, GAO–11–664...........747

A.   Liability 748
      In re Lehman Brothers Mortgage-Backed Securities
            Litigation 748
            Notes 754
            Questions 755
B.   Regulation of Credit Rating Agencies............................755
            Questions 756
VI.   Whistleblowers..756
      Wiest v. Lynch...757
      Questions...761
      Hypothetical Four 763

Chapter 13. Public Enforcement **765**
      Motivating Hypothetical..765
I.   SEC Enforcement...765
II.   Scope of SEC Enforcement 766
      In re Washington Public Power Supply System Securities
            Litigation 768
      Questions...770
III. SEC Investigations 770
      A.   Investigations and Strategy 770
            Report of Investigation Pursuant to Section 21(a) of the
                  Securities Exchange Act of 1934 and Commission
                  Statement on the Relationship of Cooperation to Agency
                  Enforcement Decisions...772
            Questions 774
            Lucent Settles SEC Enforcement Action Charging the
                  Company With $1.1 Billion Accounting Fraud 775
            Questions 776
            Hypothetical One 776
      B.   Formal Investigations and Subpoenas 777
            RNR Enterprises, Inc. v. SEC...............................778
            Questions 781
            SEC v. Dresser Industries, Inc................................781
            Notes 788
            Questions 788
            Hypothetical Two 789
IV.   Enforcement Proceedings..789
      A.   Administrative Proceedings 790
            1.   Section 21C 791
                  Questions 792
            2.   Section 15(c)(4) 792
                  Questions 793
            3.   Section 21(a) 793
            4.   Sections 12(j) & 12(k) 793
      B.   Judicial Review of Administrative Remedies............794
            KPMG, LLP v. SEC...795
            Questions 802
            Hypothetical Three 802

C.   Judicial Remedies 802
    1.   Injunctions 803
       Aaron v. SEC 803
       Notes 806
       Questions 806
    2.   Other Civil Remedies 806
       SEC v. Sargent 807
       Questions 809
       SEC v. First Pac. Bancorp 810
       Notes 813
       Questions 814
       Official Committee of Unsecured Creditors of WorldCom,
         Inc. v. SEC 814
       Questions 818
       Hypothetical Four 818
D.   Criminal Enforcement 818
    United States v. Tarallo.. 819
    Notes 825
    Questions 826

INDEX 827

TABLE OF CASES

The principal cases are in bold type.

Aaron v. SEC 768, **803**

Abell v. Potomac Insurance Co. 282

Absolute Activist Value Master Fund
Ltd. v. Ficeto 326

Abu Dhabi Commercial Bank v.
Morgan Stanley & Co., Inc. 755

Ackerberg v. Johnson, Jr. 648, 652,
657

Adams v. Standard Knitting Mills,
Inc. 690

**Affiliated Ute Citizens of Utah v.
United States** **265**

Alley v. Miramon 210

Alstom SA Sec. Litig., In re 326

Altman v. SEC 740

American High-Income Trust v.
Alliedsignal 676

Amgen, Inc. v. Connecticut Ret.
Plans and Trust Funds 267

**Apache Corp. v. New York City
Employees' Retirement
System** **708**

Arthur Children's Trust v.
Keim 310

Asadi v. G.E. Energy (U.S.A.),
LLC 762

Ashcroft v. Iqbal 264

**Asher v. Baxter International
Inc.** **239**

Barnes v. Osofsky 475

**Basic Inc. v.
Levinson** 32, **49**, 242, 268

Bastian v. Petren Resources
Corporation 288

Beecher v. Able **514**

Bell Atlantic Corp. v. Twombly 264

Binder v. Gillespie 282

Birnbaum v. Newport Steel
Corp. 206

**Blue Chip Stamps, et al. v. Manor
Drug Stores** 200, **205**

Bryan v. United States 822, 825

Burgess v. Premier Corp. 310

Busch v. Carpenter **616**

**Business Roundtable v.
SEC** **715**

Cady, Roberts & Co., In the Matter
of 336, 338

Carpenter v. United States 364

**Cendant Corp. Litigation,
In re** **215**

Central Bank of Denver v. First
Interstate Bank of Denver 290

Chapman v. Dunn 618

Charles A. Howard, In the Matter
of 451

Chevron U.S.A., Inc. v. Natural Res.
Def. Council 795

Chiarella v. United States **337**

Chris-Craft Indus., Inc. v. Piper
Aircraft Corp. 282

Compuware Corporation v. Moody's
Investors Services 755

Conley v. Gibson 264

Cort v. Ash 768

Cowin v. Bresler 210

Dirks v. SEC **344**, 352, 370

**Doran v. Petroleum Management
Corp.** **553**

**Dura Pharmaceuticals, Inc. v.
Broudo** **284**

Eichenholtz v. Brennan **519**

**Ernst & Ernst v.
Hochfelder** 229, **246**, 804

**Escott v. BarChris Construction
Corp.** **491**

Evans, United States v. 350

**Feiner v. SS & C Technologies,
Inc.** **538**

Fener v. Operating Engineers Const.
Industry and Miscellaneous
Pension Fund (Local 66) 288

Foremost-McKesson, Inc. v.
Provident Securities Co. 389

**Franchard Corporation, In the
Matter of** **84**

Freeland v. Iridium World
Communications 245

FTC v. Ruberoid Co. 800

GAF Corp. v. Heyman 94

Gaines v. Haughton 93

**Gallagher v. Abbott
Laboratories** **236**

**Garnatz v. Stifel, Nicolaus & Co.,
Inc.** **314**

Gaylord Container Corp.
Shareholders Litigation,
In re 679

Gilligan, Will & Co. v. SEC **645**

Goldberg v. Meridor 231

Goodwin v. Agassiz 334

Gould v. American-Hawaiian S. S.
Co. 690

Gould v. Ruefenacht 146

Gratz v. Claughton 339

Greater Iowa Corp. v.
McLendon 690

**Gustafson v. Alloyd Co.,
Inc.** **531**, 628

**Halliburton Co. v. Erica P. John
Fund, Inc. ("Halliburton
II")** **268**

Herman & MacLean v.
Huddleston 200

Hewlett-Packard Company, In the
Matter of 173

Higginbotham v. Baxter Int'l 256

Initial Public Offering Securities
Litigation, In re 310

International Brotherhood of
Teamsters v. Daniel 103
International Controls Corp. v.
Vesco 803
J.I. Case Co. v. Borak 687, 690
Janus Capital Group, Inc., et al.
v. First Derivative
Traders 300
Jiau, United States v. 355
John Nuveen & Co. v. Sanders 542
Joseph v. Wiles 541
Kardon v. National Gypsum
Co. 200, 206
Kaufman v. Trump's Castle
Funding 83, 245
Kenman Corp., In the Matter
of 567
Kern County Land Co. v. Occidental
Petroleum Corp. 389
Kern, In re 793
KPMG, LLP v. SEC 795
Krim v. pcOrder.com, Inc. 469
Lampf, Pleva, Lipkind, Prupis &
Petigrow v. Gilbertson 227
Landreth Timber Company v.
Landreth 142
Laperriere v. Vesta Ins. Group,
Inc. 317
Lapin v. Goldman Sachs Group,
Inc. 310
Leasco Data Processing Equipment
Corp. v. Maxwell 318
Lehman Brothers Mortgage-
Backed Securities Litigation,
In re 748
Levi Strauss & Co. Sec. Lit., In
re 540
Litwin v. Blackstone Group,
L.P. 58
Livonia Employees' Retirement
System, City of v. The Boeing
Co. 258
Longman v. Food Lion, Inc. 76
Lormand v. US Unwired Inc. 288
Lovenheim v. Iroquois Brands
Ltd. 705
Lustgraaf v. Behrens 307
Makor Issues & Rights Ltd. v.
Tellabs Inc. 257
Marine Bank v. Weaver 107
Matrixx Initiatives, Inc. v.
Siracusano 69
Matthews, United States v. 93
Merck & Co. v. Reynolds 227
Merck & Co., Inc. Securities
Litigation, In re 64
Merrill Lynch, Pierce, Fenner &
Smith, Inc. v. Dabit 202
Metge v. Baehler 306
Miller v. Thane International,
Inc. 543

Mills v. Electric Auto-Lite
Co. 690
Mizzaro v. Home Depot, Inc. 257
Morrison v. National Australia
Bank Ltd. 319, 628
Mosser v. Darrow 348
National Ass'n of Manufacturers v.
SEC 162
Newman, United States v. 351
O'Hagan, United States
v. 213, 365, 376, 825
Official Committee of Unsecured
Creditors of WorldCom, Inc. v.
SEC 814
Oil States International, Inc.,
In the Matter of 183
Omnicare, Inc. v. Laborers Dist.
Council Constr. Indus. Pension
Fund 479
Ontario Public Service Employees
Union Pension Trust Fund v.
Nortel Networks Corp. 214
Pacific Inv. Management Co.
LLC v. Mayer Brown LLP 741
Pidcock v. Sunnyland America
Inc. 313
Pinter v. Dahl 523
Piper v. Chris-Craft Industries,
Inc. 37
Pontiac Policemen's and Firemen's
Retirement System, City of v. UBS
AG 326
Reliance Elec. Co. v. Emerson Elec.
Co. 389
Reves v. Ernst & Young 148
RNR Enterprises, Inc. v.
SEC 778
Salomon Analyst Metromedia
Litigation, In re 283
Sanders v. John Nuveen & Co. 541
Santa Fe Industries, Inc., et al. v.
Green et al. 228, 367
Sawant v. Ramsey 310
Schoenbaum v. Firstbrook 318
SEC v. Barclays Bank PLC 343
SEC v. Bilzerian 806
SEC v. Chinese Consolidated
Benevolent Ass'n, Inc. 649
SEC v. Cuban 378
SEC v. Dorozhko 383
SEC v. Dresser Industries,
Inc. 781
SEC v. Edwards 122
SEC v. Fehn 92
SEC v. First City Financial
Corp. 810
SEC v. First Jersey Sec., Inc. 306
SEC v. First Pac. Bancorp 810
SEC v. Glenn W. Turner Enterprises,
Inc. 142
SEC v. Life Partners, Inc. 139

SEC v. Manor Nursing Centers, Inc. 450
SEC v. Merchant Capital, LLC **131**
SEC v. Musella 356
SEC v. Mutual Benefits Corp. **137**
SEC v. National Securities, Inc. ... 210
SEC v. O'Brien 781
SEC v. Obus 353, 361
SEC v. Ralston Purina Co. **551**, 646
SEC v. Rocklage **372**
SEC v. Rubera 126
SEC v. Sargent **807**
SEC v. SG Ltd. **108**
SEC v. Siebel Systems, Inc. **189**
SEC v. Sloan 793
SEC v. Southwest Coal & Energy Co. 450
SEC v. Texas Gulf Sulphur Co. 54, 214, 336
SEC v. Thrasher 356
SEC v. W. J. Howey Co. **98**, 118
SEC v. Wheeling-Pittsburgh Steel Corp. 788
SEC v. Zandford **211**
Semerenko v. Cendant Corp. 214
Slayton v. American Exp. Co. 245
Smith v. Ayres 210
Smolowe v. Delendo Corp. 391
Southland Sec. Corp. INSpire Ins. Solutions, Inc. 257
Stoneridge Investment Partners, LLC v. Scientific-Atlanta, Inc. **291**
Strong v. Repide **331**
Studebaker Corp. v. Gittlin 689
Tarallo, United States v. **819**
Teachers' Retirement System of Louisiana v. Hunter 288
Tellabs, Inc. v. Makor Issues & Rights, Ltd. **251**
Time Warner Inc. Sec. Litig., In re 238
TSC Industries, Inc. v. Northway 48, 51, 55, 76, 235
Tully v. Mott Supermarkets, Inc. 210
United Housing Foundation, Inc. v. Forman **115**
UnitedHealth Group Incorporated PSLRA Litigation, In re 226
Vaughn v. Teledyne, Inc. 235
Virginia Bankshares, Inc. v. Sandberg **232**, 481, 693
W. R. Grace & Co.. In the Matter of **729**
Walton v. Morgan Stanley & Co. 348
Warfield v. Alaniz **125**

Washington Public Power Supply System Securities Litigation, In re **768**
Wharf (Holdings) Limited v. United International Holdings 232
Wiest v. Lynch **757**
Williams Securities Litigation-WCG Subclass, In re 288
Williamson v. Tucker 132
Wolfson, United States v. **654**
WorldCom, Inc. Securities Litigation, In re **501**, 542
Zucco Partners, LLC v. Digimarc Corp. 256

UNIVERSITY CASEBOOK SERIES®

SECURITIES REGULATION

CASES AND ANALYSIS

FOURTH EDITION

CHAPTER 1

INTRODUCTION TO THE SECURITIES MARKETS AND SECURITIES REGULATION

MOTIVATING HYPOTHETICAL

Twenty-Four Security Inc. is a nationwide provider of corporate and personal security services. Jack, a former government agent, is the CEO of Twenty-Four. Twenty-Four has $10 billion in common stock publicly traded on the New York Stock Exchange (NYSE). Twenty-Four's common stock currently trades at a price of $50 per share. Several "sell-side" analysts working for various investment banks distribute regular opinions on Twenty-Four; most rate Twenty-Four a "Buy." Chloe, a student residing in New York, is considering whether to use $100,000 she recently inherited to purchase Twenty-Four shares through her broker, who will execute the transaction through the NYSE.

I. THE BASICS

Congress enacted the federal securities laws in the 1930s in the midst of the Great Depression. Congress' primary goal was to protect investors who were considering putting capital into the country's financial markets from abuses by company insiders and market professionals. A secondary goal was to discourage speculative frenzies among investors tempted to chase after the next big thing. The securities laws seek to protect investors by encouraging full disclosure and deterring fraud.

The federal securities laws regulate transactions involving financial instruments falling within the definition of a "security." The most prevalent types of securities include common stock, preferred stock, and bonds.

Securities transactions can be divided into two basic categories. In a "primary" transaction, a company (the "issuer") offers and sells its own securities to investors, taking the proceeds into the issuer's coffers. In a "secondary" transaction, one investor resells securities of the issuer to another investor. The issuer does not participate in the transaction. Instead, the buying investor transfers money to the selling investor. If Chloe purchases Twenty-Four Security shares through a broker who executes the transaction on the NYSE, she will purchase the shares from another investor; no money goes to Twenty-Four Security.

In securities transactions, information translates into money. Investors with an informational advantage (such as insiders of a company) can earn systematically higher returns from their trades with uninformed investors. Jack, the CEO of Twenty-Four Security, will have access to non-public information on Twenty-Four's finances,

[handwritten margin note: Goals: (1) encourage capital investment (2) discourage speculative frenzies]

1

strategic plans, and merger and acquisition opportunities. Left unregulated, Jack could buy Twenty-Four stock when the market undervalues the stock and sell stock when it is overvalued. Jack's trading advantage, however, corresponds to an informational disadvantage for Chloe, the outside investor. Any gains that Jack makes from trading come dollar-for-dollar at the expense of investors like Chloe.

The U.S. securities regime requires disclosure by those with an advantage in the markets, including, among others, insiders of corporations. The two most important federal securities laws are the Securities Act of 1933 ("Securities Act"; practitioners sometimes call it the " '33 Act") and the Securities Exchange Act of 1934 ("Exchange Act"; sometimes called the " '34 Act"). These statutes will be our main focus in this book. The Securities Act focuses on primary transactions by an issuing company selling securities to investors. The Exchange Act deals with secondary transactions between two investors in the marketplace; it also regulates securities market intermediaries, including broker-dealers and the securities exchanges. To assist in the protection of investors and the capital markets, Congress also established the Securities and Exchange Commission (SEC) when it enacted the Exchange Act. The SEC, an independent administrative agency, adopts regulations to interpret and implement the securities laws passed by Congress and also enforces those statutes and regulations.

Before exploring the federal securities laws, we first outline the most common types of securities and the markets in which investors buy and sell these securities. We then ask why people invest in securities rather than other forms of saving. Finally, we focus on valuation. At the right price almost any investment becomes attractive to investors. What determines the price an investor is willing to pay for a particular investment? What information does an investor need to calculate this price?

II. TYPES OF SECURITIES

Which investment? An investor can put money into a bank account. The investor could invest in real estate, speculating that the price of land will rise. Or, the investor may purchase publicly traded stocks or bonds in the capital markets. Securities regulation covers only a subset of available investments.

We leave the definition of a security to a more detailed analysis in Chapter 3. Some investments, however, clearly qualify. The most common form of securities investments are interests in a corporate entity. Corporations are legal entities created under state law. Most public corporations choose Delaware as their state of incorporation. Under Delaware corporate law, corporations have great flexibility in issuing different ownership interests in the corporation, including common stock, preferred stock and bonds.

How do these varying ownership interests differ? Ownership encompasses several different attributes, including rights to: 1) cash flows, 2) assets in liquidation, and 3) voting power. The last of these rights allows shareholders to elect the corporate board of directors, among other things. The diverse forms of ownership interests in a corporation allow investors to obtain different "bundles" of these rights.

Corporations enjoy great latitude in altering the general packages of rights for the different classes of securities. Nonetheless, the three basic types of securities—common, preferred, and debt—have typical characteristics as summarized in the table below.

Type of Security	Cash Flow Rights	Liquidation Rights	Voting Rights
Common	Residual and discretionary dividend	Residual and discretionary dividend	Yes
Preferred	Fixed and discretionary dividend	Medium	Contingent (e.g., if dividend not paid for certain number of quarters)
Debt	Fixed and certain interest payment	Highest	None

A. COMMON STOCK

Common stockholders enjoy no fixed monetary claim on a corporation's cash flow. Instead, common stock is "residual"—owners of common stock receive a share of corporate profits only after all other claims are satisfied (i.e., the claims of debt and preferred stockholders). Corporations may distribute profits to shareholders either by issuing dividends or by repurchasing stock from the shareholders. (Less commonly, they can also distribute assets to shareholders in liquidation.) Dividends, if declared by the board, must be distributed pro rata among a given class of shares. Stock repurchases, however, may occur through private negotiation, open market transactions, or, if for a larger number of shares, through a repurchase tender offer. Among these, only tender offers must be pro rata.

Not only are the returns to common stockholders residual, corporations are not obliged to distribute any money to their common stockholders. They can choose to keep residual returns inside the corporation's coffers as retained shareholder earnings. Distributions to common stockholders are at the board of directors' discretion. Under state corporate law, the board of directors owes fiduciary duties of loyalty and care to the common shareholders. Such duties provide a (weak) legal impetus for the board to declare a dividend if the corporation has no better use for the capital. Of course, dividends are not always in the best interests of the shareholders. Corporations with valuable investment projects that will pay off in the future may reinvest rather than paying dividends. The business judgment rule ordinarily protects a board's decision not to declare a dividend.

An interest in the residual profits of a corporation (even if distribution is discretionary) can prove quite valuable for common stockholders. Consider those who purchased common stock offered by Microsoft in its initial public offering (IPO) in 1986. An investor who purchased one share of Microsoft common (ticker: MSFT) at the IPO price of $21 per share and held onto those shares would have Microsoft shares, after nine Microsoft share splits, worth over $12,500 as of late 2014. State corporate law also gives common shareholders voting control over the corporation. Common shareholders typically receive most, if not all, of the votes to elect the board of directors. In theory, if shareholders are unhappy with a corporation's dividend policy, they can elect more generous directors. But directors can generally rely on the passivity of dispersed public shareholders; their positions are relatively secure in most public corporations.

Tax consequences also affect dividend decisions. Because publicly traded corporations pay taxes on their income, the tax on dividends represents a second tax on the same income. Until recently, corporations (with shareholders' tacit approval) would avoid the double tax by retaining earnings, eschewing dividend payments. In 2003, Congress lowered the maximum tax rate on dividends to 15% (down from the maximum ordinary income rate at the time of 38.6%), prompting many companies to begin paying dividends. Microsoft, which in the early 2000s had cash holdings of over $40 billion, began paying dividends to its shareholders in 2003 and declared a special dividend totaling $32 billion to its shareholders in 2004. In 2010, the tax on dividends was increased to 20% for some taxpayers.

Finally, common stockholders have the lowest priority claim on corporate assets in liquidation. Companies facing liquidation pay out assets according to the absolute priority rule, which puts common stockholders last among the holders of a corporation's securities. In a corporation, debtholders typically come first, receiving any assets in liquidation, up to the principal amount and unpaid interest, before common shareholders receive anything. (There is also a priority among debt holders, with secured creditors, who hold liens on specific assets, such as a drill press or a parcel of real property, getting paid first.) Preferred shares, discussed below, typically come second. The absolute priority rule stipulates that only after the contracted-for claims of debt holders and preferred shareholders are satisfied will common shareholders receive anything in liquidation. Courts sometimes deviate, however, from the absolute priority rule. Particularly in Chapter 11 bankruptcy reorganizations, shareholders may bargain for claims on the corporation's assets that would otherwise go to pay more senior securities holders. If you want to know more about bankruptcy you need to take a course in corporate reorganizations (highly recommended).

B. PREFERRED STOCK

Many corporations only have one class of equity securities: common stock. Some corporations, however, will issue another, more senior class of equity securities, generally referred to as "preferred" stock. State corporate law does not specify the characteristics of preferred stock. Indeed, many corporations will call securities with characteristics similar to preferred stock by a different name (e.g., Class A common stock or some other variant). Because the rights of preferred stock are negotiated between specific investors and corporations, preferred stocks vary greatly in their terms.

Why do some corporations issue preferred stock while others do not? Corporations typically issue preferred stock in two situations. First, relatively new startup companies will often issue preferred stock to outside investors providing capital. During the late 1990s, many would-be entrepreneurs started companies to sell dog food, books, pharmaceuticals, and a whole host of other products and services over the Internet. At the time, many of these companies seemed promising but highly risky. The Internet provided the entrepreneurs with a vast new commercial space in which to compete. That promise lured many aspiring entrepreneurs to start companies in their garages or bedrooms. To compete effectively and grab market share quickly, however, the Internet startup companies needed large and quick infusions of capital. Although some entrepreneurs provided significant financial resources out of their own pockets, many did not have the millions of dollars necessary to expand a business rapidly.

Outside investors provide a solution for the cash-strapped Internet entrepreneurs, with venture capital firms the primary source. Venture capital firms solicit funds from other investors (which the venture capitalists typically pool into a particular venture fund) and re-invest those funds into mid- and late-stage (i.e., almost ready to go public) startup companies. Venture capital firms specialize in identifying promising startup companies. After an investment is made, venture capital firms also provide management advice and business contacts for the startup companies (with potential suppliers, customers, employees, etc.). To ensure some degree of control over the direction of the company venture capital firms often obtain seats on the boards of directors of the startup companies, sometimes even a majority position.

Venture capital firms making an investment in a startup company often structure the investment as preferred stock. Investing in preferred stock gives a venture capital firm some reassurance that if the high-risk startup company performs poorly, the venture capital firm will have the ability to receive at least some of the money back before the entrepreneurs—who typically hold common stock—receive anything. In addition, preferred stock gives the venture capitalists some upside return, albeit not as great as common stock, if the startup does well. Preferred stock issued to venture capital firms frequently carries the right to convert into common stock (at a predetermined price) "convertible preferred." Convertibility allows the venture capitalist to share in the upside of the startup if it does an initial public offering (IPO). Although the dividend for preferred shares is fixed and more certain than the dividend for common shares, the residual dividend interest of common shares may be more valuable under certain circumstances. For example, imagine a company that has two classes of shares: common and preferred stock, with the preferred paying a fixed dividend of $1 per share. If the corporation earns $100 per share of common stock in net earnings per year (after the preferred shares are paid their dividends), the common stock is a much more valuable interest in the company. A conversion feature allows preferred stockholders to share in the greater financial interest by converting their preferred stock into common stock.

Preferred stock is also used by older, more established companies that need an infusion of cash. Warren Buffett, one of the most successful investors of recent times, specializes in finding undervalued companies and making a relatively large investment in them, sometimes even purchasing the entire company. Buffett (through his investment vehicle Berkshire Hathaway) has purchased, among other companies, GEICO Insurance and Dairy Queen. If Warren Buffett does not buy an entire company, he often takes a large position by investing in preferred stock. Investing in preferred stock provides Buffett with some reassurance of getting paid back his investment (it has priority over common stock) while allowing Buffett to share in much of the upside if the company does well. The usual reason an established company needs an infusion of cash—the company is in trouble—makes the reassurance provided by holding preferred stock particularly valuable.

For example, in 1989, Buffett injected $358 million into USAir in return for 9.25% of its preferred stock. Buffett hoped that the ownership of a "senior" security with a provision for dividends paid at 9.25% annually would protect him against the risks involved with investing in USAir at the time. Although the 9.25% dividend payment was not mandatory (but simply cumulated if not paid), Buffett extracted a penalty clause providing for an increased dividend (raising the dividend payment rate to between 13.25% and 14%) if the dividend was not paid when due. When USAir eventually ran into financial difficulties in the early 1990s, Berkshire Hathaway was able to collect hundreds of millions of dollars in dividends over the time period as a result of its preferred stock investment.

Why is preferred stock "preferred"? First, consider the rights to a corporation's ongoing cash flows. Common stockholders have no absolute right to cash flows, instead depending on the discretion of the board of directors to declare a dividend or stock repurchase. Common stockholders, nonetheless, may rely on the directors' fiduciary obligations to induce them to at least consider the common stockholders' interests. Preferred stockholders, like holders of corporate debt, generally enjoy no such open-ended fiduciary duty protection; they must look instead to their preferred stock contract to protect their rights. (Fiduciary duties may, however, fill in the interstices of these contractual rights.)

With respect to ongoing cash flows, preferred stock does not receive interest from the corporation, but instead is entitled to a "fixed" dividend payment. As with common stock, preferred stock gives corporations flexibility in determining the best use of scarce resources. Without the protection of fiduciary duties, preferred stock contracts typically will specify that the fixed dividend owed to preferred stockholders must be paid before common stockholders receive dividends. Moreover, any unpaid preferred stock dividends typically "cumulate" over time, meaning all arrearages must be paid before common shareholders receive any dividend. As with Berkshire Hathaway's preferred stock contract with USAir, the amount of the dividend may increase due to a penalty provision for missed dividend payments.

In liquidation, preferred stock comes before common stock. Preferred stock contracts typically specify that preferred stockholders receive any cumulated, unpaid dividends in addition to a contracted-for share of any remaining assets before common stockholders receive any payment in liquidation. Unlike common stock, preferred stock generally does not come with voting rights. As with most other aspects of securities, however, corporations and investors can tailor different packages of rights to meet their needs. Usually, preferred stock contracts will provide that if dividends to the preferred stockholders are missed for a certain number of quarters (typically two or three), then preferred stockholders will receive some voting rights to elect the board of directors. Alternatively, preferred stock contracts may specify that the preferred stockholders have the power to elect some fraction of the board of directors (e.g., two directors out of seven).

Not all preferred shares provide for dividends that cumulate if not paid (referred to a non-cumulative preferred). For such non-cumulative preferred shares, the board of directors does not need to pay all arrearages before paying a dividend to common shareholders. Some investors may negotiate for a fixed term after which the corporation must redeem the preferred shares at an agreed upon price—often set at the purchase price plus any accrued dividends if cumulative. Preferred shares without a fixed term are referred to as perpetual preferred. Banks that issue perpetual, non-cumulative, and non-convertible preferred shares may use capital obtained from the issuance as "Tier 1" capital to meet certain capital requirements under the U.S. banking laws.

C. BONDS

Bonds are a loan by investors to the corporation. Bonds may take many different forms in the public capital markets, including notes (typically shorter-term debt of a maturity period less than ten years) and indentures (longer-term bonds). The initial investment an investor makes in a bond is known as the principal amount. Unlike equity, bonds have a fixed term and the principal invested is repaid at a specified maturity date. Corporations owe bondholders fixed and certain periodic interest payments until the maturity date of the bond.

Not all bonds pay periodic interest. Zero coupon bonds pay no interest. Instead, they are sold at a discount relative to the principal amount of the bond. At the end of the maturity, the bondholders receive the full principal amount. The value of the bonds grows from the initial, discounted purchase price to the end principal payment, thereby providing an implicit interest payment equal to the growth in value of the principal amount of the bond over time. Zero coupon bonds afford issuers financial flexibility because they do not require yearly interest payments. Instead, the full amount of implicit interest—along with the principal invested—is due at the maturity date of the bond.

As a debt instrument, bonds provide investors with greater financial security than equity investments (i.e., common and preferred stock). As noted above, bondholders enjoy priority over equity in the case of liquidation. Bonds may also vary in their priority position with respect to other debt of the same issuer. Corporations may issue "senior" bonds that receive priority in payments over junior bonds. Some bondholders may also obtain a security interest in a specific asset of the corporation, providing even greater security (up to the value of the encumbered asset) for the repayment of the debt.

In theory, bondholders must all receive their principal amount as well as any interest payments owed before equity receives even a penny in liquidation. In practice, the federal bankruptcy regime furnishes a mechanism for equity to be paid even if debt is not fully paid off, a limited evasion of the absolute priority rule. Even if the absolute priority rule is followed, priority does not help bondholders if the company has insufficient assets. To avoid this unpleasant situation, bondholders protect themselves through contract. Bond covenants typically include a number of provisions to ensure that the corporation will maintain an adequate equity "cushion" to make the periodic interest payments and cover the principal owed on the bonds. Such provisions are all negotiated and therefore vary across different bonds. Typical covenants include restrictions on the ability of the corporation to pay dividends to its shareholders, sell specific assets, or exceed a specified debt-equity ratio.

A key advantage of raising capital by selling bonds is the interest deduction for federal income tax purposes. The corporation deducts from their taxable income any interest paid to the bondholders (including imputed interest for zero coupon bonds). Corporations receive no interest deduction for dividends paid to common or preferred stockholders.

As with preferred stock, the market has spawned a diverse range of bonds. In addition to zero coupon bonds, some issuers have sold perpetual bonds with no fixed maturity date to investors. Perpetual bonds provide an interest payment and are typically subordinated to other debt issued by a corporation. Depending on the specific agreement between issuer and investors, some perpetual bonds allow for cumulative interest payments (allowing the corporation to skip an interest payment, accruing the amount for later payment) and non-cumulative interest payment (allowing the corporation to skip an interest payment altogether). Not everything is up to contract. Although perpetual debt may in theory qualify an issuer for an interest deduction, issuers of perpetual debt run the risk of the IRS recharacterizing the debt as equity.

III. THE CAPITAL MARKET

Securities are bought and sold in diverse venues. A shareholder of Twenty-Four may sell the stock to her neighbor. To close the deal, the owner may transfer the stock certificates in Twenty-Four to the neighbor in exchange for cash in a face-to-face transaction.

Individually negotiated deals of this sort are unusual; most securities transactions take place through organized markets with the assistance of professional securities market intermediaries (i.e., broker-dealers). What advantages do organized markets and professional intermediaries provide to investors looking to buy or sell?

Organized markets provide investors with liquidity and transparency. Without an organized marketplace, individual investors wanting to sell a security may spend a lot of time and money finding an investor willing to purchase the security. Even if the selling investor locates a potential purchaser, the seller has no assurance that he is receiving the best price for the securities (and vice versa). In an organized market, a selling investor can quickly find investors to purchase his securities. Intermediaries may also assist in creating liquidity, standing in to purchase or sell securities when other investors are unwilling to do so. Information on the trades (and offers) of other investors also flows more easily in an organized market, providing transparency. Transparency allows investors to determine the best available prices for their desired transactions.

As noted above, securities regulation divides securities market transactions into two basic types. We explain the differences between these two markets here.

A. PRIMARY TRANSACTIONS

Primary transactions range from large multi-country offerings raising billions of dollars to smaller deals for a million dollars or less taking place solely in the United States. Companies typically turn to the capital markets when they need a large amount of money to finance a promising business project.

Large, well-established companies such as Apple often have a number of different sources of capital. Apple has enormous cash reserves built up over the years from its highly profitable iEverything business. Successful, established businesses generally do not need to access the public capital markets to finance new lines of business. Less established companies, such as Twenty-Four, must issue securities to the public capital markets if they need substantial capital to exploit growth opportunities.

Although issuers can sell securities directly to investors without the assistance of a financial institution, such offerings are rare (and typically are done as "rights" offerings to an issuer's pre-existing shareholders rather than to the general public). Instead, issuers rely on intermediaries—salespeople—to facilitate a large offering of securities. Those intermediaries—Wall Street—play a major role in both the primary and secondary market. Although we discuss the public offering process more fully in Chapter 7, we briefly describe the major players below.

Investment Banks. Investment banks help issuers offering and selling securities in most public offerings in the United States. The investment banks provide advice and financial expertise, particularly for companies selling securities to the public for the first time. In addition, investment banks frequently take on an underwriting role, assuming the financial risk that investors will not purchase the offering. In a firm commitment offering, for example, a syndicate of underwriters will purchase securities at a discount from the issuer. The underwriters then bear the full risk of being able to sell the offering to the public. The underwriters are compensated for this risk by the "spread," the difference between the discounted price they pay the issuer and the price paid by the investing public.

The structure of the investment banking business changed radically as a result of the financial crisis of 2008–2009 (the Financial Crisis). During the Financial Crisis, several major Wall Street financial firms failed, including Bear Stearns, Merrill Lynch, and Lehman Brothers. Major securities houses, such as Goldman Sachs and Morgan Stanley, converted into bank holding companies to qualify for assistance from the Federal Reserve. These bank holding companies continue to provide investment banking services. In addition, more traditional commercial banks, such as Citigroup and JPMorgan Chase, also play an increasingly important role as investment bankers in securities transactions.

Attorneys. Attorneys are ubiquitous in commercial transactions. (Good news for your career prospects!) For securities offerings, a specialized set of law firms routinely assists both issuers and investment banks in complying with the regulatory requirement for a public offering. These firms include Cravath, Swaine & Moore, Cleary Gottlieb, and Sullivan & Cromwell, among other major New York City-based law firms. The attorneys for the issuer will typically take the lead role in drafting disclosures to be filed with the SEC.

Accounting Firms. The value of an investment is determined by its expected return in the future. That return depends on the future financial performance of the business: greater future profits translate into greater returns for the investor. Past financial performance, however, can provide investors with an important glimpse into a company's financial future. Companies with fast growth in sales may be more likely to experience future growth. Companies with declining profit margins and stagnant or declining sales, in contrast, may be less promising for investors.

The importance of past financial performance in determining the value of an investment means that investors may be misled if historical financial information is inaccurate. Unscrupulous management may "cook the books" and falsify financial numbers. If sales were only $10 million for the prior quarter, a manager may make the company look better in the eyes of investors by inflating this number to $20 million with a couple of keystrokes on her computer.

Investors, however, are aware of the risk of the fraud. If investors realize that managers may falsify financial numbers, the investors will lose confidence in the reported numbers and demand a large discount when investing. Audited financial statements provide one way for companies to convince investors of the veracity of their financial disclosures. Accounting firms such as the "Big Four" of Deloitte Touche Tohmatsu, Ernst & Young, KPMG, and PricewaterhouseCoopers, provide such auditing services, as do smaller firms.

Public accounting firms rely in part on their longstanding reputations for honesty and accuracy to convince investors to accept audited financials as truthful. An accounting firm with a better reputation can attract more clients and charge higher fees. Thus, accounting firms have a strong incentive to maintain their reputations. Audits, however, are not foolproof. If the audit partner in charge cuts corners or succumbs to pressure from company management to certify falsified financials, investors will receive inaccurate information. The collapse of Arthur Andersen—formerly a "Big Five" accounting firm— was in large part due to the acquiescence of the lead Arthur Andersen partner in Enron's financial shenanigans. The subsequent criminal prosecution of Arthur Andersen for obstructing the SEC's investigation into the fall of Enron led to that firm's demise. In response, Congress enacted the Sarbanes-Oxley Act of 2002, which provided, among other things, for extensive reforms of the oversight of public company auditors in the United States (a topic we cover in Chapter 12).

Institutional Investors. Institutional investors dominate today's securities markets. Significant institutional investors include pension funds and insurance companies. Mutual funds aggregate the investment money of many smaller investors and reinvest the funds in securities. Mutual funds have two primary styles for allocating their investment dollars. Index funds allocate investors' dollars to a defined broad-based basket of securities. An S & P 500 index fund, for example, invests in a value-weighted basket of companies comprising the S & P list of America's 500 biggest companies. (This casebook's authors are long-term investors in index funds.) Actively managed funds, in contrast, research (at some cost) various investment opportunities. Although active management in theory may result in better investment opportunities, investors must pay for the privilege of active management, typically bearing much higher fund expenses than investors in index funds. The available research suggests that these greater fund expenses cause the average actively-managed fund to trail both the overall market and index funds (which generally aspire only to match the market return).

The presence of institutional investors as purchasers in the primary offering market has two countervailing consequences for the regulation of public offerings. On the one hand, institutional investors are sophisticated investors who may require less protection. On the other hand, institutional investors may cut "sweetheart" deals for themselves with issuers or underwriters. At various points in the book, we will see regulatory schemes intended to protect small investors from the big players.

B. SECONDARY TRANSACTIONS

The secondary market is closely linked to the primary market. An active secondary market allows investors to resell securities both quickly and at low cost. These aspects of a market are referred to as liquidity. Investors also favor markets with good price transparency, in which the market price will reflect the best available price for a particular security. Investors who can rely on a liquid and transparent secondary market in which to resell their securities will be more willing to purchase securities from issuers in the primary market. Without the prospect of a strong secondary market, issuers face considerable difficulty in selling securities to investors, who will demand a substantial "illiquidity" discount.

Secondary transactions between investors take place in several different venues. Some secondary transactions are negotiated one-on-one. Larger institutional investors in particular may sell and purchase large numbers of shares through a negotiated deal, called a block transaction. Smaller investors will use brokers to execute their transactions. Among large brokerage firms dealing with individual investors are Merrill Lynch (now a subsidiary of Bank of America), Charles Schwab, and E*TRADE.

There are two common types of orders in secondary markets. First, investors may place a "market" order, indicating the investor would like to purchase a specified number of shares in a company at the best available market price. Second, investors may place a "limit" order. An investor placing a limit order specifies both the number of shares as well as the limit price. Brokers are instructed not to execute the limit order until the market price reaches (or is better than) the specified limit price. Chloe, for example, could specify that she would like to purchase 1,000 shares of Twenty-Four at a price of $18 per share. Suppose the current market price of Twenty-Four is $20 per share. Chloe's order will not be executed until Twenty-Four's price falls to $18 or lower.

When a broker receives an order from a customer, the broker may attempt to match a particular trade order with trade orders submitted by the brokers' other customers. If the broker cannot make an internal match, the broker will route the order to some trading forum for execution. The three primary forms of securities markets include (1) the traditional securities exchanges, (2) Nasdaq, and (3) alternative trading systems (ATS).

1. TRADITIONAL SECURITIES EXCHANGES

The most prominent of the traditional securities exchanges is the New York Stock Exchange (NYSE). There are other securities exchanges, including the Boston Stock Exchange, the Pacific Stock Exchange, and the Philadelphia Stock Exchange. Major stock exchanges outside the United States include the London Stock Exchange, the Deutsche Bourse, and the Tokyo Stock Exchange. Securities of large, multinational companies sometimes trade in more than one securities market. Over the past decade, several major exchanges merged together. The NYSE merged with Euronext, N.V. (a European stock exchange itself formed from the merger of the Amsterdam Stock Exchange, Brussels Stock Exchange, and Paris Bourse) in 2007. Continuing the trend of consolidation, the combined entity, known as NYSE Euronext, was subsequently acquired by Intercontinental Exchange Group, Inc. in 2013.

Organized securities exchanges have historically had a physical trading floor. Although investors typically cannot interact with others directly on the trading floor of an exchange, they may do so through brokers. Trades routed to the NYSE that are not completed by the NYSE's electronic order system end up in the hands of a broker working on the trading floor at the NYSE (known as a "floor broker") for execution. Approximately 100 floor broker firms operate on the NYSE trading floor, although the number is declining as more trades are executed electronically.

Floor brokers have several options in executing their customers' trades. The NYSE maintains twenty trading posts, each manned by a specialist. A particular traded security is assigned one specialist and one trading post. Floor brokers interested in trading the security congregate around the trading post where they can obtain continuous information on the latest transaction price in the security. Floor brokers may execute trades with other brokers on the floor seeking to make the opposite transaction.

The specialist for a particular stock plays a central role in maintaining liquidity for that stock. Instead of executing an order themselves, floor brokers may employ the specialist as an agent. The specialist maintains a limit order book, listing various limit orders received from floor brokers, which consist of a desired quantity and price for the purchase or sale of a security. As the market price moves to a particular limit price, the specialist will assist in the execution of these limit orders, matching together customer orders. The specialist also maintains its own inventory of stock. When short-term imbalances result in insufficient trade volume to match opposing trades, the NYSE requires specialists to maintain liquidity by trading their own inventory in that security. The specialist must sell when other investors are unwilling to sell and must buy when other investors are unwilling to buy. Adjusting prices to correct these imbalances of supply and demand is the specialist's primary task.

2.   THE NASDAQ MARKET

Most securities transactions do not take place on a trading floor. Instead, the function of bringing together potential buyers and sellers occurs through electronic communications. The longest standing of these electronic markets is the Nasdaq market. The Nasdaq is actually three markets—the Global Select Market, the Global Market, and the Capital Market. The three tiers differ in their listing requirements, with the Global Select the most demanding. In 2006, the SEC approved Nasdaq as a national securities exchange.

Nasdaq encompasses an electronic network linking together dealers in a particular security. Such dealers, known as "market makers," hold themselves out as continuously willing to both purchase and sell a particular security—for their own account—at publicly quoted prices. For example, a market maker may hold itself out as continuously willing to purchase a block of 100 shares of Twenty-Four common stock at $19.95 per share (the bid price) and to sell 100 shares at $20.05 per share (the ask price). If Twenty-Four's shares are in fact worth $20 per share, the market maker earns a return on the ten-cent bid-ask spread between the two prices as depicted below:

$20.05 (Ask Price)

[10-cent bid-ask spread]

$19.95 (Bid Price)

Market makers do not know whether investors will accept the market makers' two-sided buy-sell quotation. If the market maker guesses wrong (e.g., sets the bid and ask prices too high), it may just get investors selling securities to the market maker (at the high price) but no investors buying. The bid-ask spread compensates the market maker for providing liquidity and bearing the risk that more informed investors in the market may take advantage of the market maker (e.g., by selling shares to the market maker when the market maker sets its bid price too high).

Several different market makers may quote prices for any one Nasdaq-listed security. Competition among these market makers helps to narrow the bid-ask spread, thereby reducing investors' trading costs. In contrast to the traditional securities exchanges, investors seeking to transact in a Nasdaq security typically deal (through their brokers) with a market maker instead of an investor seeking to make the opposite transaction. Imagine, for example, that four market makers deal in Twenty-Four's shares: Goldman Sachs (GSCO), Merrill Lynch (MLCO), Morgan Stanley (MSCO), and Rodman & Renshaw (RODM). A typical display of the available bid and ask quotes from the market makers for Twenty-Four's shares on a Nasdaq Level II Workstation will look something like this:

	Bid			Offer	
Dealer	Quantity	Price	Dealer	Quantity	Price
GSCO	20	19.90	MLCO	10	20.10
MSCO	10	19.86	MSCO	40	20.25
RODM	30	19.72	GSCO	10	20.32
MLCO	10	19.51	SBSH	20	20.42

The Nasdaq Level II Workstation will also display the last transaction price as well as "inside" bid (i.e., the highest offer to purchase price) and ask prices (i.e., the lowest offer to sell price). A list of past transactions, prices and quantities for the stock is also provided to give traders a sense of the market's "direction." The bid and ask prices and quantities displayed in the Workstation frequently change as market makers react to information about the company, its industry and the overall economy, as well as the flow of transactions. Although Goldman Sachs has the highest bid price in the above example, Morgan Stanley can easily occupy this position by increasing its bid price up to $19.95. It might do so, for example, in reaction to news that Twenty-Four's sales are going better than expected.

The NYSE and Nasdaq are the largest markets for secondary transactions in the United States. In September 2014, the average daily trading NYSE Group volume for NYSE listed firms was 1.03 billion shares (totaling to $40.9 billion average daily dollar volume). NYSEData.com Factbook (located at http://www.nyxdata.com/factbook). While the NYSE was the largest market in terms of share and dollar volume for decades, the Nasdaq has recently surpassed the NYSE. In September 2014, the average daily trading volume for the Nasdaq was 1.89 billion shares (totaling to $71.6 billion average daily dollar volume). NASDAQ Market Statistics (located at http://www.nasdaq trader.com). The NYSE remains the clear leader in terms of overall market valuation. In September 2014, the NYSE had a total domestic market capitalization of $18.8 trillion while Nasdaq had total domestic market capitalization of $6.7 trillion. Both Nasdaq and the NYSE enjoy trading volumes far greater than other exchanges in the United States.

The NYSE is not only the largest securities market in the United States in terms of market value, it also regulates securities transactions, as does the Nasdaq. As self-regulatory organizations (SROs), the NYSE and Nasdaq impose various requirements on listed companies. In addition to minimum capitalization requirements, the NYSE and Nasdaq require that listed companies have a board of directors consisting of a majority of independent directors. The NYSE and Nasdaq also provide active monitoring for securities law violations in their respective markets. Broker-dealers are overseen by the Financial Industry Regulatory Authority (FINRA). Beginning in 2010, FINRA assumed regulatory responsibility for the market surveillance and enforcement functions previously conducted by NYSE Regulation. The SEC oversees NYSE, Nasdaq, and FINRA regulation to ensure that these SROs are enforcing the securities laws and protecting investors.

3. ALTERNATIVE TRADING SYSTEMS

New electronic markets have emerged to compete with the Nasdaq and NYSE, commonly referred to as alternative trading systems (ATSs). ATSs eliminate any third-party intermediary between potential buyers and sellers of a security, such as market makers in the Nasdaq market. Among major ATSs that operated in the United States from the 1990s into the 2000s were Archipelago, Bloomberg Tradebook, and Brut. The NYSE eventually acquired Archipelago (now known as NYSE Arca, a part of IntercontinentalExchange) and Nasdaq acquired Brut.

In a typical ATS, an investor first places a limit order, indicating the price and quantity of the security in which the investor wishes to transact. Suppose Chloe wishes to purchase 100 shares of Twenty-Four at $20 per share. Upon receiving Chloe's order, the ATS will scan all of its existing limit orders from investors until it finds an investor who wants to sell 100 shares of Twenty-Four at $20 per share (or less) and matches the two investors, executing a trade. If more than one seller will take $20 per share, then the seller with the lowest price (and, if tied on price, the earlier posted time) is matched with Chloe. If no such seller exists, then the ATS will record Chloe's order in a limit order book until a matching order is received. Chloe may also cancel her order at any time.

IV. INVESTMENT DECISIONS

Investors purchase securities for a variety of reasons. Some investors may buy the stock of a company because they like the company's products. An investor may buy Disney stock because he is a big fan of Tigger. Most investors, however, make investments in order to receive even more money in the future. An investor, for example, may use $100 to purchase the stock of a company only because she believes that the stock will return a total of $110 next year through a combination of dividends and capital appreciation.

How much should an investor pay for a given investment? In some cases, the answer is straightforward. Consider how much you would pay if someone offered you an investment that "returned" $10 today (e.g., they want to sell you a $10 bill). Most rational people would not pay more than $10 for the $10 bill. In a competitive marketplace, purchasers bidding against one another will drive up the price of the $10 bill to exactly $10.

This trivial example provides a useful starting point for identifying the information that investors want. Why is it so easy to value a $10 bill? The return from the investment is certain, $10. Also, the investor receives the $10 immediately. How do other investments differ from the $10 bill? Most investments are uncertain in their expected return and will pay off only in the future. Everyone knows that a $10 bill is worth $10. But what is the expected payoff from an investment in the common stock of Twenty-Four Security?

Investors must make their best estimate of the expected return from an investment. How does an investor compare a certain amount of money today with an uncertain return of money sometime in the future? That is the essence of the investment decision. The most common financial technique used in this task is to reduce the expected return from an investment to its "present discount value" (PDV) in today's dollars. Investors can then compare an investment return's PDV with the required upfront investment to decide whether the investment is worthwhile. We begin our discussion of the valuation of securities by showing how to calculate present discount value.

A. PRESENT DISCOUNT VALUATION

Money tomorrow is worth less than the same dollar amount of money today. At the very least, an investor may take a dollar and simply put it into a bank savings account to generate more money in the future. One dollar today, when invested in a savings account at a simple interest rate of 2% per year, will grow to $1.02 in a year's time.

1. INTEREST

Why do banks pay a positive interest rate for the privilege of obtaining a depositor's money today? First, people are impatient. Most people would rather consume the same quantity and quality of a particular good today than wait until the future, all other things being equal. In the extreme, consider whether you would rather have $1,000 today or $1,000 one hundred years from now. Part of our impatience is due to the risk to our ability to consume posed by death. You can't take it with you. Although some care about future generations, most people appear to expect their descendants to fend for themselves.

Second, inflation can erode the purchasing power of cash. Cash, in and of itself, provides no direct value: What can you actually *do* with a $10 bill? Instead, money is valuable because it serves as a common unit of exchange in a market-based economy. The U.S. Treasury can alter the amount of cash in the economy simply by printing more bills. Doubling the money supply, all other things being equal, simply halves the purchasing power of a dollar. Although a nominal $1 today will still be worth $1 tomorrow, you will be able to purchase fewer goods and services tomorrow due to inflation.

Finally, a dollar in the hands of an investor today is certain. The investor can choose to spend the dollar or invest it. In contrast, money promised for some time in the future presents the risk that the investor may not in fact receive the full (or any) return. Banks may fail (although FDIC insurance minimizes this risk for the average depositor). Companies may go bankrupt. Investors, therefore, must factor in the risk of failure when valuing an investment. To induce investors to part with the sure thing represented by money today for the uncertain promise of money tomorrow, companies must compensate investors in the form of a higher promised return than they can expect from investments with less risk. If an investor can put money into a relatively safe savings account and receive a 2% annual return, the investor may invest in a risky corporate venture only if promised a 5% return.

2. PRESENT VALUE

Once we accept the proposition that money today is worth more than money tomorrow, we need to find a method to translate the value of money tomorrow into today's equivalent value.

How much would you pay today for the promise of a payment of $1.02 a year from now if the applicable interest rate were 2%? (Assume for now that the promise is risk-free.) If the interest rate is 2%, then an investor could put $1 into the bank today to receive $1.02 a year from now. Conversely, the promise of payment of $1.02 next year is worth at most $1 in today's dollars to an investor. Accordingly, $1 today is the equivalent of $1.02 next year. More generally, the PDV of any monetary value in the future is the amount of money the market would pay today to receive the future money.

Two components are needed to calculate the PDV for any particular investment. First, investors must come up with their best guess as to the value of the investment return in the future. Take, for example, an investor considering an investment of $10,000 into an oil well drilling project in return for 5% of the net profits. The investor must calculate her best guess as to the size of the net profits (e.g., $100,000 per year for the next five years) and then her return from the net profits (in this case, $5,000 per year, representing 5% of the net profits).

Second, the investor must discount the general time value of money as well as the risk inherent in the investment. If a bank promised a return of $5,000 per year for the next five years, the discount rate would likely reflect only the time value of money and not a great additional risk factor. On the other hand, investing in drilling an oil well is significantly more risky than a bank deposit. The oil well may be a dry hole. Even if oil is found, the oil may be of low quality or quantity or difficult to extract. The price of oil may change. Or, the promoters of the oil well investment may take all the profits and skip town. So the discount rate needs to reflect these risks as well.

And now a bit of math (there won't be much, we promise): To formalize the expected monetary return, imagine that an investment will provide an expected return of d_0 immediately, $d1$ in one year's time, and so on. Call the discount rate for a particular investment during a particular year rx, where $r1$ is the discount rate for the first year, $r2$ is the discount rate for the second year, and so on.

We can combine the expected return and the discount rate into the following PDV formula:

$$PVD = d_0 \; + \frac{d_1}{1 + r_1} \; + \frac{d_2}{(1 + r_1)(1 + r_2)} \; + \frac{d_3}{(1 + r_1)(1 + r_2)(1 + r_3)} \; + \;\; \cdots$$

If we assume a constant discount rate r over time, then we get (trust us here):

$$PDV = d_0 \; + \; \sum_t \frac{d_t}{(1 + r)^t}$$

HYPOTHETICAL ONE

Corporations not only issue securities; they may also invest corporate funds in securities and other investment vehicles. Suppose you are the chief financial officer of Twenty-Four Security, Inc. Although Twenty-Four will need a large amount of funds in a couple of years to finance an expansion of its security services into the Asian market, for now it just needs to find a good place to "park" its money. Suppose that Twenty-Four has $10 million cash on hand today. Calculate the present discount value of the following options.

1. Jack, Twenty-Four's CEO, will take the $10 million and put it under his mattress at home. Two years from now, he will take the money out and return it to Twenty-Four's corporate offices. Assume that Jack's mattress is quite safe and that the yearly discount rate is 5%.

2. Twenty-Four will invest the $10 million in U.S. government bonds. The bonds will mature in two years' time. They provide two interest payments of $1 million each at the end of year one and year two, and then a final payment of $10 million at the end of year two. Assume that the relevant discount rate is 5% per year.

3. Twenty-Four will purchase a "perpetuity" from the U.S. government with the $10 million. The perpetuity will provide $1 million every year indefinitely starting one year from now (but no terminal payment because the investment is perpetual). Assume that the relevant discount rate is 5% per year.

4. Twenty-Four will purchase an "annuity" from the U.S. government with the $10 million. Annuities pay a specified amount of money every year (starting in one year) for a fixed period of time (there is no terminal payment). Suppose the U.S. government annuity will pay $3 million every year for the next four years. Assume that the relevant discount rate is 5% per year.

5. Twenty-Four will use the $10 million to purchase bonds issued by Crafty Cartoons, a distributor of children's animated programs. The bonds pay no interest in years one and two (they are "zero-coupon" bonds). Instead, the bonds provide a lump sum payoff of $15 million at the end of year three. Would your answer change if the U.S. government guarantees the bonds?

B. WHAT RISKS MATTER

Most investors are risk averse; they will avoid risks unless they are compensated for it. Imagine that an investor has two possible investment opportunities, each promising an expected return of $10,000 in a year's time. Let's call them "Safe" and "Risky." Safe has little to no risk while Risky has highly variable returns. Imagine that each investment is priced at $9,000 in the market. If this were the case, all investors would choose Safe over Risky. Both result in an expected gain of $1,000 (the $10,000 return minus the cost of $9,000 to purchase the investment). Crucially, however, Safe involves less risk than Risky, thus making it more attractive to risk-averse investors.

Obviously, this is not a sustainable equilibrium. As investors shift funds to purchase Safe, its price will increase due to the greater demand. Correspondingly, the price of Risky will decrease due to the lack of any demand. Suppose that equilibrium is reached when the price of Safe is $9,500 and the price for Risky is $8,000. At these prices, Safe's high price results in a return of only 5.3% while Risky's lower price generates a return of 25%, thereby compensating the investors in Risky for the added risk.

Although uncertainties may affect almost all types of investments, not all risks are the same. Even risks of the same individual magnitude viewed in isolation may not affect the value of an investment in the same way. Investors need not remain passive when it comes to risk; they may be able to reduce the risks they face. If risk reduction is relatively cheap and readily available, the market price will not reflect a discount for bearing those risks.

Diversification provides an important avenue for investors to reduce their risks at low cost. The risks in certain investments may at least partially cancel out. Suppose we have two companies—Joe's Ice Cream Shop and Jane's Umbrella Store. Suppose that $100 invested in either Joe's or Jane's earns the following:

	Rain (50%)	**Sunny (50%)**
Joe's Ice Cream	$ 20	$200
Jane's Umbrella	$200	$ 20

An investor who puts $100 into Joe's Ice Cream can expect to earn $110 on average. But the $110 is not certain. When it rains, the return for the investment will only be $20. When it is sunny, however, the return is $200. Similarly, an investment of $100 into Jane's Umbrella will result in an average return of $110, although with a similar—*but not synchronized*—volatility.

How can a potential investor in Joe's or Jane's stock reduce the risk to which he is exposed? Imagine that the investor put $50 into both Joe's Ice Cream and Jane's Umbrella. The investor would then receive $110 when it rains ($10 from Joe, $100 from Jane) and $110 when it is sunny ($100 from Joe, $10 from Jane) from holding a portfolio of both companies.

In all three investment possibilities (all in Joe's, all in Jane's, and split 50–50 between the two companies), the *expected* return is $110. Only in the 50–50 portfolio investment, however, is the variability in the return zero. Whether it rains or shines, the investor will receive $110. Investors who construct a portfolio of companies that provide different return performance across varying states of the world reduce their risk. Big payouts are eliminated, but so are small ones, and the investor sleeps better at night.

The category of risks that can be reduced through diversification of investments is called "unsystematic risk." If a particular risk does not affect all companies in a similar manner, then companies that perform differently in response to that risk may be matched to reduce the investor's overall variability of returns. The weather affects ice cream and umbrella companies in different ways, giving rise to a diversification opportunity that allows the investor to construct a more stable portfolio of investments. Consequently, that investor will not insist upon a discount for the firm-specific risks of investing in Joe's Ice Cream or Jane's Umbrella.

Other risks cannot be so easily reduced through diversification. Such risks are known as systematic risks and affect all companies similarly, although not necessarily with the same magnitude. If the Federal Reserve raises interest rates, for example, that increase harms all companies. Growth in the number of college graduates providing skilled labor may generally help companies. The stock market as a whole will reflect those trends.

Financial economists have formalized the relationship between the required return for a particular publicly traded security and the systematic risk the security poses for investors. In one well-known asset pricing model, the Capital Asset Pricing Model (CAPM), the return for a security is a function of both the risk-free rate (Rf) (e.g., the interest rate for U.S. government treasury bonds) and the relationship of the security's return performance to the return performance of the entire stock market (Rm). We can represent the CAPM equation for the discount rate as follows:

$$R = R_f + beta(R_m - R_f)$$

The relationship between a stock's performance and the market performance is measured by "beta." A low beta indicates that the particular stock is less influenced by the movement of returns in the market as a whole. Conversely, a high beta represents a large movement of the particular stock's returns with the market returns. High betas indicate more systematic risk and correspondingly a greater discount rate for the returns. In 2004, the beta for Yahoo, Inc. was 3.228 (indicating a relatively large discount rate under the CAPM model). The beta for Coca-Cola Co., in contrast, was only 0.313 in 2004 (giving a much lower discount rate for returns in Coca-Cola Co. stock).

V.   WHO PROVIDES INFORMATION TO INVESTORS?

Investors attempting to calculate the present discounted value of a particular investment require a significant amount of information to determine both the expected return as well as the appropriate discount rate to apply to the return. How does an investor obtain this information?

Investors lacking the information necessary to value an investment are at a disadvantage in the capital markets. Corporations selling common stock to the public know more about that stock than investors. Unsuspecting investors may purchase overvalued securities from unscrupulous issuers. In the secondary market, investors with more information (including corporate officers engaged in insider trading) will enjoy systematically greater returns at the expense of uninformed investors.

The primary goal of securities regulation is to reduce outside investors' informational disadvantage. In this Part we first consider whether market actors may have an incentive to provide information to investors voluntarily. Second, we examine the case for mandatory disclosure requirements despite the presence of private market incentives to provide information.

A. THE INCENTIVE TO PROVIDE INFORMATION

Information is a valuable commodity in the capital markets. Suppose Chloe learns that Twenty-Four's new personal security products are about to be favorably reviewed by *Safe at Home* magazine. Chloe can profitably purchase Twenty-Four stock before the magazine hits the newsstand. After the public learns of the reviews, and Twenty-Four's share price rises as a result, Chloe can then sell her shares at a profit.

The value of a particular piece of information for securities trading depends on the number of potential traders with the specific information. Information that Microsoft produces Office is important for investors, but this information is already well known to almost all investors. Consequently, as we discuss in more detail below, the information is already incorporated into the price of Microsoft's common stock, so even those investors who lack the information will trade at a price that reflects it. On the other hand, a corporate officer who knows that Microsoft is about to introduce a new version of Windows—Windows 10 Plus—before any public investor knows of this information can trade profitably in Microsoft's stock before the public announcement.

Why would anyone disseminate important and non-public investment information widely to the market? To put this in another way: Given that information is costly to generate and distribute, why would anyone research and then distribute the information widely, thereby reducing the trading advantage of holding the information? To answer these questions, it may be helpful to divide information relevant to the valuation of a security into two categories: (a) information from inside the corporation (inside information) and (b) information useful in valuing the corporation that comes from outside the corporation (outside information).

Inside information encompasses all information known by anyone within a corporation that may affect the market price for the corporation's securities. Inside information includes news about the company's products, profitability, and management team, among other things.

Companies such as Twenty-Four Security have an incentive to provide their firm-specific, inside information voluntarily to the marketplace. Imagine that an array of companies seeks to sell securities to investors through primary transactions. For now, assume only that antifraud liability applies to deter misrepresentations, but disclosure is not mandatory. Some of the companies are a better investment than others. Assume that all of the companies offering securities refuse to make disclosures to prospective investors. When an investor calls to ask a question about the offering, the companies all reply, "No comment."

If you were an investor in such a situation, how much would you be willing to pay for the securities being offered by these companies? Unable to distinguish among companies, rational investors will pay the expected value approximating the average return for the group of companies. Paying greater than the average value will result in the investor systematically earning negative returns, not a stable situation in the capital markets. But not all companies are average. Some companies will provide a higher return than the average and some will provide a lower return.

Now consider the incentives of the managers of a higher value company offering securities to the market. If the managers remain silent, the higher value company will receive the average price for all companies. However, if the managers can make a credible (and low-cost) disclosure of their company's true value to investors, then the higher value company will receive substantially more for its securities. So long as antifraud liability lends credibility to a company's disclosures, the high value company will want to disclose its inside information to investors when offering securities. Once one company begins disclosing, investors, if rational, will reduce the value they assign to the companies that opt for silence. Among those companies that remain silent, those at the higher end of the valuation spectrum will then have added pressure to disclose their value to investors voluntarily, thereby increasing the amount of money investors would be willing to pay for the companies' securities.

Why might companies *not* disclose information voluntarily? First, companies may not plan on issuing securities anytime soon. Although Twenty-Four may want to convince investors that it is a good investment when it is selling common stock, Twenty-Four's managers may have fewer incentives to disclose when the company is not selling securities. A company, of course, may disclose in between offerings to foster a strong secondary market. Doing so may reduce the risk investors face by trading in the secondary market, thus reducing the costs of secondary market trading. This accrues to the benefit of the company if investors then pay more for securities sold in primary offerings.

Second, antifraud liability may not provide sufficient credibility to disclosures. Antifraud liability is imprecise. Suits are sometimes brought even when no fraud has been committed; conversely, suits are sometimes not brought when fraud has occurred. For example, few private securities fraud class actions are brought against initial public issuers offering relatively small amounts of securities. Lower value companies may take advantage of imperfections in the antifraud regime to make disclosures misrepresenting themselves as high value firms. If fraud muddies the waters, investors will be unable to distinguish among different value companies based on their disclosures. As a result, high value companies will be unable to use disclosure to distinguish themselves from the low value companies. High value companies may, instead, choose to raise money outside of the capital markets. If high value companies exit the public capital markets, only the low value companies will be left offering securities. This process reduces the average value of companies left in the market, inducing more companies to exit the markets, a downward spiral commonly known as the "lemons" problem (a reference to the market for used cars).

Third, managers may profit from a less than fully informed securities market. If the investing public knows less about an issuer's firm-specific information, managers can more easily engage in insider trading. We will see in Chapter 6 that the securities laws prohibit insider trading, but such prohibitions are imperfect. Insider trading is hard to detect. A manager who uses a friend to trade securities in only small amounts may cruise under the radar screen of the SEC. Moreover, the securities laws only prohibit trades involving a "material" informational advantage over the investing public. Managers can trade if their informational advantage does not rise to the level of materiality. If the definition of materiality (covered in Chapter 2) does not align with potential profitability, insiders may be able to exploit their informational advantages without legal consequences.

Finally, the incentive of issuers to disclose voluntarily extends only to inside information. Outside information may also create informational disparities among investors. No company operates in a vacuum. The value of Twenty-Four Security, for example, depends on: 1) the plans of its competitors to introduce competing personal security products; 2) the level of corporate espionage activity; and 3) whether regulators may impose greater safety regulations that may constrain Twenty-Four's ability to introduce new products. Numerous other factors may also affect Twenty-Four's stock price.

The market responds to these problems in a number of ways. These solutions, however, have their own problems. First, firms may turn to third parties to certify the information they disclose to the market. The reputation of the third party intermediaries may bolster the credibility of disclosure. As discussed above, underwriters typically participate in firm commitment offerings, putting their reputation on the line (as well as their own financial capital) when they sell a security. Audit firms also put their reputations on the line when they certify a company's financial statements.

High reputation underwriters and auditors earn substantial fees for their services. Companies pay this fee to "rent" the reputation of the intermediaries because they can demand a higher price when selling their securities. Despite this interest in maintaining the value of a reputation for veracity, some intermediaries may sacrifice their reputation in return for a quick gain. The fall of Arthur Andersen as a major audit firm was due in large part to the questionable actions of the lead audit partner for Enron, resulting in short-term profits in the form of more Enron-related business. We cover the regulation of auditors in Chapter 12.

Second, securities analysts provide investment information to the market, by researching both firm-specific and outside information. Buy-side analysts work for large institutional investors, providing investment analysis used in determining which investments the institutional investors should purchase or sell. Sell-side analysts, on the other hand, are employed by the large securities brokerage firms. Merrill Lynch, for example, employs many analysts covering a wide variety of industries and businesses. In addition to providing execution of order services, Merrill Lynch also sells investment advice to its brokerage customers. The advice is implicitly paid for as a portion of the broker's commission.

In the past, brokerage commissions were fixed by regulation, resulting in substantial brokerage profits. These profits were partially used to subsidize sell-side analyst research for investors. In 1975, however, brokerage commissions were deregulated, leading to intense competition. Commissions that used to run into the $100 range now run for as little as $9.95, or even lower, at some Internet brokerage sites. The sharp drop in commissions has cut into brokerage profits.

Although brokerage firms still employ substantial numbers of sell-side analysts, the funding for analysts has necessarily shifted to other sources. Many Wall Street brokerage firms turned to their growing investment banking businesses in the 1980s and 1990s to help subsidize analyst research. In return, the provision of analyst research on select companies to the marketplace became a selling point for the investment banking business. Investment banking partners would routinely tout the strength of their analysts in obtaining business from companies doing public offerings for the first time. A positive analyst report from a large Wall Street brokerage firm on a recently public Internet startup company, for example, could help bolster the stock price of the startup.

The close connection between investment banking and analyst research within the large Wall Street firms created a conflict of interest for analysts. Although investment banks represented that their analysts' research provided accurate information for investors, the analysts were compensated based on the amount of investment banking business attributable to the analysts' efforts. In the early 2000s, this conflict of interest became public as the result of an investigation by Elliot Spitzer, the New York State Attorney General. Spitzer and the SEC eventually reached a settlement with ten Wall Street investment banks. The settlement provided for a $1.4 billion settlement fund in addition to various structural reforms separating investment banking from analyst research within the investment banks.

B. THE ARGUMENT FOR MANDATORY DISCLOSURE

Although issuers have incentives to disclose information voluntarily, those incentives are not perfect. We have seen that: (a) firms not intending to issue securities may not have strong incentives to disclose; (b) antifraud liability may not ensure the veracity of disclosures; (c) managers may have a self interest in restricting disclosures (e.g., to enhance their insider trading opportunities); and (d) such disclosures will not include information emanating from outside the firm. Moreover, the intermediaries that help provide credibility to issuer disclosures, as well as the analysts that provide an independent source of information on firms, may face their own set of hurdles in maintaining the investing public's confidence.

Given the problems with voluntary disclosure, a system of mandatory disclosure may improve investor welfare. In addition, commentators have argued that a number of affirmative benefits may flow from a mandatory disclosure system. We briefly canvass some of these arguments below.

1. COORDINATION PROBLEMS

A coordination problem may discourage companies from making disclosures. Information on a particular company is more valuable if investors can use the information to compare the company against other possible investment opportunities. To the extent Twenty-Four Security performs poorly compared with other security providers, investors will pay less for Twenty-Four's shares.

Comparisons are more difficult if disclosures are not consistent. If one company defines annual revenue to include all sales made in the last fifteen months while another defines annual revenue as sales occurring in the last twelve months, then the two revenue numbers will not be comparable. Today, financial statements prepared in different countries present potential comparison problems for investors. German accounting principles, for example, permit companies to create reserves, allowing a company to shift profits from a good year to mask losses in a subsequent bad year. U.S. generally accepted accounting principles (U.S. GAAP), on the other hand, do not allow for such reserves. In addition, the U.S. securities regime does not require all companies with securities trading in U.S. markets to reconcile their accounting statements to U.S. GAAP. Instead, the U.S. securities regime allows foreign issuers to file accounting statements following international accounting standards.

The value of mandatory standardization can be exaggerated. Even if the government does not mandate one particular standard, the market may develop its own standard. Once a standard takes hold, investors will penalize issuers who fail to disclose according to the standard; non-conformity will be viewed as a signal that something is amiss with the issuer. The accounting industry, for example, develops standardized methods of accounting treatment. Financial accounting and reporting standards in the U.S. have long been primarily administered by the Financial Accounting Standards Board (FASB), a private entity.

2. AGENCY COSTS

Disclosure plays a large role in controlling agency costs within large public corporations. With accurate disclosure of a company's financial performance, outside investors can compare how well managers at a particular firm are performing relative to the managers of the firm's competitors. Of course, other factors may affect a firm's financial performance (including a poor economy, war, and other external factors). Nonetheless, a comparison with a firm's competitors controls for many such factors and provides a clearer glimpse into the quality of a firm's managers. Directors may then discipline (or terminate) managers who perform poorly.

Disclosure may also reveal the compensation, share ownership, and trading patterns of a firm's managers. Top executive officers may persuade the board of directors to award the officers exorbitant pay packages. Officers may trade on inside information. Disclosure of egregious pay packages and instances of insider trading allow shareholders to decide which managers should be replaced (through the shareholders' power to elect the board of directors). That information may also assist the SEC and private plaintiffs' attorneys in filing lawsuits against the corporate officers. Corporate officers may also face public opprobrium if their misbehavior is revealed; directors will be embarrassed by malfeasance that occurs under their watch.

Managers intent on shirking their job responsibilities or siphoning corporate resources to themselves may not voluntarily choose to disclose information concerning firm performance, executive compensation and stock trading patterns. If investors cannot completely decipher the meaning of a firm's silence on such matters (e.g., other firms may choose not to disclose information on an executive's compensation for fear that competitors may initiate a bidding war for the executive's services), then managers will be able to remain silent without suffering a large share price discount.

The agency problem may be particularly acute in the context of initial public offerings. After an issuer raises funds from an initial public offering, those in control of the issuer have many potential avenues for mischief with the funds. Companies may use the funds to pay the executives high salaries, or purchase goods and services from parties related to those in control at disadvantageous terms for the issuer. The presence of a large amount of liquid funds makes the benefit to managers from engaging in such expropriation of private benefits of control both more rewarding and easier to execute. In sum, agency costs may lead managers and promoters to disclose less information than is in the best interests of both investors and the issuer. Mandatory disclosure of items related to areas where managers can siphon value from investors (e.g., executive compensation and related-party transactions between an issuer and its managers or promoters) therefore may enhance shareholder welfare.

3. POSITIVE EXTERNALITIES

A positive externality may occur when a company makes a firm-specific disclosure to the public marketplace. Third parties unconnected with the issuer may benefit from these disclosures in at least two ways.

First, more disclosures will increase the accuracy of securities prices. The information itself may help investors value the company's business prospects. Moreover, the disclosed information may help subsidize the efforts of analysts in the stock market to research other information (acting as stepping stones to even more exhaustive research). The additional analyst-driven information may then further increase the accuracy of securities prices.

Second, firm-specific information may prove useful to competitors and other third parties. An issuer will take into account the cost to itself of providing information. The issuer will not, however, value the benefit to third parties. Indeed, in some cases, the issuer will treat a third party benefit as an affirmative cost to itself. Suppose Twenty-Four plans to invest $10 million developing a new line of video games expecting big profits, but only if Twenty-Four is the first mover into this new market niche. If competitors learn about Twenty-Four's plans, however, the competitors will have time to put together their own video games, undermining Twenty-Four's first mover advantage. Because the issuer will either ignore or treat as a cost the benefits of disclosure to competitors and other third parties, the issuer will not fully internalize all the effects from its disclosure decisions. Mandatory disclosure may force issuers to disclose information when they would not have otherwise done so voluntarily.

The issuer will not ignore the benefit of disclosure to all those who receive information. If investors value disclosure, they will reward the issuer disclosing such information through a high stock market price. Nonetheless, issuers will fail to take into account the full positive effect of their disclosure on overall stock market price accuracy and on their competitors. At the margin, will the issuer's failure to take into account these positive externalities reduce the amount of disclosure? Possibly. On the other hand, will a mandatory regulation regime result in the right level of disclosure? Will regulators correctly identify the level of disclosure that optimally accounts for improved price accuracy and benefits to competitors? Although issuers on their own may opt for too little disclosure, regulators may be inclined to require too much.

4.   DUPLICATIVE RESEARCH

Information cannot be produced for free. Investors competing with one another will have an incentive to expend large resources to obtain an informational advantage over other traders. The winner of such an information race obtains large trading profits. Those who lose the race gain little or no trading profits—the market will have already reacted to the information embedded in the large trade orders previously placed by the winner.

The "winner-take-all" nature of research leads to excessive and duplicative investment in research. When advisors for a mutual fund attempt to predict the earnings for Twenty-Four, this effort requires both time and money. An advisor may interview customers, suppliers, and other industry participants to get a sense of Twenty-Four's earnings. The advisor will also obtain data on general industry trends and review as much information as possible specific to Twenty-Four. From this information, the advisor will then spend long hours calculating future income streams. All this effort may gain a specific mutual fund a trading advantage before Twenty-Four itself announces its earnings. In comparing the performance of two funds, the fund that obtains the information first may significantly enhance its relative performance. It may not matter to society, however, whether Fidelity or Vanguard learns about an issuer's earnings one hour ahead of the other fund. If the private gain to a fund from research exceeds the social benefit, funds may engage in wasteful research races.

For information inside the issuer (firm-specific information), the issuer can discourage such wasteful battles to win the informational race. Twenty-Four represents the lowest-cost source of inside information on the value of Twenty-Four's securities. Outside investors may attempt to recreate such information only at high cost. (How can outside investors learn about a corporation's internal business plans for the future? Corporate espionage?) Moreover, many outside investors may each attempt to do so, resulting in duplicative research costs as each investor reinvents the wheel. Twenty-Four can undercut these incentives by simply disclosing its business plans publicly. Mandatory disclosure under the federal securities laws forces issuers to disclose much of their firm specific information, thereby reducing duplicative information research in the secondary market.

5.   COSTS OF MANDATORY DISCLOSURE

Notwithstanding these substantial arguments in favor of mandatory disclosure, its desirability is hardly a given. Regulators are not perfect. They make mistakes in gauging the correct level of mandatory disclosure. The behavioral biases of regulators at the SEC, for example, may cause them to ignore less visible (but nonetheless important) information in favor of more salient and recent information. Regulators may be excessively optimistic about their own abilities to provide solutions to problems in the financial markets. Tunnel vision may limit the ability of regulators to consider alternative regulatory solutions.

Perhaps more troubling than cognitive problems is the risk of agency capture. Regulators may come under the influence of wealthy and well-organized participants in the securities markets. A regulator considering her exit options after leaving the SEC may wish to establish a reputation for "reasonableness" with investment bankers, auditors, and Wall Street law firms. Even if regulators do not become captured by outside interests, the regulators may systematically select regulations designed to increase the authority and prestige of the SEC even at the expense of investor welfare. (Investors, after all, ultimately bear the cost of the regulatory regime.) As a monopolistic regulator in the United States, the SEC has little incentive to cater to the interests of investors. Even if SEC regulators make mistakes or are captured by industry participants, issuers and investors cannot opt for an alternative securities regulation regime.

C.   HOW DOES DISCLOSURE MATTER?

A key assumption underlying the debate over mandatory disclosure is that investors actually pay attention to disclosures. If disclosures were simply irrelevant to the capital markets, then imposing mandatory disclosure would squander the valuable time and money of the issuer (and therefore indirectly the funds of its shareholders). The SEC has decided that investors are most interested in financial results, management's biographies, the composition of the board of directors, and the business and properties of the issuer.

Even if investors value such information, they must still obtain, read, and digest the information in order to make an informed investment decision. Moreover, information not included in an issuer's disclosures to the market may be important to the valuation of the issuer. Information on tensions in the Middle East, for example, may be useful in valuing an oil company's stock. Investors making their own investment analyses should also incorporate such outside information. The complexity of the decision can be overwhelming.

Not surprisingly, most individual investors simply don't try. Many a corporate annual report has ended up unread in the trash can. If small investors don't take advantage of the information provided through mandatory disclosure, what is the point? Perversely, such disclosures may give an informational advantage to larger, more sophisticated investors (with enough money at stake to make study worthwhile) over the small investors who do not read the disclosures. Rather than reducing informational advantages in the capital markets, mandatory disclosure may increase them.

This paints too bleak a picture. Small investors may benefit from mandatory disclosure, even if they never glance at the unceasing stream of disclosure generated. Investors may: 1) obtain the information indirectly through the recommendations of various securities market intermediaries; and 2) benefit from the information indirectly if the information is incorporated into the stock market price for securities that trade in an "efficient market."

1.   FILTERING MECHANISMS

Investors who do not read disclosures may nonetheless learn their content and implications indirectly through securities market intermediaries. Brokers, for example, hold themselves out as providing value to investors through their access to many sources of investment-related information. In theory, brokers will review the available research on a firm, reading the firm's mandatory disclosures as well as analyst reports on the firm. Brokers will then make recommendations to individual investor clients. Through the filtering mechanism of the broker, individual investors may learn indirectly about disclosed information.

Other intermediaries assist investors who cannot spare the time to read disclosures. Mutual funds, for example, allow investors to "hire" professional money managers to allocate their investment funds. In an actively-managed mutual fund, a fund manager will research various securities in search of investment opportunities. As the fund grows larger, the fund manager can spread the cost of research across all the individual holders of the fund. Individuals with better things to do than read SEC filings can invest, with minimal effort, through a mutual fund while still benefitting from the expertise of the fund manager in picking profitable securities.

Once again, however, agency costs muddy the waters. Agency problems are not unique to managers within a corporation. Brokers may not faithfully serve the interests of their investor clients. So-called "boiler room" brokers engage in cold calls to investors, touting "can't miss" investments. More often than not, investors who purchase such investments lose while the brokers receive hefty commissions. The SEC's website quotes one cold-calling broker as stating: "You'd hammer them. I always remember this one guy, I mean, I just stayed on the phone for almost an hour, and he finally bought." Your broker may not be your friend.

Similarly, fund managers may not always have the best interests of the fund investors in mind when doing research. And they certainly do not work for free. Research has shown that equity fund managers' fees are much greater than of the fees charged by comparable pension fund managers. So your fund manager may not be your friend, either.

2.   THE EFFICIENT CAPITAL MARKET HYPOTHESIS

Despite the conflicts facing intermediaries, individual investors are not necessarily out of luck if they rely on a less than scrupulous broker or mutual fund manager. For firms whose securities are widely followed and actively traded, another mechanism may help ensure that even those investors who cannot be bothered with research are able to buy and sell securities at a price that reflects all of that information: efficient capital markets.

Financial economists developed the efficient capital markets hypothesis (ECMH) in the 1960s. The ECMH posits that the market price of an actively traded security will incorporate information related to the security. Three different versions of the ECMH align with the amount of information assumed to be incorporated into the stock market price: weak, semi-strong and strong.

a.   *Weak ECMH*

Under the weak version of the ECMH, the current market price of a security reflects the information found in all past prices for that security. If the weak version of the ECMH is true, investors cannot earn greater than normal returns by trading based on a security's past price patterns. Suppose we start with the assumption that a large drop in price is typically followed a week later by a large increase in price. The weak version of the ECMH postulates that such a systematic pattern cannot occur. Put another way, if the weak form of the ECMH is true, stock market prices follow a "random walk." Knowledge of past prices will not help investors predict whether a stock's price is headed lower or higher.

This result should not be surprising. Information on past price patterns for securities is both cheap and widely available. For example, see how long it takes you to find the recent common stock prices for The Coca-Cola Company (ticker symbol KO) at one of the many websites devoted to financial information, such as www.finance.yahoo.com.

How does it work? Suppose that thousands of traders are armed with both (a) knowledge of the systematic stock market price pattern (e.g., that a large drop is always followed by a corresponding increase), and (b) information on a large price drop for a particular company's stock, such as KO. Assume that KO's stock price drops from $45 per share to $35 per share. Everyone knows that KO's stock price will jump back up by $10 in one week, so it will soon be trading at $45 per share again. But if KO's stock price is sure to increase by $10 in a week, an investor can lock in guaranteed profits by purchasing KO stock at today's price of $35 per share. (This process is known in financial circles as "arbitrage.") Competition will quickly drive the price of KO to $45 (long before the week elapses), thereby eliminating the certain profit from trading in the stock of Coca Cola.

b. Semi-Strong ECMH

The semi-strong version of the ECMH hypothesis builds on the weak version, but it incorporates a broader range of information. Under the semi-strong hypothesis, the stock market price of an actively traded company's stock will reflect all relevant *publicly* available information. Although not all publicly available information is as easily obtained as past stock prices, by definition this category of information is broadly available to the investing public. Information that Twenty-Four Security is about to enter the personal security device market, for example, can give the holder of such information a large trading advantage in Twenty-Four stock. But that advantage persists only as long as no other investors know of Twenty-Four's imminent plans to expand its security services. Once the plans are made public, the possibility of profitable trades disappears.

What is the mechanism here? If *all* investors learn of Twenty-Four's plans simultaneously, the stock market price may simply adjust to reflect the news before any trading occurs. Even if only *some* investors learn of the plans, trades by those informed investors will quickly drive the price higher or lower, depending on the market's assessment of those plans. With increased demand for Twenty-Four's stock (assuming the entry into the personal security device market is good news), the stock market price of Twenty-Four will rise, incorporating the new information. Increased demand signals to the rest of the market that some investors believe that Twenty-Four is a good buy. Moreover, the signal is credible because the investors are putting their money on the line.

c. Strong ECMH

The strong version of the ECMH posits that the stock market price of a company incorporates all information, whether or not the information is available to the public. The mechanism? There is none—the available evidence contradicts the strong version of the ECMH. Insiders trading in their company's equity produce systematically higher returns. This outcome would be impossible if their informational advantages afforded them no trading advantages as posited by the strong version of the ECMH. So it is generally agreed that the strong version of the ECMH is false. (If it were true, of course, most securities regulation would be pointless, we would not have written this book, and you would not be taking this course.)

d. Implications of ECMH

Among the three versions of the ECMH, the semi-strong version of the ECMH has had the greatest effect on securities regulation. In particular, securities regulators have been influenced by the notion that investors who do not read a particular piece of company information may nonetheless "indirectly" receive it because the stock market price incorporates the information. For example, the SEC has allowed issuers to "incorporate by reference" their prior SEC filings in public offering disclosures (discussed in Chapter 7). The presumption is that the market has already incorporated the information in those prior filings and the price of the offered securities will reflect it. Another prominent example is the Supreme Court's decision in *Basic Inc. v. Levinson*, 485 U.S. 224 (1988), which relied in part on the notion that the capital market may incorporate disclosed information in the stock market price. The Court adopted the "fraud-on-the-market" theory, which presumes reliance even for investors who did not directly view or read a misstatement alleged to have affected a company's stock price. Defenses to the theory follow the limits of the ECMH identified by finance economists. Defendants may rebut the presumption with a showing that the market for a particular company's securities does not enjoy active trading or a substantial following of analysts. Markets without these features cannot be presumed to be informationally efficient. In 2014, the Supreme Court held in *Halliburton Co. v. Erica P. John Fund*, Inc. (excerpted in Chapter 5) that defendants may rebut the presumption by showing a lack of "price impact" from the misstatement.

Despite the influence of the semi-strong version of the ECMH on securities regulation, the theory remains controversial. Many argue that investors are frequently irrational in their investment decisions. This lack of rationality, in turn, may translate into stock market prices that do not accurately reflect all publicly available information. The most prominent version of this theory is called noise trading. Under this theory, a substantial segment of investors does not trade based on information and instead simply engages in random "noise" trades. Institutional investors, instead of arbitraging the noise away (leading to accurate securities prices), may attempt to "ride the wave" and trade with irrational trends in securities prices, hoping to cash out before the momentum fades.

More recently, both economists and legal academics have developed a growing appreciation of the fallibility of human decision making. Investors may be prone to excessive optimism, placing too much weight on their ability to make good investment choices. Investors may also ignore less salient, but nonetheless important, information and pay excessive attention to recent and more salient information. Immediately following a large stock market scandal, investors may take an overly pessimistic view of stock investments, for example. Investors may display loss aversion, placing too much weight on avoiding the realization of a loss, leading the investors to hold on too long to losing investments instead of taking their losses to help reduce their taxes. Conversely, investors may take excessive risks with newly earned money (the so-called "house" money effect).

If investors do not price securities rationally, the possibility for irrational "bubbles" (essentially, enthusiasm for stocks not grounded in realistic prospects of profit) arises. In a bubble market, stock market prices are likely to stray far from the fundamental value of the shares, i.e., the stream of dividends and capital gains the shares are likely to produce. Many point to the sharp rise of stock market prices at the end of the 1990s, particularly for Internet-related companies, followed by the rapid deflation of these prices in the early 2000s, as evidence that the U.S. securities markets suffered from such a bubble.

The possibility of stock market bubbles requires us to refine what we mean by "efficient" capital markets. One meaning of efficiency is "fundamental" efficiency. A stock market is fundamentally efficient if the prices reflect the underlying present discounted value of the return investors may expect from purchasing a security. If investors reacted rationally to information and did not suffer from any behavioral biases, the stock market would be fundamentally efficient (at least in the semi-strong sense of the ECMH).

A conclusion that the stock market is fundamentally efficient furnishes a strong basis for normative arguments against the regulation of the securities markets. If investors incorporate all available public information into stock prices then issuers, assuming no agency costs, will internalize fully the choices they make that may affect investor welfare. For example, if issuers fail to adopt the corporate governance protections that investors expect, the issuers' stock market price will take a hit, making it difficult for the issuer to raise capital. An extreme version of this argument holds that securities regulation should follow the path of state corporate law and allow issuers to choose the regulatory regime to apply to transactions in the issuers' securities. If issuers choose a regime that poorly protects investors, investors will respond by appropriately discounting the price of the issuer's shares. Issuers seeking to offer securities will therefore consider both their own welfare and that of investors in choosing a securities regime. Putting these academic arguments to one side, fundamental efficiency seems difficult to square with the dramatic fluctuations that we see in the stock market.

Even if we doubt the stock market's fundamental efficiency, the market may nonetheless be "informationally" efficient. Investors may generally have behavioral biases and other defects in processing information that lead to stock market bubbles and other forms of irrational pricing. But when new information regarding a security arrives in the market, the market may nonetheless quickly incorporate that information into the stock market. The level of stock prices may not reflect the true underlying value of companies; in an informationally efficient market the *relative* changes in stock prices may still reflect accurately the value of new information.

Suppose that Twenty-Four puts out a false press release claiming that its upcoming revenues will far exceed analysts' expectations. Even if the market is not fundamentally efficient, the market may still react to the fraudulent press release. Moreover, once the fraud is revealed, the corresponding drop in the stock market price on the revelation date may provide a good proxy for the magnitude of the fraud (along with the expected consequences of its revelation for the company). Later in the casebook, we see courts turning to an informationally efficient stock market as the best available measure of both the materiality of the fraud (meaning how important the information is to the average investor, our topic in Chapter 2) and the amount of damages (reflecting the magnitude of the fraud, covered in Chapter 5).

VI. THE REGULATORY APPARATUS

We finish our introduction to the securities markets and their regulation with (A) a brief summary of the various components of the securities laws, (B) a discussion of the Dodd-Frank Act of 2010 and the financial crisis of 2008–2009 that precipitated Dodd-Frank; (C) a survey of the SEC's role in administering the securities laws, and (D) an overview of the role of SROs in regulating the securities markets.

A. THE FEDERAL SECURITIES LAWS

Securities transactions in the United States are governed primarily by the federal securities laws. The federal securities laws comprise several pieces of legislation initially enacted during the Great Depression and amended over time. The federal securities laws include the:

- Securities Exchange Act of 1934
- Securities Act of 1933
- Investment Company Act of 1940
- Investment Advisers Act of 1940
- Trust Indenture Act of 1939
- Sarbanes-Oxley Act of 2002
- Jumpstart Our Business Startups Act of 2012

1. SECURITIES EXCHANGE ACT OF 1934

The Exchange Act primarily regulates secondary market transactions and the market professionals and institutions that facilitate such transactions. The Exchange Act, like the other securities laws, protects investors primarily through disclosure. As covered in greater detail in Chapter 4, the Exchange Act imposes periodic reporting requirements for publicly-traded companies, commonly referred to as "Exchange Act reporting issuers." Exchange Act reporting issuers must file annual Form 10–K reports and quarterly Form 10–Q reports with the SEC.

The Form 10–K and 10–Q disclosure forms include information relevant to investors, including a description of the issuer's business and properties; the directors and officers of the issuer; the ownership of the issuer; and past financial statements. Exchange Act reporting issuers must also file a Form 8–K for certain major events, such as bankruptcy or a change in control of the issuer. These disclosures must all be filed electronically with the SEC's EDGAR system, and the SEC makes these filings available to the public on its website, www.sec.gov.

Disclosures alone may not assist investors in the secondary market if issuers and their officers commit fraud. The Exchange Act tackles this problem with antifraud liability. By far the most important antifraud provision is Rule 10b–5, promulgated by the SEC under § 10(b) of the Exchange Act. Although Rule 10b–5 does not provide an explicit private cause of action for fraud, courts have developed a detailed antifraud doctrine under Rule 10b–5, prohibiting not only fraudulent disclosures (covered in Chapter 5), but also insider trading (in Chapter 6). Antifraud liability is not cheap. An expansive Rule 10b–5 regime may encourage plaintiffs' attorneys to file suits after a large drop in a firm's stock price with only minimal evidence that the firm and its officers and directors fraudulently disclosed materially misleading information. Defendants may settle even non-meritorious claims to avoid the expense of defending such a suit and the distraction on management, among other reasons. In 1995, Congress responded to the fear of frivolous suits with the passage of the Private Securities Litigation Reform Act (also covered in Chapter 5).

Fraud is not the only danger lurking in the secondary markets. Some secondary market participants may attempt to manipulate securities prices. To address this concern, the Exchange Act contains anti-manipulation provisions. Prior to the enactment of the securities laws, Congress received extensive (but less than conclusive) testimony on the presence of manipulative trades in the securities markets before the stock market crash of 1929. According to the testimony, unscrupulous traders would routinely band together to form a "stock pool." Members of the pool would buy a particular stock, generating an upward momentum in the stock price. Once the stock price rose, pool members would cash out at a profit before the stock price came back down. Section 9 of the Exchange Act now prohibits such manipulation.

The Exchange Act regulates many of the professional intermediaries that operate in the securities markets. The Exchange Act requires brokers, national securities exchanges, and municipal securities dealers, among others, to register with the SEC. Registration subjects these entities to extensive regulation by the SEC (a topic for a more advanced course in securities regulation).

The Exchange Act also regulates shareholder voting by mandating disclosure in connection with the solicitation of proxies. Congress hoped to make managers more accountable to shareholders by requiring disclosure when shareholders were asked to vote. We take up this topic in Chapter 11.

2.   SECURITIES ACT OF 1933

The Securities Act of 1933 focuses on primary market transactions. The Securities Act provides three approaches to regulating the primary market. First, the Securities Act requires issuers making a public offering to file disclosure documents containing information deemed important to investors. The two major disclosure documents are the registration statement (filed with the SEC) and the prospectus (sent to investors). The prospectus repeats the information found in Part I of the registration statement. The registration statement and prospectus contain information on the issuer's business, properties, material legal proceedings, directors and officers, ownership, and financials. The SEC has coordinated the disclosure requirements imposed by the Securities Act (for public offerings) and those imposed by the Exchange Act (for periodic filings). Under the system of "integrated disclosure" the requirements are the same for both Acts. Information is also provided on the offering itself, including the number of shares offered and the price, the underwriters involved in the offering (and their fees and discounts), and the use of the proceeds from the offering. We cover this subject in Chapter 7.

Second, the Securities Act provides for an intricate public offering procedure, often referred to as the "gun-jumping" rules, designed both to ensure that the prospectus is distributed widely to investors and that the prospectus is sent to investors before they receive other (written) information. The prohibition on giving additional information to investors is often referred to as the "quiet period" of a public offering, although the SEC has adopted a plethora of exceptions to this prohibition. These topics are also covered in Chapter 7.

Third, the Securities Act imposes heightened antifraud liability for material misstatements (and omissions creating a "half truth") in public offering documents, the topic of Chapter 8. Issuers seeking to raise capital from the market may be tempted to commit fraud to boost the proceeds from the offering. Heightened antifraud liability is intended to counter this incentive to engage in fraud.

The Securities Act also exempts certain offerings from the public offering rules. We discuss exempt offerings, including private placements, in Chapter 9. Securities sold through an exempt offering typically are restricted and the initial investors may not freely resell the restricted securities. Chapter 10 covers the provisions in the federal securities laws that allow investors, provided certain conditions are met, to resell restricted securities.

3.   INVESTMENT COMPANY ACT OF 1940 AND INVESTMENT ADVISERS ACT OF 1940

The Investment Company Act of 1940 and the Investment Advisers Act of 1940 regulate, among other things, mutual funds and their directors, managers, and advisors. The Investment Company Act requires that certain defined investment companies register with the SEC. The Investment Company Act provides specific requirements governing the responsibilities of the fund's board of directors, the capital structure of the fund, and transactions between a fund and its insiders. In addition, the Investment Company Act regulates disclosures to fund investors, including mandatory disclosures on fund objectives, risks, and performance.

The Investment Advisers Act, in turn, imposes a number of requirements on certain investment advisers. Investment advisers must register with the SEC, avoid certain types of fee arrangements, and maintain specified books and records. The Investment Advisers Act also limits advertising by investment advisors. For example, investment advisers may not use testimonials in their advertisements. We leave topics arising under these laws to more advanced courses in securities regulation.

4.   TRUST INDENTURE ACT OF 1939

The Trust Indenture Act of 1939 regulates contractual terms relating to publicly issued debt securities, including bonds, notes, and debentures above a specified dollar amount (presently $10 million). The formal agreement between the issuer and the holders of public debt securities is known as a "trust indenture." The Act specifies that the trust indenture must, among other things, provide for the appointment of a trustee to represent the public bondholders as a group. The Act also provides for the independence of the trustee as well as standards governing the conduct of the trustee. This law is generally covered in courses on corporate finance.

5. WILLIAMS ACT OF 1968

Acquirors seek to obtain control of a target corporation for a variety of reasons. An acquiror may believe that the target corporation is being poorly managed and that, under the guidance of the acquiror, the target's businesses could generate far greater profit. Once the acquiror decides to seek control of a target corporation, the acquiror can choose among a variety of transactional forms to achieve this goal. If the target's board of directors decides to resist the overtures of the acquiror, however, the acquiror's only realistic option will be to proceed through a tender offer, appealing directly to the target's shareholders. The federal securities regulation of tender offers was enacted in the Williams Act (codified as amendments to the Exchange Act) in response to hostile tender offers.

The Supreme Court has described Congress's motivation for enacting the Williams Act:

> [T]he Williams Act . . . was adopted in 1968 in response to the growing use of cash tender offers as a means for achieving corporate takeovers. Prior to the 1960's, corporate takeover attempts had typically involved either proxy solicitations, regulated under § 14 of the Securities Exchange Act, or exchange offers of securities, subject to the registration requirements of the 1933 Act. The proliferation of cash tender offers, in which publicized requests are made and intensive campaigns conducted for tenders of shares of stock at a fixed price, removed a substantial number of corporate control contests from the reach of existing disclosure requirements of the federal securities laws.

Piper v. Chris-Craft Industries, Inc., 430 U.S. 1, 22 (1977).

The Williams Act regulates tender offers for a target company's stock in three ways. First, it requires disclosure by anyone purchasing 5% or more of a public company's stock. Second, it requires disclosure by anyone making a tender offer for 5% or more of a public company's stock. Third, it regulates the tender offer process to enhance the bargaining position of target company shareholders. The Williams Act is typically covered in a mergers and acquisitions course.

6. SARBANES-OXLEY ACT OF 2002

The Sarbanes-Oxley Act of 2002 represents Congress' response to corporate scandals at Enron, WorldCom, Adelphia, Global Crossing, and Tyco, among other major publicly-held corporations that plagued the U.S. in the early 2000s. The law, a mélange of legislative reactions to the scandal du jour, provides new regulation for almost all significant players in the capital markets. Among other things, the Act establishes a quasi-governmental Public Company Accounting Oversight Board to regulate accountants along the lines of the SROs. It also prohibits auditors from performing certain non-audit consulting services for reporting issuers and requires companies to have audit committees made up exclusively of independent directors to oversee the company's relationship with its outside accountants. The Act directs the SEC to promulgate rules to encourage securities analysts to be more objective (which the SEC has done with Regulation AC). Attorneys for issuers are obligated under the Act to reveal evidence of securities law violations to the corporate board of directors. Corporate CEOs and CFOs are required to certify the information contained in their Form 10–K and 10–Q filings, as well as on the internal control structure of their companies. Finally, the Act increases the fines and criminal penalties for white-collar crime. We cover the more notable features of the Sarbanes-Oxley Act in greater detail in Chapter 12.

7. JUMPSTART OUR BUSINESS STARTUPS ACT OF 2012

Congress enacted the Jumpstart Our Business Startups Act (JOBS Act) in 2012 with the goal of increasing access to capital for emerging businesses. Proponents of the JOBS Act contended that private companies faced difficulties in raising capital due to restrictive private placement requirements (discussed in Chapter 9) and the costs imposed from the time consuming process of going public through a registered offering, with its significant liability risks (discussed in Chapters 7 and 8). For those companies that successfully sell securities in an initial public offering, the disclosure requirements, including those relating to executive compensation, imposed on public companies (discussed in Chapter 4) may prove intrusive. Those disclosure requirements are also costly, due the audit fees required to meet the various mandates of the Sarbanes-Oxley Act. Moreover, periodic disclosure requirements also expose a company to potential antifraud liability.

In response to these concerns, the JOBS Act created a new category of companies—"Emerging Growth Companies"—with a reduced level of required disclosures. We discuss the Emerging Growth Company in Chapter 4. The JOBS Act increased the threshold number of shareholders of a class of equity securities necessary before a company becomes a public company and thereby subject to the SEC's periodic disclosure filing system. We cover public company status in Chapter 4. The JOBS Act also allowed Emerging Growth Companies to "test the waters" for a potential public offering prior to filing a registration statement for the offering with the SEC. We cover Emerging Growth Companies and public offerings in Chapter 7. Finally, the JOBS Act expanded the avenues for companies to raise capital outside of a registered public offering, including modifications to the existing private placement regime under Rule 506 of the Securities Act, the addition of a new mini-public offering in § 3(b) of the Securities Act, and the creation of an entirely new form of private-public financing regime commonly known as "crowdfunding." We discuss these avenues to raise capital in Chapter 9.

B. THE FINANCIAL CRISIS AND THE DODD-FRANK ACT

Perhaps the most important event in the area of financial regulation (and indeed the economy) in the past several decades was the Financial Crisis of 2007–2008. Underlying the Financial Crisis were mortgage-backed securities based on subprime mortgages. Mortgage originators, encouraged by record low interest rates in the early 2000s, lent large amounts of money to subprime borrowers to purchase homes. Rather than hold onto subprime mortgages, mortgage originators, with the assistance of Wall Street investment banks, engaged in securitization. In the securitization process, mortgage originators sold the mortgages to so-called "special purpose vehicles" that pooled the mortgages and financed the purchase through the issuance of interests in the pool (known as residential mortgage-backed securities) to range of primarily institutional investors, including pension funds, hedge funds, and banks. In theory, securitization allowed mortgage originators to focus on the lending part of the mortgage business without worrying about liquidity. Instead of holding onto illiquid mortgages, securitization allowed mortgage originators to convert mortgages into cash, thereby allowing them to make even more home loans. As a result, mortgage originators—who bore little residual risk from the mortgages they originated—had less incentive to screen the quality of mortgage recipients. Not content with simply creating new mortgage-backed securities based on pools of underlying subprime mortgages, investment banks often took the mortgage-backed securities and combined them together to create new pools backing separate tranches of collateralized debt obligation ("CDO") securities. We discuss securitization and CDO securities in Chapter 3.

The presence of large amounts mortgage-backed securities all ultimately resting on the value of suspect subprime mortgages raised the level of systemic risk in the financial system and laid the foundation for the Financial Crisis. Broadly defined, systemic risk includes risks resulting from linkages across different institutions in a market or economy. Because of these linkages, the failure of a single entity (or subset of entities) can lead to a cascading failure across linked institutions. We discuss these linkages in greater detail in Chapter 3, but the key event triggering the crisis was the decline in value of mortgage-backed and CDO securities. Investors were surprised by a rise in the default rate for the mortgages underlying those securities, which caused the value of mortgage-backed securities to correspondingly decline. That decline, for a financial instrument previously thought to be only slightly riskier than holding Treasury bills, led to a rapid exodus from the market, further fueling the decline in the value of mortgage-backed securities.

Financial institutions left with large holdings of the now "toxic" securities then faced questions about their solvency and demands that they post greater collateral to secure their transactions. A number were unable to comply, forcing them into government-brokered rescues (Bear Stearns) or insolvency (Lehman Brothers). The resulting chilling effect on the financial markets led to a downturn in lending and investment and a worldwide "Great Recession."

In response to the Financial Crisis, Congress enacted the Dodd-Frank Act Wall Street Reform and Consumer Protection Act in 2010. Numbering over eight hundred pages in length, the Dodd-Frank Act provides a sweeping overhaul of the financial regulatory system. Most of the reforms in Dodd-Frank deal with areas outside the traditional scope of securities regulation and we largely leave these topics to other courses, providing only a brief summary here on the most important aspects of the Act. The Dodd-Frank Act focuses on improvements to bank regulation, redistributing regulatory authority. The Dodd-Frank Act also implements new regulations to provide for an orderly liquidation process for systemically important financial institutions and limits the occurrence of "too big to fail" financial institutions in the future.

To address systemic risk, the Dodd Frank Act creates a new 15 member Financial Stability Oversight Council with a focus on identifying, monitoring and addressing financial systemic risks. The Council is chaired by the Treasury Secretary and made up of regulators including the Federal Reserve Board, SEC, CFTC, Office of the Comptroller of the Currency, FDIC, Federal Housing Financing Agency, and the new Consumer Financial Protection Bureau.

The starting point of the Financial Crisis was the decisions of numerous home purchasers to borrow money (often more than they could afford) through adjustable rate subprime mortgages. Better consumer protection may reduce such ill-advised decisions. The new Consumer Financial Protection Bureau is charged with increasing the protection for consumers entering into transactions involving mortgages, credit cards, and other financial products. The Dodd-Frank Act addresses the incentive of mortgage lenders to make weak loans and shift the risk of such loans to others through securitization transaction by requiring federal banking agencies and the SEC to implement rules requiring certain companies engaged in securitization transactions to retain at least 5% of the credit risk in the issuance of asset-backed securities.

The Dodd-Frank Act addresses the potential role of hedge funds in adding to and masking the level of systemic risk in the economy. The Act requires hedge funds that manage at least $150 million in assets to register with the SEC as investment advisors. Once registered, hedge funds then come under an obligation to disclose information related to systemic risk for use by other regulators (including the new Financial Stability Oversight Council).

Other provisions in the Dodd-Frank Act relate to the SEC's core functions of disclosure regulation, investor protection, and the regulation of counterparties, intermediaries, and other institutions most relevant to the capital markets. Many of the new disclosure provisions relate to asset-backed securities (such as the mortgage-backed securities at the center of the Financial Crisis). The Dodd-Frank Act grants the SEC rulemaking authority to require issuers of asset-backed securities to disclose certain information relating to such securities, including information on specific loans within the pool of assets. We discuss the Dodd-Frank Act requirements for asset-backed securities in Chapter 7.

The Act gives the SEC specific rulemaking authority relating to shareholder voting including giving shareholders of public companies a non-binding shareholder vote on executive compensation ("say on pay" proposals) and shareholder proxy access to nominate directors. We discuss the Dodd-Frank Act's effect on shareholder voting in Chapter 11. Finally, the Act also creates a program in the SEC to encourage people to report securities violations (i.e., act as whistleblowers). We discuss this whistleblower program in Chapter 12.

C. THE SECURITIES AND EXCHANGE COMMISSION

Congress typically intervenes only sporadically in the securities market, stepping in with legislation only when there has been a crisis that captures legislators' attention. The main task of monitoring the market, enforcing the securities laws, and developing new regulations is largely left with an administrative agency: the Securities and Exchange Commission.

The SEC was established by the Securities Exchange Act of 1934. Heading the SEC are five commissioners (one of whom is appointed Chairman). Although the President appoints the commissioners, the Exchange Act requires that not more than three of the commissioners come from the same political party. Joseph Kennedy served as the SEC's first Chairman in 1934. One of Kennedy's successors was William O. Douglas, appointed SEC Chairman in 1936, more familiar to you perhaps in his later role as an Associate Justice of the U.S. Supreme Court.

The SEC is charged with administering the federal securities laws. Headquartered in Washington, D.C., the SEC also has several regional offices, the largest of which is in New York. The SEC divides its staff into several different divisions, including:

- Corporation Finance

- Trading and Markets

- Investment Management

- Enforcement

- Risk, Strategy, and Financial Innovation

The Division of Corporation Finance handles disclosure by issuers to investors, reviewing Exchange Act periodic filings (Forms 10–K, 10–Q, and 8–K). The Division of Corporation Finance also reviews the registration statements of companies doing public offerings, particularly for IPO issuers, providing comments to the issuers on the preliminary registration statements. As part of its focus on disclosure, Corporation Finance frequently reviews and proposes changes to disclosure forms and rules for approval by the Commissioners of the SEC. This division also provides guidance to companies on complying with the rules and forms.

The Division of Trading and Markets deals primarily with the regulation of the securities professionals associated with the public capital markets. As part of its function, Trading and Markets regulates, among others, broker-dealers and the self-regulatory organizations. The Division of Investment Management regulates both investment companies and investment advisors. Investment Management regulates mutual funds like those offered by Vanguard and Fidelity. The mutual fund industry has long enjoyed its reputation as one of the "cleaner" sectors of the investment industry, a notable distinction in an industry that draws more than its fair share of sleazy operators.

The Division of Enforcement investigates securities law violations. The SEC may initiate enforcement actions in federal court or conduct administrative proceedings. In criminal cases, the SEC must make a referral to the Justice Department for prosecution. (These topics are covered in greater detail in Chapter 13.)

The Division of Risk, Strategy, and Financial Innovation (known as "Risk Fin") was created in 2009 in the wake of the Financial Crisis. The new Division provides the SEC with economic and financial expertise concerning risk and economic analysis, strategic research, and financial innovation. The SEC's hope is that Risk Fin will allow the agency to keep up with the rapid innovation on Wall Street, such as the use of credit default swaps and other instruments that exacerbated the magnitude of the Financial Crisis. Risk Fin serves as a "think tank" for the SEC and integrates its work across all of the SEC's activities, from policy and rulemaking to enforcement actions.

In addition to these Divisions, the SEC has separate offices devoted to particular functions. Among the more important are the Office of the General Counsel, the Office of the Chief Accountant, the Office of International Affairs, the Office of Credit Ratings, the Office of Compliance Inspections and Examinations, and the Office of Investor Advocacy and Education. The Office of General Counsel provides legal advice to the Commissioners, drafts the opinions of the Commission in administrative proceedings, and represents the agency in the courts of appeals. The Office of the Chief Accountant provides guidance to public companies and their auditors on accounting, financial reporting, and auditing questions. Together with the Division of Corporation Finance and the Public Company Accounting Oversight Board, the Office of the Chief Accountant also monitors the accounting profession. The Office of the International Affairs takes the lead role in efforts to coordinate U.S. securities regulation with the laws of other countries, an increasingly important task as the securities markets become more and more interlinked. The Office of Credit Ratings, created as part of the Dodd-Frank Act, focuses on credit rating agencies and their procedures and methodologies. The Office of Compliance Inspections and Examinations conducts examinations of broker-dealers, investment advisers, investment companies (i.e., mutual funds), the national securities exchanges, clearing agencies, and self-regulatory organizations (including FINRA). The Office of the Investor Advocacy and Education deals with retail investor tips, complaints, and suggestions. (Call 1-800-SEC-0330 if you have a suggestion. Extra credit on the exam!). Finally, the Office of the Whistleblower processes complaints of fraud.

The SEC and its staff influence the capital markets through a variety of mechanisms. First, the SEC may engage in formal rulemaking. Corporation Finance, for example, develops regulations for securities offerings. Trading and Markets directs its attention to rulemaking affecting institutions serving the secondary markets, including broker-dealers. The commissioners of the SEC have the ultimate authority to approve new regulations after the appropriate notice and comment period for public review.

Second, the SEC brings enforcement actions. The Division of Enforcement is charged with bringing civil enforcement actions for violations of the securities laws. Enforcement actions not only punish violators of the securities laws but also deter others in the securities market from wrongdoing.

Third, the SEC's staff will sometimes issue individuals and companies a "no-action letter." A no-action letter consists of a letter requesting that the SEC's staff take a position that if the conditions as detailed in the letter are met, the staff will then recommend that no enforcement action be taken against the parties in the described transaction. The SEC's staff, in granting a no-action letter, will then respond with a letter detailing the staff's position on whether the facts specified in the original letter would warrant an enforcement action. No-action letters represent the opinion only of the SEC staff and not necessarily the view of the SEC's commissioners. Moreover, private litigants are not bound by a no-action letter and may bring suit in court based on the same fact pattern, although the court may defer to the interpretation in the no-action letter.

Finally, the SEC may influence both participants in the capital markets and the courts through its communications. Most important are the Commission's releases. Releases announce the Commission's enforcement actions, set forth the agency's interpretations of the law, propose rules and explain the rules adopted. Individual commissioners and division heads often give speeches on their views on the capital markets and securities regulation. In addition, the SEC occasionally files amicus briefs with courts adjudicating private securities lawsuits. More informally, the SEC staff answers questions on the telephone.

D. SELF-REGULATORY ORGANIZATIONS

The SEC is not the only regulator of the securities markets. Several quasi-private regulatory entities operate as an additional layer of investor protection. Among these entities are FINRA, the national securities exchanges (including the NYSE and Nasdaq), and Nationally Recognized Statistical Ratings Organizations (NRSRO) such as Moody's and Standard and Poor's. The SEC has the power to approve, disapprove or modify SRO rules as it "deems necessary or appropriate to insure the fair administration of the self-regulatory organization" under § 19 of the Exchange Act.

Established in 1939 as the National Association of Securities Dealers, FINRA regulates broker-dealers. FINRA is a private, non-profit, membership-based organization, composed of broker and securities dealer members. The Exchange Act requires that FINRA, as a self-regulatory organization, adopt rules "designed to prevent fraudulent and manipulative acts and practices, to promote just and equitable principles of trade . . . and, in general, to protect investors and the public interest." FINRA also brings enforcement actions against broker-dealers.

FINRA provides investors with a great deal of information on brokers. FINRA's "BrokerCheck" system (available at http://www.finra. org) allows any investor to examine the background and past disciplinary history of brokers registered with FINRA. FINRA also maintains an active arbitration system for customers, brokers, and brokerage firms. Most brokerage agreements provide for mandatory arbitration in case of disputes. Common investor complaints against brokers include allegations that a broker sold unsuitable securities to the investor or that the broker "churned" the investor's account to generate unwarranted trading commissions for the broker. Arbitration provides a relatively low-cost and speedy method of resolving complaints against brokers and brokerage firms. However, some question whether arbitration sacrifices consistency and fairness in adjudication to obtain these benefits.

The Nasdaq and NYSE have listing standards for companies wishing to list their shares for trading. Listed companies must meet minimum capitalization and asset requirements. Both the Nasdaq and NYSE also impose minimum corporate governance requirements, including a majority of "independent" directors. Moreover, listed companies must establish audit, executive compensation, and director nominating committees consisting entirely of independent directors.

NRSROs such as Moody's and Standard and Poor's played a prominent role in the Financial Crisis of 2008 and 2009. NRSROs routinely gave investment grade ratings to CDO bonds based on pools of mortgage-backed securities. Investors relying on such ratings were unpleasantly surprised when the systemic risk in the CDO bonds became apparent as the underlying mortgage pools lost value with the decline in housing values in the United States in the late 2000s. The Dodd-Frank Act established a new Office of Credit Ratings at the SEC focused on the regulation of Nationally Recognized Statistical Ratings Organizations. Among other things, the Act requires the SEC to promulgate rules on the procedures and methodologies of NRSROs and rules requiring disclosures for NRSROs including the assumptions behind their procedures and methodologies and the data used to determine a credit rating. We cover these rules in Chapter 12.

Another important quasi-governmental body is the Public Company Accounting Oversight Board (PCAOB) created by Congress as part of the Sarbanes-Oxley Act of 2002. The PCAOB consists of a five-member board, only two of which members may have experience as certified public accountants. A non-profit, private entity, the PCAOB is authorized under the Sarbanes-Oxley Act to oversee the audit of public companies as well as to establish requirements for auditor independence. Public accounting firms are required to register with the PCAOB. The PCAOB is funded in part from a levy imposed on all Exchange Act reporting issuers. The PCAOB conducts investigations of public accounting firms and impose sanctions. As with the other self-regulatory organizations, the PCAOB is subject to both the oversight and enforcement authority of the SEC.

———

This Chapter has introduced the common types of securities investments and the major markets for securities transactions. We have also provided a glimpse into the motivations of investors. To understand the purpose of the securities laws and to assess their effectiveness, we first need to understand why investors invest and what information investors require to make informed decisions. Investors typically will part with their hard-earned money only if they expect to receive even more money back in the future. We have explained the present discount valuation method of translating the future value of investments into today's dollars. The PDV formula is only as good as the information put into the formula. Investors require information on a company's businesses, assets, management, financials, and regulatory and competitive environment, among other things, to value accurately a company's expected cash flow and exposure to market risk. Finally, we have briefly summarized both the different components of the federal securities laws and the regulatory entities charged with enforcing and implementing those laws.

The rest of the casebook covers a number of topics important to understanding the federal securities regime governing transactions in both the primary and secondary markets. We do not attempt to be comprehensive in our coverage. Instead, we select topics that highlight the major motivations behind the securities laws and the assumptions about investor behavior embedded in those laws. Throughout the book, we emphasize the importance of disclosure as a means of reducing informational disparities in both markets. Our goal here is to help you understand the basic approaches to securities regulation.

CHAPTER 2

MATERIALITY

Rules and Statutes
—*Regulation S–K, Items 103, 303, 401, 403, 404, 406*
—*Rules 10b–5, 12b–20 of the Exchange Act*

MOTIVATING HYPOTHETICAL

Six Feet, Inc. is in the funeral business. It owns a chain of funeral homes that stretches across the U.S. and Canada and its shares are listed on the NYSE. David is the Chairman of the Board and CEO. His younger brother, Nate, is the President and COO. Although the two have worked hard together to make Six Feet the "death services" powerhouse that it is today, they have not always agreed about business strategy. David thinks that Six Feet needs to merge with another company in the funeral business to continue its growth. Nate thinks that they should continue to grow Six Feet through internal expansion.

I. WHAT MATTERS TO INVESTORS?

We learned in Chapter 1 that information is the lifeblood of the securities markets. Current and complete information about the corporation also allows shareholders to evaluate the performance of management and the board of directors. Consequently, disclosure is the focal point of federal securities regulation.

Notwithstanding the importance of disclosure to the decisions of investors, not all information will be equally relevant. The structure of the CEO's compensation package is likely to be important to most investors; the fact that the CEO enjoys fly-fishing in his spare time is not. Misleading statements regarding the compensation package are appropriately met by an SEC enforcement action and, potentially, a private class action; misleading statements about the CEO's hobbies are appropriately met by "Who cares?" Choices must be made in determining what information must be disclosed in the corporation's periodic filings and which false statements will give rise to liability.

The concept of materiality is a common threshold used in many areas to determine whether information is important enough to warrant regulation. Consider antifraud liability. Exchange Act Rule 10b–5 antifraud liability covers not only the disclosures filed with the SEC, but also voluntary disclosures such as press releases by the company and interviews provided by the CEO. The antifraud prohibition of Exchange Act Rule 10b–5 creates liability both for making "any untrue statement of a material fact" and omitting "to state a material fact necessary in order to make the statements made, in the light of the circumstances under which they were made, not misleading." So if a statement is made, there is always a duty to tell the truth, and to tell the whole truth. But even if there has been either an affirmative misleading misstatement or an omission which creates a misleading impression, the plaintiff or the SEC must also show that misleading statement or omitted fact was material. If a person has made no statement at all, we ordinarily will not reach the question of materiality because there is no general duty to volunteer information. In other words, silence is golden. The exception to this golden rule, however, is that under insider trading doctrine (the subject of Chapter 6), companies and their officers and directors have a duty to disclose all material facts before buying or selling the company's securities. Insider trading is a fraud of pure omission—the insider who trades while enjoying an informational advantage over the public is also liable under Rule 10b–5, but only if the insider's non-public information is material.

Materiality applies beyond antifraud liability. The SEC has used its rulemaking powers to make a series of ex ante determinations of what information is important to investors, and should therefore be disclosed in various SEC filings, such as the annual Form 10–K and quarterly Form 10–Q. These SEC filing requirements are contained in Regulation S–K, the focal point of the SEC integrated disclosure system. For these disclosure items, most of the discretion has been removed from the issuer and its counsel: if an item is listed in Regulation S–K, it must be disclosed, whether or not it would independently be deemed material. The SEC has determined that investors will find the required information relevant most of the time. Moreover, as we discussed in Chapter 1, a consistent set of disclosure obligations allows investors to compare firms more easily.

Although there is no general duty to disclose all material information, materiality plays an important role in applying the Regulation S–K disclosure items. Some items in the laundry list of disclosures mandated by the SEC in Regulation S–K are required only if they are "material." Item 101(a) of Regulation S–K, for example, requires issuers to disclose information on the general development of their business over the past five years as well as information pertaining to earlier periods if "material to an understanding of the general development of the business." Moreover, Regulation S–K's disclosure items do not exhaust the list of mandatory disclosures. Exchange Act Rule 12b–20 requires:

> In addition to the information expressly required to be included in a statement or report, there shall be added such further material information, if any, as may be necessary to make the required statements, in the light of the circumstances under which they are made not misleading.

Rule 408 of the Securities Act similarly prohibits misleading "half truths."

What information rises to level of materiality? The Supreme Court provided the seminal formulation of materiality in *TSC Industries, Inc. v. Northway*, 426 U.S. 438 (1976). According to *TSC Industries*, information is material if there is a "substantial likelihood that the disclosure . . . would have been viewed by the reasonable investor as having significantly altered the 'total mix' of information made available." Unfortunately, determining whether a particular morsel of information would be valued by the hypothetical "reasonable investor" is often an uncertain process. What is "reasonable?" What information would that investor consider significant? What is included in the total mix of information?

In this Chapter, we canvass how courts determine whether specific types of information are material. There is an important timing aspect to the determination of materiality. Corporate officers, with the assistance of corporate counsel, must frequently consider the materiality of corporate information they choose to disclose or not to disclose. They must make this decision knowing that their decision may be later second-guessed—first possibly a plaintiffs' attorney or the SEC, and then eventually a judge, and—in theory—a jury. If courts adopt a bright-line rule of materiality then officers and directors will have certainty that their determination of materiality will be the same as later decisionmakers. If courts adopt a more standard-based rule of materiality, officers and their lawyers will have less certainty. Indeed, in the extreme judges may apply an "I know it when I see it" test of materiality. As you consider the cases on materiality in this Chapter, consider whether the tests for materiality differ in practice from the "I know it when I see it" test.

We start with forward-looking information in Part II, dealing with future and necessarily contingent events. Then we discuss how materiality applies to historical facts in Part III. In particular, is it possible to use numerical rules of thumb to ease the uncertainty in deciding whether a particular fact is material? And what role should market reactions play in materiality determinations? In Part IV we consider how the "total mix of information" may render information immaterial even if it would be material in isolation. Finally, we conclude in Part V looking at the relationship between materiality and management integrity. Even if information is important to investors, when do privacy concerns counsel against disclosure?

II.   FORWARD-LOOKING INFORMATION

The case below outlines the general standard of materiality under the securities laws. In addition, it provides guidance in applying that standard to "forward-looking" information, i.e., disclosures regarding events that may or may not come to pass. Investors are more interested in what a company is going to do in the future than what it has done in the past. A brighter future for a company translates to higher expected earnings and a correspondingly higher return from owning the company's shares. So insights into the company's future will be eagerly digested by the markets. Why is it harder for companies and their counsel to assess the materiality of forward-looking information than historical facts?

Basic Inc. v. Levinson

485 U.S. 224 (1988).

■ BLACKMUN, J.

This case requires us to apply the materiality requirement of § 10(b) of the Securities Exchange Act of 1934 and the Securities and Exchange Commission's Rule 10b–5 in the context of preliminary corporate merger discussions. . . .

I

Prior to December 20, 1978, Basic Incorporated was a publicly traded company primarily engaged in the business of manufacturing chemical refractories for the steel industry. As early as 1965 or 1966, Combustion Engineering, Inc., a company producing mostly alumina-based refractories, expressed some interest in acquiring Basic. . . . The "Strategic Plan," dated October 25, 1976, for Combustion's Industrial Products Group included the objective: "Acquire Basic Inc. $30 million."

Beginning in September 1976, Combustion representatives had meetings and telephone conversations with Basic officers and directors, including petitioners here, concerning the possibility of a merger. During 1977 and 1978, Basic made three public statements denying that it was engaged in merger negotiations.[4] On December 18, 1978, Basic asked the New York Stock Exchange to suspend trading in its shares and issued a release stating that it had been "approached" by another company concerning a merger. On December 19, Basic's board endorsed Combustion's offer of $46 per share for its common stock, and on the following day publicly announced its approval of Combustion's tender offer for all outstanding shares.

Respondents are former Basic shareholders who sold their stock after Basic's first public statement of October 21, 1977, and before the suspension of trading in December 1978. Respondents brought a class action against Basic and its directors, asserting that the defendants issued three false or misleading public statements and thereby were in violation of § 10(b) of the 1934 Act and of Rule 10b–5. Respondents alleged that they were injured by selling Basic shares at artificially depressed prices in a market affected by petitioners' misleading statements and in reliance thereon.

The District Court . . . granted summary judgment for the defendants. It held that, as a matter of law, any misstatements were immaterial: there were no negotiations ongoing at the time of the first statement, and although negotiations were taking place when the second and third statements were issued, those negotiations were not "destined, with reasonable certainty, to become a merger agreement in principle."

The United States Court of Appeals for the Sixth Circuit . . . reversed the District Court's summary judgment, and remanded the case. The court reasoned that while petitioners were under no general

---

[4] On October 21, 1977, after heavy trading and a new high in Basic stock, the following news item appeared in the Cleveland Plain Dealer: "[Basic] President Max Muller said the company knew no reason for the stock's activity and that no negotiations were under way with any company for a merger. He said Flintkote recently denied Wall Street rumors that it would make a tender offer of $25 a share for control of the Cleveland-based maker of refractories for the steel industry."

On September 25, 1978, in reply to an inquiry from the New York Stock Exchange, Basic issued a release concerning increased activity in its stock and stated that "management is unaware of any present or pending company development that would result in the abnormally heavy trading activity and price fluctuation in company shares that have been experienced in the past few days."

On November 6, 1978, Basic issued to its shareholders a "Nine Months Report 1978." This Report stated: "With regard to the stock market activity in the Company's shares we remain unaware of any present or pending developments which would account for the high volume of trading and price fluctuations in recent months."

duty to disclose their discussions with Combustion, any statement the company voluntarily released could not be " 'so incomplete as to mislead.' " In the Court of Appeals' view, Basic's statements that no negotiations were taking place, and that it knew of no corporate developments to account for the heavy trading activity, were misleading. With respect to materiality, the court rejected the argument that preliminary merger discussions are immaterial as a matter of law, and held that "once a statement is made denying the existence of any discussions, even discussions that might not have been material in absence of the denial are material because they make the statement made untrue."

We granted certiorari, to resolve the split . . . among the Courts of Appeals as to the standard of materiality applicable to preliminary merger discussions. . . .

II

The 1934 Act was designed to protect investors against manipulation of stock prices. Underlying the adoption of extensive disclosure requirements was a legislative philosophy: "There cannot be honest markets without honest publicity. Manipulation and dishonest practices of the market place thrive upon mystery and secrecy." This Court "repeatedly has described the 'fundamental purpose' of the Act as implementing a 'philosophy of full disclosure.' "

The Court . . . explicitly has defined a standard of materiality under the securities laws, see *TSC Industries, Inc. v. Northway, Inc.*, 426 U.S. 438 (1976), concluding in the proxy-solicitation context that "[a]n omitted fact is material if there is a substantial likelihood that a reasonable shareholder would consider it important in deciding how to vote." Acknowledging that certain information concerning corporate developments could well be of "dubious significance," the Court was careful not to set too low a standard of materiality; it was concerned that a minimal standard might bring an overabundance of information within its reach, and lead management "simply to bury the shareholders in an avalanche of trivial information—a result that is hardly conducive to informed decisionmaking." It further explained that to fulfill the materiality requirement "there must be a substantial likelihood that the disclosure of the omitted fact would have been viewed by the reasonable investor as having significantly altered the 'total mix' of information made available." We now expressly adopt the *TSC Industries* standard of materiality for the § 10(b) and Rule 10b–5 context.

III

The application of this materiality standard to preliminary merger discussions is not self-evident. Where the impact of the corporate development on the target's fortune is certain and clear, the *TSC Industries* materiality definition admits straightforward application. Where, on the other hand, the event is contingent or speculative in nature, it is difficult to ascertain whether the "reasonable investor" would have considered the omitted information significant at the time. Merger negotiations, because of the ever-present possibility that the contemplated transaction will not be effectuated, fall into the latter category.[9]

A

Petitioners urge upon us a Third Circuit test for resolving this difficulty. Under this approach, preliminary merger discussions do not become material until "agreement-in-principle" as to the price and structure of the transaction has been reached between the would-be merger partners. By definition, then, information concerning any negotiations not yet at the agreement-in-principle stage could be withheld or even misrepresented without a violation of Rule 10b–5.

Three rationales have been offered in support of the "agreement-in-principle" test. The first derives from the concern expressed in *TSC Industries* that an investor not be overwhelmed by excessively detailed and trivial information, and focuses on the substantial risk that preliminary merger discussions may collapse: because such discussions are inherently tentative, disclosure of their existence itself could mislead investors and foster false optimism. The other two justifications for the agreement-in-principle standard are based on management concerns: because the requirement of "agreement-in-principle" limits the scope of disclosure obligations, it helps preserve the confidentiality of merger discussions where earlier disclosure might prejudice the negotiations; and the test also provides a usable, bright-line rule for determining when disclosure must be made.

None of these policy-based rationales, however, purports to explain why drawing the line at agreement-in-principle reflects the significance of the information upon the investor's decision. The first rationale, and the only one connected to the concerns expressed in *TSC Industries*, stands soundly rejected, even by a Court of Appeals that otherwise has accepted the wisdom of the agreement-in-principle test. "It assumes that investors are nitwits, unable to appreciate—even when told—that mergers are risky propositions up until the closing." Disclosure, and not paternalistic withholding of accurate information, is the policy chosen and expressed by Congress. We have recognized time and again, a "fundamental purpose" of the various Securities Acts, "was to substitute a philosophy of full disclosure for the philosophy of caveat emptor and thus to achieve a high standard of business ethics in the securities industry." The role of the materiality requirement is not to "attribute to investors a child-like simplicity, an inability to grasp the probabilistic significance of negotiations," but to filter out essentially useless information that a reasonable investor would not consider significant, even as part of a larger "mix" of factors to consider in making his investment decision.

The second rationale, the importance of secrecy during the early stages of merger discussions, also seems irrelevant to an assessment whether their existence is significant to the trading decision of a reasonable investor. To avoid a "bidding war" over its target, an acquiring firm often will insist that negotiations remain confidential, and at least one Court of Appeals has stated that "silence pending

---

[9]   We do not address here any other kinds of contingent or speculative information, such as earnings forecasts or projections.

settlement of the price and structure of a deal is beneficial to most investors, most of the time."

We need not ascertain, however, whether secrecy necessarily maximizes shareholder wealth—although we note that the proposition is at least disputed as a matter of theory and empirical research—for this case does not concern the timing of a disclosure; it concerns only its accuracy and completeness. We face here the narrow question whether information concerning the existence and status of preliminary merger discussions is significant to the reasonable investor's trading decision. Arguments based on the premise that some disclosure would be "premature" in a sense are more properly considered under the rubric of an issuer's duty to disclose. The "secrecy" rationale is simply inapposite to the definition of materiality.

The final justification offered in support of the agreement-in-principle test seems to be directed solely at the comfort of corporate managers. A bright-line rule indeed is easier to follow than a standard that requires the exercise of judgment in the light of all the circumstances. But ease of application alone is not an excuse for ignoring the purposes of the Securities Acts and Congress' policy decisions. Any approach that designates a single fact or occurrence as always determinative of an inherently fact-specific finding such as materiality, must necessarily be overinclusive or underinclusive. In *TSC Industries* this Court explained: "The determination [of materiality] requires delicate assessments of the inferences a 'reasonable shareholder' would draw from a given set of facts and the significance of those inferences to him. . . ."

* * *

We therefore find no valid justification for artificially excluding from the definition of materiality information concerning merger discussions, which would otherwise be considered significant to the trading decision of a reasonable investor, merely because agreement-in-principle as to price and structure has not yet been reached by the parties or their representatives.

B

The Sixth Circuit explicitly rejected the agreement-in-principle test, as we do today, but in its place adopted a rule that, if taken literally, would be equally insensitive, in our view, to the distinction between materiality and the other elements of an action under Rule 10b–5:

> When a company whose stock is publicly traded makes a statement, as Basic did, that "no negotiations" are underway, and that the corporation knows of "no reason for the stock's activity", and that "management is unaware of any present or pending corporate development that would result in the abnormally heavy trading activity", information concerning ongoing acquisition discussions becomes material by virtue of the statement denying their existence. . . .

* * *

In analyzing whether information regarding merger discussions is material such that it must be affirmatively disclosed to avoid a violation of Rule 10b–5, the discussions and their progress are the primary considerations. However, once a statement is made denying the existence of any discussions, even discussions that might not have been material in absence of the denial are material because they make the statement made untrue.

This approach, however, fails to recognize that, in order to prevail on a Rule 10b–5 claim, a plaintiff must show that the statements were misleading as to a material fact. It is not enough that a statement is false or incomplete, if the misrepresented fact is otherwise insignificant.

C

Even before this Court's decision in *TSC Industries*, the Second Circuit had explained the role of the materiality requirement of Rule 10b–5, with respect to contingent or speculative information or events, in a manner that gave that term meaning that is independent of the other provisions of the Rule. Under such circumstances, materiality "will depend at any given time upon a balancing of both the indicated probability that the event will occur and the anticipated magnitude of the event in light of the totality of the company activity." *SEC v. Texas Gulf Sulphur Co.*, 401 F.2d 849 [833] [(CA 2, 1968) (en banc).]

In a subsequent decision, the late Judge Friendly, writing for a Second Circuit panel, applied the *Texas Gulf Sulphur* probability/magnitude approach in the specific context of preliminary merger negotiations. After acknowledging that materiality is something to be determined on the basis of the particular facts of each case, he stated:

Since a merger in which it is bought out is the most important event that can occur in a small corporation's life, to wit, its death, we think that inside information, as regards a merger of this sort, can become material at an earlier stage than would be the case as regards lesser transactions—and this even though the mortality rate of mergers in such formative stages is doubtless high.

We agree with that analysis.[16]

Whether merger discussions in any particular case are material therefore depends on the facts. Generally, in order to assess the probability that the event will occur, a factfinder will need to look to indicia of interest in the transaction at the highest corporate levels. Without attempting to catalog all such possible factors, we note by way of example that board resolutions, instructions to investment bankers, and actual negotiations between principals ·or their intermediaries may serve as indicia of interest. To assess the magnitude of the transaction to the issuer of the securities allegedly manipulated, a factfinder will need to consider such facts as the size of the two corporate entities and of the potential premiums over market value. No particular event or

---

[16] The SEC in the present case endorses the highly fact-dependent probability/magnitude balancing approach of *Texas Gulf Sulphur*. It explains: "The *possibility* of a merger may have an immediate importance to investors in the company's securities even if no merger ultimately takes place." The SEC's insights are helpful, and we accord them due deference.

factor short of closing the transaction need be either necessary or sufficient by itself to render merger discussions material.[17]

As we clarify today, materiality depends on the significance the reasonable investor would place on the withheld or misrepresented information.[18] The fact-specific inquiry we endorse here is consistent with the approach a number of courts have taken in assessing the materiality of merger negotiations. Because the standard of materiality we have adopted differs from that used by both courts below, we remand the case for reconsideration of the question whether a grant of summary judgment is appropriate on this record.

* * *

NOTES

1. *The reasonable shareholder.* The Supreme Court's invocation of the "reasonable shareholder" indicates that the materiality standard is an objective one—companies do not need to worry about information relevant only to the idiosyncratic investor. Issuers are not responsible for the subjective preferences of a particular investor.

Who decides what information is material? The Supreme Court cautioned in *TSC Industries, Inc. v. Northway,* 426 U.S. 438, 450 (1976), that materiality is a mixed question of law and fact that should ordinarily be determined by the fact finder at trial. This caution is frequently ignored. Lower courts, anxious to dismiss what they perceive to be weak cases, have frequently concluded that no reasonable jury could conclude that the information misrepresented or omitted was material, thereby making dismissal or summary judgment appropriate.

2. *Forward-looking information.* Forward-looking information (sometimes called "soft" information) receives mixed treatment under the securities laws. On the one hand, the SEC has made clear that companies in the "quiet period" leading up to a public offering of securities disclose soft information only at their peril (as discussed in Chapter 7). Projections of future financial performance are particularly disfavored. The SEC's position assumes that investors are particularly vulnerable to excessively optimistic forward-looking disclosures in the public offering setting. The

---

[17] To be actionable, of course, a statement must also be misleading. Silence, absent a duty to disclose, is not misleading under Rule 10b–5. "No comment" statements are generally the functional equivalent of silence. See ... New York Stock Exchange Listed Company Manual § 202.01 (premature public announcement may properly be delayed for valid business purpose and where adequate security can be maintained). . . .

[18] We find no authority in the statute, the legislative history, or our previous decisions for varying the standard of materiality depending on who brings the action or whether insiders are alleged to have profited.

We recognize that trading (and profit making) by insiders can serve as an indication of materiality. We are not prepared to agree, however, that "[i]n cases of the disclosure of inside information to a favored few, determination of materiality has a different aspect than when the issue is, for example, an inaccuracy in a publicly disseminated press release." Devising two different standards of materiality, one for situations where insiders have traded in abrogation of their duty to disclose or abstain (or for that matter when any disclosure duty has been breached), and another covering affirmative misrepresentations by those under no duty to disclose (but under the ever-present duty not to mislead), would effectively collapse the materiality requirement into the analysis of defendant's disclosure duties.

SEC worries that because such information is inherently difficult to verify, investors are more easily lead astray.

In contrast, other areas of the securities laws recognize the importance of forward-looking information to investors and assume that investors are capable of digesting it. To induce companies to make such disclosures (and in response to the perceived risk of frivolous litigation targeting soft disclosures), Congress enacted a safe harbor for forward-looking statements as part of the Private Securities Litigation Reform Act of 1995 (covered in Chapter 5). When we revisit the issue of forward-looking information, consider how you would balance the importance of such information to investors against the risk of misleading investors.

QUESTIONS

1. Are shareholders better off if merger negotiations must be disclosed? If your answer is "no" then should companies be allowed to affirmatively misrepresent the status (or absence) of merger negotiations?

2. What prompted the misstatements at issue in the case? What could Basic have done to maintain the confidentiality of its merger negotiations with Combustion?

3. Is a judge or jury assessing the probability of an event after it has occurred likely to assign the same probability as the issuer and its counsel did when they were drafting the disclosure?

4. Was the potential merger with Basic necessarily material to Combustion shareholders?

5. Does the Court specify the threshold above which probability x magnitude becomes material?

6. Why does the Court focus on the informational needs of the "reasonable investor"? Aren't "unreasonable investors" more likely to make poor investment choices?

HYPOTHETICAL ONE

David, the CEO of Six Feet, has had several conversations with Sarah, the CEO of Dearly Departed, Inc. (Six Feet's chief competitor with a similar market share), about the possibility of merging their two companies. So far their discussions have been relatively informal, but they have discussed a merger ratio for a possible stock-for-stock merger, with Six Feet to be the survivor of the merger. They have also agreed that David would be the Chairman of the Board of the merged company and Sarah the CEO and President. (Nate, the President of Six Feet, would be looking for work!)

David and Sarah have agreed on the important terms, but David is not sure that he wants to take the deal to Six Feet's board. David and Nate hold two of the seven seats on Six Feet's board. Federico, Six Feet's Vice-President for Death Services, holds one of the other seats. He is the creative spark behind Six Feet's growth—he came up with the idea of caskets bearing the logo of the deceased's favorite sports team—and also a substantial shareholder. Federico has been wary of taking on too much risk, but he also despises Nate and would be happy to see him go. David is uncertain which way Federico will vote if the merger is presented to the board, and Federico is very influential with Six Feet's independent directors. Moreover, Six Feet and Dearly Departed have very substantial shares of the funeral services market in a number of metropolitan areas and any merger between the two could draw the scrutiny of the antitrust authorities.

David is pondering all of these variables at the time he is interviewed by The Eulogy, a magazine devoted to the funeral business. In response to the reporter's question, "Does Six Feet have any acquisitions in the pipeline?" David says "We do not currently have any major acquisitions in mind, but Six Feet is always looking for opportunities to expand if they make business sense." Does David's response contain a material omission?

III. OBJECTIVE TESTS OF MATERIALITY

Insight into future profits is what investors are most interested in, but some historical facts, such as accounting data on revenues and profits, may shed important light on a company's future course. Even historical facts can be contested, particularly in the often murky area of accounting. Rules of thumbs could help in assessing the materiality of such historical facts. In making materiality determinations, issuers, their counsel and their accountants crave certainty, which can be all too elusive. Rules of thumbs allow corporations to make their assessment of materiality without worrying that a judge or jury will come to a different conclusion later. One common rule-of-thumb holds that misstatements and omissions that account for less than 5% of earnings are presumptively immaterial. Some use a different baseline, looking to 5% of revenues or assets as the materiality threshold.

The use of rules of thumb to determine materiality provides a threshold (5%) to apply to *Basic v. Levinson's* probability x magnitude formulation in the case of contingent events. Imagine the following test: If the probability x magnitude is less than 5% of the earnings of a company, then the contingent event is not material. For historic facts, the probability is simply 1 and we can simply compare the magnitude against the 5% rule of thumb threshold.

In the following release, the SEC weighed in on the use of rules of thumb.

SEC Staff Accounting Bulletin No. 99
Release No. SAB–99 (1999).

* * *

The use of a percentage as a numerical threshold, such as 5%, may provide the basis for a preliminary assumption that—without considering all relevant circumstances—a deviation of less than the specified percentage with respect to a particular item on the registrant's financial statements is unlikely to be material. The staff has no objection to such a "rule of thumb" as an initial step in assessing materiality. But quantifying, in percentage terms, the magnitude of a misstatement is only the beginning of an analysis of materiality; it cannot appropriately be used as a substitute for a full analysis of all relevant considerations.

Materiality concerns the significance of an item to users of a registrant's financial statements. In the context of a misstatement of a financial statement item, while the "total mix" includes the size in numerical or percentage terms of the misstatement, it also includes the factual context in which the user of financial statements would view the financial statement item. The shorthand in the accounting and auditing literature for this analysis is that financial management and the auditor must consider both "quantitative" and "qualitative" factors in assessing an item's materiality.

————

Does the SEC's position in SAB No. 99 leave any room for the use of rules of thumb? Is the SEC sympathetic to the complaint of issuers that the materiality analysis is too uncertain to provide sufficient guidance for the issuers when making disclosure decisions? The Second Circuit dealt with the issue of numerical rules-of-thumb and SAB No. 99 in the following case. What qualitative factors influence the materiality determination? Can issuers apply those factors with confidence?

Litwin v. Blackstone Group, L.P.

634 F.3d 706 (2d Cir. 2011).

■ STRAUB, C., CIRCUIT JUDGE.

* * *

Lead plaintiffs . . . bring this putative securities class action on behalf of themselves and all others who purchased the common units of Blackstone at the time of its IPO. . . .

Blackstone is "a leading global alternative asset manager and provider of financial advisory services". . . . Blackstone is divided into four business segments: (1) Corporate Private Equity, which comprises its management of corporate private equity funds; (2) Real Estate, which comprises its management of general real estate funds and internationally focused real estate funds; (3) Marketable Alternative Asset Management, which comprises its management of hedge funds, mezzanine funds, senior debt vehicles, proprietary hedge funds, and publicly traded closed-end mutual funds; and (4) Financial Advisory, which comprises a variety of advisory services. The Corporate Private Equity segment constitutes approximately 37.4% of Blackstone's total assets under management ($33.1 billion of $88.4 billion). . . .

Blackstone receives a substantial portion of its revenues from two sources: (1) a 1.5% management fee on its total assets under management and (2) performance fees of 20% of the profits generated from the capital it invests on behalf of its limited partners. Under certain circumstances, when investments perform poorly, Blackstone may be subject to a "claw-back" of already paid performance fees, in other words, the required return of fees which it had already collected. . . .

Plaintiffs principally allege that, at the time of the IPO, and unbeknownst to non-insider purchasers of Blackstone common units, two of Blackstone's portfolio companies . . . were experiencing problems.

Blackstone allegedly knew of, and reasonably expected, these problems to subject it to a claw-back of performance fees and reduced performance fees, thereby materially affecting its future revenues.

FGIC Corporation

In 2003, a consortium of investors that included Blackstone purchased an 88% interest in FGIC Corp., a monoline financial guarantor, from General Electric Co. for $1.86 billion. FGIC is the parent company of Financial Guaranty, which primarily provides insurance for bonds. Although municipal bond insurance traditionally constituted the majority of Financial Guaranty's business, in the years leading up to Blackstone's IPO it began writing "insurance" on collateralized debt obligations,[2] including CDOs backed by sub-prime mortgages to higher-risk borrowers. Financial Guaranty also began writing "insurance" on residential mortgage-backed securities[3] linked to non-prime and sub-prime mortgages. This "insurance" on RMBSs and CDOs was in the form of credit default swaps.[4]

By the summer of 2007, FGIC, as a result of Financial Guaranty's underwriting practices, was exposed to billions of dollars in non-prime mortgages, with its total CDS exposure close to $13 billion. From mid-2004 through mid-2007, factors including rising interest rates, the adjustment of interest rates on sub-prime mortgages, and a substantial slowing of property-value appreciation (and in some markets, property-value depreciation) caused many borrowers to be unable to refinance their existing loans when they could not meet their payment obligations. As a result, beginning in 2005, there was a significant increase in mortgage-default rates, particularly for sub-prime mortgage loans. By early 2007, before the IPO, some of the top mortgage lenders with sub-prime mortgage exposure began revealing large losses and warned of future market losses. All of these symptoms, plaintiffs allege, provided a strong indication that the problems plaguing sub-prime lenders would generate substantial losses for FGIC on the CDSs it issued to its counterparties. This likelihood was allegedly exacerbated because, in many instances, FGIC's CDS-counterparties were able to demand accelerated payments from FGIC even before a default event occurred on the underlying referenced assets.

Blackstone's 23% equity interest in FGIC was worth approximately $331 million at the time of the IPO. Plaintiffs allege that, due to this significant interest, Blackstone was required to disclose the then-known

---

   [2]   "CDOs are diversified collections of bonds that are divided into various risk groups and then sold to investors as securities."

   [3]   RMBSs are "a type of asset-backed security—that is, a security whose value is derived from a specified pool of underlying assets. Typically, an entity (such as a bank) will buy up a large number of mortgages from other banks, assemble those mortgages into pools, securitize the pools (i.e., split them into shares that can be sold off), and then sell them, usually as bonds, to banks or other investors."

   [4]   CDSs "are contracts that provide protection against the credit risk of a particular company. The seller of a CDS agrees to pay the buyer a specific sum of money, called the notional amount, if a credit event, such as bankruptcy, occurs in the referenced company.... In exchange for this risk protection from the CDS-seller, the CDS-buyer agrees to make periodic premium payments during the course of the contract. The CDS-buyer can use the CDS to provide protection, like insurance, against the possibility that the debt instruments the buyer holds will seriously deteriorate in value because of a credit event in the referenced company."

trends, events, or uncertainties related to FGIC's business that were reasonably likely to cause Blackstone's financial information not to be indicative of future operating results. Following the IPO, in a March 10, 2008 press release, Blackstone announced its full-year and fourth-quarter 2007 earnings. The company's Corporate Private Equity segment reported 2007 revenues of $821.3 million, down 18% from 2006 revenues. "Most significantly, Blackstone reduced the value of its portfolio investment in [FGIC], . . . which accounted for $122.2 million, or 69%, of the decline in revenues for the year." Blackstone reported that its "Corporate Private Equity fourth quarter revenues of ($15.4) million were negative, as compared with revenues of $533.8 million for the fourth quarter of 2006," a change "driven primarily by decreases in the value of Blackstone's portfolio investment in [FGIC] . . . and lower net appreciation of portfolio investments in other sectors as compared with the prior year." . . . .

[The court also described allegations in the class action complaint that Blackstone failed to disclose material adverse developments relating to Blackstone's investment through its Corporate Private Equity segment in Freescale Semiconductor, Inc., a semiconductor designer and manufacturer, and allegations relating to Blackstone's real estate investments as well as various additional accounting and risk disclosure allegations].

The District Court's opinion [dismissing the complaint] primarily focused on the materiality of the alleged omissions and misstatements concerning FGIC, Freescale, and Blackstone's real estate investments. First, the District Court analyzed the relative scale or quantitative materiality of the alleged FGIC and Freescale omissions. After noting our (and the SEC's) acceptance of a 5% threshold as an appropriate "starting place" or "preliminary assumption" of immateriality, the District Court noted that "Blackstone's $331 million investment in FGIC represented a mere 0.4% of Blackstone's [total] assets under management at the time of the IPO."[7] The District Court then addressed plaintiffs' argument that the materiality of the omissions is best illustrated by the effect the eventual $122.2 million drop in value of Blackstone's FGIC investment had on Blackstone's 2007 annual revenues. The District Court found that while the decline in FGIC's investment value may have been significant relative to the Corporate Private Equity segment's annual revenues, it was quantitatively immaterial as compared with Blackstone's $3.12 billion in total revenues for 2007.[8] [The District Court similarly found that Freescale was quantitatively immaterial from the perspective of Blackstone, accounting for only 3.5% of Blackstone's total assets under management]. . . .

[R]ecognizing that a quantitative analysis is not dispositive of materiality, the District Court found that only one of the qualitative factors that we, or the SEC, often consider was present in this case. Specifically, the court found that: (1) none of the omissions concealed

---

[7]   The investment accounted for approximately 1% of the Corporate Private Equity segment's assets under management.

[8]   The District Court incorrectly stated that the "$122 million write down for FGIC was a mere 0.4% of Blackstone's $3.12 billion in annual revenue." In fact, $122 million is nearly 4% of $3.12 billion.

unlawful transactions or conduct; (2) the alleged omissions did not relate to a significant aspect of Blackstone's operations; (3) there was no significant market reaction to the public disclosure of the alleged omissions; (4) the alleged omissions did not hide a failure to meet analysts' expectations; (5) the alleged omissions did not change a loss into income or vice versa; and (6) the alleged omissions did not affect Blackstone's compliance with loan covenants or other contractual requirements. The District Court noted that the one qualitative factor it found present in this case—that the alleged omissions had the effect of increasing Blackstone's management's compensation—was not enough, by itself, to make the omissions material. Accordingly, the District Court held that the alleged omissions concerning FGIC and Freescale were immaterial as a matter of law. . . .

DISCUSSION

* * *

The primary issue before us is . . . whether Blackstone's Registration Statement and Prospectus omitted material information that Blackstone was legally required to disclose.

Required Disclosures Under Item 303 of Regulation S–K

Plaintiffs principally contend that Item 303 of SEC Regulation S–K provides the basis for Blackstone's disclosure obligation. Pursuant to Subsection (a)(3)(ii) of Item 303, a registrant must "[d]escribe any known trends or uncertainties . . . that the registrant reasonably expects will have a material . . . unfavorable impact on . . . revenues or income from continuing operations.". . . . The SEC's interpretive release regarding Item 303 clarifies that the Regulation imposes a disclosure duty "where a trend, demand, commitment, event or uncertainty is both [1] presently known to management and [2] reasonably likely to have material effects on the registrant's financial condition or results of operations.". . . .

Plaintiffs allege that the downward trend in the real estate market was already known and existing at the time of the IPO, and that the trend or uncertainty in the market was reasonably likely to have a material impact on Blackstone's financial condition. Therefore, plaintiffs have adequately pleaded a presently existing trend, event, or uncertainty, and the sole remaining issue is whether the effect of the "known" information was "reasonably likely" to be material for the purpose of Item 303 and, in turn, for the purpose of Sections 11 and 12(a)(2).

Legal Standard of Materiality

Materiality is an "inherently fact-specific finding," that is satisfied when a plaintiff alleges "a statement or omission that a reasonable investor would have considered significant in making investment decisions". . . . [W]hen a district court is presented with a Rule 12(b)(6) motion, " 'a complaint may not properly be dismissed . . . on the ground that the alleged misstatements or omissions are not material unless they are so obviously unimportant to a reasonable investor that reasonable minds could not differ on the question of their importance.' "

"[W]e have consistently rejected a formulaic approach to assessing the materiality of an alleged misrepresentation." [We have] cited with approval SEC Staff Accounting Bulletin No. 99. . . . Accordingly, a court must consider "both 'quantitative' and 'qualitative' factors in assessing an item's materiality," SAB No. 99, and that consideration should be undertaken in an integrative manner. . . .

Materiality of Omissions Related to FGIC and Freescale

* * *

While it is true that Blackstone's investments in FGIC and Freescale fall below the presumptive 5% threshold of materiality, we find that the District Court erred in its analysis of certain qualitative factors related to materiality. . . .

[T]he District Court erred in finding that the alleged omissions did not relate to a significant aspect of Blackstone's operations. In discussing "considerations that may well render material a quantitatively small misstatement," SAB No. 99 provides that "materiality . . . may turn on where [the misstatement] appears in the financial statements": "[S]ituations may arise . . . where the auditor will conclude that a matter relating to segment information is qualitatively material even though, in his or her judgment, it is quantitatively immaterial to the financial statements taken as a whole." SAB No. 99 also provides that one factor affecting qualitative materiality is whether the misstatement or omission relates to a segment that plays a "significant role" in the registrant's business. In this case, Blackstone makes clear in its offering documents that Corporate Private Equity is its flagship segment, playing a significant role in the company's history, operations, and value. . . . Because Blackstone's Corporate Private Equity segment plays such an important role in Blackstone's business and provides value to all of its other asset management and financial advisory services, a reasonable investor would almost certainly want to know information related to that segment that Blackstone reasonably expects will have a material adverse effect on its future revenues. Therefore, the alleged misstatements and omissions relating to FGIC and Freescale were plausibly material. . . .

Finally, the District Court failed to consider another relevant qualitative factor-that the omissions "mask[ ] a change in earnings or other trends." SAB No. 99. Such a possibility is precisely what the required disclosures under Item 303 aim to avoid. Here, Blackstone omitted information related to FGIC and Freescale that plaintiffs allege was reasonably likely to have a material effect on the revenues of Blackstone's Corporate Private Equity segment and, in turn, on Blackstone as a whole. Blackstone's failure to disclose that information masked a reasonably likely change in earnings, as well as the trend, event, or uncertainty that was likely to cause such a change.

All of these qualitative factors, together with the District Court's correct observation that the alleged omissions "doubtless had 'the effect of increasing management's compensation,' " show that the alleged omissions were material. Accordingly, we hold that plaintiffs have adequately pleaded that Blackstone omitted material information related to FGIC and Freescale that it was required to disclose under Item 303 of Regulation S–K. . . .

QUESTIONS

1. What qualitative factors may lead a court to find quantitatively small amounts nonetheless material? Are investors likely to weigh some of the factors more heavily?

2. How did the Second Circuit treat Blackstone's investment in FGIC (and Freescale) differently than the district court?

3. The Second Circuit stresses the importance of the Corporate Private Equity segment to Blackstone. Should we compute the 5% rule of thumb as a percentage of the income, revenues, or assets (or assets under management) of a particular important segment within an issuer, or for the issuer as a whole?

4. The Second Circuit rejects the use of a 5% rule of thumb as a threshold for materiality. Would a rule of thumb to treat items above some larger percentage, say 20%, as presumptively material be consistent with the SEC's views? Are there qualitative factors that could make such a quantitatively large misstatement nonetheless immaterial?

HYPOTHETICAL TWO

Six Feet offers financing to families that have not set aside money to pay for the burial of their loved ones. These loans, for which Six Feet charges interest well above the prime rate, have a substantial default rate. (It turns out people are less willing to pay back several thousand dollars in debt after their loved one has been buried. What's Six Feet going to do, dig them up?) Accordingly, Six Feet set aside a "loan loss" reserve for the loans that turn out to be uncollectible (the loan loss reserve is disclosed in Six Feet's financial statements). The reserve is not large, amounting to 10–15% of the outstanding loans. The loans, however, make up a substantial business segment for Six Feet, generating between 35–40% of Six Feet's profits. Moreover, the reserves have been a useful resource of "smoothing" Six Feet's earnings—typically by plus or minus 2% per year. If it looks like Six Feet may fall short of Wall Street's forecasted earnings, Arthur—Six Feet's CFO—simply dips into the loan loss reserve, declaring the reserve to be greater than needed, and adding the excess reserve to that quarter's revenue. This financial flexibility has allowed Arthur and Six Feet to meet expectations for 23 consecutive quarters. Is Six Feet's loan loss reserve practice materially misleading?

———

Are there alternatives to numerical rules of thumb? The following case identifies an external source of evidence for determining whether a reasonable shareholder would consider the contested disclosure or omission material. The case, following a common approach taken by many courts, looks to whether the company's stock price has an abnormal reaction around the date at which a public announcement is made revealing the previously undisclosed fraud or omission. For example, if prior misstatements result in investors having an overly positive view of a company, one would expect that the stock price of the company would be inflated due to the misstatements. Upon the public announcement of the previously undisclosed fraud, investors would correct for their prior optimistic view, causing the stock price to fall.

The negative stock price reaction (corrected for other factors that may cause a company's stock price to change) measures investors' views of how much the prior misstatements inflated the company's value.

Looking to the stock price reaction to a public announcement gives courts a market measure of investor assessment of the importance of the prior misstatement. Instead of relying solely on an individual judge's assessment of materiality, the market becomes the decisionmaker for what is material. Or does it? Judges still must make important decisions even when turning to the market's assessment of materiality. One important decision is the precise determination of when the stock market first learned of the previously undisclosed fraud or omission. Do you agree with the Third Circuit's approach in the following case in determining the public disclosure date?

In re Merck & Co., Inc. Securities Litigation
432 F.3d 261 (3d Cir. 2005).

■ AMBRO, T., CIRCUIT JUDGE.

Merck & Co., Inc. planned an initial public offering of its wholly owned subsidiary—Medco Health Solutions, Inc. Before the IPO was to occur, however, information about Medco's aggressive revenue-recognition policy came to light. Some details about the policy were disclosed in Merck's registration statements filed with the Securities and Exchange Commission, but a *Wall Street Journal* article reading between the lines of this disclosure precipitated a decline in Merck's stock. After further disclosures and larger declines in Merck's stock price, the Medco IPO was canceled. Union Investments Privatfonds GmbH, as lead plaintiff for a class of Merck stockholders, claims that Merck and Medco committed securities fraud under section 10(b) of the Securities Exchange Act of 1934. . . .

* * *

Merck first announced its plans for the Medco IPO in a January 2002 press release, in which Raymond Gilmartin, Merck's Chairman and CEO, said that the two companies would pursue independent strategies for success. On April 17, 2002, Merck filed its first Form S–1 with the SEC. The SEC did not approve this S–1, and Merck kept trying, finally securing SEC approval with its fifth S–1, filed on July 9. Market reaction led Merck to drop Medco's offering price, to postpone indefinitely the IPO, and finally to drop the IPO altogether.

A.   Medco's revenue-recognition policy

Medco is a pharmacy benefits manager (PBM). It saves its clients (plan sponsors) money by negotiating discount rates with pharmacies and influencing doctors to prescribe cheaper, but still therapeutically appropriate, medicines. When a customer buys drugs at a local pharmacy, the pharmacist checks with Medco to ensure that the customer is an approved beneficiary. Then the customer makes a co-payment—usually between $5 and $15—which goes directly to the pharmacy, not to Medco.

Although Medco did not handle these co-payments, it interpreted the accounting standards to allow it to recognize the co-payments as revenue.[2] But it did not disclose this revenue-recognition policy. In fact, Merck's 1999 SEC Form 10–K stated that Medco recognized revenue "for the amount billed to the plan sponsor." After Merck changed auditors, and before it began filings for the Medco IPO, it changed this language in its 2001 Form 10–K to state that revenues were "recognized based on the prescription drug price negotiated with the plan sponsor."

Merck's April 17 Form S–1 disclosed for the first time that Medco had recognized as revenue the co-payments paid by consumers, but it did not disclose the total amount of co-payments recognized. The day this S–1 was filed, Merck's stock price went up $0.03—from $55.02 to $55.05. Merck filed an amendment to its S–1 on May 21 and another on June 13.

On June 21, 2002, *The Wall Street Journal* reported that Medco had been recognizing co-payments as revenue and estimated that in 2001 $4.6 billion in co-payments had been recognized. Later disclosures would show the actual number to be $5.54 billion. The market's reaction was immediate; that day Merck's stock lost $2.22—dropping from $52.20 to $49.98. Six days later, Merck announced the postponement of the Medco IPO and indicated that it would drop Medco's offering price.

Merck filed its fourth S–1 on July 5, 2002, finally disclosing the full amount of co-payments it had recognized as revenue. The S–1 showed that Medco had recognized over $12.4 billion dollars in co-payments as revenue, $2.838 billion in 1999, $4.036 billion in 2000, and $5.537 billion in 2001. Four days later, Merck announced that it would postpone the Medco IPO indefinitely, even as it filed its last S–1, which was approved by the SEC.

Merck's stock continued to fall, reaching $45.75 on July 9, the end of the class period, and $43.57 on July 10.

* * *

B.   Does Union have a valid claim under section 10(b)?

* * *

1.   *When Merck disclosed information regarding its revenue calculations, was the disclosure material?*

* * *

Union argues that Merck's statements were material, citing the fact that Merck's stock dropped significantly when *The Wall Street Journal's* article detailing Medco's accounting practices appeared. Merck claims that because its stock price rose immediately following its initial, minimal disclosure, the disclosure was immaterial as a matter of law.

Our Court . . . has one of the "clearest commitments" to the efficient market hypothesis. Our . . . standard for measuring the materiality of

---

[2]   Merck apparently subtracted out these co-payments later, so its profit numbers were unaffected by this policy.

statements in an efficient market ... holds that "the materiality of disclosed information may be measured post hoc by looking to the movement, in the period immediately following disclosure, of the price of the firm's stock."

* * *

In this case, the disclosure occurred on April 17, and there was no negative effect on Merck's stock. *The Wall Street Journal's* article, accompanied by a significant decline in Merck's stock, appeared two months later. Union claims that this June stock decline demonstrates the materiality of the information Merck disclosed. But ... Merck's stock did not drop after the first disclosure, and that is generally when we measure the materiality of the disclosure, not two months later.

In *Basic Inc. v. Levinson*, the Supreme Court declined to resolve "how quickly and completely publicly available information is reflected in market price." ... But our Court has resolved how "quickly and completely" public information is absorbed into a firm's stock price. We have decided that this absorption occurs "in the period immediately following disclosure."

This does not mean instantaneously, of course, but in this case there was no adverse effect to Merck's stock price from the disclosure "in the period immediately following disclosure." In fact, Merck's stock continued to rise from its baseline of $55.02, including the April 17 S–1 filing date, for five trading days after the disclosure. The five-trading-day rise was followed by a five-trading-day decline, which reached a low of $54.34. Then, starting on May 1, 2002, Merck's stock remained above $55.02 until June 4. But Union expects us to ignore this one-month increase in Merck's stock price in favor of a five-day decline of little over 1%. This we will not do.

Union also argues that the April 17 disclosure was so opaque that it should not have counted as a disclosure. Although Merck disclosed that it had recognized co-payments as revenue in April, it did not disclose the sum total of those co-payments until July. This is why, Union claims, the stock price did not drop until *The Wall Street Journal's* reporter made public the estimated magnitude of the co-payment recognition. In effect, Union is arguing that investors and analysts stood in uncomprehending suspension for over two months until the *Journal* brought light to the market's darkness.

The *Journal* reporter arrived at an estimate of $4.6 billion of co-payments recognized in 2001 by using one assumption and performing one subtraction and one multiplication on the information contained in the April S–1. She determined the number of retail prescriptions filled (462 million) by subtracting home-delivery prescriptions filled (75 million) from total prescriptions filled (537 million). She then assumed an average $10 co-payment and multiplied that average co-payment by the number of retail prescriptions filled to get $4.6 billion.

The issue is whether needing this amount of mathematical proficiency to make sense of the disclosure negates the disclosure itself. ... The calculation from Merck's S–1 ... required some close reading and an assumption as to the amount of the co-payment. But the added, albeit minimal, arithmetic complexity of the calculation hardly undermines faith in an efficient market.

Union points out nonetheless that Merck was followed by many analysts, including J.P. Morgan, Morgan Stanley, and Salomon Smith Barney, who "closely examine a company's revenue and revenue growth when valuing a company's stock" in Merck's industry. The logical corollary of Union's argument then is the following rhetorical question: If these analysts—all focused on revenue—were unable for two months to make a handful of calculations, how can we presume an efficient market at all? Union is trying to have it both ways: the market understood all the good things that Merck said about its revenue but was not smart enough to understand the co-payment disclosure.[8] An efficient market for good news is an efficient market for bad news. The *Journal* reporter simply did the math on June 21; the efficient market hypothesis suggests that the market made these basic calculations months earlier.

But we do not wish to reward opaqueness. We decline to decide how many mathematical calculations are too many or how strained assumptions must be, but Merck was clearly treading a fine line with this delayed, piecemeal disclosure. It should have disclosed the amount of co-payments recognized as revenue in the April S–1; it should have disclosed this revenue-recognition policy as soon as it was adopted. Sunshine is a fine disinfectant, and Merck tried for too long to stay in the shade. The facts were disclosed, though, and it is simply too much for us to say that every analyst following Merck, one of the largest companies in the world, was in the dark.

* * *

We created a test for materiality under ... which [t]he *TSC* materiality definition "[o]rdinarily" applies, but in efficient markets materiality is defined as "information that alters the price of the firm's stock." We reached this conclusion in two steps. First, "reasonable investors" are the market. Second, information important to the market will be reflected in the stock's price. Thus, "information important to reasonable investors ... is immediately incorporated into stock prices." ...

If a company's stock trades on an efficient market, ... "the materiality of disclosed information may be measured post hoc by looking to the movement, in the period immediately following disclosure, of the price of the firm's stock."

* * *

Union failed to establish a material statement or omission by Merck, so Union did not sufficiently plead a section 10(b) violation. ... We therefore affirm the District Court's decision.

---

[8] Union needs the market to be efficient. With an efficient market it can use the fraud-on-the-market theory [Eds.: discussed in Chapter 5], which allows it to meet its section 10(b) reliance requirement. The fraud-on-the-market theory supposes that "'the price of a company's stock is determined by the available material information regarding the company and its business.'"

QUESTIONS

1. Should the lack of market movement in response to a disclosure establish the non-materiality of that disclosure? Conversely, should a significant market response be conclusive evidence of materiality?

2. Discussions of materiality by courts inevitably overlap with discussions of whether there has been a misstatement and whether there is a duty to disclose. Materiality, however, is a distinct element of all the private causes of action for fraud under the securities laws. If a company has made a misstatement, why excuse it from liability if the misstatement was not material?

3. Is the presence of securities analysts covering Merck relevant to the materiality determination?

————

Looking to the stock price reaction of a publicly traded company to the public release of previously non-public information allows judges to utilize the consensus among investors (as embodied in the market price) to assess materiality. Basing materiality on stock price reactions allows judges to avoid, at least in part, relying on their own subjective intuitions or numerical rules of thumb. Changes in stock market prices do not necessarily lead to a conclusion of materiality. Factors aside from the public release of the specific information at issue in litigation may affect a company's stock price, including changes in the macro-economy.

To screen out the effect of changes in the stock market on the stock price of a specific company, litigants will typically employ an expert witness to do an event study. In an event study, the expert will first identify an event date when new information either revealing a past misstatement or disclosing previously omitted information is made public. Suppose, for example, that a small high technology company with publicly traded common stock disclosed on June 10 previously omitted negative information on its revenues. Assuming no prior leakage of the information, the expert would select June 10 as the event date.

The expert will construct an event window, typically of 1 to 3 trading days, centered on the event date. In the case of the high technology company, a 3-day event window would run from June 9 through June 11 (assuming these days are trading days). The expert will then estimate a model of how the specific company's stock price varied in the past relative to the overall market return (using for example the Nasdaq index as a proxy for the overall market). The stock price of smaller, high technology companies, for example, typically tracks the Nasdaq index but with greater volatility. If the Nasdaq index rises by 1%, a smaller high technology company's share price may rise by 1.1%. The expert will use this model to predict how the company's stock price will vary during the event window based on how the overall market return varies during the window. If the Nasdaq index rises by 2% during the event window, for example, the expert will predict an expected return for the high technology company of 2.2%.

The expert will then obtain the actual return during the event window period for the specific company and subtract the expected return from the actual return. The difference is the "abnormal" return. Suppose for the high technology company that the actual return was 0.5% during the event window. At first glance, the positive actual return would seem to indicate that the market did not view the previously omitted information as a negative. However, this ignores the overall market movement that may mask negative investor sentiments. Given the expected return of 2.2%, the abnormal return is equal to − 1.7%—reflecting investors' negative view of the high technology company's previously omitted information.

How is a judge or jury to determine whether an abnormal return of − 1.7% indicates materiality? What if the abnormal return was in fact − 0.7% or − 2.7%? What is the materiality threshold for an abnormal return? Experts typically rely on the concept of statistical significance in determining when a particular abnormal return indicates that the information in question is material. Stock prices tend to move about randomly over time. The statistical question experts ask is whether an abnormal return, in our example − 1.7%, is due to random chance and not a reaction on the part of investors to the public disclosure of information (referred to as the "null" hypothesis). To assess the probability of random chance generating an abnormal return of − 1.7%, the expert will look at the range of past returns for the company prior to the event window. If a company's share price tends to move widely up and down over time—for example, swings of plus or minus 2% every day—then the abnormal return of − 1.7% is much more likely to be due to chance and not because the market viewed the previously omitted information as important (in other words, the expert will not be able to reject the null hypothesis). A conventional probability threshold that experts use is 5%, meaning that there is a 5% or lower chance that random chance would result in an abnormal return of a particular magnitude. Thus, if an expert concludes that the − 1.7% abnormal return for the high technology company is "significant at the 5% confidence level," this indicates that there is only a 5% or lower probability that random chance, as assessed based on the prior stock price movements of the high technology company over time, could have resulted in an abnormal return of − 1.7%.

Courts have often accepted the statistical significance of abnormal stock returns of sufficient practical magnitude as evidence of materiality for companies with publicly traded stock that trade in liquid (and efficient) secondary markets. In the case below, the Supreme Court addressed the use of statistical significance as the criterion for materiality. Importantly, the case did not involve the statistical significance of stock price movements. Instead, the case focuses on the statistical significance of an observed relationship between a pharmaceutical drug and adverse events and whether materiality should turn on whether this relationship is statistically significant.

Matrixx Initiatives, Inc. v. Siracusano

131 S.Ct. 1309 (2011).

■ SOTOMAYOR, J., delivered the opinion for a unanimous Court.

This case presents the question whether a plaintiff can state a claim for securities fraud under § 10(b) and Rule 10b–5 based on a pharmaceutical company's failure to disclose reports of adverse events associated with a product if the reports do not disclose a statistically significant number of adverse events. Respondents, plaintiffs in a securities fraud class action, allege that petitioners, Matrixx Initiatives, Inc., and three of its executives, failed to disclose reports of a possible link between its leading product, a cold remedy, and loss of smell, rendering statements made by Matrixx misleading. Matrixx contends that respondents' complaint does not adequately allege that Matrixx made a material representation or omission or that it acted with scienter because the complaint does not allege that Matrixx knew of a statistically significant number of adverse events requiring disclosure. We conclude that the materiality of adverse event reports cannot be reduced to a bright-line rule. Although in many cases reasonable investors would not consider reports of adverse events to be material information, respondents have alleged facts plausibly suggesting that reasonable investors would have viewed these particular reports as material. . . .

I

A

Matrixx develops, manufactures, and markets over-the-counter pharmaceutical products. Its core brand of products is called Zicam. . . . The active ingredient in Zicam Cold Remedy was zinc gluconate. Respondents allege that Zicam Cold Remedy accounted for approximately 70 percent of Matrixx's sales.

Respondents initiated this securities fraud class action against Matrixx on behalf of individuals who purchased Matrixx securities between October 22, 2003, and February 6, 2004. The action principally arises out of statements that Matrixx made during the class period relating to revenues and product safety. Respondents claim that Matrixx's statements were misleading in light of reports that Matrixx had received, but did not disclose, about consumers who had lost their sense of smell (a condition called anosmia) after using Zicam Cold Remedy. . . .

In 1999, Dr. Alan Hirsch, neurological director of the Smell & Taste Treatment and Research Foundation, Ltd., called Matrixx's customer service line after discovering a possible link between Zicam nasal gel and a loss of smell "in a cluster of his patients." Dr. Hirsch told a Matrixx employee that "previous studies had demonstrated that intranasal application of zinc could be problematic." He also told the employee about at least one of his patients who did not have a cold and who developed anosmia after using Zicam.

In September 2002, Timothy Clarot, Matrixx's vice president for research and development, called Miriam Linschoten, Ph.D., at the University of Colorado Health Sciences Center after receiving a complaint from a person Linschoten was treating who had lost her sense of smell after using Zicam. Clarot informed Linschoten that Matrixx had received similar complaints from other customers. Linschoten drew Clarot's attention to "previous studies linking zinc sulfate to loss of smell." Clarot gave her the impression that he had not heard of the studies. She asked Clarot whether Matrixx had done any studies of its own; he responded that it had not but that it had hired a consultant to review the product. Soon thereafter, Linschoten sent Clarot abstracts of the studies she had mentioned. . . .

By September 2003, one of Linschoten's colleagues at the University of Colorado, Dr. Bruce Jafek, had observed 10 patients suffering from anosmia after Zicam use. Linschoten and Jafek planned to present their findings at a meeting of the American Rhinologic Society in a poster presentation entitled "Zicam® Induced Anosmia." The American Rhinologic Society posted their abstract in advance of the meeting. . . .

Matrixx learned of the doctors' planned presentation. Clarot sent a letter to Dr. Jafek warning him that he did not have permission to use Matrixx's name or the names of its products. Dr. Jafek deleted the references to Zicam in the poster before presenting it to the American Rhinologic Society. . . .

Respondents allege that Matrixx made a series of public statements that were misleading in light of the foregoing information. In October 2003, after they had learned of Dr. Jafek's study and after Dr. Jafek had presented his findings to the American Rhinologic Society, Matrixx stated that Zicam was "poised for growth in the upcoming cough and cold season" and that the company had "very strong momentum." Matrixx further expressed its expectation that revenues would "be up in excess of 50% and that earnings, per share for the full year [would] be in the 25 to 30 cent range." In January 2004, Matrixx raised its revenue guidance, predicting an increase in revenues of 80 percent and earnings per share in the 33-to-38-cent range. . . .

On January 30, 2004, Dow Jones Newswires reported that the Food and Drug Administration (FDA) was "looking into complaints that an over-the-counter common-cold medicine manufactured by a unit of Matrixx Initiatives, Inc. (MTXX) may be causing some users to lose their sense of smell" in light of at least three product liability lawsuits. Matrixx's stock fell from $13.55 to $11.97 per share after the report. . . .

On February 6, 2004, the end of the class period, Good Morning America, a nationally broadcast morning news program, highlighted Dr. Jafek's findings. . . . The program reported that Dr. Jafek had discovered more than a dozen patients suffering from anosmia after using Zicam. . . . The price of Matrixx stock plummeted to $9.94 per share that same day. Zicam again issued a press release largely repeating its February 2 statement. On February 19, 2004, Matrixx filed a Form 8–K with the SEC stating that it had "convened a two-day meeting of physicians and scientists to review current information on smell disorders" in response to Dr. Jafek's presentation. According to the Form 8–K, "In the opinion of the panel, there is insufficient scientific evidence at this time to determine if zinc gluconate, when used as recommended, affects a person's ability to smell." A few weeks later, a reporter quoted Matrixx as stating that it would begin conducting "animal and human studies to further characterize these post-marketing complaints."

On the basis of these allegations, respondents claimed that Matrixx violated § 10(b) of the Securities Exchange Act and SEC Rule 10b–5 by making untrue statements of fact and failing to disclose material facts necessary to make the statements not misleading in an effort to maintain artificially high prices for Matrixx securities.

B

Matrixx moved to dismiss respondents' complaint, arguing that they had failed to plead the elements of a material misstatement or omission. . . . The District Court granted the motion to dismiss. . . . [I]t held that respondents had not alleged a "statistically significant correlation between the use of Zicam and anosmia so as to make failure to public[ly] disclose complaints and the University of Colorado study a material omission.". . . .

The Court of Appeals reversed . . . [holding] that the District Court had erred in requiring an allegation of statistical significance to establish materiality. It concluded, to the contrary, that the complaint adequately alleged "information regarding the possible link between Zicam and anosmia" that would have been significant to a reasonable investor. . . .

II

* * *

We first consider Matrixx's argument that "adverse event reports that do not reveal a statistically significant increased risk of adverse events from product use are not material information."

To prevail on a § 10(b) claim, a plaintiff must show that the defendant made a statement that was "misleading as to a material fact." In *Basic*, we held that this materiality requirement is satisfied when there is " 'a substantial likelihood that the disclosure of the omitted fact would have been viewed by the reasonable investor as having significantly altered the "total mix" of information made available.' " We were "careful not to set too low a standard of materiality," for fear that management would " 'bury the shareholders in an avalanche of trivial information.' "

Basic involved a claim that the defendant had made misleading statements denying that it was engaged in merger negotiations when it was, in fact, conducting preliminary negotiations. The defendant urged a bright-line rule that preliminary merger negotiations are material only once the parties to the negotiations reach an agreement in principle. We observed that "[a]ny approach that designates a single fact or occurrence as always determinative of an inherently fact-specific finding such as materiality, must necessarily be overinclusive or underinclusive." We thus rejected the defendant's proposed rule, explaining that it would "artificially exclud[e] from the definition of materiality information concerning merger discussions, which would otherwise be considered significant to the trading decision of a reasonable investor."

Like the defendant in *Basic*, Matrixx urges us to adopt a bright-line rule that reports of adverse events associated with a pharmaceutical company's products cannot be material absent a sufficient number of such reports to establish a statistically significant risk that the product is in fact causing the events. Absent statistical significance, Matrixx argues, adverse event reports provide only "anecdotal" evidence that "the user of a drug experienced an adverse event at some point during or following the use of that drug." Accordingly, it contends, reasonable investors would not consider such reports relevant unless they are statistically significant because only then do they "reflect a scientifically reliable basis for inferring a potential causal link between product use and the adverse event."

As in *Basic*, Matrixx's categorical rule would "artificially exclud[e]" information that "would otherwise be considered significant to the trading decision of a reasonable investor." Matrixx's argument rests on the premise that statistical significance is the only reliable indication of causation. This premise is flawed: As the SEC points out, "medical researchers ... consider multiple factors in assessing causation." Statistically significant data are not always available. For example, when an adverse event is subtle or rare, "an inability to obtain a data set of appropriate quality or quantity may preclude a finding of statistical significance." Moreover, ethical considerations may prohibit researchers from conducting randomized clinical trials to confirm a suspected causal link for the purpose of obtaining statistically significant data.

A lack of statistically significant data does not mean that medical experts have no reliable basis for inferring a causal link between a drug and adverse events. As Matrixx itself concedes, medical experts rely on other evidence to establish an inference of causation. We note that courts frequently permit expert testimony on causation based on evidence other than statistical significance. . . .

The FDA similarly does not limit the evidence it considers for purposes of assessing causation and taking regulatory action to statistically significant data. In assessing the safety risk posed by a product, the FDA considers factors such as "strength of the association," "temporal relationship of product use and the event," "consistency of findings across available data sources," "evidence of a dose-response for the effect," "biologic plausibility," "seriousness of the event relative to the disease being treated," "potential to mitigate the risk in the population," "feasibility of further study using observational or controlled clinical study designs," and "degree of benefit the product provides, including availability of other therapies.". . . .

Not only does the FDA rely on a wide range of evidence of causation, it sometimes acts on the basis of evidence that suggests, but does not prove, causation. . . . More generally, the FDA may make regulatory decisions against drugs based on postmarketing evidence that gives rise to only a suspicion of causation.

This case proves the point. In 2009, the FDA issued a warning letter to Matrixx stating that "[a] significant and growing body of evidence substantiates that the Zicam Cold Remedy intranasal products may pose a serious risk to consumers who use them." The letter cited as evidence 130 reports of anosmia the FDA had received, the fact that the FDA had received few reports of anosmia associated with other intranasal cold remedies, and "evidence in the published scientific literature that various salts of zinc can damage olfactory function in animals and humans." It did not cite statistically significant data.

Given that medical professionals and regulators act on the basis of evidence of causation that is not statistically significant, it stands to reason that in certain cases reasonable investors would as well. [A]ssessing the materiality of adverse event reports is a "fact-specific" inquiry that requires consideration of the source, content, and context of the reports. This is not to say that statistical significance (or the lack thereof) is irrelevant—only that it is not dispositive of every case.

Application of *Basic's* "total mix" standard does not mean that pharmaceutical manufacturers must disclose all reports of adverse events. Adverse event reports are daily events in the pharmaceutical industry; in 2009, the FDA entered nearly 500,000 such reports into its reporting system. The fact that a user of a drug has suffered an adverse event, standing alone, does not mean that the drug caused that event. The question remains whether a reasonable investor would have viewed the nondisclosed information " 'as having significantly altered the "total mix" of information made available.' " For the reasons just stated, the mere existence of reports of adverse events—which says nothing in and of itself about whether the drug is causing the adverse events—will not satisfy this standard. Something more is needed, but that something more is not limited to statistical significance and can come from "the source, content, and context of the reports." This contextual inquiry may reveal in some cases that reasonable investors would have viewed reports of adverse events as material even though the reports did not provide statistically significant evidence of a causal link.

* * *

Applying *Basic's* "total mix" standard in this case, we conclude that respondents have adequately pleaded materiality. This is not a case about a handful of anecdotal reports, as Matrixx suggests. Assuming the complaint's allegations to be true, as we must, Matrixx received information that plausibly indicated a reliable causal link between Zicam and anosmia. That information included reports from three medical professionals and researchers about more than 10 patients who had lost their sense of smell after using Zicam. . . . (In addition, during the class period, nine plaintiffs commenced four product liability lawsuits against Matrixx alleging a causal link between Zicam use and anosmia.) Further, Matrixx knew that Linschoten and Dr. Jafek had presented their findings about a causal link between Zicam and anosmia to a national medical conference devoted to treatment of diseases of the nose. Their presentation described a patient who experienced severe burning in his nose, followed immediately by a loss of smell, after using Zicam—suggesting a temporal relationship between Zicam use and anosmia.

Critically, both Dr. Hirsch and Linschoten had also drawn Matrixx's attention to previous studies that had demonstrated a biological causal link between intranasal application of zinc and anosmia. Before his conversation with Linschoten, Clarot, Matrixx's vice president of research and development, was seemingly unaware of these studies, and the complaint suggests that, as of the class period, Matrixx had not conducted any research of its own relating to anosmia. Accordingly, it can reasonably be inferred from the complaint that Matrixx had no basis for rejecting Dr. Jafek's findings out of hand.

We believe that these allegations suffice to "raise a reasonable expectation that discovery will reveal evidence" satisfying the materiality requirement, and to "allo[w] the court to draw the reasonable inference that the defendant is liable for the misconduct alleged. . . ." The information provided to Matrixx by medical experts revealed a plausible causal relationship between Zicam Cold Remedy and anosmia. Consumers likely would have viewed the risk associated with Zicam (possible loss of smell) as substantially outweighing the benefit of using the product (alleviating cold symptoms), particularly in light of the existence of many alternative products on the market. Importantly, Zicam Cold Remedy allegedly accounted for 70 percent of Matrixx's sales. Viewing the allegations of the complaint as a whole, the complaint alleges facts suggesting a significant risk to the commercial viability of Matrixx's leading product. . . .

Matrixx told the market that revenues were going to rise 50 and then 80 percent. Assuming the complaint's allegations to be true, however, Matrixx had information indicating a significant risk to its leading revenue-generating product. Matrixx also stated that reports indicating that Zicam caused anosmia were " 'completely unfounded and misleading' " and that " 'the safety and efficacy of zinc gluconate for the treatment of symptoms related to the common cold have been well established.' " Importantly, however, Matrixx had evidence of a biological link between Zicam's key ingredient and anosmia, and it had not conducted any studies of its own to disprove that link. In fact, as Matrixx later revealed, the scientific evidence at that time was " 'insufficient . . . to determine if zinc gluconate, when used as recommended, affects a person's ability to smell.' "

Assuming the facts to be true, these were material facts "necessary in order to make the statements made, in the light of the circumstances under which they were made, not misleading." We therefore affirm the Court of Appeals' holding that respondents adequately pleaded the element of a material misrepresentation or omission.

* * *

QUESTIONS

1. Why does the *Matrixx* Court conclude that "the materiality of adverse event reports cannot be reduced to a bright-line rule?" Why not treat a lack of a statistically significant relationship as the equivalent of no relationship?

2. The *Matrixx* Court mentions that the mere existence of adverse events does not meet the materiality standard. Instead the Court wrote: "Something more is needed." What is this something more and how should courts assess this evidence in deciding materiality for purposes of a motion to dismiss?

3. What does the *Matrixx* Court's opinion tell us about materiality and the role of a statistically significant stock price change in event studies of public disclosure?

HYPOTHETICAL THREE

David, the CEO of Six Feet, is doing a webcast for analysts, institutional investors and others interested in Six Feet's growth prospects. David tells his audience that Six Feet should enjoy 10–15% growth in revenues for the foreseeable future, as the aging baby boomer population adds to its clientele. David also tells his audience that Six Feet has been involved in government investigations for the past couple of years that may result in large penalties. The investigations relate to the past secret dumping of embalming chemicals by Six Feet employees. Six Feet's most recent Form 10–K filing made no mention of such investigations and instead stated that Six Feet faced no "material litigation or government enforcement risks." Six Feet's stock price drops 3% during the webcast on heavy trading volume. Did Six Feet make a material misstatement in its most recent Form 10–K?

IV. THE "TOTAL MIX"

Recall that in *Basic*, the Supreme Court quoted *TSC Industries, Inc. v. Northway, Inc.*, 426 U.S. 438 (1976), for the proposition that materiality requires "a substantial likelihood that the disclosure of the omitted fact would have been viewed by the reasonable investor as having significantly altered the 'total mix' of information made available." The "total mix" formulation has been an important basis upon which courts have dismissed suits that they see as non-meritorious. In the case below, the court applies one of the materiality doctrines that have grown out of the "total mix" language from *TSC Industries*: the "truth on the market" defense.

Longman v. Food Lion, Inc.

197 F.3d 675 (4th Cir. 1999).

■ NIEMEYER, P., CIRCUIT JUDGE:

On the day after ABC aired its "PrimeTime Live" television broadcast on November 5, 1992, detailing allegedly widespread unsanitary practices and labor law violations in grocery stores owned by Food Lion, Inc., the price of Food Lion's Class A stock fell approximately 11%, and the price of its Class B stock fell approximately 14%. A week later, stockholders David Longman, Jeffrey Feinman, and others who had purchased Food Lion stock during the 2¹/₂-year period before the broadcast filed these two class actions against Food Lion, which were later consolidated, alleging securities fraud under § 10(b) of the Securities Exchange Act of 1934 and Rule 10b–5 promulgated thereunder. The plaintiffs alleged that Food Lion affirmatively misled the market and failed to disclose that its earnings during the 2¹/₂-year period were artificially inflated due to its misrepresentations about and failure to disclose widespread violations of federal labor laws and pervasive, unsanitary food handling practices. They alleged that these violations and practices were attributable to Food Lion's "Effective Scheduling System," which required employees to perform certain duties within specified times at the risk of losing their jobs.

* * *

I

Food Lion is a publicly traded (over the counter) company with headquarters in Salisbury, North Carolina, that operates a chain of approximately 1,000 retail grocery stores in the southeastern part of the United States. During the relevant period, its earnings exceeded $200 million per year, and it employed about 60,000 persons.

As a management tool, Food Lion has employed a labor scheduling system, known as "Effective Scheduling," to assist department managers in scheduling their workforces based on the time that it should take an average employee to complete various tasks. While some stores have never met the goals set by the Effective Scheduling guidelines, others consistently have met those goals. In their complaints, plaintiffs alleged that the Effective Scheduling system established guidelines that were not attainable for many employees, thereby causing them to work "off the clock" without additional pay and to cut corners, including disregarding sanitary practices.

During the 2½-year "Class Period" between May 7, 1990, when Food Lion issued its 1989 Annual report, and November 5, 1992, when the PrimeTime Live broadcast aired, plaintiffs purchased stock in Food Lion, allegedly relying on its rosy statements about its relationship with its employees and the cleanliness of its stores. Plaintiffs alleged that during this period, Food Lion "reported optimistically about its future" when, in fact, its profits and optimistic outlook were dependent on a system that required its employees to violate the labor laws and to pursue unsanitary methods, facts which Food Lion failed to report.

In its 1989 Annual Report, circulated on May 7, 1990, Food Lion stated that the Human Resources Department "continues to insure that Food Lion employees receive competitive wages and excellent benefits;" that although inflation led to higher costs, "[t]hese costs were recovered primarily through improved operating efficiencies and an increased average selling price per item;" and that "[w]e will continue to pay close attention to service levels and cleanliness in our stores and believe we will achieve high marks from customers in these areas." The report said nothing about any widespread labor or sanitary problems.

During the Class Period, Food Lion continued to face and to resist the efforts of the United Food and Commercial Workers Union to organize Food Lion workers. When the union called for a boycott of Food Lion, the company issued a press release on August 30, 1990, stating:

> How ironic it is on this Labor Day weekend for a union leader to call for the destruction of more than 45,000 jobs of Food Lion employees in retaliation for their desire to remain union free. Such blatant threats and arrogant disregard of true employee free choice is the kind of coercion of employees that totally desecrates the purpose and spirit of Labor Day.

> The fact is, Food Lion opens more than 100 stores each year and adds more than 5,000 employees each year. Food Lion could not do this without offering competitive wages and excellent benefits. On average, Food Lion receives three to four applications for every available job.

About a year later, on September 11, 1991, the UFCW announced that it had filed a lengthy complaint with the Department of Labor, accusing Food Lion of widespread labor violations in tacitly encouraging employees to work "off the clock" without pay. In its press release, the union stated:

More than 37 percent of the after-tax profit of the nation's fastest-growing retail food chain, Food Lion, is derived from illegal off-the-clock work of employees.

* * *

Food Lion's profit is reported to exceed the industry average, "the complaint [filed with the Department of Labor] states," and its profit advantage is widely attributed to more efficient operations. With over one-third of its profit derived from illegal off-the-clock work, it is clear that Food Lion's profit advantage is unfairly obtained.

* * *

Food Lion could owe as much as $194 million in back wages. With liquidated damages allowed by law, its liability could be "as high as $388 million."

Food Lion responded with its own press release the same day:

Food Lion has a very clear policy against working off the clock. Employees, including managers, who have violated this policy have received discipline up to and including discharge.

This Complaint and news release by the UFCW union is simply one more example of the union's attempt to harass and coerce Food Lion management into recognizing the union without regard to the sentiments of our employees.

Food Lion employees have repeatedly rejected the UFCW union despite union efforts for more than ten years.

* * *

As has been the case in all other attacks on Food Lion by this union, the company intends to defend itself vigorously in this matter.

On the following day, Food Lion issued another press release, stating:

The UFCW's most recent claims of illegal employment practices by Food Lion and its employees insult the hard work and integrity of all Food Lion employees. Those ingredients are the key to Food Lion's success and ability to bring customers extra low prices. It is not off the clock work by employees or other illegal employment practices as the UFCW-sponsored propaganda alleges.

* * *

Food Lion denies union claims of employee mistreatment, but the public doesn't have to accept the word of either the Company or the union. Let employees and the free marketplace decide that.

* * *

Food Lion's 1991 Annual Report, circulated on June 1, 1992, referred to "continued and constant harassment of Food Lion by the

United Food and Commercial Workers Union," but it also stated more positively, "We believe that Food Lion's Extra Low Prices and its clean and conveniently located stores are especially well suited to the demands of our customers." The report quoted a store manager as saying, "Food Lion also provides job security, good wages, good working conditions and some of the best benefits in the supermarket industry." The report also included an unattributed statement that "Food Lion is one of the best-managed high growth operators in the food retailing industry." This Annual Report, like the 1989 Annual Report, did not acknowledge any widespread labor violations or sanitation problems.

Finally, in July 1992, Food Lion filed a form 10–Q with the Securities and Exchange Commission which stated:

> Management and legal counsel for the Company are currently investigating and evaluating the allegations contained in the [UFCW] Complaints. The ultimate liability, if any, which may result is not presently determinable; however, in the opinion of management, the Company has meritorious defenses to the allegations and the Company intends to defend the allegations vigorously and any liability will not have a material adverse effect on the financial condition or results of operations of the Company.

On August 3, 1993, approximately one year after this public filing (and several months after the close of the Class Period), the Department of Labor announced a settlement of the UFCW-instigated complaints against Food Lion, in which Food Lion agreed to pay $16.2 million, $8.1 million in 1993 and $8.1 million in 1994. The $16.2 million represented $13.2 million in back wages for current and former Food Lion employees and $3 million in penalties. The cost of the settlement to shareholders was 1.67 cents per share for each year, 1993 and 1994 (i.e., $8.1 million divided by the 484,000,000 shares outstanding). Experts retained by both the plaintiffs and the defendants agreed that the settlement was not material to Food Lion's earnings. Indeed, the expert for Food Lion stated that the settlement's effect on income was "de minimis."

On November 5, 1992, after all of the publicity about Food Lion's ongoing labor disputes but nine months before the Department of Labor settlement, ABC broadcast a PrimeTime Live episode about Food Lion stores, alleging widespread unsanitary practices and off-the-clock work by Food Lion employees. PrimeTime Live attributed these deficiencies to Food Lion's Effective Scheduling system. The broadcast included interviews with former and current Food Lion employees and a hidden camera investigation conducted by two ABC employees who obtained jobs at three Food Lion stores. The employees who were interviewed alleged various unsanitary business practices, including pulling meat out of a dumpster and selling it, bleaching fish and pork with Clorox "[t]o get the smell out" and then selling them, mixing rotten pork with other pork and selling it as fresh sausage, and cutting off the edge of a block of cheese that had been nibbled by rats so that the rest of the block could be sold. An employee stated that she used "fingernail polish remover to take the dates off" of products so that they could be sold after the manufacturer's date for sale had passed. . . .

Several employees described how they worked extra hours off the clock in order to be able to complete their assigned tasks. . . .

* * *

II

* * *

[A]t issue in this case [is] whether Food Lion made a false statement or omission of material fact. To establish this element, plaintiffs must point to a factual statement or omission—that is, one that is demonstrable as being true or false. Also, the statement must be false, or the omission must render public statements misleading. And finally, any statement or omission of fact must be material. Materiality is an objective concept, "involving the significance of an omitted or misrepresented fact to a reasonable investor." Thus, a fact stated or omitted is material if there is a substantial likelihood that a reasonable purchaser or seller of a security (1) would consider the fact important in deciding whether to buy or sell the security or (2) would have viewed the total mix of information made available to be significantly altered by disclosure of the fact.

These components—a factual statement or omission that is false or misleading and that is material—interact to provide a core requirement for a securities fraud claim. While opinion or puffery will often not be actionable, in particular contexts when it is both factual and material, it may be actionable. Thus, for example, a CEO's expression of "comfort" with a financial analyst's prediction of his company's future earnings was held not to be factual in that, as a future projection, it was not capable of being proved false. On the other hand, the Supreme Court has held that an opinion by board members to minority stockholders that the stock price of $42 for the purchase of their shares was a "high value" and represented a "fair" transaction could be both factual and material. See *Virginia Bankshares*, 501 U.S. at 1090–93. [Eds.: excerpted in Chapter 5] . . .

With these relevant principles in hand, we turn to the misstatements and omissions that plaintiffs in this case allege "caused" them to purchase Food Lion stock during the Class Period.

III

The essence of the plaintiffs' claim is that during the Class Period, Food Lion's earnings were "artificially inflated due to Food Lion's widespread violations of federal labor laws and pervasive unsanitary food-handling practices" and that Food Lion failed to disclose these facts and, indeed, publicly denied them. Plaintiffs contend that the true facts were "first disclosed to the public in credible fashion" when ABC News aired PrimeTime Live on November 5, 1992, presenting "an expose on Food Lion's labor and sanitation practices." . . .

A

Throughout the Class Period, Food Lion expressed, in public statements, substantial pride in the fact that its employees were well-paid and enjoyed good benefits. It claimed that it provided its employees with job security, good working conditions, and "some of the best benefits in the supermarket industry." Its Annual Reports for 1989 and

1991 and similar public statements expressed a belief that "Food Lion is one of the best-managed high growth operators in the food retailing industry."[2]

Plaintiffs claim that these rosy statements about employee compensation and benefits masked Food Lion's real labor problems that were created by its Effective Scheduling system and by the UFCW's complaint filed with the Department of Labor charging Food Lion with wage/hour violations. Plaintiffs' contention focuses on the allegation that Food Lion knew about employees being forced to work off the clock and that, even though the practice was widespread, it failed to disclose it. Because such work provided productivity from employees without compensation, the plaintiffs' theory goes, the practice illegally and artificially inflated Food Lion's earnings.

In addition, plaintiffs contend that, to the extent that the practices were made public by the UFCW and others, Food Lion's response was deceptive in explicitly denying or giving the implicit impression that it did not have significant amounts of off-the-clock work. For example, Food Lion said in response to the UFCW's complaint that it "intends to defend itself vigorously in this matter;" that the company's success was based upon the "hard work and integrity of all Food Lion employees," rather than on any "illegal employment practices;" and that "UFCW sponsored claims of extensive wage/hour violations are simply untrue." . . . Plaintiffs also point to the fact that, during this same period, Food Lion omitted to admit that its profits were substantially dependent on this off-the-clock work.

Plaintiffs' securities fraud claim cannot succeed because, despite the fact that Food Lion denied the charges, the nature of the off-the-clock claims and the claims' risk to earnings were in fact well known to the market before the PrimeTime Live broadcast, and therefore Food Lion's omissions were not material. On September 11, 1991, for instance, more than a year before the PrimeTime Live broadcast, the UFCW publicly announced that it had filed a complaint with the Department of Labor, asserting that 183 people had claimed to have illegally worked off the clock, that "[m]ore than 37 percent of the after tax profit" of Food Lion was attributable to off the clock work, and that "Food Lion could owe as much as $194 million in back wages." The union warned that Food Lion's liability could be as high as $388 million based on claims for liquidated damages. Even as Food Lion denied the claims, however, it nevertheless promised to conduct an investigation of the allegations and take appropriate action. The market had a full opportunity to evaluate these claims and to reflect their risk in the market price for Food Lion stock. The PrimeTime Live broadcast added nothing to inform the market further. Rather, it simply repeated earlier charges through experiences of seven employees.

---

[2] While not material to our holding, we note that we can find nothing in the record that would make these general statements by Food Lion, standing alone, actionable. First, these statements are immaterial puffery that is not actionable under the securities laws. Second, there is no evidence in the record that Food Lion employees were not well paid; that Food Lion did not have "some of the best benefits" in the industry; or that Food Lion was not well managed. Third, whether or not these statements are true, they do not bear on plaintiffs' claims that Food Lion forced its employees to work off the clock. Even if Food Lion's employees worked overtime without pay, they could still be well-paid compared to other employees in the industry.

Because the market was thus informed of the union's charges before PrimeTime Live aired, what PrimeTime Live disclosed was not material. Indeed, even the much larger problem alleged more than a year earlier by the union was not material. Food Lion settled all of the claims made by the union with the Department of Labor for $16.2 million, $8.1 million payable in each of 1993 and 1994. During the same period, Food Lion's earnings exceeded $200 million per year. Experts on both sides agree that this settlement, reflecting a charge of less than two cents per share for each year, was not material to Food Lion's stock price. And consistent with this conclusion, Food Lion's share price did not drop following announcement of the Department of Labor settlement. . . .

B

We turn now to the second category of alleged misstatements and omissions by Food Lion—those which related to unsanitary practices. The plaintiffs have juxtaposed Food Lion's ongoing public statements about the cleanliness of its stores with the *PrimeTime Live* broadcast which revealed allegedly widespread unsanitary practices. In its 1989 Annual Report, Food Lion stated: "We will continue to pay close attention to service levels and cleanliness in our stores and believe we will achieve high marks from customers in these areas." Similarly, in its 1991 Annual Report, Food Lion stated: "We believe that Food Lion's Extra Low Prices and its clean and conveniently located stores are especially well suited to the demands of our customers."

On their face, these statements are the kind of puffery and generalizations that reasonable investors could not have relied upon when deciding whether to buy stock. . . .

Before considering the broadcast, the district court noted that, with a few exceptions, most of the broadcast was inadmissible hearsay. None of the people who spoke were under oath or subject to cross examination. In the absence of the evidence presented by the *PrimeTime Live* broadcast, or at least most of it, the district court was left with the affidavits of Food Lion which demonstrated that it had no corporate policy, written or unwritten, that would permit or encourage unsanitary food-handling practices. The court noted that Food Lion had "an audit staff in place who conducted surprise inspections of Food Lion stores to ensure that the stores complied with health and sanitation policies." And the court concluded that Food Lion's efforts were apparently sufficient to satisfy federal, state, and local inspections which revealed that Food Lion's record was "just as good, if not better, than its competitors' inspection reports."

But even considering the entire *PrimeTime Live* broadcast, the district court stated it "still does not present evidence of widespread unsanitary conditions of which Defendants knew." It noted that "with respect to the sanitary conditions at Food Lion's 1,000 stores, the [*PrimeTime Live*] broadcast is insufficient to draw any conclusions about Food Lion's operations as a whole." The court pointed out that the broadcast was filmed at only 3 of Food Lion's almost 1,000 stores and that out of 60,000 active employees and 40,000 former employees, *PrimeTime Live* interviewed a total of 70 current and former employees, 22 of whom had left the employ of Food Lion as much as 8 years before the Class Period. The district court concluded:

[T]o the extent that there are any isolated instances of workplace errors, . . . not only is there not a substantial likelihood that the reasonable investor would consider the limited instances of workplace errors important in deciding whether to purchase Food Lion securities, but the Court also finds . . . that Defendants were taking steps to remedy these isolated problems. As a result, the Court finds that to the extent that there is any omission by Defendants in their Annual and Quarterly Reports of isolated instances of workplace errors, this omission not only is not material as required by § 10b but also could not make any affirmative statements misleading in Defendants' Annual and Quarterly Reports.

We agree with the district court that, based on the record in this case, Food Lion was not required to make public statements about the existence of various sanitation problems that were revealed from time to time. These day-to-day conditions were not shown to be material to the price of Food Lion's stock. We also agree, as earlier noted, that the public statements that it did make were no more than soft, puffing statements about clean and conveniently located stores that no reasonable investor could rely upon in buying or selling Food Lion stock. Accordingly, we conclude that Food Lion did not defraud the market with false statements or omissions of material fact as required to maintain an action under § 10(b) of the Securities Exchange Act and Rule 10b–5 promulgated thereunder.

* * *

NOTES

1.   *Bespeaks caution.* The "truth on the market" defense applied in *Food Lion* is one variation on the "total mix" doctrine. Another variation developed by the lower courts is the "bespeaks caution" doctrine. Under the "bespeaks caution" doctrine, forward-looking statements are rendered immaterial as a matter of law if they are accompanied by disclosure of risks that may preclude the forward-looking projection from coming to fruition. See, e.g., *Kaufman v. Trump's Castle Funding*, 7 F.3d 357 (3d Cir. 1993). The doctrine has been codified and expanded by Congress as a "safe harbor" for forward-looking statements, part of the Private Securities Litigation Reform Act. We discuss the forward-looking safe harbor in Chapter 5.

QUESTIONS

1.   Why did the court hold that the "off-the-clock" labor practices disclosed in the Department of Labor settlement with Food Lion were not material?

2.   Why did the court hold that the unsanitary practices of Food Lion grocery stores were not material?

3.   What is "puffery"?

HYPOTHETICAL FOUR

Six Feet has been having some problems with its employees, who are dissatisfied with what they see as low pay and depressing working conditions. The United Bereavement Workers of America has been attempting to organize the Six Feet employees. The Union and its allies in the environmental movement have been publicizing the dangers of the embalming fluid used by Six Feet, a chemical developed by Federico, Six Feet's Vice-President of Death Services. Federico believes that the embalming fluid gives the corpses "a fresher, more lifelike" appearance.

Ruth, the Vice President for Human Resources at Six Feet, issues a press release disputing the Union's claims that the embalming fluid is dangerous and stating that "Six Feet has no higher priority than the safety of its employees." Three months later, OSHA imposes a $1 million fine on Six Feet for unsafe labor conditions and bars Six Feet from any further use of Federico's embalming fluid. (OSHA reveals that Federico did no testing whatsoever to evaluate the safety of the embalming fluid.) OSHA's action fuels the frustration of Six Feet's employees, who vote to recognize the Union as their bargaining agent. The Union, after staging a costly three week strike (the bodies were piling up), manages to extract a 20% increase in wages for the Six Feet employees. Was Ruth's press release materially misleading?

V. MANAGEMENT INTEGRITY

One of the fundamental premises behind Congress's adoption of the Exchange Act was that full disclosure would make management and directors more accountable to shareholders. "Sunlight," according to that apostle of disclosure Louis Brandeis, "is said to be the best of disinfectants: electric light the most efficient policeman." Louis D. Brandeis, *Other People's Money* 92 (1913). Following this philosophy, the SEC includes a series of items in Regulation S–K (Subpart 400) relating to the competence and integrity of management. Item 401 of Regulation S–K provides for biographical information on directors and officers, including business experience for the past five years. Item 402 requires disclosure of executive compensation (including stock options). Item 404 details disclosures for transactions between the issuer and certain related parties, including family members of any director or officer.

As you read the section below, consider whether the SEC is concerned only with accountability to shareholders in mandating disclosures regarding management. Does it have other policy objectives? Keep in mind that the SEC's mandatory disclosure items are just the beginning, as additional disclosure may be necessary to avoid creating a misleading omission. Consider what statements were rendered misleading by the facts that were omitted from the filings in the case below.

In the Matter of Franchard Corporation

42 S.E.C. 163 (1964).

■ CARY, CHAIRMAN.

These are consolidated proceedings pursuant to Sections 8(c) and 8(d) of the Securities Act of 1933 to determine whether a stop order should issue suspending the effectiveness of three registration statements filed by Franchard Corporation, formerly Glickman

Corporation and whether certain post-effective amendments filed by the registrant should be declared effective. These proceedings raise important issues as to the disclosures to be required in a registration statement concerning (1) the use of substantial amounts of a company's funds for the personal benefit of its controlling person on whose business reputation public offerings of its securities were largely predicated; (2) the pledge by a dominant stockholder of his control stock; (3) the adequacy of performance of a board of directors.... In essence, we are concerned here with the role that can and should be performed by the disclosure requirements of the Securities Act in assisting investors to evaluate management....

I.   FACTS

A.   BACKGROUND

Louis J. Glickman has for many years been a large-scale real estate developer, operator and investor. From 1954, to 1960, he acquired control of real estate in this country and in Canada by means of "syndication" arrangements. These arrangements involved the acquisition by Glickman, through purchase, contract or option, of an interest in real estate; the organization of a legal entity, usually a limited partnership but in some instances a corporation, in which Glickman retained a controlling position, and in which interests were sold to the public for cash; and the acquisition by this entity of the property interest in question. Glickman conducted some of these syndication activities and certain other phases of his real estate business through a number of wholly owned corporations, the most important of which was Glickman Corporation of Nevada, now known as Venada Corporation.

In May of 1960, Glickman caused registrant to be formed in order to group under one entity most of the publicly owned corporations and limited partnerships under his control.... Registrant's stock was divided into two classes, Class A common and Class B common, with the B stockholders given the right to elect 2/3 of registrant's directors until 1971, when all outstanding B shares become A shares. Glickman established control of registrant by acquiring 450,000 of its 660,000 authorized B shares for $1 per share. He exercised a dominant role in the management of registrant's affairs as president at the time of its formation and later as its first chairman of the board.

The first of the three registration statements here involved ("1960 filing") became effective on October 12, 1960.... [The October 12, 1960 offering involved both Class A and B shares. The registrant then issued Class A shares through two additional registration statements that became effective on October 2, 1961 and then on December 1, 1961.]

B.   GLICKMAN'S WITHDRAWALS AND PLEDGES

Registrant's 1960 prospectus stated that Glickman had from time to time advanced substantial sums to the partnerships and corporations that were about to become subsidiaries of the registrant. It also said that he had advanced $211,000 to the registrant for the purpose of defraying its organization and registration costs and that this advance would be repaid without interest out of the proceeds of the public offering. On October 14, 1960—two days after the effective date of registrant's 1960 filing—Glickman began secretly to transfer funds from the registrant to Venada, his wholly owned corporation. Within 2 months the aggregate amount of these transfers amounted to $296,329. By October 2, 1961, the effective date of registrant's first 1961 filing, Glickman had made 45 withdrawals which amounted in the aggregate to $2,372,511.[8] Neither the 1961 prospectuses nor any of the effective amendments to the 1960 filing referred to these transactions.

All of registrant's prospectuses stated that Glickman owned most of its B as well as a substantial block of its A stock. On the effective date of the 1960 filing Glickman's shares were unencumbered. In the following month, however, he began to pledge his shares [to] finance his personal real estate ventures. By August 31, 1961, all of Glickman's B and much of his A stock had been pledged to banks, finance companies, and private individuals. On the effective dates of the two 1961 filings the loans secured by these pledges aggregated about $4,250,000. The effective interest rates on these loans ran as high as 24 percent annually. Glickman retained the right to vote the pledged shares in the absence of a default on the loans. The two 1961 filings made no mention of Glickman's pledges or the loans they secured.

C. ACTION OF THE BOARD OF DIRECTORS

In May 1962, the accountants who had audited the financial statements in registrant's 1960 and 1961 filings informed its directors that Glickman had from time to time diverted funds from the registrant's treasury to Venada. The directors then met with Glickman, who assured them that the withdrawals had been without wrongful intent and would not recur. Glickman agreed to repay all of the then known unauthorized withdrawals with interest at the rate of 6 percent. Registrant's directors soon discovered that Glickman had made other withdrawals, and they retained former United States District Court Judge Simon H. Rifkind to determine Glickman's liability to registrant. Glickman agreed to be bound by Judge Rifkind's determination and was continued in office.

In a report submitted on August 20, 1962, Judge Rifkind found that Glickman had on many occasions withdrawn substantial sums from registrant; that Bernard Mann, who was registrant's as well as Venada's treasurer but not a member of registrant's board of directors, was the only one of registrant's officers who had known of the withdrawals and had collaborated with Glickman in effecting them; that registrant's inadequate administrative procedures had to some extent facilitated Glickman's wrongdoing; and that all of the withdrawals had been made good with 6 percent interest. Judge Rifkind also found that 6 percent was an inadequate interest rate because Glickman and Venada had been borrowing at appreciably higher interest rates from commercial finance companies and others.

---

[8] In most instances the amounts were returned relatively soon but were followed by fresh withdrawals. The amounts owed registrant by Glickman often exceeded $1 million and on one occasion were close to $1,500,000. The withdrawals by Glickman were accomplished by transfers of funds from registrant and its subsidiaries directly to Venada and expenditures by registrant and its subsidiaries for Venada's benefit. During this period, registrant and its subsidiaries had a number of relationships with Venada which regularly required them to make payments directly to it or on its behalf. The interspersal of Glickman's unauthorized withdrawals among a large number of usual and proper disbursements on the books of registrant and its subsidiaries facilitated concealment of his activities.

On November 30, 1962, registrant's directors learned that Glickman had continued to make unauthorized withdrawals after he had promised to desist from so doing and after the issuance of the Rifkind report, that Glickman and his wife had pledged all of their shares of the registrant's stock, and that Glickman and Venada were in financial straits. Glickman and Mann thereupon resigned from all of their posts with the registrant, and Glickman sold all his B stock and some of his Class A stock to a small group of investors. Monthly cash distributions to A stockholders, which registrant had made every month since its inception, were discontinued in January 1963, and registrant changed its name from Glickman Corporation to Franchard Corporation.

II.   ALLEGED DEFICIENCIES— ACTIVITIES OF MANAGEMENT

A.   GLICKMAN'S WITHDRAWALS OF REGISTRANT'S FUNDS AND PLEDGES OF HIS SHARES

Of cardinal importance in any business is the quality of its management. Disclosures relevant to an evaluation of management are particularly pertinent where, as in this case, securities are sold largely on the personal reputation of a company's controlling person. The disclosures in these respects were materially deficient. The 1960 prospectus failed to reveal that Glickman intended to use substantial amounts of registrant's funds for the benefit of Venada, and the 1961 prospectuses made no reference to Glickman's continual diversion of substantial sums from the registrant. Glickman's pledges were not discussed in either the effective amendments to the 1960 filings or in the two 1961 filings.

In our view, these disclosures were highly material to an evaluation of the competence and reliability of registrant's management—in large measure, Glickman. In many respects, the development of disclosure standards adequate for informed appraisal of management's ability and integrity is a difficult task. How do you tell a "good" business manager from a "bad" one in a piece of paper? Managerial talent consists of personal attributes, essentially subjective in nature, that frequently defy meaningful analysis through the impersonal medium of a prospectus. Direct statements of opinion as to management's ability, which are not susceptible to objective verification, may well create an unwarranted appearance of reliability if placed in a prospectus. The integrity of management—its willingness to place its duty to public shareholders over personal interest—is an equally elusive factor for the application of disclosure standards.

Evaluation of the quality of management—to whatever extent it is possible—is an essential ingredient of informed investment decision. A need so important cannot be ignored, and in a variety of ways the disclosure requirements of the Securities Act furnish factual information to fill this need. Appraisals of competency begin with information concerning management's past business experience, which is elicited by requirements that a prospectus state the offices and positions held with the issuer by each executive officer within the last 5 years. With respect to established companies, management's past performance, as shown by comprehensive financial and other disclosures concerning the issuer's operations, furnish a guide to its future business performance. To permit judgments whether the corporation's affairs are likely to be conducted in the interest of public shareholders, the registration requirements elicit information as to the interests of insiders which may conflict with their duty of loyalty to the corporation. Disclosures are also required with respect to the remuneration and other benefits paid or proposed to be paid to management as well as material transactions between the corporation and its officers, directors, holders of more than 10 percent of its stock, and their associates.

Glickman's withdrawals were material transactions between registrant and its management, and the registration forms on which registrant's filings were made called for their disclosure. Registrant's argument that the withdrawals were not material because Glickman's undisclosed indebtedness to registrant never exceeded 1.5 percent of the gross book value of registrant's assets not only minimizes the substantial amounts of the withdrawals in relation to the stockholders' equity and the company's cash flow, but ignores the significance to prospective investors of information concerning Glickman's managerial ability and personal integrity. Registrant as such had no operating history. It concedes that the initial public offering in 1960 was made primarily, if not solely, on Glickman's name and reputation as a successful real estate investor and operator, and it is equally clear that the 1961 offerings were also predicated on his reputation. All of the prospectuses spoke of Glickman's many years of experience "in the creation and development of real estate investment opportunities' as an investor in real property for his own account." The prospectuses also made it clear that Glickman would dominate and control registrant's operations, and prospective investors in registrant's securities were, in effect, being offered an opportunity to "buy" Glickman management of real estate investments.

A description of Glickman's activities was important on several grounds. First, publication of the facts pertaining to Glickman's withdrawals of substantial funds and of his pledges of his control stock would have clearly indicated his strained financial position and his urgent need for cash in his personal real estate ventures. In the context here, these facts were as material to an evaluation of Glickman's business ability as financial statements of an established company would be to an evaluation of its management's past performance.

Second, disclosure of Glickman's continual diversion of registrant's funds to the use of Venada, his wholly owned corporation, was also germane to an evaluation of the integrity of his management. This quality is always a material factor. In the circumstances of this case the need for disclosure in this area is obvious and compelling. We have spoken of Glickman's dominance. Moreover, Venada was registrant's most important tenant and Glickman would constantly be dealing with himself on behalf of registrant in the context of pressures created by his personal strained financial condition. Even aside from the issues relating to Glickman's character, publication of the fact that he was diverting funds to Venada to bolster that company's weak financial condition was important in evaluating registrant's own operations.

Third, Glickman's need for cash as indicated by withdrawals from registrant and his substantial borrowings and pledges of registrant's shares gave him a powerful and direct motive to cause registrant to pursue policies which would permit high distribution rates and maintain a high price for registrant's A shares. The higher that price, the greater his borrowing power; a decline in that price, on the other hand, would lead to the defaults and the consequent loss of control that eventually came to pass. Since prices of cash flow real estate stocks were directly responsive to changes in cash distribution policies, and since, in any event, Glickman needed to derive as much cash as possible from registrant's operations, his financial involvements gave him a peculiarly strong personal interest in setting registrant's current cash distribution rate at the highest possible level and to overlook or to minimize the long-term impact on registrant of an unduly generous distribution policy. Investors were entitled to be apprised of these facts and such potential conflicts of interest.

Finally, the possibility of a change of control was also important to prospective investors. As we have noted, registrant's public offerings were largely predicated on Glickman's reputation as a successful real estate investor and operator. Disclosure of Glickman's secured loans, the relatively high interest rates that they bore, the secondary sources from which lenders could declare defaults would have alerted investors to the possibility of a change in the control and management of registrant and apprised them of the possible nature of any such change. . . .

We . . . cannot agree with registrant's contention that disclosure of Glickman's borrowings and pledges of registrant's stock would have been an "unwarranted revelation" of Glickman's personal affairs. An insider of a corporation that is asking the public for funds must, in return, relinquish various areas of privacy with respect to his financial affairs which impinge significantly upon the affairs of the company. That determination was made by the Congress over 30 years ago when it expressly provided in the Securities Act for disclosure of such matters as remuneration of insiders and the extent of their shareholdings in and the nature of their other material transactions with the company.

With respect to disclosure of pledged shares, registrant is not aided by pointing out that our registration forms under the Securities Act and the reports required under the Securities Exchange Act do not call for disclosure of encumbrances on a controlling stockholder's shares, and that proposals to require such disclosures in reports filed with us under the Securities Exchange Act have not been adopted.* The fact that such disclosures are not required of all issuers and their controlling persons in all cases does not negate their materiality in specific cases. The registration forms promulgated by us are guides intended to assist registrants in discharging their statutory duty of full disclosure. They are not and cannot possibly be exhaustive enumerations of each and every item material to investors in the particular circumstances relevant to a specific offering. The kaleidoscopic variety of economic life precludes any attempt at such an enumeration. The preparation of a registration statement is not satisfied, as registrant's position suggests, by a mechanical process of responding narrowly to the specific items of the applicable registration form. On the contrary, Rule 408 under the Securities Act makes clear to prospective registrants that: "In addition

---

*   [Editors' note: Such disclosure is now required by Regulation S–K, Item 403(c).]

to the information expressly required to be included in a registration statement, there shall be added such further material information, if any, as may be necessary to make the required statements in the light of the circumstances under which they were made, not misleading."

B.   ACTIVITIES OF REGISTRANT'S DIRECTORS

Another issue raised in these proceedings concerns the disclosure to be required in a prospectus regarding the adequacy of performance of managerial functions by registrant's board of directors. The Division urges that the prospectuses, by identifying the members of the board of directors, impliedly represented that they would provide oversight and direction to registrant's officers. In fact, the Division argues, the board was a nullity because the directors consistently agreed to Glickman's proposals, derived their information as to the current state of registrant's finances from Glickman's sporadic oral reports, and permitted him to fix each officer's area of responsibility.

It was obvious, however, that Glickman would exercise the dominant role in managing registrant's operations and the prospectuses contained no affirmative representations concerning the participation of the directors in registrant's affairs. Moreover, the board met regularly and received information as to registrant's affairs from Glickman and in connection with the preparation of registrant's registration statements, post-effective amendments, and periodic reports filed with us. It is clear we are not presented with a picture of total abdication of directorial responsibilities. Thus, the question posed by the Division must be whether the prospectuses were deficient in not disclosing that the directors, in overseeing the operations of the company, failed to exercise the degree of diligence which the Division believes was required of them under the circumstances in the context of the day-to-day operations of the company. We find no deficiencies in this area.

This is an issue raising fundamental considerations as to the functions of the disclosure requirements of the Securities Act. The civil liability provisions of Section 11 do establish for directors a standard of due diligence in the preparation of a registration statement—a Federal rule of directors' responsibility with respect to the completeness and accuracy of the document used in the public distribution of securities. The Act does not purport, however, to define Federal standards of directors' responsibility in the ordinary operations of business enterprises and nowhere empowers us to formulate administratively such regulatory standards.[36] The diligence required of registrant's directors in overseeing its affairs is to be evaluated in the light of the standards established by State statutory and common law.

---

[36] The deterrent effect of disclosures required by the Securities Act and other provisions of the Federal securities laws do, of course, have an impact on standards of conduct for directors. As Mr. Justice Frankfurter, a major architect of the Securities Act, stated in describing the impact of the Act: "The existence of bonuses, of excessive commissions and salaries, of preferential lists and the like, may all be open secrets among the knowing, but the knowing are few. There is a shrinking quality to such transactions; to force knowledge of them into the open is largely to restrain their happening. Many practices safely pursued in private lose their justification in public. Thus social standards newly defined gradually establish themselves as new business habits."

Moreover, representations in prospectuses or documents filed with us may also create obligations that a corporation and its directors must fulfill and thus affect management's level of performance. . . .

In our view, the application of these standards on a routine basis in the processing of registration statements would be basically incompatible with the philosophy and administration of the disclosure requirements of the Securities Act. Outright fraud or reckless indifference by directors might be readily identifiable and universally condemned. But activity short of that, which give rise to legal restraints and liabilities, invokes significant uncertainty. And for various reasons, including the complexity and diversity of business activities, the courts have exhibited a marked reluctance to interfere with good faith business judgments. The general principles reflected in statutory commandments or evolved from decisions in particular cases, while, perhaps readily articulated, furnish vague guidance for judgment in many situations. The courts are required to formulate and apply standards of directorial responsibility on the basis of a judicially developed record in the particular case in order to establish rights and liabilities in that case. . . . To generally require information in Securities Act prospectuses as to whether directors have performed their duties in accordance with the standards of responsibility required of them under State law would stretch disclosure beyond the limitations contemplated by the statutory scheme and necessitated by considerations of administrative practicality.

To be sure, we have required disclosures concerning particular transactions which have raised questions of noncompliance with State or Federal law governing business conduct. We have also required disclosures concerning directors' performance in situations involving a virtual abdication of responsibility or where the prospectus has made affirmative representations by which their performance could be tested. And these cases may not exhaust the areas where disclosure might be necessary as to activities of directors which do not comply with applicable standards. But the disclosures sought here by the staff would require evaluation of the entire conduct of a board of directors in the context of the whole business operations of a company in the light of diverse and uncertain standards. In our view, this is a function which the disclosure requirements of the Securities Act cannot effectively discharge. It would either result in self-serving generalities of little value to investors or grave uncertainties both on the part of those who must enforce and those who must comply with that Act.

* * *

NOTES

1. *Disclosure requirements.* Item 404 of Regulation S–K now requires disclosure of transactions in excess of $120,000 between the issuer and directors, officers, 5% stockholders and the family members of any of those classes. The Item is written to sweep in corporations or other entities in which those individuals have a "material" interest (defined as greater than 10% of the equity of that entity).

Still more restrictive is § 402 of the Sarbanes-Oxley Act, which prohibits loans by public companies to their executive officers and directors. In addition, § 406 of the Sarbanes-Oxley Act (implemented by the SEC in Item 406 of Regulation S–K) requires disclosure of whether the company has a code of ethics for its CEO, CFO, and controller. If the company does not have such a code of ethics, it is required to explain why not.

QUESTIONS

1. How can Glickman's withdrawals, which accounted for less than 1.5% of the gross book value of the registrant, be material?

2. At the time of the *Franchard* case, "encumbrances on a controlling stockholder's shares" was not an enumerated item required to be disclosed. What basis does the SEC have for concluding that the registrant nonetheless should have disclosed it?

3. What if Glickman had a heart condition that made him more likely than the average CEO to die or become disabled? Should this be a required disclosure in the registration statement pursuant to Rule 408 of the Securities Act?

4. Did the SEC let the Franchard directors off too lightly? Aren't the disclosures relating to the performance of directors of vital importance to investors?

HYPOTHETICAL FIVE

Six Feet rents a number of funeral homes from Keith, David's former partner, who has custody of their adopted daughter, Taylor. David (the CEO and Chairman of the Board) believes that because the rentals are at a fair market price, the lease agreements with Keith are not material. Does Six Feet need to disclose the lease agreements with Keith?

————

As *Franchard* makes clear, the securities laws will frequently require disclosure of facts that will at least make management uncomfortable. Do the securities laws require disclosure of facts that could lead to significantly more painful consequences?

In *SEC v. Fehn*, 97 F.3d 1276 (9th Cir. 1996), the Ninth Circuit rejected claims that the Fifth Amendment barred the disclosure of previous—then undiscovered—securities law violations. According to the court, "the Fifth Amendment privilege may not be invoked to resist compliance with a regulatory regime constructed to effect the State's public purposes unrelated to the enforcement of its criminal laws." The court enumerated three factors to be considered in determining whether a compelled disclosure threatens self-incrimination: "(1) whether the disclosure requirement targets a highly selective group inherently suspect of criminal activities, rather than the public generally; (2) whether the requirement involves an area permeated with criminal statutes, rather than an essentially noncriminal and regulatory area of inquiry; and (3) whether compliance would compel disclosure of information that would surely prove a significant link in a chain of evidence tending to establish [ ] guilt, rather than disclosing no inherently illegal activity." The court rejected the propositions that the securities laws were "permeated with criminal activities" or targeted "inherently illegal activities."

Fehn represents the usual judicial response to claims that the Fifth Amendment shields an individual from disclosure requirements. A notable exception to the cases requiring disclosure is *United States v. Matthews*, 787 F.2d 38 (2d Cir. 1986), which held that the omission of the fact that the defendant had been informed by the U.S. Attorney that he was likely to be indicted was not grounds for a criminal prosecution for failure to disclose the potential indictment. It is less clear that a civil enforcement action by the SEC for failure to disclose the potential indictment also would have failed.

If the criminal investigation has led to a formal indictment, disclosure is specifically required under Item 401(f)(2) of Regulation S–K. Other forms of wrongdoing have also been required to be disclosed. For example, Item 401(f)(5) of Regulation S–K requires disclosure if an officer or director has been found by a court or by the SEC to have violated the securities laws. Disclosure is also required if the officer or director filed for bankruptcy, or if he served as an executive officer of a company that filed for bankruptcy.

Note also that Item 401 limits disclosure of criminal cases and adjudications to only those occurring during the previous ten years. Earlier offenses are not addressed by the regulation. The mere fact that Item 401 does not specifically require the disclosure of earlier offenses, however, does not end the inquiry. Instead, the issuer (and other disclosing parties) must independently determine whether any earlier offenses are material for investors to obtain a complete understanding of any disclosed information, including information on criminal cases and adjudications within the previous ten years as well as any statements on the qualifications of the officers and directors. *See* Rule 408 of the Securities Act and Rule 12b–20 of the Exchange Act.

Item 401 does not require that unadjudicated civil cases against officers or directors be disclosed. Disclosure may still be required, however, if a civil lawsuit or criminal investigation substantially reflects on management integrity. Unadjudicated wrongdoing (even of a criminal nature) is generally held not to be material. Disclosure of wrongdoing may be required, however, if the issuer is proclaiming its faithfulness in obeying the law. Another important exception to the presumption of immateriality occurs when the wrongdoing involves self-dealing. For example, in a proxy case involving undisclosed bribes to foreign officials, the Ninth Circuit drew

> a sharp distinction ... between allegations of director misconduct involving a breach of trust or self-dealing—the nondisclosure of which is presumptively material—and allegations of simple breach of fiduciary duty/waste by corporate management—the nondisclosure of which is never material for § 14(a) purposes ... the distinction between "mere" bribes and bribes coupled with kickbacks to the directors makes a great deal of sense, indeed it is fundamental to a meaningful concept of materiality under § 14(a) and the preservation of state corporate law.

Gaines v. Haughton, 645 F.2d 761, 776–778 (9th Cir. 1981).

Lawsuits involving a wrongful benefit to a director or officer may be required to be disclosed as omissions of a material fact, even if they have not yet been adjudicated. Even then, the suit may not be required to be disclosed if the allegations made do not substantially undercut the directors' or officers' fitness to serve. *See, e.g., GAF Corp. v. Heyman,* 724 F.2d 727 (2d Cir. 1983) (disclosure of pending suit for breach of fiduciary duty in managing family trust not required in context of proxy fight in which the family member who filed suit was supporting the insurgent in the proxy fight). If disclosure of a pending lawsuit is required, disclosure of the basic facts will suffice; it is not necessary to concede the merits of the pending claim.

QUESTIONS

1. Is it realistic to expect company officers to disclose facts that could lead to their indictment for securities fraud? Is disclosure the real goal?

2. Can we apply the reasoning of *Fehn* to other forms of illegal activities? What if *Fehn* and the other officers of CTI were importing illegal drugs into the United States (as of yet undetected by the DEA)? Would they have to disclose this information in their Form 10–K?

HYPOTHETICAL SIX

David and Nate, the CEO and President of Six Feet respectively, have a little sister, Claire. Claire is ostensibly an employee of Six Feet, drawing a salary of $75,000 per year as David's executive assistant, but she is rarely, if ever, seen at Six Feet's headquarters. David keeps her on the payroll so that she can be covered by Six Feet's health plan. Claire's recurring trips to rehab for her drug problem are tremendously expensive, but Six Feet has remarkably generous mental health benefits included in its employee health plan. Does Six Feet need to disclose Claire's employment arrangement?

CHAPTER 3

THE DEFINITION OF A "SECURITY"

Rules and Statutes

—Sections 2(a)(1), 2(a)(3), 3(a)(3) of the Securities Act
—Sections 3(a)(10), 3(a)(14), 27 and 29 of the Exchange Act

MOTIVATING HYPOTHETICAL

Jerry and George are the two entrepreneurs behind The Soup Kitchen. The Soup Kitchen operates a chain of walk up store counters serving gourmet soup; indeed, soup so good you would put up with most anything to get a bowl. The delicious soup offered at The Soup Kitchen has engendered a cult-like following; at most locations, there is a line stretching out the door at all hours, day and night. Although The Soup Kitchen operates many of its own stores, it also sells franchises that allow individuals to open Soup Kitchen stores of their own. In order to protect The Soup Kitchen's reputation for efficient service, The Soup Kitchen requires its franchisees to enforces three simple rules:

- Pick the soup you want!
- Have your money ready!
- Move to the **extreme** left after ordering!

Failure to comply with the rules results in immediate ejection from the store. Despite these strictures, or perhaps because of them, The Soup Kitchen has been growing by leaps and bounds. Helping to fuel that growth has been The Soup Kitchen's commitment to social responsibility; the company commits 5% of its pre-tax profits to feeding the homeless. (This was George's idea; he figured it would get the "bleeding hearts" to buy more soup.)

I. DO THE SECURITIES LAWS APPLY?

A threshold question to the application of the securities laws: Is this a security? Not surprisingly, the securities laws only apply if the instrument in question is a security. (Or purports to be—the federal securities laws cover forged or nonexistent securities if, as represented by the fraudster, they fall within the statutory definition.)

The presence of a "security" in a transaction leads to a number of regulatory consequences under the Exchange Act. The most significant of these is the application of the "catch-all" antifraud Rule 10b–5 (which we will cover in detail in Chapter 5). If Rule 10b–5 applies, contractual limits on remedies are likely to be ineffective because § 29(a) voids agreements to waive compliance with any rule under the Exchange Act. Other consequences for private litigation include federal jurisdiction and nationwide service of process. Exchange Act § 27. The presence of a security also brings with it the monitoring and enforcement of the SEC and possible criminal sanctions for violations of the securities laws (covered in Chapter 13). Scam artists peddling a security risk the might of the long arm of the federal law.

The presence of a security also triggers the provisions of the Securities Act of 1933. Anyone selling a security to the public must comply with the registration, prospectus delivery and "gun-jumping" rules imposed by § 5 of that Act (the subject of Chapter 7). The public offering of a security triggers the antifraud rules of §§ 11 and 12(a)(2) (covered in Chapter 8), which are considerably more generous to plaintiffs than Rule 10b–5 or common law fraud. Parties seeking to avoid the burdens imposed on public offerings must structure their sale of securities to be eligible for complicated, and sometimes arcane, offering exemptions (the focus of Chapter 9).

A policy question lurks in the classification of an instrument as "security": *Should* the securities laws apply to the transaction in question? Why do we apply securities regulations only to certain transactions? Home purchases, for example, are not covered by the securities laws, even though they are the most substantial investment that most people make. Your savings account at the local bank, another large repository of investment dollars, is not a security. How does a "security" differ from these other investments? Because securities regulation applies only to transactions in securities, the question of "what is a security" is in many ways the same as asking "should securities regulation apply here?"

For the Congress that adopted the '33 and '34 Acts, the importance of the securities markets to the national economy was the paramount justification for federal regulation. The recent experience of the stock market crash of October 1929 and the popular association of that crash with the ensuing Great Depression were reason enough to treat securities differently from other investments. Other justifications, however, were also important. Foremost among these was the perception that state regulation, commonly referred to as "Blue Sky" regulation, had failed to protect investors from abuses by stock promoters, insiders and market professionals. This was not because the Blue Sky laws were poorly drafted, but because it was difficult for Midwestern states (whose investors were allegedly being defrauded) to exercise jurisdiction over those cheats back East. Worse yet, the regulators in New York (even though armed with the powerful Martin Act) did little to root out the bad apples.

Those rationales for federal regulation of securities are primarily historical. What justifications support the federal regulation of "securities" today? As discussed in Chapter 1, securities markets are notable for their pervasive problem of information asymmetry. Company insiders and market professionals are better equipped to value a security than outside investors. If the insiders and professionals are free to exploit that informational advantage, outsiders will be reluctant to participate in the market.

Compare the investment in a share of common stock with the purchase of a pint of peanut butter and chocolate chunk ice cream. The typical small investor will purchase 100 shares of common stock at a price of, say, $20 per share. That $2,000 may be a substantial portion of the investor's wealth. Disappointment in the investment will not be immediately apparent: The investor will learn of the company's shortcomings only in the long run when it fails to produce the expected profits, and she may not be sufficiently diversified to overcome the damage to her portfolio. To a small investor with almost all her "eggs" in one stock basket, a drop in the value of the stock's value will impose real financial hardship. The price of the pint of ice cream, by contrast, is likely to be a small expenditure for the individual. Only those who like peanut butter and chocolate will purchase at all, and disappointment in the ice cream will be apparent immediately upon tasting. Moreover, that disappointment can be remedied easily in the future by choosing another brand or another flavor, or even switching to pudding or frozen yogurt, until the individual has found a sweet treat that suits her.

Companies, in theory, could help reduce the problem of information asymmetry facing investors by volunteering disclosure, but we saw the limits of that solution in Chapter 1. And investors would face enormous collective action problems in coordinating their demands for disclosure. Moreover, lurking in the background is the suspicion that many (most?) investors are driven by irrational whimsy and infectious greed. "Greed is good"* sometimes; more often, it may lead investors to chase after phantom high returns without pausing to consider the risks behind speculative investments. Left unregulated, the markets may lead to bubbles of the sort that led to the crash of 1929 and the precipitous decline of the Nasdaq index following the Internet stock run-up of the late 1990s. Regulation of securities, in theory, helps reduce the risk to the investor. Perhaps regulation helps keep such investor frenzies in check, thereby also potentially avoiding their disruptive effects on the overall economy.

All of these reasons counsel in favor of a broad interpretation of the definition of "security" in the securities laws. Congress certainly encouraged a broad reading. Virtually identical definitions in § 2(a)(1) of the Securities Act and § 3(a)(10) of the Exchange Act include long lists of instruments ("stocks," "bonds," "fractional undivided interest in oil, gas, or other mineral right," etc.). The definitions sweep even more broadly, however, with "catch-all" provisions that capture newly-devised instruments of investment, most notably, as we shall see in the cases that follow, "investment contracts." "Investment contract" sweeps broadly to allow the SEC to go after the latest investment scam, no matter how cleverly disguised. The Supreme Court validated that expansive scope, deciding five cases implicating the definition of a security in the 40 years after the enactment of the '33 and '34 Acts; each time, the Court concluded that the instrument in question was a security. That expansive approach ended when Lewis F. Powell, Jr. joined the Court in 1972—the court rejected a broad reading of "security" in three of the four security definition cases decided during Powell's fifteen-year tenure. The next hypothetical explores the implications of the breadth of the definition of a "security."

HYPOTHETICAL ONE

Jerry, the CEO of The Soup Kitchen, wants to hire a writer to create a mail-order catalog for the upcoming holiday season. "Give the gift of soup!"

---

* Gordon Gecko famously spoke this phrase in the movie "Wall Street" (1987).

Elaine, an ex-girlfriend of Jerry's, is interested in the position. Because The Soup Kitchen is short of cash, Jerry wants to pay Elaine with several different forms of compensation. Consider whether any of the following transactions should receive the protection of the federal securities laws.

1.   Jerry pays Elaine with precious gems. Jerry tells Elaine that for every month she works at The Soup Kitchen, she will earn a two-carat diamond. After one year, Elaine takes the diamonds to a jeweler for appraisal and discovers that they are really Cubic Zirconia.

2.   Jerry pays Elaine with common stock in The Soup Kitchen. He tells Elaine that the stock is quite valuable because The Soup Kitchen "can't miss." Unfortunately, The Soup Kitchen's stock drops in value over the next year.

II.   "INVESTMENT CONTRACT"

The Supreme Court's earliest cases addressing the definition of a security involved the definition's "catch-all" provision, "investment contract." The case below sets forth the test (now known as the *Howey* test) for determining whether an instrument is an "investment contract." Given the definition of a security's role as a threshold test for the application of federal securities laws, do you think the elements of the *Howey* test capture the key factors for the application of the securities laws?

SEC v. W. J. Howey Co.
328 U.S. 293 (1946).

■ MURPHY, J.

This case involves the application of § 2[a](1) of the Securities Act of 1933 to an offering of units of a citrus grove development coupled with a contract for cultivating, marketing and remitting the net proceeds to the investor.

The Securities and Exchange Commission instituted this action to restrain the respondents from using the mails and instrumentalities of interstate commerce in the offer and sale of unregistered and nonexempt securities in violation of § 5(a) of the Act. . . .

The respondents, W. J. Howey Company and Howey-in-the-Hills Service, are Florida corporations under direct common control and management. The Howey Company owns large tracts of citrus acreage in Lake County, Florida. During the past several years it has planted about 500 acres annually, keeping half of the groves itself and offering the other half to the public "to help us finance additional development." Howey-in-the-Hills Service, Inc., is a service company engaged in cultivating and developing many of these groves, including the harvesting and marketing of the crops.

Each prospective customer is offered both a land sales contract and a service contract, after having been told that it is not feasible to invest in a grove unless service arrangements are made. While the purchaser is free to make arrangements with other service companies, the superiority of Howey-in-the-Hills Service, Inc., is stressed. Indeed, 85%

of the acreage sold during the 3-year period ending May 31, 1943, was covered by service contracts with Howey-in-the-Hills Service, Inc.

The land sales contract with the Howey Company provides for a uniform purchase price per acre or fraction thereof, varying in amount only in accordance with the number of years the particular plot has been planted with citrus trees. Upon full payment of the purchase price the land is conveyed to the purchaser by warranty deed. Purchases are usually made in narrow strips of land arranged so that an acre consists of a row of 48 trees. During the period between February 1, 1941, and May 31, 1943, 31 of the 42 persons making purchases bought less than 5 acres each. The average holding of these 31 persons was 1.33 acres and sales of as little as 0.65, 0.7 and 0.73 of an acre were made. These tracts are not separately fenced and the sole indication of several ownership is found in small land marks intelligible only through a plat book record.

The service contract, generally of a 10-year duration without option of cancellation, gives Howey-in-the-Hills Service, Inc., a leasehold interest and "full and complete" possession of the acreage. For a specified fee plus the cost of labor and materials, the company is given full discretion and authority over the cultivation of the groves and the harvest and marketing of the crops. The company is well established in the citrus business and maintains a large force of skilled personnel and a great deal of equipment, including 75 tractors, sprayer wagons, fertilizer trucks and the like. Without the consent of the company, the land owner or purchaser has no right of entry to market the crop; thus there is ordinarily no right to specific fruit. The company is accountable only for an allocation of the net profits based upon a check made at the time of picking. All the produce is pooled by the respondent companies, which do business under their own names.

The purchasers for the most part are non-residents of Florida. They are predominantly business and professional people who lack the knowledge, skill and equipment necessary for the care and cultivation of citrus trees. They are attracted by the expectation of substantial profits.... Many of these purchasers are patrons of a resort hotel owned and operated by the Howey Company in a scenic section adjacent to the groves. The hotel's advertising mentions the fine groves in the vicinity and the attention of the patrons is drawn to the groves as they are being escorted about the surrounding countryside. They are told that the groves are for sale; if they indicate an interest in the matter they are then given a sales talk.

* * *

Section 2[a](1) of the Act defines the term "security" to include the commonly known documents traded for speculation or investment. This definition also includes "securities" of a more variable character, designated by such descriptive terms as "certificate of interest or participation in any profit-sharing agreement," "investment contract" and "in general, any interest or instrument commonly known as a 'security.'" The legal issue in this case turns upon a determination of whether, under the circumstances, the land sales contract, the warranty deed and the service contract together constitute an "investment contract" within the meaning of § 2[a](1). An affirmative answer brings into operation the registration requirements of § 5(a). . . . The lower courts, in reaching a negative answer to this problem, treated the contracts and deeds as separate transactions involving no more than an ordinary real estate sale and an agreement by the seller to manage the property for the buyer.

The term "investment contract" is undefined by the Securities Act or by relevant legislative reports. But the term was common in many state "blue sky" laws in existence prior to the adoption of the federal statute and, although the term was also undefined by the state laws, it had been broadly construed by state courts so as to afford the investing public a full measure of protection. Form was disregarded for substance and emphasis was placed upon economic reality. An investment contract thus came to mean a contract or scheme for "the placing of capital or laying out of money in a way intended to secure income or profit from its employment." This definition was uniformly applied by state courts to a variety of situations where individuals were led to invest money in a common enterprise with the expectation that they would earn a profit solely through the efforts of the promoter or of some one other than themselves.

By including an investment contract within the scope of § 2[a](1) of the Securities Act, Congress was using a term the meaning of which had been crystallized by this prior judicial interpretation. It is therefore reasonable to attach that meaning to the term as used by Congress, especially since such a definition is consistent with the statutory aims. In other words, an investment contract for purposes of the Securities Act means a contract, transaction or scheme whereby a person invests his money in a common enterprise and is led to expect profits solely from the efforts of the promoter or a third party, it being immaterial whether the shares in the enterprise are evidenced by formal certificates or by nominal interests in the physical assets employed in the enterprise. . . . It permits the fulfillment of the statutory purpose of compelling full and fair disclosure relative to the issuance of "the many types of instruments that in our commercial world fall within the ordinary concept of a security." It embodies a flexible rather than a static principle, one that is capable of adaptation to meet the countless and variable schemes devised by those who seek the use of the money of others on the promise of profits.

The transactions in this case clearly involve investment contracts as so defined. The respondent companies are offering something more than fee simple interests in land, something different from a farm or orchard coupled with management services. They are offering an opportunity to contribute money and to share in the profits of a large citrus fruit enterprise managed and partly owned by respondents. They are offering this opportunity to persons who reside in distant localities and who lack the equipment and experience requisite to the cultivation, harvesting and marketing of the citrus products. Such persons have no desire to occupy the land or to develop it themselves; they are attracted solely by the prospects of a return on their investment. Indeed, individual development of the plots of land that are offered and sold would seldom be economically feasible due to their small size. Such tracts gain utility as citrus groves only when cultivated and developed as component parts of a larger area. A common enterprise managed by respondents or third parties with adequate personnel and equipment is therefore essential if the investors are to achieve their paramount aim of a return on their investments. Their respective shares in this enterprise are evidenced by land sales contracts and warranty deeds, which serve as a convenient method of determining the investors' allocable shares of the profits. The resulting transfer of rights in land is purely incidental.

Thus all the elements of a profit-seeking business venture are present here. The investors provide the capital and share in the earnings and profits; the promoters manage, control and operate the enterprise. It follows that the arrangements whereby the investors' interests are made manifest involve investment contracts, regardless of the legal terminology in which such contracts are clothed. The investment contracts in this instance take the form of land sales contracts, warranty deeds and service contracts which respondents offer to prospective investors. And respondents' failure to abide by the statutory and administrative rules in making such offerings, even though the failure result from a bona fide mistake as to the law, cannot be sanctioned under the Act.

This conclusion is unaffected by the fact that some purchasers choose not to accept the full offer of an investment contract by declining to enter into a service contract with the respondents. The Securities Act prohibits the offer as well as the sale of unregistered, non-exempt securities. Hence it is enough that the respondents merely offer the essential ingredients of an investment contract.

We reject the suggestion of the Circuit Court of Appeals that an investment contract is necessarily missing where the enterprise is not speculative or promotional in character and where the tangible interest which is sold has intrinsic value independent of the success of the enterprise as a whole. The test is whether the scheme involves an investment of money in a common enterprise with profits to come solely from the efforts of others. If that test be satisfied, it is immaterial whether the enterprise is speculative or non-speculative or whether there is a sale of property with or without intrinsic value. The statutory policy of affording broad protection to investors is not to be thwarted by unrealistic and irrelevant formulae.

* * *

NOTES

1.   *The Howey test.* The Howey test introduced here requires "a contract, transaction or scheme" and four additional elements:

1.   a person invests his money
2.   in a common enterprise and
3.   is led to expect profits
4.   solely from the efforts of the promoter or a third party.

Each of these elements has received a substantial gloss in subsequent cases, as we shall see below. In considering these four elements, keep in mind that each must be satisfied before a court will conclude that the instrument in question is a security.

2. *Sophistication and intrinsic value.* Did the Court omit important factors for defining a security? For example, should we lean toward applying the federal securities laws if the investors are unsophisticated? If so, should we say that the federal securities laws should not apply if the investors are sophisticated and do not need to protection of the securities laws? Note that the federal securities laws already provide a reduced level of protection for more sophisticated investors in the area of private placements (a topic we cover in Chapter 9).

If we are worried about unsophisticated investors, which investments pose greater risk? Investments in speculative investments without any intrinsic value are more risky than investments in things with a separate intrinsic value. If all else fails, the investment has a floor on how low it will go. If investments with intrinsic value are less risky, and therefore pose less a problem for the unsophisticated, why not use this as a factor in not treating the investment as a security? Note that this argument swayed the lower court in *Howey*, but not the Supreme Court.

QUESTIONS

1. Would the offer and sale of tracts of the orange grove—without the additional offering of the service agreement—have been a security?

2. What if the service agreement was offered by an unaffiliated company, with the services being exchanged for a cut of the oranges? Would the service agreement standing alone be a security?

3. Does it matter that the service contracts were "optional"?

4. What if the purchasers were not out-of-state tourists but instead retired and wealthy citrus tree company executives who understood the economics of the citrus fruit industry? Would this change the outcome in *Howey*?

5. Is the regulation of the sale of orange groves by the Howey Company what Congress had in mind when it enacted the securities laws? Or does *Howey* simply divert the SEC's attention away from the primary capital markets toward less important, esoteric transactions?

HYPOTHETICAL TWO

Suppose that Jerry, the CEO of The Soup Kitchen, decides that he wants to raise capital from the public capital market. He does not, however, like the prospect of federal securities regulation. Imagine, moreover, that *Howey* had come out the other way and the Supreme Court chose not to treat the offer of strips of land coupled with service contracts as investment contracts unless specifically labeled "investment contracts." After consulting with his attorney, Jackie, Jerry decides to sell "Special, Transferable Ownership Certificate Koupons" or "S.T.O.C.K." Each S.T.O.C.K. unit consists of ownership of the real property underlying one of The Soup Kitchen's retail stores and an obligatory service contract giving The Soup Kitchen the exclusive right to utilize the store. All profits from all of the stores are pooled and distributed pro rata to the S.T.O.C.K. holders. If the S.T.O.C.K. units are not investment contracts (and are not otherwise securities), how will this affect the scope of federal securities regulation?

A. "A PERSON INVESTS HIS MONEY"

The case below addresses the question of what constitutes an "investment" for purposes of the *Howey* test. Note that Justice Powell authored this opinion for the Court. Is the employment relationship at issue one that requires federal regulation? Are the securities laws well tailored to regulate that relationship?

International Brotherhood of Teamsters v. Daniel

439 U.S. 551 (1979).

■ POWELL, J.

Issue

This case presents the question whether a noncontributory, compulsory pension plan constitutes a "security" within the meaning of the Securities Act of 1933 and the Securities Exchange Act of 1934.

I

In 1954 multi-employer collective bargaining between Local 705 of the International Brotherhood of Teamsters, Chauffeurs, Warehousemen, and Helpers of America and Chicago trucking firms produced a pension plan for employees represented by the Local. The plan was compulsory and noncontributory. Employees had no choice as to participation in the plan, and did not have the option of demanding that the employer's contribution be paid directly to them as a substitute for pension eligibility. The employees paid nothing to the plan themselves. . . .

At the time respondent brought suit, employers contributed $21.50 per employee man-week and pension payments ranged from $425 to $525 a month depending on age at retirement. In order to receive a pension an employee was required to have 20 years of continuous service, including time worked before the start of the plan.

The meaning of "continuous service" is at the center of this dispute. Respondent began working as a truck driver in the Chicago area in 1950, and joined Local 705 the following year. When the plan first went into effect, respondent automatically received 5 years' credit toward the 20-year service requirement because of his earlier work experience. He retired in 1973 and applied to the plan's administrator for a pension. The administrator determined that respondent was ineligible because of a break in service between December 1960 and July 1961.[4] Respondent appealed the decision to the trustees, who affirmed. Respondent then asked the trustees to waive the continuous-service rule as it applied to him. After the trustees refused to waive the rule, respondent brought suit in federal court against the International Union (Teamsters). . . .

break in service

Respondent's complaint alleged that the Teamsters, . . . misrepresented and omitted to state material facts with respect to the value of a covered employee's interest in the pension plan. Count I of the complaint charged that these misstatements and omissions

---

[4] Respondent was laid off from December 1960 until April 1961. In addition, no contributions were paid on his behalf between April and July 1961, because of embezzlement by his employer's bookkeeper. During this 7-month period respondent could have preserved his eligibility by making the contributions himself, but he failed to do so.

constituted a fraud in connection with the sale of a security in violation of § 10(b) of the Securities Exchange Act of 1934 and the Securities and Exchange Commission's Rule 10b–5. . . . Other counts alleged violations of various labor law and common-law duties. . . .

The petitioners moved to dismiss the first two counts of the complaint on the ground that respondent had no cause of action under the Securities Acts. The District Court denied the motion. It held that respondent's interest in the Pension Fund constituted a security within the meaning of § 2[a](1) of the Securities Act, and § 3(a)(10) of the Securities Exchange Act, because the plan created an "investment contract". . . .

The order denying the motion to dismiss was certified for appeal . . . and the Court of Appeals for the Seventh Circuit affirmed. Relying on its perception of the economic realities of pension plans and various actions of Congress and the SEC with respect to such plans, the court ruled that respondent's interest in the Pension Fund was a "security." According to the court, a "sale" took place either when respondent ratified a collective-bargaining agreement embodying the Fund or when he accepted or retained covered employment instead of seeking other work. The court did not believe the subsequent enactment of the Employee Retirement Income Security Act of 1974 affected the application of the Securities Acts to pension plans, as the requirements and purposes of ERISA were perceived to be different from those of the Securities Acts.[10] We granted certiorari and now reverse.

II

"The starting point in every case involving construction of a statute is the language itself." In spite of the substantial use of employee pension plans at the time they were enacted, neither § 2[a](1) of the Securities Act nor § 3(a)(10) of the Securities Exchange Act, which defines the term "security" in considerable detail and with numerous examples, refers to pension plans of any type. Acknowledging this omission in the statutes, respondent contends that an employee's interest in a pension plan is an "investment contract," an instrument which is included in the statutory definitions of a security.

To determine whether a particular financial relationship constitutes an investment contract, "[t]he test is whether the scheme involves an investment of money in a common enterprise with profits to come solely from the efforts of others." This test is to be applied in light of "the substance—the economic realities of the transaction—rather than the names that may have been employed by the parties." Looking separately at each element of the *Howey* test, it is apparent that an employee's participation in a noncontributory, compulsory pension plan such as the Teamsters' does not comport with the commonly held understanding of an investment contract.

A.   Investment of Money

An employee who participates in a noncontributory, compulsory pension plan by definition makes no payment into the pension fund. He only accepts employment, one of the conditions of which is eligibility for

---

[10] Respondent did not have any cause of action under ERISA itself, as that Act took effect after he had retired.

a possible benefit on retirement. Respondent contends, however, that he has "invested" in the Pension Fund by permitting part of his compensation from his employer to take the form of a deferred pension benefit. By allowing his employer to pay money into the Fund, and by contributing his labor to his employer in return for these payments, respondent asserts he has made the kind of investment which the Securities Acts were intended to regulate.

In order to determine whether respondent invested in the Fund by accepting and remaining in covered employment, it is necessary to look at the entire transaction through which he obtained a chance to receive pension benefits. In every decision of this Court recognizing the presence of a "security" under the Securities Acts, the person found to have been an investor chose to give up a specific consideration in return for a separable financial interest with the characteristics of a security. In every case the purchaser gave up some tangible and definable consideration in return for an interest that had substantially the characteristics of a security.

In a pension plan such as this one, by contrast, the purported investment is a relatively insignificant part of an employee's total and indivisible compensation package. No portion of an employee's compensation other than the potential pension benefits has any of the characteristics of a security, yet these noninvestment interests cannot be segregated from the possible pension benefits. Only in the most abstract sense may it be said that an employee "exchanges" some portion of his labor in return for these possible benefits.[12] He surrenders his labor as a whole, and in return receives a compensation package that is substantially devoid of aspects resembling a security. His decision to accept and retain covered employment may have only an attenuated relationship, if any, to perceived investment possibilities of a future pension. Looking at the economic realities, it seems clear that an employee is selling his labor primarily to obtain a livelihood, not making an investment.

Respondent also argues that employer contributions on his behalf constituted his investment into the Fund. But it is inaccurate to describe these payments as having been "on behalf" of any employee. The trust agreement used employee man-weeks as a convenient way to measure an employer's overall obligation to the Fund, not as a means of measuring the employer's obligation to any particular employee. Indeed, there was no fixed relationship between contributions to the Fund and an employee's potential benefits. A pension plan with "defined benefits," such as the Local's, does not tie a qualifying employee's benefits to the time he has worked. One who has engaged in covered employment for 20 years will receive the same benefits as a person who has worked for 40, even though the latter has worked twice as long and induced a substantially larger employer contribution. Again, it ignores the economic realities to equate employer contributions with an investment by the employee.

---

[12] This is not to say that a person's "investment," in order to meet the definition of an investment contract, must take the form of cash only, rather than of goods and services.

B.   Expectation of Profits From a Common Enterprise

[The Court concluded that this element was lacking as well because most] of its income comes from employer contributions, a source in no way dependent on the efforts of the Fund's managers. . . . Not only does the greater share of a pension plan's income ordinarily come from new contributions, but unlike most entrepreneurs who manage other people's money, a plan usually can count on increased employer contributions, over which the plan itself has no control, to cover shortfalls in earnings.

* * *

IV

If any further evidence were needed to demonstrate that pension plans of the type involved are not subject to the Securities Acts, the enactment of ERISA in 1974 would put the matter to rest. Unlike the Securities Acts, ERISA deals expressly and in detail with pension plans. ERISA requires pension plans to disclose specified information to employees in a specified manner in contrast to the indefinite and uncertain disclosure obligations imposed by the antifraud provisions of the Securities Acts. Further, ERISA regulates the substantive terms of pension plans, setting standards for plan funding and limits on the eligibility requirements an employee must meet. . . . if respondent had retired after § 1053 took effect, the Fund would have been required to pay him at least a partial pension. The Securities Acts, on the other hand, do not purport to set the substantive terms of financial transactions.

The existence of this comprehensive legislation governing the use and terms of employee pension plans severely undercuts all arguments for extending the Securities Acts to noncontributory, compulsory pension plans. Congress believed that it was filling a regulatory void when it enacted ERISA, a belief which the SEC actively encouraged. Not only is the extension of the Securities Acts by the court below unsupported by the language and history of those Acts, but in light of ERISA it serves no general purpose. Whatever benefits employees might derive from the effect of the Securities Acts are now provided in more definite form through ERISA.

V

We hold that the Securities Acts do not apply to a noncontributory, compulsory pension plan. . . .

NOTES

1.   *Alternative regulatory schemes.* Both § 2(a)(1) of the Securities Act and § 3(a)(10) of the Exchange Act provide that the definition for a "security" applies "unless the context otherwise requires." In *Daniel,* the presence of an alternative federal regulatory scheme protecting investors, in this case ERISA, was cited by the Court in reaching its conclusion that the pension plan was not an investment contract. The Courts reasoned that Congress believed ERISA filled a "regulatory void," implying that the securities laws did not already cover pension plans. The Courts saw less need for the securities laws because ERISA already protects the interests of employees in a pension fund "in more definite form."

The Court emphasized the importance of an alternative regulatory scheme more strongly in *Marine Bank v. Weaver*, 455 U.S. 551 (1982), where it concluded that a certificate of deposit was not a security. The *Marine Bank* Court had this to say about federal banking regulation:

> This certificate of deposit was issued by a federally regulated bank which is subject to the comprehensive set of regulations governing the banking industry. Deposits in federally regulated banks are protected by the reserve, reporting, and inspection requirements of the federal banking law. . . . In addition, deposits are insured by the Federal Deposit Insurance Corporation. Since its formation in 1933, nearly all depositors in failing banks insured by the FDIC have received payment in full, even payment for the portions of their deposits above the amount insured. . . .

455 U.S. at 557. The presence of an alternative *federal* regulatory regime that fully protects investors strongly influenced the *Marine Bank* Court. Subsequent lower court opinions, however, have concluded that *state* regulation carries little weight in the *Howey* test.

2.   *Other pension schemes.* The pension scheme in *Daniel* was deemed not to be a security because it was mandatory and non-contributory. What about benefit plans that are voluntary and require employee contributions? The SEC takes the position that plans of this sort are securities. Sec. Act. Rel. 6281 (1981). Securities Act § 3(a)(2), however, generally exempts such plans from the registration requirements. And what about plans in between these two poles (voluntary/non-contributory and mandatory/contributory)? The SEC considers these plans not to be securities. Sec. Act. Rel. 6188 (1980).

QUESTIONS

1.   Is an employee making a "choice" with respect to a compulsory, noncontributory pension plan? Is it an "investment choice"?

2.   Consider what it means to make a choice. Implicitly, there must be a choice among different items. What are the different choice items for an investor considering whether to invest in the stock of a company like Microsoft? What are the different choice items for an employee considering a livelihood decision? If the set of choice items differs, can we say that the kind of decision (investment or not) differs as well?

3.   Why does the presence of an alternative federal regulatory scheme affect whether there is a security?

4.   What sorts of consideration count as an "investment" for purposes of the *Howey* test? Must the investor part with cash?

HYPOTHETICAL THREE

The Soup Kitchen awards its employees "profit participation units." The value of the unit is tied to the company's net earnings, with 25% of earnings paid out annually to the holders of the units (pro rata based on the number of units held). The employees' entitlement to their share of the units vests by 10% per year, reaching full vesting in year ten of employment. Participation in the profit sharing plan is not compulsory; The Soup Kitchen gives its employees the option of donating the present discounted value of the profit participation units to The Soup Kitchen's philanthropic efforts to feed the homeless. Are the profit participation units securities?

B. "[I]N A COMMON ENTERPRISE"

The *Howey* Court did not specify, for purposes of a "common enterprise," with whom the investor must have an interest in "common." Other investors? The promoter or managers of the enterprise? The following case outlines the divergent positions taken by the lower courts on the issue of commonality.

SEC v. SG Ltd.

265 F.3d 42 (1st Cir. 2001).

■ SELYA, B., CIRCUIT JUDGE.

These appeals . . . require us to determine whether virtual shares in an enterprise existing only in cyberspace fall within the purview of the federal securities laws. SG Ltd., a Dominican corporation, and its affiliate, SG Trading Ltd. asseverate that the virtual shares were part of a fantasy investment game created for the personal entertainment of Internet users, and therefore, that those shares do not implicate the federal securities laws. The Securities and Exchange Commission, plaintiff below and appellant here, counters that substance ought to prevail over form, and that merely labeling a website as a game should not negate the applicability of the securities laws.

I. BACKGROUND

The underlying litigation was spawned by SG's operation of a "StockGeneration" website offering on-line denizens an opportunity to purchase shares in eleven different "virtual companies" listed on the website's "virtual stock exchange." SG arbitrarily set the purchase and sale prices of each of these imaginary companies in biweekly "rounds," and guaranteed that investors could buy or sell any quantity of shares at posted prices. SG placed no upper limit on the amount of funds that an investor could squirrel away in its virtual offerings.

The SEC's complaint focused on shares in a particular virtual enterprise referred to by SG as the "privileged company," and so do we. SG advised potential purchasers to pay "particular attention" to shares in the privileged company and boasted that investing in those shares was a "game without any risk." To this end, its website announced that the privileged company's shares would unfailingly appreciate, boldly proclaiming that "[t]he share price of [the privileged company] is supported by the owners of SG, this is why its value constantly rises; on average at a rate of 10% monthly (this is approximately 215% annually)." To add plausibility to this representation and to allay anxiety about future pricing, SG published prices of the privileged company's shares one month in advance.

While SG conceded that a decline in the share price was theoretically possible, it assured prospective participants that "under the rules governing the fall in prices, [the share price for the privileged company] cannot fall by more than 5% in a round." To bolster this claim, it vouchsafed that shares in the privileged company were supported by several distinct revenue streams. According to SG's representations, capital inflow from new participants provided liquidity for existing participants who might choose to sell their virtual shareholdings. As a backstop, SG pledged to allocate an indeterminate portion of the profits derived from its website operations to a special reserve fund designed to maintain the price of the privileged company's shares. SG asserted that these profits emanated from four sources: (1) the collection of a 1.5% commission on each transaction conducted on its virtual stock exchange; (2) the bid-ask spread on the virtual shares; (3) the "skillful manipulation" of the share prices of eight particular imaginary companies, not including the privileged company, listed on the virtual stock exchange; and (4) SG's right to sell shares of three other virtual companies (including the privileged company). As a further hedge against adversity, SG alluded to the availability of auxiliary stabilization funds which could be tapped to ensure the continued operation of its virtual stock exchange.

SG's website contained lists of purported "big winners," an Internet bulletin board featuring testimonials from supposedly satisfied participants, and descriptions of incentive programs that held out the prospect of rewards for such activities as the referral of new participants (e.g., SG's representation that it would pay "20, 25 or 30% of the referred player's highest of the first three payments") and the establishment of affiliate websites.

At least 800 United States domiciliaries, paying real cash, purchased virtual shares in the virtual companies listed on the defendants' virtual stock exchange. In the fall of 1999, over $4,700,000 in participants' funds was deposited into a Latvian bank account in the name of SG Trading Ltd. The following spring, more than $2,700,000 was deposited in Estonian bank accounts standing in the names of SG Ltd. and SG Perfect Ltd., respectively.

In late 1999, participants began to experience difficulties in redeeming their virtual shares. On March 20, 2000, these difficulties crested; SG unilaterally suspended all pending requests to withdraw funds and sharply reduced participants' account balances in all companies except the privileged company. Two weeks later, SG peremptorily announced a reverse stock split, which caused the share prices of all companies listed on the virtual stock exchange, including the privileged company, to plummet to 1/10,000 of their previous values. At about the same time, SG stopped responding to participant requests for the return of funds, yet continued to solicit new participants through its website.

The SEC undertook an investigation into SG's activities, which culminated in the filing of a civil action in federal district court. The SEC's complaint alleged, in substance, that SG's operations constituted a fraudulent scheme in violation of the registration and antifraud provisions of the federal securities laws. The SEC sought injunctive relief, disgorgement, and civil penalties.

These appeals hinge on whether the district court erred in ruling that transactions in the privileged company's shares did not constitute transactions in securities. In the pages that follow, we explore the makeup of that particular type of security known as an investment contract; examine the district court's rationale; and apply the tripartite "investment contract" test to the facts as alleged. . . .

II. THE LEGAL LANDSCAPE

These appeals turn on whether the SEC alleged facts which, if proven, would bring this case within the jurisdictional ambit of the federal securities laws. Consequently, we focus on the type of security that the SEC alleges is apposite here: investment contracts.

* * *

B. The District Court's Rationale

We pause at this juncture to address the district court's rationale. Relying upon a dictum from *Howey* discussing "the many types of instruments that in our commercial world fall within the ordinary concept of a security," the district court drew a distinction between what it termed "commercial dealings" and what it termed "games." Characterizing purchases of the privileged company's shares as a "clearly marked and defined game," the court concluded that since that activity was not part of the commercial world, it fell beyond the jurisdictional reach of the federal securities laws. In so ruling, the court differentiated SG's operations from a classic Ponzi or pyramid scheme on the ground that those types of chicanery involved commercial dealings within a business context.

We do not gainsay the obvious correctness of the district court's observation that investment contracts lie within the commercial world. Contrary to the district court's view, however, this locution does not translate into a dichotomy between business dealings, on the one hand, and games, on the other hand, as a failsafe way for determining whether a particular financial arrangement should (or should not) be characterized as an investment contract. *Howey* remains the touchstone for ascertaining whether an investment contract exists—and the test that it prescribes must be administered without regard to nomenclature. Cf. William Shakespeare, Romeo & Juliet, act 2, sc. 2 (circa 1597) ("A rose by any other name would smell as sweet."). As long as the three-pronged *Howey* test is satisfied, the instrument must be classified as an investment contract. Once that has occurred, "it is immaterial whether the enterprise is speculative or non-speculative or whether there is a sale of property with or without intrinsic value." It is equally immaterial whether the promoter depicts the enterprise as a serious commercial venture or dubs it a game.

* * *

III. ADMINISTERING THE TRIPARTITE TEST

What remains is to analyze whether purchases of the privileged company's shares constitute investment contracts. We turn to that task, taking the three *Howey* criteria in sequence.

A. Investment of Money

The first component of the *Howey* test focuses on the investment of money. The determining factor is whether an investor "chose to give up a specific consideration in return for a separable financial interest with the characteristics of a security." We conclude that the SEC's complaint sufficiently alleges the existence of this factor.

To be sure, SG disputes the point. It argues that the individuals who purchased shares in the privileged company were not so much investing money in return for rights in the virtual shares as paying for an entertainment commodity (the opportunity to play the StockGeneration game). This argument suggests that an interesting factual issue may await resolution—whether participants were motivated primarily by a perceived investment opportunity or by the visceral excitement of playing a game. Nevertheless, this case comes to us following a dismissal under Rule 12(b)(6), and the SEC's complaint memorializes, inter alia, SG's representation that participants could "firmly expect a 10% profit monthly" on purchases of the privileged company's shares. That representation plainly supports the SEC's legal claim that participants who invested substantial amounts of money in exchange for virtual shares in the privileged company likely did so in anticipation of investment gains. Given the procedural posture of the case, no more is exigible to fulfill the first part of the *Howey* test.

B. Common Enterprise

The second component of the *Howey* test involves the existence of a common enterprise. Before diving headlong into the sea of facts, we must dispel the miasma that surrounds the appropriate legal standard.

1. **The Legal Standard.** Courts are in some disarray as to the legal rules associated with the ascertainment of a common enterprise. Many courts require a showing of horizontal commonality—a type of commonality that involves the pooling of assets from multiple investors so that all share in the profits and risks of the enterprise. Other courts have modeled the concept of common enterprise around fact patterns in which an investor's fortunes are tied to the promoter's success rather than to the fortunes of his or her fellow investors. This doctrine, known as vertical commonality, has two variants. Broad vertical commonality requires that the well-being of all investors be dependent upon the promoter's expertise. In contrast, narrow vertical commonality requires that the investors' fortunes be "interwoven with and dependent upon the efforts and success of those seeking the investment or of third parties."

Courts also differ in the steadfastness of their allegiance to a single standard of commonality. Two courts of appeals recognize only horizontal commonality. Two others adhere exclusively to broad vertical commonality.[1] The Ninth Circuit recognizes both horizontal commonality and narrow vertical commonality. To complicate matters further, four courts of appeals have accepted horizontal commonality, but have not yet ruled on whether they also will accept some form of vertical commonality. At least one of these courts, however, has explicitly rejected broad vertical commonality.

Thus far, neither the Supreme Court nor this court has authoritatively determined what type of commonality must be present to satisfy the common enterprise element.

---

[1] We note that broad vertical commonality is an expansive concept which typically overspreads other types of commonality.

First Circuit Holding

Remains circuit split undecided by U.S. Supreme Court.

The case at bar requires us to take a position on the common enterprise component of the *Howey* test. We hold that a showing of horizontal commonality—the pooling of assets from multiple investors in such a manner that all share in the profits and risks of the enterprise—satisfies the test. This holding flows naturally from the facts of *Howey*, in which the promoter commingled fruit from the investors' groves and allocated net profits based upon the production from each tract.

2. Applying the Standard. Here, the pooling element of horizontal commonality jumps off the screen. The defendants' website stated that: "The players' money is accumulated on the SG current account and is not invested anywhere, because no investment, not even the most profitable one, could possibly fully compensate for the lack of sufficiency in settling accounts with players, which lack would otherwise be more likely." Thus, as the SEC's complaint suggests, SG unambiguously represented to its clientele that participants' funds were pooled in a single account used to settle participants' on-line transactions. Therefore, pooling is established.

Of course, horizontal commonality requires more than pooling alone; it also requires that investors share in the profits and risks of the enterprise. The SEC maintains that two separate elements of SG's operations embody the necessary sharing. First, it asserts that SG was running a Ponzi or pyramid scheme dependent upon a continuous influx of new money to remain in operation,[3] and argues that such arrangements inherently involve the sharing of profit and risk among investors. Second, the SEC construes SG's promise to divert a portion of its profits from website operations to support the privileged company's shares as a bond that ties together the collective fortunes of those who have purchased the shares. While we analyze each of these theories, we note that any one of them suffices to support a finding of commonality.

We endorse the SEC's suggestion that Ponzi schemes typically satisfy the horizontal commonality standard. . . .

SG's flat 10% guaranteed return applied to all privileged company shares, expected returns were dependent upon the number of shares held, the economic assurances were based on the promoter's ability to keep the ball rolling, the investment was proclaimed to be free from risk, and participants were promised that their principal would be repaid in full upon demand. . . . we think that these facts suffice to make out horizontal commonality.

In all events, SG's promise to pay referral fees to existing participants who induced others to patronize the virtual exchange provides an alternative basis for finding horizontal commonality. The

---

[3] While the terms "Ponzi" and "pyramid" often are used interchangeably to describe financial arrangements which rob Peter to pay Paul, the two differ slightly. In Ponzi schemes—name[d] after a notorious Boston swindler, Charles Ponzi, who parlayed an initial stake of $150 into a fortune by means of an elaborate scheme featuring promissory notes yielding interest at annual rates of up to 50%—money tendered by later investors is used to pay off earlier investors. In contrast, pyramid schemes incorporate a recruiting element; they are marketing arrangements in which participants are rewarded financially based upon their ability to induce others to participate. The SEC alleges that SG's operations aptly can be characterized under either appellation.

SEC argues convincingly that this shows the existence of a pyramid scheme sufficient to satisfy the horizontal commonality standard.

* * *

StockGeneration participants who recruited new participants were promised bonuses worth 20%–30% of the recruit's payments. Taking as true the SEC's plausible allegation that the sine qua non of SG's operations was the continued net inflow of funds, the investment pool supporting the referral bonus payments was entirely dependent upon the infusion of fresh capital. Since all participants shared in the profits and risks under this pyramidal structure, it furnishes the sharing necessary to warrant a finding of horizontal commonality.

We will not paint the lily. We conclude, without serious question, that the arrangement described in the SEC's complaint fairly can be characterized as either a Ponzi or pyramid scheme, and that it provides the requisite profit-and-risk sharing to support a finding of horizontal commonality. Taking as true the SEC's allegation that SG's ability to fulfill its pecuniary guarantees was fully predicated upon the net inflow of new money, the fortunes of the participants were inextricably intertwined. As long as the privileged company continued to receive net capital infusions, existing shareholders could dip into the well of funds to draw out their profits or collect their commissions. But all of them shared the risk that new participants would not emerge, cash flow would dry up, and the underlying pool would empty.

SG's most pervervid argument against a finding of horizontal commonality consists of a denial that its operations comprise a Ponzi or pyramid scheme. It says that any such scheme requires a material misrepresentation of fact and some element of fraud or deception, and adds that those additional features are lacking here; to the contrary, the rules of StockGeneration were fully and accurately disclosed to all participants. We do not gainsay that considerable disclosure occurred. SG emphasized that new participants constituted the sole source of all financial income for its StockGeneration website.[4] Indeed, in describing the structure and mechanism of its virtual stock exchange, SG drew a colorful analogy between the privileged company's shares and an enormous card table with a mountain of money. According to SG, thousands of participants continuously threw money onto the table by purchasing shares in the privileged company, while other participants simultaneously sold their shares back to the exchange to retrieve their winnings from the table. SG remarked that the system would remain stable so long as the size of the mountain either remained constant or continued to grow.

Despite the fact that SG was relatively candid in pointing out the fragile structure of the venture, its argument lacks force. Even if we assume, for argument's sake, that misrepresentations of fact and badges of fraud are necessary for the existence of a Ponzi or pyramid scheme, the SEC's complaint contains allegations sufficient, as a matter of pleading, to establish both elements. First, the complaint alleges that SG materially misrepresented the nature of the enterprise by

---

[4] SG specifically addressed this issue on its website, declaring that: "New players: that is the only source of all financial income to any game. It does not and cannot have other sources of income. Otherwise, the game becomes unprofitable and therefore simply pointless."

concealing the fact that the supply of new participants inevitably would be exhausted, causing the scheme to implode and all existing participants to lose their money.[5] Second, the SEC's complaint plausibly characterized SG's flat guarantee of a 10% monthly return on the privileged company's shares and its assurances that it would support those shares as material misrepresentations of fact. Third, the SEC alleged that SG deceived participants by failing to disclose its intent to keep investor money for itself.

For present purposes, it is enough that the SEC's allegations, taken as true, satisfy the common enterprise component of the *Howey* test.[6]

C. Expectation of Profits Solely From the Efforts of Others

[The court concluded that investors were led to expect profits from the efforts of the promoters of the website].

* * *

QUESTIONS

1.   Do you think StockGeneration was a game or an investment? Does it matter what the participants in StockGeneration thought?

2.   Which formulation of commonality do you think best serves the purposes of the securities laws?

3.   How does broad vertical commonality differ from the prong requiring "the efforts of the promoter or a third party"?

4.   Each investor in StockGeneration had the opportunity to earn referral fees for bringing in new recruits (of up to "20%–30% of the recruit's payments"). Do these referral fees fit within the definition of horizontal commonality?

HYPOTHETICAL FOUR

George, the Chief Tasting Officer of The Soup Kitchen, has an idea for financing the company's growth while giving its franchisees incentives at the same time. George thinks the franchisees would promote the soup more aggressively if they were given exclusive rights to recruit Soup Kitchen franchisees in their geographic areas. He proposes selling "city shares" to

---

[5]   As the SEC points out, SG specifically represented on its website that SG was not a pyramid scheme that would "collapse inevitably as soon as the inflow of new players stops." It went on to state:

> This is not a pyramid. The similarities are purely superficial here. A whale might look like a fish, but there are millions of years of evolution between the two. The main fundamental difference is the lack of critical points in time, namely those of mass payments. By manipulating profit, an optimal way of spreading them in time is successfully found.

[6]   If more were needed—and we doubt that it is—SG's promise to divert a portion of profits from website operations to support share prices if the need arose also warrants a finding of horizontal commonality. Through this arrangement, SG provided participants with the opportunity to share income derived from website operations on a pro rata basis. The SEC's complaint notes these facts and alleges in substance that a percentage of participants' funds were pooled; that participants were told of their entitlement to support from this monetary pool; and that they collectively stood to gain or lose (depending on whether they received the guaranteed return on their shares). In and of themselves, these averred facts boost the SEC across the legal threshold for horizontal commonality.

franchisees, giving them the exclusive right to recruit new Soup Kitchen franchisees in their area; franchisees who recruit new franchisees will receive a portion of the franchise fee paid by the new franchisee. Owners of city shares would also receive a higher percentage of the profits from the soup that they sell. The money The Soup Kitchen raises from selling the city shares will be used for an international advertising campaign for The Soup Kitchen. Are the city shares an investment in a common enterprise?

C.   "[I]S LED TO EXPECT PROFITS"

The third element of the *Howey* test has important implications for the test as a whole. The notion that investors are "led" suggests that the actions of the promoter that induce the investor to part with his or her money will be a crucial part of the inquiry. Such an approach lends itself to the application of an objective standard: What are the reasonable expectations of the individuals to whom the instrument is offered? Do you think the purchasers of the "stock" in the case below could have reasonably expected the federal securities laws would apply to their investments?

United Housing Foundation, Inc. v. Forman
421 U.S. 837 (1975).

■ POWELL, J.

The issue in these cases is whether shares of stock entitling a purchaser to lease an apartment in Co-op City, a state subsidized and supervised nonprofit housing cooperative, are "securities" within the purview of the Securities Act of 1933 and the Securities Exchange Act of 1934.

Co-op City is a massive housing cooperative in New York City. Built between 1965 and 1971, it presently houses approximately 50,000 people on a 200-acre site containing 35 high-rise buildings and 236 town houses. The project was organized, financed, and constructed under the New York State Private Housing Finance Law. . . . In order to encourage private developers to build low-cost cooperative housing, New York provides them with large long-term, low-interest mortgage loans and substantial tax exemptions. . . . The developer . . . must agree to operate the facility "on a nonprofit basis," and he may lease apartments only to people whose incomes fall below a certain level and who have been approved by the State.

The United Housing Foundation, a nonprofit membership corporation established for the purpose of "aiding and encouraging" the creation of "adequate, safe and sanitary housing accommodations for wage earners and other persons of low or moderate income," was responsible for initiating and sponsoring the development of Co-op City. . . . UHF organized the Riverbay Corporation to own and operate the land and buildings constituting Co-op City. Riverbay, a nonprofit cooperative housing corporation, issued the stock that is the subject of this litigation. . . .

To acquire an apartment in Co-op City an eligible prospective purchaser must buy 18 shares of stock in Riverbay for each room desired. The cost per share is $25, making the total cost $450 per room, or $1,800 for a four-room apartment. The sole purpose of acquiring these shares is to enable the purchaser to occupy an apartment in Co-op City; in effect, their purchase is a recoverable deposit on an apartment. The shares are explicitly tied to the apartment: they cannot be transferred to a nontenant; nor can they be pledged or encumbered; and they descend, along with the apartment, only to a surviving spouse. No voting rights attach to the shares as such: participation in the affairs of the cooperative appertains to the apartment, with the residents of each apartment being entitled to one vote irrespective of the number of shares owned.

Any tenant who wants to terminate his occupancy, or who is forced to move out, must offer his stock to Riverbay at its initial selling price of $25 per share. . . .

In May 1965, subsequent to the completion of the initial planning, Riverbay circulated an Information Bulletin seeking to attract tenants for what would someday be apartments in Co-op City. After describing the nature and advantages of cooperative housing generally and of Co-op City in particular, the Bulletin informed prospective tenants that the total estimated cost of the project, based largely on an anticipated construction contract with [its contractor], was $283,695,550. Only a fraction of this sum, $32,795,550, was to be raised by the sale of shares to tenants. The remaining $250,900,000 was to be financed by a 40-year low-interest mortgage loan from the New York Private Housing Finance Agency. After construction of the project the mortgage payments and current operating expenses would be met by monthly rental charges paid by the tenants. While these rental charges were to vary, depending on the size, nature, and location of an apartment, the 1965 Bulletin estimated that the "average" monthly cost would be $23.02 per room, or $92.08 for a four-room apartment.

Several times during the construction of Co-op City, Riverbay, with the approval of the State Housing Commissioner, revised its contract with [its contractor] to allow for increased construction costs. In addition, Riverbay incurred other expenses that had not been reflected in the 1965 Bulletin. To meet these increased expenditures, Riverbay, with the Commissioner's approval, repeatedly secured increased mortgage loans from the State Housing Agency. Ultimately the construction loan was $125 million more than the figure estimated in the 1965 Bulletin. As a result, while the initial purchasing price remained at $450 per room, the average monthly rental charges increased periodically, reaching a figure of $39.68 per room as of July 1974.

These increases in the rental charges precipitated the present lawsuit. Respondents, 57 residents of Co-op City, sued in federal court on behalf of all 15,372 apartment owners, . . . seeking upwards of $30 million in damages, forced rental reductions, and other "appropriate" relief. . . . The heart of respondents' claim was that the 1965 Co-op City Information Bulletin falsely represented that [the contractor] would bear all subsequent cost increases due to factors such as inflation. Respondents further alleged that they were misled in their purchases of shares since the Information Bulletin failed to disclose several critical facts. On these bases, respondents asserted two claims under the fraud provisions of the federal [securities laws]. . . .

Petitioners, while denying the substance of these allegations, moved to dismiss the complaint on the ground that . . . shares of stock in Riverbay were not "securities". . . .

The District Court granted the motion to dismiss. . . .

The Court of Appeals for the Second Circuit reversed. It rested its decision on two alternative grounds. First, the court held that since the shares purchased were called "stock" the Securities Acts, which explicitly include "stock" in their definitional sections, were literally applicable. Second, the Court of Appeals concluded that the transaction was an investment contract within the meaning of the Acts and as defined by *Howey*, since there was an expectation of profits from three sources: (i) rental reductions resulting from the income produced by the commercial facilities established for the use of tenants at Co-op City; (ii) tax deductions for the portion of the monthly rental charges allocable to interest payments on the mortgage; and (iii) savings based on the fact that apartments at Co-op City cost substantially less than comparable nonsubsidized housing. . . .

In providing [the definition of a security under § 2(a)(1) of the Securities Act] Congress did not attempt to articulate the relevant economic criteria for distinguishing "securities" from "non-securities," rather, it sought to define "the term 'security' in sufficiently broad and general terms so as to include within that definition the many types of instruments that in our commercial world fall within the ordinary concept of a security." The task has fallen to the Securities and Exchange Commission, the body charged with administering the Securities Acts, and ultimately to the federal courts to decide which of the myriad financial transactions in our society come within the coverage of these statutes.

In making this determination in the present case we do not write on a clean slate. Well-settled principles enunciated by this Court establish that the shares purchased by respondents do not represent any of the "countless and variable schemes devised by those who seek the use of the money of others on the promise of profits," and therefore do not fall within "the ordinary concept of a security."

We reject at the outset any suggestion that the present transaction, evidenced by the sale of shares called "stock,"[13] must be considered a security transaction simply because the statutory definition of a security includes the words "any . . . stock." Rather we adhere to the basic principle that has guided all of the Court's decisions in this area: "(I)n searching for the meaning and scope of the word "security" in the Act(s), form should be disregarded for substance and the emphasis should be on economic reality."

The primary purpose of the Acts of 1933 and 1934 was to eliminate serious abuses in a largely unregulated securities market. The focus of the Acts is on the capital market of the enterprise system: the sale of securities to raise capital for profit-making purposes, the exchanges on which securities are traded, and the need for regulation to prevent fraud and to protect the interest of investors. Because securities

---

[13] While the record does not indicate precisely why the term "stock" was used for the instant transaction, it appears that this form is generally used as a matter of tradition and convenience.

transactions are economic in character Congress intended the application of these statutes to turn on the economic realities underlying a transaction, and not on the name appended thereto. . . .

* * *

In holding that the name given to an instrument is not dispositive, we do not suggest that the name is wholly irrelevant to the decision whether it is a security. There may be occasions when the use of a traditional name such as "stocks" or "bonds" will lead a purchaser justifiably to assume that the federal securities laws apply. This would clearly be the case when the underlying transaction embodies some of the significant characteristics typically associated with the named instrument.

In the present case respondents do not contend, nor could they, that they were misled by use of the word "stock" into believing that the federal securities laws governed their purchase. Common sense suggests that people who intend to acquire only a residential apartment in a state-subsidized cooperative, for their personal use, are not likely to believe that in reality they are purchasing investment securities simply because the transaction is evidenced by something called a share of stock. These shares have none of the characteristics "that in our commercial world fall within the ordinary concept of a security." Despite their name, they lack . . . the most common feature of stock: the right to receive "dividends contingent upon an apportionment of profits." Nor do they possess the other characteristics traditionally associated with stock: they are not negotiable; they cannot be pledged or hypothecated; they confer no voting rights in proportion to the number of shares owned; and they cannot appreciate in value. In short, the inducement to purchase was solely to acquire subsidized low-cost living space; it was not to invest for profit.

The Court of Appeals, as an alternative ground for its decision, concluded that a share in Riverbay was also an "investment contract" as defined by the Securities Acts. Respondents further argue that in any event what they agreed to purchase is "commonly known as a 'security' " within the meaning of these laws. In considering these claims we again must examine the substance—the economic realities of the transaction—rather than the names that may have been employed by the parties. We perceive no distinction, for present purposes, between an "investment contract" and an "instrument commonly known as a 'security.' " In either case, the basic test for distinguishing the transaction from other commercial dealings is "whether the scheme involves an investment of money in a common enterprise with profits to come solely from the efforts of others." *Howey*, 328 U.S. at 301.[16]

This test, in shorthand form, embodies the essential attributes that run through all of the Court's decisions defining a security. The touchstone is the presence of an investment in a common venture

---

[16]   This test speaks in terms of "profits to come solely from the efforts of others." Although the issue is not presented in this case, we note that the Court of Appeals for the Ninth Circuit has held that "the word 'solely' should not be read as a strict or literal limitation on the definition of an investment contract, but rather must be construed realistically, so as to include within the definition those schemes which involve in substance, if not form, securities." We express no view, however, as to the holding of this case.

premised on a reasonable expectation of profits to be derived from the entrepreneurial or managerial efforts of others. By profits, the Court has meant either capital appreciation resulting from the development of the initial investment . . . or a participation in earnings resulting from the use of investors' funds. . . . In such cases the investor is "attracted solely by the prospects of a return" on his investment. By contrast, when a purchaser is motivated by a desire to use or consume the item purchased—"to occupy the land or to develop it themselves," as the *Howey* Court put it—the securities laws do not apply.

Definition of profits:
① capital appreciation
② participation in earnings
not consumption

In the present case there can be no doubt that investors were attracted solely by the prospect of acquiring a place to live, and not by financial returns on their investments.

* * *

Nowhere does the Bulletin seek to attract investors by the prospect of profits resulting from the efforts of the promoters or third parties. On the contrary, the Bulletin repeatedly emphasizes the "nonprofit" nature of the endeavor. It explains that if rental charges exceed expenses the difference will be returned as a rebate, not invested for profit. It also informs purchasers that they will be unable to resell their apartments at a profit since the apartment must first be offered back to Riverbay "at the price . . . paid for it." In short, neither of the kinds of profits traditionally associated with securities was offered to respondents.

The Court of Appeals recognized that there must be an expectation of profits for these shares to be securities, and conceded that there is "no possible profit on a resale of (this) stock." The court correctly noted, however, that profit may be derived from the income yielded by an investment as well as from capital appreciation, and then proceeded to find "an expectation of 'income' in at least three ways." Two of these supposed sources of income or profits may be disposed of summarily. We turn first to the Court of Appeals' reliance on the deductibility for tax purposes of the portion of the monthly rental charge applied to interest on the mortgage. We know of no basis in law for the view that the payment of interest, with its consequent deductibility for tax purposes, constitutes income or profits. These tax benefits are nothing more than that which is available to any homeowner who pays interest on his mortgage.[20]

The Court of Appeals also found support for its concept of profits in the fact that Co-op City offered space at a cost substantially below the going rental charges for comparable housing. Again, this is an inappropriate theory of "profits" that we cannot accept. The low rent derives from the substantial financial subsidies provided by the State of New York. This benefit cannot be liquidated into cash; nor does it result from the managerial efforts of others. In a real sense, it no more embodies the attributes of income or profits than do welfare benefits, food stamps, or other government subsidies.

The final source of profit relied on by the Court of Appeals was the possibility of net income derived from the leasing by Co-op City of

---

[20] Even if these tax deductions were considered profits, they would not be the type associated with a security investment since they do not result from the managerial efforts of others.

commercial facilities, professional offices and parking spaces, and its operation of community washing machines. The income, if any, from these conveniences, all located within the common areas of the housing project, is to be used to reduce tenant rental costs. Conceptually, one might readily agree that net income from the leasing of commercial and professional facilities is the kind of profit traditionally associated with a security investment.[21] But in the present case this income—if indeed there is any is far too speculative and insubstantial to bring the entire transaction within the Securities Acts.

Initially we note that the prospect of such income as a means of offsetting rental costs is never mentioned in the Information Bulletin. Thus it is clear that investors were not attracted to Co-op City by the offer of these potential rental reductions. Moreover, nothing in the record suggests that the facilities in fact return a profit in the sense that the leasing fees are greater than the actual cost to Co-op City of the space rented. The short of the matter is that the stores and services in question were established not as a means of returning profits to tenants, but for the purpose of making essential services available for the residents of this enormous complex. . . . Undoubtedly they make Co-op City a more attractive housing opportunity, but the possibility of some rental reduction is not an "expectation of profit" in the sense found necessary in *Howey*.

There is no doubt that purchasers in this housing cooperative sought to obtain a decent home at an attractive price. But that type of economic interest characterizes every form of commercial dealing. What distinguishes a security transaction—and what is absent here—is an investment where one parts with his money in the hope of receiving profits from the efforts of others, and not where he purchases a commodity for personal consumption or living quarters for personal use.

* * *

NOTES

1.   *Real estate as a "security."* Other interests in real estate have posed difficult questions for courts grappling with the definition of investment contract. The easy case at one end of the spectrum is the purchase of land in fee simple, even if promoted as a speculative investment: any profits expected would not come "from the efforts of others." The easy case at the other end is the syndication of an office building or apartment complex. A typical syndication transaction involves a promoter selling limited partnership interests to investors. The limited partnership then purchases the office building or apartment complex. The promoter, who takes the position of general partner, often manages the real estate, paying out a portion of the rent to the limited partners over time. The limited

---

[21] The "income" derived from the rental of parking spaces and the operation of washing machines clearly was not profit for respondents since these facilities were provided exclusively for the use of tenants. Thus, when the income collected from the use of these facilities exceeds the cost of their operation the tenants simply receive the return of the initial overcharge in the form of a rent rebate. Indeed, it could be argued that the 'income' from the commercial and professional facilities is also, in effect, a rebate on the cost of goods and services purchased at these facilities since it appears likely that they are patronized almost exclusively by Co-op City residents.

partnership interests typically sold in such transactions clearly fall within the definition of investment contract.

More difficult questions are raised, however, by real estate interests between the two extremes. Consider a condominium in a resort community which the owners occupy for a portion of the year and rent out, with the assistance of the manager of the complex, for the rest of the year. The SEC takes the position that such an arrangement may constitute a security under the following circumstances:

1.   The condominiums, with any rental arrangement or other similar service, are offered and sold with emphasis on the economic benefits to the purchaser to be derived from the managerial efforts of the promoter, or a third party designated or arranged for by the promoter, from rental of the units;

2.   The offering of participation in a rental pool arrangement; and

3.   The offering of a rental or similar arrangement whereby the purchaser must hold his unit available for rental for any part of the year, must use an exclusive rental agent, or is otherwise materially restricted in his occupancy or rental of his unit.

Sec. Act Rel. 5347 (1973). This guidance provided by the SEC acts as a checklist of arrangements to avoid if the developer wants to escape the complications of the federal securities laws. Should the SEC provide more guidance to investors and promoters on the somewhat murky question of what is a security?

2.   *Crowdfunding.* Investors face an increasing number of ways to part with their money over the Internet. In recent years, a number of companies have established websites to help connect people with money with promoters seeking money to fund various business (and sometimes non-business) ideas. Perhaps the most famous of these sites is Kickstarter (www.kickstarter.com). As of the date of this edition of the casebook, almost 7 million people have pledged over $1 billion to fund almost 70,000 creative projects on Kickstarter. People give money to promoters of a project, often with a consumer focus, in return for a promise of a reward in the future. For example, the promoters of the Coolest Cooler, a cooler that also includes a Bluetooth speaker and a blender, raised over $13 million for their project in 2014. Those who pledged $165 or more were promised that they would receive, among other things, their very own Coolest Cooler once the product was ready.

One question raised by sites such as Kickstarter is whether the promoters who receive money through the site are selling a security. Certainly the people who give money to the promoter of a Kickstarter project are giving up cash. And arguably there is a common enterprise where people depend on the entrepreneurial and managerial efforts of the promoter. All the people who provide cash depend equally on the promoter to come through with the promoter's promises. One snag in applying the *Howey* test to a Kickstarter project, however, may come from the expectation of profits prong. Are those who give money to a promoter expecting profit or consumption? Even if one thinks that the people who give up cash expect consumption, does it matter that the consumption is in the future? After all, why do investors invest? To make more money in the future which can lead to more consumption (perhaps a Coolest Cooler) in the future. So what is the difference?

QUESTIONS

1. Does a Co-op share or a share of IBM better fit the traditional characteristics of "stock"? Do all stocks have the same characteristics?

2. Why does the Court also find that the Co-op shares are not investment contracts?

3. *Forman* hints at one unified approach to the definition of a security focusing on the economic realities. Should courts use the *Howey* test to determine whether the stock of particular companies counts as a security?

4. Was it a mistake to label the instrument at issue in *Forman* "stock"? What would have happened in future projects of this type if the Court had held that anything labeled "stock" fell within the definition of a security?

————

The next case addresses the question of what form the profits must take. The Court in *Forman* stated that: "By profits, the Court has meant either capital appreciation resulting from the development of the initial investment . . . or a participation in earnings resulting from the use of investors' funds." What about investments that provide a fixed return? Despite the language in *Forman*, the Court has taken a broad view of "participation in earnings."

SEC v. Edwards — participation in earnings requirement
540 U.S. 389 (2004).

■ O'CONNOR, J.

"Opportunity doesn't always knock . . . sometimes it rings." And sometimes it hangs up. So it did for the 10,000 people who invested a total of $300 million in the payphone sale-and-leaseback arrangements touted by respondent under that slogan. The Securities and Exchange Commission argues that the arrangements were investment contracts, and thus were subject to regulation under the federal securities laws. In this case, we must decide whether a moneymaking scheme is excluded from the term "investment contract" simply because the scheme offered a contractual entitlement to a fixed, rather than a variable, return.

I

Respondent Charles Edwards was the chairman, chief executive officer, and sole shareholder of ETS Payphones, Inc. ETS . . . sold payphones to the public via independent distributors. The payphones were offered packaged with a site lease, a 5-year leaseback and management agreement, and a buyback agreement. All but a tiny fraction of purchasers chose this package, although other management options were offered. The purchase price for the payphone packages was approximately $7,000. Under the leaseback and management agreement, purchasers received $82 per month, a 14% annual return. Purchasers were not involved in the day-to-day operation of the payphones they owned. ETS selected the site for the phone, installed

Profit

the equipment, arranged for connection and long-distance service, collected coin revenues, and maintained and repaired the phones. Under the buyback agreement, ETS promised to refund the full purchase price of the package at the end of the lease or within 180 days of a purchaser's request.

In its marketing materials and on its website, ETS trumpeted the "incomparable pay phone" as "an exciting business opportunity," in which recent deregulation had "open[ed] the door for profits for individual pay phone owners and operators." According to ETS, "[v]ery few business opportunities can offer the potential for ongoing revenue generation that is available in today's pay telephone industry."

The payphones did not generate enough revenue for ETS to make the payments required by the leaseback agreements, so the company depended on funds from new investors to meet its obligations. In September 2000, ETS filed for bankruptcy protection. The SEC brought this civil enforcement action the same month. It alleged that respondent and ETS had violated the registration requirements of §§ 5(a) and (c) of the Securities Act of 1933, the antifraud provisions of both § 17(a) of the Securities Act of 1933, and § 10(b) of the Securities Exchange Act of 1934. The Court of Appeals . . . held that respondent's scheme was not an investment contract, on two grounds. First, it read this Court's opinions to require that an investment contract offer either capital appreciation or a participation in the earnings of the enterprise, and thus to exclude schemes, such as respondent's, offering a fixed rate of return. Second, it held that our opinions' requirement that the return on the investment be "derived solely from the efforts of others" was not satisfied when the purchasers had a contractual entitlement to the return. We conclude that it erred on both grounds.

II

"Congress' purpose in enacting the securities laws was to regulate *investments*, in whatever form they are made and by whatever name they are called." To that end, it enacted a broad definition of "security," sufficient "to encompass virtually any instrument that might be sold as an investment." Section 2(a)(1) of the 1933 Act, and § 3(a)(10) of the 1934 Act in slightly different formulations which we have treated as essentially identical in meaning, define "security" to include "any note, stock, treasury stock, security future, bond, debenture, . . . investment contract, . . . [or any] instrument commonly known as a 'security'." "Investment contract" is not itself defined.

The test for whether a particular scheme is an investment contract was established in our decision in *SEC v. W.J. Howey* We look to "whether the scheme involves an investment of money in a common enterprise with profits to come solely from the efforts of others." . . .

In reaching that result, we first observed that when Congress included "investment contract" in the definition of security, it "was using a term the meaning of which had been crystallized" by the state courts' interpretation of their "'blue sky'" laws. The state courts had defined an investment contract as "a contract or scheme for 'the placing of capital or laying out of money in a way intended to secure income or profit from its employment,'" and had "uniformly applied" that definition to "a variety of situations where individuals were led to invest money in a common enterprise with the expectation that they would earn a profit solely through the efforts of the promoter or [a third party]." Thus, when we held that "profits" must "come solely from the efforts of others," we were speaking of the profits that investors seek on their investment, not the profits of the scheme in which they invest. We used "profits" in the sense of income or return, to include, for example, dividends, other periodic payments, or the increased value of the investment.

There is no reason to distinguish between promises of fixed returns and promises of variable returns for purposes of the test, so understood. In both cases, the investing public is attracted by representations of investment income, as purchasers were in this case by ETS' invitation to " 'watch the profits add up.' " Moreover, investments pitched as low-risk (such as those offering a "guaranteed" fixed return) are particularly attractive to individuals more vulnerable to investment fraud, including older and less sophisticated investors. Under the reading respondent advances, unscrupulous marketers of investments could evade the securities laws by picking a rate of return to promise. We will not read into the securities laws a limitation not compelled by the language that would so undermine the laws' purposes.

* * *

The Eleventh Circuit's perfunctory alternative holding, that respondent's scheme falls outside the definition because purchasers had a contractual entitlement to a return, is incorrect and inconsistent with our precedent. We are considering investment contracts. The fact that investors have bargained for a return on their investment does not mean that the return is not also expected to come solely from the efforts of others. . . .

We hold that an investment scheme promising a fixed rate of return can be an "investment contract" and thus a "security" subject to the federal securities laws.

* * *

U.S. Supreme Court holding Factually Specific.

QUESTIONS

1. Was the Court's conclusion that a guaranteed return did not exclude a financial instrument from the definition of a security consistent with the emphasis on risk reduction in *Daniel* and *Marine Bank*?

———

Consumers spending money on goods or services, such as the purchase of a car, are clearly not expecting profits. Nor are they "investing" in the ordinary sense of the word. Similarly, when a person donates money to a charity, to feed the homeless for example, the person is neither expecting profits nor investing. But what if a person decides to put money into a venture that promises a mixture of consumption and financial return or a mixture of charitable giving and financial return?

Warfield v. Alaniz

569 F.3d 1015 (9th Cir. 2009).

■ THOMAS, CIRCUIT JUDGE:

Issue

This appeal presents the question . . . of whether the charitable gift annuities sold in this case were investment contracts under federal securities law. We conclude they were, and we affirm the judgment of the district court.

Yes

I

Not only did Robert Dillie promise his investors "a gift for your lifetime and beyond," he pledged "preservation of the American way of life," "preservation of your assets," and "preservation of the American family." Unless Dillie meant to refer to the way of life perfected by the Boston swindler Charles Ponzi and his family, we can safely say that Dillie's claims were a bit overstated.

The vehicle by which Dillie was to deliver these dreams was a charitable gift annuity, sold through the Dillie-controlled Mid-America Foundation. From 1996 until 2001, the Foundation sold its charitable gift annuities through financial planners, insurance agents, and others, including the Defendants in this lawsuit.

The Foundation's marketing literature assured investors that they would receive a lifetime stream of income, with the money remaining at their death directed to a charity designated by the investor. The promotion was initially an enormous success for Dillie; the return for the investors was not. In all, the Foundation raised $55 million dollars from the sale of more than 400 charitable gift annuities. Unfortunately, the business model was simply a Ponzi scheme in which, rather than investing the investors' funds, the Foundation used the investors' funds to make annuity payments to earlier annuitants, commission payments to facilitators, and payments to Dillie and others for personal expenses (including Dillie's gambling expenses). Although it collected millions in investments, the Foundation quickly became insolvent. With a few minor exceptions, no charitable contributions were ever made, and the scheme collapsed in 2001.

Shortly after the collapse, the Securities and Exchange Commission filed a civil complaint against Dillie. The district court appointed Lawrence Warfield as Receiver for Receivership Assets in order to "prevent waste and dissipation of the assets of the Defendants to the detriment of investors." Dillie was subsequently indicted and ultimately pled guilty to several counts of wire fraud and money laundering. . . .

The Receiver filed the instant complaint seeking the return of commissions paid to agents by the Foundation for the sale of the charitable gift annuities.

* * *

II

The district court correctly held that the Foundation's charitable gift annuities were investment contracts subject to regulation as securities under Section 2(a)(1) of the Securities Act of 1933, and Section 3(a)(10) of the Securities Exchange Act of 1934.

A

* * *

[W]e note that it is undisputed that, as the district court explained:

> [T]he investors paid money to Mid-America through an irrevocable gift of cash, securities, or other assets. In return, Mid-America promised to pool the money in investments such as stocks, bonds, and money market funds, and to periodically pay each of the investors a fixed sum of money based on their individual ages and the date that payment commenced. In addition to a monthly income stream, the investors expected to receive substantial tax benefits resulting from their purchase of the CGAs.

It is also undisputed that the Foundation's literature promised that monies remaining after the named annuitants' lifetime would be directed to a charity designated by those who purchased the charitable gift annuities.

Defendants argue that the investors did not make any "investment of money" within the meaning of *Howey* because they lacked the requisite intent to realize financial gain through the transactions, and intended instead to make charitable donations. In addition, and relatedly, Defendants argue that the investors had no "expectation of profits" because the anticipated value of the gift annuities at the time of purchase was always less than the purchase amount. . . .

B

The "investment of money" prong of the *Howey* test "requires that the investor 'commit his assets to the enterprise in such a manner as to subject himself to financial loss." In *SEC v. Rubera*, 350 F.3d 1084 (9th Cir. 2003) we found this prong satisfied where investors "turned over substantial amounts of money . . . with the hope that [the investment managers' efforts] would yield financial gains." It is undisputed in this case that the purchasers of the Foundation's gift annuities "turned over substantial amounts of money" in exchange for the Foundation's promise to make annuity payments and turn funds remaining at the end of the annuitant's life over to designated charities. Furthermore, although the Foundation falsely represented that investors' accounts were "secured by the multi-million dollar assets of the Mid-America Foundation," the investors risked financial loss due to the (now realized) possibility that the Foundation would not be able to honor its promises. Defendants argue, however, that the purchasers of the Foundation's gift annuities made no investment of money because they lacked the intent to realize a financial gain and were motivated solely to make a charitable donation. We reject this argument.

At the outset, we note that, while the subjective intent of the purchasers may have some bearing on the issue of whether they entered into investment contracts, we must focus our inquiry on what the purchasers were offered or promised. Under *Howey*, courts conduct an objective inquiry into the character of the instrument or transaction offered based on what the purchasers were "led to expect." Accordingly,

Promotional material

courts have frequently examined the promotional materials associated with an instrument or transaction in determining whether an investment contract is present.

Our review of the record in this case demonstrates that the Foundation marketed its gift annuities as investments, and not merely as vehicles for philanthropy. One promotional brochure entitled "Maximizer Gift Annuity: A Gift that Offers Lifetime Income . . . and Beyond" states, under the heading "Attractive Returns," that "[y]our annuity payment is determined by your age and the amount you deposit. The older you are, the more you'll receive." The brochure goes on to list the "current average net-yield" rates. Elsewhere, under a heading titled "A Gift that Gives to the Donor," the brochure states:

> To get this same return through the stock market, [the hypothetical investor] would have had to find investments that pay dividends of 19.3%! (Even the most profitable companies rarely pay dividends of more than 5%.) The rate of return on a Mid-America Foundation "Gift Annuity" is hard to beat!

The brochure also includes a chart comparing the benefits of a $200,000 commercial annuity with a $200,000 charitable gift annuity, indicating the superiority of the charitable gift annuity in such categories as annuity rate, annual income, income tax savings, federal estate tax savings, and "partial bypass capital gains." Although the brochure also notes that the investor will "make a difference" through the purchase of the gift annuity, the brochure as a whole emphasizes the income generation and tax savings aspect of the charitable gift annuity. Indeed, a bullet point summary of the advantages of the Foundation's charitable gift annuities states: "High Rates; Tax Free Income; Capital Gains Tax Savings; Current Tax Savings; Estate Tax Free; Safe; Secure; Simple; Flexible; PAYS YOU NOW HELPS YOU MAKE A DIFFERENCE LATER."

Another brochure entitled "The Charitable Gift Annuity: Preserving Your Family Legacy . . . Now and For Generations to Come" places emphasis on the opportunity for the investor to designate family members as secondary annuitants under the scheme, noting that "[y]ou can easily include your spouse, children, or grandchildren to receive these lifetime benefits." This brochure also emphasizes the stability and security of charitable gift annuities, noting that "[a] gift annuity is one of the OLDEST and SAFEST financial instruments available." On the whole, this brochure pitches charitable gift annuities to an investor whose main concern is to provide a steady stream of income to dependents after he or she is gone. The brochure's emphasis is on the long-term income production potential of the charitable gift annuity. The fact that some purchasers may have been attracted to the gift annuities in part by the Foundation's promise to donate funds remaining after the annuitants' life to a designated charity does not alter the outcome. In sum, when the promotional materials are examined, the investment component of the annuity is evident.

Marketing methods

In addition to considering the Foundation's marketing materials, we note that the gift annuities were marketed and sold to persons who were likely to be attracted by the Foundation's promises of periodic payment of income and tax benefits. At oral argument, Defendants suggested that the charitable gift annuities were marketed solely to the

marketing strategy

elderly, who had little interest in a return on their investment. This contention is belied by the record. Not only were there relatively young investors, but some purchasers designated a much younger "second-life annuitant," often a son or daughter, who stood to receive the monthly annuity payments for the duration of his or her life after the death of the primary annuitant. In addition, to impose a requirement that the elderly must expect personally to see returns on an investment before his or her death effectively renders the "investment contract" definition inapplicable to a large portion of the population. As the Supreme Court has noted, the particular motives of investors-and the types of investment vehicles appealing to them-may vary considerably depending on the investor's stage of life. That the charitable gift annuity purchaser preferred a perceived low-risk investment yielding a stable long-term income for himself and a designated beneficiary rather than a higher risk investment should not bar the investor from the protection of the securities laws.

In sum, because under the terms of the Foundation's offer, the purchasers of the Foundation's gift annuities committed their assets in return for promised financial gain, the transactions involved satisfy the "investment of money" prong.

C

Defendants also argue that gift annuity transactions fail to satisfy the "expectation of profits" element of the *Howey* test. . . . [T]he thrust of Defendants' argument is that the "expectation of profits" prong also requires an expectation of net financial gain lacking in this case. . . . Defendants argue that because the estimated value of the gift annuities at the time of purchase was always less than the initial payment amount, the purchasers expected no net gain from the transaction. Indeed, Defendants argue that it was impossible for purchasers to see returns on their investment and that accordingly, any payments to Defendants could not constitute "profits." Defendants' argument fails.

Under the terms of the Foundation's charitable gift annuity contracts, the fixed rate at which the annuity amount was to be paid was based on the life expectancy of the purchaser. Of course, the present value of the annuity at the time of purchase, which was also based on the projected life expectancy of the purchaser, was always less than the purchase price. That fact, however, does not establish that it was impossible for the purchaser to profit from the charitable gift annuity investment. Indeed, whether or not a particular purchaser stood to see a return on his or her initial investment depended entirely on whether the investor (or the designated secondary beneficiary) lived longer than the actuarial tables predicted. Furthermore, as we discussed in the preceding section, consideration of the Foundation's promotional literature, as well as the annuity contracts themselves, demonstrates that the Foundation presented its gift annuity as opportunity for financial gain. The record indicates that for many of the annuitants, the periodic payments and tax benefits could deliver a return on the initial payment, especially when the payments paid to designated "second-life" annuitants are taken into account. Further, the purchaser may well have anticipated an increase in investment value that would accrue to the benefit of the charity. At heart, Defendants' argument under the "profits" prong closely mirrors their argument that the purchasers of gift annuities made no investment of money and fails for the same reasons discussed in our consideration of that prong.

We conclude that the structure of the charitable gift annuity contracts included an expectation of profit within the meaning of *Howey*.

* * *

QUESTIONS

1. Were the investors in *Warfield* motivated more by potential profit, or by charitable impulses? Should that matter to the question of whether their investment was a security?

2. Why did the promoters in *Warfield* target investors interested in charitable giving?

3. The present value of the annuities at issue in *Warfield* at the time of their purchase was lower than the purchase price. Purchasers of the annuities, in other words, expected a net loss from the annuities. Should the possibility of a profit (if a purchaser lives beyond her expected life span) matter in determining whether there was an expectation of a profit if the *expected* return is negative?

HYPOTHETICAL FIVE

Jerry and George persuaded their friend Kramer, who appears to be independently wealthy, to invest in The Soup Kitchen at its inception. Kramer invested $100,000 to help get The Soup Kitchen off the ground. The value of that investment has now increased exponentially, and Kramer is worried about the capital gains implications of selling his 25% stake in The Soup Kitchen. (Jerry and George are worried about the possibility their control will be diluted if Kramer sells his interest.) Jerry and George propose to create a trust—the Cosmo Fund—in exchange for Kramer's interests. The Cosmo Fund would receive 25% of The Soup Kitchen's profits. Those profits would be used to support a pet project of Kramer's, providing the homeless with work opportunities in bottle deposit arbitrage (exploiting the 5¢ differential between New York and Michigan deposits). Kramer readily agrees to the exchange.

Kramer has second thoughts about the exchange, however, after getting into a dispute with a homeless man over some Tupperware. He now wants to back out of the exchange of his interest in The Soup Kitchen, but Jerry and George refuse. Kramer now says that Jerry and George defrauded him by failing to disclose that he would not be getting a cut of the Cosmo Fund's bottle deposit arbitrage proceeds. Kramer has filed suit against The Soup Kitchen under Rule 10b–5. Did The Soup Kitchen sell Kramer a security?

D. "[S]OLELY FROM THE EFFORTS OF THE PROMOTER OR A THIRD PARTY"

The fourth element of the *Howey* test for an investment contract is whether the scheme generates returns "solely from the efforts of the promoter or a third party." In the case of out-of-state tourists purchasing strips of citrus fruit land and corresponding service contracts prohibiting the tourists from even entering the property, the profits derived from the investment are entirely due to the efforts of the operators of the service company (the promoter).

But what about situations in which the investors contribute a modicum of effort? The investors in *Howey*, for example, could have contributed not only cash for their investment, but also one day's worth of labor, during which they would get the opportunity to pick oranges for the service company. The profits no longer stem "solely" from the efforts of others. Does this minimal effort from the investors remove the scheme from the definition of *Howey*?

The fourth element of the *Howey* test has been particularly critical in determining whether an investment contract is present in two common arrangements: partnerships and franchises. These arrangements share the common feature that their investors will frequently be involved in the management of the enterprise. However, the level of control can vary considerably within these broad categories, making generalizations difficult.

Consider a franchise relationship like the one managed by The Soup Kitchen. Many retail businesses, eager to replicate what works in one location, seek to duplicate that success in other locales. The Soup Kitchen produces especially tasty mulligatawny and crab bisque and has a standard of service that attracts many customers. The Soup Kitchen, rather than opening up new lunch counters itself, seeks others to open new lunch counters. Acting as a franchisor, The Soup Kitchen may divide up various areas into distinct geographical regions. The franchisor will then sell the right to establish a new lunch counter in a particular region to a prospective franchisee for a fee, typically in the tens of thousands of dollars, as well as an ongoing royalty payment based on the lunch counter's profits.

What happens next depends on the particular franchise relationship. The franchisee typically must invest money to lease a location, build a restaurant, and get the business going. The franchisor, in turn, will spend money on national advertising campaigns and ensure that the various franchises maintain consistent product quality and lunch counter appearance. Although the franchisee typically has day-to-day control over operations at the franchisee's specific restaurant, the degree of control can vary considerably. If the franchisee invests considerable capital and enjoys only limited control (i.e., the franchisor sets the prices, hours, and provides detailed instructions for hiring employees, the decor of the restaurant and so on), is the franchise agreement a security?

One reasonably clear rule in this area is that limited partnership interests are presumed to be securities unless the limited partners exercise effective control over the enterprise. The case below applies the fourth element of the *Howey* test to a limited liability partnership.

SEC v. Merchant Capital, LLC

483 F.3d 747 (11th Cir. 2007).

■ ANDERSON, CIRCUIT JUDGE:

The SEC brought this enforcement action against defendants Steven Wyer, Kurt Beasley, and Merchant Capital, LLC ("Merchant"), alleging violations of the registration and antifraud provisions of the federal securities laws. Wyer and Beasley, through Merchant, sold interests in twenty-eight registered limited liability partnerships ("RLLPs") to 485 persons. The SEC asserted that these interests were "investment contracts" within the meaning of the federal securities laws, and that the defendants had committed securities fraud in marketing the interests. . . .

I. Facts

Wyer and Beasley formed Merchant in order to participate in the business of buying, collecting, and reselling charged-off consumer debt from financial institutions such as banks and credit card companies. . . .

When a consumer is delinquent on a credit account, the company that provided the account begins by trying to collect the debt itself. After 180 days, however, the company normally sells the debt to a wholesale purchaser. Most sales of debt occur in large pools. Some of these pools are sold at auction. Others are sold pursuant to long-term contracts with large purchasers, so-called "forward-flow contracts." Forward-flow contracts are attractive to the seller because they provide a consistent and reliable way to get rid of debt. They are attractive to the wholesaler because they provide a reliable supply and also typically guarantee that the accounts are a representative sample of the company's debt pool and that none of the debtors are deceased or bankrupt. . . .

As established at trial, the appropriate price for a pool of debt depends on the many factors that determine how likely it is that the debt in the pool will be collected. . . . Wholesalers often have proprietary computer programs that assign a weight to the various factors, assess the characteristics of the particular debt pool, and thereby estimate how valuable the pool is. . . .

* * *

Wyer and Beasley formed Merchant, with Wyer owning seventy-five percent, and Beasley twenty-five percent. Wyer and Beasley planned to raise funds through Merchant and then buy fractional shares in debt pools ultimately purchased by New Vision Financial [a wholesale debt purchaser]. New Vision would aggregate money from Merchant and other sources [and] purchase debt pools through auction and forward-flow contracts. . . . To formalize this relationship, Merchant entered into a services contract with New Vision.

Merchant began raising money in November 2001 by soliciting members of the general public to become partners. . . . Merchant employed a network of recruiters to sell the RLLP interests, and provided the recruiters with scripts. These recruiters informed potential partners that, while they would be expected to participate in the operation of their partnership, their actual duties would be limited to checking a box on ballots that would be periodically sent to them. . . .

Merchant eventually organized twenty-eight RLLPs, containing 485 partners, with a total capitalization of over $26 million. The eventual RLLP partners were all members of the general public with no demonstrated expertise in the debt purchasing business, and included a nurse, a housewife, and a railroad retiree. Each partner had a net worth of at least $250,000, and more than seventy-five percent had a net worth exceeding $500,000. Further, ninety percent of the partners self-reported business experience between "average" and "excellent." . . .

The partnerships were marketed and sold as freestanding entities. Merchant did not disclose the existence of the other partnerships or the relationship with New Vision to the RLLP partners. Despite the partnerships' formal independence, Wyer testified at trial that Merchant planned from the beginning to pool the money collected from the RLLPs in order to purchase fractional interests in debt pools owned by New Vision. . . .

Merchant prepared all the partnership materials and was the sole business contact for all of the partners. It was the only candidate for MGP ["Managing General Partner"] and was named on one-hundred percent of the ballots. Merchant thus became MGP for each of the twenty-eight RLLPs. . . .

As early as June 2002, Merchant and its principals knew that the existing partnerships were performing poorly. . . .

Despite the poor performance, no partnership replaced Merchant during the period before the SEC began its investigation. . . .

* * *

III. Status of RLLP interests under the federal securities laws

The key issue in this case is whether the RLLP interests marketed by Merchant were "investment contracts". . . . [which turns on] whether the RLLP partners were led to expect their profits solely from the efforts of Merchant.

Under this prong of *Howey*, "solely" is not interpreted restrictively. "The Supreme Court has repeatedly emphasized that economic reality is to govern over form and that the definitions of the various types of securities should not hinge on exact and literal tests." An interest thus does not fall outside the definition of investment contract merely because the purchaser has some nominal involvement with the operation of the business. Rather, "the focus is on the dependency of the investor on the entrepreneurial or managerial skills of a promoter or other party."

A general partnership interest is presumed not to be an investment contract because a general partner typically takes an active part in managing the business and therefore does not rely solely on the efforts of others. *Williamson v. Tucker*, 645 F.2d 404, 422 (5th Cir. 1981). But consistent with the substance over form principle of *Howey*, "[a] scheme which sells investments to inexperienced and unknowledgeable members of the general public cannot escape the reach of the securities laws merely by labeling itself a general partnership or joint venture." A general partnership interest may qualify as an investment contract if the general partner in fact retains little ability to control the profitability of the investment. *Williamson* recognized three situations where this would be the case:

(1) "[A]n agreement among the parties leaves so little power in the hands of the partner or venturer that the arrangement in fact distributes power as would a limited partnership,"

(2) "[T]he partner or venturer is so inexperienced and unknowledgeable in business affairs that he is incapable of intelligently exercising his partnership or venture powers,"; or

(3) "[T]he partner or venturer is so dependent on some unique entrepreneurial or managerial ability of the promoter or manager that he cannot replace the manager of the enterprise or otherwise exercise meaningful partnership or venture powers,".

Under *Williamson*, the presence of any one of these factors renders a general partnership interest an investment contract. The three factors also are not exhaustive. *Williamson* is ultimately simply a guide to determining whether the partners expected to depend solely on the efforts of others, thus satisfying the *Howey* test.

The SEC argues that the defendants should not receive the benefit of the *Williamson* presumption against investment contract status because the RLLP interests are more akin to limited partnership interests, which are routinely treated as investment contracts. It is true that an RLLP bears some similarity to a limited partnership. An RLLP partner is liable only for the amount of his or her capital contribution, plus the partner's personal acts, and is not exposed to vicarious liability for the acts of other partners or the acts of the partnership as a whole. This limitation on liability means that RLLP partners have less of an incentive to preserve control than general partners do. While general partners normally wish to preserve control because their personal assets are at risk, RLLP partners have only their investment at risk if they remain passive, and risk personal liability only if they become active.

On the other hand, it is not invariably true that partners in an RLLP, limited liability company (LLC), or limited liability partnership (LLP) lack the ability to control the profitability of their investments. The powers of partners or members in these forms of business can be altered by agreement, and may assume virtually any shape, despite the limitation on liability. . . .

It is clear in this circuit, however, that an RLLP interest is an investment contract if one of the *Williamson* factors is present. . . .

We analyze the expectations of control at the time the interest is sold, rather than at some later time after the expectations of control have developed or evolved. A post-sale delegation cannot, for example, convert a general partnership into an investment contract, if the partners had control at the beginning. As an evidentiary matter, however, we may look at how the RLLPs actually operated to answer the question of how control was allocated at the outset.

Williamson also defines the kind of evidence that is to be considered in determining the expectations of control. Consistent with *Howey's* focus on substance over form, we look at all the representations made by the promoter in marketing the interests, not just at the legal agreements underlying the sale of the interest. The ultimate issue under *Howey* is whether the partners expected to rely solely on the efforts of others, and we may rely on the totality of the circumstances surrounding the offering in making this determination.

A.   Did the arrangement in fact distribute power as would a limited partnership?

The first *Williamson* factor requires us to analyze whether "an agreement among the parties leaves so little power in the hands of the partner or venturer that the arrangement in fact distributes power as would a limited partnership." In arguing that the partners did not function as limited partners, Merchant relies primarily on the allegedly substantial powers reserved to the partners through the partnership agreement. The partnership materials informed partners that they were expected to take an active role in the business, and the agreement gave partners certain rights and powers. Partners had the ability to call meetings and hold regular quarterly meetings; the ability to participate in committees; the ability to elect the MGP; the ability to remove the MGP for cause upon a certain vote; the ability to inspect books and records; the ability to approve additional funding; the ability to amend the agreement or to dissolve the partnership upon a two-thirds vote; and the exclusive authority to approve obligations exceeding $5,000.

In the first place, the power to name the MGP was not a significant one in this case. Partners were required to turn in their ballots with their capital contribution, before their partnerships had even been formed. The power therefore reveals nothing about the partners' ability to control the business after their initial investment. Moreover, Merchant was the only option for MGP. The investors had no independent experience in the debt purchasing industry and no way of knowing about alternative MGPs. And, as a result, Merchant was named on all ballots. This power was not significant.

The partners also did not have the practical ability to remove Merchant once it was installed as MGP. First, the agreement provided for removal only for cause. This meant that Merchant could not be removed readily, and even in the case of gross incompetence, the partners would have had to litigate any unconsented removal. We have previously found that where removal is only for cause, and the investors have no other ability to impact management, the interest is an investment contract as a matter of law.

Here there were further barriers to removing Merchant. The partnership agreement required a unanimous vote of the partners. . . . [I]t is clear that such a vote, combined with removal only for cause and the factors discussed below, rendered Merchant effectively unremovable.

Compounding the legal difficulty in removing Merchant, the investors in an individual partnership were geographically dispersed, with no preexisting relationships. . . . [T]he lack of face-to-face contact among the partners exacerbated the other difficulties and rendered the supposed power to remove Merchant illusory. . . .

The next power reserved to the partners was the ability to approve all obligations over $5,000. If this power was real, it was a substantial one. The primary business of each partnership was purchasing fractionalized interests in pools of debt that generally exceeded $5,000 in value. However, as shown by Merchant's tenure as MGP, the ballot right also did not give the partners meaningful control over their investment.

First, Merchant controlled how much information appeared in the ballots, and did not submit sufficient information for the partners to be able to make meaningful decisions to approve or disapprove debt purchases. . . .

Second, besides the fact that the ballots were completely devoid of meaningful information, the partners had no way to force Merchant to heed the results of the process. . . . Merchant purchased more debt than the ballots authorized thirty times; purchased debt before ballots were sent six times; and purchased before the ten-day return period expired seventy-three times. In part because the partners had no ability to remove Merchant, they also lacked the power to force Merchant to abide by the results of the ballots.

Finally, the voting process was tilted in Merchant's favor from the very start. The partnership agreement provided that unreturned and unvoted ballots were voted in favor of management. . . . Unsurprisingly, no ballot ever went against Merchant's decisions. We therefore conclude that the voting process was a sham and did not give partners meaningful control over their investment.

Merchant insists that we are restricted to the terms of the partnership agreement in applying the first *Williamson* factor, and argues that because the approval authority was included in the terms, the district court had no choice but to conclude that it was meaningful. . . .

It is true that we are limited to assessing the expectations of control at the inception of the investment. But we are not limited to the terms of the partnership agreement in assessing those expectations of control. Post-investment events can serve as evidence of how much power partners reserved at the inception. It is difficult to imagine how a court could determine how much power the partners "in fact" retained under the agreement without looking to some extent at post-investment events. . . .

B. Were the RLLP partners so inexperienced and unknowledgeable in business affairs that they were incapable of intelligently exercising partnership or venture powers?

The second *Williamson* factor asks whether "the partner or venturer is so inexperienced and unknowledgeable in business affairs that he is incapable of intelligently exercising his partnership or venture powers." If the partner is inexperienced in "business affairs," we will find a relationship of dependency on the promoter supporting a finding of investment contract, even if the partner possesses some powers under the arrangement.

*not general
bus. exp.
→ exp in the
particular bus.*

The district court erroneously applied this factor by looking to the general business experience of the partners. *Howey* itself focused on the experience of investors in the particular business, not their general business experience. In finding that the orange grove plus service contract was an investment contract, the Court said, "[the investors] are predominantly business and professional people who lack the knowledge, skill and equipment necessary for the care and cultivation of citrus trees." . . .

In this case, the SEC presented uncontradicted evidence that the individual partners had no experience in the debt purchasing business. They were members of the general public, and included a railroad retiree, a housewife, and a nurse. Their possible general business experience is not significant in this case. They were relying solely on Merchant to operate the business, as evidenced by the fact that one-hundred percent of the partners chose Merchant as MGP. . . .

C.   Were the partners so dependent on Merchant's entrepreneurial or managerial ability that they could not replace it or otherwise exercise meaningful powers?

The third factor asks whether "the partner or venturer is so dependent on some unique entrepreneurial or managerial ability of the promoter or manager that he cannot replace the manager of the enterprise or otherwise exercise meaningful partnership or venture powers." The first *Williamson* factor analyzes the powers the partners practically retain under the arrangement with the promoter. The third factor provides that, even if the arrangement gives the partners some practical control, the instrument is an investment contract if the investors have no realistic alternative to the manager. . . .

Merchant effectively had permanent control over each partnership's assets. Merchant pooled the partnerships' assets and invested them in pools of accounts owned by New Vision. Merchant had a service contract with New Vision that gave Merchant a right to the return of debt accounts only in certain limited circumstances, or upon termination of the entire contract. Beasley admitted at trial that the partnerships had no contractual right to demand the return of the debtor accounts. Thus, even if an individual partnership managed to replace Merchant, it would find that its major assets were tied up in fractional share form in a New Vision debt pool.

* * *

The RLLPs' lack of a realistic alternative to Merchant was present from the inception of the arrangement between Merchant and the partners. Wyer admitted that he and Beasley intended from the beginning to pool capital from multiple partnerships. The partnership agreement also expressly gave Merchant the authority to contract with a third-party service. Therefore, from the beginning, RLLP partners had no realistic alternative to management by Merchant, and the third *Williamson* factor was also present.

D.   Conclusion: RLLP interests were investment contracts

For all of these reasons, the RLLP interests were investment contracts covered by the federal securities laws. The partners had the powers of limited partners, since they had no ability to remove Merchant and the purported authority to approve purchases was illusory. They were completely inexperienced in the debt purchasing industry. Finally, even if they could have removed Merchant (which they could not), they had no realistic alternative to Merchant as manager because their debt pools were in fractional form with a company whose only contractual relationship was with Merchant.

Because the RLLP interests were investment contracts, and the defendants sold the interests without filing a registration statement, the defendants violated the registration provisions of the securities laws.

* * *

QUESTIONS

1. Should the "efforts of another" inquiry focus on investors' expectations at the time of their investment or how the partnership actually operates?

2. The RLLP partners self-reported business experience between "average" and "excellent." Each partner also had a net worth of at least $250,000 (and most had a net worth above $500,000). Is evidence of the partners having general business expertise enough to show that they can exercise control? Must all of the partners have the same level of expertise?

———

The *Howey* test for an investment contract turns on whether the scheme generates returns "solely from the efforts of the promoter or a third party." We saw in *Merchant Capital* that mere "nominal involvement" on the part of investors will not negate investment contract status, despite *Howey's* use of the word "solely." Many circuit courts instead focus on the presence of entrepreneurial or managerial efforts of others. But what if an investor provides nominal efforts and the promoter of a scheme also exerts only nominal or ministerial efforts after the investment? If a third factor is important to determining investment returns unrelated to the promoter's or investor's efforts, should courts treat the *Howey* efforts of another prong as satisfied?

SEC v. Mutual Benefits Corp.
408 F.3d 737 (11th Cir. 2005).

■ Cox, Circuit Judge:

* * *

MBC is a viatical settlement provider. A viatical settlement is a transaction in which a terminally ill insured sells the benefits of his life insurance policy to a third party in return for a lump-sum cash payment equal to a percentage of the policy's face value. The purchaser of the viatical settlement realizes a profit if, when the insured dies, the policy benefits paid are greater than the purchase price, adjusted for time value. Thus, in purchasing a viatical settlement, it is of paramount importance that an accurate determination be made of the insured's expected date of death. If the insured lives longer than expected, the purchaser of the policy will realize a reduced return, or may lose money on the investment.

Viatical settlement providers, like MBC, purchase policies from individual insureds and typically sell fractionalized interests in these policies to investors. Between 1994 and 2004, over 29,000 investors nationwide invested over $1 billion in viatical settlements offered by MBC. MBC identified terminally ill insureds, negotiated purchase prices, bid on policies, and obtained life expectancy evaluations. MBC recruited doctors to evaluate the health of an insured and produce a life-expectancy evaluation. MBC also created the legal documents needed to conclude all transactions. In order to sell viatical settlements to investors, MBC solicited funds from investors directly and through agents. Following the deposit of investor funds into escrow, MBC would pay premiums, monitor the health of the insureds, collect the benefits upon death, and distribute proceeds to investors.

Investors were asked to identify a desired maturity date and submit a purchase agreement on a form provided by MBC. The promised rate of return was dependent upon the term of the investment, which in turn was determined by the life expectancy evaluation. The actual rate of return, however, depended upon the date of the insured's death. If the insured lived beyond his life expectancy, the term of the investment was extended and the premiums had to be paid either from new investor funds assigned to other policies or by additional funds from the original investors. According to MBC, projected returns were substantial. MBC told investors that the policy of a person with a life expectancy of 12 months would yield a 12% return, assuming the person died when expected; it told potential investors that the policy of a person with a life expectancy of 72 months would yield a 72% return.

MBC touted to potential investors its expertise in evaluating life expectancy, and thus its ability to make the venture successful. . . . At no time did investors or potential investors have access to insureds' medical files. Thus, they could not, on their own, engage doctors to perform life expectancy evaluations.

MBC made a profit by contracting for the right to purchase interests in life insurance policies and then selling those interests to investors at marked-up prices. A portion of the price paid by investors was set aside to pay premiums on the policy in question. MBC required investors to deposit the purchase price of the investment with an escrow agent before MBC selected a policy that fit the investment goals of the individual investor based on the price the investor wanted to pay and the life-expectancy period that the investor desired.

* * *

While MBC was supposed to perform the life expectancy evaluation prior to closing on a settlement with an insured, MBC commonly did not send the information to the doctors retained by MBC for a life expectancy evaluation until after the closing. There is evidence in the record that MBC, in fact, routinely did not receive life-expectancy evaluations until after closing. Melanie Goldberg was the person at MBC responsible for preparing the post-closing information to be sent to investors. . . . Doctors' reports were always pre-dated, she explained, because "it had to look like it was being reviewed at the time the viator was selling the policy . . . that it had to show that it was reviewed at the time the file was sold, not afterwards."

After closing on a policy, MBC assumed certain responsibilities for paying premiums due. At least 1,000 policies were held in MBC's name for the benefit of thousands of investors who purchased fractionalized interests in those policies. . . . MBC would escrow sufficient funds to pay future premiums through the date of the estimated life expectancy of a given insured, or at the discretion of MBC, longer. MBC would then seek any available disability premium waiver from the applicable insurance company. Next, MBC would establish a reserve from interest on escrowed funds and unused premiums "for payment of premiums on those policies with respect to which the insured outlives his/her projected life expectancy." MBC's affiliate, Viatical Services, Inc., would establish a "premium reserve to pay any unpaid premiums" if the reserve established by MBC and its trustee were exhausted. Lastly, the investor would be responsible for his own pro rata share. The record further reflects that MBC exercised discretion in the payment of premiums. For instance, money set aside for one set of policies was used to pay premiums for another set. A total of $4.52 million was transferred from the escrow account set up for one set of policies to an escrow account set up for another. As a result, no investor was ever asked to pay additional premiums, despite escrow deficiencies.

* * *

MBC contends that the district court erred in its conclusion that MBC's viatical settlement contracts qualify as "investment contracts" under the Securities Acts. MBC argues that we should adopt the reasoning of the court in *SEC v. Life Partners, Inc.*, 87 F.3d 536 (D.C.Cir.1996), which concluded that viatical settlement contracts are not "investment contracts" because they depend entirely upon the mortality of the insured, rather than the post-purchase managerial or entrepreneurial efforts of the viatical settlement provider.

* * *

The only real dispute concerns whether the investor's expectation of profits is based "solely on the efforts of the promoter or a third party." MBC, relying on *Life Partners*, argues that this element is "a necessarily forward-looking inquiry." MBC asks that we make a distinction between a promoter's activities prior to his having use of an investor's money and his activities after he has use of the money. This distinction was indeed made in *Life Partners*, a case involving facts similar to those presented here.

> [W]e cannot agree that the time of sale is an artificial dividing line. It is a legal construct but a significant one. If the investor's profits depend thereafter predominantly upon the promoter's efforts, then the investor may benefit from the disclosure and other requirements of the federal securities laws. But if the value of the promoter's efforts has already been impounded into the promoter's fees or into the purchase price of the investment, and if neither the promoter nor anyone

else is expected to make further efforts that will affect the outcome of the investment, then the need for federal securities regulation is greatly diminished. . . .

We see here no "venture" associated with the ownership of an insurance contract from which one's profit depends entirely upon the mortality of the insured . . .

Because no significant post-purchase activity took place here, MBC argues, the expectation of profits is not based "solely on the efforts of the promoter or a third party."

We decline to adopt the test established by the *Life Partners* court. We are not convinced that either *Howey* or *Edwards* require such a clean distinction between a promoter's activities prior to his having use of an investor's money and his activities thereafter. . . .

While it may be true that the "solely on the efforts of the promoter or a third party" prong of the *Howey* test is more easily satisfied by post-purchase activities, there is no basis for excluding pre-purchase managerial activities from the analysis. Significant pre-purchase managerial activities undertaken to insure the success of the investment may also satisfy *Howey*. Indeed, investment schemes may often involve a combination of both pre- and post-purchase managerial activities, both of which should be taken into consideration in determining whether *Howey's* test is satisfied. Courts have found investment contracts where significant efforts included the pre-purchase exercise of expertise by promoters in selecting or negotiating the price of an asset in which investors would acquire an interest.

Furthermore, while the "solely on the efforts of the promoter or a third party" prong of the *Howey* test may not be met where an investment relies predominantly on market speculation,[5] that is not the case here. The investors' expectations of profits in this case relied heavily on the pre- and post-payment efforts of the promoters in making investments in viatical settlement contracts profitable. The investors selected the "term" of their investment, and submitted completed agreement forms and money. Thereafter, MBC selected the insurance policies in which the investors' money would be placed. MBC bid on policies and negotiated purchase prices with the insureds. MBC determined how much money would be placed in escrow to cover payment of future premiums. MBC undertook to evaluate the life expectancy of the insureds-evaluations critical to the success of the venture. If MBC underestimated the insureds' life expectancy, the chances increased that the investors would realize less of a profit, or no profit at all. And, investors had no ability to assess the accuracy of representations being made by MBC or the accuracy of the life-expectancy evaluations. They could not, by reference to market trends, independently assess the prospective value of their investments in MBC's viatical settlement contracts. There were important post-purchase managerial efforts of MBC as well. Often, life-expectancy evaluations were not completed until after closing. And, after closing on

---

[5] . . . When profits depend upon market forces, public information is available to investors by which they can independently evaluate the possible success of the investment. In the case before us, investors were far more dependent on the efforts and information provided by MBC than an investor relying on the open market to produce a profit.

a policy, MBC assumed the responsibility of making premium payments. Escrow payments were collectively managed in such a manner that investors were not required to pay additional premiums. Thus, investors relied on both the pre- and post-purchase management activities of MBC to maximize the profit potential of investing in viatical settlement contracts.

MBC thus offered what amounts to a classic investment contract. Investors were offered and sold an investment in a common enterprise in which they were promised profits that were dependent on the efforts of the promoters. . . . Whether . . . the life-expectancy evaluation was actually performed before or after closing, . . . all investors here relied on the pre- and post-purchase managerial efforts of MBC to make a profit on the investment in viatical settlement contracts. The investors here relied on MBC to identify terminally ill insureds, negotiate purchase prices, pay premiums, and perform life expectancy evaluations critical to the success of the venture. The flexible test we are instructed to apply by *Howey* and *Edwards* covers these activities, qualifying MBC's viatical settlement contracts as "investment contracts" under the Securities Acts of 1933 and 1934.

* * *

QUESTIONS

1. Should it matter whether most of a promoter's significant efforts are contributed before the sale of the investment rather than after?

2. The most important factor determining the investment return for viatical settlement is the life spans of the insured parties. The investors in the pooled viatical settlements presumably had no control over the life spans and little knowledge of the particular life styles, health, etc. of any of the specific insured parties. Doesn't this factor alone make the return to investors solely through the efforts of others?

NOTES

1. *"Solely."* The lower courts have generally read the word "solely" out of the fourth element of the *Howey* standard. The cases that prompted this liberal reading involved ostensible franchise arrangements in which the investors were provided financial incentives to recruit other investors to participate in pyramid schemes. As the Ninth Circuit explained:

> Adherence to [a literal] interpretation could result in a mechanical, unduly restrictive view of what is and what is not an investment contract. It could be easy to evade by adding a requirement that the buyer contribute a modicum of effort. Thus the fact that the investors here were required to exert some efforts if a return were to be achieved should not automatically preclude a finding that the Plan or Adventure is an investment contract. To do so would not serve the purpose of the legislation. Rather we adopt a more realistic test, whether the efforts made by those other than the investor are the undeniably significant ones, those essential managerial efforts which affect the failure or success of the enterprise.

SEC v. Glenn W. Turner Enterprises, Inc., 474 F.2d 476, 482 (9th Cir. 1973).

Franchise arrangements typically require effort on the part of the franchisee. The question becomes whether the franchisee's efforts "are the undeniably significant ones" in determining whether the business will be a success. Merely labeling an essentially passive investment a franchise will not avoid the definition of "security"; courts will look through to the "economic reality" of the transaction.

HYPOTHETICAL SIX

The Soup Kitchen sells franchises to aspiring small-business owners, allowing them to open their own branches of The Soup Kitchen. The Soup Kitchen charges $100,000 each for the right to open a store in a particular geographic territory. The franchise arrangement allows The Soup Kitchen to develop a nationwide presence without having to expend much of its own capital. Nonetheless, to maintain quality and uniformity across its many planned The Soup Kitchen franchise locations, the company intends to have each franchisee sign a detailed contract specifying the layout of each lunch counter, the ingredients for the soup, rules for customers, the price of the soup, the training of employees, and lunch counter hours. Franchisees are responsible for all costs of running their lunch counters. In addition, franchisees must pay The Soup Kitchen 10% of their net profits. Is The Soup Kitchen's franchise agreement an investment contract?

III. "STOCK"

The *Howey* test for an investment contract requires courts to perform an in-depth inquiry into the substance of a transaction to determine if a security is present. "Investment contract" is only one item in the long laundry list of instruments defined as securities. The following cases address the relation between the *Howey* test for investment contract and other items on that list.

Landreth Timber Company v. Landreth

471 U.S. 681 (1985).

■ POWELL, J.

This case presents the question whether the sale of all of the stock of a company is a securities transaction subject to the antifraud provisions of the federal securities laws.

I

Respondents Ivan K. Landreth and his sons owned all of the outstanding stock of a lumber business they operated in Tonasket, Washington. The Landreth family offered their stock for sale through both Washington and out-of-state brokers. Before a purchaser was found, the company's sawmill was heavily damaged by fire. Despite the fire, the brokers continued to offer the stock for sale. Potential purchasers were advised of the damage, but were told that the mill would be completely rebuilt and modernized.

Samuel Dennis, a Massachusetts tax attorney, received a letter offering the stock for sale. On the basis of the letter's representations concerning the rebuilding plans, the predicted productivity of the mill, existing contracts, and expected profits, Dennis became interested in acquiring the stock. He talked to John Bolten, a former client who had retired to Florida, about joining him in investigating the offer. After having an audit and an inspection of the mill conducted, a stock purchase agreement was negotiated, with Dennis the purchaser of all of the common stock in the lumber company. Ivan Landreth agreed to stay on as a consultant for some time to help with the daily operations of the mill. Pursuant to the terms of the stock purchase agreement, Dennis assigned the stock he purchased to B & D Co., a corporation formed for the sole purpose of acquiring the lumber company stock. B & D then merged with the lumber company, forming petitioner Landreth Timber Co. Dennis and Bolten then acquired all of petitioner's Class A stock, representing 85% of the equity, and six other investors together owned the Class B stock, representing the remaining 15% of the equity.

After the acquisition was completed, the mill did not live up to the purchasers' expectations. Rebuilding costs exceeded earlier estimates, and new components turned out to be incompatible with existing equipment. Eventually, petitioner sold the mill at a loss and went into receivership. Petitioner then filed this suit seeking rescission of the sale of stock and $2,500,000 in damages, alleging that respondents had widely offered and then sold their stock without registering it as required by the Securities Act of 1933. Petitioner also alleged that respondents had negligently or intentionally made misrepresentations and had failed to state material facts as to the worth and prospects of the lumber company, all in violation of the Securities Exchange Act of 1934.

Respondents moved for summary judgment on the ground that the transaction was not covered by the Acts because under the so-called "sale of business" doctrine, petitioner had not purchased a "security" within the meaning of those Acts. . . .

II

* * *

As we have observed in the past, [the definition of a security under Section 2(a)(1) of the '33 Act] is quite broad and includes both instruments whose names alone carry well-settled meaning, as well as instruments of "more variable character [that] were necessarily designated by more descriptive terms," such as "investment contract" and "instrument commonly known as a 'security.'" The face of the definition shows that "stock" is considered to be a "security" within the meaning of the Acts. As we observed in *United Housing Foundation, Inc. v. Forman*, most instruments bearing such a traditional title are likely to be covered by the definition.

As we also recognized in *Forman*, the fact that instruments bear the label "stock" is not of itself sufficient to invoke the coverage of the Acts. Rather, we concluded that we must also determine whether those instruments possess "some of the significant characteristics typically associated with" stock, recognizing that when an instrument is both called "stock" and bears stock's usual characteristics, "a purchaser justifiably [may] assume that the federal securities laws apply." We identified those characteristics usually associated with common stock as (i) the right to receive dividends contingent upon an apportionment of profits; (ii) negotiability; (iii) the ability to be pledged or hypothecated; (iv) the conferring of voting rights in proportion to the number of shares owned; and (v) the capacity to appreciate in value.[2]

Under the facts of *Forman*, we concluded that the instruments at issue there were not "securities" within the meaning of the Acts. . . .

In contrast, it is undisputed that the stock involved here possesses all of the characteristics we identified in *Forman* as traditionally associated with common stock. Indeed, the District Court so found. Moreover, unlike in *Forman*, the context of the transaction involved here—the sale of stock in a corporation—is typical of the kind of context to which the Acts normally apply. It is thus much more likely here than in *Forman* that an investor would believe he was covered by the federal securities laws. Under the circumstances of this case, the plain meaning of the statutory definition mandates that the stock be treated as "securities" subject to the coverage of the Acts.

Reading the securities laws to apply to the sale of stock at issue here comports with Congress' remedial purpose in enacting the legislation to protect investors by "compelling full and fair disclosure relative to the issuance of 'the many types of instruments that in our commercial world fall within the ordinary concept of a security.'" Although we recognize that Congress did not intend to provide a comprehensive federal remedy for all fraud, we think it would improperly narrow Congress' broad definition of "security" to hold that the traditional stock at issue here falls outside the Acts' coverage.

III

Under other circumstances, we might consider the statutory analysis outlined above to be a sufficient answer compelling judgment for petitioner. Respondents urge, however, that language in our previous opinions, including *Forman*, requires that we look beyond the label "stock" and the characteristics of the instruments involved to determine whether application of the Acts is mandated by the economic substance of the transaction. . . .

A

It is fair to say that our cases have not been entirely clear on the proper method of analysis for determining when an instrument is a "security." This Court has decided a number of cases in which it looked to the economic substance of the transaction, rather than just to its form, to determine whether the Acts applied. . . .

This so-called "*Howey* test" formed the basis for the second part of our decision in *Forman*, on which respondents primarily rely. As discussed above, the first part of our decision in *Forman* concluded that the instruments at issue, while they bore the traditional label "stock," were not "securities" because they possessed none of the usual

---

[2] Although we did not so specify in *Forman*, we wish to make clear here that these characteristics are those usually associated with common stock, the kind of stock often at issue in cases involving the sale of a business. Various types of preferred stock may have different characteristics and still be covered by the Acts.

characteristics of stock. We then went on to address the argument that the instruments were "investment contracts." Applying the *Howey* test, we concluded that the instruments likewise were not "securities" by virtue of being "investment contracts" because the economic realities of the transaction showed that the purchasers had parted with their money not for the purpose of reaping profits from the efforts of others, but for the purpose of purchasing a commodity for personal consumption.

Respondents contend that *Forman* and the cases on which it was based require us to reject the view that the shares of stock at issue here may be considered "securities" because of their name and characteristics. Instead, they argue that our cases require us in every instance to look to the economic substance of the transaction to determine whether the *Howey* test has been met. According to respondents, it is clear that petitioner sought not to earn profits from the efforts of others, but to buy a company that it could manage and control. Petitioner was not a passive investor of the kind Congress intended the Acts to protect, but an active entrepreneur, who sought to "use or consume" the business purchased just as the purchasers in *Forman* sought to use the apartments they acquired after purchasing shares of stock. Thus, respondents urge that the Acts do not apply.

We disagree with respondents' interpretation of our cases. First, it is important to understand the contexts within which these cases were decided. All of the cases on which respondents rely involved unusual instruments not easily characterized as "securities." Thus, if the Acts were to apply in those cases at all, it would have to have been because the economic reality underlying the transactions indicated that the instruments were actually of a type that falls within the usual concept of a security. In the case at bar, in contrast, the instrument involved is traditional stock, plainly within the statutory definition. There is no need here, as there was in the prior cases, to look beyond the characteristics of the instrument to determine whether the Acts apply.

Contrary to respondents' implication, the Court has never foreclosed the possibility that stock could be found to be a "security" simply because it is what it purports to be. . . . Nor does *Forman* require a different result. Respondents are correct that in *Forman* we eschewed a "literal" approach that would invoke the Acts' coverage simply because the instrument carried the label "stock." *Forman* does not, however, eliminate the Court's ability to hold that an instrument is covered when its characteristics bear out the label.

Second, we would note that the *Howey* economic reality test was designed to determine whether a particular instrument is an "investment contract," not whether it fits within any of the examples listed in the statutory definition of "security." . . . Moreover, applying the *Howey* test to traditional stock and all other types of instruments listed in the statutory definition would make the Acts' enumeration of many types of instruments superfluous.

Finally, we cannot agree with respondents that the Acts were intended to cover only "passive investors" and not privately negotiated transactions involving the transfer of control to "entrepreneurs." The 1934 Act contains several provisions specifically governing tender offers, disclosure of transactions by corporate officers and principal stockholders, and the recovery of short-swing profits gained by such persons. Eliminating from the definition of "security" instruments involved in transactions where control passed to the purchaser would contravene the purposes of these provisions. Furthermore, although § 4[a](2) of the 1933 Act exempts transactions not involving any public offering from the Act's registration provisions, there is no comparable exemption from the antifraud provisions. Thus, the structure and language of the Acts refute respondents' position.

antifraud provisions apply to private s[ale] [handwritten marginalia]

* * *

IV

We also perceive strong policy reasons for not employing the sale of business doctrine under the circumstances of this case. By respondents' own admission, application of the doctrine depends in each case on whether control has passed to the purchaser. It may be argued that on the facts of this case, the doctrine is easily applied, since the transfer of 100% of a corporation's stock normally transfers control. We think even that assertion is open to some question, however, as Dennis and Bolten had no intention of running the sawmill themselves. Ivan Landreth apparently stayed on to manage the daily affairs of the business. Some commentators who support the sale of business doctrine believe that a purchaser who has the ability to exert control but chooses not to do so may deserve the Acts' protection if he is simply a passive investor not engaged in the daily management of the business. In this case, the District Court was required to undertake extensive fact-finding, and even requested supplemental facts and memoranda on the issue of control, before it was able to decide the case.

More importantly, however, if applied to this case, the sale of business doctrine would also have to be applied to cases in which less than 100% of a company's stock was sold. This inevitably would lead to difficult questions of line-drawing. The Acts' coverage would in every case depend not only on the percentage of stock transferred, but also on such factors as the number of purchasers and what provisions for voting and veto rights were agreed upon by the parties. As we explain more fully in *Gould v. Ruefenacht*, 471 U.S. 701 (1985), decided today as a companion to this case, coverage by the Acts would in most cases be unknown and unknowable to the parties at the time the stock was sold. These uncertainties attending the applicability of the Acts would hardly be in the best interests of either party to a transaction. Respondents argue that adopting petitioner's approach will increase the workload of the federal courts by converting state and common-law fraud claims into federal claims. We find more daunting, however, the prospect that parties to a transaction may never know whether they are covered by the Acts until they engage in extended discovery and litigation over a concept as often elusive as the passage of control.

V

In sum, we conclude that the stock at issue here is a "security" within the definition of the Acts, and that the sale of business doctrine does not apply. . . .

NOTES

1.   *Limited liability companies.* Limited liability companies (LLCs) are an important alternative to corporations and partnerships as an organizational form. LLCs are attractive to individuals starting a business because they combine the limited liability of the corporation with the tax advantages of the partnership's "pass through" tax treatment.

Are LLC interests securities? As a recent innovation, LLC interests are not found in the statutory definition list, so courts have turned to the investment contract analysis to answer the question. The closest available analogy is the dividing line between general and limited partnerships, with "member-managed" LLCs likely to be aligned with general partnerships and "manager-managed" LLCs lining up with limited partnerships.

QUESTIONS

1.   How does the *Landreth* Court (Powell, J.) distinguish *Forman* (Powell, J.)?

2.   How do "economic realities" influence determinations of what instruments are securities? Is there one unified test for the definition of a security?

3.   How could the parties have avoided the application of the securities laws to the sale of Landreth Timber?

HYPOTHETICAL SEVEN

Jerry and George, the CEO and Chief Tasting Officer respectively of The Soup Kitchen, have attracted a potential investor for The Soup Kitchen. Vandelay Investments is a venture capital fund that thinks The Soup Kitchen has a bright future and is anxious to invest. Vandelay, however, wants substantial control over The Soup Kitchen while it is getting established because Vandelay believes Jerry and George need a strong guiding hand. In exchange for Vandelay's investment of $20 million, The Soup Kitchen and Vandelay agree to the following terms: (1) Vandelay will receive the right to name three out of five The Soup Kitchen directors (Jerry and George will hold the other two seats); (2) the Chairman must be a Vandelay nominee; (3) Vandelay will have the right to replace Jerry and George as officers of the company; (4) Vandelay will have the right to veto any merger, sale of a majority of the company's equity, or sale of substantially all of its assets; (5) Vandelay will have the right to convert its interest into common stock if The Soup Kitchen should make an initial public offering; and (6) Vandelay will be entitled to an annual payment of $2 million, beginning three years after the agreement's inception. If the interest is labeled "preferred stock," has Vandelay purchased a security? What if it is labeled an "investment agreement"?

IV.   "NOTE"

The one financial instrument more ubiquitous than "stock" is the "note." Indeed, "note" precedes "stock" in the definitions of a security contained in § 2(a)(1) of the '33 Act and § 3(a)(10) of the '34 Act. After *Landreth* ruled that all investments labeled as stock that bear out the characteristics of stock are securities, it is fair to ask whether the same applied for notes. Are all notes that bear out the characteristics of a note (i.e., a specified interest rate, principal amount, and maturity term) securities? Tens of thousands of notes are issued each day. As the next case makes clear, only a fraction of them are securities.

Reves v. Ernst & Young

494 U.S. 56 (1990).

■ MARSHALL, J.

This case presents the question whether certain demand notes issued by the Farmers Cooperative of Arkansas and Oklahoma are "securities" within the meaning of § 3(a)(10) of the Securities Exchange Act of 1934. We conclude that they are.

I

The Co-Op is an agricultural cooperative that, at the time relevant here, had approximately 23,000 members. In order to raise money to support its general business operations, the Co-Op sold promissory notes payable on demand by the holder. Although the notes were uncollateralized and uninsured, they paid a variable rate of interest that was adjusted monthly to keep it higher than the rate paid by local financial institutions. The Co-Op offered the notes to both members and nonmembers, marketing the scheme as an "Investment Program." Advertisements for the notes, which appeared in each Co-Op newsletter, read in part: "YOUR CO-OP has more than $11,000,000 in assets to stand behind your investments. The Investment is not Federal [sic] insured but it is . . . Safe . . . Secure . . . and available when you need it." Despite these assurances, the Co-Op filed for bankruptcy in 1984. At the time of the filing, over 1,600 people held notes worth a total of $10 million.

After the Co-Op filed for bankruptcy, petitioners, a class of holders of the notes filed suit against Arthur Young & Co., the firm that had audited the Co-Op's financial statements (and the predecessor to respondent Ernst & Young). Petitioners alleged, inter alia, that Arthur Young had intentionally failed to follow generally accepted accounting principles in its audit, specifically with respect to the valuation of one of the Co-Op's major assets, a gasohol plant. Petitioners claimed that Arthur Young violated these principles in an effort to inflate the assets and net worth of the Co-Op. Petitioners maintained that, had Arthur Young properly treated the plant in its audits, they would not have purchased demand notes because the Co-Op's insolvency would have been apparent. On the basis of these allegations, petitioners claimed that Arthur Young had violated the antifraud provisions of the 1934 Act as well as Arkansas' securities laws.

II

A

This case requires us to decide whether the note issued by the Co-Op is a "security" within the meaning of the 1934 Act. . . .

The fundamental purpose undergirding the Securities Acts is "to eliminate serious abuses in a largely unregulated securities market." In defining the scope of the market that it wished to regulate, Congress painted with a broad brush. . . . Congress . . . did not attempt precisely to cabin the scope of the Securities Acts. Rather, it enacted a definition of "security" sufficiently broad to encompass virtually any instrument that might be sold as an investment.

Congress did not, however, "intend to provide a broad federal remedy for all fraud." Accordingly, "[t]he task has fallen to the Securities and Exchange Commission, the body charged with administering the Securities Acts, and ultimately to the federal courts to decide which of the myriad financial transactions in our society come within the coverage of these statutes." In discharging our duty, we are not bound by legal formalisms, but instead take account of the economics of the transaction under investigation. Congress' purpose in enacting the securities laws was to regulate investments, in whatever form they are made and by whatever name they are called.

A commitment to an examination of the economic realities of a transaction does not necessarily entail a case-by-case analysis of every instrument, however. Some instruments are obviously within the class Congress intended to regulate because they are by their nature investments. In *Landreth Timber Co. v. Landreth*, we held that an instrument bearing the name "stock" that, among other things, is negotiable, offers the possibility of capital appreciation, and carries the right to dividends contingent on the profits of a business enterprise is plainly within the class of instruments Congress intended the securities laws to cover. *Landreth Timber* does not signify a lack of concern with economic reality; rather, it signals a recognition that stock is, as a practical matter, always an investment if it has the economic characteristics traditionally associated with stock. Even if sparse exceptions to this generalization can be found, the public perception of common stock as the paradigm of a security suggests that stock, in whatever context it is sold, should be treated as within the ambit of the Acts.

We made clear in *Landreth Timber* that stock was a special case, explicitly limiting our holding to that sort of instrument. Although we refused finally to rule out a similar *per se* rule for notes, we intimated that such a rule would be unjustified. Unlike "stock," we said, " 'note' may now be viewed as a relatively broad term that encompasses instruments with widely varying characteristics, depending on whether issued in a consumer context, as commercial paper, or in some other investment context." While common stock is the quintessence of a security, and investors therefore justifiably assume that a sale of stock is covered by the Securities Acts, the same simply cannot be said of notes, which are used in a variety of settings, not all of which involve investments. Thus, the phrase "any note" should not be interpreted to mean literally "any note," but must be understood against the backdrop of what Congress was attempting to accomplish in enacting the Securities Acts.[2]

---

[2] An approach founded on economic reality rather than on a set of *per se* rules is subject to the criticism that whether a particular note is a "security" may not be entirely clear at the time it is issued. Such an approach has the corresponding advantage, though, of permitting the SEC and the courts sufficient flexibility to ensure that those who market investments are not able to escape the coverage of the Securities Acts by creating new instruments that would not be covered by a more determinate definition. One could question whether, at the expense

Because the *Landreth Timber* formula cannot sensibly be applied to notes, some other principle must be developed to define the term "note." A majority of the Courts of Appeals that have considered the issue have adopted, in varying forms, "investment versus commercial" approaches that distinguish, on the basis of all of the circumstances surrounding the transactions, notes issued in an investment context (which are "securities") from notes issued in a commercial or consumer context (which are not).

The Second Circuit's "family resemblance" approach begins with a presumption that any note with a term of more than nine months is a "security." Recognizing that not all notes are securities, however, the Second Circuit has also devised a list of notes that it has decided are obviously not securities. Accordingly, the "family resemblance" test permits an issuer to rebut the presumption that a note is a security if it can show that the note in question "bear[s] a strong family resemblance" to an item on the judicially crafted list of exceptions, or convinces the court to add a new instrument to the list.

In contrast, the Eighth and District of Columbia Circuits apply the test we created in *SEC v. W.J. Howey Co.* to determine whether an instrument is an "investment contract" to the determination whether an instrument is a "note."

We reject the approaches of those courts that have applied the *Howey* test to notes; *Howey* provides a mechanism for determining whether an instrument is an "investment contract." The demand notes here may well not be "investment contracts," but that does not mean they are not "notes." To hold that a "note" is not a "security" unless it meets a test designed for an entirely different variety of instrument "would make the Acts' enumeration of many types of instruments superfluous," and would be inconsistent with Congress' intent to regulate the entire body of instruments sold as investments.

The other two contenders—the "family resemblance" and "investment versus commercial" tests—are really two ways of formulating the same general approach. Because we think the "family resemblance" test provides a more promising framework for analysis, however, we adopt it. The test begins with the language of the statute because the Securities Acts define "security" to include "any note," we begin with a presumption that every note is a security.[3] We nonetheless recognize that this presumption cannot be irrebuttable. As we have said, Congress was concerned with regulating the investment market, not with creating a general federal cause of action for fraud. In an attempt to give more content to that dividing line, the Second Circuit has identified a list of instruments commonly denominated "notes" that

---

of the goal of clarity, Congress overvalued the goal of avoiding manipulation by the clever and dishonest. If Congress erred, however, it is for that body, and not this Court, to correct its mistake.

[3]   The Second Circuit's version of the family resemblance test provided that only notes *with a term of more than nine months* are presumed to be "securities." No presumption of any kind attached to notes of less than nine months' duration. The Second Circuit's refusal to extend the presumption to all notes was apparently founded on its interpretation of the statutory exception for notes with a maturity of nine months or less. Because we do not reach the question of how to interpret that exception, we likewise express no view on how that exception might affect the presumption that a note is a "security."

nonetheless fall without the "security" category[:] types of notes that are not "securities" include "the note delivered in consumer financing, the note secured by a mortgage on a home, the short-term note secured by a lien on a small business or some of its assets, the note evidencing a 'character' loan to a bank customer, short-term notes secured by an assignment of accounts receivable, or a note which simply formalizes an open-account debt incurred in the ordinary course of business (particularly if, as in the case of the customer of a broker, it is collateralized)") [and] "notes evidencing loans by commercial banks for current operations".

We agree that the items identified by the Second Circuit are not properly viewed as "securities." More guidance, though, is needed. It is impossible to make any meaningful inquiry into whether an instrument bears a "resemblance" to one of the instruments identified by the Second Circuit without specifying what it is about those instruments that makes *them* non-"securities." Moreover, as the Second Circuit itself has noted, its list is "not graven in stone," and is therefore capable of expansion. Thus, some standards must be developed for determining when an item should be added to the list.

An examination of the list itself makes clear what those standards should be. In creating its list, the Second Circuit was applying the same factors that this Court has held apply in deciding whether a transaction involves a "security." First, we examine the transaction to assess the motivations that would prompt a reasonable seller and buyer to enter into it. If the seller's purpose is to raise money for the general use of a business enterprise or to finance substantial investments and the buyer is interested primarily in the profit the note is expected to generate, the instrument is likely to be a "security." If the note is exchanged to facilitate the purchase and sale of a minor asset or consumer good, to correct for the seller's cash-flow difficulties, or to advance some other commercial or consumer purpose, on the other hand, the note is less sensibly described as a "security." Second, we examine the "plan of distribution" of the instrument to determine whether it is an instrument in which there is "common trading for speculation or investment." Third, we examine the reasonable expectations of the investing public: The Court will consider instruments to be "securities" on the basis of such public expectations, even where an economic analysis of the circumstances of the particular transaction might suggest that the instruments are not "securities" as used in that transaction. Finally, we examine whether some factor such as the existence of another regulatory scheme significantly reduces the risk of the instrument, thereby rendering application of the Securities Acts unnecessary.

We conclude, then, that in determining whether an instrument denominated a "note" is a "security," courts are to apply the version of the "family resemblance" test that we have articulated here: A note is presumed to be a "security," and that presumption may be rebutted only by a showing that the note bears a strong resemblance (in terms of the four factors we have identified) to one of the enumerated categories of instrument. If an instrument is not sufficiently similar to an item on the list, the decision whether another category should be added is to be made by examining the same factors.

B

Applying the family resemblance approach to this case, we have little difficulty in concluding that the notes at issue here are "securities." Ernst & Young admits that "a demand note does not closely resemble any of the Second Circuit's family resemblance examples." Nor does an examination of the four factors we have identified as being relevant to our inquiry suggest that the demand notes here are not "securities" despite their lack of similarity to any of the enumerated categories. The Co-Op sold the notes in an effort to raise capital for its general business operations, and purchasers bought them in order to earn a profit in the form of interest.[4] Indeed, one of the primary inducements offered purchasers was an interest rate constantly revised to keep it slightly above the rate paid by local banks and savings and loans. From both sides, then, the transaction is most naturally conceived as an investment in a business enterprise rather than as a purely commercial or consumer transaction.

As to the plan of distribution, the Co-Op offered the notes over an extended period to its 23,000 members, as well as to nonmembers, and more than 1,600 people held notes when the Co-Op filed for bankruptcy. To be sure, the notes were not traded on an exchange. They were, however, offered and sold to a broad segment of the public, and that is all we have held to be necessary to establish the requisite "common trading" in an instrument.

The third factor—the public's reasonable perceptions—also supports a finding that the notes in this case are "securities." We have consistently identified the fundamental essence of a "security" to be its character as an "investment." The advertisements for the notes here characterized them as "investments," and there were no countervailing factors that would have led a reasonable person to question this characterization. In these circumstances, it would be reasonable for a prospective purchaser to take the Co-Op at its word.

Finally, we find no risk-reducing factor to suggest that these instruments are not in fact securities. The notes are uncollateralized and uninsured. Moreover, . . . the notes here would escape federal regulation entirely if the Acts were held not to apply.

The court below found that "[t]he demand nature of the notes is very uncharacteristic of a security," on the theory that the virtually instant liquidity associated with demand notes is inconsistent with the risk ordinarily associated with "securities." This argument is unpersuasive. Common stock traded on a national exchange is the paradigm of a security, and it is as readily convertible into cash as is a demand note. The same is true of publicly traded corporate bonds, debentures, and any number of other instruments that are plainly within the purview of the Acts. The demand feature of a note does permit a holder to eliminate risk quickly by making a demand, but just as with publicly traded stock, the liquidity of the instrument does not eliminate risk altogether. Indeed, publicly traded stock is even more readily liquid than are demand notes, in that a demand only eliminates risk when, and if, payment is made, whereas the sale of a share of stock

---

4   We emphasize that by "profit" in the context of notes, we mean "a valuable return on an investment," which undoubtedly includes interest. . . .

through a national exchange and the receipt of the proceeds usually occur simultaneously.

We therefore hold that the notes at issue here are within the term "note" in § 3(a)(10).

III — Short-term note exception does not apply

Relying on the exception in the statute for "any note . . . which has a maturity at the time of issuance of not exceeding nine months," § 3(a)(10), respondent contends that the notes here are not "securities," even if they would otherwise qualify. Respondent cites Arkansas cases standing for the proposition that, in the context of the state statute of limitations, "[a] note payable on demand is due immediately." Respondent concludes from this rule that the "maturity" of a demand note within the meaning of § 3(a)(10) is immediate, which is, of course, less than nine months. Respondent therefore contends that the notes fall within the plain words of the exclusion and are thus not "securities."

Petitioners counter that the "plain words" of the exclusion should not govern. Petitioners cite the legislative history of a similar provision of the 1933 Act, § 3(a)(3), for the proposition that the purpose of the exclusion is to except from the coverage of the Acts only commercial paper—short-term, high quality instruments issued to fund current operations and sold only to highly sophisticated investors. Petitioners also emphasize that this Court has repeatedly held that the plain words of the definition of a "security" are not dispositive, and that we consider the economic reality of the transaction to determine whether Congress intended the Securities Acts to apply. Petitioners therefore argue, with some force, that reading the exception for short-term notes to exclude from the Acts' coverage investment notes of less than nine months' duration would be inconsistent with Congress' evident desire to permit the SEC and the courts flexibility to ensure that the Acts are not manipulated to investors' detriment. If petitioners are correct that the exclusion is intended to cover only commercial paper, these notes, which were sold in a large scale offering to unsophisticated members of the public, plainly should not fall within the exclusion.

We need not decide, however, whether petitioners' interpretation of the exception is correct, for we conclude that even if we give literal effect to the exception, the notes do not fall within its terms.

Respondent's contention that the demand notes fall within the "plain words" of the statute rests entirely upon the premise that Arkansas' statute of limitations for suits to collect demand notes is determinative of the "maturity" of the notes, as that term is used in the federal Securities Acts. The "maturity" of the notes, however, is a question of federal law. To regard States' statutes of limitations law as controlling the scope of the Securities Acts would be to hold that a particular instrument is a "security" under the 1934 Act in some States, but that the same instrument is not a "security" in others. We are unpersuaded that Congress intended the Securities Acts to apply differently to the same transactions depending on the accident of which State's law happens to apply.

* * *

Neither the law of Arkansas nor that of any other State provides an answer to the federal question, and as a matter of federal law, the words of the statute are far from "plain" with regard to whether demand notes fall within the exclusion. If it is plausible to regard a demand note as having an immediate maturity because demand could be made immediately, it is also plausible to regard the maturity of a demand note as being in excess of nine months because demand could be made many years or decades into the future. Given this ambiguity, the exclusion must be interpreted in accordance with its purpose. As we have said, we will assume for argument's sake that petitioners are incorrect in their view that the exclusion is intended to exempt only commercial paper. Respondent presents no competing view to explain why Congress would have enacted respondent's version of the exclusion, however, and the only theory that we can imagine that would support respondent's interpretation is that Congress intended to create a bright-line rule exempting from the 1934 Act's coverage all notes of less than nine months' duration, because short-term notes are, as a general rule, sufficiently safe that the Securities Acts need not apply. As we have said, however, demand notes do not necessarily have short terms. In light of Congress' broader purpose in the Acts of ensuring that investments of all descriptions be regulated to prevent fraud and abuse, we interpret the exception not to cover the demand notes at issue here. Although the result might be different if the design of the transaction suggested that both parties contemplated that demand would be made within the statutory period, that is not the case before us.

IV

For the foregoing reasons, we conclude that the demand notes at issue here fall under the "note" category of instruments that are "securities" under the 1933 and 1934 Acts. We also conclude that, even under respondent's preferred approach to § 3(a)(10)'s exclusion for short-term notes, these demand notes do not fall within the exclusion. . . .

■ REHNQUIST, C.J. with whom WHITE, O'CONNOR, and SCALIA, join, concurring in part and dissenting in part.

I join Part II of the Court's opinion, but dissent from Part III and the statements of the Court's judgment in Parts I and IV. In Part III, the Court holds that these notes were not covered by the statutory exemption for "any note . . . which has a maturity at the time of issuance of not exceeding nine months." Treating demand notes as if they were a recent development in the law of negotiable instruments, the Court says "if it is plausible to regard a demand note as having an immediate maturity because demand could be made immediately, it is also plausible to regard the maturity of a demand note as being in excess of nine months because demand could be made many years or decades into the future. Given this ambiguity, the exclusion must be interpreted in accordance with its purpose."

But the terms "note" and "maturity" did not spring full blown from the head of Congress in 1934. Neither are demand notes of recent vintage. "Note" and "maturity" have been terms of art in the legal profession for centuries, and a body of law concerning the characteristics of demand notes, including their maturity, was in existence at the time Congress passed the 1934 Act.

In construing any terms whose meanings are less than plain, we depend on the common understanding of those terms at the time of the statute's creation. Contemporaneous editions of legal dictionaries defined "maturity" as "[t]he time when a . . . note becomes due." Pursuant to the dominant consensus in the case law, instruments payable on demand were considered immediately "due" such that an action could be brought at any time without any other demand than the suit. . . .

Petitioners . . . rely, virtually exclusively, on the legislative history of § 3(a)(3) of the 1933 Act for the proposition that the term "any note" in the exemption in § 3(a)(10) of the 1934 Act encompass only notes having the character of short-term "commercial paper" exchanged among sophisticated traders. I am not altogether convinced that the legislative history of § 3(a)(3) supports that interpretation even with respect to the term "any note" in the exemption in § 3(a)(3), and to bodily transpose that legislative history to another statute has little to commend it as a method of statutory construction.

The legislative history of the 1934 Act—under which this case arises—contains nothing which would support a restrictive reading of the exemption in question. . . . Although I do not doubt that both the 1933 and 1934 Act exemptions encompass short-term commercial paper, the expansive language in the statutory provisions is strong evidence that, in the end, Congress meant for commercial paper merely to be a subset of a larger class of exempted short-term instruments.

The plausibility of imputing a restrictive reading to § 3(a)(10) from the legislative history of § 3(a)(3) is further weakened by the imperfect analogy between the two provisions in terms of both phraseology and nature. Section 3(a)(10) lacks the cryptic phrase in § 3(a)(3) which qualifies the class of instruments eligible for exemption as those arising "out of . . . current transaction[s] or the proceeds of which have been or are to be used for current transactions. . . ." While that passage somehow may strengthen an argument for limiting the exemption in § 3(a)(3) to commercial paper, its absence in § 3(a)(10) conversely militates against placing the same limitation thereon.

The exemption in § 3(a)(3) excepts the short-term instruments it covers solely from the registration requirements of the 1933 Act. The same instruments are not exempted from the 1933 Act's antifraud provisions. By contrast, the exemption in § 3(a)(10) of the 1934 Act exempts instruments encompassed thereunder from the entirety of the coverage of the 1934 Act including, conspicuously, the Act's antifraud provisions.

* * *

In sum, there is no justification for looking beyond the plain terms of § 3(a)(10), save for ascertaining the meaning of "maturity" with respect to demand notes. That inquiry reveals that the Co-Op's demand notes come within the purview of the section's exemption for short-term securities. . . .

NOTES

1. *The "family resemblance" test.* In contrast to the *Howey* test, the *Reves* "family resemblance" test for notes is a multi-factor balancing test, so an instrument need not satisfy each of the factors to be deemed a security. The open-ended nature of the test means that claims based on novel debt instruments will be difficult to resolve as a matter of law. In addition, counsel advising clients will not be able to offer as much certainty as their clients might like.

QUESTIONS

1. Do you agree with the Court that stocks are a "special case"? Are notes a "special case"?

2. What is the difference between the *Howey* and *Reves* tests?

3. Are the Coop Demand notes investment contracts under *Howey*? Why not just use *Howey* to determine whether a note is a security?

4. Why are loans made for commercial rather than general business purposes not securities?

5. Under the majority's interpretation, would a note payable in six months, renewable at the discretion of the creditor for an additional twelve months, be a security?

HYPOTHETICAL EIGHT

The Soup Kitchen has devised another scheme to raise capital to finance its growth. George, the Chief Tasting Officer, has identified a group of ten insurance companies interested in lending money to The Soup Kitchen. The consortium agrees to lend $100 million to open new Soup Kitchen lunch counters. The loan will be repaid over a ten-year term and will be secured by a mortgage on the new outlets. The interest rate is floating at prime + 5%. The loan agreement explicitly authorizes the insurance companies to transfer their interests in the loan agreement to other institutional investors. (The insurance companies may need to do this if they face liquidity problems arising from a greater-than-expected level of claims, e.g., a hurricane.) Finally, the loan agreement gives the insurance companies an option to purchase stock in The Soup Kitchen at a fixed price after the first five years of the term of the loan in exchange for a reduction in the interest rate. Is the loan agreement a security?

V. SECURITIZATION

Determining when instruments not traditionally considered securities should be deemed securities is important to stop opportunistic promoters from avoiding the application of the securities laws. Determining what is a security is also an important consideration for securitization transactions. Securitization involves the pooling of non-liquid assets and the sale of interests in the returns from this pool.

Common assets used in securitization transactions include home mortgages (including sub-prime loans), student loans, and credit card receivables. The typical securitization transaction takes the following form. An entity, often a financial institution and referred to as the 'originator,' will aggregate a large number of non-liquid assets (such as home mortgages) and sell these assets to a special purpose vehicle (SPV). The SPV will then sell interests in the stream of money from the pool (as, for example, home owners pay the interest on their home mortgages). The interests will be structured as interests directly in the profits from the pool or, alternatively, debt secured by the assets in the pool (in which case they are termed "asset-backed securities"). The interest on the asset-backed debt is paid from cash flows generated from the pool. The SPV will use the proceeds from the sale of interests in the pool or asset-backed securities to fund the initial purchase of the underlying pooled assets from the originator.

If a securitization transaction results in the issuance of interests directly in the return from a pool (such as in *Mutual Benefits* above), the *Howey* test applies to determine whether the pool interests are investment contracts. Typically investors with interests in a securitization pool stand in horizontal commonality with respect to their returns and are investing money with the expectation of profit. The more difficult issue under the *Howey* test is whether the investor's returns are solely through the efforts of others. If the investment return is not due to the originator's entrepreneurial efforts but instead to some outside factor, courts may view the solely through the efforts of others prong as lacking and conclude that the securitization interests are not securities. *Mutual Benefits*, however, suggests that the selection of the assets going into the pool will be considered an essential entrepreneurial effort.

In contrast, the question of what is a security has a clearer answer if the securitization results in the issuance of debt securities backed by the assets of the securitization pool (an asset-backed security). Asset-backed securities almost always meet the *Reves* test. First, investors in asset-backed securities do so to obtain an investment return (through the interest they receive from the securities). The SPV issuing the securities does so to raise capital to purchase the underlying pool assets. Second, the plan of distribution for asset-backed securities is often broad. Asset-backed securities are identical to one another and typically issued to large numbers of investors through an investment bank. Third, while somewhat circular, one can argue that most investors expect that the securities laws apply to asset-backed securities, particularly securitization deals sold through investment banks and marketed to investors as passive investments. Finally, there is no other regulatory scheme focused on asset-backed securities that significantly reduces the risk of such securities in a way to make the federal securities laws unnecessary.

The SEC has issued special regulations to address the application of the securities laws for asset-backed securities. In 2005, the SEC promulgated Regulation AB. Among other things, Regulation AB requires increased disclosure for asset-backed securities. We discuss these disclosure requirements in Chapter 7.

Prior to selling asset-backed securities, the SPV may structure the security to enhance its creditworthiness. Credit enhancement activities include providing additional cash collateral to the SPV, a third party guarantee for the SPV-issued debt securities (the guarantee may itself be a security under the securities laws), and dividing the SPV issued securities into different classes (such as senior and junior debt securities—leading to a higher rating for the senior securities). The originator will typically structure the SPV to ensure that the SPV's assets cannot be used to satisfy the originator's creditors if the originator becomes insolvent, known as making the SPV "bankruptcy-remote." All of this is done to raise the credit rating of the SPV, which will be obtained from a credit rating such as Moody's or Standard and Poor's. (We discuss the role of credit rating agencies in Chapter 12.) The higher the credit rating, the more investors will be willing to pay for interests in the SPV.

Securitization makes assets more saleable. Although the future interest payments from a specific home mortgage may be uncertain, the return from a large pool of similar home mortgages is much easier to quantify. Liquidity also plays a role in securitization transactions. The underlying securitized assets standing alone are illiquid. Through a securitization transaction, the holder of such illiquid assets (such as a bank selling a home mortgage through a financial institution originator) can convert the assets into cash. The bank may then turn around and lend the cash to finance even more home mortgages.

Securitization is a powerful financial tool, but the Financial Crisis of 2007–2008 revealed that it can also be a dangerous one. The chief attraction of securitization is the diversification it provides by pooling many steams of income into one package. That diversification, however, has its limits; if risks affect an asset class as a whole, securities previously thought to be safe investments may turn out to be substantially more volatile than expected. This is exactly what happened in the subprime mortgage market in 2007–2008, with disastrous consequences.

Leading up to the Financial Crisis, commercial banks took large positions in collateralized-debt obligations (CDOs) and mortgage-backed securities. CDOs are a type of structured asset-backed security that are backed by a portfolio of bonds, loans, and other assets (including mortgage-backed securities). Many hedge funds and investment banks also took large positions in CDOs and mortgage-backed securities, often using substantial leverage to finance these positions. The correlated positions of banks and hedge funds in CDOs and mortgage-backed securities created systemic risk. Any drop in the value of the underlying subprime mortgage assets had the potential of triggering margin calls for hedge funds, for example. Hedge funds, in turn, would then face pressure to liquidate their mortgage-related assets (to pay off their short-term liabilities), further depressing the price of the assets. Banks would similarly face pressure to liquidate their CDOs and mortgage-backed securities to satisfy their short-term liabilities and meet their regulatory capital requirements, further depressing the price of such assets. The declining value of CDOs and mortgage-backed securities would then further exacerbate the pressure to sell on hedge funds and banks, creating a downward spiral in the market for CDOs and mortgage-backed securities (and potentially freezing the overall credit markets).

The systemic risk in the mortgage-backed securities markets was further exacerbated by market transactions involving a particular type of derivative instrument known as a credit default swaps. A credit default swap allows two parties to exchange the risk of default of a chosen underlying instrument—for example a home mortgage or pool of home mortgages. One party agrees to pay the principal amount in the case a home mortgage defaults. The counterparty agrees to pay a stream of payments in return for the promise to receive the principal amount in case of a default. Normally, a credit default swap serves an important risk hedging function, allowing one party, that does not want to be exposed to the risk of a credit default, to shift that risk to another party who is in a better position to bear that risk. Credit default swaps serve essentially an insurance function.

In addition to using credit default swaps to hedge risks, individual speculators (primarily hedge funds) used such instruments to profit from the potential default of CDOs and mortgage-backed securities based on subprime mortgages. Once speculators realized that CDOs and mortgage-backed securities were at a high risk of default, these speculators purchased large amounts of credit default swaps from various financial institutions including Bear Stearns and American International Group, Inc. Such swaps allowed the speculators to profit from the default of such mortgage-backed securities. In addition, synthetic CDOs created solely using credit default swap derivatives and mimicking the return of an actual CDO security were an important factor in the market. Through a synthetic CDO, investors who wanted exposure to the risk and return from holding mortgage-backed CDOs could do so even when actual mortgage backed securities and CDOs were in short supply, multiplying the overall exposure in the market to a drop in CDO valuation.

Once the mounting risks behind subprime mortgages became more apparent in 2007–2008, the web of credit default swaps started to unravel. If a large counterparty were to go bankrupt, the credit default swap obligations of the counterparty would potentially become worthless. Such obligations totaled in the trillions of U.S. dollars. This would harm not only the speculators who hoped for a payment from the credit default swaps but also those institutions—including commercial and investment banks—that took out credit default swaps to hedge against holding subprime mortgage-backed securities on their balance sheets. These banks and other institutions would no longer have a hedge for the value of their mortgage-backed securities, forcing them to write down the value (under mark-to-market accounting) of these securities—leading many of these banks and institutions themselves potentially to become insolvent, thereby spreading the crisis (or what some refer to as the "contagion").

Congress responded to this meltdown during the Financial Crisis with the Dodd-Frank Act of 2010. One of the principal goals of that law is to discourage the "systemic risk" posed by the large financial institutions that typically serve as sponsors of the SPVs that issue asset-backed securities. The Dodd-Frank Act attempts to bolster the quality of the assets going into asset-backed securities by requiring "securitizers" to retain 5% of the interests created. Dodd-Frank Act § 941. The notion here is that the ability to shift risks to outside investors led to lax screening of the credit worthiness of the assets that went into asset-backed securities. By requiring originators and issuers of asset-backed securities to retain some "skin in the game," Congress hoped to foster better screening of credit risks. Certain high quality, "qualified residential mortgages" are exempted from the requirement.

Addressing the important role of derivative transactions in exacerbating the magnitude of the systemic risk associated with CDO and synthetic CDO bonds, the Dodd-Frank Act gives the SEC (together with the CFTC) regulatory authority for over-the-counter derivatives, imposing both recordkeeping and recording requirements for OTC derivative transactions and requiring that most trades involving over-the-counter derivatives—as determined by the SEC and CFTC—go through a central clearinghouse and be exchange-traded. Unlike in a derivatives transaction between two counterparties, transactions that occur through a clearinghouse shift the risk of one counterparty defaulting on its obligations under the derivatives contract away from the other counterparty and to the clearinghouse. The clearinghouse can mitigate this risk by requiring the posting of collateral and the "netting" of positions across multiple parties (e.g., if Goldman owes the clearinghouse $1,000 on one transaction and the clearinghouse owes Goldman $900 on another transaction—netting treats Goldman as owing the clearinghouse only $100 reducing the clearinghouse's exposure). Clearinghouses also assist in centralizing trade reporting, increasing transparency for such trades and providing information on the trades for the new Financial Stability Oversight Council (discussed in Chapter 1).

CHAPTER 4

DISCLOSURE AND ACCURACY

Rules and Statutes

—*Sections 12(a), 12(b), 12(g)(1), 12(g)(4), 12(g)(5), 12(j), 12(k), 13(a), 13(b), 15(d), and 21(a) of the Exchange Act*

—*Rules 10b–5, 12b–20, 12g–1, 12g–4, 12g5–1, 12h–3, 12h–6, 13a–1, 13a–11, 13a–13, 13a–14, 13a–15, 13b2–1, 13b2–2, 14a–3, 14a–9, 15d–14 of the Exchange Act*

—*Regulation FD, Regulation G, Regulation S–K*

—*Forms 8–K, 10, 10–K, 10–Q, 20–F*

—*Sarbanes-Oxley Act, Sections 304, 404, 408*

MOTIVATING HYPOTHETICAL

Michael is the founder and chief executive officer of Scranton Paper, a paper products company based in Pittsburgh. Scranton Paper is a public company with common stock trading on Nasdaq since Scranton Paper's IPO eight years ago. Those eight years have seen steady growth for Scranton Paper as it established its brand. Scranton Paper's stock price has risen accordingly; it now has approximately 5,000 shareholders and a market capitalization of $500 million. This period of steady growth for the company has required that all of the firm's profits be ploughed back into the company to finance its expansion. Michael is ready to cash in his controlling block of shares. Building the company has left him exhausted and he is ready to take a couple years off to work on his friend's beet farm. Besides, Scranton Paper really needs to affiliate itself with a major office supplies company to access the national and international distribution channels necessary to sustain Scranton Paper's growth. Michael thinks the best way for him to sell his shares and for Scranton Paper to find a distribution partner is to sell the company to one of the major office supplies companies. Michael is anxious, however, to get as much as possible for his shares just in case he decides he likes life farming beets.

I. MANDATORY DISCLOSURE AND ACCURACY

Recall from Chapter 1 the arguments for mandatory disclosure: (1) it facilitates comparable disclosures by different companies; (2) it helps reduce agency costs within the firm; (3) it helps overcome an externality problem for firms disclosing information; and (4) it reduces duplicative research by professional investors and analysts. These arguments suggest that mandatory disclosure may be necessary to bring disclosure to its socially optimal level. Congress adopted mandatory disclosure for companies with securities listed on a national securities exchange as part of the Exchange Act in 1934. Congress's chief aim was to combat what it saw as abuses by insiders in the decade leading up to the market crash of October 1929. In 1964, Congress extended mandatory disclosure to certain companies traded in the over-the-counter market.

For disclosure to be "mandatory," someone must decide what information needs to be disclosed. Congress, of course, has the power to mandate disclosures, and in some cases has exercised that power quite specifically. A recent (and controversial) example is a mandate that public companies disclose if they use certain minerals mined in the Democratic Republic of Congo in their products. If the minerals come from DRC, Congress also mandated that the companies disclose whether or not those minerals can be certified as "conflict free," i.e. not being used to fund armed groups involved in the civil war in the region. This mandate has proved quite expensive to public companies to implement, and was ultimately struck down (in part), as unconstitutional. *National Ass'n of Manufacturers v. SEC*, 748 F.3d 359 (D.C. Cir. 2014).*

In most cases, however, Congress has left the determination of disclosure mandates to the SEC. The SEC's authority over disclosure is one source of potential weakness of mandatory disclosure. Just as one can have doubts that markets will produce the optimal level of disclosure, one can doubt the ability of the SEC to hit that optimal level. The SEC tends to see disclosure as the solution for every ailment that plagues the corporate world. Every scandal is met with a new disclosure requirement; seldom does the SEC discard outdated disclosure requirements. For example, amidst considerable political fretting over "excessive" salaries in the early 1990s, the SEC required more extensive disclosure of the salaries of the top five executives of each publicly-held company. Rather than a decline in salaries, the increased disclosure correlated with an upward spiral in executive compensation as compensation consultants have pushed boards to hire above average executives at above average salaries. The result has been a "Lake Woebegone" effect, with all executives wanting to be paid at above the average scale. But the SEC was seen as "doing something." As you read the materials below, consider whether you regard mandatory disclosure as socially useful or just "doing something" about the crisis du jour.

The mandatory disclosure requirements of the Exchange Act are triggered when a firm becomes a "public company." We begin the chapter by answering the question, "What is a public company?" We turn then to these questions: When must a public company disclose? What must be disclosed

Making disclosure mandatory is one thing; making it truthful is quite another. Disclosure will do investors little good if it does not reflect reality. The agency cost problems that interfere with voluntary disclosure, however, may also lead managers to be less than truthful with mandatory disclosure. In response to that concern, the Exchange Act provides a wide variety of measures to promote accuracy by enhancing firms' corporate governance and internal controls, topics that we cover in Chapter 12.

Companies make numerous disclosures. Although many disclosures are required, companies also release information voluntarily. Public companies issue press releases and hold routine conference calls with investors and analysts. Should regulators worry about companies that disclose more information than required? What if a company discloses

---

*   As this edition went to press, that ruling had been called for rehearing (Nov.18, 2014).

information only selectively to favored investors or analysts? One fear is that an analyst may hesitate to give a company a negative rating in order to maintain the analyst's access to selective disclosures. We address the SEC's response to selective disclosure at the end of the chapter.

II. WHAT IS A "PUBLIC COMPANY?"

The overwhelming majority of companies in the United States are "private" companies. Private companies' shares are closely held by their managers and a small circle of friends and family. These investments are based, in large part, on the investors' trust in the character of the managers. That trust is based on long-standing personal relationships. Trust of this sort will be harder for firms to come by if their capital needs require them to cast a wider net in search of investors. When the firm is first seeking outside equity investment, it is likely to come from a relatively small number of venture capitalists who will subject the firm and its managers to a thorough vetting before investing. The venture capitalists will also insist on carefully detailed contracts that give them substantial control over the enterprise during this growth period.

Personal relationships and contractual protections are not a practical means of reassuring investors in a more broadly-held enterprise. The individual investor—one of perhaps thousands of investors—faces a daunting collective action problem in holding managers accountable. State corporate law helps answer the problem of creating the trust necessary to encourage investment by establishing a board of directors to protect shareholder interests and imposing an array of fiduciary duties that directors and managers owe to shareholders. But even with the mechanism of the derivative suit under corporate law to help ameliorate the collective action problem in enforcing these duties, the individual shareholder still faces a problem of information asymmetry. She simply may not have the information needed to assess whether the managers and directors are living up to the standards imposed on them by state corporate law. The cost of negotiating with management to obtain such information likely outweighs the increase in value of the shares in the individual shareholder's possession, even when the benefit to all the outstanding shares exceeds such costs. A primary purpose of the federal securities laws is to provide this information to investors in companies with broadly dispersed ownership.

A. PUBLIC COMPANY STATUS

Congress first defined the concept of "public" companies rather narrowly. Section 12(a), part of the original Exchange Act as it was adopted in 1934, prohibits broker-dealers from effecting transactions over a national securities exchange "unless a registration is effective" for that security. To accommodate constitutional concerns of the New Deal era, Congress (with a few minor exceptions) did not extend the prohibition to transactions not involving a broker-dealer. The process for registration is set forth in § 12(b) and the SEC has provided Form 10 as the basic form for registration. (Form 20–F is for foreign private issuers.)

Congress broadened the category of public companies in 1936 when it added § 15(d). That section requires companies registering securities for a sale in a public offering under the Securities Act to comply after the effective registration date of the offering with the periodic disclosure requirements of the Exchange Act at least until the next fiscal year after the effective date. Section 15(d) registrants are not required, however, to comply with the Exchange Act's requirements for proxy solicitations and tender offers under § 14, nor are their insiders subject to the reporting of stock trades and short-swing profits rules imposed by § 16 (covered in Chapter 6).

The next big expansion came in 1964, when Congress adopted § 12(g) of the Exchange Act. The constitutional concerns of the New Deal were by that time of purely historical interest. Section 12(g) accordingly omits any reliance on broker-dealers as a jurisdictional hook. Instead, it requires all issuers having a nexus to interstate commerce to register with the SEC if they have more than a threshold level of assets and a threshold number of holders of their equity securities. This provision roped in many companies whose stock traded widely in the over-the-counter market but which had not listed on a national securities exchange or completed a public offering under the Securities Act. Thus, the 1964 amendment closed a loophole strongly disliked by both the exchanges and the SEC. The thresholds set by § 12(g)(1)(A), as modified by the Jumpstart Our Business Startups Act of 2012 (JOBS Act), are set at (1) $10 million in total assets and (2) either 2,000 shareholders of record for a class of equity security, or 500 shareholders of record for a class of equity who are not accredited investors. Accredited investors include, among others, certain institutions meeting minimum total asset requirements. Natural persons with a high income ($200,000 individually or $300,000 with a spouse) or high net worth ($1 million excluding a person's primary residence) may qualify as an accredited investor. We cover the concept of accredited investors in Chapter 9. Section 12(g)(1)(B) establishes a separate public company threshold for banks and bank holding companies based on total assets exceeding a threshold of $10 million in total assets and the number of shareholders of record of a class of equity securities exceeding 2,000 persons.

The minimum levels set by § 12(g)(1) are measured as of the last day of the issuer's fiscal year, so companies wishing to avoid the status of being a public company may seek to sell assets or buy out some of their shareholders in order to avoid triggering § 12(g). (Combining the holdings of multiple owners in a trust or similar vehicle will not work—Rule 12g5–1(b)(3) directs issuers to count beneficial, rather than legal, owners, if the form of ownership is being used to circumvent the registration requirements.) Prior to the JOBS Act, private companies had to worry about stock options given to employees as compensation. If the number of employees receiving options grew too large, the company might find itself "going public" before it is ready to do an IPO. This occasionally created a problem for companies in the high-tech sector that are heavily dependent upon option-based compensation. In addition to establishing the threshold number of shareholders for public company status at 2,000 (or 500 non-accredited investors for non-bank and non-bank holding companies), the JOBS Act modified § 12(g)(5) to specify that shares "held of record" does not include securities held by persons "who received the securities pursuant to an employee compensation plan" in an exempt transaction. The exclusion in § 12(g)(5) obviates the need for private companies to worry about shares given to employees as part of an employee compensation plan. For those companies anxious to expose themselves to SEC requirements (a very small set, indeed, but Nasdaq now requires reporting status for issuers wishing to be quoted even in its lowest tier "Bulletin Board"), § 12(g) allows companies to register voluntarily even if the statutory minimums are not satisfied.

Section 12(g) sweeps in companies not listed on a national securities exchange into public company status. The most important of these companies used to trade on Nasdaq. Nasdaq originally was an over-the-counter market rather than an exchange. In August 2006, however, Nasdaq was approved as a national securities exchange for Nasdaq-listed securities. As part of the transition, Nasdaq and FINRA became self-regulatory organizations. Because of Nasdaq's shift to become a national securities exchange, Nasdaq-listed companies now must register under § 12(b) of the Exchange Act, leading to public company status without reference to the § 12(g) standards for public company status. Today, over-the-counter trading is limited to the Over the Counter Bulletin Board (OTCBB) and the "pink sheets," now known as OTC Link.

B. ESCAPING PUBLIC COMPANY STATUS

Many companies seek to avoid the exposure and expense of public status, i.e., "going dark," but that path is not an easy one. A company seeking to go dark must negate all three public company triggers: first, the company must delist if they are listed on a national securities exchange; second, the company must ensure they are not a public company under § 12(g); and third, if the company has filed a prior effective registration statement with the SEC (as part of a public offering), the company must meet the requirements of § 15(d) to suspend public company status.

To understand the difficulty of going dark, consider Scranton Paper. To avoid status as a public company, Scranton Paper would first need to delist from the Nasdaq, a national securities exchange, incurring a substantial drop in liquidity. Delisting, however, is not sufficient to avoid public company status. Scranton Paper still is a public company pursuant to § 12(g) due to its substantial assets and dispersed group of shareholders. Under Rule 12g–4, an issuer may terminate registration as a public company only if it certifies to the SEC that it has fewer than 300 shareholders of record (with termination taking effect 90 days after the certification unless the SEC specifies a shorter period). Alternatively, the issuer may show that it has fewer than 500 shareholders and less than $10 million in total assets on the last day of each of its prior three fiscal years. For a company such as Scranton Paper, with thousands of shareholders of record, reducing that number below the requisite minimum is simply not feasible. Scranton Paper can only avoid public company status through a "going private transaction" under which Scranton Paper buys back a considerable portion of its publicly-held shares, which would be an overwhelming expense. The JOBS Act modified § 12(g)(4), under which Rule 12g–4 is promulgated, to specify that banks and bank holding companies only need to reduce the number of shareholders of record for a class of equity securities below 1,200 to terminate registration under § 12(g), but no relief was provided to other companies seeking to avoid public company status.

Finally, if Scranton Paper has filed an effective registration statement with the SEC, Scranton Paper must seek to suspend public company status pursuant to § 15(d). Section 15(d) provides that issuers may suspend their public company status if they show at the beginning of a fiscal year that the company has fewer than 300 holders of record (except for the fiscal year during which the registered public offering became effective). Unlike under Rule 12g–4, § 15(d) does not provide suspension for those issuers that reduce the number of shareholders to below 500 and total assets below $10 million. The JOBS Act modified § 15(d) to specify that banks and bank holding companies only need to reduce the number of shareholders of record for a class of equity securities below 1,200 to suspend reporting under § 15(d). Note that the suspension from § 15(d) is not permanent. Instead, at the beginning of any fiscal year in which the issuer has 300 or more holders of record, the issuer once again becomes a public reporting company under § 15(d).

For foreign issuers seeking to escape the U.S. securities regime, the inability to terminate completely their public company status under § 15(d) proved problematic. Suspension for foreign private issuers from § 15(d) used to require the issuer to demonstrate that it had fewer than 300 U.S. resident holders of record at the beginning of a particular fiscal year. Once suspended, however, the issuer would have to keep track of the number of its U.S. resident investors indefinitely. Any increase to 300 or more U.S. resident investors would trigger the § 15(d) reporting duties again.

In 2007, the SEC promulgated Rule 12h–6 of the Exchange Act to provide certainty to foreign issuers seeking to terminate their relationship with the U.S. securities laws. Rule 12h–6 allows a foreign private issuer of equity securities to terminate its public company reporting obligations under § 13(a) or § 15(d) of the Exchange Act provided certain conditions are met. Among other requirements, Rule 12h–6 bases termination on a quantitative benchmark of the level of U.S. market interest in the equity securities of a foreign private issuer. The quantitative benchmark turns on the average daily trading volume of a foreign private issuer's equity securities in the United States compared with the issuer's worldwide average daily trading volume. If less than 5% of the trading volume takes place in the United States, the foreign private issuer is eligible to terminate public company status pursuant to Rule 12h–6 regardless of the number of shareholders holding the issuer's equity. As an alternative quantitative benchmark, the foreign private issuer may demonstrate that the number of shareholders of its equity is either less than 300 persons on a worldwide basis or 300 persons resident in the United States.

C. TRADING IN THE STOCK OF PRIVATE COMPANIES

The distinction between public and private companies presents a critical threshold for regulatory requirements. Public companies, as we will see, face a number of mandatory disclosure requirements among other regulatory obligations. The conventional wisdom justifying this division is that private companies are closely held and do not face the same collective action problems investors of public companies face in obtaining information and holding corporate managers accountable. But is this conventional wisdom still valid?

A growing phenomenon in the United States capital markets is the rise of trading in the stock of private companies. In early 2011, for example, Goldman Sachs announced its intention to invest $450 million of its own money into Facebook, a private company (at the time) operating a "social media" Internet site. Goldman Sachs also planned to give its clients an opportunity to invest in Facebook. Aside from the securities laws governing private placements and resales of restricted securities (covered in Chapters 9 and 10), Goldman Sachs and Facebook had to contend with the possibility that the additional investors would cause Facebook to become a public company under § 12(g).

In part a response to the concerns about public company status, Goldman Sachs suggested a particular structure to facilitate investment by its clients into Facebook indirectly. Goldman Sachs proposed establishing a special-purpose vehicle (SPV) to invest in Facebook. Under Goldman's plan, clients would purchase interests in the SPV. The SPV would then aggregate the clients' money and purchase Facebook shares with the SPV as the legal owner of the shares. Section 12(g)'s then numerical threshold (since raised to 2,000) is based on the number of shareholders who are owners "of record." Rule 12g5–1 defines securities "held of record" as those held by "each person who is identified as the owner of such securities on records of security holders maintained by or on behalf of the issuer." Suppose 50 clients purchased interests in the SPV and the SPV then purchased shares in Facebook, leaving the SPV as the owner of record in the issuer's books (as well as the books of the issuer's transfer agent). Goldman Sachs could then argue that its SPV investment structure added only a single investor toward the (then applicable) 500-person threshold of § 12(g). Rule 12g5–1(b)(3), however, provides: "If the issuer knows or has reason to know that the form of holding securities of record is used primarily to circumvent the provisions of Section 12(g) or 15(d) of the Act, the beneficial owners of such securities shall be deemed to be the record owners thereof." Ultimately, Goldman Sachs decided to restrict investors in the SPV only to clients located outside the United States.

Securities trading in pre-IPO, private company shares is a growing phenomenon. Organized trading markets have arisen on the Internet to facilitate such trades. Nasdaq Private Market connects private companies with Nasdaq's broker-dealer network. It allows private companies to limit the secondary market transactions that occur on the Nasdaq Private Market (see website at www.nasdaqprivatemarket. com). Other intermediaries in turn facilitate transactions for private companies tradable in the Nasdaq Private Market. SharesPost, a member broker-dealer of the Nasdaq Private Market, provides a platform where those interested in buying shares of private companies may connect with sellers of such shares (see website at www.shares post.com). Only accredited investors may buy the stock of private companies through SharesPost.

It is unclear how much of a problem the 2,000 record holder threshold poses for most private companies. Outside of a few, well-known companies such as Facebook, there is little interest among investors to buy and sell shares of private companies. Most private companies also typically retain a right of first refusal on employee sales of the company stock, limiting the ability of shares to enter the secondary market. Even if the number of record owners of a company's shares does cross the 2,000 threshold, § 12(g) gives issuers 120 days from the last day of its fiscal year to register with the SEC. This allows companies time to put together an initial public offering before having public company status thrust upon the company under § 12(g).

―――――――

The table below summarizes the three categories of public companies, which we will refer to collectively as "Exchange Act reporting companies," a commonly used term of art, as well as the process for terminating public company status.

Section	Trigger	Requirements	Termination
§ 12(a)	Exchange listing	- Periodic filings - Proxy rules + annual report - Tender offer rules - Insider stock transactions (§ 16)	Delisting & either (a) < 300 shareholders or (b) < 500 shareholders + < $10 m. in assets for 3 years
§ 12(g)	< 2,000 shareholders + > $10 m. in assets	- Periodic filings - Proxy rules + annual report - Tender offer rules - Insider stock transactions (§ 16)	Either (a) < 300 shareholders or (b) < 500 shareholders + < $10 m. in assets for 3 years
§ 15(d)	Registered public offering	- Periodic filings	< 300 holders + No earlier than next fiscal year after offering [Suspended unless terminated for a foreign private issuer under Rule 12h–6]

HYPOTHETICAL ONE

Scranton Paper has a subsidiary, CopyWorld, which provides photocopying services. Scranton Paper sold 20% of CopyWorld's stock in a series of private placements seven years ago. More recently, however, CopyWorld has struggled as companies moved toward the use of electronic documents. CopyWorld has had to downsize substantially in the face of this decline in demand. Currently, the subsidiary has 600 minority shareholders of record and $13 million in assets. Michael would like to avoid the cost of maintaining CopyWorld as a public company. CopyWorld owns a large copy center that has been appraised at $4 million. Michael proposes that CopyWorld sell the copy center to Scranton Paper, which will then lease the warehouse back to CopyWorld. CopyWorld would use the proceeds of the sale to buy back the shares of approximately 125 of its shareholders. Will Michael's plan to take CopyWorld private work?

III. WHEN MUST A PUBLIC COMPANY DISCLOSE?

The SEC, acting pursuant to authority conferred by Exchange Act § 13(a), requires three principal disclosure documents from public companies: Form 8–K, filed on the occurrence of specified events deemed to be of particular importance to investors; Form 10–K, filed annually; and Form 10–Q, filed quarterly. All of these forms are available to investors the same day they are filed through the SEC's EDGAR system, available at www.sec.gov.

The items required to be disclosed on these forms are drawn from the SEC's streamlined integrated disclosure system, which provides a consistent set of disclosure requirements for both the Securities and Exchange Acts. Those requirements are found in Regulation S–K (non-financial statement information) and Regulation S–X (financial statements). The different information disclosure forms contained in the securities laws then refer to specific portions of Regulations S–K and S–X. Not only do Forms 8–K, 10–K, and 10–Q reference Regulations S–K and S–X, the registration statements—Forms S–1 and S–3—for companies making a public offering (as discussed in Chapter 7) also draw from the same Regulations.

For example, consider the biographical information on the top management and directors of an issuer. Item 11(k) of Form S–1 requires the issuer to disclose information relating to its executive officers and directors. Rather than specify the required information, Item 11(k) simply references Item 401 of Regulation S–K. Likewise, Item 10 of the annual Form 10–K filing for the Exchange Act also requires disclosure concerning the issuer's executive officers and directors. Item 10 also references Items 401, 405, and 406 of Regulation S–K (among other provisions). At least for company-related information, the integrated disclosure system produces identical disclosure in these different forms.

How does the integrated disclosure system fit with our understanding of information and the securities markets? As we discussed earlier in Chapter 2 (Materiality), investors require similar information when deciding to make an investment regardless of the type of transaction. Investors buying a share of Scranton Paper in the secondary market need to know information about Scranton Paper's future plans and prospects, as well as information on its management, regulatory environment, and past financials, just as much as investors who are purchasing shares directly from Scranton Paper in a seasoned offering. The integrated disclosure system provides a common set of investment-related information.

A. FORM 8–K

In § 409 of the Sarbanes-Oxley Act, Congress gave the SEC authority to require Exchange Act reporting companies to disclose "on a rapid and current basis" material information regarding changes in a company's financial condition or operations. The 8–K, or "current" report, comes closest to requiring "real-time" disclosure; items required by Form 8–K must be made within four business days of the specified event.

The SEC has sorted events requiring current disclosure into the following sections:

1. Registrant's Business & Operations	• Entry into, a material amendment to, or termination of a "material definitive agreement," defined as contracts *outside* the ordinary course of business.
2. Financial Information	• Completion of the acquisition or disposition of assets constituting more than 10% of the registrant's total assets. • Results of operations and financial condition (if they are disclosed by press release before the filing of the 10–Q or 10–K). • Creation or triggering of an off-balance sheet arrangement. • Costs associated with exit or disposal activities, including termination benefits for employees, contract termination costs and other associated costs. • Material impairments to assets such as goodwill.
3. Securities & Trading Markets	• Receipt of a notice of delisting or a transfer of listing. • Unregistered sale of equity securities. • Material modifications to the rights of security holders.

4. Matters Related to Accountants & Financial Statements	• Changes in the company's outside auditor (and the reasons for the change). • Notice that previously issued financial statements or audit reports should no longer be relied upon.
5. Corporate Governance & Management	• A change in control of the registrant. • Departure or election/appointment of directors and principal officers. • Amendments to the articles of incorporation or bylaws. • Changes in the company's fiscal year. • Temporary suspension of trading under employee benefit plans. • Amendment to the registrant's code of ethics or the waiver of the requirements of that code. • Change in the company's shell company status. • Information related to submission of matters to a vote of the company's security holders.
6. Asset-Backed Securities (ABS)	• Certain information and computation materials related to the ABS. • Change of servicer or trustee for the ABS. • Change in credit enhancement or other external support for the ABS. • Failure to make required distributions to holders of ABS. • Certain updating disclosures related to an offering of ABS registered on Form S–3.
7. Regulation FD	• Any disclosure the issuer elects to disclose through Form 8–K to comply with Regulation FD (discussed below).

8. Other Events	• Anything that the issuer, at its option, thinks would be of importance to its security holders.
9. Financial Statements & Exhibits	• Including, among others, financial statements for businesses acquired by the registrant.

A few things to note about the Form 8–K disclosure requirements. Under § 1 of Form 8–K, only "material definitive agreements" need to be disclosed. Letters of intent for mergers or acquisitions, which generally would meet the definition of materiality under *Basic v. Levinson* (excerpted in Chapter 2), only need to be disclosed if they impose enforceable obligations. Public companies may use the Form 8–K to satisfy filing obligations arising from business combinations, such as the disclosure requirements imposed on tender offers under § 14 of the Exchange Act.

The disclosure of off-balance sheet arrangements required by § 2 of Form 8–K is an attempt to police the type of financial maneuverings that led to the downfall of Enron (a pivotal event leading to the passage of the Sarbanes-Oxley Act in 2002). The provision was adopted in response to Enron's creative efforts to shift underperforming assets and debt off its balance sheet, thereby improving how the public viewed Enron's financial health. In a typical off-balance sheet transaction, Enron would sell an underperforming asset to a "special purpose entity" partly owned by Enron. Any debt the special purposes entities incurred was also kept off of Enron's books, despite the close connection between Enron and the entities.

The requirement that "Material Impairments" of assets be disclosed under § 2 is likely to apply when a company determines that goodwill (the intangible value of a company's reputation and business contacts) put on its books in connection with an acquisition can no longer be valued at the price paid for it. Such a disclosure can be an embarrassing admission by management that the acquisition may not have worked out as hoped, hence the drop in goodwill value.

The disclosures required by § 3 relate directly to the interests of shareholders. The delisting or change in listing of a company's stock may signal lower liquidity for that stock in the future. The sale of unregistered securities generally results in the dilution of the interests of current stockholders. Finally, a change in the rights of security holders affects their interests directly, often in a negative manner.

Section 4 reflects similarly bad news for securities holders. A change in the company's outside auditor may simply reflect an effort to save money, but it also may represent a disagreement with the auditors over appropriate accounting practices. Companies changing their accountants are required to disclose not only the fact of the change, but also any disagreements they may have had with their former accountants prior to the change. Worse still for a company is a restatement of prior financial results, or a determination that results will need to be restated. Companies making disclosures of this sort typically suffer an immediate loss of credibility in the markets, not to mention a large stock price drop.

Noteworthy in § 5 is the disclosure requirement relating to a company's code of ethics. The Exchange Act does not require companies to have a code of ethics ("You can't legislate morality!"), but it does attempt to shame companies into adopting one (and sticking to it) by requiring disclosure of any such code, or an explanation of why there is none, and any waivers from that code. Form 8–K's emphasis on a company's code of ethics flows from § 406 of the Sarbanes-Oxley Act. Enron, for example, had a code of ethics prohibiting its top officers from serving as the general partner for outside limited partnerships due to the resulting conflicts of interest. The Enron board twice waived these requirements for its chief financial officer without disclosing the waivers.

The asset-backed securities disclosures of § 6 of Form 8–K were implemented by the SEC in response to a concern that the mandatory disclosure regime did not provide investors all the relevant information for issuers of asset-backed securities. Recall from Chapter 3 that asset-backed securities are instruments backed by a pool of self-liquidating financial assets.

In the SEC's ideal world, companies would make *all* of their disclosures through filings with the SEC, perhaps with an accompanying press release put out through the newswires. The agency has not yet achieved this dream, but § 8 of Form 8–K authorizes a company, at its option, to use the form to disclose anything that the company considers relevant to its security holders. Disclosure through the Form 8–K ensures broad dissemination via the EDGAR website. Unlike the mandatory items, there is no time requirement specified for optional disclosures under § 8.

In the Matter of Hewlett-Packard Company

Exchange Act Release No. 55801 (2007).

* * *

This matter involves Hewlett-Packard's failure to disclose the circumstances surrounding a board member's resignation amidst the company's controversial investigation into boardroom leaks. On May 18, 2006, HP's Board of Directors learned the findings of the company's leak investigation and voted to request the resignation of a director believed to have violated HP's policies by providing confidential information to the press. Silicon Valley venture capitalist and fellow director Thomas Perkins (not the source of the leak) voiced his strong objections to the handling of the matter, announced his resignation, and walked out of the Board meeting. Contrary to the reporting requirements of the federal securities laws, HP failed to disclose to investors the circumstances of Mr. Perkins' disagreement with the company.

* * *

HP's Leak Investigation

In or around January 2006, in response to apparent unauthorized disclosures of confidential information about HP Board meetings to the press, HP initiated an investigation to determine the source of the leaks. HP Board member Thomas Perkins, Chairman of the Board's Nominating and Governance Committee (which was responsible for, among other things, establishing board member qualifications and evaluating board operations), was generally informed of the inquiry. Mr. Perkins believed that he and HP's Chairman had agreed that, upon completion of the investigation, they would approach any individual implicated privately, obtain an assurance that it would not happen again, and inform the full Board that the matter had been resolved without identifying the source of the leak.

By April 2006, HP investigators tentatively concluded that a long-standing HP director had leaked information in connection with a January 23, 2006 press article. After consulting with HP's Chief Executive Officer, General Counsel, outside counsel, and Chairman of the Audit Committee, the Chairman of the Board determined that the leak investigation findings should be presented to the full Board.

Mr. Perkins Resigns During the May 18, 2006 Board Meeting

HP's Board of Directors met beginning at 12:30 p.m. on May 18, 2006 at HP's headquarters in Palo Alto, California. . . . At the start of the meeting, the head of HP's Audit Committee discussed the leak investigation and its findings. After some discussion, the identity of the director who provided information for the January 2006 article was revealed. The director addressed the Board, explained his actions, and left the room to permit additional deliberations. The Board discussed HP's policy on unauthorized public disclosures, and considered measures that could be taken in response to the director's actions, including asking him to resign.

During the course of the Board's deliberations, which lasted approximately 90 minutes, Mr. Perkins voiced his strong objections to the manner in which the matter was being handled. Among other things, he repeatedly told the Board that the source of the leak should have been approached "off-line" for an explanation and a warning, rather than identified to the whole Board. He affirmed his belief that the matter should have been handled confidentially by the Chairman of the Board and himself as Chairman of the Nominating and Governance Committee. He also questioned the wisdom of requesting the director to resign over what he perceived to be a relatively minor offense, noting that the director had made significant contributions to HP.

After a lengthy and heated discussion, the Board, by a secret written ballot, passed a motion to ask the director to resign from the Board. When HP's General Counsel announced the results of the vote on whether to ask the director to resign, Mr. Perkins continued to voice disagreement. As noted in the Board minutes, Mr. Perkins "restated his strong objections to the process, specifically [the Chairman's] decision to bring the matter to the full Board and the manner in which the meeting was conducted." Mr. Perkins then resigned from the Board and departed the meeting at approximately 2:00 p.m. The director identified by the leak investigation was asked to resign following the vote, but declined to resign at that time.

HP Fails to Disclose the Reasons for Mr. Perkins' Resignation

* * *

On May 22, 2006, HP filed a report on Form 8–K, pursuant to Item 5.02(b), reporting Mr. Perkins' resignation, but did not comply with Item 5.02(a) by failing to disclose that there had been a disagreement with the company. HP also filed with the Form 8–K a May 19 press release, which announced that Mr. Perkins had resigned without disclosing the circumstances of his disagreement.

HP concluded, with the advice of outside legal counsel and the General Counsel, that it need not disclose the reasons for Mr. Perkins' resignation because he merely had a disagreement with the company's Chairman, and not a disagreement with the company on a matter relating to its operations, policies, or practices. Contrary to HP's conclusion, the disagreement and the reasons for Mr. Perkins' resignation should have been disclosed, pursuant to Item 5.02(a), in the May 22 Form 8–K. Mr. Perkins resigned as a result of a disagreement with HP on the following matters: (1) the decision to present the leak investigation findings to the full Board; and (2) the decision by majority vote of the Board of Directors to ask the director identified in the leak investigation to resign. Mr. Perkins' disagreement related to important corporate governance matters and HP policies regarding handling sensitive information, and thus constituted a disagreement over HP's operations, policies or practices.

* * *

Section 13(a) of the Exchange Act and Rule 13a–11 promulgated thereunder require issuers of securities registered pursuant to Section 12 of the Exchange Act to file with the Commission current reports on Form 8–K upon the occurrence of certain events, including the departure of directors or principal officers. Item 5.02(a) of Form 8–K specifies that if a director has resigned because of a disagreement with the registrant, known to an executive officer of the registrant, on any matter relating to the registrant's operations, policies, or practices, the registrant must, among other things, disclose a brief description of the circumstances representing the disagreement that the registrant believes caused, in whole or in part, the director's resignation. In addition, the registrant must provide the resigning director with a copy of the disclosure no later than the day the company files the disclosure with the Commission. Also, the registrant must provide the director with the opportunity to furnish a response letter stating whether the director agrees with the disclosure in the registrant's Form 8–K. In the event that the registrant receives a response letter from the former director, the letter must be filed by the registrant as an amendment to its Form 8–K within two business days of its receipt. No showing of scienter is required to establish a violation of Section 13(a) of the Exchange Act.

On May 18, 2006, director Thomas Perkins resigned because of a disagreement with HP regarding the decision to present the leak investigation findings to the full Board and the decision by the Board to ask the director identified in the leak investigation to resign. The disagreement was known to HP executive officers. Mr. Perkins' disagreement with HP related to the operations, policies, or practices of HP. Consequently, HP was required by Item 5.02(a) of Form 8–K to disclose a brief description of the circumstances representing the disagreement, and was required to provide Mr. Perkins with a copy of this disclosure no later than the day of filing. By disclosing the resignation of Mr. Perkins pursuant to Item 5.02(b) in a Form 8–K filed on May 22, 2006, HP failed to disclose the circumstances of Mr. Perkins' disagreement with HP and also failed to provide the director with a copy of such a filing. As a result, HP violated Section 13(a) of the Exchange Act and Rule 13a–11 thereunder.

* * *

Accordingly, it is hereby ORDERED that Respondent HP cease and desist from committing or causing any violations and any future violations of Section 13(a) of the Exchange Act and Rule 13a–11 thereunder.

QUESTIONS

1. Do investors need to know the reasons for a director's resignation? How does this compare with the need to know the reasons for the resignation of an officer, such as the chief executive officer? Or the resignation of the company's auditor?

2. Do the 8–K disclosure requirements risk chilling candid discussion at board meetings?

3. When will a director resignation not involve a disagreement with the company over operations, policies, or practices?

HYPOTHETICAL TWO

Relations with Scranton Paper's outside auditors, Malone & Martinez, have gotten a bit rocky. Angela, Scranton Paper's CFO, has been feeling the heat from Michael over the company's earnings. Michael wants to show a consistent pattern of growth in earnings per share to justify a high price for the company in any acquisition. Unfortunately, the fundamentals of the business have not kept pace recently with Wall Street's expectations.

Angela was able to meet last quarter's numbers only by making a side deal with The Paper Clip, an office supply store. The Paper Clip agreed to purchase a huge quantity of paper to sell to its customers on a retail basis. Angela's side deal with The Paper Clip, however, allows The Paper Clip to return any paper it hasn't sold after six months if sales do not meet expectations. Despite this contingency, Angela booked all of the expected profits from the sale as part of last quarter's earnings without setting aside a sales return allowance.

Malone & Martinez is now conducting the company's annual audit and it says that booking the revenues from The Paper Clip last quarter was not consistent with U.S. generally accepted accounting principles. Moreover, Malone & Martinez says it will resign as outside auditor and go to the SEC if Scranton Paper does not restate last quarter's revenues to conform to the auditor's interpretation of GAAP. Scranton Paper's board makes it clear that it intends to fire Angela, but she resigns before they get the chance. Does Scranton Paper need to file a Form 8–K?

B. FORMS 10–K AND 10–Q

The SEC requires the most extensive disclosure on Form 10–K, which like other disclosure requirements in the securities laws, draws its specific requirements from the integrated disclosure of Regulation S–K (Items 101–103, 201, 301–305, 307–308, 401–407, 503, 601, and 701–702). Many of these items track our discussion in Chapter 2 on what information investors would desire in making an investment decision. These information items include, among others, information on a registrant's:

- Business
- Properties
- Legal Proceedings
- Market for Common Stock
- Management Discussion and Analysis of Financial Condition and Results of Operation (MD & A)
- Directors and Officers
- Executive Compensation
- Security Ownership of Certain Beneficial Owners and Management
- Certain Relationships and Related Transactions
- Principal Accounting Fees and Services

Issuers are also required to disclose the outcome of any matters submitted to a vote of their shareholders. In addition, issuers are encouraged to combine their Form 10–K, which is filed with the SEC, with the annual report that they are required to send to their shareholders under Rule 14a–3 (setting forth information those engaged in a proxy solicitation must furnish to shareholders). Recall that not all Exchange Act reporting issuers are subject to the proxy solicitation requirements of § 14. Although §§ 12(b) and 12(g) reporting issuers are subject to those rules, § 15(d) issuers are not.

Foreign private issuers with securities trading on an exchange use Form 20–F instead of Form 10–K. Since 1999, the disclosure requirements of Form 20–F closely follow the international disclosure standards promulgated by the International Organization of Securities Commissions (IOSCO). Form 20–F does not directly reference Regulation S–K, but many of the non-financial disclosure items of Form 20–F track the parallel non-financial disclosure items of Form 10–K. For financial information, companies using Form 20–F may provide information following U.S. generally accepted accounting principles (U.S. GAAP), International Financial Reporting Standards (IFRS), or provide information pursuant to another "comprehensive body of accounting principles" together with a reconciliation to U.S. GAAP. International Financial Reporting Standards are published by the International Accounting Standard Board (IASB). All listed European Union companies must follow IFRS in preparing their consolidated financial statements.

Probably the largest expense imposed by the periodic filing requirements on public companies is the audited financial statements that must be filed with the Form 10–K. The financial data required to be disclosed are specified in Regulation S–X.

The financial disclosures are supplemented by Regulation S–K Item 303, the Management Discussion and Analysis (MD & A) section. Item 303 requires a narrative discussion of the issuer's "financial condition, changes in financial condition and results of operations." The MD & A discussion goes beyond a mere explanation of the historical data provided in the financial statements and how the reporting period differed from prior periods. Companies are also required to disclose "known trends or uncertainties" that the issuer "reasonably expects" to affect the firms' liquidity, capital resources, net sales, revenues or income in the future. Although this requirement to predict the future makes managers and their legal counsel nervous, some wiggle room is left by the qualifiers that the "trends or uncertainties" be "known" and they must be "reasonably" expected to have an impact. Nonetheless, this forward-looking requirement leaves substantial room for second-guessing if a potential adverse development not disclosed by the issuer actually comes to pass. Companies may worry in particular about a private antifraud suit based on a previous forward-looking statement that has not borne out. Some comfort is provided by the forward-looking safe harbor of Exchange Act § 21E (discussed in Chapter 5) affording protection against private liability.

The quarterly Form 10–Q imposes a lighter burden than the annual Form 10–K. Most notably, the financial statements filed with the Form 10–Q need not be audited, although they must comply with GAAP. Foreign issuers are not required to file quarterly reports.

Both Forms 10–K and 10–Q must be certified by the chief executive officer and chief financial officer of the registrant. Section 302 of the Sarbanes-Oxley Act (as implemented in Rules 13a–14(a) and 15d–14(a) of the Exchange Act) requires that these officers personally certify that:

- They have reviewed the report;
- Based on the officer's knowledge, the report does not contain material misstatements or omissions;
- Based on the officer's knowledge, the financial statements "fairly present in all material respects" the issuer's results and financial condition;
- They are responsible for establishing and maintaining internal control and have:
  — Designed those controls so that material information is made known to them,
  — Evaluated the effectiveness of those controls within 90 days of the report, and
  — Presented the conclusion of their evaluation in the report;
- They have disclosed to the company's auditors and audit committee any weaknesses in those internal controls and any fraud by persons who have a significant role in the issuer's internal controls;

- Any changes to internal controls made subsequent to the evaluation are disclosed in the report.

This certification requirement does two things. First, it focuses the CEO and the CFO on the need for accuracy in reporting. These officers are unlikely to skimp on resources for financial reporting if they have to sign off on the results. Second, it reduces the ability of the CEO and CFO to claim ignorance of misstatements or omissions in the periodic reports (although they can still claim that they were not reckless in certifying). Furthermore, if they falsely certify that the report contains no misstatements or omissions, they have made an additional misstatement in certifying that the report does not contain a misstatement or omission. As a result, the certification requirement may make it harder for the CEO and CFO to evade personal liability in a private antifraud action (under Rule 10b–5 as discussed in Chapter 5) or an SEC enforcement action (the subject of Chapter 13) for material misstatements or half-truths in the Form 10–K or 10–Q.

NOTES

1. *Regulation G.* Regulation G regulates certain voluntary disclosures. Under Regulation G, adopted by the SEC pursuant to the Sarbanes Oxley Act, if public disclosure of any material information includes a non-GAAP financial measure, such as pro forma financials, the registrant must include, in the same disclosure or release, a presentation of the most directly comparable GAAP financial measure and a reconciliation of the disclosed non-GAAP financial measure to the most directly comparable GAAP financial measure. Regulation G also cautions that a non-GAAP financial measure, taken together with the accompanying information, may not misstate a material fact or omit to state a material fact necessary to make the presentation of the non-GAAP financial measure not misleading.

HYPOTHETICAL THREE

Scranton Paper's subsidiary, CopyWorld (in the business of providing photocopying services), has struggled recently due to the increasing use of electronic documents. Things may be looking up for CopyWorld, however, in its side business of drafting professional resumes. A possible rise in the unemployment rate may result in a greater number of job seekers, leading CopyWorld to shift from loss to profit. Michael, the CEO of Scranton Paper, has been keeping track of the unemployment rate and the number of job seekers and believes that CopyWorld could contribute 10% of Scranton Paper's profits next quarter. Scranton Paper's most recent Form 10–K, however, makes no mention of the likely increase in the unemployment rate in the MD & A section of its filing. Michael reasons that you cannot accurately predict future economic conditions, so the expected increase in demand for resume drafting services may not come about. Has Scranton Paper violated § 13(a) by failing to discuss the possible effects of a worsening economy on CopyWorld's profits?

C. EXECUTIVE COMPENSATION

In late 2006, and again in 2009, amid ongoing public hand wringing over the enormous pay received by top-level executives, the SEC changed the rules for disclosing executive compensation that affected, among other things, executive compensation disclosure in the annual proxy statement. Companies are now required to disclose not only the compensation of their CEOs and CFOs, but also the three other highest paid executive officers (defined as those with policy making responsibilities for a subsidiary or division).

These executive compensation disclosures include bonuses, stock and options based compensation, and retirement benefits. The SEC requires that issuers disclose the fair value of equity awards in the fiscal year measured at the grant date. If the exercise price of the option is less than the closing price of the stock on the day of issue ("in the money" options), this also must be disclosed. The value of termination and change-in-control benefits must be disclosed as well. Any "perquisites" to the named executive officers and directors must be disclosed if they aggregate more than $10,000; after that threshold is met, all perquisites must be identified and the value of every perquisite over $25,000 or 10% of all perquisites must be disclosed. Perquisites are defined as benefits (1) not integrally and directly related to the executive's job; and (2) not generally available on a non-discriminatory basis to all employees. The SEC also requires issuers to disclose a Compensation Discussion and Analysis section (CD & A), which requires a narrative discussion of the objectives and implementation of executive compensation programs and the most important factors underlying the company's compensation policies. Notably, this section must be filed with the SEC. As a result, it is subject to the certification requirements for CEOs and CFOs. Regulation S–K, Item 402.

In the wake of the Financial Crisis of 2007–2008, Congress moved to mandate further executive compensation disclosure. The Dodd-Frank Act of 2010 requires the SEC to promulgate rules expanding executive compensation disclosure in annual proxy statements sent to shareholders. Among other things, the Dodd-Frank Act focuses on the following areas:

Pay Versus Performance. The Act requires the SEC to adopt rules requiring disclosure showing "the relationship between executive compensation actually paid and the financial performance of the issuer" in the annual proxy statement. Dodd Frank Act § 953(a).

CEO Pay Disparity. The Act requires the SEC to adopt rules requiring disclosure of (A) "the median of the annual total compensation of all employees of the issuer, except the chief executive officer (or any equivalent position) of the issuer" and (B) "the annual total compensation of the chief executive officer (or any equivalent position) of the issuer." Issuers must then disclose the ratio of (A) to (B). This ratio provides a gauge of how much an issuer's CEO total compensation exceeds the median total compensation for all other employees of the issuer. Dodd Frank Act § 953(b).

Employee and Director Hedging. The Act amends § 14 of the Exchange Act to require disclosure of whether any employee or director "is permitted to purchase financial instruments . . . that are designed to hedge or offset any decrease in the market value of equity securities" granted by the issuer as compensation or that are held directly or indirectly by the employee or director. Dodd Frank Act § 955.

The Dodd-Frank executive compensation disclosure reforms are coupled with reforms affecting shareholder proxy voting. These reforms include requirements for shareholder non-binding votes on the compensation of executive officers (commonly known as "say on pay" votes), non-binding votes on golden parachute compensation agreements in a proxy solicitation related to a merger or acquisition. The Act also gives the SEC explicit authority to adopt rules to allow shareholders to nominate directors for inclusion in the issuer's own proxy solicitation materials (commonly known as "proxy access"). We discuss the Dodd-Frank Act's reforms that affect shareholder proxy voting more fully in Chapter 11.

D. EMERGING GROWTH COMPANIES

The JOBS Act of 2012 created a new category of issuers called "emerging growth companies." An emerging growth company is an issuer with total annual gross revenues of less than $1 billion (indexed for inflation) during its most recently completed fiscal year. Securities Act § 2(a)(19). Section 2(a)(19) provides that a company terminates emerging growth company status at the earliest of one of several events. First, a company ceases to be an emerging growth company on the last day of the fiscal year during which it had total annual gross revenues of $1 billion or more (indexed for inflation). Second, a company ceases to be an emerging growth company on the last day of the fiscal year following the fifth anniversary of the date of the first sale of common equity securities in a registered public offering. Third, a company ceases to be an emerging growth company on the date on which the company has issued more than $1 billion in non-convertible debt aggregated over the previous three-year period. Finally, a company ceases to be an emerging growth company the date on which the company is deemed to be a "large accelerated filer" as defined in Rule 12b–2 of the Exchange Act. Rule 12b–2 defines companies with over $700 million of worldwide equity float in the hands of non-affiliates, among other requirements, as large accelerated filers (paralleling the equity float requirement for a Well-Known Seasoned Issuer that we discuss in Chapter 7).

Emerging growth companies enjoy benefits in both areas: the public offering process and continuing obligations imposed on public companies. For public offerings, emerging growth companies can submit confidential draft registration statements to the SEC. They can also "test the waters" through pre-offering communications with certain large investors, including qualified institutional buyers and accredited institutional investors (covered in Chapter 9). The JOBS Act also reduces public offering disclosure obligations for emerging growth companies and loosens restrictions on analyst reports on emerging growth companies in a public offering. We discuss the benefits for emerging growth companies in the public offering process in Chapter 7.

Once an emerging growth company has done its IPO and become a public reporting company, the JOBS Act provides additional relief from ongoing public company requirements. First, emerging growth companies are exempt from the "say on pay" requirement that shareholders must have the ability to vote on executive compensation. Exchange Act § 14A. The JOBS Act also exempts emerging growth companies from the CEO Pay Disparity disclosures required for public companies pursuant to the Dodd-Frank Act. Third, the JOBS Act exempts emerging growth companies from certain disclosure requirements under Items 301 (selected financial data) and 303 (Management Discussion and Analysis) of Regulation S–K. Fourth, the JOBS Act exempts emerging growth companies from the requirement that an external auditor must attest to the internal controls of a public company pursuant to § 404 of the Sarbanes Oxley Act (discussed below). Finally, the JOBS Act exempts emerging growth companies from any rules promulgated by the Public Company Accounting Oversight Board requiring mandatory audit firm rotation or supplemental information to the auditor's report. An emerging growth company may opt into any of the requirements from which the JOBS Act provides an exemption.

In enacting the JOBS Act of 2012, Congress sought to reduce the burdens of going public on companies as well as the disclosure obligations imposed after they go public. The costs of going public and complying with ongoing disclosure obligations are relatively fixed in the sense that compliance costs do not scale proportionately with the market capitalization of a company. The fixed nature of compliance costs therefore imposes a greater burden on smaller companies seeking to go public. One can wonder though whether the $1 billion in total annual gross revenue ceiling for a company to qualify as an emerging growth company is too high. Zynga, Inc., a developer of FarmVille and other mobile games software, had revenues of $597.5 million in 2010, the year before its initial public offering. Zynga went public at the end of 2011, raising $1 billion in its initial public offering. Although Zynga would have qualified as an emerging growth company at the time of its IPO, it is unclear whether Zynga needed relief from the fixed cost of going public. Zynga's large offering and scale of operations and revenue put it in a better position to cover these fixed costs than many already public companies.

At the other end of the revenue spectrum, consider a small private company with revenues of only $100 million considering a public offering. Such a company will undoubtedly face large costs from going through the public offering process, and therefore benefit from the relief provided under the JOBS Act for emerging growth companies. But such a company also poses the greatest risk of fraud. Beyond fraud, investors—including in particular individual investors—may make poor investment decisions with less than full and longstanding disclosure. Unlike more established public companies that have extensive analyst coverage, emerging growth companies will typically have no analyst following, exacerbating the problem of information asymmetry.

IV. ACCURACY OF DISCLOSURE

The Exchange Act encourages accurate disclosure through both internal and external mechanisms. As we will see in Chapter 5, antifraud liability deters company officials from providing materially inaccurate disclosures. The specter of antifraud liability is bolstered by numerous other mechanisms that encourage accurate disclosures.

Most directly, the Exchange Act requires that the company "make and keep books, records, and accounts, which, in reasonable detail, accurately and fairly reflect the transactions and dispositions of the assets of the issuer." Section 13(b)(2)(A). In adopting this provision in 1977 as part of the Foreign Corrupt Practices Act, Congress drew a connection between the company's *external* disclosures regarding its financial situation and the accuracy of the company's *internal* information.

Three things are noteworthy about this requirement that the company maintain accurate books and records. First, the provision imposes strict liability—there is no knowledge, or even negligence, requirement. Inaccuracies are actionable, regardless of the company's knowledge of them. Second, there is no "materiality" qualifier—any inaccuracy, no matter how trivial, is potentially actionable. Third, (and this likely follows from the first two points), Congress provided no private right of action to enforce § 13(b)(2) and courts have not implied one. Only the SEC (and in extreme cases, the Justice Department) can enforce the provision.

Taking a "belt and suspenders" approach, Congress not only requires that companies produce the *outcome* of accurate books and records, it also mandates procedures designed to produce accurate books and records. Exchange Act § 13(b)(2)(B). A motivating force for the adoption of § 13(b)(2) was payment of bribes to foreign officials to secure contracts. The payments were—unsurprisingly—not recorded on the bribing company's books. This problem has become an enforcement priority for the SEC and the Justice Department. The following case was brought by the SEC as a cease-and-desist administrative proceeding under § 21C of the Exchange Act. We discuss § 21C proceedings at greater length in Chapter 13.

In the Matter of Oil States International, Inc.

Exchange Act Release No. 53732 (2006).

I.

The Securities and Exchange Commission deems it appropriate that cease-and-desist proceedings be, and hereby are, instituted pursuant to Section 21C of the Securities Exchange Act of 1934, against Oil States International, Inc.

II.

In anticipation of the institution of these proceedings, Respondent has submitted an Offer of Settlement which the Commission has determined to accept. Solely for the purpose of these proceedings and any other proceedings brought by or on behalf of the Commission, or to which the Commission is a party, and without admitting or denying the findings herein, except as to the Commission's jurisdiction over it and the subject matter of these proceedings, which are admitted, Respondent consents to the entry of this Order Instituting Cease-and-Desist Proceedings, Making Findings, and Imposing a Cease-and-Desist Order Pursuant to Section 21C of the Securities Exchange Act of 1934, as set forth below.

III.

* * *

This matter involves Oil States' violations of the books and records and internal controls provisions of the Foreign Corrupt Practices Act (Sections 13(b)(2)(A) and 13(b)(2)(B) of the Exchange Act), arising from certain payments made through its Hydraulic Well Control, LLC [HWC] subsidiary. Oil States, through certain employees of HWC, provided approximately $348,350 in improper payments to employees of Petróleos de Venezuela, S.A. [PDVSA], an energy company owned by the government of Venezuela. The employees were asked to participate in the scheme by a consultant for HWC, after he was requested to do so by the PDVSA employees. HWC improperly recorded the payments in its accounting books and records as ordinary business expenses, which were consolidated into those of its parent, Oil States. Oil States' internal controls failed to ensure that HWC's books and records accurately reflected the nature and purpose of these payments.

Oil States ... is a specialty provider to oil and gas drilling and production companies in the United States and in many of the world's active oil and gas producing regions, including South America. . . . HWC operates specially designed rigs and provides well site services, including workover and snubbing services, to oil and gas producers in Venezuela and other countries. . . . HWC Venezuela contributed approximately 1% of Oil States' consolidated revenues during the relevant period.

Facts

A.   Background

In 2000, HWC hired a Venezuelan consultant to interface with employees of PDVSA on behalf of HWC in the field and at the office level. . . . HWC did not investigate the background of the Consultant. . . . HWC had certain FCPA policies in place; however, HWC provided no formal training or education to the Consultant regarding the requirements of the FCPA. Further, a written contract between HWC and the Consultant failed to address compliance with the requirements of U.S. law, including the provisions of the FCPA.

In December 2003, the Consultant was approached by three PDVSA employees about a proposed "kickback" scheme. The PDVSA employees proposed that the Consultant submit inflated bills to HWC for his services and kickback the excess to the PDVSA employees. At the same time, HWC would improperly bill PDVSA for "lost rig time" on jobs.[2] If HWC did not comply with the proposed scheme, the PDVSA employees were capable of stopping or delaying HWC's work. After learning of the proposed scheme from the Consultant, three HWC Venezuela employees acceded to and facilitated the improper activity. The Consultant provided inflated invoices for his services and other documents inaccurately reflecting the amount of rig time billable to PDVSA. HWC employees incorporated these documents into HWC's books and records and HWC passed on an undetermined amount of the improper payments in inflated invoices to PDVSA.

---

[2]   "Lost rig time" is time that PDVSA contends is not properly billable to it.

B. Over-charges for Lost Rig Time

On December 10, 2003, the Consultant submitted to HWC an invoice for services that sought payment of $26,041.66, plus taxes. On December 16, 2003, the Consultant submitted to HWC an invoice for services that sought payment of $27,083.33, plus taxes. HWC paid the Consultant. HWC's payment of these invoices resulted in the first improper payments to the PDVSA employees through the consultant. Due to the difficulties in assessing lost rig time and the falsified documentation prepared by the Consultant and approved by the HWC and PDVSA employees, it is not possible to quantify the total amount of "lost rig time," if any, paid for by PDVSA during this time period.[4] . . .

C. Over-charges for Gel

In March 2004, the PDVSA employees approached the Consultant with a change in the scheme. The PDVSA employees instructed the Consultant to continue to submit inflated invoices to HWC, this time for the inclusion of "gel" (a mineral-based material that is used in drilling to control viscosity and to protect formations from drilling fluids) that had not actually been used on PDVSA jobs. The Consultant and the HWC employees agreed to continue the improper payments and, between April 2004 and November 2004, participated in five transactions involving over-charges to PDVSA for gel. During this time, HWC paid the Consultant approximately $412,000, some or all of which was used to make improper payments to the PDVSA employees. During this same time period, HWC charged PDVSA $348,350 for gel. The amount of gel legitimately charged to PDVSA is unknown.

In August 2004, HWC's Vice President of Finance in the U.S. noticed increasing contract labor (including consulting) expenses at HWC Venezuela. When he inquired into the increasing expenses, the controller at HWC Venezuela responded that the expenses were "gel-related." Despite this vague explanation, HWC's Vice President of Finance conducted no additional investigation of the issue and the scheme continued.

In December 2004, during a routine review of HWC's results while preparing the budget for the following fiscal year, HWC senior management in the U.S. discovered departures from HWC Venezuela's operating plan. Specifically, HWC management noted an unexplained narrowing of profit margins in the Venezuelan operations, which caused management to make immediate inquiry. As a result of that inquiry, the U.S. management of HWC learned of the kickback scheme. HWC reported the matter to Oil States' management, which, in turn, reported the scheme to the company's audit committee. An internal investigation conducted by Oil States uncovered no evidence that HWC or Oil States employees in the United States were aware of or sanctioned the improper payments. Upon completion of the internal investigation, Oil States terminated its relationship with the Consultant and disciplined the employees responsible for the misconduct (including dismissing two HWC Venezuela employees). Oil States also corrected its books and records, strengthened its regulatory compliance program, and reimbursed PDVSA for the improper charges. Oil States also

---

[4] "Lost rig time" is a frequently disputed calculation because there are varying legitimate but subjective reasons for billing a client for downtime during a job.

voluntarily provided their report of investigation to the Commission and the Department of Justice, and disclosed the scheme in its public filings. It then cooperated fully with the investigation conducted by the Commission staff.

D.   Violations

The FCPA, enacted in 1977, added Exchange Act Section 13(b)(2)(A) to require public companies to make and keep books, records and accounts, which, in reasonable detail, accurately and fairly reflect the transactions and dispositions of the assets of the issuer, and added Exchange Act Section 13(b)(2)(B) to require such companies to devise and maintain a system of internal accounting controls sufficient to provide reasonable assurances that: (i) transactions are executed in accordance with management's general or specific authorization; and (ii) transactions are recorded as necessary to permit preparation of financial statements in conformity with generally accepted accounting principles or any other criteria applicable to such statements, and to maintain accountability for assets.

Because HWC improperly recorded the payments to the PDVSA employees as ordinary business expenses, its books, records and accounts did not, in reasonable detail, accurately and fairly reflect its transactions and dispositions of assets.

As a result of the conduct described above, Oil States violated Section 13(b)(2)(A) of the Exchange Act.

In addition, HWC failed to take steps to ensure that the Consultant complied with the FCPA and to ensure that the nature and purpose of the payments to the PDVSA employees were accurately reflected in HWC's books and records.

As a result of the conduct described above, Oil States violated Section 13(b)(2)(B) of the Exchange Act.

* * *

NOTES

1.   *Accurate books and records.* The Exchange Act § 13(b)(2) requirement of accurate books and records is bolstered by § 13(b)(5), which states that "No person shall knowingly circumvent or knowingly fail to implement a system of internal accounting controls or knowingly falsify any book, record or account described in [§ 13(b)(2)]." Section 13(b)(4) makes clear that criminal penalties may apply for violations of § 13(b)(2)'s requirement of accurate books and records only if the violator has also run afoul of § 13(b)(5).

2.   *Incentive compensation.* Additional mechanisms for ensuring accuracy of books and records were added by the Sarbanes-Oxley Act. Recall that CEOs and CFOs are now required by Exchange Act Rule 13a–14 to certify that they have reviewed the company's internal controls on a regular basis. Another provision added by Sarbanes-Oxley intended to make officers think hard about the accuracy of company's financial statements is § 304. That section requires CEOs and CFOs to return bonus and other incentive compensation to the company for any period that the company is required to restate its financial results as a result of "misconduct." "Misconduct" is

not defined, nor is it limited to misconduct by the CEO and CFO. The Dodd-Frank Act expanded on this requirement, requiring the SEC to direct national securities exchanges to adopt listing provisions requiring companies to have "clawback" policies. Clawback policies allow companies to recover incentive-based compensation from current or former executive officers following a restatement. The trigger is material noncompliance with any financial reporting requirement during the three-year period preceding the date of the restatement. Dodd-Frank Act § 954. There is no requirement of "misconduct," and these policies can be enforced, not only by the SEC, but also by shareholders through a derivative suit on behalf of the corporation.

3. *Internal controls.* Section 404 of the Sarbanes-Oxley Act adds to the CEO/CFO certification requirement of § 302. Under § 404, managers must include a statement in the company's annual report on the manager's responsibility for the company's internal controls for financial reporting and provide an assessment of those controls. Section 404 also requires that "each registered public accounting firm that prepares or issues the audit report for the issuer" shall attest to the management's assessment of the firm's system of internal controls for financial reporting. Auditors are required to not only certify the integrity of their client's financial statements, but also assess the mechanisms that their clients have adopted to generate the financial information that goes into those statements. This auditor attestation requirement was scaled back, however, in the Dodd-Frank Act; companies with a market capitalization under $75 million are now exempt.

QUESTIONS

1.   Is it possible to bribe people without violating §§ 13(b)(2)(A) & (B)?

2.   Do prohibitions against bribing foreign officials put U.S. companies at a disadvantage relative to their foreign rivals?

3.   Do we need a legal rule instructing companies to not let their employees make bribes? Does § 13(b)(2) serve some additional purpose?

4.   What more could HWC have done to bolster its internal controls to ensure that bribe payments are reflected in the corporation information systems?

5.   Should a § 13(b) violation require a finding of scienter?

HYPOTHETICAL FOUR

The troubles for Michael, the CEO of Scranton Paper, have gone from bad to worse. Recall that Angela, the former CFO of Scranton Paper, engineered a transaction with The Paper Clip that overstated Scranton Paper's revenues. Scranton Paper's audit committee has been investigating the transaction with The Paper Clip. In the course of its investigation, the audit committee has found more mischief by Angela. It turns out that to get a shipment of high quality pulp (a key ingredient in Scranton Paper's premium paper line) delivered on time, Angela paid $75,000 to a customs official in Quebec. Needless to say, the payment does not show up in Scranton Paper's financial statements. Nor does the $500,000 slush fund from which Angela got the money for the bribe. Michael delegates all that "money stuff" to Angela and had no idea that there was a slush fund. Have any provisions of § 13(b) been violated? If so, by whom? Is § 304 of the Sarbanes-Oxley Act implicated by the bribe or the contract with The Paper Clip?

V. THE PROBLEM OF SELECTIVE DISCLOSURE

Company filings with the SEC pursuant to the mandatory disclosure system are available to anyone with access to the Web through the EDGAR system. But companies do not communicate with the investing public solely through filings required by the SEC. For most public companies, voluntary disclosures, such as press releases, analyst conferences, and investor relations personnel's responses to questions, are an equally important means of spreading news about the company. For example, most public companies will not wait for the filing of their Form 10–Q to announce their earnings for the prior quarter. Instead, the first public disclosure of that information (and the disclosure that the securities markets will respond to) will be in the form of a press release announcing the quarterly earnings followed shortly thereafter by the filing of a Form 8–K with the SEC.

Voluntary disclosures of this sort are regulated less heavily by the SEC, even though they may be considered just as material by the markets. Although most of the SEC's regulatory regime focuses on forcing companies to disclose more, voluntary disclosures pose the opposite issue of whether the securities laws should constrain the ability of issuers to disclose information. Why worry about voluntary disclosure? The SEC became concerned in the late 1990s that companies were selectively disclosing information to certain favored parties rather than disclosing the information broadly through a press release or other public media. As a result, some investors were receiving material information sooner than others. Further, the SEC was concerned that companies were currying favor with market analysts by favoring them with information not available to other investors, which may have induced the analysts to be less than objective in their opinions (giving, for example, a "Buy" recommendation when an issuer warranted only a "Hold" recommendation). Regulation FD was the SEC's response to the problem of selective disclosure.

Regulation FD covers domestic Exchange Act reporting companies (foreign issuers are exempt) and those working on the behalf of such companies ("company sources"). A company source that discloses non-public material information to certain delineated groups of "covered" persons, including broker-dealers, investment advisors, investment companies, or any investor in the company that is reasonably expected to trade on the information, must also disclose the information to the public market. This limitation was intended to exclude answers to questions posed by journalists from the reach of Regulation FD.

Also expressly excluded from the ban are persons owing "a duty of trust or confidence to the issuer (such as attorney, investment banker, or accountant)," and persons who agree to maintain the information in confidence. Such persons, as we shall see in Chapter 6, are "temporary insiders," owing a fiduciary duty to shareholders, and thus within the reach of Rule 10b–5's insider trading prohibition.

If the selective disclosure to a covered person is intentional, then the company must disclose the information simultaneously to the entire market. If non-intentional, then the company must "promptly" disclose the information to the market within 24 hours of the selective disclosure or by the time trading commences on the New York Stock Exchange, whichever is later. The corrective disclosure can be made by filing a Form 8–K with the disclosed information. Alternatively, a press release, if "reasonably designed to provide broad, non-exclusionary distribution of the information to the public," will also suffice.

Note that the prohibition against selective disclosure is imposed on the *issuer* pursuant to § 13(a)'s reporting obligations for public companies. The officer of the company who actually makes the selective disclosure is a "cause" or an "aider and abettor" of the violation by the company and therefore subject to enforcement action as well. Neither the issuer nor the officer has violated the antifraud provisions of the Exchange Act. In promulgating Regulation FD, the SEC specifically excluded private liability for violations. Only the SEC can enforce Regulation FD; the following is the first federal court case brought by the SEC to enforce the rule.

SEC v. Siebel Systems, Inc.

384 F. Supp. 2d 694 (S.D.N.Y. 2005).

■ DANIELS, G., DISTRICT JUDGE.

Plaintiff, the Securities and Exchange Commission, commenced this action, against Siebel Systems, Inc., [and] Siebel Systems's Chief Financial Officer, Kenneth Goldman. . . . The SEC charges the defendants with, *inter alia*, violations of, or aiding and abetting in the violation of, Regulation FD. . . .

* * *

Regulation FD requires an issuer to make public material information disclosed to security market professionals or holders of the issuer's securities who are reasonably likely to trade on the basis of that information. Where the issuer's selective disclosure of material nonpublic information is intentional, the issuer is to simultaneously make public disclosure. In the case of non-intentional disclosure, public disclosure must be promptly made. " 'Promptly' means as soon as reasonably practicable (but in no event after the later of 24 hours or the commencement of the next day's trading on the New York Stock Exchange) after a senior official of the issuer, . . . learns that there has been a non-intentional disclosure by the issuer or person acting on behalf of the issuer of information that the senior official knows, or is reckless in not knowing, is both material and nonpublic."

The gravamen of the complaint is that defendant Goldman made positive comments about the company's business activity levels and sales transaction pipeline at two private events on April 30th, 2003, attended by institutional investors. . . . The SEC alleges that, at these two events, Mr. Goldman privately disclosed material nonpublic information by stating that Siebel Systems's activity levels were "good" or "better," that new deals were coming back into the pipeline, that the pipeline was "building" and "growing," and that "there were some $5 million deals in Siebel's pipeline." The complaint alleges that immediately following the disclosure of this information or soon thereafter, certain attendants of the meetings and their associates made substantial purchases of shares of Siebel Systems's stock. The SEC alleges "by disclosing that Siebel's business activity levels were 'good' and 'better,' and that its sales transaction pipeline was 'growing' and 'building,' Goldman communicated to his private audiences that Siebel's business was improving as the result of new business, and that the increase in the Company's guidance for the second quarter was not simply because deals that had slipped from the first quarter were closing."

The SEC claims that these statements materially contrasted with public statements made by Thomas Siebel[3] during conference calls on April 4th and 23rd, and at an April 28th conference.... Those statements provided information about the company's "performance in the first quarter of 2003 and its expected performance in the second quarter of 2003." The SEC alleges that in these statements it was reported that: (1) Siebel Systems's first quarter results were poor because the economy was poor and because some deals that were expected to close in the previous quarter did not, *i.e.*, deals had "slipped" into the second quarter; (2) Siebel Systems's software license revenues were expected to be higher in the second quarter than in the first quarter, but the company conditioned its estimate on the performance of the overall economy; and (3) there were no indications that the existing poor economic conditions were improving.... The complaint further states that, with regard to the guidance for the second quarter of fiscal year 2003, "[t]he Company conditioned its estimate on the performance of the overall economy. It said that if the economy improved, Siebel's business would improve, and that, conversely, if the economy did not improve, then Siebel's business would not improve." The SEC alleges that the public statements "linked the Company's prospective performance to the economy's performance— that is, if the economy improved, Siebel's business would improve."

The SEC contends that "[b]ased on these disclosures, the total mix of information available to investors was that Siebel's business had performed poorly in the first quarter and would improve in the second quarter only if the economy improved." Allegedly, Mr. Goldman's "statements materially contrasted with the public statements that Thomas Siebel made during the April 4 and 23 conference calls and at the ... conference on April 28. For example, in contrast to the apocalyptic economic environment that Thomas Siebel described at the [April 28th] conference, Goldman's disclosure at the April 30 [events] were significantly more positive and upbeat. Unlike the Company's prior public disclosure about its prospective performance in the second quarter, Goldman's statements about the Company's business were not linked to or conditioned upon the performance of the economy."

The complaint further alleges that analysts, who were participating in the April 23rd conference call and the April 28th conference, "wanted to know how much of the projected increase in

---

[3]   The complaint indicates that Thomas M. Siebel is Siebel Systems's "founder and Chairman of the Board of Directors and was, until May 2004, its Chief Executive Officer."

software license revenues in the second quarter compared to the first quarter revenues was attributable to the deals that slipped from the first quarter as opposed to the Company's expectation that it would generate new business in the second quarter." The SEC alleges that when the analysts repeatedly inquired about the impact of the slipped deals on Siebel Systems's second quarter guidance, Mr. Siebel "avoided," "evaded," and "directly declined to answer the question." The SEC maintains that, publicly, "the total mix of information available to investors did not include information that would enable either analysts or investors to determine whether the increased guidance for the second quarter represented an improvement over the first quarter."

The complaint further alleges that Siebel Systems failed to file the requisite Form 8–K disclosing the material nonpublic information that Mr. Goldman had disclosed at the private meetings within the time frame specified by the SEC's rules, nor did it "disseminate that information through another method of disclosure reasonably designed to provide broad, non-exclusionary distribution of the information to the public."

* * *

VIOLATION OF REGULATION FD

The complaint alleges four nonpublic material disclosures made by Mr. Goldman which are the basis for the SEC's claims for violations of Regulation FD: (1) that there were some *five million dollar deals* in the company's pipeline for the second quarter of 2003; (2) that *new deals* were coming into the sales pipeline; (3) that the company's sales pipeline was "*growing*" or "*building*;" and (4) that the company's sales or business activity levels were "*good*" or "*better*." The complaint relies on no statements regarding specific earnings or sales figures. Defendants argue that dismissal of the complaint is warranted because the four statements at issue cannot support a conclusory allegation that these statements were either material or nonpublic.

Regulation FD does not contain definitions for the terms "material" or "nonpublic." In the SEC's release discussing the proposed adoption of the regulation, the SEC "recognize[d] that materiality judgments can be difficult." . . .

In the SEC's Adopting Release, the SEC . . . noted the frequently expressed concern that the regulation would not lead to broader dissemination of information, but would instead have a "chilling effect" on disclosure of information by the issuer. The potential chilling effect could conceivably result in the issuers "speak[ing] less often out of fear of liability based on a post hoc assessment that disclosed information was material," and "such a chilling effect result[ing] from Regulation FD [ ] would be a cost to the overall market efficiency and capital formation."

In response to this concern and in recognizing that the market is best served by more, rather than less, disclosure of information by issuers, the SEC modified the proposed Regulation FD to include certain safeguards to narrow the applicability of Regulation FD so as not to diminish the flow of information. Despite its previous acknowledgment, in the Proposing Release, that materiality judgments can be difficult, the SEC did not find that the "appropriate answer to this difficulty is to set forth a bright-line test, or an exclusive list of material items for purpose of Regulation FD." Although the SEC declined to set forth an all-inclusive list of what matters are to be deemed material, it did provide seven categories of information or events that have a higher probability of being considered material. The seven enumerated categories are:

> (1) Earnings information; (2) mergers, acquisitions, tender offers, joint ventures, or changes in assets; (3) new products or discoveries, or developments regarding customers or supplies (e.g., the acquisition or loss of a contract); (4) changes in control or in management; (5) change in auditors or auditor notification that the issuer may no longer rely on an auditor's audit report; (6) events regarding the issuer's securities—e.g., defaults on strict securities, calls of securities for redemption, repurchase plans, stock splits or changes in dividends, changes to rights of security holders, public or private sales of additional securities; and (7) bankruptcies and receiverships.

The specific matters included in the list, however, are not *per se* material.

Although Regulation FD does not contain definitions for the terms "material" or "nonpublic," the Adopting Release advises that those terms are to be defined as they have been in previous case law. With regard to the "nonpublic" element, information is nonpublic if it has not been disseminated in a manner sufficient to ensure its availability to the investing public. . . .

* * *

In applying the aforementioned principles to the case at bar, the allegations in the complaint fail to demonstrate that Regulation FD was violated. Regulation FD was never intended to be utilized in the manner attempted by the SEC under these circumstances. The statements relied upon in the complaint cannot support a conclusion that material information privately provided by Mr. Goldman was unavailable to the public. Specifically, Mr. Goldman's private statement regarding the existence of five million dollar deals in the company's pipeline for the second quarter was equivalent in substance to the information previously disclosed by Mr. Siebel. With regard to the guidance for the second quarter, Mr. Siebel stated at the April 23rd conference call:

> Our guidance and license revenue for the quarter is 120 to 140 million range. I think that we'll see lots of small deals. We'll see some medium deals. We'll see a number of deals over a million dollars. And I suspect we'll see some *greater than five*. And now that's what the mix will look like. (emphasis added).

The SEC argues that Mr. Goldman's statement, in contrast, was in the *present* tense, and hence constitutes a factually different material statement than that made by Mr. Siebel. The SEC contends that unlike Mr. Goldman's statement, Mr. Siebel's statement was in the *future* tense, and Mr. Siebel's use of the word "suspect" indicates his statement was not a present fact, but rather was forward looking.

It would appear that in examining publicly and privately disclosed information, the SEC has scrutinized, at an extremely heightened level, every particular word used in the statement, including the tense of verbs and the general syntax of each sentence. . . . Such an approach places an unreasonable burden on a company's management and spokespersons to become linguistic experts, or otherwise live in fear of violating Regulation FD should the words they use later be interpreted by the SEC as connoting even the slightest variance from the company's public statements.

Regulation FD does not require that corporate officials only utter verbatim statements that were previously publicly made. . . . To require a more demanding standard . . . could compel companies to discontinue any spontaneous communications so that the content of any intended communication may be examined by a lexicologist to ensure that the proposed statement discloses the exact information in the same form as was publicly disclosed. If Regulation FD is applied in such a manner, the very purpose of the regulation, *i.e.*, to provide the public with a broad flow of relevant investment information, would be thwarted.

Mr. Goldman's private statement regarding the existence of five million dollars deals in the company's pipeline for the second quarter was equivalent in substance to the information publicly disclosed by the company in that it conveyed the same material information. As long as the private statement conveys the same material information that the public statement publicly conveyed, Regulation FD is not implicated, and hence no greater form of disclosure, pursuant to the regulation, is required. Although Mr. Goldman's statement was not literally a word for word recitation of Mr. Siebel's disclosure, both provided the same information, and Mr. Goldman's statement did not add, contradict, or significantly alter the material information available to the general public. It therefore cannot constitute a sufficient factual basis on which to allege a nonpublic disclosure of material information in violation of Regulation FD.

Similarly unavailing are the SEC's claims that Mr. Goldman's private statements regarding new business in the pipeline and that the pipeline was "growing" or "building" was information which was not previously disclosed to the public. The SEC argues that Mr. Siebel "did not describe the status of the Company's pipeline." However, at the April 23rd conference call, a question was posed regarding the makeup of the pipeline with respect to "new versus exist[ing] customers." The verbatim transcript on which the SEC relies indicates that in response thereto, Mr. Siebel publicly stated, "every quarter will be some place between 45 and 55 percent of our business with new customers." Such a statement clearly indicated that the second quarter pipeline would include new deals.

Mr. Goldman's private description of the pipeline as "growing" or "building" provides no additional material information that was not previously publicly disclosed by the company. The complaint acknowledges Siebel Systems's April 23rd and 28th public statements that "the Company projected that its software license revenues would be in the range of $120 to $140 million, which was more than the Company's reported revenues for the first quarter." Moreover, the company publicly disclosed that the projected total revenues for the second quarter appeared to be in the 340 to 360 million dollar range, which was greater than the reported total revenues for the first quarter. Additionally, at the April 23rd conference call, Mr. Siebel explained that the anticipated increase in the license revenues was based on an analysis of the pipeline. At the April 28th conference, Mr. Siebel again explained that the projected increase was Siebel Systems's "best professional judgment based upon the pipeline with the deals that we saw . . ." Siebel Systems's public statements clearly disclosed that it was projecting an increase in revenues in the second quarter, and that this expectation was based, in part, upon an analysis of the pipeline. Based on this information, a reasonable investor would be aware that the sales pipeline was "growing" and "building." Hence Mr. Goldman's private wording, to that effect, added nothing to the total mix of information publicly available.

The SEC further alleges that Regulation FD was violated as a result of Mr. Goldman's private statements that Siebel Systems's sales or business activity levels were "good" or "better." Mr. Goldman's private statement that the activity levels were "good" or "better" was based on information available to the public since Siebel Systems publicly reported that it anticipated a future increase in the company's performance. The terms "better" and "good" are merely generalized descriptive labels based on the underlying quantitative information provided publicly by Siebel Systems. Given the detailed and specific information revealed in the company's public disclosures, Mr. Goldman's description of the company's performance and activity level as being "good" and "better" imparted no greater information to his private audiences than Siebel Systems had already disclosed to the public at large. Hence, the statements regarding the company's performance or activity levels being "good" or "better" did not alter the total mix of information already available to the reasonable investor.

The SEC maintains that Mr. Goldman's statements constituted nonpublic material information because his statements forecasted overall positive growth for the company, whereas the company's public statements avoided making such a positive affirmation. Although the SEC is not disputing that the public information was that the second quarter guidance was higher than the first quarter's actual results, the SEC asserts that this is not dispositive of whether business was improving. However, the information available to the public provides a sufficient factual basis for a reasonable investor to conclude that business was improving.

The SEC places great emphasis on the alleged actions taken by certain individuals who were in attendance at Mr. Goldman's private speaking engagements. The complaint alleges that certain attendees, and other individuals with whom they communicated, purchased Siebel Systems stock almost immediately after Mr. Goldman's private statements or soon thereafter, causing the market for Siebel Systems stock to significantly rise and for trading to surge. The SEC argues that taking these allegations as true, and drawing all reasonable inferences in its favor, leads to the conclusion that Mr. Goldman disclosed information that was both new and material.

A major factor in determining whether information is material is the importance attached to it by those who were exposed to the information as may be expressed by their reaction to the information. Although stock movement is a relevant factor to be considered in making the determination as to materiality, it is not, however, a sufficient factor alone to establish materiality.

An examination of the public and private statements do[es] not support a conclusory allegation that Mr. Goldman's statements were the disclosure of nonpublic material information. The actions taken by those in attendance at Mr. Goldman's speaking engagements, although a relevant consideration, do not change the nature or content of Mr. Goldman's statements. Regulation FD deals exclusively with the disclosure of material information. The regulation does not prohibit persons speaking on behalf of an issuer, from providing mere positive or negative characterizations, or their optimistic or pessimistic subjective general impressions, based upon or drawn from the material information available to the public. The mere fact that analysts might have considered Mr. Goldman's private statements significant is not, standing alone, a basis to infer that Regulation FD was violated.

The SEC further argues that Mr. Goldman's statements "constituted new information" because they were not "conditioned upon nor qualified by the performance of the economy," and therefore they "contrasted with the Company's prior statements and altered the total mix of information available to investors," which included, "that Siebel's business had performed poorly in the first quarter and would improve in the second quarter only if the economy improved."

It would be an unusual rule, indeed, to require that forecasts must repeatedly be accompanied by a warning that company performance might be affected by an improving or worsening economy. However, even if the potential effects of the economy constituted material information,[4] Siebel Systems had publicly disclosed that the performance of the company was linked to the performance of the economy. What Regulation FD does not require is that an individual, speaking privately on behalf of an issuer, repeat material information which has already been previously publicly proclaimed. Mr. Goldman's alleged failure to qualify his private statement about the company's performance, by linking it to, or conditioning it upon, the performance of the economy, cannot be alleged as a private disclosure of nonpublic information. Regulation FD only pertains to the required public disclosure of information, not the failure to repeat a particular public statement in private.[5]

Significantly, none of the statements challenged by the SEC falls squarely within the seven enumerated categories listed by the SEC, in the Adopting Release, as being more likely to be considered material. Applying Regulation FD in an overly aggressive manner cannot

---

[4] It is doubtful that a company's disclosure regarding its prospective performance being "linked to or conditioned upon the performance of the economy" would constitute material information. It is a fundamental and basic principle that the economy effects [sic] corporate America. Information which is so basic that a reasonable investor could be expected to know it does not constitute material facts.

[5] Although Regulation FD pertains solely to disclosure of information, the challenged communication need not be an expressed verbal or written statement. Tacit communications, such as a wink, nod, or a thumbs up or down gesture, may give rise to a Regulation FD violation.

effectively encourage full and complete public disclosure of facts reasonably deemed relevant to investment decisionmaking. It provides no clear guidance for companies to conform their conduct in compliance with Regulation FD. Instead, the enforcement of Regulation FD by excessively scrutinizing vague general comments has a potential chilling effect which can discourage, rather than, encourage public disclosure of material information.

In accepting the factual allegations in the complaint as true and drawing all reasonable inferences in the SEC's favor, the statements relied upon in the complaint fail to support its conclusory allegation that material information disclosed by Mr. Goldman in private, had not already been publicly disclosed by Siebel Systems. Accordingly, the complaint fails to sufficiently allege that Regulation FD was violated. . . .

* * *

QUESTIONS

1. Did investors other than the attendees at the meetings benefit from the Goldman's selective disclosures in any way? Are investors better off if the CFO does not speak?

2. Is there anything that Siebel could have done after the disclosures to avoid this enforcement action?

3. Did the participants who traded in Siebel stock after meeting with Goldman do anything wrong?

HYPOTHETICAL FIVE

Angela, Scranton Paper's former CFO, had caused Scranton Paper to overstate its revenues from The Paper Clip, an office supply store. Scranton Paper's auditor, Malone & Martinez, discovered the overstated revenues and demanded that Scranton Paper restate its past financial statements to correct the overstatement. Angela resigned right before the board of directors would have fired her for her role in overstating the revenues. On the day that Angela resigned, Scranton Paper issued a press release after the market closed announcing that she had resigned for "personal reasons." The press release made no mention of Malone & Martinez's demand that Scranton Paper restate its revenues. That same evening Michael, the CEO of Scranton Paper, drowned his sorrows at the local watering hole, the Paradise Lounge. "That Angela," moaned Michael to the bartender, "has ruined everything. I was going to hit a big payday when we sold Scranton Paper to a big office products conglomerate, but who will buy the company if we have to restate our earnings?" The bartender, Vikram, responded "Live and learn," as he drew Michael another beer. After serving Michael, Vikram went to the backroom, called his broker and told him that he wanted to sell short 10,000 shares of Scranton Paper. "Thanks for the tip" says Vikram after Michael leaves an extra $1 on the bar. Has Scranton Paper violated Regulation FD?

CHAPTER 5

RULE 10b–5 ANTIFRAUD

Rules and Statutes

—*Sections 9, 10(b), 18, 20(a), 21D, 21E, 27, 28 and 29 of the Exchange Act*

—*Rule 10b–5 of the Exchange Act*

MOTIVATING HYPOTHETICAL

DigitalBase, Inc. is a leading provider of computer database systems, with annual revenues of over $3 billion. Its shares are traded on the Nasdaq Capital Market. After many years of outstanding growth, DigitalBase's revenues and profits have leveled off. It has now been several years since DigitalBase's last major product introduction. Worse yet, cloud-based storage systems are starting to erode its market share. DigitalBase's CEO, Hillary, has pinned DigitalBase's hopes for future growth on developing a technological innovation, the GigaBase, which DigitalBase's research scientists believe will be able to hold several times more information than existing databases while providing greater security than the cloud. The problem is that manufacturing the GigaBase currently requires such exacting tolerances that it cannot be produced in commercial quantities at a competitive price. DigitalBase's manufacturing engineers have been working for over a year now to develop a cost-effective manufacturing process, but so far without success. Privately, DigitalBase's chief technology officer has told Hillary that he believes the odds of manufacturing the GigaBase in commercial quantities are about 50/50.

Publicly, Hillary has been relentlessly upbeat about the GigaBase. She introduced the GigaBase a year ago with the promise that it would double DigitalBase's profits. In conference calls with investment analysts since then, Hillary has repeatedly assured the analysts that progress on the GigaBase was "on schedule." Now, however, DigitalBase's chief technology officer has told Hillary that the GigaBase cannot be brought to market for at least two years, if ever. DigitalBase (reluctantly) discloses this news in its next Form 10–Q filing. DigitalBase's stock price tanks when the news is released, going from $25 per share to $15 per share in heavy trading.

I. THE ECONOMICS OF SECURITIES FRAUD AND PRIVATE RIGHTS OF ACTION

Talk is cheap. This platitude is particularly true when false talk does not lead to sanctions against the speaker. The disclosure regime imposed by the federal securities laws would provide little useful information to investors if the regime did not punish false statements by companies and their affiliates. In the worst case scenario, a failure to sanction officers who make false statements about their companies would quickly lead to the downward spiral of the "lemons effect" that we covered in Chapter 1. Truthful issuers would be driven from the market by lying companies, leading investors to ratchet downward the price they are willing to pay for the stock of the remaining, more fraudulent, pool of firms. As the "fraud" discount investors demand of all firms increases, remaining truthful firms face still greater pressure to either exit or engage in fraud themselves, eventually leading to a collapse of the market altogether. Antifraud liability checks this downward spiral.

Fraud affects the functioning of securities markets in a number of ways. Most conspicuously, fraud may influence how investors direct their capital. Firms that issue securities tend to disclose more information about their businesses in an effort to attract investors. If those disclosures are fraudulent, investors will pay an inflated price and companies will invest in projects that are not cost justified. Fraud may also allow companies to retain resources that would be better deployed elsewhere. Managers who fraudulently inflate their company's stock price may be able to invest in ill-advised empire building instead of paying cash flows to shareholders as dividends. Alternatively, managers may use fraud to keep the firm in business longer than justified when its assets should be redirected through the bankruptcy process. Investors will factor these costs into securities prices by discounting the amount that they are willing to pay for securities to reflect the risk of fraud. This discounting means that publicly-traded firms will face a higher cost of capital if capital markets are infected by fraud.

Misrepresentations by corporate managers also hurt the shareholders' ability to monitor the firm's performance and, in particular, evaluate the job the firm's managers are doing. Insofar as fraud insulates managers from scrutiny, it also may distort the market for corporate control. Poor managers may be able to discourage hostile acquirors by creating the illusion of strong performance. Managers may also have an incentive to distort prices in order to bolster their own compensation, either in the form of stock options or bonuses that are tied to the company's share price. Thus, deterring corporate misrepresentations can help make managers more accountable to shareholders.

The U.S. scheme of securities regulation deploys a variety of countermeasures to discourage fraud including third-party "gatekeepers," the topic of Chapter 12. Financial statements are audited by accounting firms, who are, in effect, "renting" their reputations to the firms that they audit. The work of the accountants is overseen by audit committees of outside directors, who also provide independent oversight of company disclosures. Rating agencies assess companies' creditworthiness. Analysts rate the credibility and completeness of company disclosures. In addition to these gatekeeper mechanisms, in Chapter 13 we cover SEC enforcement actions and criminal prosecution of fraudsters by the Justice Department and state prosecutors.

The principal focus of this chapter, private rights of action, promises additional deterrence. In fact, the SEC calls private rights of actions a "necessary supplement" to its own efforts in policing fraud. Rule 10b–5, promulgated under § 10(b) of the Exchange Act, represents the most widely used securities antifraud provision for private plaintiffs. We begin with a discussion of the implied private cause of action under Rule 10b–5, the "catch-all" antifraud provision for the federal securities laws..

A. THE RULE 10b–5 PRIVATE CAUSE OF ACTION

1. GENESIS

In the following excerpt, Milton Freeman, an SEC lawyer, explains how Rule 10b–5 was drafted and the relatively modest scope that was anticipated for the rule at its birth.

> It was one day in the year 1943, I believe. I was sitting in my office in the S.E.C. building in Philadelphia and I received a call from Jim Treanor who was then the Director of the Trading and Exchange Division. He said, "I have just been on the telephone with Paul Rowen," who was then the S.E.C. Regional Administrator in Boston, "and he has told me about the president of some company in Boston who is going around buying up the stock of his company from his own shareholders at $4.00 a share, and he has been telling them that the company is doing very badly, whereas, in fact, the earnings are going to be quadrupled and will be $2.00 a share for this coming year. Is there anything we can do about it?" So he came upstairs and I called in my secretary and I looked at Section 10(b) and I looked at Section 17 [of the Securities Act], and I put them together, and the only discussion we had there was where "in connection with the purchase or sale" should be, and we decided it should be at the end.
>
> We called the Commission and we got on the calendar, and I don't remember whether we got there that morning or after lunch. We passed a piece of paper around to all the commissioners. All the commissioners read the rule and they tossed it on the table, indicating approval. Nobody said anything except Sumner Pike who said, "Well," he said, "we are against fraud, aren't we?" That is how it happened.

Remarks of Milton Freeman, *Conference on Codification of the Federal Securities Laws*, 22 Bus. Law. 793, 922 (1967). From this rather mundane beginning, an elaborate common law of securities fraud has been created, largely by the courts, albeit with considerable encouragement from the SEC.

2. OVERLAP WITH OTHER CAUSES OF ACTION

Although broad in its scope, Rule 10b–5 of the Exchange Act does not explicitly provide a private cause of action for those injured in connection with the purchase or sale of securities. Other antifraud provisions, such as §§ 11 and 12 of the Securities Act, which we will cover in Chapter 8, do provide explicitly for private liability. Within the Exchange Act itself, §§ 9(e) and 18 provide explicit causes of action for investors who have been harmed by particular forms of securities fraud. Despite the lack of any language providing for a private cause of action in Rule 10b–5, in 1946 a federal district court recognized an implied private cause of action. *See Kardon v. National Gypsum Co.*, 69 F.Supp. 512 (E.D. Pa. 1946). Because the private cause of action under Rule 10b–5 is judicially implied, much of the doctrine surrounding Rule 10b–5 has developed through case law. As Justice Rehnquist in 1975 opined about Rule 10b–5: "[W]e deal with a judicial oak which has grown from little more than a legislative acorn." *Blue Chip Stamps, et al. v. Manor Drug Stores*, 421 U.S. 723 (1975). The existence of that cause of action was subsequently acknowledged by the Supreme Court as "beyond peradventure." *Herman & MacLean v. Huddleston*, 459 U.S. 375 (1983).

The question that lingered much longer in the courts was the relation of the Rule 10b–5 implied private cause of action to private causes of action explicitly provided for by Congress in the Securities Act and the Exchange Act. Section 11 of the Securities Act, for example, provides an explicit private cause of action for misstatements and omissions in public offering registration statements. Can a plaintiff bring suit under both § 10(b) of the Exchange Act and § 11 of the Securities Act? In *Herman & MacLean v. Huddleston et al.*, 459 U.S. 375 (1983), the Supreme Court answered in the affirmative. The Court wrote:

> Although limited in scope, § 11 places a relatively minimal burden on a plaintiff. In contrast, § 10(b) is a "catchall" antifraud provision, but it requires a plaintiff to carry a heavier burden to establish a cause of action. While a § 11 action must be brought by a purchaser of a registered security, must be based on misstatements or omissions in a registration statement, and can only be brought against certain parties, a § 10(b) action can be brought by a purchaser or seller of "*any* security" against "*any* person" who has used "*any* manipulative or deceptive device or contrivance" in connection with the purchase or sale of a security. However, a § 10(b) plaintiff carries a heavier burden than a § 11 plaintiff. Most significantly, he must prove that the defendant acted with scienter, *i.e.*, with intent to deceive, manipulate, or defraud.

> Since § 11 and § 10(b) address different types of wrongdoing, we see no reason to carve out an exception to § 10(b) for fraud occurring in a registration statement just because the same conduct may also be actionable under § 11.

The most important effect of the *Herman & MacLean* decision is to relegate the private right of action provided for in § 18 of the Exchange Act (misstatements in filings with the SEC) to the dustbin of history. Section 18's explicit cause of action is more onerous to plead and prove than the Rule 10b–5 cause of action. As a result, plaintiffs have little reason to use it. Sections 11 and 12 of the Securities Act, however, continue to play an important role in securities fraud litigation arising from public offerings.

3. SECTION 9 OF THE EXCHANGE ACT

Section 9 of the Exchange Act prohibits manipulative acts on national securities exchanges. Section 9 bans manipulative activities that are fraudulent, but allows, within regulated limits, certain activities that, despite being susceptible to manipulation, may be important to the efficient functioning of securities markets. For example, stabilization efforts by an underwriter in the context of a public offering (covered in Chapter 7) are regulated rather than banned. Generally, § 9 prohibits wash sales, matched orders, manipulative transactions, touting, tipster sheets, and other misrepresentations.

Traders engaged in a wash sale or matched orders, for example, essentially sell securities to themselves, creating an illusion of elevated trading volume. As both the buyer and the seller in a transaction, a trader in a wash sale or matched order can progressively raise the price in the transactions in the hopes of influencing the overall market price. Section 9(a)(1) prohibits wash sales and matched orders effected for "the purpose of creating a false or misleading appearance of active trading in any security registered on a national securities exchange, or a false or misleading appearance with respect to the market for any such security. . . ." "Purpose" means that the wash sale or matched order must have been done with scienter for the purpose of creating a false or misleading appearance of active trading for liability to attach.

Section 9 also regulates stabilization tactics, options, and practices affecting secondary market volatility. Section 9(a)(2) prohibits manipulative activity on national securities exchanges. In enacting § 9(a)(2), Congress intended to ban tactics used to falsely create an appearance of genuine demand in a security. There are three separate elements to a cause of action under § 9(a)(2):

- engaging in a series of transactions in any security registered on a national exchange creating actual or apparent active trading in such security, or raising or depressing the price of such security

- carrying out these transactions with scienter

- transacting for the purpose of inducing the purchase or sale of such security by others

These elements have been interpreted broadly. For example, a "series of transactions" can include bids, purchases, sales, and short sales. Courts have held that as few as three transactions constitute a "series."

Unlike § 10(b), § 9 explicitly provides both for SEC enforcement and a private right of action. Under § 9(e), the plaintiff class is limited to those who bought or sold securities on a national securities exchange at a price that was affected by market manipulation, with damages measured by the change in price.

4. OVERLAP WITH STATE LAW CAUSES OF ACTION

The Exchange Act contains a "saving clause," § 28(a), preserving state causes of action against preemption. Congress made a significant incursion into state law remedies in 1998, however, when it passed the Securities Litigation Uniform Standards Act, codified in Exchange Act § 28(f), which preempts "covered class action[s]" under state law. The provision preempts class actions under state law involving the securities of issuers, among others, that are listed on a national securities exchange whose listing standards are approved by the SEC, including the NYSE and Nasdaq. The Supreme Court has construed the Act to preempt class actions involving not only the purchase and sale of securities, but also *holding* of securities induced by misrepresentation.

See Merrill Lynch, Pierce, Fenner & Smith, Inc. v. Dabit, 547 U.S. 71 (2006). The Act excludes from preemption, however, derivative actions, as well as fraud claims based on purchases by the issuer of its own securities or recommendations by the company's board concerning mergers and tenders offers. Claims of this sort are routinely litigated in state corporate law actions.

B. THE CLASS ACTION MECHANISM

Securities transactions come in many varieties. The founders of a corporation may put seed money into the corporation in return for the initial capital stock. As the corporation grows larger, it may issue securities to a small number of relatively wealthy, sophisticated investors (individual and institutional) through a private placement. When a company (or its officers) commits fraud against a small number of investors, each investor may attempt to pursue a Rule 10b–5 or other available securities antifraud action individually.

Eventually, a growing corporation may tap the public capital markets through a public offering to thousands of investors. Once a company's securities are public, investors may buy and sell that security thousands of times every day. If a public corporation commits fraud either in a public offering or through a misleading statement (or omission) that affects secondary market trading, an individual still has a private cause of action. Such an action, however, will generally not be cost justified. Filing and pursuing a securities fraud action takes a considerable amount of time and money. For any one investor among potentially thousands who are defrauded, the benefit of pursuing a fraud action individually (based on the small number of shares the one investor purchased) is typically far outweighed by the high fixed costs of the lawsuit.

Defrauded public investors may turn instead to a class action to aggregate their common interests in a federal securities fraud lawsuit. In the typical securities fraud class action, the plaintiffs' attorney represents thousands of investors who have purchased securities during the time that a misrepresentation was distorting the security price. For fraud that affects the shares of a large public company, a class action may be the only economically feasible means for dispersed investors to pursue a legal remedy. Each of the individual investors may have a very small claim, but the aggregation of those claims can potentially sum to hundreds of millions, or billions, of dollars.

HYPOTHETICAL ONE

Recall that Hillary, the CEO of DigitalBase, promised that the new GigaBase product line would "double" DigitalBase's profits. Moreover, she reassured analysts that progress on GigaBase was "on schedule." It turns out that the release of GigaBase in fact will be delayed for at least two years (if not more). After the delay in GigaBase is revealed to the market, DigitalBase's stock price plummeted from $25 to $15 per share.

Assume that Hillary owns 20% of the outstanding voting common stock (for a total of 20 million shares). Assume that the other 80% of the stock is held by over 2000 outside investors, none of whom owns individually more than 0.1% of the stock.

1. Put yourself in the shoes of a plaintiffs' attorney. Should you file a class action against DigitalBase and Hillary based on her statements concerning GigaBase? What other information might you find useful with respect to GigaBase and Hillary to decide whether the action would be economically worthwhile?

2. Suppose you learn that DigitalBase and Hillary have a directors and officers liability insurance policy covering securities fraud actions. How does this affect your decision whether to file suit?

C. SORTING THE GOOD FROM THE BAD

As you will see in the cases that follow, the courts and Congress have worried that securities fraud class actions may fall short of optimal deterrence. Distinguishing fraud from mere business reversals is difficult. The external observer may not know whether a drop in a company's stock price is due to a prior intentional misstatement about its prospects—i.e., fraud—or a result of risky business decisions that did not pan out—i.e., misjudgment or bad luck. If unable to distinguish between the two, plaintiffs' lawyers must rely on limited, publicly available indicia when deciding whom to sue. Such indicia include SEC filings and press releases from the company, or insider trading in unusual amounts by the managers allegedly responsible for the fraud. Thus, a substantial drop in stock price following news that contradicts a previous optimistic statement may be sufficient to provoke a lawsuit. That leaves courts with the difficult task of sorting out the cases with potential merit from those with little or no merit (often referred to as "strike suits"). Courts and jurors, with hindsight, may have difficulty distinguishing knowingly false statements from unfortunate business decisions.

But see above.

If plaintiffs can withstand a motion to dismiss, defendants generally will find settlement cheaper than litigating to a jury verdict, even if the defendants believe that a jury probably would decide in their favor. Fewer than one securities fraud class action per year goes to trial. Any complaint plausible enough to get past a motion to dismiss, may be worth settling if only to avoid the costs of discovery and attorneys' fees, which can be enormous in these cases. Securities fraud class actions are expensive to defend because the critical litigation issue will often be scienter—what did the defendants know and when did they know it. The most helpful source for uncovering those facts will be the documents in the company's possession. Producing all documents relevant to the knowledge of senior executives over many months or even years can be a massive undertaking for a corporate defendant. Having produced the documents, the company can then anticipate a long series of depositions, as the plaintiffs' counsel seeks to determine whether the executives' recollections square with the documents. Furthermore, the cost in lost productivity may dwarf the expense of attorneys' fees and other direct litigation costs. Beyond the cost in executives' time, the mere existence of the class action may disrupt relationships with suppliers and customers, who will be understandably leery of dealing with a business accused of fraud.

Putting to one side the costs of litigation, the enormous potential damages also make settlement an attractive option for the company, even when it thinks it has a good prospect of prevailing at trial. The math is straightforward: A 10% chance of a $250 million judgment means that a settlement for $24.9 million makes sense. The combination of the cost of litigating securities class actions and the potential for enormous judgments means that even weak cases may produce a settlement if they are not dismissed before trial. Roughly half of all securities class actions are dismissed. Among cases that survive a motion to dismiss, roughly half settle for an amount less than a reasonable estimate of defense costs. If both weak and strong cases lead to settlements, the deterrent effect of class actions is diluted because innocent and wrongful conduct both lead to sanctions. Moreover, plaintiffs' attorneys that realize the large incentive on the part of companies and their officers to settle even weak cases will respond with the filing of an even greater number of strike suits.

These weaknesses in the system led Congress to rein in securities fraud class actions by enacting the Private Securities Litigation Reform Act of 1995 (PSLRA). Among other things the PSLRA:

- imposes a rebuttable presumption that the lead plaintiff in a class action is the shareholder with the largest financial interest in the class action litigation

- requires that plaintiffs plead with particularity facts leading to a strong inference of scienter

- imposes a stay on discovery until after the motion to dismiss is decided

- provides a safe harbor for forward-looking statements

- limits the liability of defendants not engaged in intentional fraud to their proportionate share of the harm caused

Significantly, the PSLRA has not diminished the number of lawsuits. This may be because the PSLRA did not change the measure of damages in most securities fraud cases. We will see in the damages section that this measure, an "out-of-pocket" measure intended to compensate investors, creates potentially ruinous consequences for corporations and their officers exposed to antifraud liability, particularly in the context of fraud affecting the secondary market.

As you go through the materials in this chapter on Rule 10b–5 liability, consider how the PSLRA has affected the ability of plaintiffs to file both meritorious and frivolous securities action claims.

QUESTIONS

1. Given the possibility that large damages may attract plaintiffs' attorneys to file non-meritorious suits for their settlement value, why do you think that Congress did not change the damages formula for Rule 10b–5 actions when it adopted the Private Securities Litigation Reform Act?

2. Are there any alternatives to private causes of action for deterring fraud? How do those alternatives compare to class actions?

3. Who was harmed and who benefited from the misrepresentations made by Hillary and DigitalBase? Should all of those injured have the ability to bring a private cause of action under Rule 10b–5? Who should pay the damages?

II. WHO CAN SUE UNDER RULE 10b–5?

A threshold question under Rule 10b–5 is who can bring a lawsuit against individuals and entities that have violated the rule. The SEC obviously can, but who else has standing to enforce the rule? Rule 10b–5's "in connection with" requirement limits who can sue under this rule. In addition, the lead plaintiff provision of the PSLRA gives certain investors control in a class action under the rule.

A. THE "IN CONNECTION WITH" REQUIREMENT

The question of who can sue for violations of Rule 10b–5 turns on the courts' interpretation of the clause requiring that the fraud be "in connection with the purchase or sale of any security." The following two cases address limitations on standing to bring suit based on this language. The first answers the question of whether a plaintiff must have actually purchased or sold to recover.

Blue Chip Stamps, et al. v. Manor Drug Stores
421 U.S. 723 (1975).

■ REHNQUIST, J.

This case requires us to consider whether the offerees of a stock offering, made pursuant to an antitrust consent decree and registered under the Securities Act of 1933, may maintain a private cause of action for money damages where they allege that the offeror has violated the provisions of Rule 10b–5 of the Securities and Exchange Commission, but where they have neither purchased nor sold any of the offered shares.

I

In 1963 the United States filed a civil antitrust action against Blue Chip Stamp Co. (Old Blue Chip), a company in the business of providing trading stamps to retailers, and nine retailers who owned 90% of its shares. In 1967 the action was terminated by the entry of a consent decree. The decree contemplated a plan of reorganization whereby Old Blue Chip was to be merged into a newly formed corporation, Blue Chip Stamps (New Blue Chip). The holdings of the majority shareholders of Old Blue Chip were to be reduced, and New Blue Chip, one of the petitioners here, was required under the plan to offer a substantial number of its shares of common stock to retailers who had used the stamp service in the past but who were not shareholders in the old company. Under the terms of the plan, the offering to nonshareholder users was to be proportional to past stamp usage and the shares were to be offered in units consisting of common stock and debentures.

The reorganization plan was carried out, the offering was registered with the SEC as required by the 1933 Act, and a prospectus was distributed to all offerees as required by § 5 of that Act. Somewhat more than 50% of the offered units were actually purchased. In 1970, two years after the offering, respondent, a former user of the stamp service and therefore an offeree of the 1968 offering, filed this suit. . . .

Respondent's complaint alleged, *inter alia*, that the prospectus prepared and distributed by Blue Chip in connection with the offering was materially misleading in its overly pessimistic appraisal of Blue Chip's status and future prospects. It alleged that Blue Chip intentionally made the prospectus overly pessimistic in order to discourage respondent and other members of the allegedly large class whom it represents from accepting what was intended to be a bargain offer, so that the rejected shares might later be offered to the public at a higher price. The complaint alleged that class members because of and in reliance on the false and misleading prospectus failed to purchase the offered units. . . .

The only portion of the litigation thus initiated which is before us is whether respondent may base its action on Rule 10b–5 of the Securities and Exchange Commission without having either bought or sold the securities described in the allegedly misleading prospectus. . . .

Section 10(b) of the 1934 Act does not by its terms provide an express civil remedy for its violation. Nor does the history of this provision provide any indication that Congress considered the problem of private suits under it at the time of its passage. Similarly there is no indication that the Commission in adopting Rule 10b–5 considered the question of private civil remedies under this provision.

Despite the contrast between the provisions of Rule 10b–5 and the numerous carefully drawn express civil remedies provided in the Acts of both 1933 and 1934, it was held in 1946 by the United States District Court for the Eastern District of Pennsylvania that there was an implied private right of action under the Rule. *Kardon v. National Gypsum Co.*, 69 F.Supp. 512. . . . Within a few years after the seminal *Kardon* decision, the Court of Appeals for the Second Circuit concluded that the plaintiff class for purposes of a private damage action under § 10(b) and Rule 10b–5 was limited to actual purchasers and sellers of securities. *Birnbaum v. Newport Steel Corp.*, 193 F.2d 461. . . . For the reasons hereinafter stated, we are of the opinion that *Birnbaum* was rightly decided, and that it bars respondent from maintaining this suit under Rule 10b–5.

* * *

III

The panel which decided *Birnbaum* [concluded that s]ince both § 10(b) and Rule 10b–5 proscribed only fraud "in connection with the purchase or sale" of securities, and since the history of § 10(b) revealed no congressional intention to extend a private civil remedy for money damages to other than defrauded purchasers or sellers of securities, in contrast to the express civil remedy provided by § 16(b) of the 1934 Act, the court concluded that the plaintiff class in a Rule 10b–5 action was limited to actual purchasers and sellers. . . .

In 1957 and again in 1959, the Securities and Exchange Commission sought from Congress amendment of § 10(b) to change its wording from "in connection with the purchase or sale of any security" to "in connection with the purchase or sale of, or any attempt to purchase or sell, any security." In the words of a memorandum submitted by the Commission to a congressional committee, the

purpose of the proposed change was "to make section 10(b) also
applicable to manipulative activities in connection with any attempt to
purchase or sell any security." Opposition to the amendment was based
on fears of the extension of civil liability under § 10(b) that it would
cause. Neither change was adopted by Congress.

legislative opposition to expanded liability

The longstanding acceptance by the courts, coupled with Congress'
failure to reject *Birnbaum's* reasonable interpretation of the wording of
§ 10(b), wording which is directed toward injury suffered "in connection
with the purchase or sale" of securities, argues significantly in favor of
acceptance of the *Birnbaum* rule by this Court.

* * *

While the damages suffered by purchasers and sellers pursuing a
§ 10(b) cause of action may on occasion be difficult to ascertain, in the
main such purchasers and sellers at least seek to base recovery on a
demonstrable number of shares traded. In contrast, a putative plaintiff,
who neither purchases nor sells securities but sues instead for
intangible economic injury such as loss of a noncontractual opportunity
to buy or sell, is more likely to be seeking a largely conjectural and
speculative recovery in which the number of shares involved will
depend on the plaintiff's subjective hypothesis. . . .

The principal express nonderivative private civil remedies, created
by Congress contemporaneously with the passage of § 10(b), for
violations of various provisions of the 1933 and 1934 Acts are by their
terms expressly limited to purchasers or sellers of securities. Thus
§ 11(a) of the 1933 Act confines the cause of action it grants to "any
person acquiring such security" while the remedy granted by § 12 of
that Act is limited to the "person purchasing such security." . . .

Having said all this, we would by no means be understood as
suggesting that we are able to divine from the language of § 10(b) the
express "intent of Congress" as to the contours of a private cause of
action under Rule 10b–5. When we deal with private actions under Rule
10b–5, we deal with a judicial oak which has grown from little more
than a legislative acorn. Such growth may be quite consistent with the
congressional enactment and with the role of the federal judiciary in
interpreting it, but it would be disingenuous to suggest that either
Congress in 1934 or the Securities and Exchange Commission in 1942
foreordained the present state of the law with respect to Rule 10b–5. It
is therefore proper that we consider, in addition to the factors already
discussed, what may be described as policy considerations when we
come to flesh out the portions of the law with respect to which neither
the congressional enactment nor the administrative regulations offer
conclusive guidance.

Three principal classes of potential plaintiffs are presently barred
by the *Birnbaum* rule. First are potential purchasers of shares, either
in a new offering or on the Nation's post-distribution trading markets,
who allege that they decided not to purchase because of an unduly
gloomy representation or the omission of favorable material which
made the issuer appear to be a less favorable investment vehicle than it
actually was. Second are actual shareholders in the issuer who allege
that they decided not to sell their shares because of unduly rosy
representation or a failure to disclose unfavorable material. Third are

shareholders, creditors, and perhaps others related to an issuer who suffered loss in the value of their investment due to corporate or insider activities in connection with the purchase or sale of securities which violate Rule 10b–5. It has been held that shareholder members of the second and third of these classes may frequently be able to circumvent the *Birnbaum* limitation through bringing a derivative action on behalf of the corporate issuer if the latter is itself a purchaser or seller of securities. But the first of these classes, of which respondent is a member, cannot claim the benefit of such a rule.

A great majority of the many commentators on the issue before us have taken the view that the *Birnbaum* limitation on the plaintiff class in a Rule 10b–5 action for damages is an arbitrary restriction which unreasonably prevents some deserving plaintiffs from recovering damages which have in fact been caused by violations of Rule 10b–5. The Securities and Exchange Commission has filed an amicus brief in this case espousing that same view. We have no doubt that this is indeed a disadvantage of the *Birnbaum* rule, and if it had no countervailing advantages it would be undesirable as a matter of policy, however much it might be supported by precedent and legislative history. But we are of the opinion that there are countervailing advantages to the *Birnbaum* rule, purely as a matter of policy, although those advantages are more difficult to articulate than is the disadvantage.

There has been widespread recognition that litigation under Rule 10b–5 presents a danger of vexatiousness different in degree and in kind from that which accompanies litigation in general. . . .

[I]n the field of federal securities laws governing disclosure of information even a complaint which by objective standards may have very little chance of success at trial has a settlement value to the plaintiff out of any proportion to its prospect of success at trial so long as he may prevent the suit from being resolved against him by dismissal or summary judgment. The very pendency of the lawsuit may frustrate or delay normal business activity of the defendant which is totally unrelated to the lawsuit.

* * *

The potential for possible abuse of the liberal discovery provisions of the Federal Rules of Civil Procedure may likewise exist in this type of case to a greater extent than they do in other litigation. The prospect of extensive deposition of the defendant's officers and associates and the concomitant opportunity for extensive discovery of business documents is a common occurrence in this and similar types of litigation. To the extent that this process eventually produces relevant evidence which is useful in determining the merits of the claims asserted by the parties, it bears the imprimatur of those Rules and of the many cases liberally interpreting them. But to the extent that it permits a plaintiff with a largely groundless claim to simply take up the time of a number of other people, with the right to do so representing an *in terrorem* increment of the settlement value, rather than a reasonably founded hope that the process will reveal relevant evidence, it is a social cost rather than a benefit. Yet to broadly expand the class of plaintiffs who may sue under Rule 10b–5 would appear to encourage the least appealing aspect of the use of the discovery rules.

Without the *Birnbaum* rule, an action under Rule 10b–5 will turn largely on which oral version of a series of occurrences the jury may decide to credit, and therefore no matter how improbable the allegations of the plaintiff, the case will be virtually impossible to dispose of prior to trial other than by settlement. . . .

The *Birnbaum* rule, on the other hand, permits exclusion prior to trial of those plaintiffs who were not themselves purchasers or sellers of the stock in question. The fact of purchase of stock and the fact of sale of stock are generally matters which are verifiable by documentation, and do not depend upon oral recollection, so that failure to qualify under the *Birnbaum* rule is a matter that can normally be established by the defendant either on a motion to dismiss or on a motion for summary judgment.

Obviously there is no general legal principle that courts in fashioning substantive law should do so in a manner which makes it easier, rather than more difficult, for a defendant to obtain a summary judgment. But in this type of litigation, where the mere existence of an unresolved lawsuit has settlement value to the plaintiff not only because of the possibility that he may prevail on the merits, an entirely legitimate component of settlement value, but because of the threat of extensive discovery and disruption of normal business activities which may accompany a lawsuit which is groundless in any event, but cannot be proved so before trial, such a factor is not to be totally dismissed. The *Birnbaum* rule undoubtedly excludes plaintiffs who have in fact been damaged by violations of Rule 10b–5, and to that extent it is undesirable. But it also separates in a readily demonstrable manner the group of plaintiffs who actually purchased or actually sold, and whose version of the facts is therefore more likely to be believed by the trier of fact, from the vastly larger world of potential plaintiffs who might successfully allege a claim but could seldom succeed in proving it. And this fact is one of its advantages.

[I]n the absence of the *Birnbaum* rule, it would be sufficient for a plaintiff to prove that he had failed to purchase or sell stock by reason of a defendant's violation of Rule 10b–5. . . . Plaintiff's proof would not be that he purchased or sold stock, a fact which would be capable of documentary verification in most situations, but instead that he decided *not* to purchase or sell stock. Plaintiff's entire testimony could be dependent upon uncorroborated oral evidence of many of the crucial elements of his claim, and still be sufficient to go to the jury. The jury would not even have the benefit of weighing the plaintiff's version against the defendant's version, since the elements to which the plaintiff would testify would be in many cases totally unknown and unknowable to the defendant. . . . The virtue of the *Birnbaum* rule, simply stated, in this situation, is that it limits the class of plaintiffs to those who have at least dealt in the security to which the prospectus, representation, or omission relates. And their dealing in the security, whether by way of purchase or sale, will generally be an objectively demonstrable fact in an area of the law otherwise very much dependent upon oral testimony. In the absence of the *Birnbaum* doctrine, bystanders to the securities marketing process could await developments on the sidelines without risk, claiming that inaccuracies in disclosure caused nonselling in a falling market and that unduly pessimistic predictions by the issuer followed by a rising market caused them to allow retrospectively golden opportunities to pass.

* * *

Thus we conclude that what may be called considerations of policy, which we are free to weigh in deciding this case, are by no means entirely on one side of the scale. Taken together with the precedential support for the *Birnbaum* rule over a period of more than 20 years, and the consistency of that rule with what we can glean from the intent of Congress, they lead us to conclude that it is a sound rule and should be followed.

* * *

NOTES

1. *The standing of the SEC.* Neither the SEC nor the Justice Department need to show that an actual purchaser or seller was defrauded to bring suit for violations of Rule 10b–5. *See SEC v. National Securities, Inc.*, 393 U.S. 453, 467 n. 9 (1969).

2. *Injunctive relief.* Lower courts have disagreed after *Blue Chip* on the question of whether a plaintiff must be a purchaser or seller in order to seek injunctive relief. *Compare Tully v. Mott Supermarkets, Inc.*, 540 F.2d 187, 194 (3d Cir. 1976) (allowing standing) *with Cowin v. Bresler*, 741 F.2d 410, 424–425 (D.C. Cir. 1984) (rejecting standing).

3. *Derivative actions.* Shareholders who have neither bought nor sold can bring a derivative action on behalf of the corporation if the corporation has purchased or sold securities. *See, e.g., Smith v. Ayres*, 845 F.2d 1360 (5th Cir. 1988).

4. *"Forced sellers."* The courts of appeals have also recognized standing for shareholders who have been fraudulently induced to give up their shares, for example, in a merger or liquidation. *See, e.g., Alley v. Miramon*, 614 F.2d 1372 (5th Cir. 1980).

QUESTIONS

1. How can investors be harmed by fraud if they have not engaged in a securities transaction?

2. Does eliminating non-purchasers and sellers from Rule 10b–5 actions solve the vexatious litigation problem?

HYPOTHETICAL TWO

Jesse is an avid follower of DigitalBase. Five years ago, he purchased 10,000 shares of DigitalBase at $5 per share in the hopes of large capital appreciation. At the time of Hillary's optimistic statements on the future of the GigaBase product line less than a year ago, Jesse had been planning to sell his shares at the current market price of $25 per share (to finance the renovation of his house). Hillary's optimistic statements, however, convinced Jesse to hold on to his 10,000 shares.

1. After the public revelation of significant delays in GigaBase, Jesse's stock now is worth only $15 per share. Does Jesse have standing to file suit under Rule 10b–5 against DigitalBase and Hillary?

2. Suppose in addition to holding on to his 10,000 shares, Jesse also decided to increase his DigitalBase investment by an additional 100 shares at $25 per share at the time of Hillary's optimistic statements. Does Jesse have standing to file suit under Rule 10b–5 against DigitalBase and Hillary?

The next case addresses how close the connection must be between the fraud and the requisite purchase or sale of security. Does theft, if it involves a security, give rise to a Rule 10b–5 claim?

SEC v. Zandford

535 U.S. 813 (2002).

■ STEVENS, J.

The Securities and Exchange Commission (SEC) filed a civil complaint alleging that a stockbroker violated both § 10(b) of the Securities Exchange Act of 1934 and the SEC's Rule 10b–5, by selling his customer's securities and using the proceeds for his own benefit without the customer's knowledge or consent. The question presented is whether the alleged fraudulent conduct was "in connection with the purchase or sale of any security" within the meaning of the statute and the rule.

I

Between 1987 and 1991, respondent was employed as a securities broker in the Maryland branch of a New York brokerage firm. In 1987, he persuaded William Wood, an elderly man in poor health, to open a joint investment account for himself and his mentally retarded daughter. According to the SEC's complaint, the "stated investment objectives for the account were 'safety of principal and income.'" The Woods granted respondent discretion to manage their account and a general power of attorney to engage in securities transactions for their benefit without prior approval. Relying on respondent's promise to "conservatively invest" their money, the Woods entrusted him with $419,255. Before Mr. Wood's death in 1991, all of that money was gone.

In 1991, [FINRA's predecessor] conducted a routine examination of respondent's firm and discovered that on over 25 separate occasions, money had been transferred from the Woods' account to accounts controlled by respondent. In due course, respondent was indicted in the United States District Court for the District of Maryland on 13 counts of wire fraud. The . . . count alleged that respondent sold securities in the Woods' account and then made personal use of the proceeds. . . . Each of the other counts alleged that he made wire transfers between Maryland and New York that enabled him to withdraw specified sums from the Woods' accounts. Some of those transfers involved respondent writing checks to himself from a mutual fund account held by the Woods, which required liquidating securities in order to redeem the checks. Respondent was convicted ..., sentenced to prison for 52 months, and ordered to pay $10,800 in restitution.

After respondent was indicted, the SEC filed a civil complaint in the same District Court alleging that respondent violated § 10(b) and Rule 10b–5 by engaging in a scheme to defraud the Woods and by misappropriating approximately $343,000 of the Woods' securities without their knowledge or consent. [The district court entered summary judgment against respondent. The Fourth Circuit reversed.]

The [Fourth Circuit] held that the civil complaint did not sufficiently allege the necessary connection because the sales of the Woods' securities were merely incidental to a fraud that "lay in absconding with the proceeds" of sales that were conducted in "a routine and customary fashion." ... Respondent's "scheme was simply to steal the Woods' assets" rather than to engage "in manipulation of a particular security." Ultimately, the court refused "to stretch the language of the securities fraud provisions to encompass every conversion or theft that happens to involve securities." Adopting what amounts to a "fraud on the market" theory of the statute's coverage, the court held that without some "relationship to market integrity or investor understanding," there is no violation of § 10(b).

We granted the SEC's petition for a writ of certiorari, to review the Court of Appeals' construction of the phrase "in connection with the purchase or sale of any security." ...

In its role enforcing the Act, the SEC ... has maintained that a broker who accepts payment for securities that he never intends to deliver, or who sells customer securities with intent to misappropriate the proceeds, violates § 10(b) and Rule 10b–5. This interpretation of the ambiguous text of § 10(b), in the context of formal adjudication, is entitled to deference if it is reasonable. ... While the statute must not be construed so broadly as to convert every common-law fraud that happens to involve securities into a violation of § 10(b), neither the SEC nor this Court has ever held that there must be a misrepresentation about the value of a particular security in order to run afoul of the Act.

The SEC claims respondent engaged in a fraudulent scheme in which he made sales of his customer's securities for his own benefit. Respondent submits that the sales themselves were perfectly lawful and that the subsequent misappropriation of the proceeds, though fraudulent, is not properly viewed as having the requisite connection with the sales; in his view, the alleged scheme is not materially different from a simple theft of cash or securities in an investment account. We disagree.

According to the complaint, respondent "engaged in a scheme to defraud" the Woods beginning in 1988, shortly after they opened their account, and that scheme continued throughout the 2-year period during which respondent made a series of transactions that enabled him to convert the proceeds of the sales of the Woods' securities to his own use. The securities sales and respondent's fraudulent practices were not independent events. This is not a case in which, after a lawful transaction had been consummated, a broker decided to steal the proceeds and did so. Nor is it a case in which a thief simply invested the proceeds of a routine conversion in the stock market. Rather, respondent's fraud coincided with the sales themselves.

Taking the allegations in the complaint as true, each sale was made to further respondent's fraudulent scheme; each was deceptive because it was neither authorized by, nor disclosed to, the Woods. With regard to the sales of shares in the Woods' mutual fund, respondent initiated these transactions by writing a check to himself from that account, knowing that redeeming the check would require the sale of securities. Indeed, each time respondent "exercised his power of disposition for his own benefit," that conduct, "without more," was a fraud. In the aggregate, the sales are properly viewed as a "course of business" that operated as a fraud or deceit on a stockbroker's customer. . . .

The benefit of a discretionary account is that it enables individuals, like the Woods, who lack the time, capacity, or know-how to supervise investment decisions, to delegate authority to a broker who will make decisions in their best interests without prior approval. If such individuals cannot rely on a broker to exercise that discretion for their benefit, then the account loses its added value. Moreover, any distinction between omissions and misrepresentations is illusory in the context of a broker who has a fiduciary duty to her clients. . . .

In *United States v. O'Hagan*, 521 U.S. 642 (1997), [excerpted in Chapter 6] we held that the defendant had committed fraud "in connection with" a securities transaction when he used misappropriated confidential information for trading purposes. We reasoned that "the fiduciary's fraud is consummated, not when the fiduciary gains the confidential information, but when, without disclosure to his principal, he uses the information to purchase or sell securities. The securities transaction and the breach of duty thus coincide. This is so even though the person or entity defrauded is not the other party to the trade, but is, instead, the source of the nonpublic information." The Court of Appeals distinguished *O'Hagan* by reading it to require that the misappropriated information or assets not have independent value to the client outside the securities market. We do not read *O'Hagan* as so limited. In the chief passage cited by the Court of Appeals for this proposition, we discussed the Government's position that "the misappropriation theory would not . . . apply to a case in which a person defrauded a bank into giving him a loan or embezzled cash from another, and then used the proceeds of the misdeed to purchase securities," because in that situation "the proceeds would have value to the malefactor apart from their use in a securities transaction, and the fraud would be complete as soon as the money was obtained." Even if this passage could be read to introduce a new requirement into § 10(b), it would not affect our analysis of this case, because the Woods' securities did not have value for respondent apart from their use in a securities transaction and the fraud was not complete before the sale of securities occurred.

[T]he SEC complaint describes a fraudulent scheme in which the securities transactions and breaches of fiduciary duty coincide. Those breaches were therefore "in connection with" securities sales within the meaning of § 10(b).[4] Accordingly, the judgment of the Court of Appeals is reversed, and the case is remanded for further proceedings consistent with this opinion.

NOTES

1.   *Privity and "intrinsic" value.* The broad interpretation of the "in connection with" requirement in *Zandford* supports the generally expansive reading of that phrase in the lower courts. Courts have consistently rejected the argument that the "in connection with" requirement requires contractual privity between the plaintiff and the defendant. *See, e.g., SEC v. Texas Gulf Sulphur*, 401 F.2d 833, 858–861 (2d Cir. 1968) ("Rule 10b–5 is violated whenever assertions are made, as here, in a manner reasonably calculated to influence the investing public, e.g., by means of the financial media, if such assertions are false and misleading or are so incomplete as to mislead."). Contractual privity meets the "in connection with" requirement but the requirement may be met even without privity. This conclusion's most important implications concern corporate issuers and officers, who are frequently named as defendants in Rule 10b–5 actions by plaintiffs who allege that their trades in the secondary markets were influenced by misrepresentations made by the corporate issuers and officers that go to the "intrinsic" value of the traded securities. The "intrinsic" value interpretation of the "in connection with" requirement extends to statements made that affect the stock price of other companies as well. *See Semerenko v. Cendant Corp.*, 223 F.3d 165 (3d Cir. 2000) (misstatements that affected the value of prospective merger partner are actionable). *But see Ontario Public Service Employees Union Pension Trust Fund v. Nortel Networks Corp.*, 369 F.3d 27 (2d Cir. 2004) (plaintiffs lacked standing to pursue claims against company that had a business relationship with issuer whose securities they purchased).

QUESTIONS

1.   Suppose the broker in *SEC v. Zandford* decides to sell his year-old Porsche. The broker tells the buyer that the Porsche is in "great" condition and says: "The reason for the car's great condition is that I'm a securities broker and use it only to drive back and forth to my office." In reality, the broker took the car out for racing every weekend. Shortly after the sale, the Porsche breaks down. Can the purchaser sue the broker under Rule 10b–5?

2.   Suppose a con artist fraudulently convinces an elderly couple to purchase swampland in Florida with the couple's life savings (of $1 million in cash). The con artist then uses the money to buy shares of IBM. Does the elderly couple have a Rule 10b–5 cause of action against the con artist?

3.   Suppose a broker persuades an elderly client to transfer $1 million worth of securities to a brokerage account with the broker's firm. The client instructs the broker to sell the portfolio and hold the cash until the client

---

[4]   Contrary to the Court of Appeals' prediction, our analysis does not transform every breach of fiduciary duty into a federal securities violation. If, for example, a broker embezzles cash from a client's account or takes advantage of the fiduciary relationship to induce his client into a fraudulent real estate transaction, then the fraud would not include the requisite connection to a purchase or sale of securities. Likewise if the broker told his client he was stealing the client's assets, that breach of fiduciary duty might be in connection with a sale of securities, but it would not involve a deceptive device or fraud.

decides on a new investment strategy. Broker sells the securities as instructed. Broker subsequently runs into financial difficulties. He decides to misappropriate the cash in the client's account. Does the client have a Rule 10b–5 action against the broker?

HYPOTHETICAL THREE

1.   Hillary, the CEO of DigitalBase, gives an interview to a reporter from *Digital Daily*, a blog widely read by computer types. The blog's central purpose is to keep its readers abreast of the latest developments in the technology sector. In excerpts from the interview published online, Hillary is quoted as saying that "The GigaBase is going to revolutionize information technology. Our customers will be able to store more information and access it more quickly than they ever dreamed possible." The GigaBase will create GigaData! After reading this interview, Jill, an outside investor, decides against selling her shares. She instead borrows money to pay the law school tuition bill that has recently come due. Can Jill sue under Rule 10b–5?

2.   Suppose Technology Workers of America is negotiating a labor contract with DigitalBase. The union threatens to strike, which causes the stock price to drop. The threat was a bluff—the union never had any intention of striking. Should shareholders who sold their stock in response to the strike threat (or the SEC) be able to sue the union under Rule 10b–5?

B. THE LEAD PLAINTIFF IN A CLASS ACTION

At least as important as the question of who can sue for violations of Rule 10b–5 is the question of who will represent the victims of securities fraud. In class actions, the thousands of members of the plaintiff class cannot all play a role in the controlling the litigation. Instead, the litigation is supposed to be controlled by the "lead plaintiff" under a provision that Congress added to the securities laws as part of the PSLRA. The Third Circuit discusses the application of that provision in the case below. How does the court determine who should represent the class? And how should the court determine how much to pay the attorney for the class?

In re Cendant Corp. Litigation

264 F.3d 201 (3d Cir. 2001).

■ BECKER, E., CHIEF JUDGE.

* * *

[Cendant Corporation was formed in 1997 through the merger of CUC International, Inc. and HFS Inc. Cendant's businesses included Avis, Century 21, and the Ramada and Howard Johnson hotel franchise chains. During April and July 1998, Cendant made a series of public statements announcing the restatement of several years worth of its financial statements. Cendant's stock fell from $35–5/8 in mid-April, 1998 prior to its first restatement announcement to $15–11/16 per share after the last announcement in July. Subsequent to the large stock drops, a number of securities fraud class action lawsuits were filed on behalf of investors who purchased CUC or Cendant stock during 1997.

The lawsuits named as defendants Cendant, its officers and directors, and other parties—including Ernst & Young, which had acted as CUC's independent public accountant from 1983 until the time of the creation of Cendant. . . . The District Court appointed as lead plaintiff a consortium of the three largest publicly-managed pension funds in the United States: the California Public Employees' Retirement System (CalPERS), the New York City Pension Funds (NYCPF), and the New York State Common Retirement Fund (NYSCRF) (collectively the "CalPERS Group"). The District Court also held an auction to determine the lead counsel for the plaintiffs' class action. Under the terms of the auction, candidates for lead counsel were asked to submit a bid based on the attorneys fees they were willing to accept. The District Court gave the CalPERS Group's chosen counsel the option to match what the court determined to be the lowest qualified bid.]

* * *

These are consolidated appeals from the District Court's approval of a $3.2 billion settlement of a securities fraud class action brought against Cendant Corporation and its auditors, Ernst & Young, and the Court's award of $262 million in fees to counsel for the plaintiff class. Both the settlement and the fee award are challenged in these appeals. The enormous size of both the settlement and the fee award presages a new generation of "mega cases" that will test our previously developed jurisprudence.

[The appellate court then reviewed (a) the selection of the lead plaintiff for the class action under the PSLRA, (b) the selection of the lead counsel for the class, and (c) the determination of attorney fees for the lead counsel.]

* * *

Throenle [a member of the plaintiff class] . . . argues that the members of the CalPERS Group were too conflicted to serve adequately in that capacity because they continued to hold huge amounts of Cendant stock during the Settlement negotiations. . . . Throenle's argument is based on the general assertion that a lead plaintiff who retains a substantial investment in a defendant corporation cannot adequately represent a class in a lawsuit against that corporation because this lead plaintiff will naturally be conflicted between trying to get maximum recovery for the class and trying to protect its ongoing investment in the corporation, e.g., by settling cheap or by securing corporate governance changes in lieu of cash, both of which are alleged here. . . .

Throenle's thesis is attractive. The problem with it is that Congress seems to have rejected it when it enacted the lead plaintiff provisions of the PSLRA. The Reform Act establishes a presumption that the class member "most capable of adequately representing the interests of class members" is the shareholder with the largest financial stake in the recovery sought by the class. The plaintiff with the largest stake in a given securities class action will almost invariably be a large institutional investor, and the PSLRA's legislative history expressly states that Congress anticipated and intended that such investors would serve as lead plaintiffs. We presume that Congress was aware that an institutional investor with enormous stakes in a company is highly unlikely to divest all of its holdings in that company, even after a securities class action is filed in which it is a class member.

By establishing a preference in favor of having such investors serve as lead plaintiffs, Congress must have thought that the situation present here does not inherently create an unacceptable conflict of interest. For this reason, the simple fact that the institutional investors . . . retained Cendant stock while the Settlement was negotiated is not nearly enough, standing alone, to support Throenle's claim that Lead Plaintiff was so conflicted that the Settlement should be overturned.[25]

* * *

The Reform Act establishes a two-step process for appointing a lead plaintiff: the court first identifies the presumptive lead plaintiff, and then determines whether any member of the putative class has rebutted the presumption. We begin by describing the manner in which courts charged with appointing a lead plaintiff should proceed under the PSLRA. We then measure the actions taken by the District Court against these standards.

1.   Legal Standards

a.   Identifying the Presumptive Lead Plaintiff

* * *

The section of the PSLRA that governs the appointment of the lead plaintiff is captioned "Rebuttable Presumption." The first subsection, captioned "in general," provides that "the court shall adopt a presumption that the most adequate plaintiff . . . is the person or group of persons that": (1) filed the complaint or made a motion to serve as the lead plaintiff; (2) "in the determination of the court, has the largest financial interest in the relief sought by the class;" and (3) "otherwise satisfies the requirements of Rule 23 of the Federal Rules of Civil Procedure." The next subsection, captioned "rebuttal evidence," declares that the presumption established by the previous subsection "may be rebutted only upon proof by a member of the purported plaintiff class that the presumptively most adequate plaintiff—(aa) will not fairly and adequately protect the interests of the class; or (bb) is subject to unique defenses that render such plaintiff incapable of adequately representing the class."

* * *

---

[25] . . . In economic terms, the potential conflict may be demonstrated as follows. The motivation of a rational Sell Plaintiff is simple: he wants to secure the largest possible recovery. The rational Hold Plaintiff, however, is in a more complicated situation; her goal is to reach a settlement that will maximize the combined value of her share of the settlement and the stock that she continues to hold in the defendant firm. Consequently, though a rational Sell Plaintiff would be perfectly willing to push the defendant firm one dollar short of declaring bankruptcy, a rational Hold Plaintiff rarely would be so willing because the increased value of her share of the settlement fund would almost certainly be offset by a corresponding decrease in the value of her stock. Thus, there will often be a significant conflict between the interests of Sell Plaintiffs and Hold Plaintiffs, particularly in cases where the class's expected damages are very large. . . .

The overall structure and legislative history of the statute suggest that in appointing a lead plaintiff a district court should engage in the following analysis. The initial inquiry (i.e., the determination of whether the movant with the largest interest in the case "otherwise satisfies" Rule 23) should be confined to determining whether the movant has made a prima facie showing of typicality and adequacy. The initial clause of the statute, which governs triggering the presumption, refers to determinations made by "the court," but the second, which deals with rebutting it, speaks of "proof by a member of the purported plaintiff class." This phrasing suggests that the threshold determination of whether the movant with the largest financial losses satisfies the typicality and adequacy requirements should be a product of the court's independent judgment, and that arguments by members of the purported plaintiff class as to why it does not should be considered only in the context of assessing whether the presumption has been rebutted. . . .

* * *

When making these determinations, courts should apply traditional Rule 23 principles. Thus, in inquiring whether the movant has preliminarily satisfied the typicality requirement, they should consider whether the circumstances of the movant with the largest losses "are markedly different or the legal theory upon which the claims [of that movant] are based differ[ ] from that upon which the claims of other class members will perforce be based."

In assessing whether the movant satisfies Rule 23's adequacy requirement, courts should consider whether it "has the ability and incentive to represent the claims of the class vigorously, [whether it] has obtained adequate counsel, and [whether] there is [a] conflict between [the movant's] claims and those asserted on behalf of the class." . . .

Because one of a lead plaintiff's most important functions is to "select and retain" lead counsel, one of the best ways for a court to ensure that it will fairly and adequately represent the interests of the class is to inquire whether the movant has demonstrated a willingness and ability to select competent class counsel and to negotiate a reasonable retainer agreement with that counsel. Thus, a court might conclude that the movant with the largest losses could not surmount the threshold adequacy inquiry if it lacked legal experience or sophistication, intended to select as lead counsel a firm that was plainly incapable of undertaking the representation, or had negotiated a clearly unreasonable fee agreement with its chosen counsel. We stress, however, that the question at this stage is not whether the court would "approve" that movant's choice of counsel or the terms of its retainer agreement or whether another movant may have chosen better lawyers or negotiated a better fee agreement; rather, the question is whether the choices made by the movant with the largest losses are so deficient as to demonstrate that it will not fairly and adequately represent the interests of the class, thus disqualifying it from serving as lead plaintiff at all. . . .

The PSLRA explicitly permits a "group of persons" to serve as lead plaintiff. But the goal of the Reform Act's lead plaintiff provision is to locate a person or entity whose sophistication and interest in the litigation are sufficient to permit that person or entity to function as an active agent for the class, and a group is not entitled to presumptive lead plaintiff status unless it "otherwise satisfies" Rule 23, which in turn requires that it be able to "fairly and adequately protect the interests of the class." If the court determines that the way in which a group seeking to become lead plaintiff was formed or the manner in which it is constituted would preclude it from fulfilling the tasks assigned to a lead plaintiff, the court should disqualify that movant on the grounds that it will not fairly and adequately represent the interests of the class. . . .

If, for example, a court were to determine that the movant "group" with the largest losses had been created by the efforts of lawyers hoping to ensure their eventual appointment as lead counsel, it could well conclude, based on this history, that the members of that "group" could not be counted on to monitor counsel in a sufficient manner.

Courts must also inquire whether a movant group is too large to represent the class in an adequate manner. At some point, a group becomes too large for its members to operate effectively as a single unit. When that happens, the PSLRA's goal of having an engaged lead plaintiff actively supervise the conduct of the litigation and the actions of class counsel will be impossible to achieve, and the court should conclude that such a movant does not satisfy the adequacy requirement.

Like many of the district courts that have considered this question, we do not establish a hard-and-fast rule; instead, we note only that a kind of "rule of reason prevails." We do, however, agree with the Securities and Exchange Commission that courts should generally presume that groups with more than five members are too large to work effectively.

* * *

b.   Determining Whether the Presumption Has Been Rebutted

Once a presumptive lead plaintiff is located, the court should then turn to the question whether the presumption has been rebutted. The Reform Act is quite specific on this point, providing that the presumption "may be rebutted only upon proof by a member of the purported plaintiff class that the presumptively most adequate plaintiff—(aa) will not fairly and adequately protect the interests of the class; or (bb) is subject to unique defenses that render such plaintiff incapable of adequately representing the class." This language makes two things clear. First, only class members may seek to rebut the presumption, and the court should not permit or consider any arguments by defendants or non-class members. Second, once the presumption is triggered, the question is not whether another movant might do a better job of protecting the interests of the class than the presumptive lead plaintiff; instead, the question is whether anyone can prove that the presumptive lead plaintiff will not do a "fair[ ] and adequate[ ]" job. We do not suggest that this is a low standard, but merely stress that the inquiry is not a relative one. . . .

2.   Application of the Standards Here

Under these standards, we believe that the District Court correctly identified the CalPERS Group as the presumptively most adequate plaintiff. The Group filed a motion to serve as lead plaintiff, and no party has questioned that of all the movants it has the largest financial interest in the relief sought by the Class. The District Court expressly found that the CalPERS Group satisfied Rule 23(a)'s typicality requirement. Although we have expressed concerns about certain potential conflicts of interest that might have undermined the CalPERS Group's position, we have concluded that they do not carry the day.

The District Court also found no obvious reason to doubt that a group composed of the three largest pension funds in the United States could adequately protect the class's interests. The CalPERS Group's members are legally sophisticated entities, their chosen counsel are well-qualified, and the Retainer Agreement that they negotiated was not plainly unreasonable. Moreover, although it is a group, there is no indication that the CalPERS Group was artificially created by its lawyers, and the fact that it contains three members offers no obvious reason to doubt that its members could operate effectively as a single unit. We therefore find no abuse of discretion in the District Court's determination that the CalPERS Group was the presumptive lead plaintiff.

We also conclude that the District Court was correct in holding that the CalPERS Group's presumptive lead plaintiff status had not been rebutted. Appellant Aboff and Douglas Wilson offered three reasons why the statutory presumption in favor of the CalPERS Group had been rebutted. First, Aboff and Wilson represented that "they had negotiated a reduced fee schedule with their attorneys." As we stressed above, the question at this stage is not whether Aboff and Wilson would have done a better job of securing high-quality, low-cost counsel than the CalPERS Group; the question is whether the former have put forward "proof" that the latter would "not fairly and adequately represent the class." Had Aboff and Wilson shown that: (1) their fee agreement was substantially lower than that negotiated by the CalPERS Group; (2) their chosen counsel were as qualified or more qualified than those chosen by the presumptive lead plaintiff; and (3) the CalPERS Group had no adequate explanation for why it made the choice that it did, then the presumption may have been rebutted. But this would only happen if the facts suggested that the CalPERS Group had performed inadequately in an objective sense. But Aboff and Wilson did not make this showing simply by alleging that they negotiated a lower fee; hence we hold that the District Court did not abuse its discretion in rejecting this argument.

Aboff and Wilson's second contention was that the presumption had been rebutted because "considerations other than the interests of the class might have influenced the CalPERS group when it retained its attorneys." Specifically, they alleged that "counsel for the CalPERS group had made substantial contributions to the campaign of the New York State Comptroller, who, as sole trustee of the NYSCRF [a member of the CalPERS Group], has substantial influence over the decisions of the fund," and they argued that this "created an appearance of impropriety because the contributions may have played a role in the selection of the group's counsel—a practice known as 'pay-to-play.' " We likewise find no abuse of discretion in the District Court's decision to reject this argument.

Lest we be misunderstood, we observe that actual proof of pay-to-play would constitute strong (and, quite probably, dispositive) evidence that the presumption had been rebutted. A movant that was willing to base its choice of class counsel on political contributions instead of professional considerations would, it seems to us, have quite clearly demonstrated that it would "not fairly and adequately protect the interests of the class." . . .

The problem for Aboff and Wilson is that the District Court expressly found that they had not provided evidence in support of their pay-to-play allegations, and we have no basis upon which to disagree. When pressed by the District Court, Aboff and Wilson admitted that they had no evidence that the contributions, themselves legal, had influenced the CalPERS Group's selection process. Allegations of impropriety are not proof of wrongdoing. If they were, then any class member (or lawyer seeking to be appointed lead counsel) could disable any presumptive lead plaintiff by making unsupported allegations of impropriety. We therefore hold that the District Court did not abuse its discretion in rejecting Aboff and Wilson's pay-to-play arguments.

* * *

c.   The Auction

We turn now to NYCPF's objection to the District Court's decision to employ an auction to select lead counsel. . . .

3.   Does the Reform Act Ever Permit an Auction?

The statutory section most directly on point provides that "the most adequate plaintiff shall, subject to the approval of the court, select and retain counsel to represent the class." This language makes two things clear. First, the lead plaintiff's right to select and retain counsel is not absolute—the court retains the power and the duty to supervise counsel selection and counsel retention. But second, and just as importantly, the power to "select and retain" lead counsel belongs, at least in the first instance, to the lead plaintiff, and the court's role is confined to deciding whether to "approve" that choice. Because a court-ordered auction involves the court rather than the lead plaintiff choosing lead counsel and determining the financial terms of its retention, this latter determination strongly implies that an auction is not generally permissible in a Reform Act case, at least as a matter of first resort.

This conclusion gains support when we examine the overall structure of the PSLRA's lead plaintiff section. The Reform Act contains detailed procedures for choosing the lead plaintiff, indicating that Congress attached great importance to ensuring that the right person or group is selected. The only powers expressly given to the lead plaintiff, however, are to "select and retain" counsel. If those powers are seriously limited, it would seem odd for Congress to have established such a specific means for choosing the lead plaintiff. But if the powers to "select and retain" lead counsel carry a great deal of discretion and responsibility, it makes perfect sense that Congress attached great significance to the identity of the person or group that would be making those choices.

* * *

[W]e think that the Reform Act evidences a strong presumption in favor of approving a properly-selected lead plaintiff's decisions as to counsel selection and counsel retention. When a properly-appointed lead plaintiff asks the court to approve its choice of lead counsel and of a retainer agreement, the question is not whether the court believes that the lead plaintiff could have made a better choice or gotten a better deal. Such a standard would eviscerate the Reform Act's underlying assumption that, at least in the typical case, a properly-selected lead plaintiff is likely to do as good or better job than the court at these tasks. Because of this, we think that the court's inquiry is appropriately limited to whether the lead plaintiff's selection and agreement with counsel are reasonable on their own terms.

In making this determination, courts should consider: (1) the quantum of legal experience and sophistication possessed by the lead plaintiff; (2) the manner in which the lead plaintiff chose what law firms to consider; (3) the process by which the lead plaintiff selected its final choice; (4) the qualifications and experience of counsel selected by the lead plaintiff; and (5) the evidence that the retainer agreement negotiated by the lead plaintiff was (or was not) the product of serious negotiations between the lead plaintiff and the prospective lead counsel.

* * *

Although we think . . . that an auction is impermissible in most Reform Act cases, we do not rule out the possibility that it could be validly used. If the court determines that the lead plaintiff's initial choice of counsel or negotiation of a retainer agreement is inadequate, it should clearly state why (for both the benefit of the lead plaintiff and for the record) and should direct the lead plaintiff to undertake an acceptable selection process. If the lead plaintiff's response demonstrates that it is unwilling or unable to do so, then the court will, of necessity, be required to take a more active role.

4.   Was the Auction in this Case Permissible?

We now analyze whether . . . the District Court's decision to conduct an auction was justified. . . . The District Court gave several reasons for holding an auction. First, it noted that the PSLRA makes Lead Plaintiff's decision "subject to the approval of the court." The court stressed that "given the opportunity, absent class members would try to secure the most qualified representation at the lowest cost," and then observed that, at the end of the case, it would be required to ensure that the "total attorney's fees and expenses" that it awarded to lead counsel did "not exceed a reasonable percentage of the amount of any damages and prejudgment interest actually paid to the class." The court concluded that holding an auction would aid it in making this determination and in protecting the class's interests because it would simulate the market, thus providing a "benchmark of reasonableness." Second, the District Court stated that holding an auction would have the "salutary" effect of "removing any speculative doubt" about Aboff and Wilson's pay-to-play allegations.

These reasons are not sufficient justification for holding an auction. The first (i.e., a generalized desire to hold down costs by "simulating" the market) would apply in every case, and thus cannot be enough to justify a procedure that we have concluded may only be used rarely. Further, there is no need to "simulate" the market in cases where a properly-selected lead plaintiff conducts a good-faith counsel selection process because in such cases—at least under the theory supporting the PSLRA—the fee agreed to by the lead plaintiff is the market fee.

Nor do we think that the laudable desire to dispel mere allegations of impropriety as to one member of the CalPERS Group is enough to justify holding an auction. Were it sufficient, then any disgruntled class member (or lawyer seeking to be appointed lead counsel) could disable the lead plaintiff from exercising its statutorily-conferred power by making unsupported allegations of impropriety.

* * *

For the foregoing reasons, we hold that the District Court abused its discretion by conducting an auction because its decision to do so was founded upon an erroneous understanding of the legal standards undergirding the propriety of conducting an auction under the PSLRA. With regard to counsel selection, however, this error was harmless because the counsel selected via the auction process were the same as those whom the Lead Plaintiff sought to have appointed in the first place.

* * *

The Reform Act confers on the lead plaintiff the power to "retain" lead counsel, but it also requires that the court ensure that the "total attorneys' fees and expenses awarded . . . to counsel for the plaintiff class . . . not exceed a reasonable percentage of the amount of any damages and prejudgment interest actually paid to the class." This latter provision makes clear that the court has an independent obligation to ensure the reasonableness of any fee request. The issue is the scope of this obligation.

Federal Rule of Civil Procedure 23(e) provides that no class action "shall . . . be dismissed or compromised without the approval of the court," but the detailed standards set forth for reviewing attorneys fees in this Court's earlier cases are not contained in any statute or rule. Rather, they were developed because of recognition that in the class action context there is no way for "the class" to select, retain, or monitor its lawyers in the way that an individual client would, and because of doubts that a typical lead plaintiff in the non-PSLRA context is a terribly good agent for the class. In the ordinary case, the court is the only disinterested agent capable of protecting the class from its lawyers and its primary means of doing so is by scrutinizing the lawyers' proposed fee. . . .

The Reform Act shifts the underpinnings of our class action attorneys fees jurisprudence in the securities area. As a preliminary matter, the PSLRA sets out a detailed procedure for choosing lead plaintiffs, the whole point of this process being to locate a lead plaintiff that will be an effective agent for the class. The properly-selected lead plaintiff is then charged with selecting and retaining lead counsel (subject to court approval). This regime is far different from the traditional case in which counsel is often "selected" and "retained" based on the fact that it filed the first suit. Consequently, courts have far more reason at the outset to think that counsel selection and retention were done in the best interests of the class in a typical Reform Act case than they do in other class action contexts, at least when the procedures of counsel selection employed by the lead plaintiff were adequate. . . .

We therefore believe that, under the PSLRA, courts should accord a presumption of reasonableness to any fee request submitted pursuant to a retainer agreement that was entered into between a properly-selected lead plaintiff and a properly-selected lead counsel. This presumption will ensure that the lead plaintiff, not the court, functions as the class's primary agent vis-□-vis its lawyers. Further, by rendering ex ante fee agreements more reliable, it will assist those agreements in aligning the interests of the class and its lawyers during the pendency of the litigation.

Saying that there is a presumption necessarily assumes that it can be overcome in some cases, however. First, the presumption of reasonableness would likely be abrogated entirely were the court to find that the assumptions underlying the original retainer agreement had been materially altered by significant and unusual factual and/or legal developments that could not reasonably have been foreseen at the time of the original agreement. . . .

We stress, however, that not just any factual or legal development would suffice to justify a court's decision that the presumption of reasonableness had been rebutted on grounds of changed circumstances. Uncertainties are part of any ex ante negotiation and it should be presumed that the lead plaintiff and the lead counsel took the possibility of uncertainty into account in negotiating their agreement. Thus, only unusual and unforeseeable changes, i.e., those that could not have been adequately taken into account in the negotiations, could justify a court's decision to find the presumption abrogated.

Even if the presumption of reasonableness is not undermined by changed circumstances, however, courts must still consider whether it has been rebutted. As we have noted above, there is an arguable tension between the presumption of reasonableness accorded the arrangement between the Lead Plaintiff and properly selected counsel and the duty imposed on the Court by the Reform Act, to insure "that total attorneys' fees and expenses awarded by the court to counsel for the plaintiff class shall not exceed a reasonable percentage of the amount of any damages and prejudgment interest actually paid to the class." We resolve this tension by holding that the presumption may be rebutted by a prima facie showing that the (properly submitted) retained agreement fee is clearly excessive. In terms of the policy of the Reform Act, we do not believe that candidates for lead plaintiff designation will be deterred by the understanding that their retainer fee arrangement with Lead Counsel will be subject to judicial review for clear excessiveness.

* * *

Although the foregoing discussion suggests that, in view of a presumption, whatever fee is re-submitted by Lead Counsel pursuant to the Retainer Agreement on remand has a "leg up" for approval, we cannot blind ourselves to the reality that both the fee award of $262 million under the auction and (potentially up to) $187 million under the Retainer Agreement are staggering in their size, and, on the basis of the evidence in the record, may represent compensation at an astonishing hourly rate (as well as an extraordinarily high lodestar "multiplier"). Objectors contend that the lodestar figure is approximately $8,000,000, which would mean that the multiplier would be 45.75 if lead counsel were to receive the court awarded fee, and approximately 24 if it were to receive the negotiated fee. Lead counsel counter that the $8,000,000 figure was preliminary and that the final figure will be much higher, from 50% to 100%. Even so, the multiplier would still be extremely high.

At all events, this was a simple case in terms of liability with respect to Cendant, and the case was settled at a very early stage, after little formal discovery. Thus the possibility of rebuttal of the presumption of reasonableness must be seriously considered by the District Court on remand. . . .

* * *

NOTES

1. *Cendant.* The *Cendant* case is not typical of securities fraud class actions. The size of the settlement was, at the time, the largest ever paid by an issuer in a securities fraud class action. Settlements of $10 to $30 million are much more typical.

2. *Limits on plaintiffs.* The PSLRA imposes two additional limits on lead plaintiffs in securities fraud class actions.

a.   A person may be a lead plaintiff in no more than five securities fraud class actions during any three-year period. This limit can be exceeded with the permission of the court (which is routinely granted to institutional investors who are active as lead plaintiffs);

b.   The per-share recovery of the lead plaintiff cannot be greater than that of any other member of the class, although "reasonable costs and expenses" can be awarded.

Why do you think Congress included these provisions? And, why might the latter provision discourage an investor from seeking the role of lead plaintiff?

3. *Court determination of reasonable attorneys' fees.* Courts typically follow two methods of determining reasonable attorneys' fees in securities class actions. First, courts apply the "lodestar" approach. Under the lodestar approach, courts first calculate a base attorney fee amount based on (1) the number of hours the attorneys reasonably expended on the matter and (2) the reasonable hourly market rate for attorneys with similar background and experience. Courts then apply a multiplier to this base amount, taking into account the riskiness of the litigation (i.e., the possibility that the plaintiffs' attorneys will receive nothing if there is no recovery for the class), the complexity of the case, as well as how well the attorneys performed for the class. Second, courts may instead award attorneys a percentage of the funds recovered for the class. Under a percentage approach, if the class receives no monetary recovery, the plaintiffs' attorneys also receive nothing. Even for courts that continue to follow the lodestar approach, the PSLRA places a percentage-of-the-recovery cap on the amount of damages. Under § 21D(a)(6), the attorney fees "shall not exceed a reasonable percentage of the amount of any damages and prejudgment interest actually paid to the class." Regardless of whether lodestar or a percentage-of-recovery approach is used by a court to determine the reasonableness of an attorney fee award, most fee awards typically range from 20% to 30% of the settlement amount. Larger cases typically receive smaller fee percentages.

4.   *Small losses.* The lead plaintiff presumption gives a leg up to the party making a motion for lead plaintiff with the largest financial interest in the relief sought by the class. But in order to win lead plaintiff status, an investor must first make a motion. Many large institutional investors eschew lead plaintiff status. This sometimes leads to lead plaintiffs with very small losses. In a class action filed against SPSS, Inc. in 2004 for alleged violations of § 10(b) and Rule 10b–5, the court appoint a single individual as lead plaintiff. The individual had losses of "at least $60.88" that represented the largest loss of all the members of the class seeking lead plaintiff status. Does a lead plaintiff with such small losses have adequate incentive to negotiate with and monitor the lead counsel on behalf of the class?

5.   *Plaintiffs' attorney fees.* The Third Circuit in Cendant held that the attorney fees negotiated between the lead plaintiff and the lead counsel should get a "presumption of reasonableness." Courts vary in the presumptive weight they give to the attorney fee request. A federal district court in *In re UnitedHealth Group Incorporated PSLRA Litigation*, 643 F.Supp.2d 1094, 1102 (2009) stated that: "the Court, not lead plaintiff and its lawyers, ultimately sets class action attorneys' fees. This is fully appropriate. It is, after all, the Court, not lead plaintiff, who must protect absent class members against excessive fees. The purported fee agreement may well bind lead plaintiff and its counsel-whether or not it is enforceable between them is not a question before the Court-but there is no reason at all why this two-party agreement must bind hundreds of thousands of additional, absent, plaintiffs in this class action." The *UnitedHealth* court proceeded to reduce the attorneys' fees down from a requested 11.92% of the settlement fund down to 7% of the settlement fund.

QUESTIONS

1.   Prior to the PSLRA, investors with relatively small stakes were the predominant lead plaintiffs in securities fraud class actions. Often, these lead plaintiffs had prior relationships with the law firm. Who is in charge of the litigation in such a relationship?

2.   Why does the court presume that groups with more than five members are unlikely to be effective lead plaintiffs?

3.   Courts select the lead plaintiff—from among those investors who volunteer to fill the role—based on the investors' financial stake in the litigation. How should a court determine who has the greatest financial stake in a securities fraud class action?

4.   Why might an institutional investor with a large stake in the outcome of a securities class action *not* seek the lead plaintiff position?

5. What role does the court play in reviewing attorneys' fees once a lead plaintiff has been selected under the PSLRA? If the lead plaintiff's deal with its attorneys represents the "market," what additional protection does judicial review produce?

III. ELEMENTS OF THE CAUSE OF ACTION

The elements of the Rule 10b–5 cause of action are similar to those required for common law fraud. Plaintiffs bear the burden of showing, (1) a material misstatement, (2) scienter, (3) reliance, and (4) loss causation. In this section, we cover each of these elements. As you learn about each of these requirements, consider how the PSLRA has affected the ability of private plaintiffs and their attorneys to plead and prove these elements.

[handwritten margin note: 1995 PSLRA = private securities Litigation Reform Act]

As you read the materials, note the "instrumentality of interstate commerce" requirement of Rule 10b–5. When would a securities transactions today not involve the use of an instrumentality of interstate commerce? Also keep in mind that the statute of limitations for fraud actions under the Exchange Act is the earlier of "(1) 2 years after the discovery of the facts constituting the violation; or (2) 5 years after such violation." 28 U.S.C. § 1658(b). The five-year limit is a statute of repose, which means that it is inconsistent with equitable doctrines such as tolling—five years means five years. *See Lampf, Pleva, Lipkind, Prupis & Petigrow v. Gilbertson*, 501 U.S. 350 (1991) (interpreting predecessor statute). The two-year limit, however, does not begin to run until plaintiffs have discovered the facts constituting the violation, or when a reasonably diligent plaintiff would have discovered the facts of the violation, whichever comes first. The "facts constituting the violation" are the facts a plaintiff needs to plead a claim of fraud, including scienter. *Merck & Co. v. Reynolds*, 559 U.S. 633 (2010).

[handwritten margin note: Scienter = intent or knowledge of wrongdoing]

A. MISSTATEMENT OF A MATERIAL FACT

We discussed the concept of materiality in Chapter 2. Rule 10b–5 makes unlawful the use of an untrue statement concerning a material fact or an omission that, in light of the circumstances, makes other statements misleading.

1. DECEPTION

The requirement that the plaintiff prove a misstatement of material fact plays an important role in limiting both the type of conduct that can be actionable under Rule 10b–5 and the range of potential defendants, as the cases below illustrate. Rule 10b–5 also prohibits "any device, scheme, or artifice to defraud" as well as "any act, practice, or course of business which operates or would operate as a fraud or deceit upon any person." How do these parallel prohibitions interact with the prohibition on misstatements of a material fact? Were the plaintiffs in *Santa Fe* defrauded?

Santa Fe Industries, Inc., et al. v. Green et al.

430 U.S. 462 (1977).

■ WHITE, J.

The issue in this case involves the reach and coverage of § 10(b) of the Securities Exchange Act of 1934 and Rule 10b–5 thereunder in the context of a Delaware short-form merger transaction used by the majority stockholder of a corporation to eliminate the minority interest.

I

In 1936, petitioner Santa Fe Industries, Inc., acquired control of 60% of the stock of Kirby Lumber Corp., a Delaware corporation. Through a series of purchases over the succeeding years, Santa Fe increased its control of Kirby's stock to 95%. . . . In 1974, wishing to acquire 100% ownership of Kirby, Santa Fe availed itself of § 253 of the Delaware Corporation Law, known as the "short-form merger" statute. Section 253 permits a parent corporation owning at least 90% of the stock of a subsidiary to merge with that subsidiary, upon approval by the parent's board of directors, and to make payment in cash for the shares of the minority stockholders. The statute does not require the consent of, or advance notice to, the minority stockholders. However, notice of the merger must be given within 10 days after its effective date, and any stockholder who is dissatisfied with the terms of the merger may petition the Delaware Court of Chancery for a decree ordering the surviving corporation to pay him the fair value of his shares, as determined by a court-appointed appraiser subject to review by the court.

appraisal rights

Santa Fe obtained independent appraisals of the physical assets of Kirby—land, timber, buildings, and machinery—and of Kirby's oil, gas, and mineral interests. These appraisals, together with other financial information, were submitted to Morgan Stanley & Co., an investment banking firm retained to appraise the fair market value of Kirby stock. Kirby's physical assets were appraised at $320 million (amounting to $640 for each of the 500,000 shares); Kirby's stock was valued by Morgan Stanley at $125 per share. Under the terms of the merger, minority stockholders were offered $150 per share.

The provisions of the short-form merger statute were fully complied with. The minority stockholders of Kirby were notified the day after the merger became effective and were advised of their right to obtain an appraisal in Delaware court if dissatisfied with the offer of $150 per share. They also received an information statement containing, in addition to the relevant financial data about Kirby, the appraisals of the value of Kirby's assets and the Morgan Stanley appraisal concluding that the fair market value of the stock was $125 per share.

Respondents, minority stockholders of Kirby, objected to the terms of the merger, but did not pursue their appraisal remedy in the Delaware Court of Chancery. Instead, they brought this action in federal court on behalf of the corporation and other minority stockholders, seeking to set aside the merger or to recover what they claimed to be the fair value of their shares. The amended complaint asserted that, based on the fair market value of Kirby's physical assets as revealed by the appraisal included in the information statement sent to minority shareholders, Kirby's stock was worth at least $772 per share. The complaint alleged further that . . . the purpose of the merger was to appropriate the difference between the "conceded pro rata value of the physical assets," and the offer of $150 per share—to "freez[e] out the minority stockholders at a wholly inadequate price," and that Santa Fe, knowing the appraised value of the physical assets, obtained a "fraudulent appraisal" of the stock from Morgan Stanley and offered $25 above that appraisal "in order to lull the minority stockholders into erroneously believing that [Santa Fe was] generous." This course of conduct was alleged to be "a violation of Rule 10b–5 because defendants employed a 'device, scheme, or artifice to defraud' and engaged in an 'act, practice or course of business which operates or would operate as a fraud or deceit upon any person, in connection with the purchase or sale of any security.'" . . .

The District Court dismissed the complaint for failure to state a claim upon which relief could be granted. . . .

A divided Court of Appeals for the Second Circuit reversed. It first agreed [with the district court] that there was a double aspect to the case: first, the claim that gross undervaluation of the minority stock itself violated Rule 10b–5; and second, that "without any misrepresentation or failure to disclose relevant facts, the merger itself constitutes a violation of Rule 10b–5" because it was accomplished without any corporate purpose and without prior notice to the minority stockholders. As to the first aspect of the case, the Court of Appeals did not disturb the District Court's conclusion that the complaint did not allege a material misrepresentation or nondisclosure with respect to the value of the stock; and the court declined to rule that a claim of gross undervaluation itself would suffice to make out a Rule 10b–5 case. With respect to the second aspect of the case, however, the court fundamentally disagreed with the District Court as to the reach and coverage of Rule 10b–5. The Court of Appeals' view was that, although the Rule plainly reached material misrepresentations and nondisclosures in connection with the purchase or sale of securities, neither misrepresentation nor nondisclosure was a necessary element of a Rule 10b–5 action; the Rule reached "breaches of fiduciary duty by a majority against minority shareholders without any charge of misrepresentation or lack of disclosure." . . .

We granted the petition for certiorari challenging this holding because of the importance of the issue involved to the administration of the federal securities laws. We reverse.

II

* * *

The Court of Appeals' approach to the interpretation of Rule 10b–5 is inconsistent with that taken by the Court last Term in *Ernst & Ernst v. Hochfelder*, 425 U.S. 185 (1976).

Ernst & Ernst . . . began with the principle that "[a]scertainment of congressional intent with respect to the standard of liability created by a particular section of the [1933 and 1934] Acts must . . . rest primarily on the language of that section," and then focused on the statutory language of § 10(b)—"[t]he words 'manipulative or deceptive' used in conjunction with 'device or contrivance.' " The same language and the same principle apply to this case.

To the extent that the Court of Appeals would rely on the use of the term "fraud" in Rule 10b–5 to bring within the ambit of the Rule all breaches of fiduciary duty in connection with a securities transaction, its interpretation would, like the interpretation rejected by the Court in *Ernst & Ernst*, "add a gloss to the operative language of the statute quite different from its commonly accepted meaning." . . .

The language of § 10(b) gives no indication that Congress meant to prohibit any conduct not involving manipulation or deception. Nor have we been cited to any evidence in the legislative history that would support a departure from the language of the statute. "When a statute speaks so specifically in terms of manipulation and deception, . . . and when its history reflects no more expansive intent, we are quite unwilling to extend the scope of the statute. . . ." Thus the claim of fraud and fiduciary breach in this complaint states a cause of action under any part of Rule 10b–5 only if the conduct alleged can be fairly viewed as "manipulative or deceptive" within the meaning of the statute.

III

It is our judgment that the transaction, if carried out as alleged in the complaint, was neither deceptive nor manipulative and therefore did not violate either § 10(b) of the Act or Rule 10b–5.

As we have indicated, the case comes to us on the premise that the complaint failed to allege a material misrepresentation or material failure to disclose. The finding of the District Court, undisturbed by the Court of Appeals, was that there was no "omission" or "misstatement" in the information statement accompanying the notice of merger. On the basis of the information provided, minority shareholders could either accept the price offered or reject it and seek an appraisal in the Delaware Court of Chancery. Their choice was fairly presented, and they were furnished with all relevant information on which to base their decision. . . .

IV

The language of the statute is, we think, "sufficiently clear in its context" to be dispositive here, but even if it were not, there are additional considerations that weigh heavily against permitting a cause of action under Rule 10b–5 for the breach of corporate fiduciary duty alleged in this complaint. Congress did not expressly provide a private cause of action for violations of § 10(b). Although we have recognized an implied cause of action under that section in some circumstances, we have also recognized that a private cause of action under the antifraud provisions of the Securities Exchange Act should not be implied where it is "unnecessary to ensure the fulfillment of Congress' purposes" in adopting the Act. As we noted earlier, the Court repeatedly has described the "fundamental purpose" of the Act as implementing a "philosophy of full disclosure"; once full and fair disclosure has occurred, the fairness of the terms of the transaction is at most a tangential concern of the statute. . . .

A second factor in determining whether Congress intended to create a federal cause of action in these circumstances is "whether 'the cause of action [is] one traditionally relegated to state law. . . .'" The Delaware Legislature has supplied minority shareholders with a cause of action in the Delaware Court of Chancery to recover the fair value of shares allegedly undervalued in a short-form merger. Of course, the existence of a particular state-law remedy is not dispositive of the question whether Congress meant to provide a similar federal remedy, but . . . we conclude that "it is entirely appropriate in this instance to relegate respondent and others in his situation to whatever remedy is created by state law."

The reasoning behind a holding that the complaint in this case alleged fraud under Rule 10b–5 could not be easily contained. It is difficult to imagine how a court could distinguish, for purposes of Rule 10b–5 fraud, between a majority stockholder's use of a short-form merger to eliminate the minority at an unfair price and the use of some other device, such as a long-form merger, tender offer, or liquidation, to achieve the same result; or indeed how a court could distinguish the alleged abuses in these going private transactions from other types of fiduciary self-dealing involving transactions in securities. The result would be to bring within the Rule a wide variety of corporate conduct traditionally left to state regulation. In addition to posing a "danger of vexatious litigation which could result from a widely expanded class of plaintiffs under Rule 10b–5," this extension of the federal securities laws would overlap and quite possibly interfere with state corporate law. Federal courts applying a "federal fiduciary principle" under Rule 10b–5 could be expected to depart from state fiduciary standards at least to the extent necessary to ensure uniformity within the federal system. Absent a clear indication of congressional intent, we are reluctant to federalize the substantial portion of the law of corporations that deals with transactions in securities, particularly where established state policies of corporate regulation would be overridden. "Corporations are creatures of state law, and investors commit their funds to corporate directors on the understanding that, except where federal law *expressly* requires certain responsibilities of directors with respect to stockholders, state law will govern the internal affairs of the corporation."

We thus adhere to the position that "Congress by § 10(b) did not seek to regulate transactions which constitute no more than internal corporate mismanagement." There may well be a need for uniform federal fiduciary standards to govern mergers such as that challenged in this complaint. But those standards should not be supplied by judicial extension of § 10(b) and Rule 10b–5 to "cover the corporate universe."

* * *

NOTES

1.   *State remedies.* Lower courts have found some room to evade *Santa Fe's* warning against interfering with state corporate law by permitting Rule 10b–5 actions in cases in which plaintiffs allege that they have lost their state law remedies, such as injunctive relief or appraisal, as the result of a misrepresentation by the defendants. *Goldberg v. Meridor*, 567 F.2d 209 (2d Cir. 1977).

2. *Oral misstatements. Santa Fe's* requirement of deception for Rule 10b–5 liability can be satisfied by both oral and written statements. *Wharf (Holdings) Limited v. United International Holdings*, 532 U.S. 588 (2001). *Wharf (Holdings)* also makes clear that the secret intention not to honor a promise is an actionable misstatement if the defendant intended to breach at the time the promise was made.

QUESTIONS

1. Is the Court's discussion of the intersection of state corporate law and federal securities law essential to its holding?

2. Does the Court's holding in *Santa Fe* mean that no breach of fiduciary duty can ever be a violation of Rule 10b–5?

2.   FACTS VERSUS OPINIONS

Are "just the facts, ma'am" relevant to the element of a misstatement or omission? The Supreme Court answers that evergreen question in the following—somewhat less than evergreen—opinion.

Virginia Bankshares, Inc. v. Sandberg
501 U.S. 1083 (1991).

■ SOUTER, J.

[This case arises under § 14(a) of the Securities Exchange Act of 1934 which prohibits misleading statements and omissions in connection with the solicitation of proxies. We cover the proxy rules in Chapter 11.]

The questions before us are whether a statement couched in conclusory or qualitative terms purporting to explain directors' reasons for recommending certain corporate action can be materially misleading.... We hold that knowingly false statements of reasons may be actionable even though conclusory in form....

I

In December 1986, First American Bankshares, Inc. (FABI), a bank holding company, began a "freeze-out" merger, in which the First American Bank of Virginia (Bank) eventually merged into Virginia Bankshares, Inc. (VBI), a wholly owned subsidiary of FABI. VBI owned 85% of the Bank's shares, the remaining 15% being in the hands of some 2,000 minority shareholders. FABI hired the investment banking firm of Keefe, Bruyette & Woods (KBW) to give an opinion on the appropriate price for shares of the minority holders, who would lose their interests in the Bank as a result of the merger. Based on market quotations and unverified information from FABI, KBW gave the Bank's executive committee an opinion that $42 a share would be a fair price for the minority stock. The executive committee approved the merger proposal at that price, and the full board followed suit.

Although Virginia law required only that such a merger proposal be submitted to a vote at a shareholders' meeting, and that the meeting be preceded by circulation of a statement of information to the shareholders, the directors nevertheless solicited proxies for voting on the proposal at the annual meeting set for April 21, 1987. In their solicitation, the directors urged the proposal's adoption and stated they had approved the plan because of its opportunity for the minority shareholders to achieve a "high" value, which they elsewhere described as a "fair" price, for their stock.

Although most minority shareholders gave the proxies requested, respondent Sandberg did not, and after approval of the merger she sought damages in the United States District Court for the Eastern District of Virginia from VBI, FABI, and the directors of the Bank. . . . Sandberg alleged, among other things, that the directors had not believed that the price offered was high or that the terms of the merger were fair, but had recommended the merger only because they believed they had no alternative if they wished to remain on the board. . . .

II

We consider first the actionability per se of statements of reasons, opinion, or belief. Because such a statement by definition purports to express what is consciously on the speaker's mind, we interpret the jury verdict as finding that the directors' statements of belief and opinion were made with knowledge that the directors did not hold the beliefs or opinions expressed, and we confine our discussion to statements so made. . . . Shareholders know that directors usually have knowledge and expertness far exceeding the normal investor's resources, and the directors' perceived superiority is magnified even further by the common knowledge that state law customarily obliges them to exercise their judgment in the shareholders' interest. Naturally, then, the shareowner faced with a proxy request will think it important to know the directors' beliefs about the course they recommend and their specific reasons for urging the stockholders to embrace it.

But, assuming materiality, the question remains whether statements of reasons, opinions, or beliefs are statements "with respect to . . . material fact[s]". . . . Petitioners argue that we would invite wasteful litigation of amorphous issues outside the readily provable realm of fact if we were to recognize liability here on proof that the directors did not recommend the merger for the stated reason. . . .

Attacks on the truth of directors' statements of reasons or belief . . . are factual in two senses: as statements that the directors do act for the reasons given or hold the belief stated and as statements about the subject matter of the reason or belief expressed. . . . Reasons for directors' recommendations or statements of belief are . . . characteristically matters of corporate record subject to documentation, to be supported or attacked by evidence of historical fact outside a plaintiff's control. Such evidence would include not only corporate minutes and other statements of the directors themselves, but circumstantial evidence bearing on the facts that would reasonably underlie the reasons claimed and the honesty of any statement that those reasons are the basis for a recommendation or other action, a point that becomes especially clear when the reasons or beliefs go to valuations in dollars and cents.

It is no answer to argue, as petitioners do, that the quoted statement on which liability was predicated did not express a reason in dollars and cents, but focused instead on the "indefinite and unverifiable" term, "high" value, much like the similar claim that the merger's terms were "fair" to shareholders. The objection ignores the fact that such conclusory terms in a commercial context are reasonably understood to rest on a factual basis that justifies them as accurate, the absence of which renders them misleading. Provable facts either furnish good reasons to make a conclusory commercial judgment, or they count against it, and expressions of such judgments can be uttered with knowledge of truth or falsity just like more definite statements, and defended or attacked through the orthodox evidentiary process that either substantiates their underlying justifications or tends to disprove their existence. . . . In this case, whether $42 was "high," and the proposal "fair" to the minority shareholders, depended on whether provable facts about the Bank's assets, and about actual and potential levels of operation, substantiated a value that was above, below, or more or less at the $42 figure, when assessed in accordance with recognized methods of valuation.

Respondents adduced evidence for just such facts in proving that the statement was misleading about its subject matter and a false expression of the directors' reasons. Whereas the proxy statement described the $42 price as offering a premium above both book value and market price, the evidence indicated that a calculation of the book figure based on the appreciated value of the Bank's real estate holdings eliminated any such premium. The evidence on the significance of market price showed that KBW had conceded that the market was closed, thin, and dominated by FABI, facts omitted from the statement. There was, indeed, evidence of a "going concern" value for the Bank in excess of $60 per share of common stock, another fact never disclosed. However conclusory the directors' statement may have been, then, it was open to attack by garden-variety evidence, subject neither to a plaintiff's control nor ready manufacture, and there was no undue risk of open-ended liability or uncontrollable litigation in allowing respondents the opportunity for recovery on the allegation that it was misleading to call $42 "high."

* * *

The question arises, then, whether disbelief, or undisclosed belief or motivation, standing alone, should be a sufficient basis to sustain an action . . ., absent proof by the sort of objective evidence described above that the statement also expressly or impliedly asserted something false or misleading about its subject matter. We think that proof of mere disbelief or belief undisclosed should not suffice for liability . . . and if nothing more had been required or proven in this case, we would reverse for that reason.

On the one hand, it would be rare to find a case with evidence solely of disbelief or undisclosed motivation without further proof that the statement was defective as to its subject matter. While we certainly would not hold a director's naked admission of disbelief incompetent evidence of a proxy statement's false or misleading character, such an unusual admission will not very often stand alone, and we do not substantially narrow the cause of action by requiring a plaintiff to demonstrate something false or misleading in what the statement expressly or impliedly declared about its subject.

On the other hand, to recognize liability on mere disbelief or undisclosed motive without any demonstration that the proxy statement was false or misleading about its subject would authorize . . . litigation confined solely to what one skeptical court spoke of as the "impurities" of a director's "unclean heart." . . . While it is true that the liability, if recognized, would rest on an actual, not hypothetical, psychological fact, the temptation to rest an otherwise nonexistent . . . action on psychological enquiry alone would threaten . . . strike suits and attrition by discovery. We therefore hold disbelief or undisclosed motivation, standing alone, insufficient to satisfy the element of fact that must be established. . . .

* * *

NOTES

1.   *Motives and conflicts.* Although *Virginia Bankshares* makes clear that opinions—when offered—can be actionable, the law is also clear that motives need not be disclosed if the facts are fully disclosed and the motive is neither deceptive nor manipulative. *Vaughn v. Teledyne, Inc.*, 628 F.2d 1214, 1221 (9th Cir. 1980). On the other hand, conflicts of interest generally must be disclosed to avoid a misleading omission. *TSC Industries v. Northway*, 426 U.S. 438, 453–454 n. 15 (1976).

QUESTIONS

1.   What are examples of "conclusory or qualitative" statements expressing an "opinion," "beliefs," or "reasons"?

HYPOTHETICAL FOUR

Hillary, the CEO of DigitalBase, issues a press release announcing the development of a database that is accessed through an Internet-based platform, the WebBase. The press release describes the preliminary development work that has already been done as "very promising." In fact, DigitalBase's engineers have run into serious difficulties in transmitting over the Internet data in the amounts typically stored in commercial databases. Does the press release contain a misleading statement or omission?

3.   THE DUTY TO UPDATE AND THE DUTY TO CORRECT

The next case addresses the question of whether a misstatement has to be false at the time it was made in order to state a cause of action. What if the statement was true when made, but, after some time passes, becomes false? Do corporations have a duty to update? Have the lower courts been true to the holding of *Santa Fe*?

Gallagher v. Abbott Laboratories

269 F.3d 806 (7th Cir. 2001).

■ EASTERBROOK, F., CIRCUIT JUDGE.

Year after year the Food and Drug Administration inspected the Diagnostic Division of Abbott Laboratories, found deficiencies in manufacturing quality control, and issued warnings. The Division made efforts to do better, never to the FDA's satisfaction, but until 1999 the FDA was willing to accept Abbott's promises and remedial steps. On March 17, 1999, the FDA sent Abbott another letter demanding compliance with all regulatory requirements and threatening severe consequences. This could have been read as more saber rattling— Bloomberg News revealed the letter to the financial world in June, and Abbott's stock price did not even quiver—but later developments show that it was more ominous. By September 1999 the FDA was insisting on substantial penalties plus changes in Abbott's methods of doing business. On September 29, 1999, after the markets had closed, Abbott issued a press release describing the FDA's position, asserting that Abbott was in "substantial" compliance with federal regulations, and revealing that the parties were engaged in settlement talks. Abbott's stock fell more than 6%, from $40 to $37.50, the next business day. On November 2, 1999, Abbott and the FDA resolved their differences, and a court entered a consent decree requiring Abbott to remove 125 diagnostic products from the market until it had improved its quality control and to pay a $100 million civil fine. Abbott took an accounting charge of $168 million to cover the fine and worthless inventory. The next business day Abbott's stock slumped $3.50, which together with the earlier drop implied that shareholders saw the episode as costing Abbott (in cash plus future compliance costs and lost sales) more than $5 billion. . . .

Plaintiffs in these class actions under § 10(b) of the Securities Exchange Act of 1934, and the SEC's Rule 10b–5, contend that Abbott committed fraud by deferring public revelation. . . . What sinks plaintiffs' position is their inability to identify any false statement—or for that matter any truthful statement made misleading by the omission of news about the FDA's demands.

Much of plaintiffs' argument reads as if firms have an absolute duty to disclose all information material to stock prices as soon as news comes into their possession. Yet that is not the way the securities laws work. We do not have a system of continuous disclosure. Instead firms are entitled to keep silent (about good news as well as bad news) unless positive law creates a duty to disclose. Until the Securities Act of 1933 there was no federal regulation of corporate disclosure. The 1933 Act requires firms to reveal information only when they issue securities, and the duty is owed only to persons who buy from the issuer or an underwriter distributing on its behalf; every other transaction is exempt under § 4. Section 13 of the Securities Exchange Act of 1934 adds that the SEC may require issuers to file annual and other periodic reports—with the emphasis on *periodic* rather than continuous. Section 13 and the implementing regulations contemplate that these reports will be snapshots of the corporation's status on or near the filing date, with updates due not when something "material" happens, but on the next prescribed filing date.

Regulations implementing § 13 require a comprehensive annual filing, the Form 10–K report, and less extensive quarterly supplements on Form 10–Q. The supplements need not bring up to date everything contained in the annual 10–K report; counsel for the plaintiff classes conceded at oral argument that nothing in Regulation S–K (the SEC's list of required disclosures) requires either an updating of Form 10–K reports more often than annually, or a disclosure in a quarterly Form 10–Q report of information about the firm's regulatory problems. The regulations that provide for disclosures on Form 10–Q tell us *which* items in the annual report must be updated (a subset of the full list), and how often (quarterly).

Many proposals have been made to do things differently—to junk this combination of sale-based disclosure with periodic follow-up and replace it with a system under which *issuers* rather than *securities* are registered and disclosure must be continuous. Regulation S–K goes some distance in this direction by defining identical items of disclosure for registration of stock and issuers' subsequent reports, and by authorizing the largest issuers to use their annual 10–K reports as the kernels of registration statements for new securities. But Regulation S–K does not replace periodic with continuous disclosure, and the more ambitious proposals to do this have not been adopted. . . .

Whatever may be said for and against these proposals, they must be understood as projects for legislation (and to a limited extent for the use of the SEC's rulemaking powers); judges have no authority to scoop the political branches and adopt continuous disclosure under the banner of Rule 10b–5. *Especially* not under that banner, for Rule 10b–5 condemns only fraud, and a corporation does not commit fraud by standing on its rights under a periodic-disclosure system. The Supreme Court has insisted that this judicially created right of action be used only to implement, and not to alter, the rules found in the text of the 1933 and 1934 Acts.

Trying to locate some statement that was either false or materially misleading because it did not mention the FDA's position, plaintiffs pointed in the district court to several reports filed or statements made by Abbott before November 2, 1999. [Among others, the court focused on Abbott's Form 10–K annual report for 1998 filed in March 1999.]

Plaintiffs rely principally on Item 303(a)(3)(ii) of Regulation S–K, which provides that registration statements and annual 10–K reports must reveal

> any known trends or uncertainties that have had or that the registrant reasonably expects will have a material favorable or unfavorable impact on net sales or revenues or income from continuing operations.

The FDA's letter, and its negotiating demands, are within this description, according to the plaintiff classes. We shall assume that this is so. The 10–K report did state that Abbott is "subject to comprehensive government regulation" and that "government regulatory actions can result in . . . sanctions." Plaintiffs say that this is too general in light of the FDA's letter and Abbott's continuing inability to satisfy the FDA's demands. Again we shall assume that plaintiffs are right. But there is a fundamental problem: The 10–K report was filed on March 9, 1999, and the FDA's letter is dated March 17, eight days later. Unless Abbott had a time machine, it could not have described on March 9 a letter that had yet to be written.

Attempting to surmount this temporal problem, plaintiffs insist that Abbott had a "duty to correct" the 10–K report. Yet a statement may be "corrected" only if it was incorrect when made, and nothing said as of March 9 was incorrect. In order to maintain the difference between periodic-disclosure and continuous-disclosure systems, it is essential to draw a sharp line between duties to correct and duties to update.... If, for example, the 10–K report had said that Abbott's net income for 1998 was $500 million, and the actual income was $400 million, Abbott would have had to fix the error. But if the 10–K report had projected a net income of $125 million for the first quarter of 1999, and accountants determined in May that the actual profit was only $100 million, there would have been nothing to correct; a projection is not rendered false when the world turns out otherwise. Amending the 10–K report to show the results for 1999 as they came in—or to supply a running narrative of the dispute between Abbott and the FDA—would *update* the report, not *correct* it to show Abbott's actual condition as of March 9.

Updating documents has its place in securities law. A registration statement and prospectus for a new issue of securities must be accurate when it is used to sell stock, and not just when it is filed. Material changes in a company's position thus must be reflected in a registration statement promptly. But this does not imply changes in a 10–K annual report, even when that report is used ... as the principal disclosure document. Instead of changing the 10–K report weekly or monthly, the issuer must file and distribute an addendum to that document bringing matters up to date. Anyway ... Abbott did not sell any stock to the class members during the period from March 17 to November 2, 1999....

* * *

NOTES

1. *The duty to correct and the duty to update.* Every circuit to address the question has held that issuers have a duty to correct prior misstatements, even if the statements were believed to be true when made. Courts also agree that issuers do not have a duty to correct misstatements made by third parties, unless the issuer has somehow "entangled" itself with the statements by affirming them. The duty to update prior projections, however, has spawned considerably greater disagreement. The circuits range in their positions from the Seventh Circuit's outright rejection of the duty to update in *Gallagher* to the Second Circuit's cautious acceptance of the duty to update under certain circumstances. *See, e.g., In re Time Warner Inc. Sec. Litig.*, 9 F.3d 259 (2d Cir. 1993) (holding that a duty to update arises when "a corporation is pursuing a specific business goal and announces that goal as well as an intended approach for reaching it, it may come under an obligation to disclose other approaches to reaching the goal when those approaches are under active and serious consideration.").

2. *Real time disclosure.* In § 409 of the Sarbanes-Oxley Act of 2002, Congress authorized the SEC to require "Real Time Issuer Disclosures" of material information on a "rapid and current basis" . . . as the Commission determines, by rule, is necessary or useful for the protection of investors and in the public interest." The SEC has used its authority under § 409 to expand the episodic filing requirements under Form 8–K for Exchange Act reporting issuers. Falling short of a system of continuous disclosure, the SEC both expanded the types of events that require a Form 8–K filing. The agency also shortened the deadline for most items to four days from the date of the event that triggers the Form 8–K filing requirement.

QUESTIONS

1.   Would investors be better off if companies such as Abbott Laboratories had a duty to update the disclosures in their previously filed Form 10–K?

2.   Should the issuer's duty to correct extend to misstatements made by third parties?

4.   FORWARD-LOOKING STATEMENTS

Rule 10b–5, like other liability provisions of the securities laws, requires that statements be material before they are actionable. The general rule is the same as the materiality standard we discussed in Chapter 2: Would the information be important to a reasonable investor in deciding whether to purchase or sell the security? Congress adopted a special standard, however, for "forward-looking" statements as part of the PSLRA in § 21E of the Exchange Act (and its counterpart, § 27A of the Securities Act). The following case applies that standard.

materiality ←

Asher v. Baxter International Inc.

377 F.3d 727 (7th Cir. 2004).

■ EASTERBROOK, F., CIRCUIT JUDGE.

Baxter International, a manufacturer of medical products, released its second-quarter financial results for 2002 on July 18 of that year. Sales and profits did not match analysts' expectations. Shares swiftly fell from $43 to $32. This litigation followed; plaintiffs contend that the $43 price was the result of materially misleading projections on November 5, 2001, projections that Baxter reiterated until the bad news came out on July 18, 2002. Plaintiffs want to represent a class of all investors who purchased during that time . . . in the open market. . . . [T]he district court dismissed the complaint for failure to state a claim on which relief may be granted. The court did not doubt that the allegations ordinarily would defeat a motion under Fed.R.Civ.P.12(b)(6). Still, it held, Baxter's forecasts come within the safe harbor created by the Private Securities Litigation Reform Act of 1995. The PSLRA creates rules that judges must enforce at the outset of the litigation; plaintiffs do not question the statute's application before discovery but do dispute the district court's substantive decision.

Baxter's projection, repeated many times (sometimes in documents filed with the SEC, sometimes in press releases, sometimes in executives' oral statements), was that during 2002 the business would yield revenue growth in the "low teens" compared with the prior year, earnings-per-share growth in the "mid teens," and "operational cash flow of at least $500 million." Baxter often referred to these forecasts as "our 2002 full-year commitments," which is a strange locution. No firm can make "commitments" about the future—Baxter can't compel its customers to buy more of its products—unless it plans to engage in accounting shenanigans to make the numbers come out right no matter what happens to the business. But nothing turns on the word; the district court took these "commitments" as "forward-looking statements," and plaintiffs do not quarrel with that understanding. What they do say is that the projections were too rosy, and that Baxter knew it. That charges the defendants with stupidity as much as with knavery, for the truth was bound to come out quickly, but the securities laws forbid foolish frauds along with clever ones.

According to the complaint, Baxter's projections were materially false because: (1) its Renal Division had not met its internal budgets in years; . . . (5) sales of that division's IGIV immunoglobin products had fallen short of internal predictions; and (6) in March 2002 the BioScience Division had experienced a sterility failure in the manufacture of a major product, resulting in the destruction of multiple lots and a loss exceeding $10 million. . . .

The statutory safe harbor forecloses liability if a forward-looking statement "is accompanied by meaningful cautionary statements identifying important factors that could cause actual results to differ materially from those in the forward-looking statement." The fundamental problem is that the statutory requirement of "meaningful cautionary statements" is not itself meaningful. What must the firm say? Unless it is possible to give a concrete and reliable answer, the harbor is not "safe"; yet a word such as "meaningful" resists a concrete rendition and thus makes administration of the safe harbor difficult if not impossible. It rules out a caution such as: "This is a forward-looking statement: caveat emptor." But it does not rule in any particular caution, which always may be challenged as not sufficiently "meaningful" or not pinning down the "important factors that could cause actual results to differ materially"—for if it had identified all of those factors, it would not be possible to describe the forward-looking statement itself as materially misleading. A safe harbor matters only when the firm's disclosures (including the accompanying cautionary statements) are false or misleadingly incomplete; yet whenever that condition is satisfied, one can complain that the cautionary statement must have been inadequate. The safe harbor loses its function. Yet it would be unsound to read the statute so that the safe harbor never works; then one might as well treat § 21E as defunct.

Baxter provided a number of cautionary statements throughout the class period. This one, from its 2001 Form 10–K filing—a document to which many of the firm's press releases and other statements referred—is the best illustration:

> Statements throughout this report that are not historical facts are forward-looking statements. These statements are based on the company's current expectations and involve numerous risks and uncertainties. Some of these risks and uncertainties are factors that affect all international businesses, while some

are specific to the company and the health care arenas in which it operates.

Many factors could affect the company's actual results, causing results to differ materially, from those expressed in any such forward-looking statements. These factors include, but are not limited to, interest rates; technological advances in the medical field; economic conditions; demand and market acceptance risks for new and existing products, technologies and health care services; the impact of competitive products and pricing; manufacturing capacity; new plant start-ups; global regulatory, trade and tax policies; regulatory, legal or other developments relating to the company's Series A, AF, and AX dialyzers; continued price competition; product development risks, including technological difficulties; ability to enforce patents; actions of regulatory bodies and other government authorities; reimbursement policies of government agencies; commercialization factors; results of product testing; and other factors described elsewhere in this report or in the company's other filings with the Securities and Exchange Commission. Additionally, as discussed in Item 3—"Legal Proceedings," upon the resolution of certain legal matters, the company may incur charges in excess of presently established reserves. Any such change could have a material adverse effect on the company's results of operations or cash flows in the period in which it is recorded.

* * *

The company believes that its expectations with respect to forward-looking statements are based upon reasonable assumptions within the bounds of its knowledge of its business operations, but there can be no assurance that the actual results or performance of the company will conform to any future results or performance expressed or implied by such forward-looking statements.

The district court concluded that these are "meaningful cautionary statements identifying important factors that could cause actual results to differ materially from those in the forward-looking statement." They deal with Baxter's business specifically, mentioning risks and product lines. Plaintiffs offer two responses. First they contend that the cautionary statements did not cover any of the six matters that (in plaintiffs' view) Baxter had withheld. That can't be dispositive; otherwise the statute would demand prescience. As long as the firm reveals the principal risks, the fact that some other event caused problems cannot be dispositive. Indeed, an unexpected turn of events cannot demonstrate a securities problem at all, as there cannot be "fraud by hindsight." The other response is that the cautionary statement did not follow the firm's fortunes: plants closed but the cautionary statement remained the same; sterilization failures occurred but the cautionary statement remained the same; and bad news that (plaintiffs contend) Baxter well knew in November 2001 did not cast even a shadow in the cautionary statement.

Before considering whether plaintiffs' objections defeat the safe harbor, we ask whether the cautionary statements have any bearing on Baxter's potential liability for statements in its press releases, and those its managers made orally. The press releases referred to, but did not repeat verbatim, the cautionary statements in the Form 10–K and other documents filed with the Securities and Exchange Commission. The oral statements did not do even that much. Plaintiffs say that this is fatal, because § 21E(c)(1)(A)(i) provides a safe harbor only if a written statement is "accompanied by" the meaningful caution; a statement published elsewhere differs from one that accompanies the press release. As for the oral statements: § 21E(c)(2)(A)(ii), a special rule for oral statements, provides a safe harbor only if the statement includes "that the actual results could differ materially from those projected in the forward-looking statement" and in addition:

> (i) the oral forward-looking statement is accompanied by an oral statement that additional information concerning factors that could cause actual results to differ materially from those in the forward-looking statement is contained in a readily available written document, or portion thereof;

> (ii) the accompanying oral statement referred to in clause (i) identifies the document, or portion thereof, that contains the additional information about those factors relating to the forward-looking statement; and

> (iii) the information contained in that written document is a cautionary statement that satisfies the standard established in paragraph (1)(A).

§ 21E (c)(2)(B). When speaking with analysts Baxter's executives did not provide them with all of this information, such as directions to look in the 10–K report for the full cautionary statement. It follows, plaintiffs maintain, that this suit must proceed with respect to the press releases and oral statements even if the cautionary language filed with the SEC in registration statements and other documents meets the statutory standard.

If this were a traditional securities suit—if, in other words, an investor claimed to have read or heard the statement and, not having access to the truth, relied to his detriment on the falsehood—then plaintiffs' argument would be correct. But this is not a traditional securities claim. It is a fraud-on-the-market claim. None of the plaintiffs asserts that he read any of Baxter's press releases or listened to an executive's oral statement. Instead the theory is that other people (professional traders, mutual fund managers, securities analysts) did the reading, and that they made trades or recommendations that influenced the price. In an efficient capital market, all information known to the public affects the price and thus affects every investor. *Basic Inc. v. Levinson*, 485 U.S. 224, 241–47 (1988), holds that reliance on the accuracy of the price can substitute for reliance on the accuracy of particular written or oral statements, when the statements affect the price—as they do for large and well-followed firms such as Baxter, for which there is a liquid public market. This works only to the extent that markets efficiently reflect (and thus convey to investors the economic equivalent of) all public information.

When markets are informationally efficient, it is impossible to segment information as plaintiffs propose. They ask us to say that they received (through the price) the false oral statements but not the cautionary disclosures. That can't be; only if the market is inefficient is partial transmission likely, and if the market for Baxter's stock is inefficient then this suit collapses because a fraud-on-the-market claim won't fly. An investor who invokes the fraud-on-the-market theory must acknowledge that all public information is reflected in the price, just as the Supreme Court said in *Basic*. Thus if the truth or the nature of a business risk is widely known, an incorrect statement can have no deleterious effect, and if a cautionary statement has been widely disseminated, that news too affects the price just as if that statement had been handed to each investor. If the executives' oral statements came to plaintiffs through professional traders (or analysts) and hence the price, then the cautions reached plaintiffs via the same route; market professionals are savvy enough to discount projections appropriately. Then § 21E(c)(2)(B) has been satisfied for the oral statements (and so too § 21E(c)(A)(i) for the press releases). And if the cautions did not affect the price, then the market must be inefficient and the suit fails for that reason. So we take the claim as the pleadings framed it: the market for Baxter's stock is efficient, which means that Baxter's cautionary language must be treated as if attached to every one of its oral and written statements. That leaves the question whether these statements satisfy the statutory requirement that they adequately "identify [ ] important factors that could cause actual results to differ materially from those in the forward-looking statement."

The parties agree on two propositions, each with support in decisions of other circuits. First, "boilerplate" warnings won't do; cautions must be tailored to the risks that accompany the particular projections. Second, the cautions need not identify what actually goes wrong and causes the projections to be inaccurate; prevision is not required. Unfortunately, these principles don't decide any concrete case—for that matter, the statutory language itself does not decide any concrete case. . . .

Plaintiffs say that Baxter's cautions were boilerplate, but they aren't. Statements along the lines of "all businesses are risky" or "the future lies ahead" come to nothing other than caveat emptor (which isn't enough); these statements, by contrast, at least included Baxter-specific information and highlighted some parts of the business that might cause problems. For its part, Baxter says that mentioning these business segments demonstrates that the caution is sufficient; but this also is wrong, because then any issuer could list its lines of business, say "we could have problems in any of these," and avoid liability for statements implying that no such problems were on the horizon even if the management well knew that a precipice was in sight.

What investors would like to have is a full disclosure of the assumptions and calculations behind the projections; then they could apply their own discount factors . . . however, this is not a sensible requirement. Many of the assumptions and calculations would be more useful to a firm's rivals than to its investors. Suppose, for example, that Baxter had revealed its sterility failure in the BioSciences Division, the steps it had taken to restore production, and the costs and prospects of each. Rivals could have used that information to avoid costs and hazards that had befallen Baxter, or to find solutions more quickly, and as Baxter could not have charged the rivals for this information they would have been able to undercut Baxter's price in future transactions. Baxter's shareholders would have been worse off. . . .

Another form a helpful caution might take would be the disclosure of confidence intervals. After saying that it expected growth in the low teens, Baxter might have added that events could deviate 5% in either direction (so the real projection was that growth would fall someplace between 8% and 18%); disclosure of the probability that growth will be under 10% (or over 16%) would have done much to avoid the hit stock prices took when the results for the first half of 2002 proved to be unexpectedly low. Baxter surely had developed internally some estimate of likely variance. Revealing the mean, median, and standard deviation of these internal estimates, and pinpointing the principal matters that could cause results to differ from the more likely outcome, could help to generate an accurate price for the stock. . . .

Whether or not Baxter could have made the cautions more helpful by disclosing assumptions, methods, or confidence intervals, none of these is required. The PSLRA does not require the most helpful caution; it is enough to "identify[ ] important factors that could cause actual results to differ materially from those in the forward-looking statement." This means that it is enough to point to the principal contingencies that could cause actual results to depart from the projection. The statute calls for issuers to reveal the "important factors" but not to attach probabilities to each potential bad outcome, or to reveal in detail what could go wrong; as we have said, that level of detail might hurt investors (by helping rivals) even as it improved the accuracy of stock prices. (Requiring cautions to contain elaborate detail also would defeat the goal of facilitating projections, by turning each into a form of registration statement. Undue complexity would lead issuers to shut up, and stock prices could become even less accurate. Incomplete information usually is better than none, because market professionals know other tidbits that put the news in context.) Moreover, "[i]f enterprises cannot make predictions about themselves, then securities analysts, newspaper columnists, and charlatans have protected turf. There will be predictions aplenty outside the domain of the securities acts, predictions by persons whose access to information is not as good as the issuer's. When the issuer adds its information and analysis to that assembled by outsiders, the collective assessment will be more accurate even though a given projection will be off the mark."

Yet Baxter's chosen language may fall short. There is no reason to think—at least, no reason that a court can accept at the pleading stage, before plaintiffs have access to discovery—that the items mentioned in Baxter's cautionary language were those thought at the time to be the (or any of the) "important" sources of variance. The problem is not that what actually happened went unmentioned; issuers need not anticipate all sources of deviations from expectations. Rather, the problem is that there is no reason (on this record) to conclude that Baxter mentioned those sources of variance that (at the time of the projection) were the principal or important risks. For all we can tell, the major risks Baxter knew that it faced when it made its forecasts were exactly those that, according to the complaint, came to pass, yet the cautionary statement mentioned none of them. Moreover, the cautionary language remained fixed even as the risks changed. When the sterility failure occurred in spring 2002, Baxter left both its forecasts and cautions as is. When Baxter closed the plants that (according to the complaint) were its least-cost sources of production, the forecasts and cautions continued without amendment. This raises the possibility—no greater confidence is possible before discovery—that Baxter knew of important variables that would affect its forecasts, but omitted them from the cautionary language in order to depict the projections as more certain than internal estimates at the time warranted. Thus this complaint could not be dismissed under the safe harbor, though we cannot exclude the possibility that if after discovery Baxter establishes that the cautions did reveal what were, ex ante, the major risks, the safe harbor may yet carry the day.

* * *

NOTES

1. *Bespeaks caution.* The PSLRA's forward-looking safe harbor is a codification and expansion of the judicially developed "bespeaks caution" doctrine. Under that doctrine, if:

> forecasts, opinions or projections are accompanied by meaningful cautionary statements, the forward-looking statements will not form the basis for a securities fraud claim if those statements did not affect the "total mix" of information ... provided [to] investors. In other words, cautionary language, if sufficient, renders the alleged omissions or misrepresentations immaterial as a matter of law.

Kaufman v. Trump's Castle Funding, 7 F.3d 357, 371–372 (3d Cir. 1993). Like the PSLRA's forward-looking safe harbor, the bespeaks caution doctrine only protects prospective statements, not historical facts. And also like the safe harbor, vague or boilerplate warnings will not be sufficient to protect statements from liability. Unlike the safe harbor, however, the bespeaks caution doctrine does not insulate knowingly false statements. The other important difference is that the bespeaks caution doctrine applies to statements made in connection with tender offers and initial public offerings, which are excluded from the PSLRA safe harbor.

2. *Disjunctive safe harbor requirements.* Suppose a plaintiff successfully demonstrates that the defendant acted with actual knowledge of falsity when making a misleading forward-looking statement. Can the defendant still obtain the protection of the § 21E safe harbor if the forward-looking statement is accompanied by "meaningful cautionary language"? The prevalent view among the circuits is that state of mind is irrelevant if defendants use the meaningful cautionary language prong of the § 21E safe harbor. *See Slayton v. American Exp. Co.,* 604 F.3d 758, 766 (2d Cir. 2010) ("The safe harbor is written in the disjunctive; that is, a defendant is not liable if the forward-looking statement is identified and accompanied by meaningful cautionary language or is immaterial or the plaintiff fails to prove that it was made with actual knowledge that it was false or misleading."). *But see Freeland v. Iridium World Communications,* 545 F.Supp.2d 59 (D.D.C. 2008) (concluding that cautionary language cannot be

meaningful where management had actual knowledge that a prediction was false or misleading).

QUESTIONS

1. Why did the court conclude that it could not apply the safe harbor on a motion to dismiss?

2. Given the purpose of the PSLRA to reduce frivolous litigation, how effective is the forward-looking statement safe harbor in achieving this goal if defendants find it difficult to use the safe harbor to obtain a dismissal?

3. Does the forward-looking safe harbor make it hazardous to rely on forward-looking statements? Should investors be assumed to know this?

4. Are issuers better off with the safe harbor for forward-looking statements? If so, why didn't Congress extend the same protection to all voluntary statements?

HYPOTHETICAL FIVE

Could Hillary, the CEO of DigitalBase, put out a press release containing earnings projection for DigitalBase covering the next five years so long as she includes "meaningful cautionary language" with the release and states that she is taking advantage of § 27A of the Securities Act and § 21E of the Exchange Act? Consider the following situations.

1. *Scenario One:* DigitalBase is registering for its initial public offering.

2. *Scenario Two:* DigitalBase is late in the filing of its most recent Form 10–K.

3. *Scenario Three:* DigitalBase is not required to file reports under § 13(a) or § 15(d) of the Exchange Act.

4. *Scenario Four:* Hillbert Securities provides an outside review of DigitalBase that includes earnings projections covering the next five years. What result for Hillbert under § 27A and § 21E if Hillbert is not connected in any way to DigitalBase?

B. SCIENTER

Ernst & Ernst v. Hochfelder

425 U.S. 185 (1976).

■ POWELL, J.

The issue in this case is whether an action for civil damages may lie under § 10(b) of the Securities Exchange Act of 1934, and Securities and Exchange Commission Rule 10b–5, in the absence of an allegation of intent to deceive, manipulate, or defraud on the part of the defendant.

I

* * *

[Nay, the president of a brokerage firm, embezzled investors' money for many years. Nay established a "mail rule" at his brokerage firm under which only he could open mail addressed to him which allowed him to purloin the investor funds without anyone in the brokerage firm discovering the fraudulent transfers. Ernst & Ernst was the auditor for the brokerage firm. Plaintiffs sued under § 10(b) and Rule 10b–5 alleging that Ernst & Ernst was negligent in failing to audit the brokerage firm properly.]

Respondents contended that if Ernst & Ernst had conducted a proper audit, it would have discovered this "mail rule." The existence of the rule then would have been disclosed in reports to the SEC by Ernst & Ernst as an irregular procedure that prevented an effective audit. This would have led to an investigation of Nay that would have revealed the fraudulent scheme. Respondents specifically disclaimed the existence of fraud or intentional misconduct on the part of Ernst & Ernst.

* * *

We granted certiorari to resolve the question whether a private cause of action for damages will lie under § 10(b) and Rule 10b–5 in the absence of any allegation of "scienter"—intent to deceive, manipulate, or defraud.[12] We conclude that it will not and therefore we reverse.

II

* * *

Section 10(b) makes unlawful the use or employment of "any manipulative or deceptive device or contrivance" in contravention of Commission rules. The words "manipulative or deceptive" used in conjunction with "device or contrivance" strongly suggest that § 10(b) was intended to proscribe knowing or intentional misconduct.

In its *amicus curiae* brief, however, the Commission contends that nothing in the language "manipulative or deceptive device or contrivance" limits its operation to knowing or intentional practices. In support of its view, the Commission cites the overall congressional purpose in the 1933 and 1934 Acts to protect investors against false and deceptive practices that might injure them. The Commission then reasons that since the "effect" upon investors of given conduct is the same regardless of whether the conduct is negligent or intentional, Congress must have intended to bar all such practices and not just those done knowingly or intentionally. The logic of this effect-oriented approach would impose liability for wholly faultless conduct where such conduct results in harm to investors, a result the Commission would be unlikely to support. But apart from where its logic might lead, the Commission would add a gloss to the operative language of the statute quite different from its commonly accepted meaning. The argument simply ignores the use of the words "manipulative," "device," and "contrivance"—terms that make unmistakable a congressional intent to proscribe a type of conduct quite different from negligence. Use of the

---

[12] ... In this opinion the term "scienter" refers to a mental state embracing intent to deceive, manipulate, or defraud. In certain areas of the law recklessness is considered to be a form of intentional conduct for purposes of imposing liability for some act. We need not address here the question whether, in some circumstances, reckless behavior is sufficient for civil liability under § 10(b) and Rule 10b–5. . . .

word "manipulative" is especially significant. It is and was virtually a term of art when used in connection with securities markets. It connotes intentional or willful conduct designed to deceive or defraud investors by controlling or artificially affecting the price of securities.

* * *

Neither the intended scope of § 10(b) nor the reasons for the changes in its operative language are revealed explicitly in the legislative history of the 1934 Act, which deals primarily with other aspects of the legislation. There is no indication, however, that § 10(b) was intended to proscribe conduct not involving scienter. . . .

* * *

In each instance that Congress created express civil liability in favor of purchasers or sellers of securities it clearly specified whether recovery was to be premised on knowing or intentional conduct, negligence, or entirely innocent mistake. For example, § 11 of the 1933 Act unambiguously creates a private action for damages when a registration statement includes untrue statements of material facts or fails to state material facts necessary to make the statements therein not misleading. Within the limits specified by § 11(e), the issuer of the securities is held absolutely liable for any damages resulting from such misstatement or omission. But experts such as accountants who have prepared portions of the registration statement are accorded a "due diligence" defense. In effect, this is a negligence standard. An expert may avoid civil liability with respect to the portions of the registration statement for which he was responsible by showing that "after reasonable investigation" he had "reasonable ground[s] to believe" that the statements for which he was responsible were true and there was no omission of a material fact. The express recognition of a cause of action premised on negligent behavior in § 11 stands in sharp contrast to the language of § 10(b), and significantly undercuts the Commission's argument.

We also consider it significant that each of the express civil remedies in the 1933 Act allowing recovery for negligent conduct is subject to significant procedural restrictions not applicable under § 10(b). Section 11(e) of the 1933 Act, for example, authorizes the court to require a plaintiff bringing a suit under § 11, § 12[a](2), or § 15 thereof to post a bond for costs, including attorneys' fees, and in specified circumstances to assess costs at the conclusion of the litigation. . . . These restrictions, significantly, were imposed by amendments to the 1933 Act adopted as part of the 1934 Act. . . . We think these procedural limitations indicate that the judicially created private damages remedy under § 10(b)—which has no comparable restrictions—cannot be extended, consistently with the intent of Congress, to actions premised on negligent wrongdoing. Such extension would allow causes of action covered by §§ 11, 12[a](2), and 15 to be brought instead under § 10(b) and thereby nullify the effectiveness of the carefully drawn procedural restrictions on these express actions. We would be unwilling to bring about this result absent substantial support in the legislative history, and there is none.

We have addressed, to this point, primarily the language and history of § 10(b). The Commission contends, however, that subsections (b) and (c) of Rule 10b–5 are cast in language which—if standing alone—could encompass both intentional and negligent behavior. These subsections respectively provide that it is unlawful "[t]o make any untrue statement of a material fact or to omit to state a material fact necessary in order to make the statements made, in the light of the circumstances under which they were made, not misleading ..." and "[t]o engage in any act, practice, or course of business which operates or would operate as a fraud or deceit upon any person...." Viewed in isolation the language of subsection (b), and arguably that of subsection (c), could be read as proscribing, respectively, any type of material misstatement or omission, and any course of conduct, that has the effect of defrauding investors, whether the wrongdoing was intentional or not.

We note first that such a reading cannot be harmonized with the administrative history of the Rule, a history making clear that when the Commission adopted the Rule it was intended to apply only to activities that involved scienter. More importantly, Rule 10b–5 was adopted pursuant to authority granted the Commission under § 10(b). The rulemaking power granted to an administrative agency charged with the administration of a federal statute is not the power to make law. Rather, it is " 'the power to adopt regulations to carry into effect the will of Congress as expressed by the statute.' " Thus, despite the broad view of the Rule advanced by the Commission in this case, its scope cannot exceed the power granted the Commission by Congress under § 10(b). For the reasons stated above, we think the Commission's original interpretation of Rule 10b–5 was compelled by the language and history of § 10(b) and related sections of the Acts. When a statute speaks so specifically in terms of manipulation and deception, and of implementing devices and contrivances—the commonly understood terminology of intentional wrongdoing—and when its history reflects no more expansive intent, we are quite unwilling to extend the scope of the statute to negligent conduct.

* * *

QUESTIONS

1. Why does Justice Powell say that the logic of the SEC's approach "would impose liability for wholly faultless conduct where such conduct results in harm to investors, a result the Commission would be unlikely to support"?

2. Should recklessness count as "intent to deceive, manipulate, or defraud" if the defendant had no motive to deceive?

3. The Court notes that in a § 11 action for a material misstatement (or omission where there is a duty to disclose) involving a registration statement for a public offering, Ernst & Ernst could escape liability by meeting its "due diligence" defense. To meet this defense, Ernst & Ernst must show that it was not negligent in performing its duties. Why should negligence on the part of Ernst & Ernst lead to § 11 liability but not Rule 10b–5 liability?

HYPOTHETICAL SIX

Shortly after DigitalBase discloses the problems with GigaBase, its auditor, Arthur & Young, demands that it restate its revenues for the last year. It turns out that the DigitalBase sales staff for the western U.S.— under heavy pressure from Hillary, the CEO, to maintain market share until the GigaBase comes on line—has been providing some of the distributors who sell DigitalBase's product with secret side agreements allowing the distributors to return the product if it goes unsold. DigitalBase has been booking the revenue and profit from these sales as final despite the right of return, but Arthur & Young has now stumbled across the side agreements and insists that DigitalBase restate $250 million in revenues. This creates a problem for Arthur & Young; before the revelation of the misleading revenue recognition practices, Arthur & Young certified that it had reviewed DigitalBase's financials for the past year and that they conformed to generally accepted accounting principles. When DigitalBase issues the press release announcing the restatement, its stock price drops from $15 to $10.

In conducting its review of DigitalBase, it is shown at trial that Randall, the lead partner from Arthur & Young, did not follow the industry-accepted practice of spot checking contracts with customers. If Randall had done so, it is likely that he would have uncovered the side agreements and the fact that DigitalBase was overstating its sales. Can Arthur & Young be held liable under Rule 10b–5?

––––––

In footnote twelve of the *Ernst & Ernst* opinion, Justice Powell reserved the question of whether "recklessness," as opposed to knowingly making a misstatement, would satisfy the scienter requirement. The Court has not returned to this question, but every circuit court that has addressed the question has concluded that recklessness satisfies Rule 10b–5's scienter standard. Congress flirted with codifying a scienter standard when it was drafting the PSLRA, but it instead simply adopted the pleading standard discussed in the case below.

The next case also addresses the question of how much evidence the plaintiff must put forward regarding the defendant's state of mind in order to withstand a motion to dismiss. For Rule 10b–5 (and other private claims under the Exchange Act), the PSLRA requires that complaints plead with particularity facts giving rise to a "strong inference" that the defendants had the requisite "state of mind," as codified in § 21D(b)(2) of the Exchange Act. Discovery, moreover, is stayed until after the motion to dismiss (§ 21D(b)(3)(B)), making it difficult for plaintiffs to uncover facts to meet the pleading with particularity requirement and thereby avoid dismissal. What sort of facts must a plaintiff offer to meet this heightened pleading requirement?

Tellabs, Inc. v. Makor Issues & Rights, Ltd.

551 U.S. 308 (2007).

■ GINSBURG, J.

This Court has long recognized that meritorious private actions to enforce federal antifraud securities laws are an essential supplement to criminal prosecutions and civil enforcement actions brought, respectively, by the Department of Justice and the Securities and Exchange Commission. Private securities fraud actions, however, if not adequately contained, can be employed abusively to impose substantial costs on companies and individuals whose conduct conforms to the law. As a check against abusive litigation by private parties, Congress enacted the Private Securities Litigation Reform Act of 1995.

Exacting pleading requirements are among the control measures Congress included in the PSLRA. The Act requires plaintiffs to state with particularity both the facts constituting the alleged violation, and the facts evidencing scienter, i.e., the defendant's intention "to deceive, manipulate, or defraud." This case concerns the latter requirement. As set out in § 21D(b)(2) of the PSLRA, plaintiffs must "state with particularity facts giving rise to a strong inference that the defendant acted with the required state of mind."

* * *

I

Petitioner Tellabs, Inc., manufactures specialized equipment used in fiber optic networks. During the time period relevant to this case, petitioner Richard Notebaert was Tellabs' chief executive officer and president. Respondents (Shareholders) are persons who purchased Tellabs stock between December 11, 2000, and June 19, 2001. They accuse Tellabs and Notebaert (as well as several other Tellabs executives) of engaging in a scheme to deceive the investing public about the true value of Tellabs' stock.

Beginning on December 11, 2000, the Shareholders allege, Notebaert (and by imputation Tellabs) "falsely reassured public investors, in a series of statements . . . that Tellabs was continuing to enjoy strong demand for its products and earning record revenues," when, in fact, Notebaert knew the opposite was true. From December 2000 until the spring of 2001, the Shareholders claim, Notebaert knowingly misled the public in four ways. First, he made statements indicating that demand for Tellabs' flagship networking device, the TITAN 5500, was continuing to grow, when in fact demand for that product was waning. Second, Notebaert made statements indicating that the TITAN 6500, Tellabs' next-generation networking device, was available for delivery, and that demand for that product was strong and growing, when in truth the product was not ready for delivery and demand was weak. Third, he falsely represented Tellabs' financial results for the fourth quarter of 2000 (and, in connection with those results, condoned the practice of "channel stuffing," under which Tellabs flooded its customers with unwanted products). Fourth, Notebaert made a series of overstated revenue projections, when demand for the TITAN 5500 was drying up and production of the

TITAN 6500 was behind schedule. Based on Notebaert's sunny assessments, the Shareholders contend, market analysts recommended that investors buy Tellabs' stock.

* * *

The Court of Appeals for the Seventh Circuit . . . concluded that the Shareholders had sufficiently alleged that Notebaert acted with the requisite state of mind.

The Court of Appeals recognized that the PSLRA "unequivocally raise[d] the bar for pleading scienter" by requiring plaintiffs to "plea[d] sufficient facts to create a strong inference of scienter." In evaluating whether that pleading standard is met, the Seventh Circuit said, "courts [should] examine all of the allegations in the complaint and then . . . decide whether collectively they establish such an inference." "[W]e will allow the complaint to survive," the court next and critically stated, "if it alleges facts from which, if true, a reasonable person could infer that the defendant acted with the required intent. . . . If a reasonable person could not draw such an inference from the alleged facts, the defendants are entitled to dismissal."

In adopting its standard for the survival of a complaint, the Seventh Circuit explicitly rejected a stiffer standard adopted by the Sixth Circuit, i.e., that "plaintiffs are entitled only to the most plausible of competing inferences." . . . We granted certiorari to resolve the disagreement among the Circuits on whether, and to what extent, a court must consider competing inferences in determining whether a securities fraud complaint gives rise to a "strong inference" of scienter.

II

* * *

In an ordinary civil action, the Federal Rules of Civil Procedure require only "a short and plain statement of the claim showing that the pleader is entitled to relief." Fed. Rule Civ. Proc. 8(a)(2). Although the rule encourages brevity, the complaint must say enough to give the defendant "fair notice of what the plaintiff's claim is and the grounds upon which it rests." Prior to the enactment of the PSLRA, the sufficiency of a complaint for securities fraud was governed not by Rule 8, but by the heightened pleading standard set forth in Rule 9(b). Rule 9(b) applies to "all averments of fraud or mistake"; it requires that "the circumstances constituting fraud . . . be stated with particularity" but provides that "[m]alice, intent, knowledge, and other condition of mind of a person, may be averred generally." Courts of Appeals diverged on the character of the Rule 9(b) inquiry in § 10(b) cases: Could securities fraud plaintiffs allege the requisite mental state "simply by stating that scienter existed," or were they required to allege with particularity facts giving rise to an inference of scienter? Circuits requiring plaintiffs to allege specific facts indicating scienter expressed that requirement variously. The Second Circuit's formulation was the most stringent. Securities fraud plaintiffs in that Circuit were required to "specifically plead those [facts] which they assert give rise to a strong inference that the defendants had" the requisite state of mind. The "strong inference" formulation was appropriate, the Second Circuit said, to ward off allegations of "fraud by hindsight."

Setting a uniform pleading standard for § 10(b) actions was among Congress' objectives when it enacted the PSLRA. Designed to curb perceived abuses of the § 10(b) private action—"nuisance filings, targeting of deep-pocket defendants, vexatious discovery requests and manipulation by class action lawyers,"—the PSLRA installed both substantive and procedural controls. . . . [I]n § 21D(b) of the PSLRA, Congress "impose[d] heightened pleading requirements in actions brought pursuant to § 10(b) and Rule 10b–5."

Under the PSLRA's heightened pleading instructions, any private securities complaint alleging that the defendant made a false or misleading statement must: (1) "specify each statement alleged to have been misleading [and] the reason or reasons why the statement is misleading"; and (2) "state with particularity facts giving rise to a strong inference that the defendant acted with the required state of mind." . . .

The "strong inference" standard "unequivocally raise[d] the bar for pleading scienter," and signaled Congress' purpose to promote greater uniformity among the Circuits. But "Congress did not . . . throw much light on what facts . . . suffice to create [a strong] inference," or on what "degree of imagination courts can use in divining whether" the requisite inference exists. While adopting the Second Circuit's "strong inference" standard, Congress did not codify that Circuit's case law interpreting the standard. With no clear guide from Congress other than its "inten[tion] to strengthen existing pleading requirements," Courts of Appeals have diverged again, this time in construing the term "strong inference." Among the uncertainties, should courts consider competing inferences in determining whether an inference of scienter is "strong"? Our task is to prescribe a workable construction of the "strong inference" standard, a reading geared to the PSLRA's twin goals: to curb frivolous, lawyer-driven litigation, while preserving investors' ability to recover on meritorious claims.

III

A

We establish the following prescriptions: *First,* faced with a Rule 12(b)(6) motion to dismiss a § 10(b) action, courts must, as with any motion to dismiss for failure to plead a claim on which relief can be granted, accept all factual allegations in the complaint as true. . . .

Second, courts must consider the complaint in its entirety, as well as other sources courts ordinarily examine when ruling on Rule 12(b)(6) motions to dismiss, in particular, documents incorporated into the complaint by reference, and matters of which a court may take judicial notice. The inquiry . . . is whether all of the facts alleged, taken collectively, give rise to a strong inference of scienter, not whether any individual allegation, scrutinized in isolation, meets that standard.

Third, in determining whether the pleaded facts give rise to a "strong" inference of scienter, the court must take into account plausible opposing inferences. The Seventh Circuit expressly declined to engage in such a comparative inquiry. A complaint could survive, that court said, as long as it "alleges facts from which, if true, a reasonable person could infer that the defendant acted with the required intent"; in other words, only "[i]f a reasonable person could not draw such an inference from the alleged facts" would the defendant prevail on a motion to dismiss. But in § 21D(b)(2), Congress did not merely require plaintiffs to "provide a factual basis for [their] scienter allegations," i.e., to allege facts from which an inference of scienter rationally could be drawn. Instead, Congress required plaintiffs to plead with particularity facts that give rise to a "strong"—i.e., a powerful or cogent—inference.

The strength of an inference cannot be decided in a vacuum. The inquiry is inherently comparative: How likely is it that one conclusion, as compared to others, follows from the underlying facts? To determine whether the plaintiff has alleged facts that give rise to the requisite "strong inference" of scienter, a court must consider plausible nonculpable explanations for the defendant's conduct, as well as inferences favoring the plaintiff. The inference that the defendant acted with scienter need not be irrefutable, i.e., of the "smoking-gun" genre, or even the "most plausible of competing inferences." Recall in this regard that § 21D(b)'s pleading requirements are but one constraint among many the PSLRA installed to screen out frivolous suits, while allowing meritorious actions to move forward. Yet the inference of scienter must be more than merely "reasonable" or "permissible"—it must be cogent and compelling, thus strong in light of other explanations. A complaint will survive, we hold, only if a reasonable person would deem the inference of scienter cogent and at least as compelling as any opposing inference one could draw from the facts alleged.

B

Tellabs contends that when competing inferences are considered, Notebaert's evident lack of pecuniary motive will be dispositive. The Shareholders, Tellabs stresses, did not allege that Notebaert sold any shares during the class period. While it is true that motive can be a relevant consideration, and personal financial gain may weigh heavily in favor of a scienter inference, we agree with the Seventh Circuit that the absence of a motive allegation is not fatal. As earlier stated, allegations must be considered collectively; the significance that can be ascribed to an allegation of motive, or lack thereof, depends on the entirety of the complaint.

Tellabs also maintains that several of the Shareholders' allegations are too vague or ambiguous to contribute to a strong inference of scienter. For example, the Shareholders alleged that Tellabs flooded its customers with unwanted products, a practice known as "channel stuffing." But they failed, Tellabs argues, to specify whether the channel stuffing allegedly known to Notebaert was the illegitimate kind (e.g., writing orders for products customers had not requested) or the legitimate kind (e.g., offering customers discounts as an incentive to buy). We agree that omissions and ambiguities count against inferring scienter, for plaintiffs must "state with particularity facts giving rise to a strong inference that the defendant acted with the required state of mind." We reiterate, however, that the court's job is not to scrutinize each allegation in isolation but to assess all the allegations holistically. In sum, the reviewing court must ask: When the allegations are accepted as true and taken collectively, would a reasonable person deem the inference of scienter at least as strong as any opposing inference?

* * *

■ SCALIA, J., concurring in the judgment.

I fail to see how an inference that is merely "at least as compelling as any opposing inference," can conceivably be called what the statute here at issue requires: a "strong inference." If a jade falcon were stolen from a room to which only A and B had access, could it possibly be said there was a "strong inference" that B was the thief? I think not, and I therefore think that the Court's test must fail. In my view, the test should be whether the inference of scienter (if any) is more plausible than the inference of innocence.

* * *

Congress has expressed its determination in the phrase "strong inference"; it is our job to give that phrase its normal meaning. And if we are to abandon text in favor of unexpressed purpose, as the Court does, it is inconceivable that Congress's enactment of stringent pleading requirements in the Private Securities Litigation Reform Act of 1995 somehow manifests the purpose of giving plaintiffs the edge in close cases.... There is no indication that the statute at issue here was meant to relax the ordinary rule under which a tie goes to the defendant. To the contrary, it explicitly strengthens that rule by extending it to the pleading stage of a case.

* * *

I hasten to add that, while precision of interpretation should always be pursued for its own sake, I doubt that in this instance what I deem to be the correct test will produce results much different from the Court's. How often is it that inferences are precisely in equipoise? All the more reason, I think, to read the language for what it says.

* * *

■ ALITO, J., concurring in the judgment.

* * *

In dicta ... the Court states that "omissions and ambiguities" merely "count against" inferring scienter, and that a court should consider all allegations of scienter, even nonparticularized ones, when considering whether a complaint meets the "strong inference" requirement. Not only does this interpretation contradict the clear statutory language on this point, but it undermines the particularity requirement's purpose of preventing a plaintiff from using vague or general allegations in order to get by a motion to dismiss for failure to state a claim. Allowing a plaintiff to derive benefit from such allegations would permit him to circumvent this important provision.

Furthermore, the Court's interpretation of the particularity requirement in no way distinguishes it from normal pleading review, under which a court naturally gives less weight to allegations containing "omissions and ambiguities" and more weight to allegations stating particularized facts. The particularity requirement is thus stripped of all meaning.

Questions certainly may arise as to whether certain allegations meet the statutory particularity requirement, but where that requirement is violated, the offending allegations cannot be taken into account.

II

I would also hold that a "strong inference that the defendant acted with the required state of mind" is an inference that is stronger than the inference that the defendant lacked the required state of mind.... Justice Scalia's interpretation would align the pleading test . . . with the test that is used at the summary-judgment and judgment-as-a-matter-of-law stages, whereas the Court's test would introduce a test previously unknown in civil litigation. It seems more likely that Congress meant to adopt a known quantity and thus to adopt Justice Scalia's approach.

NOTES

1. *Ties.* Justice Scalia observes in his *Tellabs* concurrence that the difference between the equal inference and preponderance standards is likely to matter in only a small fraction of cases: "How often is it that inferences are precisely in equipoise?" Is Justice Scalia correct? When courts are able to assess the probabilities of competing inferences with mathematical precision (for example 50.1% versus 49.9%), ties will be rare, as Justice Scalia suggests. Determining the probability for a particular inference is more ambiguous in practice, however, as judges must wrestle with uncertainty arising from a complicated fact pattern. Faced with two inferences of uncertain magnitude, judges may often not be sure which inference is more likely than the other, leading to a relatively large number of perceived ties.

2. *Holistic approach.* What does it mean for a court to take a holistic approach in assessing scienter allegations in the complaint? The Ninth Circuit in *Zucco Partners, LLC v. Digimarc Corp.*, 552 F.3d 981, 992 (9th Cir. 2009), stated that *Tellabs* required the court to "conduct a dual inquiry: first, we will determine whether any of the plaintiff's allegations, standing alone, are sufficient to create a strong inference of scienter; second, if no individual allegations are sufficient, we will conduct a 'holistic' review of the same allegations to determine whether the insufficient allegations combine to create a strong inference of intentional conduct or deliberate recklessness."

3. *Confidential witnesses.* Under *Tellabs*, how should courts evaluate allegations based on statements from unidentified, confidential witnesses? Plaintiffs (or more accurately plaintiffs' attorneys) often turn to confidential witnesses to meet the pleading with particularity requirement for scienter under the PSLRA. Courts have taken divergent approaches in assessing those sources. Applying *Tellabs*, Judge Easterbrook writing for the Seventh Circuit in *Higginbotham v. Baxter Int'l*, 495 F.3d 753, 757 (2007), stated that: "It is hard to see how information from anonymous sources could be deemed 'compelling' or how we could take account of plausible opposing inferences. Perhaps these confidential sources have axes to grind. Perhaps they are lying. Perhaps they don't even exist." Judge Easterbrook went on to say that: "Because it is impossible to anticipate all combinations of information that may be presented in the future, and because *Tellabs* instructs courts to evaluate the allegations in their entirety, we said above that allegations from 'confidential witnesses' must be 'discounted'" rather than ignored. Usually that discount will be steep." In contrast, the Eleventh Circuit in *Mizzaro v. Home Depot, Inc.*, 544 F.3d 1230, 1240 (11th Cir. 2008), held that "[c]onfidentiality . . . should not eviscerate the weight given if the complaint otherwise fully describes the foundation of the confidential witness's knowledge, including the position(s) held, the proximity to the offending conduct, and the relevant time frame."

4. *Collective scienter.* How are plaintiffs supposed to plead facts giving rise to a strong inference of scienter on the part of a corporate defendant? The corporation is not a real person and thus has no state of mind separate from its agents. Courts typically attribute the state of mind of individual corporate officers to the corporate entity. But what if plaintiffs are unable to demonstrate a strong inference of scienter for any individual officer? Some courts have accepted a theory of "collective scienter," allowing plaintiffs to argue that the collective knowledge of all the corporate officers and employees showed a strong inference of scienter with respect to the corporate entity. The Seventh Circuit, for example, on remand from the Supreme Court in *Tellabs*, observed:

> [I]t is possible to draw a strong inference of corporate scienter without being able to name the individuals who concocted and disseminated the fraud. Suppose General Motors announced that it had sold one million SUVs in 2006, and the actual number was zero. There would be a strong inference of corporate scienter, since so dramatic an announcement would have been approved by corporate officials sufficiently knowledgeable about the company to know that the announcement was false.

Makor Issues & Rights Ltd. v. Tellabs Inc., 513 F.3d 702, 710 (2008). *But see Southland Sec. Corp. INSpire Ins. Solutions, Inc.*, 365 F.3d 353, 366 (5th Cir. 2004) ("[W]e believe it appropriate to look to the state of mind of the individual corporate official or officials who make or issue the statement . . . rather than generally to the collective knowledge of all the corporation's officers and employees acquired in the course of their employment.").

QUESTIONS

1. Which interpretation of "strong inference"—the *Tellabs* majority's "at least as compelling as any opposing inference," or Scalia and Alito's preponderance standard—is more consistent with "the PSLRA's twin goals: to curb frivolous, lawyer-driven litigation, while preserving investors' ability to recover on meritorious claims"?

2. Is it reasonable to require the plaintiff to plead facts showing scienter before she has had access to discovery? Are sanctions appropriate if the plaintiffs' lawyer turns out to be wrong on the facts?

———

In the next case, the Seventh Circuit addresses the consequences for lawyers who fall short in pleading scienter.

City of Livonia Employees' Retirement System v. The Boeing Co.

711 F.3d 754 (7th Cir. 2013).

■ POSNER, R., CIRCUIT JUDGE

These appeals present questions—substantive, procedural, and also relating to sanctions for attorney misconduct—arising from the plaintiffs' claim that the Boeing Company, along with its chief executive officer (McNerney) and the head of its commercial aircraft division (Carson), committed securities fraud in violation of section 10(b) of the Securities Exchange Act of 1934 and SEC Rule 10b–5. The suit, filed as a class action, seek[s] hundreds of millions of dollars in damages. The district court ... dismissed the suit under Rule 12(b)(6).... The plaintiffs' appeal challenges the dismissal while the defendants' cross-appeal challenges the failure of the district court to impose sanctions on the plaintiffs' lawyers for violating Fed.R.Civ.P. 11.

* * *

The Private Securities Litigation Reform Act of 1995 altered the landscape of federal securities fraud litigation in four respects that bear on our case. First, it requires a plaintiff who is complaining about "forward-looking" statements—predictions or speculations about the future—to prove "actual knowledge" of falsity on the part of defendants, not merely reckless indifference to the danger that a statement is false.

Second, the complaint must "state with particularity facts giving rise to a *strong inference* that the defendant acted with the required state of mind," rather than a mere inference. But except with regard to "forward-looking" statements, the Act does not specify "the required state of mind," so it remains scienter.

* * *

Third, the heavy burden of pleading that the Act places on plaintiffs induces their lawyers to seek out confidential sources of information about the defendant in advance of filing a complaint—a problematic endeavor, as well illustrated by this case.

And fourth, the Act requires the district judge, even if neither side files a Rule 11 motion, to determine each party's compliance with the rule and to impose sanctions if at the end of the case he finds that the rule has been violated.

The suit is on behalf of all persons who bought common stock of Boeing between May 4 and June 22, 2009. The key allegations of the first amended complaint ... were as follows. On April 21 of that year Boeing performed a stress test on the wings of its new 787–8 Dreamliner, a plane that had not yet flown. The wings failed the test; metal strips called "stringers," designed to shift weight from the wings to the fuselage, failed to do so adequately. Yet Boeing announced on May 3 that "all structural tests required on the static airframe prior to first flight are complete" and that "the initial results [of the test] are positive" (though it also said that the data obtained in the test had not yet been fully analyzed). The implication was that the plane was on track for its "First Flight," which had been scheduled for June 30. "First

Flight," which denotes the first time a new model of an airplane flies, is an important milestone in the development of a new model, though not the final milestone—thousands of hours of additional flight testing are necessary before the plane can begin commercial operation.

In mid-May, after making some changes in the design of the stringers, Boeing conducted another test. Although the plane failed that test too, defendant McNerney stated publicly that he thought the plane would fly in June. Later defendant Carson told *Bloomberg* that the Dreamliner "definitely will fly" this month (June).

The biennial Paris Air Show began in the middle of June. Of course the Dreamliner did not fly in the show; it had never been expected to. But at the show Boeing executives made presentations concerning the Dreamliner and its development schedule. Yet on June 23, four days after the show ended, Boeing announced that the First Flight of the Dreamliner had been canceled because, Carson explained, of an "anomaly" revealed by the stringer tests. He said that Boeing had hoped to be able to solve the problem in time for a First Flight in June, but had been unable to do so. In fact the First Flight did not take place until December 2009.

When Boeing announced the cancellation of the First Flight, it also announced that the cancellation would cause a delay of unspecified length in the delivery of the Dreamliner, which many airlines had already ordered. In the two days after these announcements, Boeing's stock price dropped by more than 10 percent. The plaintiff class consists of persons who bought Boeing stock between the tests and the announcements of the cancellation and of the delay in delivery and who therefore lost money when the price dropped.

The district judge dismissed the first amended complaint . . . for failure to create a strong inference that the defendants had acted with scienter. The complaint did not indicate whether McNerney, Carson, or anyone else who had made optimistic public statements about the timing of the First Flight knew that their optimism was unfounded. The complaint was not inconsistent with the defendants having had a realistic hope that the defects in the stringers revealed by the tests could be eliminated quickly, without requiring postponement of the flight. Time may have been needed to digest the information produced by the tests and conclude from it that the First Flight would have to be delayed.

"There is no securities fraud by hindsight." The law does not require public disclosure of mere *risks* of failure. No prediction—even a prediction that the sun will rise tomorrow—has a 100 percent probability of being correct. The future is shrouded in uncertainty. If a mistaken prediction is deemed a fraud, there will be few predictions, including ones that are well grounded, as no one wants to be held hostage to an unknown future.

Any sophisticated purchaser of a product that is still on the drawing boards knows, moreover, that its market debut may be delayed, or indeed that the project may be abandoned before it yields salable product. The purchasers of the Dreamliner protected themselves against the possibility of delay in delivery by reserving the right to cancel their orders; there are no allegations regarding cancellation penalties, or for that matter penalties imposed on Boeing for delivery delays. And therefore had the defendants known before the Paris Air Show that the First Flight would have to be postponed, they would have had, so far as appears, little incentive to delay the announcement of the postponement until the show closed. True, the Paris Air Show is the industry's biggest trade show and attracts heavy media coverage. But it was not the deadline for airline companies to cancel their orders for the Dreamliner. A delay of five weeks (from May 17, the date of the second test, to June 23, the announcement of the indefinite postponement of the First Flight) would not affect cancellations. All it would do—if the defendants knew on May 17 that the First Flight would be delayed indefinitely (and this became known)—would undermine Boeing's credibility with its customers and expose the company to a multi-hundred million dollar lawsuit for securities fraud. The buyer of a $200 million dollar airplane will not overlook bad news about the plane merely because the news emerged a few days after the industry trade show rather than before or during it.

Without a motive to commit securities fraud, businessmen are unlikely to commit it. A more plausible inference than that of fraud is that the defendants, unsure whether they could fix the problem by the end of June, were reluctant to tell the world "we have a problem and maybe it will cause us to delay the First Flight and maybe not, but we're working on the problem and we hope we can fix it in time to prevent any significant delay, but we can't be sure, so stay tuned." There is a difference, famously emphasized by Kant, between a duty of truthfulness and a duty of candor, or between a lie and reticence. There is no duty of total corporate transparency—no rule that every hitch or glitch, every pratfall, in a company's operations must be disclosed in "real time," forming a running commentary, a baring of the corporate innards, day and night.

Of course the fact that a prediction *may* prove untrue does not justify representing as true a prediction that one knows, to a reasonable certainty, is false. But unless the complaint created a strong inference that McNerney and Carson, who made the allegedly false statements about the timing of the First Flight, knew they were false, there would be no fraud to impute either to them or to Boeing. No other employee of Boeing is accused of having made such statements within the scope of his employment, thereby triggering corporate liability in accordance with the doctrine of respondeat superior.

All that the first amended complaint alleged regarding what McNerney and Carson knew about the likely postponement of the First Flight was that their knowledge was confirmed by "internal e-mails" of Boeing. The reference to *internal* e-mails implied that someone inside Boeing was aiding the plaintiffs. But as no such person was identified, the judge could not determine whether such emails—without which no "strong inference" that the defendants had committed fraud was even remotely possible—existed.

Allegations concerning—in the first amended complaint merely implying—unnamed confidential sources of damaging information require a heavy discount. The sources may be ill-informed, may be acting from spite rather than knowledge, may be misrepresented, may even be nonexistent—a gimmick for obtaining discovery costly to the defendants and maybe forcing settlement or inducing more favorable settlement terms. The district judge therefore rightly refused to give any weight to the "internal e-mails" to which the complaint referred.

The judge's dismissal of the first amended complaint was without prejudice, however, and so the plaintiffs could file a second amended complaint. And they did. This one gave particulars about the confidential source (there was just one), an engineer later revealed to be Bishnujee Singh. The complaint described him as a "Boeing Senior Structural Analyst Engineer and Chief Engineer" who had worked on wing-stress tests of the Dreamliner and who as part of his job had "had direct access to, as well as first-hand knowledge of the contents of, Boeing's 787 stress test files that memorialize the results of the failed 787 wing" tests of April and May 2009. According to the complaint those files included "internal, contemporaneous communications regarding the specific results of the" tests and the engineers' analysis of the results, plus "copies of internal electronic communications to defendants McNerney and Carson . . . informing [them] that" the tests had failed and that the failure might result in a delay of the Dreamliner's First Flight. On the basis of these allegations, which were purportedly based on interview notes by an investigator (Elizabeth Stewart) retained by the plaintiffs' lawyers, the district judge denied the defendants' Rule 12(b)(6) motion to dismiss the second amended complaint.

No one had bothered to show the complaint to Singh, however, and investigation by Boeing soon revealed that the complaint's allegations concerning him could not be substantiated. Some clearly were false: He had never been employed by the company. He had been employed by a contractor for Boeing. And although the contractor had been involved in wing tests for the Dreamliner, Singh's role in or knowledge of those tests, or of any communications to the individual defendants, was and is unknown, but it is highly improbable that he either was involved in the tests or was privy to internal communications with top officials of the company.

Deposed by defendants' counsel, Singh denied virtually everything that the investigator had reported. He denied that he had been doing work for Boeing when the tests were conducted. He denied that he had ever worked on the Dreamliner 787–8, the model in question; he had worked on the 787–9, a later model. He denied having knowledge of or access to internal Boeing communications regarding the tests on the 787–8. The plaintiffs argue that he lied at his deposition because he wanted to stay in Boeing's good graces; left unexplained is why he would not have wanted to remain in those good graces when he was interviewed by the investigator.

Karim Mustafa, the lead engineer for the team working on the 787–9 of which Singh was a member, declared under oath that Boeing had restricted access to the Dreamliner test results to those with a job-related need for the information, which Singh did not have with respect to the 787–8, because he wasn't working on that model. The declaration further stated that Singh would have had to obtain Mustafa's permission as well as that of Boeing's management to obtain access to internal company files concerning engineering work on the Dreamliner, and that he did not give Singh such permission. Indeed Mustafa himself had no access to files relating to the 787–8, since his assignment was the 787–9.

On the basis of these revelations concerning the so-called confidential source, the defendants asked the judge to reconsider her denial of their motion to dismiss the second amended complaint. She reconsidered—and dismissed the complaint, this time with prejudice, precipitating the parties' appeals. She did not try to determine when Singh had been lying and when telling the truth, or whether he had never lied but the investigator had misunderstood or misrepresented what he had told her. Noting that none of the plaintiffs' lawyers had met or talked to Singh until six months after they filed the second amended complaint, even though the first amended complaint had alleged reliance on internal Boeing communications, the judge thought their failure to attempt to verify the allegations in the investigator's notes amounted to a fraud on the court.

Until Singh's deposition the plaintiffs' lawyers had vouched for the accuracy of their investigator's report. But not afterward. At oral argument the plaintiffs' counsel, by telling us that "he wouldn't do much with [Singh] at trial," admitted that Singh, because of his recantation, would not be a witness for the plaintiffs. Either he had told the investigator the same thing he said in his deposition, which would be of no help to the plaintiffs and would expose the investigator as a liar, or he had made opposite assertions on the two occasions, in which event *he* was the liar, which wouldn't help the plaintiffs either. Singh is out of the case. The plaintiffs' abandonment of their sole confidential source—their only possible source of access to a Boeing database alleged to contain emails showing that the engineers who had conducted the wing tests had realized immediately that the test results compelled cancellation of the First Flight and had informed McNerney and Carson of this—was fatal.

Without evidence from the confidential source, then, the first dismissal stood, its validity unassailable. All that changed was that the second dismissal was with prejudice, since it was obvious (and not contested) that the plaintiffs had nothing to offer by way of a third complaint. They do not ask for leave to conduct further discovery in hopes of rehabilitating their confidential source.

It remains to consider the cross-appeal, in which the defendants complain about the judge's failure to consider the imposition of Rule 11 sanctions on the plaintiffs' lawyers. The plaintiffs argue that we have no appellate jurisdiction because while the defendants, in moving to dismiss the second amended complaint, told the judge they were going to ask for the imposition of sanctions, they never filed a motion for sanctions. So there is no order denying sanctions and therefore, the plaintiffs argue, no order to take an appeal from. But this argument founders on an unusual provision of the Private Securities Litigation Reform Act: "upon final adjudication of the action, the court shall include in the record specific findings regarding compliance by each party . . . with each requirement" of Rule 11, and if a violation is found "the court shall impose sanctions" on a party or lawyer who has violated the rule. There is no requirement that the defendant have asked for the imposition of sanctions.

The defendants made clear in moving for dismissal of the second amended complaint their belief that the plaintiffs' lawyers had violated Rule 11, with which the judge's harsh criticism of the plaintiffs when she dismissed the second amended complaint indicated agreement. But in any event it would have been her duty, "upon final adjudication of the action"—which occurred when she dismissed the second amended complaint on reconsideration and entered final judgment—to determine whether to impose sanctions even if the defendants had not invited her attention to the issue. Her failure to do so made the final judgment—an appealable order, of course—vulnerable to challenge by the defendants.

The plaintiffs' lawyers had made confident assurances in their complaints about a confidential source—their only barrier to dismissal of their suit—even though none of the lawyers had spoken to the source and their investigator had acknowledged that she couldn't verify what (according to her) he had told her. She had qualms: the names the source had given her of persons to whom he reported in the Boeing chain of command were inconsistent with what she was able to learn about the chain. This should have been a red flag to the plaintiffs' lawyers. Their failure to inquire further puts one in mind of ostrich tactics—of failing to inquire for fear that the inquiry might reveal stronger evidence of *their* scienter regarding the authenticity of the confidential source than the flimsy evidence of scienter they were able to marshal against Boeing. Representations in a filing in a federal district court that are not grounded in an "inquiry reasonable under the circumstances" or that are unlikely to "have evidentiary support after a reasonable opportunity for further investigation or discovery" violate Rules 11(b) and 11(b)(3).

The plaintiffs' law firm, Robbins Geller Rudman & Dowd LLP, was criticized for misleading allegations, concerning confidential sources, made to stave off dismissal of a securities-fraud case much like this one, in [prior cases] Recidivism is relevant in assessing sanctions.

The only question is whether we should decide whether to impose Rule 11 sanctions or remand to the district court to decide. . . . The district court is in a better position than the court of appeals to calculate the dollar amount of the sanctions. It also may have additional insights into the accused lawyers' conduct, by virtue of having spent more time on the litigation than the appellate court. . . .

* * *

QUESTIONS

1. Among the alleged misstatements was the statement that Boeing's new airplane "definitely will fly." What does the court mean when it says "The future is shrouded in uncertainty"? Does this give corporations carte blanche to lie about the future? Without access to internal records, how will plaintiffs' attorneys know if corporate officers are lying or merely failing to state the obvious that the future is uncertain?

2. Plaintiffs' attorneys sometimes rely on confidential informants to establish what defendants knew at the time they made allegedly misleading statements. How long did the plaintiffs' informant, Bishnujee Singh, remain confidential?

3. Should we allow plaintiffs' attorneys to pay confidential informants a portion of any recovery they obtain either from settlement or damages at trial?

4. Should courts apply Rule 11 sanctions automatically whenever a plaintiffs' attorney fails to survive the motion to dismiss in a securities class action? Would such sanctions make plaintiffs' attorneys pay more attention to the sources they use to support their allegations of scienter?

HYPOTHETICAL SEVEN

The plaintiffs allege the following facts in their complaint against DigitalBase and Hillary, the CEO. Hillary sold 500,000 shares of stock during the class period for proceeds of $12.5 million. In addition, the financial press reported that DigitalBase was actively seeking potential merger partners in the network services sector during the class period. The plaintiffs also allege that Hillary received weekly memoranda from DigitalBase's chief technology officer updating her on the progress of the GigaBase. The plaintiffs allege (in somewhat vague terms) that these memoranda repeatedly advised Hillary of the problems with the development of the GigaBase. The plaintiffs also allege that Hillary knew that DigitalBase's existing products were generally inferior to those offered at the time by its competitors, so she must have known that DigitalBase could not be maintaining its sales levels without providing inducements. DigitalBase and Hillary file a motion to dismiss the complaint. Have the plaintiffs adequately pleaded scienter?

————

What standard applies to those elements that do not fall under the PSLRA's heightened pleading requirements? For elements that do not require heightened pleading, Rule 8(a)(2) of the Federal Rules of Civil Procedure mandates that the complaint provide "a short and plain statement of the claim showing that the pleader is entitled to relief." The Supreme Court in *Conley v. Gibson*, 355 U.S. 41, 45–46 (1957) said that Rule 8(a)(2) is designed to "give the defendant fair notice of what the . . . claim is and the ground upon which it rests." *Conley* went on to hold that "a complaint should not be dismissed for failure to state a claim unless it appears beyond doubt that the plaintiff can prove no set of facts in support of his claim which would entitle him to relief."

The Supreme Court in *Bell Atlantic Corp. v. Twombly*, 550 U.S. 544 (2007), stepped back from the *Conley* notice pleading standard, instead adopting a "plausibility" pleading standard. The Court wrote that Rule 8(a) does not require "detailed factual allegations" but does require "more than labels and conclusions, and a formulaic recitation of the elements of a cause of action will not do." The Court accordingly held that "we do not require heightened fact pleading of specifics, but only enough facts to state a claim to relief that is plausible on its face."

The Supreme Court in *Ashcroft v. Iqbal*, 556 U.S. 662 (2009), refined its *Twombly* holding. The Court in *Iqbal* observed that *Twombly* established a two-pronged approach. The Court in *Iqbal* wrote: "First, the tenet that a court must accept as true all of the allegations contained in a complaint is inapplicable to legal conclusions. Threadbare recitals of the elements of a cause of action, supported by mere conclusory statements, do not suffice." The Court then wrote: "Second, only a complaint that states a plausible claim for relief survives a motion to dismiss. Determining whether a complaint states a plausible claim for relief will, as the Court of Appeals observed, be a context-specific task that requires the reviewing court to draw on its judicial experience and common sense." The *Iqbal* Court advised that: "A claim has facial plausibility when the pleaded factual content allows the court to draw the reasonable inference that the defendant is liable for the misconduct alleged."

C. RELIANCE

The SEC need not plead or prove reliance, that is, it need not show that it (or any actual investor) relied on a misstatement in making an investment decision. By contrast, private plaintiffs must both plead and prove reliance. This requirement is sometimes called "transaction causation" in recognition of the Supreme Court's flexible interpretation of the reliance requirement. Did the plaintiffs rely in the following case?

Affiliated Ute Citizens of Utah v. United States
406 U.S. 128 (1972).

■ BLACKMUN, J.

* * *

Ute Development Corporation [UDC] was incorporated in 1958 with the stated purpose "to manage jointly with the Tribal Business Committee of the full-blood members of the Ute Indian Tribe . . . all unadjudicated or unliquidated claims against the United States, all gas, oil, and mineral rights of every kind, and all other assets not susceptible to equitable and practicable distribution to which the mixed-blood members of the said tribe . . . are now, or may hereafter become entitled . . . and to receive the proceeds therefrom and to distribute the same to the stockholders of this corporation. . . ."

[UDC issued shares of its capital stock to mixed-blood members of the Ute Indian Tribe. UDC contracted with First Security Bank of Utah (the bank) for the bank to serve as the stock transfer agent for the UDC shares, the bank to hold the stock certificates and issue receipts to the shareholders. UDC's articles provided that for the time period relevant to the case, mixed-blood shareholders seeking to sell their UDC stock must first offer the stock to other members of the Ute tribe. Only if the offer was not accepted by any member of the tribe could the stock be then sold to a nonmember.]

* * *

In February 1965 Anita R. Reyos and 84 other mixed-bloods sued the bank, two of the bank's employee-officers, John B. Gale and Verl Haslem charging violations of the Securities Exchange Act of 1934 and of Rule 10b–5 of the Securities and Exchange Commission. . . . These plaintiffs had sold UDC shares to various nonmembers including the defendants Gale and Haslem.

* * *

Defendants Gale and Haslem were the bank's assistant managers at Roosevelt. During 1963 and 1964 mixed-bloods sold 1,387 shares of UDC stock. All were sold to nonmembers of the tribe. Haslem purchased 50 of these himself and Gale purchased 63. . . . They paid cash for the shares they purchased. . . . In 1964 and 1965 UDC stock was sold by mixed-bloods at prices ranging from $300 to $700 per share. Shares were being transferred between whites, however, at prices from $500 to $700 per share.

Gale and Haslem possessed standing orders from non-Indian buyers. . . . Some of the prospective purchasers maintained deposits at the bank for the purpose of ready consummation of any transaction.

The two men received various commissions and gratuities for their services in facilitating the transfer of UDC stock from mixed-bloods to non-Indians. Gale supplied some funds as sales advances to the mixed-blood sellers. He and Haslem solicited contracts for open purchases of UDC stock and did so on bank premises and during business hours.

The District Court concluded . . . as to Gale and Haslem: The two men had devised a plan or scheme to acquire, for themselves and others, shares in UDC from mixed-bloods. In violation of their duty to make a fair disclosure, they succeeded in acquiring shares from mixed-bloods for less than fair value. As to the bank: It was put upon notice of the improper activities of its employees, Gale and Haslem, knowingly created the apparent authority on their part, and was responsible for their conduct. Its liability was joint and several with that of Gale and Haslem.

* * *

[The Court ruled that Gale, Haslem, and the bank owed a duty of disclosure to the members of the tribe selling their shares to non-Indians because their activities to encourage a market in the UDC stock among non-Indians went beyond their function as the mere transfer agent. The bank also acknowledged its duty to the tribe members in transferring their shares.]

Clearly, the Court of Appeals was right to the extent that it held that the two employees had violated Rule 10b–5; in the instances specified in that holding the record reveals a misstatement of a material fact, within the proscription of Rule 10b–5 (2), namely, that the prevailing market price of the UDC shares was the figure at which their purchases were made.

We conclude, however, that the Court of Appeals erred when it held that there was no violation of the Rule unless the record disclosed evidence of reliance on material fact misrepresentations by Gale and Haslem. We do not read Rule 10b–5 so restrictively. To be sure, the second subparagraph of the rule specifies the making of an untrue statement of a material fact and the omission to state a material fact. The first and third subparagraphs are not so restricted. These defendants' activities, outlined above, disclose, within the very language of one or the other of those subparagraphs, a "course of business" or a "device, scheme, or artifice" that operated as a fraud upon the Indian sellers. This is so because the defendants devised a plan and induced the mixed-blood holders of UDC stock to dispose of their shares without disclosing to them material facts that reasonably could have been expected to influence their decisions to sell. The individual defendants, in a distinct sense, were market makers, not only for their personal purchases constituting 8 1/3% of the sales, but for the other sales their activities produced. This being so, they possessed the affirmative duty under the Rule to disclose this fact to the mixed-blood sellers. It is no answer to urge that, as to some of the petitioners, these defendants may have made no positive representation or recommendation. The defendants may not stand mute while they facilitate the mixed-bloods' sales to those seeking to profit in the non-Indian market the defendants had developed and encouraged and with which they were fully familiar. The sellers had the right to know that the defendants were in a position to gain financially from their sales and that their shares were selling for a higher price in that market.

Under the circumstances of this case, involving primarily a failure to disclose, positive proof of reliance is not a prerequisite to recovery. All that is necessary is that the facts withheld be material in the sense that a reasonable investor might have considered them important in the making of this decision. This obligation to disclose and this withholding of a material fact establish the requisite element of causation in fact.

Gale and Haslem engaged in more than ministerial functions. Their acts were clearly within the reach of Rule 10b–5. And they were acts performed when they were obligated to act on behalf of the mixed-blood sellers. . . . The liability of the bank, of course, is coextensive with that of Gale and Haslem.

* * *

QUESTIONS

1. If the plaintiffs in a fraud by omission case had to show reliance, how could they do so?

2. Suppose that Jane, a "mixed-blood" Ute, has a time-sensitive debt that must be paid immediately. In order to pay her debts, she plans on selling 100 UDC shares to Gale and Haslem at the price of $300 per share. Assume that due to time constraints, she is simply unable to find another purchaser other than Gale and Haslem. Later, Jane learns that UDC shares are reselling among non-members at $700 per share and brings a Rule 10b–5 lawsuit against Gale and Haslem. Can Gale and Haslem argue that there is no reliance on their failure to disclose the $700 trading price among non-members?

In the next case, the Supreme Court addresses the question of reliance and class certification. The case follows a decision, *Amgen, Inc. v. Connecticut Ret. Plans and Trust Funds*, 133 S. Ct. 1184 (2013), in which the Court rejected the argument that plaintiffs should have to prove materiality in order to certify a class. The question in *Halliburton II* is how the reliance requirement applies when plaintiff seeks to certify a class based on affirmative statements made to the market generally. *Halliburton II* builds upon the Supreme Court's earlier *Basic v.*

Levinson opinion (excerpted in Chapter 2), in which the Court first established the fraud-on-the-market presumption of reliance. If the stock of a company trades in an efficient market, the price will reflect all public, material information. The fraud-on-the-market presumption assumes that investors rely on the integrity of the market price for the stock. Any material misrepresentations that affect the market price of stock trading in an efficient market will then cause the investors to purchase the shares at a price they otherwise would not have had they known of the truth. For example, a misstatement that leads the market price to increase from $100 to $110 will cause investors buying at the market price who believe the market price accurately reflects value, to purchase the shares at $110 instead of $100. *Basic* justified the fraud-on-the-market presumption:

> The presumption is ... supported by common sense and probability. Recent empirical studies have tended to confirm Congress' premise that the market price of shares traded on well-developed markets reflects all publicly available information, and, hence, any material misrepresentations. It has been noted that "it is hard to imagine that there ever is a buyer or seller who does not rely on market integrity. Who would knowingly roll the dice in a crooked crap game?" ... An investor who buys or sells stock at the price set by the market does so in reliance on the integrity of that price. Because most publicly available information is reflected in market price, an investor's reliance on any public material misrepresentations, therefore, may be presumed for purposes of a Rule 10b–5 action. . . .

As you read the *Halliburton II* opinion, consider the importance of empirical evidence from the finance literature to the Supreme Court. Does the Supreme Court in *Halliburton II* have the same view of the reliance of investors on "market integrity" as *Basic*? How can defendants rebut the presumption of reliance?

Halliburton Co. v. Erica P. John Fund, Inc. ("Halliburton II")

134 S. Ct. 2398 (2014).

■ ROBERTS, C.J.

Investors can recover damages in a private securities fraud action only if they prove that they relied on the defendant's misrepresentation in deciding to buy or sell a company's stock. In *Basic Inc. v. Levinson,* 485 U.S. 224 (1988), we held that investors could satisfy this reliance requirement by invoking a presumption that the price of stock traded in an efficient market reflects all public, material information—including material misstatements. In such a case, we concluded, anyone who buys or sells the stock at the market price may be considered to have relied on those misstatements.

We also held, however, that a defendant could rebut this presumption in a number of ways, including by showing that the alleged misrepresentation did not actually affect the stock's price—that is, that the misrepresentation had no "price impact." The questions presented are whether we should overrule or modify *Basic's* presumption of reliance and, if not, whether defendants should nonetheless be afforded an opportunity in securities class action cases to rebut the presumption at the class certification stage, by showing a lack of price impact.

I

Respondent Erica P. John Fund, Inc. (EPJ Fund) is the lead plaintiff in a putative class action against Halliburton alleging violations of section 10(b) . . . and Rule 10b–5. According to EPJ Fund, between June 3, 1999, and December 7, 2001, Halliburton made a series of misrepresentations regarding its potential liability in asbestos litigation, its expected revenue from certain construction contracts, and the anticipated benefits of its merger with another company—all in an attempt to inflate the price of its stock. Halliburton subsequently made a number of corrective disclosures, which, EPJ Fund contends, caused the company's stock price to drop and investors to lose money.

EPJ Fund moved to certify a class comprising all investors who purchased Halliburton common stock during the class period. The District Court found that the proposed class satisfied all the threshold requirements of Federal Rule of Civil Procedure 23(a): It was sufficiently numerous, there were common questions of law or fact, the representative parties' claims were typical of the class claims, and the representatives could fairly and adequately protect the interests of the class. And except for one difficulty, the court would have also concluded that the class satisfied the requirement of Rule 23(b)(3) that "the questions of law or fact common to class members predominate over any questions affecting only individual members." The difficulty was that Circuit precedent required securities fraud plaintiffs to prove "loss causation"—a causal connection between the defendants' alleged misrepresentations and the plaintiffs' economic losses—in order to invoke *Basic's* presumption of reliance and obtain class certification. EPJ Fund had not demonstrated such a connection for any of Halliburton's alleged misrepresentations, the District Court refused to certify the proposed class. The United States Court of Appeals for the Fifth Circuit affirmed the denial of class certification on the same ground.

We granted certiorari and vacated the judgment, finding nothing in "*Basic* or its logic" to justify the Fifth Circuit's requirement that securities fraud plaintiffs prove loss causation at the class certification stage in order to invoke *Basic's* presumption of reliance. "Loss causation," we explained, "addresses a matter different from whether an investor relied on a misrepresentation, presumptively or otherwise, when buying or selling a stock." We remanded the case for the lower courts to consider "any further arguments against class certification" that Halliburton had preserved.

On remand, Halliburton argued that class certification was inappropriate because the evidence it had earlier introduced to disprove loss causation also showed that none of its alleged misrepresentations had actually affected its stock price. By demonstrating the absence of any "price impact," Halliburton contended, it had rebutted *Basic's* presumption that the members of the proposed class had relied on its alleged misrepresentations simply by buying or selling its stock at the market price. And without the benefit of the *Basic* presumption, investors would have to prove reliance on an individual basis, meaning that individual issues would predominate over common ones. The District Court declined to consider Halliburton's argument.

The Fifth Circuit affirmed. . . .

We once again granted certiorari, this time to resolve a conflict among the Circuits over whether securities fraud defendants may attempt to rebut the *Basic* presumption at the class certification stage with evidence of a lack of price impact. We also accepted Halliburton's invitation to reconsider the presumption of reliance for securities fraud claims that we adopted in *Basic*.

II

Halliburton urges us to overrule *Basic*'s presumption of reliance and to instead require every securities fraud plaintiff to prove that he actually relied on the defendant's misrepresentation in deciding to buy or sell a company's stock. Before overturning a long-settled precedent, however, we require "special justification," not just an argument that the precedent was wrongly decided. Halliburton has failed to make that showing.

A

* * *

The reliance element "'ensures that there is a proper connection between a defendant's misrepresentation and a plaintiff's injury.'" The traditional (and most direct) way a plaintiff can demonstrate reliance is by showing that he was aware of a company's statement and engaged in a relevant transaction—*e.g.*, purchasing common stock—based on that specific misrepresentation."

In *Basic*, however, we recognized that requiring such direct proof of reliance "would place an unnecessarily unrealistic evidentiary burden on the Rule 10b–5 plaintiff who has traded on an impersonal market." That is because, even assuming an investor could prove that he was aware of the misrepresentation, he would still have to "show a speculative state of facts, *i.e.*, how he would have acted . . . if the misrepresentation had not been made."

We also noted that "[r]equiring proof of individualized reliance" from every securities fraud plaintiff "effectively would . . . prevent[ ] [plaintiffs] from proceeding with a class action" in Rule 10b–5 suits. If every plaintiff had to prove direct reliance on the defendant's misrepresentation, "individual issues then would . . . overwhelm[ ] the common ones," making certification under Rule 23(b)(3) inappropriate.

To address these concerns, *Basic* held that securities fraud plaintiffs can in certain circumstances satisfy the reliance element of a Rule 10b–5 action by invoking a rebuttable presumption of reliance, rather than proving direct reliance on a misrepresentation. The Court based that presumption on what is known as the "fraud-on-the-market" theory, which holds that "the market price of shares traded on well-developed markets reflects all publicly available information, and, hence, any material misrepresentations." The Court also noted that, rather than scrutinize every piece of public information about a company for himself, the typical "investor who buys or sells stock at the price set by the market does so in reliance on the integrity of that price"—the belief that it reflects all public, material information. As a result, whenever the investor buys or sells stock at the market price, his "reliance on any public material misrepresentations ... may be presumed for purposes of a Rule 10b–5 action."

Based on this theory, a plaintiff must make the following showings to demonstrate that the presumption of reliance applies in a given case: (1) that the alleged misrepresentations were publicly known, (2) that they were material, (3) that the stock traded in an efficient market, and (4) that the plaintiff traded the stock between the time the misrepresentations were made and when the truth was revealed.

At the same time, *Basic* emphasized that the presumption of reliance was rebuttable rather than conclusive. Specifically, "[a]ny showing that severs the link between the alleged misrepresentation and either the price received (or paid) by the plaintiff, or his decision to trade at a fair market price, will be sufficient to rebut the presumption of reliance." So for example, if a defendant could show that the alleged misrepresentation did not, for whatever reason, actually affect the market price, or that a plaintiff would have bought or sold the stock even had he been aware that the stock's price was tainted by fraud, then the presumption of reliance would not apply. In either of those cases, a plaintiff would have to prove that he directly relied on the defendant's misrepresentation in buying or selling the stock.

B

Halliburton contends that securities fraud plaintiffs should *always* have to prove direct reliance and that the *Basic* Court erred in allowing them to invoke a presumption of reliance instead. According to Halliburton, the *Basic* presumption contravenes congressional intent and has been undermined by subsequent developments in economic theory. Neither argument, however, so discredits *Basic* as to constitute "special justification" for overruling the decision.

* * *

Halliburton's primary argument for overruling *Basic* is that the decision rested on two premises that can no longer withstand scrutiny. The first premise concerns what is known as the "efficient capital markets hypothesis." *Basic* stated that "the market price of shares traded on well-developed markets reflects all publicly available information, and, hence, any material misrepresentations." From that statement, Halliburton concludes that the *Basic* Court espoused "a robust view of market efficiency" that is no longer tenable, for " 'overwhelming empirical evidence' now suggests that capital markets are not fundamentally efficient.' " To support this contention, Halliburton cites studies purporting to show that "public information is often not incorporated immediately (much less rationally) into market prices."

Halliburton does not, of course, maintain that capital markets are *always* inefficient. Rather, in its view, *Basic*'s fundamental error was to ignore the fact that " 'efficiency is not a binary, yes or no question.' " The markets for some securities are more efficient than the markets for others, and even a single market can process different kinds of information more or less efficiently, depending on how widely the information is disseminated and how easily it is understood. Yet *Basic,* Halliburton asserts, glossed over these nuances, assuming a false dichotomy that renders the presumption of reliance both underinclusive and overinclusive: A misrepresentation can distort a stock's market price even in a generally inefficient market, and a misrepresentation can leave a stock's market price unaffected even in a generally efficient one.

Halliburton's criticisms fail to take *Basic* on its own terms. Halliburton focuses on the debate among economists about the degree to which the market price of a company's stock reflects public information about the company—and thus the degree to which an investor can earn an abnormal, above-market return by trading on such information. That debate is not new. Indeed, the *Basic* Court acknowledged it and declined to enter the fray, declaring that "[w]e need not determine by adjudication what economists and social scientists have debated through the use of sophisticated statistical analysis and the application of economic theory." To recognize the presumption of reliance, the Court explained, was not "conclusively to adopt any particular theory of how quickly and completely publicly available information is reflected in market price." The Court instead based the presumption on the fairly modest premise that "market professionals generally consider most publicly announced material statements about companies, thereby affecting stock market prices." *Basic*'s presumption of reliance thus does not rest on a "binary" view of market efficiency. Indeed, in making the presumption rebuttable, *Basic* recognized that market efficiency is a matter of degree and accordingly made it a matter of proof.

The academic debates discussed by Halliburton have not refuted the modest premise underlying the presumption of reliance. Even the foremost critics of the efficient-capital-markets hypothesis acknowledge that public information generally affects stock prices. Halliburton also conceded as much in its reply brief and at oral argument. Debates about the precise *degree* to which stock prices accurately reflect public information are thus largely beside the point. "That the . . . price [of a stock] may be inaccurate does not detract from the fact that false statements affect it, and cause loss," which is "all that *Basic* requires." Even though the efficient capital markets hypothesis may have "garnered substantial criticism since *Basic,*" Halliburton has not identified the kind of fundamental shift in economic theory that could justify overruling a precedent on the ground that it misunderstood, or has since been overtaken by, economic realities.

Halliburton also contests a second premise underlying the *Basic* presumption: the notion that investors "invest 'in reliance on the integrity of [the market] price.'" Halliburton identifies a number of classes of investors for whom "price integrity" is supposedly "marginal or irrelevant." The primary example is the value investor, who believes that certain stocks are undervalued or overvalued and attempts to "beat the market" by buying the undervalued stocks and selling the overvalued ones. If many investors "are indifferent to prices," Halliburton contends, then courts should not presume that investors rely on the integrity of those prices and any misrepresentations incorporated into them.

But *Basic* never denied the existence of such investors. As we recently explained, *Basic* concluded only that "it is reasonable to presume that *most* investors—knowing that they have little hope of outperforming the market in the long run based solely on their analysis of publicly available information—will rely on the security's market price as an unbiased assessment of the security's value in light of all public information."

In any event, there is no reason to suppose that even Halliburton's main counterexample—the value investor—is as indifferent to the integrity of market prices as Halliburton suggests. Such an investor implicitly relies on the fact that a stock's market price will eventually reflect material information—how else could the market correction on which his profit depends occur? To be sure, the value investor "does not believe that the market price accurately reflects public information *at the time he transacts*." But to indirectly rely on a misstatement in the sense relevant for the *Basic* presumption, he need only trade stock based on the belief that the market price will incorporate public information within a reasonable period. The value investor also presumably tries to estimate *how* undervalued or overvalued a particular stock is, and such estimates can be skewed by a market price tainted by fraud.

C

The principle of *stare decisis* has " 'special force' " "in respect to statutory interpretation" because " 'Congress remains free to alter what we have done.' " So too with *Basic*'s presumption of reliance. Although the presumption is a judicially created doctrine designed to implement a judicially created cause of action, we have described the presumption as "a substantive doctrine of federal securities-fraud law." That is because it provides a way of satisfying the reliance element of the Rule 10b–5 cause of action. As with any other element of that cause of action, Congress may overturn or modify any aspect of our interpretations of the reliance requirement, including the *Basic* presumption itself. Given that possibility, we see no reason to exempt the *Basic* presumption from ordinary principles of *stare decisis*.

To buttress its case for overruling *Basic*, Halliburton contends that, in addition to being wrongly decided, the decision is inconsistent with our more recent decisions construing the Rule 10b–5 cause of action. As Halliburton notes, we have held that "we must give 'narrow dimensions . . . to a right of action Congress did not authorize when it first enacted the statute and did not expand when it revisited the law.' " Yet the *Basic* presumption, Halliburton asserts, does just the opposite, *expanding* the Rule 10b–5 cause of action.

Not so. In *Central Bank* and *Stoneridge* [eds.: excerpted below] we declined to extend Rule 10b–5 liability to entirely new categories of defendants who themselves had not made any material, public misrepresentation. Such an extension, we explained, would have eviscerated the requirement that a plaintiff prove that he relied on a misrepresentation made *by the defendant*. The *Basic* presumption does not eliminate that requirement but rather provides an alternative means of satisfying it. While the presumption makes it easier for plaintiffs to prove reliance, it does not alter the elements of the Rule 10b–5 cause of action and thus maintains the action's original legal scope.

* * *

Finally, Halliburton and its *amici* contend that, by facilitating securities class actions, the *Basic* presumption produces a number of serious and harmful consequences. Such class actions, they say, allow plaintiffs to extort large settlements from defendants for meritless claims; punish innocent shareholders, who end up having to pay settlements and judgments; impose excessive costs on businesses; and consume a disproportionately large share of judicial resources.

These concerns are more appropriately addressed to Congress, which has in fact responded, to some extent, to many of the issues raised by Halliburton and its *amici*. Congress has, for example, enacted the Private Securities Litigation Reform Act of 1995 (PSLRA), which sought to combat perceived abuses in securities litigation with heightened pleading requirements, limits on damages and attorney's fees, a "safe harbor" for certain kinds of statements, restrictions on the selection of lead plaintiffs in securities class actions, sanctions for frivolous litigation, and stays of discovery pending motions to dismiss. And to prevent plaintiffs from circumventing these restrictions by bringing securities class actions under state law in state court, Congress also enacted the Securities Litigation Uniform Standards Act of 1998, which precludes many state law class actions alleging securities fraud. Such legislation demonstrates Congress's willingness to consider policy concerns of the sort that Halliburton says should lead us to overrule *Basic*.

III

Halliburton proposes two alternatives to overruling *Basic* that would alleviate what it regards as the decision's most serious flaws. The first alternative would require plaintiffs to prove that a defendant's misrepresentation actually affected the stock price—so-called "price impact"—in order to invoke the *Basic* presumption. It should not be enough, Halliburton contends, for plaintiffs to demonstrate the general efficiency of the market in which the stock traded. Halliburton's second proposed alternative would allow defendants to rebut the presumption of reliance with evidence of a *lack* of price impact, not only at the merits stage—which all agree defendants may already do—but also before class certification.

A

As noted, to invoke the *Basic* presumption, a plaintiff must prove that: (1) the alleged misrepresentations were publicly known, (2) they were material, (3) the stock traded in an efficient market, and (4) the plaintiff traded the stock between when the misrepresentations were made and when the truth was revealed. Each of these requirements follows from the fraud-on-the-market theory underlying the presumption. If the misrepresentation was not publicly known, then it could not have distorted the stock's market price. So too if the misrepresentation was immaterial—that is, if it would not have " 'been viewed by the reasonable investor as having significantly altered the "total mix" of information made available,' "—or if the market in which the stock traded was inefficient. And if the plaintiff did not buy or sell the stock after the misrepresentation was made but before the truth was revealed, then he could not be said to have acted in reliance on a fraud-tainted price.

The first three prerequisites are directed at price impact—"whether the alleged misrepresentations affected the market price in the first place."

* * *

Halliburton argues that since the *Basic* presumption hinges on price impact, plaintiffs should be required to prove it directly in order to invoke the presumption. Proving the presumption's prerequisites, which are at best an imperfect proxy for price impact, should not suffice.

Far from a modest refinement of the *Basic* presumption, this proposal would radically alter the required showing for the reliance element of the Rule 10b–5 cause of action. What is called the *Basic* presumption actually incorporates two constituent presumptions: First, if a plaintiff shows that the defendant's misrepresentation was public and material and that the stock traded in a generally efficient market, he is entitled to a presumption that the misrepresentation affected the stock price. Second, if the plaintiff also shows that he purchased the stock at the market price during the relevant period, he is entitled to a further presumption that he purchased the stock in reliance on the defendant's misrepresentation.

By requiring plaintiffs to prove price impact directly, Halliburton's proposal would take away the first constituent presumption. Halliburton's argument for doing so is the same as its primary argument for overruling the *Basic* presumption altogether: Because market efficiency is not a yes-or-no proposition, a public, material misrepresentation might not affect a stock's price even in a generally efficient market. But as explained, *Basic* never suggested otherwise; that is why it affords defendants an opportunity to rebut the presumption by showing, among other things, that the particular misrepresentation at issue did not affect the stock's market price. For the same reasons we declined to completely jettison the *Basic* presumption, we decline to effectively jettison half of it by revising the prerequisites for invoking it.

B

Even if plaintiffs need not directly prove price impact to invoke the *Basic* presumption, Halliburton contends that defendants should at least be allowed to defeat the presumption at the class certification stage through evidence that the misrepresentation did not in fact affect the stock price. We agree.

1

There is no dispute that defendants may introduce such evidence at the merits stage to rebut the *Basic* presumption. *Basic* itself "made clear that the presumption was just that, and could be rebutted by appropriate evidence," including evidence that the asserted misrepresentation (or its correction) did not affect the market price of the defendant's stock.

Nor is there any dispute that defendants may introduce price impact evidence at the class certification stage, so long as it is for the purpose of countering a plaintiff's showing of market efficiency, rather than directly rebutting the presumption. As EPJ Fund acknowledges, "[o]f course . . . defendants can introduce evidence at class certification of lack of price impact as some evidence that the market is not efficient."

After all, plaintiffs themselves can and do introduce evidence of the *existence* of price impact in connection with "event studies"—regression analyses that seek to show that the market price of the defendant's stock tends to respond to pertinent publicly reported events. In this case, for example, EPJ Fund submitted an event study of various episodes that might have been expected to affect the price of Halliburton's stock, in order to demonstrate that the market for that stock takes account of material, public information about the company. The episodes examined by EPJ Fund's event study included one of the alleged misrepresentations that form the basis of the Fund's suit.

Defendants—like plaintiffs—may accordingly submit price impact evidence prior to class certification. What defendants may not do, EPJ Fund insists and the Court of Appeals held, is rely on that same evidence prior to class certification for the particular purpose of rebutting the presumption altogether.

This restriction makes no sense, and can readily lead to bizarre results. Suppose a defendant at the certification stage submits an event study looking at the impact on the price of its stock from six discrete events, in an effort to refute the plaintiffs' claim of general market efficiency. All agree the defendant may do this. Suppose one of the six events is the specific misrepresentation asserted by the plaintiffs. All agree that this too is perfectly acceptable. Now suppose the district court determines that, despite the defendant's study, the plaintiff has carried its burden to prove market efficiency, but that the evidence shows no price impact with respect to the specific misrepresentation challenged in the suit. The evidence at the certification stage thus shows an efficient market, on which the alleged misrepresentation had no price impact. And yet under EPJ Fund's view, the plaintiffs' action should be certified and proceed as a class action (with all that entails), even though the fraud-on-the-market theory does not apply and common reliance thus cannot be presumed.

Such a result is inconsistent with *Basic*'s own logic. Under *Basic*'s fraud-on-the-market theory, market efficiency and the other prerequisites for invoking the presumption constitute an indirect way of showing price impact. As explained, it is appropriate to allow plaintiffs to rely on this indirect proxy for price impact, rather than requiring them to prove price impact directly, given *Basic*'s rationales for recognizing a presumption of reliance in the first place.

But an indirect proxy should not preclude direct evidence when such evidence is available. As we explained in *Basic,* "[a]ny showing that severs the link between the alleged misrepresentation and . . . the price received (or paid) by the plaintiff . . . will be sufficient to rebut the presumption of reliance" because "the basis for finding that the fraud had been transmitted through market price would be gone." And without the presumption of reliance, a Rule 10b–5 suit cannot proceed as a class action: Each plaintiff would have to prove reliance individually, so common issues would not "predominate" over individual ones, as required by Rule 23(b)(3). Price impact is thus an essential precondition for any Rule 10b–5 class action. While *Basic* allows plaintiffs to establish that precondition indirectly, it does not require courts to ignore a defendant's direct, more salient evidence showing that the alleged misrepresentation did not actually affect the stock's market price and, consequently, that the *Basic* presumption does not apply.

2

The Court of Appeals relied on our decision in *Amgen* in holding that Halliburton could not introduce evidence of lack of price impact at the class certification stage. The question in *Amgen* was whether plaintiffs could be required to prove (or defendants be permitted to disprove) materiality before class certification. Even though materiality is a prerequisite for invoking the *Basic* presumption, we held that it should be left to the merits stage, because it does not bear on the predominance requirement of Rule 23(b)(3). We reasoned that materiality is an objective issue susceptible to common, classwide proof. We also noted that a failure to prove materiality would necessarily defeat every plaintiff's claim on the merits; it would not simply preclude invocation of the presumption and thereby cause individual questions of reliance to predominate over common ones. In this latter respect, we explained, materiality differs from the publicity and market efficiency prerequisites, neither of which is necessary to prove a Rule 10b–5 claim on the merits.

EPJ Fund argues that much of the foregoing could be said of price impact as well. Fair enough. But price impact differs from materiality in a crucial respect. Given that the other *Basic* prerequisites must still be proved at the class certification stage, the common issue of materiality can be left to the merits stage without risking the certification of classes in which individual issues will end up overwhelming common ones. And because materiality is a discrete issue that can be resolved in isolation from the other prerequisites, it can be wholly confined to the merits stage.

Price impact is different. The fact that a misrepresentation "was reflected in the market price at the time of [the] transaction"—that it had price impact—is "*Basic*'s fundamental premise." It thus has everything to do with the issue of predominance at the class certification stage. That is why, if reliance is to be shown through the *Basic* presumption, the publicity and market efficiency prerequisites must be proved before class certification. Without proof of those prerequisites, the fraud-on-the-market theory underlying the presumption completely collapses, rendering class certification inappropriate.

But as explained, publicity and market efficiency are nothing more than prerequisites for an indirect showing of price impact. There is no dispute that at least such indirect proof of price impact "is needed to ensure that the questions of law or fact common to the class will 'predominate.' " That is so even though such proof is also highly relevant at the merits stage.

Our choice in this case, then, is not between allowing price impact evidence at the class certification stage or relegating it to the merits. Evidence of price impact will be before the court at the certification stage in any event. The choice, rather, is between limiting the price impact inquiry before class certification to indirect evidence, or allowing consideration of direct evidence as well. As explained, we see no reason to artificially limit the inquiry at the certification stage to indirect evidence of price impact. Defendants may seek to defeat the *Basic* presumption at that stage through direct as well as indirect price impact evidence.

3

More than 25 years ago, we held that plaintiffs could satisfy the reliance element of the Rule 10b–5 cause of action by invoking a presumption that a public, material misrepresentation will distort the price of stock traded in an efficient market, and that anyone who purchases the stock at the market price may be considered to have done so in reliance on the misrepresentation. We adhere to that decision and decline to modify the prerequisites for invoking the presumption of reliance. But to maintain the consistency of the presumption with the class certification requirements of Federal Rule of Civil Procedure 23, defendants must be afforded an opportunity before class certification to defeat the presumption through evidence that an alleged misrepresentation did not actually affect the market price of the stock.

* * *

GINSBURG, J., with whom BREYER and SOTOMAYOR join, concurring.

Advancing price impact consideration from the merits stage to the certification stage may broaden the scope of discovery available at certification. But the Court recognizes that it is incumbent upon the defendant to show the absence of price impact. The Court's judgment, therefore, should impose no heavy toll on securities-fraud plaintiffs with tenable claims. On that understanding, I join the Court's opinion.

THOMAS, J., with whom SCALIA and ALITO join, concurring in the judgment.

The implied Rule 10b–5 private cause of action is "a relic of the heady days in which this Court assumed common-law powers to create causes of action." We have since ended that practice because the authority to fashion private remedies to enforce federal law belongs to Congress alone. Absent statutory authorization for a cause of action, "courts may not create one, no matter how desirable that might be as a policy matter."

Basic Inc. v. Levinson, demonstrates the wisdom of this rule. *Basic* presented the question how investors must prove the reliance element of the implied Rule 10b–5 cause of action—the requirement that the plaintiff buy or sell stock in reliance on the defendant's misstatement—when they transact on modern, impersonal securities exchanges. Were the Rule 10b–5 action statutory, the Court could have resolved this question by interpreting the statutory language. Without a statute to interpret for guidance, however, the Court began instead with a particular policy "problem": for investors in impersonal markets, the traditional reliance requirement was hard to prove and impossible to prove as common among plaintiffs bringing 10b–5 class-action suits. With the task thus framed as "resol[ving]"that " 'problem' " rather than interpreting statutory text, the Court turned to nascent economic theory and naked intuitions about investment behavior in its efforts to fashion a new, easier way to meet the reliance requirement. The result was an evidentiary presumption, based on a "fraud on the market" theory, that paved the way for class actions under Rule 10b–5.

Today we are asked to determine whether *Basic* was correctly decided. The Court suggests that it was, and that *stare decisis* demands that we preserve it. I disagree. Logic, economic realities, and our subsequent jurisprudence have undermined the foundations of the *Basic* presumption, and *stare decisis* cannot prop up the façade that remains. *Basic* should be overruled.

I

Understanding where *Basic* went wrong requires an explanation of the "reliance" requirement as traditionally understood.

* * *

The "traditional" reliance element requires a plaintiff to "sho[w] that he was aware of a company's statement and engaged in a relevant transaction . . . based on that specific misrepresentation." But investors who purchase stock from third parties on impersonal exchanges (*e.g.,* the New York Stock Exchange) often will not be aware of any particular statement made by the issuer of the security, and therefore cannot establish that they transacted based on a specific misrepresentation. Nor is the traditional reliance requirement amenable to class treatment; the inherently individualized nature of the reliance inquiry renders it impossible for a 10b–5 plaintiff to prove that common questions predominate over individual ones, making class certification improper.

* * *

II

Basic's reimagined reliance requirement was a mistake, and the passage of time has compounded its failings. First, the Court based both parts of the presumption of reliance on a questionable understanding of disputed economic theory and flawed intuitions about investor behavior.

* * *

A

Basic based the presumption of reliance on two factual assumptions. The first assumption was that, in a "well-developed market," public statements are generally "reflected" in the market price of securities. The second was that investors in such markets transact "in reliance on the integrity of that price." In other words, the Court created a presumption that a plaintiff had met the two-part, fraud-on-the-market version of the reliance requirement because, in the Court's view, "common sense and probability" suggested that each of those parts *would* be met.

In reality, both of the Court's key assumptions are highly contestable and do not provide the necessary support for *Basic*'s presumption of reliance. The first assumption—that public statements are "reflected" in the market price—was grounded in an economic theory that has garnered substantial criticism since *Basic*. The second assumption—that investors categorically rely on the integrity of the market price—is simply wrong.

1

The Court's first assumption was that "most publicly available information"—including public misstatements—"is reflected in [the] market price" of a security. The Court grounded that assumption in "empirical studies" testing a then-nascent economic theory known as the efficient capital markets hypothesis. . . .

This view of market efficiency has since lost its luster. As it turns out, even "well-developed" markets (like the New York Stock Exchange) do not uniformly incorporate information into market prices with high speed. "[F]riction in accessing public information" and the presence of "processing costs" means that "not all public information will be impounded in a security's price with the same alacrity, or perhaps with any quickness at all." For example, information that is easily digestible (merger announcements or stock splits) or especially prominent (Wall Street Journal articles) may be incorporated quickly, while information that is broadly applicable or technical (Securities and Exchange Commission filings) may be incorporated slowly or even ignored.

Further, and more importantly, "overwhelming empirical evidence" now suggests that even when markets do incorporate public information, they often fail to do so accurately. "Scores" of "efficiency-defying anomalies"—such as market swings in the absence of new information and prolonged deviations from underlying asset values—make market efficiency "more contestable than ever." Such anomalies make it difficult to tell whether, at any given moment, a stock's price accurately reflects its value as indicated by all publicly available information. In sum, economists now understand that the price impact *Basic* assumed would happen reflexively is actually far from certain even in "well-developed" markets. Thus, *Basic*'s claim that "common sense and probability" support a presumption of reliance rests on shaky footing.

2

The *Basic* Court also grounded the presumption of reliance in a second assumption: that "[a]n investor who buys or sells stock at the price set by the market does so in reliance on the integrity of that price." In other words, the Court assumed that investors transact based on the belief that the market price accurately reflects the underlying " 'value' " of the security. . . .

The Court's rather superficial analysis does not withstand scrutiny. It cannot be seriously disputed that a great many investors do *not* buy or sell stock based on a belief that the stock's price accurately reflects its value. Many investors in fact trade for the opposite reason—that is, because they think the market has under- or overvalued the stock, and they believe they can profit from that mispricing. Indeed, securities transactions often take place because the transacting parties disagree on the security's value.

Other investors trade for reasons entirely unrelated to price—for instance, to address changing liquidity needs, tax concerns, or portfolio balancing requirements. These investment decisions—made with indifference to price and thus without regard for price "integrity"—are at odds with *Basic*'s understanding of what motivates investment decisions. In short, *Basic*'s assumption that all investors rely in common on "price integrity" is simply wrong.

The majority tries (but fails) to reconcile *Basic*'s assumption about investor behavior with the reality that many investors do not behave in the way *Basic* assumed. It first asserts that *Basic* rested only on the more modest view that " '*most* investors' " rely on the integrity of a security's market price. That gloss is difficult to square with *Basic*'s plain language: "An investor who buys or sells stock at the price set by the market does so in reliance on the integrity of that price." In any event, neither *Basic* nor the majority offers anything more than a judicial hunch as evidence that even "most" investors rely on price integrity.

The majority also suggests that "there is no reason to suppose" that investors who buy stock they believe to be undervalued are "indifferent to the integrity of market prices." Such "value investor[s]," according to the majority, "implicitly rel[y] on the fact that a stock's market price will eventually reflect material information" and "presumably tr[y] to estimate *how* undervalued or overvalued a particular stock is" by reference to the market price. Whether the majority's unsupported claims about the thought processes of hypothetical investors are accurate or not, they are surely beside the point. Whatever else an investor believes about the market, he simply does not "rely on the integrity of the market price" if he does not believe that the market price accurately reflects public information *at the time he transacts.* That is, an investor cannot claim that a public misstatement induced his transaction by distorting the market price if he did not buy at that price while believing that it accurately incorporated that public information. For that sort of investor, *Basic*'s critical fiction falls apart.

* * *

III

Principles of *stare decisis* do not compel us to save *Basic*'s muddled logic and armchair economics. We have not hesitated to overrule decisions when they are "unworkable or are badly reasoned," when "the theoretical underpinnings of those decisions are called into serious question," when the decisions have become "irreconcilable" with intervening developments in "competing legal doctrines or policies," or when they are otherwise "a positive detriment to coherence and consistency in the law," Just one of these circumstances can justify our correction of bad precedent; *Basic* checks all the boxes.

In support of its decision to preserve *Basic,* the majority contends that *stare decisis* "has 'special force' 'in respect to statutory interpretation' because 'Congress remains free to alter what we have done.'" But *Basic,* of course, has nothing to do with statutory interpretation. The case concerned a judge-made evidentiary presumption for a judge-made element of the implied 10b–5 private cause of action, itself "a judicial construct that Congress did not enact in the text of the relevant statutes." We have not afforded *stare decisis* "special force" outside the context of statutory interpretation, and for good reason. In statutory cases, it is perhaps plausible that Congress watches over its enactments and will step in to fix our mistakes, so we may leave to Congress the judgment whether the interpretive question is better left "'settled'" or "'settled right.'" But this rationale is untenable when it comes to judge-made law like "implied" private causes of action, which we retain a duty to superintend. Thus, when we err in areas of judge-made law, we ought to presume that Congress expects us to correct our own mistakes—not the other way around. That duty is especially clear in the Rule 10b–5 context, where we have said that "[t]he federal courts have accepted and exercised the principal responsibility for the continuing elaboration of the scope of the 10b–5 right and the definition of the duties it imposes."

* * *

Basic took an implied cause of action and grafted on a policy-driven presumption of reliance based on nascent economic theory and personal intuitions about investment behavior. The result was an unrecognizably broad cause of action ready made for class certification. Time and experience have pointed up the error of that decision, making it all too clear that the Court's attempt to revise securities law to fit the alleged "new realities of financial markets" should have been left to Congress.

* * *

NOTES

1.   *Reliance in class actions.* The Supreme Court's relaxed "transaction causation" approach greatly eases the plaintiffs' burden in pleading the reliance element in a class action. For omissions in breach of a fiduciary duty (a species of insider trading which we will cover in greater detail in Chapter 6), *Affiliated Ute* holds that reliance is presumed if the omitted fact is material. For omissions that render statements misleading ("half-truths"), the result is less clear, with some courts requiring proof of reliance on the half-truth, *see Abell v. Potomac Insurance Co.,* 858 F.2d 1104 (5th Cir. 1988), and others applying the *Affiliated Ute* presumption. *See Chris-Craft Indus., Inc. v. Piper Aircraft Corp.,* 480 F.2d 341 (2d Cir. 1973). Affirmative misstatements are also presumed to have induced reliance if they have been disseminated into "efficient" markets under the fraud-on-the-market theory. As a result, the reliance element, which historically has made class action treatment inappropriate for common law fraud, is not a substantial barrier for Rule 10b–5 suits against companies whose securities are traded in efficient markets. The presumption does not apply, however, in markets lacking in informational efficiency, thereby excluding smaller companies in thinly-traded markets from substantial exposure to securities fraud class actions. *See Binder v. Gillespie,* 184 F.3d 1059 (9th Cir. 1999) (Fraud-on-the-market presumption does not apply to issuer whose stock was traded in the "pink sheets").

2. *Misrepresentations by third parties.* Most securities fraud class actions involve misrepresentations by an issuer that affected trading in the market for the issuer's own securities. What if third parties, such as securities analysts, publish misleading statements about the issuer's securities—can plaintiffs apply the fraud-on-the-market presumption of reliance in a Rule 10b–5 suit against the analysts? The Second Circuit said yes. *See In re Salomon Analyst Metromedia Litigation*, 544 F.3d 474, 481 (2d Cir. 2008) ("[T]he premise of [the fraud-on-the-market presumption] is that, in an efficient market, share prices reflect 'all publicly available information, and, hence, any material misrepresentations.' It thus does not matter, for purposes of establishing entitlement to the presumption, whether the misinformation was transmitted by an issuer, an analyst, or anyone else."). What if the market discounts information from an analyst more than if the information were directly from the issuer itself? So long as the market does not discount information from third parties by 100%, misstatements from third parties will affect the market price and thereby the investment decisions of investors who rely on the accuracy of the market price. At some point, however, the third party becomes too "remote" for the plaintiffs to assert reliance, as we shall see in the *Stoneridge* case, excerpted later in this chapter.

QUESTIONS

1. How does reliance fit into the class certification decision for Rule 10b–5 class actions?

2. Do *Basic* and *Halliburton II* rely on an economic theory?

3. What does it mean for an investor to rely on the "integrity of the market price"? What kinds of investors do you think rely on the "integrity of the market price"?

4. The plaintiff needs to allege loss causation and materiality in her complaint and prove those elements to win at trial, but she need not establish them at the class certification stage. Why does the plaintiff need to show reliance to certify a class?

5. How would a defendant show an absence of "price impact" from a misstatement? Does it matter that the defendant bears the burden of proof on this question?

6. How does price impact differ from materiality? From loss causation?

HYPOTHETICAL EIGHT

DigitalBase's common stock is traded on the Nasdaq Capital Market. Suppose DigitalBase decides to conduct a seasoned offering of its common stock. Several months after the offering, Jill, an outside investor, buys DigitalBase stock (that may or may not have come from the seasoned offering) on the secondary market without reading the prospectus, based solely on the secondary market price. It turns out that the prospectus contained misleading revenue numbers that overstated earnings. Can Jill recover?

1. *Scenario One:* What if Jill had bought DigitalBase stock as above, but now let's also assume that both Goldman and Fidelity know about the misstatements as a result of rumors being passed around among Wall Street insiders?

2. *Scenario Two:* Suppose Jill buys DigitalBase stock, but she does so even though she knows about the misleading financial statements because she feels the stock is undervalued despite the misstatement. Can Jill recover?

3. *Scenario Three:* What if Jill buys the DigitalBase stock because she believes it is undervalued but doesn't know about the misstatements?

D. LOSS CAUSATION

Congress codified the loss causation rule developed by the courts in § 21D(b)(4). That provision stipulates: "In any private action arising under [the Exchange Act], the plaintiff shall have the burden of proving that the act or omission of the defendant alleged to violate [the Act] caused the loss for which the plaintiff seeks to recover damages." The Supreme Court explains the loss causation requirement in the following case. How does proof of loss causation differ from proof of transaction causation and proof of damages?

Dura Pharmaceuticals, Inc. v. Broudo
544 U.S. 336 (2005).

■ BREYER, J.

A private plaintiff who claims securities fraud must prove that the defendant's fraud caused an economic loss. Exchange Act § 21D(b)(4). We consider a Ninth Circuit holding that a plaintiff can satisfy this requirement—a requirement that courts call "loss causation"—simply by alleging in the complaint and subsequently establishing that "the price" of the security "*on the date of purchase* was inflated because of the misrepresentation." In our view, the Ninth Circuit is wrong, both in respect to what a plaintiff must prove and in respect to what the plaintiffs' complaint here must allege.

I

Respondents are individuals who bought stock in Dura Pharmaceuticals, Inc., on the public securities market between April 15, 1997, and February 24, 1998. They have brought this securities fraud class action against Dura and some of its managers and directors (hereinafter Dura) in federal court. In respect to the question before us, their detailed amended . . . complaint makes substantially the following allegations:

> (1) Before and during the purchase period, Dura (or its officials) made false statements concerning both Dura's drug profits and future Food and Drug Administration (FDA) approval of a new asthmatic spray device.

> (2) In respect to drug profits, Dura falsely claimed that it expected that its drug sales would prove profitable.

> (3) In respect to the asthmatic spray device, Dura falsely claimed that it expected the FDA would soon grant its approval.

> (4) On the last day of the purchase period [of the Respondent's class action], February 24, 1998, Dura announced that its

earnings would be lower than expected, principally due to slow drug sales.

(5) The next day Dura's shares lost almost half their value (falling from about $39 per share to about $21).

(6) About eight months later (in November 1998), Dura announced that the FDA would not approve Dura's new asthmatic spray device.

(7) The next day Dura's share price temporarily fell but almost fully recovered within one week.

Most importantly, the complaint says the following (and nothing significantly more than the following) about economic losses attributable to the spray device misstatement: *"In reliance on the integrity of the market, [the plaintiffs] . . . paid artificially inflated prices for Dura securities"* and the plaintiffs suffered *"damage[s]"* thereby. (emphasis added).

* * *

The Court of Appeals for the Ninth Circuit . . . held that the complaint adequately alleged "loss causation." The Circuit wrote that "plaintiffs establish loss causation if they have shown that the price *on the date of purchase* was inflated because of the misrepresentation." (emphasis in original). It added that "the injury occurs at the time of the transaction." Since the complaint pleaded "that the price at the time of purchase was overstated," and it sufficiently identified the cause, its allegations were legally sufficient.

* * *

A

We begin with the Ninth Circuit's basic reason for finding the complaint adequate, namely, that at the end of the day plaintiffs need only "establish," *i.e.*, prove, that "the price *on the date of purchase* was inflated because of the misrepresentation." In our view, this statement of the law is wrong. Normally, in cases such as this one (*i.e.*, fraud-on-the-market cases), an inflated purchase price will not itself constitute or proximately cause the relevant economic loss.

For one thing, as a matter of pure logic, at the moment the transaction takes place, the plaintiff has suffered no loss; the inflated purchase payment is offset by ownership of a share that *at that instant* possesses equivalent value. Moreover, the logical link between the inflated share purchase price and any later economic loss is not invariably strong. Shares are normally purchased with an eye toward a later sale. But if, say, the purchaser sells the shares quickly before the relevant truth begins to leak out, the misrepresentation will not have led to any loss. If the purchaser sells later after the truth makes its way into the market place, an initially inflated purchase price *might* mean a later loss. But that is far from inevitably so. When the purchaser subsequently resells such shares, even at a lower price, that lower price may reflect, not the earlier misrepresentation, but changed economic circumstances, changed investor expectations, new industry-specific or firm-specific facts, conditions, or other events, which taken separately or together account for some or all of that lower price. (The same is true in respect to a claim that a share's higher price is lower than it would otherwise have been—a claim we do not consider here.) Other things being equal, the longer the time between purchase and sale, the more likely that this is so, *i.e.*, the more likely that other factors caused the loss.

Given the tangle of factors affecting price, the most logic alone permits us to say is that the higher purchase price will *sometimes* play a role in bringing about a future loss. It may prove to be a necessary condition of any such loss, and in that sense one might say that the inflated purchase price suggests that the misrepresentation (using language the Ninth Circuit used) "touches upon" a later economic loss. But, even if that is so, it is insufficient. To "touch upon" a loss is not to *cause* a loss, and it is the latter that the law requires.

For another thing, the Ninth Circuit's holding lacks support in precedent. Judicially implied private securities-fraud actions resemble in many (but not all) respects common-law deceit and misrepresentation actions. The common law of deceit subjects a person who "fraudulently" makes a "misrepresentation" to liability "for pecuniary loss caused" to one who justifiably relies upon that misrepresentation. And the common law has long insisted that a plaintiff in such a case show not only that had he known the truth he would not have acted but also that he suffered actual economic loss.

* * *

Finally, the Ninth Circuit's approach overlooks an important securities law objective. The securities statutes seek to maintain public confidence in the marketplace. They do so by deterring fraud, in part, through the availability of private securities fraud actions. But the statutes make these latter actions available, not to provide investors with broad insurance against market losses, but to protect them against those economic losses that misrepresentations actually cause.

The statutory provision at issue here and the paragraphs that precede it emphasize this last mentioned objective. The statute insists that securities fraud complaints "specify" each misleading statement; that they set forth the facts "on which [a] belief" that a statement is misleading was "formed"; and that they "state with particularity facts giving rise to a strong inference that the defendant acted with the required state of mind." Exchange Act § 21D(b)(1), (2). And the statute expressly imposes on plaintiffs "the burden of proving" that the defendant's misrepresentations "caused the loss for which the plaintiff seeks to recover." Exchange Act § 21D(b)(4).

The statute thereby makes clear Congress' intent to permit private securities fraud actions for recovery where, but only where, plaintiffs adequately allege and prove the traditional elements of causation and loss. By way of contrast, the Ninth Circuit's approach would allow recovery where a misrepresentation leads to an inflated purchase price but nonetheless does not proximately cause any economic loss. That is to say, it would permit recovery where these two traditional elements in fact are missing.

In sum, we find the Ninth Circuit's approach inconsistent with the law's requirement that a plaintiff prove that the defendant's misrepresentation (or other fraudulent conduct) proximately caused the plaintiff's economic loss. We need not, and do not, consider other proximate cause or loss-related questions.

B

Our holding about plaintiffs' need to *prove* proximate causation and economic loss leads us also to conclude that the plaintiffs' complaint here failed adequately to *allege* these requirements. We concede that the Federal Rules of Civil Procedure require only "a short and plain statement of the claim showing that the pleader is entitled to relief." Fed. Rule Civ. Proc. 8(a)(2). And we assume, at least for argument's sake, that neither the Rules nor the securities statutes impose any special further requirement in respect to the pleading of proximate causation or economic loss. But, even so, the "short and plain statement" must provide the defendant with "fair notice of what the plaintiff's claim is and the grounds upon which it rests." The complaint before us fails this simple test.

As we have pointed out, the plaintiffs' lengthy complaint contains only one statement that we can fairly read as describing the loss caused by the defendants' "spray device" misrepresentations. That statement says that the plaintiffs "paid artificially inflated prices for Dura's securities" and suffered "damage[s]." The statement implies that the plaintiffs' loss consisted of the "artificially inflated" purchase "prices." The complaint's failure to claim that Dura's share price fell significantly after the truth became known suggests that the plaintiffs considered the allegation of purchase price inflation alone sufficient. The complaint contains nothing that suggests otherwise.

* * *

We concede that ordinary pleading rules are not meant to impose a great burden upon a plaintiff. But it should not prove burdensome for a plaintiff who has suffered an economic loss to provide a defendant with some indication of the loss and the causal connection that the plaintiff has in mind. At the same time, allowing a plaintiff to forgo giving any indication of the economic loss and proximate cause that the plaintiff has in mind would bring about harm of the very sort the statutes seek to avoid. It would permit a plaintiff "with a largely groundless claim to simply take up the time of a number of other people, with the right to do so representing an *in terrorem* increment of the settlement value, rather than a reasonably founded hope that the [discovery] process will reveal relevant evidence." Such a rule would tend to transform a private securities action into a partial downside insurance policy.

For these reasons, we find the plaintiffs' complaint legally insufficient. We reverse the judgment of the Ninth Circuit, and we remand the case for further proceedings consistent with this opinion.

* * *

NOTES

1. *Expert witnesses.* Plaintiffs will frequently turn to expert witnesses to connect losses to the class with revelation of alleged misrepresentations (or prior omissions). Loss causation is easiest to establish when a corrective

disclosure occurs in a short period of time and the price subsequently changes by a significant amount. Difficulties can arise when experts assert that revelations leaked into the market place over time. Leakage is possible, but experts must show exactly how and when corrective information leaked into the market. Experts also run into trouble when the purported corrective disclosure is mixed with other information released by the company at the same time. If a company discloses that it had overstated revenues in the past (correcting the prior misleading disclosure) and also discloses that its CEO is departing due to health reasons (a negative piece of information unrelated to the misleading disclosure), then the expert must separate out the effects of these two disclosures to determine what portion of the stock price change is attributable to the corrective disclosure. Courts will exclude the testimony of experts who fail to "identify the mechanism by which fraud was revealed to the market" and to take into account that corrective disclosures may be mixed with the disclosure of "non-fraud related information." *In re Williams Securities Litigation-WCG Subclass*, 558 F.3d 1130, 1143 (10th Cir. 2009). *See also Fener v. Operating Engineers Const. Industry and Miscellaneous Pension Fund (Local 66)*, 579 F.3d 401 (5th Cir. 2009) ("We reject any event study that shows only how a 'stock reacted to the *entire bundle* of negative information,' rather than examining the 'evidence linking the *culpable* disclosure to the stock-price movement.' Because [plaintiffs' expert] based his study on that incorrect assumption, it cannot be used to support a finding of loss causation.").

2. *Pleading.* Loss causation is an element of the Rule 10b–5 cause of action and plaintiffs accordingly bear the burden of proof of demonstrating loss causation at trial. Most securities class actions never reach trial, however, which means that loss causation is primarily raised at the motion to dismiss stage. Defendants often make a motion to dismiss for failure to plead loss causation. The Supreme Court in *Dura* did not specify the pleading standard for loss causation. When confronted with a motion to dismiss, the circuits are split on whether plaintiffs must plead loss causation with particularity under Rule 9(b) of the Federal Rules of Civil Procedure or under the more relaxed "plausibility" pleading standard under FRCP 8(a)(2). The Fifth Circuit in *Lormand v. US Unwired Inc.*, 565 F.3d 228, 258 (2009), held that Rule 8(a)(2) requires the plaintiff to allege, in respect to loss causation, a facially 'plausible' causal relationship between the fraudulent statements or omissions and plaintiff's economic loss. . .". In contrast, the Fourth Circuit in *Teachers' Retirement System of Louisiana v. Hunter*, 477 F.3d 162, 186 (4th Cir. 2007), wrote that a "strong case can be made that because loss causation is among the 'circumstances constituting fraud for which Rule 9(b) demands particularity, loss causation should be pleaded with particularity.' "

QUESTIONS

1. In discussing the loss causation requirement, the Seventh Circuit has said that: "No social purpose would be served by encouraging everyone who suffers an investment loss because of an unanticipated change in market conditions to pick through offering memoranda with a fine-tooth comb in the hope of uncovering a misrepresentation." *Bastian v. Petren Resources Corporation*, 892 F.2d 680 (7th Cir. 1990). Wouldn't diligent searching for misrepresentations better deter fraud?

2. What purpose does the loss causation requirement serve? Would that purpose be undermined by not requiring plaintiffs to plead loss causation in their complaint?

3. Why would it be wrong "to transform a private securities action into a partial downside insurance policy"?

4. How does the Court define the "value" of a security?

5. The Court says that "it should not prove burdensome for a plaintiff who has suffered an economic loss to provide a defendant with some indication of the loss and the causal connection that the plaintiff has in mind." Do you agree? What are the potential obstacles to pleading loss causation?

IV. RULE 10b–5 DEFENDANTS

As an implied private cause of action, Rule 10b–5 does not specify potential defendants. Instead, "any person" who makes a material misstatement and meets the other requirements of the Rule 10b–5 cause of action is potentially a defendant. Assuming the plaintiff can prove all the elements of Rule 10b–5 with respect to this person, the person would face "primary" liability. What if a person does not directly make the material misstatement, or otherwise does not satisfy all the elements of Rule 10b–5? Should she nonetheless still face Rule 10b–5 liability? This question is often referred to as "secondary" liability.

Put more concretely, when DigitalBase's CEO, Hillary, puts out overly optimistic statements on its new GigaBase product, should third parties such as DigitalBase's attorneys, auditors, past underwriters, suppliers, or customers also potentially be liable under Rule 10b–5? How should courts distinguish among third parties for Rule 10b–5 secondary liability purposes?

A. SECONDARY LIABILITY

The misstatement and reliance elements of the Rule 10b–5 cause of action largely determine who can be held responsible for securities fraud. Corporate statements can be made through press releases, conference calls, SEC filings, or other means of communication. A number of entities and individuals may play a role in crafting the statements. An agent for the corporation, such as the CEO or a corporate spokesperson, may actually say the statement. A public relations firm may help draft the statement. Attorneys for the corporation may assess the statement for possible legal exposure. Wall Street investment banks interested in selling the company's securities may give advice on financial projections contained in the statement. The board of directors of the company may approve the statement before its release to the public. Who among these parties should be held liable if the statement turns out to be materially misleading?

For many years, the lower federal courts allowed plaintiffs to file claims that defendants aided and abetted the violation of Rule 10b–5. Under an aiding and abetting claim, even those who did not themselves commit the actual Rule 10b–5 violation (the "primary" violation) may be held liable to the extent the aider and abettor was reckless with regards to the existence of the primary violation and provided substantial assistance to the primary violator. The Supreme Court in *Central Bank of Denver v. First Interstate Bank of Denver*, 511 U.S. 164 (1994), faced the issue of whether Rule 10b–5 provided investors an aiding and abetting cause of action against a bank that allegedly provided assistance to a bond issuer that made misleading disclosures in a prospectus. In rejecting aiding and abetting liability under Rule 10b–5, Justice Kennedy wrote:

> [W]e look to the express private causes of action in the 1933 and 1934 Acts. In the 1933 Act, § 11 prohibits false statements or omissions of material fact in registration statements; it identifies the various categories of defendants subject to liability for a violation, but that list does not include aiders and abettors. Section 12 prohibits the sale of unregistered, nonexempt securities as well as the sale of securities by means of a material misstatement or omission; and it limits liability to those who offer or sell the security. In the 1934 Act, § 9 prohibits any person from engaging in manipulative practices such as wash sales, matched orders, and the like. Section 16 regulates short-swing trading by owners, directors, and officers. Section 18 prohibits any person from making misleading statements in reports filed with the SEC. And § 20A, added in 1988, prohibits any person from engaging in insider trading.

> This survey of the express causes of action in the securities Acts reveals that each (like § 10(b)) specifies the conduct for which defendants may be held liable. Some of the express causes of action specify categories of defendants who may be liable; others (like § 10(b)) state only that "any person" who commits one of the prohibited acts may be held liable. The important point for present purposes, however, is that none of the express causes of action in the 1934 Act further imposes liability on one who aids or abets a violation.

> From the fact that Congress did not attach private aiding and abetting liability to any of the express causes of action in the securities Acts, we can infer that Congress likely would not have attached aiding and abetting liability to § 10(b) had it provided a private § 10(b) cause of action. . . . In *Blue Chip Stamps*, we noted that it would be "anomalous to impute to Congress an intention to expand the plaintiff class for a judicially implied cause of action beyond the bounds it delineated for comparable express causes of action." . . .

> Our reasoning is confirmed by the fact that respondents' argument would impose 10b–5 aiding and abetting liability when at least one element critical for recovery under 10b–5 is absent: reliance. A plaintiff must show reliance on the defendant's misstatement or omission to recover under 10b–5. Were we to allow the aiding and abetting action proposed in this case, the defendant could be liable without any showing that the plaintiff relied upon the aider and abettor's statements or actions. Allowing plaintiffs to circumvent the

reliance requirement would disregard the careful limits on 10b–5 recovery mandated by our earlier cases.

Central Bank raised doubts as to whether the SEC could pursue aiders and abettors in its enforcement actions. Congress eliminated any uncertainty on this score, however, by adding § 20(e) to the Exchange Act as part of the PSLRA, which allows the SEC to pursue actions against "any person that knowingly provides substantial assistance to another person in violation of a provision of this title." This amendment reflects a political compromise: the SEC had its aiding-and-abetting enforcement authority restored, but with a more stringent requirement of a "knowing" state of mind.

Congress's legislative response to *Central Bank* plays a critical role in the Court's decision in the case below. Note that *Stoneridge* was written by Justice Kennedy, the author of *Central Bank*. As you read *Stoneridge*, ask yourself whether Justice Kennedy, or Justice Stevens in dissent, interprets *Central Bank* more faithfully. Who has the more persuasive argument as to the implication to be drawn from Congress's restoration of aiding and abetting authority to the SEC in the PSLRA? Finally, which interpretation better serves the policy goals of the securities laws?

Stoneridge Investment Partners, LLC v. Scientific-Atlanta, Inc.

552 U.S. 148 (2008).

■ KENNEDY J.

We consider the reach of the private right of action the Court has found implied in § 10(b) of the Securities Exchange Act of 1934, and SEC Rule 10b–5.

In this suit investors alleged losses after purchasing common stock. They sought to impose liability on entities who, acting both as customers and suppliers, agreed to arrangements that allowed the investors' company to mislead its auditor and issue a misleading financial statement affecting the stock price. We conclude the implied right of action does not reach the customer/supplier companies because the investors did not rely upon their statements or representations. . . .

I

This class-action suit by investors was filed against Charter Communications, Inc. . . .

Charter issued the financial statements and the securities in question. It was a named defendant along with some of its executives and Arthur Andersen LLP, Charter's independent auditor during the period in question. We are concerned, though, with two other defendants, respondents here. Respondents are Scientific-Atlanta, Inc., and Motorola, Inc. They were suppliers, and later customers, of Charter.

For purposes of this proceeding, we take these facts, alleged by [Stoneridge], to be true. Charter, a cable operator, engaged in a variety of fraudulent practices so its quarterly reports would meet Wall Street expectations for cable subscriber growth and operating cash flow. . . . In late 2000, Charter executives realized that, despite these efforts, the company would miss projected operating cash flow numbers by $15 to $20 million. To help meet the shortfall, Charter decided to alter its existing arrangements with respondents, Scientific-Atlanta and Motorola ["suppliers"]. [Stoneridge]'s theory as to whether Arthur Andersen was altogether misled or, on the other hand, knew the structure of the contract arrangements and was complicit to some degree, is not clear at this stage of the case. The point, however, is neither controlling nor significant for our present disposition, and in our decision we assume it was misled.

[Suppliers] supplied Charter with the digital cable converter (set top) boxes that Charter furnished to its customers. Charter arranged to overpay [suppliers] $20 for each set top box it purchased until the end of the year, with the understanding that [suppliers] would return the overpayment by purchasing advertising from Charter. The transactions, it is alleged, had no economic substance; but, because Charter would then record the advertising purchases as revenue and capitalize its purchase of the set top boxes, in violation of generally accepted accounting principles, the transactions would enable Charter to fool its auditor into approving a financial statement showing it met projected revenue and operating cash flow numbers. Respondents agreed to the arrangement.

So that Arthur Andersen would not discover the link between Charter's increased payments for the boxes and the advertising purchases, the companies drafted documents to make it appear the transactions were unrelated and conducted in the ordinary course of business. Following a request from Charter, Scientific-Atlanta sent documents to Charter stating-falsely-that it had increased production costs. It raised the price for set top boxes for the rest of 2000 by $20 per box. As for Motorola, in a written contract Charter agreed to purchase from Motorola a specific number of set top boxes and pay liquidated damages of $20 for each unit it did not take. The contract was made with the expectation Charter would fail to purchase all the units and pay Motorola the liquidated damages.

To return the additional money from the set top box sales, Scientific-Atlanta and Motorola signed contracts with Charter to purchase advertising time for a price higher than fair value. The new set top box agreements were backdated to make it appear that they were negotiated a month before the advertising agreements. The backdating was important to convey the impression that the negotiations were unconnected, a point Arthur Andersen considered necessary for separate treatment of the transactions. Charter recorded the advertising payments to inflate revenue and operating cash flow by approximately $17 million. The inflated number was shown on financial statements filed with the Securities and Exchange Commission (SEC) and reported to the public.

[Suppliers] had no role in preparing or disseminating Charter's financial statements. And their own financial statements booked the transactions as a wash, under generally accepted accounting principles. It is alleged [suppliers] knew or were in reckless disregard of Charter's intention to use the transactions to inflate its revenues and knew the resulting financial statements issued by Charter would be relied upon by research analysts and investors.

* * *

II

* * *

In *Central Bank*, the Court determined that § 10(b) liability did not extend to aiders and abettors. The Court found the scope of § 10(b) to be delimited by the text, which makes no mention of aiding and abetting liability. The Court doubted the implied § 10(b) action should extend to aiders and abettors when none of the express causes of action in the securities Acts included that liability. It added the following:

> "Were we to allow the aiding and abetting action proposed in this case, the defendant could be liable without any showing that the plaintiff relied upon the aider and abettor's statements or actions. Allowing plaintiffs to circumvent the reliance requirement would disregard the careful limits on 10b–5 recovery mandated by our earlier cases."

The decision in *Central Bank* led to calls for Congress to create an express cause of action for aiding and abetting within the Securities Exchange Act. Then-SEC Chairman Arthur Levitt, testifying before the Senate Securities Subcommittee, cited *Central Bank* and recommended that aiding and abetting liability in private claims be established. Congress did not follow this course. Instead, in [§ 20(e) of the Exchange Act, adopted as part] of the Private Securities Litigation Reform Act of 1995 (PSLRA), it directed prosecution of aiders and abettors by the SEC.

The § 10(b) implied private right of action does not extend to aiders and abettors. The conduct of a secondary actor must satisfy each of the elements or preconditions for liability; and we consider whether the allegations here are sufficient to do so.

III

The Court of Appeals concluded [Stoneridge] had not alleged that [suppliers] engaged in a deceptive act within the reach of the § 10(b) private right of action, noting that only misstatements, omissions by one who has a duty to disclose, and manipulative trading practices . . . are deceptive within the meaning of the rule. If this conclusion were read to suggest there must be a specific oral or written statement before there could be liability under § 10(b) or Rule 10b–5, it would be erroneous. Conduct itself can be deceptive, as [suppliers] concede. In this case, moreover, [suppliers]' course of conduct included both oral and written statements, such as the backdated contracts agreed to by Charter and [suppliers].

A different interpretation of the holding from the Court of Appeals opinion is that the court was stating only that any deceptive statement or act respondents made was not actionable because it did not have the requisite proximate relation to the investors' harm. That conclusion is consistent with our own determination that respondents' acts or statements were not relied upon by the investors and that, as a result, liability cannot be imposed upon respondents.

A

Reliance by the plaintiff upon the defendant's deceptive acts is an essential element of the § 10(b) private cause of action. It ensures that, for liability to arise, the "requisite causal connection between a defendant's misrepresentation and a plaintiff's injury" exists as a predicate for liability. We have found a rebuttable presumption of reliance in two different circumstances. First, if there is an omission of a material fact by one with a duty to disclose, the investor to whom the duty was owed need not provide specific proof of reliance. Second, under the fraud-on-the-market doctrine, reliance is presumed when the statements at issue become public. The public information is reflected in the market price of the security. Then it can be assumed that an investor who buys or sells stock at the market price relies upon the statement.

Neither presumption applies here. Respondents had no duty to disclose; and their deceptive acts were not communicated to the public. No member of the investing public had knowledge, either actual or presumed, of [suppliers]' deceptive acts during the relevant times. [Stoneridge], as a result, cannot show reliance upon any of [suppliers]' actions except in an indirect chain that we find too remote for liability.

B

Invoking what some courts call "scheme liability," [Stoneridge] nonetheless seeks to impose liability on [suppliers] even absent a public statement. In our view this approach does not answer the objection that [Stoneridge] did not in fact rely upon [suppliers]' own deceptive conduct.

Liability is appropriate, [Stoneridge] contends, because [suppliers] engaged in conduct with the purpose and effect of creating a false appearance of material fact to further a scheme to misrepresent Charter's revenue. The argument is that the financial statement Charter released to the public was a natural and expected consequence of [suppliers]' deceptive acts; had [suppliers] not assisted Charter, Charter's auditor would not have been fooled, and the financial statement would have been a more accurate reflection of Charter's financial condition. That causal link is sufficient, [Stoneridge] argues, to apply *Basic's* presumption of reliance to [suppliers]' acts.

In effect [Stoneridge] contends that in an efficient market investors rely not only upon the public statements relating to a security but also upon the transactions those statements reflect. Were this concept of reliance to be adopted, the implied cause of action would reach the whole marketplace in which the issuing company does business; and there is no authority for this rule.

As stated above, reliance is tied to causation, leading to the inquiry whether [suppliers]' acts were immediate or remote to the injury. In considering [Stoneridge]'s arguments, we note § 10(b) provides that the deceptive act must be "in connection with the purchase or sale of any security." Though this phrase in part defines the statute's coverage rather than causation (and so we do not evaluate the "in connection with" requirement of § 10(b) in this case), the emphasis on a purchase or sale of securities does provide some insight into the deceptive acts that concerned the enacting Congress. In all events we conclude [suppliers]' deceptive acts, which were not disclosed to the investing public, are too remote to satisfy the requirement of reliance. It was Charter, not [suppliers], that misled its auditor and filed fraudulent financial statements; nothing [suppliers] did made it necessary or inevitable for Charter to record the transactions as it did.

[Stoneridge] invokes the private cause of action under § 10(b) and seeks to apply it beyond the securities markets—the realm of financing business—to purchase and supply contracts—the realm of ordinary business operations. The latter realm is governed, for the most part, by state law. It is true that if business operations are used, as alleged here, to affect securities markets, the SEC enforcement power may reach the culpable actors. It is true as well that a dynamic, free economy presupposes a high degree of integrity in all of its parts, an integrity that must be underwritten by rules enforceable in fair, independent, accessible courts. Were the implied cause of action to be extended to the practices described here, however, there would be a risk that the federal power would be used to invite litigation beyond the immediate sphere of securities litigation and in areas already governed by functioning and effective state-law guarantees. . . . Though § 10(b) is "not 'limited to preserving the integrity of the securities markets,' " it does not reach all commercial transactions that are fraudulent and affect the price of a security in some attenuated way.

These considerations answer as well the argument that if this were a common-law action for fraud there could be a finding of reliance. Even if the assumption is correct, it is not controlling. Section 10(b) does not incorporate common-law fraud into federal law. Just as § 10(b) "is surely badly strained when construed to provide a cause of action . . . to the world at large," it should not be interpreted to provide a private cause of action against the entire marketplace in which the issuing company operates.

[Stoneridge]'s theory, moreover, would put an unsupportable interpretation on Congress' specific response to *Central Bank* in § [20(e) of the Exchange Act]. Congress amended the securities laws to provide for limited coverage of aiders and abettors. Aiding and abetting liability is authorized in actions brought by the SEC but not by private parties. [Stoneridge]'s view of primary liability makes any aider and abettor liable under § 10(b) if he or she committed a deceptive act in the process of providing assistance. Were we to adopt this construction of § 10(b), it would revive in substance the implied cause of action against all aiders and abettors except those who committed no deceptive act in the process of facilitating the fraud; and we would undermine Congress' determination that this class of defendants should be pursued by the SEC and not by private litigants.

* * *

The practical consequences of an expansion . . . provide a further reason to reject [Stoneridge]'s approach. In *Blue Chip*, the Court noted that extensive discovery and the potential for uncertainty and disruption in a lawsuit allow plaintiffs with weak claims to extort settlements from innocent companies. Adoption of [Stoneridge]'s approach would expose a new class of defendants to these risks. As noted in *Central Bank*, contracting parties might find it necessary to protect against these threats, raising the costs of doing business.

Overseas firms with no other exposure to our securities laws could be deterred from doing business here. This, in turn, may raise the cost of being a publicly traded company under our law and shift securities offerings away from domestic capital markets.

C

The history of the § 10(b) private right and the careful approach the Court has taken before proceeding without congressional direction provide further reasons to find no liability here. The § 10(b) private cause of action is a judicial construct that Congress did not enact in the text of the relevant statutes. Though the rule once may have been otherwise, it is settled that there is an implied cause of action only if the underlying statute can be interpreted to disclose the intent to create one. This is for good reason. . . . The determination of who can seek a remedy has significant consequences for the reach of federal power.

Concerns with the judicial creation of a private cause of action caution against its expansion. The decision to extend the cause of action is for Congress, not for us. Though it remains the law, the § 10(b) private right should not be extended beyond its present boundaries.

This restraint is appropriate in light of the PSLRA, which imposed heightened pleading requirements and a loss causation requirement upon "any private action" arising from the Securities Exchange Act. It is clear these requirements touch upon the implied right of action, which is now a prominent feature of federal securities regulation. Congress thus ratified the implied right of action after the Court moved away from a broad willingness to imply private rights of action. It is appropriate for us to assume that when [the PSLRA] was enacted, Congress accepted the § 10(b) private cause of action as then defined but chose to extend it no further.

IV

Secondary actors are subject to criminal penalties and civil enforcement by the SEC. . . . All secondary actors, furthermore, are not necessarily immune from private suit. The securities statutes provide an express private right of action against accountants and underwriters in certain circumstances, and the implied right of action in § 10(b) continues to cover secondary actors who commit primary violations.

Here [suppliers] were acting in concert with Charter in the ordinary course as suppliers and, as matters then evolved in the not so ordinary course, as customers. Unconventional as the arrangement was, it took place in the marketplace for goods and services, not in the investment sphere. Charter was free to do as it chose in preparing its books, conferring with its auditor, and preparing and then issuing its financial statements. In these circumstances the investors cannot be said to have relied upon any of [suppliers]' deceptive acts in the decision to purchase or sell securities; and as the requisite reliance cannot be shown, [suppliers] have no liability to [Stoneridge] under the implied right of action. This conclusion is consistent with the narrow dimensions we must give to a right of action Congress did not authorize when it first enacted the statute and did not expand when it revisited the law.

The judgment of the Court of Appeals is affirmed, and the case is remanded for further proceedings consistent with this opinion.

■ STEVENS, J., with whom SOUTER and GINSBURG join, dissenting.

* * *

What the Court fails to recognize is that this case is critically different from *Central Bank* because the bank in that case did not engage in any deceptive act and, therefore, did not itself violate § 10(b). The Court sweeps aside any distinction, remarking that holding [suppliers] liable would "reviv[e] the implied cause of action against all aiders and abettors except those who committed no deceptive act in the process of facilitating the fraud." But the fact that *Central Bank* engaged in no deceptive conduct whatsoever-in other words, that it was at most an aider and abettor-sharply distinguishes *Central Bank* from cases that do involve allegations of such conduct. . . .

The facts of this case would parallel those of *Central Bank* if [suppliers] had, for example, merely delayed sending invoices for set-top boxes to Charter. Conversely, the facts in *Central Bank* would mirror those in the case before us today if the bank had knowingly purchased real estate in wash transactions at above-market prices in order to facilitate the appraiser's overvaluation of the security. *Central Bank*, thus, poses no obstacle to [Stoneridge]'s argument that it has alleged a cause of action under § 10(b).

II

The Court's next faulty premise is that [Stoneridge] is required to allege that Scientific-Atlanta and Motorola made it "necessary or inevitable for Charter to record the transactions in the way it did," in order to demonstrate reliance. . . .

In *Basic Inc.*, we stated that "[r]eliance provides the requisite causal connection between a defendant's misrepresentation and a plaintiff's injury." The Court's view of the causation required to demonstrate reliance is unwarranted and without precedent.

In *Basic Inc.*, we held that the "fraud-on-the-market" theory provides adequate support for a presumption in private securities actions that shareholders (or former shareholders) in publicly traded companies rely on public material misstatements that affect the price of the company's stock. The holding in *Basic* is surely a sufficient response to the argument that a complaint alleging that deceptive acts which had a material effect on the price of a listed stock should be dismissed because the plaintiffs were not subjectively aware of the deception at the time of the securities' purchase or sale. This Court has not held that investors must be aware of the specific deceptive act which violates § 10(b) to demonstrate reliance.

The Court is right that a fraud-on-the-market presumption coupled with its view on causation would not support [Stoneridge]'s view of reliance. The fraud-on-the-market presumption helps investors who cannot demonstrate that they, themselves, relied on fraud that reached the market. But that presumption says nothing about causation from the other side: what an individual or corporation must do in order to have "caused" the misleading information that reached the market. The Court thus has it backwards when it first addresses the fraud-on-the-market presumption, rather than the causation required. The argument is not that the fraud-on-the-market presumption is enough standing alone, but that a correct view of causation coupled with the presumption would allow [Stoneridge] to plead reliance.

Lower courts have correctly stated that the causation necessary to demonstrate reliance is not a difficult hurdle to clear in a private right of action under § 10(b). Reliance is often equated with " 'transaction causation.' " Transaction causation, in turn, is often defined as requiring an allegation that but for the deceptive act, the plaintiff would not have entered into the securities transaction.

Even if but-for causation, standing alone, is too weak to establish reliance, [Stoneridge] has also alleged that [suppliers] proximately caused Charter's misstatement of income; [Stoneridge] has alleged that [suppliers] knew their deceptive acts would be the basis for statements that would influence the market price of Charter stock on which shareholders would rely. Thus, [suppliers]' acts had the foreseeable effect of causing [Stoneridge] to engage in the relevant securities transactions. The Restatement (Second) of Torts § 533 provides that "[t]he maker of a fraudulent misrepresentation is subject to liability . . . if the misrepresentation, although not made directly to the other, is made to a third person and the maker intends or has reason to expect that its terms will be repeated or its substance communicated to the other." The sham transactions described in the complaint in this case had the same effect on Charter's profit and loss statement as a false entry directly on its books that included $17 million of gross revenues that had not been received. And [suppliers] are alleged to have known that the outcome of their fraudulent transactions would be communicated to investors.

The Court's view of reliance is unduly stringent and unmoored from authority. The Court first says that if the [Stoneridge]'s concept of reliance is adopted the implied cause of action "would reach the whole marketplace in which the issuing company does business." The answer to that objection is, of course, that liability only attaches when the company doing business with the issuing company has itself violated § 10(b).[4] The Court next relies on what it views as a strict division between the "realm of financing business" and the "ordinary business operations." But [Stoneridge]'s position does not merge the two: A corporation engaging in a business transaction with a partner who transmits false information to the market is only liable where the corporation itself violates § 10(b). Such a rule does not invade the province of "ordinary" business transactions.

* * *

Finally, the Court relies on the course of action Congress adopted after our decision in *Central Bank* to argue that siding with [Stoneridge] on reliance would run contrary to congressional intent. . . . Congress stopped short of undoing *Central Bank* entirely, instead adopting a compromise which restored the authority of the SEC to enforce aiding and abetting liability . . . in the PSLRA. . . . This compromise surely provides no support for extending *Central Bank* in

---

[4] Because the kind of sham transactions alleged in this complaint are unquestionably isolated departures from the ordinary course of business in the American marketplace, it is hyperbolic for the Court to conclude that [Stoneridge]'s concept of reliance would authorize actions "against the entire marketplace in which the issuing company operates."

order to immunize an undefined class of actual violators of § 10(b) from liability in private litigation. Indeed, as Members of Congress—including those who rejected restoring a private cause of action against aiders and abettors—made clear, private litigation under § 10(b) continues to play a vital role in protecting the integrity of our securities markets. That Congress chose not to restore the aiding and abetting liability removed by *Central Bank* does not mean that Congress wanted to exempt from liability the broader range of conduct that today's opinion excludes.

* * *

NOTES

1. *Aiding and abetting revisited.* Congress returned to the question of aiding-and-abetting liability in 2010 in the Dodd-Frank Act. As part of that legislation, Congress empowered the SEC to pursue reckless aiders and abettors of securities fraud, thus restoring the status quo pre-*Central Bank*. Congress rejected efforts to revive private aiding-and-abetting liability, however, instead instructing the Government Accountability Office to study the question.

QUESTIONS

1. Who was more responsible for fraud (and therefore in a better position to deter the fraud)—the indenture trustee Central Bank or the *Stoneridge* suppliers? Does this difference in culpability influence the outcome of *Stoneridge*?

2. Can there be deception even if there is no misstatement or omission? Does manipulation require a misstatement or omission?

3. Would aiding-and-abetting liability allow plaintiffs to circumvent the reliance requirement?

4. What disclosure did the investors rely upon in *Stoneridge*? What role did the suppliers play in the creation of that misleading disclosure?

5. *Affiliated Ute and Halliburton II* provide presumptions of reliance in cases of pure omissions and fraud-on-the-market. Why do those presumptions not apply to the conduct of the suppliers?

6. Is the interpretive approach adopted in *Stoneridge* consistent with the approach in *Halliburton II*?

7. Do we need to cabin securities regulation from the "realm of ordinary business operations"?

—————

Stoneridge further delineated the notion of reliance introduced by *Central Bank*, but it did not address the question of who "makes" a statement for purposes of Rule 10b–5. The Supreme Court tackles that question in the following case.

Janus Capital Group, Inc., et al. v. First Derivative Traders

131 S.Ct. 2296 (2011).

■ THOMAS, J.

This case requires us to determine whether Janus Capital Management LLC (JCM), a mutual fund investment adviser, can be held liable in a private action under Rule 10b–5 for false statements included in its client mutual funds' prospectuses. . . . We conclude that JCM cannot be held liable because it did not make the statements in the prospectuses.

I

Janus Capital Group, Inc. (JCG), is a publicly traded company that created the Janus family of mutual funds. These mutual funds are organized in a Massachusetts business trust, the Janus Investment Fund. Janus Investment Fund retained JCG's wholly owned subsidiary, JCM, to be its investment adviser and administrator. JCG and JCM are the petitioners here.

Although JCG created Janus Investment Fund, Janus Investment Fund is a separate legal entity owned entirely by mutual fund investors. Janus Investment Fund has no assets apart from those owned by the investors. . . . At all times relevant to this case, all of the officers of Janus Investment Fund were also officers of JCM, but only one member of Janus Investment Fund's board of trustees was associated with JCM. . . .

As the securities laws require, Janus Investment Fund issued prospectuses describing the investment strategy and operations of its mutual funds to investors. The prospectuses for several funds represented that the funds were not suitable for market timing and can be read to suggest that JCM would implement policies to curb the practice.[1] . . . Although market timing is legal, it harms other investors in the mutual fund.

In September 2003, the Attorney General of the State of New York filed a complaint against JCG and JCM alleging that JCG entered into secret arrangements to permit market timing in several funds run by JCM. After the complaint's allegations became public, investors withdrew significant amounts of money from the Janus Investment Fund mutual funds. Because Janus Investment Fund compensated JCM based on the total value of the funds and JCM's management fees comprised a significant percentage of JCG's income, Janus Investment

---

[1] Market timing is a trading strategy that exploits time delay in mutual funds' daily valuation system. The price for buying or selling shares of a mutual fund is ordinarily determined by the next net asset value (NAV) calculation after the order is placed. The NAV calculation usually happens once a day, at the close of the major U. S. markets. Because of certain time delays, however, the values used in these calculations do not always accurately reflect the true value of the underlying assets. For example, a fund may value its foreign securities based on the price at the close of the foreign market, which may have occurred several hours before the calculation. But events might have taken place after the close of the foreign market that could be expected to affect their price. If the event were expected to increase the price of the foreign securities, a market-timing investor could buy shares of mutual fund at the artificially low NAV and sell the next day when the NAV corrects itself upward.

Fund's loss of value affected JCG's value as well. JCG's stock price fell nearly 25 percent, from $17.68 on September 2 to $13.50 on September 26.

Respondent First Derivative Traders represents a class of plaintiffs who owned JCG stock as of September 3, 2003. Its complaint asserts claims against JCG and JCM for violations of Rule 10b–5 and § 10(b) of the Securities Exchange Act of 1934. First Derivative alleges that JCG and JCM "caused mutual fund prospectuses to be issued for Janus mutual funds and made them available to the investing public, which created the misleading impression that [JCG and JCM] would implement measures to curb market timing in the Janus [mutual funds]." . . .

First Derivative contends that JCG and JCM "materially misled the investing public" and that class members relied "upon the integrity of the market price of [JCG] securities and market information relating to [JCG and JCM]." . . .

The District Court dismissed the complaint for failure to state a claim. The Court of Appeals for the Fourth Circuit reversed, holding that First Derivative had sufficiently alleged that "JCG and JCM, by participating in the writing and dissemination of the prospectuses, made the misleading statements contained in the documents." With respect to the element of reliance, the court found that investors would infer that JCM "played a role in preparing or approving the content of the Janus fund prospectuses," but that investors would not infer the same about JCG, which could be liable only as a "control person" of JCM under § 20(a).

II

We granted certiorari to address whether JCM can be held liable in a private action under Rule 10b–5 for false statements included in Janus Investment Fund's prospectuses. Under Rule 10b–5, it is unlawful for "any person, directly or indirectly, . . . [t]o make any untrue statement of a material fact" in connection with the purchase or sale of securities. To be liable, therefore, JCM must have "made" the material misstatements in the prospectuses. We hold that it did not.

A

* * *

1

One "makes" a statement by stating it. When "make" is paired with a noun expressing the action of a verb, the resulting phrase is "approximately equivalent in sense" to that verb.[6] Oxford English Dictionary 66 (def. 59) (1933) (hereinafter OED); accord, Webster's New International Dictionary 1485 (def. 43) (2d ed. 1934) ("Make followed by

---

[6] The dissent correctly notes that *Central Bank* involved secondary, not primary, liability. But for *Central Bank* to have any meaning, there must be some distinction between those who are primarily liable (and thus may be pursued in private suits) and those who are secondarily liable (and thus may not be pursued in private suits).

We draw a clean line between the two—the maker is the person or entity with ultimate authority over a statement and others are not. In contrast, the dissent's only limit on primary liability is not much of a limit at all. It would allow for primary liability whenever "[t]he specific relationships alleged . . . warrant [that] conclusion"—whatever that may mean.

a noun with the indefinite article is often nearly equivalent to the verb intransitive corresponding to that noun"). For instance, "to make a proclamation" is the approximate equivalent of "to proclaim," and "to make a promise" approximates "to promise." See 6 OED 66 (def. 59). The phrase at issue in Rule 10b–5, "[t]o make any . . . statement," is thus the approximate equivalent of "to state."

For purposes of Rule 10b–5, the maker of a statement is the person or entity with ultimate authority over the statement, including its content and whether and how to communicate it. Without control, a person or entity can merely suggest what to say, not "make" a statement in its own right. One who prepares or publishes a statement on behalf of another is not its maker. And in the ordinary case, attribution within a statement or implicit from surrounding circumstances is strong evidence that a statement was made by—and only by—the party to whom it is attributed. This rule might best be exemplified by the relationship between a speechwriter and a speaker. Even when a speechwriter drafts a speech, the content is entirely within the control of the person who delivers it. And it is the speaker who takes credit—or blame—for what is ultimately said.

This rule follows from *Central Bank*, in which we held that Rule 10b–5's private right of action does not include suits against aiders and abettors. Such suits—against entities that contribute "substantial assistance" to the making of a statement but do not actually make it— may be brought by the SEC but not by private parties. A broader reading of "make," including persons or entities without ultimate control over the content of a statement, would substantially undermine *Central Bank*. If persons or entities without control over the content of a statement could be considered primary violators who "made" the statement, then aiders and abettors would be almost nonexistent.

This interpretation is further supported by our recent decision in *Stoneridge*. There, investors sued "entities who, acting both as customers and suppliers, agreed to arrangements that allowed the investors' company to mislead its auditor and issue a misleading financial statement." We held that dismissal of the complaint was proper because the public could not have relied on the entities' undisclosed deceptive acts. Significantly, in reaching that conclusion we emphasized that "nothing [the defendants] did made it necessary or inevitable for [the company] to record the transactions as it did."[7] This emphasis suggests the rule we adopt today: that the maker of a statement is the entity with authority over the content of the statement and whether and how to communicate it. Without such authority, it is not "necessary or inevitable" that any falsehood will be contained in the statement. . . .

2

The Government contends that "make" should be defined as "create." This definition, although perhaps appropriate when "make" is directed at an object unassociated with a verb (e.g., "to make a chair"),

---

[7] We agree [with Justice Breyer's dissenting opinion] that "no one in *Stoneridge* contended that the equipment suppliers were, in fact, the makers of the cable company's misstatements." If *Stoneridge* had addressed whether the equipment suppliers were "makers," today's decision would be unnecessary. The point is that *Stoneridge's* analysis suggests that they were not.

fails to capture its meaning when directed at an object expressing the action of a verb.

Adopting the Government's definition of "make" would also lead to results inconsistent with our precedent. The Government's definition would permit private plaintiffs to sue a person who "provides the false or misleading information that another person then puts into the statement." But in *Stoneridge*, we rejected a private Rule 10b–5 suit against companies involved in deceptive transactions, even when information about those transactions was later incorporated into false public statements. We see no reason to treat participating in the drafting of a false statement differently from engaging in deceptive transactions, when each is merely an undisclosed act preceding the decision of an independent entity to make a public statement.

For its part, First Derivative suggests that the "well-recognized and uniquely close relationship between a mutual fund and its investment adviser" should inform our decision. It suggests that an investment adviser should generally be understood to be the "maker" of statements by its client mutual fund, like a playwright whose lines are delivered by an actor. We decline this invitation to disregard the corporate form. Although First Derivative and its amici persuasively argue that investment advisers exercise significant influence over their client funds it is undisputed that the corporate formalities were observed here. JCM and Janus Investment Fund remain legally separate entities, and Janus Investment Fund's board of trustees was more independent than the statute requires. Any reapportionment of liability in the securities industry in light of the close relationship between investment advisers and mutual funds is properly the responsibility of Congress and not the courts. Moreover, just as with the Government's theory, First Derivative's rule would create the broad liability that we rejected in *Stoneridge*.

Congress also has established liability in § 20(a) for "[e]very person who, directly or indirectly, controls any person liable" for violations of the securities laws. First Derivative's theory of liability based on a relationship of influence resembles the liability imposed by Congress for control. To adopt First Derivative's theory would read into Rule 10b–5 a theory of liability similar to—but broader in application than—what Congress has already created expressly elsewhere. We decline to do so.

B

Under this rule, JCM did not "make" any of the statements in the Janus Investment Fund prospectuses; Janus Investment Fund did. Only Janus Investment Fund—not JCM—bears the statutory obligation to file the prospectuses with the SEC. The SEC has recorded that Janus Investment Fund filed the prospectuses. There is no allegation that JCM in fact filed the prospectuses and falsely attributed them to Janus Investment Fund. Nor did anything on the face of the prospectuses indicate that any statements therein came from JCM rather than Janus Investment Fund—a legally independent entity with its own board of trustees.[11]

---

[11] First Derivative suggests that "indirectly" in Rule 10b–5 may broaden the meaning of "make." We disagree. The phrase "directly or indirectly" is set off by itself in Rule 10b–5 and modifies not just "to make," but also "to employ" and "to engage." We think the phrase merely

First Derivative suggests that both JCM and Janus Investment Fund might have "made" the misleading statements within the meaning of Rule 10b–5 because JCM was significantly involved in preparing the prospectuses. But this assistance, subject to the ultimate control of Janus Investment Fund, does not mean that JCM "made" any statements in the prospectuses. Although JCM, like a speechwriter, may have assisted Janus Investment Fund with crafting what Janus Investment Fund said in the prospectuses, JCM itself did not "make" those statements for purposes of Rule 10b–5.[12]. . . .

■ BREYER, J., with whom GINSBURG, SOTOMAYOR, and KAGAN join, dissenting.

* * *

The majority finds the complaint fatally flawed . . . because (1) Rule 10b–5 says that no "person" shall "directly or indirectly . . . make any untrue statement of a material fact," (2) the statements at issue appeared in the Janus Fund's prospectuses, and (3) only "the person or entity with ultimate authority over the statement, including its content and whether and how to communicate it" can "make" a false statement.

But where can the majority find legal support for the rule that it enunciates? The English language does not impose upon the word "make" boundaries of the kind the majority finds determinative. Everyday, hosts of corporate officials make statements with content that more senior officials or the board of directors have "ultimate authority" to control. . . .

Nothing in the English language prevents one from saying that several different individuals, separately or together, "make" a statement that each has a hand in producing. For example, as a matter of English, one can say that a national political party has made a statement even if the only written communication consists of uniform press releases issued in the name of local party branches; one can say that one foreign nation has made a statement even when the officials of a different nation (subject to its influence) speak about the matter; and one can say that the President has made a statement even if his press officer issues a communication, sometimes in the press officer's own name. Practical matters related to context, including control, participation, and relevant audience, help determine who "makes" a

---

clarifies that as long as a statement is made, it does not matter whether the statement was communicated directly or indirectly to the recipient. A different understanding of "indirectly" would, like a broad definition of "make," threaten to erase the line between primary violators and aiders and abettors established by *Central Bank*.

In this case, we need not define precisely what it means to communicate a "made" statement indirectly because none of the statements in the prospectuses were attributed, explicitly or implicitly, to JCM. Without attribution, there is no indication that Janus Investment Fund was quoting or otherwise repeating a statement originally "made" by JCM. More may be required to find that a person or entity made a statement indirectly, but attribution is necessary.

[12] That JCM provided access to Janus Investment Fund's prospectuses on its Web site is also not a basis for liability. Merely hosting a document on a Web site does not indicate that the hosting entity adopts the document as its own statement or exercises control over its content. . . .

statement and to whom that statement may properly be "attributed"—
at least as far as ordinary English is concerned.

* * *

The possibility of guilty management and innocent board is the
13th stroke of the new rule's clock. What is to happen when guilty
management writes a prospectus (for the board) containing materially
false statements and fools both board and public into believing they are
true? Apparently under the majority's rule, in such circumstances no
one could be found to have "ma[d]e" a materially false statement—even
though under the common law the managers would likely have been
guilty or liable (in analogous circumstances) for doing so as principals
(and not as aiders and abettors). . . .

In sum, I can find nothing in § 10(b) or in Rule 10b–5, its language,
its history, or in precedent suggesting that Congress, in enacting the
securities laws, intended a loophole of the kind that the majority's rule
may well create.

* * *

QUESTIONS

1.   How does *Janus* fit in with the Court's opinions in *Central Bank* and
Stoneridge?

2.   Why does the Court want a bright line rule to determine who "makes"
a statement for purposes of Rule 10b–5?

3.   What is the relationship of § 20(a) control person liability and the
Court's focus on "ultimate authority" in determining who makes a
misstatement?

4.   In his dissent, Justice Breyer states that the "possibility of guilty
management and innocent board is the 13th stroke of the new rule's clock."
That is a colorful image; what does Justice Breyer mean and is he correct?

HYPOTHETICAL NINE

Recall the restatement of DigitalBase's revenues, required because the
company booked as revenue contracts that were still contingent. The
plaintiffs in the DigitalBase class action have named Arthur & Young as a
defendant. In order to maximize the class period for which Arthur & Young
would share liability, the plaintiffs assert that Arthur & Young should be
liable, not only for the audited financial statements filed with DigitalBase's
10–K, but also the unaudited financial statements that DigitalBase filed
with its 10–Qs during the period that it was misstating its revenues.
Arthur & Young did not audit these interim financial statements, but it did
review them. Arthur & Young is not mentioned in the 10–Qs, and the
financial statements are explicitly labeled "unaudited." It is common
knowledge, however, that Arthur & Young is DigitalBase's auditor and
reviews its financial statements. Indeed, Arthur & Young listed
DigitalBase on its website on its representative client list. Can Arthur &
Young be held liable for the misstatements in the 10–Qs under *Janus*?

B. CONTROL PERSON LIABILITY

The rejection of aiding and abetting liability in *Central Bank* and the narrow view of primary liability taken in *Stoneridge* and *Janus* for Rule 10b–5 have revived interest in the Exchange Act's provision explicitly creating vicarious liability. Who can be subjected to liability as a "control person" under § 20(a)?

The Exchange Act does not define control. The SEC in Rule 12b–2 of the Exchange Act defines control as "the possession, direct or indirect, of the power to direct or cause the direction of the management and policies of a person, whether through the ownership of voting securities, by contract, or otherwise." (As we discuss in Chapter 7, Rule 405 of the Securities Act defines control the same way.) Courts have not always followed Rule 12b–2 in defining control. Currently there are two competing tests for § 20(a) control person liability.

All the circuits require that plaintiffs seeking to make a § 20(a) claim first demonstrate that a person (the "primary violator") violated a provision of the Exchange Act, including most importantly § 10(b) and Rule 10b–5. The circuits are split on the additional requirements for § 20(a) control person liability. The majority of the circuits follow a "potential" control test, but they vary on what is required to show potential control. The Eighth Circuit's rule requires plaintiffs to establish that the alleged control person (1) "actually participated in (i.e. exercised control over) the operations of the corporation [or person] in general" and (2) " 'possessed the power to control the specific transaction or activity upon which the primary violation is predicated, but he need not prove that this latter power was exercised.' " *Metge v. Baehler*, 762 F.2d 621 (1985). Defendants then bear the burden of showing that they "acted in good faith and did not directly or indirectly induce the act or acts constituting the violation or cause of action." Exchange Act § 20(a).

The Second, Third, and Fourth Circuits apply a "culpable participant" test. *See SEC v. First Jersey Sec., Inc.*, 101 F.3d 1450, 1472 (2d Cir. 1996). Under the culpable participant test, a plaintiff must show (1) control of the primary violator by the defendant and (2) that the alleged controlling person was a culpable participant in the specific fraud perpetrated by the primary violator. Although § 20(a) provides a good faith defense for control persons, it is unclear how a control person who is found to be a culpable participant can demonstrate good faith.

Which test better serves the goals of the Exchange Act? The more expansive "potential control" test may increase deterrence, giving potential control persons an incentive to monitor the controlled persons. A person that lacks information or the ability to affect the activities of the controlled persons, however, may not be able to deter wrongdoing. Imposing liability on such persons will simply turn them into insurers for the wrongs committed by the controlled persons. Persons deemed to be in control are not in any better position to bear the risk of wrongdoing than the parties who suffer harm from the misstatements. Indeed, the prospect of liability may lead potential control persons to avoid control, which could lead to less monitoring instead of more. Requiring culpable participation, however, may go too far in the opposite direction. Unduly limiting instances when a person with the ability to control will be held liable as a control person under § 20(a) could reduce monitoring.

Consider how the Eighth Circuit applied the potential control test in the following case. Do you agree with the approach the Eighth Circuit takes, or is the culpable participant test the better approach?

Lustgraaf v. Behrens

619 F.3d 867 (8th Cir. 2010).

■ MELLOY, M., CIRCUIT JUDGE.

This appeal concerns Appellants' claims against Appellees Sunset Financial Services, Inc. and Kansas City Life Insurance Company for damages arising out of a Ponzi scheme perpetrated by Bryan Behrens, a registered representative of Sunset and general agent of KCL. Appellants brought claims against Sunset and KCL based on theories of federal and state control-person liability and common law theories of secondary liability. The district court granted Sunset's and KCL's motions to dismiss for failure to state a claim and denied Appellants' motions for leave to file amended complaints. Appellants challenge each of these rulings. We affirm in part, reverse in part, and remand for further proceedings consistent with this opinion.

I.   Background

KCL is licensed with the Nebraska Department of Insurance to deal in sickness and accident insurance, life insurance, variable life insurance, and variable annuities. KCL also offers various investment options through Sunset, its wholly-owned subsidiary. Sunset is a broker-dealer registered with the SEC. KCL describes Sunset as an "in-house broker/dealer . . . giving agencies and producers the flexibility to offer quality life insurance as well as securities products through a single relationship." Appellants allege that Sunset markets itself as a trusted financial advisory firm with agents and representatives who can be trusted to give advice on insurance and financial matters. . . .

Appellants allege they invested money with Behrens through National Investments, Inc., an entity that Behrens controlled. In connection with these investments, Behrens sold promissory notes to Appellants, listing National Investments as the borrower. Appellants allege that Behrens took their money with the promise that he would invest it and provide them with a steady stream of income. Rather than invest the money, Behrens "misappropriated the funds for his personal use, spent the money in other ways, or simply transferred money among [Appellants] and other investors to prevent them from discovering the fraud."

* * *

[In March and July, 2009, the district court granted motions to dismiss to Sunset and KCL.]

II.   Discussion

* * *

A.   Federal Control-Person Liability

[The complaints allege] claims against Sunset and KCL for control-person liability under § 20(a) of the Securities Exchange Act of 1934. The purpose of the federal control-person statute is to "prevent people and entities from using straw parties, subsidiaries, or other agents acting on their behalf to accomplish ends that would be forbidden directly by the securities laws." To that end, the statute provides for liability of those who, subject to certain defenses, "directly or indirectly" control a primary violator of the federal securities laws. In providing for liability of controlling persons, however, Congress did not define the meaning of control. Rather, it left that task to the courts. Our Court has held that the statute . . . " 'has been interpreted as requiring only some indirect means of discipline or influence short of actual direction to hold a 'controlling person' liable.' " To meet this standard, a plaintiff must prove: (1) that a "primary violator" violated the federal securities laws; (2) that "the alleged control person actually exercised control over the general operations of the primary violator"; and (3) that "the alleged control person possessed—but did not necessarily exercise—the power to determine the specific acts or omissions upon which the underlying violation is predicated." Culpable participation by the alleged control person in the primary violation is not part of a plaintiff's prima facie case. If a plaintiff satisfies the prima facie burden, the burden shifts to the defendant to show that it "acted in good faith and did not directly or indirectly induce the act or acts constituting the violation or cause of action."

* * *

1.   Sunset

Unlike the first prong of our control-person test, where fraud is at issue, the second and third prongs involve questions of control and are therefore analyzed under our ordinary notice-pleading standard. The district court found that Appellants could not establish control-person liability against Sunset because they failed to allege facts supporting their allegations that Sunset exercised control over Behrens generally or had the ability to control Behrens with respect to the fraudulent transactions. Appellants' theory on appeal is that, as a matter of law, a plaintiff states a claim for control-person liability against a broker-dealer such as Sunset when the complaint alleges a primary violation by the broker-dealer's registered representative. . . .

Appellants allege that Behrens's fraudulent transactions took place while he was Sunset's registered representative. Sunset argues that it cannot be a control person because the fraudulent transactions took place through National Investments, a firm having no affiliation with Sunset. . . . Broker-dealers exercise considerable control over their representatives, both in the sense that their association allows representatives legal access to securities markets, and in the sense that the securities laws require broker-dealers to establish oversight systems to monitor representatives' activities. Thus, although Behrens's fraud did not take place through Sunset, it is Sunset that effectively provided Behrens access to the markets, and Sunset that had the duty to monitor his activities. Behrens could not have perpetrated his fraudulent scheme absent Appellants' belief that he had access to these markets. Sunset had the responsibility to oversee Behrens's activity with respect to his actions as a registered representative. . . .

Finally, we reject Sunset's (and KCL's) invitation to join other circuits in requiring culpable participation by a defendant in an action for control-person liability. This issue has created a circuit split. Our Court, as noted, has expressly stated that culpable participation by an alleged control person in the primary violation is not an element of the claim. Sunset and KCL argue that the passage of the PSLRA requires us to revisit the issue. We disagree. Congress designed the PSLRA, in part, to curb frivolous securities litigation by way of heightened pleading standards in fraud cases. Because federal control-person liability is dependent on control, not fraud, the heightened pleading standards instituted by the PSLRA do not provide reason to revisit our [prior] decision.

We reverse the district court's dismissal of Appellants' control-person claims against Sunset. Appellants' appeal concerning the proposed second amended complaints on this issue is therefore moot.

2. KCL

The district court found that because it dismissed Appellants' claims as to Sunset, the claims against Sunset's parent company, KCL, must also be dismissed. Appellants' argument on appeal as to KCL is similar to their argument as to Sunset; it is an argument based on the relationship of the entities. They argue that because Sunset controls Behrens, and KCL is Sunset's parent company, KCL is a controlling person as to Behrens. Without further allegations as to KCL's actual exercise of control over Behrens's general operations, § 20(a) and our case law interpreting that provision do not permit extension of control-person liability to KCL.

Although we engage in certain presumptions with respect to broker-dealers, we generally require that a plaintiff allege facts demonstrating that the alleged control person "actually exercised" control over the primary violator's general operations in order to state a claim for control-person liability. Our rule is therefore distinct from courts that only require the ability to control, regardless of whether that control was exercised. Here, the operative complaints allege that KCL wholly owned Sunset and thereby indirectly controlled Behrens. These allegations show, at most, KCL's ability to control Behrens. They fail, however, to show that KCL actually exercised control over Behrens's general operations. "Unless there are facts that indicate that the controlling shareholders were actively participating in the decisionmaking process of the [primary violator], no controlling liability can be imposed.". . . .

Appellants' proposed second amended complaints fail to cure this deficiency. The second amended complaints contain the additional allegations that: (1) Sunset and KCL operated from the same location; (2) many of Sunset's registered representatives were also agents of KCL; and (3) Sunset and KCL had shared directors and employees. These arguments fall short. First, the mere fact that the two entities shared the same office space is not an allegation of control. Nor, without explanation, is the allegation that there is some crossover in agents and representatives. The second amended complaints do not allege that overlapping agents exercised or even had the authority to control Behrens. Third, although the existence of shared directors is a factor to be considered in determining control, it is not determinative. The complaints do not ... allege the additional facts necessary to demonstrate that KCL actually exercised control over Behrens's general operations rather than merely possessed the ability to do so. Because this is a required element of Appellants' claim, we affirm the district court's denial of leave to amend.

* * *

NOTES

1. *Directors and officers.* Plaintiffs in securities fraud class actions commonly allege not only Rule 10b–5 violations, but also § 20(a) control person liability against the officers and directors of the defendant corporation. Neither directors nor officers are automatically control persons based on their position. *See Sawant v. Ramsey*, 2010 WL 3937403, at *20 ("[C]ontrol person liability is not presumed for individuals holding corporate officer status ..."); *Arthur Children's Trust v. Keim*, 994 F.2d 1390, 1396 (9th Cir. 1993) ("A director is not automatically liable as a controlling person."). Nonetheless, "[i]t is not uncommon for control 'to rest with a group of persons, such as the members of the corporation's management.'" *Arthur Children's Trust*, 994 F.2d at 1397. Finding the requisite control can be particularly difficult in the case of an outside director. Only a majority of the board can exercise control over a corporation. A single director does not have the power to control unilaterally the corporation. Whether a single director in fact has control turns on a fact-specific inquiry. Directors uninvolved in the company's business and without experience in the business are not control persons. *See Burgess v. Premier Corp.*, 727 F.2d 826, 832 (9th Cir. 1984).

2. *Pleading requirements.* The circuits are split on the pleading requirements for § 20(a) control person liability. As discussed in the *Lustgraaf* case, the Eighth Circuit, and other circuits that follow the majority approach of not requiring culpable participation, require only ordinary notice pleading. Circuits that implement the culpable participation requirement, in contrast, typically apply the PSLRA's heightened pleading standards. Under that standard, the plaintiff must plead with particularity facts giving rise to a strong inference of conscious misbehavior or recklessness on the part of the alleged control person. But there is a split even among courts within the same circuit. In the Second Circuit, which applies the culpable participation requirement for § 20(a) liability, some district courts equate culpable participation with "conscious misbehavior or recklessness." *Lapin v. Goldman Sachs Group, Inc.*, 506 F.Supp.2d 221, 246 (S.D.N.Y. 2006) These courts then proceed to require the pleading with particularity requirement under the PSLRA with respect to the control person's scienter. In contrast, in *In re Initial Public Offering Securities Litigation*, 241 F.Supp.2d 281, 396 (S.D.N.Y. 2003), Judge Scheindlin held that "culpable participation" does not require the proof of a certain state of mind and instead held that "scienter is not an essential element of a Section 20(a) claim." Accordingly, Judge Scheindlin required only notice pleading for the § 20(a) claim. One last wrinkle: Control person liability actions under § 15 of the Securities Act typically are brought for a

primary violation under §§ 11 or 12 or the Securities Act. Because neither requires scienter for a primary violation, courts have held that notice pleading suffices for a § 15 claims. *See* id. at 352.

3.   *SEC enforcement.* For many years, the SEC's ability to bring an enforcement action based on control person liability was uncertain. The Dodd-Frank Act resolves this question. Section 929P(c) of the Act amends § 20(a) of the Exchange Act to make clear that the phrase "any person" in § 20(a) includes "the Commission in any action brought under paragraph (1) or (3) of Section 21(d)." We discuss § 21(d), which gives the SEC power to pursue injunction proceedings in federal district court, in Chapter 13.

QUESTIONS

1.   Why not treat the ability to control as enough to establish a control relationship? Why does the Eighth Circuit require that the plaintiff plead facts that show that the alleged control person "actually exercised control over the general operations of the primary violator" to establish § 20(a) liability?

V.   DAMAGES

A.   OPEN MARKET DAMAGES

From an economic perspective, overall sanctions (i.e., damages in private actions plus fines imposed by the SEC plus reputational harm), multiplied by the probability that sanctions will be imposed on wrongdoers, should equal the social costs of the harm caused by fraud. Because the probability of sanctions is less than 100%—some fraudsters will get away with it—the sanction imposed needs to be greater than the harm caused by fraud.

The measure of damages in securities cases is not, however, social harm with a multiplier to reflect the probability of detection. Instead, a compensatory measure is used based on the out-of-pocket measure of damages traditionally used by tort law. That measure is the difference between price paid and the value of the security at the time of the purchase. The resulting enormous damages that would be required to compensate the victims of fraud raises the question of whether the overall level of sanctions for fraud is appropriate to the level of harm caused by the fraud.

Compensation measured by out-of-pocket damages makes sense in cases in which the corporation has fraudulently sold securities. Compensation corrects the distortion caused by fraud in two ways. First, requiring compensation to the victim discourages the corporation from committing the fraud. If the corporation has committed fraud to sell its securities its gain is likely to be roughly equivalent to the plaintiff's loss. Second, compensation discourages investors from expending resources trying to avoid fraud, termed precaution costs. Expenditures by both the perpetrator and the victim due to fraud are a social waste, so compensation makes sense in that context. The federal securities laws encourage such fraud suits by providing a very generous standard for recovery for fraud in public offerings under §§ 11 and 12 of the Securities Act, which we will study in Chapter 8. Public offering claims, however, make up only a small percentage of securities class actions.

The overwhelming majority of securities fraud class actions do not involve corporations selling securities. As you have seen in the cases in this chapter, in the typical securities fraud class action plaintiffs' attorneys sue the corporation and its officers under Rule 10b–5 of the Securities Exchange Act for alleged misrepresentations regarding the company's operations, financial performance, or future prospects that inflate the price of the company's stock in secondary trading markets such as the NYSE and the Nasdaq. Because the corporation has not sold securities (and thereby transferred wealth to itself), it has no institutional incentive to spend real resources in executing the fraud.

This type of fraud, commonly referred to as fraud on the market, also differs from what we typically consider fraud in that there is no net wealth transfer away from investors, at least in the aggregate. Instead, the wealth transfers caused by fraud on the market overwhelmingly occur between equally innocent investors. For every shareholder who *bought* at a fraudulently inflated price, another shareholder has *sold*: The buyer's individual loss is offset by the seller's gain. Assuming all traders are ignorant of the fraud, over time they will come out winners as often as losers from fraudulently distorted prices. Therefore, shareholders as a group should have no expected loss from fraud on the market, so they would have no incentive to take precautions against the fraud (even if such precautions were feasible).

Despite the fact that the corporation being sued has not gained from fraud on the market, the out-of-pocket measure promises full compensation to investors who come out on the losing end of a trade at a price distorted by misrepresentation. Those investors are entitled to recover their losses from the corporation based on its managers' misstatements. Depending on the trading volume in secondary markets, the potential recoverable damages in such suits can be a substantial percentage of the corporation's total capitalization, easily reaching hundreds of millions of dollars. With potential damages in this range, class actions are a big stick to wield against fraud. Given the somewhat arbitrary quality of these damages, based on trading volume, what is the probability of Rule 10b–5 for secondary market fraud providing the optimal level of deterrence against fraud? Or perhaps overwhelming damages are necessary because of the barriers to recovery in a Rule 10b–5 suit?

HYPOTHETICAL TEN

Consider DigitalBase's past accounting practices that led to its recent restatement. Assume that during the period when the misleading information affected the secondary market, 10 million shares of DigitalBase changed hands. Recall that the share price dropped from $15 to $10 when the restatement was announced.

1. Assume that private plaintiffs' attorneys are successful in winning a Rule 10b–5 judgment at trial based on DigitalBase's past overstatement of revenues. What is the proper out-of-pocket measure of damages? What information would you need to determine this?

2. Who was harmed by DigitalBase's overstatement of revenues in prior years?

3. Who benefited from DigitalBase's overstatement of revenues in prior years? How much did DigitalBase itself benefit?

B. FACE-TO-FACE DAMAGES

In face-to-face transactions, the court is not limited to the out-of-pocket measure. Courts, at their discretion, have applied both restitution and rescission (or rescissory damages) in Rule 10b–5 cases. Restitution requires the defendant to give the plaintiff whatever profit she made from the securities transaction giving rise to the Rule 10b–5 claim. Restitution is sometimes referred to as disgorgement.

Rescission endeavors to undo the transaction, plaintiffs are put back as close as possible to the position they would have been in had the transaction never taken place. In the case of a seller defrauding the plaintiff into buying overvalued securities, the plaintiff returns the securities and receives her purchase price back (subject to adjustments for any income the plaintiff earned while owning the securities as well as the opportunity cost of the plaintiff's money while tied up in the securities). If the plaintiff has sold the securities, the plaintiff can obtain rescissory damages. For the plaintiff who purchased overvalued securities, rescissory damages are equal to the difference between the original purchase price and the subsequent (lower) sale price, again with adjustments.

When do courts turn to restitution or rescission instead of the out-of-pocket measure of damages? In *Pidcock v. Sunnyland America Inc.*, 854 F.2d 443 (11th Cir. 1988), the Harvard family and Pidcock each owned 50% of a meat packing company. Just before selling his half to the Harvards, Pidcock asked the Harvards whether any third party buyers were interested in buying the meat pack company. The Harvards responded that there were no such third party buyers when in fact there was a buyer interested at the time. Relying on this representation, Pidcock sold his shares to the Harvards. The buyer interested at the time of Pidcock's sale did not in fact buy the meat packing company, making it difficult to determine whether the true value of Pidcock's shares at the time of his sale to the Harvards was greater than Pidcock's sale price for purposes of the out-of-pocket measure of damages in a Rule 10b–5 action. Subsequently, a different third party purchased the meat packing company at a higher price than Pidcock's sale price, thereby enriching the Harvards. The Eleventh Circuit held that district court erred in not considering the disgorgement of profits measure for Rule 10b–5 damages.

In the following case, why is the out-of-pocket measure not appropriate? What alternative measure does the court select?

Garnatz v. Stifel, Nicolaus & Co., Inc.

559 F.2d 1357 (8th Cir. 1977).

■ MATTHES, M., SENIOR CIRCUIT JUDGE.

Stifel, Nicolaus & Co., a brokerage firm, and Kingsley O. Wright, a vice-president of that firm, appeal from a judgment entered against them on a jury verdict awarding Milton W. Garnatz damages of $45,000 with interest and costs. . . . [P]laintiff's complaint was based on defendants' alleged violations of § 10(b) of the Securities Exchange Act of 1934 [and] Rule 10b–5 promulgated thereunder; . . .

I

Garnatz is a man of limited education and modest means. His familiarity with the securities markets is characteristically that of the average, individual investor, not the sophisticated trader.

In November of 1972, plaintiff attended a series of investment seminars sponsored by Stifel, Nicolaus. On the basis of representations made at those seminars and at two personal meetings with Kingsley Wright, plaintiff agreed to participate in a special bond margin account program which was purportedly designed to maximize his income while preserving his capital. The representations plaintiff specifically relied on in deciding to join in the program were: (1) that all purchases had to be approved by the board of directors of Stifel, Nicolaus; (2) that the use of a margin account entailed no risk to plaintiff's capital; (3) that the bonds purchased would not decrease more than one percent in value; (4) that the interest rate on the margin account would never exceed eight percent; and (5) that defendants' recommended purchases would be without risk. Defendants do not seriously challenge the allegation that these representations were both false and material.

Plaintiff insisted on avoiding speculation, yet most of the bonds purchased for him were either low-rated or non-rated by Standard & Poors. Although safety was a key feature of defendants' sales pitch, in order to pay the interest rate on the margin account and still provide a sufficiently attractive return, it was apparently necessary to purchase high-yield, and consequently highly-speculative bonds. At no time was any bond purchase approved by the board of directors of Stifel, Nicolaus.

Plaintiff entered into the program in late 1972. By April of 1973, the market value of Garnatz' account had declined over one percent. As a result, plaintiff was forced to relinquish all income from the bonds to pay increased margin calls. During this period, Wright repeatedly reassured Garnatz that the drop was only temporary and strongly recommended that plaintiff stay with the program, which he did. In August of 1974, the interest rate on the margin account jumped from eight percent to thirteen percent, as permitted by a change in Missouri's usury law. Garnatz does not dispute the fact that by that time he was, or should have been, on notice of the fraud.

II

The implication of a private damage remedy for violations of the federal securities laws is based partly on the notion that the abrogation of a statutorily imposed duty is tortious. Following the model of the common law tort of deceit, in § 10(b) and Rule 10b–5 actions "the defendant is liable to respond in such damages as naturally and proximately result from the fraud. . . ." Normally, federal courts measure those damages according to the out-of-pocket rule. As applied to a fraudulently induced purchase of securities, that rule provides for the recovery of the difference between the actual value of the securities and their purchase price. Recovery is also allowed for any consequential damages proximately resulting from the fraud. The rule was designed to provide plaintiffs with a compensatory recovery rather than allowing damages for a lost expectancy. It works best in the typical situation where the defendant's fraud conceals the actual value of the item purchased, yet does not affect the overall market value of that item.

Of course, the out-of-pocket rule is not a talisman. Indeed, this court has shown no hesitation in varying that measure when necessary on the facts of a given case. Our function is to fashion the remedy best suited to the harm.

In the present case, defendants urge strict application of the out-of-pocket rule. They would deny plaintiff any recovery at all, since the value of the bonds equaled their purchase price. But the fact that plaintiff got what he paid for does not mean he did not suffer any legally cognizable injury from defendants' fraud. It merely indicates that the fraud did not relate to the price of the bonds. . . .

[T]he gravamen of the present action was not whether Garnatz bought the bonds for a fair price, but that he bought at all. Absent defendants' representations regarding the safety of the program, plaintiff's express disdain for speculation undoubtedly would have precluded his participation; but the fraudulent promise of a low-cost, income-maximizing, and risk-free investment package overcame plaintiff's caution. Under these circumstances, we believe that a rescissory damage measure . . . is appropriate. Such a measure seeks to return the parties to the status quo ante the sale. In effect, the plaintiff is refunded his purchase price, reduced by any value received as a result of the fraudulent transaction. As applied to the case at bar, plaintiff can recover the decline in value of his bonds until his actual or constructive notice of the fraud, as well as any other losses properly attributable to defendants' wrongdoing. That decline in value is determined by the losses taken on bond sales plus the losses sustained on bonds held, as long as all such losses were incurred prior to the date that plaintiff knew, or should have known, of the fraud.

Some would argue, as defendants have here, that a rescissory measure of damages allows recovery of losses due to market forces rather than the defendants' conduct. We recognize that neither Stifel, Nicolaus nor Kingsley Wright caused plaintiff's bonds to decline in value. But plaintiff's purchase of these low-rated and non-rated bonds was induced by defendants' wrongful concealment of the risks normally attendant to such transactions. Those risks should therefore rightly be borne by defendants. Moreover, since plaintiff's losses were natural, proximate, and foreseeable consequences of defendants' fraud, the causative connection is sufficient. Of course, the responsibility for losses incurred after actual or constructive notice of the fraud must fall to plaintiff.

* * *

NOTES

1. *Punitive damages.* Exchange Act § 28(a) limits the amount of damages in a Rule 10b–5 claim to "actual damages," thereby excluding punitive damages. Punitive damages may be recoverable for pendent state claims of common law fraud. In the typical 10b–5 class action, however, state claims will ordinarily be preempted by the Securities Litigation Uniform Standards Act.

2. *Loss causation.* Enacted as part of the PSLRA, § 21D(b)(4) of the Exchange Act states that: "In any private action arising under this title, the plaintiff shall have the burden of proving that the act or omission of the defendant alleged to violate this title caused the loss for which the plaintiff seeks to recover damages." Restitution, however, does not focus on the plaintiff's losses but instead on the defendant's profits, which are not always the same. Similar difficulties apply for the rescission measure. The loss suffered by a plaintiff who purchases securities at their market value, such as in cases like *Garnatz*, is unclear. One could argue, nonetheless, that the plaintiff suffered loss from being induced into entering an overly risky transaction that she otherwise would never have executed.

QUESTIONS

1. Why was Garnatz not entitled to disgorgement?

2. How can investors be harmed if they got what they paid for?

3. The fraud in *Garnatz* is sometimes called "fraud in the inducement." How does the characterization of the fraud affect the damages measure? Was there loss causation in *Garnatz*?

4. Courts generally enjoy wide discretion in selecting among available Rule 10b–5 damage measurements. What principles do you think should guide this discretion?

C. PROPORTIONATE LIABILITY

The traditional rule in Rule 10b–5 actions was joint-and-several liability. Secondary defendants won an important victory in the PSLRA with the adoption of a proportionate liability provision codified in § 21D(f) of the Exchange Act. Under this provision, defendants who are found to be only reckless are required to pay only their proportionate share of the damages caused. The jury (or finder of fact) must determine the percentage of responsibility (based on conduct and causal relationship to damages) as well as whether the defendant's actions were knowing.

There are two exceptions to the general rule of proportionality, however: (1) Defendants are jointly and severally liable to a plaintiff who is entitled to damages exceeding 10% of his net worth, if the plaintiff's net worth is less than $200,000; and (2) Defendants also must make up any shortfall due to a codefendant's insolvency, which comprises up to 50% of their own liability. The far larger exception is that knowing violators continue to be jointly and severally liable for the entire judgment. The provision also makes explicit defendants' right to seek contribution from other violators, whether or not they have been named as defendants.

NOTES

1. *Proportionate liability for control persons.* Prior to the Private Securities Litigation Reform Act of 1995, control persons found liable under § 20(a) were joint and severally liable for any damages with the primary violators of an Exchange Act provision (such as § 10(b) and Rule 10b–5). Section 20(a) itself states that the control person is liable "joint and severally with and to the same extent" as the controlled primary violator. With the enactment of the PSLRA, at least one court has applied proportionate liability regime of the PSLRA to control persons liable under § 20(a). *Laperriere v. Vesta Ins. Group, Inc.*, 526 F.3d 715, 727–28 (11th Cir. 2008).

HYPOTHETICAL ELEVEN

Return to DigitalBase's reluctant disclosure in its 10–Q that the introduction of the GigaBase product will be delayed at least two years and its subsequent restatement of revenues of the prior year. Suppose that prior to these disclosures, Hillary (the CEO) engaged in insider trading, selling off ten million DigitalBase shares into the market at the pre-disclosure market price. Suppose that the out-of-pocket measure of damages for the nondisclosure is equal to $100 million. Moreover, assume that the defendants at trial are DigitalBase, Hillary, and Arthur & Young, the auditor.

1. If you were a member of the jury, how would you assign relative culpability among DigitalBase, Hillary, and Arthur & Young?

2. Assume that DigitalBase has gone bankrupt (with no remaining assets) by the time plaintiffs obtain a judgment. Hillary has left the country for an untraceable Caribbean locale, leaving Arthur & Young as the lone remaining solvent defendant. Given your assignment of culpability above, how much money can the plaintiffs recover from Arthur & Young?

3. Suppose that you, a juror, know about DigitalBase's bankrupt status and the absence of Hillary while making relative culpability assessments. How does this affect your assessment? *See* Exchange Act § 21D(f)(6).

VI. TRANSNATIONAL SECURITIES FRAUD

When Congress enacted the Exchange Act in 1934, most securities transactions took place solely within one country. Investors in New Jersey wanting to buy shares in General Motors could contact a stockbroker who would execute the transaction on the New York Stock Exchange. Today, of course, transnational securities transactions occur routinely. Many U.S. issuers list their shares for trading on foreign securities exchanges. Investors around the world may buy and sell shares in these companies on either foreign or United States exchanges.

Many foreign issuers list their shares for trading inside the U.S. Rather than have their securities, which are typically denominated in a foreign currency, trade directly in U.S. markets, foreign issuers typically will sponsor an American Depository Receipt (ADR). An ADR is a negotiable certificate that represents ownership of the shares of a foreign issuer that do not directly trade inside the United States. ADRs may be bought and sold on a U.S. securities exchange just like regular common stock. ADRs that are listed for trading on a securities exchange are termed Level II ADRs. In contrast, Level I ADRs are ADRs that are traded off-exchange in the over-the-counter market (Level I ADRs can either be formally sponsored by the foreign issuer or unsponsored). Level III ADRs are ADRs that an issuer sells in a public offering in the United States. Typically a U.S. depository institution, such as the Bank of New York, will issue and operate an ADR facility. Each ADR represents a fixed number of foreign shares. For example one ADR might represent one share common stock of the foreign issuer. While the ADR is outstanding, the depository institution will hold the underlying foreign shares. Unlike the foreign shares, the ADRs will be priced in U.S. dollars. Among other things, the depository bank will ensure that dividends from the foreign issuer are converted into U.S. dollars.

Investors interested in purchasing the shares of a foreign issuer may do so either through the purchase of ADRs (assuming ADRs have been issued for the particular foreign issuer) or the purchase of the foreign issuer's securities directly (typically on a foreign securities exchange). How far should Rule 10b–5 extend to cover material misstatements and omissions that involve a transnational securities transaction? If a foreign investor purchases a foreign issuer's securities on a foreign securities exchange, should Rule 10b–5 apply? For many years, the Second Circuit led the way in answering this question. In a series of cases, the Second Circuit devised two tests to determine when to apply Rule 10b–5 extraterritorially: the conduct and effects tests. The conduct test announced in *Leasco Data Processing Equipment Corp. v. Maxwell*, 468 F.2d 1326 (2d Cir. 1972), focused on whether enough fraudulent behavior took place in the United States to invoke Rule 10b–5, even when the securities transactions were executed outside the United States. The conduct test proved uncertain in application; activities that were merely preparatory, and thus insufficient to trigger Rule 10b–5's coverage, were murky.

The second test, the effects test, was established in *Schoenbaum v. Firstbrook*, 405 F.2d 200, 206 (2d Cir. 1968). The Second Circuit in *Schoenbaum* considered whether Rule 10b–5 reached the sale of undervalued stock in Canada that depressed the price of the issuer's stock trading on a U.S. securities exchange. The Second Circuit held that: "[T]he district court has subject matter jurisdiction over violations of the Securities Exchange Act although the transactions which are alleged to violate the Act take place outside the United States, at least when the transactions involve stock registered and listed on a national securities exchange, and are detrimental to the interests of American investors."

The world securities markets are now interlinked, which put considerable stress on the Second Circuit's effects test. If a French phone manufacturer in Paris makes a misleading statement in Paris, the statement will have an effect on the stock of domestic phone manufacturers trading on the NYSE. Does the effects test allow investors to sue the French phone manufacturer? For many courts the answer was no—not all effects satisfy *Schoenbaum* to trigger the effects test. But if disclosures that have an effect on "American security prices" (as in the example of the French phone manufacturer) fail to trigger the effects test, what is the necessary trigger? As with the conduct test, the effects test left considerable uncertainty.

Transnational securities transactions vary on three dimensions: (1) the nationality of the issuer, (2) the nationality of the investors, particularly the investors alleging a violation of Rule 10b–5, and (3) the location where a transaction is executed. Transactions that combine a foreign aspect for all three of these dimensions—a foreign issuer, foreign investor, and a foreign location of transaction—are commonly referred to as "f-cubed" litigation. Securities class actions that involved an f-cubed fact pattern posed the greatest challenge to those seeking to extend the reach of Rule 10b–5 outside the United States. Such transactions had little effect on U.S. markets, and typically minimal conduct taking place within the United States. The Supreme Court finally addressed the issue of Rule 10b–5's extraterritorial reach—and the status of the conducts and effects test—in the following case.

Morrison v. National Australia Bank Ltd.

561 U.S. 247 (2010).

■ SCALIA, J.

We decide whether § 10(b) of the Securities Exchange Act of 1934 provides a cause of action to foreign plaintiffs suing foreign and American defendants for misconduct in connection with securities traded on foreign exchanges.

I

Respondent National Australia Bank Limited was, during the relevant time, the largest bank in Australia. Its Ordinary Shares-what in America would be called "common stock"-are traded on the Australian Stock Exchange Limited and on other foreign securities exchanges, but not on any exchange in the United States. There are listed on the New York Stock Exchange, however, National's American Depositary Receipts (ADRs), which represent the right to receive a specified number of National's Ordinary Shares.

The complaint alleges the following facts, which we accept as true. In February 1998, National bought respondent HomeSide Lending, Inc., a mortgage servicing company headquartered in Florida. HomeSide's business was to receive fees for servicing mortgages (essentially the administrative tasks associated with collecting mortgage payments). The rights to receive those fees, so-called mortgage-servicing rights, can provide a valuable income stream. How valuable each of the rights is depends, in part, on the likelihood that the mortgage to which it applies will be fully repaid before it is due, terminating the need for servicing. HomeSide calculated the present value of its mortgage-servicing rights by using valuation models designed to take this likelihood into account. It recorded the value of its assets, and the numbers appeared in National's financial statements.

From 1998 until 2001, National's annual reports and other public documents touted the success of HomeSide's business. . . . But on July

5, 2001, National announced that it was writing down the value of HomeSide's assets by $450 million; and then again on September 3, by another $1.75 billion. The prices of both Ordinary Shares and ADRs slumped. . . . According to the complaint, . . . HomeSide . . . had manipulated HomeSide's financial models to make the rates of early repayment unrealistically low in order to cause the mortgage-servicing rights to appear more valuable than they really were. . . .

As relevant here, petitioners Russell Leslie Owen and Brian and Geraldine Silverlock, all Australians, purchased National's Ordinary Shares in 2000 and 2001, before the write-downs.[1] They sued National, HomeSide . . . and the three HomeSide executives in the United States District Court for the Southern District of New York for alleged violations of §§ 10(b) and 20(a) of the Securities and Exchange Act of 1934. They sought to represent a class of foreign purchasers of National's Ordinary Shares during a specified period up to the September write-down.

Respondents moved to dismiss for lack of subject-matter jurisdiction under Federal Rule of Civil Procedure 12(b)(1) and for failure to state a claim under Rule 12(b)(6). The District Court granted the motion on the former ground, finding no jurisdiction because the acts in this country were, "at most, a link in the chain of an alleged overall securities fraud scheme that culminated abroad." The Court of Appeals for the Second Circuit affirmed on similar grounds. . . .

II

Before addressing the question presented, we must correct a threshold error in the Second Circuit's analysis. It considered the extraterritorial reach of § 10(b) to raise a question of subject-matter jurisdiction, wherefore it affirmed the District Court's dismissal under Rule 12(b)(1). . . .

But to ask what conduct § 10(b) reaches is to ask what conduct § 10(b) prohibits, which is a merits question. Subject-matter jurisdiction, by contrast, "refers to a tribunal's power to hear a case." It presents an issue quite separate from the question whether the allegations the plaintiff makes entitle him to relief. The District Court here had jurisdiction . . . to adjudicate the question whether § 10(b) applies to National's conduct.

III

A

It is a "longstanding principle of American law 'that legislation of Congress, unless a contrary intent appears, is meant to apply only within the territorial jurisdiction of the United States.' " This principle represents a canon of construction, or a presumption about a statute's meaning, rather than a limit upon Congress's power to legislate. It rests on the perception that Congress ordinarily legislates with respect to domestic, not foreign matters. . . .

Despite this principle of interpretation, long and often recited in our opinions, the Second Circuit believed that, because the Exchange Act is silent as to the extraterritorial application of § 10(b), it was left to

---

[1] Robert Morrison, an American investor in National's ADRs, also brought suit, but his claims were dismissed by the District Court because he failed to allege damages. . . .

the court to "discern" whether Congress would have wanted the statute to apply. . . .

The Second Circuit . . . established that application of § 10(b) could be premised upon either some effect on American securities markets or investors or significant conduct in the United States. It later formalized these two applications into (1) an "effects test," "whether the wrongful conduct had a substantial effect in the United States or upon United States citizens," and (2) a "conduct test," "whether the wrongful conduct occurred in the United States." These became the north star of the Second Circuit's § 10(b) jurisprudence, pointing the way to what Congress would have wished. . . .

As they developed, these tests were not easy to administer. The conduct test was held to apply differently depending on whether the harmed investors were Americans or foreigners: When the alleged damages consisted of losses to American investors abroad, it was enough that acts "of material importance" performed in the United States "significantly contributed" to that result; whereas those acts must have "directly caused" the result when losses to foreigners abroad were at issue. And "merely preparatory activities in the United States" did not suffice "to trigger application of the securities laws for injury to foreigners located abroad." This required the court to distinguish between mere preparation and using the United States as a "base" for fraudulent activities in other countries. But merely satisfying the conduct test was sometimes insufficient without " 'some additional factor tipping the scales' " in favor of the application of American law. District courts have noted the difficulty of applying such vague formulations. There is no more damning indictment of the "conduct" and "effects" tests than the Second Circuit's own declaration that "the presence or absence of any single factor which was considered significant in other cases . . . is not necessarily dispositive in future cases."

* * *

Commentators have criticized the unpredictable and inconsistent application of § 10(b) to transnational cases. Some have challenged the premise underlying the Courts of Appeals' approach, namely that Congress did not consider the extraterritorial application of § 10(b) (thereby leaving it open to the courts, supposedly, to determine what Congress would have wanted). Others, more fundamentally, have noted that using congressional silence as a justification for judge-made rules violates the traditional principle that silence means no extraterritorial application.

The criticisms seem to us justified. The results of judicial-speculation-made-law-divining what Congress would have wanted if it had thought of the situation before the court-demonstrate the wisdom of the presumption against extraterritoriality. Rather than guess anew in each case, we apply the presumption in all cases, preserving a stable background against which Congress can legislate with predictable effects.

B

Rule 10b–5, the regulation under which petitioners have brought suit, was promulgated under § 10(b), and "does not extend beyond conduct encompassed by § 10(b)'s prohibition." Therefore, if § 10(b) is not extraterritorial, neither is Rule 10b–5.

On its face, § 10(b) contains nothing to suggest it applies abroad:

"It shall be unlawful for any person, directly or indirectly, by the use of any means or instrumentality of interstate commerce or of the mails, or of any facility of any national securities exchange . . . [t]o use or employ, in connection with the purchase or sale of any security registered on a national securities exchange or any security not so registered, . . . any manipulative or deceptive device or contrivance in contravention of such rules and regulations as the [Securities and Exchange] Commission may prescribe. . . ."

Petitioners and the Solicitor General contend, however, that three things indicate that § 10(b) or the Exchange Act in general has at least some extraterritorial application.

First, they point to the definition of "interstate commerce," a term used in § 10(b), which includes "trade, commerce, transportation, or communication . . . between any foreign country and any State." But "we have repeatedly held that even statutes that contain broad language in their definitions of 'commerce' that expressly refer to 'foreign commerce' do not apply abroad." The general reference to foreign commerce in the definition of "interstate commerce" does not defeat the presumption against extraterritoriality.[7]

Petitioners and the Solicitor General next point out that Congress, in describing the purposes of the Exchange Act, observed that the "prices established and offered in such transactions are generally disseminated and quoted throughout the United States and foreign countries." [§ 2(2) of the Exchange Act]. The antecedent of "such transactions," however, is found in the first sentence of the section, which declares that "transactions in securities as commonly conducted upon securities exchanges and over-the-counter markets are affected with a national public interest." [§ 2 of the Exchange Act]. Nothing suggests that this national public interest pertains to transactions conducted upon foreign exchanges and markets. The fleeting reference to the dissemination and quotation abroad of the prices of securities traded in domestic exchanges and markets cannot overcome the presumption against extraterritoriality.

Finally, there is § 30(b) of the Exchange Act which does mention the Act's extraterritorial application: "The provisions of [the Exchange Act] or of any rule or regulation thereunder shall not apply to any person insofar as he transacts a business in securities without the

---

[7]   This conclusion does not render meaningless the inclusion of "trade, commerce, transportation, or communication . . . between any foreign country and any State" in the definition of "interstate commerce." Exchange Act § 3(a)(17). For example, an issuer based abroad, whose executives approve the publication in the United States of misleading information affecting the price of the issuer's securities traded on the New York Stock Exchange, probably will make use of some instrumentality of "communication . . . between [a] foreign country and [a] State."

jurisdiction of the United States," unless he does so in violation of regulations promulgated by the Securities and Exchange Commission "to prevent . . . evasion of [the Act]." (The parties have pointed us to no regulation promulgated pursuant to § 30(b).) The Solicitor General argues that "[this] exemption would have no function if the Act did not apply in the first instance to securities transactions that occur abroad."

We are not convinced. In the first place, it would be odd for Congress to indicate the extraterritorial application of the whole Exchange Act by means of a provision imposing a condition precedent to its application abroad. And if the whole Act applied abroad, why would the Commission's enabling regulations be limited to those preventing "evasion" of the Act, rather than all those preventing "violation"? The provision seems to us directed at actions abroad that might conceal a domestic violation, or might cause what would otherwise be a domestic violation to escape on a technicality. At most, the Solicitor General's proposed inference is possible; but possible interpretations of statutory language do not override the presumption against extraterritoriality.

The Solicitor General also fails to account for § 30(a), which reads in relevant part as follows:

> "It shall be unlawful for any broker or dealer . . . to make use of the mails or of any means or instrumentality of interstate commerce for the purpose of effecting on an exchange not within or subject to the jurisdiction of the United States, any transaction in any security the issuer of which is a resident of, or is organized under the laws of, or has its principal place of business in, a place within or subject to the jurisdiction of the United States, in contravention of such rules and regulations as the Commission may prescribe. . . ."

Subsection 30(a) contains what § 10(b) lacks: a clear statement of extraterritorial effect. Its explicit provision for a specific extraterritorial application would be quite superfluous if the rest of the Exchange Act already applied to transactions on foreign exchanges-and its limitation of that application to securities of domestic issuers would be inoperative. Even if that were not true, when a statute provides for some extraterritorial application, the presumption against extraterritoriality operates to limit that provision to its terms. No one claims that § 30(a) applies here. . . .

In short, there is no affirmative indication in the Exchange Act that § 10(b) applies extraterritorially, and we therefore conclude that it does not.

IV

A

Petitioners argue that the conclusion that § 10(b) does not apply extraterritorially does not resolve this case. They contend that they seek no more than domestic application anyway, since Florida is where HomeSide and its senior executives engaged in the deceptive conduct of manipulating HomeSide's financial models; their complaint also alleged that Race and Hughes made misleading public statements there. This is less an answer to the presumption against extraterritorial application than it is an assertion-a quite valid assertion-that that presumption here (as often) is not self-evidently dispositive, but its application requires further analysis. For it is a rare case of prohibited extraterritorial application that lacks all contact with the territory of the United States. But the presumption against extraterritorial application would be a craven watchdog indeed if it retreated to its kennel whenever some domestic activity is involved in the case. . . .

[W]e think that the focus of the Exchange Act is not upon the place where the deception originated, but upon purchases and sales of securities in the United States. Section 10(b) does not punish deceptive conduct, but only deceptive conduct "in connection with the purchase or sale of any security registered on a national securities exchange or any security not so registered." Those purchase-and-sale transactions are the objects of the statute's solicitude. It is those transactions that the statute seeks to "regulate"; it is parties or prospective parties to those transactions that the statute seeks to "protec[t]". And it is in our view only transactions in securities listed on domestic exchanges, and domestic transactions in other securities, to which § 10(b) applies. . . .

The primacy of the domestic exchange is suggested by the very prologue of the Exchange Act, which sets forth as its object "[t]o provide for the regulation of securities exchanges . . . operating in interstate and foreign commerce and through the mails, to prevent inequitable and unfair practices on such exchanges. . . ." We know of no one who thought that the Act was intended to "regulat[e]" foreign securities exchanges-or indeed who even believed that under established principles of international law Congress had the power to do so. . . .

With regard to securities not registered on domestic exchanges, the exclusive focus on domestic purchases and sales is strongly confirmed by § 30(a) and (b), discussed earlier. The former extends the normal scope of the Exchange Act's prohibitions to acts effecting, in violation of rules prescribed by the Commission, a "transaction" in a United States security "on an exchange not within or subject to the jurisdiction of the United States." And the latter specifies that the Act does not apply to "any person insofar as he transacts a business in securities without the jurisdiction of the United States," unless he does so in violation of regulations promulgated by the Commission "to prevent evasion [of the Act]." Under both provisions it is the foreign location of the transaction that establishes (or reflects the presumption of) the Act's inapplicability, absent regulations by the Commission.

* * *

Finally, we reject the notion that the Exchange Act reaches conduct in this country affecting exchanges or transactions abroad . . . The probability of incompatibility with the applicable laws of other countries is so obvious that if Congress intended such foreign application "it would have addressed the subject of conflicts with foreign laws and procedures." Like the United States, foreign countries regulate their domestic securities exchanges and securities transactions occurring within their territorial jurisdiction. And the regulation of other countries often differs from ours as to what constitutes fraud, what disclosures must be made, what damages are recoverable, what discovery is available in litigation, what individual actions may be joined in a single suit, what attorney's fees are recoverable, and many other matters. The Commonwealth of Australia, the United Kingdom of

Great Britain and Northern Ireland, and the Republic of France have filed amicus briefs in this case. . . . They all complain of the interference with foreign securities regulation that application of § 10(b) abroad would produce, and urge the adoption of a clear test that will avoid that consequence. The transactional test we have adopted-whether the purchase or sale is made in the United States, or involves a security listed on a domestic exchange-meets that requirement.

B

The Solicitor General suggests a different test, which petitioners also endorse: "[A] transnational securities fraud violates [§] 10(b) when the fraud involves significant conduct in the United States that is material to the fraud's success." Neither the Solicitor General nor petitioners provide any textual support for this test. The Solicitor General sets forth a number of purposes such a test would serve: achieving a high standard of business ethics in the securities industry, ensuring honest securities markets and thereby promoting investor confidence, and preventing the United States from becoming a "Barbary Coast" for malefactors perpetrating frauds in foreign markets. But it provides no textual support for the last of these purposes, or for the first two as applied to the foreign securities industry and securities markets abroad. It is our function to give the statute the effect its language suggests, however modest that may be; not to extend it to admirable purposes it might be used to achieve.

If, moreover, one is to be attracted by the desirable consequences of the "significant and material conduct" test, one should also be repulsed by its adverse consequences. While there is no reason to believe that the United States has become the Barbary Coast for those perpetrating frauds on foreign securities markets, some fear that it has become the Shangri-La of class-action litigation for lawyers representing those allegedly cheated in foreign securities markets. . . .

* * *

Section 10(b) reaches the use of a manipulative or deceptive device or contrivance only in connection with the purchase or sale of a security listed on an American stock exchange, and the purchase or sale of any other security in the United States. This case involves no securities listed on a domestic exchange, and all aspects of the purchases complained of by those petitioners who still have live claims occurred outside the United States. Petitioners have therefore failed to state a claim on which relief can be granted. We affirm the dismissal of petitioners' complaint on this ground.

* * *

NOTES

1.   *U.S. investors trading abroad.* Although the facts of *Morrison* involve foreign purchasers buying the shares of a foreign issuer on a foreign exchange, the Court's bright-line rule focusing on the location of transaction narrows Rule 10b–5 further still. In particular, *Morrison* appears to exclude from the reach of § 10(b) and Rule 10b–5 even U.S. investors who transact in the securities of a U.S. issuer where the

transaction is consummated outside of the United States. Issuer nationality, investor nationality, and investor location are irrelevant under the *Morrison* test. Instead, what matters is the location where the securities transaction actually occurs. This territorial approach mirrors the territorial approach that the SEC takes in Regulation S with respect to § 5 of the Securities Act (discussed in Chapter 9).

2. *What is a "domestic" transaction?* When securities are bought or sold in a U.S. securities exchange, *Morrison* is clear that such transactions are domestic transactions. But what about securities that are bought or sold elsewhere? When are such transactions considered domestic? The Second Circuit in *Absolute Activist Value Master Fund Ltd. v. Ficeto*, 677 F.3d 60, 62 (2d. Cir. 2012) held that a domestic transaction for purposes of Section 10(b) and Rule 10b–5 occurs when a person incurs "irrevocable liability" or "title was transferred within the United States. " Does placing an order with a U.S.-based broker result in "irrevocable liability" within the U.S. even for securities that are purchased through a foreign securities exchange? The Second Circuit in *City of Pontiac Policemen's and Firemen's Retirement System v. UBS AG*, 725 F.3d 173 (2nd Cir. 2014) stated that purchasing securities on a foreign exchange is not domestic merely because an investor placed the purchase order with a broker located in the U.S.

3. *Dual-listed foreign issuers.* The *Morrison* Court wrote: "it is in our view only transactions in securities listed on domestic exchanges, and domestic transactions in other securities, to which § 10(b) applies." Did the Court mean securities listed on a domestic exchange only to the extent the securities are in fact traded on that domestic exchange? Or did the Court mean that once an issuer lists its securities on a domestic exchange then all transactions in the issuer's listed securities—even those that take place on foreign exchanges—are within the reach of § 10(b)? Lower courts have opted for the former. According to the court in *In re Alstom SA Sec. Litig.*, 741 F.Supp.2d 469 (S.D.N.Y. 2010): "Though isolated clauses of the opinion may be read as requiring only that a security be 'listed' on a domestic exchange for its purchase anywhere in the world to be cognizable under the federal securities laws, those excerpts read in total context compel the opposite result. For example, a crucial paragraph of *Morrison* concludes that 'it is in our view only transactions in securities listed on domestic exchanges, and domestic transactions in other securities, to which § 10(b) applies.' But the rest of the paragraph reveals a focus on where the securities transaction actually occurs. . . ."

4. *The Dodd-Frank Act.* Congress responded to *Morrison* with § 929P(b) of Dodd-Frank. That provision amends § 27 of the Exchange Act to give district courts "jurisdiction" over actions or proceedings brought by the SEC alleging a violation of the antifraud provisions of the Exchange Act involving either "conduct within the United States that constitutes significant steps in furtherance of the violation" or "conduct occurring outside the United States that has a foreseeable substantial effect within the United States." Section 929P(b) provides a similar conduct and effects test for SEC actions seeking to enforce § 17(a) of the Securities Act. Congress did not overturn *Morrison* for private § 10(b) and Rule 10b–5 actions. Instead, § 929Y of Dodd-Frank requires the SEC to solicit public comment and conduct a study to determine the extent to which private rights of action under the antifraud provisions of the Exchange Act should extend to extraterritorial transactions where there is conduct or effects within the United States.

QUESTIONS

1. Consider a transaction that does not take place on an organized securities exchange. Institutional investors located in the United States use an alternative trading system (ATS) to execute their transactions in the securities of an issuer listed for trading on the New York Stock Exchange. Suppose the ATS is physically located in the Cayman Islands and orders are accordingly matched and executed there. Do the transactions take place inside or outside the U.S.?

CHAPTER 6

INSIDER TRADING

Rules and Statutes

—Sections 10(b), 16, 20, 20A and 21A of the Exchange Act

—Rules 10b–5, 10b5–1, 10b5–2, 10b–18, 14e–3, 16a–1, 16a–2, 16a–3, 16a–4, 16b–3, 16b–6 of the Exchange Act

MOTIVATING HYPOTHETICAL

Primary World is an "expert network" firm that cultivates relationships with insiders at numerous publicly-traded high technology firms. Primary World passes what it calls "valuable insights" from these insiders to its clientele of large hedge funds (in return for a handsome fee from the hedge funds). In fact, the "valuable insights" consist of material, non-public information concerning earnings, earnings forecasts, and upcoming acquisition plans for many of the high technology firms including Amtel, a designer of computer microprocessors. Raj, a hedge fund manager, is a client of Primary World. On repeated occasions, he used information from Primary World to trade the stock of Amtel, earning significant profits on the trades. At least once, Raj avoided significant losses—selling over one million shares of Amtel right before Amtel announced a 20% drop in its earnings.

I. ECONOMICS OF INSIDER TRADING

"Insider" trading is something of a misnomer. The modern law of insider trading addresses not only trading by conventional insiders—corporate officers and directors—but also outsiders who have been given access to confidential information affecting the value of a corporation's securities. The most conspicuous members of this group include accountants, consultants, investment bankers, and lawyers. More controversially, prohibitions against insider trading now reach trading on confidential information not only in the securities of one's employer or principal, but also the securities of other companies. For example, an executive of Coca-Cola who uses secret information about a new Coke product to sell short Pepsi-Cola stock, anticipating that Pepsi would be at a competitive disadvantage in the face of Coke's blockbuster new product, would be guilty of insider trading (unless he disclosed to Coca-Cola's board his intention to trade Pepsi stock). We can therefore view modern insider trading doctrine as more generally governing which trading advantages are permissible in the securities markets. That doctrine is bolstered by Regulation FD (discussed in Chapter 4), which prohibits companies from providing non-public information to certain categories of traders.

Why prohibit insider trading? As we learned in Chapter 1, information is the lifeblood of securities markets. Insider trading is the starkest example of the profit opportunities afforded by information. Access to material information that other investors lack is the path to (relatively) risk-free profits. This fact, however, merely tells us that some investors will do better than others, that is, that insider trading will lead to transfers of wealth among investors. Why should society spend its resources deterring such transfers? Don't we have better things to worry about?

The traditional justification offered for prohibitions against insider trading is fairness: rules against insider trading protect integrity and public confidence in the stock market. There will inevitably be some information that is withheld from outsiders because companies have a variety of reasons for keeping information confidential, such as not tipping their hands to competitors. Insiders, of course, will have access to this information in the course of doing their jobs.

How does informed insider trading in the secondary markets influence outsiders? Imagine a world without insider trading prohibitions. In that world, outsiders do not know whether the share price accurately reflects the company's future prospects, but they do know that they are going to be net losers when they trade with insiders. Insider traders will only buy when they know that the stock price is too low, and they will only sell when they know the stock price is too high. Therefore, anytime an outsider trades with an insider, the outsider knows that the insider trader is taking advantage of him/her. To avoid trading losses, uninformed traders would prefer to trade only with other (equally ignorant) uninformed traders. Mispricing is inevitable (absent a requirement that the firm disclose all material information instantly), but gains and losses should average out when trading occurs between equally ignorant outsiders. In an impersonal market, however, outsiders do not know when they are trading with an insider, so insider trading imposes a transaction cost on all trading. The level of insider trading, moreover, is not fixed. Without an insider trading prohibition, the amount of insider trading as a percentage of total trading volume likely exceeds that in markets where it is prohibited (if the prohibition is enforced.)

Even if an outsider is lucky enough to avoid trading with a better-informed outsider, they cannot avoid the greater transaction costs created by insider trading. The transaction cost of insider trading is incorporated in the price of *all* trading. Market makers, like outsiders, know that they are at a disadvantage when trading with insiders, and like outsiders, they cannot know when they are trading with an insider. In order to compensate for the losses suffered by trading with an insider, market makers will increase the bid-ask spread. For example, instead of buying at $10.05 and selling at $10.10, market makers buy at $10.00 and sell at $10.15. Alternatively, they may reduce the number of shares ("depth") that they are willing to buy or sell at a quoted price. This increase in the bid-ask spread and decline in depth increases transaction costs for investors, making them less likely to buy and sell. The risk of dealing with insider traders is magnified in the options market, a favorite haven for insider traders because of the leverage it provides to the value of their information. Insider trading makes options more expensive to buy and sell, thereby further impairing liquidity.

How does insider trading affect corporate issuers? Investors are reluctant to play in what they perceive to be a rigged game. At a minimum, they must be compensated for bearing the risk that the game is fixed. Because insider trading reduces the returns from investing in the stock market, investors will discount the amount that they are willing to pay for shares to reflect the risk of insider trading. Corporations pay the price for this discounting because they receive less when they sell shares to the public. Thus, insider trading prohibitions—if effective—reduce the discount demanded by investors and the cost of capital for issuers.

Should we care about the loss in liquidity, greater bid-ask spread, and greater stock price discounts that stem from insider trading? The public confidence argument flies in the face of very high levels of investor participation in the U.S. markets even before insider trading became the subject of vigorous enforcement, starting in the 1960s. Moreover, even if insiders are prohibited from trading, the informational playing field is far from level. Not all outside investors are the same. Sophisticated, institutional investors enjoy an information advantage over most individual investors. Any informational advantage, such as one produced by astute research or the fortuitous discovery of a confidential document carelessly left on the subway, can produce a trading advantage for the holder of the information and the resulting impairment of liquidity outlined above. The securities markets are treacherous waters for uninformed investors even without the presence of insider traders.

As you read the materials in this chapter, consider the relative costs of insider trading and informed outsider trading. Are both forms of informational advantages in the secondary markets problematic? Advantages that society should prohibit? With civil sanctions? With criminal sanctions? Also consider how well the insider trading doctrine, as developed by the courts and the SEC, matches the problem of information asymmetry in the securities markets. As you will discover in reading the cases, the path of the law is seldom driven by economic analysis, and insider trading doctrine is no exception.

II.   INSIDER TRADING AT COMMON LAW

Prior to the passage of the securities laws, the primary legal remedy for insider trading was common law fraud. As you read the pre-Exchange Act case below, think about the limits of the common law rule identified by the Supreme Court. What sort of informational asymmetries are not covered by the rule? Is the law of deceit the right place to look for a prohibition against insider trading? What are the alternatives?

Strong v. Repide

213 U.S. 419 (1909).

■ PECKHAM, J.

This action . . . was brought by the plaintiff Mrs. Strong, as the owner of 800 shares of the capital stock of the Philippine Sugar Estates Development Company, Limited . . . to recover such shares from defendant (who was already the owner of 30,400 of the 42,030 shares issued by the company) on the ground that . . . defendant fraudulently concealed from plaintiff's agent, one F. Stuart Jones, facts affecting the value of the stock. . . .

In addition to his ownership of almost three fourths of the shares of the stock of the company, the defendant was one of the five directors of the company, and was elected by the board the agent and administrator general of such company, "with exclusive intervention in the management" of its general business.

* * *

[The Philippine Sugar Estates Development Company owned property in the Philippines known as the Dominican lands, and they comprised nearly one half the value of all the "friar" lands. The Philippine government made an offer to buy all of the friar lands for approximately $6 million in gold. After some negotiation with the various owners of the friar lands, the offer was increased to approximately $7.5 million.]

All the owners of all these friar lands, with the exception of the defendant, who represented his company, were willing and anxious to accept this offer and to convey the lands to the government at that price. He alone held out for a better offer while all the other owners were endeavoring to persuade him to accept the offer of the government. . . . [T]he contract for the sale was finally signed by the defendant as attorney in fact for his company, December 21, 1903. The defendant, of course, as the negotiations progressed, knew that the decision of the question lay with him, and that if he should decide to accept the last offer of the government, his decision would be the decision of his company, as he owned three fourths of its shares, and the negotiations would then go through as all the owners of the balance of the land desired it. If the sale should not be consummated, and things should remain as they were, the defendant also knew that the value of the lands and of the shares in the company would be almost nothing. . . .

While this state of things existed, and before the final offer had been made by the governor, the defendant, although still holding out for a higher price for the lands, took steps, about the middle or latter part of September, 1903, to purchase the 800 shares of stock in his company owned by Mrs. Strong, which he knew were in the possession of F. Stuart Jones, as her agent. The defendant, having decided to obtain these shares, instead of seeing Jones, who had an office next door, employed one Kauffman . . . and Kauffman employed a Mr. Sloan, a broker, who had an office some distance away, to purchase the stock for him, and told Sloan that the stock was for a member of his wife's family. Sloan communicated with the husband of Mrs. Strong, and asked if she desired to sell her stock. The husband referred him to Mr. Jones for consultation, who had the stock in his possession. Sloan did not know who wanted to buy the shares, nor did Jones when he was spoken to. Jones would not have sold at the price he did had he known it was the defendant who was purchasing, because, as he said, it would show increased value, as the defendant would not be likely to purchase more stock unless the price was going up. As the articles of incorporation . . . required a resolution of the general meeting of stockholders for the purpose of selling more than one hacienda, and as no such general meeting had been called at the time of the sale of the stock, Mr. Jones might well have supposed there was no immediate prospect of a sale of the lands being made, while, at the same time, defendant had knowledge of the probabilities thereof, which he had acquired by his conduct of the negotiations for their sale, as agent of all the shareholders, and while acting specially for them and himself.

The result of the negotiations was that Jones, on or about October 10, 1903 . . . sold the 800 shares of stock for $16,000, Mexican currency, . . . about one tenth of the amount they became worth by the sale of the lands between two and three months thereafter. In all the negotiations in regard to the purchase of the stock from Mrs. Strong, through her agent Jones, not one word of the facts affecting the value of this stock was made known to plaintiff's agent by defendant, but, on the contrary, perfect silence was kept.

* * *

If the purchase of the stock by the defendant was obtained by reason of his fraud or deceit, . . . the sale cannot stand.

* * *

The question in this case . . . is whether, under the circumstances above set forth, it was the duty of the defendant, acting in good faith, to disclose to the agent of the plaintiff the facts bearing upon or which might affect the value of the stock.

If it were conceded, for the purpose of the argument, that the ordinary relations between directors and shareholders in a business corporation are not of such a fiduciary nature as to make it the duty of a director to disclose to a shareholder the general knowledge which he may possess regarding the value of the shares of the company before he purchases any from a shareholder, yet there are cases where, by reason of the special facts, such duty exists. . . . The case before us is of the same general character. On the other hand, there [are cases holding] that no relationship of a fiduciary nature exists between a director and a shareholder in a business corporation. . . . These cases involved only the bare relationship between director and shareholder. It is here sought to make defendant responsible for his actions, not alone and simply in his character as a director, but because, in consideration of all the existing circumstances above detailed, it became the duty of the defendant, acting in good faith, to state the facts before making the purchase. That the defendant was a director of the corporation is but one of the facts upon which the liability is asserted, the existence of all the others in addition making such a combination as rendered it the plain duty of the defendant to speak. He was not only a director, but he owned three fourths of the shares of its stock, and was, at the time of the purchase of the stock, administrator general of the company, with large powers, and engaged in the negotiations which finally led to the sale of the company's lands (together with all the other friar lands) to the government at a price which very greatly enhanced the value of the stock. . . . No one knew as well as he the probability of the sale of the lands to the government. No one knew as well as he the probable price that might be obtained on such sale. The lands were the only valuable asset owned by the company. Under these circumstances, and before the negotiations for the sale were completed, the defendant employs an agent to purchase the stock, and conceals from the plaintiff's agent his own identity and his knowledge of the state of the negotiations and their probable result, with which he was familiar as the agent of the shareholders, and much of which knowledge he obtained while acting as such agent, and by reason thereof.... Concealing his identity when procuring the purchase of the stock, by his agent, was in itself strong evidence of fraud on the part of the defendant. Why did he not ask Jones, who occupied an adjoining office, if he would sell? But, by concealing his identity, he could, by such means, the more easily avoid any questions relative to the negotiations for the sale of the lands and their probable result, and could also avoid any actual misrepresentations on that subject, which he evidently thought were necessary in his case to constitute a fraud.... The whole transaction gives conclusive evidence of the overwhelming influence defendant had in the course of the negotiations as owner of a majority of the stock and as agent for the other owners, and it is clear that the final consummation was in his hands at all times. If, under all these facts, he purchased the stock from the plaintiff, the law would indeed be impotent if the sale could not be set aside or the defendant cast in damages for his fraud....

[U]nder the circumstances detailed, there was a legal obligation on the part of the defendant to make these disclosures.

* * *

NOTES

1. *Exchange transactions.* In *Strong v. Repide*, the Supreme Court follows those courts adopting the "special facts" doctrine. The "special facts" found by the Court in *Strong* amount to active concealment of the defendant's identity, thereby depriving the plaintiff-shareholder of a basis for inquiring about the transaction and the company's prospects. The Court notes, however, that the courts were not unanimous in finding a duty under such circumstances.

There was a consensus at common law, however, that a corporate insider who traded in an impersonal market on the basis of confidential information did not defraud the shareholder with whom he had traded. In the leading case of *Goodwin v. Agassiz*, 283 Mass. 358, 186 N.E. 659 (1933), the Supreme Judicial Court of Massachusetts rejected a claim that an insider commits fraud when trading over a stock exchange on the basis of confidential information. In *Goodwin*, the plaintiff-shareholder sold his shares in a mining company to two of the company's insiders, its president and general manager (who were also directors). The insiders were aware of a geologist's theory that the land owned by the company might contain valuable copper deposits. They kept this information secret, however, in order to obtain options on surrounding land that might also contain copper. Knowing that the company's stock price would rise if the theory panned out, the insiders bought heavily in the company's shares. These purchases, done over the Boston Stock Exchange, were completely anonymous—the shareholders had no idea to whom they had sold.

The court rejected the plaintiff's claim of fraud. Although the court recognized that the directors of a corporation "stand in a relation of trust to the corporation and are bound to exercise the strictest good faith in respect to its property and business," it held that directors do not "occupy the position of trustee toward individual stockholders." Thus, there was "no fiduciary relation between them and the plaintiff in the matter of the sale of his stock." The court acknowledged that the result may have been different in a face-to-face transaction, but concluded that any such duty to shareholders did not carry over to an anonymous exchange transaction.

QUESTIONS

1. Reliance is an element of common law deceit, as well as private actions under Rule 10b–5. Do you think that there was reliance by Mrs. Strong or her agent, Jones? What if the transaction had taken place over the Manila Stock Exchange?

2. How would knowledge of the identity of the purchaser (Repide) have benefited Mrs. Strong in making her decision to sell or hold?

3. How would the result change in *Strong v. Repide* if Repide, as a director and managing agent, were aware that the company was unlikely to be able to sell the friar lands, but withheld the information from Mrs. Strong (an existing shareholder) when selling her additional shares (while actively concealing his identity)? What if an unrelated third party purchased shares from Repide?

HYPOTHETICAL ONE

Consider how the state common law of insider trading (as represented by *Strong v. Repide* and *Goodwin v. Agassiz*) would apply to the Primary World hypothetical. Recall that Primary World passes confidential information obtained from officers at public companies, including Amtel, to Raj the hedge fund manager. Raj pays Primary World a fee for Primary World's services. Suppose that Jack is the CEO of Amtel. Jack has confidential information that Amtel is planning an unsolicited tender offer for its rival ARM, Inc. at a significant premium. Jack expects the price of Amtel shares to fall upon announcement of the tender offer. Jack passes the tender offer information to Primary World and then Jack instructs his own broker to sell 50% of his holdings of two million Amtel shares. (Assume the sales were negotiated with a large institutional investor who owns no Amtel shares prior to the sales). Jack also has his broker purchase ARM options with the proceeds. After receiving the information on Amtel's tender offer plans from Primary World, Raj sells his Amtel shares to the same institutional investor. Upon the announcement of Amtel's unsolicited bid for ARM, Amtel's share price drops by 10% by the end of the trading day.

1. Has Jack violated the "special facts" doctrine by purchasing ARM options or by selling his Amtel shares?

2. Has Raj violated the "special facts" doctrine with his sale of Amtel shares?

3. Suppose that Jeffrey is an outside director on ARM's board. Jeffrey had no other business relationship with ARM. Jeffrey also knows of Amtel's impending tender offer for ARM and buys a large number of ARM shares over the New York Stock Exchange prior to the announcement of the offer. Has Jeffrey violated the special facts doctrine?

III. RULE 10b–5 AND THE CLASSICAL THEORY OF INSIDER TRADING

Fast forward to the 1930s: Congress adopted the Exchange Act in 1934, largely ignoring the topic of insider trading (with the limited exception of § 16, discussed below). The SEC, after also ignoring insider trading for the first twenty-five years of its history, eventually stepped into the void, arguing that insider trading violates the antifraud prohibition of Rule 10b–5.

As you go through the cases, consider the SEC's goal in prohibiting insider trading. Is it the source of information (i.e., coming from inside or outside the traded firms) that seems important? Or is it the identity of the person engaged in the trades (an insider versus an outsider)? Or are both the source and the identity of the trader irrelevant—should maintaining a "parity" of information across all traders in the market be the central goal? The following table captures the possibilities, based on the type of trader and the source of information:

	Insider Trader	Outsider Trader
Corporate (inside) Information	Core insider	?
Outside Information	?	?

"Insider trading" typically evokes situations involving corporate insiders trading on inside corporate information. When Jack, the CEO of Amtel, attempts to sell shares in Amtel based on inside information of Amtel's upcoming acquisition of ARM, Jack is trading as a "core insider." But what about other forms of informational advantages in the market, including trades based on so-called outside information (information not obtained from the company whose securities are being traded—the "traded firm")? When Jack trades ARM options, he is capitalizing on outside information from the perspective of ARM share and option holders. And what if a non-insider, say a tippee of an insider, trades based on inside corporate information? Should outsiders be liable as well? Should the tipping insider share that liability? Should the corporation bear the responsibility of ensuring that outsiders do not receive confidential corporate information?

A. CORE INSIDERS

The SEC first pursued its insider trading theory in administrative proceedings against securities professionals with access to inside information, beginning with *Cady, Roberts & Co.*, 40 S.E.C. 907 (1961), before pressing the theory in the courts against corporate executives, most notably in *SEC v. Texas Gulf Sulphur Co.*, 401 F.2d 833 (2d Cir. 1968) (en banc), cert. denied, 394 U.S. 976 (1969). The SEC and the Justice Department had little trouble persuading the activist Second Circuit to find an insider trading prohibition in § 10(b). *Texas Gulf Sulphur* sets forth the "equal access" theory of insider trading:

> The essence of the Rule is that anyone who, trading for his own account in the securities of a corporation has "access, directly

or indirectly, to information intended to be available only for a corporate purpose and not for the personal benefit of anyone" may not take "advantage of such information knowing it is unavailable to those with whom he is dealing," i.e., the investing public. . . . Insiders, as directors or management officers are, of course, by this Rule, precluded from so unfairly dealing, but the Rule is also applicable to one possessing the information who may not be strictly termed an "insider." . . .

The core of Rule 10b–5 is the implementation of the Congressional purpose that all investors should have equal access to the rewards of participation in securities transactions. It was the intent of Congress that all members of the investing public should be subject to identical market risks, which market risks include, of course the risk that one's evaluative capacity or one's capital available to put at risk may exceed another's capacity or capital. The insiders here were not trading on an equal footing with the outside investors.

On its face, *Texas Gulf Sulphur* prohibits not only core insiders, but also outsiders, from trading based on non-public, material corporate information.

	Insider Trader	**Outsider Trader**
Corporate (inside) Information	Core insider prohibited *(Texas Gulf Sulphur)*	Outsider prohibited *(Texas Gulf Sulphur)*
Outside Information	?	?

After its successes in the Second Circuit, the SEC turned its eye toward trades based on outside information. After all, unequal access and the trading advantages it confers can come from either inside or outside the firm. Non-public information that a state regulator is about to adopt a particular video poker machine for deployment throughout the state, for example, confers a large trading advantage for purchasers of the video poker machine company's stock even though this information comes from "outside" the company. By the time of the case below, the SEC was arguing for a general theory of equality of access to information, whether or not there was a duty owed to the person on the other side of the transaction or to the source of the information.

The SEC's efforts met with more skepticism in the Supreme Court than in the Second Circuit. Where does Justice Powell find the insider trading prohibition that he incorporates into Rule 10b–5 in *Chiarella*? How does Powell's theory differ from the SEC's? And how does *Chiarella* affect *Texas Gulf Sulphur's* prohibition against outsiders trading on corporate inside information?

Chiarella v. United States

445 U.S. 222 (1980).

■ POWELL, J.

The question in this case is whether a person who learns from the confidential documents of one corporation that it is planning an attempt to secure control of a second corporation violates § 10(b) of the

Securities Exchange Act of 1934 if he fails to disclose the impending takeover before trading in the target company's securities.

<h1 style="text-align:center">I</h1>

Petitioner is a printer by trade. In 1975 and 1976, he worked as a "markup man" in the New York composing room of Pandick Press, a financial printer. Among documents that petitioner handled were five announcements of corporate takeover bids. When these documents were delivered to the printer, the identities of the acquiring and target corporations were concealed by blank spaces or false names. The true names were sent to the printer on the night of the final printing.

The petitioner, however, was able to deduce the names of the target companies before the final printing from other information contained in the documents. Without disclosing his knowledge, petitioner purchased stock in the target companies and sold the shares immediately after the takeover attempts were made public. By this method, petitioner realized a gain of slightly more than $30,000. . . . Subsequently, the Securities and Exchange Commission began an investigation of his trading activities. In May 1977, petitioner entered into a consent decree with the Commission in which he agreed to return his profits to the sellers of the shares. On the same day, he was discharged by Pandick Press.

In January 1978, petitioner was indicted on 17 counts of violating § 10(b) . . . and SEC Rule 10b–5. . . . [H]e was . . . convicted on all counts.

The Court of Appeals for the Second Circuit affirmed petitioner's conviction. We granted certiorari and we now reverse.

<h1 style="text-align:center">II</h1>

* * *

This case concerns the legal effect of the petitioner's silence. The District Court's charge permitted the jury to convict the petitioner if it found that he willfully failed to inform sellers of target company securities that he knew of a forthcoming takeover bid that would make their shares more valuable. . . .

Although the starting point of our inquiry is the language of the statute, § 10(b) does not state whether silence may constitute a manipulative or deceptive device. Section 10(b) was designed as a catch-all clause to prevent fraudulent practices. But neither the legislative history nor the statute itself affords specific guidance for the resolution of this case. When Rule 10b–5 was promulgated in 1942, the SEC did not discuss the possibility that failure to provide information might run afoul of § 10(b).

The SEC took an important step in the development of § 10(b) when it held that a broker-dealer and his firm violated that section by selling securities on the basis of undisclosed information obtained from a director of the issuer corporation who was also a registered representative of the brokerage firm. In *Cady, Roberts & Co.*, 40 S.E.C. 907 (1961), the Commission decided that a corporate insider must abstain from trading in the shares of his corporation unless he has first disclosed all material inside information known to him. The obligation to disclose or abstain derives from—

> [a]n affirmative duty to disclose material information[, which] has been traditionally imposed on corporate "insiders", particular officers, directors, or controlling stockholders. We, and the courts have consistently held that insiders must disclose material facts which are known to them by virtue of their position but which are not known to persons with whom they deal and which, if known, would affect their investment judgment.

> The Commission emphasized that the duty arose from (i) the existence of a relationship affording access to inside information intended to be available only for a corporate purpose, and (ii) the unfairness of allowing a corporate insider to take advantage of that information by trading without disclosure.[8]

> That the relationship between a corporate insider and the stockholders of his corporation gives rise to a disclosure obligation is not a novel twist of the law. At common law, misrepresentation made for the purpose of inducing reliance upon the false statement is fraudulent. But one who fails to disclose material information prior to the consummation of a transaction commits fraud only when he is under a duty to do so. And the duty to disclose arises when one party has information "that the other [party] is entitled to know because of a fiduciary or other similar relation of trust and confidence between them."[9]

* * *

Thus, administrative and judicial interpretations have established that silence in connection with the purchase or sale of securities may operate as a fraud actionable under § 10(b) despite the absence of statutory language or legislative history specifically addressing the legality of nondisclosure. But such liability is premised upon a duty to disclose arising from a relationship of trust and confidence between parties to a transaction. Application of a duty to disclose prior to trading guarantees that corporate insiders, who have an obligation to place the shareholder's welfare before their own, will not benefit personally through fraudulent use of material, nonpublic information.

III

In this case, the petitioner was convicted of violating § 10(b) although he was not a corporate insider and he received no confidential information from the target company. Moreover, the "market

---

[8] In *Cady, Roberts*, the broker-dealer was liable under § 10(b) because it received nonpublic information from a corporate insider of the issuer. Since the insider could not use the information, neither could the partners in the brokerage firm with which he was associated. The transaction in *Cady, Roberts* involved sale of stock to persons who previously may not have been shareholders in the corporation. The Commission embraced the reasoning of Judge Learned Hand that "the director or officer assumed a fiduciary relation to the buyer by the very sale; for it would be a sorry distinction to allow him to use the advantage of his position to induce the buyer into the position of a beneficiary although he was forbidden to do so once the buyer had become one." Id., at 914, n. 23, quoting *Gratz v. Claughton*, 187 F.2d 46, 49 (CA2), cert. denied, 341 U.S. 920 (1951).

[9] Restatement (Second) of Torts § 551(2)(a) (1976).

information" upon which he relied did not concern the earning power or operations of the target company, but only the plans of the acquiring company. Petitioner's use of that information was not a fraud under § 10(b) unless he was subject to an affirmative duty to disclose it before trading. In this case, the jury instructions failed to specify any such duty. In effect, the trial court instructed the jury that petitioner owed a duty to everyone; to all sellers, indeed, to the market as a whole. The jury simply was told to decide whether petitioner used material, nonpublic information at a time when "he knew other people trading in the securities market did not have access to the same information."

* * *

This reasoning suffers from two defects. First not every instance of financial unfairness constitutes fraudulent activity under § 10(b). Second, the element required to make silence fraudulent—a duty to disclose—is absent in this case. No duty could arise from petitioner's relationship with the sellers of the target company's securities, for petitioner had no prior dealings with them. He was not their agent, he was not a fiduciary, he was not a person in whom the sellers had placed their trust and confidence. He was, in fact, a complete stranger who dealt with the sellers only through impersonal market transactions.

We cannot affirm petitioner's conviction without recognizing a general duty between all participants in market transactions to forgo actions based on material, nonpublic information. Formulation of such a broad duty, which departs radically from the established doctrine that duty arises from a specific relationship between two parties, should not be undertaken absent some explicit evidence of congressional intent. . . .

[N]o such evidence emerges from the language or legislative history of § 10(b). Moreover, neither the Congress nor the Commission ever has adopted a parity-of-information rule. Instead the problems caused by misuse of market information have been addressed by detailed and sophisticated regulation that recognizes when use of market information may not harm operation of the securities markets. For example, the Williams Act limits but does not completely prohibit a tender offeror's purchases of target corporation stock before public announcement of the offer. Congress' careful action in this and other areas contrasts, and is in some tension, with the broad rule of liability we are asked to adopt in this case.

* * *

We see no basis for applying such a new and different theory of liability in this case. . . . Section 10(b) is aptly described as a catchall provision, but what it catches must be fraud. When an allegation of fraud is based upon nondisclosure, there can be no fraud absent a duty to speak. We hold that a duty to disclose under § 10(b) does not arise from the mere possession of nonpublic market information. The contrary result is without support in the legislative history of § 10(b) and would be inconsistent with the careful plan that Congress has enacted for regulation of the securities markets.

IV

* * *

[T]he United States offers an alternative theory to support petitioner's conviction. It argues that petitioner breached a duty to the acquiring corporation when he acted upon information that he obtained by virtue of his position as an employee of a printer employed by the corporation. The breach of this duty is said to support a conviction under § 10(b) for fraud perpetrated upon both the acquiring corporation and the sellers.

We need not decide whether this theory has merit for it was not submitted to the jury. . . . [T]he jury was instructed that the petitioner employed a scheme to defraud if he "did not disclose . . . material non-public information in connection with the purchases of the stock."

* * *

The judgment of the Court of Appeals is *Reversed*.

■ STEVENS, J., concurring.

* * *

I agree with the Court's determination that petitioner owed no duty of disclosure to the sellers, that his conviction rested on the erroneous premise that he did owe them such a duty, and that the judgment of the Court of Appeals must therefore be reversed.

The Court correctly does not address . . . whether the petitioner's breach of his duty of silence—a duty he unquestionably owed to his employer and to his employer's customers—could give rise to criminal liability under Rule 10b–5. Respectable arguments could be made in support of either position. On the one hand, if we assume that petitioner breached a duty to the acquiring companies that had entrusted confidential information to his employers, a legitimate argument could be made that his actions constituted "a fraud or a deceit" upon those companies "in connection with the purchase or sale of any security." On the other hand, inasmuch as those companies would not be able to recover damages from petitioner for violating Rule 10b–5 because they were neither purchasers nor sellers of target company securities, it could also be argued that no actionable violation of Rule 10b–5 had occurred. I think the Court wisely leaves the resolution of this issue for another day.

* * *

NOTES

1.   *The "classical" and "misappropriation" theories.* The theory outlined by Justice Powell in *Chiarella*, under which an insider violates Rule 10b–5 by trading in the shares of his own company without disclosing confidential information, has come to be known as the "classical" theory of insider trading. The alternative theory advanced by the government, that Chiarella had defrauded Pandick Press and its clients by using their confidential information to trade in securities, has come to be known as the "misappropriation" theory. We will return to the misappropriation theory in the *O'Hagan* case below.

2. *Rule 14e–3.* Shortly after the *Chiarella* decision, the SEC promulgated Rule 14e–3 of the Exchange Act to address the problem of non-public, material informational advantages in the context of tender offers. When any person takes substantial steps to commence a tender offer for an Exchange Act reporting company's stock, Rule 14e–3 restricts the use of non-public, material information relating to that offer. Once a tender offer is initiated, Rule 14e–3 prohibits any person (other than the potential acquirer) from trading in the target company's stock based on non-public, material information obtained from the target company, the acquirer, or an officer or director of either, among others. Unlike insider trading theories under Rule 10b–5, the prohibition of Rule 14e–3 does not require deception or the breach of a fiduciary duty.

3. *Rule 10b–18.* Although the SEC is concerned with manipulation and its adverse effects on the capital markets, there are certain necessary corporate actions that the SEC has accommodated, such as share buyback programs. The main concern with a share buyback is that the corporation may be creating an exaggerated appearance of market interest in its stock, thus "manipulating" the market. To address this concern, the SEC promulgated Rule 10b–18, which provides a safe harbor for corporations and their affiliates and/or agents from liability for manipulation under § 9(a)(2) and § 10(b). The safe harbor applies when an issuer bids for or purchases shares of its common stock and complies with the safe harbor's requirements.

There are four elements to Rule 10b–18:

- An issuer and its affiliated purchasers must use only one broker or dealer to solicit purchasers or to make bids on a single day. An issuer, however, may use more than one broker or dealer if the transaction has *not* been solicited by or for the issuer.

- An issuer bid or purchase should not constitute the day's opening transaction. In addition, no issuer purchases should be made within one-half hour of the close of trading on the national exchange.

- The bid or price paid by an issuer or its affiliate cannot exceed the current independently published bid or the last reported independent sale price.

- Excluding any block purchases, an issuer's purchases should not exceed the higher of one round lot or the number of round lots closest to 25% of the trading volume for that security.

Like other safe harbors, the Rule 10b–18 safe harbor is not the exclusive means by which an issuer can purchase its common stock. The safe harbor does, however, enable an issuer to purchase its shares while ensuring that it is not violating the manipulation prohibitions. It does not, however, protect the issuer from Rule 10b–5 claims if it has repurchased shares while in possession of material, non-public information.

4. *Disclosure.* How much disclosure is required to avoid a violation of Rule 10b–5? This question is raised by "big boy letters." Such letters are typically used in securities transactions between sophisticated institutional investors when one of the parties has access to confidential information that it does not want to disclose to the counter-party. The letters disclose that there may be confidential information, but the party from whom the information is being withheld agrees not to sue on the basis of that non-disclosure. The uninformed party also waives any claim of reliance on the non-disclosed fact. The waiver of *claims* is clearly unenforceable under Exchange Act § 29(a), but a number of courts have held that the waiver of *reliance* is effective to bar a claim by a private plaintiff. The SEC, however, is not required to show reliance in its enforcement actions, and the agency appears to view such waivers as ineffective. The SEC has entered into a settlement agreement sanctioning a bank for trading on inside information obtained in bankruptcy proceedings without disclosing the specific information. *SEC v. Barclays Bank PLC*, SEC Litigation Release No. 20132 (2007).

QUESTIONS

1. How does the theory of insider trading outlined by Justice Powell in *Chiarella* differ from the common law "special facts" doctrine of *Strong v. Repide*?

2. How does Powell's theory differ from the Second Circuit's in *Texas Gulf Sulphur*?

3. Could Pandick Press or its clients state a Rule 10b–5 cause of action against Chiarella?

4. What happened to Chiarella's relationship with Pandick Press? Does this tell us anything about the need to use Rule 10b–5 to protect Pandick Press?

HYPOTHETICAL TWO

Recall that Jack, the CEO of Amtel, ordered his broker to sell half of Jack's two million Amtel shares shortly before Amtel announced its pending tender offer for ARM. (Assume these sales were executed over the NYSE.) Jack also ordered his broker to purchase ARM call options making a substantial profit after the tender offer was announced.

1. Has Jack violated the classical theory by purchasing ARM options? By selling his Amtel shares?

2. Would Jack have violated the classical theory if he had purchased Amtel put options? (Put options give their holder the right to sell stock at a specified price even if the market price is lower.) *See* § 20(d). What if he had sold highly-leveraged Amtel "junk" bonds?

3. Suppose Amtel was selling preferred stock in a private placement while it was contemplating the ARM tender offer. Assuming nondisclosure of the tender offer, would the company have violated the classical theory? Could Amtel have purchased call options of ARM stock?

4. Suppose that Jack leaves a detailed notebook containing information on the impending acquisition on the roof of his Jaguar. The notebook falls off as Jack is pulling away. Katharina, an individual unaffiliated with Amtel or ARM, finds the notebook in the street (emblazoned with Amtel's official seal). She proceeds to sell Amtel shares short and buy call options on ARM. Has Katharina run afoul of 10b–5?

B. TIPPER/TIPPEE LIABILITY

Justice Powell adverted to the problem of individuals receiving confidential information from insiders in a footnote of *Chiarella*: "'Tippees' of corporate insiders have been held liable under § 10(b) because they have a duty not to profit from the use of inside information that they know is confidential and know or should know came from a corporate insider. The tippee's obligation has been viewed as arising from his role as a participant after the fact in the insider's breach of a fiduciary duty." How far does tippee liability extend to non-insider traders? After *Chiarella*, the insider trading doctrine can be summarized as follows:

	Insider Trader	Outsider Trader
Corporate (inside) Information	*Chiarella* Classical Insider Trading Theory	Tippee Liability?
Outside Information	?	?

The Supreme Court grappled with the question of when tippees would be liable for their trading in the case below, which features a rather unusual set of facts. Does the standard Justice Powell crafted in *Dirks* unduly constrain the SEC and the Justice Department? What policy interest is Powell protecting by adopting a standard narrower than the one urged by the SEC?

Dirks v. SEC

463 U.S. 646 (1983).

■ POWELL, J.

Petitioner Raymond Dirks received material nonpublic information from "insiders" of a corporation with which he had no connection. He disclosed this information to investors who relied on it in trading in the shares of the corporation. The question is whether Dirks violated the antifraud provisions of the federal securities laws by this disclosure.

I

In 1973, Dirks was an officer of a New York broker-dealer firm who specialized in providing investment analysis of insurance company securities to institutional investors. On March 6, Dirks received information from Ronald Secrist, a former officer of Equity Funding of America. Secrist alleged that the assets of Equity Funding, a diversified corporation primarily engaged in selling life insurance and mutual funds, were vastly overstated as the result of fraudulent corporate practices. Secrist also stated that various regulatory agencies had failed to act on similar charges made by Equity Funding employees. He urged Dirks to verify the fraud and disclose it publicly.

Dirks decided to investigate the allegations. He visited Equity Funding's headquarters in Los Angeles and interviewed several officers and employees of the corporation. The senior management denied any wrongdoing, but certain corporation employees corroborated the charges of fraud. Neither Dirks nor his firm owned or traded any Equity

Funding stock, but throughout his investigation he openly discussed the information he had obtained with a number of clients and investors. Some of these persons sold their holdings of Equity Funding securities, including five investment advisers who liquidated holdings of more than $16 million.

* * *

During the two-week period in which Dirks pursued his investigation and spread word of Secrist's charges, the price of Equity Funding stock fell from $26 per share to less than $15 per share. This led the New York Stock Exchange to halt trading on March 27. Shortly thereafter California insurance authorities impounded Equity Funding's records and uncovered evidence of the fraud. Only then did the Securities and Exchange Commission (SEC) file a complaint against Equity Funding[3] and only then, on April 2, did the *Wall Street Journal* publish a front-page story based largely on information assembled by Dirks. Equity Funding immediately went into receivership.

The SEC began an investigation into Dirks' role in the exposure of the fraud. After a hearing by an administrative law judge, the SEC found that Dirks had aided and abetted violations of . . . § 10(b) of the Securities Exchange Act of 1934 and SEC Rule 10b–5 by repeating the allegations of fraud to members of the investment community who later sold their Equity Funding stock. The SEC concluded: "Where 'tippees'— regardless of their motivation or occupation—come into possession of material 'information that they know is confidential and know or should know came from a corporate insider,' they must either publicly disclose that information or refrain from trading." Recognizing, however, that Dirks "played an important role in bringing [Equity Funding's] massive fraud to light," the SEC only censured him. (The D.C. Circuit upheld the censure imposed by the SEC.)

In view of the importance to the SEC and to the securities industry of the question presented by this case, we granted a writ of certiorari. We now reverse.

II

* * *

In examining whether Chiarella had an obligation to disclose or abstain, the Court found that there is no general duty to disclose before trading on material nonpublic information, and held that "a duty to disclose under § 10(b) does not arise from the mere possession of nonpublic market information." Such a duty arises rather from the existence of a fiduciary relationship.

* * *

---

[3]   As early as 1971, the SEC had received allegations of fraudulent accounting practices at Equity Funding. Moreover, on March 9, 1973, an official of the California Insurance Department informed the SEC's regional office in Los Angeles of Secrist's charges of fraud. Dirks himself voluntarily presented his information at the SEC's regional office beginning on March 27.

III

We were explicit in *Chiarella* in saying that there can be no duty to disclose where the person who has traded on inside information "was not [the corporation's] agent, . . . was not a fiduciary, [or] was not a person in whom the sellers [of the securities] had placed their trust and confidence." Not to require such a fiduciary relationship, we recognized, would "depar[t] radically from the established doctrine that duty arises from a specific relationship between two parties" and would amount to "recognizing a general duty between all participants in market transactions to forgo actions based on material, nonpublic information." This requirement of a specific relationship between the shareholders and the individual trading on inside information has created analytical difficulties for the SEC and courts in policing tippees who trade on inside information. Unlike insiders who have independent fiduciary duties to both the corporation and its shareholders, the typical tippee has no such relationships.[14] In view of this absence, it has been unclear how a tippee acquires the *Cady, Roberts* duty to refrain from trading on inside information.

A

The SEC's position . . . is that a tippee "inherits" the *Cady, Roberts* obligation to shareholders whenever he receives inside information from an insider:

> In tipping potential traders, Dirks breached a duty which he had assumed as a result of knowingly receiving confidential information from [Equity Funding] insiders. Tippees such as Dirks who receive non-public material information from insiders become subject to the same duty as [the] insiders. Such a tippee breaches the fiduciary duty which he assumes from the insider when the tippee knowingly transmits the information to someone who will probably trade on the basis thereof . . . Presumably, Dirks' informants were entitled to disclose the [Equity Funding] fraud in order to bring it to light and its perpetrators to justice. However, Dirks—standing in their shoes—committed a breach of the fiduciary duty which he had assumed in dealing with them, when he passed the information on to traders.

This view differs little from the view that we rejected as inconsistent with congressional intent in *Chiarella*. . . . Here, the SEC maintains that anyone who knowingly receives nonpublic material information from an insider has a fiduciary duty to disclose before trading.[15]

---

[14] Under certain circumstances, such as where corporate information is revealed legitimately to an underwriter, accountant, lawyer, or consultant working for the corporation, these outsiders may become fiduciaries of the shareholders. The basis for recognizing this fiduciary duty is not simply that such persons acquired nonpublic corporate information, but rather that they have entered into a special confidential relationship in the conduct of the business of the enterprise and are given access to information solely for corporate purposes. When such a person breaches his fiduciary relationship, he may be treated more properly as a tipper than a tippee. For such a duty to be imposed, however, the corporation must expect the outsider to keep the disclosed nonpublic information confidential, and the relationship at least must imply such a duty.

[15] Apparently, the SEC believes this case differs from *Chiarella* in that Dirks' receipt of inside information from Secrist, an insider, carried Secrist's duties with it, while *Chiarella*

In effect, the SEC's theory of tippee liability . . . appears rooted in the idea that the antifraud provisions require equal information among all traders. This conflicts with the principle set forth in *Chiarella* that only some persons, under some circumstances, will be barred from trading while in possession of material nonpublic information. . . . We reaffirm today that "[a] duty [to disclose] arises from the relationship between parties . . . and not merely from one's ability to acquire information because of his position in the market."

Imposing a duty to disclose or abstain solely because a person knowingly receives material nonpublic information from an insider and trades on it could have an inhibiting influence on the role of market analysts, which the SEC itself recognizes is necessary to the preservation of a healthy market.[17] It is commonplace for analysts to "ferret out and analyze information,"[18] and this often is done by meeting with and questioning corporate officers and others who are insiders. And information that the analysts obtain normally may be the basis for judgments as to the market worth of a corporation's securities. The analyst's judgment in this respect is made available in market letters or otherwise to clients of the firm. It is the nature of this type of information, and indeed of the markets themselves, that such information cannot be made simultaneously available to all of the corporation's stockholders or the public generally.

B

The conclusion that recipients of inside information do not invariably acquire a duty to disclose or abstain does not mean that such tippees always are free to trade on the information. The need for a ban on some tippee trading is clear. Not only are insiders forbidden by their

---

received the information without the direct involvement of an insider and thus inherited no duty to disclose or abstain. The SEC fails to explain, however, why the receipt of nonpublic information from an insider automatically carries with it the fiduciary duty of the insider. As we emphasized in *Chiarella*, mere possession of nonpublic information does not give rise to a duty to disclose or abstain; only a specific relationship does that. And we do not believe that the mere receipt of information from an insider creates such a special relationship between the tippee and the corporation's shareholders. . . .

[17] The SEC expressly recognized that "[t]he value to the entire market of [analysts'] efforts cannot be gainsaid; market efficiency in pricing is significantly enhanced by [their] initiatives to ferret out and analyze information, and thus the analyst's work redounds to the benefit of all investors." The SEC asserts that analysts remain free to obtain from management corporate information for purposes of "filling in the 'interstices in analysis'. . . ." But this rule is inherently imprecise, and imprecision prevents parties from ordering their actions in accord with legal requirements. Unless the parties have some guidance as to where the line is between permissible and impermissible disclosures and uses, neither corporate insiders nor analysts can be sure when the line is crossed.

[18] On its facts, this case is the unusual one. Dirks is an analyst in a broker-dealer firm, and he did interview management in the course of his investigation. He uncovered, however, startling information that required no analysis or exercise of judgment as to its market relevance. Nonetheless, the principle at issue here extends beyond these facts. The SEC's rule—applicable without regard to any breach by an insider—could have serious ramifications on reporting by analysts of investment views.

Despite the unusualness of Dirks' "find," the central role that he played in uncovering the fraud at Equity Funding, and that analysts in general can play in revealing information that corporations may have reason to withhold from the public, is an important one. Dirks' careful investigation brought to light a massive fraud at the corporation. And until the Equity Funding fraud was exposed, the information in the trading market was grossly inaccurate. But for Dirks' efforts, the fraud might well have gone undetected longer.

fiduciary relationship from personally using undisclosed corporate information to their advantage, but they may not give such information to an outsider for the same improper purpose of exploiting the information for their personal gain. Similarly, the transactions of those who knowingly participate with the fiduciary in such a breach are "as forbidden" as transactions "on behalf of the trustee himself." *Mosser v. Darrow*, 341 U.S. 267, 272 (1951). As the Court explained in *Mosser*, a contrary rule "would open up opportunities for devious dealings in the name of the others that the trustee could not conduct in his own." Thus, the tippee's duty to disclose or abstain is derivative from that of the insider's duty. As we noted in *Chiarella*, "[t]he tippee's obligation has been viewed as arising from his role as a participant after the fact in the insider's breach of a fiduciary duty."

Thus, some tippees must assume an insider's duty to the shareholders not because they receive inside information, but rather because it has been made available to them *improperly*. . . . Thus, a tippee assumes a fiduciary duty to the shareholders of a corporation not to trade on material nonpublic information only when the insider has breached his fiduciary duty to the shareholders by disclosing the information to the tippee and the tippee knows or should know that there has been a breach. . . . Tipping thus properly is viewed only as a means of indirectly violating the *Cady, Roberts* disclose-or-abstain rule.

C

In determining whether a tippee is under an obligation to disclose or abstain, it thus is necessary to determine whether the insider's "tip" constituted a breach of the insider's fiduciary duty. All disclosures of confidential corporate information are not inconsistent with the duty insiders owe to shareholders. In contrast to the extraordinary facts of this case, the more typical situation in which there will be a question whether disclosure violates the insider's *Cady, Roberts* duty is when insiders disclose information to analysts. In some situations, the insider will act consistently with his fiduciary duty to shareholders, and yet release of the information may affect the market. For example, it may not be clear—either to the corporate insider or to the recipient analyst—whether the information will be viewed as material nonpublic information. Corporate officials may mistakenly think the information already has been disclosed or that it is not material enough to affect the market. Whether disclosure is a breach of duty therefore depends in large part on the purpose of the disclosure. This standard was identified by the SEC itself in *Cady, Roberts*: a purpose of the securities laws was to eliminate "use of inside information for personal advantage." Thus, the test is whether the insider personally will benefit, directly or indirectly, from his disclosure. Absent some personal gain, there has been no breach of duty to stockholders. And absent a breach by the insider, there is no derivative breach.[22] . . .

---

[22] An example of a case turning on the court's determination that the disclosure did not impose any fiduciary duties on the recipient of the inside information is *Walton v. Morgan Stanley & Co.*, 623 F.2d 796 (CA2 1980). There, the defendant investment banking firm, representing one of its own corporate clients, investigated another corporation that was a possible target of a takeover bid by its client. In the course of negotiations the investment banking firm was given, on a confidential basis, unpublished material information. Subsequently, after the proposed takeover was abandoned, the firm was charged with relying on the information when it traded in the target corporation's stock. For purposes of the

The SEC argues that, if inside-trading liability does not exist when the information is transmitted for a proper purpose but is used for trading, it would be a rare situation when the parties could not fabricate some ostensibly legitimate business justification for transmitting the information. We think the SEC is unduly concerned. [Determining whether there has been a breach of duty] requires courts to focus on objective criteria, *i.e.*, whether the insider receives a direct or indirect personal benefit from the disclosure, such as a pecuniary gain or a reputational benefit that will translate into future earnings. There are objective facts and circumstances that often justify such an inference. For example, there may be a relationship between the insider and the recipient that suggests a *quid pro quo* from the latter, or an intention to benefit the particular recipient. The elements of fiduciary duty and exploitation of nonpublic information also exist when an insider makes a gift of confidential information to a trading relative or friend. The tip and trade resemble trading by the insider himself followed by a gift of the profits to the recipient.

Determining whether an insider personally benefits from a particular disclosure, a question of fact, will not always be easy for courts. But it is essential, we think, to have a guiding principle for those whose daily activities must be limited and instructed by the SEC's inside-trading rules, and we believe that there must be a breach of the insider's fiduciary duty before the tippee inherits the duty to disclose or abstain. In contrast, the rule adopted by the SEC in this case would have no limiting principle.[24]

IV

Under the inside-trading and tipping rules set forth above, we find that there was no actionable violation by Dirks. It is undisputed that Dirks himself was a stranger to Equity Funding, with no pre-existing fiduciary duty to its shareholders. He took no action, directly or indirectly, that induced the shareholders or officers of Equity Funding to repose trust or confidence in him. There was no expectation by Dirks' sources that he would keep their information in confidence. Nor did Dirks misappropriate or illegally obtain the information about Equity Funding. Unless the insiders breached their *Cady, Roberts* duty to shareholders in disclosing the nonpublic information to Dirks, he breached no duty when he passed it on to investors. . . .

It is clear that neither Secrist nor the other Equity Funding employees violated their *Cady, Roberts* duty to the corporation's shareholders by providing information to Dirks.[27] The tippers received

---

decision, it was assumed that the firm knew the information was confidential, but that it had been received in arm's-length negotiations. In the absence of any fiduciary relationship, the Court of Appeals found no basis for imposing tippee liability on the investment firm.

[24] Without legal limitations, market participants are forced to rely on the reasonableness of the SEC's litigation strategy, but that can be hazardous, as the facts of this case make plain. . . .

[27] In this Court, the SEC appears to contend that an insider invariably violates a fiduciary duty to the corporation's shareholders by transmitting nonpublic corporate information to an outsider when he has reason to believe that the outsider may use it to the disadvantage of the shareholders. "Thus, regardless of any ultimate motive to bring to public attention the derelictions at Equity Funding, Secrist breached his duty to Equity Funding shareholders." This perceived "duty" differs markedly from the one that the SEC identified in

no monetary or personal benefit for revealing Equity Funding's secrets, nor was their purpose to make a gift of valuable information to Dirks. As the facts of this case clearly indicate, the tippers were motivated by a desire to expose the fraud. In the absence of a breach of duty to shareholders by the insiders, there was no derivative breach by Dirks. Dirks therefore could not have been "a participant after the fact in [an] insider's breach of a fiduciary duty."

* * *

NOTES

1.   *Joint and several liability.* Under the *Dirks* theory, both the tipper and tippee violate Rule 10b–5 if the insider gives the outsider information for the purpose of trading. Consequently, the tipper is jointly-and-severally liable with the tippee for the tippee's profits.

2.   *Temporary insiders.* In Footnote 14 of *Dirks*, the Supreme Court explains that underwriters, accountants, lawyers, or consultants may enter into a "special confidential relationship" whereby they come under a fiduciary duty similar to insiders with respect to non-public, material information obtained through the relationship.

3.   *Tippee liability.* Conviction of the tippee is not contingent on conviction of the tipper. The Seventh Circuit explained in the course of upholding a conviction of a tippee in a case in which the tipper was acquitted:

> [I]t is not essential that the tipper know that his disclosure was improper. Where the tippee has a relationship with the insider and the tippee knows the breach to be improper, the tippee may be liable for trading on the ill-gotten information. Thus, where a tippee, for example, induces a tipper to breach her corporate duty, even if the tipper does not do so knowingly or willfully, the tippee can still be liable for trading on the improperly provided information.

United States v. Evans, 486 F.3d 315 (7th Cir. 2007).

QUESTIONS

1.   Why is "[t]he need for a ban on some tippee trading [ ] clear"?

2.   The Court in *Dirks* seems particularly concerned with preserving the flow of corporate information to outside financial analysts. What kind of investors are likely to benefit from such tips to analysts? Who (if anyone) is harmed?

Cady, Roberts and that has been the basis for federal tippee-trading rules to date. In fact, the SEC did not charge Secrist with any wrongdoing, and we do not understand the SEC to have relied on any theory of a breach of duty by Secrist in finding that Dirks breached his duty to Equity Funding's shareholders.

[T]o constitute a violation of Rule 10b–5, there must be fraud. There is no evidence that Secrist's disclosure was intended to or did in fact "deceive or defraud" anyone. Secrist certainly intended to convey relevant information that management was unlawfully concealing, and—so far as the record shows—he believed that persuading Dirks to investigate was the best way to disclose the fraud. Other efforts had proved fruitless. Under any objective standard, Secrist received no direct or indirect personal benefit from the disclosure.

The next case deals with the state of mind required for a criminal conviction for a tippee and how it relates to the elements set out by Justice Powell in *Dirks*. Does the standard set out by the Second Circuit make it too easy for tippees to avoid liability?

United States v. Newman

773 F.3d 438 (2d Cir. 2014).

■ PARKER, B., CIRCUIT JUDGE.

Defendants-appellants Todd Newman and Anthony Chiasson appeal from judgments of conviction . . . on charges of securities fraud . . .

The Government alleged that a cohort of analysts at various hedge funds and investment firms obtained material, nonpublic information from employees of publicly traded technology companies, shared it amongst each other, and subsequently passed this information to the portfolio managers at their respective companies. The Government charged Newman, a portfolio manager at Diamondback Capital Management, LLC ("Diamondback"), and Chiasson, a portfolio manager at Level Global Investors, L.P. ("Level Global"), with willfully participating in this insider trading scheme by trading in securities based on the inside information illicitly obtained by this group of analysts. On appeal, Newman and Chiasson challenge the sufficiency of the evidence as to several elements of the offense, and further argue that the district court erred in failing to instruct the jury that it must find that a tippee knew that the insider disclosed confidential information in exchange for a personal benefit.

We agree that the jury instruction was erroneous because we conclude that, in order to sustain a conviction for insider trading, the Government must prove beyond a reasonable doubt that the tippee knew that an insider disclosed confidential information *and* that he did so in exchange for a personal benefit. Moreover, we hold that the evidence was insufficient to sustain a guilty verdict against Newman and Chiasson for two reasons. *First*, the Government's evidence of any personal benefit received by the alleged insiders was insufficient to establish the tipper liability from which defendants' purported tippee liability would derive. *Second*, even assuming that the scant evidence offered on the issue of personal benefit was sufficient, which we conclude it was not, the Government presented no evidence that Newman and Chiasson knew that they were trading on information obtained from insiders in violation of those insiders' fiduciary duties.

Accordingly, we reverse the convictions of Newman and Chiasson on all counts and remand with instructions to dismiss the indictment as it pertains to them with prejudice.

BACKGROUND

This case arises from the Government's ongoing investigation into suspected insider trading activity at hedge funds. . . . At trial, the Government presented evidence that a group of financial analysts exchanged information they obtained from company insiders, both directly and more often indirectly. Specifically, the Government alleged that these analysts received information from insiders at Dell and

NVIDIA disclosing those companies' earnings numbers before they were publicly released in Dell's May 2008 and August 2008 earnings announcements and NVIDIA's May 2008 earnings announcement. These analysts then passed the inside information to their portfolio managers, including Newman and Chiasson, who, in turn, executed trades in Dell and NVIDIA stock, earning approximately $4 million and $68 million, respectively, in profits for their respective funds.

Newman and Chiasson were several steps removed from the corporate insiders and there was no evidence that either was aware of the source of the inside information. With respect to the Dell tipping chain, the evidence established that Rob Ray of Dell's investor relations department tipped information regarding Dell's consolidated earnings numbers to Sandy Goyal, an analyst at Neuberger Berman. Goyal in turn gave the information to Diamondback analyst Jesse Tortora. Tortora in turn relayed the information to his manager Newman as well as to other analysts including Level Global analyst Spyridon "Sam" Adondakis. Adondakis then passed along the Dell information to Chiasson, making Newman and Chiasson three and four levels removed from the inside tipper, respectively.

With respect to the NVIDIA tipping chain, the evidence established that Chris Choi of NVIDIA's finance unit tipped inside information to Hyung Lim, a former executive at technology companies Broadcom Corp. and Altera Corp., whom Choi knew from church. Lim passed the information to co-defendant Danny Kuo, an analyst at Whittier Trust. Kuo circulated the information to the group of analyst friends, including Tortora and Adondakis, who in turn gave the information to Newman and Chiasson, making Newman and Chiasson four levels removed from the inside tippers.

Although Ray and Choi have yet to be charged administratively, civilly, or criminally for insider trading or any other wrongdoing, the Government charged that Newman and Chiasson were criminally liable for insider trading because, as sophisticated traders, they must have known that information was disclosed by insiders in breach of a fiduciary duty, and not for any legitimate corporate purpose.

At the close of evidence, Newman and Chiasson moved for a judgment of acquittal pursuant to Federal Rule of Criminal Procedure 29. They argued that there was no evidence that the corporate insiders provided inside information in exchange for a personal benefit which is required to establish tipper liability under *Dirks v. S.E.C.*, 463 U.S. 646 (1983). Because a tippee's liability derives from the liability of the tipper, Newman and Chiasson argued that they could not be found guilty of insider trading. Newman and Chiasson also argued that, even if the corporate insiders had received a personal benefit in exchange for the inside information, there was no evidence that they knew about any such benefit. Absent such knowledge, appellants argued, they were not aware of, or participants in, the tippers' fraudulent breaches of fiduciary duties to Dell or NVIDIA, and could not be convicted of insider trading under *Dirks*. In the alternative, appellants requested that the court instruct the jury that it must find that Newman and Chiasson knew that the corporate insiders had disclosed confidential information for personal benefit in order to find them guilty.

The district court reserved decision on the Rule 29 motions. With respect to the appellants' requested jury charge, while the district court acknowledged that their position was "supportable certainly by the language of *Dirks*," it ultimately found that it was constrained by this Court's decision in *S.E.C. v. Obus*, 693 F.3d 276 (2d Cir. 2012), which listed the elements of tippee liability without enumerating knowledge of a personal benefit received by the insider as a separate element. Accordingly, the district court did not give Newman and Chiasson's proposed jury instruction. Instead, the district court gave the following instructions on the tippers' intent and the personal benefit requirement:

> Now, if you find that Mr. Ray and/or Mr. Choi had a fiduciary or other relationship of trust and confidence with their employers, then you must next consider whether the [G]overnment has proven beyond a reasonable doubt that they intentionally breached that duty of trust and confidence by disclosing material[,] nonpublic information for their own benefit.

On the issue of the appellants' knowledge, the district court instructed the jury:

> To meet its burden, the [G]overnment must also prove beyond a reasonable doubt that the defendant you are considering knew that the material, nonpublic information had been disclosed by the insider in breach of a duty of trust and confidence. The mere receipt of material, nonpublic information by a defendant, and even trading on that information, is not sufficient; he must have known that it was originally disclosed by the insider in violation of a duty of confidentiality.

On December 17, 2012, the jury returned a verdict of guilty on all counts. The district court subsequently denied the appellants' Rule 29 motions. . . .

This appeal followed.

DISCUSSION

* * *

C.   Tipping Liability

The insider trading case law . . . is not confined to insiders or misappropriators who trade for their own accounts. Courts have expanded insider trading liability to reach situations where the insider or misappropriator in possession of material nonpublic information (the "tipper") does not himself trade but discloses the information to an outsider (a "tippee") who then trades on the basis of the information before it is publicly disclosed. The elements of tipping liability are the same, regardless of whether the tipper's duty arises under the "classical" or the "misappropriation" theory.

In *Dirks*, the Supreme Court addressed the liability of a tippee analyst who received material, nonpublic information about possible fraud at an insurance company from one of the insurance company's former officers. The analyst relayed the information to some of his clients who were investors in the insurance company, and some of them, in turn, sold their shares based on the analyst's tip. The SEC charged the analyst Dirks with aiding and abetting securities fraud by relaying confidential and material inside information to people who traded the stock.

In reviewing the appeal, the Court articulated the general principle of tipping liability: "Not only are insiders forbidden by their fiduciary relationship from personally using undisclosed corporate information to their advantage, but they may not give such information to an outsider for the same improper purpose of exploiting the information for their personal gain." The test for determining whether the corporate insider has breached his fiduciary duty "is whether the insider personally will benefit, directly or indirectly, from his disclosure. Absent some personal gain, *there has been no breach of duty . . . .*"

The Supreme Court rejected the SEC's theory that a recipient of confidential information (i.e. the "tippee") must refrain from trading "whenever he receives inside information from an insider." Instead, the Court held that "[t]he tippee's duty to disclose or abstain is derivative from that of the insider's duty. Because the *tipper's* breach of fiduciary duty requires that he "personally will benefit, directly or indirectly, from his disclosure," a tippee may not be held liable in the absence of such benefit. Moreover, the Supreme Court held that a tippee may be found liable "only when the insider has breached his fiduciary duty . . . *and* the tippee knows or should know that there has been a breach." In *Dirks*, the corporate insider provided the confidential information in order to expose a fraud in the company and not for any personal benefit, and thus, the Court found that the insider had not breached his duty to the company's shareholders and that Dirks could not be held liable as tippee.

E.   *Mens Rea*

Liability for securities fraud also requires proof that the defendant acted with scienter, which is defined as "a mental state embracing intent to deceive, manipulate or defraud." In order to establish a criminal violation of the securities laws, the Government must show that the defendant acted "willfully." We have defined willfulness in this context "as a realization on the defendant's part that he was doing a wrongful act under the securities laws."

II.   The Requirements of Tippee Liability

The Government concedes that tippee liability requires proof of a personal benefit to the insider. However, the Government argues that it was not required to prove that Newman and Chiasson knew that the insiders at Dell and NVIDIA received a personal benefit in order to be found guilty of insider trading. Instead, the Government contends, consistent with the district court's instruction, that it merely needed to prove that the "defendants traded on material, nonpublic information they knew insiders had disclosed in breach of a duty of confidentiality . . ."

In support of this position, the Government cites *Dirks* for the proposition that the Supreme Court only required that the "tippee know that the tipper disclosed information in *breach of a duty.*" In addition, the Government relies on dicta in a number of our decisions post-*Dirks*, in which we have described the elements of tippee liability without specifically stating that the Government must prove that the tippee knew that the corporate insider who disclosed confidential information did so for his own personal benefit. By selectively parsing this dictum, the Government seeks to revive the absolute bar on tippee trading that the Supreme Court explicitly rejected in *Dirks*.

Although this Court has been accused of being "somewhat Delphic" in our discussion of what is required to demonstrate tippee liability, the Supreme Court was quite clear in *Dirks*. *First*, the tippee's liability derives *only* from the tipper's breach of a fiduciary duty, *not* from trading on material, non-public information. *Second*, the corporate insider has committed no breach of fiduciary duty unless he receives a personal benefit in exchange for the disclosure. *Third*, even in the presence of a tipper's breach, a tippee is liable only if he knows or should have known of the breach.

While we have not yet been presented with the question of whether the tippee's knowledge of a tipper's breach requires knowledge of the tipper's personal benefit, the answer follows naturally from *Dirks*. *Dirks* counsels us that the exchange of confidential information for personal benefit is not separate from an insider's fiduciary breach; it *is* the fiduciary breach that triggers liability for securities fraud under Rule 10b-5. For purposes of insider trading liability, the insider's disclosure of confidential information, standing alone, is not a breach. Thus, without establishing that the tippee knows of the personal benefit received by the insider in exchange for the disclosure, the Government cannot meet its burden of showing that the tippee knew of a breach.

The Government's overreliance on our prior dicta merely highlights the doctrinal novelty of its recent insider trading prosecutions, which are increasingly targeted at remote tippees many levels removed from corporate insiders. By contrast, our prior cases generally involved tippees who directly participated in the tipper's breach (and therefore had knowledge of the tipper's disclosure for personal benefit) or tippees who were explicitly apprised of the tipper's gain by an intermediary tippee. We note that the Government has not cited, nor have we found, a single case in which tippees as remote as Newman and Chiasson have been held criminally liable for insider trading.

[United States v.] Jiau, [734 F.3d 147 (2d Cir. 2013)] illustrates the importance of this distinction quite clearly. In *Jiau*, the panel was presented with the question of whether the evidence at trial was sufficient to prove that the tippers personally benefitted from their disclosure of insider information. In that context, we summarized the elements of criminal liability as follows:

> (1) the insider-tippers . . . were entrusted the duty to protect confidential information, which (2) they breached by disclosing [the information] to their tippee . . . , who (3) knew of [the tippers'] duty and (4) still used the information to trade a security or further tip the information for [the tippee's] benefit, and finally (5) the insider-tippers benefited in some way from their disclosure.

The Government relies on this language to argue that *Jiau* is merely the most recent in a string of cases in which this Court has found that a tippee, in order to be criminally liable for insider trading, need know only that an insider-tipper disclosed information in breach of a duty of confidentiality. However, we reject the Government's position that our cursory recitation of the elements in *Jiau* suggests that criminal liability may be imposed on a defendant based only on knowledge of a breach of a duty of confidentiality. In *Jiau*, the defendant knew about the benefit because she provided it. For that reason, we had no need to reach the question of whether knowledge of a breach requires that a tippee know that a personal benefit was provided to the tipper.

In light of *Dirks*, we find no support for the Government's contention that knowledge of a breach of the duty of confidentiality without knowledge of the personal benefit is sufficient to impose criminal liability. Although the Government might like the law to be different, nothing in the law requires a symmetry of information in the nation's securities markets. The Supreme Court explicitly repudiated this premise not only in *Dirks*, but in a predecessor case, *Chiarella*. . . . Thus, in both *Chiarella* and *Dirks*, the Supreme Court affirmatively established that insider trading liability is based on breaches of fiduciary duty, not on informational asymmetries. This is a critical limitation on insider trading liability that protects a corporation's interests in confidentiality while promoting efficiency in the nation's securities markets.

As noted above, *Dirks* clearly defines a breach of fiduciary duty as a breach of the duty of confidentiality in exchange for a personal benefit. Accordingly, we conclude that a tippee's knowledge of the insider's breach necessarily requires knowledge that the insider disclosed confidential information in exchange for personal benefit. In reaching this conclusion, we join every other district court to our knowledge— apart from Judge Sullivan[1]—that has confronted this question.

Our conclusion also comports with well-settled principles of substantive criminal law. [U]nder the common law, *mens rea*, which requires that the defendant know the facts that make his conduct illegal, is a necessary element in every crime. Such a requirement is particularly appropriate in insider trading cases where we have acknowledged "it is easy to imagine a . . . trader who receives a tip and is unaware that his conduct was illegal and therefore wrongful." This is also a statutory requirement, because only "willful" violations are subject to criminal provision.

In sum, we hold that to sustain an insider trading conviction against a tippee, the Government must prove each of the following elements beyond a reasonable doubt: that (1) the corporate insider was entrusted with a fiduciary duty; (2) the corporate insider breached his fiduciary duty by (a) disclosing confidential information to a tippee (b) in exchange for a personal benefit; (3) the tippee knew of the tipper's

---

[1] Although the Government argues that district court decisions in *S.E.C. v. Thrasher*, 152 F. Supp. 2d 291 (S.D.N.Y. 2001) and *S.E.C. v. Musella*, 678 F. Supp. 1060 (S.D.N.Y. 1988) support their position, these cases merely stand for the unremarkable proposition that a tippee does not need to know the details of the insider's disclosure of information. The district courts determined that the tippee did not have to know for certain how information was disclosed, nor the identity of the insiders. This is not inconsistent with a requirement that a defendant tippee understands that some benefit is being provided in return for the information.

breach, that is, he knew the information was confidential and divulged for personal benefit; and (4) the tippee still used that information to trade in a security or tip another individual for personal benefit.

In view of this conclusion, we find, reviewing the charge as a whole, that the district court's instruction failed to accurately advise the jury of the law. The district court charged the jury that the Government had to prove: (1) that the insiders had a "fiduciary or other relationship of trust and confidence" with their corporations; (2) that they "breached that duty of trust and confidence by disclosing material, nonpublic information"; (3) that they "personally benefited in some way" from the disclosure; (4) "that the defendant . . . knew the information he obtained had been disclosed in breach of a duty"; and (5) that the defendant used the information to purchase a security. Under these instructions, a reasonable juror might have concluded that a defendant could be criminally liable for insider trading merely if such defendant knew that an insider had divulged information that was required to be kept confidential. But a breach of the duty of confidentiality is not fraudulent unless the tipper acts for personal benefit, that is to say, there is no breach unless the tipper "is in effect selling the information to its recipient for cash, reciprocal information, or other things of value for himself. . . ." Thus, the district court was required to instruct the jury that the Government had to prove beyond a reasonable doubt that Newman and Chiasson knew that the tippers received a personal benefit for their disclosure.

* * *

III. Insufficiency of the Evidence

* * *

The circumstantial evidence in this case was simply too thin to warrant the inference that the corporate insiders received any personal benefit in exchange for their tips. As to the Dell tips, the Government established that Goyal and Ray were not "close" friends, but had known each other for years, having both attended business school and worked at Dell together. Further, Ray, who wanted to become a Wall Street analyst like Goyal, sought career advice and assistance from Goyal. The evidence further showed that Goyal advised Ray on a range of topics, from discussing the qualifying examination in order to become a financial analyst to editing Ray's résumé and sending it to a Wall Street recruiter, and that some of this assistance began before Ray began to provide tips about Dell's earnings. The evidence also established that Lim and Choi were "family friends" that had met through church and occasionally socialized together. The Government argues that these facts were sufficient to prove that the tippers derived some benefit from the tip. We disagree. If this was a "benefit," practically anything would qualify.

We have observed that "[p]ersonal benefit is broadly defined to include not only pecuniary gain, but also, *inter alia*, any reputational benefit that will translate into future earnings and the benefit one would obtain from simply making a gift of confidential information to a trading relative or friend." This standard, although permissive, does not suggest that the Government may prove the receipt of a personal benefit by the mere fact of a friendship, particularly of a casual or social nature. If that were true, and the Government was allowed to meet its burden by proving that two individuals were alumni of the same school or attended the same church, the personal benefit requirement would be a nullity. To the extent *Dirks* suggests that a personal benefit may be inferred from a personal relationship between the tipper and tippee, where the tippee's trades "resemble trading by the insider himself followed by a gift of the profits to the recipient," we hold that such an inference is impermissible in the absence of proof of a meaningfully close personal relationship that generates an exchange that is objective, consequential, and represents at least a potential gain of a pecuniary or similarly valuable nature. In other words . . . , this requires evidence of "a relationship between the insider and the recipient that suggests a *quid pro quo* from the latter, or an intention to benefit the [latter]."

While our case law at times emphasizes language from *Dirks* indicating that the tipper's gain need not be *immediately* pecuniary, it does not erode the fundamental insight that, in order to form the basis for a fraudulent breach, the personal benefit received in exchange for confidential information must be of some consequence. For example, in *Jiau*, we noted that at least one of the corporate insiders received something more than the ephemeral benefit of the "value[ ] [of] [Jiau's] friendship" because he also obtained access to an investment club where stock tips and insight were routinely discussed. Thus, by joining the investment club, the tipper entered into a relationship of *quid quo pro* with Jiau, and therefore had the opportunity to access information that could yield future pecuniary gain.

Here the "career advice" that Goyal gave Ray, the Dell tipper, was little more than the encouragement one would generally expect of a fellow alumnus or casual acquaintance. Crucially, Goyal testified that he would have given Ray advice without receiving information because he routinely did so for industry colleagues. Although the Government argues that the jury could have reasonably inferred from the evidence that Ray and Goyal swapped career advice for inside information, Ray himself disavowed that any such *quid pro quo* existed. Further, the evidence showed Goyal began giving Ray "career advice" over a year before Ray began providing any insider information. Thus, it would not be possible under the circumstances for a jury in a criminal trial to find beyond a reasonable doubt that Ray received a personal benefit in exchange for the disclosure of confidential information.

The evidence of personal benefit was even more scant in the NVIDIA chain. Choi and Lim were merely casual acquaintances. The evidence did not establish a history of loans or personal favors between the two. During cross examination, Lim testified that he did not provide anything of value to Choi in exchange for the information. Lim further testified that Choi did not know that Lim was trading NVIDIA stock (and in fact for the relevant period Lim did not trade stock), thus undermining any inference that Choi intended to make a "gift" of the profits earned on any transaction based on confidential information.

Even assuming that the scant evidence described above was sufficient to permit the inference of a personal benefit, which we conclude it was not, the Government presented absolutely no testimony or any other evidence that Newman and Chiasson knew that they were trading on information obtained from insiders, or that those insiders received any benefit in exchange for such disclosures, or even that Newman and Chiasson consciously avoided learning of these facts. As discussed above, the Government is required to prove beyond a reasonable doubt that Newman and Chiasson knew that the insiders received a personal benefit in exchange for disclosing confidential information.

It is largely uncontroverted that Chiasson and Newman, and even their analysts, who testified as cooperating witnesses for the Government, knew next to nothing about the insiders and nothing about what, if any, personal benefit had been provided to them. Adondakis said that he did not know what the relationship between the insider and the first-level tippee was, nor was he aware of any personal benefits exchanged for the information, nor did he communicate any such information to Chiasson. Adondakis testified that he merely told Chiasson that Goyal "was talking to someone within Dell," and that a friend of a friend of Tortora's would be getting NVIDIA information. Adondakis further testified that he did not specifically tell Chiasson that the source of the NVIDIA information worked at NVIDIA. Similarly, Tortora testified that, while he was aware Goyal received information from someone at Dell who had access to "overall" financial numbers, he was not aware of the insider's name, or position, or the circumstances of how Goyal obtained the information. Tortora further testified that he did not know whether Choi received a personal benefit for disclosing inside information regarding NVIDIA.

The Government now invites us to conclude that the jury could have found that the appellants knew the insiders disclosed the information "for some personal reason rather than for no reason at all." But the Supreme Court affirmatively rejected the premise that a tipper who discloses confidential information necessarily does so to receive a personal benefit. Moreover, it is inconceivable that a jury could conclude, beyond a reasonable doubt, that Newman and Chiasson were aware of a personal benefit, when Adondakis and Tortora, who were more intimately involved in the insider trading scheme as part of the "corrupt" analyst group, disavowed any such knowledge.

Alternatively, the Government contends that the specificity, timing, and frequency of the updates provided to Newman and Chiasson about Dell and NVIDIA were so "overwhelmingly suspicious" that they warranted various material inferences that could support a guilty verdict. Newman and Chiasson received four updates on Dell's earnings numbers in the weeks leading up to its August 2008 earnings announcement. Similarly, Newman and Chiasson received multiple updates on NVIDIA's earnings numbers between the close of the quarter and the company's earnings announcement. The Government argues that given the detailed nature and accuracy of these updates, Newman and Chiasson must have known, or deliberately avoided knowing, that the information originated with corporate insiders, *and* that those insiders disclosed the information in exchange for a personal benefit. We disagree.

Even viewed in the light most favorable to the Government, the evidence presented at trial undermined the inference of knowledge in several ways. The evidence established that analysts at hedge funds routinely estimate metrics such as revenue, gross margin, operating margin, and earnings per share through legitimate financial modeling using publicly available information and educated assumptions about industry and company trends. For example, on cross-examination, cooperating witness Goyal testified that under his financial model on Dell, when he ran the model in January 2008 without any inside information, he calculated May 2008 quarter results of $16.071 billion revenue, 18.5% gross margin, and $0.38 earnings per share. These estimates came very close to Dell's reported earnings of $16.077 billion revenue; 18.4% gross margin, and $0.38 earnings per share. Appellants also elicited testimony from the cooperating witnesses and investor relations associates that analysts routinely solicited information from companies in order to check assumptions in their models in advance of earnings announcements. Goyal testified that he frequently spoke to internal relations departments to run his model by them and ask whether his assumptions were "too high or too low" or in the "ball park," which suggests analysts routinely updated numbers in advance of the earnings announcements. Ray's supervisor confirmed that investor relations departments routinely assisted analysts with developing their models.

Moreover, the evidence established that NVIDIA and Dell's investor relations personnel routinely "leaked" earnings data in advance of quarterly earnings. Appellants introduced examples in which Dell insiders, including the head of Investor Relations, Lynn Tyson, selectively disclosed confidential quarterly financial information arguably similar to the inside information disclosed by Ray and Choi to establish relationships with financial firms who might be in a position to buy Dell's stock. For example, appellants introduced an email Tortora sent Newman summarizing a conversation he had with Tyson in which she suggested "low 12% opex [was] reasonable" for Dell's upcoming quarter and that she was "fairly confident on [operating margin] and [gross margin]."

No reasonable jury could have found beyond a reasonable doubt that Newman and Chiasson knew, or deliberately avoided knowing, that the information originated with corporate insiders. In general, information about a firm's finances could certainly be sufficiently detailed and proprietary to permit the inference that the tippee knew that the information came from an inside source. But in this case, where the financial information is of a nature regularly and accurately predicted by analyst modeling, and the tippees are several levels removed from the source, the inference that defendants knew, or should have known, that the information originated with a corporate insider is unwarranted.

Moreover, even if detail and specificity could support an inference as to the *nature* of the source, it cannot, without more, permit an inference as to that source's improper *motive* for disclosure. That is especially true here, where the evidence showed that corporate insiders at Dell and NVIDIA regularly engaged with analysts and routinely selectively disclosed the same type of information. Thus, in light of the testimony (much of which was adduced from the Government's own witnesses) about the accuracy of the analysts' estimates and the selective disclosures by the companies themselves, no rational jury would find that the tips were so overwhelmingly suspicious that Newman and Chiasson either knew or consciously avoided knowing that the information came from corporate insiders or that those insiders received any personal benefit in exchange for the disclosure.

In short, the bare facts in support of the Government's theory of the case are as consistent with an inference of innocence as one of guilt. . . . Because the Government failed to demonstrate that Newman and Chiasson had the intent to commit insider trading, it cannot sustain the convictions on either the substantive insider trading counts or the conspiracy count. Consequently, we reverse Newman and Chiasson's convictions. . . .

* * *

NOTES

1.   *Civil enforcement.* The *Newman* court mentions *SEC v. Obus*, 693 F.3d 276 (2d Cir. 2012), but rejects its application. In *Obus*, the Second Circuit held that:

> tipper liability requires that (1) the tipper had a duty to keep material non-public information confidential; (2) the tipper breached that duty by intentionally or recklessly relaying the information to a tippee who could use the information in connection with securities trading; and (3) the tipper received a personal benefit from the tip. Tippee liability requires that (1) the tipper breached a duty by tipping confidential information; (2) the tippee knew or had reason to know that the tippee improperly obtained the information (i.e., that the information was obtained through the tipper's breach); and (3) the tippee, while in knowing possession of the material non-public information, used the information by trading or by tipping for his own benefit.

Obus does not appear to require that the tippee know that the tipper received a personal benefit in disclosing the information, i.e., knowing that the information was disclosed in breach of a duty of confidentiality is sufficient.

QUESTIONS

1.   Did Newman and Chiasson have reason to believe that the information they received was disclosed in breach of a fiduciary duty?

2.   Should recklessness be sufficient to establish liability for a tippee? Does it matter how far down the chain the tippee is?

3.   What are the different states of mind that must be shown to establish tipper liability in a criminal case? A civil case? Will it be difficult to establish all three mental states or will they typically all follow in the case where a tipper receives personal benefit from a tip?

4.   What hazards does tippee liability create for hedge fund managers and other active traders?

HYPOTHETICAL THREE

Return to the Primary World hypothetical and consider various possible "chains" of information transmission.

1.   *Scenario One:* Recall the path of information involved when Raj, a hedge fund manager, sells his Amtel stock upon learning of Amtel's intent to make an unsolicited tender offer for ARM shares:

Jack (CEO of Amtel) → Primary World → Raj (who then sells)

Primary World pays Jack a regular "consulting fee" for his "insights" (that happens to include confidential information on the tender offer). Raj, in turn, pays Primary World for access to information that Primary World obtains from public company officials. Is Raj liable for insider trading?

2.   *Scenario Two:* Assume Jack has made an impermissible tip under *Dirks* through Primary World to Raj. Suppose Raj telephones his best friend Curtis, a securities analyst, and tells him that Primary World told him Amtel was planning a tender offer for ARM. "Primary World is so well connected," Raj tells Curtis.

Jack → Primary World → Raj → (via phone call from Raj) Curtis

Curtis then sells Amtel shares short. Has Curtis run afoul of *Dirks*?

3.   *Scenario Three:* Suppose Raj writes that "Primary World says sell sell sell Amtel" on a piece of paper that Raj later splits into four pieces and throws into separate dumpsters in New York City. Joel, a street person rummaging through dumpsters happens to find the four pieces and, after reconstructing the note, decides to sell Amtel short. Has Joel run afoul of *Dirks*?

Jack → Primary World → Raj → (via trash) Joel

4.   *Scenario Four:* Suppose that Raj simply overheard the information about Amtel's tender offer for ARM while in an elevator with Jack. Jack, unfortunately, has a loud voice and was talking about the deal on his cell phone. (Practice tip for future lawyers: shut up on elevators.) Raj sells his Amtel shares.

Jack → Raj

Has Raj run afoul of the *Dirks* anti-tipping rule?

IV. THE MISAPPROPRIATION THEORY

The classical insider trading theory set forth by Justice Powell in *Chiarella* and *Dirks* focuses on information obtained from inside the corporation whose stocks are traded. The contours of the doctrine can be summarized as follows:

	Insider Trader	Outsider Trader
Corporate (inside) Information	*Chiarella* Classical Theory *Dirks* temporary insiders	*Dirks* tipper-tipee liability
Outside Information	?	?

Left undecided after *Chiarella* and *Dirks* was the question of information generated outside the traded firm. Not all informational advantages in the market come from the issuer; there are many other potential sources of information. Imagine that you are an individual investor considering whether to buy Amtel stock. Who are the other outsider traders in the market? Do you think you are at a relative informational disadvantage or advantage relative to these other traders?

A wide range of outsiders trade in the secondary market. Large institutional investors—including pension funds and mutual funds— spend large sums of money on "buy-side" securities research. Institutional investors may also obtain information through close relationships with investment banks engaged in "sell-side" research. Although investment banks often will provide public research reports for all investors, favored institutional investors have greater access to the analysts, allowing them to ask questions and learn information about companies not otherwise available to the public. Other companies may also have material nonpublic information on a particular traded firm. Suppose Microsoft is about to enter the microprocessor business. The potential for added competition from Microsoft is likely material information for Amtel and other microprocessor companies. To the extent Microsoft (or its officers) trades on this information (selling Amtel stock short, for example), Microsoft and its officers enjoy a large trading advantage. Warren Buffett, "the sage of Omaha," is likely to be at a trading advantage compared to almost any individual outside investor; some investors are simply more talented than others at picking stocks.

Given the range of trading advantages among outsiders, which trading advantages should be prohibited and which allowed? Here are some possibilities:

- prohibit all non-public material informational advantages
- prohibit all "unerodable" advantages obtained through unequal access to information
- prohibit only advantages obtained through a breach of a fiduciary duty
- allow only those informational advantages obtained through the "hard work" of the trading investor
- allow all outside informational advantages

Given the harm to uninformed investors (in the form of reduced liquidity and market depth) when trading with the more informed, why not simply adopt the first alternative and ban all nonpublic material informational advantages? Why tolerate any informational advantages? Some argue that allowing investors with an informational advantage to profit gives them an incentive to research and uncover useful information about a company. Granting such investors a "property" right to their information will generate more information in the securities markets. Others focus on the "unfairness" of allowing the abuse of an "unerodable" informational advantage over uninformed investors. On this view, advantages created by skill or effort are not "unfair" and therefore should be tolerated.

A. THE MISAPPROPRIATION THEORY

Under Rule 10b–5, deciding which outside informational advantages to allow is resolved by the misappropriation theory. Remember that the Court reserved the question of the validity of the misappropriation theory in *Chiarella* because it was not presented to the jury. The SEC and the Justice Department continued to press the theory, however, which led to its eventual return to the Supreme Court. It took two cases, however, before the Court would pass on the validity of the misappropriation theory. The first case, *Carpenter v. United States*, 484 U.S. 19 (1987), was decided by a split court (4–4), which meant that the Court did not pass on the validity of the theory. That is not the only procedural quirk of *Carpenter*, however. The case came to the Supreme Court only after the Court initially voted to deny certiorari. Justice Powell prepared a draft opinion in response to that denial, in which he argued that the misappropriation theory was inconsistent with *Chiarella* and *Dirks*. According to Powell:

> [I]t is difficult to understand how any of the petitioners were guilty of criminal securities fraud. The Court of Appeals found no fiduciary relationship between any of the petitioners and the parties from whom they purchased securities. The only fiduciary duty discussed by the court is petitioner Winans' duty to [his employer]. But our previous decisions establish that the duty of an individual to his employer, alone, is insufficient to support an action under Rule 10b–5. The inquiry under that section must focus on "petitioner's relationship with the sellers of the . . . securities. . . ." . . . As the petitioners in this case had no fiduciary obligation to disclose the information before dealing in the securities, their convictions under § 10(b) and Rule 10b–5 are without support in any prior decision of this Court.

Carpenter v. United States, (Draft Dissent of Powell, J) (No. 86–422, Dec. 10, 1986) (on file at Washington & Lee University).

After Powell circulated his draft, the Court reconsidered and voted to grant certiorari. Before *Carpenter* was argued, however, Justice Powell retired. (His successor, Anthony Kennedy, was not confirmed until after the argument, which led to the 4–4 split.) Given Powell's rejection of the misappropriation theory in his draft dissent, it is reasonable to conclude that if Justice Powell had not retired when he did, the Supreme Court would have rejected the misappropriation theory in 1987.

The 4–4 split in *Carpenter*, however, left the question open. In the case that follows, the Court finally resolved the question of the validity of the misappropriation theory. The case also addresses the validity of Rule 14e–3, a rule adopted by the SEC (in the wake of the government's defeat in *Chiarella*) to combat insider trading in connection with tender offers. As you read *O'Hagan*, compare the limits of the misappropriation theory with those of the classical theory. Do you agree with Justice Powell's view or the position adopted in *O'Hagan*? Which better serves the policy interests of insider trading prohibitions? Which is more faithful to the text of § 10(b) and Congress's intention in adopting that provision? Finally, what role is left (if any) for the classical theory developed by Powell in *Chiarella* and *Dirks*?

United States v. O'Hagan

521 U.S. 642 (1997).

■ GINSBURG, J.

This case concerns the interpretation and enforcement of § 10(b) and § 14(e) of the Securities Exchange Act of 1934, and rules made by the Securities and Exchange Commission pursuant to these provisions, Rule 10b–5 and Rule 14e–3(a). . . . In particular, we address and resolve these issues: (1) Is a person who trades in securities for personal profit, using confidential information misappropriated in breach of a fiduciary duty to the source of the information, guilty of violating § 10(b) and Rule 10b–5? (2) Did the Commission exceed its rulemaking authority by adopting Rule 14e–3(a), which proscribes trading on undisclosed information in the tender offer setting, even in the absence of a duty to disclose? Our answer to the first question is yes, and to the second question, viewed in the context of this case, no.

I

Respondent James Herman O'Hagan was a partner in the law firm of Dorsey & Whitney in Minneapolis, Minnesota. In July 1988, Grand Metropolitan PLC, a company based in London, England, retained Dorsey & Whitney as local counsel to represent Grand Met regarding a potential tender offer for the common stock of the Pillsbury Company, headquartered in Minneapolis. Both Grand Met and Dorsey & Whitney took precautions to protect the confidentiality of Grand Met's tender offer plans. . . . [O]n October 4, 1988, Grand Met publicly announced its tender offer for Pillsbury stock.

On August 18, 1988, while Dorsey & Whitney was . . . representing Grand Met, O'Hagan began purchasing call options for Pillsbury stock. . . . By the end of September, he owned 2,500 unexpired Pillsbury options, apparently more than any other individual investor. O'Hagan also purchased, in September 1988, some 5,000 shares of Pillsbury common stock, at a price just under $39 per share. When Grand Met announced its tender offer in October, the price of Pillsbury stock rose to nearly $60 per share. O'Hagan then sold his Pillsbury call options and common stock, making a profit of more than $4.3 million.

The Securities and Exchange Commission initiated an investigation into O'Hagan's transactions, culminating in a 57-count indictment. The indictment alleged that O'Hagan defrauded his law firm and its client, Grand Met, by using for his own trading purposes material, nonpublic information regarding Grand Met's planned tender offer. . . . A jury convicted O'Hagan on all 57 counts, and he was sentenced to a 41-month term of imprisonment.

A divided panel of the Court of Appeals for the Eighth Circuit reversed all of O'Hagan's convictions.

* * *

II

We address first the Court of Appeals' reversal of O'Hagan's convictions under § 10(b) and Rule 10b–5.... We hold that criminal liability under § 10(b) may be predicated on the misappropriation theory.

A

* * *

Under the "traditional" or "classical theory" of insider trading liability, § 10(b) and Rule 10b–5 are violated when a corporate insider trades in the securities of his corporation on the basis of material, nonpublic information. Trading on such information qualifies as a "deceptive device" under § 10(b), we have affirmed, because "a relationship of trust and confidence [exists] between the shareholders of a corporation and those insiders who have obtained confidential information by reason of their position with that corporation." That relationship, we recognized, "gives rise to a duty to disclose [or to abstain from trading] because of the 'necessity of preventing a corporate insider from ... tak[ing] unfair advantage of ... uninformed ... stockholders.'" The classical theory applies not only to officers, directors, and other permanent insiders of a corporation, but also to attorneys, accountants, consultants, and others who temporarily become fiduciaries of a corporation.

[The "misappropriation theory" holds that a person commits fraud "in connection with" a securities transaction, and thereby violates § 10(b) and Rule 10b–5, when he misappropriates confidential information for securities trading purposes, in breach of a duty owed to the source of the information.] Under this theory, a fiduciary's undisclosed, self-serving use of a principal's information to purchase or sell securities, in breach of a duty of loyalty and confidentiality, defrauds the principal of the exclusive use of that information. In lieu of premising liability on a fiduciary relationship between company insider and purchaser or seller of the company's stock, the misappropriation theory premises liability on a fiduciary-turned-trader's deception of those who entrusted him with access to confidential information.

[handwritten margin note: not limited to "outsiders"]

The two theories are complementary, each addressing efforts to capitalize on nonpublic information through the purchase or sale of securities. The classical theory targets a corporate insider's breach of duty to shareholders with whom the insider transacts; the misappropriation theory outlaws trading on the basis of nonpublic information by a corporate "outsider" in breach of a duty owed not to a trading party, but to the source of the information. The misappropriation theory is thus designed to "protec[t] the integrity of the securities markets against abuses by 'outsiders' to a corporation who have access to confidential information that will affect th[e] corporation's security price when revealed, but who owe no fiduciary or other duty to that corporation's shareholders." ...[5]

---

[5] The Government could not have prosecuted O'Hagan under the classical theory, for O'Hagan was not an "insider" of Pillsbury, the corporation in whose stock he traded. Although an "outsider" with respect to Pillsbury, O'Hagan had an intimate association with, and was found to have traded on confidential information from, Dorsey & Whitney, counsel to tender

B

We agree with the Government that misappropriation . . . satisfies § 10(b)'s requirement that chargeable conduct involve a "deceptive device or contrivance" used "in connection with" the purchase or sale of securities. We observe, first, that misappropriators, as the Government describes them, deal in deception. A fiduciary who "[pretends] loyalty to the principal while secretly converting the principal's information for personal gain," "dupes" or defrauds the principal. . . .

A company's confidential information . . . qualifies as property to which the company has a right of exclusive use. The undisclosed misappropriation of such information, in violation of a fiduciary duty . . . constitutes fraud akin to embezzlement—"the fraudulent appropriation to one's own use of the money or goods entrusted to one's care by another." . . .

Deception through nondisclosure is central to the theory of liability for which the Government seeks recognition. . . . As counsel for the Government stated in explanation of the theory at oral argument: "To satisfy the common law rule that a trustee may not use the property that [has] been entrusted [to] him, there would have to be consent. To satisfy the requirement of the Securities Act that there be no deception, there would only have to be disclosure." See generally Restatement (Second) of Agency §§ 390, 395 (1958) (agent's disclosure obligation regarding use of confidential information).

The misappropriation theory advanced by the Government is consistent with *Santa Fe Industries, Inc. v. Green*, 430 U.S. 462 (1977), a decision underscoring that § 10(b) is not an all-purpose breach of fiduciary duty ban; rather, it trains on conduct involving manipulation or deception. . . . Full disclosure forecloses liability under the misappropriation theory: Because the deception essential to the misappropriation theory involves feigning fidelity to the source of information, if the fiduciary discloses to the source that he plans to trade on the nonpublic information, there is no "deceptive device" and thus no § 10(b) violation—although the fiduciary-turned-trader may remain liable under state law for breach of a duty of loyalty.

We turn next to the § 10(b) requirement that the misappropriator's deceptive use of information be "in connection with the purchase or sale of [a] security." This element is satisfied because the fiduciary's fraud is consummated, not when the fiduciary gains the confidential information, but when, without disclosure to his principal, he uses the information to purchase or sell securities. The securities transaction and the breach of duty thus coincide. This is so even though the person or entity defrauded is not the other party to the trade, but is, instead, the source of the nonpublic information. A misappropriator who trades on the basis of material, nonpublic information, in short, gains his advantageous market position through deception; he deceives the source of the information and simultaneously harms members of the investing public.

---

offeror Grand Met. Under the misappropriation theory, O'Hagan's securities trading does not escape Exchange Act sanction . . . simply because he was associated with, and gained nonpublic information from, the bidder, rather than the target.

The misappropriation theory targets information of a sort that misappropriators ordinarily capitalize upon to gain no-risk profits through the purchase or sale of securities. Should a misappropriator put such information to other use, the statute's prohibition would not be implicated. The theory does not catch all conceivable forms of fraud involving confidential information; rather, it catches fraudulent means of capitalizing on such information through securities transactions.

* * *

The misappropriation theory comports with § 10(b)'s language, which requires deception "in connection with the purchase or sale of any security," not deception of an identifiable purchaser or seller. The theory is also well tuned to an animating purpose of the Exchange Act: to insure honest securities markets and thereby promote investor confidence. Although informational disparity is inevitable in the securities markets, investors likely would hesitate to venture their capital in a market where trading based on misappropriated nonpublic information is unchecked by law. An investor's informational disadvantage vis-à-vis a misappropriator with material, nonpublic information stems from contrivance, not luck; it is a disadvantage that cannot be overcome with research or skill.

In sum, considering the inhibiting impact on market participation of trading on misappropriated information, and the congressional purposes underlying § 10(b), it makes scant sense to hold a lawyer like O'Hagan a § 10(b) violator if he works for a law firm representing the target of a tender offer, but not if he works for a law firm representing the bidder. The text of the statute requires no such result.[9] The misappropriation at issue here was properly made the subject of a § 10(b) charge because it meets the statutory requirement that there be "deceptive" conduct "in connection with" securities transactions.

* * *

III

We consider next the ground on which the Court of Appeals reversed O'Hagan's convictions for fraudulent trading in connection with a tender offer, in violation of § 14(e) of the Exchange Act and SEC Rule 14e–3(a). A sole question is before us as to these convictions: Did the Commission . . . exceed its rulemaking authority under § 14(e) when it adopted Rule 14e–3(a) without requiring a showing that the trading at issue entailed a breach of fiduciary duty? We hold that the Commission, in this regard and to the extent relevant to this case, did not exceed its authority.

* * *

---

[9] As noted earlier, however, the textual requirement of deception precludes § 10(b) liability when a person trading on the basis of nonpublic information has disclosed his trading plans to, or obtained authorization from, the principal—even though such conduct may affect the securities markets in the same manner as the conduct reached by the misappropriation theory. . . . [T]he fact that § 10(b) is only a partial antidote to the problems it was designed to alleviate does not call into question its prohibition of conduct that falls within its textual proscription. Moreover, once a disloyal agent discloses his imminent breach of duty, his principal may seek appropriate equitable relief under state law.

Through § 14(e) and other provisions on disclosure in the Williams Act, Congress sought to ensure that shareholders "confronted by a cash tender offer for their stock [would] not be required to respond without adequate information." . . .

* * *

As characterized by the Commission, Rule 14e–3(a) is a "disclose or abstain from trading" requirement. The Second Circuit concisely described the Rule's thrust:

> One violates Rule 14e–3(a) if he trades on the basis of material nonpublic information concerning a pending tender offer that he knows or has reason to know has been acquired "directly or indirectly" from an insider of the offeror or issuer, or someone working on their behalf. Rule 14e–3(a) is a disclosure provision. It creates a duty in those traders who fall within its ambit to abstain or disclose, *without regard to whether the trader owes a pre-existing fiduciary duty* to respect the confidentiality of the information.

In the Eighth Circuit's view, because Rule 14e–3(a) applies whether or not the trading in question breaches a fiduciary duty, the regulation exceeds the SEC's § 14(e) rulemaking authority.

* * *

The United States urges that the Eighth Circuit's reading of § 14(e) misapprehends both the Commission's authority to define fraudulent acts and the Commission's power to prevent them. "The 'defining' power," the United States submits, "would be a virtual nullity were the SEC not permitted to go beyond common law fraud (which is separately prohibited in the first [self-operative] sentence of Section 14(e))."

* * *

We need not resolve in this case whether the Commission's authority under § 14(e) to "define . . . such acts and practices as are fraudulent" is broader than the Commission's fraud-defining authority under § 10(b), for we agree with the United States that Rule 14e–3(a), as applied to cases of this genre, qualifies under § 14(e) as a "means reasonably designed to prevent" fraudulent trading on material, nonpublic information in the tender offer context.[17] A prophylactic measure, because its mission is to prevent, typically encompasses more than the core activity prohibited. . . . § 14(e)'s rulemaking authorization gives the Commission "latitude," even in the context of a term of art like "manipulative," "to regulate nondeceptive activities as a 'reasonably

---

[17] We leave for another day, when the issue requires decision, the legitimacy of Rule 14e–3(a) as applied to "warehousing," which the Government describes as "the practice by which bidders leak advance information of a tender offer to allies and encourage them to purchase the target company's stock before the bid is announced." As we observed in *Chiarella*, one of the Commission's purposes in proposing Rule 14e–3(a) was "to bar warehousing under its authority to regulate tender offers." The Government acknowledges that trading authorized by a principal breaches no fiduciary duty. The instant case, however, does not involve trading authorized by a principal; therefore, we need not here decide whether the Commission's proscription of warehousing falls within its § 14(e) authority to define or prevent fraud.

designed' means of preventing manipulative acts, without suggesting any change in the meaning of the term 'manipulative' itself." We hold, accordingly, that under § 14(e), the Commission may prohibit acts not themselves fraudulent under the common law or § 10(b), if the prohibition is "reasonably designed to prevent . . . acts and practices [that] are fraudulent."[18]

Because Congress has authorized the Commission, in § 14(e), to prescribe legislative rules, we owe the Commission's judgment "more than mere deference or weight." Therefore, in determining whether Rule 14e–3(a)'s "disclose or abstain from trading" requirement is reasonably designed to prevent fraudulent acts, we must accord the Commission's assessment "controlling weight unless [it is] arbitrary, capricious, or manifestly contrary to the statute." In this case, we conclude, the Commission's assessment is none of these.

* * *

The United States emphasizes that Rule 14e–3(a) reaches trading in which "a breach of duty is likely but difficult to prove." "Particularly in the context of a tender offer," as the Tenth Circuit recognized, "there is a fairly wide circle of people with confidential information," notably, the attorneys, investment bankers, and accountants involved in structuring the transaction. The availability of that information may lead to abuse, for "even a hint of an upcoming tender offer may send the price of the target company's stock soaring." Individuals entrusted with nonpublic information, particularly if they have no long-term loyalty to the issuer, may find the temptation to trade on that information hard to resist in view of "the very large short-term profits potentially available [to them]."

"[I]t may be possible to prove circumstantially that a person [traded on the basis of material, nonpublic information], but almost impossible to prove that the trader obtained such information in breach of a fiduciary duty owed either by the trader or by the ultimate insider source of the information." The example of a "tippee" who trades on information received from an insider illustrates the problem. Under Rule 10b–5, "a tippee assumes a fiduciary duty to the shareholders of a corporation not to trade on material nonpublic information only when the insider has breached his fiduciary duty to the shareholders by disclosing the information to the tippee and the tippee knows or should know that there has been a breach." [quoting from *Dirks*, 463 U.S., at 660]. To show that a tippee who traded on nonpublic information about a tender offer had breached a fiduciary duty would require proof not only that the insider source breached a fiduciary duty, but that the tippee knew or should have known of that breach. "Yet, in most cases, the only parties to the [information transfer] will be the insider and the alleged tippee."

In sum, it is a fair assumption that trading on the basis of material, nonpublic information will often involve a breach of a duty of confidentiality to the bidder or target company or their representatives. The SEC, cognizant of the proof problem that could enable sophisticated traders to escape responsibility, placed in Rule 14e–3(a) a "disclose or

---

[18] The Commission's power under § 10(b) is more limited.

abstain from trading" command that does not require specific proof of a breach of fiduciary duty. That prescription, we are satisfied, applied to this case, is a "means reasonably designed to prevent" fraudulent trading on material, nonpublic information in the tender offer context. Therefore, insofar as it serves to prevent the type of misappropriation charged against O'Hagan, Rule 14e–3(a) is a proper exercise of the Commission's prophylactic power under § 14(e).

* * *

NOTES

1.   *Splitting the elements.* Consider the "classic" case of insider trading in which a corporate officer, who owes a fiduciary duty to the corporation's shareholders, purchases shares from these shareholders without informing them of non-public, material information that the corporation has found a large gold deposit on its lands. In this case, the deception and breach of fiduciary duty are linked directly with the purchase transaction. The misappropriation theory breaks apart the Rule 10b–5 elements of deception and breach of a fiduciary duty. Under the misappropriation theory, neither the deception nor the breach of fiduciary duty must occur against the party trading opposite to the violator. Instead, a third party is introduced—the source of the information. If the violator breaches her fiduciary duty to the source by trading on this information to trade—without disclosure to the source—with another party then this satisfies the "in connection with" requirement. The Court's holding in *O'Hagan* validates the separation of those elements.

QUESTIONS

1.   Why did the Justice Department not pursue O'Hagan under the classical theory of insider trading set forth in *Chiarella* and *Dirks*?

2.   What if O'Hagan had told Grand Met and his law firm before the acquisition was announced that he planned to buy Pillsbury options?

3.   How does the misappropriation theory satisfy the "in connection with the purchase or sale" requirement of Rule 10b–5? If O'Hagan breached his fiduciary duty to Grand Met rather than the investors from whom he purchased, how is the fraud in connection with the purchase or sale of securities?

B. DUTY OF CONFIDENTIALITY

A common situation where a potential insider trading violation may occur involves a company officer passing on confidential corporate information to a family member with the expectation that the family member will maintain the confidence. The family member then turns around and either trades on the information or tips another who trades on the information. In this fact pattern, a tipper-tippee action against the company officer may be difficult absent a showing that the officer intended to facilitate his family member's trading, rather than simply keeping his spouse informed about his work. Instead, the SEC may opt for the misappropriation theory of insider trading.

For the misappropriation theory to apply when a family member trades securities based on confidential information obtained from a corporate officer, the family member must owe a duty of trust or confidence to the corporate officer. When can we presume that members of the same family owe each other a duty of trust or confidence? Rule 10b5–2 provides guidance on when a duty of trust or confidence may arise. The rule recognizes a duty "[w]henever a person receives or obtains material nonpublic information from his or her spouse, parent, child, or sibling." For duties that arise from a family relationship, the rule also creates a defense: "the person receiving or obtaining the information may demonstrate that no duty of trust or confidence existed with respect to the information, by establishing that he or she neither knew nor reasonably should have known that the person who was the source of the information expected that the person would keep the information confidential, because of the parties' history, pattern, or practice of sharing and maintaining confidences, and because there was no agreement or understanding to maintain the confidentiality of the information." Rule 10b5–2 establishes a presumptive duty of trust or confidence among family members and then places the burden on family members to rebut this presumption.

Consider the following circuit court case applying the misappropriation doctrine to the disclosure of non-public, material information from one family member to another. Is there deception in this case?

SEC v. Rocklage

470 F.3d 1 (1st Cir. 2006).

■ LYNCH, S., CIRCUIT JUDGE.

* * *

Mrs. Rocklage was the wife of Scott M. Rocklage. Mr. Rocklage was the Chairman and CEO of Cubist Pharmaceuticals, Inc., a publicly-traded biotechnology company. Mrs. Rocklage was not an employee of Cubist.

On December 31, 2001, Mr. Rocklage learned that one of the company's key drugs had failed its clinical trial. That afternoon, he phoned Mrs. Rocklage to discuss the trial results. . . . Before discussing the results with her, Mr. Rocklage made clear his intention that the results be kept confidential. . . . She agreed. From the time that Mr. Rocklage joined Cubist in 1994, he had routinely communicated material, nonpublic information to his wife, and she had always kept the information confidential. Based on Mrs. Rocklage's agreement, and based on their prior history of sharing nonpublic information about the company and her keeping that information confidential, Mr. Rocklage had a reasonable expectation that she would not disclose the trial results to anyone. Based on his understanding that she would keep the information confidential, Mr. Rocklage informed his wife that the clinical trial had failed. Before the results were disclosed to her, Mrs. Rocklage understood her husband's expectation of confidentiality.

Unbeknownst to her husband, Mrs. Rocklage had a preexisting understanding with her brother, defendant Beaver, that she would inform him with "a wink and a nod" if she learned significant negative news about Cubist. At the time that Mrs. Rocklage learned the negative trial results, she knew or had reason to believe that Beaver owned Cubist stock. She also knew or had reason to know her brother would trade in Cubist securities if she disclosed the nonpublic information to him.

On the evening of December 31, 2001, Mr. Rocklage discussed the failure of the drug trial in more depth with Mrs. Rocklage. He informed her that Cubist would be making a public announcement about the results, and that until that happened the results were nonpublic. . . . In effect, by her deception Mrs. Rocklage induced her husband to disclose material non-public information he would not otherwise have disclosed, and she did so with the intention of sharing this information with her brother to allow him to trade securities.

After that conversation, and on or about the evening of December 31, 2001, Mrs. Rocklage informed her husband that she planned to signal her brother to sell his stock. Mr. Rocklage urged her not to do so, and he expressed his displeasure at the idea. Nevertheless, sometime before the morning of January 2, 2002, Mrs. Rocklage called Beaver and gave him "a wink and a nod" regarding Cubist. Beaver interpreted this to mean that he should sell his Cubist stock, and so on the morning of January 2, 2002—the first possible trading day after he was tipped off—Beaver sold all of his 5,583 shares of Cubist stock. By tipping her brother, Mrs. Rocklage was providing a gift of confidential information to a relative, and so she personally benefitted.

* * *

II.

* * *

The defendants do not dispute that the complaint meets the scienter requirement, and that the disclosed information was material and nonpublic. They also do not seriously challenge the SEC's allegation that Mrs. Rocklage breached a duty she owed to her spouse under Rule 10b5–2(b)(3).

The heart of this case is thus whether the SEC's complaint has stated a claim that Mrs. Rocklage engaged in any "manipulative or deceptive device" that was "in connection with the purchase or sale of any security." In answering that question, we find it helpful to examine the issue in two parts. First, we identify exactly what "manipulative or deceptive devices" Mrs. Rocklage was alleged to have engaged in and we assess whether they were sufficiently "in connection with" a securities transaction. Second, we examine Mrs. Rocklage's pre-tip disclosure to her husband to determine whether that disclosure eliminated the deception from her actions.

1.   The Deceptive Devices

The SEC contends that Mrs. Rocklage engaged in deceptive devices, in connection with a securities transaction, when she tricked her husband into revealing confidential information to her so that she could, and did, assist her brother with the sale of his Cubist stock. We agree and think it helpful to view the devices in terms of deceptive acquisition of information and then deceptive tipping of her brother, both of which were steps in a broader scheme to enable her brother to trade in Cubist securities. The question of whether Mrs. Rocklage's disclosure makes these acts nondeceptive is a different question, which we address later.

We start with the second of these actions. Had Mrs. Rocklage never made any disclosure of her intent to tip her brother, there would have been deception in connection with a securities transaction when she did tip her brother, without her husband's consent, to enable her brother to trade in securities. Under *O'Hagan*, this would have been the case irrespective of the means by which Mrs. Rocklage acquired the information.

Still putting aside for the moment any consideration of the effects of disclosure, we turn to the other alleged deceptive action—Mrs. Rocklage's acquisition of information. Here more analysis is required. We agree that this acquisition of information was deceptive. The complaint alleges, and we must take as true, that before her husband's initial disclosure about the clinical trial, Mrs. Rocklage did absolutely nothing to correct his mistaken understanding that she would keep the trial results confidential. This was so even though Mrs. Rocklage knew that her husband had this (mis)understanding, and even though she had a preexisting arrangement to disclose certain confidential information to her brother.

The defendants argue that this acquisition of information, even if deceptive, was not "in connection with" a securities transaction. They point to language from *O'Hagan* discussing the "in connection with" requirement and explaining that "the fiduciary's fraud is consummated, not when the fiduciary gains the confidential information, but when . . . he uses the information to purchase or sell securities." In defendants' view, Mrs. Rocklage's deceptive acquisition of information was simply too far removed from her brother's sale of securities to satisfy § 10(b)'s "in connection with" requirement.

We disagree with defendants' reading of *O'Hagan* and of the "in connection with" requirement. We read the quoted sentence in *O'Hagan* as explaining when a misappropriator's deceptive scheme ends, and not as indicating when it begins. Next, *O'Hagan* had no occasion to interpret the "in connection with" requirement in a case alleging deceptive acquisition of information intended to be used in a securities transaction. The opinion does not discuss whether *O'Hagan* tricked or deceived his law firm into telling him about the tender offer, and whether while doing so he knew he would use the information for trading. The government's brief to the Supreme Court stated that "[t]he record does not indicate how [O'Hagan] first learned" about the potential tender offer. There was no claim that O'Hagan had used deception to obtain the information. On those facts, it is no surprise that the Supreme Court based liability only on O'Hagan's act of undisclosed trading itself.

Since the act of trading was itself deceptive in *O'Hagan*, the "securities transaction and the breach of duty thus coincide[d]." In this case it is true there was no such exact coincidence. But that disjunction does not mean the deception in obtaining the information was not in connection with the sale of securities.

This case differs from *O'Hagan* in that the SEC squarely alleges that Mrs. Rocklage deceptively obtained information, and that she did so as part of a preexisting scheme to assist her brother in the sale of securities. The question is how that difference is relevant to the "in connection with" requirement. . . .

* * *

[W]e think that Mrs. Rocklage's actions fit within a natural reading of the "in connection with" requirement. Mrs. Rocklage's preexisting arrangement with her brother can easily be understood as a "scheme" or "practice" or "course of business," Rule 10b–5(a), (c), whose goal was to enable her brother to trade in Cubist securities at a substantially reduced level of risk. Her deception of her husband was a natural and integral part of this scheme; she induced her husband to reveal material negative information to her about Cubist, knowing full well that in obtaining that information she would enable her brother to execute a securities transaction. She then actively facilitated a securities transaction by tipping her brother, and securities were in fact sold based on her information. These events show that her deceptive acquisition of material inside information was "in connection with" a securities transaction.

Finally, our interpretation finds further support in the investor protection purposes of § 10(b). One of the animating purposes of the statute was to "insure honest securities markets and thereby promote investor confidence." It furthers that purpose if the "in connection with" requirement reaches schemes in which one party deceptively and intentionally obtains material nonpublic information to enable another to trade with an unfair informational advantage.

2.   The Effect of Mrs. Rocklage's Pre-Tip Disclosure of her Intent to Tip her Brother

We have determined that the complaint alleges that Mrs. Rocklage engaged in a scheme involving devices that would have been deceptive in the absence of disclosure, and we have concluded that these devices were employed "in connection with" a securities transaction. We now turn to the heart of defendants' argument: whether Mrs. Rocklage's pre-tip disclosure to her husband, indicating her intent to pass the information to her brother, nonetheless means no claim of deception is stated by virtue of *O'Hagan's* language about disclosure.

The defendants' view is that a pre-tip disclosure to the source of an intention to trade or tip completely eliminates any deception involved in the transaction. They rely on *O'Hagan's* language that "if the fiduciary discloses to the source that he plans to trade on the nonpublic information, there is no 'deceptive device' and thus no § 10(b) violation." The defendants argue that *O'Hagan* put no qualifiers on what is meant by "disclos[ure] to the source" of a plan to trade on nonpublic information, and so the SEC is not free to qualify the concept.

The SEC disagrees, arguing that the disclosure referenced in *O'Hagan* must mean disclosure that is "useful" to the fiduciary's principal. The SEC draws support from a footnote in *O'Hagan* which may be read as implying that disclosure enables a source to take remedial action. See *O'Hagan*, 521 U.S. at 659 n. 9 (explaining that "once a disloyal agent discloses his imminent breach of duty, his principal may seek appropriate equitable relief under state law"). As the SEC sees it, disclosure to the source serves a useful purpose when "the source of material non-public information reasonably could be expected to, and reasonably could, prevent the unauthorized use of the information for securities trading."

Under that standard, the SEC argues, Mrs. Rocklage's disclosure was not a useful one for her source—and in this regard was unlike *O'Hagan's* hypothetical disclosure. The SEC argues this is so due to both the timing of the events and the marital relationship of the people involved. The timing of Mrs. Rocklage's disclosure that she intended to tip her brother—coming during or right before the New Year's holiday— meant that Mr. Rocklage would have had a great deal of difficulty pursuing remedial action to stop the sale of the securities. In fact, the sale was effectuated immediately at the next opening of the market. Also, the SEC argues it would be unreasonable to expect Mr. Rocklage to have risked marital discord by taking action against his wife; once she made clear she would tell her brother despite her husband's wishes, his interest may have shifted to protecting her against liability. . . .

In our view this case presents a narrower question. We start by asking about the nature of the various acts in the deceptive scheme before considering the role of and the nature of the disclosure. Unlike this case, *O'Hagan* was not a case which involved the deceptive acquisition of information. Arguably, the language in *O'Hagan* can be read to create a "safe harbor" if there is disclosure to the fiduciary principal of an intention to trade on or tip legitimately acquired information. This is because under *O'Hagan's* logic such a "safe harbor" applies, if at all, when the alleged deception is in the undisclosed trading or tipping of information. In those cases, disclosure of the intent to trade arguably will eliminate the sole source of deception. But a case of deceptive acquisition of information followed by deceptive tipping and trading is different. It makes little sense to assume that disclosure of an intention to tip using deceptively acquired information would necessarily negate the original deception.

Indeed, by framing the issues this way, we see a second important distinction between *O'Hagan* and the case at bar. *O'Hagan* was a case in which only one deceptive device was alleged: undisclosed trading on confidential information. In this case the SEC's complaint is fairly read as alleging sequential acts that could each constitute deceptive devices: (1) the acquisition of material non-public information through the deception of Mrs. Rocklage's husband, and (2) Mrs. Rocklage's use of this information to tip off her brother without her husband's consent, followed by the tippees' use of the information to trade. Perhaps, under *O'Hagan*, Mrs. Rocklage's disclosure made the second of these devices non-deceptive. But then the proper question becomes whether disclosure that negates deception as to one set of actions in a scheme necessarily renders all prior deceptive acts non-deceptive.

While that question was not directly addressed in *O'Hagan*, the opinion does offer helpful clues. In a passage that leads to a third distinction between *O'Hagan* and the fact pattern here, the Court in

O'Hagan seemed to contemplate that any liability-avoiding disclosure would come before the defendant engaged in the deceptive activity. . . . On the facts of this case, we are unwilling to say that *O'Hagan* requires us to conclude that Mrs. Rocklage's post-acquisition disclosure of her intention to tip somehow rendered her acquisition of information non-deceptive.

* * *

Once the various distinctions between this case and *O'Hagan* are understood, defendants' position is really that because some of Mrs. Rocklage's actions may have been non-deceptive, her scheme as a whole had no deceptive elements. We do not believe that *O'Hagan* requires such an understanding of § 10(b), and we in fact conclude that *O'Hagan* rejects such an understanding.

* * *

In light of her disclosure to her husband, Mrs. Rocklage's mechanism for "distributing" the information to her brother may or may not have been rendered non-deceptive by her stated intention to tip. But because of the way in which Mrs. Rocklage first acquired this information, her overall scheme was still deceptive: it had as part of it at least one deceptive device. Thus as a matter of the facts alleged in the complaint, and taking all facts and inferences in favor of the plaintiff, a § 10(b) claim is stated.

* * *

QUESTIONS

1. Why was Mrs. Rocklage's disclosure to her husband of her intention to tip her brother relevant to the court's decision?

2. What was the SEC's theory of deception?

3. Is the court's theory of deception consistent with *O'Hagan*? With *Santa Fe*?

4. Did Mr. Rocklage violate Regulation FD by disclosing the clinical trial results to Mrs. Rocklage?

———

Outside of the family context, when may a person acquire a duty of trust or confidence to a source of confidential information even where no formal fiduciary relationship exists? In Rule 10b5–2, the SEC indicated that such a duty may arise "[w]henever a person agrees to maintain information in confidence" or "[w]henever the person communicating the material nonpublic information and the person to whom it is communicated have a history, pattern, or practice of sharing confidences, such that the recipient of the information knows or reasonably should know that the person communicating the material nonpublic information expects that the recipient will maintain its confidentiality." Consider the situation of Mark Cuban, Internet entrepreneur and owner of the Dallas Mavericks basketball team, in the following case. What is required to establish a confidentiality agreement? Is it enough for a person to agree not to transmit the information to others, or must the person also agree not to use the information to trade?

SEC v. Cuban

620 F.3d 551 (5th Cir. 2010).

■ HIGGINBOTHAM, P., CIRCUIT JUDGE.

This case raises questions of the scope of liability under the misappropriation theory of insider trading. [W]e are persuaded that the case should not have been dismissed . . . and must proceed to discovery. . . .

The SEC brought this suit against Cuban alleging he violated . . . Section 10(b) and Rule 10b–5 by trading in Mamma.com stock in breach of his duty to the CEO and Mamma.com—amounting to insider trading under the misappropriation theory of liability. The core allegation is that Cuban received confidential information from the CEO of Mamma.com, a Canadian search engine company in which Cuban was a large minority stakeholder, agreed to keep the information confidential, and acknowledged he could not trade on the information. The SEC alleges that, armed with the inside information regarding a private investment of public equity (PIPE) offering, Cuban sold his stake in the company in an effort to avoid losses from the inevitable fall in Mamma.com's share price when the offering was announced.

Cuban moved to dismiss the action under Rule 9(b) and 12(b)(6). The district court found that, at most, the complaint alleged an agreement to keep the information confidential, but did not include an agreement not to trade. Finding a simple confidentiality agreement to be insufficient to create a duty to disclose or abstain from trading under the securities laws, the court granted Cuban's motion to dismiss. The SEC appeals, arguing that a confidentiality agreement creates a duty to disclose or abstain and that, regardless, the confidentiality agreement alleged in the complaint also contained an agreement not to trade on the information and that agreement would create such a duty.

* * *

While *O'Hagan* did not set the contours of a relationship of "trust and confidence" giving rise to the duty to disclose or abstain and misappropriation liability, we are tasked to determine whether Cuban had such a relationship with Mamma.com. The SEC seeks to rely on Rule 10b5–2(b)(1), which states that a person has "a duty of trust and confidence" for purposes of misappropriation liability when that person "agrees to maintain information in confidence." In dismissing the case, the district court read the complaint to allege that Cuban agreed not to disclose any confidential information but did not agree not to trade, that such a confidentiality agreement was insufficient to create a duty to disclose or abstain from trading under the misappropriation theory, and that the SEC overstepped its authority under section 10(b) in issuing Rule 10b5–2(b)(1). We differ from the district court in reading the complaint and need not reach the latter issues.

The complaint alleges that, in March 2004, Cuban acquired 600,000 shares, a 6.3% stake, of Mamma.com. Later that spring, Mamma.com decided to raise capital through a PIPE [Private Investment in Public Equity] offering on the advice of the investment bank Merriman Curhan Ford & Co. At the end of June, at Merriman's suggestion, Mamma.com decided to invite Cuban to participate in the PIPE offering. . . .

After getting in touch with Cuban on June 28, Mamma.com's CEO told Cuban he had confidential information for him and Cuban agreed to keep whatever information the CEO shared confidential. The CEO then told Cuban about the PIPE offering. Cuban became very upset "and said, among other things, that he did not like PIPEs because they dilute the existing shareholders." "At the end of the call, Cuban told the CEO 'Well, now I'm screwed. I can't sell.' ". . . . The CEO then sent Cuban a follow up email, writing " '[i]f you want more details about the private placement please contact . . . [Merriman].' "

Cuban called the Merriman representative and they spoke for eight minutes. "During that call, the salesman supplied Cuban with additional confidential details about the PIPE. In response to Cuban's questions, the salesman told him that the PIPE was being sold at a discount to the market price and that the offering included other incentives for the PIPE investors." It is a plausible inference that Cuban learned the off-market prices available to him and other PIPE participants.

With that information and one minute after speaking with the Merriman representative, Cuban called his broker and instructed him to sell his entire stake in the company. Cuban sold 10,000 shares during the evening of June 28, 2004, and the remainder during regular trading the next day. . . .

After the markets closed on June 29, Mamma.com announced the PIPE offering. The next day, Mamma.com's stock price fell 8.5% and continued to decline over the next week, eventually closing down 39% from the June 29 closing price. By selling his shares when he did, Cuban avoided over $750,000 in losses. Cuban notified the SEC that he had sold his stake in the company and publically stated that he sold his shares because Mamma.com "was conducting a PIPE, which issued shares at a discount to the prevailing market price and also would have caused his ownership position to be diluted."

In reading the complaint to allege only an agreement of confidentiality, the [district] court held that Cuban's statement that he was "screwed" because he "[could not] sell" "appears to express his belief, at least at that time, that it would be illegal for him to sell his Mamma.com shares based on the information the CEO provided." But the court stated that this statement "cannot reasonably be understood as an agreement not to sell based on the information." The court found "the complaint asserts no facts that reasonably suggest that the CEO intended to obtain from Cuban an agreement to refrain from trading on the information as opposed to an agreement merely to keep it confidential.". . . .

Reading the complaint in the light most favorable to the SEC, we reach a different conclusion. In isolation, the statement "Well, now I'm screwed. I can't sell" can plausibly be read to express Cuban's view that learning the confidences regarding the PIPE forbade his selling his stock before the offering but to express no agreement not to do so. However, after Cuban expressed the view that he could not sell to the CEO, he gained access to the confidences of the PIPE offering. . . . Cuban called [Merriman], who told Cuban "that the PIPE was being sold at a discount to the market price and that the offering included other incentives for the PIPE investors." Only after Cuban reached out to obtain this additional information, following the statement of his understanding that he could not sell, did Cuban contact his broker and sell his stake in the company.

The allegations, taken in their entirety, provide more than a plausible basis to find that the understanding between the CEO and Cuban was that he was not to trade, that it was more than a simple confidentiality agreement. . . . It is at least plausible that each of the parties understood, if only implicitly, that Mamma.com would only provide the terms and conditions of the offering to Cuban for the purpose of evaluating whether he would participate in the offering, and that Cuban could not use the information for his own personal benefit. It would require additional facts that have not been put before us for us to conclude that the parties could not plausibly have reached this shared understanding. Under Cuban's reading, he was allowed to trade on the information but prohibited from telling others-in effect providing him an exclusive license to trade on the material nonpublic information. Perhaps this was the understanding, or perhaps Cuban mislead the CEO regarding the timing of his sale in order to obtain a confidential look at the details of the PIPE.[38] We say only that on this factually sparse record, it is at least equally plausible that all sides understood there was to be no trading before the PIPE. That both Cuban and the CEO expressed the belief that Cuban could not trade appears to reinforce the plausibility of this reading.

Given the paucity of jurisprudence on the question of what constitutes a relationship of "trust and confidence" and the inherently fact-bound nature of determining whether such a duty exists, we decline to first determine or place our thumb on the scale in the district court's determination of its presence or to now draw the contours of any liability that it might bring, including the force of Rule 10b5–2(b)(1). Rather, we VACATE the judgment dismissing the case and REMAND to the court of first instance for further proceedings including discovery, consideration of summary judgment, and trial, if reached.

NOTES

1. *Trial.* In 2013, a jury cleared Cuban of insider trading. Cuban, testifying at trial, denied that he ever agreed to maintain the information relating to the PIPE offering in confidence.

---

[38] Such an arrangement would raise serious tipper/tippee liability concerns were it explicit. If the CEO knowingly gave Cuban material nonpublic information and arranged so he could trade on it, it would not be difficult for a court to infer that the CEO must have done so for some personal benefit-e.g., goodwill from a wealthy investor and large minority stakeholder. . . . This of course is not to suggest any such improprieties occurred; rather, it simply reinforces the plausibility of the interpretation of the alleged facts as evidencing an understanding that the agreement included an agreement by Cuban not to trade.

QUESTIONS

1. Why does it matter whether Cuban agreed not to trade based on confidential information? Isn't it enough that Cuban agreed not to tell others of the confidential information he obtained from Mamma.com?

2. Given the ambiguities that can often arise about the scope of a confidentiality agreement, why not assume that a general promise not to tell others presumptively includes an agreement not to trade on the information?

3. Consider the opposite presumption. Why not presume that, outside of the family context, a duty of trust or confidence regarding the use of confidential information can arise only if a person signs a written confidentiality agreement?

C. REMEDIES

Following a wave of insider trading scandals in the mid-1980s, Congress enacted the Insider Trading and Securities Fraud Enforcement Act of 1988. The Act increases sanctions for insider trading in the following ways:

- A controlling person of someone who is found liable for insider trading or tipping can be held liable for a civil penalty not exceeding the greater of $1 million or three times the profits made or losses avoided by the controlled person, if the controlling person knew, or should have known, about the violation and failed to prevent such a violation (codified in § 21A of the Exchange Act)

- The Act authorizes the SEC to pay bounties to persons who provide information that eventually leads to imposition of a civil penalty on the alleged violator of insider trading law. The informant can receive up to 10% of the penalty collected (codified in § 21A of the Exchange Act)

- The Act clarifies who has standing to bring a private cause of action based on insider trading (codified in § 20A of the Exchange Act). Section 20A authorizes contemporaneous traders to bring an action against the person who unlawfully traded on material, nonpublic information. The measure of damages in a private cause of action is the profits gained or losses avoided by the defendant (disgorgement).

HYPOTHETICAL FOUR

Return to the Primary World hypothetical. Recall that the following transactions took place:

- Jack, the CEO of Amtel, informed Primary World of Amtel's plans to make an unsolicited tender offer for all of ARM's shares

- Jack ordered his broker to sell 50% of Jack's two million Amtel shares and to purchase call options for ARM shares
- Raj, acting on a tip from Primary World on the tender offer, sells 10,000 of his own Amtel shares

Suppose that Primary World promised Jack that it will keep information on the tender offer confidential and will only use the information for later "academic" research on tender offers.

1.   Has Jack violated the misappropriation theory by purchasing ARM options? By selling his Amtel shares? Would it make a difference if the Amtel board of directors had approved Jack's transactions in advance?

2.   Has Primary World violated the misappropriation theory? Has Raj?

3.   What liability would Jack or Raj face in an action brought by the SEC? *See* Exchange Act § 21A. Would Primary World face any liability?

4.   What if Primary World announces to Jack its intention to sell Jack's information to those who will trade on the information? Can Primary World do so under the misappropriation theory? Does it matter when Primary World announces its intention; prior to when Jack gives the information or only after Jack has revealed the information?

5.   If any of these transactions violated the misappropriation theory, who has standing to bring a private right of action? *See* Exchange Act § 20A.

6.   Did Jack violate Rule 14e–3 by purchasing ARM options? By selling his Amtel shares? Did Raj?

7.   Suppose Amtel was selling preferred stock in a private placement at the time it was contemplating the ARM tender offer. Assuming nondisclosure of the tender offer, would it have violated the misappropriation theory?

———

After *O'Hagan* we are left with the following doctrinal matrix for Rule 10b–5 liability. Keep in mind that other rules interact with Rule 10b–5 to regulate informational advantages. Most important of these are Regulation FD (selective disclosures, covered in Chapter 4) and Rule 14e–3 (tender offer related information).

	Insider Trader	**Outsider Trader**
Corporate (inside) Information	*Chiarella* classical theory *Dirks* temporary insiders	*Dirks* tipper-tippee liability
Outside Information		*O'Hagan* misappropriation theory

HYPOTHETICAL FIVE

Suppose that Jack, the CEO of Amtel, learns at his bridge club that Orange, Inc. (a competing high technology company) is planning to file for bankruptcy. Assume that this is non-public, material information but also highly relevant to the stock price of Amtel. An officer of Orange carelessly happens to mention this information at the bridge club and Jack simply overheard. Can Jack buy Amtel stock while in possession of this non-public, material information? Does he violate his fiduciary duty to Amtel's shareholders by trading?

D. ALTERNATIVES TO THE MISAPPROPRIATION THEORY

Insider trading typically involves the non-disclosure of non-public material information by traders seeking to profit from the information through securities trades. Indeed, disclosure of the information may very well lead to the incorporation of the information into the market price, obviating any possible trading profits from the information. If the person making insider trades is silent, we have seen two possible ways that courts have found the person's silence deceptive and thus within the scope of Rule 10b–5. Either the person violates a fiduciary duty owed directly to the traded corporation and its shareholders (the classical theory) or the person violates a fiduciary duty, or similar duty of trust or confidence, owed to a third party source of the information (the misappropriation theory).

Some puzzles persist in the reach of the insider trading prohibition. There is no deceit if the brazen misappropriator informs the third-party source of her intent to use the source's information in securities trades. In *Rocklage*, we saw that not all disclosures to the source by the misappropriator will shield against Rule 10b–5 liability. If the misappropriator obtains the information deceptively, then disclosing an intent to trade on the information to the source shortly before trading will not necessarily undo the original deception.

What if a person simply steals the information from either the corporation or a third-party source? From a policy perspective, one justification for the misappropriation theory is that it protects the property rights of the source of the information. But if property rights underlie the misappropriation theory, why allow those who steal the information to escape insider trading liability simply because they do not owe a duty of trust or confidence to the source?

Locks and corporate security make it difficult for outsiders to break into corporate offices and rummage through files for non-public, material information. Today, a new breed of thieves have taken to the Internet to obtain corporate information, hacking into corporate servers and obtaining information without ever setting foot on corporate property. How should insider trading theory deal with hackers?

SEC v. Dorozhko

574 F.3d 42 (2d Cir. 2009).

■ CABRANES, J., CIRCUIT JUDGE.

We are asked to consider whether, in a civil enforcement lawsuit brought by the SEC under Section 10(b), computer hacking may be "deceptive" where the hacker did not breach a fiduciary duty in fraudulently obtaining material, nonpublic information used in connection with the purchase or sale of securities. For the reasons stated herein, we answer the question in the affirmative. . . .

In early October 2007, defendant Oleksandr Dorozhko, a Ukranian national and resident, opened an online trading account with

Interactive Brokers LLC and deposited $42,500 into that account. At about the same time, IMS Health, Inc. announced that it would release its third-quarter earnings during an analyst conference call scheduled for October 17, 2007 at 5 p.m.-that is, after the close of the securities markets in New York City. IMS had hired Thomson Financial, Inc. to provide investor relations and web-hosting services, which included managing the online release of IMS's earnings reports.

Beginning at 8:06 a.m. on October 17, and continuing several times during the morning and early afternoon, an anonymous computer hacker attempted to gain access to the IMS earnings report by hacking into a secure server at Thomson prior to the report's official release. At 2:15 p.m.-minutes after Thomson actually received the IMS data-that hacker successfully located and downloaded the IMS data from Thomson's secure server.

Beginning at 2:52 p.m., defendant-who had not previously used his Interactive Brokers account to trade-purchased $41,670.90 worth of IMS "put" options that would expire on October 25 and 30, 2007.[1] These purchases represented approximately 90% of all purchases of "put" options for IMS stock for the six weeks prior to October 17. In purchasing these options, which the SEC describes as "extremely risky," defendant was betting that IMS's stock price would decline precipitously (within a two-day expiration period) and significantly (by greater than 20%).

At 4:33 p.m.—slightly ahead of the analyst call—IMS announced that its earnings per share were 28% below "Street" expectations, i.e., the expectations of many Wall Street analysts. When the market opened the next morning, October 18, at 9:30 a.m., IMS's stock price sank approximately 28% almost immediately-from $29.56 to $21.20 per share. Within six minutes of the market opening, defendant had sold all of his IMS options, realizing a net profit of $286,456.59 overnight. . . .

The District Court . . . denied the SEC's request for a preliminary injunction because the SEC had not shown a likelihood of success. Specifically, the District Court ruled that computer hacking was not "deceptive" within the meaning of Section 10(b) as defined by the Supreme Court. According to the District Court, "a breach of a fiduciary duty of disclosure is a required element of any 'deceptive' device under § 10b." The District Court reasoned that since defendant was a corporate outsider with no special relationship to IMS or Thomson, he owed no fiduciary duty to either. . . .

This appeal followed. On appeal, the SEC maintains its theory that the fraud in this case consists of defendant's alleged computer hacking, which involves various misrepresentations. The SEC does not argue that defendant breached any fiduciary duties as part of his scheme. In this critical regard, we recognize that the SEC's claim against defendant-a corporate outsider who owed no fiduciary duties to the source of the information-is not based on either of the two generally accepted theories of insider trading. The SEC's claim is nonetheless

---

[1]   A "put" is "[a]n option that conveys to its holder the right, but not the obligation, to sell a specific asset at a predetermined price until a certain date. . . . Investors purchase puts in order to take advantage of a decline in the price of the asset."

based on a claim of fraud, and we turn our attention to whether this fraud is "deceptive" within the meaning of Section 10(b). . . .[3]

* * *

The District Court concluded that in *Chiarella*, *O'Hagan*, and *Zandford*, the Supreme Court developed a requirement that any "deceptive device" requires a breach of a fiduciary duty. In applying that interpretation to the instant case, the District Court ruled that "[a]lthough [defendant] may have broken the law, he is not liable in a civil action under § 10(b) because he owed no fiduciary or similar duty either to the source of his information or to those he transacted with in the market." . . . .

In our view, none of the Supreme Court opinions relied upon by the District Court-much less the sum of all three opinions-establishes a fiduciary-duty requirement as an element of every violation of Section 10(b). In *Chiarella*, *O'Hagan*, and *Zandford*, the theory of fraud was silence or nondisclosure, not an affirmative misrepresentation. The Supreme Court held that remaining silent was actionable only where there was a duty to speak, arising from a fiduciary relationship. In *Chiarella*, the Supreme Court held that there was no deception in an employee's silence because he did not have duty to speak. In *O'Hagan*, an attorney who traded on client secrets had a fiduciary duty to inform his firm that he was trading on the basis of the confidential information. Even in *Zandford*, which dealt principally with the statutory requirement that a deceptive device be used "in connection with" the purchase or sale of a security, the defendant's fraud consisted of not telling his brokerage client-to whom he owed a fiduciary duty-that he was stealing assets from the account.

Chiarella, *O'Hagan*, and *Zandford* all stand for the proposition that nondisclosure in breach of a fiduciary duty "satisfies § 10(b)'s requirement . . . [of] a 'deceptive device or contrivance,'" However, what is sufficient is not always what is necessary, and none of the Supreme Court opinions considered by the District Court require a fiduciary relationship as an element of an actionable securities claim under Section 10(b). While *Chiarella*, *O'Hagan*, and *Zandford* all dealt with fraud qua silence, an affirmative misrepresentation is a distinct species of fraud. Even if a person does not have a fiduciary duty to "disclose or abstain from trading," there is nonetheless an affirmative obligation in commercial dealings not to mislead.

In this case, the SEC has not alleged that defendant fraudulently remained silent in the face of a "duty to disclose or abstain" from trading. Rather, the SEC argues that defendant affirmatively

---

[3] In the District Court's view, "the alleged 'hacking and trading' was a 'device or contrivance' within the meaning of the statute." The District Court further observed that the scheme was "in connection with" the purchase or sale of securities because the close temporal proximity of the hacking to the trading (everything occurred in less than twenty-four hours) and the cohesiveness of the scheme (establishing the trading account, stealing the confidential information within minutes of its availability, and trading on it within minutes of the next day's opening bell) suggest that hacking into the Thomson computers was part of a single scheme to commit securities fraud. The District Court also concluded that the alleged hacking was not "manipulative" because the Supreme Court has defined that word to cover exclusively practices "intended to mislead investors by artificially affecting market activity." The parties do not challenge these conclusions in this appeal.

misrepresented himself in order to gain access to material, nonpublic information, which he then used to trade. We are aware of no precedent of the Supreme Court or our Court that forecloses or prohibits the SEC's straightforward theory of fraud. . . . Accordingly, we adopt the SEC's proposed interpretation of *Chiarella* and its progeny: "misrepresentations are fraudulent, but . . . silence is fraudulent only if there is a duty to disclose."

* * *

In its ordinary meaning, "deceptive" covers a wide spectrum of conduct involving cheating or trading in falsehoods. In light of this ordinary meaning, it is not at all surprising that Rule 10b–5 equates "deceit" with "fraud." Indeed, we have previously observed that the conduct prohibited by Section 10(b) and Rule 10b–5 "irreducibly entails some act that gives the victim a false impression."

The District Court-summarizing the SEC's allegations-described the computer hacking in this case as "employ[ing] electronic means to trick, circumvent, or bypass computer security in order to gain unauthorized access to computer systems, networks, and information . . . and to steal such data." On appeal, the SEC adds a further gloss, arguing that, in general, "[computer h]ackers either (1) 'engage in false identification and masquerade as another user['] . . . or (2) 'exploit a weakness in [an electronic] code within a program to cause the program to malfunction in a way that grants the user greater privileges.'" In our view, misrepresenting one's identity in order to gain access to information that is otherwise off limits, and then stealing that information is plainly "deceptive" within the ordinary meaning of the word. It is unclear, however, that exploiting a weakness in an electronic code to gain unauthorized access is "deceptive," rather than being mere theft. Accordingly, depending on how the hacker gained access, it seems to us entirely possible that computer hacking could be, by definition, a "deceptive device or contrivance" that is prohibited by Section 10(b) and Rule 10b–5.

However, we are hesitant to move from this general principle to a particular application without the benefit of the District Court's views as to whether the computer hacking in this case-as opposed to computer hacking in general-was "deceptive." . . . . Having established that the SEC need not demonstrate a breach of fiduciary duty, we now remand to the District Court to consider, in the first instance, whether the computer hacking in this case involved a fraudulent misrepresentation that was "deceptive" within the ordinary meaning of Section 10(b).

* * *

QUESTIONS

1. Does *Dorozhko* involve a non-disclosure of information or an affirmative misrepresentation for purposes of Rule 10b–5?

2. Is there a misrepresentation if Dorozhko enters a false account ID and password into IMS's automated computer servers if no person ever sees the ID or password?

3.   Would Dorozhko have violated Rule 10b–5 if he had simply picked the locks of IMS's corporate headquarters at night and stolen the information?

4.   Suppose Harvey, a professional thief, breaks into Amtel's offices prior to public announcement of the acquisition and uncovers information on the tender offer for ARM. Harvey then purchases ARM options the next day, eventually making $10 million from these trades. Has Harvey violated Rule 10b–5? Rule 14e–3?

V.   SECTION 16

Insider trading was a focal point for criticisms during the hearings that led to the adoption of the Exchange Act. Notwithstanding this attention, § 16 is the only section in which the 1934 Congress explicitly addressed the subject of insider trading. Section 16 takes a three-pronged approach to trading by insiders of companies with an equity security registered with the SEC pursuant to § 12 of the Exchange Act (one of the ways an issuer is deemed a "public company" as discussed in Chapter 4). First, § 16(a) requires statutory insiders (officers, defined in Rule 16a–1, directors and 10% shareholders) to report transactions in their company's equity securities within two business days of the trade. Exchange Act Rule 16a–3. Statutory insiders report by filing Form 3, for initial statements of ownership, or Form 4, for changes in ownership, with the SEC's EDGAR electronic filing system. Statutory insiders must also file an annual statement of their ownership position using Form 5 or, at their discretion, an earlier filed Form 4. The availability of Form 4 on the EDGAR system allows interested observers to track the trading patterns of statutory insiders. The availability of Form 4 filings also allows plaintiffs' attorneys to demonstrate the presence of abnormally high volumes of insider transactions as a means of meeting the pleading scienter with particularity requirement under the PSLRA (discussed in Chapter 5).

Second, § 16(b) requires the disgorgement of "short-swing" profits to the corporation by those same statutory insiders of § 12 public companies. "Short-swing" profits are defined as profits gained (or losses avoided) from a purchase followed by a sale within six months or a sale followed by a purchase within the same period. The corporation is authorized to bring suit under § 16(b) to recover an insider's short-swing profits. What is the likelihood of the statutory insiders authorizing the corporation to bring suit against themselves? Rare indeed, unless the trading insiders are no longer employed by the company. To remedy this potential problem of underenforcement, § 16(b) also authorizes shareholders to bring derivative actions on behalf of the corporation. Not surprisingly, a segment of the plaintiffs' attorney bar specializes in monitoring Form 4 filings to ferret out § 16(b) violations and bring a derivative suit to recover short swing profits. The bright-line rule nature of § 16(b) violations makes litigating such cases relatively easy for plaintiffs' attorneys.

Third, § 16(c) bans all short sales of the company's equity securities by the statutory insiders. Insiders are not allowed to bet against their company, a practice that the 1934 Congress found particularly galling. One of the justifications for prohibiting insider trading under Rule 10b–5 is that corporate insiders may find it easier to bet against the company through short sales and then sabotage the company. With the prohibition on short sales, does the argument for prohibiting insider trading become weaker?

A. SECTION 16 AND EMPLOYEE COMPENSATION

Transactions by officers and directors are relatively straightforward. The only major controversy regarding the transactions of officers and directors involves the exercise of stock options. The SEC broadened § 16 in 1991 to include options, convertible securities, and other rights relating to equity securities as "equity securities of such issuer." The expansion of the definition of "equity security" to include forms of derivative securities not only implicated reporting requirements for options, but also short-swing profits liability under § 16(b). The SEC takes the position that any acquisition or disposition of a derivative security, e.g., an option, involves either a purchase or sale.

Rules 16b–3(d)(3) and 16b–6(b), however, exempt most subsequent exercises and conversions of those derivative securities. This exemption helps reduce potential short-swing profit liability when an insider exercises options, because such a transaction is exempt and therefore does not constitute a "purchase or sale." As a result, these exemptions have eased the administration of employee benefit plans involving derivative securities. Rule 16b–3 exempts transactions between the issuer and its officers or directors in most circumstances. Tax-conditioned plans (these include a "Qualified Plan," "Excess Benefit Plan" or "Stock Purchase Plan") are exempted almost across the board; other transactions with the issuer are exempted if they are approved by the board, a committee of independent directors, or the shareholders.

One nuance regarding the application of § 16 to officers and directors is timing: Rule 16a–2 exempts transactions occurring within the six months *before* becoming an officer or a director. Transactions occurring during the six months *after* ceasing to be an officer or director are *not* exempt.

Congress added another trading restriction for officers and directors in § 306 of the Sarbanes-Oxley Act. Section 306 prohibits officers and directors from trading in the company's securities during any blackout period of more than three days during which the employees of the corporation are barred from trading the company's securities held in employee benefit plans (a "blackout period"). Any profits from prohibited trading can be recovered by the company, either directly or through a derivative action by any of the company's security holders.

B. SPECIAL ISSUES WITH LARGE BLOCK SHAREHOLDERS

Transactions by 10% shareholders can pose analytical difficulties for the determination of § 16 short swing profits. The easiest case for the application of § 16 occurs when an existing shareholder with more than 10% beneficial ownership of any class of equity securities of a public company (with securities registered pursuant to § 12) purchases common stock of the public company and then sells the common stock at a profit within a six-month period.

But what if either the purchase or sale by the 10% shareholder is not voluntary? Suppose, for example, that a 10% shareholder purchases additional shares as part of an attempted hostile takeover. The target company engineers a merger with a "White Knight" to thwart the shareholder's hostile bid. As a result of the merger agreement, the 10% shareholder is forced to exchange its shares in the public company for shares in a newly formed entity within six months of the earlier purchase date. The Supreme Court has held that a shareholder's involuntary exchange of shares as part of the merger does not itself count as a "sale." *See Kern County Land Co. v. Occidental Petroleum Corp.*, 411 U.S. 582, 600 (1973) ("We do not suggest that an exchange of stock pursuant to a merger may never result in § 16(b) liability. But the involuntary nature of Occidental's exchange [Occidental was the failed bidder-shareholder for the target company], when coupled with the absence of the possibility of speculative abuse of inside information, convinces us that § 16(b) should not apply to transactions such as this one.").

The application of § 16 to a shareholder turns on the shareholder's percentage ownership of shares. But both purchase and sale transactions may affect a shareholder's ownership percentage. When should we measure ownership for purposes of the 10% ownership threshold in § 16? Section 16(b) states that it does not apply "where such beneficial owner was not such both at the time of the purchase and sale, or the sale and purchase. . . ." Accordingly, we look to both the time of purchase and sale in assessing the 10% threshold. This formulation, however, gives rise to issues of interpretation. Suppose, for example, that a person has less than 10% ownership in a public company initially. The person purchases shares, bringing her ownership above 10% immediately after the purchase. Is the person a 10% owner at the time of the purchase? With respect to the initial purchase, the Supreme Court has answered in the negative—ownership is measured immediately before, not after, the purchase. *See Foremost-McKesson, Inc. v. Provident Securities Co.*, 423 U.S. 232, 249–250 (1976) ("We hold that, in a purchase-sale sequence, a beneficial owner must account for profits only if he was a beneficial owner 'before the purchase.' ").

Suppose instead that a person with over 10% ownership at the time of purchase of additional equity shares later engages in two sale transactions within six months of the purchase. In the first sale, the person reduces her ownership down to 9.95%. In the second sale, the person sells all her remaining shares. Is the second sale subject to § 16 short-swing profit recapture? The Supreme Court has held that while § 16 applies to the first sale, it does not apply to the second sale regardless of intent. *See Reliance Elec. Co. v. Emerson Elec. Co.*, 404 U.S. 418, 425 (1972) ("If a 'two-step' sale of a 10% owner's holdings within six months of purchase is thought to give rise to the kind of evil that Congress sought to correct through § 16(b), those transactions can be more effectively deterred by an amendment to the statute that preserves its mechanical quality than by a judicial search for the will-o'-the-wisp of an investor's 'intent' in each litigated case.").

What if groups of shareholders act in concert? Consider Shareholder A that owns 8% of the stock of a public corporation and

Shareholder B that owns 9% of the stock of the same corporation. Individually, neither would qualify as a 10% shareholder for § 16 purposes. However, Rule 16a–1(a)(1) provides that "[s]olely for purposes of determining whether a person is a beneficial owner of more than ten percent of any class of equity securities," the term "beneficial owner" means, with various exceptions, "any person who is deemed a beneficial owner pursuant to section 13(d) of the Act and the rules thereunder." Section 13(d)(3) of the Securities Exchange Act aggregates the ownership of separate shareholders "[w]hen two or more persons act as a partnership, limited partnership, syndicate, or other group for the purpose of acquiring, holding, or disposing of securities of an issuer, such syndicate or group shall be deemed a 'person' for the purposes of this subsection." If Shareholders A and B are acting together as a group with the purpose of "acquiring, holding, or disposing" the securities of a public company (typically with a common purpose to acquire or continue control over the company), their ownership is aggregated for purposes of determining the 10% threshold under § 16.

QUESTION

1.   What if two shareholders, each with a 6% ownership block in a public company, decide to act in concert to acquire 5% additional ownership (split equally between the two) in the company. Two months after the additional purchase, the two shareholders have a disagreement and no longer coordinate their actions. One month later, one of the shareholders chooses to sell the 2.5% block of shares she purchased several months earlier (bringing her individual ownership down from 8.5% back to the original 6%). Does § 16(b) apply to the sale of the 2.5% block?

C. CALCULATING SECTION 16(b) DAMAGES

Section 16(b) provides for strict liability for officers, directors, and 10% beneficial owners who purchase-sell or sell-purchase within any six month period. If insiders make only two transactions—e.g., a purchase followed by a sale of the same amount of stock—calculating profits is straightforward. But what if an insider has multiple purchases and sales during the six month period? Consider the following pattern of trades:

Date	Shares Purchased	Purchase Price	Shares Sold	Sale Price
1/1	1,000	$10		
2/1			1,000	$ 8
3/1	1,000	$12		
4/1			1,000	$13
5/1	1,000	$14		
5/15			1,000	$14.50

Looking at this pattern, note that the insider purchased a total of 3,000 shares for $36,000 and then sold 3,000 shares for $35,500 during a six-month period. Consequently, one might think that the insider lost a net $500 on her trades during the six-month period. Another way to look at how the insider performs is to look at each pair of buy-sell transactions that occur in sequence. After the first buy-sell transaction (completed on 2/1), the insider has lost a net $2,000. After the second buy-sell transaction (completed on 4/1), the insider has lost a net $1,000. And after the third buy-sell transaction (completed on 5/15) the insider has lost a net $500.

However, courts calculate damages under § 16(b) to generate the maximum possible profits possible. In *Smolowe v. Delendo Corp.*, 136 F.2d 231, 239 (2d Cir.), cert. denied, 320 U.S. 751 (1943), the Second Circuit explained:

> The statute is broadly remedial. Recovery runs not to the stockholder, but to the corporation. We must suppose that the statute was intended to be thoroughgoing, to squeeze all possible profits out of stock transactions, and thus to establish a standard so high as to prevent any conflict between the selfish interest of a fiduciary officer, director, or stockholder and the faithful performance of his duty.... The only rule whereby all possible profits can be surely recovered is that of lowest price in, highest price out—within six months—as applied by the district court.

If there are multiple purchase and sell orders in a six-month period, matching lowest price purchase orders with highest price sell orders may result in § 16 short swing profits even if an insider does not make profits on net when all transactions are taken into account. Following the "lowest price in, highest price out" methodology, the trades in the table are matched as follows:

1/1 purchase of 1,000 at $10 → 5/15 sale of 1,000 at $14.50

> (Profit = $4,500)

3/1 purchase of 1,000 at $12 → 4/1 sale of 1,000 at $13

> (Profit = $1,000)

The total profit for § 16(b) purposes is therefore $5,500.

No other matches are then made if they would result in zero or negative profits. The 5/1 purchase of 1,000 shares at $14 is not matched with the 2/1 sale of 1,000 shares at $8, which would generate a loss of $6,000, giving a net profit of-$500. The "lowest price in, highest price out" methodology therefore does not consider the insider's net investment performance during the six month statutory window, but instead focuses solely on the pairs of transactions generating the greatest profit calculation, and thus, the largest damages award.

QUESTION

1.   Although the "lowest price in, highest price out" formula maximizes profits to be disgorged, it is hard to see how an insider who is an overall loser during the statutory six-month period has been exploiting an informational advantage. If the § 16(b) profit calculation is arbitrary, why not simply impose an arbitrary damage amount (e.g., a flat $100,000 penalty)?

CHAPTER 7

PUBLIC OFFERINGS

Rules and Statutes

—*Sections 2(a)(3), 2(a)(4), 2(a)(7), 2(a)(10), 2(a)(11), 4(a)(1), 4(a)(3), 4(a)(4), 5, 7(a), 8, 10 of the Securities Act*

—*Rules 134, 135, 137, 138, 139, 153, 163, 163A, 164, 168, 169, 172, 173, 174, 193, 405, 408(b), 409, 412, 413, 415, 421, 424, 430, 430A, 430B, 430C, 431, 433, 460, 461, 462 of the Securities Act*

—*Forms S–1, S–3*

—*Regulation S–K, Items 512(a), 1100, 1104, 1111*

—*Rule 15c2–8 of the Exchange Act*

—*Regulation M, Rules 100–105*

MOTIVATING HYPOTHETICAL

J.R. is the CEO of Ewing Oil, Inc., an oil services company that has been a pioneer in hydraulic fracturing, commonly referred to in the business as "fracking." Hydraulic fracturing is a practice used to coax oil and natural gas from hard rock formations. It involves forcing large amounts of pressurized water, sand, and chemicals down the wellbore to create tiny fissures in the rock so the oil and gas can flow through the wellbore to the surface. Ewing Oil provides its services to many of the world's largest oil producers. Ray, Ewing Oil's chief engineer, has developed a new fracking process involving much higher pressures at the wellbore. Ray believes that his "turbo-fracking" process will allow for extraction of oil and gas at unprecedented depths. Ewing Oil has been closely held by the Ewing family, but it now needs a substantial amount of capital to develop Ray's turbo-fracking technology. If the company's bet on turbo-fracking pays off, J.R. believes Ewing Oil will become the dominant player in the oil services industry. To fund the expansion, J.R. is considering various financing options, including an initial public offering (IPO) of Ewing Oil common stock.

I. ECONOMICS OF PUBLIC OFFERINGS

Businesses exist to make a profit. To generate profits, businesses sell goods and services to customers in return for money. Revenues translate into profits, however, only after businesses pay for the inputs required to produce those goods and services. Costs may include expenses for employees, electricity, supplies, leases, and so on. Certain expenses go to items that provide value in the immediate future (e.g., the wages for an employee to work for the next month). Other expenses, termed capital expenses, reflect purchases of tangible assets that can be used for production for an extended period of time (e.g., a drilling rig).

Some businesses require relatively few capital assets. Consider a photography business run by a sole proprietor; she may purchase a camera and some lights. By far the greatest expense of the photographer is her own time and effort (commonly referred to as the photographer's "human capital," although not by accountants). At the other end of the spectrum are businesses requiring significant amounts of more traditional capital assets. General Motors makes automobiles and trucks, which requires significant assets in the form of factories. In addition, it purchases large amounts of steel and other raw materials.

Capital-intensive businesses may have a timing problem. Products will eventually generate revenue when sold, but businesses often must make expenditures well before the time of sale. Ewing Oil needs to spend considerable amounts of money up front to develop its turbo-fracking technology (say $200 million). The expenditure on research and development (a capital expense) will generate revenue when oil companies hire Ewing Oil to help them exploit their oil and gas reserves. That revenue stream will continue for many years after (say $20 million per year). Although the stream of revenues over time may eventually exceed the initial capital costs, a capital-intensive business initially spends far more cash than it receives (in the case of Ewing Oil, a $180 million deficit after one year).

Companies can cover such cash flow shortfalls in a variety of ways. Many smaller businesses find investment funds through either internally generated funds, such as the prior year's profits, or through investments by the founder-owners of the business. A photographer in a sole proprietorship will typically put her own money into buying a camera. As the business grows, the photographer may use some of the earnings to purchase additional gear.

Larger businesses often face capital expenditures that dwarf the resources of most individuals. Few individuals can finance the purchase of an entire automobile factory (and even if they could, they may not wish to put such a substantial portion of their wealth into one particular investment). Some larger businesses may finance a large capital expenditure out of internally generated funds. Microsoft, for example, sits on an enormous cash hoard that it can draw upon to purchase other businesses without relying on outside financing. Businesses lacking the tremendous cash flow of Microsoft have a range of external solutions to the timing problem.

Banks lend considerable sums to businesses. In exchange for the loan, banks will typically demand a security interest in the assets of the debtor-business and possibly a personal guarantee from the owners of the business. Bank debt, however, comes with constraints. As a loan, bank debt typically requires businesses to make regular interest and principal payments. For some projects, the expected stream of revenues may be uncertain and only available far into the future, if at all. In the late 1990s, entrepreneurs started a flurry of new Internet-based businesses. These startups, such as Amazon.com, promised potentially high returns, but only in the distant future and with great risk. (Most of these startups did, in fact, fail.) Such companies do not generate sufficient revenue to make interest and principal payments in the first few years after the loan is made. Banks will also often impose numerous covenants designed to protect their debt investment, including minimum debt-equity ratios and limitations on the ability of a company to spend their money.

Many businesses raise additional capital by selling equity. Unlike debt, equity capital affords the flexibility of not requiring fixed payments. As the saying goes, "Equity is soft; debt is hard." Companies that expect profits only in the distant future may find equity financing better suited to their needs. Equity, however, has a downside for the company's pre-existing owners, as bringing in more equity owners dilutes the potential upside return. If the company sells more common stock, the pre-existing common stock holders (e.g., the founders of the company) are left with a smaller proportionate share of the profits. This effect is commonly called "dilution."

Bringing outside investors into a business also poses another problem: How will the outside investors know that the business will be operated to benefit *all* the equity owners, rather than have its profits and assets diverted to the founders or managers of the firm? Businesses seeking to expand their ownership base typically will take advantage of one of the off-the-shelf organizational forms provided under state law (e.g., limited partnership, LLC, or corporation). Those forms carry with them restrictions on self-dealing by managers, which are intended to ease the concerns of potential investors. These restrictions—if effective—increase the amount investors are willing to pay for an ownership stake in the business.

In summary, a project requiring large initial expenditures with greater returns in the future is the classic motive for raising capital. Businesses have choices in raising capital. Companies may self-finance through retained earnings or they may turn to their existing shareholders for more capital contributions. Larger sums can come from a bank loan. Even larger sums can be financed through the broader capital markets. In this chapter we discuss the application of the federal securities laws to one avenue for raising capital—the decision on the part of companies to raise capital through a public offering of securities. In Chapter 9, we discuss a different option—the private placement of securities to sophisticated investors.

A. A BRIEF DESCRIPTION OF THE PUBLIC OFFERING PROCESS

Suppose that J.R. and the board of directors of Ewing Oil decide to pursue an initial public offering of common stock. What is the next step? Typically J.R. would talk to a Wall Street investment bank.

If Ewing Oil has a visible public presence and the market for IPOs is "hot," investment bankers already may have approached J.R. about a potential public offering. The market for IPOs ebbs and flows. In a slower market, or if Ewing Oil is less prominent, J.R. may need to seek out the Wall Street investment banks herself, either directly or through an intermediary such as Ewing Oil's attorneys (who may have contacts with Wall Street law firms and investment banks).

What role do investment banks play as underwriters in a public offering? First, particularly for companies going public for the first time, underwriters provide advice on the structure of the corporation, the securities to be offered, and the offering amount and price. The goal of this process is to make the firm and the offering as attractive as possible to public investors. Many startup companies develop complex capital structures and control relationships to accommodate the interests of various early-stage investors. The public capital market, in contrast, prefers straightforward capital structures, which make it easier to value the securities being offered. Consequently, IPO companies will typically have only one class of common stock. The public capital markets also favor certain corporate governance features (such as an independent board and a separate chairman and CEO), so companies going public will typically adjust their board structure to meet those expectations.

Second, investment banks help guide companies through the SEC's registration process. As you will discover in this chapter, the securities laws require companies making a public offering to file and distribute mandatory disclosure documents containing information on the company, its management, and financials as well as information related to the offering (e.g., the security being offered, the underwriters, the discount for the underwriters, the number of securities offered, and the offering price). The securities laws also restrict the ability of companies to discuss the offering or otherwise condition the market for the upcoming public offering.

Finally, underwriters are salesmen: they market the securities to the public. As repeat players in the capital markets, investment banks bring with them a wealth of contacts with institutional investors and securities dealers, which they rely on to promote demand for the offering.

1. DIFFERENT TYPES OF OFFERINGS

Issuers can access the public capital markets in a number of ways. Recent years have witnessed the rise of innovations such as Internet-based offerings and auction offerings, albeit with only limited acceptance to date. The most common type of offering continues to be the firm commitment. Below we describe briefly the firm commitment as well as three lesser-used alternatives—best efforts, direct public offerings, and the Dutch auction.

Firm Commitment. In a firm commitment, the underwriter guarantees the sale of the offering. Technically, the underwriter (or a group of underwriters forming a "syndicate") will purchase the entire offering from the issuer before turning around and reselling the securities to investors. From the issuer's standpoint, the underwriter's purchase ensures that the issuer will receive a certain amount of proceeds from the offering. The underwriter purchases the securities from the issuer at a discount to the price at which they subsequently will be offered to the public. The underwriter receives the discount for both helping to sell the offering and taking on the risk that the offering may not sell.

Consider the following example. If Ewing Oil plans on selling 10 million shares at $20 per share, the underwriter may purchase the shares from Ewing Oil at $18.60 per share, for a $1.40 underwriter's discount—often referred to as the "gross spread." Typically, the gross spread accounts for 7% of the public offering price for an initial public offering. The underwriter earns its return when it resells the shares to the public at $20 per share.

The certainty provided by a firm commitment offering may help ensure the value of the offering to both the issuer and investors. Consider Ewing Oil, which needs to raise $200 million to develop its turbo-fracking technology. A firm commitment offering ensures all investors that the company will in fact obtain the full $200 million, which makes the investment more likely to be profitable for the investors. The underwriters' commitment to purchase the entire offering may also signal the investment bankers' confidence in the issuer.

Best Efforts. An investment bank assisting in a best efforts offering agrees only to use its "best efforts" to sell the offering. Unlike a firm commitment, the investment bank does not purchase the securities. Instead, the investment bank acts purely as a selling agent, receiving a commission on each security sold. Compared to the firm commitment offering, the investment bank assumes less risk and the issuer retains more risk. If the securities do not sell, the issuer will receive smaller proceeds. The underwriter will only bear the opportunity cost of commissions unearned; it will not be stuck holding unattractive securities. Typically smaller, more speculative companies that cannot attract a firm commitment underwriting from an investment bank raise capital through best efforts public offerings.

Investors face greater risks in a best efforts offering. First, because the investment bank is not putting its own money on the line, the investors have less confidence in the securities' valuation. Investment banks in a firm commitment offering, by contrast, have a strong incentive to ensure that the offering is priced correctly, or even underpriced, lest they be left holding the securities.

Second, the issuer may not sell out the entire issue in a best efforts offering. If the offering is intended to fund the development of a new product, or the entry into a new market, obtaining only a fraction of the expected offering proceeds may jeopardize the business plan. If a new product launch requires $100 million, what good does it do to raise $25 million in a best efforts offering? To combat such fears, a variant of the best efforts offerings is the conditional best efforts offering under which the underwriters and issuer promise to rescind all sales if the offering is not sold out ("all or nothing").

Direct Public Offering. Issuers can sell securities directly to the investing public without an underwriter. The most common form of direct public offering involves an offering by a company to its existing public shareholders (referred to as a "rights" offering), but it is also possible for a company to sell to the public at large. Direct public offerings to the public at large are rare. First, many issuers lack the necessary expertise to complete a public offering (pricing, marketing, etc.). Issuers also lack a pre-existing network among securities dealers and large institutional investors. Second, investment banks play a gatekeeping role. Investors look to the investment bank to screen out poor or fraudulent offerings. With no investment bank to vouch for the offering, investors are likely to discount substantially the price they are willing to pay for the offered securities.

Dutch Auction Offering. A recent innovation in public offerings is the Dutch auction. In a Dutch auction, the issuer and underwriters do not fix a price for the offering. Instead, investors place bids for a desired number of shares at a specified price. After all the bids are placed, the issuer then chooses the highest price that will (given the range of bids) result in the offering completely selling out. So for example, imagine that Ewing Oil wants to sell 1 million shares. The following bids are made:

> Bid 1: 200,000 shares for $50 per share
>
> Bid 2: 150,000 shares for $45 per share
>
> Bid 3: 500,000 shares for $40 per share
>
> Bid 4: 150,000 shares for $35 per share
>
> Bid 5: 300,000 shares for $30 per share
>
> Bid 6: 400,000 shares for $20 per share

In this case, the market-clearing price for 1 million shares is $35 per share. At the offering price of $35 per share, the issuer will be able to sell the full 1 million shares. Put another way, the Dutch auction procedure allows the issuer to set the highest single price that will still allow it to sell all the desired shares. It also tends to result in substantially lower fees for the underwriters.

2. THE UNDERWRITERS

An important hierarchy exists among underwriters. Some well-known underwriters, such as Goldman Sachs and Morgan Stanley, stand at the top of the hierarchy. This group is often referred to as the "bulge bracket." Typically, after a successful issuance of securities, the underwriters involved will publish an advertisement known as a "tombstone" providing details of the offering. The tombstone will list all of the underwriters in a series of brackets, with the bulge bracket at the top. Placement in the different brackets depends on the reputation of the particular underwriter and the amount of the offering underwritten by the underwriter (the two concepts are linked, with bulge bracket underwriters typically underwriting the largest portions of the offering and receiving greater selling concessions relative to the other, lower-ranking underwriters participating in the offering). Higher-reputation underwriters generally participate only in offerings of more established companies.

In recent years, many new firms—in particular commercial banks—have joined the ranks of underwriters, which has reduced the cost to issuers. Competition, on the other hand, may lead individual investment bankers eager to drum up more business to sacrifice the long-term reputation of the underwriter to land the big deal at hand, even if the issuer is of questionable quality. Doing so may result in a large bonus for the individual investment banker for bringing in more business, while the reputational hit the underwriter will eventually receive once the market learns of the issuer's problems is spread across the entire firm.

3. THE UNDERWRITING PROCESS

Most public offerings are conducted as firm commitment offerings. Although in theory a single investment bank could take on the entire firm commitment offering, typically a syndicate of underwriters will share the offering. Spreading the offering out among multiple underwriters reduces the risk to any one underwriter of purchasing the securities. Although this reduces the potential profit for any one underwriter, it also reduces the risk of an unsold offering.

In the syndicate, typically one to three underwriters will take on the role of the managing underwriter. Even if an offering has more than one managing underwriter, one investment bank will still take the primary role in the offering (often referred to as the lead or book-running manager). The managing underwriter in charge of the "book" allocates the offered shares among investors. The managing underwriter will take charge of getting the issuer ready for the public offering, ensuring that the registration statement is filed and becomes effective, pricing the offering, performing due diligence for the registration statement, negotiating with the issuer on behalf of the syndicate, and managing the ultimate distribution of the securities to the public. For these extra services, the lead managing underwriter will typically take 20% or so of the gross spread. So if Ewing Oil sells shares to the underwriters at $18.60 and the IPO price is $20.00, the lead managing underwriter will receive $0.28 per share (20% of the $1.40 gross spread) for all shares sold in the offering as compensation for its role as lead manager.

Initially the managing underwriter and the issuer will sign only a non-binding letter of intent to do the public offering. The letter of intent will specify the role of the managing underwriter in the registration process and the size of the underwriting discount (i.e., the gross spread). The letter of intent often will also specify an overallotment option for the underwriters (referred to as the "Green Shoe option," after the first company to use the technique) under which underwriters, at their discretion, may expand the number of shares in the offering up to 15%. The letter of intent will not specify one critical term: the price of the offering. Pricing is left until later—just before sales commence, when the issuer and the underwriters enter into a binding underwriting agreement.

After the registration statement is filed, the managing underwriter(s) will invite other underwriters to participate in the syndicate for the firm commitment offering. To govern their relationship with each other, the members of the syndicate will sign an agreement among themselves. The agreement among underwriters will grant to the lead underwriter the authority to act on behalf of the syndicate. The agreement among underwriters will also specify each underwriter's liability for the offering, which will typically be proportionate to the amount of shares they underwrite.

Members of the syndicate are compensated out of the gross spread through a "selling concession." Typically, the selling concession is about 60% of the gross spread. For the Ewing Oil gross spread of $1.40 per share, the selling concession equals $0.84 per share. Each underwriter receives a selling concession in proportion to the number of shares that the underwriter purchases from the issuer (the underwriter's "allocation" of shares). If any of the allocated shares are sold by another underwriter or a dealer, the selling concession goes to them.

The remaining 20% of the gross spread ($0.28 per share in the Ewing Oil offering) then goes to paying various expenses arising from the offering. These expenses include the fees of the counsel for the underwriters, expenses relating to the "road show," and the costs of stabilization (covered below). The road show involves representatives from the issuer and lead underwriter traveling from city to city promoting the offering to institutional investors.

Just before the offering is made to the public, the issuer and the lead underwriter, acting on behalf of the underwriter syndicate, will finally sign a formal underwriting agreement. The underwriting agreement will set forth the terms of the offering including the number of shares to be sold by the issuer to the underwriters, the public offering price, the gross spread, and the overallotment option. The terms of the agreement are determined by bargaining and regulations. FINRA requires that underwriting fees be "reasonable." Moreover, the SEC will not declare a registration statement effective (i.e., ready for public sale) until FINRA approves the underwriting arrangement. Securities Act Rule 461. The underwriting agreement will also contain representations and warranties by the company to the underwriters, relating to, among other things, the completeness and accuracy of the information contained in the registration statement. In addition, the underwriting agreement frequently will include a provision requiring the issuer to indemnify the underwriters for certain securities law liabilities arising from the offering. (The enforceability of this provision, however, is open to question, as discussed below.)

4.   UNDERPRICING

One of the most curious aspects of the IPO market is underpricing. Companies going public for the first time on average experience a large first-day jump in their stock price from the initial public offering price. During the late 1990s, some Internet companies experienced a first-day increase of over 100%. One spectacular example, theglobe.com, an Internet website hosting company, went public at $9 per share and ended its first-day of trading at $63½ per share, trading as high as $97 on that first day. Underpricing of this sort suggests that issuers are leaving money on the table when they negotiate with the underwriters over the offering price. Issuers could price their offerings higher and obtain greater offering proceeds; rather than obtaining $9 per share for its offering, theglobe.com could have received up to $60 or so per share. Instead, the difference between the offering price and the secondary market price on the first day of trading goes to those investors lucky enough to purchase at the $9 offering price.

Underpricing is even more puzzling given the fact that offerings that have a large first-day "pop" perform relatively poorly over the first three years of the offering. (Query: Where is theglobe.com today?) Why are investors paying steep secondary market prices to buy shares that are likely to perform poorly? Underpricing is greater during "hot" issues markets when many IPOs are brought to market. One of the central advantages claimed for the Dutch auction process, described above, is the elimination of underpricing, which means that the issuer is able to capture greater proceeds from the offering. Recall that in a Dutch auction, the issuer obtains information on the market's willingness to pay for its securities from individual bids for specific quantities of securities, which allows the issuer to select the highest price that still allows it to sell out the offering. The Dutch auction is engineered to ensure that the issuer leaves no money on the table.

The Dutch auction process, while beneficial for the issuer, is less clearly good for the investing public. If underpricing results from the irrational exuberance of investors artificially driving up stock prices on the first day of trading, the Dutch auction process may simply shift the gains from that run up in prices. The irrationally exuberant will simply put in an inflated bid in the auction. The winners in a traditional offering—at the expense of the exuberant investors—are the initial IPO purchasers (often institutional investors), who purchase underpriced shares and profit by reselling these shares in the secondary market. In a Dutch auction, the issuer profits instead. Although the issuer may gain higher offering proceeds, the offering price produced by the auction may still reflect irrational frenzy, leading to an offering price exceeding the company's fundamental value. As the market cools, the secondary market price may decline just as it would under a more traditional public offering. In any event, Dutch auctions are little used.

5. CAPITAL STRUCTURE

A common misconception is that companies going public sell their entire capital stock to the public in an IPO. Suppose that Ewing Oil seeks to sell 10 million shares at $20 per share in its IPO. After a successful offering, Ewing Oil will have $200 million in gross proceeds (ignoring, for now, the gross spread and other expenses) and 10 million shares of publicly traded common stock. As depicted in the table below, the 10 million shares *could* represent the entire amount of outstanding Ewing Oil common stock. For example, a company could conduct a public offering creating the *initial* capital stock of the corporation as depicted below:

	Assets	Liabilities (Equity)
Pre-Offering	$0	$0 (from 0 shares of common stock)
Post-Offering	$200 million	$200 million (from 10 million shares of common stock sold in the public offering)

Such offerings are not common, for the simple reason that they are unlikely to succeed. Investors avoid offerings by companies with no assets, no prior owners and no operating history. A company without any operating history is simply too great a risk. Even if the initial managers of the corporation have a strong business background, investors will wonder why the initial managers have not invested any of their own money prior to the offering.

Companies typically come to an initial public offering with at least some, and often extensive, operating and financial history. With this history come assets and a pre-existing ownership base. Consider the example of Ewing Oil as depicted in the table below.

	Assets	Liabilities (Equity)
Pre-Offering	$25 million	$25 million (from 15 million outstanding shares of common stock primarily in the hands of the Ewing family)
Post-Offering	$225 million	$225 million (from 25 million outstanding shares of common stock after 10 million are sold in the public offering)

Things could get even more complicated. Suppose that in the past, the Ewing Oil business needed a quick injection of capital to overcome a short-term liquidity problem. Digger, a wealthy outside investor, provided the capital in return for preferred stock in Ewing Oil.

	Assets	Liabilities (Equity)
Pre-Offering	$35 million	$25 million (from 15 million outstanding shares of common stock primarily in the hands of the Ewing family) $10 million of preferred stock in the hands of Digger (convertible into 5 million shares of common stock)
Post-Offering	$235 million	$235 million (from 30 million outstanding shares of common stock after 10 million are sold in the public offering and Digger converts his preferred into 5 million shares of common stock)

Moreover, not all businesses are structured as corporations. Entrepreneurs can choose their organizational form under state law from among sole proprietorships, partnerships, limited liability companies and corporations. Prior to its initial public offering, for example, suppose Ewing Oil conducts its business through two separate (and interrelated) organizational forms: the limited partnership (Ewing Oil Partnership) and the corporation (Ewing Oil Management Corp.).

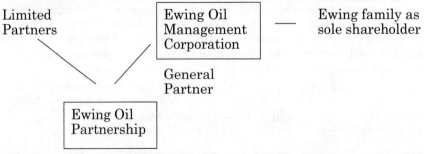

The limited partnership form allows outside investors (pre-public offering) to invest in Ewing Oil while enjoying limited liability and favorable tax treatment. Limited partnerships require one general partner to face unlimited liability, but that liability exposure can be avoided by having a corporation, here Ewing Oil Management Corp., take on the role of general partner. The Ewing family then receives their return as the shareholder of Ewing Oil Management Corp.

Although this moderately complicated structure may work for a small number of outside investors, investors in the public capital markets typically prefer a simple corporate structure—the entire business held by one formally incorporated entity—and a simple capital structure: one class of common stock. These straightforward structures make it easier for outside investors to value their potential returns. Prior to going public, the business, the lead underwriter, and attorneys will reconfigure the various ownership interests and state law entities into a single corporate form with common stock ownership.

Further changes may be necessary. Investors typically prefer companies incorporated in Delaware, the choice of most large public companies. As part of the process of reorganizing for the initial public offering, businesses incorporated in other states will typically reincorporate in Delaware.

B. PUBLIC OFFERING DISCLOSURE

The primary problem facing investors in a public offering is valuing the enterprise. Issuers and their insiders enjoy an informational advantage over outside investors. The risk for outside investors is that issuers may use this advantage to sell overvalued shares. More sophisticated investors compensate by demanding a lower price, which means issuers receive smaller proceeds than they would get if investors had full information. The net effect of information asymmetry is to raise the cost of capital for issuers.

The securities laws respond to the problem of informational advantages by requiring disclosure. The two primary disclosure documents are the registration statement and the statutory prospectus, which contains the disclosures found in Part I of the registration statement. The two documents give rise to two different levels of liability exposure (a topic covered in more detail in Chapter 8):

more complicated

Document	Use	Special Antifraud Provision
Registration Statement S-1, S-3	Filed with SEC	Section 11 Liability —Due diligence defense for non-issuer participants
Statutory Prospectus *(part I of R/S)*	Distributed to Investors	Section 12(a)(2) Liability —Reasonable care defense for sellers

For domestic companies offering securities to the public, the two basic forms for the registration statement are Forms S–1 and S–3. The information required by these registration forms can be divided into three categories: (a) transaction-related information (e.g., the offering amount, use of proceeds, underwriters, etc.), (b) company information, and (c) exhibits and undertakings. A key concept in the application of the Forms is the "public float." The SEC defines the public float as equal to the price of a company's voting and non-voting common equity (determined, among other ways, based on the price at which the company's common equity was last sold) multiplied by the number of voting and non-voting common equity shares held by non-affiliates. Affiliates are those in a control relationship with the company. We cover affiliates in Chapter 10 in our discussion of resales of securities. The forms differ both in what they require and in their eligibility requirements as follows:

- *Form S–1* is available to all issuers. Form S–1 is the most comprehensive of the disclosure documents and contains all three categories of disclosure. The prospectus under Form S–1 contains both company information and transaction-related information. Form S–1 issuers that are Exchange Act reporting issuers and current in their filings for the past twelve months may incorporate company-related information by reference from prior SEC filings, e.g., Forms 10–K, 10–Q, and 8–K (discussed in Chapter 4).

- *Form S–3* is available to issuers that have, among other situations, been a reporting company for one year, are current in their SEC filings, and have a public float over $75 million. In addition, an issuer that has been a reporting company for at least one year, and is not a shell company, may qualify for Form S–3 solely for purposes of a primary offering even if the issuer does not meet the $75 million public float requirement. Such issuers must have a class of common equity securities that is listed and registered on a national securities exchange. In addition, such issuers must limit their sales under Form S–3 in any 12-month period to a maximum of one-third of the issuer's public float. Form S–3 companies may incorporate by reference company-related information contained in prior SEC filings as well as information contained in Exchange Act reports that are filed after the effective date of the Form S–3 registration statement, known as "forward incorporation by reference." Forward incorporation by reference is particularly useful for shelf registration offerings, for which the registration statement may remain effective for a number of years.

Facilitating incorporation-by-reference is the SEC's streamlined integrated disclosure system (introduced in Chapter 4), which provides a consistent set of disclosure requirements in Regulations S–K and S–X for both the Securities and Exchange Acts. Incorporation-by-reference relies on both integrated disclosure and an assumption about how the capital markets process information. Investors in companies trading in a relatively efficient market can rely on publicly available information being reflected in the stock market price. Alternatively, for well-known companies, brokers and others who filter information on behalf of retail investors may canvass the entire array of SEC filings for a company, providing a unified assessment.

The Internet also makes it easier for investors to get information from multiple documents. Indeed, the notion of "a" document is somewhat amorphous on the Internet. If a document on the Internet hyperlinks to another document, should this be treated as one or two documents? Does it matter from the perspective of an investor if the investor has to "click" through a link to obtain more information on a potential investment, as opposed to scrolling down within the same document?

The SEC limits Form S–3 eligibility under the one-third float method to only primary offerings. Instruction 6 to General Instruction I.B.6, Form S–3. Small issuers that qualify for Form S–3 under the alternative one-third public float test may take advantage of shelf registration under Rule 415(a)(1)(x) discussed below. Allowing these issuers to incorporate future filings by reference through Form S–3 allows for automatic updating of the shelf registration statement. Issuers eligible to use Form S–3 under the one-third public float method cannot apply this eligibility to other SEC rules and regulations. For example, Rule 139's exemption for certain research reports by brokers or dealers participating in a public offering, discussed below, requires Form S–3 eligibility. Issuers eligible for Form S–3 through the one-third public float method do not qualify as Form S–3 issuers for purposes of Rule 139.

1. PLAIN ENGLISH DISCLOSURES

In the late 1990s, the SEC reformed the statutory prospectus to make it more accessible to everyday investors. Instead of turgid prose containing jargon and terms comprehensible only to financial professionals, the SEC mandated that the prospectus contain language drafted in a "clear, concise and understandable manner." Consider the following Securities Act rule governing how information is presented in the statutory prospectus:

> Rule 421—Presentation of Information in Prospectuses— Issuers can vary the order of information provided in the prospectus but must ensure that the order does not "obscure any of the required information." Information in the prospectus must be presented in a "clear, concise, and understandable manner" and follow "plain English" principles. Issuers must use "short sentences," "active voice," and avoid "legal and highly technical business terminology."

Readable prose is an admirable goal, but were the SEC's plain English reforms worth the cost? Jargon has its benefits. Some forms of highly technical phrases provide a quick and certain form of communication among those familiar with the jargon. Consider the phrase "cash flow needs will become significant in the second quarter of the upcoming fiscal year." Is "cash flow" jargon? What if we force firms to replace this language with something more understandable, but somewhat less precise such as: "We're spending more than we're taking in." Although a larger segment of investors may understand such a phrase, more sophisticated investors may glean less information if "cash flow" has a commonly understood meaning. Does plain language disclosure sacrificed depth for breadth?

II.　THE GUN-JUMPING RULES

The federal securities laws tightly regulate public offerings under a regime often referred to as the gun-jumping rules. The gun-jumping rules have three broad goals. First, the registration process focuses on two mandatory disclosure documents: a formal registration statement and a statutory prospectus. Second, the gun-jumping rules require the distribution of the statutory prospectus to both investors in the offering and other investors (for a specified period of time). Third, the gun-jumping rules restrict information about the offering if it is not part of the registration statement or prospectus.

The Securities Act divides the public offering process into three periods: the Pre-Filing Period, the Waiting Period, and the Post-Effective Period. The Pre-Filing Period ends and the Waiting Period begins when the issuer files the registration statement with the SEC. The Waiting Period gives way to the Post-Effective Period when the SEC declares the registration statement "effective."

Pre-Filing Period	Waiting Period	Post-Effective Period
	Filing of the Registration Statement	Registration Statement Effective

The three period structure of the gun-jumping rules dates back to the enactment of the Securities Act in 1933. Dramatic change came, however, in 2005 when the SEC adopted a broad ranging series of reforms ("2005 Offering Reforms") to streamline offerings by large, well-followed issuers and to update disclosure requirements to reflect changing information technology. We discuss the impact of the 2005 Offering Reforms on the gun-jumping rules throughout this chapter. Consider the SEC's rationale for the changes as provided in the Promulgating Release below.

Securities Offering Reform
Securities Act Release No. 8591.
Securities and Exchange Commission (July 19, 2005).

I.　Introduction

A.　Overview

* * *

The rules we are adopting today continue the evolution of the offering process under the Securities Act that began as far back as 1966, when Milton Cohen noted the anomaly of the structure of the disclosure rules under the Securities Act and the Exchange Act and suggested the integration of the requirements under the two statutes. Mr. Cohen's article was followed by a 1969 study led by Commissioner Francis Wheat and the Commission's Advisory Committee on Corporate Disclosure in 1977. These studies eventually led to the Commission's adoption of the integrated disclosure system, short-form registration under the Securities Act, and Securities Act Rule 415 permitting shelf registration of continuous offerings and delayed offerings.

The Commission's attention to the offering and communications processes under the Securities Act continued more recently. . . . In July 1996, the Advisory Committee on the Capital Formation and Regulatory Processes delivered its report to the Commission. Its principal recommendation was that the Securities Act registration and disclosure processes be more directly tied to the philosophy and structure of the Exchange Act through the adoption of a system of "company registration." Under company registration, the focus of Securities Act and Exchange Act registration and disclosure would move from transactions to issuers, and corollary steps would be taken to provide for disclosure and registration of individual offerings within the company registration framework. . . .

The rules we are adopting today are focused primarily on constructive, incremental changes in our regulatory structure and the offering process rather than the introduction of a far-reaching new system, as we believe that we can best achieve further integration of Securities Act and Exchange Act disclosure and processes by making adjustments in the current integrated disclosure and shelf registration systems. Further, consistent with our belief that investors and the securities markets will benefit from greater permissible communications by issuers while retaining appropriate liability for these communications, we have sought to address the need for timeliness of information for investors by building on existing statutory provisions and processes without mandating delays in the offering process that we believe would be inconsistent with the needs of issuers for timely access to the securities markets and capital.

* * *

Today's rules reflect our view that revisions to the Securities Act registration and offering procedures are appropriate in light of significant developments in the offering and capital formation procedures and can provide enhanced protection of investors under the statute. We believe that the rule changes we adopt today will:

- Facilitate greater availability of information to investors and the market with regard to all issuers;

- Eliminate barriers to open communications that have been made increasingly outmoded by technological advances;

- Reflect the increased importance of electronic dissemination of information, including the use of the Internet;

- Make the capital formation process more efficient; and

- Define more clearly both the information and the timeliness of the availability of information against which a seller's statements are evaluated for liability purposes.

* * *

B. Background

1. Advances in Technology

As we noted in the Proposing Release, significant technological advances over the last three decades have increased both the market's demand for more timely corporate disclosure and the ability of issuers to capture, process, and disseminate this information. Computers, sophisticated financial software, electronic mail, teleconferencing, videoconferencing, webcasting, and other technologies available today have replaced, to a large extent, paper, pencils, typewriters, adding machines, carbon paper, paper mail, travel, and face-to-face meetings relied on previously. The rules we are adopting today seek to recognize the integral role that technology plays in timely informing the markets and investors about important corporate information and developments.

2.   Exchange Act Reporting Standards

The role that a public issuer's Exchange Act reports play in investment decision making is a key component of the rules we are adopting today. Congress recognized that the ongoing dissemination of accurate information by issuers about themselves and their securities is essential to the effective operation of the trading markets. The Exchange Act and underlying rules have established a system of continuing disclosure about issuers that have offered securities to the public, or that have securities that are listed on a national securities exchange or are broadly held by the public. The Exchange Act rules require public issuers to make periodic disclosures at annual and quarterly intervals, with other important information reported on a more current basis. The Exchange Act specifically provides for current disclosure to maintain the timeliness and adequacy of information disclosed by issuers, and we have significantly expanded our current disclosure requirements . . .

A public issuer's Exchange Act record provides the basic source of information to the market and to potential purchasers regarding the issuer and its management, business, financial condition, and prospects. Because an issuer's Exchange Act reports and other publicly available information form the basis for the market's evaluation of the issuer and the pricing of its securities, investors in the secondary market use that information in making their investment decisions. Similarly, during a securities offering in which an issuer uses a short-form registration statement, an issuer's Exchange Act record is very often the most significant part of the information about the issuer in the registration statement.

* * *

Many of the recent changes to the Exchange Act reporting framework provide greater rigor to the process that issuers must follow in preparing their financial statements and Exchange Act reports. Senior management now must certify the material adequacy of the content of periodic Exchange Act reports. Moreover, issuers, with the involvement of senior management, now must implement and evaluate disclosure controls and procedures and internal controls over financial reporting. Further, we believe the heightened role of an issuer's board of directors and its audit committee provides a structure that can contribute to improved Exchange Act reports. . . .

We believe that the enhancements to Exchange Act reporting described above enable us to rely on these reports to a greater degree in adopting our rules to reform the securities offering process.

* * *

The concept of "company registration" informs the SEC's 2005 Offering Reforms. As the SEC noted in the Promulgating Release and as we will see in this chapter, the focus of the Securities Act is on regulating transactions. Under company registration, however, companies are the regulatory focal point. Microsoft, a large publicly-traded company, has a long history of Exchange Act filings with the SEC. Many analysts follow Microsoft and there is a rich information environment for its common stock. Whether directly or through an efficient market for Microsoft's stock, investors enjoy quite a bit of information on the value of the stock. For a company such as Microsoft, proponents of company registration would argue that the public offering process provides little benefit to investors. What is the point of additional mandatory disclosure or prospectus delivery requirements if the market already has sufficient information to value Microsoft stock? Why use the gun-jumping rules to restrict the ability of Microsoft to communicate other information if sophisticated analysts follow the company and have the ability and resources to assess additional disclosures made by Microsoft?

The SEC did not adopt company registration, but instead incorporated the intuitions behind company registration within the existing transaction-focused regulatory framework. As we go through the gun-jumping rules, consider whether attempting to account for company-level differences while staying within a transaction-focused regime adds unnecessary complexity—at least for law students attempting to learn the rules! Should the SEC instead have moved entirely to company based registration? One could imagine registering a company and then allowing the company to offer securities freely at any time with no more than a Form 8–K filing to indicate the transaction terms and a change in its outstanding capital stock after the offering. Section 28 of the Securities Act gives the SEC sweeping authority by rule or regulation to exempt "any person, security, or transaction" from any provision of the Securities Act, including the transaction focused securities offering regime. Is there some benefit to continuing to regulate specific offering transactions within the Securities Act framework?

In keeping with its incremental move toward company registration within the existing framework of the Securities Act, the SEC divided companies into four groups:

> *Non-Reporting Issuer*—issuer that is not required to file reports pursuant to § 13 or § 15(d) of the Exchange Act.

> *Unseasoned Issuer*—issuer that is required to file reports pursuant to § 13 or § 15(d) of the Exchange Act, but it does not satisfy the requirements of Form S–3 or Form F–3 for a primary offering of its securities.

> *Seasoned Issuer*—issuer that is eligible to use Form S–3 or Form F–3 to register primary offerings of securities. Primary offerings includes securities to be sold by the issuer or on its behalf, on behalf of its subsidiary, or on behalf of a person of which it is the subsidiary.

Well-Known Seasoned Issuers (WKSI)—More popularly known as "wick sees," they are defined in Rule 405. The principal requirements for WKSI status are:

- the issuer is eligible to register a primary offering of its securities on Form S–3 or Form F–3; and

- the issuer, as of a date within 60 days of the determination date, has either:

  — a minimum $700 million of common equity worldwide market value held by non-affiliates; or

  — in the registered offering in question will register only non-convertible securities, other than common equity, or will provide full and unconditional guarantees of a subsidiary's securities *provided* that the issuer previously issued $1 billion aggregate principal amount of non-convertible securities in registered offerings during the past three years. If such an issuer is eligible to register a primary offering under Form S–3 because it has a float of at least $75 million equity in the hands of non-affiliates at the determination date, the issuer can also issue common equity as a WKSI.

WKSI status is determined on a specified "determination date." The determination date is the date the issuer's most recent shelf registration statement was filed, or its most recent § 10(a)(3) amendment to a shelf registration statement, whichever is later. If the issuer has not filed a shelf registration statement then the determination date is the date of the filing of the most recent annual report on Form 10–K.

Not all of these issuers are eligible for WKSI status. Issuers are disqualified if they:

- are not current in their Exchange Act filings or late in satisfying those obligations for the preceding twelve months;

- an ineligible issuer or asset-backed issuer; or

- an investment company or business development company.

Ineligible issuers under Rule 405 include, among others, those issuers that within the past three years were a blank check or shell company or issued a registered penny stock offering are ineligible. Issuers that filed a bankruptcy petition within the past three years are also ineligible, unless they have filed an annual report with audited financial statements subsequent to their emergence from bankruptcy. Also disqualified are issuers that have violated the anti-fraud provisions of the federal securities laws during the last three years and issuers that filed a registration statement that is the subject of any pending proceeding under § 8 of the Securities Act, or has been the subject of any refusal or stop order under § 8 in the past three years. (We discuss § 8 refusal and stop orders later in the chapter.) Issuers subject to a pending proceeding under § 8A in connection with an offering are also ineligible.

What kind of company qualifies as a WKSI? Clearly, the SEC has in mind large companies with equity trading in a liquid secondary market (and a corresponding following of research analysts). Companies such as Microsoft, IBM, and McDonald's will clearly qualify for WKSI status, absent any prior securities law violations, but many medium-size companies will also qualify. WKSI-eligible issuers represented approximately 30% of listed issuers and accounted for about 95% of U.S. market capitalization in 2004.

Although the SEC classifies issuers into four groups, the primary focus of regulation during a public offering remains with the offering transaction. We turn now to the regulations governing the three time periods in an offering: the Pre-Filing Period, the Waiting Period, and the Post-Effective Period. These three time periods are defined by the application of § 5 of the Securities Act, the key provision governing the public offering process. A quick word on interstate commerce. Because the Securities Act is a federal statute, § 5 conditions its application on the "use of any means or instruments of transportation or communication in interstate commerce." That said, the scope of interstate commerce is broad, including the use of emails, faxes, telephone calls, and of course, the mail.

A. PRE-FILING PERIOD

The Pre-Filing Period runs until the registration statement is filed with the SEC. Two key provisions of § 5 of the Securities Act govern this period. Section 5(a) prohibits all sales until the registration statement becomes effective. Section 5(c) bans all offers prior to the filing of the registration statement. Once the Waiting Period commences, § 5(c) no longer applies:

| Pre-Filing Period | Waiting Period | Post-Effective Period |

§ 5(a) --- >

§ 5(c) --------------- >

1. WHAT IS AN "OFFER"

Key to understanding the Pre-Filing Period is § 5(c). Section 5(c) prohibits "offers" prior to a registration statement being filed with the SEC. The quiet period imposed on companies stems from the SEC's broad definition of the term "offer." Section 2(a)(3) of the Securities Act defines "offer," but "offer" has been expansively interpreted by SEC administrative rulings and a series of SEC Securities Act Releases.

The SEC has long held the view that the term "offer" is broader than communication including an explicit offer of securities for sale. In the SEC's view "offer" encompasses all communications that may "condition" the market for the securities. The SEC in, *In the Matter of Carl M. Loeb, Rhoades & Co.* (1959) wrote:

> The broad sweep of [the definition of an offer under § 2(a)(3)] is necessary to accomplish the statutory purposes in the light of the process of securities distribution as it exists in the United States. Securities are distributed in this country by a complex and sensitive machinery geared to accomplish nationwide

distribution of large quantities of securities with great speed. Multi-million dollar issues are often oversubscribed on the day the securities are made available for sale. This result is accomplished by a network of prior informal indications of interest or offers to buy between underwriters and dealers and between dealers and investors based upon mutual expectations that, at the moment when sales may legally be made, many prior indications will immediately materialize as purchases. It is wholly unrealistic to assume in this context that "offers" must take any particular legal form. Legal formalities come at the end to record prior understandings, but it is the procedures by which these prior understandings, embodying investment decisions, are obtained or generated which the Securities Act was intended to reform. . . .

[W]e have made clear our position that the statute prohibits issuers, underwriters and dealers from initiating a public sales campaign prior to the filing of a registration statement by means of publicity efforts which, even though not couched in terms of an express offer, condition the public mind or arouse public interest in the particular securities. . . .

We accordingly conclude that publicity, prior to the filing of a registration statement by means of public media of communication, with respect to an issuer or its securities, emanating from broker dealer firms who as underwriters or prospective underwriters have negotiated or are negotiating for a public offering of the securities of such issuer, must be presumed to set in motion or to be a part of the distribution process and therefore to involve an offer to sell or a solicitation of an offer to buy such securities prohibited by Section 5(c). . . .

Brokers and dealers properly and commendably provide their customers with a substantial amount of information concerning business and financial developments of interest to investors, including information with respect to particular securities and issuers. Section 5, nevertheless, prohibits selling efforts in connection with a proposed public distribution of securities prior to the filing of a registration statement and, as we have indicated, this prohibition includes any publicity which is in fact a part of a selling effort. Indeed, the danger to investors from publicity amounting to a selling effort may be greater in cases where an issue has "news value" since it may be easier to whip up a "speculative frenzy" concerning the offering by incomplete or misleading publicity and thus facilitate the distribution of an unsound security at inflated prices. This is precisely the evil which the Securities Act seeks to prevent.

<h1 style="text-align:center">Securities Act Release No. 3844</h1>

Securities and Exchange Commission (Oct. 8, 1957).

* * *

A basic purpose of the Securities Act of 1933 [and] the Securities Exchange Act of 1934 . . . is to require the dissemination of adequate and accurate information concerning issuers and their securities in connection with the offer and sale of securities to the public, and the publication periodically of material business and financial facts, knowledge of which is essential to an informed trading market in such securities.

There has been an increasing tendency . . . to give publicity through many media concerning corporate affairs which goes beyond the statutory requirements. This practice reflects a commendable and growing recognition on the part of industry and the investment community of the importance of informing security holders and the public generally with respect to important business and financial developments.

This trend should be encouraged. It is necessary, however, that corporate management, counsel, underwriters, dealers and public relations firms recognize that the Securities Acts impose certain responsibilities and limitations upon persons engaged in the sale of securities and that publicity and public relations activities under certain circumstances may involve violations of the securities laws and cause serious embarrassment to issuers and underwriters in connection with the timing and marketing of an issue of securities. These violations not only pose enforcement and administrative problems for the Commission, they may also give rise to civil liabilities by the seller of securities to the purchaser. . . .

* * *

It follows from the express language and the legislative history of the Securities Act that an issuer, underwriter or dealer may not legally begin a public offering or initiate a public sales campaign prior to the filing of a registration statement. It apparently is not generally understood, however, that the publication of information and statements, and publicity efforts, generally, made in advance of a proposed financing, although not couched in terms of an express offer, may in fact contribute to conditioning the public mind or arousing public interest in the issuer or in the securities of an issuer in a manner which raises a serious question whether the publicity is not in fact part of the selling effort. . . .

Example #1

An underwriter-promoter is engaged in arranging for the public financing of a mining venture to explore for a mineral which has certain possible potentialities for use in atomic research and power. While preparing a registration statement for a public offering, the underwriter-promoter distributed several thousand copies of a brochure which described in glowing generalities the future possibilities for use of the mineral and the profit potential to investors who would share in the growth prospects of a new industry. The brochure made no reference to any issuer or any security nor to any particular financing. It was sent out, however, bearing the name of the underwriting firm and obviously was designed to awaken an interest which later would be focused on the specific financing to be presented in the prospectus shortly to be sent to the same mailing list.

The distribution of the brochure under these circumstances clearly was the first step in a sales campaign to effect a public sale of the securities and as such, in the view of the Commission, violated Section 5 of the Securities Act.

Example #2

An issuer in the promotional stage intended to offer for public sale an issue of securities the proceeds of which were to be employed to explore for and develop a mineralized area. The promoters and prospective underwriter prior to the filing of the required registration statement ... arranged for a series of press releases describing the activities of the company, its proposed program of development of its properties, estimates of ore reserves and plans for a processing plant. This publicity campaign continued after the filing of a registration statement and during the period of the offering. The press releases, which could be easily reproduced and employed by dealers and salesmen engaged in the sales effort, contained representations, forecasts and quotations which could not have been supported as reliable data for inclusion in a prospectus or offering circular under the sanctions of the Act.

It is the Commission's view that issuing information of this character to the public by an issuer or underwriter through the device of the press release and the press interview is an evasion of the requirements of the Act governing selling procedures, a violation of Sections 5 and 17(a) of the Act, and that such activity subjects the seller to the risk of civil and penal sanctions and liabilities of the Act.

* * *

Example #6

* * *

The president of a company accepted, in August, an invitation to address a meeting of a security analysts' society to be held in February of the following year for the purpose of informing the membership concerning the company, its plans, its record and problems. By January a speech had been prepared together with supplemental information and data, all of which was designed to give a fairly comprehensive picture of the company, the industry in which it operates and various factors affecting its future growth. Projections of demand, operations and profits for future periods were included. The speech and the other data had been printed and it was intended that several hundred copies would be available for distribution at the meeting. In addition, since it was believed that stockholders, creditors, and perhaps customers might be interested in the talk, it was intended to mail to such persons and to a list of other selected firms and institutions copies of the material to be used at the analysts' meeting.

Later in January, a public financing by the company was authorized, preparation of a registration statement was begun and negotiation with underwriters was commenced. It soon appeared that the coming meeting of analysts, scheduled many months earlier, would be or about the time the registration statement was to be filed. This presented the question whether, in the circumstances, delivery and distribution of the speech and the supporting data to the various persons mentioned above would contravene provisions of the Securities Act.

It seemed clear that the scheduling of the speech had not been arranged in contemplation of a public offering by the issuer at or about the time of its delivery. In the circumstances, no objection was raised to the delivery of the speech at the analysts' meeting. However, since printed copies of the speech might be received by a wider audience, it was suggested that printed copies of the speech and the supporting data not be made available at the meeting nor be transmitted to other persons.

* * *

Securities Act Release No. 5180

Securities and Exchange Commission (Oct. 16, 1971).

The Commission today took note of situations when issuers whose securities are "in registration" may have [to] refuse to answer legitimate inquiries from stockholders, financial analysts, the press, or other persons concerning the company or some aspect of its business. The Commission hereby emphasizes that there is no basis in the securities acts or in any policy of the Commission which would justify the practice of non-disclosure of factual information by a publicly held company on the grounds that it has securities in registration under the Securities Act of 1933. Neither a company in registration nor its representatives should instigate publicity for the purpose of facilitating the sale of securities in a proposed offering. Further, any publication of information by a company in registration other than by means of a statutory prospectus should be limited to factual information and should not include such things as predictions, projections, forecasts or opinions with respect to value.

* * *

GUIDELINES

The Commission strongly suggests that all issuers establish internal procedures designed to avoid problems relating to the release of corporate information when in registration. As stated above, issuers and their representatives should not initiate publicity when in registration, but should nevertheless respond to legitimate inquiries for factual information about the company's financial condition and business operations. Further, care should be exercised so that, for example, predictions, projections, forecasts, estimates and opinions concerning value are not given with respect to such things, among other, as sales and earnings and value of the issuer's securities.

It has been suggested that the Commission promulgate an all-inclusive list of permissible and prohibited activities in this area. This is not feasible for the reason that determinations are based upon the particular facts of each case. However, the Commission as a matter of policy encourages the flow of factual information to shareholders and the investing public. Issuers in this regard should:

Examples

1.   Continue to advertise products and services.

2.   Continue to send out customary quarterly, annual and other periodic reports to stockholders.

3.   Continue to publish proxy statements and send out dividend notices.

4.   Continue to make announcements to the press with respect to factual business and financial development; i.e., receipt of a contract, the settlement of a strike, the opening of a plant, or similar events of interest to the community in which the business operates.

5.   Answer unsolicited telephone inquiries from stockholders, financial analysts, the press and others concerning factual information.

6.   Observe an "open door" policy in responding to unsolicited inquiries concerning factual matters from securities analysts, financial analysts, security holders, and participants in the communications field who have a legitimate interest in the corporation's affairs.

7.   Continue to hold stockholder meetings as scheduled and to answer shareholders' inquiries at stockholder meetings relating to factual matters.

In order to curtail problems in this area, issuers in this regard should avoid:

1.   Issuance of forecasts, projections, or predictions relating but not limited to revenues, income or earnings per share.

2.   Publishing opinions concerning values.

* * *

NOTES

1. *"Conditioning" the market.* The SEC actively polices efforts that may condition the market prior to the effective date of the registration statement. Leading up to the initial public offering of Salesforce.com, a provider of customer relationship management software, the CEO of Salesforce.com told a reporter that "the S.E.C. prohibits me from making any statements that would hype my I.P.O.," and the statement was subsequently released in a *New York Times* article. The CEO also discussed "the software business and his competitors" in the article. The SEC deemed these communications as conditioning the market and forced Salesforce.com to delay its initial public offering. Laurie J. Flynn and Andrew Ross Sorkin, *Salesforce.com Is Said To Delay Its Public Offering*, New York Times, May 19, 2004. Why is delaying the offer the usual remedy for § 5(c) violations? The SEC believes that delay will allow any conditioning of the market to subside.

2. *The Pre-Filing period.* When does the Pre-Filing Period begin? Once the Pre-Filing Period starts, a company and others associated with the offering may communicate about the offering or the company's future prospects only at their own peril. SEC Release No. 5180 notes that the Pre-Filing Period begins once the company is "in registration." But when does "registration" start? In Securities Act Release No. 5009 (Oct. 7, 1969), the SEC in footnote 4 provided the following guidance: " 'In registration' is used herein to mean the entire process of registration, at least from the time an issuer reaches an understanding with the broker-dealer which is to act as managing underwriter until the completion of the offering and the period of 40 or 90 days during which dealers must deliver a prospectus."

Rule 163A provides a safe harbor for the issuer clarifying when the Pre-Filing Period begins. Communications made by the issuer, or those working on behalf of an issuer (other than an underwriter or dealer participating in the offering), prior to 30 days before the filing of the registration statement with the SEC are excluded from the definition of an "offer" for purposes of § 5(c). To be eligible for the safe harbor, the communication may not mention the offering. In addition, the issuer must "take reasonable steps within its control to prevent further distribution or publication of the information during the 30-day period immediately before the issuer files the registration statement." Regulation FD's prohibition on selective disclosures (discussed in Chapter 4) applies to communications under the safe harbor.

3. *The Internet.* The growth of the Internet has provided issuers with a new medium through which to communicate with investors, posing new challenges for both the SEC and issuers. Information provided through the worldwide web is unique because different websites are interconnected through "hyperlinks." An investor accessing finance.yahoo.com, for example, may learn about a particular issuer and then click on a link to go to that issuer's homepage to continue the research. Such hyperlinks make obtaining relevant information quick and easy for investors, but do hyperlinks run afoul of the gun-jumping rules?

Rule 405 treats all non-real time electronic communication offering securities for sale as "graphic communications" and, thus, a written offer for purposes of the Securities Act. Thus, emails, videotapes, CD-ROMs, and recorded electronic version of roadshow presentations that offer securities for sale are all written offers. (Roadshows and other communications distributed electronically on a "real time" basis, however, are treated as oral communications.)

Rule 433 specifies the treatment of hyperlinks from one web page to another. Written offers are defined to include offers of the issuer's securities that are "contained on an issuer's Web site or hyperlinked by the issuer from the issuer's Web site to a third party's Web site." Rule 433(e)(1). For example, hyperlinks included within a written communication offering the issuer's securities that connect to another web site or to other information are considered part of that written communication. Rule 433 excludes "historical issuer information" contained in a separate section on the issuer's Web site from the definition of written offers unless the information was incorporated by reference, included in a prospectus of the issuer used in the offering, or otherwise used or referred to in the offering. Rule 433(e)(2).

QUESTIONS

1.   What counts as an offer?

2.   If investors eventually will receive (or have access to) a final statutory prospectus, why does it matter that they earlier obtain information that "conditions" the market?

―――――

A common theme throughout the SEC releases is the distinction between "purely factual" disclosure and disclosures that refer to the offering directly or make forecasts, projections, or predictions (so-called "soft" information). Although avoiding disclosures that refer to the offering is easy enough, how are issuers to determine if their disclosures are purely factual? Exchange Act reporting issuers must make periodic disclosures and address a constant stream of questions from analysts and the investing public. How can the reporting company balance these demands for information with the imposition of a quiet period for disclosures that are not "purely factual"?

Two safe harbors, both introduced as part of the 2005 Offering Reforms, provide some comfort for issuers. These safe harbors, described below, afford protection for regularly released business and forward-looking information.

Reporting Issuer Safe Harbor—Rule 168 of the Securities Act allows most Exchange Act reporting issuers (and those working on their behalf, other than underwriters and participating dealers) to continue the regular release of "factual business information" and "forward-looking information." Information in periodic reports (e.g., a Form 10–K) and other materials filed with the SEC are included within the safe harbor. Rule 168 provides an exemption from § 5(c)'s prohibition on offers in the Pre-Filing period. By excluding communications from the definition of an offer, the Rule also exempts communications from § 2(a)(10)'s definition of "prospectus" and thus, the application of § 5(b)(1) in the Waiting and Post-Effective periods.

Factual business information includes, among other things, factual information about the issuer and its business, advertisements of the issuer's products or services, and factual information contained in the issuer's periodic Exchange Act reports. Forward-looking information that is permitted includes financial projections, statements about the issuer management's plans and the issuer's future economic performance, and any underlying assumptions. Allowing reporting issuers the ability to disseminate certain forward-looking information during a public offering is a dramatic change from the SEC's hostile attitude toward forward-looking information set forth in the Releases above. In order to use Rule 168, the issuer must have "previously released or disseminated" the same type of information in the "ordinary course of its business" and the information must be "materially consistent in timing, manner and form" with the issuer's similar past releases or disseminations of such information. Rule 168(d). The safe harbor does not cover information relating to the offering itself.

Non-Reporting Issuer Safe Harbor—Narrower than Rule 168, Rule 169 of the Securities Act allows non-reporting issuers (i.e., most IPO issuers) to continue to disclose "factual business information." Unlike Rule 168, however, Rule 169 does not exempt forward-looking information. Underwriters and dealers participating in the offering cannot rely on Rule 169. As with Rule 168, Rule 169 provides an exemption from § 5(c)'s prohibition on offers in the Pre-Filing Period and an exclusion from § 2(a)(10)'s definition of "prospectus" for purposes of § 5(b)(1) in the Waiting and Post-Effective periods.

Rule 169 tracks Rule 168's requirements that the issuer have previously released or disseminated information of the same type in the ordinary course of business and in the same "timing, manner, and form." Rule 169 also requires that the information must have been disseminated previously to "customers and suppliers, other than in their capacities as investors or potential investors in the issuer's securities." Rule 169(d)(3). Finally, information relating to the offering is also ineligible.

Well-known seasoned issuers are given even more latitude to communicate in the Pre-Filing Period. Rule 163 exempts both oral and written communications, including offers, by or on behalf of WKSIs from § 5(c) during the Pre-Filing Period. Certain offerings, such as mergers and other business combinations, are excluded. In addition, underwriters and dealers participating in the offering are prohibited from using Rule 163. WKSIs using Rule 163 must treat such communications as "free writing prospectuses." The issuer must file any free writing prospectuses with the SEC promptly upon filing of the registration statement. Written communications must include a legend informing the investors about the formal statutory prospectus and how to get it. Regulation FD's prohibition on selective disclosures applies to Rule 163 communications.

The impact of Rule 163 is somewhat overshadowed by the expansion of the shelf registration process in the 2005 Offering Reforms. WKSIs may now file an automatic shelf registration statement that, as we discuss at the end of this chapter, allows the WKSI to register an unlimited amount of securities for an unlimited period. In effect, WKSIs who have filed an automatic shelf registration statement have skipped the Pre-Filing Period.

HYPOTHETICAL ONE

Suppose that J.R. and the Ewing Oil board of directors decide to pursue an initial public offering. The company faces a number of choices, most importantly the number of shares to sell and the price. Timing is also an issue; is the market receptive to Ewing Oil shares now or should Ewing Oil wait to obtain a better price for its shares? J.R. is concerned not only with executing a successful IPO for Ewing Oil, she is worried about the Ewing family's financial well-being. As a closely held firm, Ewing Oil stock is generally difficult, if not impossible, to resell until after the IPO. J.R. and the Ewing family hope to cash out some of their shares in the IPO and substantially more in a possible follow-on equity offering next year.

Consider whether the following actions raise any § 5(c) gun-jumping concerns during the Pre-Filing Period.

1.   *Scenario One:* Before finding an underwriter or filing a registration statement with the SEC, J.R. telephones a number of business associates from "the cartel" about investing in Ewing Oil's IPO. Among other things J.R. says, "I can get you in on the ground floor at $20 per share."

2.   *Scenario Two:* Assume that Ewing Oil is "in registration." J.R. places an ad in *World Oil* magazine touting Ewing Oil's business (Ewing Oil had run a similar ad a year earlier in other oil industry periodicals). In the ad, J.R. does not specifically mention Ewing Oil's IPO plans. Instead, the ad discusses Ewing Oil's "optimistic" view of the demand for fracking technology. Moreover, the ad also mentions the turbo-fracking technology that Ewing Oil is developing will be "coming soon" and that it will "revolutionize the industry."

3.   *Scenario Three:* J.R.'s *World Oil* ad also includes financial projections showing strong future growth in revenues and earnings for Ewing Oil. The projections end with the following statement: "Ewing Oil's strong financial future ensures that we'll be around a long time to help customers like you!"

4.   *Scenario Four:* Concerned about maintaining silence on the upcoming offering during the quiet period, J.R. orders that Ewing Oil's website make no mention of the offering or provide any form of "soft" forward-looking information or projections with respect to Ewing Oil's profitability, growth prospects, and so on. Ewing Oil's website, nonetheless, contains a set of links for investors interested in learning more about the oil services business. One link goes to www.moneyfool.com, an independent site with no financial connection to Ewing Oil. The www.moneyfool.com website provides information on investing. The website also includes an analysis of the value of Ewing Oil's upcoming offering.

2.   PUTTING TOGETHER THE OFFERING

During the Pre-Filing Period, the issuer contacts and reaches a preliminary understanding with the managing underwriter of the offering. Working together with the underwriter, counsel for the issuer, the underwriter's counsel, as well as experts (including the issuer's auditors), and the issuer then drafts the registration statement. Consider how the communications among these groups of parties are exempted from the prohibition on offers in the Pre-Filing Period.

HYPOTHETICAL TWO

1.   One of J.R.'s first decisions after deciding to take Ewing Oil public is to contact her friend Cliff, an investment banker at Barnes-Wentworth Investments. J.R. asks Cliff if Barnes-Wentworth Investments will act as the managing underwriter for the offering. J.R. discusses pricing, the number of shares, and the timing of the IPO with Cliff over the telephone. After some discussions, Cliff agrees on behalf of Barnes-Wentworth Investments to take on the position of managing underwriter. J.R. and Cliff record their tentative agreement in a letter of intent. The letter of intent omits the offering price.

2.   After agreeing to act as managing underwriter for the Ewing Oil offering, Barnes-Wentworth Investments starts putting together a

syndicate of underwriters to handle the firm commitment offering. Through a series of texts, telephone calls and emails, Cliff negotiates with representatives from twenty different investment banks (fifteen of whom eventually agree in principle to participate in the offering).

3. The five investment banks that choose not to participate as underwriters make a counter-proposal. They ask Cliff if they can participate as dealers in the offering. As dealers, they will purchase shares from one of the underwriters participating in the offering rather than directly from the issuer. Consequently, they will handle far fewer shares than each of the individual underwriters (thereby reducing their risk). The investment banks acting as dealers will earn no more than the standard dealer's commission from their sales. Cliff, on behalf of Barnes-Wentworth Investments, readily agrees to the prospective dealers' counter-proposal.

4. Barnes-Wentworth Investments sends Pam, a recent business school graduate working for Cliff, to get Ewing Oil ready for the public offering. Pam goes over Ewing Oil's books, corporate records, board minutes and other records. She also has extensive discussions with Ewing Oil's auditors, Farlow & Culver. After some thought, Pam recommends that Ewing Oil reincorporate in Delaware, adopt anti-takeover protections (including a classified board of directors), and convert all existing preferred shares into common stock. Are Pam's discussions with Farlow & Culver okay?

To reduce the tension between timely disclosure and the gun-jumping rules, the SEC has promulgated a number of safe harbor rules. Rule 135, for example, provides a safe harbor for short, factual notices of a proposed registered offering.

Consider the structure of the Rule 135 safe harbor. First, Rule 135 applies only for the issuer, any other security holder selling in the offering (e.g., if the insiders are selling some of their shares in the public offering), and those working on behalf of either of these parties. Second, Rule 135 excludes notices meeting its requirements from the definition of "offer" for purposes of § 5. What legal conclusions are avoided by escaping the definition of "offer"? During the Pre-Filing Period, § 5(c) prohibits all offers. Thus, communications meeting the requirements of Rule 135 do not run afoul of § 5(c)'s prohibition. The more general ban on sales in § 5(a), however, continues in force. As we will see when we cover the Waiting Period, § 5(b) continues with a prohibition on most written offers (included within the definition of a "prospectus"). Because Rule 135 generally excludes the communications it requires from the scope of an "offer," Rule 135 also exempts them from the definition of a prospectus for purposes of § 5(b).

Rule 135 places tight limits on the information that may be disclosed. The communication may, among other things, identify the issuer, the amount and basic terms of the offered securities, the purpose of the offering, and the anticipated timing of the offering. Outside of these narrow areas, communication is not protected under Rule 135. Notably, the underwriter cannot be identified by name (which makes it difficult for the underwriter to rely on Rule 135). On the other hand, failure to meet the terms of Rule 135 does not necessarily mean that § 5(c) has been violated. Instead, the absence of the Rule 135 safe harbor means only that issuers (and others) must contend with the uncertain definition of "offer."

Given the SEC's adoption of new safe harbors as part of the 2005 Offering Reforms under Rules 163 (for well-known seasoned issuers), 163A (prior to the 30 day period before filing of the registration statement), 168 (factual and forward-looking statements by a reporting issuer) and 169 (factual statements by a non-reporting issuer), what function does Rule 135 continue to play? Consider the situation of a non-WKSI issuing a factual notice related to the offering prior to the filing of the registration statement.

HYPOTHETICAL THREE

Excited by the prospect of Ewing Oil's upcoming public offering, J.R. puts out a press release on Ewing Oil's plans for the IPO. The press release mentions that Ewing Oil expects to raise $200 million for the offering and that the proceeds will be used to fund research and development of turbo-fracking. The press release does not mention Barnes-Wentworth Investments by name, instead only stating "a well-known, national investment bank has agreed in principle to act as our managing underwriter." Any problems?

3.   EMERGING GROWTH COMPANIES

The JOBS Act of 2012 created a new category of issuers called "emerging growth companies." An emerging growth company is an issuer with total annual gross revenues of less than $1 billion (indexed for inflation) during its most recent fiscal year. Securities Act § 2(a)(19). In Chapter 4 we examined the how the JOBS Act reduces the ongoing obligations imposed on emerging growth companies after they become public. The JOBS Act also bestows significant advantages on emerging growth companies during the public offering process.

First, emerging growth companies only need to report two years of audited financial statements in the registration statement, Securities Act § 7(a)(2), rather than the standard three years required by Form S–1. The JOBS Act also reduces disclosure obligations under Items 301 (Selected Financial Data) and Item 303 (Management Discussion & Analysis).

Second, the JOBS Act provides that emerging growth companies may submit registration statements to the SEC staff on a confidential basis. The SEC has established a secure e-mail system for issuers to use in submitting draft registration statements. Normally, at least for U.S. domestic issuers, the SEC makes all versions of filed registration statements available to the public. Keeping an initial registration statement filed with the SEC confidential gives the issuer the ability to hide information contained in the registration statement from competitors. This ability to keep proprietary information confidential— at least temporarily—is particularly important for new IPO issuers with little public information otherwise available. Confidentiality also allows issuers to withdraw from the public offering process without sending a signal of failure to the marketplace. Issuers can maintain the confidentiality of their draft registration statements until twenty-one days prior to the date on which the issuer conducts a road show at which time the issuers must file "the initial confidential submission and all amendments thereto" with the SEC. Securities Act § 6(e).

Third, the JOBS Act establishes a new "test the waters" regime for emerging growth companies. Under § 5(d) of the Securities Act, an emerging growth company and those acting on its behalf can communicate with either Qualified Institutional Buyers or institutions that are accredited investors at any time during the public offering process. Qualified Institutional Buyers include institutions that own and invest on a discretionary basis at least $100 million of securities. Institutional accredited investors include institutions with a minimum of $5 million of total assets. We discuss accredited investors in Chapter 9 and Qualified Institutional Buyers in Chapter 10.

One wrinkle for the test the waters provision is the prohibition on selective disclosures under Regulation FD that applies for Exchange Act reporting issuers. Although Regulation FD exempts certain communications that occur as part of a public offering, Regulation FD does apply to oral communications in the Pre-Filing Period. Because test the waters communications must occur selectively—only to QIBs or accredited investors—testing the waters would technically run afoul of Regulation FD. It is unclear whether the SEC will adjust Regulation FD to accommodate the new test the waters communications. In any case, Regulation FD does not apply to private companies, which are the companies most likely to avail themselves of testing the waters during an initial public offering.

Finally, the JOBS Act provides that an emerging growth company may choose to comply with any provision for which the JOBS Act would otherwise provide an exemption. JOBS Act § 107(a). Some issuers voluntarily provide three years of audited financial statements to bolster their credibility with investors.

HYPOTHETICAL FOUR

Ewing Oil had total revenues of $900 million for the prior fiscal year. Prior to filing its registration statement with the SEC, Ewing Oil proposes to make contact with a number of individuals, each with a net worth of over $10 million—sufficient wealth to be considered "accredited investors." Ewing Oil plans to discuss its upcoming offering with the accredited investors to get their opinion about possible pricing for the offering. Will the communications with the accredited investors violate § 5(c)?

B. WAITING PERIOD

After filing its registration statement with the SEC, the issuer enters into the "Waiting Period." This refers to waiting for the SEC's Division of Corporation Finance to declare the registration statement effective. Two important and separate tasks take place during the Waiting Period. First, the issuer and underwriters attempt to gauge market interest in the offering. Second, the SEC may review the registration statement before declaring it effective.

In this section, we consider (1) the process of gauging market sentiment, and (2) the process of becoming effective and the SEC enforcement powers relating to registration. During the Waiting Period, the gun-jumping rules continue to restrict issuers and their affiliates from conditioning the market, albeit in a less intrusive fashion. For companies with an active secondary trading market prior to the offering, however, it is nonetheless important to allow information to flow out to investors. We also consider here safe harbors for analyst reports, which apply throughout the public offering process.

1.   GAUGING MARKET SENTIMENT

Issuers and underwriters typically promote their offering and obtain feedback from the market during the Waiting Period. Underwriters doing a firm commitment offering are particularly keen to learn about the market's reaction to the prospective offering. Recall that in a firm commitment offering, both the underwriter's own money and (indirectly) its reputation for bringing quality, well-priced offerings to the market are on the line. Underwriters that price an offering too high will end up holding unsold allotments of securities. Those who price the offering too low may leave the issuer with smaller proceeds.

During the Pre-Filing Period, § 5(c) leaves little room to gauge market sentiment. Section 5(c) restricts all offers prior to the filing of the registration statement. As we saw above, this restriction on offers, combined with the broad definition of offers under § 2(a)(3), leads to an almost complete prohibition on communications relating to the offering in the Pre-Filing Period for non-well known seasoned issuers. (Recall though that Rule 163 allows well-known seasoned issuers to discuss the offering in the Pre-Filing Period.) With the filing of the registration statement, however, § 5(c) no longer applies. Instead, § 5(b)(1) steps in during the Waiting Period to prohibit the transmission, through interstate commerce, of any "prospectus" not meeting the requirements of the statutory prospectus as set forth in § 10 of the Securities Act. Keep in mind that § 5(a) still prohibits sales during the Waiting Period.

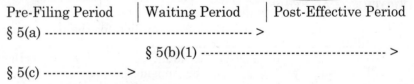

Pre-Filing Period | Waiting Period | Post-Effective Period

§ 5(a) -- >

§ 5(b)(1) --- >

§ 5(c) ----------------- >

Section 5(b)(1) prohibits the transmission of prospectuses not meeting the requirements of § 10, but permits both preliminary and final prospectuses. The definition of a prospectus under § 2(a)(10) of the Securities Act is key to understanding the extent of § 5(b)(1)'s prohibition. Although generally defining a prospectus to include all "prospectuses," § 2(a)(10) also ropes in any "notice, circular, advertisement, letter, or communication, written or by radio or television, which offers any security for sale or confirms the sale of any security." Note two things about this definition: (a) the breadth of the types of communication included and (b) the requirement that communication must either offer the security or confirm the sale of the security to qualify as a "prospectus." What types of communications "offer" the security for sale? Section 2(a)(3)'s definition of an offer continues to provide the answer.

Thus, § 2(a)(10)'s prospectus definition sweeps in all written and broadcast communications offering the security; § 5(b) then prohibits such communications if they do not comply with § 10. Section 10(b) authorizes a preliminary prospectus that complies with § 5(b)(1) in the Waiting Period. Section 10(a) defines the final prospectus that must be distributed to investors in the Post-Effective Period. To understand how this works, consider the following relationships within the Securities Act:

§ 5(b)(1)	<—	§ 2(a)(10)	<—	§ 2(a)(3)
Prohibition of prospectus not meeting § 10		Definition of prospectus		Definition of offer

In practice, § 5(b)(1) reintroduces the general prohibition on offers placed on all communications in the Pre-Filing Period, but because the prohibition is now limited to offers by means of a prospectus not complying with § 10, the restriction is not as broad as § 5(c)'s prohibition on offers during the Pre-Filing Period. Written offers in the form of a preliminary prospectus under § 10(b) are explicitly permitted. In addition, only written and broadcast communications are restricted in the Waiting Period. By negative implication, oral communications not involving a broadcast medium are permitted during the Waiting Period. Talk all you want. In addition to offers, the SEC has provided issuers with more latitude for gauging market sentiment through a number of safe harbors. These safe harbors work either to (a) include the communication as a § 10 prospectus or (b) exclude communication from the definition of a prospectus under § 2(a)(10). Which avenue the safe harbor takes is important. As we discuss in Chapter 8, communications that are deemed a § 10 prospectus face heightened liability under § 12(a)(2) for material misstatements and omissions. The following forms of communication are permitted in the Waiting Period.

a.   The Preliminary Prospectus

Under Securities Act Rule 430, the preliminary prospectus must contain essentially the same information as the final statutory prospectus, except for price-related information. Typically, the issuer and the managing underwriter will set the price just before the registration statement is declared effective. (Setting the price earlier imposes large risks on the underwriters in a firm commitment offering—what happens if the stock market declines after the price is set?) A preliminary prospectus under Rule 430 meets the requirements of § 10 only prior to the effective date and therefore may not be used in the Post-Effective Period. Exchange Act reporting issuers may also use a Rule 431 summary prospectus during the Waiting Period, but few do.

b.   The Free Writing Prospectus

Free writing prospectuses (discussed in greater detail below) complying with the requirements of Rule 433 used after the filing of the registration statement by an issuer and other offering participants, including underwriters and dealers, are treated as a § 10(b) prospectus. As a § 10(b) prospectus, a free writing prospectus satisfies § 5(b)(1)'s requirement that all prospectuses meet the requirements of § 10.

c.   The Roadshow and Other Oral Offers

Underwriters and issuers rely on oral offers to conduct "roadshows" to pitch the offering to potential investors. Such offers are not considered prospectuses under § 2(a)(10) and thus are not prohibited by § 5(b)(1). Typically conducted over a two-week period, the roadshow gives the issuer's top management and the managing underwriter the chance to sell the offering in face-to-face discussions with institutional investors nationwide. Underwriters may also make use of other oral communications. Brokers associated with the underwriters may make telephone calls to potential investors about the offering. Telephone calls are oral and therefore not prohibited by § 5(b)(1).

d.   Regularly Released Information in the Ordinary Course of Business

The ordinary course of business safe harbors under Rules 168 and 169 continue to apply in the Waiting Period. Both rules exempt communications from the scope of both § 5(c) (applicable only in the Pre-Filing Period) as well as § 2(a)(10). Once exempted from § 2(a)(10), the ordinary course of business communications are not prohibited by § 5(b)(1).

e.   "Tombstone" Advertisements

Although the Rule 135 tombstone safe harbor continues to be available in the Waiting Period, the SEC provides broader safe harbors for communications after the registration statement has been filed. Securities Act Rule 134 provides far more leeway for issuers seeking to disclose information on the offering and on their own business to the investing public. Moreover, not only the issuer, but also the underwriters, can use Rule 134.

How does Rule 134's safe harbor for "tombstone" advertisements work? When it applies, Rule 134 excludes communications from the definition of a prospectus under § 2(a)(10). (Note that the last clause of § 2(a)(10) allows the SEC to exclude written offers to sell from the definition of a prospectus.) Recall that § 5(b)(1) prohibits transmission of a prospectus that does not meet the requirements of § 10 (the formal statutory prospectus). By excluding written notices from the broad definition of a prospectus contained in § 2(a)(10), Rule 134 excludes those notices from the prohibition of § 5(b)(1). As long as no sales take place (still prohibited by § 5(a)), notices complying with Rule 134 are exempted from the gun-jumping rules. Communications under Rule 134 are also excluded from the definition of a "free writing prospectus" under Rule 405.

Rule 134 offers no protection, however, in the Pre-Filing Period. Why? Recall that § 5(c) prohibits all offers in the Pre-Filing Period. Rule 134, which only excludes communications from the definitions of a prospectus and a free writing prospectus, does not limit the reach of § 5(c), which forbids all "offers," written or oral.

What can a company disclose under Rule 134? Among other things, Rule 134 allows the disclosure of the issuer's legal identity and business location, the amount and type of security to be offered, the business of the issuer, and the price of the security. Other information about the issuer permitted includes "the address, phone number and e-mail address of the issuer's principal offices" as well as the "geographic areas in which it conducts business." Rule 134(a)(1). The names of all the underwriters, not just the managing underwriters, and their roles in the offering as well as a description of the marketing events, such as roadshow presentations, and a description of the procedures through which the underwriters will conduct the offering are permissible under Rule 134(a)(10), (11) and (12). Rule 134 also provides for disclosure of the identity of any selling security holders if included in the registration statement, the names of securities exchanges or other securities markets where the securities will be listed, and the ticker symbol. Rule 134(a)(18), (19), (20).

Reliance on Rule 134 is conditioned on the disclosure of certain information, including a boilerplate legend indicating that securities may not be sold prior to the registration statement becoming effective. Rule 134(b). The name and address of a person from whom an investor may obtain a § 10 statutory prospectus must also be disclosed. These mandatory disclosures are not required if the communication is accompanied (or preceded) by a preliminary prospectus or if the Rule 134 notice "does no more than state from whom a written prospectus meeting the requirements of § 10 of the Act may be obtained, identify the security, state the price thereof and state by whom orders will be executed." Rule 134(c).

Rule 134 does not allow the disclosure of a detailed description of the offered securities, such as a term sheet. Issuers may, however, transmit written details about the terms of the offering in a free writing prospectus during in the Waiting Period.

f.   Solicitations of Interest

Rule 134 also enables issuers to obtain indications of interest from investors. Under Rule 134(d), if a preliminary prospectus accompanies or precedes a Rule 134 communication, the communication may solicit an offer to buy or a less formal indication of interest. Rule 134(d) provides for a mandatory boilerplate legend advising the investor of his or her right to revoke the offer to buy prior to acceptance by the underwriter and that indications of interest involve no legal obligation. (Expressions of interest that are not followed by actual orders, however, may lead the underwriters to exclude the investor from subsequent offerings.)

The requirement that a preliminary prospectus precede or accompany a communication under Rules 134(c) and 134(d) is satisfied if the communication is electronic and contains an active hyperlink to that prospectus.

HYPOTHETICAL FIVE

J.R., working closely with Cliff and Barnes-Wentworth Investments, the managing underwriter for Ewing Oil's offering, filed a registration statement for Ewing Oil's offering with the SEC. J.R. is eager to take Ewing Oil's story to investors and persuade them to purchase stock in the *[handwritten: in waiting period]* upcoming IPO. Do any of the following scenarios (all during the Waiting Period) violate the gun-jumping rules?

1. *Scenario One:* J.R. and Cliff hold a series of meetings with large institutional investors interested in investing in high-growth, initial public offering stock. They fly to Boston, New York, Miami, Chicago, Los Angeles, and other cities over a couple of weeks. In each city, they make a presentation to a group of investors and answer questions.

2. *Scenario Two:* Sue Ellen, a broker working for Barnes-Wentworth Investments, learns of the upcoming Ewing Oil offering through internal communications within Barnes-Wentworth. She immediately calls her list of "favored" investors consisting of all recent college graduates from her alma mater. (She obtains this list from her school's alumni web site.) For each potential investor who takes her call (a distressingly low percentage!), she spends about five minutes touting Ewing Oil's great growth prospects, the strength of the management team, and the tendency of IPO stocks to rise quickly in price after the offering.

3. *Scenario Three:* J.R. has Ewing Oil's newly-appointed investor relations director, Holly, put together an advertisement touting the upcoming offering for placement in the *Wall Street Journal*. Among other things, the advertisement is directed at "investors who want in on the new energy economy" and states Ewing Oil's intent to sell $200 million in common stock within the next year. The ad also includes a detailed five-year projection of future profits. The advertisement does not, however, mention Barnes-Wentworth Investments.

4. *Scenario Four:* J.R. has Holly put together a "tombstone" announcement of the offering that is carried in the *Wall Street Journal*. The tombstone mentions Barnes-Wentworth Investments and Ewing Oil and has a brief description of Ewing Oil's business. In addition, the tombstone provides a summary table of the past three years audited income statements of Ewing Oil (including revenues, costs, and earnings). Finally, the advertisement includes the standard legend indicating that no sales can be made before the effective date.

5. *Scenario Five:* Sue Ellen mails out a copy of the preliminary prospectus (omitting, among other things, pricing information) to all the members of her college graduating class. She includes with the preliminary prospectus a letter stating, "I think this is a good investment that might interest you. Please call me if you want to talk further about Ewing Oil's upcoming public offering. Hook 'em Horns!"

6. *Scenario Six:* Kristin, one of the clients solicited by Sue Ellen, sends a check in the amount of $20,000 to Barnes-Wentworth Investments. With her check, Kristin sends a note indicating that she is making a "down payment" on Ewing Oil shares from the upcoming public offering.

2. FREE WRITING PROSPECTUSES

Written and broadcast communications that offer or solicit an offer to buy securities are traditionally strictly limited in the Waiting Period through the interaction of § 2(a)(10) (providing for a broad definition of prospectus) and § 5(b)(1) (§ 10 prospectus delivery requirement). One consequence of the limit on prospectuses in the Waiting Period is that issuers and underwriters seeking to communicate with investors about an offering will tend to focus on the larger, institutional investors.

Typically only the institutional investors will be invited to face-to-face meetings with the officers of the issuer and representatives from the lead underwriter at roadshow meetings. Retail investors will typically only receive communications in the form of telephone calls, if at all, from brokers associated with underwriters. Those brokers lack the full information on the offering that the corporate officers have and often are compensated on a commission basis. In sum, the institutional investors get the good stuff while retail investors end up with hard-selling brokers.

The time and expense of oral communication may limit the ability and incentive of an issuer to communicate fully with more than a select group of institutional investors. It is not worth the CEO's time to telephone each potential retail investor interested in investing only a few thousand dollars. One response to this problem is to allow more cost effective methods of communications such as written communications and video recordings of roadshows available for mass distribution over the Internet.

In the 2005 Offering Reforms, the SEC opened up mass communication with the potential of reaching more retail investors through the use of "free writing prospectuses" prior to the effective date of the registration statement. The free writing prospectus gives issuers more freedom to distribute prospectuses not meeting the requirements of a formal § 10 prospectus. Under Rule 164, a free writing prospectus that satisfies Rule 433 is treated as a § 10(b) prospectus, which means that a free writing prospectus satisfies § 5(b)(1)'s requirement that prospectuses meet the requirements of § 10. As a consequence, issuers and other offering participants, including underwriters and dealers, may send out a wide range of written (including broadcast and electronic) communications in the Waiting Period.

a. Definition of a Free Writing Prospectus

A free writing prospectus includes any written communication that offers to sell or solicits an offer to buy a security that is or will be subject to a registration statement and that does not meet the requirements of a § 10 statutory final or preliminary prospectus or a § 2(a)(10)(a) form of traditional free writing. Rule 405. Rule 405 goes on to define written communication to include written, printed, broadcast and graphic communications. Graphic communications, in turn, are defined to include "all forms of electronic media," such as e-mails, Web sites, CD-ROMS, videotapes, and "substantially similar messages widely distributed" over a variety of electronic communication networks. Significantly, the SEC excluded real-time electronic communication from the definition of graphic communication, which means that real-time electronic transmissions are "oral" communications. Included in the definition of a free writing prospectus, however, are indirect communications from the issuer to the marketplace through media sources, including interviews given by corporate officers that could be construed as offering a security.

b. Issuer Requirements

For Rule 164 to apply, the issuer or other offering participant must meet the conditions set forth in Rule 433. Rule 433 provides for different requirements depending on the type of issuer, as set forth below. (Rules 164 and 433 exclude certain ineligible issuers and transactions.)

Non-Reporting and Unseasoned Issuers—Use of free writing prospectuses is permitted only after the filing of the registration statement, so non-reporting and unseasoned issuers cannot use Rule 433 in the Pre-Filing Period. For free writing prospectuses made by the issuer or on behalf of the issuer, including any paid advertisement or publication, the free writing prospectus must be accompanied or preceded by the most recent statutory prospectus that satisfies the requirements of § 10, other than a Rule 431 summary prospectus or another free writing prospectus that is deemed a § 10(b) prospectus pursuant to Rule 433. The most recent statutory prospectus must include a price range if required. For example, in Facebook's preliminary prospectus for its initial public offering, the company stated: "We anticipate that the initial public offering rice will be between $28.00 and $35.00 per share." In fact, Facebook's IPO was priced at $38.00 per share at the effective date of the offering.

If an electronic free writing prospectus is used, issuers can deliver the statutory prospectus by simply including a hyperlink to the issuer's most recent preliminary prospectus (during the Waiting Period) or final prospectus (during the Post-Effective Period). For a free writing prospectus from a media source not affiliated with nor paid by the issuer or other offering participant, the statutory prospectus does not need to precede or accompany the media free writing prospectus. Rule 433(b)(2)(i).

Issuers that have already sent a statutory prospectus to an investor may send subsequent free writing prospectuses without including another statutory prospectus so long as there have been no material changes in the information in the previously-sent statutory prospectus. After the effective date of the registration statement, issuers must send a § 10(a) final prospectus, even if an earlier preliminary prospectus was sent to the recipient. Rule 433(b)(2)(i).

Seasoned Issuers and Well-Known Seasoned Issuers—Seasoned and well-known seasoned issuers, as well as other offering participants, may use a free writing prospectus any time after the filing of the registration statement. The filed registration statement must contain a statutory prospectus that satisfies § 10 (including a "base prospectus" under Rule 430B for shelf registrations as discussed at the end of the chapter). Unlike non-reporting and unseasoned issuers, seasoned issuers and WKSIs do not have to deliver the statutory prospectus to recipients of a free writing prospectus.

Recall that under Rule 163, a well-known seasoned issuer may also use a free writing prospectus or make oral offers prior to the filing of the registration statement. A WKSI and related offering participants do not have to deliver a statutory prospectus with the free writing prospectus. Instead, a WKSI need only provide a legend indicating where to access, or hyperlink to, the preliminary or base prospectus. The bottom line is that WKSI may therefore distribute free writing prospectuses freely throughout the public offering process, using Rule 163 in the Pre-Filing Period and Rules 164 and 433 thereafter.

c.   Disclosure, Filing and Retention Requirements

Rule 433 imposes two disclosure requirements. First, the free writing prospectus may not contain information that is inconsistent with information contained in either a filed statutory prospectus or a periodic or current report incorporated by reference into the registration statement. Rule 433(c)(1). Second, the free writing prospectus must include a specified legend indicating that the issuer has filed a registration statement with the SEC and where the recipient may obtain the preliminary or base prospectus. Rule 433(c)(2).

Rule 433 requires that certain free writing prospectuses be filed with the SEC, which means the public can access them through the SEC's EDGAR system. The issuer must file a free writing prospectus on or before the date of first use in two situations:

- Any "issuer free writing prospectus" used by any person;

- Any "issuer information" that is contained in a free writing prospectus prepared by any other person (but not information prepared by a person other than the issuer on the basis of issuer information).

Rule 433(d)(1). The issuer must also file "a description of the final terms of the issuer's securities . . . after such terms have been established." Rule 433(d)(1)(i)(C). The issuer has until two days of the "later of the date such final terms have been established for all classes of the offering and the date of first use" to file the final terms. Rule 433(d)(5).

The application of the Rule 433 filing requirement is straightforward for "issuer free writing prospectuses" which are defined to encompass all information distributed by the issuer, on behalf of the issuer, or used or referred to by the issuer. Rule 433(h)(1). Such issuer free writing prospectuses must be filed with the SEC without exception. More complicated are the filing obligations resulting from free writing prospectuses of other persons, i.e., the underwriters. Rule 433(d)(1)(i)(B) requires the issuer to file free writing prospectuses prepared by other persons that contain "issuer information." Rule 433(h)(2) defines "issuer information" as "material information about the issuer or its securities that has been provided by or on behalf of the issuer." Issuers do not need to file the free writing prospectus of other persons if the prospectus is based on, but does not directly include, issuer information. According to the SEC, "[e]xamples of this information would include information prepared by underwriters that could be, but would not be limited to, information that is proprietary to an underwriter." Securities Act Release No. 8591.

Rule 433 imposes filing obligations on persons other than the issuer. Other participants in the offering, including underwriters, must file free writing prospectuses if they are distributed in "a manner that was reasonably designed to achieve broad unrestricted dissemination" unless previously filed with the SEC. Rule 433(d)(1)(ii). What is "broad unrestricted dissemination"? The SEC tells us that "[f]ree writing prospectuses sent directly to customers of an offering participant, without regard to number, would not be broadly disseminated." Securities Act Release No. 8501.

Exception

There are exceptions to the filing requirement. Issuers and other participants can skip filing if the free writing prospectus does not contain "substantive changes from or additions to" a previously filed free writing prospectus. Rule 433(d)(3). Issuers do not need to file the free writing prospectus of other persons if the issuer information was already included in a previously filed prospectus or free writing prospectus. Rule 433(d)(4). Issuers transmitting pre-recorded versions of an electronic roadshow (considered a graphic communication) may qualify for free writing prospectus treatment under Rule 433 even if they do not file the roadshow with the SEC. Non-reporting issuers registering common equity or convertible equity securities, however, must file roadshows that qualify as written communications with the SEC unless the issuer makes a "bona fide" version of the roadshow available without restriction to any person. Rule 433(d)(8). To be "bona fide," one or more of an issuer's officers or other management personnel must make a presentation in the roadshow, among other requirements. Rule 433(h)(5).

Media sources that publish or distribute a free writing prospectus with offering information provided by the issuer or any person participating in the offering (e.g., an interview of the CEO of Ewing Oil about the upcoming IPO) are potentially exempt through the operation of Rule 433(f) from the prospectus delivery requirement for unseasoned and non-reporting issuers. Rule 433(b)(2)(i). In addition, if Rule 433(f) is complied with, the issuer or offering participant is deemed to satisfy the filing and legend requirements. Rule 433(f) requires the issuer or offering participant to meet two conditions. First, Rule 433(f)(1)(i) requires that the media source not be compensated by the issuer or other participants in the offering for the written communication or its dissemination. Second, Rule 433(f)(1)(ii) requires that the issuer or other offering participant must file with the SEC the media communication with the Rule 433(c)(2) legend within four business days of becoming aware of its publication. Alternatively, the issuer or offering participant may file a copy of all the materials provided to the media including "transcripts of interviews or similar materials." Rule 433(f)(2)(iii). The media communication does not need to be filed if the substance of the communication was already filed with the SEC. Rule 433(f)(2)(i). The issuer or other offering participant may include additional information if they believe it is needed to correct information included in the communication. Rule 433(f)(2)(ii). A legend must be included on the copy that the issuer or offering participant files with the SEC but not on the copy distributed by the media source.

One concern raised by these filing requirements is the possibility that an issuer may inadvertently fail to file by the required deadline (on or before the date of first use in the case of an issuer free writing prospectus). If that happens, the issuer risks a § 5 violation, exposing the issuer to potentially ruinous § 12(a)(1) liability (discussed in Chapter 8) if the issuer goes forward with the offering. To address this concern, the SEC allows issuers and other participants that immaterially or unintentionally miss the filing deadline for a free writing prospectus to cure the violation. Rule 164(b). The cure provision is only available if the issuer has acted in good faith and with reasonable care and issuer must cure the mistake by filing the free writing prospectus as soon as practicable after discovering the failure to file. Rule 164(c) also allows the issuer to cure an omission of the required legend in the free writing prospectus.

Finally, Rule 433(g) requires issuers and offering participants to retain any free writing prospectus that they have used for three years after the date of the initial bona fide offering of the securities if it has not been filed with the SEC. Immaterial or unintentional failure to follow the record retention requirement will not result in a violation of § 5(b)(1) so long as the issuer made a "good faith and reasonable effort" to comply with the requirement. Rule 164(d).

d.   Antifraud Liability and Regulation FD Implications

The free writing prospectus is not considered part of the formal registration statement and thus is not subject to potential § 11 antifraud liability. Nonetheless, free writing prospectuses are considered "public" communications under Rule 433(a) for purposes of § 12(a)(2) antifraud liability (as "public" is used by the Supreme Court in *Gustafson v. Alloyd Holdings*, covered in Chapter 8).

Regulation FD provides an exception for communications relating to a registered public offering. For the Pre-Filing Period safe harbors contained in Rules 163 (well-known seasoned issuer Pre-Filing offers) and 163A (greater than 30 days prior to filing exclusion) described above, the SEC provided an explicit exception to this Regulation FD exception (meaning that Regulation FD *does* apply to such communications). The SEC failed to provide a similar exception to the exception for free writing prospectuses under Rules 164 and 433. Why not? The requirements for free writing prospectuses ensure the broad dissemination of any material information. Free writing prospectuses that include new information from the issuer must be filed with the SEC on or before their first day of use. The agency posts such filings on EDGAR, thus resulting in the broad public dissemination of the information even without the mandate of Regulation FD.

HYPOTHETICAL SIX

J.R., the CEO of Ewing Oil, working closely with Cliff and Barnes-Wentworth Investments, has filed a registration statement for Ewing Oil's offering with the SEC. Do any of the following scenarios (all during the Waiting Period) violate § 5?

1.   *Scenario One:* Ewing Oil mails out a glossy pamphlet containing a photograph of J.R. and detailed information on the offering and how the offering will be "rocket fuel" propelling Ewing Oil's growth. The pamphlets are mailed to, among others, all the doctors and lawyers in Texas.

2.   *Scenario Two:* J.R. gives an interview to *Business 2.0* magazine. In the interview, J.R. discusses the offering and her hope that Ewing Oil's business will rapidly expand due to the capital provided by the offering. The *Business 2.0* article quotes the entire interview.

3.   *Scenario Three:* Cliff of Barnes-Wentworth Investments sends out an information packet on the Ewing Oil offering, including the basic terms and its own analysis of the valuation of the company, together with the preliminary prospectus to potential dealers in the offering and a select group of institutional investors that have participated in prior IPOs with

Barnes-Wentworth Investments. In constructing its valuation analysis, Barnes-Wentworth relied on detailed financial information obtained from Ewing Oil as well as discussions with Ewing Oil's chief financial officer, Bobby. Barnes-Wentworth Investments does not file the information packet with the SEC.

4. *Scenario Four:* To help drum up more interest in Ewing Oil's upcoming IPO, Cliff has Barnes-Wentworth's brokerage department mail out the same information packet from Scenario Three to all the individual investor-clients with accounts at Barnes-Wentworth.

5. *Scenario Five:* Recall that J.R. and Cliff embarked on a "road show" across the country to pitch the offering to institutional investors. Suppose that J.R. has one of the road show presentations recorded and posted as a media file on the investor relations section of Ewing Oil's website.

6. *Scenario Six:* Barnes-Wentworth Investments sends an email to its investor clients containing a hyperlink to a PDF version of Ewing Oil's preliminary prospectus. The email also contains hyperlinks to various press stories (in the *Wall Street Journal, Fortune,* etc.) discussing Ewing Oil's upcoming offering.

NOTES

1. *Term sheets.* Issuers and offering participants have not made extensive use of the freedom to communicate through written and broadcast communications provided under Rules 164 and 433. The most common Form FWP filings are term sheets, providing factual descriptions of the terms and conditions of publicly offered securities. Transmeta Corporation, for example, filed a term sheet on September 21, 2007 where it, among other things, provided that:

> Transmeta Corporation, a Delaware corporation (the "Company"). Securities Offered: Up to an aggregate of 2,000,000 shares (the "Shares") of the Company's common stock, par value $0.0001 per share (the "Common Stock") and warrants to purchase 1,000,000 shares of Common Stock (the "Warrants" and, together with the Shares, the "Securities"), to be sold in units consisting of one Share and one Warrant to purchase 0.5 shares of Common Stock for a purchase price of $6.40 per unit (the "Offering"). The Shares and Warrants will be immediately separable and will be issued separately. There will be no minimum offering amount.

Largely absent from the Form FWP filings are selling documents that expand beyond short factual description of the offering. Why have issuers and offering participants not taken greater advantage of the free writing prospectus? One explanation is the fear of antifraud liability. The exemption from § 5(b)(1) for free writing prospectuses shields the issuer and offering participants from potential § 12(a)(1) liability for a violation of § 5 (as we discuss in Chapter 8). Rule 433, however, does not protect issuers and offering participants making use of a free writing prospectus from reach of antifraud liability, which includes both Rule 10b–5 and— more worryingly— § 12(a)(2). The SEC's explicit designation of free writing prospectuses under Rule 433 as public communications brings the free writing prospectus within the scope of § 12(a)(2).

The fear of § 12(a)(2) liability is compounded by Rule 159A which allows purchasers who buy securities in the "initial distribution," even if directly from an underwriter, to sue issuers under § 12(a)(2). Issuers, as a result, have an incentive to control the public disclosures of all participants in an offering, including underwriters.

———

To summarize, issuers can make "offers" during the Waiting Period through four broad avenues not generally available during the Pre-Filing Period:

(1) oral communications; *(including over phone)*

(2) statutory prospectuses under § 10(b) (Rules 430, 431);

(3) tombstone and safe harbor statements (Rule 134, § 2(a)(10)(b)); and

(4) free writing prospectuses (Rules 164 and 433).

3. THE PROCESS OF GOING EFFECTIVE

While the issuer and managing underwriter busily seek out investors during the Waiting Period, the registration statement sits with the SEC. The issuer must wait for the registration statement to become "effective" before selling any securities to the public. Under § 8(a), a registration statement is supposed to become effective twenty days after filing. In practice, no issuer allows its registration statement to become effective automatically (other than shelf issuers, discussed below). Instead, issuers commonly file a registration statement with a Rule 473 notation, which automatically amends the registration statement until the SEC has declared it effective.

The SEC has the power under § 8(a) to accelerate the effective date of a registration statement. Typically, the issuer and the underwriters will file an acceleration request with the SEC at least two days prior to the offering's desired effective date. Rule 461 outlines the factors the SEC weighs in deciding whether to grant a request for acceleration of the effective date. Among the factors that may result in a denial of acceleration include inaccurate or inadequate information in a preliminary prospectus, failure to make a bona fide effort to conform the prospectus to the plain English requirements of Rule 421(d), a current SEC investigation of the issuer, a controlling person of the issuer, or one of the underwriters, and an objection by FINRA to the compensation to be paid to the underwriters and other broker-dealers participating in the offering. Rule 461 also stresses the importance of the "adequacy of information respecting the registrant . . . available to the public." Rule 460, in turn, states that one of the considerations in determining the adequacy of information is the distribution of the preliminary prospectus a reasonable time in advance of the anticipated effective date to each underwriter and dealer "reasonably anticipated" to be invited to participate in the offering.

Why include a delaying amendment in the registration statement pursuant to Rule 473 and wait for the SEC's approval? Why not just start selling twenty days after filing? First, under § 8(a), *any* amendment to the registration statement resets the filing date for purposes of determining when the registration statement becomes effective. Thus, issuers who intend to rely on the twenty-day effective period instead of waiting for the SEC's approval must file a complete and final registration statement twenty days prior to making their first sale. The price, of course, is one of the items that must be disclosed in the registration statement. Filing a complete registration statement would therefore require fixing the price twenty days before sale. Consider the risks of fixing the price of the offering twenty days before commencing any sales. If the price is fixed at $20, what if the price the market is willing to pay goes up to $25? What if the price the market is willing to pay goes down to $15? Recall that the underwriter is using the Waiting Period to assess investor sentiment through the roadshow. Note, however, that under Rule 430A, the issuer may, in a cash offering, file a form of the prospectus that omits price-related information as part of the registration statement. This means that the registration statement can be declared effective even before the final pricing negotiations between the issuers and the underwriters.

Second, stringent antifraud provisions apply to misstatements and omissions in the registration statement (discussed in Chapter 8). Rather than face potentially crippling antifraud lawsuits, the issuer can obtain comments from the SEC identifying deficiencies and correct them before selling to the public.

Third, issuers that do not give the SEC the time the agency deems necessary risk a formal SEC refusal or stop order. The SEC has a number of formal powers with which to stop a registration statement's effectiveness. Section 8(b) of the Securities Act gives the SEC the authority to issue a refusal order preventing a registration statement from going effective if the registration statement is "on its face incomplete or inaccurate in any material respect." To issue a refusal order, the SEC must give the issuer notice within ten days of the filing of the registration statement. Moreover, the SEC must hold a hearing within ten days of the giving of notice. The wheels of government do not spin so fast, so the refusal authority is a largely empty threat.

A more potent threat is found in § 8(d), which authorizes the SEC to issue a stop order suspending the effectiveness of a registration statement. Under § 8(d), the SEC may issue a stop order if the registration statement contains "any untrue statement of a material fact or omits to state any material fact required to be stated therein or necessary to make the statements therein not misleading." As with the refusal order under § 8(b), the § 8(d) stop order requires both notice and a hearing within fifteen days of the giving of notice. To assist the SEC in determining whether to issue a stop order, § 8(e) authorizes the SEC to investigate the issuer and underwriters. If an issuer refuses to cooperate with the SEC's investigation, that refusal can be a basis for issuing a stop order.

————

The SEC review process is relatively informal. If the SEC finds the registration statement wanting, it will typically send the issuer a comment letter. Issuers, of course, do not have to respond to the comment letter. But the SEC may refuse to accelerate effectiveness or, more drastically, initiate a formal investigation leading to a refusal or stop order. Suffice it to say that either of these events would put the issuer in a very bad light with investors.

The SEC's Division of Corporation Finance reviews some, but not all, registration statements. In 1980 the SEC adopted a policy of selective review. The SEC reviews all IPO registration statements, but only selected registration statements for seasoned offerings. On average, the review process takes a little over 40 days for IPOs. Seasoned offerings are reviewed far less frequently and for a shorter time. Non-shelf registrations on Form S–3 are reviewed less than 15% of the time and spend on average less than ten days with the SEC. *See* S.E.C., *Report of the Advisory Committee on Capital Formation and Regulatory Processes*, app. A. (1996).

4. ANALYSTS

The gun-jumping rules restrict "offers" of securities. For non-public companies doing an IPO, the gun-jumping rules are only an inconvenience. Such companies typically have no audience of public investors prior to the offering. On the other hand, for companies whose shares are trading in the secondary market, the gun-jumping rules may chill the flow of information to secondary market investors. Although investors cannot buy the registered shares until the effective date, investors can purchase economically similar (and often identical) shares on the secondary market.

The issuer is not the only source of information relating to companies traded in the market. Securities analysts—whether independent or associated with a brokerage firm—provide a constant stream of information on many publicly-traded companies. When a public company with an active secondary market and many analysts covering the company's stock does a seasoned offering, should the securities laws restrict the disclosure of these analysts' recommendations to the secondary market? The SEC's definition of an "offer" is surely broad enough to capture such recommendations, which would put analysts and their employers at risk of violating § 5.

To avoid that conclusion, the SEC provides safe harbors for the publication or distribution of "research reports" under Rules 137, 138, and 139. Research reports are defined as a written communication that "includes information, opinions, or recommendations with respect to securities of an issuer or an analysis of a security of an issuer." Rules 137(e), 138(d), 139(d). Rule 405 defines written communication to include broadcast and graphic communications (including e-mails and websites, among other forms of communication).

Rule 137 provides a safe harbor for broker-dealers not participating in the offering. If Rule 137 applies, the broker-dealer issuing a research report on a security has not made an "offer" or "participated in an offering" within the definition of "underwriter" in § 2(a)(11). Note that Rule 137 does not exclude broker-dealers from the definition of a "dealer" in § 2(a)(12) of the Securities Act, so broker-dealers excluded from the definition of an underwriter under Rule 137 still cannot take advantage of § 4(a)(1), which exempts transactions not involving any issuer, underwriter, or dealer. Rule 137, instead allows unaffiliated broker-dealers making recommendations in their regular course of business to rely on § 4(a)(3) (as interpreted by Rule 174, discussed below). The following diagram depicts the operation of Rule 137.

§ 5	<—	§ 4(a)(3)	<—	§ 2(a)(11)
Gun-Jumping		exemption		Definition of
Rules		from § 5		Underwriter
				(Rule 137)

The availability of a § 4(a)(3) exemption from § 5 does not flow automatically from the application of Rule 137. Dealers can rely on § 4(a)(3) if two conditions apply: (a) the dealer is not an underwriter and (b) the publication or distribution of research does not take place during the prospectus delivery requirement period as defined in § 4(a)(3) in conjunction with Rule 174. Rule 137 only removes the dealer from the definition of an underwriter. Even with Rule 137, a non-participating broker-dealer must take care not to publish or distribute research that may condition the market during the prospectus delivery period. Fortunately, this is not a great constraint for non-participating broker-dealers providing research for Exchange Act reporting companies. Rule 174(b) reduces the prospectus delivery period for company that is an Exchange Act reporting company immediately prior to the filing of the registration statement to zero days. The SEC apparently ignores non-participating broker-dealers publishing research on non-reporting companies during the prospectus delivery period.

How does a non-participating broker-dealer qualify for the protections of Rule 137? Rule 137 applies only to research reports that a broker-dealer publishes or distributes "in the regular course of its business." Rule 137 explicitly excludes from its coverage all broker-dealers who receive compensation from the issuer, selling security holder, or other participants in the offering. (Regular subscription fees for research are allowed under Rule 137.) Rule 137 also does not apply for securities of issuers who were a blank check company, shell company, or issuer in a penny stock offering during the past three years.

For broker-dealers participating in the distribution, the SEC provides two alternative means in Rules 138 and 139 to provide opinions on companies during the registration process. (As with Rule 137, not all companies are eligible: blank check companies, shell companies, and penny stock issuers are excluded.) First, Rule 138 provides a limited safe harbor, exempting research reports of participating broker-dealers from the definition of an "offer for sale" or "offer to sell" for purposes of § 2(a)(10) (definition of prospectus) and § 5(c) (prohibition on offers in the Pre-Filing Period). Unlike Rule 137, which is available for all issuers, Rule 138 is limited to Exchange Act reporting issuers. Rule 138 divides securities into two groups: (a) common stock and debt and preferred securities convertible into common stock; and (b) debt and preferred securities not convertible into common stock. Rule 138 gives broker-dealers a safe harbor to provide opinions on one group of securities even though the issuer is offering securities belonging to the *other* group. In order to police attempted circumventions of § 5, any broker or dealer seeking to use Rule 138 to publish research reports on a specific type of securities must have previously published or distributed research on the same types of securities in the "regular course of business." Rule 138(a)(3).

Second, Rule 139 provides a more general safe harbor for participating broker-dealers publishing research reports on Exchange

Act reporting issuers. If the requirements of Rule 139 are met, the research reports are deemed not to constitute an "offer for sale" or "offer to sell" for purposes of §§ 2(a)(10) and 5(c). Rule 139 therefore directly protects broker-dealer opinions (that otherwise may be viewed as conditioning the market) from the reach of both § 5(b) and (c).

Rule 139 has two prongs: (1) issuer-specific reports; and (2) industry reports. For issuer-specific reports, only certain issuers qualify for a Rule 139 exemption from §§ 2(a)(10) and 5(c): issuers must be eligible for Form S–3 or F–3 pursuant to the $75 million minimum public float or investment grade securities provisions of the Forms. Rule 139(a)(1)(i). A broker-dealer must publish or distribute research reports in the "regular course of its business" and not be initiating (or re-initiating after a lapse) coverage of the issuer or its securities. Rule 139(a)(1)(iii). The research reports need not, however, have been published for any minimum period of time, nor do they need to have covered the same securities being sold in the offering.

For "industry reports," the SEC allows a broker-dealer to publish or disseminate research on a broader range of issuers. Eligible issuers include all reporting issuers. Rule 139(a)(2)(i). However, greater limits are placed on the research itself. An industry report must include "similar information with respect to a substantial number of issuers in the issuer's industry or sub-industry, or . . . a comprehensive list of securities currently recommended by the broker or dealer." Rule 139(a)(2)(iii). The broker-dealer may not devote any "materially greater space or prominence" to the issuer compared with any other securities or companies. Rule 139(a)(2)(iv). Finally, the broker or dealer must publish or distribute research reports in "the regular course of its business" and "at the time of the publication or distribution of the research report, . . . include[e] similar information about the issuer or its securities in similar reports." Rule 139(a)(2)(v).

like summary prospectus

Note that broker-dealers who are participating in an offering have one additional avenue to avoid the strictures of the gun-jumping rules. Rather than look to Rules 138 or 139, the broker-dealer who is participating may attempt to treat their research report as a free writing prospectus under Rules 164 and 433. Assuming the various information, prospectus delivery (if any), filing, legending, and record retention requirements are met, participating broker-dealers may avoid the requirements of Rules 138 or 139, such as the "regular course of its business" and the "at the time of publication or distribution" requirements of Rule 139.

Another limitation on analysts' report is the "quiet period" imposed by FINRA. FINRA Rule 2711(f) prohibits managing underwriters from issuing research reports until 40 days after an initial public offering. Other broker-dealers who have participated as underwriters or dealers face a 25-day quiet period. For secondary offerings, the period is reduced to ten days and only applies to the managing underwriter. This secondary offering provision has an exception for research reports complying with Rule 139 on securities that are "actively traded" as defined by Regulation M (discussed below). Managing underwriters are also prohibited from issuing research reports for 15 days prior to, and 15 days after, the expiration of a "lock-up" agreement with company insiders. Those agreements typically expire six months after the offering.

The JOBS Act of 2012 implemented an important change in the treatment of analyst research reports. The JOBS Act of 2012 excludes analyst research reports by a broker or dealer about an emerging growth company from the definition of an offer under § 5(c) and a prospectus under § 2(a)(10) during a public offering. The exclusion covers reports even by broker and dealers participating in a public offering. Securities Act § 2(a)(3).

HYPOTHETICAL SEVEN

Ewing Oil shares are not currently publicly traded, so there are no analysts following its securities. The news of its impending public offering, however, has caused some members of the investment community to take notice of Ewing Oil. Consider whether any of these discussions of Ewing Oil's initial public offering run afoul of the gun-jumping rules.

1. *Scenario One:* Donna is a reporter for the *Dallas Morning News*. She heard of Ewing Oil's public offering from a friend who saw Ewing Oil's Rule 135 notice. After researching Ewing Oil's business, Donna writes a story on the offering as part of a general report on the high-flying IPO market. The story is published on page C1 of the *Morning News* (the market page) and includes projections on Ewing Oil's future profitability.

2. *Scenario Two:* Marilee is an analyst at Stonehurst Securities. Stonehurst regularly publishes analyst opinions on companies in various sectors. Stonehurst is not participating in the offering. Nonetheless, Marilee writes an analyst report on Ewing Oil, giving the company a "neutral" recommendation for the IPO. Stonehurst publishes the analyst report, distributing it to brokers within the company as well as to its many retail and institutional investor clients. This is, however, Stonehurst's first analyst report on Ewing Oil.

3. *Scenario Three:* Lucy is an analyst at Barnes-Wentworth Investments, the managing underwriter for Ewing Oil's offering. In preparation for the IPO, Lucy writes a research report for Ewing Oil, giving the company a "buy" recommendation for the IPO. Barnes-Wentworth publishes a summary of the report (with the buy recommendation) in its monthly newsletter sent out prior to the effective date of the offering. Ewing Oil has previously not been covered in the regular newsletter.

4. *Scenario Four:* Lucy is an analyst at Barnes-Wentworth Investments. Suppose that in the past, Ewing Oil had sold a large number of non-convertible bonds in private placements to a group of insurance companies. The insurance companies eventually resold the bonds, creating a liquid secondary market for the bonds among institutional investors well before Ewing Oil's decision to do an initial public offering of its common stock. Barnes-Wentworth Investments decides to publish a special report covering the traded bonds. Published prior to the IPO's effective date, the report summarizes Lucy's research into the bonds and her opinion that the bonds are a "good buy."

C. POST-EFFECTIVE PERIOD

Just before the registration statement goes effective, the underwriters and the issuer will typically sign a formal underwriting agreement specifying, among other things, the offering price to the public and the discount at which shares are sold to the underwriters in a firm commitment offering. After the registration statement becomes effective, § 5(a) no longer applies and the issuer and the offering participants can begin selling. In a firm commitment offering, the underwriters then purchase the discounted securities and resell them to investors. For many public offerings, the entire offering process is completed within the first day of the offering. The public offering may commence at 10 A.M. and underwriters may complete the sale of all firm commitment shares by the end of the trading day, if not earlier. For particularly "hot" IPO issues, the demand for the shares may outstrip the number of offered shares. The managing underwriter, or "book-running" underwriter, may have latitude in deciding to whom to allocate shares. Typically, larger institutional investors with repeat relationships with specific investment banks will be given preference in obtaining offered shares.

Despite the freedom to make sales in the Post-Effective Period, the issuer and others continue to face restrictions, most critically under §§ 5(b)(1) and (2).

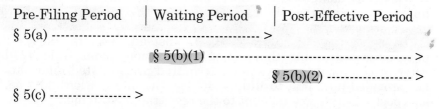

In this section we discuss: (1) forms of the statutory prospectus, (2) traditional free writing under § 2(a)(10)(a) and its relationship to § 5(b)(1), (3) the prospectus delivery requirement pursuant to §§ 5(b)(1) and (2), and (4) the updating of information contained in the statutory prospectus and registration statement.

1. FORMS OF THE FINAL PROSPECTUS

In the Post-Effective Period, issuers can no longer use Rule 430 preliminary prospectuses. Instead, the primary focus in the Post-Effective Period is on the final prospectus as provided for in § 10(a). The final statutory prospectus adds price-related information (e.g., the offering price, the underwriters' discount, etc.) to the information contained in the preliminary prospectus. Part I of the relevant registration statement form (e.g., Form S–1 or S–3 for most domestic issuers) details the required information for the final prospectus, including information on the business, properties, management, capital stock, and audited financial statements. The final prospectus may also reflect changes in the offering or revisions based on the SEC's comments on the preliminary prospectus.

Despite the focus on the § 10(a) final prospectus, there are other variants available in the Post-Effective Period. Rule 430A allows issuers to go effective with a registration statement that contains a form of the statutory prospectus that omits certain information. The 430A prospectus addresses a timing concern. As originally conceived, the final prospectus contained all the required information in one physical document. Investors would receive the entire document through the mail or directly from their broker or a dealer. Over time, the definition of a final prospectus was relaxed. Printing a physical document takes time, but issuers and underwriters typically want to set the price immediately before selling securities to the public. If the issuers and underwriters set the offering price too high, few investors will buy the securities. If the offering price is set too low, the issuer (and to a lesser extent the underwriters) leave money on the table, foregoing possibly higher proceeds.

Rule 430A of the Securities Act alleviates these timing concerns. Under Rule 430A, the final prospectus filed as part of the registration statement may omit price-related information. Rule 430A is available only for all-cash offerings, so offerings for non-cash consideration (e.g., an exchange offer for stock) cannot use Rule 430A. Rule 430A also applies to registration statements that are immediately effective upon filing with the SEC pursuant to Rule 462(e) and (f). Rule 462(e) deals with automatic shelf registration statements filed by a well-known seasoned issuer (we cover shelf registration below).

Issuers using Rule 430A must eventually file price-related information with the SEC. If the filing occurs within fifteen business days after the effective date of the registration statement, then no post-effective amendment is necessary. Instead, issuers must file a prospectus containing the pricing information under Rule 424(b)(1). After fifteen business days, if the required price-related information is not provided pursuant to Rule 424(b)(1), the information must be filed as a post-effective amendment to the registration statement.

Issuers relying on Rule 430A must also agree to the undertaking in Item 512(i) of Regulation S–K. Item 512(i) provides that for antifraud purposes (e.g., § 11 liability) price-related information filed after the effective date of the registration statement shall be deemed to be part of the registration statement as of the date the registration statement was originally declared effective. If the price-related information were instead filed as a post-effective amendment, then Item 512(i) provides for liability purposes that "each post-effective amendment that contains a form of prospectus shall be deemed to be a new registration statement relating to the securities offered therein, and the offering of such securities at that time shall be deemed to be the initial bona fide offering thereof."

While the 430A prospectus allows the issuer to go effective and itself meets the requirements of § 10 for purposes of § 5(b)(1), the issuer (and others) may not use the 430A prospectus as a § 10(a) final prospectus for other purposes. For example, in the Post-Effective Period, the free writing prospectus provision under Rule 433 requires the delivery of a § 10(a) prospectus either with or preceding the free writing prospectus for non-reporting and unseasoned issuers. Rule 433(b)(2). A 430A prospectus does not qualify for this prospectus delivery provision. As we will see below, the access-equals-delivery prospectus delivery provision under Rule 172 requires (for non-dealers) that the issuer makes a good faith and reasonable effort to file a complete § 10(a) prospectus (and not merely a 430A prospectus) with the SEC in the time specified under Rule 424. Rule 172(c)(3). Rule 424(b)(1), in turn, gives the issuer two business days after "the earlier of the date of determination of the offering price or the date it is first used after effectiveness in connection with a public offering or sales" to file the § 10(a) containing information previously omitted pursuant to Rule 430A. As we will also discuss below, traditional free writing under § 2(a)(10)(a) requires the transmission of a § 10(a) final prospectus. Section 5(b)(2)'s provision for the delivery of securities for sale also requires a final prospectus.

There are other § 10 statutory prospectuses in the Post-Effective Period. Although § 10(b) preliminary prospectuses are not valid in the Post-Effective Period, free writing prospectuses that comply with Rule 433 continue as valid § 10(b) prospectuses in the Post-Effective Period. Summary prospectuses (although little used) are also valid under Rule 431. Consequently, issuers and offering participants may freely disseminate free writing and summary prospectuses in the Post-Effective Period without violating § 5(b)(1). As with Rule 430A, a § 10(b) free writing or summary prospectus may not be used to satisfy provisions in the Post-Effective Period that require the use of a § 10(a) prospectus (including traditional free writing under § 2(a)(10)(a) and access-equals-delivery under Rule 172). The following table details the various forms of the prospectus in non-shelf offerings and their applicability to various Securities Act Post-Effective Period prospectus requirements:

Statutory Prospectus Requirement	Forms of the Prospectus (Non-Shelf)
§ 5(b)(1)	Rule 430A Prospectus Rule 431 Summary Prospectus Rule 433 Free Writing Prospectus § 10(a) Final Prospectus
§ 5(b)(2) Prospectus Delivery	§ 10(a) Final Prospectus
§ 2(a)(10)(a) Traditional Free Writing	§ 10(a) Final Prospectus
Rule 433(b)(2) Prospectus Delivery	§ 10(a) Final Prospectus
Rule 172 Access-Equals-Delivery	§ 10(a) Final Prospectus

2. TRADITIONAL FREE WRITING

In the Post-Effective Period, § 5(b)(1) prohibits written materials and broadcasts offering a security for sale (that is, a prospectus under § 2(a)(10)) unless such materials qualify as a § 10 prospectus. Both §§ 10(a) and 10(b) statutory prospectuses meet the requirements of § 5(b)(1). Section 5(b)(1) therefore allows the transmission of not only § 10(a) final statutory prospectuses but also Rule 430A prospectuses,

Rule 431 summary prospectuses, and Rule 433 free writing prospectuses.

But what about other written or broadcast offers of the securities? The definition of a prospectus under § 2(a)(10) incorporates the broad notion of offer under § 2(a)(3). Suppose an issuer or underwriter mails out materials touting the issuer's prospects as part of selling efforts after the start of the public offering. At least on its face, § 5(b)(1) appears to block the transmission of such materials in the Post-Effective Period, just as it did in the Waiting Period.

Issuers and offering participants may attempt to fit their written and broadcast offers as free writing prospectuses under Rule 433. Section 2(a)(10)(a) provides another exemption from the application of § 5(b)(1) to allow "traditional free writing." (Free writing under § 2(a)(10)(a) pre-dates and is distinct from the exemption for "free writing prospectuses" under Rules 164 and 433; we use the term "traditional free writing" to distinguish this exemption from free writing prospectuses). Section 2(a)(10)(a) removes traditional free writing from the definition of a prospectus in the Post-Effective Period as long as the traditional free writing is preceded or accompanied by a § 10(a) final statutory prospectus.

Traditional free writing potentially includes all written or broadcast offering materials which would otherwise be a prospectus not complying with § 10(a). Issuers and broker-dealers can therefore send selling documents to potential investors after the effective date as long as they also include the final statutory prospectus. Post-effective communications that fit under the traditional free writing exception contained in § 2(a)(10)(a) are not treated as free writing prospectuses. Unlike free writing prospectuses, there are no legend, filing, or record retention requirements for traditional free writing. (Recall that seasoned issuers and WKSIs do not have a prospectus delivery requirement for free writing prospectuses. Rule 433(b)(1).

3. PROSPECTUS DELIVERY REQUIREMENT

One of the primary goals of the public offering process is the creation of the mandatory disclosure documents: the registration statement and the statutory prospectus. Creation of these documents, however, can only mitigate issuers' underlying informational advantage over investors if investors receive—directly or indirectly—the information in the document. To whom, and more critically, for how long after the offering begins, must the statutory prospectus be sent?

a. The Traditional Delivery Requirement

Section 5(b) provides the cornerstone of the prospectus delivery requirement. Section 5(b)(2) requires that a § 10(a) final prospectus precede or accompany the transmission of securities for sale through an instrumentality of interstate commerce. Note that a § 10(b) statutory prospectus (such as a preliminary prospectus under Rule 430) will not meet the requirements of § 5(b)(2). Despite the straightforward prospectus delivery requirement in § 5(b)(2), the provision is of little consequence because most investors do not take physical possession of the actual security certificates (particularly for equity securities).

Instead, investors often allow their brokerage firm to hold the securities in "street name" and receive only a written confirmation of sales when purchasing securities. (Written confirmations are required by Rule 10b–10 of the Exchange Act.) Purchasing securities in street name allows investors to resell the securities quickly, with the transaction being effected by a notation in their broker's records.

The more important prospectus delivery requirement for sales of securities in public offerings is provided indirectly in the Securities Act. How indirect? Consider the following. Section 2(a)(10) defines a written confirmation of sales as a prospectus. Because the confirmation is not itself a §§ 10(a) or (b) prospectus, the transmission of the confirmation using an instrumentality of interstate commerce would violate § 5(b)(1). The prospectus delivery requirement flows from the issuer's efforts to avoid this violation of § 5(b)(1). Issuers and offering participants can avoid § 5(b)(1) by using the traditional free writing exemption from prospectus status under § 2(a)(10)(a). To satisfy the traditional free writing exemption, issuers and offering participants must precede or accompany the written confirmation of sales with a § 10(a) final statutory prospectus—resulting in prospectus delivery.

Here is the prospectus delivery requirement under § 5(b)(1), derived step-by-step:

(1) Written confirmation of sales are, without more, prospectuses under § 2(a)(10) (and must be sent under Exchange Act Rule 10b–10).

(2) Section 5(b)(1) prohibits the transmission of the written confirmation of sales since the confirmation itself is not a § 10 prospectus.

(3) Section 2(a)(10)(a) removes written confirmation of sales (and indeed other written or broadcast offers) from the definition of a prospectus if accompanied or preceded by a § 10(a) final statutory prospectus.

(4) Once § 2(a)(10)(a) removes the written confirmation of sales from the definition of a prospectus, the transmission of the confirmation no longer violates § 5(b)(1).

It is somewhat odd that investors receive the prospectus only when they receive the written confirmation of sale. If you were an investor, wouldn't you want to receive the prospectus *prior* to making your purchase decision? Perhaps realizing that the final prospectus does little good to an investor with the confirmation of sale, for non-reporting companies, Rule 15c2–8(b) requires that participating brokers send a copy of the preliminary prospectus at least 48 hours prior to the sending of the confirmation. Participating brokers comply with Rule 15c2–8(b) by sending the preliminary prospectus to all those purchasers allotted shares in the public offering.

b.   *Prospectus Delivery Period*

How long does the prospectus delivery requirement last? Section 5(b) provides no limit. Consider the cost an indefinite delivery requirement would place on secondary market transactions. Because § 5 applies to "any person," even individual investors selling securities in the secondary market (and their brokers) would have an obligation to send a statutory prospectus to purchasing investors. How would an individual investor obtain the statutory prospectus to send with the confirmation? What if the sale takes place many years after the original public offering?

Fortunately, exemptions limit the duration of the prospectus delivery requirement. Two important exemptions limit the reach of § 5(b). First, § 4(a)(1) exempts transactions not involving any "issuer, underwriter, or dealer" from § 5. Congress enacted § 4(a)(1) specifically to exempt individuals selling in ordinary secondary market transactions from the gun-jumping rules. Section 4(a)(1) exempts the vast majority of secondary market transactions. Brokers' roles in those transactions in the secondary market, if unsolicited, are exempted by § 4(a)(4).

Note that § 4(a)(1) does not exempt transactions for securities dealers; they have to find their own exemption. Section 5(b) applies broadly to all persons, so even securities dealers who did not participate in the public offering must deliver a statutory prospectus with the confirmation during the prospectus delivery period. Section 4(a)(3) provides an exemption specifically for dealers, but its availability is limited. Dealers still acting as underwriters for the offered security are not allowed to use the § 4(a)(3) exemption, so they must comply with § 5(b)'s prospectus delivery requirements. Dealers who are not underwriters but are participants in the distribution still selling an allotment from the offering may not rely on § 4(a)(3) for securities that are part of the unsold allotment. For other dealers, § 4(a)(3)—in conjunction with Rule 174—establishes time periods when § 4(a)(3) is not available. The time periods are as follows:

> 0 days—Issuer that is an Exchange Act reporting issuer immediately prior to the filing of the registration statement (i.e., an issuer subject to the reporting requirements of § 13 or § 15(d) of the Exchange Act)
>
> 25 days—Issuer whose securities will be listed on a national securities exchange as of the offering date
>
> 40 days—Issuer that does not fit any of the above categories *not* doing an initial public offering
>
> 90 days—Issuer that does not fit any of the above categories doing an initial public offering

Beyond these time periods, § 4(a)(3) exempts dealers (as long as they are not acting as underwriters selling out of an unsold allotment from the public offering) from the application of § 5(b)(1). Without § 5(b)(1) there is no longer a prospectus delivery requirement. Conversely, within the time periods when § 4(a)(3) does not apply, all dealers—whether or not participating in the offering—face a prospectus delivery requirement.

c.   Access Equals Delivery

When the Securities Act was enacted in 1933, paper documents were the primary means of communication. Although the telegraph and telephone were common by then, neither instrument provided a convenient medium to transmit a large amount of information.

Investors interested in learning the details about a particular public offering had to read the paper version of the statutory prospectus.

Even in the 1930s, however, the benefit to the investors from the prospectus delivery requirement was less than clear. The SEC can mandate that the prospectus be delivered to the door of individual investors, but it cannot make them read it. (And nobody recycled in the 1930s.) Why would an investor ignore the prospectus? For individual investors making only a small investment, the cost of reading and deciphering the prospectus—shrouded in legalese and dense with accounting figures—outweighs the potential benefit of doing so.

Even if retail investors don't read the statutory prospectus, mandatory disclosure nonetheless may protect them in one of three ways. First, the mere drafting of a disclosure document that the SEC may review encourages issuers to be truthful in their disclosures. That incentive is bolstered by the possibility of an antifraud suit under the investor-friendly standards of §§ 11 and 12(a)(2).

Second, retail investors may obtain information indirectly. Retail investors may not read the prospectus, but they may read analyst reports on the company and/or obtain advice from their brokers before investing. Both of these sources may be enlightened by the disclosures in the prospectus.

Finally, even if retail investors make no effort to digest the information, disclosure may influence the market for the offering. Most public offerings are purchased primarily by institutional investors. If institutions are not willing to purchase the securities (at least at the price range initially contemplated), the issuer and underwriters may need to reduce the price to sell out the entire offering.

How to best distribute the mandatory disclosure? Rule 172, one of the 2005 Offering Reforms, streamlines the prospectus delivery requirement through "access equals delivery" for most issuers and transactions. Rule 172(c) imposes several conditions to qualify for an exemption. Most importantly, the issuer must file a final § 10(a) statutory prospectus with the SEC (with the possible omission of certain information as provided by Rule 430A) or "make a good faith and reasonable effort to file such prospectus within the time required under Rule 424 and in the event that the issuer fails to file timely such a prospectus, the issuer files the prospectus as soon as practicable thereafter." Rule 172(c)(3). (Even if this filing condition is not satisfied, dealers can nonetheless take advantage of Rule 172. Rule 172(c)(4).)

If Rule 172(c) is satisfied, Rule 172(a) exempts written confirmations of sales from the reach of § 5(b)(1), obviating the need for broker-dealers to mail out a final prospectus with the confirmation of sales. Similarly, Rule 172(b) deems the requirement that a prospectus precede or accompany a security transmitted for sale as met for purposes of § 5(b)(2). General free writing other than the written confirmation of sales is not covered under Rule 172 and therefore falls under the traditional prospectus delivery requirement discussed above. A seasoned issuer or WKSI may avoid prospectus delivery if they instead comply with the free writing prospectus requirements under Rule 164 and 433, but the free writing prospectus is still subject to § 12(a)(2) liability.

Underwriters, brokers and dealers must send some minimal additional information along with the sales confirmation. Rule 173 requires that for transactions in which the final prospectus delivery requirement applies under Rule 174 and § 4(a)(3), participating underwriters, brokers, and dealers (or issuer if sold directly by the issuer) must either notify purchasing investors that the sale took place under an effective registration statement or provide a final prospectus. This notice informs the purchaser that they may have rights under §§ 11 and 12(a)(2). The notice must be provided not later than two business days following the completion of the sale. After the effective date of the registration statement, notices mailed under Rule 173 are exempt from § 5(b)(1) (and thus avoid the prospectus delivery requirement). Importantly, Rule 173's obligation does not flow from § 5; non-compliance with Rule 173 may lead to possible SEC enforcement, but it does not violate § 5. Compliance with Rule 173's notice requirement is not a prerequisite for the application of Rule 172's access-as-delivery. Rule 173(c).

HYPOTHETICAL EIGHT

Suppose Ewing Oil and Barnes-Wentworth Investments commence sales of the initial public offering on June 1st. Among the underwriters in the offering are Barnes-Wentworth Investments (with the largest allotment of shares) and Southfork Securities, a large investment bank based in Dallas. Southfork was allocated 400,000 Ewing Oil shares for sale. Assume that by June 3rd, Southfork has sold 300,000 shares from its allotment leaving 100,000 more shares to sell. Do any of the following run afoul of § 5?

1. *Scenario One:* Southfork summarizes the information in the Ewing Oil prospectus in a short memo with bullet points for its brokers to use in discussing the offering with their clients. Jock, one of those brokers, passes the memo along to one of his clients, Christopher.

2. *Scenario Two:* Southfork sells shares out of its remaining allotment to Christopher, an investor based in New York City. Together with the confirmation of sales, Southfork mails out a copy of the final prospectus.

3. *Scenario Three:* Simultaneously with the commencement of the offering, Ewing Oil's shares are listed on Nasdaq. Secondary market trading quickly follows. Westar Securities, a securities dealer not participating in Ewing Oil's offering, decides to sell some of its Ewing Oil common stock inventory into the market one week after the start of Ewing Oil's IPO. Westar Securities mails the stock certificates for the shares it sells to purchasing investors but does not send a statutory prospectus.

4. *Scenario Four:* Westar Securities pitches Ewing Oil common stock through cold calls to retail investors who then purchase the shares. Westar Securities acts as their broker in placing the investors' orders with a market maker in Ewing Oil stock. Westar Securities sends each purchasing investor a written confirmation, but not the statutory prospectus.

5. *Scenario Five:* Southfork issues an analyst report on Ewing Oil on June 10. At that time, Southfork still holds 50,000 shares from its allotment. The report covers a number of high-growth companies, including Ewing Oil. The report recommends Ewing Oil as a "buy" and talks glowingly about Ewing Oil's future growth prospects. The analyst report is sent to all of Southfork's customers.

6. *Scenario Six:* Suppose that Jason decides to purchase some Ewing Oil stock on the secondary market. He contacts his broker, Jock, at Southfork and instructs him to purchase 1,000 shares at the prevailing market price. Jock executes the order for Jason on June 10, sending him a written confirmation two days later, but does not include the statutory prospectus.

4.   UPDATING THE PROSPECTUS AND REGISTRATION STATEMENT

Not all public offerings sell out on the first day of the offering. "Sticky" offerings may take some time to sell. As we discuss below, issuers may also register an offering to take place over an extended period of time (a "shelf registration"). Even after the offering is initially sold, we saw in the prospectus delivery section above that under certain circumstances § 5(b) imposes a continuing obligation on dealers to send the final prospectus along with any written confirmation of sales (or provide access under Rule 172).

Information about the issuer may change after the effective date of the registration statement. The CEO of the issuer may resign. The issuer may decide to shift its business focus. The issuer may terminate its auditor and hire a new independent accountant. A company may become the target of a new lawsuit that, while unrelated to the public offering, may pose a significant contingent financial liability. For investors contemplating whether to buy the issuer's offered securities, either directly from the underwriters or in the secondary market, should it matter that the final prospectus and registration statement have become outdated?

The concept of materiality helps answer this question. Recall from Chapter 2 that materiality is defined by reference to the "total mix of information." Information that in isolation may seem important to reasonable investors loses its materiality if the market already has the information. For companies whose securities trade in an informationally efficient capital market, "new" information on the company may already be incorporated in the stock market price, making it unnecessary to update the prospectus and registration statement. Indeed, most investors would never read an updated prospectus. As a practical matter, the market price is the *only* way such new information will (indirectly) reach the investors. Consider the extent to which the efficient capital market hypothesis informs the requirements for updating the prospectus and registration statement.

a.   Updating the Prospectus

Depending on the type of issuer, the prospectus delivery requirement may extend up to 90 days after the start of the public offering for securities dealers who are not part of the underwriting syndicate. Regardless of the prospectus delivery time period, underwriters selling their allotment are required to deliver a final prospectus until their allotment is entirely sold.

Although underwriters and dealers must deliver the final prospectus, three basic duties require updating of the prospectus:

Section 10(a)(3) of the Securities Act. Under § 10(a)(3), if a prospectus is used more than nine months after the effective date of the registration statement, the information used in the prospectus may not be more than sixteen months old to the extent that the information is known or can be provided without unreasonable effort or expense.

Antifraud Liability. No explicit updating duty is specified in § 12(a)(2) or Rule 10b–5. Instead, the prospect of antifraud liability indirectly imposes an incentive for issuers to update the prospectus. If the information in a prospectus is no longer accurate, the issuer and others involved with the prospectus are potentially liable for both § 12(a)(2) and Rule 10b–5 liability.

Shelf Registration. Issuers doing a shelf registration under Rule 415 must update the prospectus to reflect any "fundamental" change to the information set forth in the registration statement pursuant to Item 512(a) of Regulation S–K. As we discuss below, Item 512(a) also requires the filing of a post-effective amendment to the registration statement.

For non-shelf registration offerings, does § 10(a)(3) provide an adequate incentive for issuers to update the prospectus? Since the prospectus delivery requirement for non-shelf public offerings may continue at most for 90 days after the commencement of the offering, § 10(a)(3)'s nine-month updating requirement has little effect. Only underwriters still selling an unsold allotment of securities are subject to the updating requirement. (The SEC takes a dim view of a non-shelf registration that continues for an extended period after the effective date of the registration statement.) Thus, § 10(a)(3) is generally important only for shelf registration offerings.

 Instead, antifraud liability provides the major incentive for updating the prospectus, principally § 12(a)(2). Section 12(a)(2) has no scienter requirement, but defendants can avoid antifraud liability if they can show that they did not know (nor could have known with "reasonable care") about the materially misleading misstatement or omission.

Another potential source of liability is § 12(a)(1). In *SEC v. Manor Nursing Centers, Inc.*, 458 F.2d 1082 (2d Cir. 1972), the Second Circuit held that a grossly misleading prospectus would violate the prospectus delivery requirement of § 5, thus potentially giving rise to a cause of action under § 12 (a)(1).

The Second Circuit's opinion in *Manor Nursing* has not attracted broad support. The Fifth Circuit in *SEC v. Southwest Coal & Energy Co.*, 624 F.2d 1312, 1318–19 (5th Cir. 1980), wrote:

> The *Manor Nursing* thesis of fraud as a basis for § 5 violations has been roundly criticized . . . § 12[a](1) provides strict liability for one who offers or sells a security in violation of § 5. Sections 11 and 12[a](2) similarly provide liability for offers or sales of securities upon misrepresentation or misleading nondisclosure of material facts, but only if the offeror cannot demonstrate that he did not know, and could not reasonably have been expected to know, of the untruth or omission. Under the *Manor Nursing* construct, however, one who proves a misrepresentation actionable under § 11 or § 12[a](2) has also

proved a violation of § 5, thus automatically establishing liability per se under § 12[a](1). Not only does this interpretation render § 11 and 12[a](2) essentially superfluous as remedial mechanisms, but it also obliterates the due diligence defense contained in these sections, plainly intended to be available to defendants in actions under the 1933 Act based on such misrepresentations or nondisclosures. Such a result could not possibly have been intended by the drafters of these provisions.

When required to update the prospectus, issuers generally prefer (if possible) to employ a process known as "stickering" under which new information is directly added (or substituted) onto the relevant page of the prospectus. Stickering has the advantage of updating only the prospectus and not the registration statement, thereby exposing the issuer only to the possibility of § 12(a)(2) and not § 11 liability for material misstatements (or omissions where there is a duty to disclose) in the updated information.

allowed b/c of Rule 424(a)

b. Updating the Registration Statement

The registration statement must be accurate as of its effective date because antifraud liability under § 11 and Rule 10b–5 is measured as of that time. In addition, the SEC may issue a stop order pursuant to § 8(d), as discussed above, if the registration statement contains misrepresentations. The SEC's authority under § 8(d), however, only reaches registration statements that contain a material misstatement at the time of the effective date. *See Charles A. Howard*, 1 S.E.C. 6 (1933). Although issuers (and other associated parties) may have a duty to correct materially false or misleading information in the registration statement at the time of the effective date, no duty exists to update previously accurate information. That is, there is no general duty to update the registration statement.

There are two major exceptions to that general rule. First, issuers using a Rule 415 shelf registration, as we will see below, must include an Item 512(a) undertaking pursuant to Regulation S–K. The Item 512(a) undertaking requires the issuer to make a post-effective amendment to the registration statement for certain events, including any § 10(a)(3) change to the prospectus, any "fundamental" change to the information set forth in the registration statement, or any material change to the plan of distribution. Rule 512 allows issuers to incorporate Exchange Act filings by reference instead of making a post-effective amendment to meet the updating requirement of Item 512(a).

Second, in certain circumstances, if the issuer updates the prospectus, the issuer also must file that updated prospectus with the SEC. Rule 424(b)(3) requires that issuers must file an updated prospectus that represents a "substantive change from or addition to" a previously filed prospectus. Once filed, the SEC will deem the prospectus to be part of the registration statement. In contrast, issuers may make non-substantive changes or additions to the prospectus through "stickering" without a new filing with the SEC.

Updating the registration statement is far more significant than stickering the prospectus. Information contained in a sticker is not considered part of the registration statement. In contrast, information filed with the SEC pursuant to Rule 424(b) is deemed part of the registration statement for purposes of § 11 antifraud liability (discussed in Chapter 8). Issuers that make a substantive change or addition to the prospectus therefore open themselves up to additional possible antifraud liability.

HYPOTHETICAL NINE

Ewing Oil's IPO registration statement has been declared effective by the SEC. In the registration statement and final prospectus, Ewing Oil disclosed that it is in the midst of negotiating a contract with a government in Asia to use Ewing Oil's turbo-fracking technology to exploit potential gas reserves. The registration statement did not include a risk factor mentioning that the government of the Asian country was unstable. Two weeks after the effective date of the registration statement, the Asian government is overthrown in a coup and, consequently, all of the contract talks have fallen through. The new regime is now in negotiations with one of Ewing Oil's major competitors. Is there any duty to update either the final prospectus or the registration statement and why?

III. PUBLIC OFFERING TRADING PRACTICES

During and immediately after a public offering, underwriters have a lot at stake in maintaining (or better yet, increasing) the market price of the offered securities. If the securities price drops precipitously during an offering, the underwriter may have trouble selling an unsold allotment. In a firm commitment offering, the underwriter bears the risk of selling the securities and thus is stuck with any unsold allotment. Downward pressure on the secondary market price can result from "flippers"—investors who purchased in the offering (at a price lower than the current secondary market price) who are looking to make a quick profit through resales—and short sellers, who are betting on a stock price decline.

Another motivation for maintaining the secondary market price is that most public offerings include an overallotment option for underwriters to expand the size of the offering. This "Green Shoe" option allows the underwriters to purchase up to an additional 15% of the offered securities at the discounted price for resale to investors at the offering price. If the price holds up, the overallotment option can mean additional profits for the underwriters. (FINRA rules prohibit the underwriter from siphoning off any of the shares from the offering for itself for subsequent resale at a higher price in the secondary market; all the offered shares must be sold at the offering price.)

A price drop after an offering commences may harm underwriters indirectly as well. Among the services underwriters provide to issuers is access to investors willing to buy the IPO stock. Large institutional investors depend on the underwriters to bring them fairly priced—or better still, underpriced—securities. If the price drops, the institutional investors that purchased in the offering will lose money and the underwriters will lose face (and, potentially, customers for future offerings). Conversely, a price rise in the aftermarket allows the underwriters' customers—the institutional IPO investors—to sell their stock to retail investors at a profit. Thus, underwriters are happy to see a price rise in the secondary market after an offering because it enhances their reputation with institutional investors.

These incentives give underwriters an interest in inflating the secondary market price by purchasing shares. How do purchases influence the market price? First, increased demand could exhaust the supply of securities that investors are willing to sell at a particular price. Different investors may have disparate beliefs about the value of the security or, alternatively, face different tax consequences from selling the securities. To induce more investors to sell, the market price must increase. Second, the presence of a large volume of purchase orders may signal to the market that informed investors have non-public information that the company is undervalued (and are acting on this information by purchasing securities). This signal will also cause the market price to rise.

Regulation M limits the ability of underwriters and issuers to influence the secondary market price of a security during an offering. The SEC explains that Regulation M "prohibit[s] activities that could artificially influence the market for the offered security, including, for example, supporting the offering price by creating the exaggerated perception of scarcity of the offered security or creating the misleading appearance of active trading in the market for the security." Securities Act Release No. 8511 (Dec. 9, 2004). Regulation M does not afford a private right of action; only the SEC can enforce it. (Section 9(e) of the Exchange Act provides a private cause of action for manipulation, but it is little used.)

A. IPO ALLOCATIONS

On December 6, 2000 the *Wall Street Journal* ran a front-page story exposing abuses in the market for initial public offerings. *See* Susan Pulliam & Randall Smith, *Seeking IPO Shares, Investors Offer to Buy More in After-Market*, Wall St. J. A1 (Dec. 6, 2000). The story revealed "tie-in" agreements between investment banks and initial investors seeking to participate in "hot" offerings. Under those agreements, initial investors would commit to buy additional shares of the offering company's stock in secondary market trading in return for allocations of shares in the IPO. As the *Wall Street Journal* related, those "[c]ommitments to buy in the after-market lock in demand for additional stock at levels above the IPO price. As such, they provide the rocket fuel that sometimes boosts IPO prices into orbit on the first trading day." This process of encouraging purchases in the aftermarket at ever-higher prices is called "laddering." The *Journal's* account of the practice essentially lays out a conspiracy between underwriters and their favored investor-customers to engage in a scheme of market manipulation. Retail investors—who end up purchasing the stock after the IPO at inflated prices—systematically lose from the manipulation.

Why would underwriters want to boost the aftermarket price? At first glance, the clear winners from a hot IPO are those initial investors who purchase at the IPO offering price, typically large institutional investors. As noted above, however, underwriters may benefit indirectly, by reducing their risk in a firm commitment offering and by enhancing their reputation among institutional investors. An alternative—and less benign from the issuer's perspective—explanation emerged from the laddering scandal. In a follow-up story on the laddering scheme, the *Journal* reported that underwriters were demanding commissions from investors favored with hot IPO allocations: "Wall Street dealers may have sought and obtained larger-than-typical trading commissions in return for giving coveted allocations of IPOs to certain investors." *See* Randall Smith & Susan Pulliam, *U.S. Probes Inflated Commissions for Hot IPOs*, Wall St. J. C1 (Dec. 7, 2000). Not surprisingly, the fallout from these revelations was severe for the investment banking industry. The SEC's investigation into the practice led to substantial settlements with many of the best-known investment banks.

If market purchases on behalf of underwriters artificially raise the price of securities, these purchases distort the true value of the securities, causing investors to pay too much. One possible regulatory response to the problem of underwriter trading practices designed to maintain or increase the secondary market price of an offered security would be a flat ban. The SEC, however, did not take such an approach. Instead, the SEC adopted a more nuanced approach in Regulation M under the Exchange Act to regulate trading practices surrounding a distribution of securities.

Regulation M balances three disparate considerations. First, not all purchases (or bids) on the part of underwriters and others associated with an offering are intended to manipulate the secondary market price. Investment banks acting as underwriters may also act as market makers for the stock in the secondary market. To serve as market makers, the banks must be able to purchase the stock at prevailing market prices to maintain market liquidity. In addition, investment banks acting as underwriters typically have a brokerage division that purchases securities on behalf of clients in unsolicited transactions.

Second, attempts to artificially influence the market price through purchases are much less likely to work for companies with a "deep" secondary market with large volumes of unrelated, independent trades. An underwriter purchasing 100,000 shares is much more likely to affect the market price for a company with an average daily trading volume of 200,000 shares than a company that trades 10 million shares daily.

Regulation M also draws a sharp distinction between efforts to raise the market price above its current level (banned market manipulation) and efforts to maintain the market price at the offering price (regulated stabilization). Although both distort the market price, the potential for distortion is greater with efforts to raise the market price. For example, consider where the market price for Ewing Oil immediately after the public offering is $20 per share. Information then reaches the market that the true value of Ewing Oil is only $17 per share. Efforts to manipulate the price upwards (if successful) can result in a price of above $20 (say $25 per share)—resulting in an overvaluation of $8 per share. With stabilization, the maximum price permitted is $20 per share (the public offering price). Thus, the potential overvaluation is only $3 per share.

B. MARKET MANIPULATION

Regulation M regulates efforts to manipulate the market price of "covered" securities. Covered securities include "any security that is the subject of a distribution, or any reference security." Regulation M defines a reference security as "a security into which a security that is the subject of a distribution ... may be converted, exchanged, or exercised or which, under the terms of the subject security, may in whole or in significant part determine the value of the subject security." Rule 100. Thus, if a company is issuing convertible bonds then the reference security is the class of common shares into which the bonds could be converted. The common shares, as reference securities, would also come under the restrictions of Regulation M as covered securities.

In order to curb market manipulation, Rules 101, 102, and 105 limit certain types of trading during the "restricted period." The restricted period is defined under Rule 100 and depends in part on the worldwide average daily trading volume (the "ADTV") for the two months, among other possible time periods, preceding the filing of the registration statement. The different possible restricted periods are as follows:

1.   For any security with an ADTV value of $100,000 or more of an issuer whose common equity securities have a public float value of $25 million or more, the period beginning on the later of one business day prior to the determination of the offering price or such time that a person becomes a distribution participant, and ending upon such person's completion of participation in the distribution; and

2.   For all other securities, the period beginning on the later of five business days prior to the determination of the offering price or such time that a person becomes a distribution participant, and ending upon such person's completion of participation in the distribution.

3.   In the case of a distribution involving a merger, acquisition, or exchange offer, the period beginning on the day proxy solicitation or offering materials are first disseminated to security holders, and ending upon the completion of the distribution.

"Distribution participant" is defined to include an "underwriter, prospective underwriter, broker, dealer, or other person who has agreed to participate or is participating in a distribution." Rule 100.

Rule 101(a) prohibits the underwriters and their affiliated purchasers from bidding for, purchasing, or inducing another to bid for or purchase a covered security during the restricted period. Exceptions are provided, however, including offers to sell or solicitations of offers to buy the securities being distributed. Rule 101(b)(9). The underwriters must be able to sell the offering, even if Rule 101 prohibits them from purchasing shares or inducing others to purchase covered securities other than the actual securities being distributed. Other notable exceptions include:

- Research falling under the safe harbors of Rule 138 or 139, even if considered an "attempt to induce any person to bid or purchase." Rule 101(b)(1).

- Stabilization transactions under Rule 104. Rule 101(b)(2).

- Bids and purchases relating to transactions in connection with the distribution (i.e., when the underwriters purchase directly from the issuer in a firm commitment offering). Rule 101(b)(8).

- De minimis transactions, defined as purchases "during the restricted period, other than by a passive market maker, that total less than 2% of the ADTV of the security being purchased." Rule 101(b)(7).

Rule 101(c)(1) provides that the restrictions of Rule 101 do not apply to certain "actively-traded securities," defined as securities with an average daily trading volume at least $1 million, issued by a company with a public float of common equity of at least $150 million. Rule 101(c)(1) reflects the view that market manipulation in a distribution of securities is less effective (and less likely) if the securities are widely traded prior to the offering.

Rule 102 provides similar bid and purchase restrictions for issuers (and selling security holders) and purchasers affiliated with them. Rule 102 parallels Rule 101 in prohibiting bids, purchases, or inducements of bids or purchases by another person of covered securities during the restricted period. Rule 102, however, provides fewer exceptions to issuers than Rule 101 affords distribution participants. Most importantly, issuers and their affiliated purchasers (other than distribution participants) are not permitted to engage in stabilization transactions under Rule 104.

Finally, Rule 105 prohibits short selling during equity offerings by persons purchasing in the offering. Certain exceptions apply. The prohibition is intended to discourage purchasers in the offering from manipulating the offering price down by selling the securities short prior to the pricing of the offering.

HYPOTHETICAL TEN

Ewing Oil and its managing underwriter Barnes-Wentworth Investments have commenced the initial public offering of 10 million shares at $20 per share. The IPO is a firm commitment underwriting with Barnes-Wentworth Investments and the other underwriters purchasing the securities from Ewing Oil at a 7% underwriters' discount. In addition, the underwriters enjoy an overallotment option of 1 million shares. The underwriters agree to purchase the firm commitment shares from Ewing Oil on the day the registration statement becomes effective. The price of the offering initially jumps up to $30 per share but then starts falling down to $25 per share on the first day of trading. Consider whether the following market activities run afoul of Regulation M.

1. *Scenario One:* During the course of the public offering, Barnes-Wentworth Investments initiates market research for Ewing Oil, issuing a "buy" recommendation for Ewing Oil securities.

2. *Scenario Two:* Suppose that Barnes-Wentworth Investments promises to allocate 100,000 additional shares of Ewing Oil's IPO to the Southern Cross Hedge Fund. Southern Cross, in turn, promises to purchase 10,000 shares of Ewing Oil in the secondary market at prices above the offering price in the first day of trading.

3. *Scenario Three:* Barnes-Wentworth Investments completes its sales of allotted Ewing Oil IPO shares two days after the offering. The shares of Ewing Oil start to sag in the secondary market to a price below the offering price. On day three, Barnes-Wentworth starts buying shares in a successful attempt to raise the market price back to a level above the offering price. On day four, Barnes-Wentworth exercises its overallotment option and then sells additional quantities of IPO shares to the market.

C. STABILIZATION

Rule 104 of Regulation M regulates efforts on the part of any person (including underwriters and purchasers affiliated with the underwriters) to stabilize the market price. Stabilization is defined to include bids and purchases with the "purpose of pegging, fixing, or maintaining the price of a security" (Rule 100). Rule 104 stabilization is the principal exception to the prohibition of Rule 101.

What types of stabilization in connection with a public offering of a security qualify under Rule 104? First, stabilization is only permitted to prevent or retard a drop in the secondary market price of a security. Purchases intended to increase the market price are not permitted. Rule 104(b). Second, Rule 104 requires that stabilization bids must give way to "any independent bid" at the same price regardless of the size of the independent bid at the time it is entered. Rule 104(c). Third, Rule 104 requires notice to the market of stabilization. Those seeking to stabilize must give prior notice to the market and disclose the purpose of the bid to the person with whom the bid is entered. In addition, the prospectus must contain a statement notifying investors of the stabilization. To facilitate monitoring of stabilization, a group attempting stabilization may also only have one stabilizing bid in a market at any one time. Rule 104(d). Finally, the stabilization price cannot be greater than the offering price. Rule 104(f). In addition, stabilization is not allowed for "at-the-market" offerings for which the price is not fixed.

Rule 104 then distinguishes between initiating and maintaining stabilization. Initiation of stabilization that occurs when the principal market for the securities is open must take place at a price no higher than the last independent transaction price if the security has traded in the principal market on that day. Similar formulations apply if the security has not traded on that day; the rule looks instead at the previous day's transaction price and the last current asking price for the stock. Persons seeking to continue with stabilization after initiation may maintain the initial stabilization price in the principal and other markets. Persons may also reduce the stabilizing price at any time. Persons may increase the stabilization price—while staying below the offering price—no higher than the highest current independent bid for the security in the principal market (if the market is open).

HYPOTHETICAL ELEVEN

Barnes-Wentworth Investments, Ewing Oil's managing underwriter, decides that maintaining the market price for Ewing Oil's common stock at near the offering price ($20 per share) after the start of the public offering would assist the efforts of the underwriters to sell out the entire offering and provide an orderly secondary market for investors. Assume that Ewing Oil common stock is listed for trading on the Nasdaq after the offering (making Nasdaq the "principal" market for Ewing Oil shares). Are the following permitted under the federal securities laws?

1.   *Scenario One:* After the Ewing Oil IPO commences, the market price sinks immediately to $15 per share (the last transaction price on Nasdaq). Barnes-Wentworth Investments commences stabilization, putting in a bid to purchase 1,000 shares of Ewing Oil at $20 per share, the IPO offering price.

2.   *Scenario Two:* After the Ewing Oil IPO commences, the market price increases dramatically to $50 per share (the last transaction price on Nasdaq). Happy, but worried that this price will not last, Barnes-Wentworth Investments puts in a stabilization bid for 1,000 shares at $50 per share.

IV. SHELF REGISTRATION

The public offering process is expensive and time consuming. Issuers must not only draft the registration statement and wait for SEC review, but they also need to take care that their communications do not run afoul of restrictions imposed during the quiet period.

How can issuers reduce the cost of the registration process? Suppose Ewing Oil registers an enormous number of shares at the time of its IPO. Can Ewing Oil then draw from this reserve of registered shares indefinitely into the future to sell additional securities into the market without a new registration? If the registration statement and prospectus are kept current, investors may already have adequate information to assess any newly-offered securities.

There are barriers, however, standing in the way of continuous registration for Ewing Oil. Section 6(a) of the Securities Act states that a "registration statement shall be deemed effective only as to the securities specified therein as proposed to be offered." The SEC in *Shawnee Chiles Syndicate*, 10 S.E.C. 109, 113 (1941), interpreted § 6(a) as prohibiting issuers from registering securities not intended to be offered immediately or in the near future. Although the precise time limit on sale is not clear, sales continuing for over a month after the effective date pose a problem.

For little-known issuers seeking to sell stock indefinitely into the future, the SEC's prohibition of indefinite registration of securities protects investors from unwise purchases of securities. Investors also enjoy other legal protections. If an issuer sells securities using an out-of-date or otherwise misleading prospectus, the issuer and those soliciting purchases on its behalf potentially face § 12(a)(2) antifraud liability.

Consider the following situations. Why should these issuers face a time limit on the effectiveness of their registration statement?

Situation 1

Ewing Oil sells 1 million convertible bonds for a total of $100 million. Each bond is convertible at any time, at the option of the bondholder, into one share of Ewing Oil common stock. At the time the bonds are sold they are priced at $100 per bond while Ewing Oil's common stock trades at $80 per share. No rational bondholder would convert at these prices. Should Ewing Oil's business take off, however, the conversion feature of the bond allows the bondholder to enjoy the upside. For example, if Ewing Oil's common stock rises to $120 per share (assume that the bond price remains constant), the bondholder will convert to obtain the higher priced shares.

The offering of convertible bonds involves two securities: (1) the bond and (2) the security into which the bonds may be converted (common stock in the case of Ewing Oil). Section 2(a)(3) of the Securities Act states (emphasis supplied):

> The issue or transfer of a right or privilege, when originally issued or transferred with a security, giving the holder of such security the right to convert such security into another security of the same issuer or of another person, or giving a right to subscribe to another security of the same issuer or of another person, which right cannot be exercised until some future date, *shall not be deemed to be an offer or sale of such other security; but the issue or transfer of such other security upon the exercise* → *sale upon conversion of such right of conversion or subscription shall be deemed a sale of such other security.*

Ewing Oil's sale of convertible bonds implicates the offer and sale of the bonds as well as the common stock into which they can be converted. Because a holder of the convertible bonds controls the timing for when to convert the bonds into common stock, the issuer cannot be sure when a "sale" of the common stock will be deemed to occur under § 2(a)(3). A holder of the convertible bond could convert immediately, leading to the need for the issuer to register the "sale" of the common stock. But because the conversion is likely to occur on a delayed basis (if at all), the issuer must also be ready to register the "sale" of the common stock into the (possibly distant) future.

Situation 2

Consider seasoned and well-known seasoned issuers. For many Form S–3 issuers, large numbers of analysts and investors follow the stock of the company. By definition, seasoned issuers and WKSIs also must comply with the Exchange Act reporting requirements (and remain current in their filings), assuring that investors and analysts receive a periodic flow of company-specific information. This means that the registration process is unlikely to provide much additional new information. Indeed, under the integrated disclosure system, much of the information contained in the registration statement will simply be incorporated by reference from the existing periodic disclosure filings (i.e., Forms 10–K, 10–Q and 8–K filings). Why force WKSI issuers to go through the entire public offering process if the market already has the WKSI's periodic disclosures?

To address these situations, among others, the SEC promulgated Rule 415 of the Securities Act to allow for shelf registration. Under shelf registration, issuers (and others) can sell registered securities for an extended period of time after the initial effective date without running afoul of the time limitation imposed by the SEC's interpretation of § 6(a).

Rule 415 provides that offerings meeting its requirements may be offered on a "continuous or delayed basis in the future." Rule 415 imposes five basic requirements. First, only certain types of offerings may qualify. These include:

- Securities which are to be offered or sold solely by or on behalf of a person or persons *other than the registrant*, a subsidiary of the registrant or a person of which the registrant is a subsidiary (Rule 415(a)(1)(i))

- Securities which are to be issued upon *conversion* of other outstanding securities (Rule 415(a)(1)(iv))

- Securities the offering of which will be *commenced promptly*, will be made on a continuous basis and may continue for a period in excess of 30 days from the date of initial effectiveness (Rule 415(a)(1)(ix))

- Securities registered (or qualified to be registered) on *Form S–3* or Form F–3 which are to be offered and sold on an immediate, continuous or delayed basis by or on behalf of the registrant, a subsidiary of the registrant or a person of which the registrant is a subsidiary (Rule 415(a)(1)(x))

Second, for non-S–3 issuers, Rule 415(a)(2) imposes a two-year time limit for shelf registration offerings falling under Rules 415(a)(1)(viii) (business combinations) and (ix) (continuous offerings to be commenced promptly). The rule leaves some wiggle room; securities for such offerings must be "reasonably expected to be offered and sold" within two years from the effective date of the registration statement. Securities sold by Form S–3 issuers under Rule 415(a)(1)(ix) or (x) are not subject to the two-year limitation. Also excluded are offerings on behalf of persons other than the registrant (e.g., a large pre-existing shareholder of the registrant) or issued upon conversion.

Third, Rule 415 requires updating of the prospectus and registration statement. Rule 415(a)(3) requires that the issuer "furnish the undertakings required by Item 512(a) of Regulation S–K" for all shelf registration offerings. Item 512(a)(1)(i) of Regulation S–K provides that the issuer will file any prospectus required under § 10(a)(3) as a post-effective amendment. Thus, if an issuer updates a prospectus used more than nine months after the effective date of the registration statement with more current information under § 10(a)(3), Item 512(a) requires the issuer to file the prospectus as an amendment to the registration statement.

Item 512(a)(1)(ii) also requires an issuer to reflect in the prospectus any "fundamental" changes in the registration statement. The issuer must file the new prospectus with the "fundamental" changes as an amendment to the registration statement. In addition, Item 512(a)(1)(iii) requires that issuers file a post-effective amendment containing any "material" change to the plan for distribution of the offering (e.g., the number of shares). For Form S–3 issuers, however, Item 512(a) excuses companies from making a post-effective amendment if the information is contained in any Exchange Act filing that is incorporated by reference into the registration statement or the information is included in a filed prospectus supplement under Rule 424(b).

The filing of a post-effective amendment to the registration statement includes the information in the registration statement for purposes of § 11 antifraud liability. Moreover, the amendment resets the effective date of the registration statement. As we discuss in Chapter 8, § 11 measures the accuracy of information in the registration statement as of the effective date, so all of the information in the registration statement must be accurate as of that date.

Can the issuer avoid the additional exposure to § 11 liability created by an amendment by opting instead for a prospectus supplement or incorporation-by-reference of the required Item 512(a) information? No—regardless of the method with which an issuer chooses to satisfy the Item 512(a) updating requirements, the issuer will still face potential § 11 liability. "Information included in a base prospectus or in an Exchange Act periodic report incorporated into a prospectus is included in the registration statement." Securities Act Release No. 8591 (July 19, 2005). Item 512(a)(5) makes clear that the prospectus supplements authorized by Rule 430B and 430C (discussed below) are also deemed to be part of the registration statement and therefore subject to § 11 liability. Only the Rule 430B prospectus supplement (for shelf registration), however, resets the registration date for the entire registration statement, and even then, only for the issuer and underwriters (thereby excluding the officers, directors and experts from new liability exposure). Rule 430B(f)(2).

Fourth, Rule 415(a)(4) provides that in an "at the market" equity offering (an offering into an existing market at the prevailing market price) by or on behalf of the issuer, the issuer may only use Rule 415(a)(1)(x) to qualify for a shelf registration. → *seasoned / WKSI*

Fifth, Rule 415(a)(5) imposes a three-year limit to shelf offerings registered under Rules 415(a)(1)(vii), (ix) (if registered on Form S–3 or F–3), and (x). Although issuers falling under Rule 415(a)(5) must re-register every three years, the burden is minimal. The issuer must file a new registration statement for those offerings, but securities registered under a prior shelf registration statement may continue to be sold until the "earlier of the effective date of the new registration statement or 180 days after the third anniversary of the initial effective date of the prior registration statement." Rule 415(a)(5)(ii)(A). In the case of a continuous offering of securities, the issuer may continue selling the securities until the effective date of the new registration statement. Rule 415(a)(5)(ii)(B). Under Rule 415(a)(6), issuers may include in a new registration statement any unsold securities covered in an earlier shelf registration statement falling under Rule 415(a)(5). Rule 415(a)(6) also allows the issuer to roll over any previously paid and unused filing fees with regard to the unsold securities to offset filing fees for the new registration statement.

(ix) = 30 days to 3-years

In addition to the basic requirements for a Rule 415 shelf registration, the SEC provides special rules for (A) automatic shelf registrations and (B) the use of a minimal "base" prospectus.

A. AUTOMATIC SHELF REGISTRATION

The SEC eases the restrictions on shelf offerings for well-known seasoned issuers. Well-known seasoned issuers can file an automatic shelf registration for most types of offerings filed on Form S–3 (sometimes referred to as a "universal shelf registration statement"). *See* Rule 405 (definition of "Automatic shelf registration statement"); Form S–3, General Instructions I.D. Rule 405. Under Rule 462, an automatic shelf registration statement, as well as any post-effective amendment, becomes effective upon filing with the SEC. The issuer need not wait for SEC review.

The automatic shelf registration statement gives well-known seasoned issuers considerable flexibility. They can register an unspecified amount of securities, only indicating the name or class of the securities. Rule 430B(a). Well-known seasoned issuers using an automatic shelf registration statement can also add additional classes of securities to the offering without filing a new registration statement. (Rule 413 requires the filing of a new registration statement to cover additional securities for most other types of offerings.) Under Rule 413(b), additional classes of securities may be added to an automatic shelf registration statement through a post-effective amendment. Drafting a post-effective amendment is a much simpler task than drafting an entire new registration statement. The ability to add an additional class of securities at a later time gives WKSIs latitude to determine the precise types and amount of securities to register, including securities of their eligible subsidiaries and secondary offerings of their securities (in the hands of insiders, for example).

Rule 415(a)(5) imposes a time limit of three years from the initial effective date for automatic shelf registration statements. In the case of an automatic shelf registration statement, the three-year re-registration requirement serves primarily a house-keeping purpose (aggregating all updates into one document) for WKSIs. A WKSI using an automatic shelf registration statement may simply file a new registration statement that becomes effective immediately upon filing under Rule 462(e). Under Rule 415(a)(6), any unsold securities and filing fees paid in connection with the unsold securities are transferred to the new automatic shelf registration. Thus, a WKSI can register an unspecified amount of a class of securities for, essentially, an unlimited time, with the ability to add on new classes of securities under Rule 413(b). WKSIs can therefore seamlessly sell any amount of securities off the shelf without delay after the filing the initial shelf registration statement. Finally, rather than pay filing fees based on the amount of securities registered up front, a WKSI can "pay-as-you-go," paying filing fees only when securities are actually sold. Rule 456(b).

In many ways, the automatic shelf registration statement for WKSIs provides the equivalent of company registration. WKSIs effectively need to only register once (with periodic house-keeping re-registrations). Although offering securities for sales will trigger various transaction-specific disclosure requirements (such as amount offered and price and price-related information), the securities regime no longer puts automatic shelf registration WKSIs through the time consuming and expensive gun-jumping rules. If company registration is a worthwhile regulatory goal, why do so for only WKSIs? Perhaps the

SEC felt the need to limit company registration to only issuers with fairly rich securities information environments.

B. THE BASE PROSPECTUS

A shelf registration issuer could simply file a complete prospectus, including price-related information, with the initial registration statement. The issuer's only obligation would then be to update the registration statement pursuant to Item 512(a) as well as to file any required prospectus supplements, such as under § 10(a)(3) of the Securities Act. In practice, issuers will often file only a minimal "base" prospectus with the initial registration statement in a shelf offering. The base prospectus omits information related to the public offering price and the underwriters, among other information. The issuer will include any omitted information from the base prospectus as part of a prospectus supplement. Rule 424(b)(2) requires that the issuer file such a prospectus supplement with the SEC "no later than the second business day following the earlier of the date of the determination of the offering price or the date it is first used after effectiveness in connection with a public offering or sales." The prospectus supplement that is filed under Rule 424(b)(2) may disclose "public offering price, description of securities, specific method of distribution or similar matters."

Rule 430B, the shelf registration corollary to Rule 430A, gives issuers considerable latitude to omit information from the base prospectus. (Rule 430C provides a "catch all" prospectus supplement provision for offerings not covered by Rules 430A and B). The following information may be omitted from the base prospectus for a shelf registration statement.

- Shelf offerings pursuant to Rule 415(a)(1)(vii) (mortgage-related securities) or (x) may omit "information that is unknown or not reasonably available to the issuer pursuant to Rule 409." Rule 430B(a). What constitutes information that is "unknown" or "not reasonably available"? Information omitted generally includes the public offering price and other price-related information, such as the underwriting discount. In addition, to the extent the issuer does not know the specific characteristics of securities to be offered on the shelf at the time of the initial filing of the registration statement, the issuer may omit such information, providing only general terms. The issuer may then include more specific details for offered securities later as part of a prospectus supplement. Other information may also qualify for omission, such as the identities of the underwriters for future takedowns off the shelf, if unknown at the time of filing of the initial registration statement.

- Shelf offerings under an automatic shelf registration statement and pursuant to Rule 415(a)(1), other than Rule 415(a)(1)(vii) or (viii), can omit information on the plan of distribution and on whether the shelf is a primary or secondary offering even if the issuer knows the information or the information is otherwise reasonably available. Rule 430B(a). The issuer may not know in

> advance which of its investors in a private placement, for example, will want to take advantage of a registered offering to resell their securities.

- Shelf offerings pursuant to Rule 415(a)(1)(i) conducted by an issuer eligible for Form S–3 or F–3 may omit the information specified in Rule 430B(a) as well as "the identities of selling security holders and amounts of securities to be registered on their behalf." This exclusion applies only for (1) an automatic shelf registration statement or (2) situations where "(i) The initial offering transaction of the securities . . . the resale of which are being registered on behalf of each of the selling security holders, was completed; (ii) The securities . . . were issued and outstanding prior to the original date of filing the registration statement covering the resale of the securities; (iii) The registration statement refers to any unnamed selling security holders in a generic manner by identifying the initial offering transaction in which the securities were sold."

Under Rule 430B, a base prospectus omitting information pursuant to the Rule would meet the requirements of § 10 for purposes of § 5(b)(1) of the Securities Act. As with Rule 430A discussed above, Rule 430B does not allow the omission of such information for a prospectus to satisfy § 10(a) for purposes of § 5(b)(2) or for the free writing exception contained in § 2(a)(10)(a). Thus, the issuer must eventually include the omitted information to transmit securities for sale (under § 5(b)(2)) or to engage in traditional free writing under § 2(a)(10)(a).

How does the omitted information eventually make its way into the prospectus? Rule 430B gives issuers flexibility in how to file the additional information through a prospectus supplement, Exchange Act report (incorporated by reference), or a post-effective amendment. Rule 430B(d). Item 512(A)(5) and Rule 430B(e) and (f) make clear that any additional information filed later, regardless of whether through incorporation-by-reference, a prospectus supplement, or a post-effective amendment, is deemed part of the registration statement. For the issuer and the underwriters, this creates a new effective date for the registration statement for § 11 antifraud liability purposes. For certain other defendants, including officers, directors, and experts, the effective date is unchanged for the other portions of the registration statement.

NOTES

1. *Underwriters.* Rule 415 creates a dilemma for underwriters. On the one hand, the shelf registration process is designed to allow issuers to sell securities quickly by relying on their prior Exchange Act filings. Speed, however, undercuts the ability of underwriters to perform due diligence on the offering, necessary if they are to avoid § 11 liability for any misstatements in the registration statement. The problems created for underwriters by this accelerated pace are explored in the *WorldCom* case, excerpted in Chapter 8.

2. *Overhang.* When a company registers securities with a shelf registration, the stock price of the company typically drops. The price drop is known as the shelf registration overhang. One explanation for shelf overhang is that the presence of a large supply hanging over the market results in a fear of substantial dilution among present stockholders, lowering the stock price. The potential sale of securities in and of itself, however, will not necessarily dilute pre-existing security holders. If a company sells common stock at a premium to the market price, the sale should increase the per share value of the pre-existing common stock. (But who would buy at a premium to the market price?) Dilution will occur only where the shares are sold at a price *lower* than the market price. But why would managers ever choose to sell for less than the market price? Only a company with serious cash flow problems would dilute shareholders this way.

An alternative explanation for market overhang is that managers can time stock sales to coincide with market overvaluation of the stock. Imagine that pre-existing shareholders cannot tell whether the market under or overvalues the stock, but managers do know. First, consider when the stock is overvalued. Those who own pre-existing stock will be less likely to obtain the benefit from selling overvalued stock (as the company will flood the market with new stock in this case). Second, consider when the stock is undervalued. The owners of pre-existing stock will then bear the entire cost of selling undervalued stock. Pre-existing shareholders, therefore, will systematically bear the cost of selling undervalued stock but miss out on selling overvalued stock—reducing their expected returns and therefore lowering the price of stock in the marketplace.

3. *Asset-backed securities.* Issuers of asset-backed securities are among the principal users of shelf registration. Indeed, mortgage backed securities warrant their own category under Rule 415(a)(vii). Asset-backed securities have also garnered their own regulatory regime. We discussed Congress's efforts to rein in asset-backed securities as part of the Dodd-Frank legislation in Chapter 3.

The SEC has also acted to provide enhanced disclosure for asset-backed securities. Regulation S–K has a separate section for disclosures by asset-backed issuers. Regulation ABS, Item 1100 et seq. of Regulation S–K, imposes detailed requirements for disclosures relating to the assets that are bundled to create these securities (Item 1111), as well as the sponsors of the securities (Item 1104). Item 1111 requires information about cash flows, such as interest rates and terms for pooled assets, but also mandates disclosure about default rates and any non-performing loans that might be included in the pool. In an effort to increase the quality of assets going into such pools, the SEC also requires a review of the assets going into the pool as provided in Rule 193. A report of that review must be included in the registration statement. Regulation S–K, Item 1111(a)(7).

HYPOTHETICAL TWELVE

Two years have passed since Ewing Oil's initial public offering (in which Ewing Oil issued eleven million shares of common at $20 per share). Ewing Oil's shares now trade on Nasdaq at around $80 per share. The Ewing family currently holds nine million Ewing Oil common shares, with eleven million in the hands of the public. Ewing Oil has been current in its Exchange Act filings over the past two years. Ewing Oil frequently has business opportunities that require it to raise capital on very short notice. Consider the following options for raising more capital.

1. *Scenario One:* Ewing Oil will issue $500 million of non-convertible bonds. J.R., the CEO of Ewing Oil, does not know when Ewing Oil will need this capital, but she hopes to be able to sell the bonds over the next six years as dictated by Ewing Oil's cash flow needs. Can Ewing Oil structure its bond offering to achieve J.R.'s goal?

2. *Scenario Two:* Suppose that six months after the initial effective date of the shelf registration described in Scenario One, J.R. is indicted for bribing foreign officials and jailed; Bobby, Ewing Oil's CFO, replaces her as CEO. If this were not a shelf registration and Ewing Oil had not yet completed its offering, what updating would Ewing Oil have to do? What about with Rule 415(a)(3)? What difference does it make?

3. *Scenario Three:* Can Ewing Oil issue $500 million of voting common stock through sales directly into Nasdaq over the next two years? Ewing Oil would prefer not to pay an underwriter's commission for the offering.

4. *Scenario Four:* Ewing Oil decides to do a shelf registration offering of common stock through Nasdaq with the assistance of Barnes-Wentworth Investments. On February 1, Ewing Oil files a Form S–3 registration statement, including a "base prospectus." The base prospectus excludes information on the offering price, underwriters, underwriting discount, and on the securities offered (referring only to an "unspecified" amount of "common stock"). Later, on June 1, Ewing Oil sells $200 million of common off the shelf. The common stock is sold at the prevailing market price of $80 per share with Barnes-Wentworth Investments acting as underwriter. On June 2, Ewing Oil files a prospectus supplement containing the previously omitted information with the SEC. Has Ewing Oil complied with Rule 415?

5. *Scenario Five:* Ewing Oil will issue $250 million of convertible bonds on a delayed basis over the next two years. Each bond (principal amount of $1000) can be converted at any time into ten shares of voting common. Assume that if all the bonds were converted today they would result in $200 million of common. The bonds' term is ten years; the conversion therefore may take place up to ten years after the bonds are sold.

6. *Scenario Six:* As noted above, the Ewing family holds nine million shares of Ewing Oil common stock. These shares are "restricted" in the sense that the securities laws prohibit the family from freely reselling the shares into the public markets absent a registration statement. (We explain why in Chapter 10.) May the Ewing family use a shelf registration covering a ten-year period for these shares?

CHAPTER 8

CIVIL LIABILITY UNDER THE SECURITIES ACT

Rules and Statutes

—*Sections 2(a)(3), 2(a)(10), 2(a)(11), 6(a), 10, 13, 15, 27, 27A of the Securities Act*

—*Rules 158, 159, 159A, 176 of the Securities Act*

MOTIVATING HYPOTHETICAL

InterTelly, Inc. was founded three years ago by two best friends, Zoe (InterTelly's CEO and chair of its board) and Elmo (InterTelly's Chief Technology Officer or "CTO"). InterTelly specializes in providing equipment to businesses enabling phone service over the Internet. To start InterTelly, Zoe and Elmo each put in $100,000 of their own money, hard work and ideas. Zoe and Elmo's initial capital carried InterTelly through its first year. By year two, InterTelly needed more capital to continue research and development. Zoe and Elmo put together their first formal business plan. That document outlined InterTelly's business, its plans for growth, its key personnel, its need and use for funds, as well as financials. After shopping their plan around to various venture capital firms, Zoe and Elmo eventually got Cadabby Capital LLC to invest $10 million in InterTelly. In return, Cadabby Capital demanded half the seats on InterTelly's board of directors as well as 40 percent of InterTelly's common stock. Now, at the end of year three, InterTelly needs more capital. InterTelly enlists Sesame Securities to be its managing underwriter for its initial public offering. The IPO distributed 10 million shares of InterTelly common stock at $20 per share. Unfortunately, InterTelly's registration statement and prospectus omitted Elmo's prior criminal conviction for commodities fraud and overstated InterTelly's earnings for the past two years.

I. PUBLIC OFFERINGS, UNCERTAINTY AND INFORMATION ASYMMETRY

Companies need capital if they want to expand into new businesses, develop new products, or launch new marketing campaigns. The public capital markets provide one source of capital. A securities offering allows a company to sell securities to a broad segment of the investing public. Most public investors prefer to remain passive and take very small positions in a large number of firms. Diversification reduces the risk of holding the securities of a particular company. This risk sharing advantage of the public capital markets, however, also heightens the potential downside for investors. Dispersed and passive investors are at the greatest risk of getting defrauded. Such investors often have the least leverage and incentive to investigate and monitor companies in their investment portfolio, thus creating a recipe for potential opportunism by insiders. Issuers (and their insiders) generally have better information than outside investors on the true risks facing a company. This is the problem of information asymmetry.

The registration process that we covered in Chapter 7 attempts to reduce information asymmetry through mandatory disclosure of material information. Companies raising capital in a public offering must persuade investors of the value of the offered securities. Although many companies disclose honestly, some issuers may misrepresent themselves to raise more capital. The civil liability provisions of the Securities Act that we will cover in this chapter are intended to ensure that the disclosures mandated by the registration process are accurate. Section 12(a)(1) guards against circumvention of the rules of the registration process. Section 11 of the Securities Act targets misstatements in the registration statement. Section 12(a)(2) of the Act provides an analogous civil antifraud provision for the public offering prospectus and statements relating to that prospectus.

II.   SECTION 11 LIABILITY

Section 11 of the Securities Act provides a civil antifraud provision for misstatements and omissions in the registration statement. As you learned in Chapter 5, plaintiffs seeking redress from an issuer and other participating parties can file a Rule 10b–5 action which mirrors in many respects the common law cause of action for deceit. Section 11 relaxes or eliminates a number of the common law requirements for fraud. The goals are to deter fraud by corporate issuers and make it easier for investors to obtain compensation. As you read through the following materials, consider the advantages plaintiffs gain from including a § 11 claim in their complaint. What limits does § 11 place on who may bring a claim?

A.   STANDING

Not all investors can bring suit under § 11. Companies making a public offering register particular securities with the SEC. The registration statement filed with the SEC covers only those securities sold as part of that specific public offering. In InterTelly's initial public offering, the company filed a registration statement covering 10 million shares of common stock at $20 per share. Because § 11 provides a cause of action only for persons "acquiring such security" sold through the registration statement, courts have interpreted § 11 as imposing a "tracing" requirement. Plaintiffs seeking to bring a § 11 claim must show that the specific shares they purchased were sold as part of the public offering under the registration statement that contained the alleged misstatement.

Tracing will be less of a problem for investors purchasing in an initial public offering, such as InterTelly's. Even then the tracing requirement may still stymie some plaintiffs. IPO companies typically will have other shares outstanding of the same class as those sold in the initial public offering. Zoe and Elmo, the founders of InterTelly, for example, obtained common stock when they initially capitalized the company. Similarly, Cadabby Capital LLC, the venture capital investor in InterTelly, purchased InterTelly common stock prior to InterTelly's initial public offering. These early investors may use Rule 144 (discussed in Chapter 10) to sell non-registered securities into the public market after the required holding period. Such sales are relatively rare, however, prior to the company making a public offering for the first time. Instead, insiders and venture capitalists that wish to sell their shares may have the shares registered as a secondary offering pursuant to the registration statement for the company's IPO. The insiders and venture capitalists that do not sell in the IPO will typically sign lock-up agreements under which they agree not to sell their non-registered shares for a certain period of time (usually six months). During this lock-up period, investors purchasing stock in the secondary market may argue that the only shares trading in the secondary markets are those registered for the IPO.

For more seasoned companies raising additional capital in a subsequent "seasoned" public offering, months or years after the IPO, § 11's tracing requirement erects a far greater hurdle. Consider how an investor of a company such as IBM would go about showing that the shares purchased in the secondary market in fact are the same shares IBM sold in its most recent public offering, rather than one of its several prior public offerings. Enterprising plaintiffs' attorneys have attempted to maneuver around the tracing requirement of § 11 with creative theories. The following case is a good example of such an attempt, as well as an illustration of the problems that modern clearing procedures create for § 11 plaintiffs. Does the tracing requirement create an unreasonable hurdle to recovery under § 11?

Krim v. pcOrder.com, Inc.

402 F.3d 489 (5th Cir. 2005).

■ HIGGINBOTHAM, P., CIRCUIT JUDGE.

Investors who purchased stock in pcOrder.com brought this consolidated securities action under Sections 11 and 15 of the Securities Act of 1933 against defendants pcOrder.com, its directors, its controlling shareholder Trilogy Software, and its investment bankers (collectively "PCOrder"), alleging that the registration statements filed with the Securities and Exchange Commission were false and misleading. The district court concluded that, with one exception, the investors lacked Section 11 standing because they could not trace their stock to the registration statements in question. . . . We affirm.

I.

PCOrder conducted an initial public offering of pcOrder.com stock on February 26, 1999, and a secondary public offering on December 7, 1999. In connection with each offering PCOrder filed a registration statement with the SEC.

Several holders of pcOrder.com stock filed multiple lawsuits against PCOrder under Section 11 of the Securities Act of 1933, which provides a right of action to "any person acquiring" shares issued pursuant to an untrue registration statement. The plaintiffs alleged that the registration statements were false and misleading. . . . The

district court consolidated the actions and appointed Lead Plaintiffs.[2]
. . .

In its October 21, 2002, order denying class certification, the district court first found that none of the Lead Plaintiffs purchased their stock during the public offerings—that is, they were "aftermarket" purchasers. However, it held that Section 11 is available not only to those who purchased their stock during the relevant public offerings, but also to aftermarket purchasers as long as the stock is "traceable" back to the relevant public offering.

The district court then considered whether Lead Plaintiffs Beebe, Dr. Burke, and Petrick could trace their stock back to either of the two public offerings. The district court found that the approximately 2.5 million shares issued in the pcOrder.com IPO were registered in a stock certificate in the name of Cede & Co., the nominee of the Depository Trust Company. The court found that, on April 19, 1999, when Beebe purchased 1000 of these "street name" shares, the pool of street name stock still contained only the IPO stock. Therefore, because all of his stock was necessarily IPO stock, Beebe was able to satisfy the traceability requirement and establish standing.

In contrast, the court concluded that standing was lacking for Dr. Burke and Petrick. By the end of June 1999 when Dr. Burke purchased 3000 shares, the court found that non-IPO shares—specifically, insider shares—had entered the street name certificate and intermingled with the IPO shares, but that IPO shares still comprised 99.85% of the pool. Subsequent to the December 7, 1999, secondary public offering, Dr. Burke made additional purchases and Petrick also purchased a number of shares at a time when IPO and SPO shares (collectively "PO stock") constituted 91% of the market. Appellants' expert acknowledged that there is no way to track individual shares within a pool once it becomes contaminated with outside shares.

In light of the intermingling of PO and non-PO stock in the market at the time of their purchases—even though PO stock was the overwhelming majority—the district court held that Dr. Burke and Petrick could not demonstrate that their shares were traceable to the public offering registration statements. In reaching this conclusion, the court considered expert testimony indicating that, given the number of shares owned by each Lead Plaintiff and the percentage of PO stock in the market, the probability that each Lead Plaintiff owned at least one share of PO stock was very nearly 100%.[6] However, the court held that this did not satisfy the traceability requirement because the "Lead Plaintiffs must demonstrate all stock for which they claim damages was

---

[2]   Bret Beebe, Dr. Gene Burke, and David Petrick were appointed Lead Plaintiffs, along with two other individuals who subsequently dropped out of the suit and are not part of this appeal.

[6]   Appellants' expert arrived at the odds of getting at least one PO (or "tainted") share using elementary principles of binomial probability. The expert treated the purchase of shares as a series of independent random draws from the stock pool (similar to flipping a weighted coin once for each share), and calculated the probability that at least one of the shares would be tainted according to the following formula: $1-(1-PO\%)^{\#shares}$, where PO% is the percentage of PO stock in the market and #shares is the number of shares owned. For example, at the end of June, when Dr. Burke had purchased 3000 shares, PO shares (specifically IPO shares) constituted 99.85% of the street name certificate. Therefore, the probability that he owned at least one PO share was $1-(1-0.9985)^{3000}$, or very nearly 100%.

actually issued pursuant to a defective statement, not just that it might have been, probably was, or most likely was, issued pursuant to a defective statement." The district court noted that, "[o]therwise, 'all persons who held stock in street name on and after the offering date could claim a proportional interest in the shares.'"

Having found that Dr. Burke and Petrick lacked Section 11 standing, the court concluded that they could not serve as class representatives and denied class certification. . . .

On May 5, 2003, the district court granted PCOrder's motion to dismiss. . . . The district court reiterated its conclusion that Beebe had standing to sue under Section 11, but that Dr. Burke and Petrick did not. . . . The court then dismissed Beebe's claim as moot because PCOrder had offered Beebe a settlement equal to his full recovery under the statute. . . .

* * *

III.

Appellants argue that Dr. Burke . . . and Petrick can establish Section 11 standing by proffering nothing more than statistics indicating a high mathematical probability, based on the number of shares purchased by each individual and the number of PO shares in the market, that at least some of their shares were issued pursuant to the challenged registration statement. We disagree.

We turn first to the language of the statute. In general, the Securities Act of 1933 "is concerned with the initial distribution of securities." Section 11 of the Securities Act, imposing civil liability for public offering of securities pursuant to a false registration statement, permits "any person acquiring such security" to sue. While Section 11's liability provisions are expansive—creating "virtually absolute" liability for corporate issuers for even innocent material misstatements—its standing provisions limit putative plaintiffs to the "narrow class of persons" consisting of "those who purchase securities that are the direct subject of the prospectus and registration statement."

The district court . . . [held] that Section 11's "language suggests a much broader class of potential plaintiffs than those who literally purchased their shares in the challenged offering." Indeed, the plain language of the statute confers standing on "any person acquiring such security," and there is no reason to categorically exclude aftermarket purchasers, "'so long as the security was indeed issued under that registration statement and not another.'" As such, aftermarket purchasers seeking standing must demonstrate the ability to "trace" their shares to the faulty registration. As one court explained:

> [T]o be able to take advantage of the lower burden of proof and almost strict liability available under § 11, a plaintiff must meet higher procedural standards. The most significant of the procedural standards is the requirement that a plaintiff be able to trace the security for which damages are claimed to the specific registration statement at issue.

[T]his traceability requirement is satisfied, as a matter of logic, when stock has only entered the market via a single offering. . . . Appellants, as aftermarket purchasers, assert that they can also demonstrate standing by showing a very high probability that they each have at least one PO share. Appellants argue that their statistical determinations, being over 50%, demonstrate by a preponderance of the evidence, that it is "more likely than not," that their shares are traceable to the public offerings in question.

We are persuaded that accepting such "statistical tracing" would impermissibly expand the statute's standing requirement. Because any share of pcOrder.com stock chosen at random in the aftermarket has at least a 90% chance of being tainted, its holder, according to Appellants' view, would have Section 11 standing.[36] In other words, every aftermarket purchaser would have standing for every share, despite the language of Section 11, limiting suit to "any person acquiring such security." As the district court found, it is "likely that any street name shareholder can make a similar claim with regard to one share." This cannot be squared with the statutory language—that is, with what Congress intended. We decline the invitation to reach further than the statute.

The fallacy of Appellants position is demonstrated with the following analogy. Taking a United States resident at random, there is a 99.83% chance that she will be from somewhere other than Wyoming. Does this high statistical likelihood alone, assuming for whatever reason there is no other information available, mean that she can avail herself of diversity jurisdiction in a suit against a Wyoming resident? Surely not.

In limiting those who can sue to "any person acquiring such security," Congress specifically conferred standing on a subset of security owners (unless . . . all shares in the market are PO shares). To allow Appellants to satisfy the tracing requirement for aftermarket standing in this case with the proffered statistical methodology would contravene the language and intent of Section 11.

Appellants urge this Court to not hew the statutory line, contending that to do so, in light of current market conditions, effectively precludes recovery under Section 11; that there is no reason to "express a preference for" the interests of defendants over plaintiffs. Appellants point out that, given the fungible nature of stocks within a street name certificate, it is virtually impossible to differentiate PO shares from non-PO shares.

However, as we have explained, Section 11 is available for anyone who purchased directly in the offering and any aftermarket purchasers who can demonstrate that their shares are traceable to the registration statement in question—e.g. when, as with Beebe, there had only been one offering at the time of purchase. When Congress enacted the

---

[36] Indeed, under Appellants' view, in any case where more than 50% of the available shares are issued pursuant to an allegedly false registration statement, all shareholders would have standing. Furthermore, even when the PO% is less than that, applying the "coin flip" methodology, *see* supra note 6, it would take relatively few shares to confer standing. For example, even if only 30% of the available shares are PO, or "tainted," shares, two shares will suffice to confer standing because there would be a 51% chance that at least one of the two shares is a PO share, i.e. $1-(1-0.30)^2 = 51\%$. (Put another way, the chance that both shares will be "clean" is $(0.70)^2$, or 49%. Therefore, the likelihood of this not being the case—i.e. that at least one share is tainted—is 51%.) When PO shares are 10% of the market, still only 7 shares are needed: $1-(1-0.10)^7 = 52\%$. Even when PO shares are only 2% of the pool, 35 shares would confer standing: $1-(1-0.02)^{35} = 51\%$.

Securities Act of 1933 it was not confronted with the widespread practice of holding stock in street name that Appellants describe as an impediment, absent our acceptance of statistical tracing, to invoking Section 11. That present market realities, given the fungibility of stock held in street name, may render Section 11 ineffective as a practical matter in some aftermarket scenarios is an issue properly addressed by Congress. It is not within our purview to rewrite the statute to take account of changed conditions. In the words of one court, Appellants' arguments may "have the sound ring of economic reality but unfortunately they merely point up the problems involved in the present scheme of statutory regulation."

It is, therefore, perhaps not surprising that we failed to locate any court, nor did Appellants point to any, that found Section 11 standing based solely on the statistical tracing theory espoused today. Given that the statute has been in existence for over 70 years and such elementary statistical calculations have been around for centuries, it is difficult to conclude that this is a coincidence. . . .

In *Barnes v. Osofsky*,[47] the Second Circuit confronted an intermingled stock pool not unlike the one we face today. In that case, two individuals challenged the settlement of a class action alleging Section 11 violations in a secondary public offering. The challengers, who purchased stock after the SPO, were unable to trace a portion of their shares to the SPO as opposed to the preexisting shares on the market. They objected to a provision of the settlement "limiting the benefits of the settlement to persons who could establish that they purchased securities issued" in the SPO. The court was not deterred by the reality that this "eliminated those who purchased after the issuance of the allegedly incomplete prospectus but could not so trace their purchases," because Section 11 "extends only to purchases of the newly registered shares." While not addressing the question before us today, *Barnes* is nonetheless instructive. Plaintiffs in that case urged a broad reading of Section 11 to cover anyone purchasing stock after the SPO— whether or not it was traceable to the SPO. Not unlike the concerns expressed by Appellants in the instant case, the plaintiffs in *Barnes* argued as follows:

> [O]nce it is agreed that § 11 is not limited to the original purchasers, to read that section as applying only to purchasers who can trace the lineage of their shares to the new offering makes the result turn on mere accident since most trading is done through brokers who neither know nor care whether they are getting [tainted] or [clean] shares. . . . [I]t is often impossible to determine whether previously traded shares are [clean] or [tainted], and that tracing is further complicated when stock is held in margin accounts in street names since many brokerage houses do not identify specific shares with particular accounts but instead treat the account as having an undivided interest in the house's position.

The court rejected these arguments and rejected the plaintiffs' broad reading of Section 11's standing requirement as "inconsistent

---

[47]   373 F.2d 269 (2d Cir.1967) (Friendly, J.).

with the over-all statutory scheme" and "contrary to the legislative history."[51] The same is true of Appellants' view today.

Here ... Congress conferred standing on those who actually purchased the tainted stock, not on the whole class of those who possibly purchased tainted shares—or, to put it another way, are at risk of having purchased tainted shares.... Appellants here cannot meet the statutory standing requirement of Section 11 merely by showing that they jumped into a potentially polluted "pool" of stock.

Appellants are surely correct in pointing out that, at some level, all evidence is "probabilistic." As we have explained, however, this does not answer the question before us today. In concluding that Appellants' attempt to "statistically trace" is incompatible with the standing requirement of Section 11, we cast no shadow on the use of statistical evidence in general. We recognize, for example, the widely accepted use of DNA evidence in criminal matters—even in capital murder trials—where proof must be beyond a reasonable doubt. While both are rooted in statistical calculations, at least two distinctions between DNA evidence and the statistics presented by Appellants come to mind. First, in most trials, DNA evidence does not stand alone. Here, Appellants have relied exclusively on a presentation of background statistics. Second, in any case, DNA evidence is more particularistic than the statistics here. DNA analysis seeks to establish a match between the DNA of a particular individual (e.g., a suspect) and a "mystery" sample (e.g., from a crime scene), essentially by quantifying and narrowing the universe of possible sources of the DNA. In contrast, Appellants' evidence merely demonstrates the probability that anyone with x number of shares will possess some tainted shares. It says nothing about the shares that one particular individual actually owns. The more particularized nature of DNA is further evident from the fact that "a nonmatch between any band of the suspect's DNA and the corresponding band of the questioned sample conclusively eliminates the suspect as the source of that sample." There is no such analog in the general statistics before us today.

Unquestionably, principles of probability are powerful tools, when deployed in appropriate tasks. Unquestionably, the statistics in this case indicate a high probability that a person purchasing a given number of shares will obtain at least one tainted share. However, these general statistics say nothing about the shares that a specific person actually owns and have no ability to separate those shares upon which standing can be based from those for which standing is improper. The task before the district court was to determine, by a preponderance of the evidence, whether and in what amount a plaintiff's shares are tainted, not whether the same number of shares drawn at random would likely include at least one tainted share. Understood in this light, statistical tracing is not up to the task at hand.

---

[51] Judge Friendly went on to note:

     Without depreciating the force of appellants' criticisms that this construction gives § 11 a rather accidental impact as between one open-market purchaser of a stock already being traded and another, we are unpersuaded that, by departing from the more natural meaning of the words, a court could come up with anything better. What appellants' arguments does suggest is that the time may have come for Congress to reexamine these two remarkable pioneering statutes in the light of thirty years' experience. . . .

In sum, aftermarket purchasers seeking Section 11 standing must demonstrate that their shares are traceable to the challenged registration statement. We are not persuaded that the statistical tracing method advanced today is sufficient to satisfy this traceability requirement.

* * *

QUESTIONS

1. Section 11 does not require plaintiffs to demonstrate any reliance on the registration statement. Does the strict tracing requirement for § 11 substitute for a reliance requirement?

2. The *Krim* court cites one of the earliest cases to impose a tracing requirement on § 11 plaintiffs, *Barnes v. Osofsky*, 373 F.2d 269 (2d Cir. 1967), In *Barnes*, Judge Henry Friendly justified the requirement by pointing to § 11(g)'s limit on damages:

> [T]he over-all limitation of § 11(g) that "In no case shall the amount recoverable under this section exceed the price at which the security was offered to the public," and the provision of § 11(e) whereby, with qualifications not here material, an underwriter's liability shall not exceed "the total price at which the securities underwritten by him and distributed to the public were offered to the public," point in the direction of limiting § 11 to purchasers of the registered shares, since otherwise their recovery would be greatly diluted when the new issue was small in relation to the trading in previously outstanding shares. . . .

Do you agree with the *Barnes* court's reading of § 11(g)? Does the tracing requirement prevent dilution of recovery at the expense of another policy goal of § 11?

HYPOTHETICAL ONE

Bird purchases 10,000 shares at $20 per share directly from Sesame Securities, the managing underwriter in InterTelly's initial public offering. Bird's shares are purchased on the day of the IPO and she received a Rule 173 notice. Recall that the registration statement and prospectus omitted Elmo's (InterTelly's CTO) prior criminal conviction for commodities fraud and overstated InterTelly's earnings for the past two years.

1. *Scenario One:* Will Bird have standing to bring a § 11 fraud suit based on the misleading statements in InterTelly's registration statement?

2. *Scenario Two:* What if Bird instead purchased her InterTelly shares two weeks after the initial public offering through her broker? Assume that the trades are executed on Nasdaq with one of several market makers quoting InterTelly's shares.

3. *Scenario Three:* Suppose that one year prior to the IPO, InterTelly's biggest shareholder, Cadabby Capital LLC, had sold 100,000 shares to a variety of investors under Rule 144. After the IPO, the shares previously sold by Cadabby Capital account for 1% of the outstanding shares trading on Nasdaq. Does this change your answer to Question 2?

B. STATUTORY DEFENDANTS

Unlike the other civil antifraud provisions of the securities laws, § 11 explicitly defines the range of potential defendants. The list includes:

(1) those who signed the registration statement (§ 11(a)(1)) including the issuer, the chief executive officer, and the chief financial officer among others (§ 6(a));

(2) directors (§ 11(a)(2), (3));

(3) various experts who prepared or certified a part of the registration statement (§ 11(a)(4));

(4) underwriters (§ 11(a)(5)); and

(5) controlling persons of any of the above (§ 15)

HYPOTHETICAL TWO

To consider the scope of § 11's delineated list of defendants, consider the following insiders from the InterTelly IPO.

Name	Position
Zoe	Chief Executive Officer & Director
Elmo	Founder & Chief Technology Officer
The Count	Treasurer & Chief Financial Officer

In addition, a number of outside participants might have played a role in making (or approving) the misstatements in InterTelly's registration statement, including:

Name	Position
Oscar	InterTelly Director
Sesame Securities	Managing Underwriter
Cadabby Capital LLC	InterTelly shareholder (40%)
Abby	Partner, Cadabby Capital & InterTelly Director
Snuffle & Gus LLP	InterTelly's Attorneys
Barkley & Grover	InterTelly's Auditor
Mumford	Senior Accountant

QUESTIONS

1.   Among the list of insider and outsider participants in the InterTelly public offering, which participants may plaintiffs potentially sue under § 11 and why?

2.   InterTelly itself is not in the list of insider and outsider participants. Can a plaintiff contemplating suing for fraud in the InterTelly public offering's registration statement also sue InterTelly under § 11?

3.   Can we sue Barkley & Grover, the auditors for InterTelly, for misstatements relating to future competitive threats contained in the risk factor section of the registration statement?

4.   A variety of professionals assisted InterTelly with its IPO. Is there anyone excluded from the list of potential § 11 defendants who *should* be liable? Why?

C.   ELEMENTS OF THE CAUSE OF ACTION

Comparing § 11 with Rule 10b–5 and state common law fraud illustrates § 11's power. Section 11, Rule 10b–5, and state common law fraud all require a showing of a material misstatement. In the securities context, as discussed in Chapter 2, materiality depends on what a reasonable investor would view as significant given the "total mix" of information available to the investor.

Other than materiality, however, the elements of a § 11 cause of action are considerably easier to satisfy than the requirements for Rule 10b–5 and common law fraud. Plaintiffs in a Rule 10b–5 or state common law fraud suit bear the burden of showing that the defendant acted with scienter. Plaintiffs must also show that the defendant's fraud caused their loss and that they relied on the misstatement (or omission where a duty to disclose exists). Section 11, on the other hand, only requires the plaintiff to show a misstatement and materiality.

Elements	Section 11	Rule 10b–5 and State Common Law Fraud
Misstatement (or omission violating a duty to disclose)	✓	✓
Materiality	✓	✓
Scienter		✓
Reliance		✓
Loss Causation	Defense	✓

The fact that scienter, reliance, and causation are not required elements of a § 11 cause of action does not necessarily mean plaintiffs may ignore these elements completely. If the issuer makes public an earnings statement covering a period of at least twelve months beginning after the effective date of the registration statement, § 11(a) provides that plaintiffs then bear the burden of demonstrating reliance.

Misstatements in the registration statement for § 11 purposes are determined as of the effective date, i.e., the information in the registration statement must be accurate on the date the SEC declares it effective. Section 11 provides for liability on "any part of the registration statement, when such part became effective." The use of the phrases "any part" and "such part" imply that different sections of the registration statement may have different effective dates. One consideration in amending the registration statement is increased antifraud liability exposure. The filing of a post-effective amendment both includes the amendment information in the registration statement and establishes a new effective date for the information for purposes of § 11 liability. (The remainder of the registration statement is still judged as of the original effective date and is not reset absent some specific provision for resetting the date.)

Issuers must amend the registration statement in certain instances. We saw in Chapter 7 that issuers doing a Rule 415 shelf registration must furnish an undertaking pursuant to Item 512(a) to file a post-effective amendment to the registration statement if, among other things, a "fundamental" change has occurred. Issuers that qualify for Form S–3, among others, may avoid a post-effective amendment to a shelf registration statement otherwise required under Item 512(a)(1)(i) (prospectuses required under § 10(a)(3)) or Item 512(a)(1)(ii) (fundamental changes) through incorporation of the information by reference to an Exchange Act filing or a prospectus supplement.

Issuers may include information in the registration statement through means other than an amendment to the registration statement. A Form S–3 issuer may rely on forward incorporation-by-reference of information filed in Exchange Act periodic filings with the SEC. Issuers may also file a prospectus supplement pursuant to Rule 424(b) to include a substantive change or addition to a previously filed prospectus. The SEC deems filings under Rule 424(b) to be part of the registration statement.

The calculation of the effective date is complicated by the SEC's 2005 Public Offering Reforms. Rule 430B allows certain shelf-registration issuers to omit specified information from the "base prospectus." When issuers eventually file a prospectus supplement with the previously omitted information with the SEC, what happens to the effective date? A prospectus supplement (a) is considered part of the registration statement and (b) resets the effective date for "that part of such registration statement relating to the securities to which such form of prospectus relates" for the issuer and underwriters. In other words, the prospectus supplement sets a new effective date for the securities in the particular shelf takedown. Rule 430B(f)(2). A shelf takedown may take place months (if not years) after the effective date of the original registration statement containing the base prospectus. The resetting of the effective date for the registration statement (at least with respect to the securities offered in the particular takedown) exposes the issuer to § 11 liability and thus gives the issuer an incentive to ensure that the part of the registration statement relating to the securities offered in the takedown is accurate at the time of the shelf takedown. The effective date does not, however, reset for the officers and directors of the issuer, or for experts. Rule 430B(f)(4).

———————

Section 11, by its terms, does not require plaintiffs to plead anything with respect to defendants' state of mind. A key advantage of § 11 for plaintiffs is that defendants generally cannot seek dismissal based on state of mind related pleadings or lack thereof, unlike Rule 10b–5, under which plaintiffs must plead state of mind with particularity (as discussed in Chapter 5). What must a plaintiff plead under § 11 with respect to an opinion?

Omnicare, Inc. v. Laborers Dist. Council Constr. Indus. Pension Fund

2015 WL 1291916.

■ KAGAN, J.

Before a company may sell securities in interstate commerce, it must file a registration statement with the Securities and Exchange Commission (SEC). If that document either "contain[s] an untrue statement of a material fact" or "omit[s] to state a material fact ... necessary to make the statements therein not misleading," a purchaser of the stock may sue for damages. Securities Act § 11. This case requires us to decide how each of those phrases applies to statements of opinion.

I

The Securities Act of 1933 ... [provides that] an issuer may offer securities to the public only after filing a registration statement. That statement must contain specified information about both the company itself and the security for sale. Beyond those required disclosures, the issuer may include additional representations of either fact or opinion.

Section 11 of the Act promotes compliance with these disclosure provisions by giving purchasers a right of action ... for material misstatements or omissions in registration statements.... Section 11 ... creates two ways to hold issuers liable for the contents of a registration statement—one focusing on what the statement says and the other on what it leaves out. Either way, the buyer need not prove (as he must to establish certain other securities offenses) that the defendant acted with any intent to deceive or defraud.

This case arises out of a registration statement that petitioner Omnicare filed in connection with a public offering of common stock. Omnicare is the nation's largest provider of pharmacy services for residents of nursing homes. Its registration statement contained (along with all mandated disclosures) analysis of the effects of various federal and state laws on its business model, including its acceptance of rebates from pharmaceutical manufacturers. Of significance here, two sentences in the registration statement expressed Omnicare's view of its compliance with legal requirements:

- "We believe our contract arrangements with other healthcare providers, our pharmaceutical suppliers and our pharmacy practices are in compliance with applicable federal and state laws."

- "We believe that our contracts with pharmaceutical manufacturers are legally and economically valid arrangements that bring value to the healthcare system and the patients that we serve."

Accompanying those legal opinions were some caveats. On the same page as the first statement above, Omnicare mentioned several state-initiated "enforcement actions against pharmaceutical manufacturers" for offering payments to pharmacies that dispensed their products; it then cautioned that the laws relating to that practice might "be interpreted in the future in a manner inconsistent with our interpretation and application." And adjacent to the second statement, Omnicare noted that the Federal Government had expressed "significant concerns" about some manufacturers' rebates to pharmacies and warned that business might suffer "if these price concessions were no longer provided."

Respondents here, pension funds that purchased Omnicare stock in the public offering (hereinafter Funds), brought suit alleging that the company's two opinion statements about legal compliance give rise to liability under § 11. Citing lawsuits that the Federal Government later pressed against Omnicare, the Funds' complaint maintained that the company's receipt of payments from drug manufacturers violated anti-kickback laws. Accordingly, the complaint asserted, Omnicare made "materially false" representations about legal compliance. And so too, the complaint continued, the company "omitted to state [material] facts necessary" to make its representations not misleading. The Funds claimed that none of Omnicare's officers and directors "possessed reasonable grounds" for thinking that the opinions offered were truthful and complete. Indeed, the complaint noted that one of Omnicare's attorneys had warned that a particular contract "carrie[d] a heightened risk" of liability under anti-kickback laws. At the same time, the Funds made clear that in light of § 11's strict liability standard, they chose to "exclude and disclaim any allegation that could be construed as alleging fraud or intentional or reckless misconduct."

* * *

We granted certiorari to consider how § 11 pertains to statements of opinion. We do so in two steps, corresponding to the two parts of § 11 and the two theories in the Funds' complaint. We initially address the Funds' claim that Omnicare made "untrue statement[s] of . . . material fact" in offering its views on legal compliance. We then take up the Funds' argument that Omnicare "omitted to state a material fact . . . necessary to make the statements [in its registration filing] not misleading." . . . [W]e see those allegations as presenting different issues. In resolving the first, we discuss when an opinion itself constitutes a factual misstatement. In analyzing the second, we address when an opinion may be rendered misleading by the omission of discrete factual representations. Because we find that the Court of Appeals applied the wrong standard, we vacate its decision.

II

The Sixth Circuit held, and the Funds now urge, that a statement of opinion that is ultimately found incorrect—even if believed at the time made—may count as an "untrue statement of a material fact." As the Funds put the point, a statement of belief may make an implicit assertion about the belief's "subject matter": To say "we believe X is true" is often to indicate that "X is in fact true." In just that way, the Funds conclude, an issuer's statement that "we believe we are following the law" conveys that "we in fact are following the law"—which is "materially false," no matter what the issuer thinks, if instead it is violating an anti-kickback statute.

But that argument wrongly conflates facts and opinions. A fact is "a thing done or existing" or "[a]n actual happening." Webster's New International Dictionary 782 (1927). An opinion is "a belief[,] a view," or a "sentiment which the mind forms of persons or things." Most important, a statement of fact ("the coffee is hot") expresses certainty about a thing, whereas a statement of opinion ("I think the coffee is hot") does not. See 7 Oxford English Dictionary 151 (1933) (an opinion "rests[s] on grounds insufficient for complete demonstration"). Indeed, that difference between the two is so ingrained in our everyday ways of speaking and thinking as to make resort to old dictionaries seem a mite silly. And Congress effectively incorporated just that distinction in § 11's first part by exposing issuers to liability not for "untrue statement[s]" full stop (which would have included ones of opinion), but only for "untrue statement[s] of . . . *fact.*"

Consider that statutory phrase's application to two hypothetical statements, couched in ways the Funds claim are equivalent. A company's CEO states: "The TVs we manufacture have the highest resolution available on the market." Or, alternatively, the CEO transforms that factual statement into one of opinion: "I *believe* " (or "I think") "the TVs we manufacture have the highest resolution available on the market." The first version would be an untrue statement of fact if a competitor had introduced a higher resolution TV a month before— even assuming the CEO had not yet learned of the new product. The CEO's assertion, after all, is not mere puffery, but a determinate, verifiable statement about her company's TVs; and the CEO, however innocently, got the facts wrong. But in the same set of circumstances, the second version would remain true. Just as she said, the CEO really did believe, when she made the statement, that her company's TVs had the sharpest picture around. And although a plaintiff could later prove that opinion erroneous, the words "I believe" themselves admitted that possibility, thus precluding liability for an untrue statement of fact. That remains the case if the CEO's opinion, as here, concerned legal compliance. If, for example, she said, "I believe our marketing practices are lawful," and actually did think that, she could not be liable for a false statement of fact—even if she afterward discovered a longtime violation of law. Once again, the statement would have been true, because all she expressed was a view, not a certainty, about legal compliance.

That still leaves some room for § 11's false-statement provision to apply to expressions of opinion. As even Omnicare acknowledges, every such statement explicitly affirms one fact: that the speaker actually holds the stated belief. For that reason, the CEO's statement about product quality ("I believe our TVs have the highest resolution available on the market") would be an untrue statement of fact—namely, the fact of her own belief—if she knew that her company's TVs only placed second. And so too the statement about legal compliance ("I believe our marketing practices are lawful") would falsely describe her own state of mind if she thought her company was breaking the law. In such cases, § 11's first part would subject the issuer to liability (assuming the misrepresentation were material).[2]

---

[2]   Our decision in *Virginia Bankshares, Inc. v. Sandberg,* 501 U.S. 1083 (1991), qualifies this statement in one respect. There, the Court considered when corporate directors' statements of opinion in a proxy solicitation give rise to liability under § 14(a) of the Securities Exchange Act, which bars conduct similar to that described in § 11. In discussing that issue, the Court raised the hypothetical possibility that a director could think he was lying while actually (*i.e.,* accidentally) telling the truth about the matter addressed in his opinion. That

In addition, some sentences that begin with opinion words like "I believe" contain embedded statements of fact . . . Suppose the CEO in our running hypothetical said: "I believe our TVs have the highest resolution available because we use a patented technology to which our competitors do not have access." That statement may be read to affirm not only the speaker's state of mind, as described above, but also an underlying fact: that the company uses a patented technology. Accordingly, liability under § 11's false-statement provision would follow (once again, assuming materiality) not only if the speaker did not hold the belief she professed but also if the supporting fact she supplied were untrue.

But the Funds cannot avail themselves of either of those ways of demonstrating liability. The two sentences to which the Funds object are pure statements of opinion: To simplify their content only a bit, Omnicare said in each that "we believe we are obeying the law." And the Funds do not contest that Omnicare's opinion was honestly held. Recall that their complaint explicitly "exclude[s] and disclaim[s]" any allegation sounding in fraud or deception. What the Funds instead claim is that Omnicare's belief turned out to be wrong—that whatever the company thought, it was in fact violating anti-kickback laws. But that allegation alone will not give rise to liability under § 11's first clause because, as we have shown, a sincere statement of pure opinion is not an "untrue statement of material fact," regardless whether an investor can ultimately prove the belief wrong. That clause, limited as it is to factual statements, does not allow investors to second-guess inherently subjective and uncertain assessments. In other words, the provision is not, as the Court of Appeals and the Funds would have it, an invitation to Monday morning quarterback an issuer's opinions.

III

A

That conclusion, however, does not end this case because the Funds also rely on § 11's omissions provision, alleging that Omnicare "omitted to state facts necessary" to make its opinion on legal compliance "not misleading." As all parties accept, whether a statement is "misleading" depends on the perspective of a reasonable investor: The inquiry (like the one into materiality) is objective. We therefore must consider when, if ever, the omission of a fact can make a statement of opinion like Omnicare's, even if literally accurate, misleading to an ordinary investor.

Omnicare claims that is just not possible. On its view, no reasonable person, in any context, can understand a pure statement of opinion to convey anything more than the speaker's own mindset. As long as an opinion is sincerely held, Omnicare argues, it cannot mislead as to any matter, regardless what related facts the speaker has omitted.

---

rare set of facts, the Court decided, would not lead to liability under § 14(a). The Court reasoned that such an inadvertently correct assessment is unlikely to cause anyone harm and that imposing liability merely for the "impurities" of a director's "unclean heart" might provoke vexatious litigation. We think the same is true (to the extent this scenario ever occurs in real life) under § 11. So if our CEO did not believe that her company's TVs had the highest resolution on the market, but (surprise!) they really did, § 11 would not impose liability for her statement.

Such statements of belief (concludes Omnicare) are thus immune from liability under § 11's second part, just as they are under its first.[4]

That claim has more than a kernel of truth. A reasonable person understands, and takes into account, the difference we have discussed above between a statement of fact and one of opinion. She recognizes the import of words like "I think" or "I believe," and grasps that they convey some lack of certainty as to the statement's content. And that may be especially so when the phrases appear in a registration statement, which the reasonable investor expects has been carefully wordsmithed to comply with the law. When reading such a document, the investor thus distinguishes between the sentences "we believe X is true" and "X is true." And because she does so, the omission of a fact that merely rebuts the latter statement fails to render the former misleading. In other words, a statement of opinion is not misleading just because external facts show the opinion to be incorrect. Reasonable investors do not understand such statements as guarantees, and § 11's omissions clause therefore does not treat them that way.

But Omnicare takes its point too far, because a reasonable investor may, depending on the circumstances, understand an opinion statement to convey facts about how the speaker has formed the opinion—or, otherwise put, about the speaker's basis for holding that view. And if the real facts are otherwise, but not provided, the opinion statement will mislead its audience. Consider an unadorned statement of opinion about legal compliance: "We believe our conduct is lawful." If the issuer makes that statement without having consulted a lawyer, it could be misleadingly incomplete. In the context of the securities market, an investor, though recognizing that legal opinions can prove wrong in the end, still likely expects such an assertion to rest on some meaningful legal inquiry—rather than, say, on mere intuition, however sincere. Similarly, if the issuer made the statement in the face of its lawyers' contrary advice, or with knowledge that the Federal Government was taking the opposite view, the investor again has cause to complain: He expects not just that the issuer believes the opinion (however irrationally), but that it fairly aligns with the information in the issuer's possession at the time.[6] Thus, if a registration statement omits material facts about the issuer's inquiry into or knowledge concerning a statement of opinion, and if those facts conflict with what a reasonable

---

[4] In a different argument that arrives at the same conclusion, Omnicare maintains that § 11, by its terms, bars only those omissions that make statements of *fact*—not opinion— misleading. The language of the omissions clause, however, is not so limited. It asks whether an omitted fact is necessary to make "statements" in "any part of the registration statement" not misleading; unlike in § 11's first clause, here the word "statements" is unmodified, thus including both fact and opinion. In any event, Omnicare's alternative interpretation succeeds merely in rephrasing the critical issue. Omnicare recognizes that every opinion statement is also a factual statement about the speaker's own belief. On Omnicare's view, the question thus becomes when, if ever, an omission can make a statement of *that fact* misleading to an ordinary investor. The following analysis applies just as well to that reformulation.

[6] The hypothetical used earlier could demonstrate the same points. Suppose the CEO, in claiming that her company's TV had the highest resolution available on the market, had failed to review any of her competitors' product specifications. Or suppose she had recently received information from industry analysts indicating that a new product had surpassed her company's on this metric. The CEO may still honestly believe in her TV's superiority. But under § 11's omissions provision, that subjective belief, in the absence of the expected inquiry or in the face of known contradictory evidence, would not insulate her from liability.

investor would take from the statement itself, then § 11's omissions clause creates liability.

An opinion statement, however, is not necessarily misleading when an issuer knows, but fails to disclose, some fact cutting the other way. Reasonable investors understand that opinions sometimes rest on a weighing of competing facts; indeed, the presence of such facts is one reason why an issuer may frame a statement as an opinion, thus conveying uncertainty. Suppose, for example, that in stating an opinion about legal compliance, the issuer did not disclose that a single junior attorney expressed doubts about a practice's legality, when six of his more senior colleagues gave a stamp of approval. That omission would not make the statement of opinion misleading, even if the minority position ultimately proved correct: A reasonable investor does not expect that *every* fact known to an issuer supports its opinion statement.

Moreover, whether an omission makes an expression of opinion misleading always depends on context. Registration statements as a class are formal documents, filed with the SEC as a legal prerequisite for selling securities to the public. Investors do not, and are right not to, expect opinions contained in those statements to reflect baseless, off-the-cuff judgments, of the kind that an individual might communicate in daily life. At the same time, an investor reads each statement within such a document, whether of fact or of opinion, in light of all its surrounding text, including hedges, disclaimers, and apparently conflicting information. And the investor takes into account the customs and practices of the relevant industry. So an omission that renders misleading a statement of opinion when viewed in a vacuum may not do so once that statement is considered, as is appropriate, in a broader frame. The reasonable investor understands a statement of opinion in its full context, and § 11 creates liability only for the omission of material facts that cannot be squared with such a fair reading. . . .[11]

And the purpose of § 11 supports this understanding of how the omissions clause maps onto opinion statements. Congress adopted § 11 to ensure that issuers "tell[ ] the whole truth" to investors. For that reason, literal accuracy is not enough: An issuer must as well desist from misleading investors by saying one thing and holding back another. Omnicare would nullify that statutory requirement for all sentences starting with the phrases "we believe" or "we think." But those magic words can preface nearly any conclusion, and the resulting statements, as we have shown, remain perfectly capable of misleading investors. Thus, Omnicare's view would punch a hole in the statute for half-truths in the form of opinion statements. And the difficulty of showing that such statements are literally false—which requires proving an issuer did not believe them—would make that opening yet more consequential: Were Omnicare right, companies would have

---

[11] . . . [W]e think Justice SCALIA's reliance on the common law's requirement of an intent to deceive is inconsistent with § 11's standard of liability. As we understand him, Justice SCALIA would limit liability for omissions under § 11 to cases in which a speaker "subjectively intend[s] the deception" arising from the omission, on the ground that the common law did the same. But § 11 discards the common law's intent requirement, making omissions unlawful—regardless of the issuer's state of mind—so long as they render statements misleading. The common law can help illuminate when an omission has that effect, but cannot change § 11's insistence on strict liability.

virtual *carte blanche* to assert opinions in registration statements free from worry about § 11. That outcome would ill-fit Congress's decision to establish a strict liability offense promoting "full and fair disclosure" of material information.

Omnicare argues, in response, that applying § 11's omissions clause in the way we have described would have "adverse policy consequences." According to Omnicare, any inquiry into the issuer's basis for holding an opinion is "hopelessly amorphous," threatening "unpredictable" and possibly "massive" liability. And because that is so, Omnicare claims, many issuers will choose not to disclose opinions at all, thus "depriving [investors] of potentially helpful information."

But first, that claim is, just as Omnicare labels it, one of "policy"; and Congress gets to make policy, not the courts. The decision Congress made, for the reasons we have indicated, was to extend § 11 liability to all statements rendered misleading by omission. In doing so, Congress no doubt made § 11 less cut-and-dry than a law prohibiting only false factual statements. Section 11's omissions clause, as applied to statements of both opinion and fact, necessarily brings the reasonable person into the analysis, and asks what she would naturally understand a statement to convey beyond its literal meaning. And for expressions of opinion, that means considering the foundation she would expect an issuer to have before making the statement. All that, however, is a feature, not a bug, of the omissions provision.

Moreover, Omnicare way overstates both the looseness of the inquiry Congress has mandated and the breadth of liability that approach threatens. As we have explained, an investor cannot state a claim by alleging only that an opinion was wrong; the complaint must as well call into question the issuer's basis for offering the opinion. And to do so, the investor cannot just say that the issuer failed to reveal its basis. Section 11's omissions clause, after all, is not a general disclosure requirement; it affords a cause of action only when an issuer's failure to include a material fact has rendered a published statement misleading. To press such a claim, an investor must allege that kind of omission— and not merely by means of conclusory assertions. To be specific: The investor must identify particular (and material) facts going to the basis for the issuer's opinion—facts about the inquiry the issuer did or did not conduct or the knowledge it did or did not have—whose omission makes the opinion statement at issue misleading to a reasonable person reading the statement fairly and in context. That is no small task for an investor.

*   *   *

Finally, we see no reason to think that liability for misleading opinions will chill disclosures useful to investors. Nothing indicates that § 11's application to misleading factual assertions in registration statements has caused such a problem. . . . That absence of fallout is unsurprising. Sellers (whether of stock or other items) have strong economic incentives to . . . well, *sell* (*i.e.,* hawk or peddle). Those market-based forces push back against any inclination to underdisclose. And to avoid exposure for omissions under § 11, an issuer need only divulge an opinion's basis, or else make clear the real tentativeness of its belief. Such ways of conveying opinions so that they do not mislead will keep valuable information flowing. And that is the only kind of information investors need. To the extent our decision today chills *misleading* opinions, that is all to the good: In enacting § 11, Congress worked to ensure better, not just more, information.

B

Our analysis on this score counsels in favor of sending the case back to the lower courts for decision. ...

In doing so, however, we reemphasize a few crucial points pertinent to the inquiry on remand. Initially, as we have said, the Funds cannot proceed without identifying one or more facts left out of Omnicare's registration statement. The Funds' recitation of the statutory language—that Omnicare "omitted to state facts necessary to make the statements made not misleading"—is not sufficient; neither is the Funds' conclusory allegation that Omnicare lacked "reasonable grounds for the belief" it stated respecting legal compliance. At oral argument, however, the Funds highlighted another, more specific allegation in their complaint: that an attorney had warned Omnicare that a particular contract "carrie[d] a heightened risk" of legal exposure under anti-kickback laws. On remand, the court must review the Funds' complaint to determine whether it adequately alleged that Omnicare had omitted that (purported) fact, or any other like it, from the registration statement. And if so, the court must determine whether the omitted fact would have been material to a reasonable investor—*i.e.,* whether "there is a substantial likelihood that a reasonable [investor] would consider it important."

Assuming the Funds clear those hurdles, the court must ask whether the alleged omission rendered Omnicare's legal compliance opinions misleading in the way described earlier—*i.e.,* because the excluded fact shows that Omnicare lacked the basis for making those statements that a reasonable investor would expect. Insofar as the omitted fact at issue is the attorney's warning, that inquiry entails consideration of such matters as the attorney's status and expertise and other legal information available to Omnicare at the time. Further, the analysis of whether Omnicare's opinion is misleading must address the statement's context. That means the court must take account of whatever facts Omnicare *did* provide about legal compliance, as well as any other hedges, disclaimers, or qualifications it included in its registration statement. The court should consider, for example, the information Omnicare offered that States had initiated enforcement actions against drug manufacturers for giving rebates to pharmacies, that the Federal Government had expressed concerns about the practice, and that the relevant laws "could "be interpreted in the future in a manner" that would harm Omnicare's business.

* * *

■ SCALIA, J., concurring.

Section 11 of the Securities Act of 1933 imposes liability where a registration statement "contain[s] an untrue statement of a material fact" or "omit[s] to state a material fact necessary to make the statements therein not misleading." I agree with the Court's discussion of what it means for an expression of opinion to state an untrue material fact. But an expression of opinion implies facts (beyond the fact that the speaker believes his opinion) only where a reasonable listener would understand it to do so. And it is only when expressions of opinion *do* imply these other facts that they can be "misleading" without the addition of other "material facts." The Court's view would count far more expressions of opinion to convey collateral facts than I— or the common law—would, and I therefore concur only in part.

The common law recognized that most listeners hear "I believe," "in my estimation," and other related phrases as *disclaiming* the assertion of a fact. Hence the (somewhat overbroad) common-law rule that a plaintiff cannot establish a misrepresentation claim "for misstatements of opinion, as distinguished from those of fact." A fraudulent misrepresentation claim based on an expression of opinion could lie for the one fact the opinion reliably conveyed: that the speaker in fact held the stated opinion. And, in some circumstances, the common law acknowledged that an expression of opinion reasonably implied "that the maker knows of no fact incompatible with his opinion." The no-facts-incompatible-with-the-opinion standard was a demanding one; it meant that a speaker's judgment had to "var[y] so far from the truth that no reasonable man in his position could have such an opinion." But without more, a listener could only reasonably interpret expressions of opinion as conveying this limited assurance of a speaker's understanding of facts.

In a few areas, the common law recognized the possibility that a listener could reasonably infer from an expression of opinion not only (1) that the speaker sincerely held it, and (2) that the speaker knew of no facts incompatible with the opinion, but also (3) that the speaker had a reasonable basis for holding the opinion. This exceptional recognition occurred only where it was "very reasonable or probable" that a listener should place special confidence in a speaker's opinion. This included two main categories, both of which were carve-outs from the general rule that "the ordinary man has a reasonable competence to form his own opinion," and "is not justified in relying [on] the . . . opinion" of another. First, expressions of opinion made in the context of a relationship of trust, such as between doctors and patients. Second, expressions of opinion made by an expert in his capacity as an expert (for example, a jeweler's statement of opinion about the value of a diamond). These exceptions allowed a listener to deal with those special expressions of opinion as though they were facts. As the leading treatise put it, "the ordinary man is free to deal in reliance upon the opinion of an expert jeweler as to the value of a diamond [or] of an attorney upon a point of law." But what reasonable person would assume that a lawyer's assessment of a diamond or a jeweler's opinion on a point of law implied an educated investigation?

The Court's expansive application of § 11's omissions clause to expressions of opinion produces a far broader field of misrepresentation; in fact, it produces almost the opposite of the common-law rule. The Court holds that a reasonable investor is right to expect a reasonable basis for *all* opinions in registration statements—for example, the conduct of a "meaningful . . . inquiry,"—unless that is sufficiently disclaimed. Take the Court's hypothetical opinion regarding legal compliance. When a disclosure statement says "we believe our conduct is lawful," the Court thinks this should be understood to suggest that a lawyer was consulted, since a reasonable investigation on this point would require consulting a lawyer. But this approach is incompatible with the common law, which had no "legal opinions are different" exception.

It is also incompatible with common sense. It seems to me strange to suggest that a statement of opinion as generic as "we believe our conduct is lawful" conveys the implied assertion of fact "we have conducted a meaningful legal investigation before espousing this opinion." It is strange to ignore the reality that a director might rely on industry practice, prior experience, or advice from regulators—rather than a meaningful legal investigation—in concluding the firm's conduct is lawful. The effect of the Court's rule is to adopt a presumption of expertise on all topics volunteered within a registration statement.

It is reasonable enough to adopt such a presumption for those matters that are required to be set forth in a registration statement. Those are matters on which the management of a corporation *are* experts. If, for example, the registration statement said "we believe that the corporation has $5,000,000 cash on hand," or "we believe the corporation has 7,500 shares of common stock outstanding," the public is entitled to assume that the management has done the necessary research, so that the asserted "belief" is undoubtedly correct. But of course a registration statement would never preface such items, within the expertise of the management, with a "we believe that." Full compliance with the law, however, is another matter. It is not specifically required to be set forth in the statement, and when management prefaces *that* volunteered information with a "we believe that," it flags the fact that this is not within our area of expertise, but we think we are in compliance.

* * *

[M]ore often, when any basis is implied at all, both sides will understand that the speaker implied a "reasonable basis," but honestly disagree on what that means. And the common law supplied a solution for this: A speaker was liable for ambiguous statements— misunderstandings—as fraudulent misrepresentations *only* where he both knew of the ambiguity *and* intended that the listener fall prey to it. . . . That his basis for belief was "objectively unreasonable" does not impart liability, so long as the belief was genuine.

This aligns with common sense. When a client receives advice from his lawyer, it is surely implicit in that advice that the lawyer has conducted a reasonable investigation—reasonable, that is, *in the lawyer's estimation.* The client is relying on the expert lawyer's judgment for the amount of investigation necessary, no less than for the legal conclusion. To be sure, if the lawyer conducts an investigation that he does not believe is adequate, he would be liable for misrepresentation. And if he conducts an investigation that he believes is adequate but is *objectively unreasonable* (and reaches an incorrect result), he may be liable for malpractice. But on the latter premise he is not liable for misrepresentation; all that was implicit in his advice was that he had conducted an investigation *he* deemed adequate. To rely on an expert's opinion is to rely on the expert's evaluation of *how much time to spend* on the question at hand.

The objective test proposed by the Court—inconsistent with the common law and common intuitions about statements of opinion— invites roundabout attacks upon expressions of opinion. Litigants seeking recompense for a corporation's expression of belief that turned out, after the fact, to be incorrect can always charge that even though the belief rested upon an investigation the corporation thought to be adequate, the investigation was not "objectively adequate."

* * *

Not to worry, says the Court. Sellers of securities need "only divulge an opinion's basis, or else make clear the real tentativeness of [their] belief [s]." One wonders what the function of "in my estimation" is, then, except as divulging such hesitation. Or what would be sufficient for the Court. "In my highly tentative estimation?" "In my estimation that, consistent with *Omnicare,* should be understood as an opinion only?" Reasonable speakers do not speak this way, and reasonable listeners do not receive opinions this way. When an expert expresses an opinion instead of stating a fact, it implies (1) that he genuinely believes the opinion, (2) that he believes his basis for the opinion is sufficient, and (most important) (3) that he is not certain of his result. Nothing more. This approach would have given lower courts and investors far more guidance and would largely have avoided the Funds' attack upon Omnicare's opinions as though Omnicare held those opinions out to be facts.

* * *

QUESTIONS

1. When is an expression of an opinion an "untrue statement of material fact"?

2. Why does the Court reject the Funds' argument that Omnicare's opinion that "we believe we are obeying the law" was a material misstatement because the underlying facts regarding Omnicare's legal compliance contradicted that opinion?

3. Under what circumstances can plaintiffs sue under § 11 for "pure statements of opinion"?

4. The Court says that "companies would have virtual carte blanche to assert opinions in registration statements free from worry about § 11" if they could insulate statements from liability by prefacing statements with "we believe." How serious is this concern?

5. What does a plaintiff need to plead to state a claim with respect to a misleading opinion? Can the plaintiff simply allege that the speaker of the opinion lacked "reasonable grounds for the belief"?

6. How does the Omnicare Court's interpretation of § 11(a) fit with the treatment of expert reports under § 11(b)?

Hypothetical Three

In the risk factors section of InterTelly's registration statement, the company discloses the possibility that future regulation of telephone service over the Internet by the Federal Communications Commission could have an adverse effect on InterTelly's business. The registration statement also states, however, that "We believe regulation by the FCC is unlikely in the current regulatory environment." One of InterTelly's directors, Oscar is a former commissioner of the FCC. At the time the registration statement was being drafted, Oscar's contacts in Washington were telling him that regulation of Internet phone service was unlikely given the current composition of the FCC, but if the political balance among the commissioners changed regulation would a real possibility because the FCC staff believed that regulation was necessary. Six months after InterTelly's public offering, two new commissioners are appointed to the FCC; shortly thereafter, the FCC issues proposed rules that would regulate phone service over the Internet. InterTelly's stock price drops $5 the day the FCC announces the proposed rules. Does InterTelly have a problem under § 11?

D. Defenses

Section 11 defendants can assert a number of defenses. A defendant who resigns and notifies the SEC of that action may obtain a defense under § 11(b)(1). Alternatively, defendants may attempt to show actual knowledge on the part of plaintiffs of the alleged fraud in the registration statement at the time the plaintiffs purchased their securities. Section 11(a). If a specific plaintiff makes a § 11 allegation, how are defendants supposed to show actual knowledge on the part of a plaintiff? Where will they obtain evidence of the plaintiff's knowledge? Expand this problem to a class action. How will defendants ascertain what knowledge each member of the class had at the time of purchase?

The most important use of actual knowledge as a defense does not require proof of the knowledge on the part of specific plaintiffs. Instead, the defense typically is employed after the issuer (or other party) makes a public announcement detailing and correcting the fraud. After such an announcement, defendants may argue the entire market "knew" of the fraud, thereby foreclosing subsequent § 11 liability. Alternatively, one could argue that once the correcting information is in the "total mix" of information in the market, the prior fraud is no longer material. We saw a version of this defense in Chapter 5 as the "truth on the market defense." This defense provides a strong impetus for potential § 11 defendants to publicly correct misstatements as soon as possible.

Section 11 lawsuits are barred after a one/three year statute of limitations imposed by § 13 of the Securities Act. Plaintiffs must file the § 11 lawsuit within one year after they find out about the fraud or should have found out about the fraud through the exercise of reasonable care (a "discovery" statute). In no case may plaintiffs bring the § 11 lawsuit more than three years after the securities were offered to the public (a "repose" statute).

1. Due Diligence Defense

By far the most important defense for § 11 defendants is the due diligence defense contained in § 11(b)(3). Issuers are excluded from the due diligence defense. Section 11 divides all other defendants into two categories: experts and non-experts. The requirement placed on each then turns on whether the alleged fraud is found in a non-expertised or expertised section of the registration statement. The most obvious example of an expertised section would be the audited financials of the issuer; the auditor serves as the expert for this portion of the registration statement. Are there other examples of experts and expertised sections?

Due Diligence Defense Requirements

(Measured at time of effective date
of the registration statement)

	Non-Expertised	Expertised
Expert	No Liability—§ 11(a)(4)	Reasonable Investigation, Reasonable Ground to Believe and Did Believe of Truth—§ 11(b)(3)(B)
Non-Expert	Reasonable Investigation, Reasonable Ground to Believe and Did Believe of Truth—§ 11(b)(3)(A)	No Reasonable Ground to Believe and Did Not Believe Untrue—§ 11(b)(3)(C)

The coarse two-by-two framework of due diligence embodied within § 11 may not completely capture the range of § 11 defendants and situations in which the defendants may find themselves during the registration process. Among the class of non-experts are top executive officers of the issuer, underwriters, outside directors of the issuer with some specific role in the offering (such as an attorney-director or underwriter-director), and outside directors with no other role. To what extent should the due diligence defense vary based on the position and role a particular non-expert defendant plays in the offering process and, more generally, in relation to the issuer?

Escott v. BarChris Construction Corp.

283 F.Supp. 643 (S.D.N.Y. 1968).

■ McLean, E., District Judge.

This is an action by purchasers of 5 1/2 per cent convertible subordinated fifteen year debentures of BarChris Construction Corporation (BarChris). . . .

The action is brought under § 11 of the Securities Act of 1933. Plaintiffs allege that the registration statement with respect to these debentures filed with the Securities and Exchange Commission, which became effective on May 16, 1961, contained material false statements and material omissions. . . .

At the time relevant here, BarChris was engaged primarily in the construction of bowling alleys. . . . The introduction of automatic pin setting machines in 1952 gave a marked stimulus to bowling. It rapidly became a popular sport, with the result that "bowling centers" began to appear throughout the country in rapidly increasing numbers. BarChris benefited from this increased interest in bowling. Its construction operations expanded rapidly. It is estimated that in 1960 BarChris installed approximately three per cent of all lanes built in the United States. . . .

BarChris's sales increased dramatically from 1956 to 1960. According to the prospectus, net sales, in round figures, in 1956 were some $800,000, in 1957 $1,300,000, in 1958 $1,700,000. In 1959 they increased to over $3,300,000, and by 1960 they had leaped to over $9,165,000. . . .

In general, BarChris's method of operation was to enter into a contract with a customer, receive from him at that time a comparatively small down payment on the purchase price, and proceed to construct and equip the bowling alley. When the work was finished and the building delivered, the customer paid the balance of the contract price in notes, payable in installments over a period of years. BarChris discounted these notes with a factor and received part of their face amount in cash. The factor held back part as a reserve. . . . [The factor, James Talcott Inc., would purchase the notes at a discount for cash and then require BarChris to guarantee a percentage of the notes sold. Initially BarChris guaranteed 25% of the notes. But under a revised "alternative" financing arrangement, BarChris eventually guaranteed 100% of the notes.]

BarChris was compelled to expend considerable sums in defraying the cost of construction before it received reimbursement. As a consequence, BarChris was in constant need of cash to finance its operations, a need which grew more pressing as operations expanded. . . . By early 1961, BarChris needed additional working capital. The proceeds of the sale of the debentures involved in this action were to be devoted, in part at least, to fill that need. . . .

The registration statement became effective on May 16. The closing of the financing took place on May 24. On that day BarChris received the net proceeds of the financing. . . .

⟐ [The court then analyzed the materiality of errors in the debenture registration statement finding, among others: (1) exaggerated 1960 sales figures in the audited financials due to the inclusion of sales of completed alleys not yet in fact sold by BarChris (and now operated by BarChris as wholly-owned subsidiaries); (2) misrepresentation that BarChris guaranteed 25% of the notes transferred to Talcott when in fact the guarantee was for 100% for most of the notes; (3) misrepresentation that all loans by corporate officers to BarChris had been repaid; (4) misrepresentation that the offering proceeds would be used to construct a new plant, develop a new equipment line, and provide working capital when in fact the proceeds were used to pay existing debt.]   ✳

The "Due Diligence" Defenses

* * *

Every defendant, except BarChris itself, to whom, as the issuer, these defenses are not available, and except Peat, Marwick, whose position rests on a different statutory provision, has pleaded these affirmative defenses. . . . As to each defendant, the question is whether he has sustained the burden of proving these defenses. . . .

Before considering the evidence, a preliminary matter should be disposed of. The defendants do not agree among themselves as to who the "experts" were or as to the parts of the registration statement which were expertised. Some defendants say that Peat, Marwick was the expert, others say that BarChris's attorneys, Perkins, Daniels, McCormack & Collins, and the underwriters' attorneys, Drinker, Biddle & Reath, were also the experts. On the first view, only those portions of the registration statement purporting to be made on Peat, Marwick's authority were expertised portions. On the other view, everything in the registration statement was within this category, because the two law firms were responsible for the entire document.

The first view is the correct one. To say that the entire registration statement is expertised because some lawyer prepared it would be an unreasonable construction of the statute. Neither the lawyer for the company nor the lawyer for the underwriters is an expert within the meaning of § 11. The only expert, in the statutory sense, was Peat, Marwick, and the only parts of the registration statement which purported to be made upon the authority of an expert were the portions which purported to be made on Peat, Marwick's authority. . . .

I turn now to the question of whether defendants have proved their due diligence defenses. The position of each defendant will be separately considered.

Russo

Russo was, to all intents and purposes, the chief executive officer of BarChris. He was a member of the executive committee. He was familiar with all aspects of the business. He was personally in charge of dealings with the factors. He acted on BarChris's behalf in making the financing agreements with Talcott and he handled the negotiations with Talcott in the spring of 1961. He talked with customers about their delinquencies.

In short, Russo knew all the relevant facts. He could not have believed that there were no untrue statements or material omissions in the prospectus. Russo has no due diligence defenses.

Vitolo and Pugliese

They were the founders of the business who stuck with it to the end. Vitolo was president and Pugliese was vice president. Despite their titles, their field of responsibility in the administration of BarChris's affairs during the period in question seems to have been less all embracing then Russo's. Pugliese in particular appears to have limited his activities to supervising the actual construction work.

Vitolo and Pugliese are each men of limited education. It is not hard to believe that for them the prospectus was difficult reading, if indeed they read it at all.

But whether it was or not is irrelevant. The liability of a director who signs a registration statement does not depend upon whether or not he read it or, if he did, whether or not he understood what he was reading.

And in any case, Vitolo and Pugliese were not as naive as they claim to be. They were members of BarChris's executive committee. At meetings of that committee BarChris's affairs were discussed at length. They must have known what was going on. Certainly they knew of the inadequacy of cash in 1961. They knew of their own large advances to the company which remained unpaid. They knew that they had agreed not to deposit their checks until the financing proceeds were received. They knew and intended that part of the proceeds were to be used to pay their own loans.

All in all, the position of Vitolo and Pugliese is not significantly different, for present purposes, from Russo's. They could not have believed that the registration statement was wholly true and that no material facts had been omitted. And in any case, there is nothing to show that they made any investigation of anything which they may not have known about or understood. They have not proved their due diligence defenses.

Kircher

Kircher was treasurer of BarChris and its chief financial officer. He is a certified public accountant and an intelligent man. He was thoroughly familiar with BarChris's financial affairs. He knew the terms of BarChris's agreements with Talcott. He knew of the customers' delinquency problem. He participated actively with Russo in May 1961 in the successful effort to hold Talcott off until the financing proceeds came in. He knew how the financing proceeds were to be applied and he saw to it that they were so applied. He arranged the officers' loans and he knew all the facts concerning them.

Moreover, as a member of the executive committee, Kircher was kept informed as to those branches of the business of which he did not have direct charge. He knew about the operation of alleys, present and prospective. . . . In brief, Kircher knew all the relevant facts.

Kircher worked on the preparation of the registration statement. He conferred with Grant and on occasion with Ballard. He supplied information to them about the company's business. He read the prospectus and understood it. He knew what it said and what it did not say.

Kircher's contention is that he had never before dealt with a registration statement, that he did not know what it should contain, and that he relied wholly on Grant, Ballard and Peat, Marwick to guide him. He claims that it was their fault, not his, if there was anything wrong with it. He says that all the facts were recorded in BarChris's books where these "experts" could have seen them if they had looked. He says that he truthfully answered all their questions. In effect, he says that if they did not know enough to ask the right questions and to give him the proper instructions, that is not his responsibility.

There is an issue of credibility here. In fact, Kircher was not frank in dealing with Grant and Ballard. He withheld information from them. But even if he had told them all the facts, this would not have constituted the due diligence contemplated by the statute. Knowing the facts, Kircher had reason to believe that the expertised portion of the prospectus, i.e., the 1960 figures, was in part incorrect. He could not shut his eyes to the facts and rely on Peat, Marwick for that portion.

As to the rest of the prospectus, knowing the facts, he did not have a reasonable ground to believe it to be true. On the contrary, he must have known that in part it was untrue. Under these circumstances, he was not entitled to sit back and place the blame on the lawyers for not advising him about it.

Kircher has not proved his due diligence defenses. . . .

Birnbaum

Birnbaum was a young lawyer, admitted to the bar in 1957, who, after brief periods of employment by two different law firms and an equally brief period of practicing in his own firm, was employed by BarChris as house counsel and assistant secretary in October 1960. Unfortunately for him, he became secretary and a director of BarChris on April 17, 1961, after the first version of the registration statement had been filed with the Securities and Exchange Commission. He signed the later amendments, thereby becoming responsible for the accuracy of the prospectus in its final form.

Although the prospectus, in its description of "management," lists Birnbaum among the "executive officers" and devotes several sentences to a recital of his career, the fact seems to be that he was not an executive officer in any real sense. He did not participate in the management of the company. As house counsel, he attended to legal matters of a routine nature. Among other things, he incorporated subsidiaries, with which BarChris was plentifully supplied. . . . He was thus aware of that aspect of the business.

Birnbaum examined contracts. . . . One of Birnbaum's more important duties, first as assistant secretary and later as full-fledged secretary, was to keep the corporate minutes of BarChris and its subsidiaries. This necessarily informed him to a considerable extent about the company's affairs. . . .

It seems probable that Birnbaum did not know of many of the inaccuracies in the prospectus. He must, however, have appreciated some of them. In any case, he made no investigation and relied on the others to get it right. . . . [H]e was entitled to rely upon Peat, Marwick for the 1960 figures, for as far as appears, he had no personal knowledge of the company's books of account or financial transactions. But he was not entitled to rely upon Kircher, Grant and Ballard for the other portions of the prospectus. As a lawyer, he should have known his obligations under the statute. He should have known that he was required to make a reasonable investigation of the truth of all the statements in the unexpertised portion of the document which he signed. Having failed to make such an investigation, he did not have reasonable ground to believe that all these statements were true. Birnbaum has not established his due diligence defenses except as to the audited 1960 figures.

Auslander

Auslander was an "outside" director, i.e., one who was not an officer of BarChris. He was chairman of the board of Valley Stream National Bank in Valley Stream, Long Island. In February 1961 Vitolo asked him to become a director of BarChris. Vitolo gave him an enthusiastic account of BarChris's progress and prospects. As an inducement, Vitolo said that when BarChris received the proceeds of a forthcoming issue of securities, it would deposit $1,000,000 in Auslander's bank.

In February and early March 1961, before accepting Vitolo's invitation, Auslander made some investigation of BarChris. He obtained Dun & Bradstreet reports which contained sales and earnings figures for periods earlier than December 31, 1960. He caused inquiry to be made of certain of BarChris's banks and was advised that they regarded BarChris favorably. He was informed that inquiry of Talcott had also produced a favorable response.

On March 3, 1961, Auslander indicated his willingness to accept a place on the board. Shortly thereafter, on March 14, Kircher sent him a copy of BarChris's annual report for 1960. Auslander observed that BarChris's auditors were Peat, Marwick. They were also the auditors for the Valley Stream National Bank. He thought well of them.

Auslander was elected a director on April 17, 1961. The registration statement in its original form had already been filed, of course without his signature. On May 10, 1961, he signed a signature page for the first amendment to the registration statement which was filed on May 11, 1961. This was a separate sheet without any document attached. Auslander did not know that it was a signature page for a registration statement. He vaguely understood that it was something "for the SEC."

Auslander attended a meeting of BarChris's directors on May 15, 1961. At that meeting he, along with the other directors, signed the signature sheet for the second amendment which constituted the registration statement in its final form. Again, this was only a separate sheet without any document attached. Auslander never saw a copy of the registration statement in its final form.

At the May 15 directors' meeting, however, Auslander did realize that what he was signing was a signature sheet to a registration statement. This was the first time that he had appreciated that fact. A copy of the registration statement in its earlier form as amended on May 11, 1961 was passed around at the meeting. Auslander glanced at it briefly. He did not read it thoroughly.

At the May 15 meeting, Russo and Vitolo stated that everything was in order and that the prospectus was correct. Auslander believed this statement.

In considering Auslander's due diligence defenses, a distinction is to be drawn between the expertised and non-expertised portions of the prospectus. As to the former, Auslander knew that Peat, Marwick had audited the 1960 figures. He believed them to be correct because he had confidence in Peat, Marwick. He had no reasonable ground to believe otherwise.

As to the non-expertised portions, however, Auslander is in a different position. He seems to have been under the impression that Peat, Marwick was responsible for all the figures. This impression was not correct, as he would have realized if he had read the prospectus carefully. Auslander made no investigation of the accuracy of the prospectus. He relied on the assurance of Vitolo and Russo, and upon the information he had received in answer to his inquiries back in February and early March. These inquiries were general ones, in the nature of a credit check. The information which he received in answer to them was also general, without specific reference to the statements in the prospectus, which was not prepared until some time thereafter.

It is true that Auslander became a director on the eve of the financing. He had little opportunity to familiarize himself with the company's affairs. The question is whether, under such circumstances, Auslander did enough to establish his due diligence defense with respect to the non-expertised portions of the prospectus. . .

Section 11 imposes liability in the first instance upon a director, no matter how new he is. He is presumed to know his responsibility when he becomes a director. He can escape liability only by using that reasonable care to investigate the facts which a prudent man would employ in the management of his own property. In my opinion, a prudent man would not act in an important matter without any knowledge of the relevant facts, in sole reliance upon representations of persons who are comparative strangers and upon general information which does not purport to cover the particular case. To say that such minimal conduct measures up to the statutory standard would, to all intents and purposes, absolve new directors from responsibility merely because they are new. This is not a sensible construction of Section 11, when one bears in mind its fundamental purpose of requiring full and truthful disclosure for the protection of investors.

I find and conclude that Auslander has not established his due diligence defense with respect to the misstatements and omissions in those portions of the prospectus other than the audited 1960 figures. . .

Grant

Grant became a director of BarChris in October 1960. His law firm was counsel to BarChris in matters pertaining to the registration of securities. Grant drafted the registration statement for the stock issue in 1959 and for the warrants in January 1961. He also drafted the registration statement for the debentures. In the preliminary division of work between him and Ballard, the underwriters' counsel, Grant took initial responsibility for preparing the registration statement, while Ballard devoted his efforts in the first instance to preparing the indenture.

Grant is sued as a director and as a signer of the registration statement. This is not an action against him for malpractice in his capacity as a lawyer. Nevertheless, in considering Grant's due diligence defenses, the unique position which he occupied cannot be disregarded. As the director most directly concerned with writing the registration statement and assuring its accuracy, more was required of him in the way of reasonable investigation than could fairly be expected of a director who had no connection with this work.

There is no valid basis for plaintiffs' accusation that Grant knew that the prospectus was false in some respects and incomplete and misleading in others. Having seen him testify at length, I am satisfied as to his integrity. I find that Grant honestly believed that the registration statement was true and that no material facts had been omitted from it.

In this belief he was mistaken, and the fact is that for all his work, he never discovered any of the errors or omissions which have been recounted at length in this opinion, with the single exception of Capitol Lanes. He knew that BarChris had not sold this alley and intended to operate it, but he appears to have been under the erroneous impression that Peat, Marwick had knowingly sanctioned its inclusion in sales because of the allegedly temporary nature of the operation.

Grant contends that a finding that he did not make a reasonable investigation would be equivalent to a holding that a lawyer for an issuing company, in order to show due diligence, must make an independent audit of the figures supplied to him by his client. I do not consider this to be a realistic statement of the issue. There were errors and omissions here which could have been detected without an audit. The question is whether, despite his failure to detect them, Grant made a reasonable effort to that end.

Much of this registration statement is a scissors and paste-pot job. Grant lifted large portions from the earlier prospectuses, modifying them in some instances to the extent that he considered necessary. But BarChris's affairs had changed for the worse by May 1961. Statements that were accurate in January were no longer accurate in May. Grant never discovered this. He accepted the assurances of Kircher and Russo that any change which might have occurred had been for the better, rather than the contrary.

It is claimed that a lawyer is entitled to rely on the statements of his client and that to require him to verify their accuracy would set an unreasonably high standard. This is too broad a generalization. It is all a matter of degree. To require an audit would obviously be unreasonable. On the other hand, to require a check of matters easily verifiable is not unreasonable. Even honest clients can make mistakes. The statute imposes liability for untrue statements regardless of whether they are intentionally untrue. The way to prevent mistakes is to test oral information by examining the original written record.

There were things which Grant could readily have checked which he did not check. For example, he was unaware of the provisions of the agreements between BarChris and Talcott. He never read them. Thus, he did not know, although he readily could have ascertained, that BarChris's contingent liability on Type B leaseback arrangements was 100 per cent, not 25 per cent. He did not appreciate that if BarChris defaulted in repurchasing delinquent customers' notes upon Talcott's demand, Talcott could accelerate all the customer paper in its hands, which amounted to over $3,000,000.

As to the backlog figure, Grant appreciated that scheduled unfilled orders on the company's books meant firm commitments, but he never asked to see the contracts which, according to the prospectus, added up to $6,905,000. Thus, he did not know that this figure was overstated by some $4,490,000. . . .

On the subject of minutes, Grant knew that minutes of certain meetings of the BarChris executive committee held in 1961 had not been written up. Kircher, who had acted as secretary at those meetings, had complete notes of them. Kircher told Grant that there was no point in writing up the minutes because the matters discussed at those meetings were purely routine. Grant did not insist that the minutes be written up, nor did he look at Kircher's notes. If he had, he would have learned that on February 27, 1961 there was an extended discussion in the executive committee meeting about customers' delinquencies, that on March 8, 1961 the committee had discussed the pros and cons of alley operation by BarChris, that on March 18, 1961 the committee was informed that BarChris was constructing or about to begin constructing twelve alleys for which it had no contracts, and that on May 13, 1961 Dreyfuss, one of the worst delinquents, had filed a [bankruptcy] petition. . . .

As far as customers' delinquencies is concerned, although Grant discussed this with Kircher, he again accepted the assurances of Kircher and Russo that no serious problem existed. He did not examine the records as to delinquencies, although BarChris maintained such a record. Any inquiry on his part of Talcott or an examination of BarChris's correspondence with Talcott in April and May 1961 would have apprised him of the true facts. . . .

Grant was entitled to rely on Peat, Marwick for the 1960 figures. He had no reasonable ground to believe them to be inaccurate. But the matters which I have mentioned were not within the expertised portion of the prospectus. As to this, Grant, was obliged to make a reasonable investigation. I am forced to find that he did not make one. . . .

The Underwriters and Coleman

The underwriters other than Drexel made no investigation of the accuracy of the prospectus. . . . They all relied upon Drexel as the "lead" underwriter.

Drexel did make an investigation. The work was in charge of Coleman, a partner of the firm, assisted by Casperson, an associate. Drexel's attorneys acted as attorneys for the entire group of underwriters. Ballard did the work, assisted by Stanton.

* * *

Like Grant, Ballard, without checking, relied on the information which he got from Kircher. He also relied on Grant who, as company counsel, presumably was familiar with its affairs. . . .

In any event, it is clear that no effectual attempt at verification was made. The question is whether due diligence required that it be made. Stated another way, is it sufficient to ask questions, to obtain answers which, if true, would be thought satisfactory, and to let it go at that, without seeking to ascertain from the records whether the answers in fact are true and complete?

I have already held that this procedure is not sufficient in Grant's case. Are underwriters in a different position, as far as due diligence is concerned?

The underwriters say that the prospectus is the company's prospectus, not theirs. Doubtless this is the way they customarily regard it. But the Securities Act makes no such distinction. The underwriters are just as responsible as the company if the prospectus is false. And prospective investors rely upon the reputation of the underwriters in deciding whether to purchase the securities. . . .

The purpose of Section 11 is to protect investors. To that end the underwriters are made responsible for the truth of the prospectus. If they may escape that responsibility by taking at face value representations made to them by the company's management, then the inclusion of underwriters among those liable under Section 11 affords the investors no additional protection. To effectuate the statute's purpose, the phrase "reasonable investigation" must be construed to require more effort on the part of the underwriters than the mere accurate reporting in the prospectus of "data presented" to them by the company. It should make no difference that this data is elicited by questions addressed to the company officers by the underwriters, or that the underwriters at the time believe that the company's officers are truthful and reliable. In order to make the underwriters' participation in this enterprise of any value to the investors, the underwriters must make some reasonable attempt to verify the data submitted to them. They may not rely solely on the company's officers or on the company's counsel. A prudent man in the management of his own property would not rely on them.

It is impossible to lay down a rigid rule suitable for every case defining the extent to which such verification must go. It is a question of degree, a matter of judgment in each case. In the present case, the underwriters' counsel made almost no attempt to verify management's representations. I hold that that was insufficient.

On the evidence in this case, I find that the underwriters' counsel did not make a reasonable investigation of the truth of those portions of the prospectus which were not made on the authority of Peat, Marwick as an expert. Drexel is bound by their failure. It is not a matter of relying upon counsel for legal advice. Here the attorneys were dealing with matters of fact. Drexel delegated to them, as its agent, the business of examining the corporate minutes and contracts. It must bear the consequences of their failure to make an adequate examination.

The other underwriters, who did nothing and relied solely on Drexel and on the lawyers, are also bound by it. It follows that although Drexel and the other underwriters believed that those portions of the prospectus were true, they had no reasonable ground for that belief, within the meaning of the statute. Hence, they have not established their due diligence defense, except as to the 1960 audited figures.[26]

* * *

Peat, Marwick

* * *

[With regard to Peat, Marwick, the court found that the auditor failed to follow generally accepted accounting standards in performing its audit. The court held that this failure to meet industry standards meant that Peat, Marwick had failed to show due diligence.]

---

[26] In view of this conclusion, it becomes unnecessary to decide whether the underwriters other than Drexel would have been protected if Drexel had established that as lead underwriter, it made a reasonable investigation.

NOTES

1. *Rule 176.* The SEC has provided some guidance on due diligence via Rule 176. Rule 176 varies the level of required due diligence based on the type of issuer, the type of security, the presence of another relationship to the issuer when the person is a director, and the type of underwriting arrangement for underwriters, among other factors. Unfortunately, Rule 176 gives little guidance on how these factors should be weighed in assessing due diligence.

QUESTIONS

1. Section 11 varies the due diligence standards for non-experts depending on whether the alleged fraud is in an expertised or non-expertised portion of the registration statement. Great importance is placed on who qualifies as an expert and what sections of the registration statement are considered expertised. Do you think attorneys drafting the registration statement should be deemed experts for the entire registration statement? Why do you think the *Escott* court rejected this approach?

2. The *Escott* court focuses on the fact that a number of defendants simply relied on the representations of BarChris insiders. What more should the defendants have done?

3. What would you have done if you were in the shoes of Birnbaum, the "young attorney" who had recently employed BarChris's house counsel, secretary, and member of the board of directors?

4. Why does the *Escott* court not require each defendant to undertake a "complete audit" of BarChris to meet his/her due diligence requirement? Wouldn't that better ferret out fraud in the registration statement?

2.   DUE DILIGENCE AND UNDERWRITERS

Reporting companies may incorporate, by reference, previously filed SEC documents. Incorporating documents by reference is quicker than drafting new ones. Information incorporated by reference, however, becomes part of the registration statement and is therefore subject to § 11 liability. Should underwriters, directors, auditors and other potential § 11 defendants bear the same due diligence responsibility for past-filed documents incorporated by reference in the registration statement? Suppose an issuer sells securities through a shelf registration. How should underwriters balance the time pressure of the shelf registration process and the need to conduct a thorough due diligence investigation of the issuer?

In re WorldCom, Inc. Securities Litigation

346 F. Supp. 2d 628 (S.D.N.Y. 2004).

■ COTE, D., DISTRICT JUDGE.

This Opinion addresses issues related to an underwriter's due diligence obligations. Following the conclusion of fact discovery, several of the parties in this consolidated securities class action arising from the collapse of WorldCom, Inc. ("WorldCom") have filed for summary judgment. . . .

It is undisputed that at least as of early 2001 WorldCom executives engaged in a secretive scheme to manipulate WorldCom's public filings concerning WorldCom's financial condition. . . .

* * *

WorldCom announced a massive restatement of its financials on June 25, 2002. It reported its intention to restate its financial statements for 2001 and the first quarter of 2002. According to that announcement, "[a]s a result of an internal audit of the company's capital expenditure accounting, it was determined that certain transfers from line cost expenses to capital accounts during this period were not made in accordance with generally accepted accounting principles (GAAP). The amount of transfers was then estimated to be over $3.8 billion. Without the improper transfers, the company estimated that it would have reported a net loss for 2001 and the first quarter of 2002. . . .

* * *

WorldCom's Accounting Strategies

* * *

Andersen [WorldCom's auditor] was unaware of the manipulation of line costs through this capitalization scheme. . . . The improper capitalization of line costs continued through the first quarter of 2002. WorldCom's internal audit department had completed its last audit of WorldCom's capital expenditures in approximately January of 2002, and had not uncovered any evidence of fraud. In May of 2002, it began another audit of the company's capital expenditures . . . and was able to uncover the transfer of line costs to capital accounts. . . .

* * *

[Prior to the public disclosure of WorldCom's accounting fraud, WorldCom sold two bond offerings in 2000 and 2001. WorldCom sold the bonds through Form S–3 shelf registration statements in both offerings. The Form S–3 statements in the two offerings incorporated audited financials from the most recent Form 10–K (the 1999 and 2000 Form 10–Ks). Andersen provided "comfort letters," as described by the court below, for the underwriters in both offerings on the accuracy of the unaudited interim financials used in the Form S–3. Eds.—The issues in the two offerings are similar; for the sake of brevity, we provide details on only the 2001 Offering.]

In February 2001 [prior to the 2001 Offering], several of the Underwriter Defendants downgraded WorldCom's credit rating due to their assessment of WorldCom's deteriorating financial condition. Then, during the weeks that followed, several of the Underwriter Defendants made a commitment to WorldCom to help it restructure its massive credit facility. In doing so, there is evidence that at least some of the Underwriter Defendants internally expressed concern again about WorldCom's financial health. WorldCom had required the banks to participate in the restructuring of the credit facility if a bank wished to play a significant role in its next bond offering, the 2001 Offering. That offering turned out to be the largest public debt offering in American

history. The Lead Plaintiff contends that the evidence of the
Underwriter Defendants' concerns about WorldCom's financial
condition in the months immediately preceding the 2001 Offering
undercuts their contention that the due diligence that they performed
in connection with the 2001 Offering was reasonable.

* * *

There is evidence that several of the Underwriter Defendants
decided to make a commitment to the restructuring of the credit facility
and to attempt to win the right to underwrite the 2001 Offering, while
at the same time reducing their own exposure to risk from holding
WorldCom debt by engaging in hedging strategies, such as credit
default swaps.

* * *

2000 Form 10–K

* * *

With respect to long-distance services, the document reported that
revenue fell in 2000 in absolute terms and as a percentage of total
WorldCom revenues. In its description of operations, line costs were
shown as a decreasing percentage of revenues for each year from 1998
to 2000, beginning with 45.3% in 1998, and ending at 39.6% in 2000.
The Form 10–K explained that the improvement was a result of
increased data and dedicated Internet traffic.

2001 Offering

Through the 2001 Offering WorldCom issued $11.9 billion worth of
notes. The May 9, 2001 registration statement and May 14, 2001
prospectus supplement for the 2001 Offering incorporated WorldCom's
2000 10–K. . . .

J.P. Morgan and [Salomon Smith Barney ("SSB")] served as co-
book runners. Each of the Underwriter Defendants for the 2001
Offering have stated that they relied on the due diligence performed by
SSB and J.P. Morgan. [Cravath, Swaine & Moore] represented the
Underwriter Defendants.

A May 16, 2001 memorandum prepared by Cravath describes the
due diligence conducted from April 19 through May 16, 2001 in
connection with the 2001 Offering. On April 23, the Underwriter
Defendants forwarded due diligence questions to WorldCom. The due
diligence for the 2001 Offering included telephone calls with WorldCom
on April 30 and May 9, and a May 9 telephone call with Andersen and
WorldCom. The due diligence inquiry also included a review of
WorldCom's board minutes, 1998 revolving credit agreement, SEC
filings, and press releases from April 19 to May 16, 2001.

* * *

On May 9, a banker from J.P. Morgan and two Cravath attorneys
spoke by telephone with Sullivan [WorldCom's CFO] . . . and with
representatives of Andersen. Andersen indicated that it had not issued
any management letters to WorldCom and that there were no
accounting concerns. WorldCom and Andersen assured J.P. Morgan

that there was nothing else material to discuss. In neither the April 30 due diligence telephone call nor the May 9 call did Sullivan disclose the . . . capitalization of line costs.

On May 9 and 16, Andersen issued comfort letters for the WorldCom first quarter 2001 financial statement. The 2001 comfort letters stand in contrast to the 2000 comfort letter [used in a WorldCom 2000 debt offering], which expressed that nothing had come to Andersen's attention to cause it to believe that "[a]ny material modifications should be made to the unaudited condensed consolidated financial statements . . ., incorporated by reference in the Registration Statement, for them to be in conformity with generally accepted accounting principles" or that "[t]he unaudited condensed consolidated financial statements . . . do not comply as to form in all material respects with the applicable accounting requirements of the Act and the related published rules and regulations." In 2001, by comparison, the letters indicated that nothing had come to Andersen's attention that caused it to believe that the financial statements "were not determined on a basis substantially consistent with that of the corresponding amounts in the audited consolidated balance sheets of WorldCom as of December 31, 2000 and 1999, and the consolidated statements of operations, shareholders' investment and cash flows for each of the three years in the period ended December 31, 2000. . . ." A J.P. Morgan banker and a Cravath attorney noticed the absence of the "negative GAAP assurance" in the 2001 comfort letter. An SSB banker noted that the issue was important to understand but advised against getting "too vocal" about it since "WorldCom's a bear to deal with on that subject."

* * *

III. *The Underwriter Defendants' Motion for Summary Judgment; The Financial Statements*

The Underwriter Defendants move for summary judgment with respect to the financial statements that were incorporated into the Registration Statements. They assert that there is no dispute that they acted reasonably in relying on Andersen's audits and comfort letters. The Underwriter Defendants contend that they were entitled to rely on WorldCom's audited financial statements and had no duty to investigate their reliability so long as they had "no reasonable ground to believe" that such financial statements contained a false statement. They also assert that they were entitled to rely in the same way on Andersen's comfort letters for the unaudited quarterly financial statements incorporated into the Registration Statements.

* * *

A. *Role of the Underwriter*

[I]n enacting Section 11, "Congress recognized that underwriters occupied a unique position that enabled them to discover and compel disclosure of essential facts about the offering. Congress believed that subjecting underwriters to the liability provisions would provide the necessary incentive to ensure their careful investigation of the offering." At the same time, Congress specifically rejected the notion of underwriters as insurers. Rather, it imposed upon underwriters the obligation to "exercise diligence of a type commensurate with the confidence, both as to integrity and competence," placed in them by those purchasing securities.

Underwriters must "exercise a high degree of care in investigation and independent verification of the company's representations." Overall, "[n]o greater reliance in our self-regulatory system is placed on any single participant in the issuance of securities than upon the underwriter." Underwriters function as "the first line of defense" with respect to material misrepresentations and omissions in registration statements. . . .

B.   *The "Due Diligence" Defenses*

* * *

Although the requirements of due diligence vary depending on whether the registration statement has been made in part or in whole on the authority of an expert, the standard for determining what constitutes a reasonable investigation and reasonable ground for belief is the same: [T]he standard of reasonableness shall be that required of a prudent man in the management of his own property.

Courts have distinguished between these two standards by labeling them the due diligence defense and the reliance defense, referring in the latter case to the reliance permitted by the statute on an expert's statement.

* * *

C.   *Accountants as Experts*

[W]hile Section 11(b) does not define the term expert or explain what sort of documents and/or work constitutes that "made on an expert's authority," it is settled that an accountant qualifies as an expert, and audited financial statements are considered expertised portions of a registration statement.

Not every auditor's opinion, however, qualifies as an expert's opinion for purposes of the Section 11 reliance defense. To distinguish among auditor's opinions, some background is in order. While financial statements are prepared by the management of a company, an accountant serving as the company's auditor may give an opinion as to whether the financial statements have been presented in conformity with GAAP. This opinion is given after the accountant has performed an audit of the company's books and records. Audits are generally completed once a year, in connection with a company's year-end financial statements. There are ten audit standards with which an auditor must comply in performing its annual audit. They are known as Generally Accepted Auditing Standards ("GAAS"). If an auditor signs a consent to have its opinion on financial statements incorporated into a company's public filings, the opinion may be shared with the public through incorporation.

Public companies are also required under the Exchange Act to file quarterly financial statements, which are referred to as interim financial statements. While not subject to an audit, interim financial statements included in Form 10–Q quarterly reports are reviewed by an independent public accountant using professional standards and procedures for conducting such reviews, as established by GAAS. The standards for the review of interim financial statements are set forth in Statement of Auditing Standards No. 71, Interim Financial Information ("SAS 71"). When a public company files a registration statement for a sale of securities, the auditor is customarily asked by underwriters to provide a comfort letter. The comfort letter will contain representations about the auditor's review of the interim financial statements. There is frequently more than one comfort letter for a transaction: an initial comfort letter, and a second or "bringdown" comfort letter issued closer to the time of closing. . . .

In an effort to encourage auditor reviews of interim financial statements, the SEC acted in 1979 to assure auditors that their review of unaudited interim financial information would not subject them to liability under Section 11. . . .

The objective of an audit is to provide a reasonable basis for expressing an opinion regarding the financial statements taken as a whole. A review of interim financial information does not provide a basis for the expression of such an opinion, because the review does not contemplate a study and evaluation of internal accounting control; tests of accounting records and of responses to inquiries by obtaining corroborating evidential matter through inspection, observation, or confirmation; and certain other procedures ordinarily performed during an audit. A review may bring to the accountant's attention significant matters affecting the interim financial information, but it does not provide assurance that the accountant will become aware of all significant matters that would be disclosed in an audit.

* * *

Underwriters may not rely on an accountant's comfort letters for interim financial statements in presenting such a defense. Comfort letters do not "expertise any portion of the registration statement that is otherwise non-expertised."

D. *Integrated Disclosure, Shelf Registration, and Rule 176*

* * *

Together, the mechanism of incorporation by reference and the expansion of shelf registration significantly reduced the time and expense necessary to prepare public offerings, thus enabling more "rapid access to today's capital markets." As the SEC recognized, these changes affected the time in which underwriters could perform their investigations of an issuer. Underwriters had weeks to perform due diligence for traditional registration statements. By contrast, under a short-form registration regime, "[p]reparation time is reduced sharply" thanks to the ability to incorporate by reference prior disclosures.

These two innovations triggered concern among underwriters. Members of the financial community worried about their ability "to undertake a reasonable investigation with respect to the adequacy of the information incorporated by reference from periodic reports filed under the Exchange Act into the short form registration statements utilized in an integrated disclosure system." . . .

Because an issuer could select among competing underwriters when offering securities through a shelf registration, some questioned whether an underwriter could "afford to devote the time and expense necessary to conduct a due diligence review before knowing whether it will handle an offering and that there may not be sufficient time to do so once it is selected." Others doubted whether they would have the chance "to apply their independent scrutiny and judgment to documents prepared by registrants many months before an offering."

[T]he SEC introduced Rule 176 in 1981 "to make explicit what circumstances may bear upon the determination of what constitutes a reasonable investigation and reasonable ground for belief as these terms are used in Section 11(b)." . . . At the time Rule 176 was finalized, the SEC took care to explain that integrated disclosure was intended to "simplify disclosure and reduce unnecessary repetition and redelivery of information," not to "modify the responsibility of underwriters and others to make a reasonable investigation." [T]he SEC advised underwriters concerned about the time pressures created by integrated disclosure to "arrange [their] due diligence procedures over time for the purpose of avoiding last minute delays in an offering environment characterized by rapid market changes." It also reminded them that an underwriter is "never compelled to proceed with an offering *until he has accomplished his due diligence*." (emphasis supplied). . . .

The SEC's intent to maintain high standards for underwriter due diligence is confirmed by its many discussions of appropriate due diligence techniques in the integrated disclosure system. In proposing Rule 176, the SEC acknowledged that different investigatory methods would be needed "in view of the compressed preparation time and the volatile nature of the capital markets." Nonetheless, it emphasized that such techniques must be *"equally thorough."* (emphasis supplied). Among the strategies recommended by the SEC were the development of a "reservoir of knowledge about the companies that may select the underwriter to distribute their securities registered on short form registration statements" through a "careful review of [periodic Exchange Act] filings on an ongoing basis," consultation of analysts' reports, and active participation in the issuer's investor relations program, especially analysts and brokers meetings.

At the time the SEC finalized the shelf registration rule two years later, it again recognized that "the techniques of conducting due diligence investigations of registrants qualified to use short form registration . . . would differ from due diligence investigations under other circumstances." Nonetheless, it stressed the use of "anticipatory and continuous due diligence programs" to augment underwriters' fulfillment of their due diligence obligations. Among other practices, the SEC approvingly noted the increased designation of one law firm to act as underwriters' counsel, which "facilitates continuous due diligence by ensuring on-going access to the registrant on the underwriters' behalf"; the holding of "Exchange Act report 'drafting sessions,'" which allow underwriters "to participate in the drafting and review of periodic disclosure documents before they are filed"; and "periodic due diligence sessions," such as meetings between prospective underwriters, their counsel, and management shortly after the release of quarterly earnings.

* * *

E.   *Case Law: Reliance Defense*

* * *

[U]nderwriters' reliance on audited financial statements may not be blind. Rather, where "red flags" regarding the reliability of an audited financial statement emerge, mere reliance on an audit will not be sufficient to ward off liability. . . .

[T]he phrase "red flags" can be used to describe . . . those facts which come to a defendant's attention that would place a reasonable party in defendant's position "on notice that the audited company was engaged in wrongdoing to the detriment of its investors." . . . Any information that "strips a defendant of his confidence in the accuracy of those portions of a registration statement premised on audited financial statements is a red flag, whether or not it relates to accounting fraud or an audit failure. . . .

* * *

1.   *Audited Financial Statements*

The Underwriter Defendants contend that they were entitled to rely on Andersen's unqualified "clean" audit opinions for WorldCom's 1999 and 2000 Form 10–Ks as expertised statements under Section 11(b)(3)(C). Their motion for summary judgment on their reliance defense is denied.

a.   *2000 Registration Statement*

The Lead Plaintiff points to one issue that it contends gave the Underwriter Defendants a reasonable ground to question the reliability of WorldCom's 1999 Form 10–K. According to the computations presented by the Lead Plaintiff, WorldCom's reported E/R ratio [Eds.— defined as the ratio of line cost expenses to revenues] was significantly lower than that of the equivalent numbers of its two closest competitors, Sprint and AT & T.[47] The Lead Plaintiff argues that, in the extremely competitive market in which WorldCom operated, that discrepancy triggered a duty to investigate such a crucial measurement of the company's health. The Lead Plaintiff has shown that there are issues of fact as to whether the Underwriter Defendants had reasonable grounds to believe that the 1999 Form 10–K was inaccurate in the lines related to the E/R ratio reflected in that filing.

The Underwriter Defendants argue that the difference in the E/R ratios was insufficient as a matter of law to put the Underwriter Defendants on notice of any accounting irregularity. In support of this, they point to the fact that this difference was publicly available information and no one else announced a belief that it suggested the existence of an accounting fraud at WorldCom.

The fact that the difference was publicly available information does not absolve the Underwriter Defendants of their duty to bring their expertise to bear on the issue. . . . If a "prudent man in the management

---

[47] WorldCom's E/R ratio was 43%. The expert for the Lead Plaintiff calculates that AT & T's equivalent ratio was 46.8% and Sprint's was 53.2%.

of his own property," upon reading the 1999 Form 10–K and being familiar with the other relevant information about the issuer's competitors would have questioned the accuracy of the figures, then those figures constituted a red flag and imposed a duty of investigation on the Underwriter Defendants. A jury would be entitled to find that this difference was of sufficient importance to have triggered a duty to investigate the reliability of the figures on which the ratio was based even though the figures had been audited.

The Underwriter Defendants contend that an audited figure can never constitute a red flag and impose a duty of investigation. This argument mischaracterizes the Lead Plaintiff's position. The Lead Plaintiff has pointed to facts extraneous to WorldCom's audited figures to argue that a reasonable person would have inquired further about the discrepancy between the audited figures and the comparable information from competitors. . . .

The Underwriter Defendants argue that the standard that should apply is whether they had "clear and direct notice" of an "accounting" problem. They argue that case law establishes that "ordinary business events" do not constitute red flags. They are wrong. There is no basis in law to find a requirement that a red flag arises only when there is "clear and direct" notice of an accounting issue. The standard under Section 11 is whether a defendant has proven that it had "no reasonable ground to believe and did not believe" that a registration statement contained material misstatements, a standard given meaning by what a "prudent man" would do in the management of his own property. Nor is the bar lowered because there is an expert's opinion on which an underwriter is entitled to rely. . . . There is no category of information which can always be ignored by an underwriter on the ground that it constitutes an ordinary business event. What is ordinary in one context may be sufficiently unusual in another to create a duty of investigation by a "prudent man."

* * *

2.   *Interim Financial Statements*

The Underwriter Defendants contend that, pursuant to Sections 11(b)(3)(A) and 12(a)(2), they were entitled to rely on Andersen's comfort letters for WorldCom's unaudited interim financial statements for the first quarter of 2000 and 2001 so long as the Lead Plaintiff is unable to show that the Underwriter Defendants were on notice of any accounting red flags. They argue that this statement of the due diligence defense is particularly appropriate because WorldCom was a seasoned issuer and the Registration Statements were part of the integrated disclosure system that allowed the Exchange Act periodic reports to be incorporated by reference. . . . They argue that in the context of integrated disclosure for shelf registrations, and as a result of SEC Rule 176, the focus is on an underwriter's continuous learning about an "industry" and reasonable reliance on other professionals, such as an issuer's auditor. As a consequence, they contend that there is no difference from the point of view of the underwriter between audited and unaudited financial statements so long as the underwriter receives an auditor's comfort letter. According to the Underwriter Defendants, so long as there are no red flags that bring the auditor's assessment into question, the receipt of a comfort letter "goes a long way to establish" due diligence with respect to all matters of accounting. . . . Finally, they argue that it is material that no amount of reasonable diligence could have uncovered the capitalization of line costs since the WorldCom management deliberately concealed it from Andersen and every other outsider and would never have given them any documents or information that would have revealed the fraud. . . .

In connection with the [2001] Offering, the Underwriter Defendants emphasize that J.P. Morgan and SSB had recently had occasion to work closely with WorldCom on other projects. The two firms had participated in the two tracking stock realignment of WorldCom announced in November 2000, and J.P. Morgan had acted as a lead manager and sole book-runner for WorldCom's $2 billion private placement in December 2000. They point to these activities as part of their continuous due diligence for WorldCom. . . .

In judging [the due diligence reasonable investigation], a jury will have to consider the non-exclusive list of factors enumerated in Rule 176. Insofar as Rule 176 is concerned, there does not appear to be any dispute that WorldCom was a "well-established" issuer, that the notes at issue were investment-grade debt securities, that SSB and J.P. Morgan assigned experienced personnel to the due diligence teams, that they spoke to the issuer's CFO and in 2001 also spoke to Andersen, that the underwriting was a firm commitment underwriting, that the underwriting was through a shelf registration, that many analysts and credit reporting agencies followed and reported on WorldCom, that the issuer and not the Underwriter Defendants had responsibility for preparing the interim financial statements, and that Andersen and not the Underwriter Defendants had responsibility for reviewing the interim financial statements.

The Lead Plaintiff has shown that there are questions of fact, however, as to whether the Underwriter Defendants conducted a reasonable investigation in either 2000 or 2001. It points to what it contends is evidence of the limited number of conversations with the issuer or its auditor, the cursory nature of the inquiries, the failure to go behind any of the almost formulaic answers given to questions, and the failure to inquire into issues of particular prominence in the Underwriter Defendants' own internal evaluations of the financial condition of the issuer or in the financial press. It argues in particular with respect to 2001, that having internally downgraded WorldCom's credit rating and having taken steps to limit their exposure as WorldCom creditors, the Underwriter Defendants were well aware that WorldCom was in a deteriorating financial position in a troubled industry, and that a reasonable investigation would have entailed a more searching inquiry than that undertaken by the Underwriter Defendants. Given the enormity of these two bond offerings, and the general deterioration in WorldCom's financial situation, at least as of the time of the 2001 Offering, they argue that a particularly probing inquiry by a prudent underwriter was warranted. These issues of fact require a jury trial.

The Underwriter Defendants have framed their summary judgment motion in a way that is incompatible with their burden of proving their due diligence defense under Section 11. They seek to restrict the inquiry on their due diligence solely to the work undertaken with respect to the interim financial statements and therefore to restrict it to a determination of whether any red flags existed that would put them on notice of a duty to make an inquiry of the interim financial statements. This formulation converts the due diligence defense into the reliance defense and balkanizes the task of due diligence.

In order to succeed with a due diligence defense, the Underwriter Defendants will have to show that they conducted a reasonable investigation of the non-expertised portions of the Registration Statements and thereafter had reasonable ground to believe that the interim financial statements were true. In assessing the reasonableness of the investigation, their receipt of the comfort letters will be important evidence, but it is insufficient by itself to establish the defense.

[A]n underwriter must conduct a reasonable investigation to prevail on the due diligence defense, even if it appears that such an investigation would have proven futile in uncovering the fraud. Without a reasonable investigation, of course, it can never be known what would have been uncovered or what additional disclosures would have been demanded.

The Underwriter Defendants argue that if they are not entitled to rely on a comfort letter, the costs of capital formation in the United States will be substantially increased since underwriters will have to hire their own accounting firms to rehash the work of the issuer's auditor. Nothing in this Opinion should be read as imposing that obligation on underwriters or the underwriting process. The term "reasonable investigation" encompasses many modes of inquiry between obtaining comfort letters from an auditor and doing little more, on one hand, and having to re-audit a company's books on the other. Nonetheless, if aggressive or unusual accounting strategies regarding significant issues come to light in the course of a reasonable investigation, a prudent underwriter may choose to consult with accounting experts to confirm that the accounting treatment is appropriate and that additional disclosure is unnecessary.

Underwriters perform a different function from auditors. They have special access to information about an issuer at a critical time in the issuer's corporate life, at a time it is seeking to raise capital. The public relies on the underwriter to obtain and verify relevant information and then make sure that essential facts are disclosed. . . . They are not being asked to duplicate the work of auditors, but to conduct a reasonable investigation. If their initial investigation leads them to question the accuracy of financial reporting, then the existence of an audit or a comfort letter will not excuse the failure to follow through with a subsequent investigation of the matter. If red flags arise from a reasonable investigation, underwriters will have to make sufficient inquiry to satisfy themselves as to the accuracy of the financial statements, and if unsatisfied, they must demand disclosure, withdraw from the underwriting process, or bear the risk of liability.

* * *

QUESTIONS

1. What is the difference, for due diligence purposes, between an audited financial statement and an unaudited financial statement accompanied by a "comfort letter" from the auditor?

2. How does a "red flag" affect the ability of a non-expert defendant to rely on the auditor for the accuracy of the audited financials?

3. What do underwriters have to do to satisfy the due diligence defense for non-expertised sections of the registration statement? Does it matter if a reasonable investigation, even if undertaken by the underwriters, would not have uncovered the alleged misstatement in the registration statement?

4. The court discusses the dilemma facing underwriters involved in shelf registration offerings incorporating information by reference from prior Exchange Act filings. The court supports the SEC's position that issuers and underwriters may accommodate the need to do due diligence for previously filed documents incorporated by reference in a registration statement by simply taking more time prior to the offering. How would such delay affect the advantages afforded by incorporation-by-reference?

5. The court notes that the SEC suggests that one solution to the compressed time frame for offerings allowed by integrated disclosure is to have the issuer maintain an ongoing relationship with a primary investment bank. What are the pros and cons of having underwriters (and other professionals) develop repeat and ongoing relationships with large public companies?

HYPOTHETICAL FOUR

InterTelly has been sued in a § 11 class action. The lawsuit alleges that the registration statement for its offering was materially misleading because it failed to disclose Elmo's (InterTelly's CTO) prior criminal conviction for commodities fraud, the likelihood that the Federal Communications Commission would regulate telephone service over the Internet, and overstated InterTelly's earnings for the last two years. In addition to InterTelly, the following players, all involved with InterTelly's initial public offering, have been named in the § 11 suit:

- Zoe, the CEO and a director
- The Count, the CFO
- Oscar, an outside director
- Sesame Securities, the managing underwriter
- Barkley & Grover, the auditor
- Cadabby Capital, a substantial shareholder

1. Zoe knew about Elmo's prior criminal conviction, but she and Elmo agreed that it did not need to be disclosed because it happened four years ago, before Zoe and Elmo even started InterTelly. Besides, Elmo got probation, so how big a deal could it have been? In her deposition, Zoe testified that she knew that there was a possibility that the FCC would regulate Internet telephone service, but she assessed the probability as very low. She also testified that she had no idea that InterTelly's financial statements were inaccurate; she relied completely on InterTelly's CFO, the

Count, who told her that he would "make sure the numbers would support a public offering." Will Zoe be able to show due diligence for the non-expertised portion? The expertised portion? What about the Count?

2. Oscar is a former commissioner of the Federal Communications Commission. Zoe invited him to join the board because he has great contacts in Washington. He attends board meetings only sporadically. In his deposition, Oscar testifies that he did not have much involvement with the registration process. He skimmed the narrative portion of the registration statement and told InterTelly's lawyers that the details in his biography were all correct. Oscar says he had no idea about Elmo's conviction. With regard to the likelihood that the FCC would regulate InterTelly's business, Oscar testifies that he discussed the issue with InterTelly's lawyers, but they told him that the possibility was too speculative to require disclosure. Oscar says he did not review the financial statements at all; he believed they were accurate because Barkley & Grover certified them. Will Oscar be able to show due diligence for the non-expertised portion? The expertised portion?

3. Sesame Securities, the managing underwriter for the offering, performed the due diligence for the underwriting syndicate. Sesame's lawyers reviewed the registration statement prepared by InterTelly's lawyers and made a number of comments on the draft. They also submitted a series of questions to Zoe, the Count, and Elmo. Among the questions posed was, "Is there any information omitted from the biographies of the officers and directors that might be material to investors?" Zoe, the Count, and Elmo all answered this question, "No." In reviewing the risk factors section, Sesame's lawyers discussed regulatory threats with the telecom industry analyst at Sesame, who thought that Congress would block any attempt by the FCC to regulate the Internet phone industry. With respect to the financial statements, Sesame had one of its analysts review the statements; the analyst said that there was nothing in the statements that raised any concerns. The plaintiffs' accounting expert testifies, however, that InterTelly had unusually high revenues for a start-up company and this was a "red flag" at the time of InterTelly's IPO. Will Sesame Securities be able to show due diligence for the non-expertised portion? The expertised portion?

4. Barkley & Grover's lead partner for the InterTelly account, Mumford, testifies that he was duped by the Count. It turns out that the Count reduced InterTelly's expenses by establishing a company, InterSub, to conduct InterTelly's research and development. InterSub (owned by the Count) funded the R & D by borrowing, securing the loan with the Count's InterTelly shares. Because the Count's shares were restricted, the bank insisted that InterTelly guarantee the loan. Mumford testifies that the Count assured him that InterSub was an independent entity and he took the Count's word for it. Moreover, Barkley & Grover's audit team checked only a sample of InterTelly's contracts and the contract with InterSub (which would have revealed the loan guarantee) was not one of the contracts selected for review. Mumford testifies that he knew nothing about InterTelly's guarantee of InterSub's loan. He also testifies that he reviewed the entire registration statement, but that he knew nothing about Elmo's prior criminal conviction, and did not have a clue about the likelihood of regulation by the FCC. The plaintiffs' accounting expert testifies in her deposition that the guarantee of InterSub's loan should have been disclosed as a contingency in InterTelly's financial statements. Will Barkley & Grover be liable for the non-expertised portion? The expertised portion?

5.   Cadabby Capital owned 40% of InterTelly's shares prior to the offering and Cadabby Capital's nominees held half of InterTelly's board seats. One of Cadabby Capital's partners, Abby, sat on InterTelly's board and the board's audit committee. Abby testifies that she had no clue that Elmo had a prior run-in with the law. She discussed the possibility of regulation by the FCC with Oscar, but she believed Oscar when he told her it was unlikely to happen. With respect to InterTelly's financial statements, Abby said that she carefully reviewed the reports prepared by Barkley & Grover each year for the audit committee and was satisfied that InterTelly's statements complied with GAAP. Abby also testifies that she and the other board members approved the contract with InterSub and that she accepted the Count's assurance that InterTelly's guarantee of the InterSub loan did not need to be disclosed in InterTelly's financial statements. Is Cadabby Capital potentially liable? Does it have any defense available to it?

E. DAMAGES

1. MEASURING § 11 DAMAGES

Unlike Rule 10b–5, § 11 clearly specifies the damages measure. For each share traceable to the registered offering, § 11 damages equal the difference between what the plaintiff paid for their shares (but not exceeding the offering price) and one of three possibilities depending on whether, and if so when, the plaintiff sold her shares:

1)   If the plaintiff sold her shares prior to the filing of suit, then the price at which the plaintiff disposed of the shares;

2)   If the plaintiff still owns her shares at the end of the suit, then the value of the shares at the time of the filing of the § 11 lawsuit; and

3)   If the plaintiff sold her shares after the filing of the suit (but before judgment), the price at which the plaintiff disposed of the shares if greater than their value at the time of the filing of the suit.

Section 11's use of the word "value" in its damages measure allows for litigants in a § 11 action to invoke a wide variety of alternatives to the market price at the time of the filing of suit. Does the court do a good job in measuring value in the case that follows?

Beecher v. Able

435 F.Supp. 397 (S.D.N.Y. 1975).

■ MOTLEY, C., DISTRICT JUDGE.

INTRODUCTION

In its Findings of Fact and Conclusions of Law . . . the court found that defendant Douglas Aircraft Company, Inc. (Douglas) had on July 12, 1966 sold $75 million of its 4 3/4 convertible debentures due July 1, 1991 under a materially false prospectus. In particular, the court found that the break-even prediction ... rendered the prospectus misleading. . . .

* * *

VALUE AS OF THE TIME OF SUIT

[T]he value of the securities at the time of suit was sharply contested at trial. [The suit was filed on October 14, 1966. The closing price of the debentures on October 14, 1966 was $75 1/2]. To establish "value," plaintiff asks the court first to look to the trading price on the day of suit and then to reduce that price by a sum which reflects the undisclosed financial crisis of defendant. At trial, plaintiff characterized the market for these debentures as free, open and sophisticated, marked by a heavy volume of trading on national exchanges. Plaintiffs relied on trading data from July to mid-October 1966 and the testimony of their expert . . ., in reaching the conclusion that market price was the best evidence of maximum fair value. The reason plaintiffs urge that market price reflects maximum fair value, as opposed to value, is because the buying public was unaware of the financial crisis gripping defendant in mid-October 1966. Thus, according to plaintiff, had the buying public been aware of the crisis they would have paid less for the security.

[The plaintiffs presented a number of points to support their argument that Douglas Aircraft Co.'s debentures would have been lower in price had the investing public known of the full extent of the "crisis" within Douglas including: (1) mounting losses; (2) "cash tightness" within Douglas; (3) the demand on the part of eight banks which had previously extended credit to Douglas for a greater interest rate as well as an infusion of equity capital among other things; (4) discussion among the banks to the effect that the management of Douglas needed "strengthening."]

* * *

In sum, plaintiff's claim that the market price of the debentures reflects a sophisticated assessment of the security's value, but that insofar as the financial plight summarized above was undisclosed, market price should be lowered to arrive at fair value. That is, had investors known of the crisis, they would simply have paid less.

The defendant urges the court to adopt a somewhat different approach from plaintiffs' in establishing "value" of the security at time of suit. Defendant contends that the market action of this offering was volatile and often unrelated to fair value. In particular defendant claims that on the date suit was filed the market price of the debenture was temporarily depressed by panic selling in response to the release of the defendant's disappointing third quarter earnings results. Thus, according to defendant, the market price of the debenture on the date of suit was not a reliable indicator of fair value. Defendant would have the court look to the optimistic long-range prospects of the defendant company and set a value which would not only off-set panic selling but which would reflect defendant's anticipated future gains, or the investment feature of the offering. . . .

[Defendants presented a number of points in support of their "panic selling" theory of value including that (1) the price of the debentures fell from well above 80 in September, 1966 to 75 1/2 at the time of the filing of suit only to rebound back to their initial levels by November 1966 and to above 100 throughout 1967; (2) Douglas enjoyed a substantial backlog of unfilled orders which would translate into higher profits in the future; and (3) banks continued to extend Douglas credit (although on stricter terms).]

* * *

As the above arguments indicate both parties for different reasons are dissatisfied with market price as conclusive evidence of value. The court is urged to look to market price and then either add or subtract a certain amount, depending on which party's claims proves more convincing. Plaintiffs through their expert conclude that fair value on the date of suit was 41. In contrast, defendant through its expert concludes that the value of the debentures on the date of suit was between 80 and 82 1/2. As noted elsewhere, closing market price on the date of suit was 75 1/2.

Case law, commentators and the parties agree that realistic value may be something other than market price, where the public is either misinformed or uninformed about important factors relating to the defendant-offeror's well being. . . . The court has previously indicated that in its view market price is merely some evidence of value. Moreover, the conclusion that "value" is not synonymous with "market price" seems clearly dictated by the plain language of Section 11(e) in which both "price" (sometimes "amount paid") and "value" are used, apparently deliberately, to connote different concepts.

After considering the above evidence offered by the parties with respect to "value" at the time of suit, the court makes the following observations and findings and reaches the following conclusions. Although the plaintiffs produced considerable evidence tending to show the unfavorable financial situation of defendant at the time of suit, the evidence does not convince the court that the situation was as desperate or life-threatening as it has been characterized by plaintiffs. More importantly, the court does not agree with plaintiffs that had investors known of the defendant's financial situation they would invariably have paid less for the debentures and that the court should set a value considerably below market price.

As the parties seem to agree, the market for these debentures was, in the main, a sophisticated market. As such, it no doubt was most interested in the long range investment and speculative features of this particular offering. The defendant's immediate financial troubles would likely be viewed as temporary rather than terminal by such a market. . . .

As defendant urged, notwithstanding the then current financial difficulties, the future of Douglas was hopeful. In particular, the substantial backlog of unfilled orders as well as the banks' continued extension of credit suggested a reasonable basis for belief in recovery. The court relies heavily on these factors in reaching the conclusion that at the time of suit the fair value of the debentures should reflect the reasonably anticipated future recovery of defendant. . . .

Defendant also argued that the value of the debentures at the time of suit was higher than market price because on that date the market price was artificially lowered due to panic selling in response to the revelation of the third quarter earnings. The evidence strongly supports the conclusion that the market price on the day of suit was characterized by panic selling. The court relies heavily on the trading data in reaching this conclusion. In particular, these data show that following the announcement of the third quarter results the market price dropped off and continued to decline at a rate in excess of the pre-revelation rate. The sharp and continued increase in volume between revelation and mid-October suggests a market reacting to news, here presumably news of the third quarter earnings. In addition to these trading data, there was convincing expert testimony which tends to confirm the conclusion that panic selling was affecting the market price at the time of suit. . . .

The court notes that, notwithstanding the fact that the market for these debentures was normally sophisticated, elements of the buying public were apparently given to irrational investment behavior and the prices during the several weeks following the revelation were substantially affected by that behavior. In the court's view, there is nothing inherently contradictory in concluding both that the market for these debentures was normally intelligent and paid a price which fairly reflects value, and that the market was occasionally irrational and paid a price below fair value.

Based on the foregoing factual findings the court concludes that market price is some evidence of fair value. Using the market price as a starting point, the court further concludes that whatever amount might rightly be subtracted to account for the temporary financial crisis of defendant at time of suit, should be off-set by adding a like amount to account for the reasonable likelihood of defendant's recovery. That is, in the court's view, with respect to value at the time of suit the defendant's financial difficulties were balanced by the defendant's probable recovery.

Finally, the court concludes that there was convincing evidence that the market price of the debentures on the day of suit was influenced by panic selling. Hence the price was somewhat below where it might have been, even in a falling market. To correct for this aberration, the court adds 9 1/2 points to the market price of 75 1/2 to establish a figure of 85 as fair value on the date of suit. It is expected that the figure of 85 as value represents a fair value of these debentures unaffected by the panic selling which along with other factors depressed the market price from 88 on September 26, 1966 to 75 1/2 on October 14, 1966.

In reaching this figure the court notes that the market fell 12 points between July 12 [the date of the debenture offering] and September 26, 1966 [the last trading date before the revelation of Douglas Aircraft's disappointing third quarter earnings results] at an average rate of .22 per day for 54 trading days. Had that rate continued for the 14 trading days September 27 to October 14, 1966 the price of the debentures would have been at approximately 84.92. Thus, 85 seems a fair value as of October 14, 1966. The 85 figure may well have obtained in a falling market, unaffected by panic selling. . . .

NOTES

1. *Loss causation defense.* Section 11(e) tells us that the damage measure depends (at least under certain circumstances) on the difference between the offering price and the value at the time of the filing of suit. As *Beecher* discusses, courts may look at a range of factors in determining this value. Section 11(e) also provides an affirmative loss causation defense that allows defendants to reduce their liability if they can prove that the depreciation of the security's value resulted from factors other than the misstatement in the registration statement. This is a switch from Rule 10b–5, under which the plaintiff bears the burden of showing loss causation.

QUESTIONS

1. Is the court correct in dismissing the plaintiff's argument that the market would have reduced the price of Douglas had it known of the negative non-public information? Among other things, the *Beecher* court notes, "the defendant's financial difficulties were balanced off by the defendant's probable recovery." But why, even if the court were correct, wouldn't negative information at least increase the *probability* of poorer financial performance and therefore warrant a reduced price for the Douglas debentures?

2. Which do you have more confidence in: the court's determination of fair value in *Beecher* or the market price of the debenture?

3. The *Beecher* court finds persuasive the notion that panic selling may have artificially depressed the price for Douglas debentures at the time of the filing of suit. Do you think that panic selling is probable in an actively-traded securities market?

HYPOTHETICAL FIVE

Consider the case where Bird purchased 100 shares from InterTelly's initial public offering at $20 per share. Assume that InterTelly's registration statement was materially misleading. Plaintiffs' attorneys filed suit against InterTelly (and other participants in the offering) six months after the IPO. At that time, InterTelly's price on Nasdaq had fallen to $10 per share. Assume that the $10 per share market price represents the "value" of InterTelly at the time of the filing of suit. What are Bird's damages in the following scenarios?

1. *Scenario One:* Bird chooses to hold onto her 100 InterTelly shares until the end of the lawsuit, at which point judgment is returned against InterTelly.

2. *Scenario Two:* Two months after the IPO (and before the filing of suit), Bird sells her shares at the then prevailing market price of $30 per share to Rosita who holds on to her shares until judgment is entered after a trial.

3. *Scenario Three:* Same as in Scenario Two, except that Bird sells to Rosita for a price of the prevailing market price of $15 per share three months after the IPO?

4. *Scenario Four:* Now suppose that Bird sells 100 shares of InterTelly to Rosita for a price of $15 per share eight months after the IPO (i.e., two months after the filing of suit). What if Bird had sold at a price of $5 per share?

2. INDEMNIFICATION, CONTRIBUTION, AND JOINT AND SEVERAL LIABILITY

Section 11 starts with the presumption that all defendants are jointly and severally liable for § 11 damages, with two statutory exceptions. First, § 11(e) limits the liability of underwriters to "the total price at which the securities underwritten by him and distributed to the public were offered to the public." Second, § 11(f)(2)(A) limits the liability of outside directors to their proportionate liability (based on their degree of wrongdoing relative to that of other defendants). Section 11(f)(2)(A) is just one of many reforms to private securities fraud litigation enacted in the Private Securities Litigation Reform Act of 1995 discussed in Chapter 5.

Outside of the statutory modifications to joint and several liability, parties may attempt to adjust their relative exposure to liability through both contract as well as implied contribution rights under § 11. Underwriters will commonly seek an agreement on the part of the issuer to indemnify the underwriters for any securities fraud liability. Should courts enforce such agreements?

Eichenholtz v. Brennan

52 F.3d 478 (3d Cir. 1995).

■ SEITZ, C., CIRCUIT JUDGE.

I.   FACTS

International Thoroughbred Breeders is a Delaware corporation in the business of buying, selling, and leasing interests in thoroughbred horses for breeding. In 1977, Garden State Racetrack burned down. In 1983, ITB proposed a plan to purchase the Garden State grounds, construct a new facility, and operate a thoroughbred and harness racing facility. ITB raised money for this undertaking through the sale of securities. . . .

Plaintiffs alleged violations of section 10(b) of the Securities and Exchange Act of 1934; Rule 10b–5; sections 11, 12[a](2), and 17(a) of the Securities Act of 1933. . . .

[A settlement agreement was reached between the plaintiffs and a subset of the defendants, including ITB. The non-settling defendants, including the underwriter for the public offerings, First Jersey, sought both contribution rights as well as enforcement of their indemnification agreement for securities liability with ITB.]

The court agrees with the non-settling defendants that under section 11 of the Securities Act of 1933, they have an express right to seek contribution for liability under that section. . . .

However, there is no express right to indemnification under the 1933 or 1934 Acts. Further, those courts that have addressed the issue have concluded that there is no implied right to indemnification under the federal securities laws. . . . This circuit has not yet addressed this issue.

As will be explained below, indemnification runs counter to the policies underlying the 1933 and 1934 Acts. In addition, there is no indication that Congress intended that indemnification be available under the Acts. . . . In drafting the Acts, Congress was not concerned with protecting the underwriters, but rather it sought to protect investors. Here, it is the underwriters, not the victims, who seek indemnification. We agree with those courts that have held that there is no implied right to seek indemnification under the federal securities laws.

In addition, in support of its right to seek indemnification from ITB, First Jersey relies on its underwriting agreements with ITB. . . .

Each of four separate underwriting agreements between ITB and First Jersey contains provisions for indemnification. In these provisions, ITB agreed to indemnify First Jersey from any and all loss, liability, claims, damage, and expense arising from any material misstatement, untrue statement, or omission in the public offering.

Generally, federal courts disallow claims for indemnification because such claims run counter to the policies underlying the federal securities acts. . . . The underlying goal of securities legislation is encouraging diligence and discouraging negligence in securities transactions. These goals are accomplished "by exposing issuers and underwriters to the substantial hazard of liability for compensatory damages."

The non-settling defendants argue that the policy of not enforcing indemnification provisions should not apply in cases, as here, where an underwriter was merely negligent, played a "de minimis" role in the public offering at issue, or was being held derivatively or vicariously liable. We disagree. . . .

As stated, the federal securities laws seek, inter alia, to encourage underwriters to conduct thorough independent investigations. Unlike contribution, contractual indemnification allows an underwriter to shift its entire liability to the issuer before any allegation of wrongdoing or a determination of fault. . . . If the court enforced an underwriter indemnification provision, it would effectively eliminate the underwriter's incentive to fulfill its investigative obligation. . . .

In addition, if the court were to allow the non-settling defendants to avoid secondary or derivative liability "merely by showing ignorance[, it] would contravene the congressional intent to protect the public, particularly unsophisticated investors, from fraudulent practices." . . . The public depends upon an underwriter's investigation and opinion, and it relies on such opinions when investing. Denying claims for indemnification would encourage underwriters to exhibit the degree of reasonable care required. . . .

We turn now to whether the bar order impermissibly impinges on the non-settling defendants' right to contribution. . . .

In general, the settlement of complex litigation before trial is favored by the federal courts. However, in multi-party litigation, settlement may be difficult. Defendants, who are willing to settle, "buy little peace through settlement unless they are assured that they will be protected against co-defendants' efforts to shift their losses through cross-claims for indemnity, contribution, and other causes related to the underlying litigation." . . . In cases involving multiple defendants, a right to contribution inhibits partial settlement.

Therefore, in order to encourage settlement in these cases, modern settlements increasingly incorporate settlement bar orders into partial settlements. "In essence, a bar order constitutes a final discharge of all obligations of the settling defendants and bars any further litigation of claims made by non-settling defendants." . . .

In the present case, the district court adopted the proportionate judgment reduction rule. It concluded that the proportionate judgment reduction is the fairest method, and the non-settling defendants will not be prejudiced by a proportionate fault reduction. We agree with the determination of the district court.

Under the proportionate judgment reduction method, the jury, in the non-settling defendants' trial, will assess the relative culpability of both settling and non-settling defendants, and the non-settling defendants will pay a commensurate percentage of the judgment. The risk of a "bad" settlement falls on the plaintiffs, who have a financial incentive to make certain that each defendant bears its share of the damages . . . the proportionate fault rule satisfies the statutory contribution goals of equity, deterrence, and the policy goal of encouraging settlement. The proportionate fault rule is the equivalent of a contribution claim; the non-settling defendants are only responsible for their portion of the liability.

We conclude that the district court did not abuse its discretion in imposing the bar order with the proportionate judgment reduction provision. . . .

QUESTIONS

1. Underwriters who demonstrate due diligence escape § 11 liability completely. Is indemnification only a concern for underwriters who fail to meet due diligence?

2. Who bears the risk under the proportionate judgment reduction method? Do the settling defendants or the plaintiffs make up the difference when the non-settling defendants' judgment is reduced?

3. Should underwriters be allowed to purchase insurance against potential § 11 liability?

HYPOTHETICAL SIX

The registration statement for InterTelly's initial public offering contained a number of misstatements, including a failure to disclose Elmo's prior criminal conviction, omissions about the likelihood of regulation by the FCC, and misstatements in the audited financial statements. Assume that the following players are involved with InterTelly's initial public offering and all have been named as defendants in a § 11 class action:

- Zoe, the CEO and a director
- The Count, the CFO
- Oscar, an outside director
- Sesame Securities, the managing underwriter
- Barkley & Grover, the auditor

1. If Sesame Securities had an enforceable indemnification contract clause with InterTelly, would the underwriter still investigate and research to verify the accuracy of disclosures in the registration statement?

2. Suppose that Zoe, the Count, and Oscar are considering settlement while Sesame Securities and Barkley & Grover are not. Why would Zoe, the Count, and Oscar worry about potential liability for contribution to Sesame Securities and Barkley & Grover?

3. Suppose that Zoe, the Count, and Oscar settle for only a small fraction of what they might owe at trial. The plaintiffs' attorneys agree to the settlement to allow them to focus their attention on the real deep pockets, Barkley & Grover and Sesame Securities. If you were a member of a jury considering contribution among the various defendants, how would you go about determining how much responsibility to assign to Barkley & Grover and Sesame Securities for the misrepresentations involving Elmo's criminal conviction, FCC regulation, and the audited financials? What information would you want to know? Is it likely such information would be available at trial?

4. Assume that, in addition to the other misstatements in the InterTelly registration statement, the filing also failed to disclose certain compensation received by Sesame Securities in connection with the offering. Specifically, Sesame Securities received "bonus" commission payments from some of its customers in exchange for receiving an allocation of InterTelly IPO shares from Sesame. InterTelly was unaware of this practice. Will InterTelly be liable for this omission in a § 11 suit? Can it recover from Sesame Securities any damages it has to pay?

III. SECTION 12(a)(1)

Unlike the other liability provisions that we have studied, § 12(a)(1) of the Securities Act is not an antifraud provision. Instead, § 12(a)(1) provides a private cause of action for violations of § 5's gun-jumping rule requirements. Violations of § 5 can occur at a number of different points in the public offering process. A company may mention the offering during the pre-filing period in a way that "conditions" the market. During the waiting period, an underwriter may send out free writing without the preliminary prospectus. After the SEC declares the registration statement effective, the issuer may fail to file the prospectus, thereby negating access equals delivery.

As you go through the materials on § 12(a)(1), consider how the various aspects of a § 12(a)(1) lawsuit differ from an antifraud suit under either § 11 of the Securities Act or Rule 10b–5 of the Exchange Act.

A. STANDING AND DEFENDANTS

The questions "Who has standing to sue?" and "Who are potential defendants?" are interconnected under § 12(a)(1). Section 12(a)(1) provides that:

> Any person who . . . offers or sells a security in violation of section 5 . . . shall be liable . . . to the person purchasing such security from him. . . .

gun-jumping rules

A person who purchases a security offered or sold in violation of § 5 therefore has standing to sue under § 12(a)(1). The class of potential defendants includes those who offer or sell to the purchasing person. In the case below, the Supreme Court defines who can be deemed to offer and sell.

Pinter v. Dahl
486 U.S. 622 (1988).

■ BLACKMUN, J.

* * *

The controversy arises out of the sale prior to 1982 of unregistered securities (fractional undivided interests in oil and gas leases) by petitioner Billy J. "B.J." Pinter to respondents Maurice Dahl and Dahl's friends, family, and business associates. Pinter is an oil and gas producer in Texas and Oklahoma, and a registered securities dealer in Texas. Dahl is a California real estate broker and investor, who, at the time of his dealings with Pinter, was a veteran of two unsuccessful oil and gas ventures. In pursuit of further investment opportunities, Dahl employed an oil field expert to locate and acquire oil and gas leases. This expert introduced Dahl to Pinter. Dahl advanced $20,000 to Pinter to acquire leases, with the understanding that they would be held in the name of Pinter's Black Gold Oil Company and that Dahl would have a right of first refusal to drill certain wells on the leasehold properties. Pinter located leases in Oklahoma, and Dahl toured the properties, often without Pinter, in order to talk to others and "get a feel for the properties." Upon examining the geology, drilling logs, and production history assembled by Pinter, Dahl concluded, in the words of the District Court, that "there was no way to lose."

After investing approximately $310,000 in the properties, Dahl told the other respondents about the venture. Except for Dahl and respondent Grantham, none of the respondents spoke to or met Pinter or toured the properties. Because of Dahl's involvement in the venture, each of the other respondents decided to invest about $7,500.

Dahl assisted his fellow investors in completing the subscription-agreement form prepared by Pinter. Each letter-contract signed by the purchaser stated that the participating interests were being sold without the benefit of registration under the Securities Act. . . . Dahl received no commission from Pinter in connection with the other respondents' purchases.

When the venture failed and their interests proved to be worthless, respondents brought suit against Pinter . . . seeking rescission under § 12[a](1) of the Securities Act for the unlawful sale of unregistered securities. . . .

The District Court, after a bench trial, granted judgment for respondent-investors. . . . A divided panel of the Court of Appeals for the Fifth Circuit affirmed. . . . [In affirming, the Court of Appeals considered whether Dahl could be considered a statutory seller under § 12(a)(1) and therefore potentially liable in contribution to Pinter, ultimately finding the Dahl was not such a statutory seller].

In determining whether Dahl may be deemed a "seller" for purposes of § 12[a](1), such that he may be held liable for the sale of unregistered securities to the other investor-respondents, we look first at the language of § 12[a](1). . . . That statute provides, in pertinent part: "Any person who . . . offers or sells a security" in violation of the registration requirement of the Securities Act "shall be liable to the person purchasing such security from him." This provision defines the class of defendants who may be subject to liability as those who offer or sell unregistered securities. But the Securities Act nowhere delineates who may be regarded as a statutory seller, and the sparse legislative history sheds no light on the issue. The courts, on their part, have not defined the term uniformly.

At the very least, however, the language of § 12[a](1) contemplates a buyer-seller relationship not unlike traditional contractual privity. Thus, it is settled that § 12[a](1) imposes liability on the owner who passed title, or other interest in the security, to the buyer for value. . . . Dahl, of course, was not a seller in this conventional sense, and therefore may be held liable only if § 12[a](1) liability extends to persons other than the person who passes title.

A

In common parlance, a person may offer or sell property without necessarily being the person who transfers title to, or other interest in, that property. We need not rely entirely on ordinary understanding of the statutory language, however, for the Securities Act defines the operative terms of § 12[a](1). Section 2[a](3) defines "sale" or "sell" to include "every contract of sale or disposition of a security or interest in a security, for value," and the terms "offer to sell," "offer for sale," or "offer" to include "every attempt or offer to dispose of, or solicitation of an offer to buy, a security or interest in a security, for value." Under these definitions, the range of persons potentially liable under § 12[a](1) is not limited to persons who pass title. The inclusion of the phrase "solicitation of an offer to buy" within the definition of "offer" brings an individual who engages in solicitation, an activity not inherently confined to the actual owner, within the scope of § 12. . . .

Determining that the activity in question falls within the definition of "offer" or "sell" in § 2[a](3), however, is only half of the analysis. The second clause of § 12[a](1), which provides that only a defendant "from" whom the plaintiff "purchased" securities may be liable, narrows the field of potential sellers.[21] Several courts and commentators have stated that the purchase requirement necessarily restricts § 12 primary liability to the owner of the security. . . . In effect, these authorities interpret the term "purchase" as complementary to only the term "sell" defined in § 2[a](3). Thus, an offeror, as defined by § 2[a](3), may incur § 12 liability only if the offeror also "sells" the security to the plaintiff, in the sense of transferring title for value. . . .

We do not read § 12[a](1) so restrictively. The purchase requirement clearly confines § 12 liability to those situations in which a sale has taken place. Thus, a prospective buyer has no recourse against

---

[21]   One important consequence of this provision is that § 12[a](1) imposes liability on only the buyer's immediate seller; remote purchasers are precluded from bringing actions against remote sellers. Thus, a buyer cannot recover against his seller's seller.

a person who touts unregistered securities to him if he does not purchase the securities. . . . The requirement, however, does not exclude solicitation from the category of activities that may render a person liable when a sale has taken place. A natural reading of the statutory language would include in the statutory seller status at least some persons who urged the buyer to purchase. For example, a securities vendor's agent who solicited the purchase would commonly be said, and would be thought by the buyer, to be among those "from" whom the buyer "purchased," even though the agent himself did not pass title. . . .

An interpretation of statutory seller that includes brokers and others who solicit offers to purchase securities furthers the purposes of the Securities Act—to promote full and fair disclosure of information to the public in the sales of securities. In order to effectuate Congress' intent that § 12[a](1) civil liability be *in terrorem* . . . the risk of its invocation should be felt by solicitors of purchases. The solicitation of a buyer is perhaps the most critical stage of the selling transaction. It is the first stage of a traditional securities sale to involve the buyer, and it is directed at producing the sale. In addition, brokers and other solicitors are well positioned to control the flow of information to a potential purchaser, and, in fact, such persons are the participants in the selling transaction who most often disseminate material information to investors. Thus, solicitation is the stage at which an investor is most likely to be injured, that is, by being persuaded to purchase securities without full and fair information. Given Congress' overriding goal of preventing this injury, we may infer that Congress intended solicitation to fall under the mantle of § 12[a](1).

Although we conclude that Congress intended § 12[a](1) liability to extend to those who solicit securities purchases, . . . Congress did not intend to impose rescission based on strict liability on a person who urges the purchase but whose motivation is solely to benefit the buyer. When a person who urges another to make a securities purchase acts merely to assist the buyer, not only is it uncommon to say that the buyer "purchased" from him, but it is also strained to describe the giving of gratuitous advice, even strongly or enthusiastically, as "soliciting." Section 2[a](3) defines an offer as a "solicitation of an offer to buy . . . for value." The person who gratuitously urges another to make a particular investment decision is not, in any meaningful sense, requesting value in exchange for his suggestion or seeking the value the titleholder will obtain in exchange for the ultimate sale. The language and purpose of § 12[a](1) suggest that liability extends only to the person who successfully solicits the purchase, motivated at least in part by a desire to serve his own financial interests or those of the securities owner. If he had such a motivation, it is fair to say that the buyer "purchased" the security from him and to align him with the owner in a rescission action.

B

Petitioner is not satisfied with extending § 12[a](1) primary liability to one who solicits securities sales for financial gain. Pinter assumes, without explication, that liability is not limited to the person who actually parts title with the securities, and urges us to validate, as the standard by which additional defendant-sellers are identified, that version of the "substantial factor" test utilized by the Fifth Circuit before the refinement espoused in this case. Under that approach, grounded in tort doctrine, a nontransferor § 12[a](1) seller is defined as one "whose participation in the buy-sell transaction is a substantial factor in causing the transaction to take place." The Court of Appeals acknowledged that Dahl would be liable as a statutory seller under this test. . . .

The deficiency of the substantial-factor test is that it divorces the analysis of seller status from any reference to the applicable statutory language and from any examination of § 12 in the context of the total statutory scheme. Those courts that have adopted the approach have not attempted to ground their analysis in the statutory language. Instead, they substitute the concept of substantial participation in the sales transaction, or proximate causation of the plaintiff's purchase, for the words "offers or sells" in § 12. The "purchase from" requirement of § 12 focuses on the defendant's relationship with the plaintiff-purchaser. The substantial-factor test, on the other hand, focuses on the defendant's degree of involvement in the securities transaction and its surrounding circumstances. Thus, although the substantial-factor test undoubtedly embraces persons who pass title and who solicit the purchase of unregistered securities as statutory sellers, the test also would extend § 12[a](1) liability to participants only remotely related to the relevant aspects of the sales transaction. Indeed, it might expose securities professionals, such as accountants and lawyers, whose involvement is only the performance of their professional services, to § 12[a](1) strict liability for rescission. The buyer does not, in any meaningful sense, "purchas[e] the security from" such a person. . . .

[T]he substantial-factor test introduces an element of uncertainty into an area that demands certainty and predictability. . . . None of the courts employing the approach has articulated what measure of participation qualifies a person for seller status, and logically sound limitations would be difficult to develop. . . . We find it particularly unlikely that Congress would have ordained *sub silentio* the imposition of strict liability on such an unpredictably defined class of defendants. . . .

C

We are unable to determine whether Dahl may be held liable as a statutory seller under § 12[a](1). The District Court explicitly found that "Dahl solicited each of the other plaintiffs (save perhaps Grantham) in connection with the offer, purchase, and receipt of their oil and gas interests." We cannot conclude that this finding was clearly erroneous. It is not clear, however, that Dahl had the kind of interest in the sales that make him liable as a statutory seller. We do know that he received no commission from Pinter in connection with the other sales, but this is not conclusive. Typically, a person who solicits the purchase will have sought or received a personal financial benefit from the sale, such as where he "anticipat[es] a share of the profits," or receives a brokerage commission. But a person who solicits the buyer's purchase in order to serve the financial interests of the owner may properly be liable under § 12[a](1) without showing that he expects to participate in the benefits the owner enjoys.

The Court of Appeals apparently concluded that Dahl was motivated entirely by a gratuitous desire to share an attractive investment opportunity with his friends and associates. This conclusion, in our view, was premature. The District Court made no findings that focused on whether Dahl urged the other purchases in order to further some financial interest of his own or of Pinter. Accordingly, further findings are necessary to assess Dahl's liability. . . .

NOTES

1. *Defendants.* Section 12(a)(1) (and § 12(a)(2) discussed below) provides one more formulation on which third parties should face liability for violations of the securities laws. Private liability under Rule 10b–5 depends on the notion of who is a "primary" violator. Liability under § 11, in contrast, extends to those persons and entities listed in § 11(a) as statutory defendants.

Section 12's approach differs from both Rule 10b–5 and § 11 in focusing on the relationship of the participating party and the investor purchasing securities. The *Pinter* Court stresses the importance of the person making contact with investors: "The solicitation of a buyer is perhaps the most critical stage of the selling transaction. It is the first stage of a traditional securities sale to involve the buyer, and it is directed at producing the sale."

Why do the approaches to secondary liability vary for the different causes of action provided in private securities laws? If solicitation is the key step in dealing with investors, why not make § 11 and Rule 10b–5 liability turn on whether a defendant engages in solicitation? If other, non-soliciting participants in an offering may still deter fraud (perhaps through their ability to monitor the issuer and influence the issuer's decision-making), why not make these other participants also liable under § 12?

QUESTIONS

1. The *Pinter* court rejects including "substantial participants" as potential § 12(a)(1) defendants in part because this class of defendants is "unpredictably defined." Is the class of defendants who help "solicit" offers more definite?

2. How do those who solicit for value compare to the list of defendants other than the issuer in § 11(a)? How do those who solicit for value compare with the old aiding and abetting liability under Rule 10b–5 and the view of defendants under Rule 10b–5 after *Stoneridge* and *Janus Capital*? What justifies the difference in potential defendants under § 12(a)(1), § 11, and Rule 10b–5?

3. As we discuss in Chapter 10, the securities laws take a broad view of what is a sale transaction. If the issuer sells to an underwriter and the underwriter resells to an ultimate purchaser, the entire chain from the issuer to the ultimate purchaser is one transaction. A § 5 violation anywhere in the transaction may then lead to potential § 12(a)(1) liability. But *Pinter* narrows who may be sued as a defendant to the seller in privity of title with the purchaser as well as those who solicit for value. Assuming no solicitation, the ultimate purchaser is limited to suing only the underwriter under § 12(a)(1). The underwriter in turn may then sue the issuer under § 12(a)(1). Should the ultimate purchaser also have the ability to sue the issuer directly (consider the application of Rule 159A and Item 512(a)(6) discussed below)?

Hypothetical Seven

Two years after InterTelly's initial public offering, Zoe decides that InterTelly needs to raise additional capital to fund a new marketing campaign. She estimates that InterTelly needs about $50 million to launch the campaign, which will focus on a large number of TV ads in which she plans to star. InterTelly will conduct the offering as a private placement exempt from § 5 pursuant to Rule 506 of Regulation D. (We cover Regulation D in Chapter 9.) Unfortunately, InterTelly's selling agent, Sesame Securities, sold the securities to investors who were not accredited and who lacked financial sophistication. Assume that InterTelly does not qualify for any other exemption from § 5's registration requirements and is liable under § 12(a)(1).

1. *Scenario One:* Recall that the following were named as defendants in the § 11 suit against InterTelly.

- Zoe, the CEO and a director
- The Count, the CFO
- Oscar, an outside director
- Sesame Securities, the managing underwriter
- Barkley & Grover, the auditor

Which of these § 11 defendants would (and would not) meet the requirements of *Pinter*?

2. *Scenario Two:* Suppose that two friends, Bert and Ernie, are investors in the InterTelly private placement. Bert learned of the private placement from Ernie. Ernie routinely passes on investment tips to Bert at their weekly tennis game. Assume that no money ever changes hands between the two (aside from Bert having to pay for lunch when he loses the tennis match again). Can InterTelly sue Ernie under § 12(a)(1) for contribution as a statutory seller?

3. *Scenario Three:* Suppose that InterTelly's attorneys, Snuffle & Gus LLP, administered the physical mailing of InterTelly's offering memorandum to all offerees. Can InterTelly sue Snuffle & Gus under § 12(a)(1) for contribution as another statutory seller? What if Snuffle & Gus included with the offering memorandum a cover letter with Snuffle & Gus's name prominently displayed at the top of the letter?

4. *Scenario Four:* What happens if the U.S. economy goes into a recession right after the investors purchase the stock from InterTelly's private placement? InterTelly's stock falls in value due to the recession; its failure to register the shares has nothing to do with the stock's decline. Can InterTelly raise the recession as a defense to rescission?

5. *Scenario Five:* Suppose that instead of holding onto his InterTelly securities purchased from the private placement at $20 per share, Bert had sold the shares at $10 per share to Kermit. Who may Kermit sue? Who may Bert sue?

B.   ELEMENTS OF THE CAUSE OF ACTION

Section 12(a)(1) works to crush out § 5 violations. Plaintiffs need only show a § 5 violation involving a security that they purchased. The plaintiff does not need to prove scienter (or even negligence), causation, reliance, or damages. Plaintiffs who demonstrate a § 5 violation then are entitled to rescission (getting their money back in exchange for the securities). Plaintiffs who have sold the securities may seek damages.

C.   DAMAGES AND DEFENSES

We saw that defendants in a § 11 antifraud action enjoyed a number of defenses. Defendants could attempt to show due diligence or that the loss in the issuer's shares was due to other causes. Should defendants in a § 12(a)(1) rescission action for a violation of § 5 enjoy similar defenses? What if an underwriter made an innocent mistake in sending out "free writing" during the waiting period? What if the stock price dropped after the offering but due to clearly unrelated reasons (e.g., a sharp spike in the price of oil)?

The short answer for § 12(a)(1) is that defendants enjoy no defenses. As with other Securities Act civil liability provisions, however, § 13 imposes a statute of limitations of one year from discovery and three years from sale.

HYPOTHETICAL EIGHT

1.   Consider Bird, an investor in the InterTelly initial public offering who bought 100 shares at $20 per share. Assume that InterTelly's underwriters failed to send a final prospectus to Bird with her confirmation and InterTelly failed to file the final prospectus with the SEC. If InterTelly's share price rises to $30, will she exercise her right to rescind under § 12(a)(1)? If InterTelly's shares drop to $10 per share, will Bird pursue her § 12(a)(1) remedy?

2.   Suppose that Rosita is another investor in the InterTelly IPO. She did receive a final prospectus with her confirmation of sale. Can she bring suit for § 12(a)(1) rescission for InterTelly's failure to send Bird a final prospectus with the confirmation of sale?

3.   Recall that Sesame Securities is the managing underwriter for InterTelly's initial public offering. Consider the following chain of transactions:

  a.   InterTelly sells to Sesame Securities at $18.60 per share

  b.   Sesame Securities sells to Bird at $20 per share

  c.   Bird sells to Kermit at $10 per share

Suppose that a § 5 violation occurred during the Waiting Period (impermissible free writing was mailed out to prospective investors without a preliminary prospectus). What damages may Bird and Kermit obtain under § 12(a)(1)?

IV. SECTION 12(a)(2) LIABILITY

Section 11 focused on misstatements in the registration statement; § 12(a)(2) provides a private cause of action for misstatements in the prospectus. Section 12(a)(2) provides in part that:

> Any person who . . . offers or sells a security . . . by the use of any means or instruments of transportation or communication in interstate commerce . . . by means of a prospectus or oral communication, which includes an untrue statement of a material fact or omits to state a material fact necessary in order to make the statements, in the light of the circumstances under which they were made, not misleading . . . shall be liable . . . to the person purchasing such security from him. . . .

Like Rule 10b–5 and § 11, § 12(a)(2) requires a material misstatement or omission and the use of an instrumentality of interstate commerce. Section § 12(a)(2) also shares many features with its sibling, § 12(a)(1). Like § 12(a)(1), only those purchasing securities have standing to sue under § 12(a)(2). Potential defendants are those who offer or sell the securities. Courts have applied the Supreme Court's § 12(a)(1) analysis in *Pinter* to determine which participating parties in an offering are involved with offering (including soliciting) and selling the securities for purposes of § 12(a)(2).

Two regulations modify the list of potential defendants under § 12(a)(2). Rule 159A defines "seller" in a primary offering of securities for purposes of § 12(a)(2) only to include the issuer of securities "sold to a person as part of the initial distribution of such securities." The issuer is deemed a seller regardless of underwriting method if the securities are offered or sold to the person through a statutory prospectus, a free writing prospectus, or "[a]ny other communication that is an offer in the offering made by the issuer to such person." Although subsequent purchasers in the secondary market are not part of the initial distribution, the first investor who purchases from an underwriter in a firm commitment offering is part of the initial distribution and pursuant to Rule 159A could sue the issuer under § 12(a)(2) even if not in direct privity of contract. Item 512(a)(6) of Regulation S–K, which is required for issuers in shelf registered offerings, provides that purchasers in the initial distribution of securities have standing to sue the issuer as a "seller" of the securities regardless of underwriting method. Unlike Rule 159A, Item 512(a)(6) expands the scope of defendants for § 12(a)(1) in addition to § 12(a)(2). Item 512(a)(6), however, applies only to shelf registration issuers while Rule 159A applies to public offerings generally.

A. THE SCOPE OF § 12(a)(2)

Although § 12(a)(2) shares similarities with other antifraud provisions and § 12(a)(1), it does differ in one important respect: Section 12(a)(2) only reaches fraud committed "by means of a prospectus or oral communication." Unfortunately, the Securities Act leaves some ambiguity in defining a prospectus. Section 2(a)(10) provides that a "prospectus" means "any prospectus, notice, circular, advertisement, letter, or communication, written or by radio or television, which offers any security for sale or confirms the sale of security. . . ." Defining prospectus to mean "any prospectus" has a certain circularity to it. Recall that the SEC traditionally has focused instead on the term "communication" in defining the scope of the "gun-jumping" rules that govern the Pre-Filing and Waiting Periods during the registration process. The agency's focus on "communication" leads to a broad interpretation of "prospectus," sweeping in virtually any written statement that could be seen as "arousing" the interest of investors in an issuer or its securities.

Complicating the matter further is § 10 of the Securities Act. Section 10 does not define a prospectus, but instead sets forth the information required for prospectuses that satisfies the requirements of § 5(b)'s prospectus delivery requirement. In short, a § 10 prospectus (or at least a § 10(a) final prospectus as well as a Rule 430 preliminary prospectus) forms Part I of the formal registration statement and contains information on the biographies of management, the composition of the board of directors, and a description of the company's business and assets, among other information.

Section 12(a)(2) thus leaves courts to puzzle over two plausible alternatives for the scope of its application:

1. Any prospectus meeting the SEC's broad interpretation of the definition contained in § 2(a)(10)

2. Only prospectuses forming Part I of the registration statement which satisfy § 10 of the Securities Act

The Supreme Court interpreted "prospectus" for purposes of § 12 in the case below. Did the Court select one of these two alternatives, or did it choose yet another interpretation for the term "prospectus"?

Gustafson v. Alloyd Co., Inc.

513 U.S. 561 (1995).

■ KENNEDY, J.

Under § 12[a](2) of the Securities Act of 1933 buyers have an express cause of action for rescission against sellers who make material misstatements or omissions "by means of a prospectus." The question presented is whether this right of rescission extends to a private, secondary transaction, on the theory that recitations in the purchase agreement are part of a "prospectus."

I

Petitioners Gustafson, McLean, and Butler (collectively Gustafson) were in 1989 the sole shareholders of Alloyd, Inc., a manufacturer of plastic packaging and automatic heat sealing equipment. Alloyd was formed, and its stock was issued, in 1961. In 1989, Gustafson decided to sell Alloyd and engaged KPMG Peat Marwick to find a buyer. In response to information distributed by KPMG, Wind Point Partners II, L.P., agreed to buy substantially all of the issued and outstanding stock through Alloyd Holdings, Inc., a new corporation formed to effect the sale of Alloyd's stock. The shareholders of Alloyd Holdings were Wind Point and a number of individual investors.

In preparation for negotiating the contract with Gustafson, Wind Point undertook an extensive analysis of the company, relying in part on a formal business review prepared by KPMG. Alloyd's practice was to take inventory at year's end, so Wind Point and KPMG considered taking an earlier inventory to use in determining the purchase price. In the end they did not do so, relying instead on certain estimates and including provisions for adjustments after the transaction closed.

On December 20, 1989, Gustafson and Alloyd Holdings executed a contract of sale. Alloyd Holdings agreed to pay Gustafson and his coshareholders $18,709,000 for the sale of the stock plus a payment of $2,122,219, which reflected the estimated increase in Alloyd's net worth from the end of the previous year, the last period for which hard financial data were available. Article IV of the purchase agreement, entitled "Representations and Warranties of the Sellers," included assurances that the company's financial statements "present fairly . . . the Company's financial condition" and that between the date of the latest balance sheet and the date the agreement was executed "there ha[d] been no material adverse change in . . . [Alloyd's] financial condition." The contract also provided that if the year-end audit and financial statements revealed a variance between estimated and actual increased value, the disappointed party would receive an adjustment.

The year-end audit of Alloyd revealed that Alloyd's actual earnings for 1989 were lower than the estimates relied upon by the parties in negotiating the adjustment amount of $2,122,219. Under the contract, the buyers had a right to recover an adjustment amount of $815,000 from the sellers. Nevertheless, on February 11, 1991, the newly formed company (now called Alloyd Co., the same as the original company) and Wind Point brought suit . . . seeking outright rescission of the contract under § 12[a](2). Alloyd (the new company) claimed that statements made by Gustafson and his coshareholders regarding the financial data of their company were inaccurate, rendering untrue the representations and warranties contained in the contract. The buyers further alleged that the contract of sale was a "prospectus," so that any misstatements contained in the agreement gave rise to liability under § 12[a](2). Pursuant to the adjustment clause, the defendants remitted to the purchasers $815,000 plus interest, but the adjustment did not cause the purchasers to drop the lawsuit. . . .

II

* * *

As this case reaches us, we must assume that the stock purchase agreement contained material misstatements of fact made by the sellers and that Gustafson would not sustain its burden of proving due care. On these assumptions, Alloyd would have a right to obtain rescission if those misstatements were made "by means of a prospectus or oral communication." The Courts of Appeals agree that the phrase "oral communication" is restricted to oral communications that relate to a prospectus. The determinative question, then, is whether the contract between Alloyd and Gustafson is a "prospectus" as the term is used in the 1933 Act.

Alloyd argues that "prospectus" is defined in a broad manner, broad enough to encompass the contract between the parties. This argument is echoed by the dissents. . . . Gustafson, by contrast, maintains that prospectus in the 1933 Act means a communication soliciting the public to purchase securities from the issuer. . . .

Three sections of the 1933 Act are critical in resolving the definitional question on which the case turns: § 2[a](10), which defines a prospectus; § 10, which sets forth the information that must be contained in a prospectus; and § 12, which imposes liability based on misstatements in a prospectus. In seeking to interpret the term "prospectus," we adopt the premise that the term should be construed, if possible, to give it a consistent meaning throughout the Act. That principle follows from our duty to construe statutes, not isolated provisions. . . .

A

We begin with § 10. . . . An examination of § 10 reveals that, whatever else "prospectus" may mean, the term is confined to a document that, absent an overriding exemption, must include the "information contained in the registration statement." By and large, only public offerings by an issuer of a security, or by controlling shareholders of an issuer, require the preparation and filing of registration statements. It follows, we conclude, that a prospectus under § 10 is confined to documents related to public offerings by an issuer or its controlling shareholders.

This much (the meaning of prospectus in § 10) seems not to be in dispute. Where the courts are in disagreement is with the implications of this proposition for the entirety of the Act, and for § 12 in particular. . . . We conclude that the term "prospectus" must have the same meaning under §§ 10 and 12. In so holding, we do not, as the dissent by Justice Ginsburg suggests, make the mistake of treating § 10 as a definitional section. . . . Instead, we find in § 10 guidance and instruction for giving the term a consistent meaning throughout the Act.

The 1933 Act, like every Act of Congress, should not be read as a series of unrelated and isolated provisions. . . . That principle applies here. If the contract before us is not a prospectus for purposes of § 10— as all must and do concede—it is not a prospectus for purposes of § 12 either.

The conclusion that prospectus has the same meaning, and refers to the same types of communications (public offers by an issuer or its controlling shareholders), in both §§ 10 and 12 is reinforced by an examination of the structure of the 1933 Act. Sections 4 and 5 of the Act together require a seller to file a registration statement and to issue a prospectus for certain defined types of sales (public offerings by an issuer, through an underwriter). Sections 7 and 10 of the Act set forth the information required in the registration statement and the prospectus. Section 11 provides for liability on account of false registration statements; § 12[a](2) for liability based on misstatements in prospectuses. Following the most natural and symmetrical reading, just as the liability imposed by § 11 flows from the requirements imposed by §§ 5 and 7 providing for the filing and content of registration statements, the liability imposed by § 12[a](2) cannot attach unless there is an obligation to distribute the prospectus in the first place (or unless there is an exemption). . . .

The primary innovation of the 1933 Act was the creation of federal duties—for the most part, registration and disclosure obligations—in connection with public offerings. . . . We are reluctant to conclude that § 12[a](2) creates vast additional liabilities that are quite independent of the new substantive obligations the Act imposes. It is more reasonable to interpret the liability provisions of the 1933 Act as designed for the primary purpose of providing remedies for violations of the obligations it had created. Indeed, §§ 11 and 12[a](1)—the statutory neighbors of § 12[a](2)—afford remedies for violations of those obligations. . . . Under our interpretation of "prospectus," § 12[a](2) in similar manner is linked to the new duties created by the Act.

On the other hand, accepting Alloyd's argument that any written offer is a prospectus under § 12 would require us to hold that the word "prospectus" in § 2 refers to a broader set of communications than the same term in § 10. . . . In the name of a plain meaning approach to statutory interpretation, the dissents discover in the Act two different species of prospectuses: formal (also called § 10) prospectuses, subject to both §§ 10 and 12, and informal prospectuses, subject only to § 12 but not to 10. . . . Nowhere in the statute, however, do the terms "formal prospectus" or "informal prospectus" appear. Instead, the Act uses one term— "prospectus" —throughout. In disagreement with the Court of Appeals and the dissenting opinions, we cannot accept the conclusion that this single operative word means one thing in one section of the Act and something quite different in another. . . .

B

Alloyd's contrary argument rests to a significant extent on § 2[a](10), or, to be more precise, on one word of that section. Section 2[a](10) provides that "[t]he term 'prospectus' means any prospectus, notice, circular, advertisement, letter, or communication, written or by radio or television, which offers any security for sale or confirms the sale of any security." Concentrating on the word "communication," Alloyd argues that any written communication that offers a security for sale is a "prospectus." Inserting its definition into § 12[a](2), Alloyd insists that a material misstatement in any communication offering a security for sale gives rise to an action for rescission, without proof of fraud by seller or reliance by the purchaser. In Alloyd's view, § 2[a](10) gives the term "prospectus" a capacious definition that, although incompatible with § 10, nevertheless governs in § 12. . . .

The word "communication," however, on which Alloyd's entire argument rests, is but one word in a list, a word Alloyd reads altogether out of context.

The relevant phrase in the definitional part of the statute must be read in its entirety, a reading which yields the interpretation that the term "prospectus" refers to a document soliciting the public to acquire securities. We find that definition controlling. Alloyd's argument that the phrase "communication, written or by radio or television," transforms any written communication offering a security for sale into a prospectus cannot consist with at least two rather sensible rules of statutory construction. First, the Court will avoid a reading which renders some words altogether redundant. . . . If "communication" included every written communication, it would render "notice, circular, advertisement, [and] letter" redundant, since each of these are forms of written communication as well. . . .

The constructional problem is resolved by the second principle Alloyd overlooks, which is that a word is known by the company it keeps (the doctrine of *noscitur a sociis*). . . . From the terms "prospectus, notice, circular, advertisement, [or] letter," it is apparent that the list refers to documents of wide dissemination. In a similar manner, the list includes communications "by radio or television," but not face-to-face or telephonic conversations. Inclusion of the term "communication" in that list suggests that it too refers to a public communication.

When the 1933 Act was drawn and adopted, the term "prospectus" was well understood to refer to a document soliciting the public to acquire securities from the issuer. . . . In this respect, the word "prospectus" is a term of art, which accounts for congressional confidence in employing what might otherwise be regarded as a partial circularity in the formal, statutory definition. . . . The use of the term "prospectus" to refer to public solicitations explains as well Congress' decision in § 12[a](2) to grant buyers a right to rescind without proof of reliance. See H.R.Rep. No. 85, 73d Cong., 1st Sess., 10 (1933) ("The statements for which [liable persons] are responsible, although they may never actually have been seen by the prospective purchaser, because of their wide dissemination, determine the market price of the security . . .").

The list of terms in § 2[a](10) prevents a seller of stock from avoiding liability by calling a soliciting document something other than a prospectus, but it does not compel the conclusion that Alloyd urges us to reach and that the dissenting opinions adopt. Instead, the term "written communication" must be read in context to refer to writings that, from a functional standpoint, are similar to the terms "notice, circular, [and] advertisement." The term includes communications held out to the public at large but that might have been thought to be outside the other words in the definitional section. . . .

D

It is understandable that Congress would provide buyers with a right to rescind, without proof of fraud or reliance, as to misstatements contained in a document prepared with care, following well-established procedures relating to investigations with due diligence and in the context of a public offering by an issuer or its controlling shareholders. It is not plausible to infer that Congress created this extensive liability for every casual communication between buyer and seller in the secondary market. It is often difficult, if not altogether impractical, for those engaged in casual communications not to omit some fact that would, if included, qualify the accuracy of a statement. Under Alloyd's view any casual communication between buyer and seller in the aftermarket could give rise to an action for rescission, with no evidence of fraud on the part of the seller or reliance on the part of the buyer. In many instances buyers in practical effect would have an option to rescind, impairing the stability of past transactions where neither fraud nor detrimental reliance on misstatements or omissions occurred. We find no basis for interpreting the statute to reach so far.

III

* * *

The legislative history of the Act concerning the precise question presented supports our interpretation with much clarity and force. Congress contemplated that § 12[a](2) would apply only to public offerings by an issuer (or a controlling shareholder). The House Report stated: "The bill affects only new offerings of securities. . . . It does not affect the ordinary redistribution of securities unless such redistribution takes on the characteristics of a new offering." The observation extended to § 12[a](2) as well. Part II, § 6 of the House Report is entitled "Civil Liabilities." It begins: "Sections 11 and 12 create and define the civil liabilities imposed by the act. . . . Fundamentally, these sections entitle the buyer of securities sold upon a registration statement . . . to sue for recovery of his purchase price." It will be recalled that as to private transactions, such as the Alloyd purchase, there will never have been a registration statement. If § 12[a](2) liability were imposed here, it would cover transactions not within the contemplated reach of the statute. . . .

* * *

In sum, the word "prospectus" is a term of art referring to a document that describes a public offering of securities by an issuer or controlling shareholder. The contract of sale, and its recitations, were not held out to the public and were not a prospectus as the term is used in the 1933 Act.

* * *

■ GINSBURG, J. with whom BREYER joins, dissenting.

A seller's misrepresentation made "by means of a prospectus or oral communication" is actionable under § 12[a](2) of the Securities Act of 1933. To limit the scope of this civil liability provision, the Court maintains that a communication qualifies as a prospectus only if made during a public offering.[1] Communications during either secondary trading or a private placement are not "prospectuses," the Court declares, and thus are not covered by § 12[a](2). . . .

To construe a legislatively defined term, courts usually start with the defining section. Section 2[a](10) defines prospectus capaciously as "any prospectus, notice, circular, advertisement, letter, or communication, written or by radio or television, which offers any security for sale or confirms the sale of any security." The items listed in the defining provision, notably "letters" and "communications," are common in private and secondary sales, as well as in public offerings. The § 2[a](10) definition thus does not confine the § 12[a](2) term "prospectus" to public offerings.

The Court bypasses § 2[a](10), and the solid support it gives the Court of Appeals' disposition. Instead of beginning at the beginning, by first attending to the definition section, the Court starts with § 10, a

---

[1] I understand the Court's definition of a public offering to encompass both transactions that must be registered under § 5 and transactions that would have been registered had the securities involved not qualified for exemption under § 3.

substantive provision. The Court correctly observes that the term "prospectus" has a circumscribed meaning in that context. A prospectus within the contemplation of § 10 is a formal document, typically a document composing part of a registration statement; a § 10 prospectus, all agree, appears only in public offerings. The Court then proceeds backward; it reads into the literally and logically prior definition section, § 2[a](10), the meaning "prospectus" has in § 10.

To justify its backward reading—proceeding from § 10 to § 2[a](10) and not the other way round—the Court states that it "cannot accept the conclusion that [the operative word 'prospectus'] means one thing in one section of the Act and something quite different in another." Our decisions, however, constantly recognize that "a characterization fitting in certain contexts may be unsuitable in others." . . .

According "prospectus" discrete meanings in § 10 and § 12[a](2) is consistent with Congress' specific instruction in § 2 that definitions apply "unless the context otherwise requires". . . . As the Court of Appeals construed the Act, § 2[a](10)'s definition of "prospectus" governs § 12[a](2), which accommodates without strain the definition's broad reach; by contrast, the specific context of § 10 requires a correspondingly specific reading of "prospectus". . . .

QUESTIONS

1. After *Gustafson*, Alloyd Holdings cannot rely on § 12(a)(2) to recover for alleged fraud in the sales contract it signed with Gustafson. What other causes of action does Alloyd Holdings have available to it? How do these causes differ?

2. Recall that § 5(b)(1) of the Securities Act makes it unlawful for any person to use the instrumentalities of interstate commerce to "carry or transmit any prospectus relating to any security with respect to which a registration statement has been filed under this Act, unless such prospectus meets the requirements of Section 10." If the word "prospectus" has one consistent meaning in the Securities Act, what does § 5(b)(1) prohibit?

3. Suppose that InterTelly does a private placement under Rule 506 for the sale of $50 million of its common stock. During the selling effort, InterTelly's representatives tell potential investors orally that InterTelly expects its new ad campaign will "increase revenues by 50%." Assuming such oral representations are materially misleading, can investors in the private placement bring suit under § 12(a)(2)?

B. IMPLICATIONS OF *GUSTAFSON*

Gustafson confines § 12(a)(2) liability to public offerings. Questions remain, however, as to who may bring suit for fraud involved in the public offering. Information disclosed in the prospectus and registration statement, for example, affects not only those investors who purchase directly from the issuer and its underwriters but also other investors in the market.

Immediately after sales of securities in a public offering commence, secondary market trading will typically begin even before all of the offered shares have been distributed. Thus, primary transactions (sales by the issuer) and secondary transactions (sales by investors) will often occur simultaneously following the start of a public offering. When one investor sells shares to another in an unsolicited broker's transaction, we have seen that §§ 4(a)(1) and 4(a)(4) of the Securities Act exempt the transaction from the prospectus delivery requirement. Nonetheless, the disclosures made in the prospectus are likely to influence the price in secondary market trading. Should investors who purchase in secondary market transactions at the time of a public offering have the ability to bring a § 12(a)(2) lawsuit for fraud in the public offering prospectus? And how does *Gustafson's* interpretation of § 12(a)(2) interact with § 11's standing requirement?

Feiner v. SS & C Technologies, Inc.

47 F.Supp. 2d 250 (D. Conn. 1999).

■ HALL, J., DISTRICT JUDGE.

This securities action arises out of an initial public offering of shares in SS & C Technologies, Inc. that was underwritten by Alex. Brown & Sons Inc. and Hambrecht & Quist LLC. The lead plaintiffs, all of whom purchased shares of SS & C during the period from May 31, 1996 through August 1, 1996, have moved . . . for an order certifying this suit as a class action. Defendants . . . argue . . . that plaintiffs' proposed class is impermissibly broad because it includes people who, having purchased shares in the aftermarket rather than in the IPO, lack standing to sue under Sections 11 and 12(a)(2) of the Securities Act of 1933. . . .

I. DISCUSSION

Defendants' contention that the class should be limited to people who purchased shares during their initial distribution is without merit. . . . [S]hareholders need not have purchased their securities directly from an issuer or statutory seller to assert a cause of action under § 11. Instead, "any purchaser has standing to sue under section 11 so long as the securities purchased can be traced back to the offering containing the allegedly defective registration statement."[2] Therefore, the fact that the proposed class in this case contains people who made aftermarket purchases of shares traceable to the registration statement,[3] as well as those who acquired their shares during the initial distribution, does not make the class overly broad. . . .

Defendants' "initial distribution" argument fails with regard to plaintiffs' § 12(a)(2) claim as well. Section 12(a)(2) does not require that shareholders purchase their securities during the initial distribution of shares, but only that plaintiffs "purchase their shares directly from a seller who makes use of a false or misleading prospectus." The statute

---

[2] Defendants' argument in the alternative that § 11 standing extends to only those plaintiffs who purchased their shares within 25 days of the IPO is similarly unavailing. Under the plain meaning of § 11 . . . plaintiff who can trace his or her purchase to an allegedly defective registration statement has standing to sue under § 11. Whether or not the purchase occurred within 25 days of the IPO is irrelevant.

[3] Because this case involves an IPO, all shares purchased in the class period are traceable to the registration statement. Therefore, the tracing requirement is necessarily satisfied for all proposed class members who made aftermarket purchases.

draws no express distinction between shares purchased in the initial distribution and shares purchased in the aftermarket. Instead, the statute requires only that a plaintiff have purchased a security, from a seller, pursuant to a misleading prospectus.

The Supreme Court's statement in *Gustafson v. Alloyd* that "§ 12(a)(2) liability [is] limited to public offerings" is not to the contrary. In *Gustafson*, the Court was drawing a distinction between public offerings and private ones, not between public offerings and aftermarket purchases. The central question in *Gustafson* was whether a purchase agreement used in connection with a private placement of securities could be considered a "prospectus" within the meaning of § 12(a)(2). The Court answered that question in the negative, holding that the term "prospectus" is "confined to documents related to public offerings by an issuer or its controlling shareholders." Therefore, the Court's statement that "§ 12(a)(2) liability [is] limited to public offerings" cannot be read to exclude aftermarket trading. By using the term "public offerings," the Court was simply distinguishing offerings in which the filing of a prospectus is required under the securities laws, i.e., public offerings, from those in which no prospectus need be filed, i.e., private placements. The Court did not go further and address the question presented here, namely whether, within the context of a public offering, § 12(a)(2) liability attaches to only the initial distribution of securities or to certain aftermarket trading as well.

This court now holds that § 12(a)(2) extends to aftermarket trading of a publicly offered security, so long as that aftermarket trading occurs "by means of a prospectus or oral communication." This is not to say that a prospectus need in fact have been delivered for a purchaser to have a § 12(a)(2) claim. Rather, all that is necessary is that delivery of a prospectus have been required under the statutory and regulatory framework. Under this framework, delivery of a prospectus is required for a fixed number of days after the registration statement becomes effective, even if the initial distribution of shares has already been completed. To limit § 12(a)(2) liability to the initial distribution would eviscerate this requirement. Under such a reading of § 12(a)(2), the statutory and regulatory framework would require that a prospectus be delivered for a certain number of days after the beginning of an offering, but would not require that the statements in that prospectus be truthful and non-deceptive. Moreover, the express language of § 12(a)(2) limits misrepresentations in connection with the sale of a security "by means of a prospectus," not "in a public offering." The court therefore rejects defendants' argument that § 12(a)(2) liability is limited to shares purchased in an initial distribution. Instead, the court holds that § 12(a)(2) liability is coextensive with the statutory and regulatory prospectus-delivery requirements.

In this case [Securities Act Rule 174(d)] required that a prospectus be delivered for all transactions in SS & C common stock by Hambrecht & Quist or Alex. Brown within 25 days of the offering date. . Any sale by an underwriter requires the delivery of a prospectus until such time as the initial distribution of shares is complete. In this case, it is undisputed that the initial distribution was complete on May 31, 1996, the first day of the IPO. Therefore, to the extent that Hambrecht & Quist or Alex. Brown made sales after this date, they did so not in their capacity as underwriters, but in their capacity as ordinary "dealers.". . . . Because the security's registration statement became effective on May 31, 1996, Hambrecht & Quist and Alex. Brown were required to deliver the prospectus any time that they sold the security up until the end of the day on June 25, 1996.

Not all members of the proposed class who purchased SS & C stock within the 25-day period have standing to bring a claim against Hambrecht & Quist or Alex. Brown under § 12(a)(2), however. Section 12(a)(2) further requires that plaintiffs "purchase their shares directly from a seller who makes use of a false or misleading prospectus." The term "seller" encompasses not only anyone who stands in privity with a purchaser, but also anyone "who successfully solicits the purchase [of a security], motivated at least in part by a desire to serve his own financial interests or those of the securities owner." In order to fall within this second category of seller, a defendant must have "actually solicited" the purchase by the plaintiffs. Therefore, a defendant's mere status as an underwriter is not sufficient to make it a seller to all purchasers for purposes of § 12(a)(2).

In this case, only certain members of the proposed class have standing to bring a § 12(a)(2) claim against Hambrecht & Quist or Alex. Brown. . . . [T]his was a "firm commitment" underwriting, i.e., one in which SS & C sold all of the shares that were issued in the IPO to the underwriters, who, in turn, sold all of the shares directly to the investing public. Because Hambrecht & Quist and Alex. Brown owned all of the shares, any sale made by either of them in the initial distribution would pass title directly to the purchaser. Therefore, any purchaser in the initial distribution stands in privity with either Hambrecht & Quist or Alex. Brown and has a § 12(a)(2) claim against them on that basis. Similarly, if either Hambrecht & Quist or Alex. Brown reacquired shares in aftermarket trading and then resold them on the aftermarket within the 25-day period, any purchaser of the resold shares would also have standing to bring a 12(a)(2) claim. In addition, to the extent that Hambrecht & Quist and Alex. Brown acted as dealers for third parties in aftermarket trading, plaintiffs who purchased from them in that capacity on or before June 25, 1996 have § 12(a)(2) standing.

Purchasers who did not acquire their shares directly from either Hambrecht & Quist or Alex. Brown, however, lack § 12(a)(2) standing. Such purchasers did not acquire their shares "directly from a seller who makes use of a false or misleading prospectus." Any argument by plaintiffs that standing to sue belongs to everyone who purchased SS & C shares within the class period is thus without merit. . . .

* * *

NOTES

1. *Aftermarket trading.* As seen in *Feiner*, courts are unwilling to extend § 12(a)(2) liability to those who purchase in secondary market transactions that do not require prospectus delivery. Some courts have been even more restrictive in interpreting the scope of § 12(a)(2) post-*Gustafson. See In re Levi Strauss & Co. Sec. Lit.*, 527 F.Supp.2d 965, 983 (N.D.Cal.2007) ("[T]he majority of the cases appear to hold that, based on *Gustafson*, § 12 is

limited to transactions purchased pursuant to a public offering and, therefore, does not extend to *any* after market transactions."). Section 11 claims, however, have been largely unaffected by *Gustafson. See Joseph v. Wiles*, 223 F.3d 1155 (10th Cir. 2000) (rejecting the argument that § 11 affords a remedy only to purchasers in the initial offering).

C. ELEMENTS OF THE CAUSE OF ACTION

Section 12(a)(2) requires plaintiffs to prove a material misstatement or omission contained in a prospectus or related oral communication, and the use of an instrumentality of interstate commerce, but not much else. Compared with Rule 10b–5, § 12(a)(2) offers a much more generous cause of action for plaintiffs. Under § 12(a)(2), plaintiffs do not need to show reliance or scienter. Although § 12(a)(2) does not explicitly mention causation, courts have treated the "by means of" phrase as requiring some showing of a causal connection between the prospectus and the purchaser's decision to buy the issuer's securities. That causation can be quite attenuated—the focus is not on individual investors, but instead on the market as a whole. *See, e.g., Sanders v. John Nuveen & Co.*, 619 F.2d 1222 (7th Cir. 1980) ("A prospectus that reports on the issuer's financial condition affects [the offering] price.")

Perhaps *Gustafson* can be better understood in light of the relative ease with which plaintiffs may pursue a § 12(a)(2) claim. The *Gustafson* Court itself mentioned a concern that every "casual communication" in the secondary market might fall under § 12(a)(2) liability if the definition of prospectus were not limited. By constraining what is a prospectus to documents used in a public offering (or, perhaps, to § 10 prospectuses), *Gustafson* limits the scope of § 12(a)(2). Arguably, limiting antifraud liability encourages persons to talk more freely.

HYPOTHETICAL NINE

Assume that two years after its IPO InterTelly, with the assistance of Sesame Securities, does a seasoned public offering for an additional 1 million shares of common stock at $30 per share. InterTelly makes a number of misleading and material misstatements in the management discussion and analysis section of the prospectus and registration statement. Consider the following purchasers of InterTelly's stock:

1. *Scenario One:* Bird buys directly from the seasoned public offering after reading the final prospectus. Can she bring a § 11 antifraud lawsuit against the issuer and its underwriters? Can she bring a § 12(a)(2) lawsuit?

2. *Scenario Two:* Ernie buys directly from the seasoned public offering and he receives a copy of the final prospectus with his confirmation of sale, but he does not read it. Can he bring a § 11 antifraud lawsuit against the issuer and its underwriters? Can he bring a § 12(a)(2) lawsuit?

3. *Scenario Three:* After the offering, Rosita buys shares of InterTelly two months after reading a copy of the prospectus she obtained from her friend, Ernie. Assume that Rosita purchases directly from Bird. Bird had earlier purchased her shares solely from the seasoned public offering. Can Rosita bring a § 11 antifraud lawsuit against the InterTelly and Sesame

Securities? Can she bring a § 12(a)(2) lawsuit? Can she bring a Rule 10b–5 lawsuit?

D. DEFENSES

As with §§ 11 and 12(a)(1), § 13's one-three year statute of limitations applies. Unlike § 12(a)(1), however, defendants in a § 12(a)(2) action may assert additional defenses. To avoid liability, defendants may attempt to demonstrate that the plaintiffs in fact knew about the untruth or omission in the prospectus. Defendants may also escape liability if they meet their burden of proof by showing that they "did not know, and in the exercise of reasonable care could not have known, of such untruth or omission."

Antifraud lawsuits related to a public offering often assert claims under both §§ 11 and 12(a)(2) because most misstatements in the registration statement will carry over to the prospectus (which is filed as part of the registration statement). A question that often arises during such suits is whether the "reasonable care" requirement is equivalent to the care required by § 11's due diligence defense. Recall that § 11 has two levels of due diligence requirement depending on whether the untruth or omission is in an expertised or non-expertised portion of the registration statement. If § 12(a)(2) tracks § 11's care requirement, which version of the due diligence test—the expertised or non-expertised form—does it follow?

> Section 12(a)(2) has a defense of reasonable care that is less demanding than the duty of due diligence imposed under Section 11. Section 12(a)(2) provides that a defendant shall not be liable if he "sustain[s] the burden of proof that he did not know, and in the exercise of reasonable care could not have known, of such untruth or omission" which is "necessary in order to make the statements, in the light of the circumstances under which they were made, not misleading."
>
> Thus, while Section 11 imposes a duty to conduct a reasonable investigation as to any portion of a registration statement not made on the authority of an expert, Section 12(a)(2) does not make any distinction based upon "expertised" statements and only requires the defendant to show that it used reasonable care. This difference is attributable to the emphasis placed on the importance of registration statements and the underwriter's vital role in assuring their accuracy. *See John Nuveen & Co. v. Sanders*, 450 U.S. 1005, 1009 (Powell, J., dissenting from denial of cert.). Because Section 11 imposes a more exacting standard, this Opinion principally addresses the law that applies to Section 11.

In re WorldCom, Inc. Securities Litigation, 346 F. Supp. 2d 628, 663–664 (S.D.N.Y. 2004).

QUESTIONS

1. How does the § 12(a)(2) defense apply to "expertised" portions of the prospectus?

2. Is there any reason to impose different standards of care under §§ 11 and 12(a)(2)?

E. DAMAGES AND LOSS CAUSATION

Section 12(a)(2) provides the same remedies as those available under § 12(a)(1): rescission, if the plaintiff still holds the security, or damages, if the plaintiff has sold the security. Rescissory damages, if the security has been sold, are measured by the difference between the plaintiff's purchase price and her sales price (adjusting downwards for any dividends or other income due to the security and upwards for interest to compensate for the time value of money).

In § 12(a)(2) suits, defendants may also attempt to show an absence of loss causation under § 12(b), providing evidence that the drop in the issuer's stock price is due to factors unrelated to the fraud. The case below assesses that defense.

Miller v. Thane International, Inc.

615 F.3d 1095 (9th Cir. 2010).

■ O'SCANNLAIN, D., CIRCUIT JUDGE:

We must decide whether a material misrepresentation in a prospectus caused actionable loss to shareholders when the price of the company's stock did not decline in the weeks immediately following disclosure of the correct information.

* * *

Section 12 liability may be avoided by way of an affirmative defense of lack of loss causation. The statute provides that if a person "proves that any portion or all of the amount recoverable under subsection (a)(2) of this section represents other than the depreciation in value of the subject security resulting from such part of the prospectus or oral communication . . . not being true or omitting to state a material fact . . . then such portion or amount . . . shall not be recoverable." Consequently, "[a] Section 12 defendant is liable only for depreciation that results directly from the misrepresentation at issue."

With the relevant statutory framework in mind, we turn now to the facts of this case. In November 2001, defendant Thane International, Inc. a company that markets consumer products through homeshopping channels, infomercials, and other similar means, and Reliant Interactive Media Corp. agreed to merge. The merger agreement provided for Reliant shareholders to receive shares of Thane for their shares of Reliant. The "imputed merger price"—the value of Reliant stock each Reliant shareholder exchanged for each Thane share—was approximately $7.00. Significantly, the prospectus Thane filed with the Securities and Exchange Commission stated that Thane stock, which had not been publicly traded previously, was "approved for quotation and trading on the NASDAQ National Market upon completion of the merger, subject to Thane's compliance with the minimum bid price requirements of $5.00 per share." Nevertheless, after the merger was consummated on May 24, 2002, Thane shares commenced trading not on the NASDAQ National Market System, but on the NASDAQ Over-the-Counter Bulletin Board.

In the nineteen days (twelve trading days) between May 24 and June 11, 2002, Thane's shares traded between $8.50 and $7.00, above the merger price that Reliant shareholders had paid. On June 24, 2002, however, the stock closed at $6.00. The next day Thane reported disappointing earnings for the fiscal year, and the stock closed at $5.25. It soon thereafter dropped below $5.00, never to rise again above that minimum price for listing on the NMS.

On August 14, 2002, Thane announced further disappointing quarterly earnings, partly caused by a slump in the industry. It also reported that it had originally delayed listing on the NMS in order to time it with a secondary public offering, but that recent business developments had put listing on the NMS on hold. Thane shares tumbled to $1.95 by August 16, 2002. In February 2004, Thane bought out existing shareholders at a price of $0.35 per share.

In September 2002, a class of individual Reliant investors who acquired shares of Thane in the merger filed suit against Thane . . . the investors alleged that Thane's pre-merger prospectus contained materially misleading representations because it implied that Thane shares would list on the NMS.

* * *

[T]he investors advance two arguments that the district court erred as a matter of law in finding an absence of loss causation.

The investors first argue that the district court's award of judgment to Thane on loss causation is foreclosed [by] our [prior] holding in the investors' favor on materiality. . . .

But loss causation and materiality are different concepts in the statutory scheme. Indeed, the statute provides a loss causation defense even when there are materially misleading representations. If a ruling on materiality foreclosed an affirmative defense of loss causation, that affirmative defense would be . . . "a nullity."

Moreover, the materiality inquiry concerns whether a "reasonable investor" *would* consider a particular misstatement important. By contrast, the loss causation inquiry assesses whether a particular misstatement *actually* resulted in loss. It is historical and context-dependent. . . .

* * *

The investors also contend that the district court improperly found that Thane's stock price impounded the failure to list on the NMS before it fell below the merger price.

* * *

Turning to the merits, the question is whether the district court clearly erred in holding that Thane established the absence of loss causation. Because the stock price movements are undisputed, we focus on whether the district court clearly erred in finding that the Thane stock price could impound the fact of listing on the OTCBB instead of the NMS in the nineteen-day period before the price dropped below the merger price the investors paid for the stock.

The record contains substantial evidence supporting the district court's finding. Thane's expert stated that Thane's stock price could and did impound information about Thane during this nineteen-day period, including the listing on the OTCBB, which was disseminated on Internet bulletin board postings even though no analysts covered Thane.... The investors also argue that the fact that the stock traded on low volume, a mere 55,300 shares, in the nineteen days before it dropped below the merger price undermines the expert's conclusion. Low volume, however, does not necessarily indicate an unreliable market price. Rather, it could indicate that the market price is in equilibrium because neither buyers nor sellers believe they can profit by acting. In fact, the investors' own account supports this version of events: they stated that they decided to hold on to their shares for investment reasons, not because low volume prevented them from selling their shares.

In any event, even the investors' expert admitted that Thane's stock price could absorb information. We recognized as much in [our prior ruling] when we said that Thane's stock price slump in August "was compounded by the company's failure to find and market the 'hit' product it had hoped to find." Moreover, the stock price "tumbled" approximately forty-six percent in response to the August 2002 earnings report, which paralleled the identical percentage drop in earnings compared to the same quarter in the prior year, and the difference between listing on the OTCBB instead of the NMS is simpler to decode than an earnings report, as even one of the investors admitted.

The investors argue that this August 2002 earnings report disclosed additional information about the misleading representation and management's integrity, namely that management "intentionally" did not list on the NMS. Although the investors do not spell out their position, they appear to argue that focusing on the changes in price in the first nineteen days is inappropriate because some of the truth regarding the misleading representation was not publicly available until the August 2002 earnings report.

The August 2002 earnings report, however, reiterated information that was obvious immediately after the merger, namely, that Thane was not going to be listed on the NMS because of market conditions. Even the investors' expert testified that the market was aware of Thane's nonlisting at the outset of the merger, long before the August 2002 earnings report, and it was obvious that Thane could not list on the NMS in August because its stock price was below the $5 minimum. Moreover, the August 2002 earnings report is not, as investors argue, a "mea culpa" that undermined management's integrity for the first time. That integrity was undermined, if at all, by the failure to list on the NMS. The earnings report did not provide evidence that such failure, involving a decision not to list even though Thane's stock was approved to do so, was any more "intentional" than it had been in the days immediately subsequent to the merger.

It is true that listing on the NMS is superior to listing on the OTCBB, ... but that is irrelevant. The question at issue here is whether listing on the OTCBB instead of the NMS actually caused the investors' losses. The investors ask us to reason from hypothetical and expected consequences. But predictions are not proof of what actually happened. The investors' own expert testified that listing on the OTCBB instead of the NMS would not necessarily reduce Thane's stock price.

* * *

QUESTIONS

1. How can a misstatement be material and yet not suffice to show loss causation? Is this consistent with the efficient capital market hypothesis?

2. Who bears the burden of proof on loss causation in a § 12(a)(2) case? How did that party meet that burden in *Miller*?

HYPOTHETICAL TEN

InterTelly's seasoned public offering for 1 million shares at $30 per share took place on January 1. InterTelly makes a number of material misstatements about its future earnings expectations in the management discussion and analysis section of the prospectus.

Rumors started circulating soon after the offering about a potential earnings shortfall at InterTelly. However, InterTelly waited until February 1 to release lower earnings projections. On the same date, *Telecom World* magazine released a story on the rapidly shrinking market for Internet phone gear (InterTelly's primary source of revenue). Also on February 1, the Federal Reserve Chairman testified before Congress that the economy was doing better than expected. On February 5, several prominent plaintiffs' attorneys filed class action lawsuits under §§ 11 and 12(a)(2) against InterTelly.

Assume that InterTelly's shares, although listed on Nasdaq, have a relatively low trading volume. In addition, only one analyst (from Sesame Securities) covers InterTelly. InterTelly's share price displays this pattern:

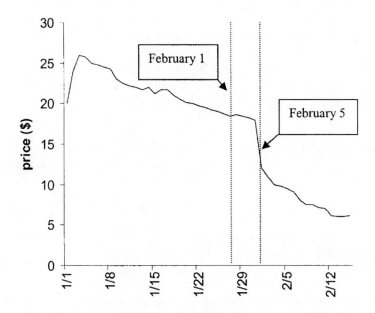

If you are the plaintiff, what arguments do you make regarding loss causation? If you are the defendant what can you argue about loss causation? What additional information would you like to know?

CHAPTER 9

EXEMPT OFFERINGS

Rules and Statutes

—*Sections 3(a)(11), 3(b), 4(a)(2) , 4(a)(6), 4A of the Securities Act*

—*Sections 3(a)(80) of the Exchange Act*

—*Rules 135c, 147, 152, 155 of the Securities Act*

—*Regulation A, Rules 251–263*

—*Regulation S, Rules 901–905*

—*Regulation D, Rules 500–508*

MOTIVATING HYPOTHETICAL

Trendy, Inc. is a manufacturer of trendy fruit juice drinks. Trendy's most popular product is a low calorie lime-flavored drink known as Lean Green. Lean Green has enjoyed wild success in Trendy's home region of the Pacific Northwest. Trendy hopes to expand the campaign for Lean Green into several cities outside the Pacific Northwest. Such a campaign, however, is costly, involving both advertising and expanding Trendy's distribution network. Privately held, Trendy does not have the cash on hand to finance the expansion. Kim, the CEO of Trendy, does not feel the time is right for a large-scale public offering. Nor does she want to obtain the required funds (upwards of $10 million) by borrowing from a bank.

I. INTRODUCTION

Companies have a variety of choices to raise capital, but each comes with constraints. Bank loans typically require steady payments of interest. In addition, many banks will impose operating restrictions on the company such as maximum debt-equity ratios and covenants against certain forms of investments by the company. At the other extreme, companies may go directly to the public and offer securities broadly. As we saw in Chapters 7 and 8, public offerings face stringent and costly regulation under the Securities Act. Issuers engaged in a public offering face mandatory disclosure (the registration statement and statutory prospectus), the gun-jumping rules of § 5, and heightened antifraud liability under §§ 11 and 12(a)(2) of the Securities Act.

Notwithstanding these requirements, the public offering process is not "one size fits all." Smaller reporting companies get some streamlining of disclosure obligations on Form S–K. Foreign issuers face less disclosure burden when filing Forms F–1 or F–3. Nonetheless, the gun-jumping rules and antifraud liability provisions of the public offering process remain for these issuers along with their corresponding costs and delays. Although Form S–3 issuers get some relief from the burden of the gun-jumping rules through shelf registration, shelf offerings still face stringent antifraud liability.

Should issuers be allowed to sell securities to investors with less regulation? The rigorous protection afforded to investors in the public registration process results in some issuers simply choosing not to sell securities to investors, instead turning to alternative forms of financing or eschewing an otherwise profitable business venture. Public investors then lose the opportunity to invest in such companies.

Moreover, not all investors require the same level of protection. Investors may benefit from mandatory disclosures if the investors are unable or unwilling to negotiate for disclosure on their own. If many investors stand in a similar position, collective action problems may undermine efforts to obtain information. Similarly, the gun-jumping rules benefit less sophisticated investors the most, as they are presumably more vulnerable to over-optimism and other biases that may lead them to focus on company advertising materials at the expense of hard financial facts. Sophisticated institutional investors purchasing securities through negotiated transactions with issuers require less protection; they can demand information from the issuer and have the expertise to evaluate that information.

The securities laws recognize the high costs of public offerings and that the benefits may vary depending on the issuer's and investors' situations. Issuers selling securities are afforded a number of exemptions from § 5. In this chapter we discuss exempt offerings under the following provisions of the Securities Act:

- Section 4(a)(2)
- Regulation D
- Section 3(b)(2) and Regulation A
- Section 4(a)(6)
- Section 3(a)(11) and Rule 147
- Regulation S

As we go through each type of exempt offering, assess the balance taken between securities regulation's cost and investor protection. Given the array of exemptions, also consider whether any type of offering dominates from the issuer's perspective. Or do the exempt offerings vary in costs and benefits depending on the situation? Also consider whether the presence of so many exempt offerings undermines the public offering process. Why would an issuer choose to undergo the public offering process if it can raise capital less expensively through one of the exempt offerings?

II.   SECTION 4(a)(2) OFFERINGS

Section 4(a)(2) of the Securities Act exempts "transactions by an issuer not involving any public offering" from § 5. Although the term "issuer" is relatively straightforward (defined under § 2(a)(4) of the Securities Act) and the effect of receiving an exemption from § 5 is also clear (i.e., the issuer does not have to follow the gun-jumping or prospectus delivery rules), the term "public offering" is less clear. How narrowly targeted must an offering be to be "non-public"?

The Supreme Court and the SEC have generally eschewed a plain meaning approach to defining "public" under § 4(a)(2). Instead, the definition has turned on the more fundamental question of the purposes of the securities laws and whether the costs of registering an offering are outweighed by its benefits. The question of what constitutes a "public" offering therefore involves many of the same issues with which we wrestled earlier in defining "security."

In 1935, the SEC's General Counsel issued an opinion enumerating factors relating to whether an offering is "public." Those factors include:

- the number of offerees
- the relationship of the offerees to each other and to the issuer
- the number of units offered
- the size of the offering
- the manner of the offering

Securities Act Release No. 285 (Jan. 24, 1935). Is the SEC's General Counsel's test consistent with the standards set forth in the following Supreme Court opinion?

SEC v. Ralston Purina Co.
346 U.S. 119 (1953).

■ CLARK, J.

Section [4(a)(2)] of the Securities Act of 1933 exempts "transactions by an issuer not involving any public offering" from the registration requirements of § 5. We must decide whether Ralston Purina's offerings of treasury stock to its "key employees" are within this exemption. . . .

Ralston Purina manufactures and distributes various feed and cereal products. Its processing and distribution facilities are scattered throughout the United States and Canada, staffed by some 7,000 employees. At least since 1911 the company has had a policy of encouraging stock ownership among its employees; more particularly, since 1942 it has made authorized but unissued common shares available to some of them. Between 1947 and 1951, the period covered by the record in this case, Ralston Purina sold nearly $2,000,000 of stock to employees without registration and in so doing made use of the mails.

In each of these years, a corporate resolution authorized the sale of common stock "to employees * * * who shall, without any solicitation by the Company or its officers or employees, inquire of any of them as to how to purchase common stock of Ralston Purina Company." A memorandum sent to branch and store managers after the resolution was adopted, advised that "The only employees to whom this stock will be available will be those who take the initiative and are interested in buying stock at present market prices." Among those responding to these offers were employees with the duties of artist, bakeshop foreman, chow loading foreman, clerical assistant, copywriter, electrician, stock clerk, mill office clerk, order credit trainee, production trainee, stenographer, and veterinarian. . . . No records were kept of those to whom the offers were made; the estimated number in 1951 was 500.

The company bottoms its exemption claim on the classification of all offerees as "key employees" in its organization. Its position on trial was that "A key employee * * * is not confined to an organization chart. It would include an individual who is eligible for promotion, an individual who especially influences others or who advises others, a person whom the employees look to in some special way, an individual, of course, who carries some special responsibility, who is sympathetic to management and who is ambitious and who the management feels is likely to be promoted to a greater responsibility." That an offering to all of its employees would be public is conceded.

The Securities Act nowhere defines the scope of [§ 4(a)(2)'s] private offering exemption. Nor is the legislative history of much help in staking out its boundaries. . . .

Decisions under comparable exemptions in the English Companies Acts and state "blue sky" laws, the statutory antecedents of federal securities legislation have made one thing clear—to be public, an offer need not be open to the whole world. . . .

Exemption from the registration requirements of the Securities Act is the question. The design of the statute is to protect investors by promoting full disclosure of information thought necessary to informed investment decisions. The natural way to interpret the private offering exemption is in light of the statutory purpose. Since exempt transactions are those as to which "there is no practical need for * * * (the bill's) application," the applicability of § [4(a)(2)] should turn on whether the particular class of persons affected need the protection of the Act. An offering to those who are shown to be able to fend for themselves is a transaction "not involving any public offering."

The Commission would have us go one step further and hold that "an offering to a substantial number of the public" is not exempt under § [4(a)(2)]. We are advised that "whatever the special circumstances, the Commission has consistently interpreted the exemption as being inapplicable when a large number of offerees is involved." But the statute would seem to apply to a "public offering" whether to few or many. It may well be that offerings to a substantial number of persons would rarely be exempt. Indeed nothing prevents the commission, in enforcing the statute, from using some kind of numerical test in deciding when to investigate particular exemption claims. But there is no warrant for superimposing a quantity limit on private offerings as a matter of statutory interpretation.

The exemption, as we construe it, does not deprive corporate employees, as a class, of the safeguards of the Act. We agree that some employee offerings may come within § [4(a)(2)], e.g., one made to executive personnel who because of their position have access to the same kind of information that the act would make available in the form of a registration statement. Absent such a showing of special circumstances, employees are just as much members of the investing "public" as any of their neighbors in the community. . . .

Keeping in mind the broadly remedial purposes of federal securities legislation, imposition of the burden of proof on an issuer who would plead the exemption seems to us fair and reasonable. . . . [O]nce it is seen that the exemption question turns on the knowledge of the offerees, the issuer's motives, laudable though they may be, fade into irrelevance. The focus of inquiry should be on the need of the offerees for the protections afforded by registration. The employees here were not shown to have access to the kind of information which registration would disclose. The obvious opportunities for pressure and imposition make it advisable that they be entitled to compliance with § 5.

Reversed.

Questions

1. Why did Ralston Purina concede that a general offering of its stock to all its employees would be public?

2. Why would Ralston Purina want to sell stock to its own employees? Why did it define its "key employees" as it did?

3. Under the Court's interpretation, can we say definitively that an offering to ten is private? Or that an offering to 1,000 is public?

4. What types of investors can "fend for themselves"?

5. Who bears the burden of proof to show whether an exemption from § 5 applies?

Doran v. Petroleum Management Corp.

545 F.2d 893 (5th Cir. 1977).

■ GOLDBERG, I., CIRCUIT JUDGE.

In this case a sophisticated investor who purchased a limited partnership interest in an oil drilling venture seeks to rescind. The question raised is whether the sale was part of a private offering exempted by § 4[(a)](2) of the Securities Act of 1933 from the registration requirements of that Act. We hold that in the absence of findings of fact that each offeree had been furnished information about the issuer that a registration statement would have disclosed or that each offeree had effective access to such information, the district court erred in concluding that the offering was a private placement. Accordingly, we reverse and remand.

I.   Facts

Prior to July 1970, Petroleum Management Corporation (PMC) organized a California limited partnership for the purpose of drilling and operating four wells in Wyoming. . . .

As found by the district court, PMC contacted only four other persons with respect to possible participation in the partnership. All but the plaintiff declined.

During the late summer of 1970, plaintiff William H. Doran, Jr., received a telephone call from a California securities broker previously known to him. The broker, Phillip Kendrick, advised Doran of the opportunity to become a "special participant" in the partnership. PMC then sent Doran the drilling logs and technical maps of the proposed drilling area. PMC informed Doran that two of the proposed four wells had already been completed. Doran agreed to become a "special participant" in the Wyoming drilling program. In consideration for his partnership share, Doran agreed to contribute $125,000 toward the partnership. . . .

[The Wyoming Oil and Gas Conservation Commission ordered PMC's wells sealed for almost year as punishment for PMC's deliberate overproduction of oil in violation of the Commission's production allowances. Even after the wells were re-opened, they produced less income. As a result, Doran obtained less from his investment than expected, leading him to default on a note taken out to finance his purchase of special participant interests in PMC.]

* * *

II. The Private Offering Exemption

No registration statement was filed with any federal or state regulatory body in connection with the defendants' offering of securities. Along with two other factors that we may take as established that the defendants sold or offered to sell these securities, and that the defendants used interstate transportation or communication in connection with the sale or offer of sale the plaintiff thus states a prima facie case for a violation of the federal securities laws.

The defendants do not contest the existence of the elements of plaintiff's prima facie case but raise an affirmative defense that the relevant transactions came within the exemption from registration found in § 4[(a)](2). Specifically, they contend that the offering of securities was not a public offering. The defendants, who of course bear the burden of proving this affirmative defense, must therefore show that the offering was private.

This court has in the past identified four factors relevant to whether an offering qualifies for the exemption. The consideration of these factors, along with the policies embodied in the 1933 Act, structure the inquiry. The relevant factors include the number of offerees and their relationship to each other and the issuer, the number of units offered, the size of the offering, and the manner of the offering. Consideration of these factors need not exhaust the inquiry, nor is one factor's weighing heavily in favor of the private status of the offering sufficient to ensure the availability of the exemption. Rather, these factors serve as guideposts to the court in attempting to determine whether subjecting the offering to registration requirements would further the purposes of the 1933 Act.

The term "private offering" is not defined in the Securities Act of 1933. The scope of the § 4[(a)](2) private offering exemption must therefore be determined by reference to the legislative purposes of the Act. In *SEC v. Ralston Purina Co.*, the SEC had sought to enjoin a corporation's offer of unregistered stock to its employees, and the Court grappled with the corporation's defense that the offering came within the private placement exemption. The Court began by looking to the statutory purpose:

> Since exempt transactions are those as to which "there is no practical need for . . . (the bill's) application," the applicability of (§4[(a)](2)) should turn on whether the particular class of persons affected need the protection of the Act. An offering to

those who are shown to be able to fend for themselves is a transaction "not involving any public offering."

According to the Court, the purpose of the Act was "to protect investors by promoting full disclosure of information thought necessary to informed investment decisions." It therefore followed that "the exemption question turns on the knowledge of the offerees." That formulation remains the touchstone of the inquiry into the scope of the private offering exemption. It is most nearly reflected in the first of the four factors: the number of offerees and their relationship to each other and to the issuer.

In the case at bar, the defendants may have demonstrated the presence of the latter three factors. A small number of units offered, relatively modest financial stakes, and an offering characterized by personal contact between the issuer and offerees free of public advertising or intermediaries such as investment bankers or securities exchanges these aspects of the instant transaction aid the defendants' search for a § 4[(a)](2) exemption.

Nevertheless, with respect to the first, most critical, and conceptually most problematic factor, the record does not permit us to agree that the defendants have proved that they are entitled to the limited sanctuary afforded by § 4[(a)](2). We must examine more closely the importance of demonstrating both the number of offerees and their relationship to the issuer in order to see why the defendants have not yet gained the § 4[(a)](2)exemption.

A.   The Number of Offerees

Establishing the number of persons involved in an offering is important both in order to ascertain the magnitude of the offering and in order to determine the characteristics and knowledge of the persons thus identified.

The number of offerees, not the number of purchasers, is the relevant figure in considering the number of persons involved in an offering. A private placement claimant's failure to adduce any evidence regarding the number of offerees will be fatal to the claim. The number of offerees is not itself a decisive factor in determining the availability of the private offering exemption. Just as an offering to few may be public, so an offering to many may be private. . . . In the case at bar, the record indicates that eight investors were offered limited partnership shares in the drilling program a total that would be entirely consistent with a finding that the offering was private.

* * *

[I]n considering the need of the offerees for the protection that registration would have afforded we must look beyond Doran's interests to those of all his fellow offerees. Even the offeree-plaintiff's 20–20 vision with respect to the facts underlying the security would not save the exemption if any one of his fellow offerees was in a blind.

B.   The Offerees' Relationship to the Issuer

Since *SEC v. Ralston*, courts have sought to determine the need of offerees for the protections afforded by registration by focusing on the relationship between offerees and issuer and more particularly on the information available to the offerees by virtue of that relationship. Once the offerees have been identified, it is possible to investigate their relationship to the issuer.

1. The role of investment sophistication

The lower court's finding that Doran was a sophisticated investor is amply supported by the record, as is the sophistication of the other offerees. Doran holds a petroleum engineering degree from Texas A & M University. His net worth is in excess of $1,000,000. His holdings of approximately twenty-six oil and gas properties are valued at $850,000.

Nevertheless, evidence of a high degree of business or legal sophistication on the part of all offerees does not suffice to bring the offering within the private placement exemption . . . "if the plaintiffs did not possess the information requisite for a registration statement, they could not bring their sophisticated knowledge of business affairs to bear in deciding whether or not to invest. . . ." Sophistication is not a substitute for access to the information that registration would disclose . . . although the evidence of the offerees' expertise "is certainly favorable to the defendants, the level of sophistication will not carry the point. In this context, the relationship between the promoters and the purchasers and the 'access to the kind of information which registration would disclose' become highly relevant factors."[10]

In short, there must be sufficient basis of accurate information upon which the sophisticated investor may exercise his skills. Just as a scientist cannot be without his specimens, so the shrewdest investor's acuity will be blunted without specifications about the issuer. For an investor to be invested with exemptive status he must have the required data for judgment.

2. The requirement of available information

The interplay between two factors, the relationship between offerees and issuer and the offerees' access to information that registration would disclose, has been a matter of some conceptual and terminological difficulty. For purposes of this discussion, we shall adopt the following conventions: We shall refer to offerees who have not been furnished registration information directly, but who are in a position relative to the issuer to obtain the information registration would provide, as having "access" to such information. By a position of access we mean a relationship based on factors such as employment, family, or economic bargaining power that enables the offeree effectively to obtain such information. When offerees, regardless of whether they occupy a position of access, have been furnished with the information a registration statement would provide, we shall say merely that such information has been disclosed. When the offerees have access to or there has been disclosure of the information registration would provide, we shall say that such information was available.

The requirement that all offerees have available the information registration would provide has been firmly established by this court as a necessary condition of gaining the private offering exemption. Our decisions have been predicated upon *Ralston Purina*, where the

---

[10] We do not intimate that evidence of the offerees' sophistication is required in all cases to establish a private offering exemption under § 4[(a)](2). . . .

Supreme Court held that in the absence of a showing that the "key employees" to whom a corporation offered its common stock had knowledge obviating the need for registration, the offering did not qualify for the private offering exemption. The Court said that an employee offering would come within the exemption if it were shown that the employees were "executive personnel who because of their position have access to the same kind of information that the act would make available in the form of a registration statement." . . .

Because the district court . . . inferred from evidence of Doran's sophistication that his purchase of a partnership share was incident to a private offering, we must remand so that the lower court may determine the extent of the information available to each offeree.

More specifically, we shall require on remand that the defendants demonstrate that all offerees, whatever their expertise, had available the information a registration statement would have afforded a prospective investor in a public offering. Such a showing is not independently sufficient to establish that the offering qualified for the private placement exemption, but it is necessary to gain the exemption and is to be weighed along with the sophistication and number of the offerees, the number of units offered, and the size and manner of the offering. Because in this case these latter factors weigh heavily in favor of the private offering exemption, satisfaction of the necessary condition regarding the availability of relevant information to the offerees would compel the conclusion that this offering fell within the exemption. . . .

C.   On Remand: The Issuer-Offeree Relationship

In determining on remand the extent of the information available to the offerees, the district court must keep in mind that the "availability" of information means either disclosure of or effective access to the relevant information. The relationship between issuer and offeree is most critical when the issuer relies on the latter route.

To begin with, if the defendants could prove that all offerees were actually furnished the information a registration statement would have provided, whether the offerees occupied a position of access pre-existing such disclosure would not be dispositive of the status of the offering. If disclosure were proved and if, as here, the remaining factors such as the manner of the offering and the investment sophistication of the offerees weigh heavily in favor of the private status of the offering, the absence of a privileged relationship between offeree and issuer would not preclude a finding that the offering was private. Any other conclusion . . . would conflict with the policies of the [§ 4(a)(2)] exemption.

Alternatively it might be shown that the offeree had access to the files and record of the company that contained the relevant information. Such access might be afforded merely by the position of the offeree or by the issuer's promise to open appropriate files and records to the offeree as well as to answer inquiries regarding material information. In either case, the relationship between offeree and issuer now becomes critical, for it must be shown that the offeree could realistically have been expected to take advantage of his access to ascertain the relevant information.[12] Similarly the investment sophistication of the offeree assumes added importance, for it is important that he could have been expected to ask the right questions and seek out the relevant information.

In sum, both the relationship between issuer and offeree and the latter's investment sophistication are critical when the issuer or another relies on the offeree's "access" rather than the issuer's "disclosure" to come within the exemption. . . .

* * *

Once the alternative means of coming within the private placement exemption are clearly separated, we can appreciate the proper role to be accorded the requirement that the offerees occupy a privileged or "insider" status relative to the issuer. That is to say, when the issuer relies on "access" absent actual disclosure, he must show that the offerees occupied a privileged position relative to the issuer that afforded them an opportunity for effective access to the information registration would otherwise provide.[18] When the issuer relies on actual disclosure to come within the exemption, he need not demonstrate that the offerees held such a privileged position. Although mere disclosure is not a sufficient condition for establishing the availability of the private offering exemption, and a court will weigh other factors such as the manner of the offering and the investment sophistication of the offerees, the "insider" status of the offerees is not a necessary condition of obtaining the exemption.

* * *

QUESTIONS

1. How does the *Doran* court tie *Ralston Purina* to the 1935 SEC General Counsel Opinion's factors?

2. What test does the *Doran* court use to determine whether an offering qualifies for § 4(a)(2)?

3. Would the *Doran* court treat an outside investor that had considerable financial resources and represented the only possible source of financing for the issuer as having "access" to information similar to that in a registration statement?

---

[12] For example, the offeree's ability to compel the issuer to make good his promise may depend on the offeree's bargaining power or on his family or employment relationship to the issuer.

[18] That all offerees are in certain respects "insiders" does not ensure that the issuer will gain the private placement exemption. An insider may be an insider with respect to fiscal matters of the company, but an outsider with respect to a particular issue of securities. He may know much about the financial structure of the company but his position may nonetheless not allow him access to a few vital facts pertaining to the transaction at issue. If Doran had effective access to all information that registration would provide, he would be a transactional insider. That is all we require regarding the availability of information. If, on the other hand, his inside knowledge was incomplete or his access ineffective, he would be a transactional outsider despite the fact that we might consider him an "insider" for other purposes.

4. What happens to the offering if Doran is sophisticated and he is given full access to information, but one of the offerees (who did not eventually purchase) was not given the same information or was not sophisticated?

5. How important is sophistication to the court? Would a completely unsophisticated offeree qualify for the exemption?

HYPOTHETICAL ONE

1. *Scenario One:* Trendy decides to move forward with a private placement offering structured to meet the requirements of § 4(a)(2). Trendy identifies all the retirees from Grist, a local toothpaste factory, and sends invitations to learn more about Trendy to the 300 retirees. All the offerees are given the opportunity to go hiking with Kim, the CEO of Trendy, and discuss the offering. Ten (relatively-fit) retirees take the hike, each spending about two hours discussing Trendy's business and future prospects. All ten hikers decide to purchase (sending their checks in the mail) and Trendy raises $10 million from the offering (selling 10,000 shares of common stock to the ten investors in aggregate). Does Trendy's offering comply with § 4(a)(2)?

2. *Scenario Two:* What if Trendy instead offers and sells securities through an unregistered offering to 30 members of the "Rich Inheritors" club? All members of the club are over 21 and have a net worth of over $100 million inherited entirely from their parents. The 30 club members are each afforded the same opportunity to go hiking with Kim to discuss the offering and all 30 (indolent and rich, but fit) investors each spend two hours hiking with Kim. All 30 purchase shares in the offering.

3. *Scenario Three:* Same as Scenario Two, except Trendy offers and sells to 30 members of the "Poor Professors" club. Each member is a tenured finance professor with a net worth of under $100,000. None of the professors are fit enough to hike, so Kim spends two hours drinking lattés with them.

III. REGULATION D

Although some offerings clearly fall within § 4(a)(2), substantial areas of uncertainty remain. Founders setting up a corporation and putting in cash in exchange for the corporation's initial capital stock are certainly within the scope of § 4(a)(2). When the corporation accepts first-round investments from venture capitalists, do these transactions also fall within the ambit of § 4(a)(2)? If the venture capitalists can "fend for themselves" and have access to information equivalent to that provided in the registration statement then § 4(a)(2) exempts the transaction from § 5. Suppose, however, that the growing corporation then turns to other groups of investors including: (a) family and friends; (b) wealthy individuals; and (c) smaller institutional investors. Will the offering to these investors also fall under § 4(a)(2)?

The penalty for guessing incorrectly stings. If § 4(a)(2) does not apply, § 5 applies (absent another exemption). If the issuer is not exempt from § 5, then the issuer will face possible § 12(a)(1) liability. Recall that § 12(a)(1) does not require a showing of scienter, causation, reliance or even a material misstatement or omission. Instead, § 12(a)(1) imposes strict liability for violations of § 5. The harshness of the § 12(a)(1) remedy deters issuers from making a private placement unless they are confident of their exemption from § 5.

To provide issuers greater certainty in private placements, the SEC promulgated Regulation D of the Securities Act (Rules 500–508). Rule 506 provides a safe harbor for the § 4(a)(2) exemption. Although Regulation D does not eliminate all uncertainty, it is far more predictable than § 4(a)(2). Consider the interaction of Regulation D and § 4(a)(2). Assuming that Regulation D is somewhat narrower than § 4(a)(2), how does the safe harbor rule affect the structuring of private placements? If you were the CEO of a corporation contemplating a private placement, under what circumstances would you step outside the boundaries of Regulation D and "push the envelope" of what the law allows under § 4(a)(2)?

The starting point to understanding Regulation D is Rules 504, 505, and 506. These rules set forth the requirements for the three basic exemptions under Regulation D. Although we started our discussion with § 4(a)(2), only Rule 506 is a § 4(a)(2) exemption. Offerings under Rules 504 and 505 fall under § 3(b)(1) of the Securities Act, which allows the SEC to exempt from § 5 offerings up to $5 million. Two other provisions establish the framework for Regulation D. Rule 501 provides definitions used throughout Regulation D. Rule 502 sets forth the various requirements incorporated in the three offering exemptions found in Rules 504–506.

The three types of Regulation D offerings differ in the eligibility of certain issuers to use the exemptions. Rule 506 is open to all issuers. Rule 505 excludes investment companies. Rules 505 and 506 also disqualify certain issuers involved in a past securities laws violation. Rule 504 prohibits not only investment companies and "blank check" companies, but also Exchange Act reporting issuers. The exclusion of Exchange Act reporting issuers limits Rule 504 offerings to smaller companies without a liquid secondary trading market. Excluding blank check companies prevents smaller, development stage companies without a specific business plan or purpose from using Rule 504. The following table summarizes the exclusions from Regulation D.

	Rule 504 (§ 3(b)(1))	Rule 505 (§ 3(b)(1))	Rule 506 (§ 4(a)(2))
Excluded Issuers	Not '34 Act Co. Not Investment Co. Not Blank Check Co.	Not Investment Co. Disqualification (505(b)(2)(iii))	Disqualification per Dodd-Frank Act

Regulation D offerings under Rules 504–506 also differ with respect to the following categories:

- aggregate offering price
- purchasers
- general solicitation
- disclosure
- resale restrictions

We examine each criterion in turn. As you read the materials, see if you can figure out why Rule 506 offerings dominate by far the other two *[handwritten margin notes: "aggregation: issuer must reduce the offering price ceiling at current offering by the amount of securities sold in the preceding 12 months preceding the offering amount to either ① 504 or 505 — cr amount offer mele (va) section 5"]*

exemptions under Regulation D (well over 90%, both in number and dollar amount).

A. AGGREGATE OFFERING PRICE

The most conspicuous difference among the various Regulation D exemptions is the offering amount allowed, i.e., "aggregate offering price." Under Rule 504, issuers may sell up to $1 million of securities, under Rule 505, issuers may sell up to $5 million of securities, and under Rule 506, issuers may sell an unlimited amount.

Constraining the aggregate offering price limits the potential scope of a Regulation D offering. Smaller offerings are less likely to involve widespread public selling efforts. Individual retail investors are therefore also unlikely to invest in such smaller offerings.

The aggregate offering price limitations provoke two questions. Why might an issuer prefer a Rule 504 or 505 offering over a Rule 506 offering, which does not limit the offering amount? The answer, of course, is that the requirements for a Rule 506 private placement are more restrictive.

Second, what prevents an issuer from simply doing repeated Rule 504 or 505 offerings to evade the offering price limitation? For example, a corporation could sell $5 million on May 1, $5 million on June 1, $5 million on June 15, etc. This strategy is thwarted by aggregation rules that determine the aggregate offering price for Rules 504 and 505. Under both Rules, issuers must reduce the offering price ceiling—$1 million for Rule 504 and $5 million for Rule 505—by the amount of securities sold in the twelve months preceding the offering pursuant to either (1) an offering under § 3(b) of the Securities Act (which includes both Rule 504 and 505 offerings), or (2) an offering made in violation of § 5. Thus, a corporation that sold $5 million of securities on May 1 under Rule 505 would have its aggregate offering price ceiling Rule 504 and 505 offerings limited to $0 until May 1 of the next year.

HYPOTHETICAL TWO

Trendy decides to do a Regulation D offering to raise capital for its contemplated expansion of the marketing and distribution of Trendy's Lean Green drink.

1. *Scenario One:* Suppose that Trendy raises $1 million per month over a five-month period from January 2015 to May 2015. Sales are made to 25 unsophisticated purchasers. Do any of the three Regulation D offering types exempt Trendy from § 5?

2. *Scenario Two:* After raising $5 million from January 2015 to May 2015, on February 1, 2016, Trendy decides to engage in a new round of financing. Trendy seeks to raise an additional $5 million quickly in an exempt offering to twenty unsophisticated purchasers. Can Trendy sell securities under any of the Regulation D exemptions?

3. *Scenario Three:* Suppose that earlier in June 2014, Trendy sold $10 million of common stock attempting to use § 4(a)(2). Trendy made the mistake of selling to 25 investors without providing either information or access. How does this 2014 offering affect Trendy's January to May, 2015 sale of securities in Scenario One?

B. PURCHASERS

The SEC's central concern with unregistered offerings is the broad-based sales of securities to the general public. Many public investors lack investment sophistication, leading them to purchase overvalued securities. In addition, public investors may feed off of each other's excessive optimism, driving the price of overvalued securities still higher. Regulation D addresses this concern by restricting purchasers.

First, Regulation D limits the number of purchasers. Rules 505 and 506 limit offerings to a maximum of 35 purchasers. Rule 504, however, does not limit the number of purchasers, instead relying on the $1 million aggregate offering price to indirectly constrain the scope of the offering.

The 35-purchaser ceiling under Rules 505 and 506 has an enormous loophole. Rule 501(e) excludes certain investors from the count of purchasers. For example, under Rule 501(e)(1)(i) any "relative, spouse or relative of the spouse of a purchaser who has the same principal residence as the purchaser" is not counted as a separate purchaser. More importantly, Rule 501(e)(1)(iv) excludes "accredited investors" from the purchaser tally. Because of the accredited investor exclusion, Rules 505 and 506 allow sales to an unlimited number of "accredited investors" plus not more than 35 persons who are not "accredited investors." In practice, most offerings are sold exclusively to accredited investors.

Who counts as an accredited investor? Many of the categories involve large entities and institutions, including banks, broker-dealers, and insurance companies. Trusts, partnerships, and corporations also qualify if they have a minimum of $5 million in total assets, among other requirements. In addition, Rule 501(a) defines three additional categories of accredited investors:

- Rule 501(a)(4): Any director, executive officer, or general partner of the issuer of the securities.

- Rule 501(a)(5): Any natural person whose individual net worth, or joint net worth with that person's spouse, at the time of his purchase exceeds $1,000,000.

- Rule 501(a)(6): Any natural person whose individual income exceeded $200,000 in each of the two most recent years or whose joint income with his/her spouse exceeded $300,000 in each of those years and has a reasonable expectation of reaching the same income level in the current year.

The concept of accredited investors is central to Regulation D. Because accredited investors are excluded from the calculation of the number of purchasers, issuers may sell to an unlimited number of accredited investors under Rules 505 and 506. Although Rule 505's separate aggregate offering price limit of $5 million constrains such offerings, Rule 506 has no such limit. In theory, therefore, an issuer may sell an unlimited amount of securities under Rule 506 (i.e., into the billions of dollars) to an unlimited number of accredited investors.

Outside of Regulation D, Securities Act§ 4(a)(5) exempts offers and sales to accredited investors from § 5. Offerings under § 4(a)(5) are limited to the $5 million limit established under § 3(b)(1). Issuers or anyone acting on behalf of the issuer may not engage in "advertising or public solicitation." Section 4(a)(5) also requires that issuers file a notice of the transaction with the SEC. The SEC requires issuers selling pursuant to § 4(a)(5) to file notice on Form D. Presumably because of the $5 million limit, issuers rarely rely on § 4(a)(5) exclusively as an exemption from § 5.

Issuers typically rely on placement agents to provide access to pre-screened pools of accredited investors. Placement agents maintain databases of potential accredited investors, typically determining accredited status using information found in suitability questionnaires filled out by the investors. But what if an investor lies or makes a mistake on the questionnaire? Rule 501(a) provides that the issuer need only "reasonably" believe that an investor falls in one of the specified categories of accredited investors.

Even accredited investors have a limited appetite for privately placed securities. The chief constraint on that appetite is that securities sold through Regulation D are "restricted": Resales are limited from the date of investment unless the securities are registered under § 5 or the selling investor finds an exemption from § 5. Rule 144, covered in Chapter 10, provides such an exemption, allowing resales of restricted securities after a specified holding period of six months (for reporting issuers) or one year (for non-reporting issuers). If the accredited investors decide to rebalance their portfolios, or need to raise cash for some other reason, the investors will be unable to sell the restricted securities immediately.

Regulation D did not originally provide for inflation adjustment for the income and net worth tests for individuals to become accredited investors. Since the income and net worth numerical thresholds were implemented in April 1982, inflation has substantially eroded those limits. One million dollars in 1982 is the equivalent of $2.43 million in 2015, so the $1 million net worth eligibility requirement is effectively less than half of what it was when Regulation D was introduced. Failing to adjust for inflation has allowed an ever-expanding group of individuals to qualify as accredited investors. The net worth test, moreover, did not take into account the mix of assets that go into a person's net worth. Should a person whose net worth consists entirely of marketable securities be treated differently from a person whose net worth consists almost entirely of the person's house?

In 2010, Congress stepped in to compel the SEC to revise its accredited investor definition. The Dodd-Frank Act requires the SEC to adopt rules adjusting the $1 million net worth test for a natural person to become an accredited investor to exclude the "value of the primary residence of such national person." Dodd-Frank Act § 413(a). Congress also required that an investor's primary residence be excluded under the net worth test. Beyond the $1 million net worth test, the Dodd-Frank Act instructs that SEC to undertake a review of the definition of an accredited investor as applied to natural persons to determine whether the definition should be adjusted "for the protection of investors, in the public interest, and in light of the economy." Dodd-Frank Act § 413(b). Starting in 2014, the Act requires the SEC to undertake a subsequent review of the accredited investor definition "in its entirety" at least once every four years thereafter.

In early 2012, the SEC adopted a rule adjusting the net worth test for a natural person accredited investor under Rule 501(a)(5). The SEC also provided parallel adjustments to the definition of accredited investor under Rule 215 that defines the terms accredited investor under § 2(a)(15) of the Securities Act for purposes of the § 4(a)(5) exemption. Under the new rule, both equity and liability in the investor's primary residence are excluded, unless the liability exceeds the fair market value of the home.

HYPOTHETICAL THREE

Trendy decides to do a Regulation D offering under Rule 505 to raise capital for its contemplated expansion of the marketing and distribution of Trendy's Lean Green drink. Suppose that Trendy raises $1 million per month over a five-month period from January 2015 to May 2015. Sales are made to 35 unsophisticated purchasers. Trendy also makes sales to the following investors. Do these additional sales create any problems under Regulation D?

1.   *Scenario One:* Trendy sells securities in the offering to all of its executive vice presidents, including to Alan, the VP for drink research and Laura, the VP for human resources.

2.   *Scenario Two:* Trendy sells securities in the offering to Dale. Dale is a retiree who has a stock portfolio of $1.1 million; the entire portfolio is invested in index funds and Dale has no other significant assets or debts. Dale lives off the dividends from the portfolio (along with limited sales of capital) to pay for monthly expenses. (Dale lives in San Francisco where rents can run up to $3,000 per month for his one-bedroom apartment.) Dale has no other source of income, but enjoys golfing.

3.   *Scenario Three:* Trendy sells securities to Beth. Beth has a Ph.D. in financial economics from the University of California, Berkeley. Beth worked only one year for Morgan Stanley before being fired for insider trading. During that year, however, Beth made $2,000,000 from her trading efforts and has a net worth today of $700,000 (after paying stiff civil penalties to the SEC). Beth now froths milk for cappuccinos and makes $15.00 an hour.

4.   *Scenario Four:* What if Beth shares an apartment with Andrei, one of the 35 unsophisticated purchasers in the offering. If Beth and Andrei are simply good friends (but nothing more), does Beth count as a purchaser, thereby increasing the total to 36 purchasers?

5.   *Scenario Five:* Trendy sells securities to the Trendy Investment Partnership. TIP was formed a month prior to Trendy's offering and has 50 partners. None of the partners, individually, is an accredited investor. TIP's total net assets are $1 million.

––––––––

In comparing the three Regulation D offerings, issuers face a tradeoff between the restrictions on the aggregate offering price and the number of purchasers. Rule 504 imposes no limit on purchasers but restricts offerings to $1 million. Rule 505, in contrast, restricts the number of non-accredited purchasers to 35 (plus an unlimited number of accredited purchasers) and allows offerings of up to $5 million.

What of Rule 506? At first glance, Rule 506 dominates Rule 505 from the issuers' perspective. Under Rule 506, an issuer may sell to up to 35 purchasers with no aggregate offering price limit. But Rule 506 offerings face an additional regulatory constraint not present for Rule 504 or 505 offerings: Rule 506 purchasers who are not accredited investors must also meet a sophistication requirement. Purchasers must have "such knowledge and experience in financial and business matters that he is capable of evaluating the merits and risks of the prospective investment, or the issuer reasonably believes immediately prior to making any sale that such purchaser comes within this description." Rule 506(b)(2)(ii)

How are issuers supposed to determine whether an investor (alone or with a purchaser representative) is able to evaluate the merits and risks of an investment? One could imagine issuers looking to factors such as:

- Wealth and income (much like for accredited investor status for individuals)
- Experience (general business or more specific to securities investment?)
- Education
- Present investment status (well-diversified or not)
- Performance on an investment test (much like qualifying for a driver's license)

Among these factors, which ones are mostly likely to correlate with an investor's ability to assess the merits and risks of investments? How expensive would it be for an issuer to administer such a screen for sophistication? What risk would the issuer run that a court or the SEC may later question the accuracy and reasonableness of the screen? In practice, because Rule 506's sophistication requirement is somewhat vague, many Rule 506 offerings exclude non-accredited investors altogether and sell only to accredited investors.

The following table summarizes the tradeoff between aggregate offering price and purchaser restrictions for the three types of Regulation D offerings:

	Rule 504 (§ 3(b)(1))	Rule 505 (§ 3(b)(1))	Rule 506 (§ 4(a) (2))
Aggregate Offering Price	≤ $1 million (Rules 504(b)(2), 501(c)) Prior 12 mo. and during offering aggregation with § 3(b) offerings and § 5(a) violations	≤ $5 million (Rules 505(b)(2)(i), 501(c)) Prior 12 mo. and during offering aggregation with § 3(b) offerings and § 5(a) violations	Unlimited

Number of Purchasers	No limit on purchasers	≤ 35 non-accredited Purchasers; Unlimited accredited purchasers (Rules 505(b)(2)(ii), 501(a), 501(e))	≤ 35 non-accredited Purchasers; Unlimited accredited purchasers (Rules 506(b)(2)(i), 501(a), 501(e)) Sophistication requirement (Rules 506(b)(2)(ii), 501(h))

HYPOTHETICAL FOUR

1. *Scenario One:* Trendy decides to raise $20 million through a common stock offering under Rule 506 of Regulation D. Among the purchasers is Howard, who is not an accredited investor. Howard spent a year and a half in business school studying the financial markets, before dropping out. Howard presently sells cool drinks from a street side vending stand in Manhattan. Do Howard's purchases jeopardize Trendy's Rule 506 exemption?

2. *Scenario Two:* Suppose that Howard turns to his friend Nicole, an investment banker, to help him with his investment decisions. Do Howard's purchases jeopardize the Rule 506 exemption?

3. *Scenario Three:* What if Nicole, Howard's potential purchaser representative, is also a director of Trendy, Inc.?

C. GENERAL SOLICITATION

Regulation D's restrictions on the number and sophistication of *purchasers* do not necessarily address § 4(a)(2)'s concern for *offerees*. Broad-based offerings to the general public may lead the public in to a "frenzy," overwhelming the valuations of sophisticated investors.

To address this concern, Regulation D addresses "offerees" separately from purchasers. Rule 502(c) bans general solicitations and advertising. This ban applies to both Rule 505 and 506(b) offerings. Rule 504 exempts issuers from Rule 502(c) if the issuer meets certain state law offering requirements. Rule 504 issuers may avoid the general solicitation ban of Rule 502(c) if the issuer sells exclusively in a state that provides for the registration of the securities under state law and also requires the public filing and delivery to investors of a "substantive disclosure document" prior to sale. Rule 504(b)(1)(i)–(iii).

In certain areas, the application of Rule 502(c) is clear. Suppose an issuer decides to run television commercials publicizing an upcoming private placement under Rule 506(b). This clearly would count as general advertising. Including a disclaimer in the advertisement restricting the solicitation to an arbitrary subset of the general public will not change this result. Suppose the placement agent for the issuer (typically an investment bank assisting with the private placement) creates a glossy offering pamphlet for the private placement and mails the pamphlet out to the following groups:

- all redheads in the United States
- all residents of Ann Arbor, Michigan
- all students taking civil procedure at NYU Law School

Although these groups are restricted, they do not create any meaningful restriction in the sense of culling out investors based on sophistication or ability to "fend for themselves."

The harder question arises with respect to investors who are selected at least somewhat based on their financial sophistication or wealth (from which sophistication perhaps can be assumed?). Consider the following groups:

- all executive officers of the *Fortune 500* companies
- all finance professors in the United States
- the 50 wealthiest people in the United States as identified in *Forbes*

Would an unsolicited mailing of an offering pamphlet to these investors run afoul of the prohibition on general solicitations?

In the Matter of Kenman Corp.

S.E.C., [1984–1985 Transfer Binder] Fed. Sec. L. Rep. (CCH) ¶ 83,767 (Apr. 19, 1985).

* * *

During certain times from on or about August 29, 1983 through May 15, 1984, Kenman Securities and Kenman [the parent corporation of Kenman Securities] participated in two limited partnerships offerings. Missiondale Palms Associates ("Missiondale") is a Utah limited partnership organized in August 1983 to acquire an apartment complex in Tucson, Arizona. Kenman is the general partner of Missiondale. From on or about August 29, 1983, Kenman through Kenman Securities sold limited partnership interests in Missiondale to 39 investors who invested a total of $875,000. No registration statement under the Securities Act was filed with the Commission or is in effect concerning the Missiondale limited partnership interests.

Orem Dairy Queen Associates ("Orem Associates") is a Utah limited partnership organized in January 1984 to acquire land and a franchise for a Dairy Queen restaurant and to construct and operate the restaurant in Orem, Utah. Kenman is the general partner of Orem Associates. From on or about January 13, 1984, Kenman through Kenman Securities sold limited partnership interests in Orem Associates to 25 investors who invested a total of $280,000. No registration statement was filed with the Commission or is in effect concerning the Orem Associates limited partnership interests. A Form D was filed with the Commission with respect to the Orem Associates offering, on or about March 2, 1984, which offering was made pursuant to Rule 506 of Regulation D.

In early 1983, Kenman and Kenman Securities mailed information concerning Missiondale to an unknown number of persons. This information included a one page cover letter, a four page promotional document and a reply card to request a personal sales meeting with Kenman's president. Kenman and Kenman Securities also mailed similar information concerning Orem Associates to an unknown number of persons in early 1984.

Persons to whom Kenman and Kenman Securities sent materials were chosen from six sources. First, they utilized a list of persons who had participated in prior offerings by them. Second, they reviewed the annual reports of fifty "Fortune 500" companies and obtained the names of executive officers. The third source was a list of names of persons who had previously invested $10,000 or more in real estate offerings by issuers other than Kenman. This list was purchased by Kenman from a third party. The fourth source was a list of physicians in the State of California. The fifth source was a list of managerial engineers employed by Hughes Aircraft Company or by similar companies. Sixth, Kenman obtained a copy of the Morris County, New Jersey Industrial Directory and selected names of the presidents of certain listed companies.

Kenman and Kenman Securities did not keep sufficiently detailed records to identify the specific persons or the actual number of persons to whom information was sent concerning the Missiondale and the Orem Associates offerings. However, information concerning the offerings were sent to a number of persons on a list of names compiled from these sources. . . .

* * *

Based on the foregoing, the Commission finds that Kenman and Kenman Securities willfully violated Sections 5(a) and 5(c) of the Securities Act in that they offered and sold limited partnership interests in Missiondale and Orem Associates when no registration statement was filed with the Commission or was in effect and no exemption from registration was available.

* * *

Kenman and Kenman Securities relied on the exemption from registration under Section 4[a](2) of the Securities Act with respect to the Missiondale and Orem Associates offerings. In addition, the Orem Associates offering was structured to qualify under the "safe harbor" provided by Rule 506 of Regulation D.

An offering pursuant to Rule 506 must comply with Rules 501 through 503 of Regulation D. Rule 502(c) precludes the offer and sale of securities "by any form of general solicitation or general advertisement. . . ." Section 4[a](2) of the Securities Act provides an exemption from registration for "transactions by an issuer not involving any public offering." The exemption from registration under Section 4[a](2) is not available to an issuer that is engaged in a general solicitation or general advertising.

The Commission concludes that Kenman and Kenman Securities engaged in general solicitations[6] and therefore the exemptions from

---

[6] In determining what constitutes a general solicitation, the Commission's Division of Corporation Finance has underscored the existence and substance of pre-existing relationships between the issuer and those being solicited. Kenman admits that persons who received the Orem Associates mailings had no pre-existing relationship with Kenman. These persons were selected only because their names were on lists that were purchased or created by Kenman. Although the make-up of the lists may indicate that the persons themselves have some degree of investment sophistication or financial well-being, utilization of lists of thousands of persons

registration under Section 4[a](2) with respect to the Missiondale and Orem Associates offerings and the safe harbor of Rule 506 of Regulation D with respect to the Orem Associates offering were not available.

* * *

QUESTIONS

1.   What result if Kenman had only sold to those investors that had purchased before from Kenman?

2.   The *Kenman* decision states: "The exemption from registration under Section 4[a](2) is not available to an issuer that is engaged in a general solicitation or general advertising." Is this consistent with *Ralston Purina* and *Doran*?

———

SEC No-Action Letter Mineral Lands Research & Marketing Corporation

Publicly Available December 4, 1985.

LETTER TO SEC
March 21, 1985

Office of Chief Counsel
Division of Corporation Finance
Securities and Exchange Commission
450 Fifth Street, N.W.
Washington, D.C. 20549

Gentlemen:

We are writing on behalf of our client Mineral Lands Research & Marketing Corporation for your advice concerning a proposed offering of the Company's securities without registration under the Securities Act of 1933 in reliance on the exemption contained in Rule 504 of Regulation D promulgated under the Act.

BACKGROUND

The Company was formed for the purpose of locating, identifying and acquiring mineral properties with a view to selling, developing or joint venturing the properties. The Company proposes to raise up to $500,000 through the sale of its equity securities in reliance upon the exemption from registration contained in Rule 504. The Company does not intend to rely on the exemption from the application of the provisions of Rule 502(c) and (d) contained in Rule 504(b)(1). Potential investors will be provided with a disclosure document containing substantially the same information as would be included in a

---

with no pre-existing relationship to the offeror clearly does not comply with the limitation of Rule 502(c) on the manner of solicitation. Here, Kenman mailed information concerning Orem Associates not only to previous Kenman investors, but to an unknown number of persons with whom Kenman had no prior contact or relationship.

Registration Statement on Form S–18 under the Act. All sales will be effected through the officers and directors of the Company who will not receive any commissions or any other additional remuneration in connection with the sales. It is anticipated that most of the offers and sales will be made through one officer and director of the Company to individuals with whom he has a prior existing business relationship, although a limited number of offers and sales are anticipated to be made through other officers and directors. This officer and director is a licensed insurance broker and is the owner of a sole proprietorship through which he sells a variety of insurance and financial products. He proposes to offer the Company's securities to up to 600 of his existing clientele and anticipates that each investor will purchase between $500 and $2,000 of the Company's securities. It is likely that most of the investors will neither qualify as "accredited investors" within the meaning of Rule 501(a) of Regulation D nor be sophisticated investors.

DISCUSSION

Rule 502(c) of Regulation D provides as a condition to the availability of the Rule 504 exemption that "neither the issuer nor any person acting on its behalf shall offer or sell the securities by any form of general solicitation or general advertising." Although there is no limitation on the number of offerees or purchasers involved in offerings pursuant to Rule 504 as there is with offerings pursuant to Rules 505 and 506, the Commission has indicated "that depending on the actual circumstances, offerings made to such large numbers of purchasers may involve a violation of the prohibitions against general solicitation and general advertising."

The Staff of the Commission has taken the position that the mailing of a written offer by an issuer to up to 330 persons having a pre-existing relationship with the general partner of the issuer would not exceed the terms of Rule 502(c). The Staff also noted, however, that the general partner had determined that the investment was suitable for the proposed investors and that they had the requisite sophistication. Although this latter condition will most likely not be satisfied as to a majority, if not all, of the investors in the Company's proposed offering, we nonetheless believe that the proposed manner of offering by the Company would not constitute general advertising or general solicitation because most of the offerees are a limited group with whom an officer and director of the issuer has a pre-existing business relationship and Rule 504 does not require that the investment be suitable for the purchaser or that the purchaser be sophisticated.

REQUEST

We respectfully request that the Division concur with our opinion and advise us that it would not recommend any action to the Commission if the Company proceeds with the offering of securities described above. We understand that such a position would be based upon the facts and circumstances described in this letter and that any different facts or conditions might require a different response.

* * *

[Eds.—In the typical no-action letter, the SEC staff's response follows immediately after the requesting letter as set forth below:]

SEC LETTER

* * *

You have requested that the Division take a no-action position with respect to the availability of an exemption from Regulation D. As the Commission stated in its adopting release for Regulation D, the staff will not issue no-action letters with respect to transactions under Regulation D. Your letter does, however, present an interpretive issue to which we will respond. That question concerns the application of Rule 502(c) to the Company's proposal to offer securities to persons with whom officers and directors of the Company have prior business relationships.

The class of offerees includes 600 persons who are existing clients of an officer who is an insurance broker. It is your view that the proposed manner of offering would not constitute general advertising or solicitation because most of the offerees consist of a limited group with whom an officer and director of the issuer has pre-existing business relationships.

The Division agrees with your view that the existence of relationships between an issuer and offerees is an important factor in determining whether offers violate Rule 502(c). The types of relationships with offerees that may be important in establishing that a general solicitation has not taken place are those that would enable the issuer (or a person acting on its behalf) to be aware of the financial circumstances or sophistication of the persons with whom the relationship exists or that otherwise are of some substance and duration. As your letter does not include sufficient facts to enable us to make a determination whether the type of relationship contemplated is present, the Division is unable to express a view on this matter.

* * *

_____

How do brokerage firms acting as placement agents in a private placement obtain the requisite pre-existing relationships with investors? The SEC in a series of no-action letters has indicated that brokerage firms may actively solicit investors with a general interest in investing in private placements. *See* EF Hutton, SEC No-Action Letter (Dec. 3, 1985); Bateman Eichler, Hill Richards, SEC No-Action Letter (Dec. 3, 1985). The solicitation may not mention any particular private placement offering. Moreover, the solicitations must take place a sufficient amount of time prior to any contemplated offering to enable the brokerage firm to assess the sophistication of the investors. On-line offeree questionnaires followed by screening on the part of brokerage firms are acceptable. *See* IPOnet, SEC No-Action Letter (July 26, 1996).

_____

The JOBS Act, enacted in 2012, directed the SEC to adopt rules removing the Rule 502(c) prohibition against general solicitation and general advertising. Congress ordered the repeal of the general solicitation ban, however, only for Rule 506 offerings sold solely to accredited investors. In 2013, the SEC implemented Congress's directive to permit general solicitation if all of the investors in a Rule 506 offering are accredited investors. Issuers relying on the new rule must take reasonable steps to verify that the purchasers are accredited investors. The changes are found in Rule 506(c).

The JOBS Act and Rule 506(c) do not eliminate the prohibition on general solicitation altogether. The prohibition still applies to all Rule 505 offerings as well as Rule 506(b) offerings if not all purchasers are accredited. Issuers are therefore faced with a choice. They can structure their offerings to sell only to accredited investors, thereby avoiding general solicitation prohibition. This option under Rule 506(c) comes with a cost, however, as it requires that the issuer verify the accredited investor status of participants in the offering. The second option, under Rule 506(b), does not allow for general solicitation, but it does allow the issuer to rely on self-verification of accredited investor status by participants in the offering. To date, most issuers have chosen Rule 506(b), apparently preferring self-verification over the opportunity to engage in a general solicitation.

HYPOTHETICAL FIVE

Trendy moves forward with a Rule 506 offering to raise $10 million for its expansion campaign for the Lean Green drink. Eager to find investors for the offering, Kim, the CEO of Trendy, employs West Securities to help sell the offering. Mark, the managing partner of West Securities, is working to sell the securities. Are these sales practices permissible under Rule 502(c)?

1. *Scenario One:* Mark walks up and down his alma mater's health club locker room, the Yale Club in New York, telling everyone about his offering, passing out offering circulars, and collecting purchase requests. Assume that Mark, a gregarious fellow, knows everyone in the health club on a first-name basis.

2. *Scenario Two:* Suppose Trendy tells West Securities that it will reduce its offering down to $5 million in order to fit within Rule 505. Mark again goes to solicit interest from among his friends at the health club.

3. *Scenario Three:* Mark goes to the financial district in Boston and drops in unannounced at the offices of large mutual fund managers for Fidelity, Scudder, Dreyfus, and other prominent mutual funds (all very sophisticated investors). Mark again passes out offering circulars and collects purchase requests. Mark only knows of the mutual fund managers by reputation, having seen their names repeatedly in the *Wall Street Journal*.

4. *Scenario Four:* Trendy completes a Rule 506(b) offering on January 1 for $10 million in common stock, selling to ten accredited investors and twenty sophisticated purchasers (none of whom are accredited). Later in the year, Trendy makes a Rule 505 offering for $4 million of common stock from July 1 to July 30, selling to 30 unsophisticated purchasers. Trendy makes another Rule 505 offering for $1 million of common stock from

December 1 to December 15 of the same year, selling to five unsophisticated purchasers. If Trendy engaged in general solicitation in its January Rule 506 offering, but not in the later two Rule 505 offerings, does that affect the other two offerings? (Assume no integration of the offerings.)

D. DISCLOSURE

The public offering process focuses on the registration statement and statutory prospectus. These documents are intended to reduce the informational advantage that issuers have over public investors. Of course, no one forces an investor to purchase securities in an offering. Investors can always simply walk away if an issuer does not provide information. Nonetheless, in the public offering context, mandatory disclosure may be justified if some investors lack the sophistication to recognize the importance of disclosure. Similarly, if a large number of investors invest in an offering, no one investor may expend the resources to bargain with the issuer to obtain disclosure. If the issuer is the least cost provider of information—e.g., on firm-specific information relating to the issuer itself—then forcing the issuer to make such disclosure may benefit all investors.

Do these same arguments apply for a private placement to a small number of sophisticated investors? Instead of many retail investors clamoring for the latest IPO stock, picture instead ten mutual funds, a hedge fund, and an insurance company considering whether to purchase securities in a private placement. Part of the rationale behind *Ralston Purina's* "fend for themselves" formulation is that for some types of investors, the stringent protections of the securities laws are unnecessary (or at least not cost-justified).

Private placements under Regulation D do not entirely eliminate disclosure. Rule 502(b) divides Regulation D along two dimensions: (1) the type of investor (accredited or not) and (2) the type of offering (Rule 504 v. Rule 505 or 506). Based on this division, the following disclosure is mandated:

	Non-Accredited Investor	**Accredited Investor**
Rule 504 Offering	No specific disclosure required	No specific disclosure required
Rule 505 or 506 Offering	Specific disclosure required by Rule 502(b)(2)	No specific disclosure required

Issuers do not need to provide any disclosure to accredited investors pursuant to Rule 502(b)(1). Issuers making a Rule 504 offering also face no mandatory disclosure requirements, at least under the federal securities laws, although they may face state securities registration requirements. Rule 502(b)(1). For Rule 505 or 506 offerings to a non-accredited investor, the type of disclosure mandated under Rule 502(b)(2) then varies based on: (1) the type of issuer and (2) the size of the offering.

	Non-Exchange Act Reporting Company	**Exchange Act Reporting Company**
Offerings up to $2 million	Non-financial info under Rule 502(b)(2)(i)(A) Financial info under Rule 502(b)(2)(i)(B)(1)	Rule 502(b)(2)(ii)
Offerings up to $7.5 million	Non-financial info under Rule 502(b)(2)(i)(A) Financial info under Rule 502(b)(2)(i)(B)(2)	Same as above
Offerings over $7.5 million	Non-financial info under Rule 502(b)(2)(i)(A) Financial info under Rule 502(b)(2)(i)(B)(3)	Same as above

The disclosure for Exchange Act reporting issuers does not vary by offering amount. Instead, Exchange Act reporting issuers have a choice. They may either provide a combination of the most recent annual report, the definitive proxy statement, and (only if requested by the purchaser in writing) the most recent Form 10–K or just the most recent Form 10–K if it contains the information found in the annual report. Rule 502(b)(2)(ii)(A) & (B). In either case, issuers must also disclose any more recent Exchange Act filings made since those filings. Also, issuers must provide "a brief description of the securities being offered, the use of the proceeds from the offering, and any material changes in the issuer's affairs that are not disclosed in the documents furnished." Rule 502(b)(2)(ii)(C).

For non-Exchange Act reporting issuers, Rule 502(b)(2)(i)(A) provides for the same non-financial disclosure regardless of offering amount. Rule 502(b)(2)(i)(A) makes reference to the "same kind" of information contained in Part I of the registration statement used in a public offering.

The offering amount becomes important only for disclosure of financial information by non-Exchange Act reporting issuers. Rules 502(b)(2)(i)(B)(1) through (3) mandate different levels of financial disclosure. Generally, as the offering amount increases, the level of financial disclosure increases (with a greater audit requirement). Students can trace the requirements through the following referenced forms:

- Up to $2 million: Article 8 of Regulation S–X (except only the issuer's balance sheet must be audited).

- Up to $7.5 million: Financial statement information contained in Form S–1 for smaller reporting companies (except only the audited balance sheet is required if obtaining audited financial statements takes "unreasonable effort or expense").

- Over $7.5 million: Financial statement information contained in the public offering registration statement (except only the audited balance sheet is required if

obtaining   audited   financial   statements   takes
"unreasonable effort or expense").

In addition, Rule 502(b) provides a catchall provision to ensure that
non-accredited investors receive notice of information given to
accredited investors. The issuer must give non-accredited investors a
brief written description of "any material written information
concerning the offering that has been provided by the issuer to any
accredited investor" not already given to the non-accredited investors.
Rule 502(b)(2)(iv). Also, if the non-accredited investor provides a
written request for the information, the issuer must furnish the
information to the non-accredited investor within a reasonable time
prior to the purchase.

The issuer must also give each purchaser the "opportunity to ask
questions and receive answers" relating to the offering. Rule
502(b)(2)(v). The issuer must also supply any additional information
necessary to verify the accuracy of the specific mandatory disclosure
items in Rules 502(b)(2)(i) and (ii) upon the request of any purchaser
provided the "issuer possesses or can acquire without unreasonable
effort or expense" the information.

HYPOTHETICAL SIX

Kim, the CEO of Trendy Inc., wants your advice regarding disclosure
for Trendy's upcoming Rule 506 private placement of $10 million in
common stock. She has the following questions.

1. If Trendy sells only to accredited investors, what information must
Trendy disclose?

2. What information should Trendy disclose voluntarily to the accredited
investors?

E. RESALE RESTRICTIONS

Securities sold through Regulation D generally cannot be freely
resold with one exception. Investors that purchase securities sold
through a Rule 504 offering that complies with the state law
registration requirement specified by Rule 504(b)(1) may freely resell
the securities. A liquid public secondary market is possible immediately
after a Rule 504 offering. The small size of the Rule 504 offering
(limited to $1 million) and state law restrictions may, however, limit the
development of any secondary market in the Rule 504 securities.

For Rule 505 and 506 offerings, Rule 502(d) explicitly restricts
resales. Regulation D securities "have the status of securities acquired
in a transaction under section 4[a](2) of the Act and cannot be resold
without registration under the Act or an exemption therefrom." Rule
502(d). Not only are the securities sold through Regulation D so-called
"restricted securities," but Rule 502(d) imposes a requirement that the
issuer take reasonable care to discourage investors from reselling the
securities (at least under circumstances in which the purchasers would
be deemed "underwriters" under § 2(a)(11)). Among other things, the
issuer can disclose in writing the unregistered status of the securities
and place a legend on the securities indicating that they have not been

registered under the Securities Act, although this is not the exclusive means by which resale can be restricted.

One difficulty created by Regulation D's "restricted" securities is that the Securities Act does not regulate securities, but instead focuses on transactions. Consider the application of § 4(a)(1)'s exemption from § 5. As long as the *transaction* does not involve an issuer, underwriter, or dealer, investors may freely resell even a restricted security even though the security has never been registered for a public offering. As we will see in Chapter 10, the key concept for resales is whether the investor is acting as an underwriter for the issuer. If the investor has underwriter status, the § 4(a)(1) exemption is unavailable, thereby rendering any resale subject to the registration requirements of § 5.

What is the downside of owning a restricted security? Investors hope for a positive future return when they purchase a security. Securities provide a return directly through dividends. In addition, a security holder may also benefit through capital appreciation. Many companies, however, do not pay dividends—particularly high growth companies—because earnings are plowed back into building the business. As a company's anticipated profits grow, so does its stock price. Investors can exploit this capital appreciation by selling their securities. Restrictions on resale, therefore, severely impinge the ability of investors to realize their capital appreciation. Investors interested in diversifying their portfolio cannot do so if resale is restricted. As we will see in Chapter 10, investors can resell even restricted securities, but those avenues are limited. Consequently, private placement investors typically require an illiquidity discount to induce them to purchase.

HYPOTHETICAL SEVEN

What would be wrong with permanently prohibiting the resale of "restricted" securities without registration by the issuer? Consider the effect of an indefinite ban on resales in the following two scenarios.

1. *Scenario One:* Trendy, Inc. issues $10 million of common stock in a private placement. Trendy is not listed on an exchange. Few investors know much about Trendy's business or finances.

2. *Scenario Two:* Megasoft, Inc. issues $10 million of common stock in a private placement. Megasoft's common stock trades on the NYSE; it has a market capitalization of $200 billion. Several analysts follow Megasoft and regularly issue opinions evaluating its common stock.

F. INTEGRATION

Issuers must reduce the aggregate offering price ceiling for Rule 504 and Rule 505 offerings to account for prior offerings under § 3(b) and in violation of § 5. The reduction in the aggregate offering price ceiling prevents issuers from easily avoiding the offering amount limitation through multiple, separate offerings closely spaced in time.

Issuers may devise other strategies to divide offerings artificially to evade other Regulation D requirements. For example, both Rule 505 and Rule 506 offerings impose a limit of 35 purchasers. An issuer may divide an offering for $10 million to 60 purchasers into two parts—

selling $5 million to 30 purchasers in two "separate" offerings—to avoid the 35-purchaser limit.

Or, suppose an issuer seeks to sell $9 million of securities to 40 accredited investors with whom the issuer has a pre-existing relationship, and $1 million to twenty individual investors with whom the issuer has no pre-existing relationship. Such an offering would violate Rule 502(c)'s prohibition on general solicitation due to the presence of the individual investors. Nonetheless, the issuer could seek to characterize the offering as two separate offerings: one offering of $9 million to the 40 accredited investors with the preexisting relationship under Rule 506; and a second offering of $1 million to the twenty individual investors under Rule 504, to which the general solicitation ban does not apply (assuming state law registration requirements are met). Left unconstrained, issuers would be free to break apart transactions, evading many of Regulation D's limitations.

The integration doctrine restrains the ability of issuers to recharacterize offerings strategically. Several factors are relevant in determining whether seemingly separate offers and sales should be treated as one transaction (integrated). These factors are:

- whether the sales are part of a single plan of financing
- whether the sales involve issuance of the same class of securities
- whether the sales have been made at or about the same time
- whether the same type of consideration is received
- whether the sales are made for the same general purpose

Securities Act Release No. 4552 (November 6, 1962)

To provide greater certainty for issuers, the SEC in Regulation D provides a safe harbor from integration under Rule 502(a). Rule 502(a) applies six months prior to the start of the offering and six months after the *end* of the offering. To illustrate, imagine that a Regulation D private placement occurs from 7/1/11 to 8/1/11 as depicted below:

```
<——————    |              | ———————>
Minus          Start          End            Plus
6 months       Offering       Offering       6 months
1/1/15         7/1/15         8/1/15         2/1/16
```

Two time periods are important for the Rule 502(a) safe harbor: (a) the *safe harbor window* stretching from the beginning of the pre-offering six month period to the end of the post-offering six month period (1/1/15 to 2/1/15 in the diagram above) and (b) the *six-month periods window* consisting of the pre-offering and post-offering six month periods but not the time period of the offering itself (1/1/15 to 7/1/15 and 8/1/15 to 2/1/16 in the diagram above).

Sales outside the *safe harbor window* are deemed separate from the Regulation D offering, with one exception. During the *six-month periods window*, if the issuer offers or sells securities that "are of the same or similar class as those offered or sold under Regulation D," then the issuer loses the safe harbor entirely.

HYPOTHETICAL EIGHT

1. *Scenario One:* Trendy is contemplating a private placement to raise $10 million to fund its Lean Green drink expansion campaign. Trendy wants to raise this money through sales using a broker-dealer that has contacts with 35 individual investors (non-accredited but sophisticated) who want in the aggregate to purchase $5 million of common stock. Trendy also plans on making cold calls to 35 individual investors (assume accredited) to sell the remaining $5 million of common stock. If there were no integration doctrine, how could Trendy structure its transactions within Regulation D, allowing it to raise all this money in the next month?

2. *Scenario Two:* Suppose Trendy instead decides to do the following two offerings:

On January 1, Trendy conducts a Rule 505 offering of preferred stock sold through its brokers to investors with whom the company has a pre-existing relationship. The offering raises $5 million and the proceeds are used to expand its Lean Green production facilities. Thirty purchasers (non-accredited) participate in the offering.

Exactly two years later, Trendy decides to hire a new marketing consultant and engage in a new marketing campaign for Lean Green. To fund the campaign, Trendy conducts a private placement under Rule 506 for $10 million of bonds to ten purchasers (non-accredited) in return for the purchasers' marketing efforts.

3. *Scenario Three:* Suppose Kim reads Rule 502(a) and decides to structure the following series of transactions:

On 1/1 Trendy makes a Rule 504 offering for $1 million of common stock selling to ten individual purchasers (non-accredited and unsophisticated) through broker-dealers who have pre-existing relationships with the purchasers. The offer closes on 1/1 and is all cash. The proceeds are used to expand the Lean Green production facilities.

On 3/1 Trendy makes a Rule 506 offering for $10 million of common stock, selling to 35 individual purchasers (non-accredited) through broker-dealers with pre-existing relationships with the purchasers. The offer closes on 3/1 and is all cash. The proceeds are also used to expand the Lean Green production facilities.

Trendy on 11/1 decides to conduct a Rule 505 offering, selling $4 million of common stock to 25 former law students with whom the CEO has pre-existing relationships (all took the CEO's securities regulation class a few years ago but alas remain unsophisticated). The offering is all in cash and the proceeds are used to fund a new office building for Trendy's executive officers.

Are there any problems with these offerings?

G. INNOCENT AND INSIGNIFICANT MISTAKES

To err is human; fortunately Regulation D forgives (some) mistakes. Under Rule 508, failure to comply with a requirement for a

Rule 504, 505, or 506 offering will not necessarily result in a loss of exemptions for an offer or sale to a particular individual or entity.

Recall that in our study of the gun-jumping rules for registered public offerings, we did not see an explicit "insignificant and innocent" defense for issuers. Issuers that inadvertently condition the market in the Pre-Filing Period or innocently include additional free writing with the preliminary prospectus in the Waiting Period violate § 5 unless they comply with one of the various safe harbors. Moreover, a defect in the offer or sale of securities to *one* investor would taint the offering for all investors, with the consequence that the entire transaction would violate § 5. Section 12(a)(1) then provides a strict liability private cause of action for all those who purchased securities sold in the offering. Even if the mistake is innocent or trivial, investors can rescind their purchases, recovering their full purchase price under § 12(a)(1).

Given the SEC's hard stance with regard to registered offerings, why does Regulation D excuse insignificant and innocent mistakes? Indeed, in some ways, mistakes are harder to justify in a Regulation D offering. Because Regulation D is relatively bright-line, issuers have an easier time complying. Does Rule 508 result in issuers taking a lax approach to complying with Regulation D requirements?

One possible justification for Rule 508 is that the average investor in a Regulation D offering is more sophisticated compared with investors in a public offering. Presumably such sophisticated investors are able to "fend for themselves" and thus do not necessarily need the full gamut of securities law protections.

Although more generous than the gun-jumping rules, Rule 508's forgiveness is limited in several respects. First, Rule 508 does not shield the issuer from SEC enforcement actions. The SEC may bring an enforcement action against the issuer for violation of § 5 under § 20 of the Securities Act. Rule 508 only shields the issuer from private actions under § 12(a)(1).

Second, Rule 508 limits excuse to those situations where "failure to comply did not pertain to a term, condition or requirement directly intended to protect that particular individual or entity." Thus, if the issuer failed to deliver the required disclosure under Rule 502(b) to a particular investor and that investor sues for violation of § 5, the issuer cannot rely on Rule 508 to cure the defect in its use of Regulation D. If *other* investors (who did receive the information under Rule 502(b)) complain about the lack of information given to a particular investor, however, the issuer may then invoke Rule 508 to bar the claim of these other investors.

Third, even if the failure to comply was not related to a requirement directly intended to protect the particular investor suing, Rule 508 will also be unavailable to the issuer unless the failure to comply was "insignificant with respect to the offering as a whole." This exclusion has real teeth; certain types of failures to comply are defined by the SEC as significant, thereby making Rule 508 inapplicable. The failures relate to the following (as listed in Rule 508(a)(2)):

- the general solicitation prohibition (Rule 502(c))
- the aggregate offering price limitation (Rules 504(b)(2), 505(b)(2)(i))

- the limit on the number of purchasers (Rules 505(b)(2)(ii) and 506(b)(2)(i))

Finally, Rule 508(a)(3) requires that "[a] good faith and reasonable attempt was made to comply with all applicable terms, conditions, and requirements of Rule 504, 505 or 506."

HYPOTHETICAL NINE

Trendy conducts a private placement for $10 million of common stock under Rule 506, selling to five large hedge funds (all accredited investors with pre-existing relationships with Trendy and the placement agent for the offering) and 36 sophisticated, non-accredited purchasers (all lower-level Trendy employees). Two of the non-accredited purchasers tell Trendy that they are cousins and live in the same house. Consider how Rule 508 may apply to the following circumstances.

1.   *Scenario One:* It turns out that the cousins are not in fact cousins, but just friends (and they lied on their offeree questionnaire about their status). The hedge funds sue under § 12(a)(1) to rescind their purchases.

2.   *Scenario Two:* Suppose instead that Trendy simply forgot to mail the required disclosures under Rule 502(b) to the cousins. The cousins eventually get the information after they make their purchases. The hedge funds sue under § 12(a)(1) to rescind their purchases.

3.   *Scenario Three:* Suppose that one of the non-accredited investors was not an employee and had no pre-existing relationship with Trendy. The hedge funds sue under § 12(a)(1) to rescind their purchases.

H. DISQUALIFICATION

In 2013 the SEC promulgated rules to implement disqualification for Rule 506 pursuant to Dodd-Frank. Rule 506(d)'s disqualification is based on the presence of specified bad acts on the part of two groups of potential participants in the private placement.

- The issuer, including any predecessors or any affiliated issuer (termed the "issuer" here)

- Key individuals and entities connected with the issuer or the offering (termed the "related participants" here). These include any director or officer of the issuer, beneficial owner of 20 percent or more of any class of its equity securities, and any promoter of the issuer presently connected with it in any capacity. Also included is any person that is paid for the solicitation of purchasers in connection with the Rule 506 offering (including typically the private placement agent assisting the issuer in the offering) as well partner, director, or officer of the soliciting agent.

The presence of a bad act on the part of the issuer or a related participant results in the issuer losing the exemption under Rule 506. Rule 506(d)(1) thus punishes the issuer for associating with related participants that have engaged in prior bad acts.

For the issuer and related participants in a Rule 506 private placement, an important subset of bad acts includes past securities-related wrongdoings. The past securities-related wrongdoing must be in connection with the purchase or sale of any security, relate to a false filing with the SEC, or involve the "conduct of the business of an underwriter, broker, dealer, municipal securities dealer, investment adviser or paid solicitor of purchasers of securities." Rule 506(d) disqualification follows if the bad act has led to (among other consequences):

- A conviction for any felony or misdemeanor related to the purchase or sale of securities in the ten years prior to the sale of securities under Rule 506 involving the past securities-related wrongdoing. For issuers, including predecessors or any affiliated issuers, the time period is shortened to five years prior to the sale of securities under Rule 506. *See* Rule 506(d)(1)(i).

- A court order, judgment, or decree entered within five years of the sale of securities under Rule 506 restraining or enjoining the individual or entity from engaging or continuing to engage in any conduct or practice related to the past securities-related wrongdoing. *See* Rule 506(d)(1)(ii).

Outside of these specific past securities-related wrongdoings, issuers are also disqualified from Rule 506 if either the issuer or related participant, is subject to one of the following restrictions:

- A final order from state securities commissions, a state authority that supervises or examines financial institutions, a state insurance commission, an "appropriate" federal banking agency, the U.S. Commodity Futures Trading Commission, or the National Credit Union Administration that, among others, bars the specific party from association with the other regulator, bars the specific party from engaging in the business of securities, insurance or banking, or "[c]onstitutes a final order based on a violation of any law or regulation that prohibits fraudulent, manipulative, or deceptive conduct entered within ten years before such sale." Rule 506(d)(1)(iii).

- Certain SEC orders that, among others, at the time of the sale of securities under Rule 506, suspends of revokes the specific party's registration as a broker, dealer, municipal securities dealer, or investment advisor or otherwise limits their activities. Rule 506(d)(1)(iv).

- An SEC order entered into within five years of the sale of securities under Rule 506 that orders the specific party to "cease and desist from committing or causing a violation or future violation of" any scienter-based antifraud provision of the federal securities laws (including Rule 10b–5) or § 5 of the Securities Act. Rule 506(d)(1)(v).

- A suspension or expulsion from membership in FINRA or a national securities exchange "for any act or omission to act constituting conduct inconsistent with just and equitable principles of trade." Rule 506(d)(1)(vi). This restriction also covers individuals who are barred from associating with a member for such conduct.

- "[A] stop or refusal order under § 8 [entered within five years of the Rule 506 sale] or is at the time of the Rule 506 sale of securities the subject of an SEC investigation or proceeding to determine whether a stop order should be issued. Rule 506(d)(1)(vii).

Rule 506 gives discretion to the SEC to waive the disqualification if "the Commission determines that it is not necessary under the circumstances that an exemption be denied." Rule 506(d)(2)(ii). In addition, the issuer may avoid disqualification if: "the issuer establishes that it did not know and, in the exercise of reasonable care, could not have known that a disqualification existed under [Rule 506(d)(1)]." Rule 506(d)(2)(iv). The instructions to Rule 506(d)(2)(iv) then state: "An issuer will not be able to establish that it has exercised reasonable care unless it has made, in light of the circumstances, factual inquiry into whether any disqualifications exist. The nature and scope of the factual inquiry will vary based on the facts and circumstances concerning, among other things, the issuer and the other offering participants."

Rule 505 also provides for disqualification based on similar, but somewhat narrower grounds, than Rule 506(d). Rule 505 does not specify the circumstances when issuers are disqualified from using the exemption, but instead references the disqualifiers contained in Rule 262 of Regulation A. Rule 505(b)(2)(iii). Note that Rule 504 does not contain a disqualification provision. Registered public offerings are also available to all issuers without disqualification.

In addition to these specific disqualification provisions, Rule 507 applies a general disqualification from the use of Rules 504, 505, and 506. The disqualification provision under Rule 507 is narrow, focusing solely on issuers that in the past have failed to comply with the notice filing requirement of Rule 503.

The SEC used its authority to waive disqualification upon a showing of "good cause" in the following SEC administrative order.

Order Under Rule 506(d) of the Securities Act of 1933 Granting a Waiver of the Rule 506(d)(1)(ii) Disqualification Provision In the Matter of Bank of America, N.A. and Merrill Lynch, Pierce, Fenner & Smith, Inc.

S.E.C. Rel. No. 9421 (Nov. 25, 2014).

* * *

Bank of America, N.A. and Merrill Lynch, Pierce, Fenner & Smith Inc. (the "Respondents"), submitted a letter dated November 18, 2014, requesting that the Securities and Exchange Commission (the "Commission") grant a waiver of disqualification under Rule 506(d)(1)(ii) of Regulation D . . . upon entry of the final judgment (the "Judgment") by the United States District Court for the Western District of North Carolina Charlotte Division. The Judgment enjoins the Respondents from committing violations of Sections 17(a)(2) and (3), and Section 5(b)(1) of the Securities Act of 1933.

Rule 506(d)(2)(ii) of Regulation D provides that disqualification "shall not apply. . . upon a showing of good cause and without prejudice to any other action by the Commission, if the Commission determines that it is not necessary under the circumstances that an exemption be denied." The Commission has determined that as part of the Rule 506(d)(2)(ii) showing of good cause, the Respondents will comply with the following:

A.   Retain, at Respondents' expense and within sixty (60) days of the issuance of this Order, a qualified independent consultant (the "Consultant") not unacceptable to the Staff. Respondents shall require the Consultant to conduct a comprehensive review of the policies and procedures relating to compliance with Rule 506 of Regulation D by Respondents and the subsidiaries of Respondents conducting any activities that would otherwise be disqualified pursuant to the Judgment (together with Respondents, the "Rule 506 Entities").

B.   Cooperate fully with the Consultant, including providing the Consultant with access to the Rule 506 Entities' files, books, records, and personnel as reasonably requested for the review, obtaining the cooperation of employees or other persons under Respondents' control, and permitting the Consultant to engage such assistance (whether clerical, legal, technological, or of any other expert nature) as necessary to achieve the purposes of the retention.

C.   Require the Consultant to complete its review and submit a written preliminary report ("Preliminary Report") to the Respondents and Commission staff within three hundred and sixty (360) days of the issuance of this Order. . . .

D.   Within one hundred and eighty (180) days of receipt of the Preliminary Report, adopt and implement all recommendations contained in the Preliminary Report. . . .

E.   Within one hundred and eighty (180) days from the date of the Respondents' implementation of the recommendations contained in the Preliminary Report, require the Consultant to submit a final written report ("Final Report") to the Respondents, including their principal executive officers and principal legal officers, and Commission staff. The Consultant shall certify in the Final Report that the Respondents have implemented the recommendations contained in the Preliminary Report and that the Respondent's policies and procedures designed to ensure compliance by the Rule 506 Entities with their obligations under Rule 506 of Regulation D are reasonably designed to achieve their stated purpose.

F.   On or after the date that the Respondents have adopted and implemented all recommendations referenced in paragraph D of this Order, and in no event earlier than the date when the Final Report is delivered pursuant to paragraph E of this Order, the Respondents may apply to the Commission for a waiver covering the remaining 30 months in the disqualification period that are not covered by this Order.

G.   Require the Consultant to enter into an agreement that provides that for the period of engagement and for a period of two years from completion of the engagement, the Consultant shall not enter into any employment, consultant, attorney-client, auditing or other professional relationship with the Rule 506 Entities, or any of their present or former affiliates, directors, officers, employees, or agents acting in their capacity as such. . . .

H.   To ensure the independence of the Consultant, Respondents shall not have the authority to terminate the Consultant without prior written approval of Commission staff and shall compensate the Consultant and persons engaged to assist the Consultant for services rendered pursuant to this Order at their reasonable and customary rates.

Based on the foregoing, Commission has determined that pursuant to Rule 506(d)(2)(ii) of Regulation D under the Securities Act a showing of good cause has been made that it is not necessary under the circumstances that the exemptions be denied.

* * *

QUESTIONS

1.   Why did Bank of America and Merrill Lynch need to cooperate with the SEC's "good cause" conditions to obtain a waiver from disqualification?

2.   Is the SEC getting "two bites at the apple" through the "good cause" provision? Presumably the SEC got the sanctions the court deemed appropriate in the underlying case against Bank of America and Merrill Lynch. Why should the SEC then get to impose further remedial requirements on the bad actor as a condition for the waiver under Rule 506(d)(2)(ii)?

I.   OTHER ASPECTS OF REGULATION D

1.   STATE SECURITIES REGULATION

Long before the enactment of the Securities Act of 1933 and the Securities Exchange Act of 1934, states imposed "Blue Sky" regulations, starting with Kansas in 1911. Today states vary widely in their methods of regulation. Some states, such as New York, do not require registration of securities (except for securities sold in real estate or intrastate offerings) and instead impose only antifraud liability. Other states, including California, Texas, and Wisconsin, require issuers to meet a merit test, prohibiting issuers from offering or selling securities that failed to meet certain substantive criteria (and thus are deemed "unfair" for investors). Most states combine disclosure with limited merit review. Although the predominant number of states model their Blue Sky laws after the Uniform Securities Act of 1956 and the Revised Uniform Securities Act of 1985, with variations across different states, the model codes do not specify a single method of securities regulation.

Instead, the "uniform" acts allow states to pick and choose from among antifraud liability, disclosure, and merit regulation options.

The diversity of regulatory approaches among the states forced issuers selling securities in multiple states to spend time and resources to comply with each states' securities registration requirements. In 1996, Congress narrowed the scope of state securities regulation with the National Securities Markets Improvement Act of 1996 (NSMIA). Certain "covered securities," including securities listed or approved for listing on the NYSE, AMEX and Nasdaq are exempted from state securities registration requirements. Covered securities also include securities issued in an exempt offering under Rule 506. Consequently, states may not require the registration of securities offered and sold under Rule 506. States may nonetheless require that Rule 506 issuers notify the states of the offering and to impose a notification fee. Although NSMIA bars state registration of certain securities, states can continue to investigate and enforce their antifraud laws.

Under NSMIA, covered securities do not include securities exempt from registration pursuant to Rules 504 or 505 of Regulation D. State Blue Sky regulation may potentially apply to Rule 504 and 505 offerings as a result. Covered securities also do not include securities offered and sold under § 3(a)(11) of the intrastate offering exemption. We discuss the intrastate offering exemption later in the chapter.

Despite the potential application of Blue Sky registration requirements to Rule 504 and 505 offerings, most states have adopted exemptions from registration. The states vary in their requirements for an exemption. Several states have moved over the past decade to adopt the Uniform Securities Act of 2002. Under the 2002 Act, states provide for an exemption from state registration for all sales and offers to institutional investors. The 2002 Act also provides an exemption for sales to 25 or fewer investors in a 12-month period so long as the issuer restricts advertisement of the offering, pays commissions only to registered broker-dealers or agents, and makes sales only to those whom the issuer reasonably believes has investment intent. The 25 or fewer investor exemption does not impose any sophistication, net worth, income, or other requirement on the investors.

2.   RULE 504

Rule 504 excuses issuers from the requirements imposed under Rules 505 and 506, including the general solicitation ban (Rule 502(c)), disclosure (Rule 502(b)), and resale restriction (Rule 502(d)). An issuer complying with Rule 504 may solicit offers broadly without disclosing any information. Investors purchasing through a Rule 504 offering, moreover, may immediately resell the securities into the public secondary markets. Issuers complying with Rule 504 can essentially engage in a mini public offering.

There are two caveats, however, to this observation. First, Rule 504 is limited in its aggregate offering price to $1 million and it excludes Exchange Act reporting issuers. The mini public offering allowable under Rule 504 therefore is primarily of use for small, less well-followed issuers that need to raise small amounts of capital. The ability to engage in general solicitation and avoid disclosure may not matter if only more sophisticated investors participate in the market for such offerings. Sophisticated investors will presumably demand disclosure and will have the wherewithal to fend for themselves despite receiving a general solicitation, but are such investors interested in such small-scale offerings?

Second, issuers seeking to use Rule 504 to avoid the general solicitation and resale restrictions of Regulation D must meet certain requirements related to state law registration requirements. First, the issuer may sell securities in states, such as California, that provide for state registration of the securities and the "public filing and delivery to investors of a substantive disclosure document before sale." Issuers that sell securities in "accordance with those state provisions" may avoid the application of Rule 502(c) (general solicitation) and Rule 502(d) (resale restrictions). Rule 504(b)(1)(i). Second, issuers may also sell in states that have no state registration requirement, such as New York, so long as they comply with the registration and public filing and delivery requirements of another state, such as California. Issuers must ensure that "the disclosure document is delivered before sale to all purchasers (including those in the states that have no such procedure)." Rule 504(b)(1)(ii). Third, issuers may make sales "[e]xclusively according to state law exemptions from registration that permit general solicitation and general advertising so long as sales are made only to 'accredited investors' as defined in Rule 501(a)." Rule 504(b)(1)(iii).

3.   FORM D

Rule 503 requires that issuers engaged in a Rule 504, 505, or 506 offering file a Form D with the SEC. The issuer has until the fifteenth day after the start of the offering to file Form D. No immediate penalty results if an issuer fails to file Form D. Rule 507, however, provides that an issuer may not use Regulation D if it is subject to an order, judgment, or decree by any court enjoining it from violating Rule 503.

Form D contains basic information on the issuer and the offering, including the promoters of the offering, 10% beneficial owners, and the executive officers and directors of the issuer, broker-dealers assisting with the offering and their commission, the minimum investment required of an investor, and the offering price, the number of investors, expenses, and use of proceeds.

4.   EXCHANGE ACT FILING

Exchange Act reporting issuers of equity securities in an unregistered offering must also file a Form 8–K with the SEC. Item 3.02(a) of Form 8–K provides that the issuer must report the information specified in Item 701 of Regulation S–K, including information on the securities sold, the underwriters and other purchasers, the consideration received for the securities, the use of proceeds, and the exemption claimed from § 5. If the equity securities sold in the unregistered offering account for less than 1% of the outstanding equity securities of the same class, Item 3.02(b) exempts the issuer from the Form 8–K filing requirement (an even more generous exemption applies for small business issuers). All Exchange Act reporting issuers, including those exempt under Form 8–K, must provide similar information on unregistered sales of securities in their periodic Form 10–K and 10–Q filings unless already reported in a prior filing. Because the Form 8–K filing requirement applies to all unregistered sales, issuers must file a Form 8–K not only for Regulation D offerings, but also for § 4(a)(2), intrastate, Regulation S, and other offerings exempt from § 5.

J. THE PRIVATE PLACEMENT PROCESS

Although the legal requirements for a private placement are complicated, many issuers successfully sell securities through a private placement under § 4(a)(2) or Regulation D. How does the typical private placement work? This depends on the size of the offering. If a company sells securities to its top officers, the offering will typically take place under § 4(a)(2) without much formality.

If the company is offering securities to outside investors, the issuer will hire a placement agent to assist in the offering. Most private placements are done as best efforts offerings under which the placement agent is compensated through a commission for each security sold in the offering and reimbursed for expenses.

The placement agent, much like an underwriter in a registered public offering, will first review the business and finances of the issuer. One goal of this initial review is to give the placement agent the opportunity to develop a "due diligence" package to give to investors who are considering the offering. The review will also result in a plan of financing. This recommendation may include timing, types of securities, and amounts to be raised through a private placement. In some cases, a third party rating agency may then rate the issuer and the offered securities (particularly debt).

Once a plan of financing is agreed upon and the issuer moves forward with a private placement, the placement agent will also help write up a private placement memorandum. No specific SEC form dictates the exact contents of the private placement memorandum, although Rule 502(b) specifies what information must be included. The memorandum typically contains similar information to a public offering statutory prospectus, detailing the issuer's business, properties, management, and financials. The requirements of the securities laws aside, most sophisticated investors in the private placement market will simply avoid offerings that lack a private placement memorandum containing this standardized information.

Once the private placement memorandum is ready, the placement agent will begin marketing the offering. This involves contacting investors with whom the agent has a pre-existing relationship (complying with the general solicitation prohibition in Regulation D). For issuers unfamiliar with the private placement market, the placement agent will guide the issuer toward investors most likely to participate in the offering and provide advice on how best to sell the offering. The placement agent may also set up roadshow meetings between the issuers and investors. Investors, for their part, may look to the placement agent to screen issuers, recommending only viable, worthwhile investments. The due diligence package created by the placement agent will also assist investors in valuing the private placement.

Investors wishing to participate in the offering may then negotiate terms with the issuer. In a bond offering, for example, investors will focus particular attention on the covenants in the bond indenture. Such terms may include maximum debt-equity ratios, restrictions on dividends, and so on. Once investors make the decision to purchase, the private placement agent will assist with the execution of the subscription agreements and the transfer of money and securities.

———

Section 4(a)(2) and Regulation D provide the most important set of exemptions from § 5's registration requirement. We finish our coverage of offering exemptions with four additional exemptions from registration: Regulation A, Crowdfunding, the intrastate offering exemption under § 3(a)(11) and Rule 147 of the Securities Act, and Regulation S.

Given the availability of § 4(a)(2) and Regulation D, why have Congress and the SEC provided these additional exemptions? Section 4(a)(2) and Regulation D focus primarily on the needs of the investors (i.e., are the investors able to fend for themselves), the relatively small scope of the offering, and the selling efforts. What additional factors may lead Congress and the SEC to exempt offerings from § 5? Paramount are: (1) the needs of small business issuers; (2) the presence of an alternative regulatory regime (state-based securities regulation); and (3) the importance of national boundaries and the need to respect the authority of other countries.

IV. REGULATION A

Small business issuers enjoy a number of routes to raise capital in the securities markets with relaxed disclosure requirements and regulations. For "emerging growth companies" doing public offerings, the JOBS Act eases the burden of disclosure requirements as we discuss in Chapter 7. Although emerging growth companies must comply with § 5's gun-jumping regime, less stringent disclosure reduces the cost of preparing the registration statement for a public offering.

Non-Exchange Act reporting companies (typically smaller issuers with fewer than 2,000 shareholders or less than $10 million in assets) may also take advantage of Rule 504 to do a public offering of securities that can be freely resold. Rule 504, however, imposes a $1 million limit on the aggregate offering price and requires issuers to comply with state law registration requirements in order to avoid the general solicitation and resale limitations of Regulation D. Rules 502(c) and (d).

Standing in between registered public offerings on the one hand, and Rule 504 on the other, is Regulation A, promulgated pursuant to § 3(b)(2) of the Securities Act. Like offerings under Rule 504 and§ 5, Regulation A allows for the free resale of securities, which creates the possibility of a liquid secondary market following an offering.

Until recently, Regulation A was of little economic significance, hamstrung by a $5 million ceiling on the offering amount. Issuers were also put off by the time and expense of complying with Regulation A's gun jumping rules and disclosure requirements. Finally, issuers seeking to use Regulation A were required to comply with state "Blue Sky" securities law requirements in every state in which securities were offered and sold. As a consequence, Regulation A was largely ignored.

Congress boosted the appeal of Regulation A as part of the JOBS Act of 2012. Viewing the $5 million ceiling as inadequate, Congress raised the statutory exemption authority to $50 million. Section 3(b)(5) provides for SEC review of the offering amount limitation every 2 years to determine whether to increase the amount. Another key change for Regulation A is Securities Act § 3(b)(4), which provides for ongoing periodic disclosure after the offering. Rather than piggyback onto the existing disclosure regime, Congress instructed the SEC to create a new set of disclosure rules for Regulation A issuers.

The SEC implemented this new exemption authority in 2015. The so-called "Regulation A+" adopts a two-tier regime. The first, Tier 1, largely carries forward the prior Regulation A regime, albeit with a more generous $20 million limit in any twelve-month period. The second tier, Tier 2, provides for offerings of up to $50 million in any twelve-month period. We briefly summarize here the main contours of Regulation A offerings, highlighting the regulatory differences between Tier 1 and Tier 2.

A note on Regulation A's terminology: Regulation A is a mini-public offering. Consequently, many of the terms used in Regulation A have direct counterparts from the registered public offering process. Issuers file an offering statement (registration statement) with the SEC of which a key part is the offering circular (prospectus). Issuers go through a three time period sequences in a Regulation A offering, going from the time prior to the filing of the offering statement with the SEC (the Pre-Filing Period), to the period during which the issuer waits for the SEC to declare the offering statement qualified (the equivalent of effectiveness for a registration statement) (the Waiting Period), to the period after the SEC has qualified the offering statement and sales may commence (the Post-Qualification Period).

A. ELIGIBLE ISSUERS AND SECURITIES

Only issuers organized under the laws of the United States or Canada that have their principal place of business in those countries may take advantage of the Regulation A exemptions from § 5. Rule 251(b). In addition, certain issuers are ineligible, including Exchange Act reporting issuers, blank check companies, and certain investment companies. Rule 251(b). Issuers that have the registration of a security revoked for failing to comply with the federal securities laws pursuant to § 12(j) of the Exchange Act within five years before the filing of the offering statement cannot use Regulation A. Rule 251(b)(6). Issuers that have previously issued securities under a Regulation A but that have failed to file with the SEC the required reports under Regulation A pursuant to Rule 257 (discussed below) during the two years preceding the filing of a new Regulation A offering statement are also ineligible. Rule 251(b)(7).

Regulation A is also limited to certain "eligible" securities, such as equity and debt (including debt that is convertible into equity). Regulation A explicitly excludes asset-backed securities. Rule 261(c).

In addition to issuer sales of securities, Regulation A also provides a limited means for resale by investors (termed "selling securityholders") who cannot freely resell their securities into the public capital markets. (Holders of such restricted securities are typically insiders and others who purchased the securities from the company in a private placement.) Rule 251(a)(1) and (a)(2).

B. "BAD ACTOR" DISQUALIFICATION

Regulation A has a disqualifying provision in Rule 262 that tracks the disqualification provision in Rule 506(d), targeting bad acts by two groups of potential participants in a Regulation A offering:

- The issuer, including any predecessors or any affiliated issuer (termed the "issuer" here).

- Key individuals and entities connected with the issuer or the offering (termed "related participants" here). These include any director or officer of the issuer, beneficial owner of 20 percent or more of any class of its voting equity securities, and any promoter of the issuer presently connected with it in any capacity. Also included is any person that is paid to solicit purchasers in connection with the offering (typically a broker-dealer assisting the issuer in the offering) as well partner, director, or officer of the soliciting agent.

Rule 262 then delineates a list of bad acts similar to the list of bad acts in Rule 506(d). The past wrongdoing must be in connection with the purchase or sale of any security, relate to a false filing with the SEC, or involve the "conduct of the business of an underwriter, broker, dealer, municipal securities dealer, investment adviser or paid solicitor of purchasers of securities." Rule 262 disqualification follows if the bad act has led to (among other consequences):

- A conviction for any felony or misdemeanor in the ten years prior to the Regulation A filing. For issuers, the time period is shortened to five years. Rule 262(a)(1).

- A court order, judgment, or decree entered within five years of the Regulation A filing restraining or enjoining the individual or entity from engaging or continuing to engage in any conduct or practice related to the past wrongdoing. Rule 262(a)(2).

Beyond these specific past securities-related violations, issuers are also disqualified under Rule 262 if either the issuer or related participant is subject to one of the following restrictions:

- A final order from state securities commissions, a state authority that supervises or examines financial institutions, a state insurance commission, an "appropriate" federal banking agency, the U.S. Commodity Futures Trading Commission, or the National Credit Union Administration that, among others, bars the specific party from association with the other regulator, bars the specific party from engaging in the business of securities, insurance or banking, or "[c]onstitutes a final order based on a violation of any law or regulation that prohibits fraudulent, manipulative, or deceptive conduct entered within ten years before such filing of the offering statement." Rule 262(a)(3).

- Certain SEC orders that at the time of the Regulation A filing, suspend or revoke the party's registration as a broker, dealer, municipal securities dealer, or investment advisor or otherwise limits their activities. Rule 262(a)(4).

- An SEC order entered into within five years of the Regulation A filing that orders the specific party to "cease and desist from committing or causing a violation or future violation of" any scienter-based antifraud provision of the federal securities laws (including Rule 10b–5) or § 5 of the Securities Act. Rule 262(a)(5).

- A suspension or expulsion from FINRA or a national securities exchange "for any act or omission to act constituting conduct inconsistent with just and equitable principles of trade." Rule 262(a)(6). This restriction also covers individuals who are barred from associating with a member for such conduct.

- "Has filed (as a registrant or issuer), or was or was named as an underwriter in, any registration statement or offering statement filed with the Commission that, within five years before the filing of the offering statement, was the subject of a refusal order, stop order, or order suspending the Regulation A exemption, or is, at the time of such filing, the subject of an investigation or proceeding to determine whether a stop order or suspension order should be issued." Rule 262(a)(7).

Rule 262 gives discretion to the SEC to waive the disqualification. Rule 262(b)(2). In addition, the issuer may avoid disqualification if: "the issuer establishes that it did not know and, in the exercise of reasonable care, could not have known that a disqualification existed under [Rule 262(a)]." Rule 262(b)(4). The instructions to Rule 262(b)(4) then state: "An issuer will not be able to establish that it has exercised reasonable care unless it has made, in light of the circumstances, factual inquiry into whether any disqualifications exist."

In comparing Regulation A with a registered public offering or a Rule 504 offering, note that both Rule 504 and Regulation A are only available to non-Exchange Act reporting companies. Rule 504, however, does not contain a disqualification provision. Registered public offerings are available to all issuers without regard to reporting status and without any disqualification.

HYPOTHETICAL TEN

Imagine that Frauds-R-Us, Inc., a non-Exchange Act reporting issuer, seeks capital to expand its short term loan business located in New Jersey. Frauds-R-Us had previously attempted to make a registered initial public offering a year ago. After the filing of the registration statement for the IPO, CorpFin suggested that the company provide more detailed biographical descriptions for the directors and top officers of the company.

Frauds-R-Us refused, choosing instead to wait out the twenty-day period for its registration statement to become effective. Thereafter, the SEC gave notice, held a hearing, and issued a stop order pursuant to § 8(d) suspending the effectiveness of the registration statement. Now, a year later, Frauds-R-Us is attempting to raise capital once more from the public capital markets, this time armed with the full biography of its directors and officers.

1. Can Frauds-R-Us do a Tier 2 Regulation A offering for $40 million?

2. Can Frauds-R-Us go back and register for an initial public offering for $100 million?

C. AGGREGATE OFFERING PRICE

Regulation A is promulgated under § 3(b)(2) of the Securities Act which sets an upper limit of $50 million on offerings (subject to the SEC's periodic review of that limit). Accordingly, Regulation A establishes two aggregate offering price ceilings. In a Tier 1 offering, issuers may sell up to $20 million. As we discuss in Chapter 10, securities that were not initially sold through a public offering (restricted securities) as well as securities held by affiliates (those in a control relationship with the issuer) may not generally be resold in the public capital markets without complying with § 5 of the Securities Act. Unlike Regulation D, Regulation A allows selling securityholders to sell their restricted securities in a transaction exempt from § 5. Of the $20 million limit for a Tier 1 offering, investors may sell up to $6 million. (So if investors use the Regulation A offering to resell $6 million of securities that otherwise would have to comply with § 5, the issuer may sell up to $14 million in a Tier 1 Regulation A offering). In a Tier 2 offering, issuers may sell up to $50 million in any 12-month period. Of this $50 million, investors can sell up to $15 million in secondary sales.

As with Regulation D, the $20 and $50 million aggregate offering price limits are reduced based on all securities sold within a twelve-month "look back" window before the start of the offering and during the offering itself. Unlike Regulation D, however, only securities sold pursuant to Regulation A are counted against the aggregate offering price. Compare this with the aggregate offering price for Rule 504 and 505 offerings; under those Regulation D exemptions, the aggregate offering price limit is reduced by securities sold under § 3(b) as well as violations of § 5. Regulation A is therefore more lenient in allowing issuers to engage in multiple prior § 3(b) (but not Regulation A) offerings, without reducing the maximum amount of proceeds that can be derived from a Regulation A offering.

The SEC added another offering amount restriction for secondary securities sales if an issuer is selling in an initial Regulation A offering. The worry is that pre-offering investors holding restricted securities may use Regulation A as a backdoor method of selling. For that initial offering, and any subsequent sales in a Regulation A offering for one year following the qualification date of the issuer's first Regulation A offering, investors cannot exceed 30% of the aggregate offering price for that offering. After twelve months from the first Regulation A offering, this 30% limit only applies to affiliate resales through Regulation A.

The table below compares Regulation A to registered public offerings (which have no offering price limit) and Rule 504.

	Public Offering	Regulation A	Rule 504
Offering Price Limitation	None	Tier 1: $20 million (No more than $6 million from selling securityholders) Tier 2: $50 million (No more than $15 million from selling securityholders)	$1 million Not available for selling securityholders
Aggregation	None	Prior 12-month aggregation with Reg. A offerings only (Rule 251(a)(1))	Prior 12-month aggregation with § 3(b) offerings and § 5(a) violations (Rule 504(b)(2))

HYPOTHETICAL ELEVEN

Trendy Inc. decides to make the following series of offerings (each taking place in one day). Assume that the offerings are for distinct and separate purposes (e.g., research and development, construction of Lean Green factory, advertising) and will not be integrated:

January 1: Sale of $3 million of common stock under Rule 506 to 30 accredited individual investors (all making more than $400,000 per year).

February 1: Sale of $20 million of common stock under a Tier 2 Regulation A together with $15 million of common stock sold by selling securityholders. Assume this is Trendy's first Regulation A offering.

December 1: Sale of $2 million of securities under Rule 505 of Regulation D to 30 non-accredited investors.

The January 1st offering under Rule 506 was sold using broad-based solicitations to reach investors. Neither Trendy nor its placement agent verified the accredited investor status of the January 1st investors but instead "took them at their word." Are the offers exempt from § 5?

D. INVESTORS

Regulation A offerings are open to all investors. Perhaps out of a fear that this may result in retail investors getting in over their heads and losing money invested in risky private companies, the SEC limits how much an investor can invest in a Tier 2 offering. In a Tier 2 offering, the SEC limits the amount that a non-accredited natural person can purchase to no more than 10% of the greater of the investor's annual income and net worth as determined according to Rule 501 of Regulation D. Rule 251(d)(2)(i)(C)(1). For an investor with a net worth of $100,000, Regulation A thus limits the amount the investor can lose in any one offering to $10,000 (assuming the 10% of net worth is the applicable threshold for the particular investor). For non-accredited entities, the 10% limit is applied based on an entity's annual revenues and net assets. Rule 251(d)(2)(i)(C)(2). Accredited investors are not limited. The limit only applies to issuers not listed on a national securities exchange upon qualification.

The limit on how much an investor may invest in a particular Regulation A offering gives some assurance that the investor can absorb potential losses. Note that analogous investment limits also apply to crowdfunding. According to § 4(a)(6), the aggregate amount sold to an investor cannot exceed the greater $2,000 or 5 percent of the annual income or net worth of such investor or 10 percent of the annual income or net worth, depending on whether the investor's annual income or net worth is less or more than $100,000. Absent any limitation on the types of investors who can invest, these limits protect unsophisticated purchasers from getting in over their heads. But what of investors who invest in multiple Regulation A offerings? If a retail investor invests in 10% of her net worth separately in five different Regulation A offerings, the investor will have 50% of her net worth at risk in a number of relatively risky Regulation A securities. Is this an acceptable amount of risk for a retail investor?

What happens if an investor lies about her net worth or assets to the issuer? Regulation A allows issuers to rely on an investor's representations, as long as the issuer does not know that the investor is making a misrepresentation. Rule 251(d)(2)(i)(D). Left open is what happens if the issuer does not explicitly know at the time of the sale the representation is untrue, but has information that casts doubt on the veracity of the representation. Does Rule 251(d)(2)(i)(D) shield issuers from unreasonably relying on the issuer's representations? Note the difference with the verification requirement imposed on issuers of an investor's accredited investor status for issuers using general solicitation pursuant to Rule 506(c) under Regulation D.

There is no investment limit for investors in a Tier 1 offering. Typically issuers opting for Tier 1 will be smaller and less well known. Don't such issuers pose the greatest risk to investors? Even in a Tier 2 offering, accredited investors do not face any investment limit, thus allowing them to invest their entire net worth in a single offering.

E. DISCLOSURE

1. OFFERING

Regulation A imposes mandatory offering disclosure requirements: the offering statement and offering circular, roughly analogous to the registration statement and statutory prospectus, respectively.

Offering Statement: Securities Act Form 1–A sets forth the contents of the Regulation A offering statement. Part I of Form 1–A contains information specific to Regulation A, including the issuer's eligibility to use Regulation A, whether the offering is Tier 1 or 2, whether significant participants in the offering are subject to the disqualification provision of Rule

262, the type of securities offered and the price and amount of the offering, the amount of the offering attributable to selling securityholders, and the jurisdictions in which securities are to be offered. Form 1–A also requires the disclosure of any unregistered securities sold by the issuer (or any of its predecessors or affiliated issuers) within one year prior to the filing of the Form 1–A. Rule 252(a) also provides that issuers must include additional material information "necessary to make the required statements, in the light of the circumstances under which they are made, not misleading." The SEC requires that the "issuer, its principal executive offering, principal financial officer, principal accounting officer, and a majority of the members of its board of directors" must sign the offering statement. Rule 252(c).

Offering Circular: Rule 253(a) states that the offering circular "must include the information required by Form 1–A for offering circulars." The information contained in the offering circular (contained in Part II of Form 1–A) resembles that of the statutory prospectus used in a registered public offering. The required categories of information include, among others:

- Risk Factors
- Dilution
- Plan of Distribution and Selling Securityholders
- Use of Proceeds to Issuer
- Description of Business
- Description of Property
- Management's Discussion and Analysis of Financial Condition and Results of Operations (or the "MD&A")
- Directors, Executive Officers and Significant Employees
- Compensation of Directors and Executive Officers
- Security Ownership of Management and Certain Securityholders
- Interest of Management and Others in Certain Transactions
- Description of Securities Being Offered
- Certain Financial Statement Information

These categories track the information found in the statutory prospectus in a registered public offering (discussed in Chapter 7). One key difference is that the required financial disclosure is less demanding. Both Tier 1 and Tier 2 issuers must file balance sheets, income statements, cash flows, and other financial statements for the two most recently completed fiscal years. U.S. issuers must follow U.S. Generally Accepted Accounting Principles (US GAAP) in preparing their financial statements. Canadian issuers may use either US GAAP or International Financial Reporting Standards (IFRS) adopted by the International Accounting Standards Board (IASB). Tier 2 issuers must file audited financial statements. There is no audit requirement for a

Tier 1 issuer's financial statements, subject to one exception. If the Tier 1 issuer obtained an audit of its financial statements for other purposes and the audit meets specified standards, then the Tier 1 issuer must file audited financial statements.

Within 30 days after terminating or completing a Regulation A offering, Tier 1 issuers must file a Form 1–Z exit report. Rule 257(a). Among other things, Form 1–Z requires the disclosure of the portion of sales by the issuer and the portion sold by selling securityholders. Tier 2 issuers can disclose this information either on Part I of Form 1–Z or as part of their annual report, whichever is filed first.

HYPOTHETICAL TWELVE

Trendy plans to sell $20 million of common stock through a Tier 1 offering. After consulting with her attorneys and reading through Form 1–A, Kim, the CEO of Trendy, is reluctant to pay the cost of having the company's financials audited in preparation for the offering. Nonetheless, Kim ultimately agrees with Trendy's investment bank (acting as the placement agent for the offering), that obtaining audited financials for Trendy's past three years would be a good idea for the offering. Why did the investment bank recommend this?

2.   PERIODIC REPORTING

A key advantage for private companies that sell securities in a Regulation D private placement is that the sale does not necessarily trigger public company status. If the Regulation D offering results in an increase in the total assets of the private company and the number of shareholders sufficient to cross the public company thresholds contained in § 12(g) of the Exchange Act then the private company must register as a public company. So long as the issuer remains below the § 12(g) numerical threshold, however, Regulation D allows a private company to raise capital without triggering the burdens of public company status. Those requirements include the periodic disclosure requirements we covered in Chapter 4, such as the annual Form 10–K and quarterly Form 10–Q filing requirements.

Regulation A differs from Regulation D in that an unlimited number of non-accredited investors may purchase in a Regulation A offering. Moreover, investors who purchase in a Regulation A offering may resell their shares immediately without restriction. Those resales may generate a secondary market for the securities of even a private company. Unlike a Regulation D private placement, a secondary market may develop quickly for shares sold through a Regulation A offering.

Is a secondary market likely to develop for the shares of a private company, which by definition has a relatively low amount of assets and shareholders? (If the total asset size crosses $10 million and the number of shareholders cross the thresholds set in § 12(g) then the private company will have to register as a public company.)

To address concerns about uninformed investors, the SEC provides for ongoing disclosures for Tier 2 issuers that have sold securities through a Regulation A offering. These requirements are similar to, but more limited than the periodic disclosure requirements imposed on public companies. Rule 257(b). These include:

- Form 1–K annual reports (the analogue of Form 10–K annual reports). Form 1–K permits issuers to incorporate by reference certain information previously filed on EDGAR. Form 1–K includes information on business operations for the previous three fiscal years, transactions with related persons, beneficial ownership of voting securities by executive officers, directors and 10% owners, identities of directors and significant employees with a description of their business experience, executive compensation data for the most recent fiscal year for the three highest paid officers or directors, management discussion and analysis of certain matters, and two years of audited financial statements. Form 10–K annual reports, by contrast, require audited statements of income, cash flows, and owner's equity for the three most recent fiscal years as well as audited balance sheets as of the end of each of the two most recent fiscal years.

- Form 1–SA semi-annual reports (the analogue of Form 10–Q quarterly reports). Form 1–SA primarily consists of financial statements and management discussion and analysis disclosures. Financial statements disclosed under Form 1–SA are not required to be audited. Note that Form 10–Q similarly provides for the disclosure of non-audited financial statements.

- Form 1–U current reports (the analogue of Form 8–K current reports). The SEC requires that Tier 2 issuers submit Form 1–U current reports upon certain triggering events including bankruptcy or receivership, fundamental changes in the nature of business, material modification to the rights of securityholders, and the unregistered sale of securities. Form 1–U would be required to be filed within four business days after the occurrence of any triggering event. Form 1–U also allows for incorporation by reference.

The SEC suspends the duty to file ongoing reports for Tier 2 issuers that meet certain requirements. Rule 257(d). Ongoing disclosure is suspended for:

- Exchange Act Reporting Issuers. Rule 257(d)(1). The suspension is automatic and immediate for a Tier 2 issuer that becomes an Exchange Act reporting issuer.

- Issuers where the number of holders of record of the class of securities that was sold under Regulation A drops below 300 (or 1,200 for certain banks and bank holdings companies). Rule 257(d)(2). To suspend disclosure, the issuer must file an exit report under Form 1–Z and the issuer must have filed all reports due pursuant to Rule 257(b) before the Form 1–Z filing for the most recent three fiscal years the portion of the current year preceding the Form 1–Z filing date or the period since the issuer became subject to reporting, whichever is shorter. Rule 257(d)(2). In addition, the issuer may not suspend reporting for any particular fiscal year under Rule 257(d)(2) if "(i) [d]uring that fiscal year a Tier 2 offering statement was qualified; (ii) [t]he issuer has not filed an annual report under this rule or the Exchange Act for the fiscal year in which a Tier 2 offering statement was qualified; or (iii) Offers or sales of securities of that class are being made pursuant to a Tier 2 Regulation A offering." Rule 257(d)(4). Assuming an issuer satisfies the requirements for suspension under Rule 257(d)(2), the suspension is immediate.

Termination of ongoing Regulation A disclosure requirements may be more appropriate than suspension for some issuers. Accordingly, Rule 257(e) provides for the termination of the duty to file Regulation A ongoing reports. In particular, if the issuer suspends initially because it becomes an Exchange Act reporting issuer under Rule 257(d)(1) and then subsequently the issuer terminates or suspends its duty to file Exchange Act reports (e.g., because the issuer becomes a private company), then the issuer's Regulation A ongoing disclosure obligations are terminated under Rule 257(e) if the issuer is also eligible to suspend the issuer's duty to file reports under Rule 257(d)(2).

F. Regulation A Gun Jumping

Much like the public offering process, Regulation A imposes a similar controlled process. The gun jumping rules of Regulation A focus on two key events: (1) the filing of the offering statement with the SEC and (2) the "qualification" of the offering statement (corresponding to the effective date for a registered public offering), after which sales may commence to the general public. Using these two events, we can divide the time periods for a Regulation A offering into three time periods (corresponding to the public offering process): (1) the Pre-Filing Period; (2) Waiting Period; and (3) Post-Qualification period.

Pre-Filing Period	Waiting Period	Post-Qualification Period
Filing	Qualification	

As we go through each Regulation A offering period, consider how the restrictions on offers differ from § 5's gun jumping rules.

1. Pre-Filing Period

At first glance, the rules governing the Pre-Filing Period for a Regulation A offering seem analogous to the Pre-Filing Period under § 5. No sales are permitted in the Pre-Filing Period. Rule 251(d)(2). Under Rule 251(d)(1)(i), "no offers of securities shall be made unless an offering statement has been filed with the Commission." Rule 255, however, creates a major exception to this prohibition on offers in the Pre-Filing Period, allowing issuers to "test the waters" and determine the appetite of investors for the offering. Rule 255(a) provides that: "At any time before the qualification of an offering statement . . . an issuer or any person authorized to act on behalf of an issuer may communicate orally or in writing to determine whether there is any interest in a contemplated securities offering." Rule 255(a) makes clear that no binding commitment can be made until the offering is qualified.

To take advantage of testing the waters, the SEC requires that the communication meet certain conditions. Among other things, the communication must contain a disclaimer of any binding commitment or sale prior to qualification. Rule 255(b)(3). Rule 255(a) also makes clear that: "Such communications are deemed to be an offer of a security for sale for purposes of the antifraud provisions of the federal securities laws." Testing the waters communications are thus subject to potential Rule 10b–5 and § 12(a)(2) liability.

One concern is the possibility of opportunistic testing of the waters. Consider the following scenario. An issuer could (a) initiate a Regulation A offering; (b) test the waters, thereby priming the market for the company's securities; (c) withdraw the Regulation A offering (leading to an "abandoned Regulation A offering"); and finally, (d) commence a full blown public offering. To the extent investors are in fact misled by the initial, non-regulated disclosures, Regulation A could provide a backdoor way for issuers to condition the market for a § 5 public offering.

To check these opportunistic behaviors, the SEC limits abandoned Regulation A offerings. Recall that issuers offering or selling securities in sequential offerings always face the possibility of integration. Any abandoned Regulation A offering followed by a registered public offering would thus pose the risk that any solicitations made as part of the Regulation A offering would be integrated with the later registered public offering which causes the non-Exchange Act reporting issuer to violate § 5(c) and face possible § 12(a)(1) liability. In Rule 255(e), the SEC addresses this possibility in two ways. First, if the testing the water solicitation of an abandoned Regulation A offering was directed only to qualified institutional buyers (a term we cover more formally in Chapter 10, but for now, large institutional investors) and institutional accredited investors permitted under § 5(d) of the Securities Act, then the abandoned Regulation A offering would not be integrated with any subsequent registered public offering. Second, if the issuer tested the waters with others besides qualified institutional buyers and institutional accredited investors then integration is a possibility unless the issuer "waits at least 30 calendar days between the last such solicitation of interest in the Regulation A offering and the filing of a registration statement." Rule 255(e).

Issuers that have not sold securities in a prior Regulation A offering may worry about compliance with the Regulation A disclosure requirements. To address this concern, Regulation A gives issuers that have not previously sold securities under Regulation A or a registered public offering a non-public review of a draft offering statement before the filing of the offering statement with the SEC. Rule 252(d).

HYPOTHETICAL THIRTEEN

1. Suppose Kim, the CEO of Trendy, decides to have Trendy do a Regulation A offering. Kim is uncertain about the potential market for Trendy's stock and the possible offering price. Prior to filing the offering statement, she decides to contact a couple dozen institutional investors to gauge their interest in Trendy. In her conversations with the institutional investors, Kim conveys her positive forecasts for Trendy's earnings growth over the next several years. She tells them a Regulation A offering would

act as the "rocket fuel" to launch Trendy's earnings even further upward. Is there anything wrong with Kim's conversations with the institutional investors?

2. Assume that Kim intended all along to do a registered public offering. To test the waters for the public offering, she first had Trendy initiate a Regulation A offering (testing the waters through broad based mailings directed to retail investors). Trendy then withdrew its Regulation A offering. After 25 days, Trendy then commenced its registered public offering. Have Trendy and Kim violated § 5?

2. WAITING PERIOD

After the offering statement is filed with the SEC, the issuer enters into the Waiting Period Sales are still prohibited. Rule 251(d)(2), but issuers may make oral offers as well as written offers pursuant to Rule 254. Rule 251(d)(1)(ii). Rule 254 provides for a "preliminary" offering circular containing the same information as the final offering circular but excluding price related information (e.g., the offering price, underwriting discounts and commissions, etc.). In addition, as in the Pre-Filing Period, testing the waters communication under Rule 255 can continue in the Waiting Period. Rule 251(d)(1)(ii).

Although Regulation A does not provide a free writing prospectus analogue to Rule 433, testing the waters under Rule 255 allows issuers to make written offers in the Waiting Period. The issuer must include a copy of the preliminary offering circular with the Rule 255 communication (and a URL where the offering statement can be accessed); unlike for free writing prospectuses, there is no filing (or alternatively record keeping) requirement. Rule 255(b).

HYPOTHETICAL FOURTEEN

Suppose that Trendy continues with its Regulation A offering. It files an offering circular and engages in testing the waters through broad-based mailings directed to retail investors. Is this permitted?

3. POST-QUALIFICATION PERIOD

Unlike § 6(a)'s twenty calendar day delay from filing to the effective date for registered public offerings, Regulation A provides that qualification of the offering statement will occur only when the SEC gives its approval. Rule 252(e).

After the offering statement has been qualified, sales can begin. Rule 251(d)(2)(i). Issuers and those communicating on behalf of the issuers may no longer test the waters under Rule 255. Instead Rule 251(d)(1)(iii) states that: "Offers may be made after the offering statement has been qualified, but any written offers must be accompanied with or preceded by the most recent offering circular filed with the Commission for such offering." An offering circular must accompany any offer in the Post-Qualification Period, but the issuer need not provide a URL where the offering statement may be found.

Regulation A also imposes an offering circular delivery requirement in the Post-Qualification Period for sales (similar to the prospectus delivery requirement in the Post-Effective Period). Rule 251(d)(2)(ii).

Issuers and underwriters must deliver an offering circular within two business days. Sales by a dealer within 90 calendar days after qualification also require delivery of a final offering circular. As with Rule 174, the SEC does not require delivery of the final offering circular by a dealer after 25 calendar days if the Regulation A issuer lists the security on a registered national securities exchange. In addition, issuers required to file ongoing reports pursuant to Rule 257(b) do not have to deliver the final offering circular. As discussed above, Rule 257(b) imposes ongoing reporting requirements for issuers that have sold securities in a prior Tier 2 Regulation A offering.

To satisfy the delivery requirement for the final offering circular, the SEC adopted an "access equals delivery" model, similar to the one for registered offerings under the Rule 172. Upon qualification of the offering statement, sales of Regulation A securities may occur without a final offering circular physically accompanying a security for sale, provided the final offering circular is available on EDGAR. Rule 251(d)(2)(ii)(E).

One can wonder how useful receiving the final offering circular will be to an investor who receives the document "not later than two business days following the completion of such sale." Recognizing that information is more useful to investors prior to the sale, the SEC also requires that a preliminary offering circular be delivered prior to sale for issuers not currently filing reports pursuant to Rule 257(b). Rule 251(d)(2)(i)(B). Those issuers must send a preliminary offering circular 48 hours before the sale to "any person that before the qualification of the offering statement had indicated an interest in purchase securities in the offering." Rule 251(d)(2)(i)(B).

HYPOTHETICAL FIFTEEN

Trendy's offering statement is now qualified. Twenty days after qualification, Jones Securities, a securities dealer not participating in Trendy's Regulation A offering, decides to purchase some Trendy stock on the secondary market. Two days later, Jones Securities sells these shares into the open market to several individual investors and mails a confirmation of sales (and nothing else). Any problem with this?

G. CONTINUOUS OFFERINGS

The SEC allows both continuous and delayed offerings under Regulation A in certain circumstances, along the lines of shelf-registered public offerings. Regulation A allows those other than the issuer (or a company connected in a subsidiary relationship with the issuer) to sell securities on a continuous or delayed basis. Rule 251(d)(3)(i)(A). For example, an individual venture capitalist that holds restricted securities of an issuer purchased through a prior Regulation D private placement may sell securities on a continuous or delayed basis through a Regulation A offering. Issuers may also sell securities on a continuous or delayed basis as part of a dividend or interest reinvestment plan or an employee benefit plan. Rule 251(d)(3)(i)(B). The issuer may use Regulation A to issue securities upon the exercise of outstanding options, warrants, or rights, Rule 251(d)(3)(i)(C), and conversion of other outstanding securities. Rule 251(d)(3)(i)(D). If an issuer has debt securities outstanding that are, at the option of the debtholders, convertible into the issuer's equity, then the issuer may keep the underlying equity registered under Regulation A to facilitate rapid conversion. Issuers may also issue securities under Regulation A on a continuous or delayed basis if securities are pledged as collateral. Rule 251(d)(3)(i)(E).

Unlike shelf registration under Rule 415, Regulation A limits the ability of issuers to sell securities directly to investors on a continuous or delayed basis. In particular, Regulation A provides that: "Securities the offering of which will be commenced within two calendar days after the qualification date, will be made on a continuous basis, may continue for a period in excess of 30 calendar days from the date of initial qualification, and will be offered in an amount that, at the time the offering statement is qualified, is reasonably expected to be offered and sold within two years from the initial qualification date." Rule 251(d)(3)(i)(F). As with shelf registration, Regulation A imposes offering statement updating requirements for issuer continuous offerings. Rule 251(d)(3)(i)(F). Issuers cannot use Regulation A to sell securities on a delayed basis as Form S–3 issuers are able to do under Rule 415. The SEC also does not allow "at the market" offerings under Regulation A. Rule 251(d)(3)(ii). The SEC excluded "at the market offerings," due to concerns that an offering sold at fluctuating market prices might create problems keeping those offerings within Regulation A's maximum offering size limits.

H. Insignificant Deviations

Regulation A excuses some failures to comply with its terms. Rule 260 provides that failures to comply are excused if three conditions are satisfied:

- The failure to comply did not relate to a provision of Regulation A directly intended to protect that particular individual or entity.

- The failure to comply with Regulation A was "insignificant with respect to the offering as a whole." Failure to follow Rules 251(a) (Tier 1 and Tier 2 aggregate offering price and sales limitations and limits on secondary sales in first year), 251(b) (eligible issuers), 251(d)(1) (restriction on offers) and 251(d)(3) (continuous or delayed offerings) are defined as significant to the offering as a whole. Thus, failure to comply with these provisions cannot be excused.

- A good faith and reasonable attempt was made to comply with all applicable terms, conditions and requirements of Regulation A. Rule 260(a)(3).

As with Regulation D's Rule 508, Rule 260 does not shield persons failing to comply with Regulation A from SEC enforcement action under § 20 of the Securities Act. Rule 260(b).

HYPOTHETICAL SIXTEEN

Consider the following errors in Trendy's Regulation A offering and whether they might potentially be treated as insignificant deviations under Rule 260.

1.   Trendy's attorneys made a mistake. It turns out that Trendy in fact is required to make periodic disclosures as an Exchange Act reporting company because it has over $10 million in net assets and more than 2,000 shareholders.

2.   Trendy's placement agents make a mistake and Trendy sells $50.1 million through its Tier 2 Regulation A offering.

3.   Trendy fails to send a copy of the preliminary offering circular to Emma, a purchaser in the Regulation A offering who had indicated interest in the offering prior to the qualification date, before Emma's purchase of securities in the offering. Later, in the Post-Qualification Period, Trendy finally mails her a copy of the final offering circular.

I.   ANTIFRAUD LIABILITY

An important consideration for issuers considering a Regulation A offering is antifraud liability. Rule 10b–5 applies to fraud in connection with the purchase or sale of securities and therefore applies to misleading statements and omissions in the offering circular, offering statement, and other documents used in the Regulation A offering.

From Chapter 8, we saw that § 11 (registration statement) and § 12(a)(2) (prospectus) provided heightened antifraud liability for documents used in a public offering under § 5. Because Regulation A involves an offering statement and not a registration statement, § 11 does not apply.

Section 3(b)(2)(D) of the Securities Act stipulates that § 12(a)(2) liability applies to any person offering or selling Regulation A securities. Consistent with this provision, sellers have liability under § 12(a)(2) for any offer or sale by means of an offering circular or oral statement that includes a material misleading statement.

J.   INTEGRATION

Recall that sales will be integrated if they:

- are part of a single plan of financing;
- involve issuance of the same class of securities;
- have been made at or about the same time;
- are made for the same general purpose; and
- involve the same type of consideration.

Securities Act Release No. 4552 (November 6, 1962). No one factor is controlling, so integration under this test can be uncertain.

Regulation A provides its own safe harbor from integration that offers considerable assurance because it is "two sided." If the terms of Rule 251(c) of Regulation A are met, then the Regulation A offering will not be integrated with another offering. Symmetrically, the other offering will also not have the Regulation A offering integrated into it. Thus, the Regulation A protects both offerings from integration.

How do we get this result? Rule 251(c) states that: "Offers and sales made in reliance on this Regulation A will not be integrated with. . . ." This language implies that no integration will take place between the Regulation A offering and the other offers and sales. In contrast, note that Rule 502(a) of Regulation D states that if its terms are met, then the other offers and sales "will not be considered part of that Regulation D offering." Rule 502(a) does not say that the Regulation D offering will not be integrated into the other offering. Thus, while Regulation A provides a two sided anti-integration safe harbor, Regulation D's safe harbor protects only one side.

Among the offerings covered under Rule 251(c), note the following that are protected against integration with a Regulation A offering:

- Prior offers or sales of securities. Rule 251(c)(1).

- Subsequent offers or sales of securities that are:
    - registered under the Securities Act except as provided in Rule 255(e). Rule 251(c)(2)(i).
    - exempt under Rule 701 (an exemption from § 5 for companies selling securities to their own employees, directors, officers, among others). Rule 251(c)(2)(ii).
    - made pursuant to an employee benefit plan. Rule 251(c)(2)(iii).
    - exempt under Regulation S (an exemption from § 5 for securities sold outside the United States). Rule 251(c)(2)(iv).
    - made more than six months after the completion of the Regulation A offering. Rule 251(c)(2)(v).
    - exempt under § 4(a)(6) of the Securities Act. Rule 251(c)(2)(vi).

Compared with the Regulation D safe harbor (Rule 502(a)), Regulation A provides a narrower time frame during which the integration safe harbor does not apply (and hence, a broader safe harbor). Any offering *prior* to the Regulation A offering is exempt from integration. Thus, even though Regulation D offerings have their own safe harbor from integration under Rule 502(a), an issuer may offer and sell securities pursuant to a Regulation D exemption and then immediately upon completion of the Regulation D offering begin a Regulation A offering. Because the Regulation D offering is prior to the Regulation A offering, Rule 251(c)(1) provides a two-way integration safe harbor that protects both offerings from integration.

HYPOTHETICAL SEVENTEEN

Trendy makes the following offerings:

1/1 to 1/30: Sale of $5 million of common stock pursuant to Rule 505 to 25 unsophisticated purchasers to fund expansion of the Lean Green product.

2/1 to 2/28: Testing the waters offers for a $48 million Tier 2 offering of common stock pursuant to Regulation A. On 3/1, the offering statement is filed with the SEC. On 4/1, sales begin and by 4/15 all $48 million of common stock has been sold. Proceeds will be used to fund expansion of the Lean Green product.

Should the two offerings be integrated?

K. STATE SECURITIES LAW REQUIREMENTS

Prior to the SEC's adoption of the new Regulation A in 2015, state securities regulators regulated Regulation A offerings three different ways. First, many states required pre-offering review of a Regulation A offering. In recent years, state securities regulators have introduced a coordinated review process allowing an issuer to satisfy this review requirement for multiple states more easily. Second, many states require the filing of offering material. Third, states have state-law based antifraud provisions that apply to offering materials and other offering-related communications.

In Regulation A the SEC provided that Tier 1 offerings remain subject to all three aspects of state securities regulation. The SEC exempted Tier 2 offerings from state pre-offering review, however, by defining purchasers in Tier 2 offerings as "qualified purchasers" for purposes of § 18(b)(3) of the Securities Act, which limits state regulatory authority. Rule 256. States retain the power to require the filing of offering materials and to enforce state antifraud laws even for a Tier 2 offering. The SEC justified this partial preemption of state regulation based on the more stringent disclosure requirements and ongoing reporting obligations imposed on Tier 2 issuers.

V. CROWDFUNDING

As part of the JOBS Act of 2012, Congress enacted the Capital Raising Online While Deterring Fraud and Unethical Non-Disclosure Act of 2012 (the CROWDFUND Act). Crowdfunding has its roots outside of the formal capital markets, with the rise of the Internet. The Internet allowed groups of people to pooled their money through websites, such as kickstarter.com, to fund various artistic and other creative endeavors. People typically contributed money without regard to investment return, for projects such as the development of a video game, the filming of documentaries, or the writing of a first novel. In return for their funding, project sponsors typically promised contributors copies of the completed video game, a digital download of the finished documentary film, or first edition copies of their book.

The JOBS Act piggybacks on the concept of groups of individuals pooling their money informally to provide a new, less regulated method for companies to raise capital. The crowdfunding exemption from § 5 is found in § 4(a)(6) of the Securities Act. Unlike § 4(a)(2) or Rule 506, the JOBS Act does not restrict the types of investors who may participate in crowdfunding, so retail investors are welcome to invest.

The JOBS Act does, however, limit the quantity that both issuers can sell and investors can buy. The JOBS Act limits issuers to no more than $1 million in crowdfunding sales during any 12-month period.

Section 4(a)(6)(A). Section 4A(h) of the Securities Act provides that the SEC must adjust the $1 million threshold at least every five years to account for inflation. The $1 million limit parallels the $1 million aggregate offering price limitation in Rule 504 and severely limits the appeal of crowdfunding for most established issuers. Consequently, we predict that typically only smaller, lesser-known companies—for example new Internet startups—will take advantage of crowdfunding.

The JOBS Act also limits the aggregate amount that may be sold by all issuers to any particular investor during a 12-month period. Section 4(a)(6)(B) creates two separate individual investor limits. The first limit is defined as "the greater of $2,000 or 5 percent of the annual income or net worth of such investor, as applicable, if either the annual income or the net worth of the investor is less than $100,000." For example, if an investor has an annual income of $50,000 and a net worth of $25,000 then the first limit would equal $2,500 (5% of $50,000). The second limit is defined as "10 percent of the annual income or net worth of such investor, as applicable, not to exceed a maximum aggregate amount sold of $100,000, if either the annual income or net worth of the investor is equal to or more than $100,000." For the investor with an annual income of $50,000 and a net worth of $500,000, the second limit equals $50,000. Notably, the individual investor's limit is aggregated during any 12-month period for all issuers using the § 4(a)(6) crowdfunding exemption. Section 4A(h) of the Securities Act provides that the SEC must adjust the dollar amounts in § 4(a)(6)(B) over time "in accordance with any rules of the Commission under this title regarding the calculation of the income and net worth, respectively, of an accredited investor."

Note that the crowdfunding limit on the amount that all issuers may sell to a particular investor in a 12-month period does not distinguish between retail and institutional investors. Institutional investors are unlikely to have much interest in crowdfunding. It simply is not worth the effort for institutional investors to research and investigate a new investment if the maximum investment is $100,000. As a result, retail investors will likely dominate crowdfunding.

Given the likely composition of the crowdfunding market, individual retail investors purchasing securities from relatively unknown startup companies, at best, face highly risky investment choices without the information or sophistication to make informed decisions. At worst, retail investors will face a sea of fraudsters. Congress's solution to this dilemma was to employ third party gatekeepers. The JOBS Act requires that issuers selling based on the crowdfunding exemption must rely on either a broker or a "funding portal." Securities Act § 4(a)(6)(C). Funding portals are defined "as an intermediary in a transaction involving the offer or sale of securities for the account of others, solely pursuant to section 4[a](6)." Exchange Act § 3(a)(80). Section 3(a)(80) excludes those who offer investment advice or recommendations, engage in solicitations relating to the securities offered, or compensate others for such solicitations. In addition, those who hold, manage, possess, or otherwise handle investor funds or securities cannot act as a funding portal. Given this list of exclusions, what can a funding portal do? At a minimum, a funding portal may act as a venue for issuers and investors to find one another and enter into securities transactions. Presumably, a web-based funding portal may therefore list the issuers seeking crowdfunding. A web-based funding portal also may advertise itself generally to investors seeking a location to participate in crowdfunding transactions, as long as it does not solicit investors for any particular offering.

Section 4A imposes a number of requirements on brokers and funding portals that seek to act as an intermediary in § 4(a)(6) crowdfunding transactions. First, the broker or funding portal must register with the SEC and applicable self-regulatory organization (FINRA in the case of brokers). Securities Act § 4A(a)(1), (2). The broker or funding portal must also provide investors with disclosures, as well as investor education materials as the SEC determines appropriate. Securities Act § 4A(a)(3). What form will these investor education materials take? Would it be too negative to point out that IPO investors in Facebook lost more than 25% of their value in the first week of trading after the IPO and that crowdfunding investors may potentially experience even greater losses? Should education materials report on the actual performance of all prior crowdfunding investments made through a specific broker or funding portal in the past year (including median, mean, and variance)? Or should the investor education materials simply contain platitudes about the fact that investments in equity are not as safe as putting money in an FDIC-insured bank account?

The JOBS Act goes beyond disclosure and investor education. In keeping with the view of brokers and funding portals as gatekeepers, § 4A requires these intermediaries to ensure that each investor reviews the investor-education information. Securities Act § 4A(a)(4)(A). Will a signed certification from the investor be enough? Many investors may sign even if they haven't read the investor education materials. Or does the broker or funding portal need to monitor the investor to make sure they actually read the investor education materials? Moreover, § 4A(a)(4)(B) requires that the broker or funding portal "positively affirms that the investor understands that the investor is risking the loss of the entire investment, and that the investor could bear such a loss."

Section 4A also imposes an investor test requirement. Most investor screens, such as the accredited investor standard, rely on objective metrics based on assets, amount invested in securities, net worth, and income to distinguish among investors. In contrast, § 4(A) requires that the broker or funding portal ensures that investors can answer questions demonstrating an understanding of the risks of investing in startups and illiquidity. Securities Act § 4A(a)(4)(C). Should the questions on such a test include questions about the efficient capital markets hypothesis and basic knowledge on the time value of money? Should they be multiple choice? Once we go down the path of requiring investors to take tests, should the SEC or FINRA centralize such tests, essentially licensing investors to participate in crowdfunding? Or can each broker or funding portal make up its own questions to test investors?

Not content with requiring investor testing, Congress also directly imposes investigation requirements on brokers and funding portals. Section 4A requires the brokers and funding portals must take measures to reduce the risk of fraud. This includes obtaining background checks as well as checking the securities enforcement regulatory history of the officers, directors and twenty percent equity holders of issuers. Securities Act § 4A(a)(5).

Investors care greatly whether an issuer raises enough capital to follow through on its business plans. If a company needs $1 million to open a new factory and the company raises only $700,000, investors may worry that the factory will not open and the company will use the $700,000 for other purposes. Addressing this fear, § 4A(a)(7) requires that a broker or funding portal transmit offering proceeds from a crowdfunding offering only when the aggregate capital raised is equal to or exceeds the target offering amount (as established by the issuer). Investors can also cancel their commitment to invest for such time period as the SEC through rulemaking deems appropriate.

Brokers and funding portals must also make efforts to ensure that investors do not exceed the § 4A individual investor limits described above (§ 4A(a)(8)), protect the private of information collected from investors (§ 4A(a)(9)), and not compensate promoters and others for providing the broker or funding portal with personal identifying information of any potential investors (§ 4A(a)(10)). Directors, officers, or partners of a broker or funding portal must not have any financial interest in an issuer using the broker or funding portal's services. Securities Act § 4A(a)(11).

Crowdfunding poses a dilemma for securities regulators. Its explicit goal is to increase capital market access for those companies, typically small and unknown startups, that otherwise would have difficulty getting raising capital. Yet in inviting small and unknown startups, crowdfunding also invites fraudsters and con artists eager to bilk unsophisticated investors of their money. Will disclosures, investor tests, and background checks adequately offset the increased risk of fraud posed by those issuers that self-select themselves into the crowdfunding market (i.e., those issuers unable to raise capital through more traditional means from institutional investors)?

A. DISCLOSURE

Section 4A imposes a number of disclosure requirements directly on issuers selling in a crowdfunding transaction. Issuers must make information available to investors, potential investors, the broker or funding portal intermediary assisting in the crowdfunding, and the SEC. Required disclosures include identifying information on the issuer (including its physical and website addresses), the names of directors, officers, and shareholders with more than 20 percent of the shares of the issuer, the intended use of proceeds, the target offering amount, the price (or method to determine the price provided that investors will be provided the final price in writing prior to sale), a description of the issuer's business and anticipated business plan, and certain information on the financial condition of the issuer (varying based on the specific target offering amount thresholds adjusted for inflation). Securities Act § 4A(b)(1)(A)-(G). Business plans typically include earnings projections for the issuer; investors in a crowdfunding transaction may therefore receive more mandatory disclosure than investors in a registered public offering that does not require any earnings projections in the registration statement.

A crowdfunding issuer must also provide a description of its ownership and capital stock. As part of this disclosure, issuers must disclose the terms of the securities being offered, how the exercise of rights by the principal shareholders could harm the crowdfunding investors, how the offered securities are being valued, and the risks to investors from minority ownership in the issuer and the risks associated with corporate actions such as potential dilution. Securities Act § 4A(b)(1)(H).

B. LIMITS ON ISSUER COMMUNICATION

Issuers are prohibited from advertising the terms of an offering using the crowdfunding exemption except for notices that direct investors to a funding portal or broker. Securities Act § 4A(b)(2). The limitation on advertisements containing the terms of the offering appears less stringent than the limits provided under the gun-jumping rules for a registered public offering. For example, if an issuer sends one-on-one communications to specific investors prior to sale commencing, is this allowable because such communications are not advertisements? If an issuer sends out a broad advertisement that mentions the offering generally without discussing specific terms is this allowable because "terms of the offering" are not mentioned? We will have to wait for SEC rulemaking to clarify the limits on issuer crowdfunding communications. Regulation FD would limit selective disclosures to potential investors, but it only applies to Exchange Act reporting issuers, who are unlikely to avail themselves of the crowdfunding exemption. Private companies may communicate selectively without regard to Regulation FD (*see* Chapter 4).

Issuers are also limited in their ability to hire others to promote a crowdfunding transaction. Section 4A(b)(3) requires issuers disclose compensation paid to brokers or funding portals for promoting the offering. What are the limits of this provision? May an issuer hire a third party to promote its offering outside of communication channels provided by a broker or funding portal, or would that constitute impermissible advertising?

C. PERIODIC DISCLOSURES

Issuers must file with the SEC and provide to investors "reports of the results of operations and financial statements of the issuer" at least annually. The JOBS Act also empowers the SEC to require disclosures and create exceptions as well as termination dates. Securities Act § 4A(b)(4). The ongoing disclosure obligation creates a substantial distinctive to rely on crowdfunding. A private company that chooses to raise capital through a private placement faces no ongoing disclosure obligations after the close of the offering.

D. ANTIFRAUD LIABILITY

Rule 10b–5 applies to crowdfunding transactions, as it does to all transactions in connection with the purchase or sale of securities that use an instrumentality of interstate commerce. Nonetheless, Congress also adopted heightened antifraud liability for crowdfunding transactions—most likely in response to the types of investors (retail) and issuers (smaller, lesser-known) that will participate in crowdfunding. To help ensure the accuracy of information disclosed in a crowdfunding offering, Congress enacted a private antifraud liability provisions specifically for crowdfunding.

Crowdfunding antifraud liability closely follows § 12(a)(2) liability as its model. Like § 12(a)(2), only those who purchase securities have standing to bring a private suit under § 4A(c). Section 4A(c) provides that a person who purchases securities in a § 4(a)(6) transaction may bring a private action against an "issuer." Unlike § 12(a)(2), however, § 4A(c) provides an expanded list of possible defendants. Although only an "issuer" may be a defendant, § 4A(c)(3) defines an issuer to include directors, CEOs, CFOs, and "any person who offers or sells the security in such offering." Securities Act § 4A(c)(3).

Like § 12(a)(2), § 4A(c) provides liability if an issuer makes "an untrue statement of a material fact or omits to state a material fact required to be stated or necessary in order to make the statements, in the light of the circumstances under which they were made, not misleading" as part of an offering or sale of securities under § 4(a)(6). Also like § 12(a)(2), § 4A(c) does not impose a scienter or reliance requirement as part of the plaintiff's cause of action. Moreover, § 4A(c) does not require plaintiffs to demonstrate loss causation.

Several defenses are available to issuers. Purchasers that knew of the untruth or omission at the time of the offer or sale are barred. Securities Act § 4A(c)(2)(A). Section 4A(c)(1)(B) also provides that § 12(b)'s loss causation defense applies to the § 4A(c) private actions. Section 4A(c)(2)(B) provides for a reasonable care defense for the issuer. The statute of limitations provision of § 13 applies. Securities Act § 4A(c)(1)(B). Finally, § 4A(c) provides similar remedies. Purchasers receive rescission as their remedy, adjusted for any income received, or damages if they no longer own the securities.

E. RESALES

As we saw in our discussion of § 4(a)(2) and Regulation D, investors who purchase securities through an exemption from § 5 are limited in their ability to resell these securities. These privately placed securities are referred to as "restricted" securities because of restrictions on resale. On the one hand, the resale restrictions reduce the value of the securities to the investors. Without the ability to resell, investors cannot convert these securities into cash and will demand an illiquidity discount. On the other hand, the resale restrictions help protect the public offering process. If investors can immediately resell freely after an exempt offering, issuers will avoid public offerings.

Congress followed the path taken for other forms of exempt offerings by imposing resale restrictions on crowdfunding securities. Securities sold pursuant to § 4(a)(6) cannot be resold by the purchaser for one year. Securities Act § 4A(e). Section 4A(e) provides several exceptions from the restriction on resales, allowing sales back to the issuer, to accredited investors, sales through a registered public offering, sales to family members, among other circumstances.

The 1-year limitation on resale may not be the most important limitation on resales. Only smaller, little-known issuers are likely to take advantage of crowdfunding. Moreover, issuers can raise only up to $1 million in a 12-month period using crowdfunding. The volume of securities sold by a typical crowdfunding issuer generally will be insufficient to support a liquid trading market, even after the 1-year holding period expires. Without such a market, retail investors will have difficulty reselling their securities. Retail investors will hope that the issuer eventually sells a large number of shares in a registered public offering, thereby creating a liquid market.

F. DISQUALIFICATION

The JOBS Act provides for disqualification through SEC rulemaking of issuers, brokers, and funding portals, "substantially similar" to the disqualification provision contained in Rule 262 of Regulation A. JOBS Act § 302(d). Disqualification under Rule 262 is based on the presence of specified bad acts, including being the subject of an SEC proceeding or examination under § 8 of the Securities Act or the subject of a stop or refusal order within five years of the first sale of securities (in the case of disqualification under the JOBS Act—the first sale of crowdfunding securities). Other bad acts include being convicted of any felony or misdemeanor in connection with the purchase or sale of any security or involving a "false filing" with the SEC within five years prior to the first sale of securities or being subject to any "order, judgment, or decree of any court of competent jurisdiction" entered within five years of the first sale of securities that enjoins the issuer from making a false filing with the SEC.

In addition to Rule 262 disqualification, Congress added two other circumstances that SEC rulemaking should treat as a disqualifying. First, persons are disqualified if they are subject to certain orders from specified state regulatory authorities, a federal banking regulatory agency, or the National Credit Union Administration. JOBS Act § 302(d)(2)(B). These orders include, among others, bars on persons from associating with an entity regulated by one of these agencies.

Congress has moved increasingly toward using ex post disqualification after a securities law violation to protect investors from future violations. The move is somewhat piecemeal. As we have seen, Congress recently implemented disqualification as part of Rule 506 (enacted as part of Dodd Frank Act of 2010) and for the new crowdfunding regime (enacted as part of the JOBS Act of 2012). Other funding avenues do not have disqualification, however, including § 4(a)(2) private placements and registered public offerings. Will disqualification in certain types of funding simply channel fraudsters to other types of offering that lack a disqualification provision?

G. PUBLIC COMPANY STATUS

We saw in Chapter 4 that private companies seeking to raise capital through exempt offerings must worry about becoming a public company even without an initial public offering. The JOBS Act of 2012 greatly alleviated the risk of becoming a creeping public company by: (1) increasing the threshold number of shareholders of record of a class of equity to become a public company from 500 to 2,000 (or 500 non-accredited investors); and (2) excluding employees from the shareholders of record tally if they receive equity securities through exempt transactions pursuant to an employee compensation plan.

Crowdfunding poses a heightened risk to startups of becoming a public company. Assuming total assets of a startup company are above $10 million, the startup must worry that crowdfunding is likely to attract a relative large number of retail investors, each purchasing a relatively small number of shares. For purposes of avoiding public company status, it is much better to have one institutional investor purchase 200,000 shares than to have 2,000 retail investors each purchase 100 shares. The fear of public company status may chill the use of crowdfunding by startups. Congress addressed this concern by requiring the SEC to engage in rulemaking to specify that securities acquired under a § 4(a)(6) crowdfunding offering are excluded from the provisions of § 12(g) of the Exchange Act and thus the numerical shareholder threshold to become a public company. Exchange Act § 12(g)(6).

HYPOTHETICAL EIGHTEEN

Redeye, Inc. is a startup company based in New York City that manufactures highly caffeinated energy drinks. Jeff, the CEO, founder, and sole shareholder of Redeye, hopes to break out of the Northeast region and market Redeye's energy drinks out on the West Coast in direct competition with Trendy, Inc. Redeye is a low budget operation and Jeff calculates that Redeye needs only $500,000 to start an Internet-based word-of-mouth campaign to raise awareness of Redeye on the West Coast. What are the pros and cons of crowdfunding for Redeye? What alternatives methods of raising capital would you suggest to Jeff?

VI. INTRASTATE OFFERINGS

Section 5 of the Securities Act reaches broadly to regulate all offers and sales of securities involving interstate commerce. Even for a securities offering that takes place exclusively in one state, issuers and those working on the issuers' behalf can run afoul of § 5 if they use a telephone, the mail, or other instruments of interstate commerce.

Despite the reach of § 5 to offerings essentially intrastate in character, there are reasons to exempt such offerings from the registration requirements. Intrastate offerings are often smaller in scope and are sold to investors that have a general knowledge of the local companies offering the securities, reducing the need for the heavy regulatory intervention of § 5. Offerings that take place solely within one state may have less effect on the confidence of investors in the national securities marketplace. Finally, state "Blue Sky" securities regulation, discussed earlier in the chapter, provides a substitute for federal securities regulation. Particularly if the offering is sold in only one state, state regulators have both a greater incentive to police the offering (all the investors are within their jurisdiction) and a greater ability to do so. The National Securities Markets Improvement Act of

1996 preempts state securities registration requirements for "covered securities." The definition of covered securities, however, does not include securities offered and sold under § 3(a)(11), allowing for state "Blue Sky" regulation of securities sold pursuant to the intrastate offering exemption.

We start with a discussion of the intrastate offering exemption under § 3(a)(11). We then discuss the safe harbor for intrastate offerings in Rule 147.

A. SECTION 3(a)(11) OFFERINGS

Section 3(a)(11) of the Securities Act exempts from § 5 securities sold as "part of an issue offered and sold only to persons resident within a single State or Territory, where the issuer of such security is a person resident and doing business within or, if a corporation, incorporated by and doing business within, such State or Territory." Consider the SEC's view of the scope of § 3(a)(11) in the following release. Despite the presence of possible state securities regulation, the SEC has generally construed § 3(a)(11) narrowly. Why do you think the SEC has taken this attitude toward the intrastate exemption?

Securities Act Release No. 4434
Securities and Exchange Commission (Dec. 6, 1961).

* * *

The legislative history of the Securities Act clearly shows that [the § 3(a)(11)] exemption was designed to apply only to local financing that may practicably be consummated in its entirety within the State or Territory in which the issuer is both incorporated and doing business. . . .

"Issue" Concept

A basic condition of the exemption is that the entire issue of securities be offered and sold exclusively to residents of the state in question. Consequently, an offer to a non-resident which is considered a part of the intrastate issue will render the exemption unavailable to the entire offering.

Whether an offering is "a part of an issue", that is, whether it is an integrated part of an offering previously made or proposed to be made, is a question of fact and depends essentially upon whether the offerings are a related part of a plan or program. Thus, the exemption should not be relied upon in combination with another exemption for the different parts of a single issue where a part is offered or sold to non-residents. . . .

[S]ince the exemption is designed to cover only those security distributions, which, as a whole, are essentially local in character, it is clear that the phrase "sold only to persons resident" as used in Section 3(a)(11) cannot refer merely to the initial sales by the issuing corporation to its underwriters, or even the subsequent resales by the underwriters to distributing dealers. To give effect to the fundamental purpose of the exemption, it is necessary that the entire issue of securities shall be offered and sold to, and come to rest only in the hands of residents within the state. If any part of the issue is offered or sold to a non-resident, the exemption is unavailable not only for the securities so sold, but for all securities forming a part of the issue, including those sold to residents. It is incumbent upon the issuer, underwriter, dealers and other persons connected with the offering to make sure that it does not become an interstate distribution through resales. It is understood to be customary for such persons to obtain assurances that purchases are not made with a view to resale to non-residents.

Doing Business Within the State

In view of the local character of the Section 3(a)(11) exemption, the requirement that the issuer be doing business in the state can only be satisfied by the performance of substantial operational activities in the state of incorporation. The doing business requirement is not met by functions in the particular state such as bookkeeping, stock record and similar activities or by offering securities in the state. Thus, the exemption would be unavailable to an offering by a company made in the state of its incorporation of undivided fractional oil and gas interests located in other states even though the company conducted other business in the state of its incorporation. While the person creating the fractional interests is technically the "issuer" as defined in Section 2[a](4) of the Act, the purchaser of such security obtains no interest in the issuer's separate business within the state. Similarly, an intrastate exemption would not be available to a "local" mortgage company offering interests in out-of-state mortgages which are sold under circumstances to constitute them investment contracts. . . .

If the proceeds of the offering are to be used primarily for the purpose of a new business conducted outside of the state of incorporation and unrelated to some incidental business locally conducted, the exemption should not be relied upon. So also, a Section 3(a)(11) exemption should not be relied upon for each of a series of corporations organized in different states where there is in fact and purpose a single business enterprise or financial venture whether or not it is planned to merge or consolidate the various corporations at a later date.

Residence Within the State

Section 3(a)(11) requires that the entire issue be confined to a single state in which the issuer, the offerees and the purchasers are residents. Mere presence in the state is not sufficient to constitute residence as in the case of military personnel at a military post. The mere obtaining of formal representations of residence and agreements not to resell to non-residents or agreements that sales are void if the purchaser is a non-resident should not be relied upon without more as establishing the availability of the exemption.

An offering may be so large that its success as a local offering appears doubtful from the outset. . . .

A secondary offering by a controlling person in the issuer's state of incorporation may be made in reliance on a Section 3(a)(11) exemption provided the exemption would be available to the issuer for a primary offering in that state. It is not essential that the controlling person be a resident of the issuer's state of incorporation.

Resales

From these general principles it follows that if during the course of distribution any underwriter, any distributing dealer (whether or not a member of the formal selling or distributing group), or any dealer or other person purchasing securities from a distributing dealer for resale were to offer or sell such securities to a non-resident, the exemption would be defeated. In other words, Section 3(a)(11) contemplates that the exemption is applicable only if the entire issue is distributed pursuant to the statutory conditions. Consequently, any offers or sales to a non-resident in connection with the distribution of the issue would destroy the exemption as to all securities which are a part of that issue, including those sold to residents regardless of whether such sales are made directly to non-residents or indirectly through residents who as part of the distribution thereafter sell to non-residents. . . .

This is not to suggest, however, that securities which have actually come to rest in the hands of resident investors, such as persons purchasing without a view to further distribution or resale to non-residents, may not in due course be resold by such persons, whether directly or through dealers or brokers, to non-residents without in any way affecting the exemption. The relevance of any such resales consists only of the evidentiary light which they might cast upon the factual question whether the securities had in fact come to rest in the hands of resident investors. If the securities are resold but a short time after their acquisition to a non-resident this fact, although not conclusive, might support an inference that the original offering had not come to rest in the state, and that the resale therefore constituted a part of the process of primary distribution; a stronger inference would arise if the purchaser involved were a security dealer. It may be noted that the non-residence of the underwriter or dealer is not pertinent as long as the ultimate distribution is solely to residents of the state. . . .

Conclusion

In conclusion, the fact should be stressed that Section 3(a)(11) is designed to apply only to distributions genuinely local in character. From a practical point of view, the provisions of that section can exempt only issues which in reality represent local financing by local industries, carried out through local investment. Any distribution not of this type raises a serious question as to the availability of Section 3(a)(11). Consequently, any dealer proposing to participate in the distribution of an issue claimed to be exempt under Section 3(a)(11) should examine the character of the transaction and the proposed or actual manner of its execution by all persons concerned with it with the greatest care to satisfy himself that the distribution will not, or did not, exceed the limitations of the exemption. Otherwise the dealer, even though his own sales may be carefully confined to resident purchasers, may subject himself to serious risk of civil liability under Section 12[a](1) of the Act for selling without prior registration a security not in fact entitled to exemption from registration. In Release No. 4386, we noted that the quick commencement of trading and prompt resale of portions of the issue to non-residents raises a serious question whether the entire issue has, in fact, come to rest in the hands of investors resident in the state of the initial offering.

Busch v. Carpenter

827 F.2d 653 (10th Cir. 1987).

■ SEYMOUR, S., CIRCUIT JUDGE.

Paul and Linda Busch brought this action under [§ 12 of the Securities Act] against Craig Carpenter, George Jensen, and Ronald Burnett to recover the purchase price of shares of stock in Sonic Petroleum, Inc. Plaintiffs alleged that the stock had not been registered as required by [§ 5(a)], and that the stock did not qualify for the intrastate offering exemption set out in [§ 3(a)(11)].[1] . . . The parties filed cross motions for summary judgment, and the district court granted judgment for defendants. We affirm in part, reverse in part, and remand for further proceedings.

I.

BACKGROUND

The undisputed facts are briefly as follows. Sonic was incorporated in Utah on October 2, 1980. The three defendants were officers and directors of Sonic at its inception. Carpenter was president until May 1981, and a director and officer through June 26, 1981, the date on which plaintiffs bought their shares. Jensen was vice president and a director through June 26. Burnett was secretary and a director until May 1981. During October and November of 1980, Sonic publicly offered and sold shares of Sonic stock to Utah residents through Olsen & Company, Inc. Although Sonic complied with Utah state registration requirements, it did not file a registration statement under federal securities law, relying on the exemption from registration provided for intrastate offerings. Sonic, which had no prior operating history at the time of this offering, was incorporated in Utah and purportedly organized to acquire, extract, and market natural resources such as oil, gas, and coal. Although the company had not undertaken this activity in Utah or anywhere else, it maintained its corporate office, books, and records in Utah at the time of the initial offering. It is not disputed that the offering of 25,000,000 shares of Sonic was sold for $500,000 entirely to Utah residents.

In late March or early April of 1981, Carpenter was contacted by William Mason, an Illinois oil and gas promoter, about a merger of Sonic with Mason's operations in Illinois. Sonic and Mason reached an agreement, effective May 25, 1981, under which Sonic issued Mason a controlling block of stock and acquired an Illinois drilling corporation privately owned by Mason. Carpenter, Jensen, Mason, Mason's wife, and their son were officers and directors of the new company, which was renamed Mason Oil Co., Inc. Burnett had resigned his positions with Sonic at the shareholders meeting on the proposed merger, and he took no part in the operation of Mason Oil. Shortly after Mason Oil was formed, William Mason drew $351,126 from the remainder of the

---

[1] Plaintiffs also alleged that defendants had violated Rule 147, which is a "safe harbor" provision establishing the circumstances in which the SEC will not challenge the applicability of the intrastate offering exemption. The district court held that defendants' failure to comply with Rule 147 did not preclude them from establishing that they were nonetheless entitled to the exemption. Plaintiffs do not raise this ruling as error on appeal.

$435,000 net proceeds of the original Sonic offering and deposited it in Illinois. This money was not used in Utah.

In May 1981, Mason and Carpenter set up Norbil Investments, a brokerage account in Utah, so that Mason and his friends could buy shares of the company's stock. Plaintiffs, who are California residents, bought their stock through Norbil. Plaintiffs also presented evidence of purchases through Norbil of stock by other non-residents between May and August 1981.

II.
THE INTRASTATE OFFERING EXEMPTION

* * *

Congress . . . recognized that the protections of the 1933 Act were not essential for those securities that could be supervised effectively by the states. . . .

* * *

A.   Coming to Rest

The district court ruled that the resale of stock to non-residents occurred after the issued securities had come to rest in Utah and concluded that the public offering was therefore consummated in Utah within the meaning of section 3(a)(11). On appeal, plaintiffs contend that the court's ruling was erroneous and that the circumstances of the resale defeated the intrastate exemption.

In order to fall within the intrastate exemption, initial sales to state residents must be bona fide. The intrastate exemption becomes unavailable whenever sales or purchases by an issuer, an intermediary, or a subsequent purchaser circumvent the federal securities laws. The SEC has consistently maintained that a distribution of securities must have "actually come to rest in the hands of resident investors—persons purchasing for investment and not with a view to further distribution or for purposes of resale." We agree.

During the proceedings below, plaintiffs contended that the resale to non-residents within seven months of the initial offering in and of itself precluded the application of the intrastate offering exemption. The Amicus [the SEC] raises a new argument on appeal, contending that because defendants had the burden to show their right to the exemption, they had the burden below to present evidence that the original buyers bought with investment intent. The [SEC] argues that without such a showing, summary judgment for defendants was improper. . . .

We reject the [SEC's] argument. The intrastate offering exemption requires that the issue be "offered and sold only to persons resident within a single State." In our view, a seller seeking summary judgment makes a prima facie showing that the offering was consummated within a state by showing that the stock was sold only to residents of that state. We disagree with [the SEC] that, in order to be entitled to summary judgment, the issuer should be required to disprove all the possible circumstances that might establish the stock has not come to rest. It seems more logical to us to impose on the other party the burden of producing some contrary evidence on this issue when the seller claiming the exemption has satisfied the facial requirement of the statute. In the face of defendants' undisputed showing that all of the original buyers were Utah residents, plaintiffs were therefore required to produce evidence that the stock had not come to rest but had been sold to people who intended to resell it out of state.

The evidence fails to suggest that any of Sonic's publicly offered shares were issued under questionable circumstances. Carpenter and Mason did not know each other until their initial conversation in the spring of 1981. . . . Moreover, the interstate purchases by Mason and others of freely trading shares several months after the completion of the intrastate offering do not, without more, impugn the investment intent of the original buyers or otherwise imply an effort to evade the federal securities laws. Norbil served as a conduit for over-the-counter purchases made by Olsen & Company on behalf of Mason and various acquaintances. Although Carpenter did collect from buyers, pay Olsen, and transfer the stock certificates to their new owners, there is simply no indication that those who sold through Norbil had not originally purchased their stock for investment purposes. . . . Accordingly, the trial court did not err in concluding that no genuine question of fact was raised on whether the issue had come to rest in the hands of Utah residents.

B. Doing Business

Plaintiffs alternatively contend that defendants were not entitled to the intrastate offering exemption because the corporate issuer was not doing business in Utah as required by section 3(a)(11). There is no dispute that the newly formed company, not yet operational, maintained its offices, books, and records in Salt Lake City. The decisive issue concerns whether, under the circumstances of this case, Sonic's failure to invest a portion of the proceeds from its initial public offering in Utah could defeat the intrastate exemption.

Although neither the statute nor its legislative history defines the doing business requirement, courts have uniformly held that it refers to activity that actually generates revenue within an issuer's home state. The leading case is *Chapman v. Dunn*, 414 F.2d 153 (6th Cir.1969), which involved a company that maintained its offices and issued stock in Michigan while operating its sole productive venture, an oil and gas business, in Ohio. The *Chapman* court reasoned that "doing business" in the context of securities regulation connotes substantially more activity than that which would warrant exercising personal jurisdiction in ordinary civil suits. Effective supervision of stock offerings, the court added, can entail on-site inspections, familiarity with local economic conditions, and sometimes reliance upon judicial process. State oversight of business operations located elsewhere could often prove cumbersome, costly, and ineffective. The *Chapman* court therefore approved the SEC's view that the intrastate exemption applies only in cases of local financing for local industries. The court held that "doing business" refers to income-producing activity, and that an issuer must conduct a "predominant amount" of that activity within its home state.

* * *

[A]n issuer cannot claim the exemption simply by opening an office in a particular state. Conducting substantially all income-producing operations elsewhere defeats the exemption, as do the plans of recently organized companies to invest the net proceeds of initial public offerings only in other states. Doing business under the 1933 Act means more than maintaining an office, books, and records in one state.

Viewing the evidence and drawing reasonable inferences most favorably to plaintiffs, a fact issue exists regarding . . . Sonic's plans for the use of proceeds. . . . Here the corporation never did more than maintain its office, books, and records in Utah. This was not sufficient to make a prima facie showing of compliance with the intrastate offering exemption. While its prospectus stated that no more than twenty percent of all proceeds would be used outside of Utah, Sonic nonetheless transferred essentially all of its assets to Mason in Illinois. The record contains no evidence, moreover, of any prior efforts whatever at locating investment opportunities within Utah. These considerations support a reasonable inference that Sonic may have been intending all along to invest its assets outside the state. Although Carpenter and Mason may have been strangers to one another, this fact alone fails to dispel the possibility that Sonic had been seeking and perhaps investigating other business operations out of state. If so, and we intimate no view on this unresolved fact question, the intrastate exemption would be unavailable.

We are not persuaded by defendants' argument that Sonic did business in Utah when its public offering was consummated, that its stated purpose was to do business within that state, and that the company should not be penalized for reorganizing its operations at a later date. We have already noted that under the Act, doing business means more than opening an office at the time of a public offering. The issue is not whether a newly formed company performs such minimal corporate functions within a state, but whether subsequent proceeds are to be employed in that same state. A newly formed company may not claim the exemption while planning covertly to invest the proceeds of a local offering in other states. . . . Accordingly, we conclude that a genuine issue of material fact exists precluding summary judgment in favor of all defendants.

* * *

IV.

CONCLUSION

In view of our conclusion that fact questions exist on whether the company was doing business in Utah within the ambit of the intrastate exemption and as to Carpenter's liability for any violation of the Act, we reverse in part and remand for further proceedings. . . .

QUESTIONS

1. Who bears the burden of demonstrating that all the purchasers of securities under § 3(a)(11) are residents of the same state?

2.   Sonic was initially incorporated in Utah and had its office, corporate books, etc. there. Why didn't this establish that Sonic was resident and doing business in Utah?

3.   What if Sonic had substantial income producing activities in Utah but intended to use the proceeds from the offering to drill for gas in Nevada?

———

Although the intent behind § 3(a)(11) is straightforward (exempting local financing for local businesses from federal securities registration requirements), the application of § 3(a)(11) is more ambiguous. Consider the following concepts important in determining the application of § 3(a)(11):

- Issuer Resident and Doing Business in a State
- Investors Resident in a State
  - When are sales to investors outside the states integrated?
  - When do securities sold to investors within the state "come to rest"?

Section 3(a)(11) defines none of these items with precision. Instead, we are left with somewhat vague standards. The SEC in Securities Act Release 4552, for example, put forth a multi-prong test for integration. We are told that two offerings may be integrated and treated as one to the extent the two offerings have the same general purpose, plan of financing, consideration, and are close in time to one another. Release 4552 does not tell us, however, how to balance these factors if they do not all point in the same direction.

Similarly, if investors within the state resell their securities to out-of-state investors, does this result in a loss of the exemption? The answer depends on whether the in-state investors had "investment intent." Although the passage of time (in particular over two years) before a resale suggests initial investment intent, the SEC does not favor reliance upon the mere passage of time as evidence of investment intent. Consider how you would resolve these ambiguities in the following hypothetical.

HYPOTHETICAL NINETEEN

Assume that Trendy is based in San Francisco, CA. On January 1 it sold $50 million worth of common stock through a private placement to 30 sophisticated purchasers and accredited investors across the United States pursuant to Rule 506 of Regulation D. Trendy used the $50 million to construct a soft drink manufacturing plant in Los Angeles, CA. On August 1, Trendy then sold an additional $20 million of common stock solely to California investors. Trendy used the proceeds from the offering to finish construction of the manufacturing plant.

1.   If Trendy's January 1 and August 1 offerings are integrated, what effect does that have on the § 3(a)(11) offering?

2.   Will the two offerings be integrated? Do any safe harbors protect against integration?

3. Assume that on July 31, Trendy had $20 million in cash that it could use either to finish construction of the factory or invest in a new research and development facility located in Arizona. Rather than make this choice, Trendy conducts an intrastate offering of common stock to California residents, raising an additional $20 million in cash. Trendy directs the proceeds from the intrastate offering to finance the construction of the factory. Trendy simultaneously directs the $20 million in cash it had on hand prior to the intrastate offering to build the R & D facility in Arizona. Does this jeopardize the § 3(a)(11) exemption?

B. RULE 147

To bring certainty to issuers wanting to raise capital through an intrastate offering, the SEC promulgated Rule 147 in 1974. Like Rule 506, Rule 147 is not exclusive. Issuers that fail to meet the terms of Rule 147 may still rely on § 3(a)(11). Given the relative certainty of Rule 147, however, few issuers would purposely seek to test the limits of § 3(a)(11). Consider the following SEC Release announcing the adoption of Rule 147.

Exchange Act Release No. 5450
Securities and Exchange Commission (Jan. 7, 1974).

The Securities and Exchange Commission today adopted Rule 147 which defines certain terms in, and clarified certain conditions of, Section 3(a)(11) of the Securities Act of 1933. . . .

Background and Purpose

* * *

Section 3(a)(11) was intended to allow issuers with localized operations to sell securities as part of a plan of local financing. Congress apparently believed that a company whose operations are restricted to one area should be able to raise money from investors in the immediate vicinity without having to register the securities with a federal agency. In theory, the investors would be protected both by their proximity to the issuer and by state regulation. Rule 147 reflects this Congressional intent and is limited in its application to transactions where state regulation will be most effective. The Commission has consistently taken the position that the exemption applies only to local financing provided by local investors for local companies. To satisfy the exemption, the entire issue must be offered and sold exclusively to residents of the state in which the issuer is resident and doing business. An offer or sale of part of the issue to a single non-resident will destroy the exemption for the entire issue.

The Transaction Concept

Although the intrastate offering exemption is contained in Section 3 of the Act, which Section is phrased in terms of exempt "securities" rather than "transactions", the legislative history and Commission and judicial interpretations indicate that the exemption covers only specific transactions and not the securities themselves. Rule 147 reflects this interpretation.

The "Part of an Issue" Concept

The determination of what constitutes "part of an issue" for purposes of the exemption, i.e. what should be "integrated", has traditionally been dependent on the facts involved in each case.

In this connection, the Commission generally has deemed intrastate offerings to be "integrated" with those registered or private offerings of the same class of securities made by the issuer at or about the same time. . . .

As adopted, the rule provides in Subparagraph (b)(2) that, for purposes of the rule only, certain offers and sales of securities, discussed below, will be deemed not to be part of an issue and therefore not be integrated, but the rule does not otherwise define "part of an issue." Accordingly, as to offers and sales not within (b)(2), issuers who want to rely on Rule 147 will have to determine whether their offers and sales are part of an issue by applying the five factor [integration test].

The "Person Resident Within" Concept

The object of the Section 3(a)(11) exemption, i.e., to restrict the offering to persons within the same locality as the issuer who are, by reason of their proximity, likely to be familiar with the issuer and protected by the state law governing the issuer, is best served by interpreting the residence requirement narrowly. In addition, the determination of whether all parts of the issue have been sold only to residents can be made only after the securities have "come to rest" within the state or territory. Rule 147 retains these concepts, but provides more objective standards for determining when a person is considered a resident within a state for purposes of the rule and when securities have come to rest within a state.

The "Doing Business Within" Requirement

Because the primary purpose of the intrastate exemption was to allow an essentially local business to raise money within the state where the investors would be likely to be familiar with the business and with the management, the doing business requirement has traditionally been viewed strictly. First, not only should the business be located within the state, but the principal or predominant business must be carried on there. Second, substantially all of the proceeds of the offering must be put to use within the local area.

Rule 147 reinforces these requirements by providing specific percentage amounts of business that must be conducted within the state, and of proceeds from the offering that must be spent in connection with such business. In addition, the rule requires that the principal office of the issuer be within the state.

Synopsis of Rule 147

1. Preliminary Notes

The first preliminary note to the rule indicates that the rule does not raise any presumption that the Section 3(a)(11) exemption would not be available for transactions which do not satisfy all of the provisions of the rule.

As initially proposed, the rule was intended not to be available for secondary transactions. In order to make this clear, the fourth preliminary note indicates that the rule is available only for transactions by an issuer and that the rule is not available for secondary transactions. However, in accordance with long standing administrative interpretations of Section 3(a)(11), the intrastate offering exemption may be available for secondary offers and sales by controlling persons of the issuer, if the exemption would have been available to the issuer.

2.   Transactions Covered—Rule 147(a)

Paragraph (a) of the rule provides that offers, offers to sell, offers for sale and sales of securities that meet all the conditions of the rule will be deemed to come within the exemption provided by Section 3(a)(11). Those conditions are: (1) the issuer must be resident and doing business within the state or territory in which the securities are offered and sold (Rule 147(c)); (2) the offerees and purchasers must be resident within such state or territory (Rule 147(d)); (3) resales for a period of 9 months after the last sale which is part of an issue must be limited as provided (Rule 147(e) and (f)). In addition, the revised rule provides that certain offers and sales of securities by or for the issuers will be deemed not "part of an issue" for purposes of the rule only (Rule 147(b)).

3.   "Part of an Issue"—Rule 147(b)

Subparagraph (b)(1) of the rule provides that all securities of the issuer which are part of an issue must be offered, offered for sale or sold only in accordance with all of the terms of the rule. For the purposes of the rule only, subparagraph (b)(2) provides that all securities of the issuer offered, offered for sale or sold pursuant to the exemptions provided under Section 3 or 4[a](2) of the Act or registered pursuant to the Act, prior to or subsequent to the six month period immediately preceding or subsequent to any offer, offer to sell, offer for sale or sale pursuant to Rule 147 will be deemed not part of an issue provided that there are no offers, offers to sell or sales of securities of the same or similar class by or for the issuer during either of these six month periods. If there have been offers or sales during the six months, then in order to determine what constitutes part of an issue, reference should be made to the five traditional integration factors. . . .

4.   Nature of the Issuer—Rule 147(C)—"Person Resident Within"—
      Rule 147(C)(1)

Subparagraph (c)(1) of the rule defines the situation in which issuers would be deemed to be "resident within" a state or territory. A corporation, limited partnership or business trust must be incorporated or organized pursuant to the laws of such state or territory. Section 3(a)(11) provides specifically that a corporate issuer must be incorporated in the state. . . .

5.   Nature of the Issuer—Rule 147(C)—Doing Business Within—Rule
      147(C)(2)

Subparagraph (c)(2) of the rule provides that the issuer will be deemed to be "doing business within" a state or territory in which the offers and sales are to be made if: (1) at least 80 percent of its gross revenues and those of its subsidiaries on a consolidated basis (a) for its most recent fiscal year (if the first offer of any part of the issue is made during the first six months of the issuer's current fiscal year) or (b) for the subsequent six month period, or for the twelve months ended with that period (if the first offer of any part of the issue is made during the last six months of the issuer's current fiscal year) were derived from the operation of a business or property located in or rendering of services within the state or territory; (2) at least 80 percent of the issuer's assets and those of its subsidiaries on a consolidated basis at the end of the most recent fiscal semi-annual period prior to the first offer of any part of the issue are located within such state or territory; (3) at least 80 percent of the net proceeds to the issuer from the sales made pursuant to the rule are intended to be and are used in connection with the operation of a business or property or the rendering of services within such state or territory; and (4) the issuer's principal office is located in the state or territory.

* * *

The provisions of paragraph (c) are intended to assure that the issuer is primarily a local business. . . . The following examples demonstrate the manner in which these standards would be interpreted:

Example 1. X corporation is incorporated in State A and has its only warehouse, only manufacturing plant and only office in that state. X's only business is selling products throughout the United States and Canada through mail order catalogs. X annually mails catalogs and order forms from its office to residents of most states and several provinces of Canada. All orders are filled at and products shipped from X's warehouse to customers throughout the United States and Canada. All the products shipped are manufactured by X at its plant in State A. These activities are X's sole source of revenues.

Question. Is X deriving more than 80 percent of its gross revenues from the "operation of a business or . . . rendering of services" within State A?

Interpretive Response. Yes, this aspect of the "doing business within" standard is satisfied.

Example 2. Assume the same facts as Example 1, except that X has no manufacturing plant and purchases the products it sells from corporations located in other states.

Question. Is X deriving more than 80 percent of its gross revenues from the "operation of a business or . . . rendering of services" within State A?

Interpretive Response. Yes, this aspect of the "doing business within" standard is satisfied.

* * *

6.   Offerees and Purchasers: Persons Resident—Rule 147(d)

Paragraph (d) of the rule provides that offers and sales may be made only to persons resident within the state or territory. An individual offeree or purchaser of any part of an issue would be deemed to be a person resident within the state or territory if such person has his principal residence in the state or territory. Temporary residence, such as that of many persons in the military service, would not satisfy the provisions of paragraph (d). In addition, if a person purchases securities on behalf of other persons, the residence of those persons must satisfy paragraph (d). If the offeree or purchaser is a business organization its residence will be deemed the state or territory in which it has its principal office, unless it is an entity organized for the specific purpose of acquiring securities in the offering, in which case it will be deemed to be a resident of a state only if all of the beneficial owners of interests in such entity are residents of the state.

As initially proposed, subparagraph (d)(2) provided that an individual, in order to be deemed a resident, must have his principal residence in the state and must not have any present intention of moving his principal residence to another state. The Commission believes that it would be difficult to determine a person's intentions, and accordingly, has deleted the latter requirement. In addition, as initially proposed, the rule would have deemed the residence of a business organization to be the state in which it was incorporated or otherwise organized. The Commission believes that the location of a company's principal office is more of an indication of its local character for purposes of the offeree residence provision of the rule than is its state of incorporation. Section 3(a)(11) requires that an issuer corporation be incorporated within the state, but there is no similar requirement in the statute for a corporation that is an offeree or purchaser.

7. Limitations on Resales—Rule 147(e)

Paragraph (e) of the rule provides that during the period in which securities that are part of an issue are being offered and sold and for a period of nine months from the date of the last sale by the issuer of any part of the issue, resales of any part of the issue by any person shall be made only to persons resident within the same state or territory. This provides objective standards for determining when an issue "comes to rest." The rule as initially proposed limited both reoffers and resales during a twelve month period after the last sale by the issuer of any part of the issue. However, the Commission believes that it would be difficult for an issuer to prohibit or even learn of reoffers. Thus, the limitation on reoffers would be impractical because, if any purchaser made a reoffer outside of such state or territory, the issuer would lose the exemption provided by the rule. In addition, the Commission determined that a shorter period would satisfy the coming to rest test for purposes of the rule. Thus, the twelve month period has been reduced to nine months.

Persons who acquire securities from issuers in transactions complying with the rule would acquire unregistered securities that could only be reoffered and resold pursuant to an exemption from the registration provisions of the Act. . . .

8. Precautions Against Interstate Offers and Sales—Rule 147(f)

Paragraph (f) of the rule requires issuers to take steps to preserve the exemption provided by the rule, since any resale of any part of the issue before it comes to rest within the state to persons resident in another state or territory will, under the Act, be in violation of Section

5. The required steps are: (i) placing a legend on the certificate or other document evidencing the security stating that the securities have not been registered under the Act and setting forth the limitations on resale contained in paragraph (e); (ii) issuing stop transfer instructions to the issuer's transfer agent, if any, with respect to the securities, or, if the issuer transfers its own securities, making a notation in the appropriate records of the issuer; and (iii) obtaining a written representation from each purchaser as to his residence. Where persons other than the issuer are reselling securities of the issuer during the time period specified in paragraph (e) of the rule, the issuer would, if the securities are presented for transfer, be required to take steps (i) and (ii). In addition, the rule requires that the issuer disclose in writing the limitations on resale imposed by paragraph (e) and the provisions of subsections (f)(1)(i) and (ii) and subparagraph (f)(2).

Operation of Rule 147

* * *

The rule is a nonexclusive rule. However, persons who choose to rely on Section 3(a)(11) without complying with all the conditions of the rule would have the burden of establishing that they have complied with the judicial and administrative interpretations of Section 3(a)(11) in effect at the time of the offering. The Commission also emphasizes that the exemption provided by Section 3(a)(11) is not an exemption from the civil liability provisions of Section 12[a](2) or the anti-fraud provisions of Section 17 of the Act or of Section 10(b) of the Securities Exchange Act of 1934. The Commission further emphasizes that Rule 147 is available only for transactions by issuers and is not available for secondary offerings.

* * *

HYPOTHETICAL TWENTY

1. Trendy sells $20 million of common stock in an intrastate offering solely to California residents. Incorporated and headquartered in California, Trendy plans to use the proceeds to finance additional drink-related research and development at its lab located in Berkeley, CA. Research expenditures typically include purchasing a large amount of raw materials from around the globe (e.g., exotic plant roots, etc. to use in formulating new drinks). Assume that at least 50% of the proceeds will be used to purchase these raw materials for use in the Berkeley lab. Does the offering comply with Rule 147?

2. What if Trendy, in conducting the $20 million intrastate offering, circulates an offering memorandum rife with inaccuracies relating to the background of Trendy's officers and directors?

3. Kim, the CEO of Trendy, is also its largest shareholder. Kim decides to cash out some of her holdings. If Kim were simply to sell her securities through a broker into the national securities markets, she would run afoul of § 5. Instead, Kim seeks to sell her securities in a broad-based offering solely to residents of California using ads placed in the *Los Angeles Times*. Would this offering be covered by Rule 147?

4. Mitu, a purchaser of the securities in Trendy's California intrastate offering, suddenly finds out that he needs a new car three months after making his investment. Mitu liquidates his Trendy holdings (his only liquid asset) to purchase the car, selling the securities to his brother-in-law in New York.

5. In conducting an intrastate offering under Rule 147, Trendy makes a mistake. It fails to check for the residency of one out of 500 investors in its offerings. As it turns out, the one investor recently moved to Arizona. Does Trendy's offering still qualify under Rule 147?

VII. REGULATION S

Up to now, we have focused on domestic issuers and investors, but the United States is only one among over a hundred countries with an organized securities market. Securities transactions may span a number of different countries. Imagine a German investor purchasing the securities of a Japanese corporation through a transaction on the New York Stock Exchange. Or an investor in Iowa may go onto the Internet and purchase shares in an Italian corporation on the London Stock Exchange.

When a securities transaction cuts across national borders, which country should regulate that transaction? Presently, each country decides for itself whether to apply its securities laws to a transaction. Germany may choose to regulate in order to protect investors residing in Germany. Similarly, the United States may intervene to protect the integrity of the U.S. capital markets. If multiple countries intervene to regulate the same transaction, issuers and others participating in the offering face potentially duplicative regulation, raising costs without increasing the level of investor protection. Worse yet, some regulations may conflict. One country may require issuers to disclose certain types of information while another country may impose a "quiet period."

For primary offerings of securities, the United States follows a largely territorial approach to regulation. Section 5 covers all transactions involving an offer or sale of securities through interstate commerce. A transaction completely outside the United States, and therefore not involving interstate commerce, will not implicate § 5. But the reach of the definition of interstate commerce is broad. Suppose an issuer in France selling securities to investors located in Paris advertises the offering in a French newspaper. The French newspaper is distributed in France, but is also sold in the United States. The distribution of the ad through the circulation of the French newspaper into the United States implicates interstate commerce and thus, § 5.

The SEC provides an exemption under Regulation S of the Securities Act that defines the scope of § 5. Consider the merits of taking an expansive view of the reach of U.S. securities laws. Why not apply the U.S. regime to securities transactions taking place in France, Japan, and Brazil if investors in the U.S. are affected by such transactions?

A. BASIC REGULATION S REQUIREMENTS

Regulation S removes certain "offshore" offers and sales from the definition of offers and sales for purposes of § 5, effectively exempting those transactions from § 5. Exemption from § 5 does not exempt issuers or securities transactions from the entire scope of U.S. securities regulation. An exemption from § 5 frees the issuers from the gun-jumping rules and the heightened public offering antifraud provisions of § 11, but it does not exempt the issuer from, among other regulations, Rule 10b–5 antifraud liability.* The Supreme Court in *Morrison v. National Australia Bank Ltd.*, 130 S.Ct. 2869 (2010) (excerpted in Chapter 5), ruled against the extraterritorial application of Rule 10b–5, holding that "Section 10(b) reaches the use of a manipulative or deceptive device or contrivance only in connection with the purchase or sale of a security listed on an American stock exchange, and the purchase or sale of any other security in the United States."

Rule 901 of Regulation S provides the actual exemption, exempting offers and sales from § 5 if they are "outside the United States." Whether a securities transaction is deemed to be outside the United States depends on whether the transaction falls into one of the three categories: Category 1, 2, and 3 offerings. The SEC explains its "territorial" approach:

> The registration of securities is intended to protect the U.S. capital markets and investors purchasing in the U.S. market. Principles of comity and the reasonable expectations of participants in the global markets justify reliance on laws applicable in jurisdictions outside the United States to define requirements for transactions effected offshore. The territorial approach recognizes the primacy of the laws in which a market is located. As investors choose their markets, they choose the laws and regulations applicable in such markets.

Offshore Offers and Sales, Securities Act Release No. 6863 (1990).

As with many provisions of the Securities Act, many of the nuances of Regulation S are found in its definitional provisions, Rule 902. We list key defined terms and their associated Rule 902 provision below:

Designated Offshore Securities Market—Rule 902(b)

Directed Selling Efforts—Rule 902(c)

Distributor—Rule 902(d)

Distribution Compliance Period—Rule 902(f)

Offering Restrictions—Rule 902(g)

Offshore Transaction—Rule 902(h)

Substantial U.S. Market Interest—Rule 902(j)

U.S. Person—Rule 902(k)

Two basic requirements are imposed on all three offering categories. All offerings must take place through an "offshore

---

*   Arguably, under *Gustafson v. Alloyd Co.*, 513 U.S. 561 (1995), § 12(a)(2) also applies to an unregistered public offering. If so, then Regulation S does not protect issuers engaged in public offerings abroad from § 12(a)(2) liability, if the offering is within the jurisdictional scope of the Securities Act.

transaction" and involve no "directed selling efforts" into the U.S. Consider each requirement in turn.

1.   OFFSHORE TRANSACTION

Offshore transactions involve transactions where offers are not made to a "person in the United States." Rule 902(h). Geography is key to an offshore transaction. A person may be a U.S. citizen or resident, but if she receives an offer while on vacation in Bangalore, this qualifies as an offer outside the United States. Not only must offers take place outside the United States, the actual purchase transaction must occur offshore as well. Rule 902(h) provides two alternative means for the purchase transaction to qualify as offshore. First, the buyer is "outside the United States or the seller and any person acting on its behalf reasonably believe that the buyer is outside the United States" at the time of origination of the buy order. Alternatively, the transaction is executed on an "established foreign securities exchange."

The offshore transaction requirement embodies Regulation S's focus on territoriality. As a necessary (but not sufficient) condition of obtaining the Regulation S exemption, either the buyer must be actually outside the U.S. or the transaction must be executed on an established foreign securities exchange. The SEC explains that the buyer's location:

> . . . clearly and objectively provides evidence of the offshore nature of the transaction. The requirement that the buyer itself, rather than its agent, be outside the United States reduces evidentiary difficulties and problems in administering the Regulation, both for regulators and private parties attempting to ensure compliance with the conditions of the safe harbor. Second, the buyer's location outside the United States supports the expectation that the buyer is or should be aware that the transaction is not subject to registration under the Securities Act.

Securities Act Release No. 6863 (April 24, 1990).

HYPOTHETICAL TWENTY-ONE

Suppose that Trendy Inc. (a U.S.-incorporated issuer) is still searching for new sources of capital. Trendy has already engaged in a series of private placements, a Regulation A offerings, and an intrastate offering. The prior financing has helped launch Trendy's marketing campaign for the Lean Green drink. Now, Trendy wants to expand Lean Green internationally (first throughout North America and then into Europe and Asia). Kim, the CEO of Trendy, worries that Trendy may have exhausted the supply of investors in the United States. Instead, Kim wants to sell Trendy common stock in a series of public offerings in Germany and France. Kim hopes to conduct the offerings pursuant to Regulation S. Which of the following are "offshore" transactions?

1.   *Scenario One:* Trendy, Inc. offers and sells securities to investors in Topeka, Kansas.

2.   *Scenario Two:* Trendy makes all offers and sales to German citizens in Germany.

3. *Scenario Three:* Trendy attempts to make all offers and sales to German citizens in Germany. United States citizens from Kansas vacationing in Hamburg, Germany, however, happen to obtain and read some of the offering documents. The Kansas investors, while still in Germany, purchase securities directly from German distributors working on behalf of Trendy.

4. *Scenario Four:* Investors in Kansas decide to purchase securities in Trendy, Inc. after tasting the Lean Green drink. They instruct their broker to purchase common shares. The broker, without the knowledge of the investors, executes the orders through the Frankfurt Stock Exchange. Among the Trendy shares purchased are securities recently sold by Trendy into the German market pursuant to Regulation S.

2.   NO DIRECTED SELLING EFFORTS

For securities sold through Regulation S, Rule 902(c) defines "directed selling efforts" as "any activity undertaken for the purpose of, or that could reasonably be expected to have the effect of, conditioning the market." Rule 902(c) provides that conditioning the market includes "placing an advertisement in a publication 'with a general circulation in the United States' that refers to the offering of securities being made in reliance upon this Regulation S." Publications with general circulation include "any publication that is printed primarily for distribution in the United States" or had an average circulation in the U.S. of 15,000 or more copies per issue for the preceding twelve months.

In considering the scope of Rule 902(c), recall the broad definition given to "conditioning the market" in the gun-jumping rules (*see* Chapter 7). Efforts designed to raise investor interest in the issuer, even if they do not mention the issuer or offering explicitly (but instead discuss the general industry and mention the underwriter for example) may be considered as conditioning the market. In addition, the SEC takes a dim view of references to forward-looking information, including earnings projections, treating such non-"factual" disclosures as likely to condition the market. Although the SEC provides various exemptions and safe harbors for communications from treatment as an "offer" or "prospectus" during the public offering process, the SEC continues to maintain a broad view of "conditioning the market."

Several forms of communications are excluded from the definition of directed selling efforts. Among the excluded communications are advertisements required to be published under U.S. or foreign law (or pursuant to the rules of a self-regulatory organization such as the NYSE), provided that the advertisements include no more information than legally required and provides a boilerplate statement that the securities may not be offered or sold in the U.S. (or to a U.S. person, if the offering is under Category 2 or 3). Rule 902(c)(3)(ii) also provides that a tombstone advertisement of the offering (with very limited disclosure) in a publication with general circulation in the U.S. will not count as a directed selling effort.

The SEC provides the following guidance for companies on disclosure directed into the U.S. during a Regulation S offering:

> An isolated, limited contact with the United States generally will not constitute directed selling efforts that result in a loss

of the safe harbor for the entire offering. The Regulation likewise is not intended to inhibit routine activities conducted in the United States for purposes other than inducing the purchase or sale of the securities being distributed abroad, such as routine advertising and corporate communications. The dissemination of routine information of the character and content normally published by a company, and unrelated to a securities selling effort, generally would not be directed selling efforts under the Regulation. For example, press releases regarding the financial results of the issuer or the occurrence of material events with respect to the issuer generally will not be deemed to be "directed selling efforts."

Similarly, the Regulation is not intended to limit or interfere with news stories or other bona fide journalistic activities, or otherwise hinder the flow of normal corporate news regarding foreign issuers. Access by journalists for publications with a general circulation in the United States to offshore press conferences, press releases and meetings with company press spokespersons in which an offshore offering or tender offer is discussed need not be limited where the information is made available to the foreign and U.S. press generally and is not intended to induce purchases of securities by persons in the United States or tenders of securities by U.S. holders in the case of exchange offers.

Securities Act Release No. 6863 (April 24, 1990).

HYPOTHETICAL TWENTY-TWO

Trendy is moving forward with a Regulation S offering of its common stock in Germany. Consider the following communications from Trendy and whether they may be considered as directed selling efforts into the United States.

1. Trendy takes out an advertisement in the *Wall Street Journal* that has the following statement:

Trendy is a worldwide leader in the alternative drink market. Trendy's Lean Green drink both refreshes the soul and helps line the pockets of Trendy's investors. We project increasing long-term profits (at over a 25% annual rate of growth) for Trendy's investors over the next ten years. To be a Trendy investor is to be a well-satisfied investor.

2. Trendy advertises the offering in the European edition of the *Investor Times*. The U.S. edition of the *Investor Times* does not include the Trendy advertisement. Some copies of the European edition, however (representing less than 1% of the circulation of the European edition) make their way into the United States in the hands of business travelers flying into the U.S. from Europe.

B. CATEGORIES OF REGULATION S OFFERINGS

Whether an offering is considered to be outside the United States depends on whether the offering falls under one of the three categories of offerings exempted by Regulation S. In broad terms, the three categories are divided based on the risk that an offering will (a) catch the initial interest of investors in the U.S. and (b) result in eventual flowback of the securities into the U.S. securities markets.

1.   CATEGORY 1 (RULE 903(b)(1))

Category 1 offerings face the fewest restrictions under Regulation S. Issuers eligible for a Category 1 offering only need to meet the basic offshore transaction and no directed selling efforts requirements discussed above to qualify for the exemption. The SEC believes that Category 1 offerings pose the least risk of generating U.S. interest in the offering or flowback of securities into the U.S.

Several types of offerings qualify as Category 1 offerings. Consider the two most important types of Category 1 offerings. First, offerings involving *foreign* issuers that reasonably believe at the start of the offering that "no substantial U.S. market interest" exists in the class of securities offered or sold qualify as Category 1 offerings.

Rule 902(j) defines the term "substantial U.S. market interest." For equity securities, a substantial U.S. market interest exists if the securities exchanges and inter-dealer quotation systems in the U.S. in aggregate represent the single largest market for the class of securities measured for a period defined as "the shorter of the issuer's prior fiscal year or the period since the issuer's incorporation." Substantial U.S. market interest also exists if 20% or more of all trading in the class of equity securities took place in the United States (in a securities exchange or inter-dealer quotation systems) and less than 55% of trading took place in a securities market of a single foreign country for the same period of time.

Second, securities sold through an "overseas directed offering" may also qualify as a Category 1 offering. Among other types of offerings, overseas-directed offerings include offerings by a *foreign* issuer into a single foreign country to the residents of that country. Domestic issuers may qualify for a Category 1 offering only if they sell non-convertible debt securities, denominated in a foreign currency, through an overseas directed offering. The direct offering must comply with local laws, customary practices, and document requirements of the single foreign country (*see* Rule 903(b)(1)(ii)).

A common feature of these two offerings is the low likelihood that securities will flow from their initial overseas marketplace back into the United States. If no substantial interest exists in the U.S. for the securities, investors seeking to sell securities into the U.S. will face low liquidity and large price discounts from those few investors willing to purchase the securities. Thus, flowback is likely to be minimal. Similarly, if the securities are sold in a directed manner into one market to foreign residents, an active trading market will likely arise (or may already exist) in that foreign market. Liquidity begets liquidity; because investors seek liquidity for their trades, investors will gravitate toward this foreign marketplace.

HYPOTHETICAL TWENTY-THREE

1.   Trendy is incorporated in the U.S. and conducts most of its business in the U.S. Assume nonetheless that the secondary market with the highest

volume for Trendy's common stock is the Frankfurt Stock Exchange. Over 90% of the secondary market transactions in Trendy common stock take place in the Frankfurt Stock Exchange. Trendy seeks to raise additional capital through a Regulation S offering in Europe of common stock. Does Trendy qualify for Category 1?

2. Bland, Ltd., Trendy's major European competitor based in London and incorporated in the United Kingdom, makes an offering of common stock entirely in Japan conforming to Japanese securities laws. Bland's major secondary market is the NYSE with over 80% of stock trading taking place there. Does Bland qualify for Category 1?

2. CATEGORY 2 OFFERINGS (RULE 903(b)(2))

For companies with a substantial U.S. market interest that want to sell their securities in more than one country, most offerings of domestic and foreign issuers fall into Category 2 or 3. Whether an offering is eligible for Category 2 depends on the answer to three questions: (a) Is the issuer foreign or domestic? (b) Is it an Exchange Act reporting issuer? and (c) Is the issuer offering debt or equity?

Foreign issuers present less risk that an offering of securities overseas will find their way into the U.S. More information is generally available on an Exchange Act reporting issuer, reducing the harm to investors if there is flowback to the U.S. On the other hand, Exchange Act reporting status means that there is a secondary market for the issuer's shares in the U.S., heightening the risk of flowback into the U.S. and the impact from any fraud in the offering on U.S. markets, even if the fraud occurs overseas. Finally, debt securities pose less risk to investors. Because the returns from debt investments are more predictable than equity, the harm to investors from the lack of information provided by registration, even for securities that eventually flow back into the U.S., is diminished. Moreover, secondary debt markets are primarily institutional, so debt sold overseas is less likely to make its way into the hands of U.S. retail investors.

Combining these three factors, the following table details the eligibility for Category 2 status for those offerings that cannot qualify under Category 1. Category 3 acts as a catchall. Offerings that fail to meet either Category 1 or 2 are automatically considered Category 3 offerings:

	Exchange Act reporting issuer	**Non-Exchange Act reporting issuer**
Foreign issuer	Equity—Category 2	Equity—Category 3
	Debt—Category 2	Debt—Category 2
Domestic issuer	Equity—Category 3	Equity—Category 3
	Debt—Category 2	Debt—Category 3

Note that domestic issuers are only eligible for Category 2 if they are an Exchange Act reporting issuer *and* making a debt offering abroad.

Category 2 issuers must meet several requirements during the "distribution compliance period." Rule 902(f) defines the distribution compliance period as commencing from the *later* of: (a) when securities are first offered pursuant to Regulation S to persons other than distributors; or (b) the date the offering closes. All offers and sales by a distributor of securities from an unsold allotment or subscription are also deemed, regardless of timing, as occurring during the distribution compliance period.

As with Category 1 offerings, Category 2 offerings must comply with the basic offshore offering and no directed selling efforts requirements. In addition to the basic requirements, Category 2 offerings must also comply with "transactional restrictions" for a 40-day distribution compliance period. Under the transactional restrictions, offers and sales may not be made to a U.S. person or for the account or benefit of a U.S. person. Distributors are excluded from this prohibition, allowing sales to U.S.-based distributors. Rule 902(d) defines a distributor as "any underwriter, dealer, or other person who participates, pursuant to a contractual arrangement, in the distribution of the securities offered or sold in reliance on this Regulation S." If a distributor sells securities to another distributor or dealer, the distributor must send notice to the purchaser that the purchaser is under the same restrictions or offers that apply to the selling distributor.

"U.S. Person" is defined in Rule 902(k). Consider the interaction of the "U.S. Person" definition with the definition of an offshore transaction discussed above. Offshore transactions are defined as offers "not made to a person in the United States." Rule 902(h). Whether a person is "in the United States" for purposes of an offshore transaction is defined by a person's actions (i.e., whether they physically leave the U.S.). A U.S. Person by contrast, is defined by status (i.e., whether a person is a resident of the United States). Thus, an issuer (or distributor) making a Category 2 offering could not offer or sell securities to an investor resident in Kansas who happens to be in Germany. Although the investor would not be in the United States, the investor would still be a U.S. Person.

To enhance compliance with the transactional restrictions, Category 2 offerings must also comply with "offering restrictions," as defined by Rule 902(g). First, the offering restrictions apply for the duration of the 40-day distribution compliance period.

Second, the offering restrictions require that distributors agree in writing that all offers and sales during the distribution compliance period will occur through exempt transactions under Regulation S, some other exemption from registration, or through a registered offering under § 5. Distributors must also agree not to engage in hedging transactions for the duration of the distribution compliance period. Hedging transactions are contemporaneous transactions designed to shift the economic risk of ownership of Regulation S offered securities into the United States while formally keeping ownership outside the United States. For example, U.S. investors could engage in an equity swap with foreign holders of a Regulation S-offered security. Under the swap, the foreign investors would maintain formal ownership of the Regulation S security but receive a return based on some other security (or basket of securities such as the S & P 500 index). The U.S. investor, in turn, would receive the return from ownership of the Regulation S security and owe the foreign investors the return on the other security or basket of securities. If allowed, such hedging transactions would transfer the economic risk of ownership of Regulation S securities into the United States.

Third, the offering restrictions require a disclaimer stating that the securities are unregistered and may not be offered or sold in the United States or to a U.S. person except through an exemption from registration or registration under § 5. The disclaimer must be included in the offering prospectus and advertisements for the offering.

HYPOTHETICAL TWENTY-FOUR

Bland, Inc. (Trendy's London-based competitor) is an Exchange Act reporting company whose major secondary market is the New York Stock Exchange. Bland hires Morimoto Securities of Tokyo as its placement agent. Under their agreement, Morimoto Securities will first purchase the shares from Bland at a discount and resell the shares to investors in a firm commitment offering. Morimoto plans to offer the stock throughout Asia, selling to both securities dealers and to a few select institutional investors. Suppose that the offering commences on June 1 when Morimoto purchases 10 million shares of Bland common stock. Morimoto begins offers to investors on June 2, selling the shares over a period of three weeks.

1. *Scenario One:* Morimoto Securities offers and sells Bland common stock to investors throughout Asia. For which category of Regulation S offering do the offers and sales qualify?

2. *Scenario Two:* Morimoto Securities sells Bland common stock to the fabulously wealthy Mr. Gates (a resident of Seattle and former chairman of a major U.S. investment bank) who happens to be visiting in Japan during the offering. Gates purchases Bland stock while still in Japan.

3. *Scenario Three:* Morimoto Securities sells Bland securities to a Japanese incorporated entity, Bland Investor Ltd. Bland Investor was incorporated just prior to the offering. Bland Investor has only one shareholder, the fabulously wealthy Mr. Gates.

3. CATEGORY 3 OFFERINGS (RULE 903(b)(3))

Category 3 offerings provide a catchall form of Regulation S offering for issuers unable to qualify for the other two categories of offerings. U.S. issuers seeking to sell equity fall under Category 3 regardless of their Exchange Act reporting status. Non-Exchange Act reporting foreign issuers selling equity securities also fall under Category 3 if they cannot qualify under Category 1.

Category 3 securities represent the greatest risk of flowback into the United States. Flowback risk derives from securities that: (a) are more likely to gravitate to the U.S. market. U.S. issuers mainly fall in Category 3) and/or (b) pose greater potential harm to investors (due to the lack of information on non-Exchange Act reporting issuers).

As with Category 1 and 2 offerings, Category 3 issuers must comply with the basic requirements of and offshore offering and no directed selling efforts. In addition to the two basic requirements, Regulation S imposes on Category 3 offerings the same offering restrictions as Category 2, albeit with a different distribution compliance period. For offerings of debt securities, the offering restrictions extend for the same 40-day distribution compliance period as Category 2. For equity offerings, the offering restrictions apply for a one-year distribution compliance period, shortened to six months for U.S. reporting issuers.

Category 3 offerings then face additional requirements depending on whether the offering is for debt or equity. Debt securities face fewer restrictions for a shorter period because the risk of flowback is lower for the primarily institutional debt market. Three transactional restrictions apply to debt securities during the 40-day distribution compliance period. First, offers and sales must not be made to a U.S. person or for the account or benefit of a U.S. person. Second, in transactions where a distributor sells securities to another distributor or dealer, the distributor must notify the purchaser that the purchaser is under the same restrictions that apply to the selling distributor. Lastly, the debt securities must be in the form of a temporary global security. The issuer may not exchange the temporary global security for definitive securities until after the expiration of the 40-day compliance period. The issuer is also prohibited from making the exchange for a definitive security unless the requesting investor (excluding distributors) certifies that she is either not a U.S. person or that she purchased the securities through a transaction exempt from the registration requirements of § 5.

In the case of equity securities, several transactional restrictions apply during the six-month or one-year distribution compliance periods. First, offers and sales may not be made to a U.S. person or for the account or benefit of a U.S. person. Second, in transactions in which a distributor sells securities to another distributor or dealer, the distributor must notify the purchaser that the purchaser is under the same restrictions that apply to the selling distributor. Finally, offers and sales made prior to the expiration of the distribution compliance period must meet several additional requirements:

Purchaser Certification (Rule 903(b)(3)(iii)(B)(1)). The purchaser of the Regulation S securities (excluding a distributor) must certify that the purchaser is not a U.S. person and is not acquiring the securities for the account of a U.S. person. Alternatively, the purchaser may certify that the purchase occurred through a transaction exempt from the registration requirements.

Purchaser Contract Obligations (Rule 903(b)(3)(iii)(B)(2)). The issuer is required to obtain the purchaser's contractual consent to various purchaser restrictions. Purchasers must agree to resell any purchased Category 3 securities only in accordance with Regulation S, some other exemption from registration, or through registration under § 5. Purchasers also must agree not to engage in any hedging transactions with the Regulation S securities unless in compliance with the Securities Act.

Legend (Rule 903(b)(3)(iii)(B)(3)). The issuers must place a legend on the securities stating that the securities may be transferred only under the resale provisions of Regulation S, another exemption from registration, or registration under § 5. The legend must also state that hedging transactions may not take place unless in compliance with the Securities Act. Many foreign stock exchanges will not allow listing of securities with a legend restricting transferability.

Transfer Restrictions (Rule 903(b)(3)(iii)(B)(4)). Issuers must agree (either by contract or within the corporate charter or bylaws) to not register the transfer of securities that take place outside the scope of Regulation S, some other exemption to registration, or a registered offering under § 5. If foreign law prohibits issuers from refusing to register a transfer of securities, issuers may opt instead to implement alternative procedures to protect against prohibited resales (including the legend as detailed in Rule 903(b)(3)(iii)(B)(3)).

HYPOTHETICAL TWENTY-FIVE

For the following problems, assume that Trendy is an Exchange Act reporting company whose major secondary market is the New York Stock Exchange. Trendy hires Sprout Securities of Brussels as its placement agent. Under their agreement, Sprout Securities will act as a selling agent for Trendy using its best efforts for a commission. Sprout plans on offering the stock throughout Europe through sales to both securities dealers and to a few select institutional investors. Suppose that the offering commences on June 1 for 10 million shares of Trendy Inc. Sprout Securities immediately places 5 million of the shares. The other 5 million, however, are more difficult to place. The offering finally closes (with all the shares sold) on July 1.

1. Sprout offers and sells common stock to investors throughout Europe. For which category of Regulation S does this offering qualify?

2. Lexa, an investor living in Germany, purchased shares directly from Sprout Securities on June 1. Lexa holds the securities for a week and then sells them back to Sprout (acting as a market maker for Trendy's common stock). Sprout Securities then turns around and sells the securities to Hwa-Jin, an investor living in Korea, on July 10.

3. As part of Trendy's offering of common stock in Brussels, Sprout Securities advertises the offering throughout Belgium. Sales are made to all manner of investors, including mailroom clerks, chow delivery foremen and secretaries. Trendy raises $20 million from the offering. Assuming Regulation S applies, is this legal under the federal securities laws?

C. INTEGRATION

Despite the availability of Regulation S, U.S. issuers face substantial costs when raising capital abroad. Not only are the transaction costs (such as international travel and communication) higher, but the issuer also faces a new array of laws for each country where securities are offered and sold. U.S. issuers will therefore be selective in raising capital abroad. For example, a U.S. issuer with a significant business presence in another country may offer and sell securities in that country to build loyalty among investor-customers and to gain greater influence over government regulators.

U.S. issuers may also sell securities abroad when the size of the offering exceeds the ability of the U.S. capital market to absorb it. In such cases, the issuer may have a U.S. tranche (typically under

Regulation D and Rule 144A) and a series of other tranches of securities for different countries under Regulation S. Typically, the different tranches are offered simultaneously.

Those simultaneous offerings would ordinarily raise concerns that the different tranches will be integrated. Integration of the Regulation D offering (sold to U.S. investors) with the Regulation S tranches will result in a loss of the Regulation S exemption. Likewise, the presence of unsophisticated investors (and possibly general solicitation) in the offshore tranche will destroy the Regulation D exemption.

The SEC provides comfort to issuers worried about integration. Rather than establish a safe harbor against integration, the SEC went one step further. The SEC simply stated that integration would not occur: "Offshore transactions made in compliance with Regulation S will not be integrated with registered domestic offerings or domestic offerings that satisfy the requirements for an exemption from registration under the Securities Act, even if undertaken contemporaneously." Securities Act Release No. 6863 (April 24, 1990).

D. RESALES

As we will discuss in Chapter 10, resales after an exempt transaction are not necessarily exempt from § 5. Investors reselling soon after the exempt offering run the risk of being classified as underwriters. Investors who are deemed "underwriters" are considered part of the issuer's primary transaction and therefore cannot qualify for the § 4(a)(1) exemption from § 5.

Rule 905 of the Securities Act makes clear that equity securities of domestic U.S. issuers acquired from the issuer, a distributor in the offering or an affiliate in a transaction covered under Rule 901 or 903 are "restricted securities" as provided for in Rule 144. Rule 905 further specifies that the securities remain restricted securities even if acquired through an exempt resale pursuant to Rule 901 or Rule 904. Because of the restricted status of Regulation S securities, investors cannot resell equity securities of domestic issuers without an exemption from § 5 (such as Rules 144 or 144A) or registration under § 5.

Rule 905 closed off a Regulation S loophole. Purchasers of securities sold in a Regulation S offering resold the securities back into the U.S. after the distribution compliance period. Prior to the adoption of Rule 905, the distribution compliance period for equity securities (even those of domestic issuers) was only 40 days. The combination of a short distribution compliance period, combined with resales commencing after the expiration of the period, led to rapid resales of Regulation S securities back into the U.S. The SEC ultimately adopted Rule 905 to stop such resales, at least for equity securities of domestic issuers. What is less clear is what happens for resales of securities sold by foreign issuers and debt securities of domestic issuers. After the distribution compliance period, may investors resell these securities into the United States? Even after a 40-day distribution compliance period—as in the case of an Exchange Act reporting foreign issuer selling equity securities?

This question drove the promulgation of Rule 905:

The commenters also noted that if equity securities issued by these foreign companies are deemed restricted securities, the issuers in essence would be applying to their offshore offerings many of the standard practices used in U.S. private placements. The certification and purchaser agreement requirements would impose a significant burden on foreign issuers that wish to conduct public offerings in their home jurisdictions. In addition, many foreign stock exchanges will not permit trading of legended securities. The commenters asserted that the legending and stop transfer restrictions, as well as to a lesser extent the disclosure and certification requirements that would be imposed by the rule, would impede both public offerings and trading in those securities on offshore public markets that do not accept legended stock for trading. As a result, the classification of foreign equity securities as "restricted" could create a strong disincentive for foreign companies to list their securities on U.S. markets.

Securities Act Release No. 7505 (February 17, 1998).

Rule 904 provides a special resale provision for Regulation S securities. First, Rule 904 specifies a class of person who may use Rule 904's resale exemption. This class includes "any person other than the issuer, a distributor, any of their respective affiliates . . . or any person acting on behalf of any of the foregoing." Affiliates, however, do not include any officer or director of the issuer who is an affiliate solely from his or her position as an officer or director.

Second, Rule 904 imposes a number of requirements to qualify the resale for an exemption from § 5. Exempt resales involve the same basic requirements as the issuer exemptions under Regulation S. No "directed selling efforts" may be made inside the United States by the selling investor, the selling investor's affiliates or agents. Offshore transactions are more limited for resales than they are for initial sales. The buyer must be reasonably believed to be outside of the United States or the sale must take place on a "designated offshore securities market." Under Rule 902(b), the SEC may label a foreign securities market (exchange or non-exchange market) as a designated offshore securities market. Designated offshore securities markets include the London Stock Exchange, the Frankfurt Stock Exchange, and the Tokyo Stock Exchange, and many others. The SEC frequently adds new securities exchanges to the list of designated offshore securities market. Among factors the SEC considers in providing such a designation are: foreign law, the "community" of brokers, dealers, and other securities professionals and their operating history within the country, government and self-regulatory oversight, and the presence of an organized clearance and settlement system. The offer or sale must take place through an "offshore transaction."

Additional requirements apply if the selling investors are securities dealers or persons otherwise receiving selling concessions (i.e., the persons either receive a commission or purchased the securities at a discount from a participant in the offering) and the distribution compliance period has not expired. For such resales, the selling investor (or any person acting on behalf of the selling investor) must not be aware that the offeree or buyer is a U.S. person. If the purchaser is a dealer when he or she resells the securities, the selling investor must notify the purchaser that the securities can only be sold during the distribution compliance period in compliance with Regulation S, some other exemption from § 5's registration requirements, or through a registered offering.

Additional requirements are also placed on officers or directors (deemed affiliates by virtue of their positions) who resell Regulation S securities. No selling concession may be paid by the officer or director other than the usual and customary broker's commission.

Although Rule 904 provides a special resale provision for Regulation S securities and Regulation S securities are "restricted," there are alternative avenues for resale. As discussed in the next chapter, investors holding unregistered securities may still be able to resell the securities if the investors are deemed not to be "underwriters," thus enabling the investors to take advantage of § 4(a)(1)'s exemption from § 5.

E. GLOBAL REGULATION S OFFERINGS

Many large securities offerings now are offered and sold concurrently in several securities markets around the world. A German automobile company may seek to raise $1 billion to finance the manufacture of hybrid vehicles. To do so, the German company may decide to offer senior secured notes in the following amounts: $400 million in the United States, $200 million in South America, and the remaining $400 million in Europe. Spreading an offering across different countries in separate "tranches" helps ensure adequate investor appetite for large offerings of securities.

Issuers will typically offer and sell the U.S. tranche of securities pursuant to Rule 144A (covered in Chapter 10). Technically such an offering involves an initial sale by the issuer on a firm commitment basis to a broker-dealer under a § 4(a)(2) or Regulation D exemption from § 5. The placement agent will then turn around and resell the securities to "qualified institutional buyers," primarily large institutional investors, pursuant to the resale exemption in Rule 144A. Issuers will use Regulation S to offer and sell the non-U.S. tranches of securities. The anti-integration provision of Regulation S allows the issuer to make concurrent Rule 144A/Regulation S offerings. Although securities sold abroad under Regulation S escape the registration requirements of § 5, issuers and other participants must still comply with the applicable securities laws of the markets in which they offer and sell securities.

CHAPTER 10

SECONDARY MARKET TRANSACTIONS

Rules and Statutes

—*Sections 2(a)(11), 2(a)(12), 4(a)(1), 4(a)(2), 4(a)(3), 4(a)(4) of the Securities Act*

—*Rules 144, 144A, 405 of the Securities Act*

—*Rules 12g3–2, 15c2–11 of the Exchange Act*

MOTIVATING HYPOTHETICAL

Skipper is the CEO of Island Tours, Inc. The company, based in Hawaii, provides tourists with three-hour boat tours of the Hawaiian Islands. Formed ten years ago, Island Tours has sold common stock in a series of private placements to its own officers (including Skipper) as well as three "angel investors" based in California (including Howell, the heir to the Hatchet-Cuckoo Oil empire). Currently, Skipper owns 40% of Island Tours outstanding common stock and Howell owns 2% of the common stock. Both purchased all of their stock in Island Tours' earlier private placements. Three years ago, Island Tours went public with an offering of $100 million of common stock. Island Tours stock is publicly traded on Nasdaq. Due to better-than-expected popularity of its tours, Island Tours common stock price has been increasing rapidly. Eager to take advantage of the recent price increase and diversify their holdings, both Skipper and Howell would like to sell some of their common stock into the public markets.

I. INTRODUCTION

Why do investors purchase securities? For most people, securities are simply a means of storing and building wealth. Investors are willing to part with money today to buy securities in the hope of receiving even more money in the future. Securities can provide a return, in the form of dividends in the case of stock, or interest payments in the case of bonds. For years, AT&T's common stock was favored by those seeking a steady return and a relatively predictable stream of dividends. Not all common stock pays dividends. Growth companies are able to attract investors who seek return in the form of capital gains. Even some shareholders holding dividend-paying stocks may need to cash out quickly and, therefore, prefer a more immediate way of getting a return from their investment. Investors interested in cashing out may turn to the secondary securities markets.

The secondary securities markets provide investors liquidity, matching prospective sellers with potential buyers. The securities markets, however, differ from other markets. In most markets, buyers deal directly with sellers or the sellers' agents. So a student purchasing a book typically deals with a bookstore (working as the consignment agent for the book publisher). One could imagine a similar structure for the securities markets, with purchasers interacting directly with sellers. And for some transactions, typically involving large block trades, purchasers do in fact negotiate directly with sellers. But, for most secondary market transactions, direct negotiations between purchasers and sellers are simply impractical. The capital markets provide a mechanism to bring together potential sellers and purchasers of securities quickly and at low cost. With a large number of potential buyers and sellers, an investor will have confidence that she can transact at the prevailing market price quickly and at a minimal cost.

How do markets foster liquidity? Historically markets have relied on direct interpersonal communications to facilitate transactions. The NYSE, for example, provides a physical market space (the trading floor) where brokers interact with one another. On the trading floor, brokers literally shout out orders to one another to buy and sell securities. Although somewhat chaotic, this "open outcry system" allows the market price to adjust rapidly to new information. To ensure the liquidity of its listed securities, the NYSE also provides for "specialists." Specialists facilitate the matching of brokers seeking to buy and sell securities on behalf of their customer. The specialists also stand ready as dealers to buy or sell the stock when no one else will.

Most markets today, however, do not rely on brokers interacting at a physical location. Instead, computers and electronic communication allow traders to be brought together, in a virtual sense, from all over the world. In the largest of these computerized markets, Nasdaq, securities dealers hold themselves out to the public as being willing, continuously during the trading day, to buy and sell securities for their own account at particular prices. Such dealers are known as market makers. The price at which the market maker buys securities (the bid price) is always set below the price at which the market maker is willing to sell securities (the ask price). For example, Minnow Financial may act as a market maker for Island Tours, Inc. Suppose Minnow Financial, in its capacity as a market maker, posts on the Nasdaq quotation system that it is willing to sell 100 shares of Island Tours for $100 and buy 100 shares for $99.75. Minnow Financial then makes money on the "spread" of a quarter per share between the selling price of $100 and the buying price of $99.75. (For actively traded securities, the spread is usually much narrower than this.) On the Nasdaq, any single security may have multiple market makers all competing with one another based on the spread. This competition reduces transaction costs for investors seeking to buy or sell securities on Nasdaq. Nasdaq's primary competitor, the NYSE is moving increasingly into electronic trading through the development of its so-called "hybrid" market, allowing automatic electronic execution of orders while retaining a role for specialists and floor brokers.

Not all securities may enter into the public secondary capital market in the United States. Section 5 of the Securities Act applies not only to any "person" but also to all transactions. Thus, no transactions may occur even after the effective date of a registration statement without complying with § 5. Section 5 continues to apply indefinitely— i.e., it is not limited to the public offering period. If securities are sold using interstate commerce without a current registration statement and a formal statutory prospectus, there is a § 5 violation. Section 5 applies, by its terms, even if both the buyer and seller of the securities have no affiliation with the corporation and no ability to force registration or generate an up-to-date statutory prospectus.

But of course the story does not end here. Applying § 5 indefinitely to secondary transactions would dry up liquidity. Secondary market transactions are made possible through the exemptions from § 5, namely §§ 4(a)(1) and 4(a)(4). Section 4(a)(1) exempts transactions from § 5 so long as no "issuer, underwriter, or dealer" is present in the transaction. Section 4(a)(4) exempts unsolicited broker's transactions. Sections 4(a)(1) and 4(a)(4) create the necessary breathing space for the vast majority of secondary market transactions to take place. Determining the scope of secondary market trading therefore requires an examination of §§ 4(a)(1) and 4(a)(4).

II.   TRANSACTION AND UNDERWRITER?

Understanding the interplay between § 5 and the § 4(a)(1) exemption requires two analytical steps. First, we need to determine the scope of the "transaction." Section 5 applies to a transaction, as does the § 4(a) (1) exemption. Once we have identified the transaction, we need to determine whether an issuer, underwriter, or dealer is participating in the transaction. If an issuer or underwriter participates in the transaction, then the entire transaction loses the § 4(a)(1) exemption and thus must comply with § 5.

Consider first the definition of a transaction. Here history matters. It is universally understood a registered public offering is a discrete transaction. Any subsequent resales by the initial investors who purchased from underwriters or participating dealers are separate transactions. Those initial investors can resell immediately using the § 4(a)(1) exemption, which facilitates a public secondary market for the securities. (Affiliates of the issuer face a different set of restrictions; leave them to one side for now.)

By contrast, the scope of the transaction is defined differently for a private placement; no registration statement has been filed. Imagine a private placement under § 4(a)(2) from Island Tours to an initial sophisticated and informed investor, Lovey. Typically, a placement agent, here Wentworth Investments, will assist the issuer in the private placement. The diagram below depicts the transaction.

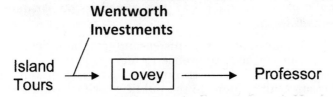

What is the status of a subsequent resale by Lovey to the Professor of the "restricted" securities she purchased in the private placement? That question depends on whether Lovey is treated as an "underwriter." If she is, her resales may be treated as part of the issuer's transaction— i.e., the initial private placement—which may jeopardize that transaction's exemption from registration.

Under § 2(a)(11) any person who does the following is an underwriter:

- purchases from an issuer with a view to, or offers or sells for an issuer in connection with, the distribution of any security
- participates or has a direct or indirect participation in any such undertaking
- participates or has a participation in the direct or indirect underwriting of any such undertaking

Obviously, Wall Street investment banks assisting an issuer in a public offering of securities fall within the underwriter definition. Both firm commitment (in which an investment bank purchases the securities at a discount with the intent of reselling them) and best efforts (in which the investment bank acts as an agent selling the securities on behalf of the issuer) bring the investment bank within the definition of underwriter. Such offerings need to be registered under § 5. Section 2(a)(11), however, captures far more than Wall Street investment banks as "underwriters."

Understanding the treatment of resales under the Securities Act requires us to recognize that Wentworth Investments is not the only possible underwriter under § 2(a)(11) in the above diagram. Lovey may also act as an underwriter for Island Tours if Lovey purchased her securities with a "view to" their "distribution." If Lovey is an underwriter then the securities did not "come to rest" with her. Instead, Lovey is a conduit for the securities and the Professor is the ultimate purchaser from Island Tours. That makes Lovey is an underwriter, and what otherwise would have been two separate transactions 1) Island Tours to Lovey and 2) Lovey to the Professor, becomes one transaction: Island Tours to the Professor. Is that transaction exempt from § 5?

Consider whether § 4(a)(1) applies to the transaction. Lovey's status as an underwriter collapses the sale from Island Tours through Lovey to the Professor into one transaction. But Lovey's status as an underwriter also means that the § 4(a)(1) exemption does not apply because both an issuer and an underwriter are participating in this transaction. Moreover, because it is all one transaction, Island Tours must now also worry that the Professor does not fit within the issuer's original §4(a)(2) exemption from § 5. That would be a concern, if, for example, the Professor is not sophisticated or did not receive disclosure. If the Professor does not fit within the private placement exemption, then Island Tours may have violated § 5 because it failed to file a registration statement.

History does not matter for this second question. Section 5 applies to any transaction without reference to any prior transaction. Suppose Microsoft sold common stock through a registered public offering in 1986. Any resales subsequent to the public offering would be considered separate transactions (and generally exempt under § 4(a)(1)). In 2015, suppose Microsoft repurchases some of this common stock, waits one week, and then resells the shares. Even though the stock was previously sold in a registered public offering back in 1986, § 5 still applies to the 2015 Microsoft transaction. An issuer (Microsoft) is present in the 2015 transaction, so the transaction will not qualify for the § 4(a)(1) exemption from § 5. Microsoft will have to find another exemption from § 5 (such as § 4(a)(2)) or register pursuant to § 5. The 1986 registration statement by which the stock was previously sold does not apply to the 2015 transaction. This "memory-less" property of § 5's application to transactions will be important in understanding why affiliate resales generally are not eligible for § 4(a)(1). Consequently, affiliates must comply with § 5 or find another exemption

The following case provides some guidance on when courts will conclude that an investor (such as Lovey in our hypothetical) has purchased with a "view to" the "distribution" of securities for the issuer, thus making that investor an "underwriter."

Gilligan, Will & Co. v. SEC

267 F.2d 461 (2d Cir. 1959).

■ LUMBARD, J., CIRCUIT JUDGE.

The question for decision is whether Gilligan, Will & Co. and its partners, James Gilligan and William Will, were underwriters with respect to the distribution of Crowell-Collier Publishing Company securities and as such willfully violated the Securities Act of 1933 by acquiring and distributing debentures and common stock which were not registered. For reasons which are discussed below, this question turns on whether the issue was a "public offering" as those words are used in the Act.

* * *

We hold that there was substantial evidence to justify the findings and conclusions of the Commission that the issue was a public offering and that petitioners were underwriters. . . .

The principal and essential purpose of the 1933 Act is to protect investors by requiring registration with the Commission of certain information concerning securities offered for sale. For reasons which will be developed, the crucial provisions of law in this case are § 5 of the 1933 Act which makes it unlawful for anyone, by any interstate communication or use of the mails, to sell or deliver any security unless a registration statement is in effect; and § 4[(a)](1) which exempts from this prohibition "transactions by any person other than issuer, underwriter, or dealer" and § 4[(a)](2) which exempts "transactions by an issuer not involving any public offering."

* * *

On July 6, 1955, Elliott & Company agreed with Crowell-Collier to try to sell privately, without registration, $3,000,000 of Crowell-Collier 5% debentures, convertible at any time into common stock at $5 a share, and [the] Elliott firm received an option on an additional $1,000,000 of debentures. Edward L. Elliott, a partner in Elliott & Company, advised Gilligan [of Gilligan, Will & Co.] of this agreement. He told Gilligan that Gilligan could purchase, but only for investment, as much of the $3,000,000 as he wished. . . . Gilligan was told by Elliott that Crowell-Collier had "turned the corner" and was then operating on a profitable basis. ... Gilligan agreed to purchase $100,000 of debentures for his own account. ...

On August 10, 1955 the $100,000 debentures were delivered to Gilligan, Will & Co., which sent a letter to Crowell-Collier stating: "that said debentures are being purchased for investment and that the undersigned has no present intention of distributing the same."

In May 1956, after Gilligan noticed that the advertising in Crowell-Collier magazines was not increasing, he decided to convert his debentures into common stock and to sell the stock. Later in May [Gilligan and others] sold the stock at a profit on the American Stock Exchange. ...

Petitioners assert that they were not "underwriters" within the meaning of the exemption provided by ... § 4[(a)](1). Since § 2[a](11) defines an "underwriter" as "any person who has purchased from an issuer with a view to * * * the distribution of any security" and since a "distribution" requires a "public offering," the question is whether there was a "public offering." Petitioners ... assert that whether there was a "distribution" must be judged solely by their own acts and intention, and not by the acts or intention of the issuer or others. In other words they claim that whether the total offering was in fact public, their purchases and resales may be found to be exempt on the ground that they were not underwriters if their own resales did not amount to a public offering.

In the view we take of this case we need not decide whether, if the petitioners had purchased with a view to only such resales as would not amount to a distribution or public offering, their acts would be exempt even though the issue was in fact a public offering. We find that the resales contemplated and executed by petitioners were themselves a distribution or public offering as the latter term has been defined by the Supreme Court, and we therefore find that petitioners were underwriters and that their transactions were not exempt under § 4[(a)](1).

In *S.E.C. v. Ralston Purina Co.*, 1953, 346 U.S. 119, the Supreme Court considered the exemptions provided by § [4(a)(2)] ... defin[ing] the standard to be applied in determining whether an issue is a public offering. It held that the governing fact is whether the persons to whom the offering is made are in such a position with respect to the issuer that they either actually have such information as a registration would have disclosed, or have access to such information. The stipulation of facts here expressly states that the purchasers "were not supplied with material information of the scope and character contemplated by the Securities Act nor were the purchasers in such a relation to the issuer as to have access to such information concerning the company and its affairs."

* * *

The Commission also found that "The sales by Gilligan and registrant of the underlying common stock on the American Stock Exchange in May 1956, clearly constituted a public distribution." Petitioners contest this conclusion on the ground that since the conversion and sales occurred more than ten months after the purchase of the debentures the Commission was bound to find that the debentures so converted had been held for investment, and that the sales were therefore exempt under § 4[(a)](1) since made by a person other than an issuer, underwriter or dealer. Petitioners concede that if such sales were intended at the time of purchase, the debentures would not then have been held as investments; but it argues that the stipulation reveals that the sales were undertaken only after a change of the issuer's circumstances as a result of which petitioners, acting as prudent investors, thought it wise to sell. The catalytic circumstances were the failure, noted by Gilligan, of Crowell-Collier to increase its advertising space as he had anticipated that it would. We agree with the Commission that in the circumstances here presented the intention to retain the debentures only if Crowell-Collier continued to operate profitably was equivalent to a "purchased * * * with a view to * * * distribution" within the statutory definition of underwriters in § 2[a](11). To hold otherwise would be to permit a dealer who speculatively purchases an unregistered security in the hope that the financially weak issuer had, as is stipulated here, "turned the corner," to unload on the unadvised public what he later determines to be an unsound investment without the disclosure sought by the securities laws, although it is in precisely such circumstances that disclosure is most necessary and desirable. The Commission was within its discretion in finding on this stipulation that petitioners bought "with a view to distribution" despite the ten months of holding.

* * *

NOTES

1. *Broker-dealers.* Gilligan's status as an affiliated person of a broker-dealer is irrelevant to the court's holding that he was an underwriter. It is clear that anyone who purchases securities from an issuer with a view to their distribution is an "underwriter," even if he or she is not employed by a broker-dealer.

QUESTIONS

1. If the issuer's changed circumstances (such as a downturn in profits) do not qualify as a change that would exclude the investor from status as an underwriter, what sort of changed circumstance would be consistent with having "investment intent" at the time the securities were initially purchased?

2. Suppose Gilligan resold his shares to Wentworth Investments, a Wall Street investment bank, within days of purchasing them from Crowell-Collier. Wentworth Investments signs a letter stipulating that "said debentures are being purchased for investment and the undersigned has no present intention of distributing the same." Has Gilligan violated § 5?

———

Gilligan, Will makes two points. First, *Gilligan, Will* provides guidance on the "changed circumstances" that will allow an investor to claim that she did not purchase securities with a "view to" the resale of such securities. Investors who did not purchase with a "view to" resale are not underwriters under § 2(a)(11), thus making § 4(a)(1)'s exemption from § 5 potentially available. A change in the circumstances of the issuer (e.g., a downturn in the issuer's business) will not allow the investor to resell without being deemed an underwriter. Instead, courts focus on the reselling investor's changed circumstances.

What types of changed circumstances are consistent with "investment intent"? The passage of time may indicate that the investor initially held with investment intent, but has now changed her mind. Courts use a two-year holding period rule of thumb in determining whether the "securities have come to rest," and therefore the initial purchaser did not initially purchase with a "view to" the securities resale. After a three-year holding period the presumption of investment intent becomes "conclusive." *Ackerberg v. Johnson, Jr.*, 892 F.2d 1328 (8th Cir. 1989). Alternatively, even without the passage of time, an investor may provide evidence of her initial investment intent by showing an unexpected change in circumstances that led her to change her investment plans. An investor, for example, could argue that an unexpected need to purchase a new car required her to liquidate her portfolio of restricted securities.

Second, *Gilligan, Will* connects the term "distribution" in the definition of an underwriter in § 2(a)(11) with the term "public offering" in § 4(a)(2) as defined by *Ralston Purina*. If the term "distribution" is equivalent to a "public offering," can a reselling investor sell to investors able to "fend for themselves" without becoming an underwriter? The ABA Committee on Federal Regulation of Securities has referred to such a resale as a "secondary private placement." We consider this connection in greater depth later in the chapter when we discuss the § 4 (a)(1 ½) exemption.

Consider the "view to" aspect of the definition of an underwriter and the investment intent test in the following hypothetical.

HYPOTHETICAL ONE

Suppose that Desert Tours Inc., a competitor of Island Tours, has not yet gone public. Desert Tours has raised capital exclusively through private placements of common stock to accredited investors. Consider the following resales by those accredited investors.

1. *Scenario One:* Gilligan purchased 2,000 shares of Desert Tours for a total of $200,000 in one of the private placements. At the time of the offering, Gilligan believed that Desert Tours was a highly speculative investment. Over the first few months after the private placement, Desert Tours made far greater profits than expected. (It turns out that people were clamoring to ride through the desert on a horse with no name). Six months after his purchase, Gilligan is sure his stock is now worth a lot more than what he paid for it. Can he cash in by reselling his shares to retail investors in the secondary market?

2. *Scenario Two:* Suppose that Gilligan purchased $200,000 in a Desert Tours private placement a week ago. A hurricane two days ago has badly eroded the foundation of Gilligan's beachfront cottage; his contractor estimates that rebuilding the foundation will cost $200,000. The contractor insists on payment up front in cash. (Gilligan has been somewhat slow with

payment in the past.) Can Gilligan sell his Desert Tours stock to pay his contractor?

3.   *Scenario Three:* Mary Ann purchased 2,000 shares of Desert Tours for a total of $200,000. Assume that she obtained an offering circular at the time of the private placement giving detailed information on Desert Tour's business and finances. Three years have passed since Mary Ann purchased shares in the private placement. She would now like to resell her shares in the secondary market. Desert Tours—a highly secretive company—has made no disclosures since the private placement. Can Mary Ann sell?

———

Section 2(a)(11)'s definition of underwriter extends beyond those who purchase from the issuer with a view to reselling the securities; it also includes those who offer or sell for the issuer and those who otherwise "participate" in the offering. The *Chinese Consolidated* case below demonstrates the breadth of this definition. It also demonstrates the Securities Act's focus on transactions rather than issuers and securities. What does this transactional focus mean for the operation of §§ 5 and 4(a)(1)?

SEC v. Chinese Consolidated Benevolent Ass'n, Inc.

120 F.2d 738 (2d Cir. 1941).

■ HAND, L., CIRCUIT JUDGE.

The Securities and Exchange Commission seeks to enjoin the defendant from the use of any instruments of interstate commerce or of the mails in disposing, or attempting to dispose, of Chinese Government bonds for which no registration statements has ever been made.

The defendant is a New York corporation organized for benevolent purposes having a membership of 25,000 Chinese. On September 1, 1937, the Republic of China authorized the issuance of $500,000,000 in 5% bonds. In October, 1937, the defendant set up a committee which has had no official or contractual relation with the Chinese government for the purpose of:

(a) Uniting the Chinese in aiding the Chinese people and government in their difficulties.

(b) Soliciting and receiving funds from members of Chinese communities in New York, New Jersey and Connecticut, as well as from the general public in those states, for transmission to China for general relief.

All the members of the committee were Chinese and resided in New York City. Through mass meetings, advertising in newspapers distributed through the mails, and personal appeals, the committee urged the members of Chinese communities in New York, New Jersey and Connecticut to purchase the Chinese government bonds referred to and offered to accept funds from prospective purchasers for delivery to the Bank of China in New York as agent for the purchasers. At the request of individual purchasers and for their convenience the committee received some $600,000 to be used for acquiring the bonds, and delivered the moneys to the New York agency of the Bank of China, together with written applications by the respective purchasers for the bonds which they desired to buy. The New York agency transmitted the funds to its branch in Hong Kong with instructions to make the purchases for the account of the various customers. The Hong Kong bank returned the bonds by mail to the New York branch which in turn forwarded them by mail to the purchasers at their mailing addresses, which, in some cases, were in care of the defendant at its headquarters in New York. Neither the committee, nor any of its members, has ever made a charge for their activities or received any compensation from any source. The Bank of China has acted as an agent in the transactions and has not solicited the purchase of bonds or the business involved in transmitting the funds for that purpose.

No registration statement under the Securities Act has ever been made covering any of the Chinese bonds advertised for sale. Nevertheless the defendant has been a medium through which over $600,000 has been collected from would-be purchasers and through which bonds in that amount have been sold to residents of New York, New Jersey and Connecticut.

* * *

We think that the defendant has violated Section 5(a) of the Securities Act when read in connection with Section 2[a](3) because it engaged in selling unregistered securities issued by the Chinese government when it solicited offers to buy the securities "for value." The solicitation of offers to buy the unregistered bonds, either with or without compensation, brought defendant's activities literally within the prohibition of the statute. Whether the Chinese government as issuer authorized the solicitation, or merely availed itself of gratuitous and even unknown acts on the part of the defendant whereby written offers to buy, and the funds collected for payment, were transmitted to the Chinese banks does not affect the meaning of the statutory provisions which are quite explicit. In either case the solicitation was equally for the benefit of the Chinese government and broadly speaking was for the issuer in connection with the distribution of the bonds.

* * *

Under Section 4[(a)](1) the defendant is not exempt from registration requirements if it is "an underwriter." . . . Though the defendant solicited the orders, obtained the cash from the purchasers and caused both to be forwarded so as to procure the bonds, it is nevertheless contended that its acts could not have been for the Chinese government because it had no contractual arrangement or even understanding with the latter. But the aim of the Securities Act is to have information available for investors. This objective will be defeated if buying orders can be solicited which result in uninformed and improvident purchases. It can make no difference as regards the policy of the act whether an issuer has solicited orders through an agent, or has merely taken advantage of the services of a person interested for patriotic reasons in securing offers to buy. The aim of the issuer is to promote the distribution of the securities, and of the Securities Act is to protect the public by requiring that it be furnished with adequate information upon which to make investments. Accordingly the words "(sell) for an issuer in connection with the distribution of any security" ought to be read as covering continual solicitations, such as the defendant was engaged in, which normally would result in a distribution of issues of unregistered securities within the United States. Here a series of events were set in motion by the solicitation of offers to buy which culminated in a distribution to buy which culminated in a distribution that was initiated by the defendant. We hold that the defendant acted as an underwriter. . . .

Section 4[(a)](1) was intended to exempt only trading transactions between individual investors with relation to securities already issued and not to exempt distributions by issuers. The words of the exemption in Section 4[(a)](1) are: "Transaction by any person other than an issuer, underwriter, or dealer; * * * ". The issuer in this case was the Republic of China. The complete transaction included not only solicitation by the defendant of offers to buy, but the offers themselves, the transmission of the offers and the purchase money through the banks to the Chinese government, the acceptance by that government of the offers and the delivery of the bonds to the purchaser or the defendant as his agent. Even if the defendant is not itself "an issuer, underwriter, or dealer" it was participating in a transaction with an issuer, to wit, the Chinese Government. The argument on behalf of the defendant incorrectly assumes that Section 4[(a)](1) applies to the component parts of the entire transaction we have mentioned and thus exempts defendant unless it is an underwriter for the Chinese Republic. Section 5(a)(1), however, broadly prohibits sales of securities irrespective of the character of the person making them. The exemption is limited to "transactions" by persons other than "issuers, underwriters or dealers". It does not in terms or by fair implication protect those who are engaged in steps necessary to the distribution of security issues. To give Section 4[(a)](1) the construction urged by the defendant would afford a ready method of thwarting the policy of the law and evading its provisions. . . .

It is unreasonable to conjure up all the difficulties that might arise if every attempt to suggest investment in a foreign bond issue were to be treated as a sale requiring a registration statement under the Act. This is a case where there was systematic continuous solicitation, followed by collection and remission of funds to purchase the securities, and ultimate distribution of the bonds in the United States through defendant's aid. We do not think results should be determined by the mere passage of title to the securities in China. . . .

* * *

QUESTIONS

1. The Association did not have a contract with the Chinese government, did not accept any money and was not considered an agent for the government. Nonetheless, the court held that the Association was acting "for the issuer." Does this stretch the definition of underwriter in § 2(a)(11) too far?

2. Would the result change if the Association had not collected or transmitted any money, but simply urged people to send money directly to the Bank of China for investment in the bonds?

3. What if the *Wall Street Journal's* editorial page opines that the bonds are not only a good investment but also a good way of showing America's support for China? Would the *Journal* be part of the issuer's distribution?

We have seen the importance of the underwriter concept in determining whether a resale transaction is part of an issuer's private placement. Deeming a resale transaction as separate from the issuer's private placement allows most investors (but not affiliates, as we discuss below) to resell using the § 4(a)(1) exemption from § 5. But what about resales by those initial investors who purchase after an issuer sells securities through a registered public offering?

In a registered public offering, the "distribution" involves the sale of securities from the issuer to underwriters (in a firm commitment offering) and then to the initial investors purchasing from underwriters and dealers participating in the offering. This view of "distribution" corresponds to the SEC's focus on the "initial distribution" in defining the scope of liability in Rule 159A (for § 12(a)(2)) and Item 512(a)(6) of Regulation S–K (for § 12(a)(1) & (2)). Resale transactions that occur after the initial investors take ownership of securities in a public offering take place after the initial distribution and thus are separate from the public offering. Moreover, because the resales are not part of the issuer's initial distribution, the initial investors are not underwriters. Without an issuer or underwriter present, the initial investors (excluding affiliates of the issuer) selling in the secondary market may take advantage of the § 4(a)(1) exemption from § 5. Allowing free resales in the secondary market is, of course, one of the advantages to issuers of selling through a registered public offering.

One loose end: The plain language of § 4(a)(1) suggests that it is not available if there is a "dealer" in the transaction, and § 2(a)(12) defines "dealers" to include brokers. Does this reading defeat the application of § 4(a)(1) to any transaction involving a broker, even in the secondary market? The short answer is no. Here is the Eighth Circuit's response to the argument that the presence of a broker in a privately-negotiated transaction was sufficient to defeat the application of the § 4(a)(1) exemption.

> While it is true that § 4[(a)](1) exempts transactions and not individuals, the mere involvement of a broker, qua broker, in a secondary transaction by persons other than an issuer, underwriter or dealer, is insufficient to vitiate the exemption. . . . Were its involvement enough to deny the § 4[(a)](1) exemption to persons not issuers, underwriters or dealers, few secondary transactions involving the resale of restricted securities would be exempt under § 4[(a)](1).

Ackerberg v. Johnson, Jr., 892 F.2d 1328, 1334 n.4 (8th Cir. 1989).

III. CONTROL PERSONS' RESALES

"Control persons" of issuers face greater regulation than other investors. Control persons can be liable for the actions of those under their control. Securities Act § 15. And as we saw in Chapter 6, insiders (a broader set of individuals that may include control persons under certain circumstances) face various prohibitions on insider trading.

In addition to insider trading prohibitions, control persons, absent an exemption, must register their sale of securities under the Securities Act. Why? First, like any other investor, the control person may be an underwriter for the issuer if the control person purchases with a "view to" reselling in a "distribution" of the securities. With certain changes in circumstances or a sufficient holding period, courts will not treat the control person as an underwriter for the issuer.

Second, even if a control person is not an underwriter for the issuer, the control person's resale transaction may nonetheless involve an underwriter. Recall that § 5 by its terms applies to *all* offers and sales of securities. This is the "memory-less" property of § 5 we discussed earlier in the Chapter. Without more, ordinary secondary market transactions would become subject to § 5's registration requirements. But § 4(a)(1) exempts most ordinary secondary market transactions from § 5. Control persons, however, do not qualify for § 4(a)(1) if they sell securities with the assistance of an intermediary (or sell through an intermediary to another investor) because § 2(a)(11) makes the intermediary an underwriter. The presence of an underwriter in the transaction destroys the § 4(a)(1) exemption for the entire transaction (*see Chinese Consolidated*) and all those participating in the transaction, including control persons. Thus, without an exemption, the control person must register its offer and sales of securities ("control securities") pursuant to § 5.

A. UNDERWRITERS FOR CONTROL PERSONS

What is the statutory basis for concluding that control persons are subject to the registration requirements of § 5? The definition of underwriter under § 2(a)(11) primarily focuses on the relationship with the issuer. The last sentence of § 2(a)(11) deals with the control persons:

> As used in this paragraph the term "issuer" shall include, in addition to an issuer, any person directly or indirectly controlling or controlled by the issuer, or any person under direct or indirect common control with the issuer.

Thus, for purposes of § 2(a)(11) the term "issuer" includes control persons. In determining whether a person is acting as an underwriter, we need to consider whether the person is selling or offering securities for a control person (or otherwise participating in such sales). Control persons are not deemed, however, to be issuers for other provisions, including most critically § 4(a)(1).

Why subject control persons to the registration requirements imposed on issuers if the control person relies on an underwriter? Consider the following hypothetical.

HYPOTHETICAL TWO

Skipper is the CEO of Island Tours and owns 40% of the outstanding common stock. Skipper rules Island Tours with an iron hand, making all major policy decisions and dominating the nominees he has chosen as directors. Skipper, of course, is also the chairman of the board.

1. Suppose that Skipper decides to resell 1 million of his own Island Tours shares on the Nasdaq. Skipper plans to sell the shares in many transactions over time so as to minimize his sales' effect on the stock price. How do Skipper's sales affect public investors?

2. Recall that Howell is the other major shareholder of Island Tours, with 2% of the outstanding common stock. Suppose that Howell is an Island Tours director. Howell's board position affords him access to many internal details about Island Tours. Howell decides to sell 10,000 shares of Island Tours on the Nasdaq. Do Howell's sales raise any concerns?

Section 2(a)(11)'s definition of "underwriter" recognizes the informational advantages enjoyed by control persons. How does this definitional twist limit control persons reselling their securities?

United States v. Wolfson

405 F.2d 779 (2d Cir. 1968).

■ WOODBURY, P., SENIOR CIRCUIT JUDGE.

It was stipulated at the trial that at all relevant times there were 2,510,000 shares of Continental Enterprises, Inc., issued and outstanding. The evidence is clear, indeed is not disputed, that of these the appellant Louis E. Wolfson himself with members of his immediate family and his right hand man and first lieutenant, the appellant Elkin B. Gerbert, owned 1,149,775 or in excess of 40%. The balance of the stock was in the hands of approximately 5,000 outside shareholders. The government's undisputed evidence at the trial was that between August 1, 1960, and January 31, 1962, Wolfson himself sold 404,150 shares of Continental through six brokerage houses. . . .

[T]here is ample evidence that . . . as the largest individual shareholder [Wolfson] was Continental's guiding spirit in that the officers of the corporation were subject to his direction and control and that no corporate policy decisions were made without his knowledge and consent. Indeed Wolfson admitted as much on the stand. No registration statement was in effect as to Continental; its stock was traded over-the-counter.

The appellants do not dispute the foregoing basic facts. They took the position at the trial that they had no idea . . . that there was any provision of law requiring registration of a security before its distribution by a controlling person to the public. On the stand in their defense they took the position that they operated at a level of corporate finance far above such "details" as the securities laws; as to whether a particular stock must be registered. They asserted and their counsel argued to the jury that they were much too busy with large affairs to concern themselves with such minor matters and attributed the fault of failure to register to subordinates in the Wolfson organization and to failure of the brokers to give notice of the need. Obviously in finding the appellants guilty the jury rejected this defense, if indeed, it is any defense at all.

* * *

The appellants argue that they come within [the § 4[(a)](1)] exemption for they are not issuers, underwriters or dealers. At first blush there would appear to be some merit in this argument. The immediate difficulty with it, however, is that § 4[(a)](1) by its terms exempts only "transactions," not classes of persons and ignores § 2[a](11) of the Act which defines an "underwriter". . . .

In short, the brokers provided outlets for the stock of issuers and thus were underwriters. Wherefore the stock was sold in "transactions by underwriters" which are not within the exemption of § 4[(a)](1). . . .

But the appellants contend that the brokers in this case cannot be classified as underwriters because their part in the sales transactions came within § 4[(a)](4), which exempts "brokers' transactions executed upon customers' orders on any exchange or in the over-the-counter market but not the solicitation of such orders."[1] The answer to this contention is that § 4[(a)](4) was designed only to exempt the brokers' part in security transactions. Control persons must find their own exemptions.

There is nothing inherently unreasonable for a broker to claim the exemption of § 4[(a)](4) when he is unaware that his customer's part in the transaction is not exempt. . . . It will hardly do for the appellants to say that because they kept the true facts from the brokers they can take advantage of the exemption the brokers gained thereby.

* * *

QUESTIONS

1. What if Wolfson had simply sold 400,000 shares in a negotiated transaction with Warren, a sophisticated (and extremely successful) investor from Omaha, Nebraska? Assume that the negotiation and sale is all done without the assistance of a third party.

2. Section 4(a)(1) is a "transaction" exemption. If the transaction meets the requirements of § 4(a)(1), then all involved are exempt from § 5 registration requirements. Does the court take the same approach with § 4(a)(4)'s exemption from § 5?

3. In discussing § 4(a)(4)'s exemption for unsolicited broker's transaction, the court implies that a broker may have difficulty in relying on the exemption if the broker knows his customer does not qualify for an exemption. How does this interpretation fit the language of § 4(a)(4)?

B. SECTION 4(a)(1 ½) EXEMPTION

Wolfson holds that the operation of § 2(a)(11) in combination with §§ 4(a)(1) and 5, places a registration obligation on control persons seeking to resell their securities. *Wolfson*, combined with *Gilligan*, also leads us to a second conclusion. Whenever a control person resells securities, we must undertake two separate analyses. First, as we do with non-control persons, we ask whether the control person is acting as an underwriter for the issuer. For this first inquiry, there is no distinction between control and non-control persons who purchase from

---

[1]   It is undisputed that the brokers involved in this case did not solicit orders from the appellants.

the issuer and resell their securities with a view to the distribution of the securities ("restricted securities"). In either case, § 4(a)(1) is not available if the initial purchaser is acting as an underwriter for the issuer. So control persons must avoid acting as an underwriter purchasing with a view to distribution for their resales. For investors who are not control persons, this is the only inquiry. The diagram below depicts the first inquiry, with Island Tours (issuer), Skipper (control person), and Mary Ann (outside investor). If Skipper purchases securities from Island Tours and then resells the securities to Mary Ann, is Skipper an underwriter for Island Tours?

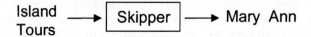

A second inquiry is required, however, for control persons even when the control person is not an underwriter for the issuer. The definition of underwriter in § 2(a)(11) requires us to ask whether a third party is acting as an underwriter for the control person. A third party can serve as the control person's underwriter in at least two circumstances. First, an intermediary may assist the control person in the resale (e.g., a brokerage firm, such as Wentworth Investments). Second, an investor, here Mary Ann, may purchase from the control person; Mary Ann may then resell the securities to another investor, such as the Professor. If Mary Ann's purchase-resale is with a "view to" the "distribution" of the securities then Mary Ann may be deemed an underwriter for Skipper, the control person. The diagram below depicts the second inquiry and its focus on these two possible underwriters for a control person.

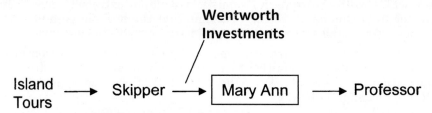

Even if the control person is reselling securities years after purchasing them from the issuer in a private placement (or alternatively, securities purchased through a registered public offering or in the secondary markets), the control person potentially faces registration requirements under § 5 for these "control securities" due to this second inquiry. As we saw in Chapter 7, however, registration for a public offering can be time-consuming and expensive. Moreover, not all control persons may have the power to force registration by the issuer. The definition of control person found in Rule 405 is not based on the power to force registration but can be read more broadly. Thus, control persons would like to avoid registration if possible.

The key to avoiding the registration requirement is the status of the intermediary facilitating the control person's sales. If the intermediary assisting the control person is not an underwriter, and no other underwriter for the control person is present, then the control person can rely on § 4(a)(1). How do we avoid the conclusion that the intermediary is an "underwriter"? We saw in Chapter 9 that certain transactions may not require the protections afforded by the public registration process. Under § 4(a)(2), issuers can make private placements to investors able to "fend for themselves." Courts have created a similar doctrinal framework for control person resales to investors able to fend for themselves. Although the private placement exemption under § 4(a)(2) is available only to issuers, the same rationale (that investors do not need the protection of registration) applies to control person resales to sophisticated investors.

The doctrinal hook for this analysis is the so-called § 4(a)(1 ½) exemption. Technically, there is no § 4(a)(1 ½) exemption. Instead, the § 4(a)(1 ½) exemption is a § 4(a)(1) exemption (with its emphasis on the definition of an underwriter) informed by § 4(a)(2)'s distinction between public and private offerings. *See Ackerberg v. Johnson, Jr.*, 892 F.2d 1328 (8th Cir. 1989). If the control person is selling to an investor with the ability to fend for himself, there is no "distribution" within the meaning of § 2(a)(11), and therefore no "underwriter" in the control person's transaction. The § 4(a)(1) exemption is then available to the control person.

The following hypothetical lays out the difference between the two underwriter inquiries that must be made for resales by control persons and the application of the § 4(a)(1 ½) analysis to those sales.

HYPOTHETICAL THREE

Suppose that Skipper, the CEO and majority shareholder of Island Tours, purchases 100,000 shares from Island Tours at a price of $10 per share as part of a broader Rule 506 private placement. Skipper himself is an accredited investor. In the Rule 506 offering, Island Tours sold to ten other accredited investors and 35 sophisticated non-accredited purchasers. Consider how the securities laws apply to the following transactions.

1. *Scenario One:* One month after purchasing his shares in the private placement, Skipper—ignoring the advice of Island Tours' general counsel that it is too soon to resell—wants to resell the 100,000 shares to five individual investors. Each investor has a Ph.D. in finance (specializing in the valuation of island tour companies—a fairly narrow niche). Skipper provides each investor with detailed information on Island Tours. None of the five individual investors, however, qualifies as an accredited investor under Regulation D. Skipper takes care to ensure that no third party assists him in the sales.

2. *Scenario Two:* After holding the 100,000 shares for four years, Skipper sells the stock through his broker, Minnow Financial, to a large number of retail investors. Minnow does not solicit the retail investors' orders.

3. *Scenario Three:* Skipper holds on to the shares he purchased in the private placement. He also buys 50,000 more shares on Nasdaq (assume these shares can be traced back to Island Tour's initial public offering). A week after his purchase, Skipper has a change of heart and instructs Minnow Financial to resell those shares on the Nasdaq.

IV. RULE 144

The materials above demonstrate that boundaries of the definition of underwriter are murky. Although the investment intent test provides some guidance on whether the investors purchased the securities with a "view to" the resale of the securities, the application of the test is challenging, particularly for resales occurring less than two years from their initial purchase. Moreover, the SEC has long disfavored the focus of the investment intent test on the circumstances of the investor seeking to resell unregistered securities. Instead, the SEC argues that the permissibility of resales should focus more on the amount of information on the issuer available in the secondary market.

Investors may also seek to escape underwriter status through sales not involving a "distribution" of the securities. In determining whether the seller is an underwriter, courts equate "distribution" with "public offering" and look to *Ralston Purina* in determining whether the purchasers of the securities are able to "fend for themselves." As with the investment test, the scope of what constitutes a public offering is somewhat amorphous.

To provide greater clarity and to shift the focus of resales onto the availability of information about the issuer, in 1972 the SEC promulgated Rule 144 as a safe harbor for resales from § 5's registration requirements. The following excerpt comes from the SEC release promulgating Rule 144:

> [T]he rule as adopted is not exclusive. However, persons who offer or sell restricted securities without complying with Rule 144 are hereby put on notice by the Commission that in view of the broad remedial purposes of the Act and of public policy which strongly supports registration, they will have a substantial burden of proof in establishing that an exemption from registration is available for such offers or sales. . . .

> Moreover, with respect to restricted securities acquired after the effective date of the rule, the staff will not issue "no-action" letters relating to resales of such securities. Further, in connection with such resales the Commission hereby puts all persons including brokers and attorneys on notice that the "change in circumstances" concept should no longer be considered as one of the factors in determining whether a person is an underwriter. . . . [T]he "change in circumstances" concept in the Commission's opinion fails to meet the objectives of the Act, since the circumstances of the seller are unrelated to the need of investors for the protections afforded by the registration and other provisions of the Act.

Securities Act Release No. 5223 (Jan. 11, 1972).

Complying with Rule 144 exempts the party in question from being deemed an underwriter under § 2(a)(11). Why does this matter? Recall that § 4(a)(1) exempts transaction from § 5's registration requirements but only if an "underwriter" is not present. By excluding certain parties from underwriter status, Rule 144 makes § 4(a)(1) available.

Rule 144's application varies based on two factors: (1) the presence of an "affiliate" and (2) the presence of "restricted" or "unrestricted" securities. Rule 144(a)(1) defines an "affiliate" as "a person that directly, or indirectly through one or more intermediaries, controls, or is controlled by, or is under common control with, such issuer." Note the relationship of this language with the last sentence of § 2(a)(11). Rule 144(a)(3) includes in its definition of "restricted" security a security "acquired directly or indirectly from the issuer, or from an affiliate of the issuer, in a transaction or chain of transactions not involving any public offering," or acquired in a transaction in which Section 502(d) applies (e.g., Rule 505 or Rule 506 offerings).

For resales involving either (1) a non-affiliate selling restricted securities or (2) an affiliate (or someone selling on behalf of the affiliate) selling either restricted or unrestricted securities, Rule 144 may provide relief from underwriter status. Consider the following situations.

Any person who sells restricted securities for her own account. If the person who resells restricted securities is considered an underwriter, then the transaction will not qualify for § 4(a)(1) and, absent some other exemption, must comply with the requirements of § 5. On the other hand, if Rule 144 applies, the reselling party is deemed not to be an underwriter. To the extent the separate resale transaction does not otherwise involve an issuer, underwriter, or dealer, the reselling party may take advantage of § 4(a)(1)'s exemption from § 5. Both non-affiliates (Rule 144(b)(1)) and affiliates (Rule 144(b)(2)) may use Rule 144 to avoid status as an underwriter (either for the issuer or for an affiliate).

Any person who sells restricted or unrestricted securities for the account of an affiliate. If a person sells restricted or even unrestricted securities (i.e., securities that were registered for a public offering in the past) on behalf of the account of an affiliate, the person may be considered an underwriter under § 2(a)(11). A broker assisting an affiliate in the affiliate's resales, for example, may fall under the underwriter definition. Once the person is an underwriter, § 4(a)(1)'s exemption no longer is available, exposing the transaction to § 5, as we saw in *Wolfson.* Complying with Rule 144 allows the person selling on behalf of the affiliate to escape underwriter status (Rule 144(b)(2)). If the transaction does not otherwise involve an issuer, underwriter, or dealer, then § 4(a)(1) exempts the entire affiliate resale transaction from § 5.

Sellers must meet a number of requirements to qualify for Rule 144's exemption from underwriter status. As we go through the requirements, consider whether investors in the secondary market are sufficiently protected by Rule 144's conditions. Does your opinion differ based on the type of issuer? For example, Exchange Act reporting issuers already must comply with periodic disclosure requirements (i.e., Forms 10–K, 10–Q and 8–K). Exchange Act reporting issuers also tend to be larger with a more active secondary market. Such issuers are more likely to be followed by analysts and institutional investors. We will see that Rule 144 makes distinctions based on whether the issuer is an Exchange Act reporting company. Should Rule 144 make further distinctions—for example, between WKSIs and non-WKSIs?

The basic requirements of Rule 144 fall into two categories:

- Current Public Information (Rule 144(c))
- Holding Period for Restricted Securities (Rule 144(d))

Because the information requirements are easier to understand in light of the holding periods, we explain the holding period requirement first. As we discuss each of these requirements, consider how they vary depending on (1) whether the issuer of the securities is an Exchange Act reporting issuer; and (2) whether the reseller is a non-affiliate or affiliate (or a person selling on behalf of an affiliate). After discussing the basic Rule 144 requirements, we turn to the additional requirements imposed only on affiliate resales (and resales on an affiliate's behalf).

A. HOLDING PERIOD FOR RESTRICTED SECURITIES

Rule 144(d) imposes a holding period for restricted securities. The holding period runs from the later of the acquisition of the securities from (1) the issuer or (2) an affiliate of the issuer. The SEC provides the following rationale for the requirement:

> [A] holding period prior to resale is essential, among other reasons, to assure that those persons who buy under a claim of a section 4[(a)](2) exemption have assumed the economic risks of investment, and therefore, are not acting as conduits for sale to the public of unregistered securities, directly or indirectly, on behalf of an issuer. It should be noted that there is nothing in section 2[a](11) which places a time limit on a person's status as an underwriter. The public has the same need for protection afforded by registration whether the securities are distributed shortly after their purchase or after a considerable length of time.

Securities Act Release 5223 (Jan. 11, 1972).

When originally enacted, the holding period in Rule 144(d) was set at two years. In 1997, the SEC reduced the holding period down to one year. The SEC in 2008 further shortened the holding period for Exchange Act reporting issuers to six months. Rule 144(d)(1)(i). (The issuer must have been reporting for at least 90 days immediately before the Rule 144 resale.) For non-reporting issuers, the holding period is one year. Rule 144(d)(1)(ii).

Note that the holding period only applies to restricted securities. For unrestricted securities—e.g., securities sold through a prior public offering—there is no holding period required by Rule 144. But wait a second. If the securities are unrestricted, why do we need Rule 144 at all? Why not go directly to § 4(a)(1), which exempts most secondary market transactions after a public offering? The answer lies in the treatment of affiliates under Rule 144. Recall from *Wolfson* that if an intermediary assists the control person in the distribution of securities, even if unrestricted, the assisting person is considered an underwriter under § 2(a)(11). With the presence of an underwriter in the transaction, the control person is unable to rely on § 4(a)(1) to avoid § 5's registration requirements—control persons always need to be worried about avoiding a distribution. The control person must therefore turn to either the § 4(a)(1 ½) exemption or Rule 144 to avoid a distribution of their "control securities." Holding periods are not relevant for sales by controlling persons of securities that were previously publicly traded. Rule 144, therefore, does not require any additional holding period for sales by affiliates. Affiliates must comply with the holding period requirement, however, if they acquired their shares from the issuer pursuant to § 4(a)(2) or some other exemption from § 5.

Also note how the holding period is measured. Rule 144(d) states that the holding period is measured from "the later of the date of the acquisition of the securities from the issuer or from an affiliate of the issuer, and any resale of such securities. . . ." The focus of Rule 144(d) on the when securities are acquired from "the issuer, or from an affiliate of the issuer" implicitly allows subsequent non-affiliate holders to "tack" on the holding period of the initial acquirer from the issuer or affiliate. Rule 144(d) also applies special rules for tacking in non-sale situations. For example, the holding period for securities acquired through a gift is calculated from their initial acquisition by the donor. Rule 144(d)(3)(v).

B. Current Public Information

Understanding the information requirement of Rule 144 requires (1) assessing when the information requirement applies and (2) determining the information required.

1. Applicability

The application of the information requirement for Rule 144 turns on whether an affiliate or non-affiliate seeks the exemption from § 5 for the resale. Affiliates (and those selling on behalf of affiliates) must always satisfy the information requirement. Rule 144(b)(2),(3).

For non-affiliates, Rule 144 imposes the information requirement only for Exchange Act reporting issuers. Rule 144(b)(1)(i). The information requirement for non-affiliates reselling the securities of Exchange Act reporting issuers terminates after a one-year holding period. We refer to this as the *information* period to distinguish it from the Rule 144(d) holding period discussed above. The one-year information period is measured from "the later of the date the securities were acquired from the issuer or from an affiliate of the issuer." Rule 144(b)(1)(i). There is no information requirement for non-affiliates reselling securities of non-Exchange Act reporting issuers. Rule 144(b)(1)(ii).

At first glance, the application of the information requirement for non-affiliates seems backward. Rule 144(b)(1)(i) tells us that a non-affiliate reselling the securities of a *reporting* issuer must comply with the information requirements of Rule 144(c) until the expiration of the one-year information period. Rule 144(b)(1)(ii), on the other hand, states that a non-affiliate reselling the securities of a *non-reporting* issuer has no information requirements.

Why is there no information requirement for non-reporting issuers? Presumably the market knows little about such issuers, especially when compared to reporting issuers. The answer lies with the application of the Rule 144(d) holding period. Because of the six month holding period under Rule 144(d), non-affiliates reselling the securities of reporting issuers must comply with the information requirements of Rule 144(c) for resales between six months and one-year after the initial purchase from the issuer. In contrast, non-affiliates reselling the securities of non-reporting issuers may not resell at all until after Rule 144(d)'s one-year holding period expires. After the one-year Rule 144(d) holding period, non-affiliates may resell freely the securities of both reporting and non-reporting issuers without restriction. That includes the elimination of the information requirement.

2. INFORMATION REQUIRED

Rule 144(c) requires that "current public information" be available. Information is deemed available to investors for an Exchange Act reporting issuer if: (1) the issuer has been an Exchange Act reporting company for at least 90 days immediately preceding the sale of the securities; and (2) the issuer has been current in its Exchange Act periodic disclosure filings for the past twelve months. Rule 144(c)(1). How will an investor attempting to resell securities know whether an Exchange Act reporting issuer has met its disclosure obligations? The Note to Rule 144(c) provides that the investor may rely upon a statement from the issuer that it has complied with the periodic reporting requirements.

When applicable (e.g., affiliate resales), non-Exchange Act reporting issuers must make available the information specified in Rule 15c2–11(a)(5)(i)–(xiv) and (xvi) of the Exchange Act. Rule 144(c)(2). Rule 15c2–11 refers to the information broker-dealers must keep on hand (and reasonably current) with respect to companies on which the broker-dealers publish a quotation or submit a price quotation in "any quotation medium." The information includes, among other things, the name of the corporation, the state of incorporation, the number of shares or total amount of securities outstanding as of the end of the issuer's most recent fiscal year, the most recent balance sheet, profit and loss, and retained earnings statements, and similar financial information is required for the two preceding fiscal years as well, assuming the issuer or its predecessor has been in existence. Non-Exchange Act reporting issuers that wish to encourage a liquid secondary market for their shares in the over-the-counter market will voluntarily supply the required Rule 15c2–11 information to broker-dealers acting as market makers in the stock. (Recall that market makers continuously publish bid and ask quotations for stocks in which they make a market).

The following table diagrams the interaction of the information requirement and the holding periods under Rule 144(b)(1)(i) and (ii) and Rule 144(d). Note that affiliate resales, when permissible under Rule 144(d), must comply with not only the information requirements of Rule 144 but also the volume limits (Rule 144(e)), manner of sale (Rule 144(f)), and notice (Rule 144(h)) requirements that we discuss below (collectively referred to in the table as "all 144 requirements").

	Less than 6 mos.	**6 mos. to 1 year**	**1 year or more**
Non-Affiliate and Reporting Issue	No Resales (144(d)(1)(i))	Resales allowed but 144(c) information applies (144(d)(1)(i))	No restrictions on resales
Non-Affiliate and Non-Reporting Issuer	No Resales (144(d)(1)(ii))	No Resales (144(d)(1)(ii))	No restrictions on resales
Affiliate (or for the account of an Affiliate) and Reporting Issuer	No Resales of restricted securities (144(d)(1)(i)) Resales of unrestricted securities allowed but must comply with all 144 requirements	Resales allowed but must comply with all 144 requirements	Resales allowed but must comply with all 144 requirements
Affiliate (or for the account of an Affiliate) and Non-Reporting Issuer	No Resales of restricted securities (144(d)(1)(i)) Resales of unrestricted securities allowed but must comply with all 144 requirements	No Resales of restricted securities (144(d)(1)(i)) Resales of unrestricted securities allowed but must comply with all 144 requirements	Resales of unrestricted securities allowed but must comply with all 144 requirements

HYPOTHETICAL FOUR

Island Tours has been an Exchange Act reporting company since going public three years ago. Island Tours recently sold an additional $5 million of common stock through a Regulation D private placement to several accredited investors. In the private placement, Skipper, the CEO, purchased 100,000 shares at $10 per share and Mary Ann, an outside investor with no other affiliation with Island Tours, also purchased 100,000 shares. Does Rule 144 permit the following resales?

1. *Scenario One:* Mary Ann wants to resell on Nasdaq the 100,000 shares three months after the private placement. Can she do this?

2. *Scenario Two:* Mary Ann wants to resell her 100,000 shares thirteen months after the private placement. Assume that Island Tours is currently tardy in filing its latest Form 10–K.

3.   *Scenario Three:* Assume Mary Ann purchased her 100,000 shares from the private placement five months ago. Mary Ann gives the shares to her friend, Gilligan, to help him pay for the repairs to his beach house. Gilligan sells the shares two months later.

4.   *Scenario Four:* After holding the 100,000 shares he purchased in Island Tours' private placement for fourteen months, Skipper resells them to the Professor, an outside investor, through unsolicited broker's transactions. Island Tours has not yet filed its latest Form 10–K, which was due two months ago. Is that sale valid under Rule 144?

5.   *Scenario Five:* After holding the 100,000 shares he purchased in Island Tours' private placement for fourteen months, Skipper resells them to the Professor, an outside investor, through unsolicited broker's transactions. Island Tours is current in all its SEC filings. What if, one month later, the Professor resells the securities to other outside investors on Nasdaq?

6.   *Scenario Six:* Skipper purchases 1,000 shares of Island Tours on Nasdaq. One week later, Skipper has second thoughts about the purchase and resells them through an unsolicited broker's transaction on Nasdaq. Assume that Island Tours is current with all its Exchange Act filings.

————

Rule 144 presents the possibility that non-affiliate investors who own restricted securities of private companies may eventually (after one year) resell the securities freely in the secondary market without any requirements. Such resales would expose secondary market investors to the risk of purchasing securities without any current public information. This risk, however, may be more apparent than real. Restricted securities for a private company are unlikely to flow into the secondary markets through Rule 144 resales in large volume because a private company will not have a large market capitalization. Moreover, to the extent the number of shareholders of record of a class of the company's equity securities crosses 2,000 and the total assets of the company exceeds $10 million, the private company will become public under § 12(g) of the Exchange Act, triggering periodic filing requirements (as discussed in Chapter 4).

The private issuer will care about the number of shareholders holding its stock and the possibility of crossing the 2,000-shareholder threshold for public company status. Most restricted securities contain a "legend" restricting resales imposed by the issuer. The SEC tells investors that seek to use Rule 144 to resell restricted securities the following: "Only a transfer agent can remove a restrictive legend. But the transfer agent won't remove the legend unless you've obtained the consent of the issuer—usually in the form of an opinion letter from the issuer's counsel—that the restricted legend can be removed. Unless this happens, the transfer agent doesn't have the authority to remove the legend and execute the trade in the marketplace." SEC, Rule 144: Selling Restricted and Control Securities (available at http://www.sec.gov/investor/pubs/rule144.htm).

C. ADDITIONAL REQUIREMENTS FOR AFFILIATE RESALES

Rule 144 provides non-affiliates a relatively certain and trouble-free method of reselling restricted securities. Non-affiliates reselling restricted securities of Exchange Act reporting issuers need only wait the requisite six month holding period from when the initial purchase occurred from the issuer and ensure that the information requirements of Rule 144(c) are met for the initial one-year information period after initial purchase from the issuer. Non-affiliates reselling restricted securities of non-Exchange Act reporting issuers do not even have to meet the information requirement, but still must comply with the Rule 144(d) one-year holding period. Non-affiliates may tack the holding period of prior non-affiliate purchasers to their holding period.

Affiliates, and those selling control securities on their behalf, face additional restrictions, including: (1) limits on the amount sold, (2) restrictions on the manner of sale, and (3) a notice requirement.

1. LIMITATION ON AMOUNT OF SECURITIES SOLD

Rule 144(e) restricts the amount of affiliate resales of restricted and unrestricted securities that may occur in a three-month period. Rule 144(e)(1) provides that the limit is the greatest of:

(i)   one percent of the outstanding shares or units of the same class of securities,

(ii) the average weekly reported trading volume of the same class of securities during the four calendar weeks preceding the filing of notice of the sale with the SEC, or

(iii) for debt securities, ten percent of the principal amount of the debt tranche.

Note that the volume limit is based on a company's entire secondary market trading volume. Thus affiliates of larger, more liquid issuers can sell a greater amount of securities. Debt is subject to a special rule because debt, unlike equity, typically is sold in separate tranches. Each tranche is identifiable based on the maturity date, among other distinguishing characteristics. Because debt securities do not aggregate together in one class in the same way as common stock, applying tests based on the total trading volume or outstanding units would result in a much lower cap for debt. Rule 144(e)(2) adjusts for this difference by providing for a higher volume limit (ten percent of the tranche) for debt.

Why limit the volume of sales by affiliates? Consider the following excerpt from the SEC release promulgating Rule 144:

It is consistent with the rationale of the Act that Section 4[(a)](1) be interpreted to permit only routine trading transactions as distinguished from distributions. Therefore, a person reselling securities under Section 4[(a)](1) of the Act must sell the securities in such limited quantities and in such a manner so as not to disrupt the trading markets. The larger the amount of securities involved, the more likely it is that such resales may involve methods of offering and amounts of compensation usually associated with a distribution rather than routine trading transactions. Thus, solicitation of buy orders or the payment of extra compensation are not permitted by the rule.

Securities Act Release No. 33–5223 (Jan. 11, 1972).

The SEC's first justification for the volume limit in Rule 144 is a fear that a large number of securities entering the market at once will disrupt the market. A large sale of securities may cause the stock price, at least temporarily, to drop. Rule 144's volume limitation may help avoid such a shock to the market. This rationale is not without problems. Large block sales of previously registered securities are not restricted by Rule 144, non-affiliates may sell an unlimited amount of securities into the public securities markets. Moreover, the risk of a large stock price drop from a large block sale is unclear. Sellers have a natural incentive not to cause the stock price to drop precipitously as they sell their shares because it will reduce the proceeds from their sales. They will therefore try to disguise their sales by breaking them up among a number of brokers or spacing them out over time.

The second rationale is that the sale of a large amount of securities at once increases the likelihood that the reselling investors may use tactics associated with public offerings—including offering brokers greater commissions and attempting to condition the market with overly positive information on the company. Limiting the size of an offering may therefore indirectly limit the incentive to use public offering tactics.

HYPOTHETICAL FIVE

To raise additional capital, Island Tours sold an additional $5 million of common stock through a Regulation D private placement six months after its public offering. Island Tours now has 10 million shares of common stock outstanding. The average weekly trading volume of Island Tours has consistently been around 125,000 shares at about $10 per share.

1.   *Scenario One:* Skipper purchased 100,000 shares in Island Tours' recent private placement. Suppose that along with the shares in the private placement, Skipper also purchased 100,000 unrestricted shares on Nasdaq. Skipper now proposes reselling all 200,000 into the market through unsolicited broker's transactions using Minnow Financial.

2.   *Scenario Two:* Same facts as Scenario One, except now Skipper decides to resell only his 100,000 restricted shares through unsolicited brokers' transactions on Nasdaq. At about the same time, Skipper resells the 100,000 unrestricted shares to Howell, a member of the board of directors and 2% shareholder of Island Tours. Minnow Financial facilitates Skipper's sale to Howell.

2.   MANNER OF SALE

Rule 144(f) carefully limits the means by which an affiliate can resell equity securities into the secondary market. The SEC does not restrict the manner of sale for debt securities. Rule 144(f)(3)(ii). Affiliates (and those selling on behalf of affiliates) can only sell equity: (1) through unsolicited "brokers' transactions" as provided for in § 4(a)(4); (2) directly to a "market maker" as defined in § 3(a)(38) of the Exchange Act; or (3) in a "riskless principal transaction." Recall from

Chapter 1 that market makers are dealers who continuously offer quotations in specific securities, holding themselves out to the general secondary market as being willing to buy or sell the securities at specified buy and sell prices. In a riskless principal transaction, a securities dealer fulfills a sale (or buy) order from an investor by buying (or selling) the security for the dealer's own account (hence a "principal" transaction). The dealer also enters into a concurrent and opposite second principal transaction to remove the risk of the first principal transaction. Although technically involving two principal transactions (the purchase from the selling investor and the sale to another dealer or other investor), the riskless principal transaction in substance puts the securities dealer in the same riskless position as a broker acting as an agent facilitating a transaction.

Rule 144(g) interprets unsolicited "brokers' transaction" in § 4(a)(4). Brokers may not solicit orders. Rule 144(g)(3). Moreover, the broker may (1) do "no more than execute the order or orders to sell the securities as agent" and (2) receive "no more than the usual and customary broker's commission." Rule 144(g)(1), (2). Rule 144(g) provides some exceptions to the general prohibition on solicitations. Among other things, brokers may inquire of customers who have indicated an "unsolicited bona fide interest in the securities within the preceding 10 business days." Rule 144(g)(3)(ii). A broker may also post bid and ask quotations in an inter-dealer quotation system or an alternative trading system if certain specified requirements are met. Rule 144(g)(3)(iii), (iv).

Rule 144(g) imposes additional requirements for unsolicited brokers' transactions. Brokers must inquire into the circumstances of the sale transaction in order to determine whether the affiliate is engaged in a distribution. A reasonable inquiry includes (but is not limited to) looking at the Form 144 filing required of affiliates disclosing the expected amount of securities to be sold under Rule 144. In addition, the broker needs to determine the length of time the affiliate has held the securities, how the affiliate acquired the securities, whether the affiliate intends to sell additional securities of the same class, and if the affiliate has made any solicitations.

HYPOTHETICAL SIX

Imagine that you are a broker working for Minnow Financial. You receive a large flow of orders from many different investors. You receive an order from Skipper, the CEO of Island Tours, to sell unregistered common stock purchased in Island Tours' private placement of seven months ago. The securities all bear a Rule 502(d) restricted legend.

1.   Suppose that Minnow Financial maintains a list of customers that have indicated within the past ten days that they would like to purchase the stock of "high-growth, high-risk startup companies." Minnow Financial records the names of only those customers who have purchased similar securities in the past from the brokerage. Can the broker receiving the sale order from Skipper contact the customers on the list and sell them the Island Tours restricted stock?

3.   NOTICE OF PROPOSED SALE

Affiliates (and those selling on their behalf) must file a Form 144 with the SEC. The SEC makes Form 144 available to the public. If the securities trade on a national securities exchange, affiliates must also file the Form 144 with the principal exchange on which the securities are admitted for trading. Rule 144(h). Form 144 requires affiliates to disclose their identity, their relationship with the issuer, the date and nature of the acquisition transactions through which the selling shareholder acquired the securities to be sold, information on all securities of the issuer that the investor sold during the past three months, the name and address of each broker and market maker through whom securities are to be sold, and the proposed amounts of securities to be sold through each broker and market maker. Affiliates need not file, however, if, for any given three month period, they do not exceed 5,000 shares for an aggregate sale price less than or equal to $50,000.

Affiliates must file the Form 144 when they place the first sale order with a broker or execute the trade directly with a market maker. Rule 144(f). Because the disclosure is for prospective trades and must be filed when the trade is actually executed, the Form 144 may indicate more shares than the actual amount sold, but affiliates filing a Form 144 must have a bona fide intention to sell the securities within a reasonable time after filing the form.

D.   OTHER CONSIDERATIONS

The SEC in its notes to Rule 144 makes clear that the Rule, working through the definition of an underwriter and § 4(a)(1), provides an exemption only from § 5's registration requirements. There is no exemption from antifraud liability. Of course, antifraud liability geared to specific public offering documents (§ 11 for the registration statement and § 12(a)(2) for the prospectus) does not apply. Rule 10b–5, however, continues to apply to any materially misleading disclosures in communications relating to the sale of securities under Rule 144.

E.   IMPLICATIONS

The SEC's 2008 reduction of the holding period for restricted securities of Exchange Act reporting companies makes private placements a more attractive alternative to public offerings. Public offerings allow immediate resale to any investor but require enhanced disclosure (the registration statement and prospectus), the application of the gun-jumping rules, and heightened civil liability. A private placement under Rule 506 avoids all of these headaches. Issuers may sell an unlimited amount of securities to a select number of accredited investors under Rule 506. There is no additional disclosure requirement for a Rule 506 offering to accredited investors. Moreover, the gun-jumping rules and the heightened civil liability provisions of §§ 11 and 12(a)(2) do not apply to private placements. Because Rule 144 allows the initial accredited investors to resell the securities freely after only six months, they will demand little if any liquidity discount relative to a public offering. Given the reduced regulatory burden and the minimal discounting for a private placement, expect reporting issuers to increase their use of private placements in the future.

V.   RULE 144A

Rule 144 is not the only safe harbor exempting resales from § 5. Rule 144A provides another avenue to resell securities, albeit to a restricted set of investors. Through a combination of Regulation D and Rule 144A, issuers can sell a large amount of securities without registering under § 5, but still allowing immediate resales. Today, Rule 144A offerings total hundreds of billions annually, with a particular emphasis on debt and convertible debt securities.

Rule 144A exempts resales by two types of sellers. First, Rule 144A(b) covers offers and sales by a person other than an issuer or dealer. If the conditions of Rule 144A(d) are met, then Rule 144A(b) provides that the offers or sales are not a "distribution" of securities. Consequently, the person offering the securities is not an underwriter, which makes § 4(a)(1) available (as with Rule 144).

Rule 144A(c) exempts securities dealers. To the extent the terms of Rule 144A are met, securities dealers are deemed not to be participating in a distribution within the meaning of section 4(a)(3)(C) of the Act. In addition, the dealers are excluded from the definition of underwriter. Finally, the securities are also not deemed to be "offered to the public" under § 4(a)(3)(A). The combination of these provisions allows the dealer to rely on the § 4(a)(3) exemption.

Why do issuers, investment banks, and securities lawyers commonly refer to a Rule 144A "offering"? Technically, Rule 144A exempts only resales. Issuers cannot rely on Rule 144A to protect primary transactions from the reach of § 5. How does the Rule 144A resale exemption facilitate primary sale of securities by issuers?

Here's how it works in practice:

- The issuer sells the securities under § 4(a)(2) or Rule 506 of Regulation D to an investment bank (a dealer, commonly called the "initial purchaser");

- The investment bank—relying on Rule 144A(c)—then resells the securities to a broad range of large institutional investors, known as "qualified institutional buyers," or more commonly, QIBs.

Combining Rule 144A with an initial private placement allows issuers to sell enormous amounts of securities through an investment bank to many sophisticated institutional investors. Unlike an offering solely under § 4(a)(2) or Rule 506, combining a private placement with Rule 144A allows the initial purchaser in the offering to resell the securities, as long as the subsequent purchasers are institutional investors.

Rule 144A(e) makes clear that the issuer need not worry about the subsequent resales to QIBs: "Offers and sales of securities pursuant to this section shall be deemed not to affect the availability of any exemption or safe harbor relating to any previous or subsequent offer or sale of such securities by the issuer or any prior or subsequent holder thereof." Rule 144A(e) thus protects prior and subsequent parties from integration with a specific Rule 144A transaction. When an issuer sells to a placement agent under Rule 506 who in turn resells quickly to QIBs under Rule 144A, the immediate resale does not affect the issuer's initial Rule 506 sale to the placement agent.

Rule 144A(d) sets forth four basic requirements:

(A) Sales must be to a qualified institutional buyer

(B) Purchasers must be notified of the exemption

(C) Non-fungibility

(D) Disclosure

We consider each of the requirements in turn.

A. SALES TO A QUALIFIED INSTITUTIONAL BUYER

Rule 144A(d)(1) requires that all sales be made only to qualified institutional buyers or those the seller reasonably believes to be qualified institutional buyers. Qualified institutional buyers are defined to include an entity (investing for their own account or for the accounts of other QIBs) that in the aggregate owns and invests on a discretionary basis $100 million or more in securities of companies unaffiliated with the QIB. Rule 144A(a)(1). Insurance companies, investment companies, corporations, and partnerships, among others, are included. The $100 million threshold represents a presumption on the part of the SEC that institutions with such a large portfolio will have extensive financial sophistication and experience.

Additional requirements are imposed on banks, which must not only meet the $100 million requirement, but also have an audited net worth of $25 million to be considered qualified institutional buyers. This restriction reflects the federal deposit insurance that banks enjoy, which means that banks are effectively putting public funds at risk.

By contrast, securities dealers are given greater latitude under Rule 144A. In order to qualify as QIBs, securities dealers need only own or invest on a discretionary basis $10 million in the aggregate of securities. In addition, securities dealers acting in a "riskless principal" transaction for a QIB also qualify for QIB status. In a riskless principal transaction, the broker-dealer is simultaneously acquiring a security from one entity and selling the same security to another entity. Although title to the security does momentarily lie with the broker-dealer, the broker-dealer is essentially acting as an agent for the two parties ultimately selling and buying the security. Dealers acting as intermediaries in a riskless principal transaction "grease the wheels" to bring together potential buyers and sellers.

Straightforward on its face, Rule 144A(d)(1) is noteworthy for what it does not require. Unlike Regulation D, which bans general solicitations under certain circumstances, Rule 144A(d)(1) only requires that sales be made to qualified institutional buyers. Sellers may approach any qualified institutional buyer even without a pre-existing relationship. Pursuant to the JOBS Act of 2012, Congress directed the SEC to modify Rule 144A to allow offers to all investors, including non-QIBs. Although the seller must reasonably believe that *purchasers* are QIBs, the JOBS Act allows sellers to engage in general solicitation and advertising in an effort to contact QIBs. The SEC implemented this directive by deleting all references to "offer" and "offeree" in Rule

144A(d)(1). Resales under Rule 144A can now be promoted through general solicitation, as long as the purchasers are limited to QIBs.

B. PURCHASER AWARENESS OF EXEMPTION

Rule 144A(d)(2) requires that the seller take reasonable steps to ensure that the purchaser knows that the sale is made in reliance on Rule 144A. Such steps include placing a legend on the securities indicating (1) their restricted status; and (2) that resales may only take place through registration or an exemption from § 5. Issuers will also obtain a restricted CUSIP identifier for the securities. A CUSIP is assigned to financial instruments, providing a unique identifier for any particular stock, bond, etc. Issuers will also include a similar statement in the private placement memorandum for the Regulation D/Rule 144A offering.

C. FUNGIBILITY

Only certain types of securities qualify for Rule 144A. Issuers cannot offer or sell securities of the same class as securities listed on a national securities exchange. Rule 144A(d)(3). So issuers who have their common stock listed on a national exchange cannot sell common stock under Rule 144A. How to work around this restriction? One possibility would be to issue a new series of preferred stock. More commonly, however, exchange-listed issuers issue a class of debt securities convertible into the exchange-traded common stock. Rule 144A(d)(3), however, limits this potential loophole by excluding convertible securities that allow investors to convert into securities listed on a national securities exchange, *unless* the effective conversion premium is at least ten percent. The conversion premium greatly reduces the chance of rapid conversion into the underlying listed or quoted stock. The conversion premium ensures that conversion will only take place (if at all) in the future if the price of the listed or quoted securities rises by more than ten percent.

D. DISCLOSURE

Rule 144A(d)(4) imposes disclosure requirements, although Exchange Act reporting issuers are exempt. For other issuers, Rule 144A(d)(4) requires that the holder of the securities as well as any prospective purchaser have the right, on their request, to obtain specified information from the issuer.

The specified information under Rule 144A(d)(4) must be "reasonably current" and include "a very brief statement of the nature of the business of the issuer and the products and services it offers; and the issuer's most recent balance sheet and profit and loss and retained earnings statements, and similar financial statements for such part of the two preceding fiscal years as the issuer has been in operation (the financial statements should be audited to the extent reasonably available)." On its face, Rule 144A(d)(4)'s information requirement is unusual in the duration of the obligation. Sellers seeking to use Rule 144A must ensure that the issuer is willing to provide the specified information essentially indefinitely. The SEC, however, did not believe this information requirement would impose a significant burden:

Many foreign issuers that will be subject to the requirement . . . will have securities traded in established offshore markets, and already will have made the required information publicly available in such markets. Even for domestic issuers, the required information represents only a portion of that which would be necessary before a U.S. broker or dealer could submit for publication a quotation for the securities of such an issuer in a quotation medium in the United States. The Commission expects that the kinds of information commonly furnished under Rule 12g3–2(b) by foreign private issuers almost invariably would satisfy the information requirement and that foreign private issuers who wish their securities to be Rule 144A-eligible will simply obtain a Rule 12g3–2(b) exemption on a voluntary basis. Financial statements meeting the timing requirements of the issuer's home country or principal trading markets would be considered sufficiently current for purposes of the information requirement of the Rule.

Securities Act Release No. 6862 (April 23, 1990).

Even if the cost were low, why would an issuer agree to continue to provide such reasonably current information well after the initial sale of the securities? Consider what happens to an issuer that refuses to provide such information to subsequent purchasers in the resale market. The initial purchaser will then be unable to use Rule 144A to subsequently resell, thereby chilling the secondary market. The initial investors, in turn, will discount the amount they are willing to pay the issuer for the securities, reflecting an illiquidity premium. The issuer's own best interests, therefore, will lead the issuer to contract with investors to provide for an on-going right to disclosure.

Indeed, despite the relatively narrow reach of Rule 144A(d)(4)'s disclosure requirement, most issuers engaged in a Rule 144A offering will voluntarily disclose in an offering circular. The offering circular will not only advise investors of the use of the Rule 144A exemption from § 5, but will also disclose information similar to that found in the registration statement, including audited financial statements and a description of the business, properties, management, and shareholders. Issuers disclose not because of any legal mandate, but because the market demands the information. Issuers that do not disclose will suffer a large "information asymmetry" discount or, in the extreme, find their securities unmarketable.

HYPOTHETICAL SEVEN

Island Tours wants to raise additional capital to expand its operations internationally to provide tours in Aruba and the Maldives. Island Tours' common stock has traded on Nasdaq since its IPO three years ago. Skipper, the CEO of Island Tours, does not want to expose the company (or himself) to potential § 11 liability from the offering. Island Tours turns to you for advice. Consider the following possible scenarios:

1. *Scenario One:* Island Tours proposes to sell $50 million of a new class of preferred stock to about ten large mutual funds. Island Tours cold calls 100 mutual funds (assume that all are QIBs) as potential purchasers and provides each mutual fund with some basic information on Island Tours and three years worth of audited financials. Can Island Tours sell to the mutual funds under Rule 144A?

2. *Scenario Two:* Island Tours proposes to sell $50 million of a new class of preferred stock. Island Tours first sells the preferred stock to Wentworth Investments, a large Wall Street investment bank (an accredited investor) under Rule 506. Wentworth Investments turns around and resells the shares almost immediately to fifty large mutual funds (all QIBs). Wentworth Investments does not have a pre-existing relationship with each QIB. Each mutual fund is informed of the Rule 144A exemption. Can Island Tours sell to the mutual funds through Wentworth Investments?

3. *Scenario Three:* Same as Scenario Two. Suppose that Wentworth Investments instead resells immediately to Lovey, an accredited investor who individually owns and invest on a discretionary basis over $1 billion in securities. Wentworth Investments does not enjoy a pre-existing relationship with Lovey.

E. RESALES

After an initial Rule 144A transaction, how are subsequent resales treated? Suppose Island Tours sells securities to Wentworth Investments in a Rule 506 private placement. The investment bank resells immediately to Minnow Financial, a QIB, through a valid Rule 144A exemption. Minnow Financial turns around and subsequently resells to Lovey, an individual and thus not a QIB.

Island Tours → **Wentworth Investments** → **Minnow Financial** → **Lovey**

Although Rule 144A itself does not impose subsequent resale restrictions, the preliminary notes to Rule 144A make clear that securities resold through Rule 144A continue to be classified as restricted securities. Minnow Financial' resales to Lovey may therefore take place but only if the resales are registered under § 5 or qualify for an exemption from § 5.

Minnow Financial in the above example may resell to Lovey after a six month holding period pursuant to Rule 144. (This assumes that Minnow is not an affiliate of Island Tours.) Minnow Financial could also immediately sell to a QIB, assuming the other requirements of Rule 144A are met. Alternatively, Minnow Financial could negotiate for registration rights from Island Tours, giving Minnow the right to get Island Tours to register the shares for resale.

Absent registration under § 5, Minnow Financial's quickest and most certain method of reselling securities is through Rule 144A to other QIBs. Although the SEC reduced the holding period under Rule 144, investors must still bear investment risk for six months before taking advantage of Rule 144 resales. Liquidity is important to investors. Even qualified institutional buyers may hesitate (or demand a significant discount) unless the securities can be resold eventually in the public markets. The ability to resell to other QIBs creates a "super"-secondary market of only QIBs for unregistered securities sold through Rule 144A. Note that Lovey is not able to participate in this 144A secondary market regardless of her sophistication or wealth.

The fact that Rule 144A allows resales to other QIBs does not ensure that a secondary market will arise. Bringing together potential buyers and sellers in an organized market setting is costly. Moreover, because of the limited number of QIBs, such a market is necessarily not as deep as the public capital markets. The SEC originally envisioned that Rule 144A resales would take place through electronic trading systems and, in particular, through the automated PORTAL trading system ("Private Offerings, Resale and Trading through Automated Linkages"). Clearance and settlement of trade on the PORTAL system take place through the Depository Trust Company. In practice, relatively few Rule 144A securities are actually traded using the automated PORTAL system.

The Sarbanes-Oxley Act, however, by discouraging many firms from entering the public equity markets, has fueled the market's demand for alternative trading venues for Rule 144A securities. Wall Street investment banks responded to the desire for liquidity through the creation of proprietary trading systems specifically geared toward resales of restricted securities among qualified institutional buyers pursuant to Rule 144A. In 2007, Nasdaq revamped its PORTAL trading system to provide a computerized system for secondary market trading for stocks issued under Rule 144A. As of late 2007, a number of Wall Street firms, agreed to cooperate with Nasdaq's PORTAL efforts (in a coalition termed the "PORTAL alliance"). The liquidity of the PORTAL system was further enhanced in 2009 when the Depository Trust Company (DTC) made all Rule 144A securities eligible for its clearing and settlement services.

Companies relying on the PORTAL system to provide liquidity for their unregistered shares must take care to avoid other triggers for public company status under the U.S. securities laws. As we discussed in Chapter 4, even a company that never sells through a registered public offering may be deemed a public company if it has more than $10 million in total assets and at least 2,000 shareholders of class of equity securities under Section 12(g) and Rule 12g–1 of the Exchange Act. The consequence of achieving public company status is that the company then has to comply with the periodic disclosure requirements, Regulation FD, and other requirements imposed by the Exchange Act, as well as the governance requirements imposed pursuant to the Sarbanes-Oxley Act. DTC now tracks the holders of Rule 144A securities deposited with it to ensure that the number of shareholders holding equity does not exceed 1,999.

Rule 144A is not an exclusive safe harbor. Despite the focus in Rule 144A on the type of security (i.e., whether the security is fungible with one traded on a national securities exchange), ultimately the Securities Act focuses on transactions. Purchasers of securities under Rule 144A can eventually resell the securities freely through Rule 144 after meeting either the six month or one year holding period requirement. Once resold through Rule 144, the Rule 144A securities may then be freely resold in the public secondary market without restriction. Regulation S also allows QIBs to resell securities purchased in a Rule 144A transaction offshore to persons outside the United States.

HYPOTHETICAL EIGHT

Island Tours, an Exchange Act reporting issuer, wants to raise additional capital to open a tropical resort, Castaway Island. Island Tours' common stock has traded on Nasdaq since its IPO three years ago. Island Tours hires Wentworth Investments to act as its selling agent. Through Wentworth Investments, Island Tours sells $50 million of a new class of preferred shares to 10 accredited purchasers under Rule 506. Lovey, one of the accredited purchasers, bought $1 million in the offering. (Lovey has a net worth of $1 billion.) Consider the following scenarios:

1. *Scenario One:* Two days after the offering, Lovey cold calls Jonas Capital Group (a qualified institutional buyer) and Jonas agrees to purchase all of her preferred shares in Island Tours. Is this okay?

2. *Scenario Two:* Lovey sells to Jonas Capital Group three months after she purchases the securities from Island Tours. Jonas in turn sells the securities to Grumby Insurance (also a QIB) the next week. Any problems?

3. *Scenario Three:* Same as Scenario Two. Suppose Jonas Capital Group sells the securities instead to the Professor, an academic earning $50,000 a year with a net worth of $900,000, the next day. Any problems?

4. *Scenario Four:* Suppose Island Tours instead issued $10 million of common stock through a Rule 506 offering to ten accredited investors (including Lovey). Can Lovey sell $1 million of the common stock purchased in the Rule 506 offering to Jonas (a QIB) under Rule 144A?

F. RULE 144A AND REGISTRATION UNDER THE SECURITIES ACT

Although Rule 144 allows qualified institutional buyers to resell securities eventually into the broader secondary market, QIBs often demand registration rights from issuers. Registration rights allow QIBs to force the issuer to register the Rule 144A shares for immediate resale through a secondary public offering.

What are the benefits of providing registration rights? Restricted securities, as we have seen above, are illiquid. Despite the availability of the PORTAL system, most QIBs prefer to resell into the broader secondary markets. Securities sold without an accompanying registration rights agreement receive a discount from investors. Mutual funds and insurance companies are also limited in their ability to invest in illiquid securities. An open-end mutual fund, for example, may hold no more than 15 percent of the fund's assets in illiquid securities. The SEC has made clear, however, that Rule 144A securities are not necessarily considered illiquid for purposes of determining the 15 percent ceiling for mutual funds. *See* Securities Act Release No. 6862 (April 23, 1990). Nonetheless, providing for registration rights allows QIBs to invest more in Regulation D/Rule 144A offerings.

One method for issuers to register securities initially sold through a Rule 144A offering is through shelf registration. Rule 415(a)(1)(i) allows for the shelf registration of secondary offerings of shares. Typically, the issuer will agree as part of the primary offering to QIBs to maintain the shelf registration for six months or one year, depending on the company's reporting status, after which QIBs may turn to Rule 144 to resell the restricted securities. A more common method for issuers to give effect to a registration rights agreement is through a public exchange offer. In the exchange offer, identical registered securities are exchanged for the restricted Rule 144A securities. The SEC has, however, confined the use of such exchange offers for U.S. issuers to non-convertible debt securities and investment grade preferred stock. *See, e.g.*, SEC No-Action Letter, Exxon Capital Holding Corp. (available May 13, 1988).

If issuers are willing to grant QIBs registration rights, why not simply sell the securities through a public offering in the first place rather than through Rule 144A? First, registration rights are often limited. Issuers may, for example, provide for a delayed effective date to give themselves time before investors may exercise the registration rights. Second, courts have held that the initial Rule 144A offering and any subsequent public exchange offering are considered separate, non-integrated transaction. *See American High-Income Trust v. Alliedsignal*, 329 F. Supp. 2d 534 (S.D.N.Y. 2004). The offering memorandum used in the Rule 144A transaction is thus not a "prospectus" for purposes of § 12(a)(2) liability. Neither the issuer nor any of the placement agents will face §§ 11 or 12(a)(2) liability for misstatements relating to the initial Rule 144A private placement, although Rule 10b–5 continues to apply. Although issuers may face Securities Act liability for a subsequent public exchange offering (when and if such an offering occurs), placement agents are not liable if they do not participate in the exchange.

CHAPTER 11

FEDERAL REGULATION OF SHAREHOLDER VOTING

Rules and Statutes

—*Sections 14(a), 14A, 27 of the Exchange Act*

—*Rule 14a–1 through Rule 14a–18, 14a–21, 14n–1 through 14n–3 of the Exchange Act*

—*Schedules 14A, 14N of the Exchange Act*

MOTIVATING HYPOTHETICAL

Sterling Cooper Worldwide is a major advertising agency with its headquarters in New York, NY. Since its founding twenty years ago, Sterling Cooper has enjoyed phenomenal growth. Two years ago, Sterling Cooper went public with an offering of its common stock. Sterling Cooper shares trade on the American Stock Exchange; the company currently has a market capitalization of $500 million and over 1,000 shareholders. Don, the CEO and Chairman of Sterling Cooper, owns 10% of the outstanding stock. The board of Sterling Cooper consists of seven directors including Don, Lane (the CFO), and five outside directors. Betty, an individual investor living in Rye, NY, owns 100 shares of Sterling Cooper as part of her portfolio.

I. INTRODUCTION

Corporations range from small businesses with one shareholder to large multi-national conglomerates with thousands of shareholders. In theory, shareholders are the residual "owners" of the corporation. After all other claimants, including employees, suppliers, and creditors, are paid what they are owed, shareholders receive the residual profits (or bear the residual loss, but only to the extent of their investment).

Although corporations enjoy considerable freedom under state corporate law to allocate voting power among their equity holders, generally the lowest priority class of securities in a corporation (i.e., common stock) retains voting power. Through their votes, shareholders elect the board of directors of a corporation. The board controls the operation of the corporation, including the choice of its top executive officers.

Most directors of large, public corporations are elected annually at the shareholders meeting. Shareholders also vote to approve certain major transactions, such as a statutory merger with another corporation. Corporate officers and directors may also ask shareholders to vote to ratify certain transactions in which the officers and directors have a conflict of interest. In certain jurisdictions, shareholders also vote to ratify the company's choice of outside auditor.

Although shareholders are entitled to cast their votes at the annual shareholder meeting, most shareholders do not attend the meeting. If you owned only 100 shares of Sterling Cooper, would you fly to the company's headquarters in New York to attend the annual meeting? Most shareholders vote by proxy, completing a proxy card (referred to as a "form of proxy") and allowing a proxy (typically the incumbent directors) to vote their shares.

How does a typical proxy vote take place? First, the issuer identifies shareholders eligible to vote. To be eligible, shareholders must be shareholders as of the "record date." The board of directors usually sets the record date up to a couple of months before the meeting date. Complicating matters, most investors who own shares through brokerage accounts are not the owners of record. Instead, the shares are held in "street name" with the brokerage firms listed as the legal owners of the shares. Brokerage firms are required to send the proxy card to the shareholders whose shares are held in street name so the shareholders can vote their shares. Tabulation companies collect the proxies. Once collected, the tabulation company certifies the proxies and tabulates the results.

Shareholder voting is not cheap. Those seeking shareholders' votes must bring the issue to the shareholders' attention. The officers and directors of a corporation enjoy privileges of incumbency in capturing the shareholders' attention. They have immediate access to the shareholders of record of the corporation (through the corporate transfer agent). This allows managers to identify those shareholders not holding their shares in street name, typically larger, institutional owners who carry more weight in determining a vote. More importantly, the directors distribute their proxy statement to the shareholders at the corporation's expense. Outsiders nominating an opposing slate of candidates for the board of directors (or some other voting issue for shareholders) must generally bear the cost of mailing out separate proxy solicitations. As we discuss in this chapter, in certain circumstances, shareholders may nominate directors or place proposals on the company's own proxy statement. Outsiders must also lobby directly, "wining and dining" large shareholders to persuade them to vote for the alternate slate of directors. State corporate law allows reimbursement of such expenses incurred by outsiders only if the outsiders win control of the board *and* obtain a shareholder vote approving such reimbursement. Moreover, those "soliciting" a proxy face both disclosure requirements and antifraud liability under the federal securities laws, further raising insurgent costs.

Compounding the high costs of getting shareholders to vote on a particular issue is rational apathy. Suppose Betty, the shareholder with 100 shares of Sterling Cooper, must choose between Sterling Cooper's slate of directors and some competing slate. Reading disclosures and deciding how to vote takes time and effort. Even if Betty does vote, her vote is unlikely to matter. What are the chances that her 100 shares, out of a total of 50 million shares, will be pivotal? From Betty's perspective, her 100 share investment may not justify her time and attention. Betty, if she is like many individual investors, may simply throw proxy solicitations in the recycling bin.

In this chapter we discuss the basic federal securities regulatory framework governing the solicitation of proxies. We focus particularly on the election of directors involving a potential corporate change of control. We then examine the present scope of shareholder voting power. If shareholders are the residual owners of the firm, should they have more voting power? And who should decide the allocation of power within a corporation? As part of this discussion, we assess the ability of shareholders to insert their own proposals on the company's proxy statement under Rule 14a–8 and nominate directors for the board under Rule 14a–11.

II. SOLICITATION OF PROXIES

State corporate law allocates power between shareholders and the board of directors. As noted above, shareholders of large public corporations typically have the right only to elect directors, approve certain major corporate transactions, and ratify transactions in which a director or officer has a conflict of interest. Outside of these episodic votes, shareholders have little say in the corporation's affairs.

When outsiders seek to elect a competing slate of nominees as directors, we call that a "proxy contest." During the 1950s, insurgents turned to proxy contests as a device to replace the directors and thereby take control of the corporation. Although typically roundly defeated, insurgents occasionally succeeded. Robert Young, for example, wrested control of the New York Central Railroad from the Vanderbilt family through a proxy contest in 1954. By the 1970s, however, proxy contests fell into disuse, displaced by tender offers, which allowed a bidder to purchase shares outright from public investors rather than simply obtaining their votes. Among other advantages of the tender offer, investors are much more likely to tender their shares to an unknown bidder (particularly if offered cash) than they are to vote for an unknown insurgent's nominees in a proxy contest. If an unknown insurgent wins a proxy contest, investors who still own shares will have to live with the consequences on share value. At least the prior incumbent managers are something of a known quantity.

The use of defensive tactics to thwart hostile tender offers has resulted in a resurgence of proxy contests. Companies now deploy "poison pills" that threaten to dilute the interest of a hostile bidder if the bidder crosses a certain threshold of share ownership. For a hostile bidder to succeed in a tender offer, the bidder must first obtain board approval to redeem the poison pill. The Delaware Chancery Court explains the strategy:

> When poison pills became prevalent, would-be acquirors resorted to proxy contests as a method of obtaining indirectly that which they could no longer get through a tender offer. By taking out the target company's board through a proxy fight or a consent solicitation, the acquiror could obtain control of the board room, redeem the pill, and open the way for consummation of its tender offer.

In re Gaylord Container Corp. Shareholders Litigation, 753 A.2d 462, 482 (Del. Ch. 2000).

The federal securities regulatory scheme only applies to proxy solicitations that occur for companies required to register their securities under Exchange Act § 12. Recall from Chapter 4 that this section requires companies to register if they have securities listed on a national securities exchange (§ 12(a)) or $10 million in total assets and 2,000 shareholders (§ 12(g) and Rule 12g–1). Throughout the proxy rules, companies with securities registered under § 12 with respect to which proxies are solicited are referred to as the "registrant." Companies required to make Exchange Act reporting filings solely pursuant to § 15(d) are not subject to the proxy rules.

For registrants, § 14(a) of the Exchange Act and its accompanying rules regulate the proxy solicitation process. That regulatory scheme is triggered when a person "solicit[s] any proxy." Section 14(a). If a solicitation has occurred then the proxy rules contained in Rule 14a–3 through Rule 14a–15 apply, absent an exemption. We start with the threshold issue of what counts as a "solicitation."

A. WHAT IS A "SOLICITATION"?

What counts as a proxy solicitation? Consider Paul, the head of the Manhattan Public Employee Retirement System (MPERS), a large shareholder of Sterling Cooper. Paul has nominated a competing slate of candidates for election to Sterling Cooper's board. Paul calls up dozens of institutional investors holding Sterling Cooper stock and asks them for their proxy to vote for his candidates. Paul's communications clearly constitute a solicitation of a proxy under the definition of a solicitation in Rule 14a–1(*l*).

The definition of solicitation is much broader than explicit communications intended to obtain an actual proxy for voting purposes. Rule 14a–1(*l*) of the Exchange Act treats any communication "under circumstances reasonably calculated to result in the procurement, withholding or revocation of a proxy" as a solicitation. Rule 14a–1(f) defines "proxy" to include not only "every proxy" but also "consent or authorization" where "consent or authorization may take the form of failure to object or to dissent." The Rule 14a–1(*l*) definition of a "solicitation" of a proxy extends to communications by third parties who are not seeking the power to vote proxies on a particular voting issue. The SEC has stated that "statements made for the purpose of inducing security holders to give, revoke, or withhold a proxy . . . by any person who has solicited or intends to solicit proxies . . . may involve a solicitation within the meaning of the regulation, depending upon the particular facts and circumstances." Securities and Exchange Commission, Adoption of Amendments to Proxy Rules, Exchange Act Release No. 5276 (Jan. 17, 1956). Under particular facts and circumstances, investors discussing how to vote, presumably influencing the views of one another and perhaps other investors, may be engaged in a proxy solicitation.

Once a communication is considered a proxy solicitation, the communicating party faces a number of requirements. Absent an exemption, the soliciting party may need to file a preliminary proxy statement with the SEC, wait for SEC approval, and then mail a formal proxy statement to those privy to the communications. In addition to mailing and filing costs and delay, this regime discourages communications by investors wishing to remain anonymous. Because proxy statements are required to be filed with the SEC, the registrant and other shareholders are able to determine not only the identity of communicating parties but also the substance of such communications. Moreover, because Rule 14a–9's antifraud prohibitions apply to all proxy solicitations, investors also face the specter of potential antifraud liability. Incumbent management may bring a suit for violation of the proxy rules as part of its defense against a proxy contest. Such a suit may impose costs on insurgents and stir up doubt among shareholders about the insurgent. Rule 14a–9 suits are a two-way street. Insurgent shareholders may also bring a Rule 14a–9 action against the incumbent directors for fraud in the incumbents' proxy statement.

The SEC narrows the broad definition of a solicitation under Rule 14a–1(*l*) through a number of exemptions. There are two basic categories of exemptions. The first category, contained in Rule 14a–1(*l*)(2), removes the communication completely from the definition of a proxy solicitation. Rule 14a–1(*l*)(2)(iv), for example, excludes from the definition of a proxy solicitation public announcements by shareholders who do not otherwise engage in a proxy solicitation on how they intend to vote, including public speeches, press releases, and newspaper advertisements. Because of the exclusion, communicating parties are shielded from Rule 14a–9's antifraud prohibitions as well as the other proxy requirements. If Paul can convince Cosgrove Investments to vote in favor of MPERS' candidates, Cosgrove can announce its intentions through a newspaper advertisement, which may persuade other shareholders to join Paul's cause. Because such an announcement is excluded from the definition of a solicitation under Rule 14a–1(*l*)(2)(iv), Cosgrove does not face any proxy rule-related costs or potential liability.

The second category of exemptions, found in Rule 14a–2, does not remove communication from the definition of a solicitation but instead exempts the solicitation from the application of a subset of the proxy rules. Rule 14a–2(a)(6), for example, allows "tombstone"-like advertisements about a proxy solicitation. Under Rule 14a–2(a)(6), solicitations made through "a newspaper advertisement which informs security holders of a source from which they may obtain copies of a proxy statement, form of proxy and any other soliciting material" and that do no more than: (i) name the registrant, (ii) state the reason for the advertisement, and (iii) identify the proposal or proposals are not required to comply with Rules 14a–3 through 14a–15.

Similarly, Rule 14a–2(b) exempts certain solicitations from some of the proxy rules, including, critically, the disclosure requirements. The exemption is not all-inclusive. In particular, Rule 14a–9's antifraud prohibition continues to apply. Rule 14a–2(b)(1) exempts solicitations by a person who does not seek "the power to act as proxy for a security holder and does not furnish or otherwise request, or act on behalf of a person who furnishes or requests, a form of revocation, abstention, consent or authorization." Not everyone can use Rule 14a–2(b)(1); officers or directors of the registrant and nominees to the board of directors "for whose election as a director proxies are solicited" cannot rely on the exemption. Also excluded is any person who would "receive a benefit from a successful solicitation that would not be shared pro rata by all other holders of the same class of securities." In parallel with the

Rule 14a–2(b)(1) exemption, Rule 14a–2(b)(2) exempts solicitations if "the total number of persons solicited is not more than ten." The registrant is excluded from this exemption.

HYPOTHETICAL ONE

Paul, the head of MPERS, is contemplating a proxy contest, putting up his own competing slate of nominees for election to Sterling Cooper's board of directors. Consider whether any of the following communications constitute a proxy solicitation.

1. Paul telephones nine institutional investors. In the phone calls, he discusses at length the reasons that the institutional investors should give him their proxy to vote for his nominees to the board.

2. Campbell Capital, one of the institutional investors that received a phone call from Paul, telephones Holloway Investments to confer regarding the proxy contest. Both Campbell Capital and Holloway are large shareholders of Sterling Cooper.

3. After some consideration, Campbell Capital decides to support Paul's slate of nominees. To give Paul an added boost, Campbell posts its decision on its publicly available web page.

4. The *New York Times* publishes an editorial extolling the virtues of Paul and his insurgent slate of board nominees. The editorial is published at the same time shareholders receive proxy solicitations from Paul and from Sterling Cooper's incumbent management.

B. PROXY DISCLOSURE

Proxy regulation, like the rest of the federal securities regime, focuses primarily on disclosure. We discuss two aspects of the proxy disclosure regime: (1) the disclosure and filing requirements for the "proxy statement" sent to shareholders whose proxy is being solicited and (2) the ability of parties to engage in proxy solicitations prior to furnishing the proxy statement, "testing the waters" before launching a full-blown proxy contest.

1. DISCLOSURE AND FILING REQUIREMENTS

Rule 14a–3(a) prohibits solicitations before a formal proxy statement containing information specified by the SEC is delivered to the solicited shareholder, either concurrently with or prior to the solicitation. For those seeking to obtain the actual proxy from shareholders, shareholders must receive a "form of the proxy" as specified in Rule 14a–4. The form of the proxy must set forth in bold-face whether the proxy solicitation is on behalf of the board of directors or some other party and must specify separately each voting item as well as boxes for approval, disapproval, or abstention.

The formal proxy disclosure comes in two flavors: the preliminary and definitive proxy statements, as defined in Schedule 14A. For certain routine voting issues, only a definitive proxy statement is required. If the registrant is soliciting proxies for an annual meeting and the only voting issues involve the election of directors, the election, approval, or ratification of accountants, or other routine matters, the registrant only needs to file a definitive proxy statement with the SEC no later than the first date such materials are sent to shareholders. Rule 14a–6(b).

For all other voting issues, the registrant and other parties soliciting proxies must first file a preliminary proxy statement with the SEC at least ten calendar days prior to the date the definitive proxy statement is first sent or given to security holders. Even for routine matters, such as the election of directors, if the "registrant comments upon or refers to a solicitation in opposition in connection with the meeting in its proxy material" then the registrant must also meet the preliminary proxy statement filing requirement. Rule 14a–6(a). Unless marked as confidential, information in the preliminary proxy statement is available online through the SEC's EDGAR system.

Although parties may solicit proxies once a preliminary proxy statement has been delivered, parties may not deliver a form of proxy, consent or authorization to any security holder unless the security holder has received a definitive proxy statement. Those seeking to obtain proxies must wait until the definitive proxy statement is filed with the SEC.

In theory, soliciting parties may begin using a definitive proxy ten days after filing the preliminary proxy statement. The soliciting party does not need to wait for SEC approval before soliciting with the definitive proxy statement, but must file the definitive proxy statement with the SEC. Rule 14a–6(b). In practice, the registrant and other soliciting parties will typically wait for SEC approval of the preliminary proxy before proceeding with the definitive proxy statement. For certain voting issues, particularly mergers, the soliciting parties will give the SEC considerably more than ten days to review the proxy statement.

Why wait for SEC approval? The SEC staff often provides comments on the preliminary proxy statement, which can take as long as six to eight weeks. Waiting for SEC approval provides soliciting parties some degree of comfort that their proxy statement satisfies disclosure requirements and does not violate Rule 14a–9, although SEC approval does not afford a safe harbor from a later Rule 14a–9 action. Moreover, ignoring the SEC's comments runs the risk of a possible SEC enforcement action. Note the similarity here with the practice of delaying the effective date for a registration statement during the waiting period to allow for SEC review in the public offering process discussed in Chapter 7.

Schedule 14A requires a number of disclosures. For registrants seeking proxies relating to the election of directors at the annual meeting, Schedule 14A requires that the proxy statement disclose, among other things:

- date, time, and place of the meeting of shareholders (Item 1)
- the persons making the solicitation (Item 4)
- voting securities (Item 6)
- ownership of certain beneficial owners holding more than 5% of any class of the registrant's voting securities (Item 6)
- director nominees and officers of the registrant (Item 7)

- audit, nominating and compensation committees of the board of directors, including whether the members of the audit and nominating committees are independent (Item 7)
- compensation of directors and officers (Item 8)

Schedule 14A, like other mandatory disclosure documents under the federal securities laws, incorporates by reference a number of items in Regulations S–K and S–X. Item 8 of Schedule 14A, for example, deals with the compensation of directors and executive officers and makes explicit reference to Item 402 of Regulation S–K. Item 11(l) of Form S–1, dealing with executive compensation (*see* Chapter 7 on public offerings), likewise references Item 402 of Regulation S–K.

Schedule 14A places fewer disclosure requirements on insurgents putting forth a competing slate of nominees. Such insurgents do not need to present information on the registrant's directors and officers of the registrant (including compensation) or board committees. Shareholders already receive that information in the management's own proxy statement. Only information on the insurgent's own nominees to the board is required.

For registrants seeking a shareholder vote for certain major corporate events and transactions other than election of directors, Schedule 14A requires additional disclosure related to the events and transactions. These include:

- Authorization or Issuance of Securities Otherwise than for Exchange (Item 11)
- Modification or Exchange of Securities (Item 12)
- Mergers, Consolidations, Acquisitions and Similar Matters (Item 14)
- Acquisition or Disposition of Property (Item 15)

Together with the required proxy statement, solicitations on behalf of the registrant relating to an annual meeting at which directors are to be elected must be accompanied or preceded by an annual report to security holders. Rule 14a–3(b) mandates specific information that must be included in the annual report, including audited financial statements.

For communications relating to a proxy vote not excluded under the definitional provision for a solicitation in Rule 14a–1(l) or otherwise exempt under Rule 14a–2, Rule 14a–3(f) provides a special exemption from the proxy statement delivery requirement, for any "communication . . . appearing in a broadcast media, newspaper, magazine or other bona fide publication disseminated on a regular basis." Rule 14a–3(f)'s exemption has two prerequisites. First, no form of proxy may be provided to the security holder in connection with the communication. Second, at the time the communication is made, a definitive proxy statement relating to the solicitation must have been filed with the SEC under Rule 14a–6(b).

Consider the purpose of Rule 14a–3(f). Imagine that an insurgent wishes to advertise her views on a proxy contest in the *Wall Street Journal*. Because the insurgent is soliciting a proxy (with large institutional investors for example), the insurgent will not qualify for the Rule 14a–1(*l*)(2)(iv) exclusion for public communications on the vote. The insurgent will, absent anything else, have to distribute a copy of the proxy statement either together with the *Wall Street Journal* or prior to the delivery of the newspaper to every recipient under Rule 14a–3. The prohibitive cost of delivering those proxy statements would likely eliminate all public communication by the insurgent. Company officials would face a similar requirement, but they can use corporate funds to pay the cost of distributing the proxy statement. Rule 14a–3(f) eliminates the otherwise prohibitive cost to insurgents of delivering the proxy statement to all those receiving a public solicitation. Rule 14a–9's antifraud prohibition, however, continues to apply.

2.   TESTING THE WATERS

For activist shareholders seeking to dislodge an incumbent board through a proxy contest, the cost and delay associated with drafting a proxy statement and awaiting SEC clearance for the definitive proxy statement may deter many from launching a contest in the first place. Consider a potential insurgent weighing whether to launch a contest without knowing how shareholders might react to such a contest. If shareholders are receptive, a proxy contest may have a decent chance of dislodging the incumbent directors or pressuring them to change corporate policies. On the other hand, if shareholders are not receptive a proxy contest is a waste of time and money.

Assessing shareholders' interest in a proxy contest, therefore, is important in reducing the risk facing insurgents. The proxy rules provide several avenues for insurgents to "test the waters." In order to be useful, "testing the waters" must be available before the insurgent undertakes the expense of drafting and filing the proxy statement. As we discussed above, Rule 14a–2(b)(2) exempts solicitations of ten or fewer shareholders from most of the proxy rules. For many public companies, the top ten institutional investors own a sizeable fraction of the outstanding shares. The option of communicating with just the top ten institutions, therefore, may provide potential insurgents with vital information on their likelihood of success.

Rule 14a–12 significantly expands the ability of the registrant and potential insurgents, to "test the waters" through communications prior to furnishing a proxy statement to shareholders. Solicitations under Rule 14a–12 may be either oral or written. In the case of written communications, the soliciting parties must identify participants in the solicitation (e.g., the insurgent) as well as describe "their direct or indirect interests, by security holdings or otherwise" in the registrant. Rule 14a–12(a)(1)(i). Soliciting parties must also include with written solicitations a "prominent legend in clear, plain language advising security holders to read the proxy statement when it is available. . . ." Rule 14a–12(a)(1)(ii).

Oral solicitations do not require the delivery of a proxy statement under Rule 14a–12. This opens up the possibility that soliciting parties may shift from written to oral communications. However, telephone scripts, presentation materials, and electronic communications are written communications for purposes of Rule 14a–12.

Any soliciting materials "published, sent or given to security holders" pursuant to Rule 14a–12(a) must be filed with the SEC no later than the first date on which the information is disseminated to the security holders. Rule 14a–12(b). Whether solicitations under Rule 14a–12 take place through oral or written communications, a form of proxy (i.e., a proxy voting card) may not be given to any shareholder receiving a solicitation under Rule 14a–12 until the shareholder has also received a definitive proxy statement under Rule 14a–3(a).

Rule 14a–12 has opened up the proxy solicitation process prior to the furnishing of a proxy statement. At the same time, electronic communication over the Internet (including web sites, message boards, and emails) has drastically reduced the cost of communication. Lower costs combined with a more relaxed regulatory attitude under Rule 14a–12 have given rise to increased communication regarding proxy contests and reduced barriers for insurgents seeking to wage a proxy contest. In an early example, Travis Street Partners LLC, an investment fund, used the Internet in a proxy contest to elect three directors to the ICO Inc. board. Travis Street used its web page and message board to keep interested parties informed of its proxy campaign. Not only did Travis Street keep investors informed about the contest, the Internet provided Travis Street with valuable information on potential supporters who registered their email addresses and other contact information on Travis Street's web page.

Until recently, proxy contests were exceedingly rare. Insurgents faced high costs in identifying large shareholders. Even when large shareholders were identified, insurgents faced SEC review of all communication with the shareholders as potential proxy solicitations. In addition, almost all such contests failed, with incumbent directors retaining their seats. Today, an insurgent putting forth a competing slate of director nominees may make oral and written solicitations even before filing a preliminary proxy statement with the SEC under Rule 14a–12. Incumbents receive no formal notice of the outsider's efforts to drum up support for a proxy contest until the outsider files the preliminary proxy statement with the SEC. Insurgents may also persuade large institutional investors to join their efforts to displace the incumbents. Large institutional investors can publicly announce their intentions on the proxy contest vote pursuant to Rule 14a–1(*l*) without triggering the proxy rules. The insurgent may also take out newspaper ads and make other forms of public communication under Rule 14a–3(f) without distributing a proxy statement. Two significant barriers remain. Insurgents who individually or together with a group beneficially own more than 5% of the target company's stock must disclose their holdings and intentions under § 13(d) of the Exchange Act. Rule 14a–9 antifraud liability also applies to all proxy solicitations.

HYPOTHETICAL TWO

Paul of MPERS has not yet filed a definitive proxy statement with the SEC. Nonetheless, the financial markets are buzzing with rumors of Paul's impending proxy contest for control of Sterling Cooper's board. Which proxy solicitation requirements apply to the following communications?

1. *Scenario One:* Paul sends out a short letter to all the major institutional investor shareholders of Sterling Cooper. The letter describes at length the lack of cost controls at Sterling Cooper and the drinking problem of Don, the CEO, who was recently arrested for drunk driving.

Paul does not mention the identities of his competing slate of directors, but does state: "I am presently assembling a team of highly respected nominees to Sterling Cooper's board and will provide more information later with the definitive proxy statement."

2.   *Scenario Two:* What if Paul also mails out a detailed proposal for how he would turn Sterling Cooper's business around to the company's ten largest outside shareholders? The mailing contains confidential information about Paul's proposed business strategy.

3.   *Scenario Three:* What if Paul, instead of sending out the letter to selected institutional investors, publishes it in the *Wall Street Journal*?

C. RULE 14a–9 ANTIFRAUD LIABILITY

As with the other areas of the securities laws, the proxy rules provide for antifraud liability to ensure the veracity of disclosed information. Rule 14a–9's scope is limited to solicitations subject to § 14(a). Neither Rule 14a–9 nor § 14(a) explicitly provide a private cause of action. Should courts nonetheless recognize a cause of action to enforce Rule 14a–9 and § 14(a)?

J.I. Case Co. v. Borak
377 U.S. 426 (1964).

■ CLARK, J.

This is a civil action brought by respondent, a stockholder of petitioner J. I. Case Company, charging deprivation of the pre-emptive rights of respondent and other shareholders by reason by a merger between Case and the American Tractor Corporation. It is alleged that the merger was effected through the circulation of a false and misleading proxy statement by those proposing the merger. . . . We consider only the question of whether § 27 of the [Exchange] Act authorizes a federal cause of action for rescission or damages to a corporate stockholder with respect to a consummated merger which was authorized pursuant to the use of a proxy statement alleged to contain false and misleading statements violative of § 14(a) of the Act. . . .

I.

Respondent, the owner of 2,000 shares of common stock of Case acquired prior to the merger, brought this suit . . . seeking to enjoin a proposed merger between Case and the American Tractor Corporation (ATC) on various grounds, including . . . misrepresentations contained in the material circulated to obtain proxies. . . . They alleged: that petitioners, or their predecessors, solicited or permitted their names to be used in the solicitation of proxies of Case stockholders for use at a special stockholders' meeting at which the proposed merger with ATC was to be voted upon; that the proxy solicitation material so circulated was false and misleading in violation of § 14(a) of the Act and Rule 14a–9 which the Commission had promulgated thereunder; that the merger was approved at the meeting by a small margin of votes and was thereafter consummated; that the merger would not have been approved but for the false and misleading statements in the proxy solicitation material; and that Case stockholders were damaged thereby. The respondent sought judgment holding the merger void and damages for himself and all other stockholders similarly situated, as well as such further relief "as equity shall require."

* * *

II.

It appears clear that private parties have a right under § 27 to bring suit for violation of § 14(a) of the Act. Indeed, this section specifically grants the appropriate District Courts jurisdiction over "all suits in equity and actions at law brought to enforce any liability or duty created" under the Act. The petitioners make no concessions, however, emphasizing that Congress made no specific reference to a private right of action in § 14(a); that, in any event, the right . . . should be limited to prospective relief only. . . .

III.

* * *

The purpose of § 14(a) is to prevent management or others from obtaining authorization for corporate action by means of deceptive or inadequate disclosure in proxy solicitation. The section stemmed from the congressional belief that "(f)air corporate suffrage is an important right that should attach to every equity security bought on a public exchange." It was intended to "control the conditions under which proxies may be solicited with a view to preventing the recurrence of abuses which * * * (had) frustrated the free exercise of the voting rights of stockholders." "Too often proxies are solicited without explanation to the stockholder of the real nature of the questions for which authority to cast his vote is sought." These broad remedial purposes are evidenced in the language of the section which makes it "unlawful for any person * * * to solicit or to permit the use of his name to solicit any proxy or consent or authorization in respect of any security * * * registered on any national securities exchange in contravention of such rules and regulations as the Commission may prescribe as necessary or appropriate in the public interest or for the protection of investors." While this language makes no specific reference to a private right of action, among its chief purposes is "the protection of investors," which certainly implies the availability of judicial relief where necessary to achieve that result. . . .

[T]he possibility of civil damages or injunctive relief serves as a most effective weapon in the enforcement of the proxy requirements. The Commission advises that it examines over 2,000 proxy statements annually and each of them must necessarily be expedited. Time does not permit an independent examination of the facts set out in the proxy material and this results in the Commission's acceptance of the representations contained therein at their face value, unless contrary to other material on file with it. Indeed, on the allegations of respondent's complaint, the proxy material failed to disclose alleged unlawful market manipulation of the stock of ATC, and this unlawful manipulation would not have been apparent to the Commission until after the merger.

We, therefore, believe that under the circumstances here it is the duty of the courts to be alert to provide such remedies as are necessary to make effective the congressional purpose. . . .

It is for the federal courts "to adjust their remedies so as to grant the necessary relief" where federally secured rights are invaded. "And it is also well settled that where legal rights have been invaded, and a federal statute provides for a general right to sue for such invasion, federal courts may use any available remedy to make good the wrong done." Section 27 grants the District Courts jurisdiction "of all suits in equity and actions at law brought to enforce any liability or duty created by this title * * *."

Nor do we find merit in the contention that such remedies are limited to prospective relief. . . . [I]f federal jurisdiction were limited to the granting of declaratory relief, victims of deceptive proxy statements would be obliged to go into state courts for remedial relief. And if the law of the State happened to attach no responsibility to the use of misleading proxy statements, the whole purpose of the section might be frustrated. Furthermore, the hurdles that the victim might face (such as separate suits, . . . security for expenses statutes, bringing in all parties necessary for complete relief, etc.) might well prove insuperable to effective relief.

IV.

Our finding that federal courts have the power to grant all necessary remedial relief is not to be construed as any indication of what we believe to be the necessary and appropriate relief in this case. We are concerned here only with a determination that federal jurisdiction for this purpose does exist. Whatever remedy is necessary must await the trial on the merits. . . .

* * *

QUESTIONS

1. The Court points to the goal of "protection of investors" as implying "the availability of judicial relief where necessary to achieve that result." Is this rationale too broad? Do the securities laws have goals other than investor protection?

2. Why would it be costly for shareholders to go to state court to seek damages and other relief for fraud in the proxy statement?

3. Is *Borak* consistent with Court's later concern in *Blue Chip*, *Virginia Bankshares*, *Gustafson*, and *Central Bank of Denver* over speculative and frivolous lawsuits?

———

The *Borak* Court dealt with the ability of a shareholder to bring a private cause of action under Rule 14a–9. What about the registrant itself? Can the incumbent board authorize the corporation to sue insurgent shareholders for violating Rule 14a–9? What about for a violation of the other proxy rules? Courts have generally held that the registrant can bring suit to obtain equitable remedies for violations of the proxy rules. *See Studebaker Corp. v. Gittlin*, 360 F.2d 692, 695 (2d

Cir. 1966); *Greater Iowa Corp. v. McLendon*, 378 F.2d 783, 794 (8th Cir. 1967). Allowing the registrant to sue to enforce the proxy rules reduces the burden on the SEC to police proxies. Moreover, the registrant will have better information than the SEC as to the use of proxies relating to the registrant's own securities. The incumbent board of directors, however, may use corporate funds to harass insurgents to raise the cost of a proxy contest, thereby further entrenching the incumbents.

Borak did not address the state of mind plaintiffs need to show to bring a Rule 14a–9 cause of action. Should there be strict liability for false proxy solicitations under Rule 14a–9? Or should liability require a showing of negligence, recklessness, or actual knowledge of the falsehood? Courts have rejected the strict liability approach, but they are split on whether the state of mind required should be negligence, *see, e.g., Gould v. American-Hawaiian S. S. Co.*, 535 F.2d 761 (3d Cir. 1976) (negligence sufficient for outside directors), or scienter, *see Adams v. Standard Knitting Mills, Inc.*, 623 F.2d 422 (6th Cir. 1980) (requiring scienter for accountants).

The Supreme Court in *Borak* also did not decide what causal connection between fraud in a proxy solicitation and harm to shareholders engaged in a vote was required to establish liability. Should plaintiffs have to establish that each shareholder read the fraudulent proxy solicitation and changed their vote in reliance on the solicitation?

Mills v. Electric Auto-Lite Co.

396 U.S. 375 (1970).

■ HARLAN, J.

This case requires us to consider a basic aspect of the implied private right of action for violation of § 14(a) of the Securities Exchange Act of 1934 recognized by this Court in *J. I. Case Co. v. Borak*, 377 U.S. 426 (1964). As in *Borak* the asserted wrong is that a corporate merger was accomplished through the use of a proxy statement that was materially false or misleading. The question with which we deal is what causal relationship must be shown between such a statement and the merger to establish a cause of action based on the violation of the Act.

I

Petitioners were shareholders of the Electric Auto-Lite Company until 1963, when it was merged into Mergenthaler Linotype Company. They brought suit on the day before the shareholders' meeting at which the vote was to take place on the merger against Auto-Lite, Mergenthaler, and a third company, American Manufacturing Company, Inc. The complaint sought an injunction against the voting by Auto-Lite's management of all proxies obtained by means of an allegedly misleading proxy solicitation; however, it did not seek a temporary restraining order, and the voting went ahead as scheduled the following day. Several months later petitioners filed an amended complaint, seeking to have the merger set aside and to obtain such other relief as might be proper.

[Petitioners] alleged that the proxy statement sent out by the Auto-Lite management to solicit shareholders' votes in favor of the merger was misleading, in violation of § 14(a) of the Act and SEC Rule 14a–9 thereunder. Petitioners recited that before the merger Mergenthaler owned over 50% of the outstanding shares of Auto-Lite common stock, and had been in control of Auto-Lite for two years. American Manufacturing in turn owned about one-third of the outstanding shares of Mergenthaler, and for two years had been in voting control of Mergenthaler and, through it, of Auto-Lite. Petitioners charged that in light of these circumstances the proxy statement was misleading in that it told Auto-Lite shareholders that their board of directors recommended approval of the merger without also informing them that all 11 of Auto-Lite's directors were nominees of Mergenthaler and were under the "control and domination of Mergenthaler." . . .

On petitioners' motion for summary judgment ... the District Court for the Northern District of Illinois ruled as a matter of law that the claimed defect in the proxy statement was, in light of the circumstances in which the statement was made, a material omission. The District Court concluded, from its reading of the *Borak* opinion, that it had to hold a hearing on the issue whether there was "a causal connection between the finding that there has been a violation of the disclosure requirements of § 14(a) and the alleged injury to the plaintiffs" before it could consider what remedies would be appropriate.

After holding such a hearing, the court found that under the terms of the merger agreement, an affirmative vote of two-thirds of the Auto-Lite shares was required for approval of the merger, and that the respondent companies owned and controlled about 54% of the outstanding shares. Therefore, to obtain authorization of the merger, respondents had to secure the approval of a substantial number of the minority shareholders. At the stockholders' meeting, approximately 950,000 shares, out of 1,160,000 shares outstanding, were voted in favor of the merger. This included 317,000 votes obtained by proxy from the minority shareholders, votes that were "necessary and indispensable to the approval of the merger." The District Court concluded that a causal relationship had thus been shown. . . .

[R]espondents took an interlocutory appeal to the Court of Appeals for the Seventh Circuit. That court affirmed the District Court's conclusion that the proxy statement was materially deficient, but reversed on the question of causation. The court acknowledged that, if an injunction had been sought a sufficient time before the stockholders' meeting, "corrective measures would have been appropriate." However, since this suit was brought too late for preventive action, the courts had to determine "whether the misleading statement and omission caused the submission of sufficient proxies," as a prerequisite to a determination of liability under the Act. If the respondents could show, "by a preponderance of probabilities, that the merger would have received a sufficient vote even if the proxy statement had not been misleading in the respect found," petitioners would be entitled to no relief of any kind.

The Court of Appeals acknowledged that this test corresponds to the common-law fraud test of whether the injured party relied on the misrepresentation. However, rightly concluding that "(r)eliance by thousands of individuals, as here, can scarcely be inquired into," the court ruled that the issue was to be determined by proof of the fairness of the terms of the merger. If respondents could show that the merger had merit and was fair to the minority shareholders, the trial court would be justified in concluding that a sufficient number of shareholders would have approved the merger had there been no deficiency in the proxy statement. In that case respondents would be entitled to a judgment in their favor.

* * *

II

As we stressed in *Borak*, § 14(a) stemmed from a congressional belief that "(f)air corporate suffrage is an important right that should attach to every equity security bought on a public exchange." The provision was intended to promote "the free exercise of the voting rights of stockholders" by ensuring that proxies would be solicited with "explanation to the stockholder of the real nature of the questions for which authority to cast his vote is sought." The decision below, by permitting all liability to be foreclosed on the basis of a finding that the merger was fair, would allow the stockholders to be by-passed, at least where the only legal challenge to the merger is a suit for retrospective relief after the meeting has been held. A judicial appraisal of the merger's merits could be substituted for the actual and informed vote of the stockholders.

The result would be to insulate from private redress an entire category of proxy violations—those relating to matters other than the terms of the merger. Even outrageous misrepresentations in a proxy solicitation, if they did not relate to the terms of the transaction, would give rise to no cause of action under § 14(a). Particularly if carried over to enforcement actions by the Securities and Exchange Commission itself, such a result would subvert the congressional purpose of ensuring full and fair disclosure to shareholders.

Further, recognition of the fairness of the merger as a complete defense would confront small shareholders with an additional obstacle to making a successful challenge to a proposal recommended through a defective proxy statement. The risk that they would be unable to rebut the corporation's evidence of the fairness of the proposal, and thus to establish their cause of action, would be bound to discourage such shareholders from the private enforcement of the proxy rules that "provides a necessary supplement to Commission action."

Such a frustration of the congressional policy is not required by anything in the wording of the statute or in our opinion in the *Borak* case. . . . Use of a solicitation that is materially misleading is itself a violation of law, as the Court of Appeals recognized in stating that injunctive relief would be available to remedy such a defect if sought prior to the stockholders' meeting. In *Borak*, which came to this Court on a dismissal of the complaint, the Court limited its inquiry to whether a violation of § 14(a) gives rise to "a federal cause of action for rescission or damages." . . . In the present case there has been a hearing specifically directed to the causation problem. The question before the Court is whether the facts found on the basis of that hearing are sufficient in law to establish petitioners' cause of action, and we conclude that they are.

Where the misstatement or omission in a proxy statement has been shown to be "material," as it was found to be here, that determination itself indubitably embodies a conclusion that the defect was of such a character that it might have been considered important by a reasonable shareholder who was in the process of deciding how to vote. This requirement that the defect have a significant propensity to affect the voting process is found in the express terms of Rule 14a–9, and it adequately serves the purpose of ensuring that a cause of action cannot be established by proof of a defect so trivial, or so unrelated to the transaction for which approval is sought, that correction of the defect or imposition of liability would not further the interests protected by § 14(a).

In this case, where the misleading aspect of the solicitation involved failure to reveal a serious conflict of interest on the part of the directors, the Court of Appeals concluded that the crucial question in determining materiality was "whether the minority shareholders were sufficiently alerted to the board's relationship to their adversary to be on their guard." An adequate disclosure of this relationship would have warned the stockholders to give more careful scrutiny to the terms of the merger than they might to one recommended by an entirely disinterested board. Thus, the failure to make such a disclosure was found to be a material defect "as a matter of law," thwarting the informed decision at which the statute aims, regardless of whether the terms of the merger were such that a reasonable stockholder would have approved the transaction after more careful analysis.

There is no need to supplement this requirement, as did the Court of Appeals, with a requirement of proof of whether the defect actually had a decisive effect on the voting. Where there has been a finding of materiality, a shareholder has made a sufficient showing of causal relationship between the violation and the injury for which he seeks redress if, as here, he proves that the proxy solicitation itself, rather than the particular defect in the solicitation materials, was an essential link in the accomplishment of the transaction. This objective test will avoid the impracticalities of determining how many votes were affected, and, by resolving doubts in favor of those the statute is designed to protect, will effectuate the congressional policy of ensuring that the shareholders are able to make an informed choice when they are consulted on corporate transactions.[7]

* * *

NOTES

1. *Virginia Bankshares.* The *Mills* Court reserved the question of whether a § 14(a) cause of action would lie if the proxy solicitation was not an "essential link" to the completion of the transaction alleged to have harmed the shareholder-plaintiffs. The Supreme Court answered that question in *Virginia Bankshares, Inc. v. Sandberg*, 501 U.S. 1083 (1991), rejecting plaintiffs' "speculative" causation argument that the directors would have wanted to avoid bad public relations from proceeding with a

---

[7] We need not decide in this case whether causation could be shown where the management controls a sufficient number of shares to approve the transaction without any votes from the minority. . . .

merger without minority shareholder approval, even though such approval was not required under state law. The *Virginia Bankshares* Court reserved the question whether § 14(a) provides a cause of action for state remedies, such as appraisal rights, lost as a result of a misleading proxy solicitation. Lower courts have generally held that it does.

QUESTIONS

1. If a court determines that the terms of a merger are "fair," why should shareholders have an antifraud claim? What is the loss to shareholders from any misstatement or omission in the proxy solicitation materials if they received "fair" terms?

2. What, in addition to materiality, is required to show causation? How does the Court's holding in *Electric Auto-Lite* differ from the Court's views on the relationship of materiality to loss causation for purposes of Rule 10b–5 in *Dura Pharmaceuticals v. Broudo* (excerpted in Chapter 5)?

3. What sort of "impracticalities" are avoided through the Court's use of materiality in determining whether causation exists for a § 14(a) claim? What does *Electric Auto-Lite* have in common with the *Halliburton II* case (excerpted in Chapter 5)?

4. In rejecting the court of appeals' hypothetical vote approach, the Court worried that § 14(a)'s goal "full and fair disclosure to shareholders" would be subverted "if carried over to enforcement actions by the Securities and Exchange Commission itself." Should the same standards apply to both SEC and private rights of action? Do you agree with the SEC that private rights of action are a necessary supplement to the SEC's enforcement efforts in this area?

D. MANAGING THE COSTS OF PROXY SOLICITATIONS

The federal proxy regime aims to ensure that all shareholders have equal and fair access to vote; the tools used to accomplish this goal, however, have their costs. Insurgents who nominate a competing slate for the board of directors or who seek to influence the shareholder vote on whether to ratify a merger, for example, face mandatory disclosure requirements under Schedule 14A as well as potential antifraud liability under § 14(a) and Rule 14a–9. Even those who are not active insurgents, but instead merely want to discuss an upcoming proxy vote with other shareholders, may potentially fall under the definition of a proxy solicitation under Rule 14a–1(*l*) and thereby become subject to mandatory disclosure and antifraud liability. Although there are exceptions, understanding these exceptions likely requires the assistance of an attorney.

The costs for an insurgent are not limited to the costs of complying with the federal securities regime. Consider what other costs might affect an insurgent waging a proxy contest to change the board of directors. At a minimum, insurgents must communicate with shareholders. Although broad based communications to all the shareholders may have some effect, insurgents often will focus their efforts on the shareholders with the largest holdings.

HYPOTHETICAL THREE

Paul, the head of MPERS, has decided to proceed with a proxy contest to nominate a competing slate of nominees to Sterling Cooper's board. Paul has filed the required Schedule 14A and now seeks to communicate directly with Sterling Cooper's shareholders. You are Paul's advisor, and he asks you what his next steps should be.

1.   COMMUNICATING WITH SHAREHOLDERS

One of the major costs facing shareholders attempting to solicit proxies during a vote is the cost of identifying and communicating with other shareholders. The securities laws mandate disclosure regarding principal shareholders through several mechanisms:

- Section 16(a) of the Exchange Act—Beneficial owners of more than 10 percent of any class of any equity security of companies that are required to register under § 12 and must file any changes in ownership on Form 4.

- Beneficial owners of "more than five percent of any class of the registrant's voting securities" (as defined in Item 403 of Regulation S–K) must be identified in multiple securities filing documents, including the annual Form 10–K, the proxy statement under Schedule 14A, and the registration statement under Form S–1.

- Williams Act—Under § 13(d) of the Exchange Act, shareholders that hold more than 5 percent of any class of equity (either individually or working in concert with a group) must file a Schedule 13D, publicly disclosing their share ownership.

These disclosure rules allow insurgents to easily identify shareholders with over 5 percent beneficial ownership. Most public corporations, however, have few shareholders with more than 5 percent. Even when there is such a shareholder, the shareholder may already have close ties with management and hold seats on the board of directors, making the shareholder unlikely to support any insurgent proxy contest. Identifying smaller shareholders will not be so easy, but may nonetheless be crucial to an insurgent. For an insurgent to have a chance at dislodging incumbent board members, the insurgent must obtain the support of a wide range of medium-sized institutional investors.

Consider the top four beneficial owners of Sterling Cooper as disclosed in the company's most recent proxy statement:

Name and Address of Beneficial Ownership	Amount and Nature of Beneficial Ownership	Percent of Class
Don Draper	2,462,500	9.85%
Holloway Investments	1,725,000	6.90%
Roger Sterling	1,400,000	5.60%
Bertram Cooper	1,162,500	4.25%

As reported in the proxy statement, two of the four large block shareholders, Don Draper and Roger Sterling, are both founders and employees of Sterling Cooper, and Don is also the CEO and sits on the board. Neither Don nor Roger would be likely to vote for any insurgent. The largest outside shareholder, Holloway Investments, has no reported ties with Sterling Cooper other than its share ownership. Bertram Cooper is the former CEO of Sterling Cooper; like Holloway Investments, it is difficult to predict how he would vote in a proxy contest. Although former CEOs generally are sympathetic with current managers, Bertram has specific grievances with the management of Sterling Cooper. To overcome the votes in the hands of Don and Roger as well as the tendency of most public shareholders to side with management, an insurgent would have to find more shareholders than just Holloway Investments and Bertram to change the Sterling Cooper board of directors.

The corporation itself is the lowest cost source for identifying the corporation's shareholders of record. Rule 14a–7 of the Exchange Act requires the corporation to assist the security holder in communicating with the other shareholders in certain circumstances. Upon a request by a security holder under Rule 14a–7, the corporation must either mail the security holder's soliciting materials or provide a security holder with a list consisting of all the shareholders of record. The requesting security holder does not get a free ride, however; the corporation is entitled to "reasonable expenses" from the requesting security holder. For a typical public company, the expenses can total close to $20,000.

A corporation that chooses to mail out an insurgent's materials to shareholders under Rule 14a–7 can thereby avoid providing the identity of its shareholders to the insurgent. If an insurgent wants to communicate directly with larger shareholders, obtaining the shareholders' names is critical. Insurgents have other means of uncovering shareholder identity. Institutional investment managers who exercise investment discretion over accounts holding certain specified § 13(f) equity securities with an aggregate fair market value of $100 million are required to file a Form 13–F detailing their holdings of these securities. The SEC publishes an update to the list of § 13(f) securities on a quarterly basis. Form 13–F filings do not cover all shareholders, however, disclosing only institutional investment managers. Private data sources, such as Thomson Reuters, also provide ownership and contact information for institutional shareholders of public corporations. Finally, state corporate law may afford access to the company's shareholder list, although the insurgent may need to file suit to get it.

Even when insurgents know the identities of the major shareholders, communicating with them can be quite costly. Insurgents that use Rule 14a–7 may have the corporation mail packets of written materials to shareholders. Written materials, however, are rarely effective in convincing a shareholder to take sides with an insurgent against management. If you were a busy investment manager and received a written package from an unknown shareholder about a possible proxy contest involving one of the companies in your portfolio, what would you do? Would you even bother to read the materials? Insurgents typically focus instead on more targeted communication with certain larger institutional investors, including public pension funds and socially responsible funds that often are more willing to oppose incumbent managers.

Even after identifying important institutional investors, an insurgent must then identify who makes decisions with respect to proxy votes. Although some institutions decide internally how to vote their shares, many institutions obtain advice on how to vote from proxy voting services such as Institutional Shareholder Services Inc. (ISS). Persuading ISS to support an insurgent's campaign, substantially promotes their prospects of success.

Establishing communication with influential shareholders is only the first step toward obtaining votes. Insurgents, particularly if unknown to shareholders, must convince often skeptical shareholders to side with them. To do so, insurgents must expend considerable resources communicating with a handful of shareholders. Obtaining the public support of some of these large shareholders as well as positive press reports may garner support from other shareholders.

In recent years, shareholder voting has undergone dramatic changes that reduce the costs of waging a proxy contest. In 2007, the SEC adopted a "notice and access" electronic proxy delivery system, available generally for proxy solicitations other than those relating to business combinations. Exchange Act Rule 14a–16. Under the voluntary notice and access system, public companies may choose to provide proxy materials, including the proxy statement, annual report, and form of proxy, through an Internet posting available for investors. An issuer that opts for electronic delivery must mail notice to shareholders at least 40 days in advance of the annual meeting informing the shareholders of the Internet availability of proxy materials (e.g., posted at the issuer's website), among other things. Issuers may also supply the form of the proxy card on the website and have investors execute the proxy card online as long as the issuer ensures that the investors have access to the proxy statement and annual report online as well. Issuers must send investors either hard copies or an email of the proxy material upon request.

Significantly, the SEC also made a similar "notice and access" electronic delivery system available to soliciting persons other than the issuer, such as insurgents waging a proxy contest. Electronic delivery of the proxy materials coupled with electronic proxy voting potentially may greatly reduce the expense facing dissidents in a proxy contest as well as increase the likelihood that the dissidents will receive a positive response from dispersed shareholders (who otherwise may simply discard mailed proxy materials).

Market developments have also bolstered dissident shareholders. Shareholder activists recently have made use of vote buying to magnify their voting power in proxy contests. Some activists will borrow shares from other investors in order to vote them in a specific proxy contest. Other activists will take a long position in shares (to obtain the voting power), while hedging the economic risk of this long position through equity swaps and other techniques. Dissidents sponsoring a proxy contest may either buy votes themselves or rely on the support of other activists (typically hedge funds) purchasing votes.

Instead of a high stakes proxy contests for the entire board, dissidents may seek to use "short slate" proxy contests in which the dissidents nominate less than a full slate of directors. Through a short slate contest, the dissident typically seeks to put only a minority number of directors onto the board of directors. Shareholder activists may use short slate contests as leverage in negotiating for corporate policy changes without threatening the current management's control of the corporation. Carl Icahn, for example, commenced a short slate proxy contest in 2007 to nominate a minority of directors to the board of Motorola, Inc. as part of his efforts to force Motorola to buy back $20 billion of its shares. Icahn represented his short slate campaign as a move to "demand accountability" from Motorola's board. Even with ISS' support, Icahn lost. In other situations, however, shareholder activists armed with the threat to nominate a short slate have obtained settlements from the targeted companies. Consequently, shareholder activists have been waging short slate proxy contests with increasing frequency.

2.   MANAGEMENT DEFENSIVE TACTICS

Incumbent managers are unlikely to remain passive when confronted with a proxy contest or opposition to a merger; managers will also lobby major shareholders. Under state law, these lobbying efforts are typically reimbursed by the company.

Managers may also adopt additional defensive tactics to stymie insurgents in a proxy contest. The first and more common countermeasure is the implementation of the so called "classified" or "staggered" board. Directors in a staggered board are typically elected for staggered three-year terms. At any one annual meeting, shareholders may only elect one-third of the board. A proxy contest to change the control of a corporation therefore requires two consecutive campaigns to win control. Adopting a classified board, however, typically requires shareholder approval, which is unlikely to be forthcoming, particularly in the midst of a proxy contest. Thus, this defensive measure must have been adopted well in advance of the proxy contest, typically before a company does its initial public offering.

Second, managers may attempt to change the date of the annual meeting, delaying the meeting to forestall a change of control through a proxy contest. Changing the meeting date after the establishment of a record date may invalidate proxies already collected by the insurgents. The insurgent must then re-solicit shareholders to obtain a new set of proxies for the later meeting date. State corporate law, however, limits the ability of managers to change the meeting date if the change is intended to entrench incumbents.

Third, managers may inflict legal costs on insurgents. Section 14(a) and Rule 14a–9 provide antifraud liability for material misstatements and half-truths in proxy solicitations. In theory, antifraud liability promotes accuracy, enabling shareholders to make informed voting decisions. In practice, antifraud liability may have a more pernicious impact on insurgents waging proxy contests. As a defensive tactic, management may bring a lawsuit against an insurgent for providing a materially misleading proxy statement. Even if the proxy statement is not deficient, the prospect of having to defend a lawsuit raises the costs and imposes potential delay on an insurgent.

3. REIMBURSEMENT OF EXPENSES

Proxy contests are costly. An insurgent who brings a contest to replace the directors out of a desire to increase the value of the corporation is acting on behalf of all the shareholders. State corporate law, however, generally does not provide for mandatory reimbursement of insurgents. Instead, insurgents are reimbursed only if they win control over the board of directors and thereby are able to obtain board approval for reimbursement. Reimbursement must also be ratified by the other shareholders. Shareholder activists who bring a proxy contest and fail to win control are not reimbursed by the corporation for their expenses under state corporate law, even if they secure corporate governance reforms. Similarly, activists who solicit proxies opposing a management-sponsored proposal (e.g., a merger) are not reimbursed by the corporation even if their opposition benefits all shareholders.

Why should the corporation reimburse expenses? Payments from the corporation represent a pro rata reduction in value for all shareholders. So the real issue is whether the group of all shareholders should pay for the activists' efforts. If the activist's efforts benefits all shareholders in bringing a contest (e.g., replacing underperforming managers), then reimbursement makes sense.

Why not reimburse *all* proxy solicitations, whether or not there is a change in control? Lack of reimbursement deters activists from potentially value-enhancing solicitations. Without reimbursement, such activists bear all the costs of engaging in proxy solicitations, but capture only a small part of the benefit. Not all activists, however, will act in the best interests of all the shareholders. A universal reimbursement rule would require that corporate money be used to subsidize activists engaged in self-interested solicitations.

Although state corporate law generally does not treat insurgents very generously, the SEC has forced corporations to support shareholder activists indirectly through the proxy rules. We discuss this support next as part of the broader discussion of how much power over the corporation should the securities law give to shareholders.

III. SHAREHOLDER DEMOCRACY

Shareholders of publicly-held corporations have little influence over corporate policy. Shareholders vote infrequently; everyday business decisions, as well as fundamental questions of business strategy, are vested with the board of directors under state corporate law.

This separation between ownership and control brings many benefits for investors. Dispersed investors in the public markets typically do not want to expend time or effort monitoring managers or setting corporate policy. Giving investors greater say in the corporation will not change corporate policy very much if investors are rationally apathetic. More perniciously, some shareholders may use additional power to hold the company hostage, extracting side payments at the expense of the other shareholders. Passive shareholders may prefer to keep shareholders out of the day-to-day operation of the corporation.

Separating ownership and control, however, leads to the possibility that the managers may pursue their own agenda at the expense of shareholders. State corporate law tries to keep management in check by giving shareholders the power to elect directors. Agency costs within the corporation are also limited by court review of business decisions (within the limits of the business judgment rule) and the possibility of a hostile takeover.

Within that framework, shareholder voting has the potential to play an important role in controlling corporate agency costs. Shareholders (particularly those with only small ownership interests) are, however, unlikely to expend much energy in deciding how to vote. Shareholders with small interests will view their vote as unlikely to be pivotal, making it even less likely that they will spend time or energy on deciding how to vote.

In thinking about shareholder voting, two issues are paramount. First, which issues should be put to a shareholder vote? Rational apathy among shareholders leaves open the risk that a small group of shareholders may use the shareholder voting process to promote their own narrow self-interest. A shareholder may gain from the publicity surrounding a shareholder vote, even if it does not benefit other shareholders. Managers may also pay off a more active shareholder to ward off a possible shareholder vote, again at the expense of the group of all shareholders. Many potential shareholder issue proposals, discussed below, never reach an actual vote. Instead, the shareholder sponsor will negotiate an informal settlement with the corporation's management. Should we ban such settlements? If we do, we will also be banning value-increasing corporate governance changes adopted voluntarily by managers as part of such a settlement.

Second, what role should the SEC play in reducing the costs of shareholder voting? The SEC's primary regulatory tool is disclosure. Is disclosure enough? Should the SEC intervene more actively to reduce the agency costs in firms facing dispersed shareholders?

A. SHAREHOLDER PROPOSALS

In response to the high cost of shareholder voting, the SEC promulgated Rule 14a–8 to promote shareholder "democracy." Rule 14a–8 allows shareholders to piggyback certain types of proposals onto the management's proxy statement for the annual shareholder meeting. If the shareholder proposal and its sponsor meet all of Rule 14a–8's requirements, companies must include the proposal in the company's own proxy statement and include it on the company's proxy. Shareholders cannot, however, use Rule 14a–8 to nominate their own slate of directors or propose a merger. Insurgents waging a proxy contest must find their own means to communicate with shareholders.

Shareholders proposals typically deal with matters involving far smaller sums of money. Some typical proposals:

- Remove a corporation's poison pill takeover defensive device

- Include more diversity on the board of directors

- Expand the company's equal employment policies

- Report on or improve the corporation's labor standards

At first glance, the proxy rules appear generous to shareholder-sponsored issue proposals. Unlike other SEC rules we have examined in this casebook, Rule 14a–8 is written in "plain English." (The rules were revised when the SEC was making "plain English" a priority for company filings. The SEC quickly lost interest in the project. Query: Would drafting the rest of the securities laws in the same format make them more comprehensible?) Rule 14a–8(a), for example, describes shareholder proposals as follows: "A shareholder proposal is your recommendation or requirement that the company and/or its board of directors take action, which you intend to present at a meeting of the company's shareholders. Your proposal should state as clearly as possible the course of action that you believe the company should follow."

Rule 14a–8 imposes both eligibility and procedural requirements on sponsors of shareholder proposals. The Rule also excludes certain types of proposals altogether. Dropping out of the coverage of Rule 14a–8 does not necessarily mean the end of the road for a proposal. The shareholder sponsor can always solicit proxies on its own for the proposal. Doing so, however, will require the sponsor to incur the costs of distribution. Although the Internet drastically reduces such costs, this has not proved to be a viable alternative to the Rule 14a–8 process.

1. ELIGIBILITY AND PROCEDURAL REQUIREMENTS

Rule 14a–8 sets eligibility requirements for shareholders wishing to include a shareholder proposal. Sponsors must be the record or beneficial owner of at least 1% or $2,000 of the outstanding securities entitled to vote, and they must have held that amount continuously for at least one year prior to the date the proposal is submitted to the company. Sponsors must continue to hold onto these securities through the date of the shareholders' meeting (Rule 14a–8(b)). For most publicly-held corporations, the relevant constraint will be the $2,000 in share holding. For example, Sterling Cooper, a relatively small public corporation, has a market capitalization of $500 million, with 25 million outstanding shares. Shareholders attempting to meet the 1% requirement would need to hold $5 million worth of Sterling Cooper common shares. The $2,000 threshold is considerably easier to meet; a Sterling Cooper shareholder would only need to hold 100 shares.

Eligible shareholders must then meet several procedural requirements:

- Sponsors may make only one proposal per shareholders' meeting. Rule 14a–8(c).
- The proposal must not exceed 500 words. Rule 14a–8(d).
- Sponsors must submit the proposal to the company no later than 120 days prior to the calendar date corresponding to when the company sent out its proxy statement for the previous year's annual meeting. Rule 14a–8(e).
- Sponsors (or their representatives) must appear at the annual shareholder meeting. Rule 14a–8(h).

The company bears the burden of proof if it rejects a shareholder proposal. Rule 14a–8(g). If the company believes that a proposal or its sponsor violates any of the eligibility or procedural requirements, the company generally must notify the sponsor of the deficiency and allow the sponsor to correct the deficiency. Rule 14a–8(f). If the deficiency cannot be remedied (e.g., if the proposal was submitted after the 120 days deadline) then the company does not need to give notice to the sponsor before rejecting the proposal.

Companies that intend to include a statement opposing the shareholder proposal in the company proxy statement must send the opposing statement to the sponsor of the proposal no later than 30 calendar days before they file the definitive proxy statement. Rule 14a–8(m). Rule 14a–8(m) tells shareholder sponsors that "if you believe that the company's opposition to your proposal contains materially false or misleading statements that may violate our anti-fraud rule, Rule 14a–9, you should promptly send to the Commission staff and the company a letter explaining the reasons for your view."

2.   SUBSTANTIVE EXCLUSIONS

Rule 14a–8 limits the type of proposal that must be included in the company's proxy. Recall that Rule 14a–8 is designed to reduce the cost to shareholders of communicating with other shareholders over issues of importance to all shareholders. Allowing proposals furthering a personal grievance would be unlikely to advance this goal. Suppose a shareholder is unhappy with some of Sterling Cooper's clients because she has invested in those clients' competitors. Allowing that one shareholder to vent her unhappiness in Sterling Cooper's proxy statement would probably not increase shareholder welfare.

Rule 14a–8(i) accordingly allows the company to exclude the following proposals that are unlikely to appeal to most shareholders:

- Personal grievance, special interest proposals. Rule 14a–8(i)(4).

- Irrelevant proposals—"If the proposal relates to operations which account for less than 5 percent of the company's total assets at the end of its most recent fiscal year, and for less than 5 percent of its net earnings and gross sales for its most recent fiscal year, and is not otherwise significantly related to the company's business." Rule 14a–8(i)(5).

- Proposals where the corporation lacks the power or authority to implement the proposal. Rule 14a–8(i)(6).

Rule 14a–8 also screens out proposals unlikely to add to overall shareholder welfare because they have already been proposed or are in the process of being dealt with as follows:

- Proposals that have been substantially implemented. Rule 14a–8(i)(10).

- Proposals that substantially duplicate another proposal already on the company's proxy statement. Rule 14a–8(i)(11).

- Resubmitted proposals that were submitted in the past and received little support. Rule 14a–8(i)(12).

Rule 14a–8(i)(12) provides a numerical standard for excluding previously-submitted proposals. If more than three calendar years have passed since the last time a proposal dealing with "substantially the same subject matter" as a prior proposal was included in the company's proxy then the resubmitted proposal is not excludable under Rule 14a–8(i)(12). If three calendar years or less have passed, then Rule 14a–8(i)(12) blocks the resubmitted proposal if the proposal received less than the following thresholds:

3% of the vote if proposed once within the preceding five calendar years;

6% of the vote on its last submission to shareholders if proposed twice previously within the preceding five calendar years; or

10% of the vote on its last submission to shareholders if proposed three times or more previously within the preceding five calendar years.

Proposals that deal with specific corporate policy decisions (and have not already been submitted or otherwise dealt with), on the other hand, are likely to affect the welfare of all shareholders and thus capture the interest of shareholders as a group. One could imagine a regime in which shareholders have more direct voting control over day-to-day corporate policy decisions. State corporate law, however, has generally avoided this course, instead vesting management control of the corporation in the directors. This separation of ownership (in the shareholders) and control (in the officers and directors) allows shareholders to remain passive. The separation of ownership and control therefore appeals to investors seeking a return without having to expend time or resources thinking about corporate policy.

Rule 14a–8 recognizes the desire of shareholders to remain passive and the allocation of authority to the officers and directors by generally blocking proposals that may undermine this division of power under state corporate law. In particular, Rule 14a–8 blocks:

- Proposals that are improper under state law. Rule 14a–8(i)(1).

Proposals that mandate that the board of directors take a specific policy direction (e.g., stipulating that Sterling Cooper avoid certain clients) would be prohibited under state corporate law. Shareholders avoid the Rule 14a–8(i)(1) prohibition for proposals improper under state law by framing their proposals as recommendations, which the SEC considers proper under state law. For example, sponsors will simply *suggest* that a corporation remove its poison pill, rather than demanding its removal.

What impact do precatory proposals have on corporate directors? If a proposal is couched as a suggestion, why should directors pay it any heed? Directors may implement voluntarily a proposal that receives a lot of votes to avoid damaging publicity. Outside directors in particular, may feel obliged to support a proposal that obtains a majority of shareholder votes even if it is only a recommendation. Outside directors interested in their own reputations may not care for the spotlight of media attention surrounding a proxy proposal. If the proposal is renewed, more opportunities are created to establish communication links and relationships between shareholders that may encourage more action by the shareholders. A takeover proposal or proxy contest, for example, may become easier after an issue proposal garners substantial support. Finally, managers seeking to maximize shareholder welfare may be unaware of how popular a proposal is until shareholders vote in its favor. Once made aware of the popularity, managers may voluntarily adopt the proposal.

Rule 14a–8 also blocks:

- Proposals that deal with "ordinary business operations." Rule 14a–8(i)(7).

- Proposals relating to the amount of dividends. Rule 14a–8(i)(13).

- Proposals relating to the election to the board of directors. Rule 14a–8(i)(8).

- Proposals that otherwise conflict with a voting proposal put forward by the company. Rule 14a–8(i)(9).

A sponsor may attempt to craft a proposal outside of the scope of ordinary business operations. For example, a sponsor may propose that the corporation establish a committee to examine the human rights policies of countries in which the corporation does business. Proposals that do not involve "ordinary business operations" may nonetheless be deemed irrelevant from the corporate perspective under Rule 14a–8(i)(5).

Finally, some proposals are excluded as violations of law generally or the proxy rules specifically:

- Proposal if implemented would violate "any state, federal, or foreign law to which it is subject." Rule 14a–8(i)(2).

- Proposal conflicts with any of the proxy rules, including Rule 14a–9's antifraud prohibition. Rule 14a–8(i)(3).

HYPOTHETICAL FOUR

Bertram, a former CEO of Sterling Cooper, has held 4.25% of Sterling Cooper's stock since its founding. He is unhappy with Sterling Cooper's current management and is considering submitting a proposal for inclusion in Sterling Cooper's proxy statement. Consider the following scenarios.

1. *Scenario One:* Bertram submits a proposal mandating that the corporation sever ties with clients that produce cigarettes. Bertram believes doing so will enhance profits because Sterling Cooper will be perceived as a more socially responsible company.

2. *Scenario Two:* Bertram submits a proposal that Sterling Cooper should make a special payment of $1 million to its former CEOs for their long years of service to the company.

3. *Scenario Three:* Bertram submits a proposal recommending that the board of directors study its nomination procedures for directors and assess how diversity can be increased among nominees to the board. Two years ago, Peggy (unrelated to Bertram) submitted a proposal requesting that

Sterling Cooper's board study increasing female representation on the board. The proposal received only 2% of the vote.

4. *Scenario Four:* Bertram submits the following proposal: "Sterling Cooper makes too much profit at the expense of the health of people who buy cigarettes that Sterling Cooper advertises in developing countries. We recommend that Sterling Cooper commission a study on the impact of smoking on the health of consumers."

————

What is left after excluding this list of prohibited subject matters? Shareholders are caught in a bind between the requirements that proposals not be irrelevant (Rule 14a–8(i)(5)) and be within the scope of the corporation's authority (Rule 14a–8(i)(6)) on the one hand, and the requirements that the proposal not deal with "ordinary business operations" (Rule 14a–8(i)(7)) and not otherwise be improper under state law (Rule 14a–8(i)(1)). Most relevant proposals within the corporation's authority are also likely to be proposals that are improper under state law and deal with "ordinary business operations."

The *Lovenheim* case addresses whether a proposal is relevant to a corporation. Rule 14a–8(i)(5) provides both a bright-line numerical cutoff and also a looser standard to determine whether the proposal is "not otherwise significantly related to the company's business." Does the cutoff or the standard control?

Lovenheim v. Iroquois Brands Ltd.

618 F.Supp. 554 (D.D.C. 1985).

■ GASCH, O., DISTRICT JUDGE

I.   BACKGROUND

This matter is now before the Court on plaintiff's motion for preliminary injunction. Plaintiff Peter C. Lovenheim, owner of two hundred shares of common stock in Iroquois Brands, Ltd. (hereinafter "Iroquois/Delaware"), seeks to bar Iroquois/Delaware from excluding from the proxy materials being sent to all shareholders in preparation for an upcoming shareholder meeting information concerning a proposed resolution he intends to offer at the meeting. Mr. Lovenheim's proposed resolution relates to the procedure used to force-feed geese for production of paté de foie gras in France,[2] a type of paté imported by Iroquois/Delaware. Specifically, his resolution calls upon the Directors of Iroquois/Delaware to:

---

[2]   Paté de foie gras is made from the liver of geese. According to Mr. Lovenheim's affidavit, force-feeding is frequently used in order to expand the liver and thereby produce a larger quantity of paté. Mr. Lovenheim's affidavit also contains a description of the force-feeding process:

Force-feeding usually begins when the geese are four months old. On some farms where feeding is mechanized, the bird's body and wings are placed in a metal brace and its neck is stretched. Through a funnel inserted 10–12 inches down the throat of the goose, a machine pumps up to 400 grams of corn-based mash into its stomach. An elastic band around the goose's throat prevents regurgitation. When feeding is manual, a handler uses a funnel and stick to force the mash down.

Plaintiff contends that such force-feeding is a form of cruelty to animals.

form a committee to study the methods by which its French supplier produces paté de foie gras, and report to the shareholders its findings and opinions, based on expert consultation, on whether this production method causes undue distress, pain or suffering to the animals involved and, if so, whether further distribution of this product should be discontinued until a more humane production method is developed.

Mr. Lovenheim's right to compel Iroquois/Delaware to insert information concerning his proposal in the proxy materials turns on the applicability of section 14(a) of the Securities Exchange Act of 1934 and the shareholder proposal rule promulgated by the Securities and Exchange Commission Rule 14a–8. . . .

Iroquois/Delaware has refused to allow information concerning Mr. Lovenheim's proposal to be included in proxy materials being sent in connection with the next annual shareholders meeting. In doing so, Iroquois/Delaware relies on an exception to the general requirement of Rule 14a–8, Rule 14a–8[i](5). That exception provides that an issuer of securities "may omit a proposal and any statement in support thereof" from its proxy statement and form of proxy:

> if the proposal relates to operations which account for less than 5 percent of the issuer's total assets at the end of its most recent fiscal year, and for less than 5 percent of its net earnings and gross sales for its most recent fiscal year, and is not otherwise significantly related to the issuer's business.

Rule 14a–8[i](5).

* * *

II. LIKELIHOOD OF PLAINTIFF PREVAILING ON MERITS

* * *

Iroquois/Delaware's reliance on the argument that this exception applies is based on the following information contained in the affidavit of its president: Iroquois/Delaware has annual revenues of $141 million with $6 million in annual profits and $78 million in assets. In contrast, its paté de foie gras sales were just $79,000 last year, representing a net loss on paté sales of $3,121. Iroquois/Delaware has only $34,000 in assets related to paté. Thus none of the company's net earnings and less than .05 percent of its assets are implicated by plaintiff's proposal. These levels are obviously far below the five percent threshold set forth in the first portion of the exception claimed by Iroquois/Delaware.

Plaintiff does not contest that his proposed resolution relates to a matter of little economic significance to Iroquois/Delaware. Nevertheless he contends that the Rule 14a–8[i](5) exception is not applicable as it cannot be said that his proposal "is not otherwise significantly related to the issuer's business" as is required by the final portion of that exception. In other words, plaintiff's argument that Rule 14a–8 does not permit omission of his proposal rests on the assertion that the rule and statute on which it is based do not permit omission merely because a proposal is not economically significant where a proposal has "ethical or social significance."[8]

Iroquois/Delaware challenges plaintiff's view that ethical and social proposals cannot be excluded even if they do not meet the economic or five percent test. Instead, Iroquois/Delaware views the exception solely in economic terms as permitting omission of any proposals relating to a de minimis share of assets and profits. Iroquois/Delaware asserts that since corporations are economic entities, only an economic test is appropriate.

The Court would note that the applicability of the Rule 14a–8[i](5) exception to Mr. Lovenheim's proposal represents a close question given the lack of clarity in the exception itself. In effect, plaintiff relies on the word "otherwise," suggesting that it indicates the drafters of the rule intended that other noneconomic tests of significance be used. Iroquois/Delaware relies on the fact that the rule examines other significance in relation to the issuer's business. Because of the apparent ambiguity of the rule, the Court considers the history of the shareholder proposal rule in determining the proper interpretation of the most recent version of that rule.

Prior to 1983, paragraph 14a–8[i](5) excluded proposals "not significantly related to the issuer's business" but did not contain an objective economic significance test such as the five percent of sales, assets, and earnings specified in the first part of the current version. Although a series of SEC decisions through 1976 allowing issuers to exclude proposals challenging compliance with the Arab economic boycott of Israel allowed exclusion if the issuer did less than one percent of their business with Arab countries or Israel, the Commission stated later in 1976 that it did "not believe that subparagraph [i](5) should be hinged solely on the economic relativity of a proposal." Thus the Commission required inclusion "in many situations in which the related business comprised less than one percent" of the company's revenues, profits or assets "where the proposal has raised *policy questions* important enough to be considered 'significantly related' to the issuer's business."

As indicated above, the 1983 revision adopted the five percent test of economic significance in an effort to create a more objective standard. Nevertheless, in adopting this standard, the Commission stated that proposals will be includable notwithstanding their "failure to reach the specified economic thresholds if a significant relationship to the issuer's business is demonstrated on the face of the resolution or supporting statement." Thus it seems clear based on the history of the rule that

---

[8] The assertion that the proposal is significant in an ethical and social sense relies on plaintiff's argument that "the very availability of a market for products that may be obtained through the inhumane force-feeding of geese cannot help but contribute to the continuation of such treatment." Plaintiff's brief characterizes the humane treatment of animals as among the foundations of western culture and cites in support of this view the Seven Laws of Noah, an animal protection statute enacted by the Massachusetts Bay Colony in 1641, numerous federal statutes enacted since 1877, and animal protection laws existing in all fifty states and the District of Columbia. An additional indication of the significance of plaintiff's proposal is the support of such leading organizations in the field of animal care as the American Society for the Prevention of Cruelty to Animals and The Humane Society of the United States for measures aimed at discontinuing use of force-feeding.

"the meaning of 'significantly related' is not *limited* to economic significance."

* * *

[T]he Court cannot ignore the history of the rule which reveals no decision by the Commission to limit the determination to the economic criteria relied on by Iroquois/Delaware. The Court therefore holds that in light of the ethical and social significance of plaintiff's proposal and the fact that it implicates significant levels of sales, plaintiff has shown a likelihood of prevailing on the merits with regard to the issue of whether his proposal is "otherwise significantly related" to Iroquois/Delaware's business.[16]

* * *

QUESTIONS

1.   If a proposal deals with an aspect of a company that accounts for less than 5% of the business, is it still possible for such a proposal to have economic significance to the company and its shareholders?

2.   What limit is there on the phrase "otherwise significantly related" in Rule 14a–8(i)(5) if it includes items of non-economic significance?

3.   What if the plaintiff in *Lovenheim* also owns shares in Sterling Cooper (which has not been involved in any paté de foie gras advertising) and the plaintiff seeks to include the same proposal on the Sterling Cooper proxy statement?

4.   Why not allow issue proposals under Rule 14a–8 that are not significantly related to a company's business? Shouldn't shareholders be allowed to use their own corporation as a medium of communication?

———

Even if a proposal is relevant to a corporation, the proposal may nonetheless implicate only the corporation's "ordinary business operations" and thus face exclusion under Rule 14a–8(i)(7). What types of corporate actions count as "ordinary business operations"? The court in *Apache Corp.* ruled on a proposal that dealt with both an important social policy and as well as the operations of a corporation. Is such a proposal excludable under Rule 14a–8(i)(7)?

Apache Corp. v. New York City Employees' Retirement System

621 F. Supp. 2d 444 (S.D. Tex. 2008).

■ MILLER, G., DISTRICT JUDGE.

Pending before the court are plaintiff Apache Corporation's Original Complaint seeking a declaratory judgment. . . . For the reasons

---

[16] The result would, of course, be different if plaintiff's proposal was ethically significant in the abstract but had no meaningful relationship to the business of Iroquois/Delaware as Iroquois/Delaware was not engaged in the business of importing paté de foie gras.

discussed below, the court finds that Apache properly excluded defendants' proposal from proxy materials mailed to Apache's shareholders. . . .

BACKGROUND

Apache . . . is an independent energy company. . . . Defendants New York City Employees' Retirement System [et al.], and Office of the Comptroller of the City of New York are five New York pension funds and New York's chief fiscal and chief auditing officer, the custodian and trustee of the Funds.

On October 29, 2007, NYC Comptroller submitted . . . a shareholder proposal for inclusion in the company's proxy statement to be mailed in advance of Apache's May 8, 2008, annual shareholders' meeting. The Proposal reads:

SEXUAL ORIENTATION

Submitted By William C. Thompson, Jr., Comptroller, City of New York, on behalf of the Boards of Trustees of the New York City Pension Funds

WHEREAS, corporations with non-discrimination policies relating to sexual orientation have a competitive advantage to recruit and retain employees from the widest talent pool;

Employment discrimination on the basis of sexual orientation diminishes employee morale and productivity;

The company has an interest in preventing discrimination and resolving complaints internally so as to avoid costly litigation and damage its reputation as an equal opportunity employer;

Atlanta, Seattle, Los Angeles, and San Francisco have adopted legislation restricting business with companies that do not guaranteed equal treatment for lesbian and gay employees and similar legislation is pending in other jurisdictions;

The company has operations in and makes sales to institutions in states and cities which prohibit discrimination on the basis of sexual orientation;

A recent National Gay and Lesbian Taskforce study has found that 16%–44% of gay men and lesbians in twenty cities nationwide experienced workplace harassment or discrimination based on their sexual orientation;

National public opinion polls consistently find more than three-quarters of the American people support equal rights in the workplace for gay men, lesbians, and bisexuals;

A number of Fortune 500 corporations have implemented non-discrimination policies encompassing the following principles:

1) Discrimination based on sexual orientation and gender identity will be prohibited in the company's employment policy statement.

2) The company's non-discrimination policy will be distributed to all employees.

3) There shall be no discrimination based on any employee's actual or perceived health condition, status, or disability.

4) There shall be no discrimination in the allocation of employee benefits on the basis of sexual orientation or gender identity.

5) Sexual orientation and gender identity issues will be included in corporate employee diversity and sensitivity programs.

6) There shall be no discrimination in the recognition of employee groups based on sexual orientation or gender identity.

7) Corporate advertising policy will avoid the use of negative stereotypes based on sexual orientation or gender identity.

8) There shall be no discrimination in corporate advertising and marketing policy based on sexual orientation or gender identity.

9) There shall be no discrimination in the sale of goods and services based on sexual orientation or gender identity, and

10) There shall be no policy barring on corporate charitable contributions to groups and organizations based on sexual orientation.

RESOLVED: The Shareholders request that management implement equal employment opportunity policies based on the aforementioned principles prohibiting discrimination based on sexual orientation and gender identity.

STATEMENT: By implementing policies prohibiting discrimination based on sexual orientation and gender identity, the Company will ensure a respectful and supportive atmosphere for all employees and enhance its competitive edge by joining the growing ranks of companies guaranteeing equal opportunity for all employees.

Apache refused to include the proposal in its proxy materials and on January 3, 2008, pursuant to Rule 14a–8(j), Apache requested a no-action letter from the Securities and Exchange Commission's Division of Corporation Finance. . . . On March 5, 2008, the SEC's Division of Corporation Finance issued a no-action letter.

* * *

ANALYSIS

* * *

Apache seeks to exclude the Proposal based on the Rule 14a–8(i)(7) exception. . . . Rule 14a–8(i)(7) permits exclusion of a proposal if it "deals with a matter relating to the company's ordinary business operations." The term "ordinary business operations" escapes formal definition. To gleam its scope, courts look to SEC guidance and state law. In adopting Rule 14a–8(i)(7), the SEC stated:

* * * only "business matters that are mundane in nature and do not involve any substantial policy" considerations may be omitted under the "ordinary business" exception.

The policy underlying the ordinary business exclusion rests on two central considerations. The first relates to the subject matter of the proposal. Certain tasks are so fundamental to management's ability to run a company on a day-to-day basis that they could not, as a practical matter, be subject to direct shareholder oversight. Examples include the management of the workforce, such as the hiring, promotion, and termination of employees, decisions on production quality and quantity, and the retention of suppliers. However, proposals relating to such matters but focusing on sufficiently significant social policy issues (e.g., significant discrimination matters) generally would not be considered to be excludable, because the proposals would transcend the day-to-day business matters and raise policy issues so significant that it would be appropriate for a shareholder vote.

The second consideration relates to the degree to which the proposal seeks to "micro-manage" the company by probing too deeply into matters of a complex nature upon which shareholders, as a group, would not be in a position to make an informed judgment. This consideration may come into play in a number of circumstances, such as where the proposal involves intricate detail, or seeks to impose specific time-frames or methods for implementing complex policies.

Amendments to Rules on Shareholder Proposals ("1998 Release"). As to the second factor, the SEC explained that the determination "will be made on a case-by-case basis, taking into account factors such as the nature of the proposal and the circumstances of the company to which it is directed."

A clear reading of the *1998 Release* informs this court's analysis. To read the guidance as directing proper exclusion of shareholder proposals only when those proposals do not implicate a significant social policy would make much of the statement superfluous and most of the no-action letters presented to the court by the parties incorrect. Because such a directive cannot be gleamed from the release language, the court finds that it must first determine whether the Proposal implicates a significant policy issue. A proposal that does not concern a significant policy issue but nevertheless implicates the ordinary business operations of a company is properly excludable under Rule 14a–8(i)(7). However, a proposal concerning the ordinary business operations of a company that implicates a significant policy issue is only excludable under Rule 14a–8(i)(7) if it "seeks to 'micro-manage' the company by probing too deeply into matters of a complex nature upon which shareholders, as a group, would not be in a position to make an informed judgment." As one court explained, "management cannot exercise its specialized talents effectively if corporate investors assert the power to dictate the minutiae of daily business decisions."

The court now turns to the Proposal. The "resolved" paragraph provides, "The Shareholders request that management implement equal employment opportunity policies based on the aforementioned principles prohibiting discrimination based on sexual orientation and gender identity." NYC Comptroller now argues that the enumerated principles merely illustrate how various Fortune 500 corporations implemented non-discrimination policies. Nevertheless, a plain reading dictates the construction of the request. The shareholders seek that the company implement policies based on a list of principles. It is those principles that determine the employment opportunity policies, and not vice versa. Specifically, Apache directs the court to the following principles:

> Principle (4) There shall be no discrimination in the allocation of employee benefits on the basis of sexual orientation or gender identity;

> Principle (7) Corporate advertising policy will avoid the use of negative stereotypes based on sexual orientation or gender identity;

> Principle (8) There shall be no discrimination in corporate advertising and marketing policy based on sexual orientation or gender identity;

> Principle (9) There shall be no discrimination in the sale of goods and services based on sexual orientation or gender identity; and,

> Principle (10) There shall be no policy barring on corporate charitable contributions to groups and organizations based on sexual orientation.

With these in mind, the Proposal seeks to have Apache implement policies incorporating sexual orientation and gender identity into the company's employee benefits allocation, corporate advertising and marketing activities, sales activities, and charitable contributions.

Undoubtedly, advertising and marketing, sale of goods and services, and charitable contributions are ordinary business matters. Yet, NYC Comptroller, through the Proposal, seeks to have Apache implement equal employment opportunity policies which incorporate anti-discrimination directives based on sexual orientation and gender identity into such activities. The court finds that only principles one through six are directed at discrimination in employment. To consider the remaining four principles as implicating employment discrimination would be a far stretch. Instead, principles seven through ten aim at discrimination in Apache's business conduct as it relates to advertising, marketing, sales, and charitable contributions. Therefore, because these principles do not implicate the social policy underlying the Proposal, and because the Proposal must be read with all of its parts, the Proposal is properly excludable under Rule 14a–8(i)(7).

Even were the court to find that principles seven through ten implicate the underlying social policy, the Proposal seeks to micromanage the company to an unacceptable degree. Shareholders, as a group, are not sufficiently involved in the day-to-day operations of Apache's business to fully appreciate its complex nature. For example, shareholders, as a group, are not positioned to make informed judgments as to the propriety of certain sales and purchases. Similarly, the complex implications stemming from the proposed principle forbidding discrimination in the sale of goods and services based on sexual orientation or gender identity preclude provident judgment on the part of the shareholders. It would be imprudent to effectively cede control over such day-to-day decisions, traditionally within the purview of a company's executives and officers, to the shareholders. The aforementioned concerns are enhanced by the principle's implicit requirement that Apache determine whether its customers and suppliers discriminate on the basis of sexual orientation or gender identity. Such an inquiry is impractical and unreasonable, and the determination as to its propriety should properly remain with the company's management.

CONCLUSION

For the foregoing reasons, the court finds that pursuant to Rule 14a–8(i)(7), Apache properly excluded the Proposal from the proxy statement mailed to its shareholders.

* * *

QUESTIONS

1. Where is the line between "business matters that are mundane in nature" and issues that "involve [a] substantial policy"?

2. Why did the court find that non-discrimination policies relating to advertising and marketing, sale of goods and services, and charitable contributions do not qualify as significant social policy issues for purposes of determining whether the proposal at issue is excludable?

3. How could the pension funds alter their proposal to make it more likely to be included?

4. Should corporations be allowed to opt out of Rule 14a–8 shareholder issue proposals through their articles of incorporation?

HYPOTHETICAL FIVE

Bertram, who has held 4.25% of Sterling Cooper's stock since its founding, has some proposals that he thinks Sterling Cooper's board of directors should study. Will Sterling Cooper succeed in obtaining a no-action letter from the SEC if it seeks to exclude from the company's annual proxy statement the following proposals?

1. *Proposal One:* RESOLVED: "The board should examine the negative impact of the public's perception of the company's role in cigarette advertising."

2. *Proposal Two:* RESOLVED: "The board should study the feasibility of changes in Sterling Cooper's salary scale. In particular we request the board establish a board committee to study increasing salaries for workers making less than $100,000 per year by 10% and decreasing the pay of all other workers by 5%. A more equitable wage scale will not only increase employee morale but also reduce greater societal unrest, thereby strengthening the moral fabric of this nation."

3. *Proposal Three:* RESOLVED: "The board should establish a board committee charged with ensuring that the company does not take on excessive risks that could threaten its solvency."

B. SEC AUTHORITY OVER SHAREHOLDER VOTING

A key concern in the shareholder proposal process under Rule 14a–8 is the need to reconcile federal disclosure requirements with state corporate law. Rule 14a–8(i)(1) prohibits proposals that are not valid under applicable state law. Traditionally the division of power and authority within a corporation is at the core of state corporate law. The SEC, nonetheless, has required corporations to include a number of shareholders proposals that deal with the incumbent directors' control over the corporation. These include proposals (couched as recommendations) to declassify a staggered board of directors, include more diversity on the board, and remove a poison pill.

Should the SEC get more involved in dictating the corporate governance of publicly-held firms? The SEC's role in determining how corporations should allocate power among managers and shareholders has grown significantly with the enactment of the Sarbanes-Oxley Act in 2002 and the Dodd-Frank Act in 2010. Sarbanes-Oxley intrudes directly on a publicly-held firm's corporate governance in a variety of ways, which we canvass in Chapter 12. The Dodd-Frank Act contains provisions that focus on shareholder voting.

1. PROXY ACCESS

The Dodd-Frank Act authorizes the SEC to give shareholders access to the company's proxy for their own nominees. Historically, outside insurgents could launch a full-blown contest with their own proxy statement to elect a competing slate to a company's board of directors, but as discussed above, such contests are quite costly and correspondingly rare. The Dodd-Frank Act authorized the SEC to allow shareholders to nominate candidates for director directly on the company's proxy without the expense of a proxy contest using a separate proxy statement. Dodd-Frank Act, § 971.

The SEC implemented that authority through Rule 14a–11. Rule 14a–11 empowered shareholders (and shareholder groups) who have held at least 3% of the company's stock for three years to nominate directors and have those nominees included in the company's proxy statement and ballot. The rule did not provide an alternative to a full-fledged proxy contest, however, as shareholders could only nominate 25% of the board (or the greatest whole number below 25%) with a minimum of one. If different shareholders exceeded this limit with their separate nominees, the shareholder with the largest holdings was given priority in accessing the company's proxy statement.

The SEC also amended Rule 14a–8(i)(8) to facilitate shareholder proposals requiring companies to provide for proxy access in the company's governing documents. Rule 14a–8(i)(8) allows shareholders to submit proposals to expand the proxy access procedures beyond those required by Rule 14a–11. Possible proposals might include lower ownership thresholds, shorter holding periods, or a greater number of nominees.

The SEC adopted Rule 14a–11 over the heated objections of corporate management. Groups representing management then challenged the rule in court, and the SEC stayed the rule pending the resolution of that case. The D.C. Circuit vacated Rule 14a–11 in the following opinion.

Business Roundtable v. SEC

647 F.3d 1144 (D.C. Cir. 2011).

■ GINSBURG, D. CIRCUIT JUDGE.

The Business Roundtable and the Chamber of Commerce of the United States, each of which has corporate members that issue publicly traded securities, petition for review of Exchange Act Rule 14a–11. The rule requires public companies to provide shareholders with information about, and their ability to vote for, shareholder-nominated candidates for the board of directors. The petitioners argue the Securities and Exchange Commission promulgated the rule in violation of the Administrative Procedure Act, because, among other reasons, the Commission failed adequately to consider the rule's effect upon efficiency, competition, and capital formation, as required by Section 3(f) of the Exchange Act. . . . For these reasons and more, we grant the petition for review and vacate the rule.

I.   Background

The proxy process is the principal means by which shareholders of a publicly traded corporation elect the company's board of directors. Typically, incumbent directors nominate a candidate for each vacancy prior to the election, which is held at the company's annual meeting. Before the meeting the company puts information about each nominee in the set of "proxy materials"—usually comprising a proxy voting card and a proxy statement—it distributes to all shareholders. . . . A shareholder who wishes to nominate a different candidate may separately file his own proxy statement and solicit votes from shareholders, thereby initiating a "proxy contest."

Rule 14a–11 provides shareholders an alternative path for nominating and electing directors. Concerned the current process impedes the expression of shareholders' right under state corporation laws to nominate and elect directors, the Commission proposed the rule, and adopted it with the goal of ensuring "the proxy process functions, as nearly as possible, as a replacement for an actual in-person meeting of shareholders." . . . The rule requires a company subject to the Exchange Act proxy rules . . . to include in its proxy materials "the name of a person or persons nominated by a [qualifying] shareholder or group of shareholders for election to the board of directors."

* * *

A company that receives notice from an eligible shareholder or group must include the proffered information about the shareholder(s) and his nominee(s) in its proxy statement and include the nominee(s) on the proxy voting card.

The Commission did place certain limitations upon the application of Rule 14a–11. The rule does not apply if applicable state law or a company's governing documents "prohibit shareholders from nominating a candidate for election as a director." Nor may a shareholder use Rule 14a–11 if he is holding the company's securities with the intent of effecting a change of control of the company. The company is not required to include in its proxy materials more than one shareholder nominee or the number of nominees, if more than one, equal to 25 percent of the number of directors on the board.

The Commission concluded that Rule 14a–11 could create "potential benefits of improved board and company performance and shareholder value" sufficient to "justify [its] potential costs." The agency rejected proposals to let each company's board or a majority of its shareholders decide whether to incorporate Rule 14a–11 in its bylaws, saying that "exclusive reliance on private ordering under State law would not be as effective and efficient" in facilitating shareholders' right to nominate and elect directors. . . . The two Commissioners voting against the rule faulted the Commission on both theoretical and empirical grounds.

* * *

II.   Analysis

Under the APA, we will set aside agency action that is "arbitrary, capricious, an abuse of discretion, or otherwise not in accordance with law." We must assure ourselves the agency has "examine[d] the relevant data and articulate[d] a satisfactory explanation for its action including a rational connection between the facts found and the choices made." The Commission also has a "statutory obligation to determine as best it can the economic implications of the rule."

Indeed, the Commission has a unique obligation to consider the effect of a new rule upon "efficiency, competition, and capital formation," Exchange Act § 3(f), and its failure to "apprise itself—and hence the public and the Congress—of the economic consequences of a proposed regulation" makes promulgation of the rule arbitrary and capricious and not in accordance with law.

The petitioners argue the Commission acted arbitrarily and capriciously here because it neglected its statutory responsibility to determine the likely economic consequences of Rule 14a–11 and to connect those consequences to efficiency, competition, and capital formation. . . .

We agree with the petitioners and hold the Commission acted arbitrarily and capriciously for having failed . . . adequately to assess the economic effects of a new rule. Here the Commission inconsistently and opportunistically framed the costs and benefits of the rule; failed adequately to quantify the certain costs or to explain why those costs could not be quantified; neglected to support its predictive judgments; contradicted itself; and failed to respond to substantial problems raised by commenters. . . .

A.   Consideration of Economic Consequences

In the Adopting Release, the Commission predicted Rule 14a–11 would lead to "[d]irect cost savings" for shareholders in part due to "reduced printing and postage costs" and reduced expenditures for advertising compared to those of a "traditional" proxy contest. The Commission also identified some intangible, or at least less readily quantifiable, benefits, principally that the rule "will mitigate collective action and free-rider concerns," which can discourage a shareholder from exercising his right to nominate a director in a traditional proxy contest, and "has the potential of creating the benefit of improved board performance and enhanced shareholder value." The Commission anticipated the rule would also impose costs upon companies and shareholders related to "the preparation of required disclosure, printing and mailing . . ., and [to] additional solicitations," and could have "adverse effects on company and board performance," for example, by distracting management. The Commission nonetheless concluded the rule would promote the "efficiency of the economy on the whole," and the benefits of the rule would "justify the costs" of the rule.

The petitioners contend the Commission neglected both to quantify the costs companies would incur opposing shareholder nominees and to substantiate the rule's predicted benefits. They also argue the Commission failed to consider the consequences of union and state pension funds using the rule and failed properly to evaluate the frequency with which shareholders would initiate election contests.

1. Consideration of Costs and Benefits

In the Adopting Release, the Commission recognized "company boards may be motivated by the issues at stake to expend significant resources to challenge shareholder director nominees." Nonetheless, the Commission believed a company's solicitation and campaign costs "may be limited by two factors": first, "to the extent that the directors' fiduciary duties prevent them from using corporate funds to resist shareholder director nominations for no good-faith corporate purpose," they may decide "simply [to] include the shareholder director nominees . . . in the company's proxy materials"; and second, the "requisite ownership threshold and holding period" would "limit the number of shareholder director nominations that a board may receive, consider, and possibly contest."

The petitioners object that the Commission failed to appreciate the intensity with which issuers would oppose nominees and arbitrarily dismissed the probability that directors would conclude their fiduciary duties required them to support their own nominees. The petitioners also argue it was arbitrary for the Commission not to estimate the costs of solicitation and campaigning that companies would incur to oppose candidates nominated by shareholders, which costs commenters expected to be quite large. The Chamber of Commerce submitted a comment predicting boards would incur substantial expenditures opposing shareholder nominees through "significant media and public relations efforts, advertising . . ., mass mailings, and other communication efforts, as well as the hiring of outside advisors and the expenditure of significant time and effort by the company's employees." It pointed out that in recent proxy contests at larger companies costs "ranged from $14 million to $4 million" and at smaller companies "from $3 million to $800,000." In its brief the Commission maintains it did consider the commenters' estimates of the costs, but reasonably explained why those costs "may prove less than these estimates."

We agree with the petitioners that the Commission's prediction directors might choose not to oppose shareholder nominees had no basis beyond mere speculation. Although it is possible that a board, consistent with its fiduciary duties, might forgo expending resources to oppose a shareholder nominee—for example, if it believes the cost of opposition would exceed the cost to the company of the board's preferred candidate losing the election, discounted by the probability of that happening—the Commission has presented no evidence that such forbearance is ever seen in practice. To the contrary, the American Bar Association Committee on Federal Regulation of Securities commented:

> If the [shareholder] nominee is determined [by the board] not to be as appropriate a candidate as those to be nominated by the board's independent nominating committee . . ., then the board will be compelled by its fiduciary duty to make an appropriate effort to oppose the nominee, as boards now do in traditional proxy contests.

The Commission's second point, that the required minimum amount and duration of share ownership will limit the number of directors nominated under the new rule, is a reason to expect election contests to be infrequent; it says nothing about the amount a company will spend on solicitation and campaign costs when there is a contested election. Although the Commission acknowledged that companies may expend resources to oppose shareholder nominees, it did nothing to estimate and quantify the costs it expected companies to incur; nor did it claim estimating those costs was not possible, for empirical evidence about expenditures in traditional proxy contests was readily available. Because the agency failed to "make tough choices about which of the competing estimates is most plausible, [or] to hazard a guess as to which is correct," we believe it neglected its statutory obligation to assess the economic consequences of its rule.

The petitioners also maintain, and we agree, the Commission relied upon insufficient empirical data when it concluded that Rule 14a–11 will improve board performance and increase shareholder value by facilitating the election of dissident shareholder nominees. The Commission acknowledged the numerous studies submitted by commenters that reached the opposite result. One commenter, for example, submitted an empirical study showing that "when dissident directors win board seats, those firms underperform peers by 19 to 40% over the two years following the proxy contest." The Commission completely discounted those studies "because of questions raised by subsequent studies, limitations acknowledged by the studies' authors, or [its] own concerns about the studies' methodology or scope."

The Commission instead relied exclusively and heavily upon two relatively unpersuasive studies, one concerning the effect of "hybrid boards" (which include some dissident directors) and the other concerning the effect of proxy contests in general, upon shareholder value. Indeed, the Commission "recognize[d] the limitations of the [hybrid board] study," and noted "its long-term findings on shareholder value creation are difficult to interpret." In view of the admittedly (and at best) "mixed" empirical evidence, we think the Commission has not sufficiently supported its conclusion that increasing the potential for election of directors nominated by shareholders will result in improved board and company performance and shareholder value.

Moreover, as petitioners point out, the Commission discounted the costs of Rule 14a–11—but not the benefits—as a mere artifact of the state law right of shareholders to elect directors. For example, with reference to the potential costs of Rule 14a–11, such as management distraction and reduction in the time a board spends "on strategic and long-term thinking," the Commission thought it "important to note that these costs are associated with the traditional State law right to nominate and elect directors, and are not costs incurred for including shareholder nominees for director in the company's proxy materials." As we have said before, this type of reasoning, which fails to view a cost at the margin, is illogical and, in an economic analysis, unacceptable.

2.   Shareholders with Special Interests

The petitioners next argue the Commission acted arbitrarily and capriciously by "entirely fail[ing] to consider an important aspect of the problem," to wit, how union and state pension funds might use Rule 14a–11. Commenters expressed concern that these employee benefit funds would impose costs upon companies by using Rule 14a–11 as leverage to gain concessions, such as additional benefits for unionized employees, unrelated to shareholder value. The Commission insists it did consider this problem, albeit not *in haec verba*, along the way to its conclusion that "the totality of the evidence and economic theory" both indicate the rule "has the potential of creating the benefit of improved board performance and enhanced shareholder value." Specifically, the Commission recognized "companies could be negatively affected if shareholders use the new rules to promote their narrow interests at the expense of other shareholders," but reasoned these potential costs "may be limited" because the ownership and holding requirements would "allow the use of the rule by only holders who demonstrated a significant, long-term commitment to the company," and who would therefore be less likely to act in a way that would diminish shareholder value. The Commission also noted costs may be limited because other shareholders may be alerted, through the disclosure requirements, "to the narrow interests of the nominating shareholder."

The petitioners also contend the Commission failed to respond to the costs companies would incur even when a shareholder nominee is not ultimately elected. These costs may be incurred either by a board succumbing to the demands, unrelated to increasing value, of a special interest shareholder threatening to nominate a director, or by opposing and defeating such nominee(s). The Commission did not completely ignore these potential costs, but neither did it adequately address them.

Notwithstanding the ownership and holding requirements, there is good reason to believe institutional investors with special interests will be able to use the rule and, as more than one commenter noted, "public and union pension funds" are the institutional investors "most likely to make use of proxy access." Nonetheless, the Commission failed to respond to comments arguing that investors with a special interest, such as unions and state and local governments whose interests in jobs may well be greater than their interest in share value, can be expected to pursue self-interested objectives rather than the goal of maximizing shareholder value, and will likely cause companies to incur costs even when their nominee is unlikely to be elected. By ducking serious evaluation of the costs that could be imposed upon companies from use of the rule by shareholders representing special interests, particularly union and government pension funds, we think the Commission acted arbitrarily.

3.   Frequency of Election Contests

In the Proposing Release, the Commission estimated 269 companies per year, comprising 208 companies reporting under the Exchange Act and 61 registered investment companies, would receive nominations pursuant to Rule 14a–11. In the Adopting Release, however, the Commission reduced that estimate to 51, comprising only 45 reporting companies and 6 investment companies, in view of "the additional eligibility requirements" the Commission adopted in the final version of Rule 14a–11. (As originally proposed, Rule 14a–11 would have required a nominating shareholder to have held the securities for only one year rather than the three years required in the final rule.) In revising its estimate, the Commission also newly relied upon "[t]he number of contested elections and board-related shareholder proposals" in a recent year, which it believed was "a better indicator of how many shareholders might submit a nomination" than were the data upon which it had based its estimate in the Proposing Release.

The petitioners argue the Commission's revised estimate unreasonably departs from the estimate used in the Proposing Release, conflicts with its assertion the rule facilitates elections contests, and undermines its reliance upon frequent use of Rule 14a–11 to estimate the amount by which shareholders will benefit from "direct printing and mailing cost savings." The petitioners also contend the estimate is inconsistent with the Commission's prediction shareholders will initiate 147 proposals per year under Rule 14a–8, a rule not challenged here.*

The Commission was not unreasonable in predicting investors will use Rule 14a–11 less frequently than traditional proxy contests have been used in the past. As Commission counsel pointed out at oral argument, there would still be some traditional proxy contests; the total number of efforts by shareholders to nominate and elect directors will surely be greater when shareholders have two paths rather than one open to them. In any event, the final estimated frequency (51) with which shareholders will use Rule 14a–11 does not clearly conflict with the higher estimate in the Proposing Release (269), or the estimate of proposals under Rule 14a–8 (147), both of which were based upon looser eligibility standards.

In weighing the rule's costs and benefits, however, the Commission arbitrarily ignored the effect of the final rule upon the total number of election contests. That is, the Adopting Release does not address whether and to what extent Rule 14a–11 will take the place of traditional proxy contests. Without this crucial datum, the Commission has no way of knowing whether the rule will facilitate enough election contests to be of net benefit.

We also agree with the petitioners that the Commission's discussion of the estimated frequency of nominations under Rule 14a–11 is internally inconsistent and therefore arbitrary. In discussing its benefits, the Commission predicted nominating shareholders would realize "[d]irect cost savings" from not having to print or mail their own proxy materials. These savings would "remove a disincentive for

---

* The Commission simultaneously amended Rule 14a–8 to prevent companies from excluding from their proxy materials shareholder proposals to establish a procedure for shareholders to nominate directors.

shareholders to submit their own director nominations" and otherwise facilitate election contests. The Commission then cited comment letters predicting the number of elections contested under Rule 14a–11 would be quite high. One of the comments reported, based upon the proposed rule and a survey of directors, that approximately 15 percent of all companies with shares listed on exchanges, that is, "hundreds" of public companies, expected a shareholder or group of shareholders to nominate a director using the new rule. Thus, the Commission anticipated frequent use of Rule 14a–11 when estimating benefits, but assumed infrequent use when estimating costs.

* * *

III. Conclusion

For the foregoing reasons, we hold the Commission was arbitrary and capricious in promulgating Rule 14a–11. Accordingly, we have no occasion to address the petitioners' First Amendment challenge to the rule. The petition is granted and the rule is hereby

Vacated.

NOTES

1. *What comes next?* The SEC has not revisited the question of proxy access since *Business Roundtable* vacated Rule 14a–11 in 2011.

2. *Shareholder proxy access proposals.* Pursuant to Rule 14a-8(i)(8), shareholders at several companies have submitted precatory issue proposals requesting that the company submit a bylaw amendment implementing proxy access for shareholders to approve. If the company submits such a bylaw amendment and a majority of shares approve it, the company would then allow certain shareholders to nominate a certain fraction (typically a maximum of 20%) of the board of directors. The proposals frequently come with minimum ownership requirements, such as 3% of the outstanding shares, and a minimum holding period, such as 3 years. In 2013, Hewlett Packard shareholders voted a majority of outstanding shares in favor of a proposal to amend Hewlett Packard's bylaws to permit proxy access. Subsequent to the vote, Hewlett Packard implemented proxy access. More recently, the Comptroller of the City of New York submitted Rule 14a–8 proxy access proposals to 75 U.S. public companies for the 2015 proxy season as part of its Boardroom Accountability Project.

QUESTIONS

1. What costs did the SEC ignore in adopting Rule 14a–11?

2. How was the SEC inconsistent in assessing the costs and benefits of Rule 14a–11?

3. Rule 14a–11 requires 3% ownership of voting securities as the threshold for eligibility. Why not use a 1% threshold or a 10% threshold?

4. What kind of investor is most likely to be able to satisfy the eligibility requirements of Rule 14a–11?

5. Rule 14a–11 allows eligible shareholders to nominate only a limited number of directors. Why limit the number of shareholder nominees?

6. Rule 14a–8(i)(8) allows shareholders to make proposals to broaden proxy access, but shareholders are not allowed to narrow it. Should shareholders be given the right to curtail proxy access? If shareholders were given that right, would Rule 14a–11 have been more likely to withstand challenge?

7. If Congress thought proxy access was desirable, why did it not mandate it in the Dodd-Frank Act instead of delegating rulemaking authority to the SEC?

2. SAY ON PAY

The Dodd-Frank Act also sought to enhance shareholder power over executive compensation. Exchange Act § 14A. The SEC implemented that directive by requiring companies to conduct an advisory vote of shareholders on the pay packages of top executives at least once every three years. Rule 14a–21(a). The pay of directors, however, is not subject to an advisory vote. The pay to be approved is for the named executive officers of the company, as defined in Item 402(a)(3) of Regulation S–K. The compensation of these executives is subject to enhanced disclosure in the Compensation Discussion and Analysis section of the proxy statement, discussed in Chapter 4. That disclosure now must also address whether (and if so, how) the company has considered the results of the most recent say-on-pay vote in determining compensation policies and decisions. The instructions to Rule 14a–21 provide this sample resolution:

> RESOLVED, that the compensation paid to the company's named executive officers, as disclosed pursuant to Item 402 of Regulation S–K, including the Compensation Discussion and Analysis, compensation tables and narrative discussion is hereby APPROVED.

The example is not exclusive; companies can use other formulations for their shareholder resolutions.

The initial results of the say on pay votes showed that shareholders were approving the compensation packages for 98.5% of the companies. Even though almost all say on pay votes to date have resulted in approval of executive compensation, the mere prospect of a say on pay vote may change the amount and form (e.g., base pay versus incentive pay) of pay presented to shareholders for a vote. A number of companies, moreover, were able to secure approval only after modifying their compensation packages. A handful of derivative lawsuits were also filed against the directors of companies that were subject to a no vote, despite § 14A's stipulation that the law is not intended to change the fiduciary duties of directors with respect to executive compensation.

Section 14A requires companies to conduct a separate shareholder advisory vote, which must be held at least once every 6 years, to determine how often (every 1, 2, or 3 years) an issuer will conduct a shareholder advisory vote on executive compensation. Rule 14a–21(b). Shareholders must have four choices: every year, every other year, every third year, or abstain, although the company is allowed to make a recommendation to shareholders.

Section 14A also requires a shareholder advisory vote on "golden parachute" payments made to executives displaced in connection with mergers and acquisitions. Future employment arrangements are not considered compensation related to the subject transaction. If a company has made its "golden parachute" provisions subject to a shareholder vote as part of the say on pay approval process, it need not provide a vote in connection with the transaction. Rule 14a–21(c).

QUESTIONS

1. Should say on pay votes be mandatory rather than advisory? Why should the board of directors of a public company pay attention to a "mere" advisory vote?

2. Section 14A leaves it to the shareholders of a company to vote on the issue of how frequently to hold say on pay votes. Should the SEC instead mandate that companies with higher pay packages be subject to more frequent say on pay votes?

3. Should shareholders be allowed to opt out permanently from say on pay votes?

CHAPTER 12

Gatekeepers

Rules and Statutes

—*Sections 4C, 10A, 13(k), 15E, 21F of the Exchange Act*
—*Rules 10A–1 to 3 and 21F–1 to 5 of the Exchange Act*
—*SEC Rules of Practice 102(e), 205*

MOTIVATING HYPOTHETICAL

Parks & Recreation, Inc. (P & R) maintains city parks for an annual fee. P & R has been a public company trading on the Nasdaq Capital Market since its initial public offering eight years ago. Those eight years have seen steady growth for P & R as it established its reputation for maintaining pristine parks. P & R's reputation allowed it to obtain the business of many municipalities tired of maintaining their own parks. This period of steady growth for P & R has required that all of the firm's profits be ploughed back into the company to finance its expansion. As a result, P & R's shareholders have yet to receive any dividends and some of them are becoming impatient. Leslie, the founder, CEO, and Chairman of the board of P & R, is starting to feel the heat. The Haverford Fund, a hedge fund that has taken a big stake in P & R, is pressuring the P & R board to put the company up for sale. Leslie needs to show improved profits—and free cash flow to support a dividend—to ensure she keeps her position.

I. Gatekeeping

We have seen throughout the book the emphasis that Congress and the SEC have put on disclosure in promoting efficient capital markets. Disclosure does not promote market efficiency, however, if it is inaccurate. As we have seen in Chapters 5 and 8, material misstatements by corporate officers give rise to private rights of action against those officers and the corporation they serve. Private lawsuits are bolstered by government enforcement efforts from the SEC and the Justice Department, the subject of Chapter 13. Despite this array of antifraud enforcement, fraud is still with us. Is there anything else we can do to keep corporate officers honest?

One answer is to relax requirements for private causes of action against officers and the corporation, which is the approach taken in §§ 11 and 12(a)(2) of the Securities Act with respect to public offerings. Congress and the Supreme Court, however, have been tightening the requirements that apply to lawsuits brought under the main antifraud provision of the securities laws, § 10(b) of the Exchange Act. Relaxing the standards for private suits opens the door for abuses, principally frivolous suits filed for their *in terrorem* settlement value.

Perhaps we should give the SEC greater funding for more government enforcement? Any initiative to increase the SEC's funding faces an uphill battle in Congress, which has been inconsistent with its funding of the SEC's budget. Congress is quite generous in the wake of a major financial scandal; less so in a bull market. Moreover, SEC enforcement has its downsides, as we discuss in Chapter 13. Critics complain that the agency is complacent, that it is too cozy with industry, that it chases headlines, and that its lawyer-driven culture leaves it without the financial sophistication to understand the markets.

So what's the alternative? Faced with persistent cycles of fraud, Congress and the SEC have looked to recruit secondary actors to help police the accuracy of disclosure. "Secondary actors" do not directly violate the antifraud provisions of the securities laws, but instead provide substantial assistance to primary actors engaged in fraud. The idea is to use affiliated parties and business contacts of the corporation who have the power to dissuade fraud by corporate officers. The classic definition of gatekeeper focuses on service providers that customarily assist companies with securities transactions. Why do we call them "gatekeepers"? Gatekeepers are thought to be in a position to influence, using their special status to prevent wrongdoing by companies. To call someone a gatekeeper assumes that they have: (1) the capacity to identify fraud; and (2) the ability to stop it before investors are harmed.

Who qualifies as a gatekeeper? Gatekeepers obviously include accountants and attorneys, but credit rating agencies and others can also fit in this category. These professionals act as intermediaries between investors and companies, verifying or certifying the accuracy of corporate disclosure. To be sure, many of these professionals are loathe to concede that they play such a verification role. Perhaps they resist because the label "gatekeeper" appears to be an invitation for Congress and the SEC to regulate the gatekeeper's business, or worse yet, impose liability on them.

Economic incentives push some institutions to play a gatekeeping role. A familiar example of this form of gatekeeping is the role that underwriters play in vouching for companies making public offerings. As we discussed in Chapter 7, underwriters are renting their reputations to corporate issuers when they act as intermediaries to investors. Accounting firms, too, put their reputations on the line when they certify a company's financial statements. Accounting firms with a reputation for integrity can charge more for their certification services. That gives accounting firms an incentive to protect their reputations through vigorous screening for accounting problems.

Economic incentives do not always work so neatly. Individual partners within an accounting firm, for example, may make decisions to further their own personal welfare at the expense of the accounting firm as a whole. Such a self-serving partner may choose to ignore accounting problems at a large client of the partner in order to maintain the partner's compensation, even if this action may endanger the overall reputation of the accounting firm.

To address the weaknesses with economic incentives and to enlist those without an economic incentive, but capable of playing a gatekeeping role, Congress and the SEC have expanded the role of gatekeepers over time. Sometimes the role is legally mandated, as with the requirement of an independent audit for a public company's financial statements. Other times, however, the recruitment of a secondary party is indirect; the secondary party's monitoring is induced by the threat of private liability or SEC enforcement action if the monitor fails to uncover and check the fraud. Underwriters, for example, are compelled to stand behind the integrity of registration statements for public offerings by potential § 11 liability. (We covered the underwriter's role in Chapters 7 & 8, so we will not rehash that discussion here.) The debate over aiding-and-abetting liability under § 10(b), covered in Chapter 5, is largely an argument about the role that gatekeeping should play.

One risk in imposing liability on secondary actors is that it will dilute the deterrent effect of sanctions targeting the primary wrongdoer. If plaintiffs' attorneys can extract large settlements from secondary actors, they have less incentive to pursue the primary wrongdoer, which may undermine deterrence.

In this chapter, we look at the roles played by secondary actors in promoting the accuracy of corporate disclosure. As you look at the roles played by these secondary actors, ask yourself about their capacity to play a gatekeeping role. Do they have access to accurate information about the corporation? If they have access, can they prevent corporate officers from engaging in fraud? If they are able, do they have private incentives to play that role? Can lawmakers and regulators effectively influence those incentives to induce the secondary actor to play a gatekeeping role? At what cost?

II.   OUTSIDE DIRECTORS

Boards of public companies consist of both insiders, almost invariably including the chief executive officer, and outside directors. Outside directors often are drawn from top officers of other corporations, former politicians, and an occasional university president or head of a foundation. Outside directors of public companies typically receive six-figure annual compensation, often in the form of company stock, or stock options for their services. Directors of successful companies also often receive invitations to serve as directors on more company boards. These incentives push corporate directors to view their primary role as maximizing shareholder value. That goal is best served by outside directors acting as advisors to the company's CEO on strategic issues, bringing their wealth of business experience to bear in solving the company's problems and identifying new opportunities. Directors are inclined to view themselves as being part of a team that includes corporate management, working together to increase profits.

Notwithstanding this perception that directors are part of the team with management, it is quite clear that under state corporate law, the board of directors alone exercises ultimate authority over the business and affairs of the corporation. Corporate officers work for the board. Officers exercise only the authority delegated to them by the board, and are accountable to the board. If the board is dissatisfied with the performance of any corporate officer, it can terminate that officer. This power to terminate is one that corporate boards have exercised with increasing frequency over the last twenty years. Underperforming or unethical CEOs are much more likely to be shown the door than they used to be.

Congress has sought to harness that power of the board to promote compliance with the securities laws. In particular, the federal securities laws enlist outside directors in the battle against fraud. Recall from Chapter 8 that directors are among the category of enumerated defendants for § 11 of the Securities Act. Outside directors can also be held liable under § 10(b) of the Exchange Act if they make material misstatements on behalf of the corporation, or potentially as control persons under § 20(a) of the Exchange Act if they take an active role in directing the affairs of the corporation beyond that of the typical outside director.

More recently, Congress has tinkered with the makeup of public company boards. Those efforts made substantial inroads into corporate governance, an area traditionally governed by state corporate law. The Sarbanes-Oxley Act of 2002 began the trend, requiring companies listed on national securities exchanges to have an audit committee consisting of a majority of independent directors. Sarbanes-Oxley Act § 301. The NYSE requires that independent directors make up the majority of the board of a listed company. NYSE Listed Company Manual § 303A.01. Independent directors are a subset of outside directors. The NYSE provides stringent, bright-line interpretations of which outside directors qualify as independent. These rules bar most business relationships between the independent director and the company. NYSE Listed Company Manual § 303A.02. Former employees cannot be deemed independent for at least five years after their employment has ceased.

The Dodd-Frank Act makes further incursions into corporate governance. Section 972 of the Act requires that companies disclose whether the same person holds both the CEO and chairman of the board positions, and explain why the position is combined or not. Section 952 requires the SEC to direct, by rule, the national securities exchanges and national securities associations to prohibit the listing of equity securities unless the compensation committees of the companies' boards are made up exclusively of independent directors. The independence requirement for the board compensation committee parallels the independence requirement for the board audit committee implemented as part of the Sarbanes-Oxley Act (discussed later in this chapter). Moreover, § 952 imposes a variety of responsibilities on compensation committees. For example, compensation committees must be directly responsible for hiring and supervising compensation consultants.

These incursions of federal securities laws into state corporate law indirectly encourage outside directors to play a role in ensuring a public corporation's compliance with the federal securities laws. The SEC has also brought enforcement actions against outside directors for failing to ensure accuracy in corporate disclosures. The case excerpted below, *W.R. Grace*, was a rather controversial effort by the SEC. Do you think the SEC was justified in bringing this case against an outside director?

A procedural note: *W.R. Grace* was brought by the SEC as a report of investigation under § 21(a) of the Exchange Act. As we discuss in Chapter 13, the SEC can use administrative proceedings to pursue those who violate the Exchange Act and the SEC's rules and regulations. An investigation pursuant to § 21(a) represents one of the SEC's more informal and least threatening means of enforcing the securities laws, resulting in no penalties, constraints on future actions, or formal censure. Instead, the SEC issues a public report detailing violations of the securities laws.

In the Matter of W. R. Grace & Co.
Exchange Act Release No. 39157 (1997).

The staff of the Division of Enforcement has conducted an investigation into whether W. R. Grace & Co. (WRG) violated certain provisions of the federal securities laws and whether certain former officers and directors of WRG contributed to any such violations. . . .

In the Administrative Order against WRG, the Commission found that WRG, in its 1992 annual report on Form 10–K and its 1993 proxy statement, did not fully disclose the substantial retirement benefits it had agreed to provide J. Peter Grace, Jr., effective at his retirement as chief executive officer on December 31, 1992. . . . As a result, WRG violated Sections 13(a) and 14(a) of the Exchange Act and Rules 13a–1, 14a–3 and 14a–9 thereunder.

The Commission is issuing this Report of Investigation [under § 21(a)] to emphasize the affirmative responsibilities of corporate officers and directors to ensure that the shareholders whom they serve receive accurate and complete disclosure of information required by the proxy solicitation and periodic reporting provisions of the federal securities laws. Officers and directors who review, approve, or sign their company's proxy statements or periodic reports must take steps to ensure the accuracy and completeness of the statements contained therein, especially as they concern those matters within their particular knowledge or expertise. To fulfill this responsibility, officers and directors must be vigilant in exercising their authority throughout the disclosure process.

In this case, both Grace, Jr., then the chairman of WRG's board of directors, and J. P. Bolduc, then WRG's chief executive officer and a member of WRG's board of directors, knew of Grace, Jr.'s substantial retirement benefits. . . . Eben Pyne, a non-management member of the board, also was aware of Grace, Jr.'s benefits. . . . [T]hese officers and directors reviewed all or portions of the relevant documents, and all but Pyne signed the relevant reports. Although the record does not demonstrate that Bolduc, [and] Pyne acted in bad faith, the Commission concludes that they did not fulfill their obligations under the federal securities laws. Bolduc [and] Pyne, each assumed, without taking the steps necessary to confirm their assumptions, that WRG's procedures would produce drafts of disclosure documents describing all matters that required disclosure.[5] Each also assumed, without taking steps necessary to confirm their assumptions, that other corporate officers, including counsel, had conducted full and informed reviews of the drafts. Bolduc [and] Pyne each had a responsibility to go beyond the

---

[5] Indeed, this matter demonstrates that corporate disclosure mechanisms cannot compensate for the failures of individuals. WRG's procedures failed because, among other reasons, Grace, Jr. did not disclose some of his retirement benefits . . . in questionnaires which WRG distributed to officers and directors to gather information for disclosure in WRG's proxy statements and periodic reports.

established procedures to inquire into the reasons for non-disclosure of information of which they were aware.

* * *

III. Grace, Jr., Bolduc, and Pyne Failed to Take Steps to Ensure that Grace, Jr.'s Retirement Benefits were Fully Disclosed.

During the latter part of 1992, Grace, Jr.'s health was deteriorating. Pursuant to delegated authority from WRG's board of directors, WRG's Compensation, Employee Benefits and Stock Incentive Committee entered into negotiations with Grace, Jr., which resulted in his retirement from WRG as its chief executive officer, effective on December 31, 1992. Pyne, then chairman of the Compensation Committee, met several times with Grace, Jr. during November and December 1992. The negotiations resulted in an agreement in principle with respect to Grace, Jr.'s proposed retirement benefits. Among the provisions of this agreement in principle was an understanding that Grace, Jr. would continue to receive in retirement various substantial perquisites which he had received while chief executive officer. On December 7, 1992, WRG's board of directors approved Grace, Jr.'s proposed retirement benefits.

Subsequently, Grace, Jr. and Pyne, on behalf of WRG, executed a letter agreement dated December 21, 1992, which reflected the terms of this agreement in principle.[8] . . . Pursuant to this provision of the Retirement Agreement, Grace, Jr. received the following benefits, among others, from WRG in 1993: (a) continued use of a Company-owned and maintained apartment with a market value estimated by WRG to be in excess of $3 million, with services of a cook, who was a WRG employee; (b) use of a company limousine and driver on a 24 hour basis; (c) the services of full-time secretaries and administrative assistants; (d) the use of corporate aircraft for personal and business travel; (e) home nursing services; and (f) security services.

While there was general knowledge within management that Grace, Jr.'s Retirement Agreement provided for the continuation of benefits that he had received before retirement, specific information about Grace, Jr.'s benefits was not generally available to WRG's management. Only non-management directors were involved in the negotiation or approval of Grace, Jr.'s retirement benefits. . . . However, Grace, Jr. and Pyne met with Bolduc in December 1992 to discuss Grace, Jr.'s retirement benefits after the negotiations over these benefits were completed. At that time, Bolduc became aware of each of the "other benefits" that WRG was providing to Grace, Jr.

The Company provided Grace, Jr. with directors' and officers' questionnaires in the course of preparing its 1992 Form 10–K and 1993 proxy statement and its 1993 Form 10–K and 1994 proxy statement. These questionnaires contained questions asking whether Grace, Jr. received certain benefits from the Company during the preceding year, including, among other things, use of Company property, including apartments; housing and other living expenses (including domestic

---

8   Bolduc and Pyne each assert that they assumed that this letter agreement, because it was drafted by WRG's legal counsel, would receive full consideration in WRG's disclosure process.

service) provided at his principal and/or vacation residence; and other perquisites. Grace, Jr. incorrectly responded "no" to these questions.

The final version of WRG's 1993 proxy statement contained language discussing Grace, Jr.'s Retirement Agreement, including a statement that Grace, Jr. would receive "certain other benefits." WRG filed the Retirement Agreement as an exhibit to its 1992 Form 10–K, but did not further describe Grace, Jr.'s "other benefits," nor did WRG disclose the costs of providing them in any of its proxy statements or periodic reports filed with the Commission before 1995.[10]

Because WRG's senior management was excluded from the negotiation and approval of Grace, Jr.'s retirement benefits, WRG's disclosure counsel made arrangements for Pyne to review the executive compensation section of WRG's draft 1993 proxy statement, and Pyne did so. Bolduc, in his capacity as WRG's CEO, reviewed drafts of WRG's 1993 proxy statement and signed WRG's 1992 Form 10–K, which incorporated the proxy statement's section on executive compensation by reference. Grace, Jr., in his capacity as chairman, also signed the 1992 Form 10–K. Although Grace, Jr., Bolduc, and Pyne knew about the "other benefits" WRG had agreed to provide Grace, Jr. upon his retirement, they did not question the absence of information about these "other benefits" in WRG's disclosure of Grace, Jr.'s retirement benefits. Even if Bolduc and Pyne, as each asserted, assumed that WRG's legal counsel (whose office had participated in drafting the Retirement Agreement) had considered the adequacy of the disclosure concerning Grace, Jr.'s benefits, they should not have relied upon that assumption. They should have raised the issue of disclosure of Grace, Jr.'s "other benefits," for example, by discussing the issue specifically with disclosure counsel, telling counsel exactly what they knew about the benefits, and asking specifically whether the benefits should be disclosed.[11] As a result, WRG's 1992 Form 10–K and 1993 proxy statement failed to disclose specific information about the "other benefits."

* * *

V. CONCLUSION

Serving as an officer or director of a public company is a privilege which carries with it substantial obligations. If an officer or director knows or should know that his or her company's statements concerning particular issues are inadequate or incomplete, he or she has an obligation to correct that failure. An officer or director may rely upon the company's procedures for determining what disclosure is required

---

[10] After information concerning Grace, Jr.'s "other benefits" became public, WRG disclosed in its 1995 proxy statement that the benefits provided to Grace, Jr. pursuant to the "other benefits" provision cost the Company $3,601,500 in fiscal year 1993, of which approximately $2,700,000 was attributable to Grace, Jr.'s having access to corporate aircraft.

[11] This might have established that counsel was not in fact fully informed about these benefits or that Grace, Jr. had incorrectly filled out his D & O questionnaires regarding these benefits.

only if he or she has a reasonable basis for believing that those procedures have resulted in full consideration of those issues.[16]

Grace, Jr., Bolduc [and] Pyne ... did not fulfill their obligations under the federal securities laws. Grace, Jr., Bolduc, and Pyne knew or should have known that Grace, Jr.'s retirement benefits were not fully disclosed in drafts of WRG's 1993 proxy statement and 1992 Form 10–K. ... As noted, Grace, Jr. failed to identify information relating to [this issue] in his D & O questionnaires. Grace, Jr., Bolduc, [and] Pyne, given their positions as directors or senior officers and their particular knowledge of these transactions, should have inquired as to whether the securities laws required disclosure of this information. This inquiry could have included seeking the specific and fully informed advice of counsel. If they were not reasonably satisfied as to the answers they received, they should have insisted that the documents be corrected before they were filed with the Commission.[17]

WRG's violations resulted, in part, from its corporate culture, which reflected Grace, Jr.'s substantial influence over the Company.[18] Given this circumstance, Bolduc [and] Pyne ... should have been more attentive to issues concerning disclosure of information relating to Grace, Jr.... Bolduc [and] Pyne ... did not adequately follow through on fostering accurate and complete disclosure, which should have been their touchstone as members of WRG's board of directors or as officers of WRG.

Since Grace, Jr.'s death, WRG has substantially revised the composition of its board of directors. Because of the unique circumstances presented here (including the death of Grace, Jr.), the Commission has determined not to issue cease-and-desist orders or take other action against Bolduc [and] Pyne ... in this matter. However, the Commission remains resolved to take enforcement action, where appropriate, against individual directors and officers who have violated or caused violations of the federal securities laws.

DISSENT OF COMMISSIONER STEVEN M.H. WALLMAN

The Section 21(a) report In the Matter of W.R. Grace & Co articulates a certain legal standard, and then applies that standard to these facts. I take issue with that standard specifically to the extent it suggests that officers and directors must ensure the accuracy and completeness of company disclosures. Moreover, I do not agree that, when the appropriate legal standard is applied to the particular facts of this case as described in the Report itself, there has been a violation of law on the part of the ... individuals cited.

Certain of the disclosures of W.R. Grace & Co. relating to perquisites ... were not in compliance with applicable requirements.

---

[16] Procedures or mechanisms established to identify and address disclosure issues are effective only if individuals in positions to affect the disclosure process are vigilant in exercising their responsibilities.

[17] Bolduc [and] Pyne ... would each bear this responsibility even if, as each asserted, each assumed that WRG's internal mechanisms for preparing the relevant disclosure documents, including review of counsel, would address these issues.

[18] There is some evidence that Bolduc recognized that Grace, Jr. exercised a degree of influence over WRG which was inappropriate for a public corporation and attempted to limit that influence.

The Company has consented to the issuance of a cease and desist order with respect to these matters.

As for individual liability, the record suggests that were J. Peter Grace, Jr. still alive, further examination as to whether he was a cause of the Company's improper disclosures would be in order. But in attempting to find other individuals who were responsible for the Company's conduct, I disagree with the Commission's conclusion that, on this record, J.P. Bolduc [and] Eben Pyne . . . failed to fulfill their obligations under the federal securities laws.[20] To conclude otherwise is to impose strict liability for such a disclosure failure—which simply is not the law.

In this case, as stated in the Report, Grace, Jr. exerted an unusual amount of control over the Company. But the Company also had policies and procedures in place designed to satisfy the Company's disclosure obligations. The Company prepared and distributed appropriate director and officer questionnaires requesting information concerning, specifically, the receipt of perquisites and other benefits. . . . The Company also surveyed the chief financial officers of the Company's operating units for the same information. Draft documents were circulated among senior management (including Bolduc) and members of the board for their review and comment. A substantial number of people were involved in the creation or review of the relevant disclosure documents. From the record, there do not appear to have been any red flags or warnings to indicate that this system—which included the employment of respected and competent securities counsel—was breaking down, or was inadequate to produce documents that would comply with the federal securities laws. Yet, even though appropriate procedures were in place, and followed, insufficient disclosures were made. . . .

Whether disclosure of certain matters is required under the federal securities laws is a legal (or mixed legal and factual) determination that ultimately has to be made by counsel after being informed of the relevant facts. Bolduc [and] Pyne . . . were aware of the documents relevant to the . . . questioned disclosures at issue in this case: the retirement agreement with Grace, Jr. . . . The existence of these documents also was known to various attorneys in the [WRG] Office of Legal Counsel [OLC]—the office whose job it was to prepare disclosure in accordance with legal requirements, and the same office that drafted these documents. . . .

* * *

The two questioned disclosures in this case both turn on fine line legal interpretations. Bolduc [and] Pyne . . . were not lawyers; they were not versed in SEC line item disclosure requirements; they were not possibly capable of making the fine judgment calls on whether disclosure of the items at issue here was sufficient or warranted. These decisions were the domain of counsel. Bolduc [and] Pyne were not in a position to second-guess this type of disclosure and had every right to

---

[20] I understand that Grace, Jr. received compensation and perquisites that many believe were inappropriate, and that many believe the board or others in management should have taken action to reduce those benefits. But we at the Commission do not administer the corporate law, which is the proper venue for those complaints.

rely on a system designed to produce appropriate disclosure. If there were any attorneys in OLC who were unsure, or unaware, of the significance, or specifics, of the terms of . . . the retirement agreement . . . and clarification was needed to make a determination of what the law required in terms of disclosure, then it was the responsibility of those attorneys to ask the appropriate questions.

The issue then is simple: did legal counsel have the necessary facts to do the job that was required—and if not, did these . . . individuals know (or, perhaps, should these . . . individuals have known) that counsel did not have the necessary facts.

It is clear that disclosure counsel in particular was well aware of the facts regarding Grace, Jr.'s retirement package since he was supplied with an actual copy of the retirement agreement—an agreement filed publicly as an exhibit to the Company's Form 10–K. The agreement specifically provided that:

> All other benefits and arrangements currently provided [Grace, Jr.] as chief executive officer (including, but not limited to, the use of office space and corporate aircraft) will continue to be provided to [him].

There was no change in the benefits being granted Grace, Jr. from previous years—what he received as CEO he was to continue to receive in retirement. Disclosure counsel, knowing these facts, then apparently made the determination that the description of these continued benefits as certain other benefits was adequate disclosure under Item 402(h) of Regulation S–K, and presented drafts with that disclosure to Bolduc and Pyne.

Bolduc and Pyne knew that disclosure counsel had reviewed this certain other benefits language and the retirement agreement and appeared to be in possession of all relevant facts, including that Grace, Jr. was now retired. Bolduc and Pyne relied on disclosure counsel to make the legal determination as to what the law required regarding disclosure of the retirement agreement, including the level of detail regarding disclosure of any specific terms or conditions. Given the plain language of both the disclosure and the relevant portion of the retirement agreement, I fail to see where the red flag exists that would require non-lawyers to question the explicit determinations of their disclosure counsel as to the level of disclosure detail.

Moreover, details regarding the benefits in question—all of which Grace, Jr. had been receiving while he was still Chief Executive Officer—were not disclosed in previous filings with the Commission made prior to his retirement. I would venture to say that many securities lawyers would not know that the Company's summary disclosure of these very same benefits in a later filing would somehow now be inadequate because of Grace, Jr.'s retirement and change in status from executive officer and director to non-employee director/consultant. In fact, I would suspect that most securities lawyers would believe that less, not more, disclosure would be required upon such a change. It is simply not the law to require non-securities law experts to guess at the legal significance from a federal securities law disclosure standpoint of such a change in status and, therefore, be required to question the articulated judgment of their disclosure counsel and the resultant level of disclosure.

* * *

If the facts were different, it might be possible to conclude that these . . . individuals knew or had reason to know that the process had not worked appropriately, and there then might be reason to impose upon them a duty of inquiry that might rise to the level of querying and second-guessing counsel's judgments and disclosures. Examples might include knowing that Grace, Jr. had intentionally or otherwise not completed his questionnaire properly, or the presence of past mistakes or omissions in the Company's disclosure documents that would have alerted them to the fact that their disclosure process was failing. But those are not the facts of this record or as stated in the Report.

The Commission is understandably wary about pursuing lawyers for their legal judgments. I share that wariness and believe that when professionals—whether lawyers, accountants or others—are acting in their capacity as such they must be given the opportunity to exercise their professional judgment without fear that a mistake, no matter how innocent—or difference of judgment with the Commission—will result in their being viewed as having violated the federal securities laws. We need to recognize that in those circumstances where such judgments are made, there simply may be no person that will be individually liable. Holding the client liable for not questioning the legal judgment of counsel is not the answer.

If the Commission believes it has a case against these . . . individuals, then it should have brought it. The record, however, did not support any such case. There is a well-known maxim: bad facts make bad law. Here, we have bad circumstances. . . .

QUESTIONS

1. Why do you think the SEC did not impose a more stringent sanction on Bolduc, the CEO of WRG, and Pyne, an outside director? Why did Bolduc and Pyne consent to the entry of the order? Why was the company treated more harshly than the individuals?

2. Should an outside director like Pyne be responsible for mistakes in the company's disclosure?

3. Should it matter that Grace Jr. "dominated" the company? If so, how?

4. Commissioner Wallman is troubled by what he sees as the SEC second-guessing Bolduc and Pyne for relying on the company's lawyers to determine the company's disclosure. Should the advice of counsel be a defense to an SEC enforcement action?

5. Was the retirement package provided to Grace, Jr. material to an assessment of W.R. Grace?

HYPOTHETICAL ONE

Ann is an outside director of Parks & Recreation, Inc. Ann was the college roommate of Leslie, the CEO and founder of P & R, and now works as a nurse. Ann has served as a director of P & R since the company's IPO several years ago. Ann has recently learned from Leslie that P & R's auditor, Dwyer & Ludgate, is getting "suspicious" about how P & R records revenues received from its municipality-customers. Apparently, many of the municipalities have run into hard times and have been slow in remitting payment to P & R, sometimes failing to make payments for several years. Leslie tells Ann, "not to worry though—we still book the revenue as actually coming in because state governments always bail out any small town that goes under." Leslie asks Ann to keep this information confidential as a "friend." What would you do if you were Ann?

III. THE INDEPENDENT AUDITOR

The SEC requires that the financial statements filed with the Form 10–K be audited by an independent accounting firm. Exchange Act Rule 13a–1. In addition, an independent accounting firm must review the interim financial statements that the company files with its Form 10–Q. Regulation S–X Rule 10–01(d). Virtually all large public companies employ as their auditors one of the "Big Four" accounting firms: Deloitte Touche Tohmatsu, Ernst & Young, KPMG and PricewaterhouseCoopers. Accounting firms are regulated by state boards of accountancy in each state in which they practice, and are also subject to the codes of conduct of the American Institute of Certified Public Accountants. Accounting firms providing services to public companies are also subject to regulation under the federal securities laws.

Auditors of public companies must register with the Public Company Accounting Oversight Board (generally known by its acronym PCAOB, or more fun, but less linear, the "Peekaboo"), and are subject to discipline by that entity. The PCAOB, a non-profit corporation, is a quasi-governmental regulator created by the Sarbanes-Oxley Act. The PCAOB is responsible for the supervision and discipline of public accountants, subject to the oversight of the SEC.

Audits of public companies must be conducted in accordance with standards laid down by the PCAOB. The PCAOB requires auditors to plan and perform the audit to obtain reasonable assurance of whether the financial statements are free of material misstatement (whether caused by error or fraud). For public companies with market capitalization in excess of $75 million, auditors must determine whether effective internal control over financial reporting was maintained in all material respects. The goal of the audit is for the auditor to come to an opinion on the fairness of the company's financial statements. Do they present, in all material respects, the financial position, results of operations, and cash flows in conformity with generally accepted accounting principles? PCAOB, Statement on Auditing Standards No. 1, AU § 110.01.

In addition to the oversight provided by the PCAOB, public company auditors are also subject to discipline by the SEC. Because the audit firms certify the financial statements to the SEC, they subject themselves to discipline by the SEC under the agency's rules of practice, Rule 102(e). As part of the Sarbanes-Oxley Act, Congress codified the SEC's authority under Rule 102(e) to discipline accountants in § 4C of the Exchange Act. Accountants may be barred from practicing before the SEC if they are found:

(i) Not to possess the requisite qualifications to represent others;

(ii) To be lacking in character or integrity or to have engaged in unethical or improper professional conduct; or

(iii) To have willfully violated, or willfully aided and abetted the violation of any provision of the Federal securities laws or the rules and regulations thereunder.

Exchange Act § 4C. Section 4C goes on to define "improper professional conduct" as "intentional or knowing conduct, including reckless conduct, that results in a violation of applicable professional standards" as well as negligent conduct in the form of either "a single instance of highly unreasonable conduct" or "repeated instances of unreasonable conduct." Notably, "practice" before the SEC is defined to include not only appearances in administrative proceedings before the SEC, but also the provision of advice to companies regarding documents that will be filed with the SEC. SEC Rule of Practice 205.2.

The "Big Four" used to be known as the "Big Five" accounting firms. The demise of the fifth member of the "Big Five"—Arthur Andersen—as a result of its involvement in the accounting fraud at Enron, led to the inclusion of an elaborate set of requirements for auditors in the Sarbanes-Oxley Act, most of which are administered by the PCAOB. The provision most directly traceable to Arthur Andersen's demise is 18 U.S.C. § 1520, which makes it a criminal offense to destroy corporate audit records.

Regulation of auditing also extends to the issuer's corporate governance. Under § 10A(m) of the Exchange Act, the retention, compensation and oversight of the company's external auditor must be entrusted to an audit committee of the board of directors. The audit committee also has the authority to hire its own advisors (typically legal counsel) at the company's expense. The auditors must report to the audit committee "critical accounting policies and practices," alternative treatments of financial information discussed with management and any other "material written communications" between the auditor and management. The audit committee is also responsible for approving any non-audit services (now strictly limited, as discussed below) provided by the company's auditor. Finally, the audit committee is charged with establishing procedures for dealing with complaints relating to auditing and internal controls. As we discuss below, "whistleblowers" who make such complaints are protected from retaliation by both civil and criminal sanctions against those who retaliate.

Only independent directors can serve on the audit committee. Exchange Act § 10A(m). This means that the only compensation the director can receive from the company is the director's fee—no consulting or other employment arrangements are permitted. The SEC has bolstered this independence requirement with a disclosure requirement, Regulation S–K Item 309, relating to the expertise of the audit committee. Item 309 requires the company to disclose whether any member of the audit committee qualifies as a "financial expert," which requires either experience as an accountant or an accounting officer, or experience supervising an accounting officer or overseeing public accountants. Listing requirements for the NYSE and Nasdaq require financial literacy for *all* audit committee members.

In addition to creating a new regulatory and oversight apparatus, Congress also imposed new responsibilities on auditors. Recall from Chapter 4 that § 404 of the Sarbanes-Oxley Act requires auditors to attest to management's report on the adequacy of the company's internal control over financial reporting. This provision has been singled out as substantially increasing audit costs. In response to those increased audit costs, the auditor attestation requirement was scaled back in the Dodd-Frank Act, which now exempts companies with a market capitalization under $75 million.

Congress has also charged auditors with ferreting out fraud. Auditors must adopt procedures to detect "illegal acts that would have a direct and material effect" on financial statements and identify material related party transactions. Exchange Act § 10A(a)(1). Auditors are also required to evaluate the ability of the client to continue as a going concern through its next fiscal year. These duties were added to existing responsibilities to report illegal acts to management and the audit committee or entire board of directors. Exchange Act § 10A(b). A board of directors receiving such a report must notify the SEC; if it fails to do so, the audit firm must provide notice to the SEC itself. (A similar "whistleblowing" requirement, minus the requirement of a report to the SEC, is imposed on lawyers by the SEC's Rules of Practice, discussed below.) Finally, Exchange Act Rule 13b2–2 prohibits officers and directors of the issuer from misleading the auditor in connection with any filing to be made with the SEC.

Congress also bolstered auditor independence in the Sarbanes-Oxley Act. Congress worried that the lure of lucrative contracts for other services would lead auditors to knuckle under to management pressure, thereby compromising the integrity of the audit. Consequently, auditors are now banned from providing a broad array of services to their audit clients, including: bookkeeping, designing financial systems, appraisal and valuation services, actuarial services, internal auditing functions, management and human resources services, investment services and legal services. Exchange Act § 10A(g). Auditors may still provide, among other things, tax planning advice to their clients so long as they obtain prior approval from the audit committee. The PCAOB is authorized to ban the provision of other services as well.

Audit firms are also required by § 10A(j) to rotate the partner in charge of the audit for each client at least once every five years. Too familiar a relationship between the partner and company executives can compromise independence. In the same vein, § 10A(*l*) bans audit firms from auditing companies whose CEOs, CFOs, or controllers were employed by the audit firm and that employee participated in the audit of the company during the prior year.

HYPOTHETICAL TWO

Dwyer & Ludgate, the accounting firm for Parks & Recreation, Inc., is worried about a possible blight to Dwyer & Ludgate's reputation from financial shenanigans at P & R involving Tom, the CFO of P & R. Dwyer & Ludgate recently got a call from the SEC's Division of Enforcement. One of Dwyer & Ludgate's junior accountants for the P & R engagement, Chris, has been talking to the government. Chris has told the Enforcement Division that he came across a bank statement from Pawnee Bank for a $500,000 account when he was working on the P & R audit. When he asked Tom about the account and why it did not appear on P & R's balance sheet, Tom told him not to worry about it, that it was a "temporary" account, and that it would soon be consolidated with P & R's primary account. Chris was worried, however, and raised it with the partner in charge of the P & R audit, Wendy. Wendy raised the issue with Leslie, the CEO of P & R, who told her "not to worry about it because Tom always gets the money stuff sorted out before the time we need to file." Wendy then told Chris that if Tom told him that it would be taken care of, it would be taken care of, and that he should not be harassing the CFO of such an important client. Dwyer & Ludgate signed off on the audit without qualification and Leslie (CEO) and Tom (CFO) both certified the 10–K with financial statements that did not reflect the $500,000 account. The Enforcement Division says that it is now considering action against Dwyer & Ludgate and Wendy. Does Wendy have a problem?

IV. THE ROLE OF LAWYERS IN ENFORCING THE SECURITIES LAWS

Attorneys' work implicates the securities laws at various points. Lawyers assist corporations with various types of securities transactions, such as public offerings, private placements, and mergers and acquisitions. Attorneys also play key roles in preparing Form 10–Ks, 10–Qs, and 8–Ks and advising on disclosure issues for voluntary disclosures, such as press releases and conference calls. Of course, they also represent clients in formal proceedings, both in court and before the SEC.

Attorneys sometimes provide written legal opinions to advise corporate clients on the best method of carrying out transactions. They may also provide opinions to issuers in connection with the validity of a securities issuance, which may be a prerequisite to closing an offering. For public offerings in particular, lawyers play a key role in the due diligence process, reviewing the registration statement and prospectus for accuracy and completeness. Recall from *Escott* (excerpted in Chapter 8) the expectation that counsel for the company and the underwriter will play leading roles in thoroughly investigating the issuer's business and management.

Given the key role played by lawyers in securities transactions, it is no surprise that lawyers, like accountants, are subject to regulation under the federal securities laws, in addition to the legal ethics rules administered by the state bar authorities. The SEC has the authority to censure and suspend lawyers who practice before it under the SEC's Rule of Practice 102(e), which has largely been codified in § 4C of the Exchange Act. As with accountants, "practice" before the SEC includes not only appearances in administrative proceedings before the SEC, but also the provision of advice to companies regarding documents that will be filed with the SEC. SEC Rule of Practice 205.2. Thus, legal advice to a registrant that the SEC subsequently determines to have been incorrect can be potentially career ending for the securities lawyer. Few companies would be willing to hire a corporate lawyer who cannot provide advice on SEC filings. That possibility no doubt deters many lawyers from offering advice that pushes the boundaries of the law.

This draconian authority under Rule 102(e) has been used exceedingly sparingly. The most common basis for excluding a lawyer from practice before the SEC has been a prior disbarment by state bar authorities. The SEC has the authority, however, to determine for itself that a lawyer has violated applicable state ethics rules. *Altman v. SEC*, 666 F.3d 1322 (D.C. Cir. 2011) (upholding SEC order barring lawyer from practice before agency for violation of New York Disciplinary Rules). Lawyers can also be found to have "caused" a public company's violation of § 13(a) of the Exchange Act, thereby exposing the lawyer to an injunction or a cease and desist order. Such a finding is hardly likely to enhance a corporate lawyer's career prospects.

The "whistleblowing" obligations of lawyers are somewhat less stringent than those imposed on accountants. Section 307 of Sarbanes-Oxley directed the SEC to establish rules "setting forth minimum standards of professional conduct for attorneys appearing and practicing before the Commission." The SEC responded with Rule of Practice 205. Lawyers are required to report material violations of state or federal securities law and material breaches of fiduciary duty to the company's chief legal officer (i.e., the company's general counsel) or to both the chief legal officer and the chief executive officer. SEC Rule of Practice 205.3(b)(1). The chief legal officer is then required to investigate and cause the company to take an appropriate response if she determines that there has been a material violation. The chief legal officer is required to report back to the lawyer initiating the investigation. Rule 205.3(b)(2). If the lawyer believes that the company's response is insufficient, the lawyer must report the problem to the company's audit committee, any other board committee consisting solely of independent directors, the entire board, or a "qualified legal compliance committee," if the issuer has established one. Rule 205.3(b)(3), (c). The "qualified legal compliance committee" must have at least one member of the audit committee and two or more independent directors. The lawyer *may* reveal confidential information to the SEC without the issuer's consent to "prevent the issuer from committing a material violation that is likely to cause substantial injury to the financial interest or property of the issuer or investors" or to rectify the consequences of such violation that has already occurred, if the attorney's services were used to facilitate the violation. The lawyer may also disclose to the SEC to prevent the issuer from committing perjury in a SEC investigation or enforcement action. Rule 205.3(d).

QUESTIONS

1. What are the implications of the observation by an SEC Commissioner that "in securities matters (other than those where advocacy is clearly proper) the attorney will have to function in a manner more akin to that of the auditors than to that of the advocate"? Sommer, *The Emerging*

Responsibilities of the Securities Lawyer, 1973–1974 Fed. Sec. L. Rep. (CCH) ¶ 79,61 at 83,689, 83,690 (1974).

2. Who is the securities lawyer's client? Management? The board of directors? Current shareholders? Prospective shareholders? The company?

3. Is the SEC the appropriate authority to supervise the conduct of lawyers? Is this role consistent with the agency's enforcement obligations?

HYPOTHETICAL THREE

Ron is a partner at the law firm of Gergich & Meagle, outside counsel for Parks & Recreation, Inc. In drafting the Form 10–K for P & R, Ron discovers that right before his departure, Tom (the former CFO of P & R who was recently terminated due to financial shenanigans) withdrew $10 million from P & R's corporate bank account and spent the entire amount on a fun-filled night in Atlantic City. Ron reports the matter to Justin, P & R's general counsel. Justin thanks Ron and tells him that the company knows about the theft but wants to keep things "quiet" in the upcoming Form 10–K to give the company a chance to "make up" the $10 million deficit before the markets find out. Justin tells Ron specifically not to report this information to P & R's audit committee but to keep the information to himself. Justin concludes by telling Ron: "Parks & Recreation is one of Gergich & Meagle's best clients; I'm sure you want to keep it that way." What should Ron do (if anything)?

———

The following case arises out the collapse of Refco, a commodities brokerage firm. Refco's primary outside counsel, Joseph Collins was convicted by a federal jury of securities and wire fraud. The indictment alleged that Collins schemed with the executives of Refco to conceal $2.4 billion in debt. According to the prosecution, Collins brought more than $40 million in billings to his law firm, Mayer Brown LLP, from his representation of Refco. The following opinion addresses the securities class action claims brought under Rule 10b–5 against Collins and Mayer Brown LLP.

Pacific Inv. Management Co. LLC v. Mayer Brown LLP

603 F.3d 144 (2d Cir. 2010).

■ CABRANES, J., CIRCUIT JUDGE.

This appeal presents [the question] whether, under § 10(b) of the Securities Exchange Act of 1934 and Securities and Exchange Commission Rule 10b–5, a corporation's outside counsel can be liable for false statements that those attorneys allegedly create, but which were not attributed to the law firm or its attorneys at the time the statements were disseminated. . . .

Plaintiffs-appellants, Pacific Investment Management Company LLC and RH Capital Associates LLC appeal from a judgment dismissing their claims against defendants-appellees Mayer Brown LLP, a law firm, and Joseph P. Collins, a former partner at Mayer

Brown. Plaintiffs alleged that defendants violated federal securities laws in the course of representing the now-bankrupt brokerage firm Refco Inc. Specifically, they claimed that defendants (1) facilitated fraudulent transactions between Refco and third parties for the purpose of concealing Refco's uncollectible debt and (2) drafted portions of Refco's security offering documents that contained false information. Although defendants allegedly created false statements that investors relied upon, all of those statements were attributed to Refco, and not Mayer Brown or Collins, at the time of dissemination.

We hold that a secondary actor can be held liable in a private damages action brought pursuant to Rule 10b–5(b) only for false statements attributed to the secondary-actor defendant at the time of dissemination. Absent attribution, plaintiffs cannot show that they relied on defendants' *own* false statements, and participation in the creation of those statements amounts, at most, to aiding and abetting securities fraud. . . .

BACKGROUND

* * *

This case arises from the 2005 collapse of Refco, which was once one of the world's largest providers of brokerage and clearing services in the international derivatives, currency, and futures markets. According to plaintiffs, Mayer Brown served as Refco's primary outside counsel from 1994 until the company's collapse. Collins, a partner at Mayer Brown, was the firm's primary contact with Refco and the billing partner in charge of the Refco account. Refco was a lucrative client for Mayer Brown and Collins' largest personal client.

As part of its business model, Refco extended credit to its customers so that they could trade on "margin"—*i.e.*, trade in securities with money borrowed from Refco. In the late 1990s, Refco customers suffered massive trading losses and consequently were unable to repay hundreds of millions of dollars of margin loans extended by Refco. Concerned that properly accounting for these debts as "write-offs" would threaten the company's survival, Refco, allegedly with the help of defendants, arranged a series of sham transactions designed to conceal the losses.

Specifically, plaintiffs allege that Refco transferred its uncollectible debts to Refco Group Holdings, Inc. [RGHI]—an entity controlled by Refco's Chief Executive Officer—in exchange for a receivable purportedly owed from RGHI to Refco. Recognizing that a large debt owed to it by a related entity would arouse suspicion with investors and regulators, Refco, allegedly with the help of defendants, engaged in a series of sham loan transactions at the end of each quarter and each fiscal year to pay off the RGHI receivable. It did so by loaning money to third parties, who then loaned the same amount to RGHI, which in turn used the funds to pay off Refco's receivable. Days after the fiscal period closed, all of the loans were repaid and the third parties were paid a fee for their participation in the scheme. The result of these circular transactions was that, at the end of financial periods, Refco reported receivables owed to it by various third parties rather than the related entity RGHI.

Mayer Brown and Collins participated in seventeen of these sham loan transactions between 2000 and 2005, representing both Refco and RGHI. According to plaintiffs, defendants' involvement included negotiating the terms of the loans, drafting and revising the documents relating to the loans, transmitting the documents to the participants, and retaining custody of and distributing the executed copies of the documents.

Plaintiffs also allege that defendants are responsible for false statements appearing in three Refco documents: (1) an Offering Memorandum for an unregistered bond offering in July 2004), (2) a Registration Statement for a subsequent registered bond offering, and (3) a Registration Statement for Refco's initial public offering of common stock in August 2005. Each of these documents contained false or misleading statements because they failed to disclose the true nature of Refco's financial condition, which had been concealed, in part, through the loan transactions described above.

Defendants allegedly participated in the creation of the false statements contained in each of the documents identified above. Collins and other Mayer Brown attorneys allegedly reviewed and revised portions of the Offering Memorandum and attended drafting sessions. Collins and another Mayer Brown attorney also personally drafted the Management Discussion & Analysis portion of the Offering Memorandum, which, according to plaintiffs, discussed Refco's business and financial condition in a way that defendants knew to be false. The Offering Memorandum was used as the foundation for the Registration Statement, which was substantially similar in content. According to plaintiffs, defendants further assisted in the preparation of the Registration Statement by reviewing comment letters from the SEC and participating in drafting sessions. Finally, plaintiffs allege that defendants were directly involved in reviewing and drafting the IPO Registration Statement because they received, and presumably reviewed, the SEC's comments on that filing.

Both the Offering Memorandum and the IPO Registration Statement note that Mayer Brown represented Refco in connection with those transactions. The Registration Statement does not mention Mayer Brown. None of the documents specifically attribute any of the information contained therein to Mayer Brown or Collins.

Plaintiffs, who purchased securities from Refco during the period that defendants were allegedly engaging in fraud, commenced this action after Refco declared bankruptcy in 2005. They asserted claims for violation of § 10(b) of the Exchange Act and Rule 10b–5. . . .

The District Court dismissed plaintiffs' claims. . . . With respect to plaintiffs' claim that defendants violated Rule 10b–5(b) by drafting and revising portions of Refco's public documents, the Court found that no statements in those documents were attributed to defendants and that plaintiffs had therefore alleged conduct akin to aiding and abetting, for which securities laws provide no private right of action. . . .

DISCUSSION

I. Plaintiffs' Rule 10b–5(b) Claim

Plaintiffs assert that the District Court erred in holding that attorneys who participate in the drafting of false statements cannot be liable in a private damages action if the statements are not attributed to those attorneys at the time of dissemination. Along with the SEC as *amicus curiae*, plaintiffs argue that attribution is only one means by which attorneys and other secondary actors can incur liability for securities fraud. They urge us to adopt a "creator standard" and hold that a defendant can be liable for *creating* a false statement that investors rely on, regardless of whether that statement is attributed to the defendant at the time of dissemination. . . .

Defendants respond that, under our precedents, attorneys who participate in the drafting of false statements cannot be liable absent explicit attribution at the time of dissemination. Without attribution, defendants contend, secondary actors do not commit a primary violation of Rule 10b–5(b) and their conduct amounts, at most, to aiding and abetting.

* * *

1.   Attribution Is Consistent with *Stoneridge*

The Supreme Court has never directly addressed whether attribution at the time of dissemination is required for secondary actors to be liable in a private damages action brought pursuant to Rule 10b–5. Nevertheless, the Court's recent decision in *Stoneridge* is instructive.

The Supreme Court's focus on reliance in *Stoneridge* favors a rule, such as attribution, that is designed to preserve that element of the private right of action available under Rule 10b–5. In *Stoneridge*, . . . [t]he Court held that plaintiffs' claims failed as a matter of law because plaintiffs could not demonstrate that they "rel[ied] upon [defendants'] *own* deceptive conduct" and because "[i]t was [the issuing firm] Charter, not [defendants], that misled its auditor and filed fraudulent financial statements." We think that reasoning is consistent with an attribution requirement in the context of claims based on false statements. If a plaintiff must rely on a secondary actor's *own* deceptive conduct to state a claim under Rule 10b–5(a) and (c), it stands to reason that a plaintiff must also rely on a secondary actor's *own* deceptive statements—and not on statements conveyed to the public through another source and not attributed to the defendant—to state a claim under Rule 10b–5(b).

More generally, *Stoneridge* stands for the proposition that reliance is the critical element in private actions under Rule 10b–5. This general proposition, applied to the specific issue of secondary actor liability, further supports an attribution requirement. Attribution is necessary to show reliance. Where statements are publicly attributed to a well-known national law or accounting firm, buyers and sellers of securities (and the market generally) are more likely to credit the accuracy of those statements. Because of the firm's imprimatur, individuals may be comforted by the supposedly impartial assessment and, accordingly, be induced to purchase a particular security. Without explicit attribution to the firm, however, reliance on that firm's participation can only be shown through "an indirect chain . . . too remote for liability."

2.   Attribution Is Consistent with Our "Bright Line" Approach

* * *

A bright line rule such as an attribution requirement also has many benefits in application. An attribution requirement is relatively easy for district courts to apply and avoids protracted litigation and discovery aimed at learning the identity of each person or entity that had some connection, however tenuous, to the creation of an allegedly false statement. Furthermore, as the Supreme Court has explained, securities law is "an area that demands certainty and predictability." Uncertainty can lead to many undesirable consequences, "[f]or example, newer and smaller companies may find it difficult to obtain advice from professionals. A professional may fear that a newer or smaller company may not survive and that business failure would generate securities litigation against the professional, among others." Uncertainty also increases the costs of doing business and raising capital. A creator standard would inevitably lead to uncertainty regarding the scope of Rule 10b–5 liability and potentially deter beneficial conduct.

C.   Application of the Attribution Requirement

Applying the attribution standard to the alleged false and misleading statements in this case, we conclude that the District Court properly dismissed plaintiffs' Rule 10b–5(b) claims against Mayer Brown and Collins. No statements in the Offering Memorandum, the Registration Statement, or the IPO Registration Statement are attributed to Collins, and he is not even mentioned by name in any of those documents. Accordingly, plaintiffs cannot show reliance on any of Collins' statements.

The Offering Memorandum and the IPO Registration Statement note that Mayer Brown, among other counsel, represented Refco in connection with those transactions but neither document attributes any particular statements to Mayer Brown. Mayer Brown is not identified as the author of any portion of the documents. Nor can the mere mention of the firm's representation of Refco be considered an "articulated statement" by Mayer Brown adopting Refco's statements as its own. Absent such attribution, plaintiffs cannot show reliance on any statements of Mayer Brown.

* * *

We recognize that, after *Stoneridge*, it is somewhat unclear how the deceptive conduct of a secondary actor could be communicated to the public and yet remain "deceptive." What is clear from *Stoneridge*, however, is that the mere fact that the ultimate result of a secondary actor's deceptive course of conduct is communicated to the public through a company's financial statements is insufficient to show reliance on the secondary actor's *own* deceptive conduct. Because that is all plaintiffs have alleged here, we are bound by the Supreme Court's holding in *Stoneridge*.

Furthermore, nothing about Mayer Brown's or Collins' actions made it necessary or inevitable that Refco would mislead investors. As the District Court aptly noted, unlike in *Stoneridge*, "the Mayer Brown Defendants were not even the counter-party to the fraudulent transactions; they merely participated in drafting the documents to effect those transactions." We therefore agree that, "[a]s was the case in *Stoneridge*, it was Refco, not the Mayer Brown Defendants, that filed fraudulent financial statements; nothing the Mayer Brown Defendants did made it necessary or inevitable for Refco to record the transactions as it did."

* * *

QUESTIONS

1. Mayer Brown's partner, Collins, went to jail for his work with Refco, but he and the firm are excused from civil liability. Does this make sense from a policy perspective? Is it fair that investors should have a more difficult time recovering than a prosecutor has in obtaining a conviction?

2. Should lawyers be required to certify the narrative disclosures in a company's SEC filings, such as the Management's Discussion and Analysis section? The financial statements?

3. How does the Supreme Court's subsequent *Janus Capital* decision (excerpted in Chapter 5) affect Rule 10b–5 liability exposure for attorneys and law firms like Collins and Mayer Brown LLP?

V. CREDIT RATING AGENCIES

Standard & Poor's, Moody's Investors Service, Inc., and Fitch, Inc. have all been designated by the SEC as nationally recognized statistical rating organizations (NRSROs). They rate the creditworthiness of corporate issuers, as well as specific securities issuances. Prior to the Financial Crisis, classification by the SEC as an NRSRO meant that securities highly rated by these credit ratings agencies could be purchased by institutional investors who were limited to holding only "safe" investments. In the Financial Crisis, however, it turned out that many of these investments were not so safe, particularly the mortgage-backed securities discussed in Chapter 3. In enacting the Dodd-Frank Act, Congress specifically found that:

> Credit rating agencies, including nationally recognized statistical rating organizations, play a critical "gatekeeper" role in the debt market that is functionally similar to that of securities analysts, who evaluate the quality of securities in the equity market, and auditors, who review the financial statements of firms. Such role justifies a similar level of public oversight and accountability.

Dodd-Frank Act § 931(2). We cover in this section "the public oversight and accountability" imposed on credit rating agencies by Congress and the SEC. Before we get into the regulations, however, a brief note on the economic role played by the credit rating agencies. The following excerpt from a report by the Government Accountability Office provides a useful summary of the role that credit rating agencies play and the impact that they have on financial markets.

Securities Fraud Liability of Secondary Actors, GAO–11–664

U.S. Government Accountability Office (July 21, 2011).

The [Exchange] Act defines a credit rating as an assessment of the creditworthiness of an obligor as an entity or with respect to specific securities or money market instruments. Section 3(a)(60). In the past few decades, credit ratings have assumed increasing importance in the financial markets, in large part due to their use in law and regulation. In 1975, the SEC first used the term National Recognized Statistical Rating Organization (NRSRO) to describe those rating agencies whose ratings could be relied upon to determine capital charges for different types of debt securities broker-dealers held. Since then, the SEC has used the NRSRO designation in a number of regulations. Issuers seek credit ratings for a number of reasons, such as to improve the marketability or pricing of their financial obligations, or to satisfy investors, lenders, or counterparties. Institutional investors, such as mutual funds, pension funds, and insurance companies are among the largest owners of debt securities in the United States and are substantial users of credit ratings. Retail participation in the debt markets generally takes place indirectly through these fiduciaries. Institutional investors may use credit ratings as one of several inputs to their own internal credit assessments and investment analysis. Broker-dealers that make recommendations and sell securities to their clients also use ratings.

Academic literature suggests that credit ratings affect financial markets both by providing information to investors and other market participants and by their use in regulations. Studies find that obtaining a credit rating generally increases a firm's access to capital markets and that firms with credit ratings have capital structures different from those of firms without them. Some studies suggest that firms adjust their capital structure to achieve a particular credit rating. One explanation of these relationships is that credit rating agencies have access to private information about the issuers and issues they rate, and the ratings they assign incorporate this information. Thus, ratings are a mechanism for communicating this otherwise unavailable information to market participants. The appropriate role of credit rating agencies has become increasingly controversial in the wake of the recent financial crisis. The performance of the three largest NRSROs in rating subprime residential mortgage-backed securities and related securities raised questions about the accuracy of their ratings generally, the integrity of the ratings process, and investor reliance on NRSRO ratings for investment decisions.

———

As the GAO report makes clear, credit rating agencies are economically important. They are also quite controversial. Why? One reason is that the ratings provided by the agencies proved of dubious accuracy during the Financial Crisis. The ratings attached to mortgage-backed securities and collateralized-debt obligations proved to be wildly optimistic, as many AAA-rated securities plunged in value as the subprime mortgage market collapsed. Moreover, downgrades of the credit ratings for those instruments tended to lag behind the deterioration of their market value.

Credit ratings are also suspect for structural reasons. Credit rating agencies have traditionally not done any factual verification of the information that their rating models depend on. That information is obtained from the issuer and simply "plugged" into the models credit rating agencies use to determine future default risk.

Even more disturbing, however, are the conflicts of interest inherent in the credit rating agencies' business models. Credit rating agencies provide advice to companies issuing securities on how to enhance the ratings for the securities that they plan to issue. Yet more suspect, credit rating agencies are not paid by the users of credit ratings, but instead, by the issuers of the securities rated. Moreover, credit rating agencies must compete to attract the business of issuers. These conflicts of interest for credit rating agencies bring into question their objectivity. Do credit rating agencies skew their ratings to attract business from issuers?

A. LIABILITY

In the following case, plaintiffs argue that credit rating agencies are effectively working on behalf of corporate issuers. The plaintiffs' goal was to push the boundaries of the list of statutory defendants under § 11 of the Securities Act (covered in Chapter 8). Should credit rating agencies be included in § 11's strict liability regime? What factors should be considered in making this determination?

In re Lehman Brothers Mortgage-Backed Securities Litigation
650 F.3d 167 (2d Cir. 2011).

■ RAGGI, R., CIRCUIT JUDGE.

* * *

Plaintiffs appeal from judgments of the United States District Court, dismissing their class-action complaints seeking to hold defendants ... Standard & Poor's, Moody's Investors Service, Inc., and/or Fitch, Inc. (collectively, "Rating Agencies"), liable as underwriters ... for misstatements or omissions in securities offering documents in violation of § 11.... Plaintiffs submit that the Rating Agencies are "underwriters" as defined by § 2(a)(11) because they helped structure securities transactions to achieve desired ratings....

I. *Background*

A. *The Securities Offerings*

1. *Mortgage Pass-Through Certificates*

In the period from 2005 to 2007, plaintiffs and similarly situated persons purchased approximately $155 billion worth of mortgage pass-through certificates registered with the Securities and Exchange Commission entitling them to distributions from underlying pools of mortgages. To create such certificates, a "sponsor" originates or acquires mortgages. Next, the loans are sold to a "depositor" that securitizes the loans—meaning, in effect, that the depositor secures the rights to cash flows from the loans so that those rights can be sold to investors. The loans are then placed in issuing trusts, which collect the principal and interest payments made by the individual mortgage borrowers and, in turn, pay out distributions to the purchasers of the mortgage pass-through certificates. Finally, different risk levels, or "tranches" of risk, are created by using various types of credit enhancement, such as subordinating lower tranches to absorb losses first, overcollateralizing the loan pools in excess of the bond amount, or creating an excess spread fund to cover the difference between the interest collected from borrowers and amounts owed to investors.[1] Each tranche is denominated by a credit rating—in these cases issued by one or more Rating Agencies—determined by the seniority level and the expected loss of the loan pool. Finally, the depositor sells the certificates to underwriters, who then offer them to investors.

Many of the certificates here at issue received AAA ratings, the "safest" tranche supposedly least likely to default. Investment-grade ratings were crucial to the certificates' sale because many institutional investors must purchase investment-grade securities. Moreover, some senior certificates' sales were conditioned on the receipt of AAA ratings.

2. *Plaintiffs' Purchase of Certificates*

The Plaintiffs bought certificates in . . . offerings . . . that were sponsored by Lehman Brothers Holdings, Inc. (LBHI) and underwritten by Lehman Brothers, Inc., with Structured Asset Securities Corporation, a wholly-owned LBHI entity, acting as depositor. The certificates were issued pursuant to one of two registration statements, initially filed with the SEC on September 16, 2005, and August 8, 2006, respectively. . . .

B. *Rating Agencies' Alleged Role in the Offerings*

In the transactions described above, plaintiffs allege that the Rating Agencies, which ordinarily serve as passive evaluators of credit risk, exceeded their traditional roles by actively aiding in the structuring and securitization process. Specifically, plaintiffs allege that issuing banks engaged particular Rating Agencies through a "ratings shopping" process, whereby the Rating Agencies reviewed loan-level data for a mortgage pool and provided preliminary ratings. The banks then negotiated with the Rating Agencies regarding the amount of credit enhancements and percentage of AAA certificates for each mortgage pool. By thus "play[ing] the agencies off one another" and choosing the agency offering the highest percentage of AAA certificates with the least amount of credit enhancements, the banks purportedly "engender[ed] a race to the bottom in terms of rating quality."

During and after this negotiation, the Rating Agencies engaged in an "iterative process" with the banks, providing "feedback" on which combinations of loans and credit enhancements would generate particular ratings. In the course of this dialogue, issuers adjusted the certificates' structures until they achieved desired ratings. As one

---

[1]   Subordinating the bonds creates a tiered structure known as a "waterfall." Losses from mortgage defaults, delinquencies, or other factors are allocated in reverse seniority, with junior tranches incurring losses first until their interests are reduced to zero.

Moody's officer described the process: "You start with a rating and build a deal around a rating." Plaintiffs submit that the Rating Agencies thus helped determine the composition of loan pools, the certificates' structures, and the amount and kinds of credit enhancement for particular tranches.

Toward this end, the Rating Agencies allegedly provided their modeling tools to the banks' traders to help them pre-determine the combinations of credit enhancements and loans needed to achieve specific ratings. S & P's LEVELS or SPIRES models, and Moody's M-3 model, analyzed fifty to eighty different loan characteristics in estimating the number and extent of likely loan defaults. Based on these factors, the models calculated the amount of credit enhancement required for a specific pool of loans to receive a AAA rating. According to the Plaintiffs, LBHI used the modeling data in determining bidding prices for loans. Moody's and S & P also received loan—level files and advised Lehman on appropriate loan prices. The Rating Agencies, however, had purportedly failed to update their models to reflect accurately the higher risks of certain underlying loans, such as subprime, interest-only, and negative amortization mortgages.[2] The models also failed to account for deteriorating loan origination standards. As a result, plaintiffs complain that the certificates' AAA or investment-grade ratings did not accurately represent their risk.

C. *District Court Proceedings*

During the 2008 mortgage crisis, the Rating Agencies downgraded plaintiffs' AAA or investment-grade certificates, causing their values to decline. Plaintiffs proceeded to sue various entities involved in their offerings.

* * *

All plaintiffs allege that the Rating Agencies that rated their certificates are "underwriters" as defined in § 2(a)(11) and, therefore, are strictly liable pursuant to § 11(a)(5) for misstatements and omissions in the certificates' offering documents. . . .

* * *

The term "underwriter" is defined in [§ 2(a)(11)] as:

> any person who has purchased from an issuer with a view to, or offers or sells for an issuer in connection with, the distribution of any security, or participates or has a direct or indirect participation in any such undertaking, or participates or has a participation in the direct or indirect underwriting of any such undertaking.

Plaintiffs submit that the Rating Agencies qualify as underwriters because they structured the certificates here at issue to achieve desired ratings, which was a necessary predicate to the securities' distribution

---

[2] Subprime mortgages are loans made to borrowers with poor credit histories, "creating a high risk of default." An interest-only loan allows borrowers to pay only the interest for a stated period "in return for significantly larger payments later." A negative amortization loan involves increases in the principal balance when monthly payments are insufficient to pay accruing interest. Plaintiffs allege that S & P developed an updated ratings model in 2004 that covered these new mortgage products, but it was never implemented.

in the market. We are not persuaded. The plain language of the statute limits liability to persons who participate in the purchase, offer, or sale of securities for distribution. While such participation may be indirect as well as direct, the statute does not reach further to identify as underwriters persons who provide services that facilitate a securities offering, but who do not themselves participate in the statutorily specified distribution-related activities.

1. *Underwriter Liability Requires Participation in Activities Involving the Distribution of Securities to the Public*

a. *The Statute's Plain Language*

To interpret the statutory definition of "underwriter," we begin, as we must, with the statute's text, considering the ordinary meaning of Congress's chosen language as informed by its punctuation.

Applying these principles here, we conclude that common to all categories of persons identified as "underwriters" by the plain language of § 2(a)(11) is activity related to the actual distribution of securities. With respect to the first two categories of persons qualifying as "underwriters"—those who (1) purchase from an issuer or (2) offer or sell for an issuer—this is evidenced by the fact that the distribution requirement is set off from the two antecedent activities by a comma. Indeed, this interpretation is especially warranted here because the first category, persons "purchasing from an issuer with a view to," is incomplete unless read in conjunction with "the distribution of any security."

With respect to the last two categories of persons qualifying as "underwriters," their connection to the activity of distribution is evidenced by use of the phrase "such undertaking," which plainly references the aforesaid purchases, offers, or sales relating to the distribution of securities.

Thus, to qualify as an underwriter under the participation prongs of the statutory definition, a person must participate, directly or indirectly, in purchasing securities from an issuer with a view to distribution, in offering or selling securities for an issuer in connection with a distribution, or in the underwriting of such an offering. Nothing in the statute's text supports expanding the definition of underwriter to reach persons not themselves participating in such purchases, offers, or sales, but whose actions may facilitate the participation of others in such undertakings.

* * *

[N]othing in plaintiffs' complaints suggest that the Rating Agencies explicitly assumed the responsibilities of underwriters. Plaintiffs' allegations that the Rating Agencies assumed the historic role of underwriters by evaluating loan data and assisting in the creation of the securities falls well short of alleging that the Agencies—explicitly, or otherwise—participated in the *distribution* of the securities. Indeed, . . . all of the certificate transactions here at issue involved traditional underwriters other than the Rating Agencies.

* * *

c.   *Legislative History and Purpose*

Even if we were to identify ambiguity in the text or in our prior case law, which we do not, an examination of § 11's legislative history and purpose reinforces our holding that the Rating Agencies do not qualify as 'underwriters.' . . .

A House Report explains that "underwriter" was "defined broadly enough to include not only the ordinary underwriter, who for a commission promises to see that an issue is disposed of at a certain price, but also . . . the person who purchases an issue outright with the idea of then selling that issue to the public." Additionally, the definition encompassed "two other groups of persons who perform functions, similar in character, in the distribution:" (1) underwriters of the underwriter, and (2) "participants in the underwriting or outright purchase . . . who are given a certain share or interest." A later House Report states that changes were made to exclude from the definition those who merely furnish an underwriter money, and to adopt a test "of participation in the underwriting undertaking rather than that of a mere interest in it."

By focusing on persons playing roles similar to those disposing of or reselling securities, or those participating in such actions, these reports indicate that "congressional intent was to include as underwriters all persons who might *operate as conduits* for securities being placed into the hands of the investing public." In short, Congress did not intend for strict underwriter liability to extend to persons merely *interested in* a distribution by virtue of their provision of non-distribution services to an offeror.

"Indeed, the strict liability nature of the statutory cause of action suggests the opposite." As we have previously noted, § 11 ensures accurate disclosures in registration statements by imposing *in terrorem* liability on a limited list of persons. To be sure, "direct or indirect participation" in underwriting subjects a person to strict liability. But the participation must be in the statutorily enumerated distributional activities, not in non-distributional activities that may facilitate the eventual distribution by others. This approach avoids the implausible result of transforming every lawyer, accountant, and other professional whose work is theoretically "necessary" to bringing a security to market into an "underwriter" subject to strict liability under § 11, a dramatic outcome that Congress provided no sign of intending. Rather, the legislative history signals that § 11 was designed to impose its exacting standards regarding the provision of accurate and complete information only on the people (or entities) responsible for distributing securities to the public, that is, on those engaged in the public offering.

In sum, we conclude that the text, case law, legislative history, and purpose of the statute demonstrate that Congress intended the participation clause of the underwriter definition to reach those who participate in purchasing securities with a view towards distribution, or in offering or selling securities for an issuer in connection with a distribution, but not further.

2. *Application of Underwriter Definition to Defendants' Alleged Conduct*

With this understanding of the scope of § 11 liability, we consider plaintiffs' challenge to the dismissal of their complaints against the Rating Agencies. . . . Applying the underwriter definition on *de novo* review, we conclude that plaintiffs failed to allege facts sufficient to state a plausible § 11 claim against the Rating Agency defendants.

The complaints contain extensive descriptions of the Rating Agencies' activities in structuring the certificate transactions, dictating the kinds and quantity of loans or credit enhancements needed for desired ratings, and providing modeling tools to traders to pre-structure loan pools. Plaintiffs submit that these allegations demonstrate that the Rating Agencies played a necessary role in the securities' distribution because (1) their ratings translated opaque financial products into understandable risk levels, (2) institutional investors were required to buy investment-grade securities, and (3) offerings were conditioned on senior tranches receiving AAA ratings. We disagree . . . structuring or creating securities does not constitute the requisite participation in underwriting.

As the district court in this case explained, even assuming, as we must, that the Rating Agencies "had a good deal to do with the composition and characteristics of the pools of mortgage loans and the credit enhancements of the [c]ertificates that ultimately were sold," plaintiffs failed to allege that defendants "participated in the relevant" undertaking: that of purchasing securities from the issuer with a view towards distribution, or selling or offering securities for the issuer in connection with a distribution. The Rating Agencies' efforts in creating and structuring certificates occurred during the initial stages of securitization, not during efforts to disperse certificates to investors.

The fact that the market needed ratings to understand structured financial products or that particular ratings were essential to the certificates' eventual sale does not change the analysis. While it is certainly true that some investors will refrain from buying securities that do not bear a AAA rating, and that some banks will decline to assume the risk of pursuing a public offering unless a security receives a high credit rating, plaintiffs, once again, fail to demonstrate that the Rating Agencies were involved in a statutorily listed distributional activity.

The rating issued by a Rating Agency speaks merely to the Agency's opinion of the creditworthiness of a particular security. In other words, it is the sort of expert opinion classically evaluated under the "expert" provision of § 11, not under the "underwriter" provision. Indeed, each offering document explained that the assigned credit rating was "not a recommendation to buy, sell or hold securities and may be subject to revision or withdrawal at any time."

Furthermore, expanding § 11 to cover the conduct of the Rating Agencies would contradict that section's specific enumeration of liable parties, which does not include a number of persons necessary to the creation of securities, such as banks that originated the underlying loans, traders who structured the transactions, or experts who did not consent to being named. Because plaintiffs' theory would render these narrowly drawn categories meaningless and contradict well-settled canons of statutory construction, we decline to adopt it. Rather, we conclude that the mere structuring or creation of securities does not constitute participation in statutory underwriting. . . .

Contrary to plaintiffs' assertion, this conclusion will not absolve rating agencies of all liability for their roles in fraudulent securities offerings. As plaintiffs acknowledged at oral argument, they may bring securities fraud claims against the Rating Agencies pursuant to § 10(b) of the Securities Exchange Act of 1934, although liability under that section is, of course, subject to scienter, reliance, and loss causation requirements not applicable to § 11 claims. It is precisely because § 11 "give[s] rise to liability more readily," however, that it is applies "more narrowly" than § 10(b).

In sum, because plaintiffs failed to plead facts sufficient to bring the Rating Agencies within the statutory definition of underwriter, their § 11 claims against these defendants were properly dismissed.

* * *

NOTES

1.   *Expert liability and credit rating agencies.* The *Lehman Brothers* court mentioned that the credit rating agencies' ratings disclosed in the registration statement are "the sort of expert opinion classically evaluated under the 'expert' provision of § 11." Section 11(a)(4) allows plaintiffs to name experts as defendants in a § 11 action with respect to specific expertised sections of the registration statement. Prior to the Dodd-Frank Act, however, Rule 436(g) of the Securities Act provided that "the security rating assigned to a class of debt securities, a class of convertible debt securities, or a class of preferred stock by a nationally recognized statistical rating organization . . . shall not be considered a part of the registration statement prepared or certified by a person within the meaning of [§] 11 of the Act." Section 939G of the Dodd-Frank Act explicitly rescinded Rule 436(g). As a result, credit rating agencies that consent to have their credit ratings disclosed as part of the registration statement now face liability as experts under § 11(a)(4) for material misstatements or omissions relating to the credit ratings. Perhaps not surprisingly, the credit rating agencies refused to give their consent to be named as experts, the debt markets temporarily froze, and the SEC declared a moratorium on its rule requiring the disclosure of credit ratings.

The Dodd-Frank Act also makes a number of changes to the Exchange Act intended to increase potential liability for credit rating agencies. The law specifically provides that the enforcement and penalty provisions of the 1934 Act "apply to statements made by a credit rating agency in the same manner and to the same extent as such provisions apply to statements made by a registered public accounting firm or a securities analyst under the securities laws." Exchange Act § 15E(m)(1). Dodd-Frank also modifies the requisite "state of mind" for private securities fraud actions against a credit rating agency. An investor or other plaintiff may now satisfy pleading standards by stating facts giving rise to a strong inference that the credit rating agency knowingly or recklessly failed to conduct a reasonable investigation of the rated security or the credit rating agency failed to obtain reasonable verification of such factual elements from a competent party independent of the issuer. Exchange Act § 21D(b)(2). The Dodd-Frank Act also excludes ratings from the forward-looking safe harbor of the PSLRA. Exchange Act § 15E(m)(1).

One lingering issue with respect to the liability of credit rating agencies is whether their ratings are expressions of opinions entitled to First Amendment protection. Courts are divided on this question. *Compare Compuware Corporation v. Moody's Investors Services*, 499 F.3d 520, 530 (6th Cir. 2007) (actual malice required in breach of contract action against credit rating agency) *with Abu Dhabi Commercial Bank v. Morgan Stanley & Co., Inc.*, 651 F. Supp. 2d 155 (S.D.N.Y. 2009) (no First Amendment protection for rating circulated only to a small group of investors).

QUESTIONS

1. Where is the line between "distributional" and "non-distributional" activities in an offering?

2. Would making credit rating agencies liable for misstatements in the registration statement reduce information asymmetry for investors in a public offering? At what cost?

B. REGULATION OF CREDIT RATING AGENCIES

Not satisfied with increasing credit rating agencies' liability exposure, Congress also stepped up the regulation of NRSROs in the Dodd-Frank Act. That legislation came on the heels of the Credit Rating Agency Reform Act of 2006, which added § 15E to the Exchange Act. The 2006 Act authorized the SEC to adopt rules to limit the effects of NRSROs conflicts of interest, but expressly denied the SEC authority over "the substance of credit ratings or the procedures or methodologies by which and NRSRO determines credit ratings." Exchange Act § 15E(c)(2).

The Dodd-Frank Act did not undo this restriction, but it did increase the SEC's enforcement authority over NRSROs, including the establishment of an Office of Credit Ratings. Exchange Act § 15E(p). The law also requires NRSROs to establish effective internal control structures, Exchange Act § 15E(c)(3), and requires greater disclosure of rating methodology and performance. Exchange Act § 15E(q)–(s). Credit rating agencies now must also disclose any third party due diligence that they are relying on in rating a security. Exchange Act § 15E(s)(4). Finally, Congress regulated the corporate governance of credit rating agencies, mandating independent board of directors for NRSROs. Exchange Act § 15E(t).

Congress also acted to reduce the influence of credit ratings. The Dodd-Frank Act requires the SEC (and other federal agencies) to review existing regulations that require the use of an assessment of the credit-worthiness of a security and remove any reference or the requirement of reliance on credit ratings and substitute in such regulations an appropriate standard of credit-worthiness. Dodd-Frank Act § 939A.

QUESTIONS

1. Should the current business model of credit rating agencies be replaced by a model in which investors pay for subscriptions? A government rating agency?

2. What problems are created by reducing regulatory reliance on credit ratings? Are there any adequate substitutes?

VI. WHISTLEBLOWERS

Company employees who blow the whistle on fraud at their employers attract a lot of attention from the press and politicians. Sherron Watkins at Enron and Cynthia Cooper at WorldCom were mid-level employees who played critical roles in bringing the frauds at those two companies to light. Not surprisingly, Congress included provisions in the Sarbanes-Oxley Act protecting whistleblowers who come forward with information relating to corporate wrongdoing. When Congress returned to securities regulation reform with the Dodd-Frank Act, it created large incentives for whistleblowers to curtail corporate fraud.

Why are whistleblowers so popular with Congress? Whistleblower are perhaps not, strictly speaking, gatekeepers because they generally do not have the power to prevent fraud by withholding their cooperation. Whistleblowers, however, have one advantage over the categories of gatekeepers that we have discussed above in their access to information. Whistleblowers are typically insiders, with a level of access to information that outside professionals will seldom have. The biggest challenge for a high-level corporate executive in carrying out a fraud of any substantial scope or duration is keeping subordinates in the dark. Of course, even if subordinates are privy to the fraudulent scheme, the CEO or CFO engaged in fraud may be able to keep his or her subordinates silent through intimidation. The threat of firing is a pretty substantial factor influencing even honest employees from reporting what they know to the company's board of directors, notwithstanding their fiduciary obligation to do so.

It is this threat of intimidation that Congress attempted to tackle with the whistleblowing provisions in the Sarbanes-Oxley Act. Public companies are prohibited from discriminating against employees who provide information about fraud at the corporation to federal agencies, Congress, or their supervisors. 18 U.S.C. § 1514A(a). Claims of discrimination first must be presented to the Occupational Safety and Health Administration (OSHA), which is part of the Department of Labor, within 90 days of the violation. 18 U.S.C. § 1514A(b). Individuals who are not granted relief by OSHA can file suit in federal court. 18 U.S.C. § 1514A(b)(1). Remedies include backpay, reinstatement, and attorneys' fees. 18 U.S.C. § 1514A(c). The Justice Department can also pursue criminal prosecutions for violations. 18 U.S.C. § 1513(e).

The case below discusses the Sarbanes-Oxley whistleblower provision. Does the provision give sufficient protection to employees who try to disclose wrongdoing?

Wiest v. Lynch

2011 WL 2923860 (E.D.Pa. 2011).

■ PRATTER, G., DISTRICT JUDGE.

Jeffrey Wiest has sued his former employer, Tyco Electronics Corp. (Tyco), along with a number of Tyco officers and management-level employees namely, Thomas Lynch, Terrence Curtin, Charles Post, and Charles Dougherty. . . . Mr. Wiest alleges that the Defendants violated the anti-retaliation provision of the Sarbanes-Oxley Act of 2002 by retaliating and discriminating against him after he engaged in allegedly protected activity. . . .

The Defendants have moved to dismiss the entire Complaint. For the reasons set forth below, their motion will be granted.

* * *

Mr. Wiest is a former employee of Tyco. Before his termination in April 2010, Mr. Wiest had worked for 31 years in Tyco's accounts payable department. Throughout his employment, Mr. Wiest had consistently received high ratings in his job performance reviews, especially in the areas of "integrity" and "ethics and values." He received an "impact bonus" in July 2008 for his "significant achievements and continuing focus on 'doing the right thing.'"

Tyco is a wholly-owned subsidiary of Tyco Electronics Ltd. (Tyco Ltd.), a publicly traded Swiss corporation. Until 2007, Tyco Ltd. was a subsidiary of Tyco International, Ltd. (Tyco International). Tyco Ltd. was separated from Tyco International in the wake of a highly-publicized 2002 corporate scandal involving Tyco International's former CEO, Dennis Kozlowski, that resulted in Mr. Kozlowski's 2005 conviction for allegedly receiving $81 million in unauthorized bonuses. The last several years of Mr. Wiest's employment at Tyco were allegedly extremely stressful as a result of the Kozlowski scandal, pressure to reduce costs, and Mr. Wiest's personal medical issues.

Beginning in mid-2007, Mr. Wiest refused to process certain event expenditures that he felt were improper because they did not meet reimbursement or payment standards set by the accounting department, violated rules and regulations promulgated by the Securities and Exchange Commission or tax laws and regulations, or otherwise raised ethical concerns. Among the expenses Mr. Wiest refused to process without further review of the proper tax or accounting treatment were expenses associated with [an event] at the Atlantis Resort in the Bahamas (the Atlantis event). Mr. Wiest sent email communications to his supervisors regarding the need for further tax or accounting analyses of the expenses. . . . Plaintiff was particularly concerned because he felt that there were similarities between some of the expenses . . . and the type of expenditures for which Mr. Kozlowski was eventually prosecuted.

After further review of the expenses associated with the Atlantis event, Tyco's tax department found that the event costs had been improperly categorized as business expenses, and instead would have to be treated as award income to the employees who attended the event. Tyco's management decided to go ahead with the event, treat the costs as award income to the attendees, and cover the resulting tax liability by "grossing up" the attendees' bonuses.[2]

* * *

Apparently, Mr. Wiest continued to express his concerns regarding various other expenditures until September 2009, when he began to suspect that individuals on Tyco's management team were frustrated with his challenges to event expenditures, especially the head of the business unit that hosted the Atlantis [event], Defendant Charles Dougherty. Mr. Wiest alleges that his suspicion was bolstered when he noticed that his co-workers and supervisors were acting differently around him, and Susan Wallace of Tyco's human resources department called him in for a meeting on September 17, 2009. During the meeting, Ms. Wallace informed Mr. Wiest that she was initiating an investigation into allegations that he had: (1) failed to properly report baseball tickets he had received from Mr. Hofsass in August 2009 as a vendor gift in violation of company policy; (2) made sexually suggestive comments to co-workers; and (3) engaged in an improper relationship with another Tyco employee ten years earlier. Mr. Wiest questioned the seriousness of the allegations, but was not allowed to respond to the allegations during the meeting. He was also unable to receive any additional information from Mr. Hofsass.

On September 29, 2009, after inquiring about the status of the investigation, Mr. Wiest was told that "it was at a very serious stage." The next morning, he was told that he should not bother with a scheduled performance review. As a result of the stress of the investigation, Mr. Wiest says he went home sick later that day, and went on medical leave until he was terminated seven months later, on April 1, 2010.

Mr. Wiest filed an administrative complaint with the Occupational Safety and Health Administration on November 24, 2009, alleging that the Defendants had violated 18 U.S.C. § 1514A by retaliating against him for engaging in protected activity. The Secretary of Labor made no final determination within 180 days of the date Mr. Wiest filed his administrative complaint. Mr. Wiest filed suit in federal court on July 7, 2010.

* * *

DISCUSSION

I.   SOX Retaliation Claim

Mr. Wiest alleges that the Defendants' investigation of the allegations of past misconduct by him was a retaliatory unfavorable personnel action taken by them in response to his alleged protected activities of challenging certain payment requests and refusing to process the challenged requests.

* * *

---

[2]   To "gross up" an employee's bonus means to pay the employee "an additional amount of cash beyond the value of the [award income] in order to cover [the employee's] tax liability."

In order to state a prima facie case under § 1514A, a plaintiff must allege that (1) he engaged in protected activity; (2) the defendants "knew or suspected, actually or constructively," that he had engaged in the protected activity; (3) he suffered an unfavorable personnel action; and (4) the protected activity was a contributing factor in the unfavorable personnel action. The Defendants argue that Mr. Wiest has failed to plead sufficient facts to establish any of the four required elements for a prima facie case. Because the Court concludes that Mr. Wiest has failed to plead sufficient facts to support a finding that he engaged in protected activity, the other three elements will not be discussed, and Mr. Wiest's SOX claim will be dismissed.

SOX protects an employee who has "provided information" to a supervisor regarding conduct that the employee "reasonably believes" violates one of the specific provisions enumerated in § 1514A. For a communication to be protected, it must "definitively and specifically" relate to one of the statutes or rules listed in § 1514A. Although the employee does not have to cite a specific code provision or prove that a violation actually occurred, the employee's communication must express "an objectively reasonable belief there has been shareholder fraud." This requires that the employee's communication do more than merely allege that wrongdoing has occurred. Instead, the employee's communication must convey that his concern with any alleged misconduct is linked to "an objectively reasonable belief that the company intentionally misrepresented or omitted certain facts to investors, which were material and which risked loss." Furthermore, to constitute protected activity, the plaintiff's communication must provide information that reflects a reasonable belief of an existing violation.

In order to determine whether an employee made a protected communication, a court must look to what the employee actually communicated to the employer at the time the alleged SOX violation occurred. Mr. Wiest has attached to his complaint emails that he sent to his supervisors in connection with [the Atlantis and other events] in which he expressed his concerns regarding the tax or accounting treatment and approval process for associated costs. In deciding whether Mr. Wiest has sufficiently pleaded that he engaged in protected activity, the Court will consider whether the content of the emails, which are the only communications alleged in the complaint, interpreted in the light most favorable to him, gives rise to a reasonable inference that he provided information to his supervisors that "definitively and specifically" conveyed his "objectively reasonable" belief that conduct constituting shareholder fraud had either taken place or was in progress.

1.   June 3, 2008 Email

On June 3, 2008, Defendant Lynch allegedly approved an expenditure of approximately $350,000 in connection with the Atlantis event. The same day, Mr. Wiest sent his supervisor, Mr. Hofsass, an email addressing Mr. Wiest's concerns regarding the proper tax and accounting treatment of the approved expenses. The body of the email is quoted here in full:

Doug,

In order to be sure all costs associated with the referenced event are recorded properly and therefore also treated correctly for tax purposes, we want to be sure the following areas are reviewed and addressed (perhaps by the relevant tax department resources):

- As submitted, the costs are charged entirely to advertising expense, which seems inappropriate and does not address the issue of breaking out the meals and entertainment portions which we feel would fall into the 50% deductibility classification for tax purposes.

- There appears to be over 40 spouses/guests attending and the applicable costs (i.e. meals, entertainment, etc.) need to be separately detailed so they can be recorded as income to the employees attending this event.

- The business purpose for the event must be clearly stated.

- The expenses should be reviewed for potential disallowance by a taxing authority based on excessive/extravagant spend levels (for example room rates range from $475 to $1095 per night and several of the items detailed on the listing of entertainment expenses may also raise issues).

Mr. Wiest also provided Mr. Hofsass with a copy of the detailed invoice for the event, adding a list he prepared of "Select Bahama Events That Could Be Considered Extravagant." On its face, the list did not contain any information that would give rise to a reasonable inference that Mr. Wiest was asserting any fraudulent activity had occurred or was ongoing or that he was suspicious in such regard. Instead, it simply sets forth the items and how much each item cost. Mr. Wiest's email was forwarded to Marc Vestal of the Tyco tax department, who apparently agreed to review any tax issues. Except for an email sent to Mr. Vestal with a link to a web page containing information about the Atlantis event, Mr. Wiest has not referenced in his complaint any other emails that he sent concerning the Atlantis event. Likewise, he has not alleged that he sent additional emails or had additional discussions with his supervisors about his concerns regarding proper accounting and tax treatment.

The Court cannot describe Mr. Wiest's communications as providing information "definitively and specifically" conveying a reasonable belief that conduct constituting shareholder fraud had either taken place or was in progress. The email he sent Mr. Hofsass does not suggest that Mr. Wiest suspected that a decision not to conduct further tax review of the expenses had been made intentionally. A fair reading of Mr. Wiest's email demonstrates that he only recommends that the tax department review the areas listed in the email. Based on Mr. Wiest's attached exhibits, it appears that his advice was indeed followed. Nothing in the email would allow the Court to draw a reasonable inference that Mr. Wiest's concern about proper tax and accounting treatment was connected in any way to a concern about shareholder fraud, as required for a showing that Mr. Wiest had engaged in activity protected under § 1514A. Furthermore, Mr. Wiest's email does not support a reasonable inference that he was expressing a belief that any type of fraudulent behavior in violation of SOX had occurred or was in progress. Mr. Wiest's communications simply provided information and suggestions to ensure proper tax and accounting treatment of the Atlantis event expenses. As such, then, they did not rise to the level of "definitively and specifically" conveying a reasonable belief that a violation of the laws and regulations listed in § 1514A was taking place, notwithstanding Mr. Wiest's conclusory assertion in the complaint that he had made "protected disclosures relating to fraudulent accounting practice, attempted shareholder fraud, and lack of compliance with United States Generally Accepted Accounting Principles (GAAP)."

* * *

Finally, Mr. Wiest alleges that after the tax department review resulted in the costs of the Atlantis event being treated as award income to the attending employees, the Defendants then improperly "grossed up" the attendees' bonuses to cover the employees' tax liability, a practice which Mr. Wiest is at pains to point out that the prosecutor in the Kozlowski case had found to be an unacceptable means of "avoid[ing] taxes when there is no benefit to the company." However, although Mr. Wiest has attached emails that were forwarded to him containing the calculations for grossing up the bonuses, he has not alleged that he reported his concerns about the impropriety of grossing up the bonuses to anyone at the time that the bonuses were being calculated or awarded. Thus, Mr. Wiest's allegation regarding his concern over the grossed up bonuses also fails to support a finding that he engaged in protected activity within the meaning of § 1514A.

The Court concludes that Mr. Wiest has failed to make a sufficient factual showing to support a reasonable inference that . . . his email communications relating to the Atlantis event expenses . . . constituted protected activity under § 1514A.

* * *

For the foregoing reasons, the Court concludes that Mr. Wiest has failed to allege sufficient facts that would permit a reasonable inference that he engaged in protected activity within the meaning of § 1514A. Thus, he has failed to state a cause of action under SOX.

* * *

QUESTIONS

1. Does the whistleblowing provision of the Sarbanes-Oxley Act put too heavy a burden on employees to allege fraud? If you were a corporate employee, how comfortable would you be alleging to your superior that a colleague was engaged in fraud (which would include that your colleague acted with scienter)?

2. If you were Wiest's superior, would you have understood Wiest to be alleging fraud in his email, or merely identifying mistakes that need correction?

———

Congress upped the ante for whistleblowers when it enacted the Dodd-Frank Act. The Dodd-Frank Act added a new provision to the Exchange Act, § 21F, entitled "Securities Whistleblower Incentives and Protection." Whistleblowers are defined as any individual or group of individuals "who provide[ ] information relating to a violation of the securities laws to the Commission, in a manner established, by rule or regulation, by the Commission." Exchange Act § 21F(a)(6). Congress instructed the SEC to establish a whistleblower program, which the SEC has implemented through its Office of the Whistleblower. That office received over 3,000 complaints in 2013. Congress also authorized the SEC to pay an award to eligible whistleblowers who voluntarily provide the agency with original information about a violation of the federal securities laws that leads to a successful enforcement action. Rule 21F–1. Awards are only paid if the enforcement action leads to sanctions exceeding $1 million. Rule 21F–3. Awards are potentially substantial, however, with bounties ranging between 10 and 30 percent of the sanction obtained by the SEC. Rule 21F–5. Compliance and audit personnel, however, are excluded from receiving awards. Rule 21F–4(b)(4)(iii)(B). In 2013, the SEC made three awards.

The Dodd-Frank Act also expands protection for whistleblowers. Employers are prohibited from discharging, demoting, suspending, threatening, harassing, or otherwise discriminating against a whistleblower "because of any lawful act done by the whistleblower" in (1) providing information to the SEC, (2) assisting in any SEC investigation or action related to such information, or (3) "in making disclosures that are required or protected under" any securities law or regulation. Exchange Act § 21F(h)(1)(A). Adding teeth to this prohibition, whistleblowers alleging a violation of the anti-retaliation provisions can bring a private cause of action against their employers, Exchange Act § 21F(h)(1)(B), with remedies including reinstatement, double back pay, and attorneys' fees. Exchange Act § 21F(h)(1)(C). Unlike the Sarbanes-Oxley whistleblower provision, employees need not exhaust their administrative remedies with OSHA before filing suit. The SEC can also enforce the anti-retaliation provisions. Rule 21F–2(b)(2).

Noticeably absent from the Dodd-Frank whistleblower provision is any requirement that the whistleblower internally report to corporate superiors (including the board of directors) or any protection for whistleblowers who internally report. Reports to the SEC and other government agencies are eligible for awards and protection from retaliation, but employees who report wrongdoing to corporate superiors are not covered by the statute. *Asadi v. G.E. Energy (U.S.A.), LLC*, 720 F.3d 620 (5th Cir. 2013). Recall that Sarbanes-Oxley mandated that public companies set up internal whistleblowing systems. Critics of the Dodd-Frank provision worry that it will undermine the elaborate and expensive internal compliance systems that corporations set up to comply with Sarbanes-Oxley's whistleblower provisions. If any employee can score a big payday by reporting fraud to the SEC, why bother with the company's audit committee?

HYPOTHETICAL FOUR

April works as the administrative assistant for Leslie, the CEO and founder of Parks and Recreation, Inc. One day, while bringing in Leslie's mail, April noticed a document on Leslie's desk entitled "confidential." Curious, April glanced over the document and realized that the document described P & R's recent efforts to retain key employees through the use of backdated option awards. The document describes P & R's recent award of options that were actually granted on March 1 (when the market price of P & R's stock was $100 per share) but were backdated to February 1 with an exercise price set equal to P & R's stock price on February 1 ($70 per share). A part-time MBA student, April, realized that backdating allowed P & R to provide a hidden, in-the-money profit to their recipients while allowing P & R to record a lower compensation expense for the options in P & R's financial statements. The total amount of the reduced option compensation expense equals roughly $2 million. April desperately needs to keep her $50,000 per year job to pay for her part-time MBA courses (and to fund her garage band). What are April's incentives to report what she saw to others within P & R or to the SEC (or other regulatory authorities)? Would you blow the whistle if you were April?

CHAPTER 13

PUBLIC ENFORCEMENT

Rules and Statutes

—*Sections 17(a), 20, 24 of the Securities Act*

—*Sections 10(b), 12(j), 12(k), 15(c)(4), 21, 21B, 21C, 21F, 25, 32 of the Exchange Act*

—*Rules 10b–5, 14e–3, 15c2–11 of the Exchange Act*

—*Section 308 of the Sarbanes Oxley Act*

—*18 U.S.C. §§ 1348, 1349, 1350*

MOTIVATING HYPOTHETICAL

Lost Travel provides unique vacation packages at a premium price. Hugo is the CEO of Lost Travel, a public company with common stock listed on the New York Stock Exchange. Lost Travel expanded rapidly over the past several years through the sale of extended tours of uncharted islands in the Pacific. Lost Travel's robust revenues have induced several Wall Street analysts to give its common stock a "buy" rating. As a result, Lost Travel's stock price has risen substantially.

Unbeknownst to Creative Accounts, Lost Travel's auditors, Hugo manipulated sales to show more tours than Lost actually booked, frequently double counting the same vacation trip. (There . . . and back!) The manipulation resulted in significantly overstated revenues in Lost Travel's financial statements over the past two years.

I. SEC ENFORCEMENT

We saw in Chapters 5 and 8 that private litigation plays a large role in the enforcement of the securities laws in the United States, particularly through class actions. Most countries do not follow the example of the United States. Instead, the primary mechanism of enforcement in most countries is through public enforcement.

In the United States, the public enforcement of the federal securities laws is left largely to the SEC and FINRA. The individual states also enforce state securities laws. The National Securities Market Improvement Act of 1996 preempts state securities laws from applying to most securities offerings, including offerings of nationally traded securities and offering of the securities of registered investment companies (including mutual funds). Despite the broad preemption, the National Securities Market Improvement Act allows states to continue bringing antifraud actions for "fraud or deceit" relating to securities. The states, most notably New York, have pursued a number of high profile securities-related enforcement actions.

The SEC's Division of Enforcement investigates possible violations of the securities laws. The Division of Enforcement also prosecutes civil enforcement suits in federal court and in administrative proceedings within the SEC. The Division of Enforcement staff is divided between the SEC's home office in Washington, D.C., and the SEC's regional offices throughout the United States.

In this Chapter we first discuss the scope of SEC enforcement power relative to private enforcement of the securities laws. We then follow the SEC enforcement process chronologically. We discuss how the SEC investigates possible violations of the securities laws. Most investigations start informally and, if the evidence warrants, transform into formal investigations upon the order by majority vote of the SEC Commissioners. We examine how the SEC pursues enforcement proceedings. The SEC faces a choice whether to bring a formal action through administrative proceedings or in federal district court. Most litigants facing an SEC enforcement action settle with the SEC. The SEC also refers more serious cases to the Justice Department for criminal prosecution.

II. SCOPE OF SEC ENFORCEMENT

Unlike private enforcement, SEC enforcement potentially covers all aspects of the securities regime. The SEC has the power to bring an enforcement action against any person, including entities, who violate the securities laws. Many provisions of the securities law are not accompanied by a private right of action, which means that only the SEC can enforce them. For example, only the SEC may enforce Regulation FD and the filing requirements under the periodic disclosure system (including Form 10–K, 10–Q, and 8–K disclosures). In Chapter 4, we saw some of the administrative proceedings available only to the SEC in the course of examining the Exchange Act's disclosure requirements, including the books and records provision of § 13(b)(2) of the Exchange Act.

Why does the United States rely on both public and private enforcement of the securities laws? Incentives are one concern. Although most SEC staffers are undoubtedly public spirited, they are typically compensated with a fixed, relatively low, salary. Moreover, any penalties obtained from SEC litigation either go into the U.S. Treasury or in certain cases, are given back to investors through Fair Fund provisions. In contrast, private plaintiffs' attorneys who drive securities class actions have strong monetary incentives to bring such actions. Private plaintiffs' attorneys are compensated with a high percentage of any recovery for the class (typically ranging from 10 to 25%). Of course, as we discuss in Chapter 5, critics allege that this private incentive may lead some plaintiffs' attorney to file suits simply to extort a settlement.

Another concern arises from the public choice literature: the possibility that SEC enforcement may be overly influenced by concentrated interest groups, particularly large financial institutions. A close connection exists between the SEC's Division of Enforcement and large financial institutions. SEC Directors of Enforcement routinely move on to careers on Wall Street after leaving the SEC. Gary Lynch, a Director in the 1980s, went on to work as the Vice Chairman and Chief Legal Officer of Morgan Stanley. Richard Walker, another former head of SEC enforcement who resigned in 2001, worked as the general counsel of Deutsche Bank AG. Stephen Cutler, another former Director who resigned in 2005, went on to work as the General Counsel of JP Morgan Chase & Company. This close connection between the SEC and industry motivated Congress to require, as part of the Dodd-Frank Act, that the U.S. Government Accountability Office study SEC staff turnover. Dodd-Frank Act § 968.

The SEC has been criticized for enforcement complacency. The SEC, for example, faced a congressional probe for its failure to uncover the Ponzi scheme involving Bernard Madoff and Bernard L. Madoff Investment Securities LLC. Over a sixteen-year period, the SEC received six credible warnings relating to Madoff. Although the SEC examined Bernard L. Madoff Investment Securities LLC repeatedly in the 1990s and 2000s and interviewed Madoff at least twice, the SEC did not uncover his US $50 billion Ponzi scheme until 2008. The SEC Inspector General, concluded that "despite numerous credible and detailed complaints, the SEC never properly examined or investigated Madoff's trading and never took the necessary, but basic, steps to determine if Madoff was operating a Ponzi scheme." SEC, Office of Inspector General, Investigation of Failure of the SEC to Uncover Bernard Madoff's Ponzi Scheme (Case No. OIG–509) (Aug 31, 2009).

The SEC also failed to take prompt action against R. Allen Stanford's Ponzi scheme. A 2010 report from the SEC's Inspector General concluded that the SEC's Fort Worth office had information that Stanford was operating a Ponzi scheme as early as 1997. The SEC did not initiate meaningful investigations until late 2005. During those eight years "the potential fraud grew exponentially, from $250 million to $1.5 billion." SEC Office of Inspector General, Report of Investigation, Investigation of the SEC's Response to Concerns Regarding Robert Allen Stanford's Alleged Ponzi Scheme dated March 31, 2010. The SEC's Inspector General:

> also found that the former head of Enforcement in Fort Worth, who played a significant role in multiple decisions over the years to quash investigations of Stanford, sought to represent Stanford on three separate occasions after he left the Commission, and in fact represented Stanford briefly in 2006 before he was informed by the SEC Ethics Office that it was improper to do so.

In response in part to the perception that the SEC moved too slowly investigating Madoff and Stanford, the Division of Enforcement added a new "Office of Market Intelligence" in 2010. The Office of Market Intelligence centralizes the collection, analysis, and monitoring of the numerous tips, complaints, and referrals given to the SEC. The Division of Enforcement also added new units to focus specifically on asset management, market abuse, structured financial products, foreign corrupt practices, and municipal securities and public pensions.

Given the limitations of public enforcement, an important question is to what extent private enforcement is allowed to overlap with public enforcement. Chapters 5 and 8 discuss private causes of action under Rule 10b–5 of the Exchange Act and §§ 11 and 12 of the Securities Act. Those causes of action are limited by either stringent pleading or standing requirements.

The next case addresses whether private litigants have a private cause of action to enforce § 17(a) of the Securities Act. The language of Rule 10b–5 tracks § 17(a), which targets (1) any "device, scheme, or artifice to defraud," (2) any "untrue statement of a material fact or any omission to state a material fact necessary in order to make the statements made, in light of the circumstances under which they were made, not misleading," and (3) any "transaction, practice, or course of business which operates or would operate as a fraud or deceit upon the purchaser." Unlike the private causes of action under Rule 10b–5 or §§ 11 and 12, § 17(a) covers not only sales of securities but also offers. Moreover, in the context of an SEC civil enforcement action, the Supreme Court in *Aaron v. SEC*, 446 U.S. 680 (1980), held that the SEC only needs to show negligence on the part of defendants for purposes of § 17(a)(2) or (3). Should private litigants be allowed to bring private actions under § 17(a)? Would such private actions supplement public enforcement or provide plaintiffs' attorneys with a weapon for extortion?

In re Washington Public Power Supply System Securities Litigation

823 F.2d 1349 (9th Cir. 1987, en banc).

■ HALL, C. CIRCUIT JUDGE.

     * * *

Between 1977 and 1981, the Washington Public Power Supply System (WPPSS) sold bonds with a face value of $2.25 billion to finance construction of two nuclear power plants. In 1982 WPPSS ceased construction of these plants and thereafter defaulted on the bond payments. In 1983 plaintiffs-appellants, purchasers of WPPSS bonds, filed a class action, on behalf of themselves and all others who purchased the bonds ... against WPPSS and nearly 200 other defendants alleging that the bonds were sold "on false pretenses" in violation of both federal and state securities laws. ...

[W]e address the following question: Will a private action lie under section 17(a) of the Securities Act of 1933?

        * * *

The Supreme Court, in *Cort v. Ash*, 422 U.S. 66 (1975), set out the analysis to be applied in determining whether a private remedy is implicit in a statute not expressly providing one:

> First, is the plaintiff "one of the class for whose especial benefit the statute was enacted," that is, does the statute create a federal right in favor of the plaintiff? Second, is there any indication of legislative intent, explicit or implicit, either to create such a remedy or to deny one? Third, is it consistent with the underlying purposes of the legislative scheme to imply such a remedy for the plaintiff? And finally, is the cause of action one traditionally relegated to state law, in an area basically the concern of the States, so that it would be inappropriate to infer a cause of action based solely on federal law?

* * *

We first examine the language of section 17(a) in light of the legislative history and statutory structure of the Securities Act of 1933. The language of section 17(a) reveals no intent to create a private remedy. It merely represents a general censure of fraudulent practices. Indeed, Congress provided the Securities Exchange Commission (SEC) with specific procedures to enforce section 17(a) in sections 20 and 24, indicating that Congress did not intend to create private remedies under section 17(a), but rather that Congress sought to supplement the protections afforded to investors under sections 5, 11, and 12 by giving the Commission the power to deal with flagrant cases of abuse by means of sections 17, 20, and 24. . . .

Even if the first factor were satisfied, we find that the plaintiffs have failed to clear the second and the third *Cort v. Ash* hurdles, that is, plaintiffs have failed to provide evidence of legislative intent to create or reaffirm a private remedy under section 17(a) and plaintiffs have failed to show that such a private remedy would be consistent with the purposes underlying the legislative scheme of which section 17(a) is a part. . . .

In face of the plain language of section 17(a), there is no reason to infer a private remedy in favor of some individuals where "Congress, rather than drafting the legislation 'with an unmistakable focus on the benefited class,' instead has framed the statute simply as a general prohibition." Moreover, Congress' inclusion of sections 11 and 12 of the Securities Act shows that when Congress wished to provide a private damages remedy, it knew how to do it and it did so expressly. Plaintiffs point out that all of the antifraud provisions of the Securities Act are specifically designed to protect investors. . . . However . . . barring private actions under section 17(a) would not "inexorably result in a number of alleged fraudulent practices going undetected by the authorities and unremedied." Plaintiffs here can pursue (and indeed are pursuing) the defendants under section 10(b) of the Securities Exchange Act of 1934. In fact, the very availability of that avenue of relief has persuaded some courts not to imply a private right of action under section 17(a).

There simply is no indication, explicit or implicit, of legislative intent to create a private right of action under section 17(a). . . . The House Committee Report, in a section entitled "Civil Liabilities," indicates that sections 11 and 12 were intended to be the exclusive private remedies under the Act and that imposition of a "greater responsibility" than that provided by sections 11 and 12 "would unnecessarily restrain the conscientious administration of honest business with no compensating advantage to the public.". . . .

Implying a private right of action under section 17(a) is also inconsistent with the statutory scheme of the Securities Act. The presence of express civil remedies within the same act militates against a finding of Congressional intent to imply further remedies. . . .

[I]mplying a private action under section 17(a) attributes to Congress the rather bizarre intention of enabling a purchaser to avoid the statute of limitations and other procedural limitations which it explicitly provided would apply to private actions under sections 11 and

12. If Congress had intended to provide a private remedy under section 17(a), sections 11 and 12 would be "entirely superfluous" and "[t]he complex scheme which Congress wove in the express civil liability sections would be totally undermined."

* * *

QUESTIONS

1. Congress provided express causes of action in §§ 9 and 18 of the Exchange Act. How would the implied private right of action under Rule 10b–5 and § 10(b) of the Exchange Act (discussed in Chapter 5) fare under the *Cort v. Ash* test?

2. Does public or private enforcement of the securities laws better protect investors and the capital markets? Does overlapping enforcement offer advantages relative to purely public, or purely private, enforcement of the securities laws?

————

Even where public and private enforcement overlap, such as under Rule 10b–5, Congress has given public enforcement greater latitude. For example, the U.S. Supreme Court eliminated aiding and abetting liability for Rule 10b–5 actions in *Central Bank* (discussed in Chapter 5). As part of the Private Securities Litigation Reform Act of 1995, Congress restored aiding and abetting liability, but only for SEC enforcement actions. Exchange Act § 20(e). Similarly, the U.S. Supreme Court held Rule 10b–5 does not extend to reach fraudulent securities transaction that take place outside the United States in *Morrison v. National Australia Bank* (excerpted in Chapter 5). As part of the Dodd-Frank Act of 2010, Congress provided that the SEC may bring a Rule 10b–5 (as well as a § 17(a)) cause of action in federal court where there is either conduct in the United States that "constitutes significant steps in furtherance of the violation" or conduct outside the United States that has "a foreseeable substantial effect within the United States." Dodd-Frank Act § 929P(b).

III. SEC INVESTIGATIONS

A. INVESTIGATIONS AND STRATEGY

The starting point in the SEC enforcement process is the identification of enforcement targets. The SEC relies on many sources to gather intelligence on potential violations. The SEC's Office of Investor Education and Advocacy provides a means for investors to transmit their concerns and problems with securities transactions and professionals. The SEC provides several on-line forms on its website (at www.sec.gov/complaint/tipscomplaints.html) for investors to make complaints relating to mutual funds, brokerage accounts, 401(k) accounts, insider trading, among others. The SEC also receives information from self-regulatory organizations including the national securities exchanges. The New York Stock Exchange Regulation's Market Surveillance division monitors the trading of NYSE and Amex-listed securities for abuses, including insider trading. The NYSE either will refer abuses to the NYSE Regulation Enforcement division or to the SEC. The Public Company Accounting Oversight Board can also refer possible securities law violations to the SEC. The SEC also receives information and referrals from state securities regulators as well as members of Congress acting on behalf of their constituents.

Companies often discover possible securities law issues through their own internal investigations and voluntarily inform the SEC of such issues. Voluntary disclosure may lead the SEC to be more lenient with the company than if the SEC were to learn of the issue through other sources, including employee whistleblowers. Tips may come not only from employees (or ex-employees) but also from disgruntled ex-spouses of key employees. The Dodd-Frank Act enhances whistleblower protection and financial incentives, which we discuss in Chapter 12. The SEC also learns of possible securities law violations through its review of company filings, news reports, and the filing of private securities class actions. Short sellers may also provide information to the SEC, hoping to drive down the price of a security.

Once a possible securities law violation is identified, the SEC must determine whether to open an investigation. Due to limited SEC resources, not all possible securities law violations lead to an investigation. The SEC ranks potential violations based on whether the violations are in an area of enforcement priority, the magnitude of the potential violations, and the resources required to investigate the potential violations. Once an informal inquiry commences, the SEC ordinarily keeps such preliminary investigations confidential. Moreover, even the targets of the inquiry do not have the right to be notified. Subjects of the investigation are likely to learn about the inquiry soon enough, however, as the SEC Enforcement staff will be seeking voluntary cooperation (generally informal interviews and document requests) from both the targets of the investigation and others who may have relevant information. After that first contact, companies frequently disclose investigations in press releases or in a filing, such as a Form 8–K or 10–K. A pending investigation may have significant collateral consequences. For example, the company's auditors may be unwilling to certify the company's financial statements until the investigation is resolved. Without certified accounting statements, the company cannot file its Form 10–K, which puts the company at risk of delisting. Many investigations never get beyond the informal stage, either because the staff determines that no violations have occurred or because the target of investigation agrees to take certain actions (including, for example, a restatement of its past financials in the case of accounting problems).

The report of investigation below outlines what the SEC expects from the targets of its investigations. It is followed by an SEC press release explaining the consequences of a failure to cooperate. How likely is it that a corporation will choose not to cooperate with an SEC investigation? If a corporation is a possible target of an SEC investigation, what advantages does it gain from undertaking its own voluntary internal investigation and remedial efforts?

Report of Investigation Pursuant to Section 21(a) of the Securities Exchange Act of 1934 and Commission Statement on the Relationship of Cooperation to Agency Enforcement Decisions

Exchange Act Rel. No. 44969 (2001).

Today, we commence and settle a cease-and-desist proceeding against Gisela de Leon-Meredith, former controller of a public company's subsidiary. Our order finds that Meredith caused the parent company's books and records to be inaccurate and its periodic reports misstated, and then covered up those facts.

We are not taking action against the parent company, given the nature of the conduct and the company's responses. Within a week of learning about the apparent misconduct, the company's internal auditors had conducted a preliminary review and had advised company management who, in turn, advised the Board's audit committee, that Meredith had caused the company's books and records to be inaccurate and its financial reports to be misstated. The full Board was advised and authorized the company to hire an outside law firm to conduct a thorough inquiry. Four days later, Meredith was dismissed, as were two other employees who, in the company's view, had inadequately supervised Meredith; a day later, the company disclosed publicly and to us that its financial statements would be restated. The price of the company's shares did not decline after the announcement or after the restatement was published. The company pledged and gave complete cooperation to our staff. It provided the staff with all information relevant to the underlying violations. Among other things, the company produced the details of its internal investigation, including notes and transcripts of interviews of Meredith and others; and it did not invoke the attorney-client privilege, work product protection or other privileges or protections with respect to any facts uncovered in the investigation.

The company also strengthened its financial reporting processes to address Meredith's conduct—developing a detailed closing process for the subsidiary's accounting personnel, consolidating subsidiary accounting functions under a parent company CPA, hiring three new CPAs for the accounting department responsible for preparing the subsidiary's financial statements, redesigning the subsidiary's minimum annual audit requirements, and requiring the parent company's controller to interview and approve all senior accounting personnel in its subsidiaries' reporting processes.

Our willingness to credit such behavior in deciding whether and how to take enforcement action benefits investors as well as our enforcement program. When businesses seek out, self-report and rectify illegal conduct, and otherwise cooperate with Commission staff, large expenditures of government and shareholder resources can be avoided and investors can benefit more promptly. . . .

[T]he paramount issue in every enforcement judgment is, and must be, what best protects investors. There is no single, or constant, answer to that question. Self-policing, self-reporting, remediation and cooperation with law enforcement authorities, among other things, are unquestionably important in promoting investors' best interests. But, so too are vigorous enforcement and the imposition of appropriate sanctions where the law has been violated. Indeed, there may be circumstances where conduct is so egregious, and harm so great, that no amount of cooperation or other mitigating conduct can justify a decision not to bring any enforcement action at all. In the end, no set of criteria can, or should, be strictly applied in every situation to which they may be applicable.

* * *

In brief form, we set forth below some of the criteria we will consider in determining whether, and how much, to credit self-policing, self-reporting, remediation and cooperation—from the extraordinary step of taking no enforcement action to bringing reduced charges, seeking lighter sanctions, or including mitigating language in documents we use to announce and resolve enforcement actions.

1.   What is the nature of the misconduct involved? Did it result from inadvertence, honest mistake, simple negligence, reckless or deliberate indifference to indicia of wrongful conduct, willful misconduct or unadorned venality? Were the company's auditors misled?

2.   How did the misconduct arise? Is it the result of pressure placed on employees to achieve specific results, or a tone of lawlessness set by those in control of the company? What compliance procedures were in place to prevent the misconduct now uncovered? Why did those procedures fail to stop or inhibit the wrongful conduct?

3.   Where in the organization did the misconduct occur? How high up in the chain of command was knowledge of, or participation in, the misconduct? Did senior personnel participate in, or turn a blind eye toward, obvious indicia of misconduct? How systemic was the behavior? Is it symptomatic of the way the entity does business, or was it isolated?

4.   How long did the misconduct last? Was it a one-quarter, or one-time, event, or did it last several years? In the case of a public company, did the misconduct occur before the company went public? Did it facilitate the company's ability to go public?

5.   How much harm has the misconduct inflicted upon investors and other corporate constituencies? Did the share price of the company's stock drop significantly upon its discovery and disclosure?

6.   How was the misconduct detected and who uncovered it?

7.   How long after discovery of the misconduct did it take to implement an effective response?

8.   What steps did the company take upon learning of the misconduct? Did the company immediately stop the misconduct? Are persons responsible for any misconduct still with the company? If so, are they still in the same positions? Did the company promptly, completely and effectively disclose the existence of the misconduct to the public, to regulators and to self-regulators? Did the company cooperate completely with appropriate regulatory and law enforcement bodies? Did the company identify what additional related misconduct is likely to have occurred? Did the company take steps to identify the extent of damage to investors and other corporate constituencies? Did

the company appropriately recompense those adversely affected by the conduct?

9.   What processes did the company follow to resolve many of these issues and ferret out necessary information? Were the Audit Committee and the Board of Directors fully informed? If so, when?

10. Did the company commit to learn the truth, fully and expeditiously? Did it do a thorough review of the nature, extent, origins and consequences of the conduct and related behavior? Did management, the Board or committees consisting solely of outside directors oversee the review? Did company employees or outside persons perform the review? If outside persons, had they done other work for the company? Where the review was conducted by outside counsel, had management previously engaged such counsel? Were scope limitations placed on the review? If so, what were they?

11. Did the company promptly make available to our staff the results of its review and provide sufficient documentation reflecting its response to the situation? Did the company identify possible violative conduct and evidence with sufficient precision to facilitate prompt enforcement actions against those who violated the law? Did the company produce a thorough and probing written report detailing the findings of its review? Did the company voluntarily disclose information our staff did not directly request and otherwise might not have uncovered? Did the company ask its employees to cooperate with our staff and make all reasonable efforts to secure such cooperation?

12. What assurances are there that the conduct is unlikely to recur? Did the company adopt and ensure enforcement of new and more effective internal controls and procedures designed to prevent a recurrence of the misconduct? Did the company provide our staff with sufficient information for it to evaluate the company's measures to correct the situation and ensure that the conduct does not recur?

13. Is the company the same company in which the misconduct occurred, or has it changed through a merger or bankruptcy reorganization?

We hope that this Report of Investigation and Commission Statement will further encourage self-policing efforts and will promote more self-reporting, remediation and cooperation with the Commission staff. . . .

QUESTIONS

1.   Should the SEC factor a defendant's decision to assert the attorney-client privilege in determining the appropriate level of sanctions?

2.   Why is the period of time over which the misconduct occurred relevant in determining the appropriate sanction?

3.   Is the drop in the company's share price upon disclosure of the wrongdoing a relevant consideration in determining the appropriate level of sanctions?

Lucent Settles SEC Enforcement Action Charging the Company With $1.1 Billion Accounting Fraud
Press Release 2004–67.

Washington, D.C., May 17, 2004—The Securities and Exchange Commission today charged Lucent Technologies Inc. with securities fraud, and violations of the reporting, books and records and internal control provisions of the federal securities laws. The SEC also charged nine current and former Lucent officers, executives and employees, and one former Winstar Communications Inc. officer with securities fraud and aiding and abetting Lucent's violations of the federal securities laws. The SEC's complaint alleges that Lucent fraudulently and improperly recognized approximately $1.148 billion of revenue and $470 million in pre-tax income during its fiscal year 2000.

Lucent and three of the former Lucent employees agreed to settle the case without admitting or denying the allegations. As part of the settlement, Lucent agreed to pay a $25 million penalty for its lack of cooperation.

"Companies whose actions delay, hinder or undermine SEC investigations will not succeed," said Paul Berger, Associate Director of Enforcement. "Stiff sanctions and exposure of their conduct will serve as a reminder to companies that only genuine cooperation serves the best interests of investors."

The SEC's complaint alleges that Lucent's violations of generally accepted accounting principles (GAAP) were due to the fraudulent and reckless actions of the defendants and deficient internal controls that led to numerous accounting errors by others. In their drive to realize revenue, meet internal sales targets and/or obtain sales bonuses, the complaint alleges, defendants . . . improperly granted, and/or failed to disclose, various side agreements, credits and other incentives to induce Lucent's customers to purchase the company's products. These extra-contractual commitments were made in at least ten transactions in fiscal 2000, and Lucent violated GAAP by recognizing revenue on these transactions both in circumstances: (a) where it could not be recognized under GAAP; and (b) by recording the revenue earlier than was permitted under GAAP.

In carrying out their fraudulent conduct, according to the complaint, these Lucent officers, executives and employees violated and circumvented Lucent's internal accounting controls, falsified documents, hid side agreements with customers, failed to inform personnel in Lucent's corporate finance and accounting structure of the existence of the extra-contractual commitments or, in some instances, took steps to affirmatively mislead them.

* * *

Lucent's Lack of Cooperation

Lucent's penalty for its failure to cooperate is based on the following conduct.

Throughout the investigation, Lucent provided incomplete document production, producing key documents after the testimony of relevant witnesses, and failed to ensure that a relevant document was preserved and produced pursuant to a subpoena. As a result, the staff's ability to conduct an efficient and comprehensive investigation was impeded.

After reaching an agreement in principle with the staff to settle the case, Lucent's former Chairman/CEO and outside counsel agreed to an interview with Fortune magazine. During the interview, Lucent's counsel characterized Lucent's fraudulent booking of the $125 million software pool agreement between Lucent and Winstar as a "failure of communication," thus denying that an accounting fraud had occurred. Lucent's statements were made after Lucent had agreed in principle to settle this case without admitting or denying the allegations concerning, among other things, the Winstar transaction. Lucent's public statements undermined both the spirit and letter of its agreement in principle with the staff.

After reaching an agreement in principle with the staff to settle the case, and without being required to do so by state law or its corporate charter, Lucent expanded the scope of employees that could be indemnified against the consequences of this SEC enforcement action. Such conduct is contrary to the public interest.

Lucent also failed over a period of time to provide timely and full disclosure to the staff on a key issue concerning indemnification of employees. Failure to provide accurate and complete disclosure to the staff undermines the integrity of SEC investigations.

* * *

QUESTIONS

1. How should Lucent have responded to the news that it was under SEC investigation?

2. What provision of § 21(a) of the Exchange Act, which gives the SEC authority to conduct investigations, authorizes penalties for non-cooperation?

3. Why does the SEC insist that settling companies not deny the allegations in the SEC's complaint?

4. Should the SEC sanction companies more severely if the companies indemnify their employees for costs relating to an SEC investigation?

HYPOTHETICAL ONE

Lost Travel has landed in hot water. After extensive investigation, the *Wall Street Journal* recently ran a story on Lost Travel's irregular accounting practices that resulted in significantly overstated revenue numbers over the past two years. The story resulted in the resignation of Kate, the CFO of Lost Travel. Hugo, the CEO of Lost Travel, calls you, having just received a phone call from a staff attorney at the SEC's Division of Enforcement. The enforcement attorney told Hugo that they would like to talk to him informally about an unusual trading pattern in Lost Travel's stock right before the *Wall Street Journal* story and Kate's resignation. Hugo is in a panic; his stock options in Lost Travel have plummeted. He asks you how to make this problem go away quickly and easily. What advice do you give him?

B. FORMAL INVESTIGATIONS AND SUBPOENAS

As noted above, most investigations are concluded by a settlement after the staff's informal investigation. If the target refuses to cooperate with the staff's informal investigation, the Enforcement staff typically will seek the Commission's approval of a formal investigation (also ordinarily non-public). Alternatively, the Commission has delegated authority to commence a formal investigation to the Director of the SEC's Enforcement Division.

Section 21(a) of the Exchange Act authorizes the SEC to investigate "as it deems necessary to determine whether any person has violated, is violating, or is about to violate any provision of this title, the rules or regulations thereunder, [the rules and regulations of SROs], and may require or permit any person to file with it a statement in writing, under oath or otherwise as the Commission shall determine, as to all the facts and circumstances concerning the matter to be investigated." Once the Commission votes to begin a formal investigation under § 21(a), the Enforcement staff has the power "to administer oaths and affirmations, subpoena witnesses, compel their attendance, take evidence, and require the production of any books, papers, correspondence, memoranda, or other records which the Commission deems relevant or material to the inquiry." Exchange Act § 21(b). The power to issue administrative subpoenas under § 21(b) includes both documents and testimony. Subpoenas can be particularly useful in getting third parties, who may have had business dealings with the target, to provide testimony.

Recipients of an SEC administrative subpoena will receive the formal order of investigation. From the formal order, the recipient may determine the scope of the investigation and, sometimes, the targets of the investigation. In addition to answering the SEC's questions, a person testifying pursuant to a subpoena is allowed to make a statement on the record after the examination.

An SEC administrative subpoena, standing alone, does not compel a person to appear and provide testimony. The recipient of a subpoena can simply choose not to appear. The SEC has no direct power to enforce its administrative subpoenas, but it does have tools to encourage compliance. First, the SEC may take the refusal to comply with an administrative subpoena as a signal of culpability and respond by ramping up its investigation. The SEC may also impose harsher civil penalties or choose to refer the case to the Justice Department for criminal proceedings. Second, the SEC may go to district court to get an order mandating compliance with the administrative subpoena if the recipient of the subpoena refuses to comply voluntarily. Exchange Act § 21(c). A judicial order to comply with a subpoena is backed up by the court's power of contempt. Under the interpretation of § 21(c) in the case below, what would an impermissible use of the SEC's subpoena power look like?

RNR Enterprises, Inc. v. SEC

122 F.3d 93 (2d Cir. 1997).

■ JACOBS, D. CIRCUIT JUDGE.

Respondent-appellant Richard K. Wells challenges the enforceability of an administrative subpoena served on him and a company he controls pursuant to a Formal Order of the SEC that opened an investigation into a particular industry, but did not name either Wells or his company.

In July 1996, the SEC moved in the Southern District of New York for an order enforcing previously issued subpoenas against Wells; Robert J. Carlo; and RNR Enterprises, Inc. A subpoena *ad testificandum* . . . directed that Wells appear to give testimony in the Matter of Certain Sales of Unregistered Securities of Telecommunications Technology Ventures, an investigation "pursuant to a formal order issued by the Securities and Exchange Commission under the authority of Section 20(a) of the Securities Act of 1933 and Section 21(a) of the Securities Exchange Act of 1934."

The Formal Order identified in the subpoena was issued by the SEC in July 1994. In relevant part, the Formal Order recited that information known to the SEC tended to show the following things:

- that there had been possible violations of federal securities laws in connection with the offering and sale of securities in "ventures that acquire licenses for, or develop or operate transmission facilities of, or otherwise concern, Specialized Mobile Radio . . . and similar telecommunications technologies that are subject to licensing by the United States Federal Communications Commission."

- specifically, that from 1988 to the present, certain persons had offered such "Telecommunications Technology Securities" without filing the requisite registration statements with the SEC; obtained money or property by means of untrue statements or misleading omissions of material fact, made in connection with the offer, purchase or sale of such securities; or effected transactions in such securities without first registering as brokers or dealers.

The Formal Order directed that "a private investigation be conducted to determine whether any persons have engaged, are engaged, or are about to engage, in any of the [alleged] acts, practices, or courses of business, or in any acts, practices, or courses of business of similar purport or object," and it authorized two designated SEC officers to (among other things) "subpoena witnesses and compel their attendance" for the purposes of the investigation. . . .

In support of its enforcement motion, the SEC filed a declaration written by an SEC attorney, which:

- identified Wells as the Chairman and Chief Executive Officer of RNR;

- described the business of RNR as the acquisition and development of "specialized mobile radio properties";

- recited the determination by Commission staff "that Respondents might have information relevant to the Investigation";

- represented that the subpoenas sought "testimony that will assist the Commission in determining whether there have been violations of the federal securities laws as described in the Formal Order," specifically, that the SEC needed the testimony of all three respondents in order to obtain information concerning RNR's 1995 offering of $5 million of unregistered securities to the public;

- and reported that Wells had appeared and answered some of the SEC's initial questions, but stopped answering questions on the advice of counsel, and later refused to appear and testify.

* * *

II

The courts' role in a proceeding to enforce an administrative subpoena is extremely limited. To win judicial enforcement of an administrative subpoena, the SEC must show [1] that the investigation will be conducted pursuant to a legitimate purpose, [2] that the inquiry may be relevant to the purpose, [3] that the information sought is not already within the Commissioner's possession, and [4] that the administrative steps required have been followed.

[A] governmental investigation into corporate matters may be of such a sweeping nature and so unrelated to the matter properly under inquiry as to exceed the investigatory power. However, it is sufficient if the inquiry is within the authority of the agency, the demand is not too indefinite and the information sought is reasonably relevant. The respondent opposing enforcement must shoulder the burden of showing that the subpoena is unreasonable or was issued in bad faith or for an improper purpose, or that compliance would be unnecessarily burdensome.

Construing his arguments liberally, Wells challenges the legitimacy of the investigation, the relevance of his testimony to it, and the SEC's good faith, and asserts violations of due process and the APA. His claims are without merit.

The Formal Order indicates that it was issued because the SEC had information suggesting that securities laws had been violated in connection with the offering and sale of "Telecommunications Technology Securities." The Formal Order reflects a legitimate investigatory purpose.

Moreover, the information sought by the subpoena is relevant to that investigation. We defer to the agency's appraisal of relevancy, which must be accepted so long as it is not obviously wrong. . . . We measure the relevance of the sought-after information against the general purposes of the agency's investigation, which necessarily presupposes an inquiry into the permissible range of investigation under the statute. An affidavit from a governmental official is sufficient to establish a prima facie showing that these requirements have been met.

The Formal Order does not name Wells or RNR, but it does describe companies of a specific and discrete type—a category that includes RNR—and specifies as one reason for the investigation the possible offerings by such companies of unregistered securities. The SEC's allegations concerning RNR's Offering confirm that an inquiry into the offering is within the scope of the Formal Order. Wells has not carried his burden of showing that the subpoena was unreasonable. Although Wells describes in a conclusory fashion the alleged improprieties by SEC personnel, he has altogether failed to demonstrate that the subpoena was sought in bad faith.

Wells contends that his due process rights were violated because the Formal Order (i) did not name RNR, (ii) predated the establishment of RNR and (iii) improperly "encompasses an entire industry." These arguments notwithstanding, the procedures followed by the SEC in Wells' case are authorized. The statute and regulations do not preclude an industry-wide administrative investigation of possible securities law violations where, as set forth in the Formal Order, information before the SEC shows that violations of federal securities laws may have occurred on an industry-wide basis. Nor do they require that the order authorizing the investigation target by name a specific company or person suspected of violating securities laws. The SEC often undertakes investigations into suspicious securities transactions without any knowledge of which of the parties involved may have violated the law. Additionally, there is no requirement that the scope of the investigation be limited to companies that existed before the Formal Order was issued where (as here) the Formal Order expressly provided that the investigation would encompass persons who "are about to engage" in the alleged acts, and the Order remained in effect at the time the subpoenas were issued.

Moreover, [d]ue process does not require notice, either actual or constructive, of an administrative investigation into possible violations of the securities laws. . . .

As we have discussed, the investigation authorized by the Formal Order in this case is within the SEC's authority; the inquiry into possible securities violations related to the Offering falls within the scope of the Formal Order; the information sought by the subpoena served on Wells is relevant to the purpose of the investigation authorized by the Formal Order; and Wells has not shown that the subpoena was unreasonable or issued in bad faith. Neither the securities laws nor the Constitution impose a distinct requirement that, before issuing the subpoena, the SEC issue a Formal Order authorizing by name an investigation of RNR or Wells.

[Eds.—Wells subsequently ignored the court order enforcing the SEC's administrative subpoenas. The District Court Judge ordered Wells incarcerated. Wells was released from jail only upon his bond that he would comply with the court order to respond to the SEC's administrative subpoenas.]

* * *

QUESTIONS

1. Is it reasonable of the SEC to investigate an entire industry for possible violations of the securities laws? Is it likely to be a good use of enforcement resources?

2. Should § 21 of the Exchange Act be amended to require the SEC to show probable cause that a violation of the securities laws has occurred in order to have its subpoenas enforced?

3. Does the ability of the target of an SEC administrative subpoena to challenge the enforceability of the subpoena in court for bad faith or an improper purpose adequately protect the target from overreaching by the SEC?

———

The following case raises the issue of overlapping SEC and Justice Department investigations. It is not unusual for the SEC to be investigating at the same time as a grand jury is considering a possible indictment. Testimony from an SEC investigation can be used against the witness, not only in the SEC proceeding, but also in a criminal case or in private litigation, such as a class action. (The testimony may be obtainable under the Freedom of Information Act after the SEC has concluded its investigation if the witness does not seek confidential treatment.) Private parties cannot directly free ride on the SEC's investigative efforts—§ 21(g) of the Exchange Act requires SEC permission for any private action to be consolidated with an SEC injunctive action. The SEC rarely grants permission.

SEC administrative proceedings are civil rather than criminal, so the rights afforded criminal defendants do not apply, but witnesses are afforded some protections by the SEC's Rules of Practice. Witnesses giving testimony under oath as part of a formal investigation may be accompanied by counsel (and witnesses cannot be compelled to testify at all in an informal investigation). Moreover, the Fifth Amendment privilege against self-incrimination can be asserted in response to inquiries by the SEC. If a witness invokes his Fifth Amendment right, however, an adverse inference can be drawn against him in the SEC proceeding (but not in any parallel criminal action). In addition, the Fifth Amendment does not protect an individual from having to disclose records that belong to the corporation, even if those records would tend to incriminate the individual. Nor does the Fifth Amendment give the target of an investigation the right to block subpoenas directed to third parties (or even be notified of those subpoenas). *SEC v. O'Brien*, 467 U.S. 735 (1984). As you read the following case, consider whether cooperation between the SEC and the Justice Department poses risks for the rights of the targets of their investigations.

SEC v. Dresser Industries, Inc.

628 F.2d 1368 (D.C. Cir. 1980).

■ WRIGHT, J. SKELLY, CHIEF JUDGE.

Dresser Industries, Inc. appeals from a decision of the District Court requiring obedience to a subpoena *duces tecum* issued by the

Securities and Exchange Commission on April 21, 1978, and denying Dresser's motion to quash the subpoena. The subpoena was issued in connection with an SEC investigation into Dresser's use of corporate funds to make what are euphemistically called "questionable foreign payments," and into the adequacy of Dresser's disclosures of such payments under the securities laws. [Eds.:—a subpoena *duces tecum* is a subpoena for the production of evidence, including documents and other tangible evidence.]

The principal issue facing this en banc court is whether Dresser is entitled to special protection against this SEC subpoena because of a parallel investigation into the same questionable foreign payments now being conducted by a federal grand jury under the guidance of the United States Department of Justice. Dresser argues principally that the SEC subpoena abuses the civil discovery process of the SEC for the purpose of criminal discovery and infringes the role of the grand jury in independently investigating allegations of criminal wrongdoing. . . .

I.   BACKGROUND

A.   *Origin of the Investigations*

Illegal and questionable corporate payments surfaced as a major public problem in late 1973, when several major scandals implicated prominent American corporations in improper use of corporate funds to influence government officials in the United States and foreign countries. . . . SEC investigation revealed that many corporate officials were falsifying financial records to shield questionable foreign and domestic payments from exposure to the public and even, in many cases, to corporate directors and accountants.

* * *

[T]he problem of questionable foreign payments proved so widespread that the SEC devised a "Voluntary Disclosure Program" to encourage corporations to conduct investigations of their past conduct and make appropriate disclosures without direct SEC coercion. Participation in the Voluntary Disclosure Program would not insulate a corporation from an SEC enforcement action, but the Commission would be less likely to exercise its discretion to initiate enforcement actions against participants. The most important elements of the Voluntary Disclosure Program were (1) an independent committee of the corporation would conduct a thorough investigation into questionable foreign and domestic payments made by the corporation; (2) the committee would disclose the results of this investigation to the board of directors in full; (3) the corporation would disclose the substance of the report to the public and the SEC on Form 8–K; and (4) the corporation would issue a policy statement prohibiting future questionable and illegal payments and maintenance of false or incomplete records in connection with them. Except in "egregious cases" the SEC would not require that public disclosures include specific names, dates, and places. Rather, the disclosures might be "generic" in form. Thus companies participating in the Voluntary Disclosure Program would ordinarily be spared the consequences to their employees, property, and business that might result from public disclosure of specific instances of foreign bribery or kickbacks. However, companies participating in the Voluntary Disclosure Program had to agree to grant SEC requests for access to the final report and to the unexpurgated underlying documentations.

B. *The Dresser Investigations*

On January 27, 1976 an attorney and other representatives of Dresser met with members of the SEC staff to discuss a proposed filing. At the meeting Dresser agreed to conduct an internal inquiry into questionable foreign payments, in accordance with the terms of the Voluntary Disclosure Program. The next day Dresser submitted a Form 8–K describing, in generic terms, one questionable foreign payment. On November 11, 1976 Dresser filed a second Form 8–K reporting the results of the internal investigation. On February 10, 1977 the company supplemented this report with a third Form 8–K concerning a questionable payment not reported in the earlier reports. The reports concerned Dresser's foreign activities after November 1, 1973. All disclosures were in generic, not specific, terms.

As part of its general monitoring program the SEC staff requested access to the documents underlying Dresser's report. On July 15, 1977 Dresser refused to grant such access. The company argued that allowing the staff to make notes or copies might subject its documents to public disclosure through the Freedom of Information Act. Dresser stated that such disclosure could endanger certain of its employees working abroad. During the ensuing discussions with the staff Dresser attempted to impose conditions of confidentiality upon any SEC examination of its documents, but the staff did not agree. Instead, it issued a recommendation to the Commission for a formal order of investigation in the Dresser case. This recommendation was predicated on the staff's conclusions that Dresser:

1. may have used corporate funds for non-corporate purposes;

2. may have made false and misleading statements concerning the existence of and circumstances surrounding material obligations of Dresser to certain foreign governments and to other entities; and

3. may have made false entries and caused false entries to be made upon the books and records of Dresser, and its affiliates and subsidiaries with respect to, among other things, payments to foreign government officials.

Moreover, the staff reported that Dresser's proxy soliciting materials, reports, and statements may have been misleading with respect to the potential risks involved in its conduct of business through questionable foreign payments, and may have included false statements in connection with such payments. Dresser vigorously opposed issuance of an order of investigation.

Meanwhile, the Department of Justice had established a task force on transnational payments to investigate possible criminal violations arising from illegal foreign payments. Two SEC attorneys participated in the task force. In the summer of 1977 the Justice task force requested access to SEC files on the approximately 400 companies, including Dresser, that had participated in the Voluntary Disclosure Program. Pursuant to Commission authorization the SEC staff transmitted all such files to the Justice task force in August 1977. After its preliminary investigation of the Form 8–K's submitted by Dresser under the Voluntary Disclosure Program, Justice presented Dresser's case to a grand jury in the District of Columbia on January 25, 1978. . . . [T]he District of Columbia grand jury subpoenaed Dresser's documents on April 21, 1978. At roughly the same time the SEC issued a formal order of private investigation, authorizing the staff to subpoena the documents and to obtain other relevant evidence. Pursuant to that order the staff issued a subpoena *duces tecum*, returnable on May 4, 1978. This subpoena covered substantially the same documents and materials subpoenaed by the grand jury, and more. Dresser did not respond to the subpoena. . . . On June 30, 1978, the District Court issued a memorandum opinion and order rejecting all of Dresser's objections to the SEC subpoena and requiring Dresser to comply with the subpoena within ten days after notice from the SEC. . . . This appeal followed.

* * *

II. GENERAL PRINCIPLES

A. *Parallel Investigations*

The civil and regulatory laws of the United States frequently overlap with the criminal laws, creating the possibility of parallel civil and criminal proceedings, either successive or simultaneous. In the absence of substantial prejudice to the rights of the parties involved, such parallel proceedings are unobjectionable under our jurisprudence.

The Constitution, therefore, does not ordinarily require a stay of civil proceedings pending the outcome of criminal proceedings. Nevertheless, a court may decide in its discretion to stay civil proceedings, postpone civil discovery, or impose protective orders and conditions "when the interests of justice seem ( ) to require such action, sometimes at the request of the prosecution, . . . sometimes at the request of the defense." The court must make such determinations in the light of the particular circumstances of the case. Other than where there is specific evidence of agency bad faith or malicious governmental tactics, the strongest case for deferring civil proceedings until after completion of criminal proceedings is where a party under indictment for a serious offense is required to defend a civil or administrative action involving the same matter. The noncriminal proceeding, if not deferred, might undermine the party's Fifth Amendment privilege against self-incrimination, expand rights of criminal discovery beyond the limits of Federal Rule of Criminal Procedure 16(b), expose the basis of the defense to the prosecution in advance of criminal trial, or otherwise prejudice the case. If delay of the noncriminal proceeding would not seriously injure the public interest, a court may be justified in deferring it. . . . In some such cases, however, the courts may adequately protect the government and the private party by merely deferring civil discovery or entering an appropriate protective order. The case at bar is a far weaker one for staying the administrative investigation. No indictment has been returned; no Fifth Amendment privilege is threatened; Rule 16(b) has not come into effect; and the SEC subpoena does not require Dresser to reveal the basis for its defense.

B.   *SEC Investigations*

The case at bar concerns enforcement of the securities laws of the United States. . . . These statutes explicitly empower the SEC to investigate possible infractions of the securities laws with a view to both civil and criminal enforcement, and to transmit the fruits of its investigations to Justice in the event of potential criminal proceedings. . . . Under the . . . '34 Act the SEC may "transmit such evidence as may be available concerning such acts or practices . . . to the Attorney General, who may, in his discretion, institute the necessary criminal proceedings under this chapter." The '33 Act is to similar effect.

Effective enforcement of the securities laws requires that the SEC and Justice be able to investigate possible violations simultaneously. . . . If the SEC suspects that a company has violated the securities laws, it must be able to respond quickly: it must be able to obtain relevant information concerning the alleged violation and to seek prompt judicial redress if necessary. Similarly, Justice must act quickly if it suspects that the laws have been broken. Grand jury investigations take time, as do criminal prosecutions. If Justice moves too slowly the statute of limitations may run, witnesses may die or move away, memories may fade, or enforcement resources may be diverted. The SEC cannot always wait for Justice to complete the criminal proceedings if it is to obtain the necessary prompt civil remedy; neither can Justice always await the conclusion of the civil proceeding without endangering its criminal case. Thus we should not block parallel investigations by these agencies in the absence of "special circumstances" in which the nature of the proceedings demonstrably prejudices substantial rights of the investigated party or of the government.

* * *

The investigation of Dresser based as it was on the staff's conclusion that Dresser may have engaged in conduct seriously contravening the securities laws falls squarely within the Commission's explicit investigatory authority. . . . Since the validity of summonses or subpoenas "depend(s) ultimately on whether they were among those authorized by Congress," we conclude that this subpoena is enforceable. . . .

Fulfillment of the SEC's civil enforcement responsibilities requires this conclusion. . . . [T]he SEC must often act quickly, lest the false or incomplete statements of corporations mislead investors and infect the markets. Thus the Commission must be able to investigate possible securities infractions and undertake civil enforcement actions even after Justice has begun a criminal investigation. For the SEC to stay its hand might well defeat its purpose.

* * *

No one would suggest that the grand jurors, unassisted by accountants, lawyers, or others schooled in the arcana of corporate financial accounting, could sift through the masses of Dresser's corporate documents and arrive at a coherent picture of the company's foreign payments and disclosure practices. In this area, as in many areas of great complexity, the grand jurors are assisted guided and influenced, in fact not only by the United States Attorneys assigned to the investigation, but also by experts provided by the federal regulatory agencies with experience in the particular subject areas. This expert assistance is permitted under Rule 6(e), and it promotes the efficiency and rationality of the criminal investigative process. In this case two SEC agents have been assigned to Justice's task force on transnational payments to assist in the investigation of companies possibly involved in illegal foreign payments. There can be little doubt that the grand jury's deliberations will be influenced by the work of these SEC agents. Any additional influence that might arise as a result of enforcement of the SEC subpoena and transmittal of documents to Justice thereafter is likely to be inconsequential.

We conclude that the danger that enforcement of this subpoena might infringe the role of the grand jury is too speculative and remote at this point to justify so extreme an action as denying enforcement of this subpoena.

In essence, Dresser has launched this attack on the parallel SEC and Justice proceedings in order to obtain protection against the bare SEC proceeding, which it fears will result in public disclosure of sensitive corporate documents. The prejudice Dresser claims it will suffer from the parallel nature of the proceedings is speculative and undefined if indeed Dresser would suffer any prejudice from it at all. Any entitlement to confidential treatment of its documents must arise under the laws pertaining to the SEC; the fortuity of a parallel grand jury investigation cannot expand Dresser's rights in this SEC enforcement action. . . .

IV. COOPERATION BETWEEN SEC AND JUSTICE

Congress understands and approves of the "close working relationship" between the agencies in their investigative capacities. . . . Congress manifestly did not intend that the SEC be forbidden to share information with Justice at this stage of the investigation. . . . In view of Congress' concern that the agencies share information "at the earliest stage of any investigation in order to insure that the evidence needed for a criminal prosecution does not become stale," and that the agencies avoid "a costly duplication of effort," it would be unreasonable to prevent a sharing of information at this point in the investigation. . . . Where the agency has a legitimate noncriminal purpose for the investigation, it acts in good faith even if it might use the information gained in the investigation for criminal enforcement purposes as well. In the present case the SEC plainly has a legitimate noncriminal purpose for its investigation of Dresser. It follows that the investigation is in good faith, in the absence of complicating factors. There is, therefore, no reason to impose a protective order [barring the SEC from sharing information with Justice.]

* * *

Allowing early participation in the case by the United States Attorney minimizes statute of limitations problems. The more time a United States Attorney has, the easier it is for him to become familiar with the complex facts of a securities fraud case, to prepare the case, and to present it to a grand jury before expiration of the applicable statute of limitations. Earlier initiation of criminal proceedings moreover is consistent with a defendant's right to a speedy trial. . . . On the other side of the balance, the . . . concern for preserving the limitations on criminal discovery is largely irrelevant at this stage of the proceedings. . . . Thus this would be an inappropriate situation to impose a "prophylactic" rule against cooperation between the agencies. We believe the courts can prevent any injustice that may arise in the particular circumstances of parallel investigations in the future.

V. OTHER ISSUES

* * *

Dresser argues that the District Court erred in granting judgment for the SEC without permitting Dresser to conduct discovery into the propriety of the SEC investigation. Although the precise nature of Dresser's desired discovery is not clear, the company apparently would investigate: (1) the SEC criminal referral and the concurrent criminal investigation, with a view to the possibility that the SEC has proceeded in bad faith; (2) the ethical propriety of SEC agents' participation in the criminal investigation; (3) the existence of an SEC commitment of confidentiality; and (4) the basis for the SEC staff's decision to request a formal investigation of Dresser.

We recognize that discovery may be available in some subpoena enforcement proceedings where the circumstances indicate that further information is necessary for the courts to discharge their duty. . . . However, district courts must be cautious in granting such discovery rights, lest they transform subpoena enforcement proceedings into exhaustive inquisitions into the practices of the regulatory agencies. Discovery should be permitted only where the respondent is able to distinguish himself from "the class of the ordinary (respondent)," by citing special circumstances that raise doubts about the agency's good faith. Even then, district courts must limit discovery to the minimum necessary in the interests of justice by requiring specific interrogatories or affidavits rather than "full-dress discovery and trial."

We conclude that the District Court acted within its discretion in denying Dresser discovery in this case, and that it properly granted judgment to the SEC on the record before it. . . . Dresser's suggestion that the order of investigation is improper because there was no "likelihood that a violation has been or is about to be committed," does not distinguish Dresser from any other recalcitrant subpoena respondent. At this stage of the investigation neither this court nor the SEC could know whether Dresser has violated the law. The Commission's discretion concerning which potential violators to investigate is, while not unbounded, extremely broad. Dresser has suggested no improper motive for the SEC investigation, Dresser's bare protestations of innocence do not suffice to call the SEC's bona fides into question.

* * *

NOTES

1. *Parallel proceedings.* The usual pattern when the Justice Department has decided to prosecute someone for a securities violation is a coordinated announcement of the criminal indictment and the SEC's enforcement action. The SEC—as a matter of discretion and with the consent of the court—will then typically stay its action until the criminal case has been resolved. If the defendant is convicted, collateral estoppel gives the SEC an easy case. If the defendant is acquitted, the SEC gets another bite at the apple with the lower preponderance of the evidence standard for civil cases.

2. *Subpoena enforcement.* Enforcement of SEC administrative subpoenas will be denied if the target of the subpoena can demonstrate that the agency is investigating in "bad faith." For a rare example of a target successfully challenging the enforcement of an SEC subpoena, *see SEC v. Wheeling-Pittsburgh Steel Corp.*, 648 F.2d 118 (3d Cir. 1981) (en banc), in which the target of the investigation alleged that the SEC's investigation was prompted by pressure from an influential Senator. Under the circumstances, the appellate court held that the target was entitled to discovery on the issue of the agency's purpose in bringing the investigation.

3. *The Foreign Corrupt Practices Act.* The mid-1970s scandal over bribes paid by U.S. companies to foreign officials led Congress to adopt § 13(b)(2) of the Exchange Act, requiring accurate books and records (discussed in Chapter 4). Few companies were disclosing the existence of slush funds to pay bribes on their balance sheets. It also led Congress to prohibit directly the payment of bribes in § 30A of the Exchange Act. The latter provision sits rather oddly in the securities laws, as it has no apparent connection to the protection of investors or the regulation of the securities markets. Nonetheless, the SEC is charged with civil enforcement of the provision. The Justice Department enforces criminal violations of the law. After little enforcement for the first thirty years after its enactment, this anti-bribery provision has become a priority for both the SEC and Justice Department in recent years.

QUESTIONS

1. *Dresser* describes the SEC's efforts in the 1970s to push firms toward adopting internal corporate procedures for "investigation, disclosure, and prevention of illegal corporate payments." Eventually the SEC devised a "Voluntary Disclosure Program" to encourage corporations to conduct investigations of their past conduct and make appropriate disclosures without direct SEC coercion. Are changes in a company's corporate governance an appropriate area for SEC enforcement? Use of the court's equitable powers? Does it infringe on state corporate law? Shareholder democracy?

2. Would it make sense to consolidate criminal and civil enforcement in one agency?

3. Why does the SEC insist on seeing the documents underlying a corporation's internal investigation?

4. Why is the court concerned that granting a defendant discovery rights could "transform subpoena enforcement into exhaustive inquisitions into the practices of the regulatory agencies"? Doesn't the public have the right to know how the SEC conducts its investigations?

HYPOTHETICAL TWO

Kate, the former Chief Financial Officer of Lost Travel, resigned after the *Wall Street Journal* uncovered Lost Travel's overstated revenues. The SEC has subpoenaed Hugo's (the CEO of Lost Travel) email records. Hugo is worried about handing over an email that he sent to Kate telling her to "do whatever you have to do to find another $400,000 in revenues." Does Hugo have to turn over his email?

IV. ENFORCEMENT PROCEEDINGS

After completing its investigation (whether formal or informal), the SEC faces a number of options. The SEC can simply terminate the investigation. The SEC may also, in the case of a willful violation, refer the investigation to the U.S. Department of Justice to commence criminal prosecution. In the case of criminal prosecution, the SEC will typically assist officials at the Department of Justice. The SEC may also choose to proceed with civil enforcement proceedings where the SEC brings formal charges against the targets of investigation. The Commission must authorize the initiation of enforcement proceedings by a majority vote. The SEC may bring charges either by filing a complaint in federal district court or in an administrative proceeding before an administrative law judge.

Before the commencement of enforcement proceedings, the SEC typically (at its discretion) gives the target of the investigation notice of the findings of the investigation, the substance of the charges, and the staff's recommendation for enforcement proceedings in what is commonly referred to as a "Wells Notice." The target of investigation ordinarily will be allowed to present its side of the case directly to the Commissioners in the form of a "Wells submission." A Wells submission is an opportunity to explain why the violation alleged by the staff was inadvertent or not in bad faith, or that the staff has incorrectly interpreted the requirements of the law. In providing their Wells submission, targets under investigation are able to argue that charges should not be brought (or that only reduced charges should be brought) as well as propose a settlement before the SEC formally charges the target with a violation of the securities laws. Not all targets of investigation who receive a Wells Notice choose to respond to the SEC with a Wells submission. The Wells submission is neither privileged nor confidential. Perhaps most importantly, the Wells submission is discoverable by plaintiffs in private litigation against the target of investigation.

Most SEC enforcement proceedings do not entail any actual proceedings. Instead, the SEC will simultaneously announce publicly an enforcement proceeding and a settlement. Settlements of enforcement proceedings result in either an order in either an administrative proceeding (a "consent order") or an injunctive action in district court (a "consent decree"). Both the initiation and settlement of administrative proceedings and court actions require Commission approval. The SEC reports consent orders and consent decrees through litigation releases (available on the SEC's website at www.sec.gov). Typically, the defendant will consent to the judgment, and pay a penalty, but neither admit nor deny the allegations in the SEC's complaint.

Why are most SEC formal investigations and prospective enforcement proceedings settled? Targets of investigation are eager to avoid: (1) the continuing harm to their reputation from having their misconduct aired in litigation with the SEC; (2) the enormous expense of litigating against the resources of the federal government; (3) a referral to the Department of Justice for possible criminal prosecution; and (4) the ruinous potential private liability that could come from the collateral estoppel effect of an adverse judgment. Plaintiffs' attorneys are likely to "piggyback" on an SEC victory with a securities fraud class action. As you have seen above, consent orders and consent decrees routinely contain a stipulation that the subject of the order or decree is not admitting to the wrongdoing, so the target is free to relitigate the facts in any private action. A standard clause in SEC settlement agreements, however, makes it a term of the agreement that the settling party will not deny publicly any allegation in the SEC's complaint. A public denial of wrongdoing will likely provoke a motion by the SEC to vacate the settlement (followed by a prompt retraction of the denial by the settling party).

The SEC brings civil enforcement suits in federal court when the SEC seeks injunctions (typically orders prohibiting future violations of the securities laws), civil money penalties, and disgorgement of illegal profits. The SEC may also seek a federal court order to bar and suspend individuals from acting as officers or directors of public companies.

The SEC also may bring enforcement actions as administrative proceedings before an administrative law judge. Through an administrative proceeding, the SEC may obtain a cease-and-desist order, which can include both an order for disgorgement of ill-gotten gains and civil penalties. The SEC also uses administrative proceedings to bring action against certain regulated entities, including broker-dealers, investment advisors, and their employees. Such actions include administrative proceedings to revoke or suspend registration. For employees, the SEC may seek to bar or suspend the individuals from employment with a broker-dealer or investment advisor.

A. ADMINISTRATIVE PROCEEDINGS

The SEC has a range of internal administrative proceedings available to it to address violations of the securities laws. Those proceedings carry with them a diverse range of sanctions. The table below summarizes the principal proceedings available under the Exchange Act for violations relating to disclosure by public companies and the sanctions available in each.

Section	Proceeding	Sanctions
21C	Cease-and-desist	– Temporary orders – Cease-and-desist order from violating securities laws – Disgorgement – Civil penalties – Officer and Director bar from public companies
15(c)(4)	Disclosure violations	– Order to stop disclosure violations
21(a)	Report of investigation	– Public announcement of violation of securities laws
12(j) & (k)	Trading suspensions	– Halt trading for ten days or indefinitely

1. SECTION 21C

Section 21C of the Exchange Act, and its counterpart § 8A of the Securities Act, give the SEC considerable flexibility to impose a cease and desist order on any person who is "violating, has violated, or is about to violate any provision" of the Exchange Act or any SEC rule or regulation promulgated under the Act. Although the SEC can choose at its discretion among an array of alternate proceedings to enforce the securities laws, the SEC relies primarily on cease and desist proceedings under § 21C.

Although defendants are entitled to notice and an administrative hearing, the SEC does not face the delay of going through the courts to obtain the initial cease and desist order. The SEC's Division of Enforcement can proceed in an administrative proceeding, initially before an SEC Administrative Law Judge, with review by the Commission itself (and subsequent review in the courts of appeals, discussed below). The federal rules of civil procedure do not apply in SEC administrative hearings; instead, the proceedings are governed by the agency's more flexible rules of practice.

In a § 21C proceeding against a person directly committing a securities law violation, the Division only needs to show that a person "is violating, has violated, or is about to violate" the Exchange Act. For "other persons" who contribute to the violation, the SEC must show that the "other person . . . is, was, or would be a cause of the violation, due to an act or omission the person knew or should have known would contribute to such violation." The cease and desist order may simply order the wrongdoer to "cease committing or causing such violation." If the SEC also seeks to order the wrongdoer to cease and desist from engaging in "any future violation of the same provision," the SEC may need to show a likelihood of future violation (as discussed below in the *KPMG* case).

Despite the minimal burden imposed on the SEC to make its case (and the home court advantage), the cease-and-desist proceeding nonetheless makes significant sanctions available to the SEC. The order that the respondent "cease and desist" from violating the securities laws is backed by the threat of civil penalties and an injunction in court if the subject of the order fails to comply. In addition, the SEC has the power in a § 21C proceeding to order the disgorgement of funds procured as a result of the violation. Section 21C(e). The Dodd-Frank Act authorized the SEC to impose civil penalties in a § 21C proceeding. Section 21B sets forth the applicable penalties in three tiers ranging from $5,000 to $500,000. Finally, if the SEC determines that the respondent has violated § 10(b)'s antifraud prohibition, it can use a § 21C proceeding to bar that person from serving as an officer or director of a public company if it also determines that "the conduct of that person demonstrates unfitness to serve as an officer or director." Section 21C(f).

The SEC has the power to issue temporary orders requiring the respondent to stop the violation and to prevent the dissipation of assets pending the outcome of a § 21C proceeding. Section 21C(c). The SEC can issue temporary cease and desist orders if the agency determines that the violation is "likely to result in significant dissipation or conversion of assets, significant harm to investors, or substantial harm to the public interest." The temporary order requires notice to the respondent and a hearing before the Commission, unless the Commission determines that "notice and hearing prior to entry [of the temporary order] would be impracticable or contrary to the public interest." This authority allows the SEC to move quickly if it has concerns that a respondent may try to hide assets before the proceeding can be concluded.

QUESTIONS

1.   How does disgorgement differ from damages and civil penalties?

2.   What benefit does the SEC gain from first obtaining a § 21C cease-and-desist order instead of going directly to court?

3.   How often will the SEC determine that a person it has found guilty of fraud under § 10(b) is nonetheless fit to serve as an officer or director?

2.   SECTION 15(c)(4)

Section 15(c)(4) allows for an SEC administrative proceeding for violations of §§ 12, 13, 14, and 15(d) of the Exchange Act, covering, among other things, the periodic disclosure requirements for public companies and the proxy solicitation requirements (covered in Chapter 11). The SEC may use § 15(c)(4) to bring an action against the issuer or any person who may have violated one of those provisions, as well as "any person who was a cause of the failure to comply." This authority allows the SEC to sanction not only the employees of the issuer (including its officers and directors), but also outside accountants and lawyers if they are the "cause" of a misleading or late filing. The power to sanction individuals gives the SEC substantial negotiating leverage, as officers and directors may be quite happy to agree to settlements sanctioning the issuer if they can escape being named in the order as individual violators.

The § 15(c)(4) proceeding is limited, however, when compared with the cease-and-desist proceeding available to the SEC under § 21C. (Congress adopted § 21C as an amendment to the Exchange Act long

SECTION IVENFORCEMENT PROCEEDINGS**793**

after § 15(c)(4) was adopted.) Section 15(c)(4) provides for no civil penalties or sanctions. Instead, under § 15(c)(4), the SEC may publish its findings and issue an order requiring compliance to remedy the violation under §§ 12, 13, 14, and 15(d) of the Exchange Act. Once a § 15(c)(4) order is in place, the SEC must go to federal district court if a respondent violates the order to obtain a court order compelling obedience. Only if the respondent violates the court order is the more serious sanction of contempt available. By contrast, the SEC can immediately seek civil penalties in court if the terms of a § 21C cease-and-desist order are violated. Moreover, the § 15(c)(4) proceeding does not afford the disgorgement remedy and officer and director bar provided by the § 21C proceeding. Compared with § 21C, the substantive scope of the types of violations the SEC may address is also limited. The SEC has held that § 15(c)(4), unlike § 21C, does not give the SEC the power to impose compliance orders dealing with future violations. *See In re Kern*, 50 S.E.C. 596, 598 (1991).

QUESTIONS

1. Given the availability of a § 21C cease-and-desist proceeding, why would the SEC ever use a § 15(c)(4) proceeding to pursue a violation of §§ 12, 13, 14, and 15(d) of the Exchange Act?

3.   SECTION 21(a)

Section 21(a) gives the SEC broad authority to investigate any person who may have violated (or is about to violate) the Exchange Act or the rules of one of the self-regulatory organizations (SROs), such as FINRA, or to secure information "to serve as a basis for recommending further legislation concerning the matters to which this title relates." The report authorized by § 21(a) can be used to publicize violations or to outline problems that may require additional legislation or regulation. It also can be used, however, to publicize violations of the law in cases where the SEC determines that further sanctions are not warranted. The § 21(a) report is the least stringent sanction available to the SEC— no penalties, no constraints on future action, not even a formal censure. As used in this setting, a § 21(a) report amounts to little more than a public scolding by the Commission. Occasionally, however, respondents agree to governance reforms as part of an agreed-upon § 21(a) report.

4.   SECTIONS 12(j) & 12(k)

The SEC can take direct steps to limit the harm caused to investors by misstatements or selective disclosures. Section 12(k) of the Exchange Act allows the SEC to suspend trading in any security for up to ten days if the agency determines "that the public interest and the protection of investors so require." The SEC is authorized to halt trading for longer periods under § 12(j) of the Exchange Act, but that provision requires the SEC to provide notice and a hearing to the issuer before trading can be halted. An attempt by the SEC to circumvent the notice and hearing requirements of § 12(j) by issuing repeated ten-day suspensions under § 12(k) was rebuffed by the Supreme Court in *SEC v. Sloan*, 436 U.S. 103 (1978). The SEC has bootstrapped the effectiveness of § 12(k), however, by promulgating Rule 15c2–11, which prohibits broker-dealers from initiating or resuming trading in a public company if it does not have current information on that company. The SEC has used § 12(k) to suspend trading in "shell" companies (firms with few or no assets or operations) that have not filed their periodic reports. After the ten-day suspension, Rule 15c2–11 steps in to stop broker-dealers from *resuming* trades in the securities of companies with inadequate current information. Thus, creative rulemaking has allowed the SEC to replace a portion of the authority it was denied in *Sloan*.

Section 12(k) also gives the SEC authority to adopt emergency orders to "alter, supplement, suspend, or impose requirements or restrictions" to, among other things, "maintain or restore fair and orderly securities markets." As the Financial Crisis unfolded, the SEC adopted an emergency order in July 2008 prohibiting naked short sales of the stock of 19 financial firms, including Fannie Mae and Freddie Mac. The emergency order eventually lapsed in August 2008. Short sales involve sales by parties of securities the parties do not actually own. In an "ordinary" short sales transaction, the shorting party borrows shares from an intermediary (usually a broker) and sells the borrowed shares at the current market price. The shorting party then repurchases the shares later in time at the market price for the later date and returns the shares to the lending intermediary. If the securities price between the time of the initial sale and eventual repurchase drops, the shorting party earns a profit. Short selling therefore provides a method for shorting parties to bet that the price for a specific security will fall. So-called "naked" short sales involves short-selling shares without first borrowing the shares. Because naked short sellers do not first borrow the security, their ability to sell short is much greater than an ordinary short seller. The SEC subsequently used its emergency order authority under § 12(k) to adopt an order temporarily prohibiting all (including not only naked but also ordinary) short sales of 799 banks, insurance companies, and securities firms. SEC, Emergency Order Pursuant to Section 12(k)(2) of the Securities Exchange Act of 1934 Taking Action to Respond to Market Developments, Exchange Act Rel. No. 34–58592 (Sept. 18, 2008).

The emergency short sale prohibitions of 2008 addressed the SEC's concern that certain investors, including in particular hedge funds, were driving the stock price of financial issuers artificially lower, disconnecting the price of the stock from its "true price valuation." The SEC also expressed concern that a low stock price may cause investors to lose confidence in the covered financial institutions, exacerbating the financial crisis. The SEC's ban, however, was not without its critics. Several argued that short sales, including naked short sales, serve a critical function in incorporating new information into stock prices and ensuring stock market accuracy and efficiency. A ban on short sales, under this view, simply results in less informative stock prices and greater stock market price volatility as a result. Eventually, on October 14, 2008, the SEC adopted Rule 10b–21 of the Exchange Act, permanently prohibiting naked (but not ordinary) short sales.

B. JUDICIAL REVIEW OF ADMINISTRATIVE REMEDIES

SEC orders arising from the agency's administrative proceedings are subject to review either in the court of appeals for the circuit in which the "person aggrieved by a final order of the Commission . . . resides or has his principal place of business, or for the District of Columbia Circuit." Exchange Act § 25(a)(1). Thus, litigants challenging the SEC have a limited choice of fora in which to do so. The D.C. Circuit has delivered a number of key losses for the SEC on points of administrative law (including the *Business Roundtable* decision, excerpted in Chapter 11) so it is a popular choice for litigants challenging the agency's decisions. Whatever the forum, the SEC enjoys the presumption that its factual findings are correct: "The findings of the Commission as to the facts, if supported by substantial evidence are conclusive." Exchange Act § 25(a)(4). And the agency's interpretation of the law will ordinarily be afforded deference under *Chevron U.S.A., Inc. v. Natural Res. Def. Council*, 467 U.S. 837 (1984), so challenges to SEC action face an uphill battle.

The *KPMG* case below addresses the standards for judicial review of the SEC's administrative actions. It involves a rather nuanced application of the principle that the auditor must be "independent" of the company. The American Institute of Certified Public Accountants (AICPA), the national professional organization for certified public accountants, promulgates a Code of Professional Conduct to govern accountants. Section 302 of the Code provides, in part, that:

A member in public practice shall not

(1) Perform for a contingent fee any professional services for, or receive such a fee from a client for whom the member or the member's firm performs,

(a) an audit or review of a financial statement. . . .

The *KPMG* opinion also addresses the appropriate standard for cease-and-desist orders under § 21C. Are enforcement proceedings the appropriate means for regulating the accounting profession? Should respondents be afforded greater procedural protections?

KPMG, LLP v. SEC

289 F.3d 109 (D.C. Cir. 2002).

■ ROGERS, J., CIRCUIT JUDGE.

KPMG, LLP challenges a cease-and-desist order entered by the Securities and Exchange Commission, pursuant to Section 21C(a) of the Securities Exchange Act, on the basis of several violations of the securities laws and regulations. KPMG principally contends that the Commission lacks authority to turn the ancillary authority provided by Section 21C into an independent basis to sanction accountants, failed to give fair notice of its novel interpretation of Rule 302 of the Code of Professional Conduct of the American Institute of Certified Public Accountants ("AICPA"), and adopted an improper presumption in concluding there was a sufficient risk of future violations warranting a cease-and-desist remedy. KPMG also contends that the cease-and-desist order is overbroad and vague. We hold that although KPMG did not have fair notice of the Commission's interpretation of AICPA Rule 302, the Commission properly could use a negligence standard to enforce violations of the Exchange Act and Commission rules under Section 21C. . . .

I.

The Commission issued the cease-and-desist order following an evidentiary hearing that commenced, based on allegations by the Division of Enforcement and the Office of the Chief Accountant, with the issuance on December 4, 1997, of an order instituting a proceeding under Commission Rule of Practice 102(e) and Section 21C of the Exchange Act. . . .

[KPMG lent money to the four founding principals of BayMark, a financial and business consulting firm, and granted BayMark and its subsidiaries, including KPMG BayMark Strategies, the rights to use the "KPMG" name in return for a royalty fee of five percent of BayMark's quarterly consolidated fee income. The SEC Office of the Chief Accountant (OCA), upon becoming aware of KPMG's arrangement with BayMark, warned KPMG against having BayMark provide consulting services to KPMG's audit clients.]

Notwithstanding this warning, on November 3, 1995, Strategies entered into an agreement with PORTA—a long-standing KPMG audit client facing financial difficulties—to provide "turnaround services" and assist it with financing. Leonard Sturm, KPMG's engagement partner for PORTA's 1994 audit, had introduced PORTA to BayMark. Under the agreement between PORTA and Strategies, one of BayMark's founding principals, Edward Olson, would be Chief Operating Officer of PORTA and Strategies would receive a management fee of $250,000 and a "success fee" based on a percentage of PORTA's earnings, disposed inventory, and restructured debt. On November 9, 1995, PORTA's Board of Directors elected Olson president and Chief Operating Officer of the company.

Sturm became aware that PORTA was engaging BayMark and contacted [KPMG's Department of Professional Practice, "DPP"] to determine whether it was okay for BayMark to provide services to an audit client. [Chris Trattou, a KPMG senior manager] indicated that it was okay and that the Commission had no objection to it. Once Sturm learned that Olson was an officer of PORTA, he inquired again as to whether there were any independence concerns with the audit. Trattou discussed the matter with Michael Conway, the partner in charge of the DPP; they disagreed as to the propriety of the arrangement, with Conway . . . expressing concern.

After several meetings in December 1995 between Conway . . . and OCA staff, OCA staff indicated that in order to resolve its independence concerns, KPMG would need to drop the KPMG initials from the BayMark parties' names, eliminate the royalty fee arrangement, and bring about the repayment of the $400,000 in loans made to the BayMark principals. Conway agreed to undertake negotiations with BayMark to make these changes. Although Conway alerted OCA staff to the existence of six dual engagements where KPMG was the auditor of record and BayMark had contracts with those clients, Conway did not inform OCA staff of the detailed entanglements involved with PORTA, i.e., the outstanding loan to Olson, Olson's status as an officer of PORTA and a principal of BayMark, and the success fee arrangement.

The evidence also showed that sometime before December 27, 1995, Trattou called Sturm with an answer to Sturm's earlier independence inquiries. Trattou indicated that the Commission was aware of the PORTA situation and that the KPMG audit of PORTA could proceed. On December 27, 1995, PORTA signed KPMG's engagement letter to conduct its 1995 audit. When OCA staff discovered the PORTA audit, it informed Conway that KPMG was not independent from PORTA because none of the structural changes to the BayMark strategic alliance had been implemented and a loan was outstanding to Olson who was part of PORTA's management. By letter of June 21, 1996, OCA advised PORTA that KPMG's independence had been compromised and that PORTA's audited financial statements included in its 1995 annual report would be considered unaudited and not in compliance with federal securities laws.

* * *

The Commission ... concluded, on the basis of KPMG's debtor/creditor relationship with Olson and its right to share in Strategies' "success" fee, that KPMG's independence was impaired under [generally accepted accounting standards]. Noting that KPMG admitted that the loan to Olson impaired its independence under GAAS, the Commission characterized the violation as a "serious" mistake that arose from KPMG's failure to exercise ordinary care to maintain its independence. Further, the Commission interpreted AICPA Rule 302 to "flatly prohibit[ ] an auditor from 'perfor[ming] for a contingent fee any professional services for, or receiv[ing] such a fee' from a client," and found that KPMG violated Rule 302 by receiving such a fee. The Commission concluded that "these relationships, whether considered individually or collectively, impaired [KPMG's] independence." Because of these impairments, the Commission concluded that KPMG violated Rule 2–02(b)(1) of Regulation S–X, which requires that the accountant's report "state whether the audit was made in accordance with generally accepted auditing standards." In addition, the Commission concluded that PORTA violated Section 13(a) of the Exchange Act, and Rule 13a–1, which requires issuers to file reports certified by independent public accountants. The Commission repeated that each of the two impairments (the debtor/creditor relationship and the contingency fee arrangement) "considered on its own, compromised [KPMG's] independence and each is sufficient, on its own, to support our finding of violations of Section 13(a) and Rule 13a–1," and "[s]imilarly, each impairment is sufficient, standing alone, to compromise independence under GAAS and to support our finding of violation of Rule 2–02(b)(1)."

Turning to the question of the appropriate sanctions for the violations, the Commission concluded that under Section 21C it could issue a cease-and-desist order for negligent conduct that causes a primary violation of the securities laws and regulations, and that KPMG had acted negligently in determining that it was independent from PORTA. As a result, the Commission issued a cease-and-desist order to KPMG because it acted negligently, which resulted in its primary violation of Rule 2–02(b) of Regulation S–X, and in its being a cause of PORTA's violations of Section 13(a) of the Exchange Act, and

Rule 13a–1. The Commission denied KPMG's motion for reconsideration and KPMG appealed to the court.

In Part II, we address KPMG's challenges to the determinations underlying the Commission's decision to issue a cease-and-desist order. In Part III, we address KPMG's challenges to the cease-and-desist order.

II.

KPMG contends that . . . it lacked fair notice of the Commission's interpretation of AICPA Rule 302 prohibiting the receipt of contingent fees. . . . KPMG also contends that negligence is an impermissible basis for a cease-and-desist order against accountants who cause a violation of securities laws or regulations. . . .

A.

* * *

[The SEC's interpretation of AICPA Rule 302 was at odds with AICPA's interpretation. AICPA rejected the SEC's interpretation of Rule 302 because "BayMark was not an accounting firm, and thus not a 'member in public practice,' and because the royalty BayMark was committed to pay KPMG was not linked to the attainment of any 'specified finding or result' and its amount was not 'dependent upon the finding or result' of any professional or other service." The Court reasoned that, at the very least, KPMG lacked any notice of the SEC's novel interpretation of Rule 302. Thus, as a matter of due process, the Court held "that the Commission erred in finding that KPMG had violated AICPA Rule 302 as a result of its arrangement with BayMark and BayMark's arrangement with PORTA."]

* * *

C.

KPMG also challenges the propriety of a negligence standard under Section 21C. . . . KPMG's contention that the Commission cannot use Section 21C "to bootstrap" its authority to regulate accountants fails on several grounds. First, Rule 102(e) provides that the Commission may sanction accountants in a particular manner. The rule provided at the time of the administrative proceeding that the Commission could "deny, temporarily or permanently, the privilege of appearing or practicing before it" to any accountant who had "engaged in unethical or improper professional conduct" or "willfully violated . . . any provision of the Federal securities laws." No such barring order was entered here, and there is nothing in the rule itself to indicate that it is the exclusive means for addressing accountants' conduct. KPMG's contention that the Commission viewed Rule 102(e) to be the exclusive basis for disciplinary actions against accountants is an overstatement. . . .

Second, the premise of KPMG's view that the Commission's invocation of Section 21C is no more than a way to circumvent the scienter requirement of Rule 102(e) is flawed. There is no support for the position that the culpability standards governing Rule 102(e) proceedings can be applied with equal force in Section 21C proceedings. The nature of the two proceedings is different. As the Commission points out, "one is a professional disciplinary proceeding designed to protect the integrity of the Commission's process while the other is a law enforcement proceeding," each involving "fundamentally different remedies. . . ."

* * *

Moreover, the Commission was virtually compelled by Congress' choice of language in enacting Section 21C to interpret the phrase "an act or omission the person knew or should have known would contribute to such violation" as setting a negligence standard. KPMG contends that the court should give no deference to the Commission's interpretation of Section 21C as regulating accounting negligence as it is an unexplained and unsupportable usurpation of authority. Yet the plain language of Section 21C invokes, as the Commission stated, "classic negligence language."

* * *

III.

KPMG challenges the cease-and-desist order as improper on a variety of grounds, only one of which we conclude has apparent merit. . . .

* * *

The Commission's cease-and-desist order required that KPMG cease and desist from committing present or future violations of Rule 2–02(b) of Regulation S–X, or being the cause of any present or future violation of Section 13(a) of the Exchange Act or Rule 13a–1 thereunder due to an act or omission that KPMG knows or should know will contribute to such violation, by having any transactions, interests or relationships that would impair its independence under Rule 2–01 of Regulation S–X or under GAAS. In addressing KPMG's challenges to the order, our review of the Commission's choice of a sanction is limited by both the Administrative Procedure Act and Supreme Court precedent. The APA limits our inquiry to whether the Commission's sanction was "arbitrary, capricious, an abuse of discretion, or otherwise not in accordance with law." The Supreme Court has long instructed that the Commission's choice of sanction shall not be disturbed by the court unless the sanction is either "unwarranted in law or is without justification in fact."

A.

KPMG contends that the cease-and-desist order is overbroad because it bears no reasonable relation to the violations found. KPMG also contends that the order is unduly vague because by prohibiting all relationships that violate GAAS, the order incorporates broad, open-ended standards that require interpretation and exposes KPMG to the possibility of punishment for making good-faith but incorrect judgments about compliance. Neither contention is persuasive.

Section 21C authorizes the entry of a cease-and-desist order to prohibit "any future violation of the same provision" found to have been violated in the instant case. The provisions at issue are . . . Section 13(a) of the Exchange Act, and Rule 13a–1 promulgated thereunder. There is, consequently, no "sweeping order to obey the law" as KPMG contends, because the terms of the order are limited to these provisions. Further, the Commission stated that the order "extends only to violative acts 'the threat of which in the future is indicated because of their similarity or relation to those [past] unlawful acts.'" The order thus extends only to a subset of the violations comprehended by the rules and statutory provisions involved, namely those that are independence related. By concluding that the seriousness of KPMG's misconduct, combined with the flaws in its mode of assessing independence, created a serious risk of future independence-impairing relationships beyond the two circumstances at issue, the Commission justified an order aimed at preventing violations flowing from a broader array of independence impairments than the precise ones found. In so doing, it cannot be said that the order has "no reasonable relation to the unlawful practices found to exist."

* * *

Neither is there any requirement on the part of the Commission to tailor its order more narrowly to specific types of violations of the provisions involved. The "any future violation" language in Section 21C makes this clear and the "reasonable relationship" requirement does not impose such a limit. As the Supreme Court observed in *FTC v. Ruberoid Co.*, 343 U.S. 470, 72 (1952), cease-and-desist authority is "not limited to prohibiting the illegal practice in the precise form in which it is found to have existed in the past. If the Commission is to attain the objectives Congress envisioned, it cannot be required to confine its road block to the narrow lane the transgressor has traveled; it must be allowed effectively to close all roads to the prohibited goal, so that its order may not be by-passed with impunity." What KPMG would appear to suggest is required—namely an order so narrow that in the absence of copy-cat violations there would be no possibility of a violation of the order—ignores the expansive language used by Congress. . . .

KPMG's challenge to the cease-and-desist order on vagueness grounds is similarly without merit. KPMG contends that because GAAS standards are "vague and open-ended" the Commission could not properly enjoin compliance with broad prohibitions that require subjective interpretation and complex judgments over which reasonable professionals may disagree. This court has observed . . . that cease-and-desist orders should be "sufficiently clear and precise to avoid raising serious questions as to their meaning and application." KPMG nevertheless fails to show that such serious questions will necessarily arise to its detriment.

Section 21C allows for the order to enjoin the "causing [of] such violation and any future violation of the same provision, rule, or regulation." That is all the order did; it ordered KPMG to "cease and desist from committing any violation or future violation of . . . Section 13(a) of the Securities Exchange Act of 1934 or Rule 13a–1 thereunder." The order merely tracks the statutory language and inserts the relevant provisions. Further, although GAAS may be a complex scheme and reasonable professionals may differ as to its application to discrete sets of facts, it is not a set of indefinite and open-ended standards subject to the whims of the Commission. Rather, as with most provisions of the law, there are broad areas of clarity an instances closer to the line where there will be some doubt. The rule, as amended, effective February 2001, includes examples of when independence will be found lacking, and while non-exclusive, the examples nonetheless inform the general standard.... If KPMG has a disagreement with the Commission as to its interpretation of a GAAS standard, it will have the opportunity to make the case for its interpretation in any contempt proceeding the Commission may institute to adjudicate an alleged violation of the order.

B.

More problematic, however, is KPMG's contention that in entering the cease-and-desist order, the Commission created an improper presumption that a past violation is sufficient evidence of "some risk" of future violation, and applied it in an arbitrary and capricious manner whereby it is, "in essence, irrebutable," ignoring KPMG's evidence of serious remediation and the ALJ's finding there was no future threat of harm. In seeking reconsideration by the Commission, KPMG argued that the Commission had failed to comply with the standard that it had established for issuance of a cease-and-desist order—namely some likelihood of future violation based on proof of some continuing or threatened conduct by KPMG creating an increased likelihood of future violations—and that there was no such evidence. The plain language of Section 21C, as well as the legislative history, undermine KPMG's contention that the Commission erred in proceeding on the basis of a lower risk of future violation than is required for an injunction. However, the precise manner in which the standard is met is unclear from the Commission's analysis on reconsideration.

In its original opinion, the Commission acknowledged that:

> in imposing sanctions, we traditionally have balanced a variety of mitigating and aggravating circumstances, such as the harm caused by the violations, the seriousness of the violations, the extent of the wrongdoer's unjust enrichment, and the wrongdoer's disciplinary record. The questions this case poses are whether, as a matter of either statutory command or in the exercise of our broad discretion, we will require some showing of likelihood of future violations before issuing a cease-and-desist order, and how that showing may be made.

The Commission had stated that a single violation sufficed to show the necessary likelihood. On reconsideration, the Commission explained that, consistent with the history leading up to the enactment of Section 21C, it had applied a standard for showing a risk of future violations that was significantly less than that required for an injunction. To the Commission, "although 'some risk' of future violations is necessary, it need not be very great to warrant issuing a cease-and-desist order and that in the ordinary case and absent evidence to the contrary, a finding of past violation raises a sufficient risk of future violation." Disclaiming that issuance of a cease-and-desist order is "automatic" on a finding of past violation, the Commission stated that "[a]long with the risk of future violations, we will continue to consider our traditional factors in determining whether a cease-and-desist order is an appropriate sanction based on the entire record."

The Commission proceeded to reject KPMG's argument that the violative conduct was isolated, inadvertent, and unconnected to any ongoing conduct or engagement. Rather, the Commission explained, that although "the isolated nature of the violations tended to counsel against relief . . . we did not, and do not, consider the lack of care at senior levels that attended the independence determinations in this case to have been merely inadvertent or to be 'unconnected' to any ongoing conduct or engagement." The risk of future violations arises here, the Commission explained, "from the manifestly inadequate level of scrutiny given to independence issues and [KPMG's] consistent failure to recognize the seriousness of this misconduct." The Commission then noted that the loan to Olson, an officer of a registrant, was, in the words of a witness, "an absolute blatant out-and-out violation" of GAAS.

* * *

IV.

Accordingly, because KPMG lacked fair notice of the Commission's interpretation of AICPA Rule 302, we reverse the Commission's finding that the "success" fee/royalty arrangement violated that rule. . . . We affirm the Commission's determination that negligence is an appropriate basis for violations underlying a Section 21C cease-and-desist order, and reject KPMG's contentions that the order is overbroad and vague. . . .

QUESTIONS

1.   Do you agree that a negligence standard is a sufficient basis for the entry of a cease-and-desist order against "other persons" who "contribute to such violation" under § 21C?

2.   Why wasn't the SEC's cease-and-desist order against KPMG void for overbreadth?

3.   Why wasn't the SEC's cease-and-desist order against KPMG void for vagueness?

4.   Does the opportunity to dispute the SEC's interpretation of law in a contempt proceeding adequately protect KPMG?

HYPOTHETICAL THREE

Creative Accounts is the accounting firm for Lost Travel. Kate, the former CFO of Lost Travel, had maintained a secret slush fund of $500,000 from which she paid bribes to foreign officials to facilitate Lost Travel's unique vacation opportunities. Daniel, a junior accountant at Creative Accounts, spilled the beans to the SEC on the audit partner at Creative Accounts for Lost Travel, John, for ignoring Kate's slush fund in the course of the audit. What sanctions can the SEC apply to John and Creative Accounts in a § 21C proceeding?

C. JUDICIAL REMEDIES

For more serious violations of the securities laws, the SEC has traditionally been more likely to seek relief in federal district court. The

SEC has a broad range of sanctions available to it, including court injunctions against future violations, corporate governance reforms, disgorgement and civil penalties. In an extreme case, the SEC has even succeeded in having a new board of directors appointed by the court. *See International Controls Corp. v. Vesco*, 490 F.2d 1334 (2d Cir. 1974) (approving appointment of interim board of directors). Although § 21C provides for disgorgement from auditors who violate their whistleblowing duties, the SEC may seek disgorgement more generally from any defendant under a court's equitable powers. In choosing to pursue a judicial remedy, the SEC gives up the home court advantage and speed—as courts are slower than administrative proceedings.

1. INJUNCTIONS

Section 21(d)(1) of the Exchange Act and its counterpart, § 20(b) of the Securities Act, authorize the SEC to file an action in the appropriate district court to enjoin violations of the securities laws, regulations thereunder, and the rules of the SROs. The SEC does not need to show irreparable injury or the inadequacy of other remedies in order to obtain an injunction. The *Aaron* case below addresses the question of the state of mind that the SEC must show when it seeks to halt the fraudulent sale of securities. *Aaron* involves the SEC's motion for an injunction based on violations of the antifraud provisions found in § 17(a) of the Securities Act and Rule 10b–5 and § 10(b) of the Exchange Act.

Aaron v. SEC

446 U.S. 680 (1980).

■ STEWART, J.

The issue in this case is whether the Securities and Exchange Commission is required to establish scienter as an element of a civil enforcement action to enjoin violations of Section 17(a) of the Securities Act of 1933, Section 10(b) of the Securities Exchange Act of 1934, and Commission Rule 10b–5 promulgated under that section of the 1934 Act.

I

When the events giving rise to this enforcement proceeding occurred, the petitioner was a managerial employee at E. L. Aaron & Co., a registered broker-dealer with its principal office in New York City. Among other responsibilities at the firm, the petitioner was charged with supervising the sales made by its registered representatives and maintaining the so-called "due diligence" files for those securities in which the firm served as a market maker. One such security was the common stock of Lawn-A-Mat Chemical & Equipment Corp., a company engaged in the business of selling lawn-care franchises and supplying its franchisees with products and equipment.

Between November 1974 and September 1975, two registered representatives of the firm, Norman Schreiber and Donald Cainson, conducted a sales campaign in which they repeatedly made false and misleading statements in an effort to solicit orders for the purchase of Lawn-A-Mat common stock. . . .

Upon receiving several complaints from prospective investors, an officer of Lawn-A-Mat informed Schreiber and Cainson that their statements were false and misleading and requested them to cease making such statements. This request went unheeded. Thereafter, Milton Kean, an attorney representing Lawn-A-Mat, communicated with the petitioner twice by telephone. In these conversations, Kean informed the petitioner that Schreiber and Cainson were making false and misleading statements and described the substance of what they were saying. The petitioner, in addition to being so informed by Kean, had reason to know that the statements were false, since he knew that the reports in Lawn-A-Mat's due diligence file indicated a deteriorating financial condition and revealed no plans for manufacturing a new car and tractor. Although assuring Kean that the misrepresentations would cease, the petitioner took no affirmative steps to prevent their recurrence. The petitioner's only response to the telephone calls was to inform Cainson of Kean's complaint and to direct him to communicate with Kean. Otherwise, the petitioner did nothing to prevent the two registered representatives under his direct supervision from continuing to make false and misleading statements in promoting Lawn-A-Mat common stock.

In February 1976, the Commission filed a complaint in the District Court for the Southern District of New York against the petitioner and seven other defendants in connection with the offer and sale of Lawn-A-Mat common stock. In seeking preliminary and final injunctive relief pursuant to § 20(b) of the 1933 Act and § 21(d) of the 1934 Act, the Commission alleged that the petitioner had violated and aided and abetted violations of three provisions—§ 17(a) of the 1933 Act, § 10(b) of the 1934 Act, and Commission Rule 10b–5 promulgated under that section of the 1934 Act.

The gravamen of the charges against the petitioner was that he knew or had reason to know that the employees under his supervision were engaged in fraudulent practices, but failed to take adequate steps to prevent those practices from continuing.

* * *

We granted certiorari to resolve the conflict in the federal courts as to whether the Commission is required to establish scienter—an intent on the part of the defendant to deceive, manipulate, or defraud[5]—as an element of a Commission enforcement action to enjoin violations of § 17(a), § 10(b), and Rule 10b–5.

II

* * *

The issue here is whether the Commission in seeking injunctive relief either under § 20(b) for violations of § 17(a), or under § 21(d) for violations of § 10(b) or Rule 10b–5, is required to establish scienter. Resolution of that issue could depend upon (1) the substantive

---

[5] The term "scienter" is used throughout this opinion, as it was in *Ernst & Ernst v. Hochfelder*, 425 U.S. 185, 194, n. 12, to refer to "a mental state embracing intent to deceive, manipulate, or defraud." We have no occasion here to address the question, reserved in *Hochfelder*, whether, under some circumstances, scienter may also include reckless behavior.

provisions of § 17(a), § 10(b), and Rule 10b–5, or (2) the statutory provisions authorizing injunctive relief "upon a proper showing," § 20(b) and § 21(d). We turn to an examination of each to determine the extent to which they may require proof of scienter.

[The court held that scienter is a necessary element of a violation of § 10(b) and Rule 10b–5 based on its prior holding in *Ernst & Ernst v. Hochfelder*, excerpted in Chapter 5. In contrast, while the Court found that the language of § 17(a)(1) requires scienter, the Court held that scienter was not required under either § 17(a)(2) or § 17(a)(3).]

* * *

There remains to be determined whether the provisions authorizing injunctive relief, § 20(b) of the 1933 Act and § 21(d) of the 1934 Act, modify the substantive provisions at issue in this case so far as scienter is concerned.

The language and legislative history of § 20(b) and § 21(d) both indicate that Congress intended neither to add to nor to detract from the requisite showing of scienter under the substantive provisions at issue. Sections 20(b) and 21(d) provide that the Commission may seek injunctive relief whenever it appears that a person "is engaged or [is] about to engage in any acts or practices" constituting a violation of the 1933 or 1934 Acts or regulations promulgated thereunder and that, "upon a proper showing," a district court shall grant the injunction. The elements of "a proper showing" thus include, at a minimum, proof that a person is engaged in or is about to engage in a substantive violation of either one of the Acts or of the regulations promulgated thereunder. Accordingly, when scienter is an element of the substantive violation sought to be enjoined, it must be proved before an injunction may issue. But with respect to those provisions such as § 17(a)(2) and § 17(a)(3), which may be violated even in the absence of scienter, nothing on the face of § 20(b) or § 21(d) purports to impose an independent requirement of scienter. And there is nothing in the legislative history of either provision to suggest a contrary legislative intent.

This is not to say, however, that scienter has no bearing at all on whether a district court should enjoin a person violating or about to violate § 17(a)(2) or § 17(a)(3). In cases where the Commission is seeking to enjoin a person "about to engage in any acts or practices which . . . will constitute" a violation of those provisions, the Commission must establish a sufficient evidentiary predicate to show that such future violation may occur. An important factor in this regard is the degree of intentional wrongdoing evident in a defendant's past conduct. Moreover, as the Commission recognizes, a district court may consider scienter or lack of it as one of the aggravating or mitigating factors to be taken into account in exercising its equitable discretion in deciding whether or not to grant injunctive relief. And the proper exercise of equitable discretion is necessary to ensure a "nice adjustment and reconciliation between the public interest and private needs."

III

For the reasons stated in this opinion, we hold that the Commission is required to establish scienter as an element of a civil enforcement action to enjoin violations of § 17(a)(1) of the 1933 Act, § 10(b) of the 1934 Act, and Rule 10b–5 promulgated under that section of the 1934 Act. We further hold that the Commission need not establish scienter as an element of an action to enjoin violations of § 17(a)(2) and § 17(a)(3) of the 1933 Act. . . .

NOTES

1. *Section 17(a).* Section 17(a) is one of the few provisions of the Securities Act that applies to aftermarket sales of securities, as well as their distribution from issuers and their affiliates. The Court's opinion in *Aaron*, allowing the SEC to get an injunction for negligent conduct under §§ 17(a)(2) & (a)(3), has made § 17 a mainstay of SEC enforcement actions. Section 17 applies only to any person engaged in the "offer and sale of any security," which excludes purchasers as defendants. Thus, the SEC only needs to resort to Exchange Act § 10(b) and Rule 10b–5 when the defendant has committed fraud in the *purchase* of securities (a considerably less common phenomenon). Private plaintiffs have not been so fortunate, as most courts have followed *Washington Power*, excerpted above, in holding that § 17 does not create a private cause of action.

2. *Collateral consequences.* The most important collateral consequence of an injunction is the reputational hit that the defendant will take when the injunction is announced. The SEC prolongs this effect on one's reputation by requiring disclosure an injunction against violating the securities laws entered within the last ten years under Regulation S–K Item 401, which is incorporated by reference into a variety of required SEC filings. SEC cease-and-desist orders also must be disclosed. An injunction also triggers a variety of "bad boy" disqualifiers for certain non-registered offerings. Rule 506 of the Securities Act, for example, precludes issuers from relying on the private placement safe harbor if they have recently been enjoined from violating the antifraud provisions of the securities laws.

QUESTIONS

1. What state of mind must the SEC show to get an injunction for violations of substantive provisions that impose strict liability, such as § 5 of the Securities Act?

2. Is there a policy basis for distinguishing fraud in the purchase of securities (which requires scienter under Rule 10b–5 of the Exchange Act) from fraud in the sale of securities (which does not require scienter under §§ 17(a)(2) and (3) of the Securities Act)?

3. Why would Congress specify varying requirements for state of mind in the different provisions of § 17?

2.   OTHER CIVIL REMEDIES

The other remedies available to the SEC in court go well beyond an injunction against future violations. The agency can also seek disgorgement of any ill-gotten gains from the defendant and a range of civil penalties. Disgorgement orders stick with defendants—they are not dischargeable in bankruptcy if the violation involved fraudulently obtaining money. *SEC v. Bilzerian,* 153 F.3d 1278 (11th Cir. 1998). In addition, the SEC can seek to bar a defendant from serving as an officer or director of a public company. The next two cases address the standards for awarding the various forms of relief available to the SEC.

Sargent deals with Rule 14e–3, promulgated under § 14(e) of the Exchange Act (discussed more fully in Chapter 6). Rule 14e–3 prohibits trades based on material, nonpublic information pertaining to a tender offer if the trading party knows or should know that the information derives from either the acquirer or target company or someone working on behalf of either entity. At issue in the *Sargent* case is the heightened civil penalties for insider trading violations under the Insider Trading and Securities Fraud Enforcement Act of 1988.

SEC v. Sargent

329 F.3d 34 (1st Cir. 2003).

■ TORRUELLA, J., CIRCUIT JUDGE.

Defendant-appellee Dennis J. Shepard illegally shared confidential information regarding an upcoming tender offer with defendant-appellee Michael G. Sargent, who profited by using the information to trade in the target's stock. Sargent recommended the target's stock to co-defendant Robert Scharn, who also realized profits on the trades. In a civil enforcement action brought by plaintiff-appellant Securities and Exchange Commission against Shepard and Sargent, a jury found the defendants liable for violating Section 14(e) of the Securities Exchange Act, and Rule 14e–3 thereunder. As a remedy, the district court disgorged the defendants of the illicit profits. The SEC appeals the district court's denial of injunctive relief . . . and civil penalties. After careful review, we affirm.

I.   Facts

In 1994, Purolator Products, a publicly held manufacturer of automotive parts, was the target of acquisition efforts by Mark IV Industries, Incorporated. Defendant Shepard and J. Anthony Aldrich (against whom the Commission did not file a complaint) were the sole shareholders of a consulting firm. Aldrich, a member of the board of directors for the target, had nonpublic information that Purolator and Mark IV were involved in negotiations regarding Mark IV's acquisition proposal. In July 1994, Aldrich shared the information with Shepard. Shepard agreed not to disclose the information and indicated that he understood his obligation to maintain its confidentiality.

On Saturday, September 10, 1994, Shepard told Sargent, his friend and dentist, that Aldrich was on the Purolator board and he stated, "I am aware of a company right now that is probably going to be bought," but "even if I had the money I can't buy stock in this company because I am too close to the situation." The following Monday, Sargent contacted his broker and asked him to do some research on Purolator. Sargent thereafter purchased a total of 20,400 shares of Purolator. Sargent also notified his close friend Scharn of his purchases in Purolator. Scharn then purchased 5,000 shares of Purolator. Within a few days of the tender offer announcement, Sargent sold all of his Purolator stock at a profit of $141,768. Scharn sold his shares at a profit of $33,100.

The SEC filed the current action in March 1996, charging Shepard, Sargent, Scharn, and a fourth defendant with tipping and/or trading in violation of Exchange Act Section 10(b), Rule 10b–5, Section 14(e), and Rule 14e–3 and seeking injunctive relief, disgorgement, prejudgment interest, and civil penalties. The . . . jury found Shepard and Sargent liable for violations of Section 14(e) and Rule 14e–3 but did not find them liable for violations of Section 10(b) and Rule 10b–5. The jury found Scharn not liable on all counts.

On March 27, 2002, the district court issued an amended final judgment ordering Sargent and Shepard jointly and severally liable for disgorgement of Sargent's and Scharn's trading profits, a total of $174,868. The court declined to enter an injunction against future violations. The court also refused to order the defendants to pay prejudgment interest on the disgorgement amount and to assess penalties pursuant to the Insider Trading and Securities Fraud Enforcement Act of 1988, codified in Section 21A(a) of the Exchange Act. This appeal of the district court's denial of an injunction, interest, and penalties followed.

* * *

The SEC argues that the district court relied on an erroneous legal standard in refusing to grant an injunction against future violations of securities laws. The agency claims that the court believed that defendants must pose a "relatively imminent" threat of recidivism in order to justify permanent injunctive relief. We disagree, finding instead that the district court reached the proper conclusion under the correct standard.

The Securities and Exchange Act permits the SEC to seek an injunction in federal district court to prevent violations of securities laws. Section 21(d). Such an injunction is appropriate where there is, "at a minimum, proof that a person is engaged in or is about to engage in a substantive violation of either one of the Acts or of the regulations promulgated thereunder." This court has upheld issuance of injunctions in cases where future violations were likely. . . .

The reasonable likelihood of future violations is typically assessed by looking at several factors, none of which is determinative. Courts consider, among other things, the nature of the violation, including its egregiousness and its isolated or repeated nature, as well as whether the defendants will, owing to their occupation, be in a position to violate again. The courts also take into account whether the defendants have recognized the wrongfulness of their conduct.

Under these factors, the district court acted within its discretion in denying an injunction with respect to Shepard. Shepard disclosed confidential information to Sargent, but this was a first-time violation. As the SEC admits, Shepard's violation was not an egregious one, particularly where he neither traded on the information himself nor derived any direct personal profit. Further, his current position as president of a web-casting company does not put him in a position where future violations are likely. We therefore affirm the denial of an injunction against Shepard.

With respect to Sargent, there was also no abuse of discretion on the part of the district court in denying an injunction. Sargent's violation was isolated and unsophisticated: he simply put two and two together and, based on a casual conversation, invested in one company without attempting to conceal his trades. Sargent is unlikely to be privy to insider information either through his occupation as a dentist or because of his wife's position as a consultant. Further, Sargent's acceptance of the jury verdict without further appeal is sufficient acknowledgment of the wrongfulness of his conduct. The district court's denial of an injunction against Sargent is affirmed.

* * *

V. Civil Penalties

Finally, the SEC seeks reversal of the denial of Congressionally-provided civil penalties, which can amount to a maximum of three times the illicit profits realized (or losses avoided), and are intended to "penalize [the] defendant for . . . illegal conduct." In evaluating whether or not to assess civil penalties, a court may take seven factors into account, such as: (1) the egregiousness of the violations; (2) the isolated or repeated nature of the violations; (3) the defendant's financial worth; (4) whether the defendant concealed his trading; (5) what other penalties arise as the result of the defendant's conduct; and (6) whether the defendant is employed in the securities industry.

Applying these factors, we find no reason to reverse the district court with regard to civil penalties for Shepard. Shepard's violations consisted of a one-time tip to Sargent, and, as stated above, he did not personally realize any trades or direct profit. He, therefore, is left $174,868 worse off than he was prior to the activity for which he is liable. Further, he is not directly involved in the securities business, and he cooperated with and responded honestly to authorities. Finally, Shepard's financial net worth is not so high as to require civil penalties.

Applying the . . . factors to Sargent, we also find that the district court acted within its discretion in refusing to assess civil penalties. Sargent was an outsider who made no efforts to conceal his isolated transaction, which involved trading in the same stock during a short period of time and, as discussed in part III above, was not an egregious violation of securities laws. He is not employed in the securities industry. While he may have a high net worth, that factor alone does not merit reversal of the district court's denial of civil penalties. Further, Sargent was criminally convicted for his actions, and the sanction imposed in the criminal case—a year's probation and a $5,000 fine—also tempers the need for an additional monetary penalty.

* * *

QUESTIONS

1. The SEC argued that the lower court inappropriately applied a "relatively imminent threat" test to determine whether to grant the SEC an injunction. The First Circuit said that an injunction is appropriate "where future violations were likely." How do the two tests differ?

2. The First Circuit's test for issuing a securities law injunction focuses on the possibility of future misconduct. Does this focus undermine deterrence?

3. Why should the application of civil penalties turn on net worth? We don't apply a financial net worth test to determine the appropriate fine for a speeding ticket. How do securities violations differ?

———

The SEC has traditionally attempted to restore ill-gotten gains disgorged by defendants to defrauded investors when possible. If it is not possible to identify the victims, the money goes to the U.S. Treasury. Note that plaintiffs' attorneys are not a priority. Section 21(d)(4) of the Exchange Act prohibits the payment of disgorged funds "as payment for attorneys' fees or expenses incurred by private parties seeking distribution of the disgorged funds."

The practice of distributing money to victims has been expanded by the "Fair Funds for Investors" provision of the Sarbanes-Oxley Act. Prior to the Sarbanes-Oxley Act, only disgorgement was eligible for investor compensation. Any civil penalties imposed by the SEC would go to the U.S. Treasury. Section 308 of the Sarbanes-Oxley Act provides that if the SEC obtains an order requiring disgorgement (or settlement agreeing to disgorgement) in any judicial or administrative enforcement action, then the SEC can direct any civil penalty to be "added to and become part of the disgorgement fund for the benefit of the victims of such violation." The Dodd-Frank Act enhances the SEC's discretion; the agency can now direct civil penalties to such a fund, whether or not there is an order of disgorgement.

Although Congress has expanded the range of funds the SEC can use to compensate investors, the SEC is not required to establish a Fair Fund for investor compensation. Establishing a Fair Fund is solely at the SEC's discretion and the SEC can choose instead to direct that civil penalties go to the U.S. Treasury.

Measuring the amount to be disgorged can sometimes be difficult. The SEC must show that "its disgorgement figure reasonably approximates the amount of unjust enrichment," but a showing of "actual profits on the tainted transactions at least presumptively" satisfies the government's burden, at which point the burden shifts to the defendant to show why his actual profits are not equivalent to his unjust enrichment. *SEC v. First City Financial Corp.*, 890 F.2d 1215, 1232 (D.C. Cir. 1989). This measurement issue creates the possibility for dueling econometric experts. Consider the court's measure of disgorgement in the following case.

SEC v. First Pac. Bancorp

142 F.3d 1186 (9th Cir. 1998).

■ FERNANDEZ, F., CIRCUIT JUDGE.

The Securities and Exchange Commission brought a civil enforcement action against Leonard S. Sands, First Pacific Bancorp, and PacVen Inc. for violations of the antifraud, filing and disclosure provisions of the federal securities laws. The district court granted partial summary judgment in favor of the SEC on three of its claims. After a bench trial, the court ruled in favor of the SEC on all of its remaining claims. Sands, Bancorp and PacVen appeal the district court's grant of partial summary judgment. They also appeal the court's final judgment, which permanently enjoins them from future violations of the securities laws, orders them to disgorge $688,000 plus prejudgment interest, and permanently bars Sands from acting as an officer or director of a public company. We affirm.

BACKGROUND

Sands was the chairman of the board, chief executive officer and corporate counsel of Bancorp, . . . a bank holding company, and owned 54% of its common stock. Sands was also the chairman of the board and corporate counsel of First Pacific Bank, Inc. (Bank), the wholly owned subsidiary of Bancorp and its major asset. In addition, Sands was the president and the CEO of PacVen, a Nevada "blank check," also known as "shell," corporation formed for the purpose of merging with or acquiring other companies.

Beginning in the early 1980s, state and federal regulators repeatedly rated the Bank "unsatisfactory" because of its inadequate capital, earnings and liquidity, and because of its increasing amounts of classified assets and past due loans. In the late 1980s, Bancorp and Sands engaged in several financial transactions designed to raise additional capital for the failing Bank. They committed various securities law violations in the process.

The transaction which underlies most of the issues in this appeal was the Bancorp's 1987 public offering of securities. In April of 1987, it commenced a "mini-max" public offering with the intention of downstreaming its proceeds to the financially troubled Bank. Under the terms of the offering, Bancorp was required to sell a minimum of 750 "units," at $2,000 each, on an all-or-nothing basis by August 12, 1987. The underwriter later extended the deadline to October 10, 1987. If all 750 units were not sold by the deadline, the offering was to be cancelled and the funds were to be returned to the investors. . . .

On October 9, 1987, $1,688,000 was forwarded to the escrow agent for investment in the Bancorp offering, but of those funds, $1,000,000 was in the form of a check. . . . That check was later returned unpaid. Also, $500,000 had been raised in a public offering by PacVen in July of 1987, and was fraudulently diverted by Sands into the Bancorp offering. Thus, Bancorp only succeeded in raising $688,000 by the deadline, and only $188,000 of the funds came from bona fide investors.

However, Sands and Bancorp did not return the funds to the investors as they had promised in the Prospectus, but instead continued with the offering. On December 30, 1987, the date the offering was scheduled to close, Sands purchased 500 of the Bancorp units, paying $1,000,000 of his own funds. That purchase brought the total amount to $1,688,000. The offering was then closed and the proceeds were delivered to the Bank.

Among other things, the SEC sought to have Sands, Bancorp and PacVen disgorge the $688,000 raised in the Bancorp offering from outside investors. . . .

* * *

A.   DISGORGEMENT

Sands . . . claims that . . . he should not have been ordered to disgorge $688,000. . . .

* * *

(2)   The disgorgement order against Sands

The district court has broad equity powers to order the disgorgement of "ill-gotten gains" obtained through the violation of the securities laws. Disgorgement is designed to deprive a wrongdoer of unjust enrichment, and to deter others from violating securities laws by making violations unprofitable. Further, where two or more individuals or entities collaborate or have a close relationship in engaging in the violations of the securities laws, they have been held jointly and severally liable for the disgorgement of illegally obtained proceeds. Sands played the principal role in the fraudulent activities in connection with the Bancorp offering. He fraudulently diverted $500,000 from PacVen and later invested his own funds in order to close an offering that had already failed to meet the minimum requirement. As the chairman of the board, the CEO and the majority shareholder of Bancorp, and as the president and the CEO of PacVen, Sands clearly enjoyed a "close relationship" with those corporate codefendants. It was appropriate to hold Sands and his corporate codefendants jointly and severally liable for their jointly undertaken violations of the securities laws.

Sands argues that he should not have been ordered to disgorge the proceeds of the offering because he received no personal financial benefit as a result of that offering. We reject the argument. The infusion of capital from the Bancorp offering put off a bank failure and enabled the Bank to remain in operation for two and a half more years. During that time, Sands engaged in what the district court's findings characterized as "milking the asset," by paying himself hundreds of thousands of dollars in salaries, commissions, and consulting, management and legal fees. . . . The FDIC inspector found that Sands was paying himself excessive compensation, which amounted to two or three times what a CEO of a comparable, well-managed institution would receive. . . . Thus, Sands received substantial personal benefit from the infusion of the illegally obtained proceeds from the Bancorp offering into the failing Bank, which justified the district court's order directing Sands to disgorge those proceeds.[6]

* * *

---

[6] The district court was not required to trace every dollar of the offering proceeds fraudulently retained by Sands. The amount he was ordered to disgorge had to be only "a reasonable approximation of profits causally connected to the violation." Nor does the fact that Sands' scheme ultimately failed and he lost $1,000,000 of his own funds release him from his obligations toward the defrauded investors. As Judge Friendly once stated in a securities manipulation case, there is "no reason why, in determining how much should be disgorged in a case where defendants have manipulated securities so as to mulct the public, the court must give them credit for the fact that they had not succeeded in unloading all their purchases at the time when the scheme collapsed."

B. OFFICER AND DIRECTOR BAR

Sands earnestly argues that he should not have been "permanently and unconditionally prohibited from acting as an officer or director of [a public company]." We . . . agree with the district court that protection of the public justifies the bar. . . .

The district court has broad equitable powers to fashion appropriate relief for violations of the federal securities laws, which include the power to order an officer and director bar. In addition to the court's inherent equitable powers, the Securities Enforcement Remedies and Penny Stock Reform Act of 1990 authorizes the court to order an officer and director bar "if the person's conduct demonstrates substantial unfitness to serve as an officer or director." § 21(d)(2). In determining whether to order the bar, a court may consider: "(1) the 'egregiousness' of the underlying securities law violation; (2) the defendant's 'repeat offender' status; (3) the defendant's 'role' or position when he engaged in the fraud; (4) the defendant's degree of scienter; (5) the defendant's economic stake in the violation; and (6) the likelihood that misconduct will recur."

The district court considered those factors, and found that Sands' "securities violations are egregious; he caused the collapse of a federally insured bank; he attempted to stymie banking regulators from doing their jobs; he is a recidivist; and the fraudulent conduct he committed occurred while serving in a corporate or fiduciary capacity." The district court also found that Sands had a high level of scienter, that he engaged in ongoing and recurrent violations, that he had failed to assume any responsibility for his violations of law, that he utterly failed to recognize the wrongful nature of his conduct, and that there was a strong likelihood of future violations. We see no error in those detailed findings. . . .

CONCLUSION

Sands, a sophisticated businessman and a lawyer, has engaged in numerous activities in violation of the securities laws and basic notions of right and wrong. He perpetuated a number of frauds upon investors and regulators. We need not sort out whether his principles are just plain wrong, or whether he is afflicted with akrasia, or whether there is some other explanation for his actions. What is clear is that he, along with Bancorp and PacVen, must disgorge the amounts that the unwitting investors were relieved of. Equally clear, the district court properly barred him from assuming a position from which he could inflict similar wrongs in the future.

AFFIRMED

NOTES

1. *Remedies.* The SEC's enforcement arsenal was supplemented by the Sarbanes-Oxley Act. Exchange Act § 21C(c) allows the SEC to ask a court to temporarily freeze assets to prevent a company from making "extraordinary payments" to its officers and directors. This adds to the SEC's authority under § 21(d) to seek preliminary injunctive relief against persons who may be violating or about to violate the federal securities laws. The SEC can also seek to bar a person from participating in future penny

stock offerings if their misconduct involved a penny stock offering (an investment sector well known for its serial fraudsters). Section 21(d)(6). The standard for the SEC to seek a directors and officers bar was changed from "substantial unfitness" to simply "unfitness." Finally, § 21(d)(5) authorizes the SEC to "seek, and Federal court may grant, any equitable relief that may be appropriate or necessary for the benefit of investors." This affirms the courts' longstanding practice of exercising their inherent equitable powers to fashion appropriate remedies.

In addition to the remedies outlined here, the SEC has a whole pantheon of remedies available for use against investment professionals, such as broker-dealers, investment companies and investment advisors. Most of these remedies are available in both administrative and court proceedings.

QUESTIONS

1. As an investor, why would you care whether a public offering is conducted on a "mini-max" basis?

2. What is "akrasia"?

3. Is investor compensation the best use of the money recovered by the SEC? Would the money be better spent funding more SEC enforcement attorneys?

4. How should a court determine whether an equitable remedy sought by the SEC is "appropriate or necessary for the benefit of investors"?

When the SEC creates a disgorgement fund or Fair Fund, there will often be different classes of investors who have lost money due to the underlying securities law violations. If a company overstates its revenue numbers, this will make the company appear more valuable not only to stockholders but also to investors who purchase the junior and senior debt of the company. How should the SEC distinguish among these different classes of investors in deciding who gets compensated? Consider the SEC's plan of distribution for the Fair Fund arising out of an SEC enforcement action against WorldCom for accounting fraud that commenced in the early 2000s.

Official Committee of Unsecured Creditors of WorldCom, Inc. v. SEC

467 F.3d 73 (2d Cir. 2006).

■ SOTOMAYOR, S., CIRCUIT JUDGE.

Appellant Official Committee of Unsecured Creditors of WorldCom, Inc. appeals from an order of the United States District Court for the Southern District of New York approving a plan by the Securities and Exchange Commission to distribute money to the victims of WorldCom, Inc.'s securities fraud. The SEC prepared a distribution plan pursuant to the "Fair Funds for Investors" provision of the Sarbanes-Oxley Act of 2002 under which the SEC would distribute to defrauded investors the money it collected through the settlement of its civil enforcement action against WorldCom. The Committee, which was not a party to the litigation below, argues that the distribution plan wrongfully excluded certain categories of creditors and that the district court, had it applied the correct standard of review, would have rejected these exclusions. We . . . hold that the district court correctly reviewed the SEC's plan for fairness and reasonableness and did not abuse its discretion in approving it.

BACKGROUND

On June 25, 2002, WorldCom announced its intention to restate its financial results for all four quarters of 2001 and the first quarter of 2002 because of accounting irregularities. One day later, the SEC filed a civil complaint against WorldCom in the United States District Court . . . It alleged that WorldCom had overstated its income by $9 billion between 1999 and the first quarter of 2002 and in doing so violated various federal securities laws. On July 21, 2002, WorldCom filed for bankruptcy under Chapter 11 of the Bankruptcy Code. On July 29, 2002, the United States Trustee appointed the Committee to represent WorldCom's unsecured creditors. . . .

On July 7, 2003, the district court approved a final settlement between WorldCom and the SEC under which the company would pay a civil penalty of $750 million. The settlement included a nominal disgorgement of $1, which triggered the Fair Fund provision, allowing the civil penalty to be added to the disgorgement fund and distributed to defrauded investors. . . .

On April 15, 2004, after WorldCom emerged from bankruptcy, the SEC sought the district court's approval of its plan to distribute the funds. Because there was not enough money to compensate all the victims of WorldCom's fraud, the plan excluded several groups of investors. In particular, it excluded investors who recovered thirty-six cents or more on the dollar under the Chapter 11 reorganization plan or through the sale of their securities, and investors who made a net profit on their combined purchases or sales of WorldCom securities during the period in which the fraud occurred. On July 20, 2004, having found the plan "fair and reasonable," the district court approved it.

DISCUSSION

* * *

According to the Committee, the district court extended inappropriate deference to the SEC when it approved the Fair Fund distribution . . . We hold that the "fair and reasonable" standard of review applied by the district court is the appropriate one for Fair Fund distribution plans. We also hold that the district court did not abuse its discretion in approving the plan. . . .

A.   Disgorgement Funds and Fair Funds

District courts possess broad equitable discretion to craft remedies for violations of the Exchange Act. Within this discretion, district courts may require wrongdoers to disgorge fraudulently obtained profits. . . .

Finding that disgorgement insufficiently deters securities laws violations because it merely restores the status quo ante, Congress enacted the Securities Enforcement Remedies Act and Penny Stock

Reform Act of 1990. . . . As the House Report on the Remedies Act noted,

> Disgorgement merely requires the return of wrongfully obtained profits; it does not result in any actual economic penalty or act as a financial disincentive to engage in securities fraud. . . . The Committee therefore concluded that authority to seek or impose substantial money penalties, in addition to disgorgement of profits, is necessary for the deterrence of securities law violations. . . .

. . . . The Remedies Act permits the SEC, in addition to seeking disgorgement of ill-gotten profits, to seek civil penalties of generally up to the amount of the gross pecuniary gain from the securities fraud.

Prior to Sarbanes-Oxley, civil penalties obtained pursuant to the Remedies Act were paid to the Treasury, and thus were unavailable to injured investors. Sarbanes-Oxley's Fair Fund provision provides the SEC with flexibility by permitting it to distribute civil penalties among defrauded investors by adding the civil penalties to the disgorgement fund. . . . Thus, as with disgorged profits, the SEC may now, if it chooses, use civil penalties that it sought for the purposes of deterrence to compensate injured investors.

B.   The Appropriate Standard of Review for Fair Fund Distributions

As the district court noted, the standard of review for Fair Fund distribution plans is a question of first impression, ... The Committee contends that the district court should not have reviewed the Fair Fund distribution plan under the "fair and reasonable" standard for disgorgement plans . . . because the goal of Fair Fund distributions is compensation of victims rather than deterrence of future wrongdoing. The district court, it argues, should have "performed an independent review of the proposed plan." . . . .

For the reasons that follow, we conclude that enactment of the Fair Fund provision has not substantially changed the SEC's role in determining how to distribute the proceeds of a securities fraud.

First, as we have explained, although the SEC's purpose in seeking disgorgement of ill-gotten profits has always been deterrence, courts allow it to distribute the proceeds of disgorgement actions as compensation to injured investors. Deterrence is also the SEC's goal in seeking civil penalties and the Fair Fund provision does no more than permit civil penalties subsequently to be distributed in the same way as disgorged profits. The Committee overreads the Fair Fund provision's mention of "the benefit of the victims" as changing the SEC's role in distributing funds to injured investors, when instead the language merely empowers the SEC to do with civil penalties what it has long done with disgorged profits. The Fair Fund provision expands the ambit of penalty payments that the SEC has the discretion to distribute. Nothing indicates that the addition of civil penalties to a disgorgement fund changes the SEC's role in determining how the payments should be distributed.

Second, as the SEC correctly observes, even after the enactment of the Fair Fund provision, the decision remains in the hands of the SEC whether to distribute civil penalties to victims at all. Even if the Fair Fund provision explicitly mentions compensation, the fact that the SEC is not required to distribute Fair Fund proceeds to injured investors belies the Committee's assertion that the Fair Fund provision makes compensation the primary purpose of the distribution or compels a district court to conduct an independent review of the SEC's plan. Rather, the Fair Fund provision indicates that the SEC has the same discretion when distributing Fair Fund proceeds that it has when distributing only disgorged profits.

Finally, the . . . Committee argues that compensation is not within the SEC's expertise, and thus that the "fair and reasonable" standard of review affords it inappropriate deference. The SEC's claim to expertise here, however, comes from the fact that it is fulfilling a role assigned to it by statute. We have long understood that the SEC's charge to enforce the securities laws carries with it the discretion to determine how to distribute recovered profits among injured investors. The Fair Fund provision merely increases the funds that the SEC may distribute and in no way changes the SEC's role. We therefore reject the Committee's contention that the SEC acts outside the scope of its expertise and deserves less deference when it prepares a plan to distribute civil penalties along with disgorged profits.

C.   The District Court's Approval of the Fair Fund Distribution

[W]e also hold that . . . our review of the district court's exercise of its equitable powers in approving the plan is for abuse of discretion. We conclude that the district court did not abuse its discretion in approving the plan, and thus we reject the Committee's challenges.

First, the Committee argues that the distribution plan should not have excluded investors whose aggregated sales and purchases of WorldCom securities over the relevant time period resulted in a net profit. . . . [A]s the district court observed, "[w]hen funds are limited, hard choices must be made." It is clear that the SEC considered carefully how best to apportion limited funds among the many injured investors before deciding to exclude this category of investors. . . .

Second, the Committee objects to the exclusion of creditors who recovered more than thirty-six cents on the dollar either in the bankruptcy proceeding or through the sale of their WorldCom securities. In reviewing the Committee's objection to this exclusion, the district court observed that "it is fair and reasonable that the limited funds available for distribution not be directed to those who have already recovered more than the approximately thirty-six cents on the dollar recovered by general creditors, and rather be used to increase the still-considerably smaller recovery of those covered by the proposed Distribution Plan." As the SEC notes, without the exclusion, those creditors who already recovered more than others in the bankruptcy proceeding would also have stood to collect from the Fair Fund, at the expense of those creditors who received less in the bankruptcy proceedings and shareholders who had thus far received nothing.

The Committee argues that this exclusion "flies in the face of the strong public policy that puts the rights of bondholders ahead of those of shareholders." In the Committee's view, excluding creditors who already recovered more than general unsecured creditors would "undermine time-honored principles of the Bankruptcy Code, . . . a result Congress could not have intended." We recognize . . . that there is tension between the priority assigned to claims under the Bankruptcy Code and the Fair Fund provision, which empowers the SEC to distribute funds among injured investors outside the bankruptcy proceeding. We see no indication in the Fair Fund provision, however, that the SEC must follow the Bankruptcy Code's claim priorities when developing a distribution plan. In the absence of such an indication, it is not our role to mitigate this tension.

The district court was required only to determine that the SEC's distribution plan fairly and reasonably distributed the limited Fair Fund proceeds among the potential claimants. We are satisfied that it did not abuse its discretion in so finding. . . .

QUESTIONS

1. If compensation is the goal of the Fair Funds provision, why did Congress not require that all disgorgement and civil penalties be distributed to defrauded investors?

2. If deterrence is the goal, why does it matter how the SEC distributes disgorgement money? Why not require the SEC to distribute funds pro rata to all investors?

3. Is it appropriate for the SEC to violate the absolute priority rule in distributing funds to defrauded investors?

HYPOTHETICAL FOUR

Lost Travel has a number of problems that may get it, its officers, and its auditors into hot water with the SEC. These include: (1) Lost Travel's overstatement of revenues in its financial statements over the past two years; (2) Kate's payment while she was the CFO of Lost Travel of bribes to foreign officials; and (3) the secret $500,000 slush fund from which she paid the bribes. Lost Travel's audited financial statements, filed with its Form 10–K, show neither the bribes nor the slush fund. Hugo (the CEO), Kate, and Creative Accounts all certified the financial statements. The SEC has now brought an action in district court, naming Lost Travel, Hugo, and Kate as defendants. What remedies are appropriate? And which defendants should be liable for those remedies?

D. CRIMINAL ENFORCEMENT

Criminal sanctions are an essential component of enforcement. For the hard-core fraudster, only the threat of hard time will deter misconduct, particularly in light of the enormous pecuniary rewards from committing fraud. The threat of jail time is also important in dissuading the executives of public companies from wrongdoing. Consider the financial controller, who is under pressure from the CEO to meet Wall Street's earnings expectations for the company. In the absence of jail time as a deterrent, a financial controller may be tempted to reclassify a current expense as a capital investment, thereby shifting the accounting cost of the expense into future years, thereby raising current earnings. Doing so will solidify the controller's standing with the CEO and increase the share price at least temporarily, raising the value of the controller's stock options. The fraud may go undetected, leaving the controller to enjoy the profits from his exercised options. If the fraud is uncovered, civil penalties will sting, but they may not provide a large ex ante deterrent once they are discounted by the low probability of detection. Criminal sanctions substantially raise the expected cost of securities law violations.

Section 21(d) of the Exchange Act authorizes the SEC to refer criminal violations of the securities laws to the U.S. Attorney General for prosecution. In recent years, the Justice Department has brought several high profile criminal proceedings. Bernard Madoff is one example. Madoff pleaded guilty to, among other things, fraud under Rule 10b–5, mail and wire fraud, and money laundering in 2009. Madoff received a 150-year sentence in prison. As part of his guilty plea, Madoff admitted: "As I engaged in my fraud, I knew what I was doing was wrong, indeed criminal. When I began the Ponzi scheme, I believed it would end shortly and I would be able to extricate myself and my clients from the scheme." Madoff's excuse is a familiar one; most fraudsters believe they can turn things around before their fraud comes to light.

Defendants can commit criminal offenses while attempting to hold off governmental investigations. Although Martha Stewart faced insider trading charges for allegedly selling her shares of ImClone Systems. based on non-public, material information, Stewart was eventually convicted and imprisoned, not for securities fraud, but for obstruction of justice and lying to investigators.

Section 32(a) of the Exchange Act makes it a criminal offense to "willfully violate[ ] any provision [of the Exchange Act] or any rule or regulation thereunder" or to "willfully and knowingly make[ ], or cause[ ] to be made, any statement in any application, report, or document required to be filed under [the Exchange Act] ... which statement was false or misleading with respect to any material fact." Stiff penalties await those convicted: up to $5,000,000 in fines and twenty years' imprisonment for natural persons, and $25,000,000 in fines for corporations. A defendant can avoid imprisonment (but not fines), however, "if he proves that he had no knowledge of such rule or regulation." What do "willfully" and "knowingly" mean in this context? How do they differ?

United States v. Tarallo

380 F.3d 1174 (9th Cir. 2004).

■ GRABER, S., CIRCUIT JUDGE.

Defendant Aldo Tarallo appeals his convictions on six counts of securities fraud, in violation of Exchange Act §§ 10(b) and 32 and Rule 10b–5.... [W]e hold that a defendant may commit securities fraud "willfully" in violation of § 32 and Rule 10b–5 even if the defendant did not know at the time of the acts that the conduct violated the law. We further hold that a defendant may commit securities fraud "willfully" by intentionally acting with reckless disregard for the truth of material misleading statements....

FACTUAL AND PROCEDURAL BACKGROUND

Defendant and two co-defendants, David Colvin and John Larson, together participated in a fraudulent telemarketing scheme. Colvin owned several companies used in the scheme, including Intellinet, Inc., and Larson was Intellinet's sales manager. Defendant was hired by Intellinet as a telemarketer, and he participated in the fraud from April 1997 until February 20, 1998. Defendant and others solicited those called to invest in various businesses whose value and operations were fictitious. These purported businesses included Medical Advantage, Inc., Lamelli Medical Technology, Inc., and R.A.C. International, Inc. . . .

Defendant and his co-defendants falsely represented to potential investors that Medical Advantage operated independent weight loss clinics around the country and had a projected 1997 revenue of $8.2 million, and that C. Everett Koop and Tom Brokaw supported or were affiliated with the company. Defendant and his co-defendants falsely represented to potential investors that Lamelli had developed a detoxification system that could detoxify a person of all alcohol or drugs in 15 minutes, that the system had won FDA approval, and that $187 million in revenue was expected to be generated by this alleged invention in 1998. Defendant and his co-defendants falsely represented to potential investors that R.A.C. had generated $2.3 million in revenue in 1997 from sales of motor oil, car batteries, and tools, and that the company projected for 1998 revenues of approximately $3.5 million.

Defendant and his co-defendants told potential investors that they would be investing by means of promissory notes, which would be held in a "trust" for a fixed term of between 90 and 180 days. In return, the investors would receive 12 percent interest per annum and shares of "restricted stock" in the company. Defendant told investors that the company's Initial Public Offering ("IPO") would occur on or before the date on which the promissory note was to mature, at which point investors could (at their option) either receive back their invested principal or use it to purchase shares offered in the IPO. Instead of holding the invested funds in trust as promised, however, Colvin and others used those funds for the benefit of Colvin, Larson, Defendant, and their associates, and the investors never saw their money again.

After a nine-day trial, a jury convicted Defendant on six counts of securities fraud. . . . Defendant timely appealed.

DISCUSSION

Defendant [argues] on appeal [that] there was insufficient evidence to support the fraud convictions; [and] (C) the district court erred in instructing the jury;

A.   Evidence Supporting the Fraud Convictions

* * *

[A] defendant may be convicted of committing securities fraud only if the government proves specific intent to defraud, mislead, or deceive.

Defendant argues that there was insufficient evidence that he knew that the statements he made to potential investors were false. If he did not even know that the statements were false, of course, he could not have had the specific intent to defraud. He points out that Colvin and Larson distributed typewritten scripts for salespeople to use during sales calls, and he asserts that the investment materials they provided to Defendant (and passed along to investors) were sophisticated and were not recognizably false. In essence, Defendant claims that no evidence at trial established that he was anything other than an innocent who was duped right along with the investors.

The record does not support Defendant's claim. A reasonable factfinder could have found beyond a reasonable doubt that Defendant knew of the fraudulent nature of the scheme in which he was participating.

For example, the jury was presented with evidence that Defendant knew that it was a lie to assure investors that their money was guaranteed and risk-free because it was held in a "trust" until the IPO occurred. For example, Crew testified that Defendant told him that his investment would be held in a trust and that, after the IPO, he could receive his principal back with interest, or else receive shares in the company. However, Defendant received paychecks from Sierra Ridge Management Trust, which was one of the trusts for which Defendant solicited investors. Agent Goldman testified that, after being arrested and Mirandized, Defendant admitted that he knew he was being paid out of the same "trust" companies that investors' money was being deposited. Paul Coynes, who worked with Defendant as a telemarketer, also testified for the prosecution. Coynes explained that he realized after a time that it was impossible for the money he was soliciting to be held safely in a trust:

> [W]e told people that all the money went into the trust company. And at some point it became clear to me how ridiculous that was because we were getting paid a commission, the sales manager was getting paid a commission, and the owner of the company was obviously living a decent life-style and that money had to come from somewhere.

A juror could reasonably conclude from this evidence that Defendant knew that the "trusts" were not actually safe, but were being raided for payroll.

The jury also heard evidence that Defendant lied to potential investors about where he was located, telling them during telephone conversations that he was in a different office from Colvin, an office that did not exist. Investor-victim John Wiedmer testified that Defendant told him that he was in a Washington, D.C., office, while Colvin was in California. Wiedmer testified that this statement influenced his decision to invest because it made the publishing company Defendant was pitching sound like "a pretty big operation," and that representation added some credence to the legitimacy of the enterprise. . . .

The foregoing evidence supported the jury's finding beyond a reasonable doubt that Defendant knew of the fraudulent nature of the telemarketing scheme and that he acted with the intent to defraud.

* * *

C. Jury Instructions

Defendant claims several errors in the jury instructions relating to the fraud counts as to which there was sufficient evidence.

* * *

2. Instructions equating "willfully" and "knowingly."

Defendant was charged with, and convicted of, securities fraud under Exchange Act § 32 and under Rule 10b–5, which was promulgated under the authority of § 10(b). Section 32(a) states:

> (a) Willful violations; false and misleading statements
>
> Any person who *willfully* violates any provision of this chapter . . . , or any rule or regulation thereunder . . ., or any person who *willfully and knowingly* makes, or causes to be made, any statement in any application, report, or document required to be filed under this chapter or any rule or regulation thereunder . . . which statement was false or misleading with respect to any material fact, shall upon conviction be fined not more than $5,000,000, or imprisoned not more than 20 years, or both, except that when such person is a person other than a natural person, a fine not exceeding $25,000,000 may be imposed; but no person shall be subject to imprisonment under this section for the violation of any rule or regulation if he proves that he had no knowledge of such rule or regulation. (emphases added).

The district court instructed the jury on "knowingly" and "willfully" as follows:

> Each of the crimes charged in the indictment requires proof beyond a reasonable doubt that the defendant acted knowingly. An act is done knowingly if the defendant is aware of the act and does not act or fail to act through ignorance, mistake, or accident.
>
> The government is not required to prove that the defendant knew that his acts or omissions were unlawful. Thus, for example, to prove a defendant guilty of securities fraud . . . based on making a false or misleading representation, the government must prove beyond a reasonable doubt that the defendant knew the representation was false or was made with reckless indifference to its truth or falsity, but it need not prove that in making the representation the defendant knew he was committing securities fraud . . . or any other criminal offense.
>
> In these statutes, willfully has the same meaning as knowingly.

Defendant argues that the court erred by instructing that "willfully" and "knowingly" mean the same thing, and by instructing that the government did not have to prove that defendant knew that his conduct was unlawful. He argues that the "willful" instruction runs afoul of *Bryan v. United States*, 524 U.S. 184, 191–92 (1998), in which the Supreme Court stated:

> As a general matter, when used in the criminal context, a "willful" act is one undertaken with a "bad purpose." In other words, in order to establish a "willful" violation of a statute, "the Government must prove that the defendant acted with knowledge that his conduct was unlawful."

Because § 32 requires a showing of "willfulness," Defendant argues, it was error to instruct the jury that Defendant could be convicted even if the jury found that he did not know that his conduct was unlawful.

As an initial matter, we note that the district court did err in this instruction, although not in the way that Defendant claims. As quoted above, the district court instructed that "[e]ach of the crimes charged in the indictment requires proof beyond a reasonable doubt that the defendant acted knowingly." However, § 32(a) states that a person who "willfully" violates any provision of the chapter or any rule or regulation promulgated thereunder is subject to criminal penalty. "Knowingly" is not a required element. "Knowingly" is an element for the conviction of any individual who "makes, or causes to be made, any statement in any application, report, or document required to be filed under this chapter or any rule or regulation thereunder. . . ." As § 32 makes clear, such a person must be found to have engaged in the proscribed conduct "willfully and knowingly."

The conduct for which Defendant was indicted, tried, and convicted did not involve the filing of an application, report, or document required by the securities laws. Instead, his conduct was covered by Rule 10b–5. That conduct clearly falls under the first provision of § 32(a), which requires only that the act be done "willfully," but does not require that the act be done "knowingly." Therefore, the district court's instruction that "[e]ach of the crimes charged in the indictment requires proof beyond a reasonable doubt that the defendant acted knowingly" was erroneous.

However, the district court then went on to equate "willfully" with "knowingly." The district court's error in including "knowingly" in the instructions is therefore harmless so long as the definition the court provided for knowingly and willfully satisfies the statutory definition of "willfully." We turn now to that question.

The Supreme Court has taken pains to observe that the word "willful" "is a word of many meanings" and that "its construction is often influenced by its context." We must consider, then, the context in which "willfully" is found in the securities fraud statutes. The question is whether the securities fraud statutes' use of the term "willfully" means that a defendant can be convicted of securities fraud only if he or she knows that the charged conduct is unlawful, or whether "willfully" simply means what the district court instructed it means: "knowingly" in the sense that the defendant intends those actions and that they are not the product of accident or mistake.

Defendant's argument-that willfulness requires that he knew that he was breaking the law at the time he made his false statements—has been previously rejected by this and other courts. The Second Circuit explained that "[t]he language makes one point entirely clear. A person can willfully violate an SEC rule even if he does not know of its existence. This conclusion follows from the difference between the standard for violation of the statute or a rule or regulation, to wit, 'willfully,' and that for false or misleading statements, namely willfully and knowingly.'" . . . Adopting the reasoning of the Second Circuit, we "accept[ed] this with the qualifications, doubtless intended by the author, that the act be wrongful under the securities laws and that the knowingly wrongful act involve a significant risk of effecting the violation that has occurred."

* * *

Even were we not bound by our existing precedent, we would reach the same result. The final clause of § 32(a) provides that "no person shall be subject to imprisonment under this section for the violation of any rule or regulation if he proves that he had no knowledge of such rule or regulation." The opening sentence of subsection (a) explains that "[a]ny person who *willfully* violates any provision of this chapter . . . or any rule or regulation thereunder . . ." commits a crime. (emphasis added). If "willfully" meant "with knowledge that one's conduct violates a rule or regulation," the last clause proscribing imprisonment—but not a fine—in cases where a defendant did not know of the rule or regulation would be nonsensical: If willfully meant "with knowledge that one is breaking the law," there would be no need to proscribe imprisonment (but permit imposition of a fine) for someone who acted without knowing that he or she was violating a rule or regulation. Such a person could not have been convicted in the first place.

Under our jurisprudence, then, "willfully" as it is used in § 32(a) means intentionally undertaking an act that one knows to be wrongful; "willfully" in this context does not require that the actor know specifically that the conduct was unlawful. The district court's instructions correctly informed the jury that it had to find that defendant intentionally undertook such an act:

> [T]o prove a defendant guilty of securities fraud or mail fraud based on making a false or misleading representation, the government must prove beyond a reasonable doubt that the defendant knew the representation was false or was made with reckless indifference to its truth or falsity, but it need not prove that in making the representation the defendant knew he was committing securities fraud, mail fraud, or any other criminal offense.

The district court's instructions thus required the jury to find that Defendant had made statements that he knew at the time were false, or else made them with a reckless disregard for whether they were false. The district court therefore required the jury to find that Defendant undertook acts that he knew at the time to be wrongful, meeting the standard for defining "willfully" in this circuit. The district court's importation of the term "knowingly" into the jury instructions was harmless beyond a reasonable doubt, because the court equated "knowingly" with "willfully," and the court's definition properly explained "willfully."

3. *Recklessness standard for securities fraud.*

As discussed above, the district court instructed the jury that it could convict Defendant of . . . securities fraud if it found that he had made a false statement, which was a representation that either "(a) was then known to be untrue by the person making or causing it to be made or (b) was made or caused to be made with reckless indifference as to its truth or falsity." Defendant argues that the recklessness portion of the instruction was error. . . .

The comment to Ninth Circuit Model Jury Instruction 9.7 (2000) states that reckless disregard for truth or falsity is sufficient to sustain a conviction for securities fraud.... Defendant argues that the comment incorrectly describes the law to be applied in this case, because ... the Supreme Court's decision in *United States v. O'Hagan*, 521 U.S. 642 (1997), stands for the proposition that recklessness is insufficient to sustain a criminal conviction for securities fraud. In *O'Hagan*, the Supreme Court said that, in order to convict a defendant of securities fraud, the government must prove that the defendant "willfully" violated Rule 10b–5. Defendant again cites *Bryan* for the proposition that willfulness requires actual knowledge and argues that recklessness cannot satisfy this requirement.

Defendant's argument fails.... [R]ecklessness is adequate to support a conviction for securities fraud.... As we explained above, "willfully" in the context of § 32 is best understood to mean "voluntarily and knowingly wrongful," not "with the intent to violate the law." We find no error in the recklessness instruction.

* * *

NOTES

1. *Sarbanes-Oxley criminal offenses.* Apparently not satisfied with the criminal penalties provided by § 32(a) for violations of the general antifraud provision in § 10(b) of the Exchange Act, Congress added a separate securities fraud offense to the federal criminal code as part of the Sarbanes-Oxley Act:

> Whoever knowingly executes, or attempts to execute, a scheme or artifice—
>
> (1) to defraud any person in connection with any security of [a reporting company]; or
>
> (2) to obtain, by means of false or fraudulent pretenses, representations, or promises, any money or property in connection with the purchase or sale of any security of [a reporting company];
>
> shall be fined under this title, or imprisoned not more than 25 years, or both.

18 U.S.C. § 1348. Also added was a provision making attempts and conspiracies punishable to the same extent as the underlying crime. 18 U.S.C. § 1349. A final provision requires certification of financial statements by CEOs and CFOs that "the periodic report containing the financial statements fully complies with the requirements of section 13(a) or 15(d) of the Securities Exchange Act ... and that information contained in the periodic report fairly presents, in all material respects, the financial condition and results of operations of the issuer." Violators of the certification provisions "knowing that the periodic report accompanying the statement does not comport with all the requirements set forth in this section shall be fined not more than $1,000,000 or imprisoned not more than 10 years, or both." More serious sanctions of a $5,000,000 fine and/or 20 years in prison are available for a defendant who "willfully certifies any statement ... knowing that the periodic report accompanying the statement does not comport with all the requirements set forth in this section." 18 U.S.C. § 1350.

QUESTIONS

1. Does the defendant have to have the intent to violate the law to act "willfully"?

2. How do we know when an act is wrongful?

3. How do the criminal penalties under 18 U.S.C. § 1348 for fraud differ from penalties for criminal violations of the general antifraud provision in § 10(b) under Exchange Act§ 32(a)?

4. How do the criminal penalties under 18 U.S.C. § 1350 for violation of § 302 of the Sarbanes-Oxley Act differ from penalties for criminal violations of Rule 13a–14 under Exchange Act§ 32(a)?

INDEX

References are to Pages

ACCOUNTING AND AUDITING
Arthur Andersen collapse, 11
Big Four and Big Five firms, 737
Capital expenses, 393
Capital market roles, 10
Comfort letters from auditors, 509, 511
Conflicts of interest, 738
Criminal liabilities of auditors, 737
FASB
    See also Financial Accounting
        Standards Board, this
        index
    Regulatory authority, 25
Financial statement audits, 10, 736
Financial statements, audited and
    unaudited, 509, 511
Form 10–K filings, this index
Audits, 736
Form 8–K filings, auditor information,
    172
    Certification requirements, 771
Gatekeepers, accountants as
    Generally, 726, 736
    Dodd-Frank requirements, 738
    Whistleblower duties, 738
Generally accepted accounting principles,
    25
Generally Accepted Auditing Standards,
    505
Independent auditor standards, 736
International Financial Reporting
    Standards, 177
International vs US accounting
    standards, 25
Mark-to-market accounting, 159
PCAOB
    See also Public Company
        Accounting Oversight
        Board, this index
    Registration, 736
    Regulation, 37
Registration requirements, 44
Regulatory reforms, 11
Reputations of, 10, 726
Rule 10b–5 antifraud liability of auditors,
    289
Rules of practice before SEC, 739
Sarbanes-Oxley Act
Reforms, 737
Regulations, 37
SEC regulatory authority, 11, 41
Smoothing practices, 63
Standard accounting principles, 25
State regulation, 736
Valuation roles, 10
Whistleblower duties, 738

ACCURACY OF DISCLOSURES
    Generally, 161 et seq., 182

Books and records, 183
Foreign Corrupt Practices Act violations,
    184
Policy considerations, 198
Rule 10b–5, this index
Selective disclosure problems, 188 et seq.

ACQUISITIONS
Control Contests, this index
Mergers, this index

ADELPHIA SCANDAL
Sarbanes-Oxley Act, 37

ADVERTISING
Investment Advisers Act restrictions, 36

ADVISERS
Investment Advisers Act, this index

AGENCY COSTS
Brokers, agency costs of, 29
Disclosure regulations controlling, 25
Disclosure requirements as control
    measure, 161
Voting rights to control, 699

AIDERS AND ABETTORS
Dodd-Frank Act, 299
Gatekeeper duties, aider and abettor
    liability reinforcing, 727
Rule 10b–5, this index
Private Securities Litigation Reform Act,
    770
Public vs private enforcement, 770

ALTERNATIVE TRADING SYSTEMS
    (ATS)
    Generally, 15
Rule 10b–5 applicability, 327

AMERICAN DEPOSITORY
    RECEIPTS (ADR)
Generally, 317

ANALYSTS
Financial Industry Regulatory Authority
    restrictions on reports, 439
Gun-jumping rules, analysts restrictions,
    437
Information production, 24
Investment Advisers Act, this index
Investment banks, analyst research
    connections, 24

ANTI-FRAUD
See Fraud, this index

ARBITRAGE
Generally, 30

ASSET-BACKED SECURITIES
    See also Securitization, this index
Shelf registrations, 465

ATTORNEYS
Capital market roles, 10
Class actions
    Auctions, 221
    Fee awards, 224, 226
    Pay-to-play, 221
Disclosure regulations, Sarbanes-Oxley
    Act, 37
Fee awards
    Class actions, 224, 226
    Lodestar calculations, 225
Gatekeeper duties
    Generally, 726, 739, 746 et
        seq.
    Private rights of action against
        attorneys, 741
    Sarbanes-Oxley standards, 740
    Whistleblowing obligations, 740
Opinion letters, 739
Private actions against, 741
Private actions, attorneys' roles in
    bringing, 766
Rule 10b–5 antifraud liability, 289
Rules of practice before SEC, 739
Sarbanes-Oxley Act
    Disclosure regulations, 37
    Gatekeeper duties, 740
SEC supervisorial authority, 739
Whistleblowing obligations, 740

AUCTIONS
See Dutch Auctions, this index

AUDITS
See Accounting and Auditing, this index

BENEFICIAL OWNERS
Generally, 695

BESPEAKS CAUTION DOCTRINE
Forward-looking statements, 83, 245
Private Securities Litigation Reform Act,
    245

BIRNBAUM RULE
Rule 10b–5 antifraud, 208

BLUE SKY REGULATION
Generally, 96, 584
See also State Securities Regulations, this
    index

BOARDS OF DIRECTORS
See Directors, this index

BONDS
See also Securities, Instruments
    Regulated as, this index
Perpetual bonds, 8
Priorities of creditors, 4, 7
Trust Indenture Act, 36
Zero coupon bonds, 7

BOOKS AND RECORDS
Materiality of discrepancies, 183

BROKER-DEALERS
Agency costs of utilizing, 29
Analyst research, 24

Boiler room brokers, 29
Capital market, roles in, 8
Churning, 43
Commissions, deregulation, 24
Conflicts of interest, 30
Deregulation of commissions, 24
Disclosure filtering functions, 29
Exempt offerings, brokers' roles, 571
Fees, 30
Filtering of disclosures, 29
Financial Industry Regulatory Authority
    regulatory responsibility, 15, 43
Floor brokers, 12
Investment bank activities, 24
Market makers
    Generally, 13
    Initial public offer trading, 453
Private offerings, brokers' roles, 571
Proxy solicitations, brokers' roles, 678
Resales of exempt securities
Brokers for reselling control persons, 655
Rule 144A sales, 669
Rule 144 sales
    Generally, 658 et seq.
    See also Resales of Exempt
        Offerings, this index
Rule 144A sales
    Generally, 669
    See also Resales of Exempt
        Offerings, this index
Rule 10b–5 antifraud liability, 211
Securities Exchange Act regulation, 35
Specialists, 12, 642

CAPITAL ASSET PRICING MODEL
    (CAPM)
Generally, 20

CAPITAL MARKET
    Generally, 8
    See also Markets, this index
Accounting firms' roles, 10
Arbitrage, 30
Asymmetric information problems, 467
Attorneys' roles, 10
Broker-dealers' roles, 8
Bubbles, 32
Efficiency and fundamental efficiency, 32
Efficient Capital Markets Hypothesis, this
    index
Fraud-on-the-market theory, 32
Information, this index
Informational efficiency, 33
Institutional investors' roles, 11
Intermediaries, 9
Investment banks' roles, 9
Investment decisions, 15
Liquidity advantages, 9
Manipulation of Markets, this index
Materiality of information, stock price
    reaction as measurement, 64, 68
Primary market transactions, 9
Private Securities Litigation Reform Act,
    this index
Rights offerings to pre-existing
    shareholders, 9

Secondary Markets, this index
Spread, 10
Syndicates of underwriters, 9
Transparency advantages, 9
Underwriters' roles, 9

CAPITAL STRUCTURE
Generally, 401

CAPTURE
Regulatory, 28

CAUSATION
Loss causation
    Fraud-on-the-market rule, 270
    Materiality and, 544, 694
    Rule 10b–5 liability, 284, 316
    Section 11 liability, 477, 518
    Section 12(a)(2) liability, 543
Materiality, loss causation and, 544, 694
Proxy solicitations, fraud liability, 690, 694
Reliance-causation relationship, 294
Rule 10b–5
    Damages, loss causation, 284, 316
    Transaction causation, 265
Section 11 liability
    Loss causation, 477
    Loss causation defense, 518
Section 12(a)(2) liability
    Loss causation, 543
Transaction causation
    Reliance relationship, 298
    Rule 10b–5 antifraud, 265

CEASE AND DESIST PROCEEDINGS
Generally, 772, 791
Judicial review, 795

CERTIFICATES OF DEPOSIT
Security laws applicability, 106

CIVIL ACTIONS
See Private Civil Actions, this index

CLASS ACTIONS
Attorneys
    Auctions to select, 221
    Fee awards, 224, 226
    Pay-to-play, 221
Birnbaum rule, 208
Certifications
    Loss causation, 269
    Reliance, 289
Conflicts of interest of lead plaintiffs, 216, 220
Damages, Rule 10b–5 antifraud, 311
f-cubed litigation, 319
Institutional investors as lead plaintiffs, 216
Lead plaintiffs
    Generally, 215 et seq.
    Conflicts of interest, 216, 220
    Institutional investors as, 216
    Rebuttable presumptions, 217, 220
    Rule 10b–5 antifraud, 215
Loss causation certifications, 269
Pay-to-play counsel selection, 221

Private Securities Litigation Reform Act
    reforms, 204
Reliance
    Generally, 282
    Certifications, 289
Rule 10b–5
    Generally, 202
    Damages, 311
    Strike suits, 203
Strike suits, 203
Typicality requirement, 217

CLAWBACK POLICIES
Executive compensation, 187
Mutual fund management fees, 58

COLLATERALIZED DEBT OBLIGATION (CDO)
Financial crisis of 2008–2009, 38

COMMERCIAL BANKS
Investment banks distinguished, 10

COMMON ENTERPRISE
Security laws applicability, 107

COMMON LAW INSIDER TRADING
Generally, 331
Reliance, 335

COMMON STOCK
Generally, 3
Classes of stock, 4
Dividends, 3
Preferred stock compared, 4
Priorities, 4
Residual dividend interests, 5
Voting rights of holders, 4

COMPENSATION
Executive Compensation, this index
Stock Options, this index

COMPENSATION DISCUSSION AND ANALYSIS SECTION (CD & A)
Generally, 180

COMPUTER HACKERS
Deceptive practices, 385
Insider trading violations, 383

CONCLUSORY STATEMENTS
Rule 10b–5 antifraud, 232

CONDOMINIUMS
Security laws applicability, 121

CONFIDENTIAL INFORMATION
Agreement to maintain confidentiality
    Generally, 381
    Insider trading, 378
Determination as to confidentiality
    status, 378
Fiduciary's duty to protect, 367, 373

CONFLICTS OF INTEREST
    See also Related-Party
        Transactions, this index
Audit committees, 737
Auditors, 738

Brokers, 30
Class action lead plaintiffs, 216, 219
Credit rating agencies, 755
Disclosure regulations, 26

CONGRESSIONAL INTENT
Exempt intrastate offerings, 617
Federal securities regulation, 96
Insider trading, Section 16, 387
Private rights of action, 296, 536
Private Securities Litigation Reform Act,
    34, 216

CONTRIBUTION
Rule 10b–5 control person liability, 316
Securities Act Section 11 liability, 519
Underwriters' contractual contribution
    rights, 519

CONTROL
Separation between ownership and
    control, 699

CONTROL CONTESTS
Disclosure regulations, 37
Proxy contests
    Securities Exchange Act
        regulations, 37
    Tender offers compared, 679
Tender offers, 679
Williams Act, this index

CONTROL PERSONS
Ability to control vs actual control, 310
Culpable participant test, 306
Definition, 306
Directors as, 310, 728
Dodd-Frank Act, 311
Informational advantages enjoyed by, 654
Insiders as, 652
Intermediaries of, 656, 660
Issuers, control persons as, 653
Management, control persons within, 309
Officers as, 310
Parent and subsidiary company
    relationships, 309
Pleading requirements, 310
Potential control test, 306
Presumptive liability, 309
Private Securities Litigation Reform Act,
    proportionate liability, 316
Resales of exempt securities
        Generally, 652
        Brokers for control persons, 655
        Informational advantages enjoyed
            by control persons, 654
        Issuers, control persons as, 653
        Rule 144 safe harbor, 660
        Section 4(1) exemption, 655
        Underwriters as control persons,
            653
        Underwriters for control persons,
            653
Rule 10b–5 antifraud
        Generally, 306
        Proportionate liability, 316
Scienter, 310

SEC enforcement, 311
Securities Exchange Act Section 20(a)
        liability
            Generally, 301, 303
            Vicarious liability, 306
State control person tests, 307
Ultimate authority, 304, 305
Underwriters as control persons, 653
Underwriters for control persons, 653
Vicarious liability
        Culpable participant test, 306
        Good faith defense, 306
        Potential control test, 306

COOPERATIVE HOUSING
Security laws applicability, 115, 122

CORPORATE GOVERNANCE
Director nominations by shareholder,
    proxy access rights, 714
Dodd-Frank reforms, 714
Eligibility of shareholder issue proposals,
    701
Form 8–K filings, 175
Gatekeeper Regulation, this index
Golden parachute arrangements, advisory
    votes on, 182, 722
Independent director requirements, 44
Issue proposals by shareholders, 700
Political issues, shareholder proposals
    addressing, 705, 709
Procedural requirements for shareholder
    issue proposals, 701
Proxy access rights for shareholder
    nominations of directors, 714
Proxy Solicitations, this index
Relevance standards limiting shareholder
    issue proposals, 705, 709
Sarbanes-Oxley Act reforms, 674, 714
Say on pay rules, 182, 722
SEC proxy access rules, 714
SEC supervision of shareholder voting,
    714
Securities Exchange Act requirements,
    162
Self-regulatory organization
    requirements, 43
Shareholder democracy, 699
Shareholder nominations of directors,
    proxy access rights, 714
Stock price relationship, 32
Whistleblowers, this index

CORRECTIVE DISCLOSURES
Form 8–K filings, 189

COSTS
Agency Costs, this index
Mandatory disclosure, 28
Proxy Solicitations, this index
Public offering registration, 458

CREDIT DEFAULT SWAPS
        Generally, 59, 158
Risk hedging functions, 158

CREDIT RATING AGENCIES
Conflicts of interest, 755

Dodd-Frank reforms
    Generally, 747, 754
    Conflicts of interest, 755
Expert liability, 754
Financial crisis of 2008–2009, 43
Forward-looking statements, 755
Gatekeeper duties
    Generally, 726
    Dodd-Frank reforms, 747, 754
    Expert liability, 754
    Liabilities, 748
    SEC oversight authority, 747
Liabilities, 748
Mortgage-backed securities, ratings
    failures
    Generally, 746
    Private civil actions, 748
Nationally Recognized Statistical Ratings
    Organizations, 43, 746
Private civil actions, 748
Regulation, 755
SEC ratings of the agencies, 746
SEC supervisorial authority, 755
Systemic risk analyses, 44
Underwriter status, 748

CRIMINAL ENFORCEMENT
    Generally, 818
    See also Justice Department, this
        index
Auditors, 737
Fines, 819
Fifth Amendment Privilege, this index
Imprisonment, 819
Investigations, overlapping, by SEC and
    Justice, 781
Madoff scandal, 819
Sarbanes-Oxley Act, 825
Willful and knowing violations, 819

CUSTOMERS OF ISSUERS
Rule 10b–5 secondary liability, 291

DAMAGES
Class actions, 311
Disgorgement, this index
Face-to-face transactions, 313
Fraud in the inducement, 316
Insider trading, Section 16 violations, 390
Loss causation, 284, 316
Private Civil Actions, this index
Punitive damages, Rule 10b–5 antifraud,
    316
Rule 10b–5, this index
Section 11 liability, 514
Section 12(a)(1) liability, 529
Section 12(a)(2) liability, 543

DEBT
    See also Bonds, this index
Securities and debt arrangements
    distinguished, 147

DECEPTION
    See also Fraud-on-the-Market, this
        index
Computer hackers' devices, 383, 385

Definition, 385
Fraud and deceit compared, 385
Insider trading, deception aspects, 376
Intent to deceive, 246
Misstatements or omissions and, 299
Rule 10b–5 antifraud
    Generally, 227
    Motive to deceive, 235
Scienter, this index

DEFINITIONS
Arbitrage, 30
Beneficial owner, 695
Big boy letter, 342
Boiler room broker, 29
Bond, 7
Bubble, 32
Bulge bracket, 398
Capital expenses, 393
CAPM, 20
CDO, 39
CDS, 59
Churning, 43
Common stock, 3
Control person, 306
Core insiders, 336
Deceptive practice, 385
Dilution, 395
ECMH, 30
Efficiency, 32
FASB, 25
FINRA, 15
Floor broker, 12
Forward-looking, 49
Fundamental efficiency, 32
GAAP, 25
GAAS, 505
Gatekeeper, 726
Going dark, 164
Green Shoe option, 399, 452
Gun-jumping, 35
House money, 32
IFRS, 177
Informational efficiency, 33
Initial public offerings, 5
Inside information, 329
Interest, 16
Investment bank, 9
IPO, 5
ISS, 697
Key employee, 552
Legend, 664
Lemons problem, 23
Market maker, 13
Materiality, this index
MD & A, 178
Noise trade, 32
Non-reporting issuer, 409
NRSRO, 43
Offer, 411
Overhang price drop, 464
Owners of record, 167
PCAOB, 736
PDV, 16
Perpetual bond, 8
PIPE, 378

PORTAL, 674
Positive externality, 26
Present value, 16
Priority, 8
Private offering, 554
Privity, 214
Prospectus, 531, 532, 534
Proxy solicitation, 680
PSLRA, 204
Public Companies, this index
Public offering, 536, 550
Put option, 384
QIB, 669
RMBS, 59
Roadshow, 426
Scienter, 247, 804
Seasoned issuers, 409
SEC, 2
Securities, Instruments Regulated as, this
    index
Shelf registration, 449
Smoothing of earnings, 63
Soft information, 55
Solicitation, 680
Sophisticated investor, 556
Specialist, 642
Spread, 10
SRO, 15
Stabilization, 457
Statutory insider, 387
Strike suits, 203
Systemic risk, 39
Temporary insider, 188
Tombstone advertisement, 426
Underwriter, 9, 649
Unseasoned issuers, 409
Unsystematic risk, 19
Warehousing of stock, 369
Well-known seasoned issuer, 410
Whistleblower, 762
WKSI, 410
Zero coupon bond, 7

DEREGULATION
Brokers' commissions, 24

DILUTION
Shelf registrations, 465

DIRECTORS
    See also Management, this index
Audit committees
    Conflicts of interest, 737
    Independent directors on, 737
    Sarbanes-Oxley Act requirements,
        738, 737
Business judgment rule protection, 3
Classified boards, 698
Conflicts of interest, 737
Control person liabilities, 728
Control person status, 309
Dividends policies, 3
Dodd-Frank Act requirements, 728
Fiduciary duties, 3, 6
Form 8–K reports of resignations and
    terminations, 173

Gatekeeper duties of outside directors,
    727 et seq.
Independent directors
    Generally, 44
    Audit committees, 737
    Outside directors distinguished, 728
Insider Trading, this index
Management alliances, 728
Officer relationships to, 728
Outside directors
    Dodd-Frank Act requirements, 728
    Gatekeeper duties, 727 et seq.
    Gatekeeper liabilities, 728
    Independent directors
        distinguished, 728
    SEC enforcement actions against,
        728
Replacements of directors, public
    enforcement judicial remedies, 803
Rule 10b–5 control person liability
    Generally, 306
    Proportionate liability, 316
Sarbanes-Oxley Act, audit committee
    standards, 728, 737
SEC bar orders, 813
SEC enforcement actions against outside
    directors, 728
Shareholder elections, 678
Shareholder nominations of directors,
    proxy access rights, 714
Staggered boards, 698

DISCLOSURE REGULATIONS
    Generally, 24 et seq., 161 et
        seq.
    See also Information, this index
Accounting principle standards, 25
Accuracy of Disclosures, this index
Agency cost control through, 25, 161
Argument for, 24
Attorneys, Sarbanes-Oxley Act, 37
Comparisons of financial statements, 25
Compensation Discussion and Analysis,
    180
Competitor benefits, 26
Conflicts of interest, 26
Control disputes, 37
Coordination problems inhibiting
    disclosures, 25
Correction duties, Rule 10b–5 antifraud,
    235
Costs of mandatory disclosure, 28
EDGAR website dissemination, 173
Efficient capital markets hypothesis as
    factor, 32
Executive compensation, 26, 162, 179
Exempt offerings
    Public offerings distinguished, 573
    Regulation D, 573
    Rule 144A resales of, 671
Federal statute policies, 2
Fifth Amendment privilege conflicts, 92
Filings, proxy solicitations, 682
Filtering disclosures, 29
Financial Accounting Standards Board
    regulatory authority, 25

Financial statement comparisons, 25
Foreign Corrupt Practices Act violations,
    184
Form S–1 filings, 64
Form S–K public offerings, 549
Fraud-on-the-market theory, 32
Gatekeeper regulation compared, 725
Generally accepted accounting principles,
    25
Gun-Jumping Rules, this index
How disclosure matters,28
Incorporation by reference of past filings,
    404, 501
Insider trading, Section 16 reports
        Generally, 387
        See also Insider Trading, this index
Integrated Disclosure, this index
Intermediaries, use in filtering
    disclosures, 29
International vs US accounting
    standards, 25
Investment Company Act, 36
Materiality, this index
Mergers and acquisitions, 37
Past filings, incorporation of by reference,
    404, 501
Plain English disclosures, public offerings,
    405
Policy considerations, 162, 725
Positive externalities, 26
Principal disclosure documents, 169
Proprietary information, 26
Prospectuses, 35, 403
Proxy solicitations
        Generally, 682
        See also Proxy Solicitations,
            this index
        Costs, 678
        Filings, 682
Public company status triggering, 162
Public offering rules, 35, 403
Public vs exempt offerings, 573
Rationale, 24
Real-time disclosure, 170, 239
Regulation G, 179
Related-party transactions
        Generally, 26
        Materiality, 85, 91
Relevance of disclosures, 28
Rule 144A resales of exempt securities,
    671
Sarbanes-Oxley Act, 37
Securities law violations, 92
Selective Disclosure, this index
Small vs sophisticated investor benefits,
    29
Standard accounting principles, 25
Update duties, 235
What disclosure matters, 47
Williams Act, 37

DISCOUNT
Present discount value, 16, 44

DISCOVERY
Federal rules, 208

Private Securities Litigation Reform Act
    restrictions, 204, 251, 252

DISGORGEMENT
Dodd-Frank Act, 810
Fair Fund distributions, 816
Rule 10b–5, 313
Sarbanes-Oxley Act, 810
Victims of wrongdoing, distributions to,
    814

DIVERSIFICATION
Risk reduction, 19

DIVIDENDS
Common stock, 3
Cumulative, 6
Directors' control over, 3
Penalties for nonpayment, 6
Preferred stock, 6
Residual dividend interests, 5
Tax consequences, 4

DODD-FRANK ACT
Accounting and auditing, 738
Aider and abettor liability, 299
Civil penalties in SEC enforcement, 792
Conflicts of interest, credit rating
    agencies, 755
Control person liability, SEC enforcement,
    310
Corporate governance, 714
Credit rating agency reforms
        Generally, 747, 754
        Conflicts of interest, 755
Credit risk regulations, 40
Directors, board composition
    requirements, 728
Disgorgement, 806, 810
Executive compensation
        Clawbacks, 187
        Disclosures, 179
Exempt offerings
        Disqualifications, 580
        Regulation D, 560, 563
Financial crisis of 2008–2009, 39
Financial Stability Oversight Council
    creation, 40
Golden parachute arrangements, advisory
    votes on, 182, 722
Hedge fund regulations, 40
Judicial remedies, 806, 810
Mortgage regulations, 40
Proxy access rules, 714
Public enforcement civil penalties, 792
Rule 10b–5 antifraud, extraterritorial
    application, 327
Say on pay rules, 182, 722
Scope of Act, 39
SEC enforcement
        Control person liability, 311
        Proxy access rules, 715
        Reforms, 40
Shareholder nominations of directors,
    proxy access rights, 714
Shareholder voting requirements, 40
Systemic risk discouragement, 159

Voting requirements, 40
Whistleblower programs, 40
Whistleblower protections, 761

DUE DILIGENCE DEFENSE
Comfort letters from auditors, 509, 511
Rule 176, 501
Rule 10b–5 antifraud, 248
Securities Act Section 11 liability
        Generally, 490 et seq.
           Rule 176, 501
           Shelf registrations, 501
           Underwriters, 501
Underwriters, 501

DUTCH AUCTIONS
        Generally, 396, 397
Advantages, 401

ECONOMIC CONSIDERATIONS
Fraud and Rule 10b–5 liability, 197
Insider trading, 329
Public offerings
        Generally, 393
        Exempt offerings compared, 548

EDGAR WEBSITE
Information dissemination, 173
Insider trading, Section 16 reports, 387
Proxy solicitations, 682

**EFFICIENT CAPITAL MARKETS
     HYPOTHESIS (ECMH)**
        Generally, 30
Disclosure effects presumptions, 32
Efficiency and fundamental efficiency, 32
Efficient markets, materiality in, 67
Fundamental efficiency, 32
Informational efficiency, 33
Materiality determinations, stock price
     reaction as measurement, 64, 68
Materiality in efficient markets, 67
Stock price reaction as measurement of
     materiality, 64, 68

ELECTRONIC COMMUNICATIONS
EDGAR website, this index
Internet, this index
Secondary market transactions, 12

EMPLOYEES
Compensation, this index
Executive Compensation, this index
Key employees, 552
Stock sales to as public offerings, 550
Whistleblowers, this index

ENFORCEMENT
Criminal Enforcement, this index
Private Civil Actions, this index
Public Enforcement, this index

ENRON SCANDAL
Arthur Andersen collapse, 11
Big Four and Big Five accounting firms,
     737
Off-balance sheet arrangements, 172
Sarbanes-Oxley Act, 37

EXCHANGE ACT
See Securities Exchange Act, this index

EXECUTIVE COMPENSATION
Clawback policies, 187
Compensation Discussion and Analysis,
     180
Disclosure regulations, 26, 162, 179
Dodd-Frank Act disclosures, 180
Form 10–K filings, 729
Golden parachutes, Dodd-Frank Act
     requirement of advisory votes on,
     182, 722
Pay versus performance rules, 179
Retirement benefits, Form 10–K filings,
     729
Sarbanes-Oxley Act disclosures, 179
Say on pay rules, 182, 722
Voting on, 182, 722

EXEMPT OFFERINGS
        Generally, 549 et seq.
Aggregate offering price, Regulation D
     distinctions, 561
Brokers' roles, 571
Categories of Regulation S offerings, 631
Congressional intent, intrastate offerings,
     617
Directed selling efforts, Regulation S, 630
Disclosure regulations
     Exempt vs public offerings, 573
     Regulation D, 573
Disqualifications
     Regulation D, 580
Dodd-Frank Act
     Disqualifications, 580
     Regulation D, 563
Eligibility, Regulation D, 560
Employees, sales to as public offerings,
     550
Exchange Act filings, Regulation D, 586
Form D filings, 586
General solicitations, Regulation D, 566
Global Regulation S offerings, 640
Integration, Regulation D, 576
Integration of offshore and domestic
     orders
     Global Regulation S offerings, 640
     Regulation S, 637
Intrastate offerings
        Generally, 611 et seq.
     Congressional intent, 616
     Policy considerations, 588
     Resale limitations, 625
     Rule 147, 621
Section 3(a)(11), 613
Legend restrictions on resales, 664
No action letters, Regulation D, 569
No directed selling efforts rule,
     Regulation S, 630
Offshore sales
        Generally, 627 et seq.
     Regulation S, below
Policy considerations, 588
Private offerings
        Generally, 550 et seq.

Section 4(2), below
Term defined, 554
Private placement process, Regulation D, 587
Public offerings compared, 549
Public offerings distinguished, 550
Purchaser standards, Regulation D, 562
Registration rights of Rule 144A qualified institutional buyers, 675
Regulation A
    Generally, 588
    Aggregate offering price, 592
    Antifraud liability, 603
    "Bad actor" disqualification, 590
    Continuous offerings, 601
    Disclosure, 594
    Eligible issuers and securities, 589
    Gun jumping, 598
    Insignificant deviations, 602
    Integration, 603
    Investors, 593
    Policy considerations, 588
    Small business issuers, 588
    State securities law requirements, 605
Regulation D
    Generally, 559
    Accredited investors, 562
    Aggregate offering price distinctions, 560
    Disclosure regulations, 573
    Disqualifications, 580
    Dodd-Frank Act, 563
    Eligibility, 560
    Exchange Act filings, 586
    Form D filings, 586
    Form 10–K reports, 574
    General solicitations, 566
    Integration, 576
    No action letters, 569
    Private placement process, 587
    Private rights of actions for violations, 579
    Purchaser standards, 562
    Resale restrictions, 575
    Safe harbor, 560
    Section 4(2) distinguished, 559
    Sophisticate purchasers, 561
    State securities laws applicability, 584
    Three kinds of exemptions, 560
    Venture capital activities, 559
Regulation S
    Generally, 627 et seq.
    Categories of offerings, 631
    Directed selling efforts, 630
    Global Regulation S offerings, 640
    Integration of offshore and domestic orders
        Generally, 637
        Global Regulation S offerings, 640
    No directed selling efforts rule, 630
    Offshore transactions, 629
    Policy considerations, 588
    Resales, 638

Resale limitations
    See also Resales of Exempt Offerings, this index
    Intrastate offerings, 625
    Regulation D, 575
    Regulation S, 638
    Rule 504 offerings, 585
Restrictions on purchases amounting to private vs public offering, 552
Rule 147, intrastate offerings, 621
Rule 504 offerings, 585
Rule 144 sales
    Generally, 658 et seq.
    See also Resales of Exempt Offerings, this index
Rule 144A sales
    Generally, 669
    See also Resales of Exempt Offerings, this index
Sarbanes-Oxley Act impact on Rule 144A resales of exempt securities, 674
Scope of public offerings and exemptions, 550
Section 4(2)
    Generally, 550 et seq.
    Private offering, term defined, 554
    Regulation D distinguished, 559
    Sophisticated investors, 556, 557
    Special participant purchasers, 552
Section 3(a)(11) offerings, 613
Securities Act exemptions, 36
Small business issuers, Regulation A, 588
Sophisticate purchasers
    Regulation D, 561
Sophisticated investors
    Section 4(2), 556, 557
Special participant purchasers, Section 4(2), 552
State securities laws applicability, Regulation D, 584
Uniform Securities Act of 1985, 584
Venture capital activities, Regulation D, 559

EXPENSES
See Costs, this index

EXPERT WITNESSES
Rule 10b–5 loss issues, 287
Stock pricing, event studies, 68

EXTERNALITIES
Positive externalities, 26

FACE-TO-FACE TRANSACTIONS
Rule 10b–5 damages, 313
Stock exchange intermediation distinguished, 8

FACT AND LAW QUESTIONS
Materiality of information, 55

FIDUCIARY DUTIES
Confidential information, fiduciary's duty to protect, 367, 373
Directors, 3, 6
Insider trading
    Misappropriation theory, 364

Special facts doctrine, 334
Reliance, breach claims, 282
Rule 10b–5 duties distinguished, 214

FIFTH AMENDMENT PRIVILEGE
Disclosure mandates, 92
Form S–K filings, 92, 782
SEC investigations, 781

**FINANCIAL ACCOUNTING
    STANDARDS BOARD (FASB)**
Regulatory authority, 25

FINANCIAL CRISIS OF 2008–2009
Generally, 38
Causes, 39
Collateralized debt obligation, 39
Credit rating agencies' failures, 746
Dodd-Frank Act, 39
Investment banks impacted, 9
Mortgage-backed securities, 38
Ratings organizations, 43
Securitization practices, 38
Special purpose vehicles, 39
Systemic risk, 39
Toxic securities, 39

**FINANCIAL INDUSTRY
    REGULATORY AUTHORITY
    (FINRA)**
BrokerCheck system, 43
Broker-dealer regulations, 15, 43
Enforcement authority
        Generally, 765
        See also Public Enforcement, this
            index
Public offering regulations, 400
Underwriter regulations, 399, 452

**FINANCIAL STABILITY OVERSIGHT
    COUNCIL**
Generally, 160
Creation, 40

FINANCIAL STATEMENTS
Accounting and Auditing, this index
Audited and unaudited, 509, 511
Audits, 10, 736
Comparisons, 25
Form 10–Q filings, 178

FIXED RETURNS ARRANGEMENTS
Security laws applicability, 122

**FOREIGN CORRUPT PRACTICES
    ACT**
Generally, 186
Disclosures of violations, 184, 788

FOREIGN ISSUERS
American Depository Receipts, 317
Dual-listed, 326
f-cubed litigation, 319
Form 10–K filings, 178
Global Regulation S offerings, 640
Public company status, 164
Regulation S exemptions
        Generally, 627 et seq.

See also Exempt Offerings, this
    index
Transnational securities fraud, 317 et seq.

FORGED SECURITIES
Security laws applicability, 95

FORM 8–K FILINGS
Generally, 34, 170
Auditor information, 172
Contents, 170
Corporate governance matters, 175
Corrective disclosures, 189
Director resignations and terminations,
    173
Exempt offerings filing requirements,
    Regulation D, 586
Fifth Amendment privilege issues, 782
Materiality standards, 71, 172
Off-balance sheet arrangements, 172
Principal disclosure documents, 170
Public enforcement of filing requirements,
    766
Real-time disclosures, 170, 239
Sarbanes Oxley Act, 170

FORM 10–K FILINGS
Generally, 34, 177
Audit requirements, 736
Beneficial owner identifications, 695
Certification requirements, 771
Certifications of officers, 179
Contents, 178
Executive compensation, 729
Exempt offerings, 574
Foreign issuers, 177
Form 10–Q distinguished, 178
Integrated disclosure, 177
Management Discussion and Analysis
    (MD & A), 178

Materiality of information, 47, 65
Principal disclosure documents, 69
Public enforcement of filing requirements,
    766
Regulation S–K, 177
Sarbanes-Oxley Act certifications, 37
Underwriter reliance, 508

FORM 10–Q FILINGS
Generally, 34, 177
Certifications of officers, 179
Contents, 178
Corrective statements, 236
Earnings statements, 188
Financial statements, 178
Form 10–K distinguished, 178
Materiality of information, 47, 79
Principal disclosure documents, 169
Public enforcement of filing requirements,
    766
Regulation S–K, 177
Sarbanes-Oxley Act certifications, 38
Updating of information, 237

FORM S–1 FILINGS
Materiality of information, 64

FORM S–K FILINGS
Fifth Amendment privilege conflicts, 92
Related-party transactions, 91

**FORWARD-LOOKING
     INFORMATION**
Bespeaks caution doctrine, 83, 240
Credit rating agencies, 755
Gun-jumping rules, 418
Knowing falsehoods, 245
Materiality, 48, 238
Merger plans, 51
Quiet period releases, 55
Rule 10b–5 antifraud, 239, 245
Soft nature of, 55

FRANCHISE PURCHASES
Security laws applicability, 130, 137

FRAUD
          See also Deception, this index
Antifraud rules, policy considerations, 725
Catch-all antifraud Rule, 95
Causation, this index
Common law and Rule 10b–5 fraud
          actions compared, 227
Damages, this index
Deceit compared, 385
f-cubed litigation, 319
Inducement, fraud in, damages, 316
Information provision, 22
Insider trading, common law fraud
               Generally, 331
               Reliance, 335
Manipulation of Markets, this index
Markets, fraud-on-the-market theory, 32
Materiality, this index
National Securities Market Improvement
          Act, public enforcement, 765
Policy considerations, antifraud rules, 725
Private rights of action, proxy solicitation
          fraud, 689
Prospectuses
               Generally, 432
               Rescission claim based on, 531
Proxy solicitations, 678
Public enforcement
               See also Public Enforcement,
                    this index
               National Securities Market
                    Improvement Act, public
                    enforcement, 765
Punitive damages, 316
Registration statements, strict liability,
          752
Reliance, insider trading common law
          fraud, 335
Rule 14a–9
               Generally, 687
               See also Proxy Solicitations, this
                    index
Rule 10b–5
               See also Rule 10b–5, this
                    index
               Common law fraud actions
                    compared, 227
Scienter, this index

Securities Act
               Generally, 35
               Section 11 liability, 477
               Section 17(a), public vs private
                    enforcement, 768
Standing to sue. See Private Civil Actions,
          this index
Strict liability, registration statements,
          752
Transnational securities fraud, 317 et seq.

FRAUD-ON-THE-MARKET
Loss causation, 270
Materiality of information, 67
Presumptive reliance, 294
Truth on the market defense, 76, 83

GATEKEEPER REGULATION
               Generally, 725 et seq.
Accountants
               Generally, 726, 736
               Dodd-Frank requirements, 738
               Whistleblower duties, 738
Aider and abettor liabilities of
               gatekeepers, 727
Attorneys
               Generally, 726, 739, 746 et
                    seq.
               Private rights of action against
                    attorneys, 741
               Sarbanes-Oxley standards, 740
               SEC supervisorial authority, 739
               Whistleblowing obligations, 740
Credit rating agencies
               Generally, 726, 746
               Dodd-Frank reforms, 747, 754
               Expert liability, 754
               Liabilities, 748
               SEC oversight authority, 747
Definition of gatekeeper, 726
Disclosure regulation compared, 725
Dodd-Frank Act
               Credit rating agencies, 754
               Whistleblowers, 40, 761
Employee whistleblowers, 756
Enhancements of gatekeepers' roles, 727
Expert liability, credit rating agencies,
          754
Incentives, whistleblowers', 762
Incentives enhancing gatekeepers' roles,
          727
Liabilities
               Aiding and abetting, 727
               Credit rating agencies, 748, 754
               Outside directors, 728
               Rule 10b–5 fraud liability compared,
                    725
Outside directors
               Generally, 727 et seq.
               Liabilities, 728
Policy considerations, 725, 727
Private rights of action against attorneys,
          741
Private rights of action compared, 725
Protected communications of
               whistleblowers, 758, 759

Rule 10b–5 fraud liability compared, 725
Sarbanes-Oxley Act
        Attorneys, 740
        Whistleblower protections, 756
SEC enforcement compared, 725
SEC oversight authority
        Attorneys, 739
        Credit rating agencies, 747
Underwriters as gatekeepers, 726
Whistleblowers
                Generally, 756
        See also Whistleblowers, this index

**GENERALLY ACCEPTED
        ACCOUNTING PRINCIPLES
        (GAAP)**
US standards, 25

**GENERALLY ACCEPTED AUDITING
        STANDARDS (GAAS)**
Generally, 505

GLOBAL CROSSING SCANDAL
Sarbanes-Oxley Act, 37

GOLDEN PARACHUTES
Dodd-Frank Act requirement of advisory
        votes on, 182, 723

GOVERNANCE
See Corporate Governance, this index

GUN-JUMPING RULES
2005 reforms
                Generally, 406
        Forward-looking information, 418
        Safe harbors, 418, 426
Allocations by underwriters, 441
Analysts restrictions, 437
Company registration proposals, 409
Conditioning the market, 416
Deliveries of prospectuses, 444
Financial Industry Regulatory Authority
        restrictions on analysts' reports, 441
Firm commitment offerings, 441
Forward-looking information, 418
Free writing prospectuses, 425, 428
Gauging market sentiment, 424
        Generally, 405 et seq.
Goals, 405
Going effective process, 435
In-registration status, 415
Internet, impact on public issue disclosure
        rules, 417
Internet communication of free writing
        prospectuses, 428
Offer, term defined, 411
Overview, 406
Post-effective period, 441
Pre-filing period, 411
Process of going effective, 435
Prospectuses, this index
Putting together the offering, 420
Registration statement filings, 406
Registration statements, updating, 449
Roadshow activities, 426
Safe harbors, 418, 426
Secondary market impacts, 437

Soft information, 418
Solicitations of interest, 427
Tombstone advertising, 398, 426
Traditional free writing, 443
Underwriters' allocations, 441
Updating the prospectuses and
        registration statements, 449
Waiting period, 423 et seq.

HEDGE FUNDS
Dodd-Frank Act regulations, 40
Shareholder voting activities, 697

HOWEY TEST
Security laws applicability, 98, 156

IMPLIED CIVIL LIABILITY
See Private Civil Actions, this index

INCORPORATION BY REFERENCE
        Generally, 404, 501
Integrated disclosure, 404, 450

INDEMNIFICATION
Securities Act Section 11 liability, 519
Underwriter agreements, 399

INDUCEMENT, FRAUD IN
Damages, 316

INFLATION
Valuation affects, 16

INFORMATION
                Generally, 20 et seq.
        See also Accuracy of Disclosures,
                this index; Disclosure
                Regulations, this index
Agency costs control through disclosure,
        161
Analyst research, 24
Asymmetric information problems, public
        offerings, 467
Bounties paid by SEC for insider trading
        information, 381
Competitor benefits from disclosures, 26
Computer hacking, insider trading on
        information developed from, 383
Confidential Information, this index
Control persons, informational
        advantages enjoyed by, 654
Coordination problems inhibiting
        disclosures, 25
Correction duties, Rule 10b–5 antifraud,
        235
Duplicative information, 27
EDGAR website dissemination, 173
Efficient Capital Markets Hypothesis, this
        index
Exploitation of informational advantages,
        23
Fact vs opinion statements, Rule 10b–5
        antifraud, 232
Filtering disclosures, 29
Forward-Looking Information, 55
Fraud liability, 22
Generally accepted accounting principles,
        25

How disclosure matters, 28
Importance of, 1
Incentives to provide, 21
Inside information
    Generally, 329
    See also Confidential
      Information, this index;
      Insider Trading, this
      index
    Advantages of insiders, 1
    Computer hacking, information
      developed from, 383
    Definition, 329
    Outside information compared, 21
    Stolen information, 383
Insider trading activities, SEC bounties
    for information re, 381
Intermediaries, use in filtering
    disclosures, 29
International vs US accounting
    standards, 25
Irrationality factors affecting
    investments, 32
Lemons problem, 23
Management integrity information,
    materiality, 84
Materiality levels
    Generally, 23
    See also Materiality, this index
Noise trades, 32
Omnicare and Section 11, 479
Opinions as, Rule 10b–5 antifraud, 232
Outside and inside information compared,
    21
Positive externalities, 26
Proprietary information, disclosure
    regulations, 26
Public offerings, asymmetric information
    problems, 467
Relevance of disclosures, 28
Resales of exempt securities, Rule 144
    information requirements, 662
Rule 144 information requirements,
    resales of exempt securities, 661
Rule 10b–5 antifraud, fact vs opinion
    statements, 232
Secondary markets, information
    advantages, 21
Secret information, materiality, 52
Selective disclosure problems, 188 et seq.
Small vs sophisticated investor benefits
    from disclosures, 29
Soft information, 55
Stolen information, insider trading, 383
Update duties, Rule 10b–5 antifraud, 235
Value of, 26

INITIAL PUBLIC OFFERINGS (IPO)
    Generally, 5
    See also Public Offerings, this index
Allocations, IPO, 452
Allocations by underwriters, 441
Conditioning the market, 416
Exempt Offerings, this index
Gun-jumping rules, impacts vs
    established issuers, 437

Hot offerings agreements, 453
Materiality of information re, 64
Regulation M, manipulation of markets
    Generally, 454
    Stabilization activities, 457
Stabilization activities, 457
Underpricing phenomenon, 400

INJUNCTIONS
Private rights of action, 210
Public enforcement, 803

INSIDER TRADING
    Generally, 329
    See also Regulation FD, this index
Agreement to maintain confidentiality of
    information, misappropriation
    theory, 378
Big boy letter defenses, Rule 10b–5
    claims, 342
Black-out periods, Section 16 prohibitions,
    388
Bounties paid by SEC for insider trading
    information, 381
Civil penalties, 381
Classical theory
    Generally, 336 et seq.
    Misappropriation theory compared,
      341, 362, 371
Common law fraud
    Generally, 331
    Reliance, 335
Computer hacking, information developed
    from, 383
Confidential nature of inside information,
    378
Control persons as insiders, 652
Core insiders, SEC enforcement, 336
Damages, Section 16 violations, 390
Deceptive acts, misappropriation theory,
    376
Disclosure defenses, Rule 10b–5 claims,
    342
Doctrinal matrix, Rule 10b–5 claims, 382
Duty of silence, Rule 10b–5 claims, 341
Duty to speak, Rule 10b–5 claims, 340
Economics, 329
Equal access theory, Rule 10b–5 claims,
    336
Exploitation by insiders of informational
    advantages, 23
External vs internal tips,
    misappropriation theory, 362
Family members as tippees, 370
Fiduciary duties
    Misappropriation theory, 364
    Special facts doctrine, 334
Information access advantages, 1
Information as inside, 329
Insider Trading and Securities Fraud
    Enforcement Act of 1988
      Generally, 381
      Civil penalties, 807
Joint and several liability, tippers and
    tippees, 350
Judicial remedies, 807

Large block shareholders, Section 16, 388

Merger plan information, Rule 10b–5 claims, 337

Misappropriation theory

> Generally, 362 et seq.

> Agreement to maintain confidentiality of information, 378

> Classical theory compared, 341, 362, 371

> Computer hacking, information developed from, 383

> Confidential nature of inside information, 378

> Deceptive acts, 376

> External vs internal tips, 362

> Family members as tippees, 370

> Fiduciary duty violations, 364

> Private civil actions by contemporaneous traders, 381

> Scienter, 373

> Stolen information, 383

> Third-party tippees, 370

> Tippee liability, 370

> Validity questions, 364

Outside and inside information compared, 21

Outsiders with insider status, 329

Policy considerations, 329

Private causes of action, 34

Private civil actions by contemporaneous traders, 381

Public enforcement judicial remedies, 807

Reliance

> Generally, 282

> Common law fraud, 335

Rule 10b–5 claims

> Generally, 336 et seq.

> Big boy letter defenses, 342

> Core insiders, 336

> Disclosure defenses, 342

> Doctrinal matrix, 382

> Duty of silence, 341

> Duty to speak questions, 340

> Equal access theory, 336

> Family members tippees, 370

> Merger plan information, 337

> Share repurchase programs, 342

> Temporary insiders, 350

> Tipper/tippee liability, 344

Rule 14e–3 claims

Tender offer information, 342, 364, 369, 382

Scienter, misappropriation theory, 373

SEC responses

> Generally, 336

> Bounties for whistleblowers, 381

> Enforcement against core insiders, 336

Secondary markets, information advantages, 21

Section 16

> Generally, 387

> Black-out periods, 388

> Congressional intent, 387

> Damages for violations, 390

> Large block shareholders, 388

> Reports by statutory insiders, 387

> Short sales by insiders, 387

> Short swing profits disgorgement, 387

> Stock option exercises, 388

Share repurchase programs, Rule 10b–5 claims, 342

Short sales by insiders, Section 16, 387

Short swing profits disgorgement, Section 16, 387

Special facts doctrine, 334

Statutory insiders, Section 16 violations, 387

Stock option exercises, Section 16 reports, 388

Stolen information, misappropriation theory, 383

Temporary insiders

> Generally, 188

> Rule 10b–5 claims, 350

Tender offer related information, 342, 364, 382

Third-party tippees, misappropriation theory, 370

Tippee liability, misappropriation theory, 370

Tipper/tippee liability, Rule 10b–5 claims, 344

Traditional insiders, 329

INSIDER TRADING AND SECURITIES FRAUD ENFORCEMENT ACT OF 1988

> Generally, 381

Civil penalties, 807

INSTITUTIONAL INVESTORS

> See also Qualified Institutional Buyers, this index

Capital market roles, 11

Class actions, institutional investors as lead plaintiffs, 216

Proxy contest roles, 687

Rule 144A resales of exempt securities

> Generally, 670

> Registration rights of qualified institutional buyers, 675

Super-secondary market for qualified institutional buyers, 674

Underwriter relationships, 452

INSTITUTIONAL SHAREHOLDER SERVICES (ISS)

Proxy voting services, 697

INTEGRATED DISCLOSURE

> Generally, 35, 506, 512

Form 10–K, 177

Incorporation by references of prior disclosures, 404, 450

Regulation S–K, 48, 170

Regulation S–X, 169

SEC adoption, 406

Shelf registration, 509

INTEGRATION OF EXEMPT OFFERINGS
Offshore and domestic orders
Global Regulation S offerings, 640
Regulation S, 637
Regulation D, 576

INTENT
Congressional Intent, this index
Deceptive intent
Generally, 246
Rule 10b–5, 247
Investment intent test, resales of exempt securities, 658
Manipulation of markets, 200, 246

INTEREST
Generally, 16

INTERMEDIARIES
Broker-dealers as, 670
Capital market, 9
Control persons, intermediaries of, 656, 660
Disclosures. intermediaries, use in filtering, 29
Face-to-face and stock exchange intermediated trades distinguished, 8
Filtering of information through, 29
Gatekeeper obligations, 726
Investment Banks, this index
Securities Exchange Act regulation
Generally, 2
Professional intermediaries, 35
Underwriter status of, 653, 656

INTERNAL CONTROLS
Sarbanes-Oxley Act, 187

INTERNATIONAL FINANCIAL REPORTING STANDARDS (IFRS)
Generally, 177

INTERNET
Computer Hackers, this index
Free writing prospectuses, 428
Proxy solicitations, internet use, 686
Public issue disclosure rules impacted, 417
Public offerings, internet-based, 396
Virtual shares in cyberspace enterprises, securities regulations applicability, 108

INVESTMENT
Accredited investors, 562
Arbitrage, 30
Bubbles, 32
Capital Market, this index
Decisions, 15
Definition of security, investment test, 103
Disclosures, small vs sophisticated investor benefits, 29
House money effect, 32
Information, this index

Institutional Investors, this index
Investment intent presumptions
Generally, 648
See also Securities, Instruments Regulated as, this index
Irrationality factors affecting investments, 32
Materiality determinations, reasonable investor standard, 48
Noise trades, 32
Resales of exempt securities
Investment intent test, 658
Rule 144A investor restrictions, 669
Rule 144A investor restrictions on resales of exempt securities, 669
Securities, Instruments Regulated as, this index
Small vs sophisticated investor benefits from disclosures, 29
Sophisticated Investors, this index

INVESTMENT ADVISERS
Rule 10b–5 antifraud, 300

INVESTMENT ADVISERS ACT
Generally, 36
Advertising restrictions, 36
Analysts regulation, 36
Mutual fund regulations, 36

INVESTMENT BANKS
See also Underwriters, this index
Analyst research connections, 24
Brokers acting as, 24
Capital market roles, 9
Commercial banks distinguished, 10
Financial crisis of 2008–2009 impacts, 10
Public offerings roles, 396

INVESTMENT COMPANY ACT
Generally, 36
Disclosure regulations, 36
Mutual fund regulations, 36
Organization requirements, 36
SEC registrations, 36

INVESTMENT CONTRACTS
Security laws applicability, 96

ISSUERS
Control persons as, 653
Customers of issuers, secondary liability, 291
Dual-listed foreign issuers, 326
Exempt Offerings, this index
Foreign Issuers, this index
Non-reporting issuers, 409
Public Offerings, this index
Representations and warranties, 400
Seasoned issuers, 409
Shelf Registrations, this index
Small business issuers, Regulation A exempt offerings, 587
Suppliers to issuers, secondary liability, 291
Unseasoned issuers, 409
Warranties to underwriters, 400
Well-known seasoned issuers

Generally, 410
Shelf registration, 462

JOINT AND SEVERAL LIABILITY
Insider trading tippers and tippees, 350
Securities Act Section 11 liability, 519

JUDICIAL REMEDIES
See Public Enforcement, this index

JUDICIAL REVIEW
Generally, 715, 794
See also Public Enforcement, this
index
Cease and desist orders, 795

JURISDICTION
Doing business in context of securities
regulations, 617
Extraterritoriality presumptions, 321
Federal jurisdiction over securities acts
violations
Generally, 96, 110, 116,
689
See also Securities,
Instruments Regulated
as, this index
Offshore actions, 318, 320, 323
Private Civil Actions, this index
Rule 10b–5, extraterritorial application
Generally, 319
Dodd-Frank Act, 326

JUSTICE DEPARTMENT
See Criminal Enforcement, this
index
Investigations, SEC/Justice cooperation,
781
Overlapping SEC/Justice Department
investigations, 781
SEC referrals, 789

LAW AND FACT QUESTIONS
Materiality of information, 55

LAWYERS
See Attorneys, this index

LEAD PLAINTIFFS
See Class Actions, this index

LEGENDS
Exempt securities, legend restrictions on
resales, 664

LIMIT ORDERS
Secondary market transactions, 11

LIMITATIONS OF ACTIONS
Rule 10b–5 antifraud, 227

LIMITED LIABILITY COMPANIES
Interests in, security laws applicability,
147

LIMITED PARTNERSHIPS
Interests in security laws applicability,
130

LIQUIDITY
Capital market advantages, 9
Secondary market transactions
Generally, 11
Floor brokers' roles, 12

LOSS CAUSATION
See Causation, this index

MADOFF SCANDAL
Criminal enforcement, 819
SEC investigation failures, 767

MANAGEMENT
See also Control Persons, this index
Control persons within, 309
Directors as management, 728
Individual shareholders, management
deals with, 700
Insider Trading, this index
Integrity, materiality of information as to,
84
Proxy solicitations, management
defensive tactics, 698

**MANAGEMENT DISCUSSION AND
ANALYSIS (MD & A)**
Generally, 178

MANIPULATION OF MARKETS
See also Deception, this index;
Fraud-on-the-Market, this
index
Hot offerings agreements, 453
Intent to manipulate, 200, 246
Misstatements or omissions and, 299
Private rights of action, 200
Regulation M
Generally, 454, 455
Stabilization activities, 457
Rule 10b–5, manipulative motives, 235
Rule 10b–18, share repurchase programs,
342
Scienter, this index
Secondary markets, underwriters'
activities, 452
SEC's rulemaking authority to prevent,
369
Securities Exchange Act provisions, 34
Share repurchase programs, 342
Stabilization activities, 457
Stock market crash of 1929 causes, 35
Underwriters' activities on secondary
markets, 452
Warehousing of stock subject to tender
offer, 369

MARKET ORDERS
Secondary market transactions, 11

MARKETS
See also Capital Market, this index
Primary market transactions, 9
Public offerings, gauging market
sentiment, 424
Secondary Markets, this index
Stock Exchanges, this index

MATERIALITY
Generally, 47 et seq.
Adverse events reports
Generally, 69
Bright-line rules, 72, 75
Books and records discrepancies, 183
Bright-line rules
Generally, 53
Adverse events reports, 72, 75
Consistency rules, 48
Denials, 54
Efficient markets, materiality in, 67
Five percent rule, 57, 63
Form 8–K filings, 71, 172
Form 10–K filings, 65
Form 10–Q filings, 79
Form S–1 filings, 64
Forms 10–K and 10–Q filings, 48
Forward looking information
Merger plans as, 51, 52
Forward-looking information
Generally, 49, 239
Soft nature of, 55
Fraud-on-the-market theory, 67
Half truths masking changes in business, 62
Half-truths, 48
Information, materiality levels, 23
Initial public offerings, 64
Labor relations problems, 76, 83
Law and fact questions, 55
Loss causation relationship, 544, 694
Management integrity information, 84
Market reactions affecting determinations, 49
Merger discussions
Generally, 49
Forward looking information, 51
Misleading material, 48
Objective tests
Generally, 57 et seq.
Five percent rule, 57, 63
Significant role in business, 62
Opinion with reference to Virginia Bankshares, 481
Probability/magnitude approach, 54
Prospectuses, 85, 89
Puffery, 81
Qualitative materiality, 62
Quantitative materiality, 60
Reasonable investor standard, 48
Reasonable shareholder standard, 52, 55
Registration statements, 64
Regulation S–K
Generally, 48, 61
Management integrity, 84
Regulatory problems, 76, 83
Related-party transactions, 85, 91
Rule 10b–5, misstatement of material fact requirement, 227
Rule of thumb
Generally, 57, 63
SEC, 57
Secrecy rationale, 52
Section 12(a)(2) litigation, 544
Securities Exchange Act standards, 48

Securities law violations, 92
Soft nature of forward-looking information, 55
Stock price reaction as measurement, 64, 68
Substantial likelihood standard, 48, 57, 80
Total mix approach, 76
Truth on the market defense, 76, 83
What matters to investors, 47

MERGERS
See also Control Contests, this index
Disclosure regulations, 37
Fraud liability, proxy solicitations, 687
Insider trading on merger plan information, 337
Materiality of information re preliminary discussions, 48
Parent-subsidiary, Rule 10b–5 antifraud claims, 228
Proxy solicitations
Fraud liability, 687
Securities Exchange Act regulations, 37
Rule 10b–5 claims
Generally, 228
Insider trading on merger plan information, 337
Shareholder voting rights, 678
Short-form mergers, 228
Williams Act, this index

MISAPPROPRIATION THEORY
See Insider Trading, this index

MORTGAGE-BACKED SECURITIES
Credit rating agencies' failures, 746
Financial crisis of 2008–2009, 38

MOTIVES
Opinions, motives for, 235

MUTUAL FUNDS
Generally, 11
See also Institutional Investors, this index
Disclosure filtering functions, 29
Hedge Funds, this index
Investment Advisers Act regulations, 36
Investment Company Act regulations, 36

NATIONAL SECURITIES MARKETS IMPROVEMENT ACT
State regulation, 584, 613, 765

NATIONALLY RECOGNIZED STATISTICAL RATINGS ORGANIZATIONS (NRSRO)
Generally, 43

NONEXISTENT SECURITIES
Security laws applicability, 95

NOTES
Definition of security, implications of use of term, 147

OFF-BALANCE SHEET ARRANGEMENTS
Form 8–K filings, 172

OFFERINGS
Private Offerings, this index
Public Offerings, this index

OFFICERS
See also Management, this index
Certifications of Form 10–K and 10–Q filings, 38
Control person status, 309
Directors, officer relationships to, 728
Insider trading, Section 16 reports
Generally, 387
See also Insider Trading, this index
Rule 10b–5 control person liability
Generally, 306
Proportionate liability, 316
SEC bar orders, 813

OFFSHORE ISSUES
Generally, 627 et seq.
See also Exempt Offerings, this index
Federal jurisdiction over securities acts violations, 318, 320, 323
Integration of offshore and domestic orders
Global Regulation S offerings, 640
Regulation S offerings, 637

OPINION LETTERS
Attorneys, 739

OPINIONS
Motives for, 235
Omnicare, 479
Rule 10b–5, fact vs opinion statements, 232

OPTIONS
Put options, 384
Stock Options, this index
Underwriters' Green Shoe options, 399, 452

OWNERS OF RECORD
Generally, 167

OWNERSHIP
See also Agency Costs, this index; Shareholders, this index
Attributes, 2
Separation between ownership and control, 699

PARENT AND SUBSIDIARY COMPANIES
Control person issues, 309
Mergers, Rule 10b–5 antifraud claims, 228

PAY-TO-PLAY
Class action counsel selection, 221

PLEADING
Control person liability, 310

Private Securities Litigation Reform Act, this index

POLICY CONSIDERATIONS
Accuracy of disclosures, 198
Antifraud rules, 725
Disclosure regulations, 162, 725
Exempt vs public offerings, 549
Gatekeeper-based regulatory theories, 725, 727
Insider trading, 329
Private rights of action, 725
Resales of exempt securities, Rule 144, 668

PONZI AND PYRAMID SCHEMES
Security laws applicability, 113, 125

PORTAL TRADING SYSTEM
Generally, 674

PREFERRED STOCK
Generally, 4
Classes of stock, 4
Common stock compared, 4
Conversion rights, 5
Convertibility, 5
Dividends, 5
Participating preferred, 6
Priorities, 4, 6
Voting rights of holders, 7

PRESENT DISCOUNT VALUE (PDV)
Generally, 16, 44

PRESUMPTIONS
Class actions
Counsel fee awards, reasonableness of, 224, 226
Lead plaintiff qualifications, rebuttable presumptions, 217, 220
Control person liability, 309
Efficient capital market hypothesis, disclosure effects presumptions, 32
Extraterritoriality of jurisdiction, 321
Fraud-on-the-market, presumptive reliance, 294
Investment intent, 648
Reliance
Generally, 224,
Securities regulations applicability, 133, 150

PRICE
See also Valuation, this index
Efficient capital markets hypothesis, 30
Event studies, stock pricing, 68
Manipulation of Markets, this index
Prospectuses, price statements, 441
Public offerings, maintaining secondary market prices, 452
Public offerings, under pricing, 400
Shelf registrations, overhang price drops, 464
Under pricing of public offerings, 400

PRIMARY MARKETS
Exempt Offerings, this index
Public Offerings, this index
Secondary markets distinguished, 1

PRIORITIES
Generally, 8
Bonds, 7
Common stock holders, 3
Creditors, 4
Participating preferred, 6
Preferred stock, 4, 5

PRIVATE CIVIL ACTIONS
See also Public Enforcement, this index
Aiders and abettors
Public enforcement compared, 770
Rule 10b–5 antifraud, 294
Attorneys
Liabilities, 741
Roles in bringing actions, 766
Class actions, Rule 10b–5, 202
Communications subject to prospectus rules, Section 12(a)(2) liability, 531, 536
Congressional intent, 296, 536
Contemporaneous traders' claims against trading insiders, 381
Contribution, Section 11 liability, 519
Credit rating agencies, mortgage-backed securities ratings, 748
Damages
Section 11 liability, 514
Section 12(a)(1) liability, 529
Section 12(a)(2) liability, 543
Defendants
Section 11 liability, statutory defendants, 476
Section 12(a)(1) liability, 522
Defenses
Section 12(a)(1) liability, 529
Section 12(a)(2) liability, 542
Securities Act Section 11 liability, 490 et seq.
Development, 199
Due diligence defense
Rule 176, 501
Section 11 liability
Generally, 490 et seq.
Rule 176, 501
Shelf registrations, 501
Underwriters, 501
Elements of action
Section 11 liability, 477
Section 12(a)(1) liability, 529
Section 12(a)(2) liability, 541
Forced seller claims, Rule 10b–5, 210
Foreign plaintiffs, Rule 10b–5, 319
Fraud
Proxy solicitations, 689
Rule 10b–5, below
Section 11 liability, 477
Gatekeeper regulation compared, 725
Gun-jumping rules, Section 12(a)(1) liability, 522

Implied and explicit rights, 200
Indemnification, Section 11 liability, 519
Injunctive relief, Rule 10b–5 antifraud, 210
Insider trading
Generally, 34
Contemporaneous traders' claims, 381
Joint and several liability, Section 11, 519
Loss causation
Section 11 liability, 477, 518
Section 12(a)(2) liability, 543
Manipulation, 200
Materiality, Section 12(a)(2) liability, 544
Mortgage-backed securities ratings, credit rating agencies, 748
Policy considerations
Generally, 725
Public vs private enforcement, 766
Private Securities Litigation Reform Act reforms, 204
Prospectuses subject to Section 12(a)(2) liability, 534
Proxy solicitation fraud, 689
Public enforcement compared
Generally, 765
Aiding and abetting liability, 770
Policy considerations, 766
Public Enforcement, this index
Registration statement fraud, Section 11 liability, 468, 491
Regulation D exempt offering violations, 579
Reliance
Rule 10b–5 antifraud, 265
Section 11 liability, 508
Rescission
Section 12(a)(1) liability, 529
Section 12(a)(2) liability, 543
Rule 10b–5
Generally, 34, 197 et seq.
See also Rule 10b–5, this index
Defendants, 289
Section 12(a)(1) liability compared, 527
SEC investigation evidence use in, 781
Secondary liability
Control Persons, this index
Rule 10b–5, this index
Secondary market purchasers' claims, Section 12(a)(2), 537
Section 11 liability
Generally, 468 et seq.
Contribution, 519
Damages, 514
Defenses, 490 et seq.
Due diligence defense
Generally, 490 et seq.
Rule 176, 501
Shelf registrations, 501
Underwriters, 501
Elements of action, 477
Fraud, 477
Indemnification, 519

Joint and several liability, 519
Loss causation, 477
Loss causation defense, 518
Opinions, 479
Registration statement fraud, 491
Registration statements, 468
Reliance defense, 508
Rule 176, due diligence defense, 501
Section 12(a)(1) liability compared, 527
Section 12(a)(2) liability compared, 530
Shelf registrations, due diligence defense, 501
Standing, 468
Statutory defendants, 476
Underwriters, due diligence defense, 501
Section 12(a)(1) liability
Generally, 522
Damages, 529
Defendants, 522
Defenses, 529
Elements of action, 529
Gun-jumping rules, 522
Rescission, 529
Rule 10b–5 liability compared, 527
Section 11 liability compared, 527
Section 12(a)(2) liability compared, 530
Standing, 522
Substantial participant, 525, 527
Section 12(a)(2) liability
Generally, 530 et seq.
Communications subject to prospectus rules, 531, 536
Damages, 543
Defenses, 542
Elements of action, 541
Loss causation, 543
Materiality, 544
Prospectus misstatements, 530
Prospectuses subject to, 534
Rescission, 543
Scope of liability, 530
Secondary market purchasers' claims, 537
Section 11 liability compared, 530
Section 12(a)(1) liability compared, 530
Standing, 537
Securities Act violations
Generally, 467 et seq.
Congressional intent, 536
Fraud, 199
Section 11 liability, above
Section 17(a) frauds, 768
Securities Exchange Act, Section 9 manipulation, 200
Standing to sue
Rule 10b–5 antifraud, 205
Section 11 liability, 468
Section 12(a)(1) liability, 522
Section 12(a)(2) liability, 537
State law causes of action, 201

Statutory defendants, Section 11 liability, 476
Substantial participant, Section 12(a)(1) liability, 525, 527
Whistleblowers, civil suits for discrimination, 756

PRIVATE COMPANIES
Public companies distinguished, 163
Public companies going dark, 164
Special-purpose vehicle as, 167
Trading in stock of, 167

PRIVATE INVESTMENT OF PUBLIC EQUITY (PIPE) OFFERINGS
Generally, 378

PRIVATE LIABILITY
Regulation FD, 188

PRIVATE OFFERINGS
Generally, 550 et seq.
See also Exempt Offerings, this index
Brokers' roles, 571
Definition, 554
PORTAL trading system, 674
Public offerings compared, 549
Restrictions on purchases amounting to private vs public offering, 552
Section 4(2), 554

PRIVATE SECURITIES LITIGATION REFORM ACT (PSLRA)
Generally, 204
Aiding and abetting liability, 770
Bespeaks caution doctrine, 245
Confidential witnesses as sources of pleading assertions, 256
Congressional Intent, 217
Congressional intent, 35
Control persons, proportionate liability, 316
Discovery restrictions, 204, 251, 252
Forward-looking safe harbor, 245
Heightened pleading standards, 251
Lead plaintiff designations, 215
Pleading
Confidential witnesses as sources of pleading assertions, 256
State of mind, 251
Proportionate liability, control persons, 316
Rule 10b–5
Control persons, 316
Proportionate liability, 316
Secondary liability, 291
Secondary liability, 291

PROFIT
Expectation of profits, security laws applicability, 115, 122

PROPORTIONATE LIABILITY
Rule 10b–5 control person liability, 316

PROPRIETARY INFORMATION
Disclosure regulations, 26

PROSPECTUSES
Antifraud liability, 432
Base prospectuses, shelf registrations, 463
Communications subject to prospectus
    rules, Section 12(a)(2) liability, 531,
    536
Definition, 531, 532, 534
Deliveries, 444
Final prospectuses, 441
Fraud liability
        Generally, 433
        Rescission claim, 531
Free writing prospectuses, 425, 428
Internet communication of free writing
    prospectuses, 428
Materiality of information, 85, 89
Out-of-date, 458
Preliminary prospectuses, 425
Price statements, 441
Private rights of action for misstatements,
    Section 12(a)(2) liability, 530
Public offering disclosures, 403
Rescission claim based on prospectus
    fraud, 531
Roadshow activities, 426
Rule 10b–5 antifraud, 205
Section 12(a)(2) liability
        Generally, 534
        Communications subject to
            prospectus rules, 531, 536
        Misstatements, 530
Securities Exchange Act requirements, 35
Shelf registrations
        See also Shelf Registrations,
            this index
        Base prospectuses, 463
Statutory prospectuses, 426
Summary prospectuses, 425
Traditional free writing, 443

PROXY SOLICITATIONS
        Generally, 679 et seq.
        See also Voting Rights, this index
Access rights, shareholder nominations of
    directors, 714
Brokers' roles, 678
Causation
        Fraud liability, 690, 694
Communication costs
        Generally, 695
        Internet use, 686
Contests, proxy, 679
        Generally, 678, 694
        Communication costs, 695
        Internet use, 686
        Management defensive tactics, 698
        Managing costs, 694
        Reimbursement, 699
Disclosure requirements
        Generally, 682
        Costs, 678
        EDGAR publication, 683
        Filings, 682
        Preliminary statements, 682
        SEC approvals, 683
        Testing the waters, 685

Dodd-Frank proxy access rules, 714
EDGAR publication, 683
Eligibility of shareholder issue proposals,
    701
Expenses. Costs, above
Federal regulations applicability, 680
Fraud liability
        Generally, 687
        Causation, 690, 694
        Costs, 678
        Merger votes, 687
        Private rights of action, 689
Hedge fund voting activities, 697
Institutional investor roles, 687
Internet communication, 686
Issue proposals by shareholders, 700
Management defensive tactics, costs, 698
Managing costs, 694
Merger votes, fraud liability, 687
Political issues, shareholder proposals
        addressing, 705, 709
Preliminary statements, disclosure
        requirements, 682
Private rights of action, fraud liability,
    689
Procedural requirements for shareholder
        issue proposals, 701
Proxy voting services, 697
Registered vs unregistered securities, 680
Reimbursement of costs, 699
Relevance standards limiting shareholder
        issue proposals, 705, 709
Rule 14a–9 antifraud liability. Fraud
        liability, above
Rule 10b–5 antifraud, 232
Scope of federal regulations, 680
SEC approvals, 683
SEC proxy access rules, 714
SEC supervision of shareholder voting,
    714
Securities Exchange Act regulations, 37
Shareholder nominations of directors,
        proxy access rights, 714
Short slate proxy contests, 698
Solicitation, definition of term, 680
Submissions of proxies, 678
Tender offers, proxy contests compared,
    679
Testing the waters, 685
Voting by proxies, 678
Voting services, 697

PUBLIC COMPANIES
        Generally, 163
Disclosure regulations, public company
        status triggering, 162
Foreign issuers, 164
Going dark, 164
Owners of record, 167
Private companies distinguished, 163
Securities Exchange Act, 163
Special-purpose vehicles designed to
        avoid, public company status, 167

PUBLIC COMPANY ACCOUNTING OVERSIGHT BOARD (PCAOB)
Organization, 44
Registration requirements, 44
Registrations of auditors, 736
Self-Regulatory Organizations compared, 37

PUBLIC ENFORCEMENT
Generally, 765 et seq.
See also Private Civil Actions, this index
Administrative proceedings
Generally, 790 et seq.
Cease and desist orders, below
Civil penalties, 791
Dodd-Frank Act civil penalties, 792
Sanctions, 791
Securities Exchange Act
Section 21(a), 793
Section 15(c)(4), 792
Section 21C, 791
Sections 12(j) and (k), 793
Self-regulatory organization rules violations, 793
Aiding and abetting liability, private vs public enforcement, 770
Asset freezes, 813
Bar orders, 813
Bounties for insider trading information, 381
Cease and desist orders
Generally, 772, 791
Judicial review, 795
Civil penalties, 792
Computer hackers, insider trading violations, 383
Control person liability
See also Control Persons, this index
Dodd-Frank Act, 311
Decisions to enforce, 789
Directors, outside director liabilities, 728
Distribution by underwriters of unregistered securities, 645, 649
Dodd-Frank Act
Civil penalties, 792
Control person liability, 311
Remedies, 806, 810
Federal preemption, 765
Fifth Amendment protections, 781
Financial Industry Regulatory Authority, 765
Formal investigations, 777
Gatekeeper regulation compared, 725
In connection with purchase or sale, Rule 10b–5 antifraud, 210
Injunctions, 803
Insider trading
Core insiders, 336
Judicial remedies, 806
Judicial remedies
Generally, 794, 802 et seq.
Asset freezes, 813
Bar orders, 793
Cease and desist orders, 795

Director replacements, 803
Disgorgement, 810
Dodd-Frank Act, 810
Fair Fund distributions, 816
Injunctions, 803
Insider trading, 806
Sarbanes-Oxley Act, 810
Securities Enforcement Remedies and Penny Stock Reform Act, 813
National Securities Market Improvement Act, 765
Outside director liabilities, 728
Overlapping SEC/Justice Department investigations, 781
Policy considerations, private vs public enforcement, 766
Private civil actions, SEC investigation evidence use in, 781
Private enforcement compared
Generally, 765
Aiding and abetting liability, 770
Policy considerations, 766
Registration requirements, 645, 649
Regulation D exempt offering violations, 579
Regulation FD, 188, 766
Reliance
Rule 10b–5 antifraud, 265
Rule 10b–5 antifraud
In connection with purchase or sale, 210
Reliance, 265
Sanctions, administrative proceedings, 791
Sarbanes-Oxley Act remedies
Generally, 810
Asset freezes, 813
Scienter, 803
Scope of SEC authority, 766
SEC Division of Enforcement, 766
SEC investigations
Generally, 770 et seq.
Commission votes to litigate, 789
Criminal prosecutions, use of evidence in, 781
Fifth Amendment protections, 781
Form 8-K disclosures of investigations, 771
Formal investigations, 777
Informal investigations, 771
Justice/SEC cooperation, 781
Overlapping SEC/Justice Department investigations, 781
Private civil actions, use of evidence in, 781
Referrals to Justice, 789
Self-reporting and enforcement proceedings decisions, 772
Settlements, 775, 790
Subpoenas, 777, 788
Voluntary Disclosure Program, 782
Wells notices, 789
Securities Act Section 17(a) frauds, 768

Securities Enforcement Remedies and
    Penny Stock Reform Act, 813
Securities Exchange Act
    Section 21(a), 793
    Section 15(c)(4), 792
    Section 21C, 791
    Sections 12(j) and (k), 793
Self-regulatory organization rules
    violations, administrative
    proceedings, 793
Self-reporting and enforcement
    proceedings decisions, 772
Settlements, 775, 790
Subpoenas, 777, 788
Unregistered securities distributions, 645,
    649
Wells notices, 789

PUBLIC OFFERINGS
    See also Primary Markets, this
        index
All or nothing offerings, 397
Allocations, IPO, 452
Allocations by underwriters, 441
Antifraud liability, 36
Asymmetric information problems, 467
Capital structure and, 401
Company registration proposals, 409
Conditioning the market, 416
Costs, 458
Definition, 536, 550
Deliveries of prospectuses, 444
Disclosure regulations
    Generally, 35, 403
    Exempt vs public offerings, 572
    Prospectuses, 403
Discounts, 399
Dutch auctions
    Generally, 396, 397
    Advantages, 401
Economics of
    Generally, 393
    Exempt offerings compared, 549
Employees, sales to as, 550
Exempt Offerings, this index
Fees paid to underwriters, 400
Financial Industry Regulatory Authority
    Regulations, 400
    Restrictions on analysts' reports,
        439
Firm commitment offerings
    Generally, 396
    All or nothing offerings, 397
    Gun-jumping rules, 441
    Rights offerings, 397
    Underwriter risks, 452
    Underwriters' roles, 396
Flippers, 452
Form S–K disclosures, 549
Free writing prospectuses, 425, 428
Gauging market sentiment, 424
    Generally, 393 et seq.
Going effective process, 435
Green Shoe options, 399, 452
Gun-jumping
    Generally, 35

See also Gun-Jumping Rules, this
    index
Indefinite registration, 458
Initial Public Offerings, this index
In-registration status, 415
Internet, impact on public issue disclosure
    rules, 417
Internet communication of free writing
    prospectuses, 428
Internet-base offerings, 396
Investment banks' roles, 396
Letter of intent, 399
Maintaining secondary market prices, 452
Non-reporting issuers, 409
Offer, term defined, 411
Out-of-date prospectuses, 458
Plain English disclosures, 405
Post-effective period, 441
Pre-filing period, 411
Price statements in prospectuses, 441
Pricing, 400
Private Civil Actions, this index
Private investment of public equity
    (PIPE) offering, 378
Procedures, overview, 395
Process of going effective, 435
Prospectuses
            Generally, 35, 403
        See also Prospectuses, this
            index
    Fraud, rescission claim based on,
        531
Putting together the offering, 420
Registration
    Costs, 458
    Exempt Offerings, this index
    Exempt securities, registration
        rights of Rule 144A qualified
        institutional buyers, 675
    Filings, 406
    Fraud
        Section 11 liability, 491
        Strict liability, 752
    Incorporation by reference of past
        filings, 404, 501
    Indefinite, 458
    Materiality of information, 64
    Post-effective period, 441
    Pre-filing period, 411
    Qualified institutional buyers of
        Rule 144A exempt securities,
        675
    Section 11 liability, 468
    Shelf Registrations, this index
    Strict liability for fraud, 752
    Updating, 449
    Waiting period, 423 et seq.
Representations to underwriters, 400
Rescission claim based on prospectus
    fraud, 531
Rights offerings, 397
Roadshow activities, 426
Scope of public offerings and exemptions,
    550
Seasoned issuers, 409

Secondary markets, maintaining prices in, 452
Securities Act, 35
Selling concessions, 399
Shelf Registrations, this index
Short seller activities, 452
Small companies, Form S–K disclosures, 549
Soft information, 418
Solicitations of interest, 427
Strict liability, registration statement fraud, 752
Tombstone advertising, 398, 426
Trading practices, 452
Traditional free writing, 443
2005 Offering Reforms
    Generally, 406
    See also Gun-Jumping Rules, this index
Underpricing phenomenon, 400
Underwriters' roles
    Generally, 396, 399
    Allocations, 441
    Firm commitment offerings, 396
Unseasoned issuers, 409
Updating registrations, 449
Updating the prospectuses and registration statements, 449
Waiting period, 423 et seq.
Warranties to underwriters, 400
Well-known seasoned issuers
    Generally, 410
    Shelf registration, 462

PUFFERY
Materiality determinations, 81

QUALIFIED INSTITUTIONAL BUYERS (QIB)
    Generally, 669
    See also Institutional Investors, this index
Rule 144A resales of exempt securities
    Generally, 670
    Registration rights of QIBs, 675
Super-secondary market, 674

QUALITATIVE STATEMENTS
Rule 10b–5 antifraud, 232

QUIET PERIOD
Forward-looking information releases, 55

RATING AGENCIES
See Credit Rating Agencies, this index

REAL-TIME DISCLOSURES
Sarbanes-Oxley Act, 239

RECKLESS MISSTATEMENTS
Rule 10b–5 antifraud, 247, 249

REFORMS
See Regulatory Reforms, this index

REGISTRATION STATEMENTS
See Public Offerings, this index

REGULATION
    Generally, 33 et seq.
Capture of regulators, 28
Components of federal securities laws, 34
Credit rating agencies, 755
Disclosure Regulations, this index
Dodd-Frank Act, this index
Financial Stability Oversight Council, this index
Investment Advisers Act, this index
Investment Company Act, this index
Public Company Accounting Oversight Board, 37
Reforms. See Regulatory Reforms, this index
Reporting Requirements, this index
Sarbanes-Oxley Act, this index
Securities Act, this index
Securities and Exchange Commission, this index
Securities Exchange Act, this index
Trust Indenture Act, 36
Voting regulations, 35

REGULATION A
See Exempt Offerings, this index

REGULATION AB
Securitization, securities laws applicability, 157

REGULATION D
See Exempt Offerings, this index

REGULATION FD
    Generally, 382
    See also Insider Trading, this index
Insider trading, 382
Private liability, 188
Public enforcement, 766
Public enforcement of filing requirements, 766
SEC enforcement, 188
Selective disclosure, 188, 196
Wink or nod, 195

REGULATION G
Sarbanes-Oxley Act, 179

REGULATION M
    Generally, 454
    See also Manipulation of Markets, this index
Stabilization activities, 457

REGULATION S
See Exempt Offerings, this index

REGULATION S–K
Asset-backed securities, shelf registrations, 465
Form 10–K and 10–Q filings, 177
Integrated disclosure, 169
Management integrity information, materiality, 84
Materiality of information
    Generally, 47, 61

Management integrity information, 84

Shelf registrations, asset-backed securities, 465

Updating of information, 237

REGULATION S–X
Integrated disclosure, 169

REGULATORY CAPTURE
Generally, 28

REGULATORY PROBLEMS
Disclosures, Rule 10b–5 antifraud, 235

REGULATORY REFORMS
Accounting firms, 11
Class actions, 204
Credit rating agencies
    Generally, 747, 754
    Conflicts of interest, 755
Dodd-Frank Act, this index
Gun-jumping rules
    Generally, 406
    Forward-looking information, 418
    Safe harbors, 418, 426
Private Securities Litigation Reform Act, this index
Sarbanes-Oxley Act, this index
Securities Enforcement Remedies and Penny Stock Reform Act, 813
Securitization systemic risks, 159

RELATED-PARTY TRANSACTIONS
    See also Conflicts of Interest, this index
Disclosure regulations
    Generally, 26
    Materiality, 85, 91
Form S–K filings, 91

RELIANCE
Causation relationship, 294
Class actions
    Generally, 282
    Certifications, 289
Fiduciary duty breach claims, 282
Fraud-on-the-market, presumptive reliance, 294
Insider trading, 282
Presumptions
    Generally, 224,
Rule 10b–5 antifraud
    Generally, 265
    Third party misrepresentations, 283
Third party misrepresentations, duty to correct, 283
Transaction causation relationship, 298

REPORTING REQUIREMENTS
Disclosure Regulations, this index
Financial Statements, this index
Form 8–K Filings, this index
Form 10–K Filings, this index
Form 10–Q Filings, this index

RESALES OF EXEMPT OFFERINGS
    Generally, 641 et seq.

See also Exempt Offerings, this index
Affiliate resales, Rule 144, 664
Broker-dealers, Rule 144A sales, 669
Brokers for reselling control persons, 655
Burden of proving exempt status, Rule 144 sales, 658
Control person resales
    Generally, 652
    Brokers for control persons, 655
    Informational advantages enjoyed by control persons, 654
    Issuers, control persons as, 653
    Rule 144 safe harbor, 660
    Section 4(1) exemption, 655
    Underwriters as control persons, 653
    Underwriters for control persons, 653
CUSIPs, Rule 144A sales, 671
Disclosure requirements, Rule 144A sales, 671
Holding period for restricted securities, Rule 144 sales, 660
Information requirements, Rule 144 sales, 662
Informational advantages enjoyed by control persons, 654
Institutional investors
    Registration rights of qualified institutional buyers, 675
    Rule 144A sales
        Generally, 670
        Registration rights of qualified institutional buyers, 675
Intrastate exempt offerings, 625
Investment intent test, 658
Investor restricted sales, Rule 144A, 669
Issuers, control persons as, 653
Legend restrictions on resales, 664
Notices, Rule 144 sales, 668
Policy considerations, Rule 144 sales, 668
PORTAL trading system, 674
Purchaser awareness of Rule 144A sale status, 671
Qualified institutional buyers, Rule 144A sales
    Generally, 670
    Registration rights of QIBs, 675
Qualifying securities, Rule 144A sales, 670
Regulation D, 575
Regulation S offerings, 638
Restricted securities, holding period for, 660
Rule 504, 585
Rule 144 sales
    Generally, 658 et seq.
    Affiliate resales, 664
    Amount of affiliate resales, 665
    Burden of proving exempt status, 658
    Control persons, 660
    Holding period for restricted securities, 660
    Information requirements, 662

Manner of affiliate resales, 666
Notice of proposed sales by affiliate resales, 668
Policy considerations, 668
Restricted securities holding period for, 660
Rule 144A sales
Broker-dealers, 669
CUSIPs, 671
Disclosure requirements, 671
Institutional investors
Generally, 670
Registration rights of qualified institutional buyers, 675
Investor restrictions, 669
PORTAL trading system, 674
Purchaser awareness of sale status, 671
Qualified institutional buyers
Generally, 670
Registration rights of QIBs, 675
Qualifying securities, 670
Registration rights of qualified institutional buyers, 675
Sarbanes-Oxley Act impact, 674
Subsequent resales, 673
Sarbanes-Oxley Act impact on Rule 144A sales, 674
Subsequent Rule 144A resales, 673
Underwriter distributions of unregistered securities, 645, 649
Underwriter transactions, 643
Underwriters as control persons, 653
Underwriters for control persons, 653

RESCISSION
See Private Civil Actions, this index

RESTITUTION
Rule 10b–5 antifraud, 313

REVES TEST
Definition of security, 148, 156

REVISED UNIFORM SECURITIES ACT OF 1985
Exempt offerings, 584

RISK
Credit default swaps, risk hedging functions, 158
Credit risk, Dodd-Frank Act regulations, 40
Diversification to reduce, 19
SEC, risk expertise, 42
Securitization practices, risk distributions, 38
Systemic risk
Dodd-Frank Act reforms, 159
Financial crisis of 2008–2009, 39
Ratings organization analyses, 43
Underwriters, firm commitment offerings, 452
Unsystematic risk, 19
Valuation affects, 18

RULE 144 SALES
Generally, 658 et seq.
See also Resales of Exempt Offerings, this index

RULE 144A SALES
Generally, 669
See also Resales of Exempt Offerings, this index

RULE 10B–5
Generally, 197
Accountants, 289
Aiders and abettors
Generally, 289
Dodd-Frank Act aiding and abetting liability, 299
Private rights of action, 293
Alternative trading system transactions, 327
Attorney fee awards, class actions, 224, 226
Attorney liability, 289
Authority of SEC to adopt, 249
Birnbaum rule, 208
Broker activities, 211
Burden of proof, 289
Causation
Loss causation, 284
Transaction causation, 265
Class actions
Generally, 202
See also Class Actions, this index
Damages, 311
Strike suits, 203
Common law fraud actions compared, 227
Conclusory statements, 232
Control person liability
Generally, 306
Proportionate liability, 316
Correction duties, 235
Customers of issuers, secondary liability, 291
Damages
Generally, 311
Disgorgement, 313
Face-to-face transactions, 313
Fraud in the inducement, 316
Loss causation, 316
Open market damages, 311
Out-of-pocket measure, 311
Punitive damages, 316
Restitution, 313
State claims, 316
Deceit and fraud compared, 385
Deception, 227
Deceptive motives, 235
Defendants
Generally, 289 et seq.
Aiders and abettors, 289
Control person liability, above
Dodd-Frank Act aiding and abetting liability, 299
Investment advisers, 300
Primary violations, 289

Secondary liability, below

Development of private rights of action, 199

Disgorgement, 313

Dodd-Frank Act, extraterritorial application, 326

Due diligence defense, 248

Economics of security fraud, 197

Elements of cause of action
    Generally, 227 et seq.
    Burden of proof, 289
    Conclusory or qualitative' statements, 235
    Conclusory statements, 232
    Correction duties, 235
    Deception, 227
    Deceptive motives, 235
    Fact vs opinion statements, 232
    Forward-looking statements, 239
    Instrumentality of interstate commerce, 227
    Intent to deceive, 247
    Loss causation, 284
    Manipulative motives, 235
    Materiality, 227
    Misstatement of material fact, 227
    Motives, deceptive nor manipulative, 235
    Opinions, 232
    Qualitative statements, 232
    Reckless misstatements, 247, 249
    Regulatory problem disclosures, 236
    Reliance, 265
    Scienter, 246 et seq.
    Third party misrepresentations, duty to correct
        Generally, 238
        Reliance, 283
    Transaction causation, 265
    Update duties, 235

Expert witnesses on loss issues, 287

Extraterritorial application
    Generally, 319
    Dodd-Frank Act, 326

Face-to-face transaction damages, 313

Fact vs opinion statements, 232

f-cubed litigation, 319

Fiduciary breaches distinguished, 213

Forced seller claims, private rights of action, 210

Foreign plaintiffs, 319

Forward-looking statements, 239

Fraud in the inducement damages, 316

Fraud on the market, 268

Gatekeeper regulation compared, 725

In connection with purchase or sale
    Insider trading by third-party tippee, 374
    Private rights of action, 204
    SEC enforcement, 210

Injunctive relief, private rights of action, 210

Insider trading claims
    Generally, 336 et seq.
    See also Insider Trading, this index

Instrumentality of interstate commerce requirement, 227

Intent to deceive, 247

Intrinsic value, statements going to, 214

Investment advisers, 300

Joint-and-several liability, 316

Jurisdiction, extraterritorial application
    Generally, 319
    Dodd-Frank Act, 326

Limitations of actions, 227

Loss causation
    Generally, 284
    Damages, 316

Manipulative motives, 235

Materiality, 227

Mergers, 228

Misstatement of material fact, 227

Motives, deceptive nor manipulative, 235

Nexus of fraud to purchase or sale, private rights of action, 211

Open market damages, 311

Opinions, 232

Out-of-pocket measure of damages, 311

Primary violations, 289

Private causes of action
    Generally, 34
    See also Class Actions, this index

Private rights of action
    Generally, 197 et seq.
    Aiders and abettors, 293
    Birnbaum rule, 208
    Class actions, 202
    Defendants, 289
    Development, 199
    Forced seller claims, 210
    Foreign plaintiffs, 319
    Genesis, 199
    In connection with purchase or sale, 205
    Injunctive relief, 210
    Intrinsic value, statements going to, 214
    Nexus of fraud to purchase or sale, 211
    Private Securities Litigation Reform Act reforms, 204
    Privity, 214
    Related causes of action, 199
    Reliance, 265
    Secondary liability, 293
    Standing to sue, 205
    State law causes of action, 201
    Strike suits, 203

Private Securities Litigation Reform Act
    Proportionate liability, 316
    Reforms, 204
    Secondary liability, 291

Privity, private rights of action, 214

Proportionate liability, secondary defendants, 316

Prospectuses, 205

Proxy solicitations, 232

Punitive damages, 316

Qualitative statements, 232

Reckless misstatements, 247, 249

Regulatory problem disclosures, 236

Related causes of action, 199
Reliance, SEC enforcement, 265
Restitution, 313
Scienter, 246 et seq.
SEC enforcement, in connection with
    purchase or sale, 210
Secondary defendants, proportionate
    liability, 316
Secondary liability
        Generally, 289 et seq.
        Aiders and abettors, 289
        Customers, 291
        Dodd-Frank Act aiding and abetting
            liability, 299
        Investment advisers, 300
        Primary violations, 289
        Private rights of action, 293
        Private Securities Litigation Reform
            Act, 291
        Suppliers, 291
        Who makes the statement, 299
Securities Act fraud prohibitions
    compared
        Generally, 200
        Section 17(a), 768
Securities Litigation Uniform Standards
    Act, state claims, 316
Standing to sue, private rights of action,
    205
State claims
        Generally, 201
        Securities Litigation Uniform
            Standards Act, 316
Suppliers to issuers, secondary liability,
    291
Third party misrepresentations, duty to
    correct
        Generally, 238
        Reliance, 283
Transaction causation
        Generally, 265
Transnational securities fraud, 317 et seq.
Underwriters, 289
Update duties, 235
Who makes the statement, 299

**SALE/LEASEBACK
    ARRANGEMENTS**
Security laws applicability, 122

SARBANES-OXLEY ACT
        Generally, 37
Accounting firm regulations, 37
Accounting practices, 737
Adelphia scandal, 37
Attorneys, disclosure regulations, 37
Audit committee standards, 728, 737
Certifications of Form 10–K and 10–Q
    filings, 38
Corporate governance reforms, 674, 714
Criminal enforcement, 825
Disclosure regulations, attorneys, 37
Disgorgement remedy, 810
Enron scandal, 37
Executive compensation disclosures, 179

Exempt securities Rule 144A resales to
    avoid, 674
Fair Fund distributions, 816
Form 8–K filings, 170
Global Crossing scandal, 37
Internal controls, 187
Judicial remedies, 810
Public Company Accounting Oversight
    Board, 37
Real-time disclosures, 239
Regulation G, 179
Rule 144A resales of exempt securities to
    avoid, 674
SEC rulemaking authority, 37
Tyco scandal, 37
Whistleblower protections, 756
WorldCom scandal, 37

SCIENTER
Collective scienter, 256
Control person liability, 310
Definition, 247, 804
Holistic approach to scienter allegations,
    256
Insider trading, misappropriation theory,
    373
Public enforcement, 803
Rule 10b–5 antifraud, 246 et seq.

**SCOPE OF SECURITIES
    REGULATION**
See Securities, Instruments Regulated as,
    this index

SECONDARY LIABILITY
Aiders and Abettors, this index
Control Persons, this index
Vicarious liability, 306, 307

SECONDARY MARKETS
        Generally, 11, 641 et seq.
        See also Stock Exchanges, this
            index
Electronic communications, 12
Exempt offering resales
        Generally, 575
        See also Resales of Exempt
            Offerings, this index
Floor brokers, 12
Gun-jumping rules, secondary market
    impacts, 437
Information advantages, 21
Limit orders, 12
Liquidity
        Generally, 11, 641
        Floor brokers' roles, 12
Market makers
        Generally, 13
        Initial public offer trading, 453
Market orders, 11
Primary and secondary transactions
    distinguished, 1
Public distributions of unregistered stock,
    646
Public offering Section 12(a)(2) liability,
    secondary purchasers' claims, 537
Public offering trading practices, 452

Resale restrictions
    Generally, 575
    See also Resales of Exempt
        Offerings, this index
Securities Act limitation on issues traded
    in, 642
Short-term imbalances, 12
Specialists, 12, 642
Stabilization activities, 457
Super-secondary market for qualified
    institutional buyers, 674
Traditional securities exchanges, 12
Transparency, 11
Underwriter distributions of unregistered
    securities, 645, 649
Underwriter transactions, 643

SECRET INFORMATION
Materiality, secrecy rationale, 52

SECURITIES, INSTRUMENTS
    REGULATED AS
    Generally, 95
Broad interpretation rationale, 97
Catch-all antifraud Rule, 95
Certificates of deposit, 107
Common enterprise interests, 108
Condominiums, 121
Consumption elements, 124
Cooperative housing sales, 115, 122
Debt arrangements distinguished, 147
Expectation of profits, 115, 122
Family resemblance test, 150, 156
Fixed returns arrangements, 122
Forged securities, 95
Franchise purchases
    Generally, 130
    Nominal involvements, 137
Home purchases
    Generally, 96
    Condominiums, 121
    Co-op housing, 115
Howey test, 98, 156
Investment contracts, 96
Investment test, 103
Led to expect profits test, 115, 122
Limited liability company interests, 147
Limited partnership interests, 130
Nonexistent securities, 95
Note, implications of use of term, 147
Policy questions underlying
    determinations, 96
Ponzi and pyramid schemes, 113, 125
Regulation AB, 157
Regulatory consequences of
    determinations, 95
Reves test, 148, 156
Sale/leaseback arrangements, 122
Securitization practices, 156
Solely from the efforts of another
    Generally, 129
    Nominal involvements, 137
Stock, implications of use of term, 142
Supreme Court decisions, 98
Types of securities, 2
Viatical settlements, 137

Virtual shares in cyberspace enterprises,
    108

SECURITIES ACT
Antifraud liability, 36
Components of federal securities laws, 34
Congressional intent
    Generally, 96
    Private rights of action, 536
Enactment, 1
Exempt Offerings, this index
Federal preemption of state regulation,
    584
Fraud prohibitions, Exchange Act Rule
    10b–5 compared, 200
Gun-jumping rules
    Generally, 35
    See also Gun-Jumping Rules, this
        index
Private rights of action
    Generally, 467 et seq.
    See also Private Civil Actions,
        this index
    Congressional intent, 536
Prospectuses, 35
Public distributions of unregistered stock,
    646
Registration
    See also Public Offerings, this
        index
    Public distributions of unregistered
        stock, 646
    Underwriter distributions of
        unregistered securities, 645,
        649
Regulation D exempt offerings, Rule 504,
    585
Regulatory focus, 35
Resales of Exempt Offerings, this index
Rule 144 sales
    Generally, 658 et seq.
    See also Resales of Exempt
        Offerings, this index
Rule 144A sales
    Generally, 669
    See also Resales of Exempt
        Offerings, this index
SEC filings, 35
Secondary markets trading limitations
    Generally, 642
    See also Secondary Markets, this
        index
Section 4(2) exempt offerings, 550
State regulation, federal preemption, 584
Underwriter distributions of unregistered
    securities, 645, 649

SECURITIES ANALYSTS
See Analysts, this index

SECURITIES AND EXCHANGE
    COMMISSION (SEC)
    Generally, 41
Accounting firms regulation, 11, 42
Attorneys, supervisorial authority of
    commission, 739

Attorneys' and accountants' rules of
        practice before SEC, 739
Bar orders, 813
Company registration proposals, 409
Corporate governance, supervision of
        shareholder voting, 714
Creation, 2
Credit rating agencies
        SEC ratings of the agencies, 746
        SEC supervisorial authority, 755
Division of Enforcement, 766
Dodd-Frank Act reforms, 40
Enforcement authority
                Generally, 41, 42, 765 et
                        seq.
                See also Public Enforcement,
                        this index
                Decisions to enforce, 789
                Division of Enforcement, 766
                Investigations, below
                Scope, 766
Fifth Amendment protections in
        investigations, 781
Form D filings, exempt offerings, 586
Form 8–K Filings, this index
Form 10–K Filings, this index
Form 10–Q Filings, this index
Formal investigations, 777
Incorporation by reference of past filings,
        404, 501
Independent nature of agency, 41
Informal investigations, 771
Insider trading responses, 336
Integrated disclosure adoption, 406
Investigations
                Generally, 770 et seq.
                Public Enforcement, this index
Investment Company Act registrations,
        36
Judicial review of actions, 715
Justice Department referrals for
        prosecution, 42
Litigation, 42, 43
Madoff investigation failures, 767
Manipulation of markets, rulemaking
        authority to prevent, 369
Materiality of information, rule of thumb,
        57
No action letters, 569
Organization, 41
Overlapping SEC/Justice Department
        investigations, 781
Past filings
        Incorporation by reference of, 404,
                501
Political independence, 41
Proxy access rules, 714
Proxy Solicitations, this index
Public Offerings, this index
Regional offices, 41
Regulatory authority
        Accounting firms regulation, 11, 42
        Enforcement authority, above
        Rule 10b–5 adoption, 248
        Sarbanes-Oxley Act, 37
Reporting Requirements, this index

Responsibilities of commission, 41
Risk expertise, 42
Rule 10b–5
        Generally, 34
        Authority of SEC to adopt, 249
        Development, 199
Sarbanes-Oxley Act rulemaking
        authority, 37
Securities Act filings, 35
Self-regulatory organization oversight
        authority, 15, 43
Self-reporting and enforcement
        proceedings decisions, 772
Shareholder voting, supervision of, 714
Subpoenas, 777, 788
Supervisorial authority, credit rating
        agencies, 755
Voluntary Disclosure Program, 782
2005 Offering Reforms
        Generally, 406
        Gun-Jumping Rules, 406

SECURITIES ENFORCEMENT
        REMEDIES AND PENNY
        STOCK REFORM ACT
Public enforcement judicial remedies, 813

SECURITIES EXCHANGE ACT
        Generally, 34
Broker regulation of, 35
Components of federal securities laws, 34
Congressional intent, 96
Corporate governance standards, 162
Enactment, 1
Exempt offerings, Exchange Act filing
        requirements, 586
Federal preemption of state regulation,
        584
Form 8–K Filings, this index
Form 10–K Filings, this index
Form 10–Q Filings, this index
Intermediaries, regulation, 2, 35
Manipulation of Markets, this index
Materiality standards, 48
Private rights of action, Section 9
        manipulation, 200
Private Securities Litigation Reform Act,
        this index
Professional intermediaries, regulation,
        35
Prospectuses, 35
Proxy solicitation regulations, 37
Public companies, 163
Public enforcement
        Section 21(a), 793
        Section 15(c)(4), 792
        Section 21C, 791
        Sections 12(j) and (k), 793
Reporting requirements, 34
Resales of Exempt Offerings, this index
Rule 144 sales
        Generally, 658 et seq.
        See also Resales of Exempt
                Offerings, this index
Rule 144A sales
        Generally, 669

See also Resales of Exempt
    Offerings, this index
Rule 10b–5, this index
Section 16 insider trading
    Generally, 387
    See also Insider Trading, this index
State regulation, federal preemption, 584
Stock exchange regulation, 35
Voting regulations, 35
Williams Act, this index

SECURITIES LITIGATION
**   UNIFORM STANDARDS ACT**
**   (SLUSA)**
Federal preemption, 201
Rule 10b–5 class actions, 316

SECURITIZATION
Credit default swaps use, 158
Dodd-Frank Act, systemic risk reforms,
    159
Financial crisis of 2008–2009, 38
Mortgage-backed securities, ratings
    failures
        Generally, 746
        Private civil actions, 748
Regulation AB, 157
Risk distributions, 38
Securities laws applicability to
    securitization practices, 156
Skin in the game rules, 159
Systemic risk, 159

SELECTIVE DISCLOSURE
Generally, 188 et seq.
Regulation FD, 188, 195

SELF-REGULATORY
**   ORGANIZATIONS (SRO)**
Generally, 43
Corporate governance standards, 44
Independent director requirements, 44
Nationally Recognized Statistical Ratings
    Organizations, 43
Public Company Accounting Oversight
    Board, this index
Public Company Accounting Oversight
    Board compared, 37
Public enforcement of rules violations, 793
SEC oversight, 15, 44
Stock exchanges acting as, 15

SETTLEMENT
Public enforcement, 775, 790

SHARE REPURCHASE PROGRAMS
Insider trading, Rule 10b–5 claims, 342
Manipulation safe harbor, 342

SHAREHOLDERS
Generally, 677 et seq.
    See also Agency Costs, this index
Agency costs controls, 699
Beneficial owner status, 695
Contests, proxy, 679
Controlling, Rule 10b–5 liability
    Generally, 306
    Proportionate liability, 316

Corporate Governance, this index
Director elections, 678
Dodd-Frank proxy access rules, 714
Eligibility of shareholder issue proposals,
    701
Golden parachute arrangements, advisory
    votes on, 182, 722
Hedge fund voting activities, 697
Individual shareholders, management
    deals with, 700
Insider trading by large block
    shareholders, Section 16
    restrictions, 388
Issue proposals by shareholders, 700
Management deals with individual
    shareholders, 700
Mergers, voting rights, 678
Nominations of directors, proxy access
    rights, 715
Ownership attributes, 2
Political issues, shareholder proposals
    addressing, 705, 709
Procedural requirements for shareholder
    issue proposals, 701
Proxies, voting by, 678
Proxy Solicitations, this index
Proxy voting services, 697
Relevance standards limiting shareholder
    issue proposals, 705, 709
Rule 10b–5 control person liability
    Generally, 306
    Proportionate liability, 316
Say on pay rules, 182, 722
SEC proxy access rules, 714
SEC supervision of voting, 714
Separation between ownership and
    control, 699
Short slate proxy contests, 698
Tender offers, proxy contests compared,
    679
Voting rights
        See also Voting Rights, this
            index
    Common stock holders, 4
    Preferred stock holders, 6

SHELF REGISTRATIONS
Generally, 458
Asset-backed securities, Regulation S–K
    disclosures, 465
Automatic, 462
Base prospectuses, 463
Definition, 449
Dilution, 465
Due diligence defense, Securities Act
    Section 11 liability, 501
Integrated disclosure, 509
Overhang price drops, 464
Regulation S–K disclosures, asset-backed
    securities, 465
Securities Act Section 11 liability, due
    diligence defense, 501
Underwriters' dilemma, 464
Well-known seasoned issuers, 462

SHORT SALES
Insiders', Section 16 prohibitions, 387
Public offerings, short seller activities, 452
Put options, 384

SHORT-TERM IMBALANCES
Secondary market transactions, 12

SMALL BUSINESS ISSUERS
Regulation A exempt offerings, 588

SOFT INFORMATION
Gun-jumping rules, 418

SOPHISTICATED INVESTORS
See also Qualified Institutional Buyers, this index
Definition, 556
Exempt offerings, Section 4(2), 556

SPECIAL FACTS DOCTRINE
Insider trading, 334

SPECIALISTS
Generally, 12, 642

SPECIAL-PURPOSE VEHICLES (SPV)
Generally, 157
See also Securitization, this index
Financial crisis of 2008–2009, 39
Off-balance sheet arrangements, 172
Private company treatment, 167

STANDING
See Private Civil Actions, this index

STATE REGULATION
Accounting and auditing services regulation, 736
Control persons, state theories, 306
Defects in, 96
Exempt offerings, Regulation D, 584
Federal preemption
Generally, 584, 613
Public enforcement, 765
Intrastate offerings exempt from federal regulations
Generally, 612 et seq.
See also Exempt Offerings, this index
National Securities Markets Improvement Act, 584, 613
Private rights of action, 201

STOCK
Corporate governance practices, price relationship, 33
Definition of security, implications of use of term, 142
Dilution of value, 395

STOCK EXCHANGES
Generally, 12
See also Secondary Markets, this index
Alternative trading systems, Rule 10b–5 applicability, 327

American Depository Receipts, 317
Face-to-face transactions distinguished, 8
PORTAL trading system, 674
Private companies, trading in stock of, 167
Public Offerings, this index
Resales of Exempt Offerings, this index
Rule 10b–5 applicability, alternative trading systems, 327
Secondary markets generally, 641
Securities Exchange Act regulation, 35
Traditional securities exchanges, 12

STOCK MARKET CRASH OF 1929
Manipulation of stock prices as a cause, 35

STOCK OPTIONS
Insiders' exercises, Section 16 reports, 388

STRIKE SUITS
Generally, 203

SUPPLIERS
Rule 10b–5 secondary liability, 291

SYSTEMIC RISK
Financial crisis of 2008–2009, 39

TAX CONSEQUENCES
Dividends, 4

TENDER OFFERS
Insider trading on offer related information, 342, 364, 382
Pro rata, 3
Proxy contests compared, 679
Warehousing of stock subject to, 369
Williams Act regulations, 37

TESTING THE WATERS
Proxy solicitation disclosure requirements, 685

THIRD PARTY MISREPRESENTATIONS
Generally, 238
Reliance, 283

TIPPER/TIPPEE LIABILITY
See Insider Trading, this index

TOXIC SECURITIES
Financial crisis of 2008–2009, 39

TRANSACTION CAUSATION
See Causation, this index

TRANSNATIONAL SECURITIES FRAUD
Foreign issuers, 317 et seq.

TRANSPARENCY
Capital market advantages, 9, 11

TRUST INDENTURE ACT
Generally, 36

TYCO SCANDAL
Sarbanes-Oxley Act, 37

TYPES OF SECURITIES
Generally, 2
See also Securities, Instruments
Regulated as, this index
Bonds, 7
Classes of stock, 4
Common stock, 3
Conversion rights, 5
Preferred stock, 4

UNDERWRITERS
Generally, 398
See also Investment Banks, this
index
Allocations, 441
Allocations of initial public offerings, 452
Book-running underwriters, 441
Bulge bracket, 398
Capital market roles, 9
Contribution rights, contractual, 519
Control persons
Underwriters as, 653
Underwriters for, 653
Credit rating agencies, underwriter
status, 748
Definition, 649
Distribution of unregistered securities,
645, 649
Due diligence defense, Section 11 liability,
501
Fees, 399
Financial Industry Regulatory Authority
regulations, 400, 452
Financial statements, reliance on, 509,
511
Firm commitment offerings
Gun-jumping rules, 441
Risks, 452
Form 10–K filings reliance as Securities
Act Section 16 defense, 508
Gatekeeper duties, 726
Green Shoe options, 399, 452
Indemnification agreements, 400
Initial public offerings allocations, 452
Institutional investor relationships, 452
Issuer's representations and warranties,
400
Managing underwriters, 399
Private Civil Actions, this index
Process of underwriting, 399
Public offering roles
Generally, 396
Firm commitment offerings, 396
Reputational value, 398
Risks, firm commitment offerings, 452
Rule 144 sales
Generally, 658 et seq.
See also Resales of Exempt
Offerings, this index
Rule 144A sales
Generally, 669
See also Resales of Exempt
Offerings, this index
Rule 10b–5 antifraud liability, 289
Secondary markets, underwriter
transactions in, 642

Section 11 liability, due diligence defense,
501
Selling concessions, 399
Shelf registrations, underwriters'
dilemma, 463
Syndicates, 9, 399

UNIFORM SECURITIES ACT OF 1985
Exempt offerings, 584

VALUATION
Accounting firms' roles, 10
Agency costs, 25
Capital Asset Pricing Model, 20
Corporate governance, stock price
relationship, 33
Dilution, 395
Efficient Capital Markets Hypothesis, this
index
Inflation effects, 16
Information, value of, 26
Interest effects, 16
Intrinsic value, Rule 10b–5 claims based
on statements going to, 214
Investment decisions, 15
Manipulation of Markets, this index
Mark-to-market accounting, 159
Money, 16
Present discount value, 16, 44
Present value, 16
Risks effecting, 18
Rule 10b–5 antifraud, statements going to
intrinsic value, 214
Securities Act Section 11 damages, 514
Underwriters, reputational value, 398

VENTURE CAPITAL FIRMS
Generally, 5
Regulation D exempt offerings, 559

VIATICAL SETTLEMENTS
Security laws applicability, 137

VICARIOUS LIABILITY
Generally, 306, 307
Control Persons, this index

VOLUNTARY DISCLOSURE
Selective disclosure problems, 188 et seq.

VOTING RIGHTS
Generally, 677 et seq.
Agency costs controls, 699
Buying votes, 698
Classified boards, 698
Common stock holders, 4
Contests, proxy, 679
Director elections, 678
Dodd-Frank Act
Generally, 40
Proxy access rules, 714
Eligibility of shareholder issue proposals,
701
Executive compensation, say on pay rules,
182, 722
Golden parachute arrangements, advisory
votes on, 182, 722
Hedge fund voting activities, 697

Issue proposals by shareholders, 700
Mergers, 678
Political issues, shareholder proposals
    addressing, 705, 709
Preferred stock holders, 6
Procedural requirements for shareholder
    issue proposals, 701
Proxies, voting by, 678
Proxy Solicitations, this index
Proxy voting services, 697
Relevance standards limiting shareholder
    issue proposals, 705, 709
Say on pay rules, 182, 722
SEC proxy access rules, 714
SEC supervision, 714
Securities Exchange Act regulations, 35
Shareholder nominations of directors,
    proxy access rights, 714
Short slate proxy contests, 698
Staggered boards, 698
Tender offers, proxy contests compared,
    679

WHAT IS A SECURITY
See Securities, Instruments Regulated as,
    this index

WHISTLEBLOWERS
    See also Gatekeeper Regulation,
        this index
Accountants, 738
Attorneys, 740
Bounties paid by SEC for information re
    insider trading activities, 381
Civil suits for discrimination, 756
Discrimination, 756
Dodd-Frank protections, 40, 762
Employee whistleblowers, 756
Incentives, 762
Insider trading activities, SEC bounties
    for information re, 381
OSHA protections, 756
Protected communications, 758, 759
Retaliation, 756
Sarbanes-Oxley Act protections, 756

WILLIAMS ACT
    Generally, 37
Beneficial owner identifications, 695
Disclosure regulations, 37
Tender offer regulations, 37, 37

WORLDCOM SCANDAL
Sarbanes-Oxley Act, 37